THE OXFORD HANDBOOK OF

MUSIC AND MEDIEVALISM

THE OXFORD HANDBOOK OF

MUSIC AND

MEDIEVALISM

Edited by
STEPHEN C. MEYER

and

KIRSTEN YRI

OXFORD
UNIVERSITY PRESS

Oxford University Press is a department of the University of Oxford. It furthers
the University's objective of excellence in research, scholarship, and education
by publishing worldwide. Oxford is a registered trade mark of Oxford University
Press in the UK and certain other countries.

Published in the United States of America by Oxford University Press
198 Madison Avenue, New York, NY 10016, United States of America.

Library of Congress Control Number: 2019955815

ISBN 978-0-19-065844-1

1 3 5 7 9 8 6 4 2

Printed by Sheridan Books, Inc., United States of America

Acknowledgments

This handbook began as an idea for a small collection of essays on medievalism in music. That it grew to include thirty-three essays is a testament not only to a growing field, but also to the confidence Oxford placed in us as editors. We wish to thank Oxford University Press, in particular, Editor in Chief Suzanne Ryan, and Assistant Editor Lauralee Yeary, for their stewardship, their continuous support and enthusiasm for the project. For the Handbook's production, we are indebted to Lakshmanan Sethuraman and his team. Thanks also go to two Laurier students, Anthea Conway-White and Bridget Ramzy for their diligence with musical examples and citations. Finally, our deepest gratitude extends to the authors for their contributions, for their commitment to the project, and for their patience and cooperation during the editorial process.

In developing this project and bringing it to completion, the editors have benefitted from the advice and insights of numerous friends, colleagues, and students. In addition to the contributors (many of whom provided valuable ideas about the shape of the handbook as a whole), we would like to thank Rebekah Ahrendt, Jenny Doctor, Sarah Fuller, Andreas Giger, Ashley Greathouse, Thomas Grey, Brian Hart, and Annette Kreutziger-Herr.

We would also like to acknowledge the invaluable support that our families have given to us. We would especially like to thank our partners, Eileen Strempel and Andreas Kitzmann, for their loving encouragement.

Contents

SECTION 2 PERFORMING THE MIDDLE AGES

SECTION 3 MEDIEVALISM AND COMPOSITIONAL PRACTICE IN THE TWENTIETH CENTURY

SECTION 4   REIMAGINING THE MEDIEVAL WOMAN

SECTION 5   ECHOES OF THE MIDDLE AGES IN FOLK, ROCK, AND METAL

SECTION 6   MEDIEVALISM OF THE SCREEN

Notes on Contributors

Jennifer Bain is a professor of music and Associate Dean of Research for the Faculty of Arts and Social Sciences at Dalhousie University. Named to the Royal Society of Canada's College of New Scholars, Artists and Scientists of, she has received numerous grants from the Social Sciences and Humanities Research Council of Canada.Her publications focus on the reception and analysis of medieval music and the development of digital chant research tools and her book *Hildegard of Bingen and Musical Reception: The Modern Revival of a Medieval Composer*, was published by Cambridge University Press in 2015.

Edward Breen is the coordinator of the music department at the City Literary Institute, London, and a regular contributor to *Gramophone Magazine*. He studies the early music revival of the 1960s and 1970s with an emphasis on musicians who worked with David Munrow.

Caitlin Vaughn Carlos is a visiting assistant professor at the University of Redlands, where she teaches courses for music majors as well as general education courses. She is currently completing her PhD in musicology at the University of California, Los Angeles. Her research focus is on nostalgia and pastoral imagery in British and American rock music of the early 1970s. She holds an MA in historical musicology from the University of Southern California and an MM in voice performance from the University of Redlands.

David Clem teaches courses in music history and film music as an instructor of music history at the Greatbatch School of Music, Houghton College, in Houghton, New York. He has published on the role of music in filmic adaptations. His research interests include intersections between philosophy, cultural criticism, and musical multimedia. This includes taking hermeneutic approaches to analyzing film and opera and the study of preexisting music that is recontextualized in multimedia settings.

Lisa Colton is a reader in musicology at the University of Huddersfield and the author of *Angel Song: Medieval English Music in History* (Routledge, 2017). Her research focuses on medieval music, on twentieth-century British composers, and on aspects of music, gender, and sexuality. Recent publications include a book chapter on medievalism in the soundtrack to *The Wicker Man* (*Recomposing the Past: Early Music on Stage and Screen*, Routledge, 2018) and a chapter on "Physical and Conceptual Boundaries in English Devotional Music, 1250–1500" (*Devotional Interaction in Medieval Britain and Its Afterlives*, Brill, 2018).

James Cook is a lecturer in early music at the University of Edinburgh. He works on music of the fourteenth to sixteenth centuries and has written for journals such as *Music & Letters* and *Early Music*. He also investigates the representation of early music in film, television, and video games, most recently coediting *Recomposing the Past: Representations of Early Music on Stage and Screen*. Outside the university, James serves as membership secretary for the Society for Renaissance Studies and is a scholar in residence for the Binchois Consort.

Karen M. Cook is assistant professor of music history at the Hartt School, the University of Hartford. She specializes in late medieval music theory and notation, with current book projects including a monograph on the development of ever-smaller rhythmic note values. She also focuses on the intersections of music and identity in media such as television and video games, with special regard to musical medievalism. Recent and forthcoming works appear in *Studies in Medievalism, Music in the Role-Playing Game: Heroes & Harmonies, The Medieval Disability Sourcebook,* and *postmedieval.*

James Deaville is a professor at the School for Studies in Art & Culture: Music at Carleton University. He has published in the *Journal of the American Musicological Society, Journal of the Society for American Music, American Music, Journal of Musicological Research,* and *Music and Politics* and has contributed to books published by Oxford, Cambridge, and Routledge, among others. He also edited *Music in Television: Channels of Listening* (Routledge, 2011) and coedited *Music and the Broadcast Experience* with Christina Baade (Oxford, 2016). He is currently coediting the *Oxford Handbook of Music and Advertising* and is working on a monograph about music in cinematic trailers.

Elizabeth Dister received her PhD in music from Washington University in St. Louis in 2015. Her research focuses on French music and politics in the twentieth century, in particular on musical representations of Joan of Arc in the 1930s and 1940s. She works at Webster University's Faculty Development Center, where she focuses on teaching and learning issues related to student engagement and motivation and creates programming for faculty on topics such as teaching and technology, engaged learning, and inclusive teaching.

Laura Dolp is an associate professor at Montclair State University. Her interdisciplinary research explores the historical agency of music as a site of human transformation, including music and spirituality, the interrelation of music and social spaces, mapping and musical practices, and the poetics of the natural world. She is the editor of *Arvo Pärt's White Light: Media, Culture, Politics* (Cambridge University Press, 2017) and a coauthor for *The Cambridge Companion to Arvo Pärt* (2012) and *Artistic Citizenship: Artistry, Social Responsibility, and Ethical Praxis* (Oxford University Press, 2016). Her research also appears in *19th-Century Music* and *Journal of Musicological Research.*

Barbara Eichner is a senior lecturer in music at Oxford Brookes University. Her work in nineteenth-century German music focuses on questions of nationalism, historicism, and identity; she is the author of *History in Mighty Sounds: Musical Constructions of German National Identity, 1848–1914* (2012) as well as articles and chapters about the music of Richard Wagner. In her other research area, she investigates monastic music in the early modern era.

Gillian L. Gower received her PhD from the University of California, Los Angeles, in 2016 and is currently Interim Program and Research Developer at the UCLA Center for the Study of Women. Her research mainly focuses on the intersections between power, gender, and sacred music in late medieval England, with a particular focus on queenship. She has also written about cultural depictions of British queens in postmedieval contexts, including popular music and music for stage and screen.

Donald Greig began his career as a lecturer in film studies before becoming a professional singer. Over the past thirty years, he has sung with numerous early music ensembles and is particularly associated with The Orlando Consort, of which he is a founding member, and The Tallis Scholars, with whom he sang for over twenty-five years. He has created several projects for The Orlando Consort, including a soundtrack of music from the lifetime of Joan of Arc to accompany screenings of Dreyer's *La Passion de Jeanne d'Arc*. The project was the basis of his doctorate in music at the University of Nottingham where he is currently an Honorary Research Fellow. He has published articles in *Screen* and *Early Music* and has contributed chapters to various academic publications.

Ross Hagen is an assistant professor of music studies at Utah Valley University in Orem, Utah. He holds a PhD and an MM in musicology from the University of Colorado at Boulder. Dr. Hagen's research interests include black metal, music fan cultures, twentieth/twenty-first century avant-garde music, and music and ritual. He is a coeditor of the upcoming volume *Medievalism and Metal Music Studies: Throwing Down the Gauntlet*. In addition to his academic work, Dr. Hagen is an active composer and performer of electroacoustic music, and extreme metal.

John Haines is a professor of music and medieval studies at the University of Toronto. He has published on early music and its modern reception in a variety of journals, both musicological—from *Early Music History* to *Popular Music*—and nonmusicological—from *Scriptorium* to *The Sixteenth Century Journal*. Recent books include *Music in Films on the Middle Ages: Authenticity vs. Fantasy* (Cambridge, 2014) and *Chants du diable, chants du peuple: voyage en musique dans le Moyen Âge* (Brepols, 2018).

Diana R. Hallman is an associate professor at the University of Kentucky. She centers her musicological research in nineteenth-century French opera and cultural history, with a particular focus on French grand opera and the composer Fromental Halévy. She is the author of the book *Opera, Liberalism, and Antisemitism in Nineteenth-Century*

France: The Politics of Halévy's La Juive (Cambridge, 2002, 2007), as well as articles in *The Cambridge Companion to Grand Opera* (2003), *Music, Theater, and Cultural Transfer: Paris, 1830–1914* (2009), *Le Concours du Prix de Rome de la musique* (2011), *Jewishness and the Arts* (forthcoming, 2020), and *Histoire de l'opéra français* (2020). Current projects include a study of social-political representation in *opéra comique* of the July Monarchy and the preparation of a multi-authored edited collection to be titled *America in the French Imaginary.*

Deborah Heckert teaches in the Department of Music at Stony Brook University. She is the author of *Composing History: National Identities and the English Masque Revival, 1860–1925* and has essays in the volumes *Elgar and His World* and *British Music and Modernism, 1995–1960.* Her current research interests focus on British modernism in the early decades of the twentieth century, the role of history in the identity politics of the English musical renaissance, and the intersections between British music and the visual arts.

Alexis Luko is an associate professor of music in the School for Studies in Art and Culture and the College of the Humanities at Carleton University in Ottawa, Canada. She holds a PhD from McGill University and previously worked as a visiting professor at the Eastman School of Music and the College Music Department at the University of Rochester. She is a musicologist specializing in film music, opera, music of the Middle Ages and Renaissance, and early music analysis. Her book *Sonatas, Screams, and Silence: Music and Sound in the Films of Ingmar Bergman* was published in 2016 by Routledge.

Stephen C. Meyer holds a PhD from Stony Brook University and worked for many years in the Department of Art and Music Histories at Syracuse University. He is currently a professor of musicology at the College-Conservatory of Music of the University of Cincinnati. He is the author of *Carl Maria von Weber and the Search for a German Opera* (Indiana University Press, 2003) and *Epic Sound: Music in Postwar Hollywood Biblical Films* (Indiana University Press, 2014) and the editor of *Music in Epic Film: Listening to Spectacle* (Routledge, 2016). In addition, he has published articles in numerous scholarly journals, including the *Journal of the American Musicological Society, 19th-Century Music, The Musical Quarterly,* and the *Cambridge Opera Journal.* From 2014 until 2018, he also served as the editor in chief of the *Journal of Music History Pedagogy.*

Balázs Mikusi holds a PhD from Cornell University and has been the head of music at National Széchényi Library in Budapest since 2009. He navigates a double career as a musicologist and music librarian. From 2016 to 2019 Mikusi served as both president of the Hungarian Musicological Society and Vice President of the International Association of Music Libraries. . He has published research articles in *Nineteenth-Century Music, Eighteenth-Century Music, Journal of Musicological Research, Ad Parnassum, The Musical Times, Mozart Jahrbuch,* and *Haydn Studien* and is at work on two monographs about the history of secular part songs in Germany ca. 1780–ca. 1815 and Joseph Haydn's personal music collection, respectively.

Elinor Olin is a member of the music history faculty at Northern Illinois University. Her research has focused on melodrama, nineteenth-century opera, and cultural nationalism in France. She has written articles for *19th-Century Music*, *The Journal of Musicological Research*, *MLA Notes*, and publications of the Lyric Opera of Chicago. Dr. Olin led the Santa Fe Opera Seminars between 2014 and 2018, and is the founder of Opera Immersion Seminars. She has read papers at meetings of the American Musicological Society and the Musicological Society of Australia, and has been an invited speaker at international conferences at Oxford University and the University of Nottingham. She has presented workshops and lectures for the Lyric Opera of Chicago, Chicago Symphony, Grant Park Music Festival, and Ars Musica Chicago.

Nils Holger Petersen is an associate professor emeritus of church history at the University of Copenhagen, with a research focus on medieval liturgy, music and drama, and their receptions in the postmedieval world. He is the main editor for the book series *Ritus et Artes: Traditions and Transformations* (Brepols) and an area editor for music for the *Encyclopedia of the Bible and Its Reception* (De Gruyter, 2009–). He has been involved in many international research collaborations and was project leader for an international project on medieval saints and their cultural receptions under the *European Science Foundation* (2011–2014).

Liana Püschel is a teaching assistant of musicology at Università degli studi di Torino, Humanities Faculty. Her research focuses on the relationship between music and literature in the works of composers of the late nineteenth century. In June 2017, she was awarded the prize Una vita nella musica, in the category Young Musicologist. Püschel is currently participating in an e-learning project on music and cinema at Università degli studi di Torino.

Michael S. Richardson is an assistant professor of musicology at the University of St. Thomas in Houston, Texas. He completed his PhD in music history and theory at Stony Brook University in 2016, and he received a DAAD grant to conduct dissertation research in Germany for the 2012–2013 academic year under the guidance of Annette Kreutziger-Herr. His research interests include late eighteenth- and nineteenth-century German, French, and Russian opera, nineteenth-century European folklorism and nationalism, and medievalism and medieval music reception. His forthcoming monograph, *Medievalism and Nationalism in Early Nineteenth-Century German Opera: Euryanthe to Lohengrin*, will be published in 2020.

Jacob Sagrans is a musicologist and performer who specializes in the early music revival, sacred choral music, musical medievalism, and music and gender. He holds a PhD in musicology from McGill University, where he wrote his dissertation on "Early Music and the Choir of King's College, Cambridge, 1958 to 2015." He has taught at Boston conservatory at Berklee, McGill University, Tufts University, and Brown

University. He is also a member of Coro Allegro, Boston's acclaimed LGBTQ+ and allied classical chorus.

Laura K. T. Stokes is the performing arts librarian at Brown University, where she has also been a visiting lecturer in music. She holds a PhD in musicology from Indiana University: her dissertation is titled "Music and Cultural Politics during the Reign of Friedrich Wilhelm IV of Prussia." Her research focuses on music and politics, music for public ritual, performance history, publishing history, nineteenth-century medievalism, and women in music, as well as Fanny Hensel, Felix Mendelssohn, and Giacomo Meyerbeer. She is the author of *Fanny Hensel: A Research and Information Guide* (Routledge, 2019), and her essay on Felix Mendelssohn's *Deutsche Liturgie* will appear in *Rethinking Mendelssohn* (Oxford, forthcoming).

Anne Stone is an associate professor of musicology at the Graduate Center of the City University of New York. Her medieval research centers on song manuscripts, the cultural and intellectual history of music writing, and the, relationship of song to late-medieval poetic subjectivity and autobiography. Her twentieth-century research considers medievalism in the work of modernist composers. She is currently a member of the editorial team preparing a new edition of the complete works of Guillaume de Machaut and is writing a book provisionally called *Reading Late Medieval Song*.

Marie Sumner Lott is an associate professor of music history at Georgia State University in Atlanta. She is the author of *The Social Worlds of Nineteenth-Century Chamber Music: Composers, Consumers, Communities* (University of Illinois Press, 2015). In addition to several essays in book-length collections published by Cambridge University Press, Orpheus Editions, and the University of Rochester Press, she has published articles and reviews on the music of Carl Czerny, Louise Farrenc, the Schumanns, and Johannes Brahms in peer-reviewed journals such as *Ad Parnassum*, the *Journal of Musicological Research*, and *MLA Notes*.

Simon Trafford is a lecturer in medieval history at the Institute of Historical Research, University of London. His principal research interests lie in the history and archaeology of northwestern Europe in the early Middle Ages, but he is also interested in usage and appropriation of the medieval by popular culture from the nineteenth century to the present. He is convener of the University of London Interdisciplinary Seminar on Medievalism and has published widely on the representation of the Middle Ages in pop music, especially Viking metal.

Scott R. Troyer is an independent scholar and administrator working the the Cincinnati area. His MM thesis, entitled "Layers of Meaning: Intertextuality in Early Anabaptist Song," received the University of Cincinnati's Distinguished Master's Thesis award in the humanities category and was submitted to the 2018 Midwestern Association of Graduate Schools distinguished master's thesis competition on behalf of the university. His primary research interests concern music–text relationships and musical references in the sixteenth century. In 2017, he worked as a musical analyst for the Citations: The

Renaissance Imitation Mass project creating a searchable online database of musical citations in the imitation mass repertoire.

Elizabeth Randell Upton is an associate professor of musicology at the University of California, Los Angeles. She is the author of *Music and Performance in the Later Middle Ages* (Palgrave, 2012), which identified and examined evidence about social context, performers, and the listening experience in fourteenth- and early fifteenth-century music by Du Fay and others. Her new book project explores the influence of popular music and folk music revivals of the 1950s and 1960s on the early music revival of the 1980s in the United Kingdom and the United States.

Aleksandra Vojčić is an associate professor of music theory at the University of Michigan and former faculty member at the Juilliard School. Her primary research interests are rhythm and meter, focusing on the music of the long twentieth century. Lectures and papers have been presented and published in the United Kingdom, Lithuania, Austria, and the United States. Abroad, her work has been published by the Lithuanian Academy of Music and Theater, Gesellschaft für Musiktheorie, Kunstuniversität Graz, Cambridge Scholars Publishing, and Cambridge University Press. In the United States, her articles have appeared in *Perspectives of New Music*, *Theoria*, and *Current Musicology*. She is currently working on a monograph titled *Rhythmic Form: Structure and Process in 20th-Century Repertoire* (under review at Oxford University Press).

Kirsten Yri is an associate professor of musicology at Wilfrid Laurier University. She has maintained an interest in medievalism since her dissertation, "Medieval Uncloistered: Uses of Medieval Music in Late Twentieth-Century Culture." She has published a series of articles on the medieval music revival in *Early Music*, *American Music*, *Women and Music*, and *A Companion to Guillaume de Machaut*. Her articles on medievalism and rock music appear in *Current Musicology*, *Intersections*, *Popular Music*, and *postmedieval*. She is currently writing a monograph on the musical aesthetic of parody in works by Carl Orff.

INTRODUCTION

KIRSTEN YRI AND STEPHEN C. MEYER

MEDIEVALISM—broadly construed as retrospective immersion in the images, sounds, narratives, and ideologies of the European Middle Ages—has left a powerful mark in both art music and popular music culture of the nineteenth and twentieth centuries. Although scholars across the humanities have been studying this phenomenon in art, film, theater, literature, and historiography and there is now an impressive bibliography of works on the subject, musicology has been slower to participate in this scholarly endeavor. One explanation is that musicology has tended to organize itself chronologically and geographically, producing a disciplinary environment in which the medievalism of Wagner's *Lohengrin* (for example) is disconnected from the study of medieval chant or medievalism in Arvo Pärt's *Miserere*. The fact that the various musical genres in which medievalism is manifest (e.g., rock, fantasy film, video games, nineteenth-century opera, mid-century twentieth-century modernist works) each have their own specialized technical, musical, and theoretical knowledge makes dialogue and intellectual exchange even more difficult. This handbook provides a snapshot of the growing field of music and medievalism. Its contents develop new critical insights that venture outside chronological and geographical boundaries and provide a capstone and point of departure for future scholarship on music and medievalism.

The publication of this handbook is motivated in part by the rapid growth in the scholarly study of medievalism over the past several decades. No publication has contributed more to this growth than *Studies in Medievalism*, the annual journal that has recently published its twenty-seventh volume. Each issue of this journal—as many readers of this handbook will know—is given its own distinct title; the first two volumes, for example, were devoted to "Medievalism in England" and "Medievalism in America," respectively. Although every emerging academic field must to some degree stake out its own distinct corner of the academic landscape, the fact that four of the twenty-seven volumes of *Studies in Medievalism* bear titles that reference questions of definition testifies to the special importance that this topic has had in the field.[1] Medievalism, we might say, is inherently self-reflective, informed by questions of self-identity that supply much of its intellectual energy.

One of the most important of these questions concerns the distinction between *medievalism* and *medieval studies* and the extent to which such a distinction is possible and/or desirable. It would seem that the difference between the two terms has to do with both form and intentionality. Medieval studies is essentially an academic term and finds its most natural expression in books and articles that are dedicated to establishing historical knowledge about the "real" Middle Ages. Medievalism, by contrast, seems to encompass a much broader range of cultural forms, including not only written materials, but also buildings, paintings, set designs, and music. In this regard, medievalism could be viewed as a cultural phenomenon or style, with its medieval cultural forms classified as *medievalist*. With regard to literary works, the distinction between these two classifications appears at first to be relatively clear. The philological efforts of J. R. R. Tolkien and other scholars to establish the authoritative text of *Sir Gawain and the Green Knight*, on the one hand, would be an example of medieval studies. Edward Bulwer-Lytton's fantasy reimagination of medieval England in his 1848 historical novel *Harold, the Last of the Saxons*, on the other hand, belongs clearly in the category of medievalism.

Beginning in the postwar period and accelerating through the 1980s and 1990s, however, scholars of medieval studies began to recognize that positivist scholarship on the Middle Ages was inevitably informed by the political, nationalist, religious agendas or the subjective experiences of those doing the inquiries. The acceptance of medievalism as an academic discipline thus acknowledges multiple discourses of the Middle Ages, various histories, if you will, going so far as to understand its recovery as one embroiled as much in contextual modes as in scientific methods. Thus, scholars began to see that the academic discipline of medieval studies overlapped in large part with the more "fictional" versions of the Middle Ages against which they were distinguished. The sections on the medieval period in Michelet's *Histoire de France*—to take a concrete example—could be viewed as an example of medieval studies since they were grounded in the "scientific" methodologies of source studies.[2] But Michelet's account is so powerfully shaped by ideology that it approaches the form and tone of a novel, suggesting that the medieval sections of the *Histoire de France* should be more properly categorized as examples of medievalism. Sir Walter Scott's *Ivanhoe* (to take an opposing example) engages in medievalism. And yet, although nearly all the characters in Scott's novel are imaginary, his work reveals a deep and rich understanding of late twelfth-century England; a case could be made that *Ivanhoe* (or at least certain sections of it) approaches a form of medieval studies.

What makes the discussion of the divide between medieval studies and medievalism more complicated in the discipline of musicology and music history particularly is the fact that, especially for music written prior to 1200, little is definitive in terms of providing a record of medieval sound. The notational systems used in the Middle Ages lack basic information concerning instruments, scope of ensemble, and sometimes even melodic shape, harmony, rhythm, or meter. Although musicians from the nineteenth century (the period with which our handbook begins) had some access to musical materials from the Middle Ages, few could read medieval musical notation or understand the concepts contained in medieval musical treatises. Especially during this period, the realization of medieval music was always at least to some extent a work of fantasy. The semantic ambiguity of musical notation stands in marked contrast to the status of medieval literature. Although there will always be gaps in context, meaning, and/or linguistic use, literary texts from the Middle Ages can offer significantly more information to later periods than their musical counterparts. The recovery and performance of medieval music—to put this in terms of the dichotomies that we are discussing here—has never fit completely securely under the aegis of medieval studies.

The work of the Benedictine monks of Solesmes provides an instructive example of this insecurity. Their efforts to recover the music of the early church were surely informed by a desire to establish authentic historical knowledge about Gregorian chant, and in this sense we might subsume it under the category of medieval studies. But as Katherine Bergeron and others have pointed out, the work of the monks also reflected the political and ideological tensions of the nineteenth and early twentieth centuries.[3] Like A. W. Pugin's medievalist designs for the houses of Parliament, the typefaces of the *Liber usualis* represented a repurposing of medieval forms for use in the present: In this sense they are perfect examples of medievalism. The monks of Solesmes were hardly the only scholars interested in preserving and transmitting medieval music. Scholars and performing musicians from the nineteenth century to the present day have made enormous efforts to understand all aspects of medieval musical notation and to establish critical editions of musical texts: Many of these efforts were far more scientific than those employed at Solesmes. They have used information gleaned from literature and the visual arts in an effort to establish authentic performance practices of medieval music. As in literary studies and other fields, however, musicologists increasingly understood this recovery work as inextricably bound up with questions of contemporary ideology and aesthetics; in this sense, it functions simply as another form of medievalism.

Questions about authenticity and intentionality also inform the distinction between *neomedievalism* and medievalism, a distinction that is central to much of the recent scholarship in this field. Even within the essays of this collection (let alone across the field more generally), the term is used in various ways and with varying degrees of centrality. Neomedievalist works might be understood as those which reference and reuse medievalist forms, not those of the Middle Ages themselves; in this sense we may regard neomedievalism as synonymous with *two-storied medievalism*.[4] With its references to *Beowulf* and other works of medieval literature, to take one example, J. R. R. Tolkien's legendarium can be understood as an example of medievalism. Role-playing games such as Dungeons & Dragons or Magic, by contrast, refer (albeit in a general way) back to Tolkien and earlier examples of medievalism. Largely unconcerned with the original medieval phenomena, they can be classified as examples of neomedievalism. As with the distinction between medieval studies and medievalism, however, that between medievalism and neomedievalism seems much less secure when it is applied to specific musical forms. As the contributions to this handbook attest, the very nature of the medieval music revival on recordings has resulted in significant points of contact between art music and musicians in the popular and film music industries. Here again, questions of intentionality and form blur the boundaries between classifications. While many ensembles seek to faithfully reconstruct a medieval musical work or moment in medieval history, rock bands and film composers, who follow the different rules of their genres, frequently borrow, reinvent, or reinterpret medieval figures not necessarily to narrate the past, but to draw connections to the present. Looking beyond the high/low divide that is often erected to distinguish popular music and film music from medieval music or music in the academy, we may consider the medieval musical allusions in both popular culture and historically informed medieval music in terms of the medievalism/neomedievalism divide. The Pagan bands that Scott Troyer discusses in his contribution to this volume, for example, often appropriate texts from the Middle Ages "directly," and in this sense they function as examples of medievalism. The fact that they so frequently reference medievalist fantasies that have little or no grounding in historical texts, however, would lead us to classify them as neomedievalist. The 2009 Margarethe von Trotta film *Vision—Aus dem Leben der Hildegard von Bingen* that Jennifer Bain discusses in her contribution to this handbook provides another example of the fluid border between medievalism and neomedievalism. Based as it is on the biography of the most famous medieval female composer, the film references many concrete details from the real Middle Ages. The emergence of Hildegard as an iconic figure in the history of medieval music is very much indebted to the work of many scholars, and her compositions were a key part of the early music revival and the historically informed performance movement of the 1970s, 1980s, and 1990s. But the film also builds on medievalist tropes concerning music, nature, and spirituality; in this sense it is as neomedievalist as other films that are less historically grounded. Indeed, a similar kind of classificatory ambiguity haunts other musical works and genres discussed in this handbook. As with the boundary between medieval studies and medievalism, therefore, that between medievalism and neomedievalism is difficult, if not impossible, to determine.

The fluidity and the contested nature of these boundaries help to account for another distinctive characteristic of medievalism, namely, the number of taxonomies that the field has generated. One of the most influential of these taxonomies has been the list of "Ten Little Middle Ages" that Umberto Eco included as part of his 1973 essay, "Dreaming of the Middle Ages"; indeed, references to this work appear in many of the essays in this collection.[5] Eco was primarily interested in the purposes for which medieval images and ideas were deployed in postmedieval texts; the categories of his taxonomy therefore articulate distinct rhetorical functions. The Middle Ages of "national identities," for example (the sixth of Eco's "Ten Little Middle Ages"), would include a diverse group of novels, paintings, quasi-academic collections of folk songs, and other materials that evoke the Middle Ages to buttress the sense of a distinct nationhood. In presenting this taxonomy, Eco is for the most part following an overtly deconstructionist agenda, setting up the "little Middle Ages" to expose their artificiality. His eighth category—"of philological construction"—stands in opposition to the rest by insisting on a kind of authority, a truth against which to compare the remaining nine Middle Ages. Herein lies the largest shift in medievalism since the 1990s: Authors (including contributors to this handbook) now use Eco's taxonomy as a point of departure and recognize that the engagement with the Middle Ages may not always require historical accuracy. In those cases, it makes little sense to test its authenticity against authority.

For the contributors to this handbook, Eco's classificatory system has perhaps been less important than the fourfold taxonomy included by Annette Kreutziger-Herr in her entry "Medievalism" for *Oxford Music Online*.[6] Building on the four models of medieval reception proposed by Francis Gentry and Ulrich Müller, Kreutziger-Herr identifies four forms of medievalism[7]:

> 1) productive, creative medievalism, in which topics, themes, forms, works of art, and individuals of the Middle Ages are formed into a new work of art; 2) reproductive medievalism, in which medieval works are reconstructed through musical performance or renovation (of a painting or a building) and perceived to be authentic; 3) scientific medievalism, in which authors, works, events, or facts are studied and explained with methodologies regarded as authentic within the diversity of medieval studies; 4) political and ideological medievalism, in which works, themes, ideas or persons are exploited for political reasons.[8]

If Eco's taxonomy places the emphasis on the rhetorical function of medievalist works, Kreutziger-Herr's classification moves this emphasis toward methodology. As she herself points out, the borders between the categories of her taxonomy are extraordinarily fluid. Individual works frequently partake of more than one type of medievalism, and different interpreters may classify the same work in different ways.

Either of these taxonomies—or, indeed, another of our own invention—might conceivably have functioned as a means to organize this handbook. Instead, we have chosen to group the essays into sections on the basis of the historical periods, themes, or genres that they share. We begin the handbook with a section on nineteenth-century medievalist music and the ideological assumptions by which this music was informed. Our decision to begin with the music of the nineteenth century (and not that of some other period) needs explanation. If medievalism is most broadly understood as the postmedieval borrowing of medieval ideas, narratives, images, and sounds, then it might be said to have begun at the end of the Middle Ages themselves (whenever that might have been). By this definition, Dürer's 1512 portrait of Charlemagne might be considered a medievalist work, as would Pierre Corneille's 1653 drama *Pertharite, roi des Lombards* (loosely based on the history of a seventh-century Lombard king). Correspondingly, certain seventeenth- or eighteenth-century musical works, such as Handel's 1725 opera *Rodelinda, Regina de Langobardi* (whose libretto was based on the Corneille drama just referenced), could also be regarded as medievalist. For the purposes of this handbook, however, we have chosen to exclude these earlier works and instead to begin with the nineteenth century. The early years of this century, as Richard Utz explains in his essay "*Medievalitas Fugit*: Medievalism and Temporality," saw the emergence of a *modern temporality*—a sense of the Middle Ages as a distinct Other that could be investigated with new science-like methodologies.[9] In this sense, questions about the chronological boundaries of medievalism are bound up with a second distinction of the self-referential questions that we articulated in the opening paragraphs of this introduction, concerning the distinction between medievalism and medieval studies. The nineteenth century witnessed the beginnings of scholarly attempts to recover (or reconstruct) the historical materials of medieval music. As Laura K. T. Stokes shows, nineteenth-century medievalists worked to differentiate their scholarly enterprise from the more "fanciful" image of medievalism; the attempts of nineteenth-century historians and theorists to "reconstruct" medieval music mark a clear break with earlier forms of medievalism. In terms of our previous discussion, their work could be seen as an effort to bring the philological approaches of literary studies into the field of music.

The scholarly scientific work of reconstruction functioned in a fascinating and complex dialogue with musical compositions intended in various ways to evoke or represent the medieval period. In part because "authentic" examples of actual medieval music were not yet widely available, references to the Middle Ages in these works tended to rely more on literary themes and other extramusical references. To use terms from Kreutziger-Herr's taxonomy, then, we could say that the medievalism of the nineteenth century was largely *creative*. Although some composers were interested in using medieval melodies in their works, medieval references were far more likely to be produced by more general markers such as modal harmonies, melodic simplicity, rhythmic consistency, and parallelisms. In this sense, the approach that Kreutziger-Herr calls *scientific medievalism* played a less important role in the nineteenth century than it did in the musical culture of later periods. This does not mean, however, that medievalism itself was unimportant: quite the contrary, in fact. Readers of this handbook hardly need to be reminded of the diverse ways in which nineteenth-century artists, architects, novelists, and poets embraced texts and images of the Middle Ages, from Tennyson's *Idylls of the King* to the rebuilding of the Cologne Cathedral, from Sir Walter Scott's *Ivanhoe* to the paintings of the Pre-Raphaelites. Despite the relative paucity of authentic medieval musical texts, then, it is hardly surprising that nineteenth-century composers should also be interested in expressing the character of the Middle Ages and in using medievalist themes to further their aesthetic and ideological goals.

Needless to say, these aesthetic and ideological goals were quite diverse. As was the case in the arts, many nineteenth-century composers were deeply invested in the legacy of the Middle Ages as an expression of national or regional identity, while for others, medievalism was bound up with nostalgia for a lost Catholic or imperial unity. Some engaged with medieval images as part of a romantic escape from modernity, while some used medieval themes or settings as a means of commenting on contemporary social or political structures. The essays in the first section of this handbook take up some of these complex "deployments" of the Middle Ages in the nineteenth century. As we might expect, many of these essays concern opera, arguably the most popular musical form of the nineteenth century and the one in which the connections to the other arts are most apparent. In their contributions to this handbook, Michael S. Richardson and Elinor Olin consider two works (*Genoveva* and *Le Roi d'Ys*, respectively) to reveal crucial and perhaps unexpected ways in which medievalism functioned in nineteenth-century opera. Diana R. Hallman takes up the vital role that medievalism played in French grand opera, while Liana Püschel and Barbara Eichner discuss different forms of medievalism in the works of Verdi and Wagner, respectively. In her contribution to this handbook, Marie Sumner Lott discusses the intersection between medievalism and bourgeois ideologies, while Balázs Mikusi considers the changing role that medievalism played in the works of Franz Liszt. Taken together, the essays of Section 1 testify to the remarkable breadth of medievalism in the musical culture of the nineteenth century, a period before the real music of the Middle Ages was widely known or understood.

At first glance, the essays in Section 2 of this handbook seem to have little in common with those of the first. The topic of this section, "Performing the Middle Ages," points to the revival and reconstruction of medieval music in the twentieth century. As performers and scholars of medieval music will already know, the first wave of the medieval music revival sparked a pursuit for authenticity that matched the professionalization of the discipline of medieval music within the academy. Painstaking theoretical and editorial work (what Kreutziger-Herr would characterize as scientific medievalism) was central both to performers and to academicians during this period, in which the pursuit of authenticity, that is, fidelity to the score, the performance tradition, and, of course, the intentions of the composer (insofar as these could be determined), was the paramount concern. A new stage in the development of these approaches was marked by the 1988 publication of Nicholas Kenyon's symposium *Authenticity and Early Music*, some of whose contributors questioned whether such authenticity was even possible or, indeed, how valuable it was.[10] Questions about performance practice—which paralleled and contributed to broader deconstructionist and poststructuralist trends in the academy—began to dominate musicological discourse on this topic. Richard Taruskin, for example, denied the possibility of historical performance as authentic reconstruction, suggesting that the attention to composer's intentions and original instruments has obscured what is in fact a very modern practice.[11] Daniel Leech-Wilkinson's book, *The Modern Invention of Medieval Music*—which highlighted the inescapably modern interventions involved in restoring medieval music traditions—was also instrumental in shifting understandings of medieval performance.[12] As Leech-Wilkinson showed, personality, culture, and taste were at least as important as concrete evidence in the reconstruction of medieval music.

In this sense, the revival of medieval music may be as embedded in the ideologies of the producers as the romantic medievalism of the nineteenth century.[13] The particular sound and aesthetic that King's College developed for their Lessons and Carols services (discussed by Jacob Sagrans in his contribution to this handbook) provides a case example of the ways in which an ideological investment in historicism and English nationalism functioned in a purportedly medievalist setting. As Sagrans notes, the Lessons and Carols services built on the authority of medieval tradition to create a sense of identity, serving distinctly twentieth-century national agendas and suggesting modes of belonging defined by race, religion, and gender. The medievalism of these King's College services is thus better classified as an example of what Kreutziger-Herr describes as *reproductive* medievalism.

Although music historians and performers freely acknowledge the presentism of their engagement with the past, this acknowledgment has not resulted in a rejection of historically informed performances; rather, it merely acknowledges that performances of medieval music can be free to serve contemporary, artistic, functional, and popular needs as well. As Edward Breen notes in his essay for this handbook, for example, David Munrow's efforts to recreate medieval music clearly reflect the influence of the folk revival of the 1950s and 1960s. The medieval sound developed by David Munrow and others was, in turn, refracted onto the 1970s folk-rock genre and beyond. The revival of medieval music, in short, unfolded in a complex dialogue with twentieth-century forms and genres, even when (or especially when) the link to modernity was disavowed. The Orlando Consort's score for Carl Theodor Dreyer's silent film *La Passion de Jeanne d'Arc*, discussed by Donald Greig in his contribution to this handbook, can be understood in these terms, as an effort to combine historical awareness and creativity in order to "import" medieval music into a twentieth-century genre. The film is acclaimed for more than its historical reconstruction of the life and trial of the medieval figure—its creative and artistic vision, forged in the aesthetics of modernism, were also central to the film's success. The consort's soundtrack for the film—which integrates historically and regionally appropriate music into a contemporary artistic aesthetic—mirrors and reinforces this vision by creating a musical medievalism that both embraces and questions historical alterity.

The enormous scholarly efforts to recover, edit, and interpret the music of the Middle Ages may not have solved questions about authentic performance practice; indeed, the end result of the "authenticity wars" of the 1970s, 1980s, and 1990s may have been simply to show us that authenticity is a chimerical goal. The influence of these scholarly efforts on twentieth-century composition, however, was undeniable. Carl Orff's choral works—to take one example—were informed, in part, by Rudolf von Ficker's scholarship on Gothic polyphony, as well as the sound of organum as it was reconstructed at the end of the 1920s. Arvo Pärt's tintinnabuli technique also shows some indebtedness to medieval sacred music and the sounds of early music. On a more general level, medieval concepts of rhythm—including but not limited to proportionality and isorhythmic ideas—influenced a wide range of composers, even while others were attracted to modal harmonies or certain aspects of the texture of medieval music. As composers became more informed by real medieval compositional techniques or musical practices, they found more diverse ways to engage with the idea of the Middle Ages. Section 3 of this handbook focuses on twentieth-century works created with these medievalist techniques in mind.

The musical medievalism of works such as *Carmina Burana* and *A Ceremony of Carols* is reinforced by the incorporation of texts from the Middle Ages. But twentieth-century musical medievalism is not always so overt. In some cases, composers who were attracted to particular aspects of medieval composition—for example, lack of harmonic direction or rhythmic modes—could incorporate these aspects into their own compositional idiom, mixing them seamlessly with "modern" compositional ideas so that they became an intrinsic part of the composer's individual language. Works created in this manner do not necessarily purport to be medieval, but they do claim to be informed by real medieval compositional techniques or ideas. While certainly something of the medieval idiom might be said to remain and, indeed, even be audible in these cases, the nature of these medievalist references is transformed. In this sense, these works evince the self-reflective quality that we have identified as a more general feature of medievalism.

In both a technical and a semantic sense, therefore, twentieth-century composers seemed to be referencing the Middle Ages in radically new ways, and the medievalist music of this period frequently sounds much different than that produced in the previous century. Indeed, as Kirsten Yri points out in her essay on Orff's *Carmina Burana*, twentieth-century composers could employ musical medievalism to counter the well-worn tradition of romanticism. But if the means by which twentieth-century composers incorporated the medieval into their works differed from those pursued by their counterparts in the previous period, their ideological goals remained in some cases quite similar. As Lisa Colton shows in her contribution, composer Margaret Lucy Wilkins's exploration of medieval compositional techniques allowed her to distance her musical language from modernity. Ralph Vaughan Williams, whose *Mass in G minor* forms the subject of Deborah Heckert's contribution, turned to the Middle Ages to articulate a sense of national identity. If the romantic critique of modernity was a central part of nineteenth-century medievalism, so too was the medievalism of composers such as Pärt and Tavener a means of countering the modernist enterprise to articulate a space for spirituality and reflection. In her essay, Laura Dolp provides a detailed account of this process as it unfolded in Pärt's oeuvre. Aleksandra Vojčić and Anne Stone take somewhat different approaches to the topic of medievalism in twentieth-century compositional practices by focusing on the legacy of a specific medieval codex (in the case of Vojčić) and a specific medieval figure (in the case of Stone). In the music of the twentieth century, then, just as in that of the nineteenth century, medieval ideas and images were used for a diverse and even contradictory set of goals. The Middle Ages might answer the more general call for simplicity and directness, but they were just as often used in connection with modernist complexity. As many of the essays from this section show, the desire for a music of the future inevitably intersected with a yearning for the music of the past.

This desire for a music of the future has been frequently bound up with the desire for social transformation, and in this sense, medievalism can be inherently ideological. The essays of Section 4 take up some of these ideological ramifications by focusing on four female figures: Hildegard of Bingen (in the essay by Jennifer Bain), Joan of Arc (in Elizabeth Dister's contribution), Queen Dagmar (in the essay by Nils Holger Petersen), and the Lady of Courtly Love (in Gillian L. Gower's contribution). These essays illustrate some of the diverse ways in which compensatory history, nationalism, romanticism, and feminist interests have impacted the way the Middle Ages and medieval women are reimagined in our culture. The connections between female figures, romanticism, and nationalism certainly play a role in the reception of music dedicated to Queen Dagmar and Joan of Arc, who offered inspiration and solace during the Nazi occupations of Denmark and France, respectively. The figure of Hildegard von Bingen—who is often constructed as a feminine mystic battling against the strictures of the Catholic

Church—takes on a more iconoclastic role. Viewed as an Enlightened figure, Hildegard is frequently understood as a scientific medical practitioner and healer, and her music is therefore aligned with the natural world. A very different image emerges with the figure of Guinevere, who takes on the guise of an idealized feminine consort at the same time that she embodies a threat to the dominant order. Taken together, then, the essays of Section 4 illustrate the diverse ways in which music intersects with the figure of the medieval woman.

The essays in Section 5—which concern echoes of the Middle Ages in folk, rock, and metal—are but a small number of papers that address this topic. As we intimated previously, the increased availability of early music recordings and antiquarian interests had an important impact on the genres of folk and folk-rock music during the 1960s, especially with regard to texture and timbre. Folk-rock bands Steeleye Span, Pentangle, and Amazing Blondel were among those that drew on traditional styles and modes associated with the Middle Ages, even playing medieval or archaic instruments. Gryphon, Gentle Giant, and Yes were among the progressive rock bands that followed suit, creating a discernible medieval influence that Edward Macan termed *medievalist rock*.[14] Tracing the specifically medieval echoes in the popular music of the late twentieth and twenty-first centuries, however, is made more difficult by the fact that these echoes tend to commingle with references to music from other historical eras. As Susan Fast has shown in a seminal essay for medievalism in rock music, allusions to Tudor music and the Renaissance more generally are caught up in the "conflation of all pre-modern music into one very distant Other" that is still described as medievalism.[15] Developing this thread, Elizabeth Randell Upton notes (in her contribution to this handbook) that even baroque music and the harpsichord can signal a form of nostalgia that parallels the longing for a medieval Other. In music that was arguably mainstream, this interest in the medieval Other peaked with rock bands like Led Zeppelin. As Caitlin Carlos shows in her contribution to this handbook, Led Zeppelin embraced the fantasy world of *The Lord of the Rings* in their concept albums and their lyrics to voice resistance to the destructive "progress" of modernity. For bands from the late 1960s and early 1970s, Carlos notes, the Shire represented the British pastoral landscape and offered a nostalgic pursuit of timelessness.

This form of medievalism, defined by nostalgia and antimodernism, appeared to dissipate during the 1980s, but that is only because it was transmuted to the metal and Goth subgenres of rock that were less visible to the mainstream. As Ross Hagen, Simon Trafford, and Scott R. Troyer all acknowledge, the Gothic rock band Dead Can Dance continued the antimodernist trend in the 1980s, exploding countless genres (e.g., New Age, neofolk, *Mittelalter* rock, doom and Goth metal, Viking metal, and Pagan metal) that engage in more complex ways with medieval imagery and its musical world. Dead Can Dance introduced world music elements into their mix, setting off a range of ethnomedieval engagements that might include Sheila Chandra and Djur Djura and that are certainly transformed in the ethnomedievalism (and eco-activism) of Pagan folk-rock bands discussed by Scott R. Troyer.[16] The backdrop for Troyer's discussion of the German band Faun is the German *Mittelalter* rock scene of Schandmaul, Saltatio

Mortis, and Corvus Corax, whose medieval-inspired folk rock shares an audience with fans from the metal genre for its visual imagery, its virtuosity and linearity, its intensity, and, now largely amplified, acoustic instruments. Here, too, the engagement with sounds that signify a broader geographical definition of the European Middle Ages can be heard, a gesture that is perhaps inspired by Dead Can Dance's reach into the East.

Such incursions frequently engage in more complex ways with medieval imagery and its musical world, playing with medievalism at a metadiscursive level. Some of the musicians active in Viking metal, as Simon Trafford notes in his contribution, have rejected the nationalist imagery of medievalism that was associated with the some of the earlier northern European bands. Viking metal's inclusion of texts and symbols designed to reach a wider geographical region and ethnic base appears to be part of trend toward transnationalism in the neofolk and Pagan metal scenes if Corvus Corax's releases of *Sverker* and *Gimlie* are any indication. Medievalism in the recent metal and Goth genres is also self-reflective about the ways in which they use gendered images. In the bands discussed by Ross Hagen, for instance, the courtly love tradition is deconstructed and problematized in an aesthetic called *beauty and the beast*, and Trafford notes the masculine warrior image of Viking metal as one form of transgression against "civil" society. In this sense, the bands discussed by Ross, Trafford, and Troyer seem to respond directly to cultural tensions that are specific to the late twentieth and early twenty-first centuries. Another is the rejection of Christian religion, whether as an outright dismissal (as in Pagan folk, Viking metal, Gothic rock, and doom metal) or as an exploration of spirituality that is divorced from religious dogma (folk rock and medieval rock). The medievalist activity of rock bands today, moreover, shares some of the imagery of disillusionment and anticapitalism that characterized much of the medievalist music from the more chronologically distant romantic period. In opposition to these earlier works, however, these bands play a fundamental role in questioning grand narratives of nationalism, gender, and religion. In this sense, their aesthetics exemplify the self-reflexivity that we have identified as one of the key characteristics of medievalism in all its diverse manifestations.

Section 6 explores another important site for twentieth and twenty-first century medievalism: film and screen media. The essays in this section concern a wide variety of forms: from cinematic genres such as fantasy, art film, epic, and horror to television and video games. It is hardly surprising that this generic diversity (as well as the diversity in the settings in which the various screen narratives unfold) should also be reflected in accompanying music. In both historical and fantastic cinematic allusions to the Middle Ages, music plays a vital role in creating both a sense of identification and a sense of historical distance. Film composers may draw on aural signifiers (such as the *evil medieval* trope that James Deaville discusses in his contribution to this handbook) in ways to amplify the identification with negative values in a narrative. The use of music by Wagner or by Orff in a film like *Excalibur* (discussed by David Clem in his essay) might be understood as a form of neomedievalism, while the medievalism of Howard Shore's score for the Lord of the Rings films (discussed by Stephen C. Meyer) may have more to do with deep structures than with surface features. In her contribution, Alexis

Luko considers the role of medievalism in two contrasting films from Ingmar Bergman, while John Haines covers the diverse deployments of medievalism in Disney films and the ways in which these forms intersect with corporate franchising. If there is a single factor that unites all the medievalist music discussed in this section, it has to do with the paramount role that music plays in the onscreen narrative flow. In these films, as well as in *Game of Thrones*, discussed by James Cook, and the Harry Potter video games (the topic of Karen M. Cook's contribution) music must be simultaneously distancing and immersive: articulating a sense of Otherness even as it pulls the viewer/player into an alternate world.

In assembling this handbook, our goal has not been to provide a comprehensive overview of music and medievalism; such a task would entail an entire series of handbooks rather than a single volume. What we have attempted to articulate instead is medievalism's potential as a theoretical framework. In terms of both methodology and content, we have cast a broad net, to bring forth a group of essays that showcase some of the diverse approaches and topics that contemporary scholars are pursuing within this growing field. But although our net is broad, it still leaves much to be captured. Our readers will immediately identify numerous examples of music and medievalism that are not touched on in this handbook. One of the most regrettable is the absence of scholarship that takes up musical medievalism generated in regions of the world outside Europe and North America, as well as a lack of scholarship that considers people of color. The gaps between the strands of our net—if we are allowed to develop this metaphor— are all too apparent. While acknowledging these gaps, however, it is our hope that readers will also consider the strands themselves: the links that tie various expressions of medieval-inspired art music, film music, popular music, and historically informed performance together.

Notes

1. *Studies in Medievalism* XVII (2009): "Defining Medievalism(s)"; *Studies in Medievalism* XVIII (2010): "Defining Medievalism(s) II"; *Studies in Medievalism* XIX (2011): "Defining Neomedievalism(s)"; *Studies in Medievalism* XIX (2011): "Defining Neomedievalism(s)." All these volumes are edited by Karl Fugelso and are published by Boydell & Brewer (Rochester, NY).

2. Michelet published his monumental *Historie de France* in nineteen volumes over the period 1833–1867. Volumes 2–6 concern the Middle Ages.

3. Katherine Bergeron, *Decadent Enchantments: The Revival of Gregorian Chant at Solesmes* (Berkeley: University of California Press, 1998).

4. Edward Haymes coined the term in his article "Two-Storied Medievalism in Wagner's *Die Meistersinger von Nürnberg*," *Studies in Medievalism* 3 (1991): 505–513. See also the two *Studies in Medievalism* volumes, "Defining NeoMedievalism," cited previously.

5. Umberto Eco, "Dreaming of the Middle Ages," in *Faith in Fakes: Travels in Hyperreality*, trans. William Weaver (London: Vintage, 1998), 61–72.

6. Annette Kreutziger-Herr, "Medievalism," *Oxford Music Online*, accessed April 12, 2018, http://www.oxfordmusiconline.com.libproxy.wlu.ca/grovemusic/view/10.1093/gmo/ 9781561592630.001.0001/omo-9781561592630-e-0002261008?rskey=petrOY&result=1.

Although the essays of our collection constitute an integrated whole, they are also designed to be read independently. For this reason, then, we have elected to preserve the references and descriptions to this taxonomy within individual essays, even though this material to some extent recapitulates the description that we offer here.

7. Francis Gentry and Ulrich Müller, "The Reception of the Middle Ages in Germany: An Overview," *Studies in Medievalism* 3, no. 4 (Spring 1991): 399–422.

8. Kreutziger-Herr, "Medievalism."

9. Richard Utz, "*Medievalitas Fugit*: Medievalism and Temporality," *Studies in Medievalism* XVIII (2010): "Defining Medievalism(s) II," ed. Karl Fugelso, 31–43, here 32. For a discussion of the medieval Other in musicology, see Annette Kreutziger-Herr, "Postmodern Middle Ages: Medieval Music at the Dawn of the Twenty-First Century," *Florilegium* 15 (1998): 187–205; and Susan Fast, "Days of Future Passed: Rock, Pop and the Yearning for the Middle Ages," in *Mittelalter-Sehnsucht? Texte des interdisziplinären Symposions zur musikalischen Mittelalterrezeption an der Universität Heidelberg, April 1998*, ed. Annette Kreutziger-Herr and Dorothea Redepenning (Kiel: Wissenschaftsverlag Vauk, 2000), 35–56.

10. Nicholas Kenyon, ed. *Authenticity and Early Music: A Symposium* (New York: Oxford University Press, 1988).

11. Taruskin's essays collected in *Text and Act: Essays on Music and Performance* (New York: Oxford University Press, 1995) were especially influential.

12. Daniel Leech-Wilkinson, *The Modern Invention of Medieval Music: Scholarship, Ideology, Performance* (Cambridge: Cambridge University Press, 2002).

13. The bibliography at the end of this handbook provides an overview of the rich scholarship on the modern revival of medieval music.

14. Edward Macan, *Rocking the Classics, English Progressive Rock and the Counterculture* (Oxford: Oxford University Press, 1997), 135.

15. Susan Fast, "Days of Future Passed: Rock, Pop, and the Yearning for the Middle Ages," in *Mittelalter-Sehnsucht? Texte des interdisziplinären Symposions zur musikalischen Mittelalterrezeption an der Universität Heidelberg, April 1998*, ed. Annette Kreutziger-Herr and Dorothea Redepenning (Kiel: Wissenschaftsverlat, 2000), 39.

16. See Chandra's *Weaving My Ancestors' Voices* (1992) and *The Zen Kiss* (1994); and Djura's *A Yemma* (1990) and *Voice of Silence* (1993). These are discussed by Timothy Taylor in *Global Pop: World Music, World Markets* (London: Routledge, 1997).

ROMANTICIZING THE MEDIEVAL: THE LONGING FOR THE MIDDLE AGES IN THE NINETEENTH CENTURY

CHAPTER 1

··

MEDIEVALISMS IN EARLY NINETEENTH-CENTURY GERMAN MUSICAL THOUGHT

··

LAURA K. T. STOKES

NINETEENTH-CENTURY scholars went to no small effort to differentiate the academically respectable field of medieval studies from popular medievalism.[1] Medievalism conventionally implied the fanciful, the fictionalized, the imaginative, or something artfully constructed, while medieval studies indicated the weight of historical facts, research, positivistic manuscript-based methods, and objective truth. It was clear which side the academy would prefer. In the process of enhancing the scholarly reputation of medieval studies in the late nineteenth century, writers whose medieval histories exhibited romanticizing or overtly interpretive tendencies were dismissed or forgotten.[2] Yet the attempt to strongly differentiate medieval studies from medievalism is problematic; from today's perspective, this cannot be a simple matter of differences of source material and narrative construction. As Annette Kreutziger-Herr clarifies in her article on the topic, medieval studies—by virtue of the practices through which it constructed its subject matter—was never purely objective and academic and could ultimately be understood as a form of medievalism. In turn, medievalism was just as likely to be informed by "academic" studies of the Middle Ages as by the "fictionalized" constructions of the era. Medieval studies and medievalism, to put this a different way, continually permeate one another.[3]

This entwining of medieval studies and medievalism was also (not surprisingly) found in early nineteenth-century musical scholarship. The scholarly study of medieval music was in a nascent phase; thus—in part because of the scarcity of and problems with deciphering sources of medieval music—its approach to music and composers from the distant past was marked by a flexible combination of objective and subjective discourse.[4] Although the reception of any music inevitably involves mediation, medieval music both required and invited a high degree of interpretation and even creative intervention—not least because of the relative paucity of sources, unfamiliarity of the notation, and the less than fully documented performance practices. The reception of this music is necessarily a story of constructed transmission from the earliest collections of medieval song; since the sources that have survived typically date from well after the original time of composition, contact with this music has been highly mediated from the time of its earliest surviving records.[5] In addition, although the early nineteenth century was the period of development and implementation of philological and text-critical methodologies, not all writers and scholars immediately took up these methods. These methods, moreover, left open many questions of interpretation concerning the text (or music) and its significance.

Medievalism in its many forms was a powerful intellectual current across Europe in the late eighteenth and early nineteenth centuries; one only need turn to the novels of Sir Walter Scott (1771–1832), the Gothic revival in architecture, or the writings of François-René de Chateaubriand (1768–1848) and Madame de Staël (1766–1817) for oft-cited examples. Some scholars, however, have suggested that medievalism took on a particular character in Germanic lands in the post-Napoleonic era. W. D. Robson-Scott, among others, has argued that medievalism was bound up with the "reawakening of the national spirit" as the German nation(s) emerged from years of invasion and occupation by the French.[6] The trauma of the Napoleonic Wars and resulting disillusionment with the social and cultural promises of the Enlightenment transformed people's relationship with history in particular ways in German territories; the devastation wrought on the German landscape during the wars was perceived not only as damage to (or negation of) material artifacts and lives by an outside and unnatural force, but also as the destruction of human memory.[7] The task of uncovering, reconstructing, and reading artifacts from the past to revive (or ignite for the first time) a sense of the specificity and contingency of German history became the task of "patriotic intellectuals," who were to encourage "the people to see themselves as Germans."[8]

The nature of nineteenth-century German medievalism, however, was manifold, thus eluding any attempt to (in David Blackbourne's words) "anatomize the 'German mind'" through a singular definition.[9] Although there is a tendency in musical scholarship to associate German medievalism with German nationalism in an uncomplicated way, an understanding of the diversity in early nineteenth-century German medievalisms leads to a broader palette of interpretive possibilities. There were many medievalisms, including some that were not particularly nationalistic—and, of course, there was a wide range of nationalisms as well.[10] Although certain strands of early nineteenth-century German nationalist medievalism were later turned toward deeply troubling purposes (for example, the appropriation of medievalism by the Nazis), early nineteenth-century German medievalism and German nationalism formed a complex relationship, into which individual writers and musicians fit in unique ways. The historian David Barclay has constructed a taxonomy that engages this interplay of medievalisms and nationalisms; in it, he distinguishes five types of medievalism in nineteenth-century Germany: cosmopolitan, Christian-German, national-liberal, escapist, and official.[11] The first type—cosmopolitan medievalism—predated the Napoleonic Wars; Barclay sees it essentially as "innocent of nationalist enthusiasm."[12] Christian-German medievalism, in Barclay's scheme, appeared after 1806 and centered on a rejection of French ideas and values (especially those that led to revolution) and a focus on the medieval as a means by which to glorify religion. When it takes on a political cast, this strand of medievalism tends to be highly conservative. Barclay discerns, however, that there were also links between liberal thinkers and medievalism; for example, Gothic monuments could be perceived as instances of the historical collective achievements of the German people. Escapist medievalism was the use of the medieval as a means of rejecting industrialization and urban mass society with its concomitant political unrest (this strand is best represented by Ludwig II of Bavaria and his castle, Neuschwanstein). Official medievalism, in Barclay's view, came into effect largely after 1871 with the coalescing of the German Empire; this involved the use of medieval imagery to promote the empire as legitimate and unified through a long-standing history.

All of Barclay's types have an overt or implicit political or ideological element, which forms a point of contact with another taxonomy that will be important to my discussion, namely, the classification of medievalisms in music that Kreutziger-Herr delineates in the essay referred to above. Kreutziger-Herr describes four different modes or forms of medievalism, namely: productive, reproductive, scientific, and political. Although apparently objective—or at least not intentionally imaginative—writing about medieval music appears to fit comfortably into a "scientific" mode of medievalism, elements of productive and reproductive medievalism can also be located in nineteenth-century scholarship, particularly when such scholarship "translates" medieval music and its world for a contemporary audience. Early nineteenth-century German scholarship about medieval music can be understood through both Barclay's and Kreutziger-Herr's taxonomical systems simultaneously. Barclay presents his political medievalisms as self-contained; interplay between them occurs, however, in many instances of nineteenth-century music, writing, and art. Barclay's medievalisms (all of which fit into Kreutziger-Herr's political category) also necessarily engage with at least one of Kreutziger-Herr's three other modes of medievalism (productive, reproductive, or scientific).

While not necessarily comprehensive for all work that was done on medieval music in the nineteenth century, these taxonomies of medievalism clarify ways in which medieval music could bear manifold and possibly mutually exclusive meanings for different constituencies. In the remainder of this essay, I will examine works by three German-language writers on medieval music—Anton Friedrich Justus Thibaut, Raphael Georg Kiesewetter, and Friedrich Heinrich von der Hagen—to illustrate an array of approaches to and objectives for the study of medieval music.[13] A nationalistic perspective is overtly present only in the case of Hagen's writing. Kiesewetter takes an evolving and somewhat ambiguous position on nationalist sentiment, and it is difficult to detect any hint of nationalism in Thibaut's musical writings. In all cases, however, the presence of medieval music performs some kind of social, spiritual, or intellectual work, which may thus enfold an implicitly political message, even if that message is not nationalistic.

Examination of these writer's works thus demonstrates a range of potential meanings carried by the medieval in Germanic areas in the aftermath of the Wars of Liberation.

Medieval Music: An Imprecise Definition

Although there was a great deal of interest during the first half of the nineteenth century in what is now termed medieval music, there was no consensus as to the chronological borders of the Middle Ages and no commonly understood definition of it as a music-historiographical period. These ambiguities were also present in the history of the arts more generally. A great deal has been written on the topic of exactly when historians of the arts began to differentiate between a medieval and a Renaissance period as distinct historical-aesthetic entities.[14] Although a concept existed as early as the fourteenth century of an era that followed and was separate from antiquity (*media tempora*), its chronological boundaries, especially the termination point, remained under debate.[15] One can trace the origins of the term Renaissance from the historian Jules Michelet to the art historian Jacob Burckhardt; in music history, August Wilhelm Ambros—influenced by Burckhardt—is generally credited as the first to differentiate a period of the Renaissance, in the third volume of his history of music (1868).[16] Before Ambros, the widespread music-historical understanding—at least in Germany—was of a long medieval period, sometimes termed the Gothic period, which included much of what is now considered Renaissance music. In 1826, for example, an anonymous German author termed the year 1555 "the Middle Ages of music."[17] The period now understood as the Renaissance was also sometimes called "the second part of the Middle Ages."[18] Indeed, Kiesewetter's essay "Ueber den weltlichen und volksmässigen Gesang im Mittelalter" (On secular and folk music of the Middle Ages) discusses music from the twelfth through the sixteenth centuries, implying through the title that he included sixteenth-century music under the rubric of Middle Ages; the author terms this time span "the long period of the Middle Ages."[19] Thus, the concept of a long Middle Ages is widely applicable to German historical music studies in the early nineteenth century.

Thibaut's *Über Reinheit der Tonkunst*

Anton Justus Friedrich Thibaut's life (1772–1840) was divided between his professional activities as a professor at the University of Heidelberg—where he was a respected scholar of pandect law—and his no-less-absorbing activities as the organizer of a well-known amateur *Musikverein* (singing society) and writer on music. The singing society, which attracted luminaries including Robert Schumann, Felix Mendelssohn, Jean Paul,

G. W. F. Hegel, and Carl Friedrich Zelter, gathered regularly in Thibaut's home for evenings of performing largely sacred works in a sober and devotional atmosphere.[20]

Although less remembered today, Thibaut and his writings on early music were well regarded and widely read in the nineteenth century. *Über Reinheit der Tonkunst* (*On Purity in Music*) was first published in 1825; this was quickly followed by a greatly revised and enlarged second edition in 1826. This second edition became the basis for numerous other German editions; it ran to at least seven editions in Germany in the nineteenth century, a scholarly edition appeared in 1907, and there were two nineteenth-century translations into English.[21] This proliferation of editions confirms the widespread interest that it generated. Schumann used quotations from *Über Reinheit der Tonkunst* as mottoes under the masthead of the *Neue Zeitschrift für Musik* eight times between 1835 and 1837 (i.e., long after he left Heidelberg), which shows not only his deep engagement with and absorption of Thibaut's thought, but also a desire to disseminate it to his audience.[22] Schumann later made reference to Thibaut in the foreword to the second edition of *Album für die Jugend* (1850), recommending Thibaut's book as future reading material for the young player.

Thibaut's goal in writing about early music was to awaken interest in it for its moral and spiritual power. For this reason, he was primarily concerned with sacred, specifically church, music.[23] There is little in the way of a nationalistically oriented agenda in evidence. Although *Über Reinheit der Tonkunst* is, with reason, now mostly seen as a participant in the nineteenth-century Palestrina revival (which itself, in light of the long medieval period, is part of medievalism), an often-overlooked aspect of this work is Thibaut's fascination with the music of early Christianity.[24] The opening of the first chapter of the 1825 edition asserts the existence of not one but two periods in which church music reached the highest state of perfection: the first five centuries after Christ and later in the fifteenth and sixteenth centuries, culminating in the works of Palestrina.[25] The music of the early church, that is, its *first* music, per Thibaut, has a power to affect the human soul that reaches beyond anything in the contemporary church. He says of it,

> there are the most pressing reasons to keep the original music of each church pure and unaltered.... It is an indisputable truth, that songs that innocently and simply come forth from an exalted and deeply moved soul have an indescribable magic that never grows old.[26]

This indescribable power inherent in the early music of the church, a power of purity and innocence that is the effusion of an exalted soul, suggests that Thibaut sees in this music the potential for a needed and longed-for source of spiritual renewal. Such a modern-day renewal would include, as an effect, an end to sectarianism; Thibaut, himself a Protestant, suggests that Protestant churches would benefit from taking up some of the oldest music (in his understanding) of the church, even though this music—namely, Gregorian and Ambrosian chant—was, by the nineteenth century, generally associated with Catholicism. The power of this music, for Thibaut, is not in its theological or dogmatic significance, but in its historical associations with ardent and uncomplicated religious feelings. He says,

> Only through the return to older [music] will the Protestant churches overcome the spirit of sectarianism, and each individual church should strive to incorporate the truly exemplary music of all other churches.... thus, those in the Protestant churches should return to Ambrosian and Gregorian songs, and adopt the best of them. Indeed these songs, which originated from the purest exaltation, are one of the most beautiful inheritances from the older church, and they should also be preserved by the Protestants, since their church will in this way be more connected to a venerable past, and so will acquire more honor in the eyes of the people.[27]

A problem remains for Thibaut, however: Precisely this music is inaccessible and/or indecipherable. Gregorian and Ambrosian chant as it has been transmitted through the Catholic Church is in a state of decay, he says, even in the Sistine Chapel; thus, a turn to the music of the contemporary Catholic Church will not do.[28] He holds out a modicum of hope for recovery of the original music through two tactics: first, the deciphering of a manuscript at the monastery of St. Gall, which Thibaut believes to hold the entirety of original Gregorian chant intact; and second, the close examination of Greek and Russian Orthodox Church music, which Thibaut believes represents a tradition that remained unbroken from the second and third centuries CE to the nineteenth century.[29] Regardless of whether these tactics could have produced Thibaut's desired results, it is notable that his approach to recovering or reconstructing early music is not bounded by national or denominational considerations, but demonstrates a measure of cosmopolitanism in the service of Christian renewal (perhaps combining elements of Barclay's cosmopolitan medievalism and Christian-German medievalism). Yet he also yearns for authenticity in rediscovering both the musical text and the spiritual content of early music (touching on Kreutziger-Herr's category of reproductive medievalism).

Thibaut does not include any examples or transcriptions of the early Christian (pre-Palestrina) music that he discusses, although he did own collections of Gregorian chant and other early church music, which he greatly valued.[30] His goal was not to provide new readings of medieval musical texts, but rather to shed light on this music's imagined spiritual meaning and effect and to encourage others to embrace it. To him, the earliest church music—that is, medieval music—remains a nexus of longing and desire, not just for the music itself, but also for the spiritual power associated with the fervor of a unified and uncorrupted religion.

Thibaut's book ignited controversy in the musical press, a central component of which was a multipart critique by Hans Georg Nägeli that appeared in six consecutive issues of the *Literatur-Blatt* (a child publication of the *Morgenblatt für gebildete Stände* from the publisher Cotta) in 1825.[31] A focal point of Nägeli's criticism was that Thibaut's emphasis on the old at the expense of the new served to inhibit musical progress; Nägeli also faulted Thibaut, however, for overlooking what he believed to be the most important historical period in church music: the Reformation and its associated German composers.[32] The critique and Thibaut's response (along with other pertinent commentary) were republished in a volume entitled *Der Streit zwischen der Alten und Neuen Musik* (The Conflict between Old and New Music), which leaned strongly toward Nägeli's position.[33] In the preface, the anonymous editor declared that the effect of Thibaut's book was to "inhibit...if not kill" musical progress in Germany and suggested that Thibaut's views were not only "wrong" but also "un-German."[34] It is clear that Thibaut's contemporaries discerned, and in some cases were outraged by, his lack of nationalistic feeling in his views on the long medieval period in music. Yet the enduring popularity of Thibaut's book over the course of the nineteenth century indicates that his cosmopolitan ideas—which enfolded a search after a certain authenticity in spiritual and musical reproduction—continued to have traction in at least some musical circles.

Kiesewetter on the Music of the Middle Ages

Although Thibaut's correspondent Raphael Georg Kiesewetter (1773–1850) was an amateur musician and music scholar, his contributions to musical life in his resident city of Vienna as well as to the emerging discipline of musicology throughout Europe were monumental.[35] A court administrator by profession, he entered the Austrian Army in 1794, rose through numerous positions in the government, including direction of the chancellery, and was elevated to the nobility in 1843.[36] Outside his military and governmental career, however, Kiesewetter focused his talents and energies on music. One of the founding members of the Gesellschaft der Musikfreunde, he was voted its vice president in 1821, a position he retained for more than twenty years.[37] Kiesewetter also held a series of private historical concerts in his home that focused on seventeenth- and eighteenth-century music.[38] He played the flute, bassoon, and guitar and possessed a fine bass voice. Kiesewetter is remembered today, however, for his prolific and wide-ranging writing on music; his books and essays span in subject matter from tuning systems to general music history, biography, and even Arabic music.[39]

In his *Geschichte der europäisch-abendländischen oder unserer heutigen Musik* (History of European-occidental or our Current Music) (1834), Kiesewetter included a substantial amount of (what we would now call) medieval music history in a monograph intended for a broad, nonspecialist readership.[40] Because of the progressive framework of his history—in which the past is examined to explain the present—his concept can be seen as ultimately deriving from the Enlightenment models (i.e., the music histories written by Charles Burney and Johann Nikolaus Forkel) with which he was intimately acquainted.[41] His scientific approach to his material leads him to focus on the specifics of music theory and interpretation of musical notation. Kiesewetter's musical judgments presuppose the existence of absolute standards of musical taste and excellence, rather than demonstrating any hint of cultural relativism. And by these standards, much music of the medieval period does not hold up well.

Table 1.1 The "Epochs" in Kiesewetter's *Geschichte der europäisch-abendlän-dischen Musik*

Chapter	Central figure/figures	Years (all CE)
Introduction	[None: on the origins of Christian church music]	"From the beginning of the Christian calendar to the end of the ninth century."[42]
I	Hucbald	901–1000
II	Guido	1001–1100
III	"Without names."[43]	1101–1200
IV	Franco	1201–1300
V	Marchettus and de Muris	1300–1380
VI	Dufay	1380–1450
VII	Ockenheim [Ockeghem]	1450–1480
VII	Josquin	1480–1520
IX	Hadrian Willaert [Adrian Willaert]	1520–1560
X	Palestrina	1560–1600
XI	Montiverde [Monteverdi]	1600–1640
XII	Carissimi	1640–1680
XIII	Scarlatti [Alessandro Scarlatti]	1680–1725
XIV	"Epoch of the Modern Neapolitan School. Leo and Durante"	1725–1760
XV	Gluck	1760–1780
XVI	Haydn and Mozart	1780–1800
XVII	Beethoven and Rossini	1800–1832

Kiesewetter's framework is postulated in a series of "epochs," most of which center around one or two "great men" (they are all men; see Table 1.1).

Kiesewetter's stated reason for this approach is to separate the history of music from other types of history, including from political history. He says,

> I am of the opinion, that art, in its fate, creates its own historical periods, which as a rule, do not align with the history of the world in general or of particular states, nor does it have anything in common with them. Art, which is the common property of humanity, does not cohere with the political divisions of Empires. And division according to artistic schools (in those periods, that is, in which we can even speak of such things) is in music history the most useless and specious of them all, while the boundaries of real or purported schools according to time and place, indeed in part their existence as such, may be difficult or impossible to ascertain, and while this division all-too-often puts the historian in a quandary, especially in the absence of reliable and complete information, that at the cost of his own conviction and thus also the truth, [he must] accept or augment data, in order to force everything into a predetermined compartment.[44]

This music history is thus—in theory—entirely self-contained and should reject any hint of nationally oriented thinking. (In practice, Kiesewetter does not manage to exclude political and social history completely.[45]) Although the surface structure consists of a series of individuals who contribute to the long-term "progress" of music history, Kiesewetter has a secondary but nonetheless crucial agenda: namely, to trace the history of the development of compositional techniques, with a focus on tonality, harmony, and counterpoint. This agenda generates a framework that enables his history to proceed without reference to anything outside music (for the most part). With an end goal in mind of contemporary compositional techniques and language, it becomes possible to view music history as progressing. This forms the basis of Kiesewetter's aesthetic judgments; he views developments that lead toward modern compositional language and techniques more positively than those that do not. Kiesewetter considers harmony the defining characteristic of "our"—that is, of European—music, which he differentiates from ancient Greek music or Asian music.[46] He therefore evaluates theorists and composers primarily in terms of their contributions to the development of counterpoint and harmony. For example, Marchettus of Padua and Johannes de Muris are praised for banning parallel consonances, the Netherlands school (headed by Dufay) is lauded for its "advanced counterpoint," and an important effect of early music printing was that it promoted progress of "harmonic art."[47]

Kiesewetter's pronouncements on early medieval music (as opposed to medieval theory), however, are noticeably negative. He indicates that there was a disconnect between theory and practice, in which composers and practicing musicians should have taken up the ideas of theorists, but failed to do so:

> These already-mentioned teachers [i.e., Franco of Cologne, Marchettus of Padua, and Johannes de Muris] had not only already put the *mensura* in good order, but also left behind very good (if insufficient) rules for harmony—or, as they called it, discant—and in such a way prepared the path by which art very soon should have progressed to greater and more significant perfection. That this was not, in fact, the consequence, can only be explained in that it was typical in earlier times to see music more as an object of scholarship than as art, and to treat it accordingly.[48]

Regardless of whether this statement is logical (is it really likely that developments in theory had nothing to do with practice?), it enables Kiesewetter to treat early medieval music dismissively while still embracing theory for its potential to lead to later musical developments. Of the few composers and compositions he is aware of from the time before Dufay, he has little good to say. Although he includes an example of a three-voice work by Adam de la Halle in an appendix, for example, he casts doubt on the idea that Adam wrote the counterpoint himself, and at any rate, he does not think that the music could have been enjoyable, even in its own time.[49] When it comes to Guillaume de Machaut, Kiesewetter is outright mocking. For many years, he writes, he understood a Gloria by Machaut to be nothing but the work of a "brash dilettante" who "decided once to dabble in composition"; thus, he was startled to learn that this Mass was actually performed for a royal audience.[50] Francesco Landini's music, according to Kiesewetter, is characterized primarily by "the immoderate use of a kind of syncopation," although he is given credit for managing to avoid parallel fifths and octaves.[51] These depictions suggest that Kiesewetter believed early medieval composers, on the whole, to be hopelessly flailing in their attempts to discover how music "should" be composed.[52] Only when he gets to Dufay and the composers of the Netherlands school does Kiesewetter begin to view the music more positively; this improvement is, specifically, a result of their use of counterpoint.[53]

Despite Kiesewetter's strongly negative aesthetic reaction to medieval music, he nonetheless included several examples of it in the final section of his *Geschichte*, called "Die ältesten Monumente eines figurirten Contrapunctes" (The Oldest Monuments of Figured Counterpoint). Here appear works by the much-maligned de la Halle and Machaut, along with a chanson by an unnamed composer, a canzona from Landini, and excerpts from masses by Dufay, Eloy (i.e., Eloy d'Amerval), Vincentius (i.e., Guillaume) Faugues, and Ockeghem. In most of these examples, Kiesewetter presents a replica of the "original" notation and then its *Entzifferung* (decoding or deciphering); although he may not have enjoyed medieval music sonically, it appears that he took intellectual, scientific pleasure in puzzling out the unfamiliar notation.

In a review in *Eutonia*, Kiesewetter's *Geschichte* was praised for its avoidance of national or provincial divisions and focus on progress in musical art and scholarship, as well as its accessibility to a wide audience.[54] Nonetheless, Kiesewetter's book—like Thibaut's—was criticized for a lack of an adequate amount of German-oriented content, including its minimal discussion of the composers Walther, Senfl, and Luther.[55] The final chapters of Kiesewetter's book came under particular fire for their perceived neglect of current German composers. The *Eutonia* reviewer wrote scathingly, "The great changes in the German musical world in the last twenty years are completely unknown to him; he [Kiesewetter] is only a Viennese scholastic; he does not understand his German Fatherland; he is not really a German."[56] Although Kiesewetter had attempted to avoid the national and political in his *Geschichte*, that lack itself was seen as a refusal to engage; perhaps intended as cosmopolitanism, his work could nevertheless be perceived as a form of escapism.

Kiesewetter changed his mind about at least some medieval music a few years later, as is seen in his essay "Ueber den weltlichen und volksmässigen Gesang im Mittelalter."[57] Here he discusses secular music of the medieval period—including that of the troubadours and trouvères, a topic that was largely passed over in his *Geschichte*, with its focus on harmonic developments. His take on troubadour and trouvère music is noticeably more positive than his views on medieval music in his *Geschichte*; this is thanks to the "natural" (i.e., not rule-bound) qualities of this music and its close relationship to folk music. The essay traces the course of secular song up to the development of monody at the end of the sixteenth century.

Here, Kiesewetter comments substantially on how the music of the Middle Ages had been and would best be transcribed for and conveyed to a nineteenth-century audience. He notes that in Burney's *History of Music*, five troubadour songs had been presented in modern notation with the addition of piano accompaniment and text translation into English. Indeed, the type of translation of medieval notation that Burney undertook was a typical and well-respected practice in eighteenth-century musical scholarship.[58]

Kiesewetter nonetheless distances himself from this practice, saying that these melodies were not composed with harmony in mind, and therefore the addition of modern harmony is "forced."[59] He notes, moreover, that "the least artfully-enhanced interpretation of the notation of the earlier periods is, in my opinion, the one that comes closest to the truth," indicating that Kiesewetter perceives his goal in examining music to be the pursuit of objectivity.[60] Nonetheless, Kiesewetter acknowledges a continued need for and practice of editorial intervention and mediation between this music and the reader: "The translator must, therefore, allow himself certain liberties, more often having to do with the poetic meter than the significance of the figures; to add in caesuras, pauses, and breaths that are not shown in the original, etc."[61] He also suggests that troubadour melodies are written in tonal language (major and minor) and show a tendency toward modulation to the dominant.[62] Thus, although Kiesewetter rejects some aspects of his predecessors' tendency to translate medieval music into a modern guise, his approach to the transcription and editing of music retains elements of mediation and interpretation, and he explains formal-harmonic structures in terms of eighteenth- and nineteenth-century music theory—perhaps an extension of his tendency to view music history in general as leading toward contemporary compositional techniques.

Kiesewetter approaches medieval music as an object of intellectual interest and a step in the development of modern music. Kiesewetter's take on medieval music lacks the spiritual and religious dimension, as well as the emotional longing and nostalgia, found in Thibaut's writing; instead of looking to the past for a model, he examines the past to show how it led to the present. When it comes to the musical texts, even while he distances himself from the approach of scholars who preceded him (who dramatically altered medieval music to make it more approachable to a contemporary public), he admits the need for editorial intervention. In short, although on the surface Kiesewetter has a scientific and reproductive take on medieval music (in terms of Kreutziger-Herr's taxonomy), there are distinct elements of the productive and creative in his approach, particularly with editing practices and the narrative framework of development of compositional techniques.

Although the existence of Friedrich Heinrich von der Hagen's research on the music of the *Minnesinger* (which I will discuss in the following section) had been reported by the music scholar Andreas Kretzschmer as early as 1827, Kiesewetter was apparently unaware of it in 1838.[63] Kiesewetter states that "we would all like to believe, as German patriots," that the music of *Minnesingers* was not inferior to that of the troubadours, but (Kiesewetter believes) no trace of *Minnesinger* music is to be found.[64] His self-identification here as a German patriot adds an intriguing element to his otherwise generally nonnationalistic orientation toward medieval music history—although it may also have been a response to the earlier critical assertion that he was not really a German. Although Kiesewetter wished to construct a music history that was independent of political history, he could not avoid the problem that nineteenth-century music-historical scholarship itself was intimately bound up with contemporary politics. That the connection to patriotic feeling would appear with Kiesewetter's mention of the *Minnesinger* is perhaps not a coincidence; with the publication of Hagen's multivolume tome on the *Minnesinger*, this particular corner of medieval musical studies became tied to an overtly German nationalistic outlook.

Friedrich Heinrich von der Hagen, Professor Fischer, and *Minnesang*

Friedrich Heinrich von der Hagen (1780–1856) made his name as a Germanist and philologist, not as a music scholar; nonetheless, his influence on nineteenth-century musical life, both through his early translations of the *Nibelungenlied* and through his multi-volume edition of *Minnesang*, was extensive. Hagen was educated in law and worked in the legal profession in Berlin for some years before giving it up to pursue an academic position in early German literature, an area of long-standing interest for him. Although he did not join the military during the Napoleonic Wars, he demonstrated an increasingly patriotic attitude in his private and public writings during that time.[65] During a research trip in 1816–1817 (supported by the Prussian government), meetings with nationalistic and religious colleagues solidified his self-identification as a conservative Prussian Protestant.[66] From 1824 until his death in 1856, he was a professor of German language and literature at the University of Berlin (now Humboldt University); he also published numerous translations of Middle High German and Nordic literature. His 1838 compendium of *Minnesang*, entitled *Minnesinger: Deutsche Liederdichter des zwölften, dreizehnten und vierzehnten Jahrhunderts*, was intended as a complete edition of *Minnesinger* poetry from the twelfth through the fourteenth centuries. This work marks another shift in the study of medieval music in Germany toward an overtly Christian-German perspective (to use Barclay's taxonomy), underpinned by scientific methodologies, that in many ways presages the later official medievalism of the German Empire.

Hagen was not the first to publish an edition of *Minnesinger* poetry, although his approach was broader than that of his predecessors and, significantly, this edition was the first to attempt to engage with and explicate the music of *Minnesang*. In 1758–1759, the Swiss philologist Johann Jakob Bodmer had published a two-volume *Sammlung von Minnesingern aus dem schwæbischen Zeitpuncte*, based on the texts included in the Manesse Codex, which was at that time held at the (then) Royal Library in Paris. Next, in 1803, Ludwig Tieck published a newly edited *Minnelieder aus dem schwäbischen Zeitalter*. Based to some extent on Bodmer's earlier work, Tieck's edition found a degree of popular success and a wide readership that the previous edition of *Minnelieder* had not.[67]

Hagen's 1838 edition included not only the *Minnesinger* texts found in the Manesse Codex, but also the Jena, Heidelberg, and Weingartner manuscripts, as well as a Neithart manuscript that was in Hagen's own possession.[68] The sheer scope of Hagen's work on Middle High German lyric poetry has never been equaled; it remains a reference for the study of *Minnesang* to this day.[69] The first three volumes encompass the poetic texts; the fourth volume includes biographical information on the *Minnesinger* (as well as text-critical remarks), ten pages of lithograph reproductions of manuscript pages, most of which appear to include music notation, thirty melodies found in the Jena manuscript, forty melodies found in Hagen's own manuscript, an essay by the music scholar Professor Fischer ("Ueber die Musik der Minnesinger"), and three of the melodies arranged with piano accompaniment and transcribed into modern notation.[70]

The introductory pages of Hagen's work illustrate the underlying nationalistic and promonarchical perspective. Hagen had again received direct financial support from the Prussian government for the travel involved in the project, which is acknowledged both through the dedication (which is to Friedrich Wilhelm III of Prussia) and through the address to the king that follows.[71] Hagen describes an intense vision of the cultural-historical entity he is trying to convey through this work, which is a deeply nationalistic, promonarchical image of a Germany organized through a strictly differentiated social hierarchy, relating backward and forward through time to the current ruling houses of Prussia and Austria:

> The picture of the old splendor of the German Fatherland, particularly rich and vivid, appears in these manifold voices of the most meaningful and active Life, as their direct expression. Here enters—in the most powerful, most brilliant, and most fateful time of the Holy Roman-German Empire, the Hohenstaufens (close allies of Your Majesty's Hohenzollern ancestors), through the tortuous intermediate realm until the establishment of the Habsburg Empire—a choir of nearly two hundred singers, all enthusiastic for *Minne*, in the highest and holiest as well as the carefree, secular sense, for the beauty of women and of spring, as well as for the Holy Sepulcher, for lord and Fatherland, for native culture and custom, for all the joys and sorrows of life, to transfigure pain to glory through song. After the Emperor, who is the highest head of worldly glory, the representatives of the entire great Empire follow here in a long immeasurable parade: kings, dukes, margraves, landgraves, princes, counts, barons, nobles, knightly vassals, secular clergy, monastic brothers, bourgeois masters, to the traveling singers and players, who were also often knights.[72]

The social hierarchy depicted here excludes the lowest social classes; Hagen considers *Minnesang* the inheritance of the nobility. The celebratory image of the parade, headed by the emperor and including a long train of noble musicians, is reminiscent of the tradition of festive entrance parades, which had for centuries been a component of the celebration of major dynastic events for European monarchies.[73] In this way, Hagen's imaginative description links the publication of his compendium of poetic texts to the ongoing viability of the Prussian and Austrian monarchies; Hagen's edition itself becomes a kind of dynastic event.

Hagen also reinforces the consciousness that the *Minnesang* genre is *musical* (and not just poetic) in the introduction, in a section called "Presentation, Song."[74] He notes the "inseparable relationship of the melodies and the construction of the [text] strophes" and sketches the connections between word syllabification, pronunciation, and the number of notes per word likely found in *Minnelieder*, as well as the generic interchange between sacred and secular music.[75] He also notes that *Minnesang* was composed in the church modes, linking *Minnesang* and contemporary German Protestant chorales.[76]

Further details of interpretation of the musical notation are left to the essay by Fischer, found in the fourth volume. Fischer (perhaps unknowingly echoing Kiesewetter) notes that *Minnesinger* music is not likely to be pleasing to contemporary tastes, even when it is embellished with an accompaniment.[77] He contextualizes *Minnelieder* music in a discussion of text–music relations in general, with particular attention to rhythmic values and both musical and poetic meter. Fischer then endeavors to explain the notation found in the *Minnelied* manuscripts. Since the manuscripts exhibit differing notational practices, no single interpretation of individual signs will suffice; even the same sign may have variant meanings in different contexts or manuscripts. The manuscripts also document differing aspects of the music: for example, there may or may not be clefs, and formal repetitions may or may not be indicated. When the same *Minnesang* appears in different manuscripts, Hagen (and possibly his collaborator) compared them for alternative readings. Fischer concludes that, in many cases, aspects of musical rhythm and meter in *Minnesang* directly reflected the poetic meter of the text. Three of the melodies that were included in the pages of manuscript lithographs are given as examples in modern notation with piano accompaniment (which is in no way independent of the text); metrical and rhythmic aspects of the melody are worked out according to the text. The goal of the musical essay as a whole is to encourage composers to pay more attention to the historical aspects of song composition, rather than to pursue virtuosity, and to pay greater heed to poetic form in their musical settings.[78]

Although the bulk of Hagen's edition consisted of *Minnesinger* poetry, it was nonetheless prominently and positively noted in the musical press. C. F. Becker suggested that composers make use of it to "warm and inspire their imaginations."[79] G. W. Fink was even more effusive in his praise, which makes explicit the role that Hagen's work was to play in awakening German national feeling, specifically among musicians:

> It is right for a German musician of our time at a minimum to acquire a general picture of our Fatherland's old and venerable singers, who from the higher oaks of dawning groves, under which they sleep in honored memory, in the immortal glory of ghostly sounding voices, like us, are awakened.
>
> As much from that time (like their castles, sunken in ruins) of a unified Germany (which has become almost like a fairy tale) as is necessary for us to elevate the memory of our father-singers, is presented here, in brief, to the friends of music, so that no one can be ensnared by the delusion that our German Fatherland at any time cultivated music and song any less than any other peoples of the earth.[80]

Thus, Hagen's work was received as a force to awaken German national-musical feeling and to cultivate awareness and pride in Germany's (unified) music history. This epitomizes the overlap between medieval studies and medievalism that I described: Hagen's approach is based on manuscript studies and philological, text-critical methodologies, but this is in the service of a highly imaginative and political outcome, that of reviving a sense of German history and identity.

Conclusions

....

This exploration of these writers' works has illustrated a range (although far from a comprehensive one!) of possible responses to medieval music found within a brief time span of a decade and a half (1825–1838) in the early nineteenth century. Following Kreutziger-Herr's formulation, each of these authors constructs a different kind of subject out of medieval music. Without attempting to categorize these individuals and their work rigidly, it is clear that different forms of medievalism came together in their thinking. Blending the frameworks constructed by Kreutziger-Herr and Barclay, one can find elements of Christian-German medievalism in Thibaut's writing, but also cosmopolitanism and reproductive medievalism (although without, sad to say, the ability to execute the reproductions he longs for). In Kiesewetter's work, we find a tendency toward reproductive and scientific medievalism, but also creative, interpretive elements, elements of liberalism (with his view that art belongs to humanity and of the importance of folk music for art song), and perhaps even escapism in his attempt to reject social and political aspects of music history. Kiesewetter's *Geschichte* also illustrates the dangers of judging the past by present-day criteria. Hagen demonstrates both scientific and Christian-German, conservative-nationalistic medievalism; he best epitomizes the idea of the "reawakening of the national spirit" that Robson-Scott considered the essence of the nineteenth-century German approach to history. Indeed, Hagen, with his relationship to the ruling house of Prussia, presages the official medievalism that would become part of the public relations toolkit of the German Reich. But political motivation stemming from the rulers of the various German nations was not the only cause of the slow move toward nationalism in medieval studies; the critical press also played a role in pushing authors to make a public declaration of their German patriotism.

The wide-ranging potential significances of medievalism found in writing on music suggest that the same approach could be effectively applied to nineteenth-century medievalist music. After all, nineteenth-century composers took up medieval topics with enthusiasm; Wagner's operas are only the most famous of a large repertoire of opera, song, and even instrumental music that engaged with the musical culture of the long Middle Ages. Exploration of these works through the lens of one or more medievalisms could potentially open up a new interpretive domain and enrich our ideas of how nineteenth-century composers engaged with the distant past.

Notes

1. Kathleen Biddick, *The Shock of Medievalism* (Durham, NC: Duke University Press, 1998), 1–2.
2. Ibid., 3.
3. Annette Kreutziger-Herr, "Medievalism," *Oxford Music Online*, accessed July 13, 2017, http://www.oxfordmusiconline.com/subscriber/article/grove/music/2261008. For a discussion of Kreutziger-Herr's entry, see the introduction to this handbook.

4. John Haines, *Eight Centuries of Troubadours and Trouvères: The Changing Identity of Medieval Music, Musical Performance and Reception* (Cambridge: Cambridge University Press, 2004), 160.

5. Ibid., 14–18.

6. W. D. Robson-Scott, *The Literary Background of the Gothic Revival in Germany: A Chapter in the History of Taste* (Oxford: Clarendon Press, 1965), 301.

7. Peter Fritzsche, *Stranded in the Present: Modern Time and the Melancholy of History* (Cambridge, MA: Harvard University Press, 2004), 93–94.

8. Ibid., 123. I would argue that this tendency does not equate to the notion, previously common in German historical scholarship, of the *Sonderweg*. The *Sonderweg* idea indicates that the Germanic focus on traditional culture and *Bildung* led to a lack of bourgeois political and civic engagement, which allowed for the rise of fascism in the twentieth century. The *Sonderweg* construct has more recently been dismissed; see Pamela M. Potter, *Art of Suppression: Confronting the Nazi Past in Histories of the Visual and Performing Arts* (Oakland: University of California Press, 2016), 178–179. In addition, the nineteenth-century authors discussed in this essay were all politically engaged, either in their music writing or in their nonmusical careers, thus contradicting the notion that a focus on the past led to a disregard for present-day political concerns.

9. David Blackbourn and Geoff Eley, *The Peculiarities of German History: Bourgeois Society and Politics in Nineteenth-Century Germany* (Oxford: Oxford University Press, 1984), 161.

10. For further reading on the complex nature of early nineteenth-century German nationalism, see Matthew Levinger, *Enlightened Nationalism: The Transformation of Prussian Political Culture 1806–1848* (Oxford: Oxford University Press, 2000).

11. David E. Barclay, "Medievalism and Nationalism in Nineteenth-Century Germany," in *Medievalism in Europe*, ed. Leslie J. Workman, *Studies in Medievalism* V (Cambridge: Brewer, 1994), 5–22.

12. Ibid., 7.

13. Along with Hagen's collaborator, Professor Fischer.

14. See, for example, Jessie Ann Owens, "Music Historiography and the Definition of 'Renaissance,'" *Notes* 47, no. 2 (1990): 305–330; James Haar, "Music of the Renaissance as Viewed by the Romantics," in *Music and Context: Essays for John M. Ward*, ed. Ann Dhu Shapiro (Cambridge, MA: Harvard University Press, 1985), 126–144; and Andrew Kirkman, "'Under Such Heavy Chains': The Discovery and Evaluation of Late Medieval Music before Ambros," *19th-Century Music* 24, no. 1 (2000): 89–112.

15. Annette Kreutziger-Herr, *Ein Traum vom Mittelalter: Die Wiederentdeckung mittelalterlicher Musik in der Neuzeit* (Köln: Böhlau Verlag, 2003), 90–91. Kreutziger-Herr mentions a case (without citation) of the French Revolution itself being named as the endpoint of the Middle Ages.

16. Owens, "Music Historiography," 305. In the process of examining materials for this essay, however, I discovered that François-Joseph Fétis had used this terminology in 1834, in a review of Kiesewetter's book *Geschichte der europäisch-abendländischen oder unserer heutigen Musik*; "Littérature musicale: Revue de nouveautés: 1, *Geschichte der europæisch-abendlœndischen...*," *Revue musicale* VIII, 31 (August 5, 1834): 243: "Les travaux du savant musicien, auteur de l'*Histoire de la musique de l'Euope occidentale*, ont eu principalement le Moyen-Âge et la renaissance pour object." It is not clear where Fétis would have placed the boundary of the Renaissance, however, since Kiesewetter's *Geschichte* does not use the term Renaissance and covers music history continuously until 1832. In addition, Michelet's

Histoire de France (Paris: Hachette, 1835–1867) includes a discussion of Martin Luther's music, which he calls the "true heart of the Renaissance," Michelet, *Histoire*, vol. 8, 108–109. This volume of the *Histoire* was published in 1855, thus postdating Fétis's comment, but this strengthens the case that the concept of a music-historical Renaissance was established in France several decades before it reached Germany.

17. *Der Streit zwischen der Alten und Neuen Musik* (Breslau: Förster, 1826), 113: "Es kann diese Zeit [1555] das Mittelalter der Musik genannt werden." This book, discussed below in the section on Thibaut's *Über Reinheit der Tonkunst*, is a compilation of the debates over Thibaut's book; the section quoted, however, appears to have been written by the anonymous compiler.

18. Kreutziger-Herr, *Ein Traum vom Mittelalter*, 94.

19. Raphael Georg Kiesewetter, "Ueber den weltlichen und volksmässigen Gesang im Mittelalter," *Allgemeine musikalische Zeitung* XL, 15 (April 11, 1838): 233: "die lange Periode des Mittelalters."

20. Martin Staehelin, "Anton Friedrich Justus Thibaut und die Musikgeschichte," *Heidelberger Jahrbücher* XXXIV (1990): 41.

21. These editions are Heidelberg: J. C. B. Mohr, 1825, 1826, 1851, 1861, 1873, 1884, and 1893; W. H. Gladstone's translation of the 1825 edition (London: Murray, 1877), John Broadhouse's translation of the 1826 edition (London: Reeves, [1882]), and Raimond Heuler's scholarly edition (Paderborn: Ferdinand Schöningh, 1907). Heuler's dating of the first edition to 1824 is based on a misreading of the Goethe–Zelter correspondence; Zelter discussed Thibaut's book in a letter from December 1825.

22. These mottoes are found in the following issues of the *Neue Zeitschrift für Musik*: July 24, 1835; August 7, 1835; January 8, 1836; February 9, 1836; November 18, 1836; September 15, 1837; October 10, 1837; and October 13, 1837.

23. Thibaut does express interest in and respect for "national songs," but this interest encompasses a range of nationalities, including Jewish, Greek, English, Scottish, Russian, Danish, etc. See Thibaut (1826), 12 and 74–93.

24. Staehelin, "Anton Friedrich Justus Thibaut und die Musikgeschichte," 42. Although Staehelin mentions the convergences between E. T. A. Hoffmann's views, especially as expressed in his 1814 "Alte und neue Kirchenmusik," and Thibaut's views, the extent of Hoffmann's influence on Thibaut is not clear. Thibaut does not specifically refer to Hoffmann in *Über Reinheit der Tonkunst*, although he does mention several other contemporary writers on music.

25. Thibaut *Über Reinheit der Tonkunst* (1825), 7.

26. Thibaut *Über Reinheit der Tonkunst* (1826), 11–12. "Aber auch abgesehen davon waren die dringendsten Gründe vorhanden, die Urchoräle jeder Kirche rein und unverletzt zu erhalten.…immer wird es doch eine unbestreitbare Wahrheit bleiben, daß Gesänge, welche unschuldig und einfach aus einem begeisterten, tiefbewegten Gemüth hervorgingen, einen nie veraltenden, unbeschreiblichen Zauber haben."

27. Ibid., 25–27. "Allein bei der Rückkehr zum Alten sollte auch aus den protestantischen Kirchen aller Sectengeist verschwinden, und jede einzelne Kirche sollte sich beeifern, die wahrhaft musterhaften Gesänge aller anderen aufzunehmen.…so sollte man in protestantischen Kirchen auch auf die Ambrosianischen und Gregorianischen Gesänge zurückgehen, und sich die vorzüglichsten derselben aneignen. Denn diese Gesänge, aus der reinsten Begeisterung entstanden, sind eine der schönsten Überlieferungen der älteren Kirche, welche auch von der Protestanten wie ein Heiligtum bewahrt werden sollte, weil

ihre Kirche sich dadurch mehr mit einem ehrwürdigen Alterthume in Verbindung setzten, und so für das Volk noch mehr Würde bekommen würde."

28. Ibid., 14.

29. Thibaut was not alone in this belief about the St. Gall manuscript; see Katherine Bergeron, *Decadent Enchantments: The Revival of Gregorian Chant at Solesmes* (Berkeley: University of California Press, 1998), 72–74. On Orthodox music, see Thibaut *Über Reinheit der Tonkunst* (1826), 7, 29–30.

30. See the *Verzeichniss der von dem verstorbenen Grossh. Badischen Prof. der Rechte und Geheimenrathe Dr. Anton Friedrich Justus Thibaut zu Heidelberg hinterlassenen Musiksammlung* (Heidelberg: Groos, 1842), 34–35.

31. Hans Georg Nägeli, "Zeichen der Zeit im Gebiete der Musik," *Literatur-Blatt* (October 28, 1825; November 1, 1825; November 4, 1825; November 8, 1825; November 11, 1825; and November 15, 1825). Thibaut countered with a rebuttal in the same publication on December 6, 1825.

32. Nägeli, "Zeichen der Zeit" (November 4, 1825): 351–352.

33. *Der Streit zwischen der Alte und Neue Musik* (Breslau: Förster, 1826).

34. *Streit*, I: Thibaut's book would "das Fortschreiten der Deutschen in der wahren und rechten Kunst nichts weniger als fördernd, sondern vielmehr hemmend, wenn nicht gar tödtend." Further on, the anonymous editor calls Thibaut's point of view "diese falsche, undeutsche Ansicht" (*Streit*, IV). It is worth noting that the publisher of this book was also a publisher of new compositions; thus, this firm had a pecuniary interest in new musical works achieving popularity.

35. On Thibaut and Kiesewetter's correspondence, see Herfrid Kier, *Raphael Georg Kiesewetter (1773-1850): Wegbereiter des musikalischen Historismus*, Studien zur Musikgeschichte des 19. Jahrhunderts, Bd. 13 (Regensburg: Bosse, 1968), 242–243. It is unlikely that Thibaut and Kiesewetter ever met, and although they had a cordial professional relationship, there was very little agreement in their views.

36. Kier, *Raphael Georg Kiesewetter*, 17.

37. Ibid., 29.

38. Ibid., 31.

39. See Kier, *Raphael Georg Kiesewetter*, 97–166, for an annotated list of Kiesewetter's publications on musical subjects.

40. R. G. Kiesewetter, *Geschichte der europäisch-abendländischen oder unsrer heutigen Musik: Darstellung ihres Ursprunges, ihres Wachsthumes und ihrer stufenweise Entwicklung; Von dem ersten Jahrhundert des Christenthumes bis auf unsre Zeit* (Leipzig: Breitkopf & Härtel, 1834). This was translated into English by Robert Müller in 1848 with the title *History of the Modern Music of Western Europe: From the First Century of the Christian Era to the Present Day* (London: Newby, 1848).

41. Kirkman, "The Discovery and Evaluation," 103.

42. Kiesewetter, *Geschichte*, 1.

43. Ibid., 26: "Ohne Namen." In the 1848 English translation, Robert Müller gives this chapter heading a more pointed meaning: "Not distinguished by the name of any particular individual."

44. Ibid., 10: "Ich bin der Meinung, dass die Kunst in ihren Schicksalen sich selbst ihre eigenen Geschichtperioden bildet, welche in der Regel mit jenen der allgemeinen Welt- und der besonderen Staatengeschichte nicht zusammen treffen, auch mit diesen in der That nichts gemein haben; dass die Kunst, ein Gemeingut der Menschheit, auch mit der politischen Eintheilung der Reiche nicht zusammenhängt, und dass die Eintheilung nach Kunstschulen

(in jenen Perioden nämlich, wo von solchen nur überhaupt eine Rede seyn kann) in der Geschichte der Musik die unbrauchbarste und trügerischeste von allen ist, weil die Gränzen der (wirklichen oder vorgeblichen) Schulen nach Zeit und Ort, ja zum Theil deren Existenz, als solcher, schwer oder gar nicht zu erweise seyn möchte, und weil diese Eintheilung den Historiker allzu oft in die Verlegenheit setzt, zumal bei Mangel zuverlässiger und vollständiger Nachrichten, auf Kosten der eigenen Ueberzeugung, somit auch der Wahrheit, Data anzunehmen oder zu ergänzen, um nur Alles in eines der vorgezeichneten Fächer zu zwängen."

45. For example, he acknowledges that court and papal patronage had a significant effect on artistic movements in the sixteenth century; Kiesewetter, *Geschichte*, 54–57, 64–66.

46. Ibid., 8: "Diese von uns so genannte Harmonie...ist ganz und allein unsrer Musik eigen."

47. Ibid., 39, 46, and 56.

48. Ibid., 42: "diese eben genannten Lehrer [Franco, Marchettus, and de Muris] nicht bloß die Mensur sehr wohl geordnet, sondern auch für die Harmonie, oder (wie sie es nannten) für den Diskants, schon gute, wenn auch nicht genügend Regeln hinterlassen, und solchergestalt die Bahn ziemlich geebnet hatten, auf welcher die Kunst sehr bald weiter und zu bedeutender Vollkommenheit hätte gefördert werden sollen. Dass dies in der That noch nicht erfolgt war, lässt sich nur daraus erklären, dass man von Alters her gewöhnt war, die Musik mehr als einen Gegenstand der Gelehrtheit, mehr als Wissenschaft, denn als Kunst anzusehen, und demgemäss zu behandeln."

49. Ibid., 37.

50. Ibid., 40–41: "Ich habe es, so lange ich es kenne, für das Machwerk eines kecken Dilettanten gehalten, der...sich irgend einmal vermass, sich auch noch in einer musikalischen Composition zu versuchen."

51. Ibid., 41: "Bemerkenswerth ist daran der unmässige Gebrauch einer Art von Syncopation."

52. Since Kiesewetter thought of the Middle Ages as extending through the sixteenth century, he regarded Machaut and Landini as early medieval composers.

53. Ibid., 46. Kreutziger-Herr (*Ein Traum vom Mittelalter*, 115–118) suggests that Kiesewetter's disregard for Léonin and Pérotin's roles in the development of counterpoint stemmed from a desire to downplay the accomplishments of French medieval composers; she points out that both John Hawkins in his *General History of the Science and Practice of Music* (1776) and Ernst Ludwig Gerber in his *Historisches-biographisches Lexikon* (1790–1792) mention Léonin and Pérotin; thus, they were already known to music historians. However, their roles in the development of polyphony were misunderstood: Hawkins is not clear on the definition of *organum* and suggests that Léonin may have instead been an "organist;" Gerber notes that Pérotin was a "*Kontrapunktist*" but then translates "*Descanter*" as "*Singmeister*" (or singing-master). Indeed, Léonin and Pérotin were not well known for their role in the development of polyphony until Charles Edmond Coussemaker's 1864 edition of the Anonymous IV treatise. Thus Kiesewetter, writing in the 1830s, can perhaps be excused for his disregard of Léonin and Pérotin as polyphonists. That is not to say that Kiesewetter did not engage in subtle nationalism in his other writings; see, for example, his 1829 essay, "Die Verdienst der Niederlander um die Tonkunst," in which Kiesewetter makes a point that Franco of Cologne was German and not, as previously believed, French. (*Verhandelingen over de vraag Welke verdiensten hebben zich de Nederlanders vooral in de 14°, 15° en 16° eeuw in het vak der toonkunst verworven; en in hoe verre kunnen de Nederlandsche kunstenaars van dien tijd, die zich naar Italien begeven hebben, invloed gehad hebben op de muzijkscholen, die zich kort daarn a in Italien hebben gevormd?* [Amsterdam: Muller, 1829], 6.)

54. "Ueber geschichtliche Werke der Musik," *Eutonia* X (1837): 225–226.

55. The reviewer perceives Kiesewetter's neglect of early Lutheran composers as stemming from his (Kiesewetter's) Roman Catholicism; "Ueber geschichtliche," 226. The reviewer's view of Catholicism, however, does not seem to have directly led to the accusation that Kiesewetter was "not really a German" (below), which stems more from Kiesewetter's disregard of contemporary German composers. (The same reviewer generously praises Kiesewetter's treatment of St. Gregory and Palestrina.) Certainly, confessional identities were gradually rehardening in early nineteenth-century Germany (in contrast to the relative tolerance of the late eighteenth century), but confessional strife and confession-based nationalism had not yet reached the peak that would occur in the later nineteenth-century *Kulturkampf*. Some major Protestant political figures, including Friedrich Wilhelm IV of Prussia, exhibited a conciliatory attitude toward Catholics, not least because the Catholic Rhineland had been enfolded into Prussia as a result of the Congress of Vienna. In addition, many well-regarded early nineteenth-century Protestant composers were fascinated by Catholic music. See Joel F. Harrington and Helmut Walser Smith, "Confessionalization, Community, and State-Building in Germany, 1555–1870," *The Journal of Modern History* 69, no. 1 (March 1997); and James Garratt, *Palestrina and the German Romantic Imagination: Interpreting Historicism in Nineteenth-Century Music* (Cambridge: Cambridge University Press, 2002), especially chap. 3: "The Protestant Palestrina Revival."

56. Ibid., 227–228: "Ihm ist die große Veränderung in der deutschen Musikwelt seit 20 Jahren wie steinfremd; er ist nur ein Wiener Stubengelehrter; er kennt sein deutsches Vaterland nicht; er ist kein eigentlicher Deutscher."

57. See n20.

58. Haines, *Eight Centuries of Troubadours*, 89.

59. Kiesewetter, "Ueber den weltlichen," 240.

60. Ibid., 240: "Die am wenigsten gekünstelte Auslegung der Notation jener frühern Periode ist meines Erachtens diejenige, die sich am meister der Wahrheit nähert."

61. Ibid., 240: "Die Uebersetzer mussten daher wohl in vielen Stellen sich gleichergestalt Freiheiten gestatten, oft mehr das poetische Metrum, als die Geltung der Figur berücksichtigen; Einschnitte, Pausen oder Suspirien unterschieben, wo dergleichen im Originale nicht angezeigt sind u.s.w."

62. Ibid., 241.

63. [Andreas] Kretschmer, "Treie Aufsätze. Ueber deutsche Musik des Mittelalters," *Berliner allgemeine musikalische Zeitung* 4, no. 17 (April 24, 1827): 129.

64. Kiesewetter, "Ueber den weltlichen," 234: "Bekanntlich ist von den Melodieen unserer Minnesänger (Zeit- und Kunstgenossen der Troubadours) bisher keine Spur aufgefunden worden … vielleicht (wir wollen es als deutsch Patrioten gern glauben) haben sie [i.e., the Minnesinger] den Troubadours an Kunst, Geschmack und Erfindung, auch in musikalischer Beziehung nicht nachgestanden."

65. Eckhard Grunewald, *Friedrich Heinrich von der Hagen 1780–1856: Ein Beitrag zu Frühgeschichte der Germanistik* (Berlin: de Gruyter, 1988), 21–22.

66. Ibid., 23.

67. Kreutziger-Herr, *Ein Traum vom Mittelalter*, 67.

68. The Manesse Codex was still in Paris at that time, although it is now held at the University of Heidelberg. On the philological approach in Hagen's edition, see Grunewald, *Friedrich Heinrich von der Hagen*, 185–199.

69. Grunewald, *Friedrich Heinrich von der Hagen*, 196.

70. Ibid., 423, indicates that the author of the essay is an "E. Fischer," without additional details. This may be Gottfried Emil Fischer (1791–1841), author of *Ueber Gesang- und Gesangsunterricht* (Berlin: Oehmigke, 1831).

71. Grunewald, *Friedrich Heinrich von der Hagen*, 191.

72. Friedrich Heinrich von der Hagen, *Minnesinger: Deutsche Liederdichter des zwölften, dreizehnten und vierzehnten Jahrhunderts*, Bd. 1 (Leipzig: Barth, 1838), [viii–ix]: "Das Bild der alten Herrlichkeit des Deutschen Vaterlandes erscheint in diesen manigfaltigen Stimmen des sinn- und thatvollsten Lebens, als dessen unmittelbarster Ausdruck, vor allen reich und anschaulich. Hier tritt in der mächtigsten, glänzendsten und verhängnisvollsten Zeit des heiligen Römisch-Deutschen Kaiserreichs, unter den, den nahen Hohenzollernschen Ahnherren Euer Majestät befreundeten Hohenstaufen, durch das verworrene Zwischenreich hin bis zur Herstellung unter den Habsburgern, ein Chor von beinahe zweihundert Sängern auf, Alle begeistert für Minne, im höchsten und heiligen, wie im heitern, weltlichen Sinn, für Frauen- und Frühlingsschöne, wie für das heilige Grab, für Fürsten und Vaterland, für heimische Zucht und Sitte, für alle Freuden und Leiden des Lebens, im Liede auch das Weh zur Wonne verklärend:—im langen unabsehbaren Zuge, nach dem höchsten Haupte der Weltherrlichkeit, dem Kaiser, folgen hier die Vertreter des gesammten großen Reichs, Könige, Herzöge, Markgrafen, Landgrafen, Fürsten, Grafen, Freiherren, Edle, ritterliche Dienstmannen, Weltgeistliche, Klosterbrüder, bürgerliche Meister, bis zu den fahrenden Singern und Spielleuten, welche auch oft zugleich Ritter waren."

73. See Edmund A. Bowles, *Musical Ensembles in Festival Books 1500–1800: An Iconographical & Documentary Survey*, Studies in Music 103 (Ann Arbor, MI: UMI Research Press, 1989).

74. Hagen, Bd. 1, XXXVIII: "Vortrag, Gesa[n]g" (misspelling in the original).

75. Ibid., XXXVIII: "die unzertrennliche Verbindung der Sangweise und des Strophenbaus," and XXXVIII–XXXIX.

76. Ibid., XXXIX.

77. Ibid., Bd. 4, 853.

78. Ibid., Bd. 4, 862.

79. C. F. Becker, "Literatur: Die Minnesinger des 12., 13. und 14. Jahrhunderts," *Neue Zeitschrift für Musik* XIII, 28 (October 3, 1840): 111.

80. G. W. Fink, "*Minnesinger. Deutsche Liederdichter des zwölften, dreizehnten und vierzehnten Jahrhunderts*" (review), *Allgemeine musikalische Zeitung* 43, no. 46 (November 17, 1841): 937: "Es gebührt einem teutschen Musiker unserer Zeit, mindestens ein allgemeines Bild von jenen altehrwürdigen Vaterlandssängern zu gewinnen, die von höheren Eichen dämmernder Haine, als wir, umrauscht wurden, unter denen sie schlafen in der Ehre des Andenkens, im unvergänglichen Ruhme geisterhaft tönender Stimmen. Nur so viel aus jener, gleich ihren Burgen, in Ruinen gesunkenen Zeit eines fast märchenhaft gewordenen vereinten Teutschthums, als uns zur Erhebung des Gedächtnisses an unsere Sängerväter durchaus nothwendig ist, werde hier den Musikfreunden in Kürze dargelegt, damit Niemand sich von dem Wahn umgarnen lasse, als habe unser teutsches Vaterland zu irgend einer Zeit Ton- und Gesangeslust weniger gepflegt, wie irgend ein anderes Volk der Erde."

CHAPTER 2

FROM KNIGHT ERRANT TO FAMILY MAN

Romantic Medievalism in Brahms's Romanzen aus L. Tiecks Magelone, *op. 33 (1865–1869)*

MARIE SUMNER LOTT

JOHANNES BRAHMS (1833–1897) composed romantic medievalist works throughout his life. His first published work, the Piano Sonata in C Major (1853), includes "an old German *Minnelied*" at the beginning of the Andante second movement, and one of his last compositions, the F-major "Romance" composed in 1893 and published in his op. 118 set of *Klavierstücke*, invokes the medieval romance tradition of the troubadours, as filtered through earlier piano romances.[1] Between these two works, Brahms set ostensibly medieval or *altdeutsch* texts in songs and choruses as well as newer poetry filled with chivalric and courtly images to create works filled with romantic longing, resignation, and nostalgia.[2] Like the artists, musicians, and writers who came before him, Brahms understood the Middle Ages as a period filled with possibilities. For nineteenth-century creators and their audiences, this era represented a world on the cusp of change, sometimes portrayed as a kind of Eden before the fall, but more often depicted as a complicated world mirroring the struggles of the present. For Brahms and his contemporaries, evoking the medieval era in newly created works offered an opportunity to examine current social and political issues from a safe temporal distance.

Brahms's most prolonged engagement with medievalism occurred in the 1860s, a decade in which he saw both tragedies and triumphs in his personal and professional life. He visited Vienna, where the city's most respected musicians and critics embraced his music, and the success of *Ein deutsches Requiem* (A German Requiem) catapulted him to national fame; but the initial reception of his first piano concerto was mixed, at best, and he was continually overlooked for a permanent position in his hometown of Hamburg. Brahms also mourned the death of his mother in 1865, his intense relationship with Clara Schumann experienced many ups and downs, and his brief courtship and engagement to Agathe von Siebold ended when he callously broke off their affair, apparently telling her, "I cannot be bound."[3] The coincidence of these events has led some previous scholars to treat the medievalist works of the 1860s, especially the dramatic cantata *Rinaldo* (op. 50, 1869), in purely personal terms, as musical autobiography expressing Brahms's decision at the beginning of the decade to renounce marriage and pursue a monkish bachelor's life in service to art.[4] But Brahms's medievalist works, like all his music, reach beyond his personal circumstances to address the broader public and express communally held ideals, in addition to any personal, private expressions of love and allegiance they may convey.[5]

In the contemporaneous song cycle *Romanzen aus L. Tiecks Magelone* (op. 33, 1865–1869), Brahms provides a rich musical exploration of one man's journey from youthful naiveté and insecurity to maturity and self-knowledge. The song cycle sets poems from Ludwig Tieck's *Liebesgeschichte der schönen Magelone und des Grafen Peter von Provence* (Romance of the Fair Magelone and Count Peter of Provence), first published in 1797 and reissued in the collection *Phantasus* of 1812. The story takes place in a medieval atmosphere of chivalry and courtly love. Peter, a young knight, is inspired by a traveling minstrel's song to leave the comfort of his family's castle to seek his fortune in a faraway land. Peter sees the beautiful Magelone, princess of Naples, at a tournament and falls instantly in love with her; he woos her in song and they elope to return to his homeland. When they are separated through implausible events on the journey, they both lament their fate and pledge to live and die true to their love for one another. They are reunited at the end of the work—again, through implausible, but not fantastical, circumstances—and the tale ends happily. Each chapter of Tieck's brief story ends with a song sung by the protagonist or another character in the narrative. Brahms set fifteen of the eighteen song texts and published them in Tieck's original order; Rieter-Biedermann released Songs 1–6 in 1865 and Songs 7–15 in 1869.[6]

This narrative of adventure and self-discovery clearly resonated with Brahms (in his thirties at the time of composition) and his own coming of age, but it also speaks to a nearly universal experience of personal growth and development in modern society. In fact, the main outline of Tieck's folk tale follows the basic structure of the late eighteenth-century and early nineteenth-century *Bildungsroman*, or novel of development, first made famous by Goethe's *Wilhelm Meisters Lehrjahre* (William Meister's Years of Apprenticeship, 1795–1796).[7] But, as the first section of this essay will explain, it also belongs to a later group of romantic reactions to and critiques of that genre and the supposed culture of conformity it came to represent. By the time Brahms encountered the tale, the "king of romanticism" had become a man out of step with the artistic and political currents of his day.[8] When Tieck died in 1853, he was eulogized as a great theater director and one of the leading lights of a bygone era.[9] In the 1850s and 1860s, new trends in German literary life reflected the disappointments of the mostly failed revolutions of 1848 and the social changes brought by industrialization and urbanization in the new era. The analysis of Brahms's song cycle that follows shows how Brahms's music offers a reconciliation between the past and the present, between romanticism and realism. As in some of his other works from this period, Brahms adopts medievalist or "chivalric" musical gestures and other archaizing features in the first half of the cycle to connect the narrative's portrayal of youth and possibilities to early romantic notions of the medieval as a wellspring of artistic renewal.[10] The second half of the cycle then abandons those archaisms in favor of a more unaffected style rooted in later nineteenth-century song traditions and appropriate to the work's overarching narrative of growth and increasing security. In this way, Brahms updates Tieck's early romantic fairy tale for the new age, using the techniques of later nineteenth-century realism to make the revolutionary ideals represented by romantic medievalism applicable for a new generation of artists and their audiences.

The Middle Ages in Romantic and Realist Literature

As previous scholars have noted, Brahms was an avid reader and a devotee of authors associated with German romanticism as it flourished in literature and philosophy ca. 1790 to 1820. Brahms's library, documented by Kurt Hofmann, contained many volumes by Novalis (the pseudonym of Georg Philipp Friedrich Freiherr von Hardenberg), Jean Paul (Johann Paul Friedrich Richter), and E. T. A. Hoffmann. During the 1850s, Brahms occasionally signed compositions and letters "Joh. Kreisler Jun." (Johannes Kreisler, junior), associating himself with Hoffmann's tragic fictional *Kapellmeister*.[11] But few studies of Brahms and his music in the first half of his professional life (ca. 1850 to 1869) take into account the wider context of his fascination with these early nineteenth-century authors.[12] Scholars have, by and large, failed to acknowledge that romanticism as represented by these figures and even by later romantics had fallen well out of fashion in the German literary world by the time Brahms began to incorporate their ideas into his own mature artworks. As early as the 1830s, writers associated with the Young Germany movement decried what they understood as romanticism's apolitical concerns, its emphasis on the metaphysical rather than the immediate needs of present-day society.[13] Writing of the then sixty-two-year-old Tieck, Heinrich Heine noted, "A certain feeble-mindedness is and ever was to be observed in him. This want of decision is only too perceptible in all that he did or wrote. Certainly there is no independent character in his works. His first manner shows him a mere nothing, his second as a true and trusty squire of the Schlegels, and his third as an imitator of Goethe."[14] That Heine published this essay describing Tieck's work in the past tense while Tieck was still active as the court theater director in Dresden and as a writer and theater critic speaks to the open hostilities between the older and younger generations during the Vormärz era.

In the 1850s–1860s, when Brahms began his public career as a pianist and composer, poetic realism became the primary artistic and literary movement in German-speaking regions. Like their Young German predecessors, realist authors sought to replace romanticism's focus on the fantastical and ideal with a more grounded attention to everyday life.

Theodor Storm and Gottfried Keller would be the standard-bearers for the new style, and Brahms owned volumes by both authors, in addition to a wide selection of other medievalist novels, novellas, and collections produced after 1850. Thus, to really understand Brahms's medievalism, we must investigate both the origins and cultural context of the texts that he chose to set, such as Tieck's Magelone poems, and the literary culture of the later decades in which he developed his compositional voice and in which his works were first heard by the public.

Tieck's *Liebesgeschichte der schönen Magelone* combines elements from two related traditions within German romanticism. Based on a French romance first transmitted in German in a sixteenth-century chapbook, or *Volksbuch*, it clearly belongs to the artistic folk-tale or fairy-tale tradition that proliferated at the turn of the century.[15] Because the story concerns a young man's journey of self-discovery, it also draws on the model of the *Bildungsroman*. Tieck's generation responded to Goethe's Wilhelm Meister novels with a mixture of reverence and disgust; the notion of a work that could so aptly mirror the inner life of a subject and express the experience of that person's self-cultivation and maturation made it a model that would be imitated throughout the century by German, French, and English writers. But the triumph of commerce over poetry that Novalis would rail against in his critique of the work as "a novel against the romantic" also prompted the younger generation to create an alternative in the so-called *Kunstlerroman*, a novel based on the development of an artist or poet and his philosophy of art. Novalis's own (unfinished) *Heinrich von Ofterdingen*, published posthumously in 1802, offers just such an alternative. Tieck collaborated with Wilhelm Heinrich Wackenroder on a similar artistic treatise in novel form, *Herzensergießungen eines kunstliebenden Klosterbruders* (Outpourings of an Art-loving Friar, 1797), and contributed his own version in *Franz Sternbalds Wanderungen* (Franz Sternbald's Wanderings, 1798). All these novels of self-discovery share a literary structure comprising a series of episodes or encounters, a focus on the inner life and thought of the protagonist (often at the expense of forward-moving plot development), and interpolated songs or poems. The later reactions also share an emphasis on northern European medieval and Renaissance art, in opposition to the focus on classical Greek and Roman models in works by Goethe and Schiller. Works like these communicated the central tenets of romanticism also being espoused by the Schlegel brothers in their journal *Athenaeum*.

The romantics loved what they knew of the Middle Ages, and their work to revive and revitalize public interest in this period continued to influence later authors for several decades. In addition to stories, novels, and plays set in a fantasy-tinged Middle Ages, Tieck edited a collection of *Minnelieder* (*Minnelieder aus dem Swäbischen Zeitalter*, 1803), translating them from the Middle High German of their original sources into modern German and smoothing out the language so that they would be accessible to the average poetry reader of the 1800s. His other medievalist collections and compilations, such as his translation of Ulrich von Liechtenstein's *Frauendienst* (1812), stories based on the legend of the song contest at the Wartburg (*Der Tannenhäuser*, 1812), and tales from the *Niebelungenlied* (*Siegfrieds Jugend* and *Siegfried der Drachentöter*, both from 1804), similarly addressed the German reading public rather than scholars, making aspects of ancient German history available to a wider populace.[16]

A direct descendent of these early romantic medievalist works was Joseph Victor von Scheffel's novel *Ekkehard* (1855), based on the life of Ekkehard II, a monk and poet at the Abbey of St. Gall during the tenth century. *Ekkehard* has been described as the most popular historical novel of the nineteenth century; it was continually in print into the twentieth century, with new editions and translations released every decade.[17] Brahms owned this and two of Scheffel's other medievalist works: a collection of poems titled *Frau Aventiure: Lieder aus Heinrich von Ofterdingens Zeit* (Lady Adventure: Songs from the Time of Heinrich von Ofterdingen, 1863) and the novel *Juniperus: Geschichte eines Kreuzfahrers* (Juniperus: History of a Crusader, 1871). Scheffel's novels privilege stories about hearth and home and celebrate the middle-class values of economy, humility, piety, and domesticity, but they also convey a sense of resignation typical of the later, postromantic approach to the distant past. Sheffel's works imply that the major significant individuals have already lived and that history has passed over the author/reader.[18]

Authors active in the second half of the century embraced poetic realism to express the ambiguity and uncertainty of a generation coming to terms with new political and social realities in the wake of the 1848 uprisings throughout Europe.[19] Their works, which are frequently set in the distant past, are less purely escapist than Scheffel's novels, with more frequent and overt commentary on contemporary concerns; many of their works openly criticize bourgeois prejudices and the materialism of modern urban life. The role of the artist in society is a central issue, as is the conflict between idealism and pragmatism. Gottfried Keller's *Der grüne Heinrich* (Green Henry, 1854–1855, revised 1879–1880) exemplifies the poetic realist approach to the *Bildungsroman* and the social concerns that characterized literature and other artworks of the post-1848 era, such as Brahms's *Magelone Romanzen*. It traces the development of a young man of "above-average sensibility" from youthful innocence and idealism to a resigned practicality and from artistic egocentrism to a life in service to the community. As with other novels in this tradition, though, the ending of *Der grüne Heinrich* is ambivalent, colored with resignation rather than triumph. Henry's mother dies alone while he travels from city to city in search of artistic fulfillment (in the later version he arrives home just in time to say a last goodbye). After returning to his hometown, he lives out his days alone as well, working as a civil servant. He remains unmarried despite having a strong attraction to a local girl who returns his affection but agrees to a platonic relationship, both seeming to sacrifice personal, private happiness to honor their public duty. Thus, to a certain extent, Keller's novel embraces the broad outlines of the *Bildungsroman* as Goethe's descendants understood it, though with a more earnest sense of duty and consequences than Wilhelm Meister and with a less manifesto-like tone than Novalis's *Heinrich von Ofterdingen* or Tieck's *Franz Sternbald*.

In this and other realist works, the central conflicts appear irreconcilable, so that the protagonists must find a way to live in the world that is, rather than attempt to create a world as they wish it to be. This feature is the key difference between authors from the early romantic school and the later generation of authors who rejected it. Seeing in the past the foundations of a more perfect future, Tieck, Novalis, and Scott presented a vision of the Middle Ages that could serve as inspiration for present-day authors, artists, and citizens. In the later works of the realists, however, a historical setting and the use of reminiscence and framing narratives combine to create distance between the reader, author, and story. Stories are told in the third person, and multiple reminders of the storytelling mode constantly reinforce for the reader that the narrator is merely conveying information obtained elsewhere—in a found manuscript or as a secondhand story told to him by a witness. In his medievalist works of the 1860s, Brahms, a young man finding his own way in the world, much like the protagonists of the novellas discussed here, explores the relationship between the past and the present and between romanticism's focus on the ideal and realism's focus on the pragmatic. His *Magelone Romanzen* offers an optimistic reconciliation between the two traditions.

Romantic Medievalist Fantasies in Brahms's *Magelone Romanzen*, Songs 1–8

The fifteen songs of the *Magelone Romanzen* group neatly into two halves arranged around a central turning point (no. 8) that encapsulates the crux of the musical narrative.[20] Songs 1–7 describe Peter of Provence's decision to leave home in search of adventure (nos. 1 and 2), the awakening of his love for the princess Magelone and their courtship through a series of songs he writes for her (nos. 3, 4, and 5), anticipation of meeting her in person (no. 6), and then their time together (no. 7). Several of these songs contain clear markers of chivalric medievalism, particularly the first two songs, "Keinen hat es noch gereut" (No one has yet regretted it) and "Traun! Bogen und Pfeil" (Truly, bow and arrow are fit for the foe), as discussed by Bellman.[21] These examples of *local color* suggest the setting for the drama that unfolds in the rest of the work, but they also provide telling portrayals of the protagonist's unrealistic, fairy-tale-based expectations for his journey as well as his inexperience. For example, the first song in Peter's voice, no. 2, presents a bravado-filled paean to war and war games such as medieval tournaments. Tieck (as narrator) describes it as an "old German song" that Peter remembers and sings on his travels. As Bellman has noted, Brahms's setting uses movement from tonic to subtonic (♭VII) to emphasize the song's other-timely quality and to give it an almost primitive vigor. Other features highlight the two-dimensional understanding of good and evil in the text. The expressive marking *Kräftig* (strongly, robustly) encourages the singer and pianist to put great energy into the opening section that describes the "wretched foe" (mm. 1–16) with accented downbeats, a staccato bass line replete with octave doublings, and a *forte* dynamic. The vocal line's choppy leaping motives and dotted rhythms give it a jaunty, celebratory style, and the doubling of this line in the piano's right-hand part increases the loud, boisterous atmosphere. The subsequent section (mm. 17–28) describing the "noble soul" of the hero provides contrast by moving from C minor to the relative major (E♭) and by introducing horn fifths to illustrate the nobility mentioned in the text. The four-measure phrase is then repeated down a step in D♭ (♭VII again) and extended to transition to G major in preparation for the return of tonic in m. 29. The vocal line is more widely spaced here than in the opening section, containing dotted fanfare rhythms on triadic chord tones in each measure. This section contains no seventh chords or passing dissonances, and the lack of clear functional harmonies increases its archaism and associations with the long-ago days of chivalry.

Despite the apparent confidence and vitality of the chivalric style in the opening two songs, the overarching narrative of this half of the work tells of Peter's insecurity and his search for a personal identity that will guide him into and through adulthood. The collection of pretended identities in these songs goes well beyond the heroic vigor of the chivalric style to include other kinds of archaism and compositional devices not overtly connected to topical medievalist features. Nos. 4 and 5, for example, convey poems that Peter wrote to woo Magelone and sent to her via her nurse. They show the protagonist establishing his pedigree and writing to persuade Magelone of his love and devotion. As performances of courtly love, they enact Peter's attempts to portray himself in a particular (stereotypical?) style borrowed from fairy tales. No. 4, "Liebe kam aus fernen Landen" (Venus came from a faraway land), affects a simple, folklike style to relate a tale of the goddess of love encountering a mortal who has never loved before and ensnaring him in her bonds.[22] The main motive of the voice's melody, doubled an octave below in the piano's left hand, traces a chain of falling leaps followed by a descending scale to create a folklike simplicity (see Example 2.1a). Brahms's off-beat chordal accompaniment in the piano's right hand contributes to the naive effect appropriate to this evocation of romantic troubadours. As the poem's speaker feels the power of love for the first time, his desire for fame and fortune falls away; he despairs of ever escaping Venus's bonds. Brahms sets this new section in F major, a third away from the song's tonic D♭, and provides a more complex, almost theatrical piano part (mm. 38–47, see Example 2.1b). The rippling triplets and soaring melody in the accompaniment paint the imagery of the text ("all my

EXAMPLE 2.1A Brahms, "Liebe kam aus fernen Landen," op. 33/4, mm. 1–4.

EXAMPLE 2.1B Brahms, "Liebe kam aus fernen Landen," op. 33/4, mm. 38–41.

desires fled into the blue firmament"). Brahms's expressive markings throughout this "Poco vivace e sempre animato" section (Cresc. ed animato in m. 39; Sempre animato in m. 48) indicate the heightened level of emotion and almost panic of the text, which the repetition of the initial vocal motive a whole tone higher amplifies (it starts on C in m. 38 and on D in m. 40). When the opening melody and texture return in a soft dynamic in m. 72 (marked "Tempo I") and in the home key of D♭ major, the poetic speaker's complete submission to Love/Venus is clear.

The song represents a multilayered performance of medieval courtly love. In the context of the story, Peter creates an analogy to his own devotion, his whole-hearted submission to love and to his beloved Magelone. But it also demonstrates his (and Tieck's) familiarity with the language of courtly love and noble poetry, particularly in the last stanza when the speaker (in a musical line associated with Venus/Love) notes that "if your only love does not love you, only sickness and bitter death are left." As readers of Tieck's tale would know, Peter sent this love song to Magelone with a precious ring to prove that he belonged to a distinguished family with aristocratic lineage. This performance of good breeding and education extends to the language and style of the poem.[23] Brahms's setting of the text in his song cycle performs a similar kind of ventriloquism, particularly in the straightforward, folkish style of the opening melody. Eighteenth-century collections of folk song and medieval romances included what the editor or author considered an appropriate accompaniment in the modern style and regularized melodies and rhythms to fit the song aesthetic of the day. Brahms's triadic accompaniment, simple bass line, and symmetrical melody recall key aspects of the popular song style in these collections, demonstrating Brahms's own pedigree as a sophisticated music collector and educated reader.

In the companion to this troubadour romance, "So willst du des Armen" (Will you then take pity on a poor man?), Peter takes on the role of an ardent suitor, casting aside the reserved, allusive style of the previous song. Having received word that she returns his affection, he proposes to Magelone in the message to which this song and another ring are attached. Brahms sets the text to accentuate the differences between courtly love, which revels in unrequited longing for an inaccessible beloved in artful metaphor-filled poems and songs, and the promise of erotic fulfillment brought by romantic love between equals in the real world. No. 5 reverses every possible musical element of no. 4, from the key scheme (D♭–F–D♭ in no. 4; F–D♭–F in no. 5) to the tempo markings (Andante in no. 4, Allegro in no. 5) and accompaniment textures. Whereas the troubadour song of no. 4 unfolds gradually over four and a half minutes with nested *a b a* forms within its overall rounded structure, no. 5 runs its course in less than two minutes, barreling forward with hardly a pause between phrases. The accompaniment is filled with repeated chords that give the whole texture a ringing, triumphant quality, especially in the outer sections (mm. 1–19 and 70–89), where triplet rhythms add to the enthusiastic energy. The style of the short setting suggests that, having made his decision, Peter cannot wait another second to consummate his union with Magelone.

The first half of the cycle constantly switches between songs like these meant to be read and heard (in the context of Tieck's narrative) as performances and songs that Peter sings in private moments to explore his own emotions and reactions with no audience to hear him. These two song types stand in direct contrast to each other, as Brahms set the private songs in more complex formal structures with a nearly virtuosic singing style and more involved accompaniments. John Daverio likened these extended songs (nos. 3, 6, and 8) to operatic arias because they contain two contrasting sections familiar from the two-part slow/fast aria tradition of early romantic opera.[24] For example, no. 3 describes Peter's confused emotions prompted by seeing (and immediately falling in love with) Magelone at a tournament; it communicates the protagonist's bewilderment and inexperience via form and surface features.

The A section begins with an eight-measure piano prelude that foreshadows the melody of the first strophe. The vocal line employs an earnest, legato style filled with yearning sighs and decorative turns in the vocal line; the piano part's rolled chords imitate the lute with which Peter accompanies himself, and the soft dynamic of the whole conveys an intimate, reflective atmosphere. In mm. 21–24, the texture changes briefly to a more staccato style with clipped, syllabic declamation; Peter seems to interrupt himself when he realizes that the pleasure of love comes with the pain of separation or potential rejection, but in m. 25 the accompaniment reintroduces the expressive motive associated earlier with the first line's "sorrow and joy," as though his subconscious mind recalls that longing. The remainder of the A section repeats this alternation from short, choppy, chordal motives to legato lines in euphonious parallel thirds. The B section, marked Vivace and beginning in ⁶⁄₈ meter, effects an abrupt change of tone. Brahms introduces a syllabic martial style that suggests Peter attempting to pull himself together at the same time that he asks, "How is it that in my dreams my thoughts veer up and down?" Over dominant harmonies and long tones, Peter exclaims, Cherubino-like, "I hardly know myself!" By the end of the song, he has convinced himself that happiness can only be achieved through a union with the beloved, and the confident martial style returns with gusto (mm. 86–106), culminating in a showily ornamented cadence at the words "hope and happiness." The overall effect of the song is an artfully chaotic collection of emotions and images that reflect the young protagonist's first experience of romantic love.

No. 8, "Wir müssen uns trennen" (We must part, beloved lute), articulates the main turning point in the cycle. It presents Peter saying farewell to his lute and, by extension, to the artistic identity of his youth and taking up his armor and weapons in preparation to leave Naples with Magelone. (They have decided, impulsively, to elope to thwart her father's plan to marry her to another knight.) The song contrasts two significant icons of medievalism and, perhaps, competing ideals of masculinity in nineteenth-century culture. As a troubadour, Peter embodies the main medieval character type that inspired the revival of interest in medieval poetry and song. In painting and costume, in architecture and literature, troubadours and their Teutonic cousins (*Minnesinger*) inspired romantic creators to experiment with new techniques and to rebel against the dominant aesthetic ideals of the eighteenth century (balance, symmetry, logical order motivated by reverence of classical models) to create more immediate, personal forms of expression.[25] Thus, despite the seemingly conservative associations of looking back to an ancient art form for inspiration and renewal, references to the troubadour type and to lyrical romances actually go hand in hand with the revolutionary spirit prevalent in the romantic generation. In such works, the counterweight to the troubadour is the knight (or the crusader, a figure who appears in many artworks of the nineteenth century, including operas, oratorios, and cantatas). Warfare and war games such as jousting formed the second significant aspect of medieval culture in the romantic imagination, as the explosion of Crusades histories and plays about knights (*Ritterdrama*) in the late eighteenth century demonstrates.[26]

The juxtaposition of these two types in the *Schöne Magelone* tale—the troubadour as artist-hero and the crusader as pious warrior—allowed Tieck and Brahms to propose a reconciliation between them and to offer an alternative model wherein a strong, virile subject can demonstrate artistic subtlety and understanding. Despite the apparent archaism of the text, which addresses Peter's lute, lance, and steel armor, this song provides a powerful analogy for modern-day (i.e., nineteenth-century) men. Peter's decision to give up the avocations of his youth (lute-playing, sporting competitions) brings him to the realization that he now has adult responsibilities and can no longer selfishly pursue only his own aims. Brahms's musical setting dramatizes this realization and loss of innocence with a mournful, nostalgic style in the outer sections—the first section (A, mm. 1–19) addresses the lute with a fond farewell, and the final section (A′, mm. 72–84) addresses the night to ask for its protection. The musical style of these sections features long legato vocal lines with arch-shaped phrases, and each one begins with staccato arpeggios in the piano that imitate the sound of a plucked lute accompaniment, but the phrase lengths within this seemingly simple song defy easy periodization. Each phrase ends off-tonic, and the only dominant/tonic motion occurs at the beginning of phrases (m. 3 and m. 14) or in the middle of phrases, where it seems like passing motion rather than closure (see Example 2.2). The song opens with two measures of piano chords that set a tense mood without foreshadowing the vocal melody, and then the singer enters with a six-measure phrase that moves from the tonic G♭ through B♭ minor to cadence on F major (VII in the context of tonic G♭ minor, V of the subsequent phrase's B♭ minor). The contrasting phrase (b, mm. 9–13) introduces a new piano motive in the right hand, a menacing tremor of thirty-second notes at the end of the first and third beats that pervades the texture for the rest of the A section. This unsettled atmosphere throughout the A section suggests that however determined the protagonist might be in

EXAMPLE 2.2 Brahms, "Wir müssen uns trennen," op. 33/8, mm. 8–12.

Ich   zie - he zum Strei - te, zum Rau - be hin-aus,   und hab   ich die Beu - te, dann flieg   ich nach Haus.

his decision, the thought of taking on this unprecedented responsibility causes some anxiety. When this music returns at the end of the song, though, Peter's increased resolve and confidence are communicated by the return of the nostalgic melody and lute accompaniment without the thirty-second-note tremor and with greater tonal clarity. The left-hand part of the piano accompaniment now plays on the beat, as opposed to its earlier off-beat eighth notes, giving the reprise a more assured, secure texture. At the end of the song, the original vocal melody is extended from six to eight measures; the repetition of "already the morning smiles on us" leads to a strong cadence in Gb major at m. 82.

The middle section (B, mm. 20–71) addresses Peter's weapons ("Come, dear weapons, often donned for sport, now defend my happiness") and conveys the protagonist's enthusiastic acceptance of this new challenge. Still enjoying the fantasy of adventure, Peter sings in increasingly intense metaphors of struggle and perseverance: plunging into the waves of adversity and delighting in the prospect of shedding his noble blood to defend his "precious property" (Magelone, presumably). The musical setting reflects this mounting excitement and impatience through variations in the accompaniment's textures and rhythms as well as the ascending pitch level of the vocal line. With each successive stanza, the musical texture thickens from the simple triadic half notes and quarter notes of mm. 20–31 to octave triplets with added dissonance in mm. 32–48 and, finally, alternating triplets between the two hands that ratchet up the energy of this section through the rhetorical question, "Who lacks courage for that?" Meanwhile, the long crescendo and overall ascending trajectory of the vocal line culminate in a triumphant rising arpeggio and fermata over dominant harmony at the end of the section (mm. 47–48). Despite the eagerness of the text and its setting, the overall effect of this B section is increased stability, perhaps reflecting Peter's growth and the dependability that he will attempt to develop in the coming days. Especially in comparison to the A section, the phrase rhythms here are more regular, with symmetrical, four-measure antecedents and consequents marked by predictable, goal-directed harmonies. Thus, though the music returns to the nostalgic style of the opening A section for the last five lines of text, Peter has already accepted his new duty and can already contemplate happy memories of former pleasures without the anxiety that shadowed their loss in the first section of the song.

A Realist's Depiction of Love and Marriage, Songs 9–15

After this turning point (the acceptance of adult responsibility expressed in no. 8), the songs in the second half of the cycle turn from a romantic vision of medieval heroism and courtly love to a realist exploration of everyday emotions and experiences in a more modern idiom. In this second half of the cycle, the chivalric and archaic markers of some earlier songs fall away, and the folk song–influenced aesthetic of the nineteenth-century Lied takes over. The majority of songs in the second half are in modified strophic forms with structural returns of opening material at the ends of songs, a formal approach that creates a unified, consistent expression for this section of the cycle. Each of the songs in this second half deals with one emotion or reaction rather than the chaotic mixture of feelings evident in earlier songs, particularly in nos. 3 and 6. The second half contains no *operatic* forms, and all of Peter's songs in this part of the cycle are framed as Peter's solitary inward reflections, with the exception of the intimate lullaby no. 9, which Peter sings to Magelone as she falls asleep next to him. Whereas the first half of the cycle gives the overall effect of a young man trying on a series of different identities and personas (warrior, troubadour, nobleman), Peter's songs in the second half create the impression of a more self-assured and singular persona, the persona of the husband.

In the second half of the cycle, Peter sings two slow, longing-filled songs about Magelone and his love for her, and both embrace simpler musical and textual styles appropriate to a modern (late nineteenth-century) art song setting. No. 9, "Ruhe Süßliebchen" (Rest, sweet beloved), is a lullaby in A♭ major, the same key in which he first expressed the dawning of his love for the princess in no. 3. Brahms divides each of the three eight-line stanzas into two sections with distinctive melodies (*a b*), and over the course of the song he varies the music of *a* in each of its appearances, while the melody of *b* remains constant (see Example 2.3).[27] The melody of *b*, the refrain, begins with a memorable rising motive from the beginning of the piano introduction, and its prominence and constancy give each stanza a large-scale antecedent/consequent relationship so that the varied *a* melody seems to relax into the *b* melody in each iteration.[28] Brahms connects the two halves of each stanza by continuing the piano figuration from the *a* section into the refrain; thus, although the melody of *b* is constant (like Peter's love and devotion), the accompaniment changes to reflect the sentiment of the stanza as a whole (as he contemplates his love and beloved from different perspectives). As Heather Platt has noted, this connection between phrases is intensified by the harmonic language of *a*, which is sung over dominant harmonies with no structural cadences in tonic.[29] The first strongly articulated cadence underpins the final phrase of the refrain, "forever I am yours" in mm. 39–41. The *a* melody descends through the octave from E♭5 to E♭4; that gradual descent expresses the calming, soothing intent of the text in addition to creating a strong sense of arrival when the *b* melody enters with its familiar motif. The *b* melody consists of a series of simple rising and falling arpeggios first introduced by the piano at the

EXAMPLE 2.3 Comparison of melodic returns in Brahms, "Ruhe, Süßliebchen," op. 33/9.

beginning of the song, and each four-note phrase ends with a half step that increases the sensation of tension and release at the downbeat. The song's sensuous melodic style, particularly in the refrain, encapsulates the lived experience of romantic or even erotic love, as opposed to Peter's earlier imaginings.[30] As a genre, the lullaby's associations with daily routines and the rhythms of family life, including childrearing, make it a suitable song type to represent Peter's new social role and focus on everyday life in the here and now.

That focus continues in Peter's lament after the lovers' separation. (When a bird steals Magelone's rings, Peter gets into a boat to chase it across the sea; he becomes lost in a storm and is washed ashore in a foreign land.) No. 12, "Muß es eine Trennung geben" (Must there be a parting), is the simplest song in the cycle and Peter's most concentrated expression of a single emotion. Brahms set the short text of four four-line stanzas in a straightforward strophic form, with the first strophe in G minor repeated exactly and the third and fourth strophes altered to reflect the doleful questions and answers of the text. Throughout the song, the vocal melody is more consistent than any of Peter's other songs in the cycle, and the piano's constant rolling accompaniment of descending arpeggios gives the piece a unified sound that is only disrupted in mm. 22–27 (see Example 2.4a). At that point, in the third strophe, both the vocal line and the accompaniment are altered slightly for the wistful phrase, "If I had remained unloved, I would have a glimmer of hope." The piano's arpeggios give way to stacked thirds in the right hand over reiterated chord roots in the bass (the phrase occurs over a broad V–I progression). The vocal line's rhythms are shorter with a more syllabic text setting in this strophe (compare Example 2.4a to Example 2.4b), and the sequenced motive on D in mm. 22–23 and on G in mm. 25–26 underlines a move to tonic major. The introduction of the major tonic here prompts a change in harmony for the fourth strophe; though the vocal melody is an exact repetition of mm. 1–13, the piano accompaniment begins on C minor (iv) rather than tonic and moves through G minor before cadencing in G major at m. 43. These deft changes of melody and harmony lend expressive power to the song's repetitions, which might otherwise become monotonous. As in the lullaby (no. 9), this lament uses a straightforward structure and familiar musical gestures to communicate Peter's growth. With the hushed repetition of the line, "secretly my heart is breaking," we sense that Peter is ruminating on his situation and has resigned himself to his fate, much as the protagonists of contemporaneous realist literary works did. The quiet close in G major suggests an acceptance of the loss that has come with his great love and adventure.

The second half of the song cycle introduces outside perspectives into the work for the first time since the minstrel's song in no. 1. In Tieck's tale, nos. 11 and 13 belong to Magelone and the Muslim princess Sulima, respectively, and Tieck describes the text of the final song, no. 15 ("Treue Liebe"), as a duet that Peter and Magelone sing each year on their anniversary. The sudden appearance of these external voices in a work that has, until this point, focused on Peter's own thoughts and feelings highlights the ambiguity

EXAMPLE 2.4A Brahms, "Muß es seine Trennung geben," op. 33/12, mm. 1–4.

EXAMPLE 2.4B Brahms, "Muß es seine Trennung geben," op. 33/12, mm. 21–27.

of the work's genre and expressive purpose. We could interpret this incorporation of new points of view in terms of Peter's journey of self-discovery, as indications of his ability to think outside his own desires or his increasing empathy and ability to consider the needs of others and his relationship to a broader community. That said, some songs in the second half of the cycle appear to engage Tieck's framing narrative more obviously than those in the first half, because overt references to events told only in the narrative and not in the songs themselves make the second half harder to follow without some indication of the narrative context. (For that reason, some performers added a connecting text between songs, and the publisher Rieter-Biedermann sought to issue a version of the cycle with an explanatory poem; I will return to this point in the next section.) The sudden intrusion of a character's name, Sulima, as the title of no. 13 begs further explanation, because this is the only instance in the song cycle when a character is named.

The text of no. 13 describes chattering nightingales, whispering trees, and a pining heart longing for kisses in a light musical style that communicates untroubled naiveté. Brahms's setting contains no obvious exoticism or local color in its musical surface, but several features provide a sort of secondary exoticism in their presentation of the Muslim girl's innocence and lack of sophistication. The song's bright E major tonality is an abrupt shift from the flat-side minor keys of the preceding songs (nos. 10–12 in C minor, F minor, and G minor), and the style is cloyingly simple in comparison to the previous songs. The skipping rhythms, light texture, and triadic harmonies of the song's piano introduction convey a youthful vitality, and the Vivace tempo marking combines with the performance indication of "Zart, heimlich" (delicate, secretive) to create an atmosphere of carefree diversion. The musical materials consist of just two themes: a repeated A melody (mm. 12–14, heard again in mm. 59–72) and a longer B melody (mm. 26–47 and 73–94). Each section cadences cleanly in tonic and is followed by a piano interlude or postlude based on the opening introduction. In the context of Tieck's narrative, the trusting naiveté of the song and its text, whose speaker (Sulima) eagerly awaits her beloved (Peter) who she believes will sweep her away to a life of love and contentment, is both sad and touching. The piano postlude ends with the same "vamp-like" circular motive that began the song and runs continuously throughout it, evoking the image of Sulima on her balcony, reaching the end of her song and starting over again all night without pause, waiting for the young man who will never come for her.

Sulima and her music clearly stand apart from the more intense and nuanced sentiments associated with both Peter's and Magelone's longing and depth of feeling, as presented in nos. 9, 11, and 12. She provides a mirror of Peter's earlier youthful self, his naiveté and idealized notions of love and adventure. Her charming innocence may engage subtle tropes of the exotic female temptress and the sensuous pleasures that the East represented to European audiences, but without musical markers of exotic or orientalist *topoi*, the effect here is muted. Here, as in his contemporaneous cantata *Rinaldo*, Brahms carefully avoids what had become accepted procedures for evoking orientalist eroticism in opera and other musical works.[31] Brahms's use of a title for this song, however, ensures that the listener/performer will associate its innocence and simplicity with an outside character, rather than with the main pair of lovers. The song suggests a troubled, beleaguered man's attraction to a seemingly uncomplicated, accessible younger woman and transcends the specific narrative context to convey a common reaction to marital difficulties. Conjuring up the image of an exotic Eastern character with the name Sulima, while simultaneously representing her in a familiar, even banal, Western musical style, Brahms offers an ironic take on the trope of the oriental seductress. In distancing his work from the exotic allure of contemporaneous stage productions and tone poems that offered more titillating representations of the Middle Ages and of the Middle East, Brahms focused the narrative of his song cycle on tangible, present-day domestic concerns.

Tieck's Narrative, Brahms's Narrative, and a Reconciliation

Despite his own decision to closely associate these songs with Tieck's story by placing the phrase "from L. Tieck's fair Magelone" in the title, Brahms was ambivalent about the relationship between his work and Tieck's medievalist narrative in later years. In 1870, nearly a decade after his composition of the earliest songs and five years after the publication of the first half, Brahms wrote to his friend, the music critic Adolf Schubring: "About the Magelone Romances, one need not think too much of a connection, or even of the story. It was only out of a German thoroughness that I composed [them all] down to the last number."[32] When Jakob Rieter-Biedermann suggested adding connecting text to the work to clarify the narrative context when he prepared a reprint in 1875, Brahms objected, suggesting sarcastically that the text itself (a poem by Otto Schlotke) should be bound in gold leaf and read "by every good member of the Schanzengarten household each Sunday before the sermon."[33] He continued, "But it has nothing to do with my songs, just as little as the whole Rittergeschichte. Don't let it be printed!!!"[34] Two months later, he wrote again to Rieter that the cycle "has absolutely nothing to do with the Phantasus and the Liebesgeschichte vom Peter. Really, I have merely set the words to music, and no one should be concerned over the landscape."[35] Brahms made these comments in the 1870s, after he had established himself in Vienna. His 1869–1870 exchange of letters with Schubring discusses the recent premiere of his cantata *Rinaldo* and mentions Brahms's search for a suitable opera or oratorio text. Dramatic music, as well as the lukewarm reception of Brahms's early experiments in that vein, was obviously very much on his mind at that point. Five years later, Brahms's main compositional activities had narrowed somewhat to focus on instrumental music, nondramatic choral works, and songs, and the composer increasingly directed his energy toward established domestic and concert hall venues and the genres and forms associated with them. Brahms's insistence that the *Magelone Romanzen* should be considered as a collection of songs rather than a generically ambiguous musical rendering of Tieck's story is consistent with the professional identity that he cultivated in the 1870s and 1880s. That Tieck had fallen out of favor in the literary world and that the *Schöne Magelone* never enjoyed the broad popularity that Tieck's *Melusine* and *Genoveva* had may have been factors, as well as Brahms's interest in classical literature and folk materials as demonstrated by his library holdings and text settings.[36]

In addition to these considerations, Brahms surely was also thinking about practical matters of performance and reception for the songs, as Loges has discussed. In the 1860s it was still highly unusual to perform songs from a collection or cycle one after the other, and the song recital that is a standard feature of concert life today did not become common until the last quarter of the century. Brahms's close friends and associates, Julius Stockhausen, to whom he dedicated the *Magelone Romanzen*, and Amalie Joachim, established this practice through their own performances and those of their pupils.[37] Stockhausen was one of the first professional singers to regularly program complete song cycles by Robert Schumann and Franz Schubert, though this practice was not without controversy.[38] Brahms's biographer Max Kalbeck notes that Stockhausen and Joachim both performed the entire *Magelone Romanzen* occasionally, while also noting that Brahms apparently objected to this practice.[39] Many critics of the nineteenth century report that performing an entire evening of songs, let alone songs by a single composer and from a single collection, risked tiring or boring audiences used to more heterogeneous programs that mixed vocal works with chamber music and piano solos or duos.

But what if we read this song cycle and its texts more literally and take Brahms at his word when he says that the songs have nothing to do with Tieck's tale, that we should not be overly worried about the landscape? Is it possible that the second half of the cycle, in particular, expresses a linear narrative other than the one envisioned by Tieck, perhaps one more rooted in recent realist prose works of the 1850s–1860s? On their own, nos. 9 through 15 tell a story of marital dissatisfaction, temptation or infidelity, and reconciliation.[40] After a blissful union and lullaby, the protagonist immediately sings of hardships (no. 10: "nothing goes well…I am a lost soul"), then laments the loss of happiness (no. 11: "how quickly vanishes the brightness…our life swims away like a wave…we awake to depths of pain," and no. 12: "in secrecy my heart is breaking"). As noted, these songs contain no chivalric style markers or archaisms; in the modern style of a folk-inflected Lied, these songs "merely set the text," as Brahms says, without local color effects that would connect them to Tieck's narrative.

In her insightful study of Brahms's song collections, Inge van Rij notes that Tieck excerpted several of the poems from his *Schöne Magelone* and published them with individual titles as a cycle called *Des Jünglings Liebe* (The Young Man's Love).[41] Tieck's repackaging of the poems places them in a more modern, realistic scenario, emphasizing the universal or timeless sentiments they convey rather than the medievalism of the original context. For example, Tieck omitted the poem "Traun! Bogen und Pfeil," which van Rij describes as "one of the few poems from Tieck's collection specifically to evoke the chivalric context of the original tale."[42] In the lyric cycle, Tieck gives the poem originally associated with Sulima the title "Lockung" (Enticement). Van Rij acknowledges that, while the existence of the lyric cycle allows for a reading of the poems and perhaps the song cycle outside the context of the original narrative, several features indicate that Brahms specifically chose to associate his work with the romantic story *Schöne Magelone*. Brahms gave this title as the source of the poems in his published score, he chose to set a poem from the original tale that Tieck omitted from the lyric cycle, and he designated no. 13 "Sulima," calling attention to the specific situation of this song in the narrative as a song sung by that character. Although he titled his no. 10 song "Verzweiflung" (Desperation), the same title Tieck gives this poem, Brahms may have been unaware of the lyric version of the poems and arrived at this title based solely on his own interpretation of the text. Nonetheless, Brahms's musical settings in the second half of his cycle seem to reinforce their connection to everyday life, as opposed to his more obviously medievalist and archaic settings of the songs in the first half.

Brahms's ambivalence about this song cycle and the relationship between his settings and the original tale may reflect similar doubt about the romantic ideology of earlier decades. The literary and philosophical works of the romantics clearly appealed to him, and he would continue to set the works of these poets as songs and choruses into his later years. But here and in the cantata *Rinaldo*, we can hear Brahms struggling to find a reconciliation between the revolutionary fervor and idealism of Tieck and his generation, on the one hand, and the realistic pragmatism of his own day on the other.

Brahms's setting of the final song in the cycle, "Treue Liebe dauert lange" (True love endures), offers insight into his middle path between the extremes of these two ideologies (romanticism and realism). Tieck titled this song "Treue" (Faithfulness) in his lyric cycle, and Brahms's rearrangement of the poem's text suggests that he interpreted the final poem of the tale in similar terms. Although Brahms repeated phrases, lines, and stanzas in earlier settings of the *Magelone Romanzen*, this song is the only one in which he rearranged lines to create a new structure in the finished product. Brahms's version creates a rounded song form (A B A′) that aligns with an art song aesthetic appropriate for the private, often domestic, performances associated with the genre and brings together ideals that Tieck's version seems to place in opposition (true love and pleasure). Tieck's text for no. 15 divides into two starkly contrasting sections. The first half of the poem comprises three four-line stanzas, alternating eight- and seven-syllable lines in a trochaic meter (long–short, or strong–weak) with a predictable *abab cdcd* rhyme scheme, much like the simpler texts encountered earlier in the cycle. It describes in a closed, complete way the value and longevity of true love, which overcomes "menacing dense hosts, tempting to inconstancy" and dispels improper thoughts by looking toward a promising future ("the cheerful glance of spring"). This portion of the text seems designed for a straightforward setting in an *a b a* form and encourages a sentimental or touching style, which Brahms provides in his opening A section (mm. 1–53, see Example 2.5). The song begins with a hymnlike or folkish melody in E♭ major. The voice's syllabic, diatonic setting with half notes in common time evokes a peaceful, unhurried reflection on the nature of true love. The phrase rhythm provides comfortable regularity with a four-measure piano introduction that closes on a half cadence, followed by two eight-measure phrases clearly articulated in four-measure antecedent/consequent pairs. The chordal accompaniment suggests a tranquil, domestic environment; it is easy to hear this opening section in the context of a middle-class parlor or house concert.

The second half of Tieck's text is one long stanza of varied line lengths, with several "lines" consisting of a single three-syllable word and others as long as ten syllables. It has the chaotic, ecstatic style seen in some of the early poems in the cycle, particularly those associated with Peter's desire for adventure (no. 1, the minstrel's song) or his emotional confusion (no. 3, his first flourishing of love; no. 6, the anticipation of meeting Magelone). In those earlier texts, Brahms embraced the contrasts with musical settings that emphasized a diversity of styles, with changes of meter and tempo, a colorful harmonic palette, and varied rhythms and textures to differentiate the text's sections. In this song, though, he smooths out the disruptions by grouping Tieck's short three-syllable lines into longer

EXAMPLE 2.5 Brahms, "Treue Liebe," op. 33/15, mm. 1–8.

spans set as four-measure musical phrases and then repeating some text to create a nested *a b a'* form for the B section (mm. 54–104) that matches and balances the A section in length and structure. Each of the three subsections here closes with a strong cadence that stops musical time—with a fermata at m. 60 and m. 104 and with a full measure of static dominant harmony (with the leading tone in the voice) at m. 72, followed by a rest. These definitive closing gestures make Brahms's imposed tripartite form clear for the listener and performer and provide multiple climactic points to express the joy and fulfillment described in the text. Several aspects of this section's opening phrase, though, emphasize continuity with the previous section. The duple-meter "Lebhaft" ("lively") B section does present an immediate contrast with the triple-meter "Ziemlich langsam" ("somewhat slowly") A section, but both are in E♭ major, and the preceding section closes with a half cadence on B♭7, which clearly connects these sections harmonically. The piano's triplet figuration at the beginning of the B section continues the triplet rhythms of the prior measures. This musical setting clarifies that the pleasure celebrated in the B section is the direct outcome of the long-suffering, tried-and-true love described in the A section.

These two connected sections would be enough to express that notion, but Brahms goes a step further by creating a third section to close the song and the cycle as a whole (A′, mm. 105–116). Here the opening music and text of line 1 ("True love endures long") return to usher in a final repetition of the last lines of the text ("Let it be parted from sorrow…lovely, blessed, heavenly pleasure!") now set to the A section's sentimental, slow-tempo melody. In this way, Brahms closes the song cycle with a kind of moral that applies specifically to the second half, read as a cautionary tale about the temptation of infidelity, and to the entire work, read as a musical *Bildungsroman* that brings the listener and performer from a highly romanticized, medievalist vision of youthful adventure and idealized first love to a realist, modern depiction of maturity and self-knowledge. Unlike the realist fiction and poetry of his day, though, Brahms retains the optimistic outlook evident in the early romantic works of Tieck's generation, thereby reconciling the two traditions and expressing, perhaps, his own hopes for the realization of the romantic ideal in his lifetime and in his life's work.

Acknowledgments

The author would like to thank Heather Platt and Reuben Philips for their instructive comments on earlier versions of this chapter and to acknowledge the support of a GSU Provost's Faculty Fellowship in the 2016–2017 academic year.

Notes

1. On the Andante movements of the early piano sonatas, see George Bozarth, "Brahms's *Lieder ohne Worte*: The 'Poetic' Andantes of the Piano Sonatas," in *Brahms Studies: Analytical and Historical Perspectives*, ed. G. Bozarth (Oxford: Clarendon, 1990), 345–378; and Janice Dickensheets, "The Nineteenth-Century Sonata Cycle as Novel: A Topical and Literary Analysis of the Second Piano Sonata of Johannes Brahms" (DMA diss., University

of Northern Colorado, 2004). On Brahms's piano romance, see Marie Sumner Lott, "Romantic Medievalism in the Piano Romances of Clara and Robert Schumann and Brahms," *American Brahms Society Newsletter* 33, no. 1 (2015): 1–8.

2. Daniel Beller-McKenna, "Between 'Sehnsucht' and Nostalgia: Brahms's 'Lieder und Romanzen' for Women's Chorus, op. 44," *Ars Lyrica* 19 (2010): 129–152; Natasha Loges, "How to Make a 'Volkslied': Early Models in the Songs of Johannes Brahms," *Music and Letters* 93, no. 3 (2012): 316–349.

3. Styra Avins, *Johannes Brahms, Life and Letters* (Oxford: Oxford University Press, 1998), 751–752. Avins notes that we have no documentary evidence of the breakup except for Agathe's later memoir, a semifictional story she wrote for her children after Brahms's death (*In Memoriam J.B.*).

4. This interpretive tradition began with Brahms's first biographer Max Kalbeck. See Carol A. Hess, "'Als wahres volles Menschenbild': Brahms's *Rinaldo* and Autobiographical Allusion," *Brahms Studies* 2 (1998): 63–89.

5. This sort of dual purpose or address is evident throughout Brahms's output; see especially Paul Berry, *Brahms among Friends: Listening, Performance, and the Rhetoric of Allusion* (New York: Oxford University Press, 2014); and Dillon Parmer, "Musical Meaning for the Few: Instances of Private Reception in the Music of Brahms," *Current Musicology* 83 (Spring 2007): 109–130.

6. Brahms chose not to set the introductory song addressed to the reader, but did set each song from Chapters 1–14; he also did not set the two songs of Chapters 15 and 16. According to George Bozarth, Brahms composed Songs 1–4 in 1861 and Songs 5–6 in 1862, and McCorkle notes that Brahms offered these songs to Breitkopf und Härtel (who refused them) in October 1864. Bozarth also dates subsequent songs in the cycle to 1861–1862 (Songs 12 and 13), gives no date for Song 11, and gives a range of 1861–1865 for Song 8. Bozarth, "The Lieder of Johannes Brahms, 1868–71: Studies in Chronology and Compositional Process" (PhD diss., Princeton University, 1978); and Margit McCorkle, *Johannes Brahms Thematisch-Bibliographisches Werkverzeichnis* (Munich: Henle, 1984), 113.

7. Goethe's novel depicts this quest in an ironic, even mocking, light. Wilhelm eventually ends up in a secret society, "The Tower," that, it turns out, has been controlling his experiences along this journey of self-discovery all along. As literary scholar Nicholas Saul has noted, "The novel's frequent reception—critics speak of Wilhelm Meister's brothers—is thus a chain of productive misunderstandings." Nicholas Saul, "Aesthetic Humanism (1790–1830)," in *The Cambridge History of German Literature*, ed. Helen Watanabe-O'Kelly (Cambridge: Cambridge University Press, 1997), 202–271, quote from 217. On the *Bildungsroman* and its impact on literary culture of the early nineteenth century, see Franco Moretti, *The Way of the World: The Bildungsroman in European Culture*, rev. 2nd ed. (London: Verso, 2000).

8. See "Tieck, Ludwig (1773–1853)," in *Nineteenth-Century Literature Criticism*, ed. Laurie Lanzen Harris and Sheila Fitzgerald, vol. 5 (Farmington Hills, MI: Gale, 1984), 510–533.

9. Tieck's younger contemporary, the dramatist C. Friedrich Hebbel, coined the moniker "König der Romantik" in his obituary, and biographers have used it ever since. See Armin Gebhardt, *Ludwig Tieck: Leben und Gesamtwerk des "Königs der Romantik"* (Marburg: Tectum, 1997); and Klaus Günzel, *König der Romantik: Das Leben des Dichters Ludwig Tieck in Briefen, Selbstzeugnissen und Berichten* (Berlin: Wunderlich, 1985).

10. Jonathan Bellman, "Aus alten Märchen: The Chivalric Style of Schumann and Brahms," *Journal of Musicology* 13 (1995): 117–135.

11. Antonio Baldassarre, "Johannes Brahms and Johannes Kreisler: Creativity and Aesthetics of the Young Brahms Illustrated by the 'Piano Trio in B Major' Opus 8," *Acta Musicologica* 72, no. 2 (2000): 145–167.

12. In an otherwise excellent account of the performance traditions surrounding the *Magelone Romanzen*, Natasha Loges describes the novella with songs and poems primarily as an earlier romantic genre, saying that it "had largely vanished in Brahms's day, although it had enjoyed popularity earlier in the century." In fact, the novella continued to be the primary genre for innovative prose fiction through the end of the nineteenth century, though the emphasis on songs did wane. Loges cites later examples by Keller and Storm in a footnote but does not discuss their impact on Brahms and his generation. Natasha Loges, "The Limits of the Lied: Brahms's *Magelone-Romanzen*, op. 33," in *Brahms in the Home and the Concert Hall: Between Private and Public Performance*, ed. Katy Hamilton and Natasha Loges (Cambridge: Cambridge University Press, 2014), 300–323, quote from 312.

13. Tieck, who had become increasingly conservative in his own political and social outlook, published harsh criticisms of the new movement, engaging in a literary combat that would color reception of his work into the twentieth century.

14. Heine, excerpt from *De l'Allemagne* (1835), as quoted in *Nineteenth-Century Literature Criticism*, vol. 5 (Farmington Hills, MI: Gale, 1984), 514. Fetzer notes that "the first generation of German literary historians writing on romanticism (1870–1930) likewise viewed [Tieck] from an unfavorable and unflattering perspective: a competent craftsman rather than an inspired artist, a writer rather than a poet, and by consensus a catalyst but not an original genius." John Francis Fetzer, "Ludwig Tieck" in George Stade (ed.), *European Writers: The Romantic Century* vol. 5 (New York: Charles Scribner's Sons, 1983), 233–260, quote from p. 233.

15. Tieck's *Blonde Eckbert* (1797) is his most famous fairy tale, though the plays *Der gestiefelte Kater* (*Puss in Boots*, 1797) and *Ritter Blaubart* (*The Knight Bluebeard*, 1796) also engage the fairy-tale tradition being developed by Fouqué, Brentano, and others.

16. As Angelika Koller points out, Tieck's collection is aimed at the popular reader, though only about 25 percent of the German population was literate at this time. Angelika Koller, *Minnesang-Rezeption um 1800: Falldarstellungen zu den Romantikern und ihren Zeitgenossen und Exkurse zu ausgewählten Sachfragen* (Frankfurt am Main: Lang, 1992).

17. Markus Bernauer, "The Historical Novel and Historical Romances," in *Romantic Prose Fiction*, ed. M. Engel, B. Dieterle, and G. Gilespie (Amsterdam: Benjamin, 2008), 296–324.

18. Gail Finney, "Revolution, Resignation, Realism, 1830–1890," in *Cambridge History of German Literature*, ed. Helen Watanabe-O'Kelly (Cambridge: Cambridge University Press, 1997), 272–326.

19. The poetic realists of Germany differed in approach from the contemporaneous social realists in France, Britain, and Russia (e.g., Stendhal, Balzac, Thackery, Tolstoy). Whereas social realism "depicts individuals confronting social institutions against a panoramic background of history-making contemporaneous events," German poetic realists (Storm, Keller, Freytag) "focus on private activities of small groups of people in provincial regions…much of it set in the distant past." Gail Finney, "Poetic Realism, 1848–1890," in *European Writers: The Romantic Century*, ed. George Stade (New York: Scribner's, 1983), 6:913–942, quote from 913.

20. In his theory of the novella, Tieck identified the *Wendepunkt* (turning point) as a key feature of the genre. He defined it as the event that "suddenly and unexpectedly inverted the whole course of the action" (as quoted in Annette Simonis, "Turning Points in the

Nineteenth-Century Novella: Poetic Negotiations and the Representation of Social Rituals," in *Turning Points: Concepts and Narratives of Change in Literature and Other Media*, ed. Ansgar Nünning and Kai Marcel Sicks [Berlin: De Gruyter, 2012], 61), which is often the event that moves the narrative from the real to the fantastic (or "marvelous"). Later realists such as Gustav Freytag and C. F. Meyer spent considerable time and energy theorizing the turning point and its use in the novellas of their day. Simonis, "Turning Points in the Nineteenth-Century Novella," 59–71, quote from 63.

21. Bellman, "The Chivalric Style of Schumann and Brahms," 120.

22. Bellman suggests that no. 4 "hint[s] at a Baroque ground bass" (Bellman, "The Chivalric Style of Schumann and Brahms," 119). The song does not present a series of variations over a recurring bass, but it does evoke fugal subjects and similar repeatable melodies, such as the famous "Canon in D" by Johann Pachelbel, whose first measure Brahms's melody closely resembles.

23. As noted, Tieck edited a collection of German secular songs from the Middle Ages published in 1803 as *Minnelieder aus dem Swäbische Zeitalter*. (Tieck's collection contains only the texts of the songs, because the *Minnelieder* melodies do not survive in the sources to which he had access.) See Koller, *Minnesang-Rezeption um 1800*; and Annette Kreutziger-Herr, *Ein Traum vom Mittelalter: Die Wiederentdeckung mittelalterlicher Musik in der Neuzeit* (Berlin: Böhlau, 2003).

24. John Daverio, "Brahms's *Magelone Romanzen* and the 'Romantic Imperative,'" *Journal of Musicology* 7, no. 3 (1989): 357–359. Daverio never mentions the operatic romance in his discussion of this work and seems to use the term *operatic* to convey the difference between longer, more formally complex, and virtuosic songs (nos. 3, 6, 8, and 15) and the shorter, strophic, folklike or Lied-like songs that dominate the cycle. In the nineteenth century, though, composers including Meyerbeer and Weber frequently used the term *romance* or *romanza* to indicate a diegetic song, especially in operas set in the distant past. This usage follows an earlier French tradition, as described by Daniel Heartz, "The Beginnings of the Operatic Romance: Rousseau, Sedaine, and Monsigny," *Eighteenth-Century Studies* 15, no. 2 (1982): 149–178.

25. The connection between medievalism and artistic renewal is evident, for example, in Wordsworth and Coleridge's collection *Lyrical Ballads* (1797, revised and expanded 1800), whose poems were inspired by and are meant to evoke the rustic bardic poetry of Britain's distant past and folk traditions, and in the romantic reception of poetry by "Ossian" (James MacPherson writing as a medieval Scottish bard).

26. Elizabeth Siberry, *The New Crusaders: Images of the Crusades in the 19th and Early 20th Centuries* (Aldershot, UK: Ashgate, 2000). A close third in importance and interest was the rise in Middle Ages–inspired mystical Catholicism.

27. Many composers set this poem to music in the nineteenth century, including Louis Spohr, Franz Lachner, Wilhelm Berger, A. B. Marx, and Luise Reichardt. Loges notes that at least thirty settings were produced between 1830 and 1900 (Loges, "The Limits of the Lied," 315).

28. My reading of this form differs from that offered by Natasha Loges, who analyzes the song as a more rondo-like A B A′ C A″ and notes that "the sections are progressively more technically demanding…creating an impression of a considerable mental journey rather than a simple lullaby." I propose that this mental journey and the musical style that suggests it reflect Peter's mature contemplation of a realistic domestic life. Loges, "The Limits of the Lied," 319.

29. Heather Platt, "Text–Music Relationships in the Lieder of Johannes Brahms" (PhD diss., City University of New York, 1992), especially 277–286 and 150–160.

30. Platt, citing Peter Jost, suggests that "Peter may have more on his mind than putting Magelone to sleep" (Platt, "Text–Music Relationships," 283). This reading of the text makes sense in the context of the surrounding narrative: At the beginning of the next chapter, Peter loosens Magelone's garments because it seems to him that her breathing has become labored, and "her beautiful white bosom emerge[s] from her concealing robes."

31. Ralph P. Locke, *Musical Exoticism: Images and Reflections* (Cambridge: Cambridge University Press, 2009), especially 25–42 and 175–213; and James Parakilas, "The Soldier and the Exotic: Operatic Variations on a Themes of Racial Encounter," *Opera Quarterly* 10, no. 2–3 (1993): 33–56 and 43–69.

32. "Bei den Magelonene-Romanzen braucht man wohl nich viel an einen Zusammenhang, und gar mit der Erzählung zu denken. Es ist wohl nur etwas deutsche Gründlichkeit, daß ich bis zur letzten Nummer komponierte." *Johannes Brahms, Briefe an Joseph Viktor Widmann, Ellen und Ferdinand Detter, Adolf Schubring*, ed. Max Kalbeck (Berlin: Deutschen Brahms-Gesellschaft, 1915). Brahms overstates the case here, because he did not compose settings of all Tieck's poems. (He omitted three of Tieck's eighteen poems, as noted previously.)

33. Rieter owned an estate in Winterthur known as the Schanzengarten, and Brahms stayed there on several occasions. Most discussions of the *Magelone Romanzen* quote only the second half of this passage ("it has nothing to do with my songs"). Brahms's assessment of the moralizing tone in Schlotke's text and his seeming dismissal of it suggests that the quality of the text may have had as much of an impact on Brahms's refusal to associate his work with Schlotke's poem as his ambivalence about the song cycle's narrativity.

34. "Den verbindenden Text bitte schön mit Goldschnitt binden zu lassen und im Schanzengarten jeden Sonntag vor der Predigt den werten Hausgenossen vorlesen zu lassen.—Mit meinen "Liedern" aber hat er nichts zu tun, so wenig wie die ganze Rittergeschichte! Ja nicht drucken lassen!!!" *Johannes Brahms im Briefwechsel mit Breitkopf & Härtel, Bartolf Senff, J. Rieter-Biedermann, C.F. Peters, E. W. Fritzsch und Robert Lienau*, ed. Wilhelm Altmann (Berlin: Deutsche Brahms-Gesellschaft, 1921), 250.

35. "Das ist alles recht gut und schön, aber meine ["Magelonen"-]Musik hat nun einmal durchaus nichts mit dem 'Phantasus' und der Liebesgeschichte vom Peter zu tun. Ich habe wirklich bloß die Worte in Musik gesetzt, und es geht neimand dabei die Lanschaft oder das Hospital oder sonst was an." Ibid., 256.

36. Whereas Brahms favored more recent popular poems and accessible folk or folkish texts in his solo songs (Georg Daumer, Klaus Groth, Karl Lemke, etc.), all of his large-scale choral works except *Rinaldo* set poems in a classical tradition—Hölderlin (*Schicksalslied*), Goethe (*Alto Rhapsody, Gesang der Parzen*), Schiller (*Nänie*)—or religious and biblical texts (Ave Maria, *Begräbnisgesang, Triumphlied, Deutsches Requiem*). *Rinaldo* sets a romantic medievalist text written by Goethe in 1812.

37. Loges, "The Limits of the Lied," 307–311.

38. Brahms and Stockhausen performed together on several occasions, including a concert tour in German and Danish cities in 1868, and they presented selections from the *Magelone Romanzen* in 1862 and 1868.

39. See the extended footnote on pages 428–429 of Kalbeck, *Johannes Brahms* I (Berlin: Deutsche Brahms-Gesellschaft, 1904).

40. Although no. 11 sets a text intended as Magelone's lament, nothing in the poem or in the presentation of the song in print suggests a change of poetic voice, so without the framing

narrative of the original tale, one could easily hear this as a continuation of the protagonist's (Peter's) responses to his situation.

41. Inge van Rij, *Brahms's Song Collections* (Cambridge: Cambridge University Press, 2006), 85–91. The lyric cycle was included in a three-volume collection of Tieck's poems published in Dresden by P. G. Hilscher in 1821–1823.

42. Van Rij, *Brahms's Song Collections*, 11–12. She continues, "By omitting this poem and the first [the preface's poem addressing the reader], Tieck creates a logical narrative progression, from youthful *Wanderlust* to first love, to doubt, to despair, to reunion and the return of stability. Moreover, the new poetic group can be understood without the context of the specific story of Peter and Magelone and its medieval setting [...] the emphasis is on the general and universal rather than the specific and remote."

CHAPTER 3

LISZT'S MEDIEVALIST MODERNISM

BALÁZS MIKUSI

As a composer writing in the nineteenth century, Franz Liszt is typically considered one of the most progressive musicians of his time, one who, more than any of his contemporaries, "hurled his lance into the infinite space of the future."[1] Nonetheless, Liszt was no less invested in the music of the past than any of his less revolutionary-minded colleagues and even severely criticized conservatories for failing to appreciate "old art as an indispensable stirrup for the present."[2] This latter interest in the past is reflected in both Liszt's biography and his worklist and is characterized by a keen interest in the outstanding achievements of the baroque (especially J. S. Bach, whom he considered the "Thomas Aquinas of Music"), the vocal polyphony of the Renaissance (Palestrina, in particular), and the vocal monophony of the Middle Ages (which his generation primarily knew in a somewhat corrupted repertory of Gregorian chant).[3]

Liszt's Authentic–Ecclesiastical–Liturgical Hunt

Liszt's largest-scale attempt at a historical tableau, the oratorio *Die Legende von der heiligen Elisabeth*, reveals his pursuit of "authentic" melodies attached to the medieval figure, St. Elisabeth (1207–1231). As Liszt points out in a concluding remark appended to the full score, thanks to advice he received from several colleagues in Hungary, he managed to identify two melodies (in Liszt's original German: *Motive*) "which have stood, since old times, in traditional, ecclesiastical, and historical connection with St. Elisabeth." Example 3.1 shows one of these.

Liszt also identified two other borrowed *Volksmelodien*, the historicity of which he evidently viewed with more suspicion: a Hungarian folk melody recommended by the violinist Ede Reményi (which Liszt specifically uses as a leitmotif related to the character

EXAMPLE 3.1 "Quasi stella matutina."

of the Hungarian magnate) and a pilgrim's song "ostensibly from the time of the cru-sades" proposed by Alexander Wilhelm Gottschalg, cantor in Tiefurt near Weimar. In fact, the style of the latter two melodies leaves no doubt about their more recent origins (in the nineteenth and the eighteenth centuries, respectively), but the pedigrees of the first two are also not as spotless as the composer might have hoped for. "Szent Örsébet asszony" was published (as Liszt correctly notes) in the 1695 collection *Lyra coelestis*, but lacking any earlier traces of it, one tends to assume that it was in fact written by the editor György Náray specifically for his publication. And even the antiphon "Quasi stella matutina" (originally sung, as the composer remarks, "in festo, sanctae Elisabeth") is not fully authentic, insofar as it actually belonged to the feast of Saint Elisabeth of Portugal, rather than of Hungary.

Whether or not Liszt succeeded in embedding in his oratorio truly authentic musical quotations, the crucial point is that he made a serious effort to do so. As Nicolas Dufetel has recently explored in some detail, the composer contacted many more friends and colleagues than those mentioned in his appendix and launched a true "authentic–ecclesiastical–liturgical hunt" for appropriate musical relics.[4] And, at least from the lis-tener's point of view, his quest was by no means in vain: apart from the stylistically more or less contemporary Hungarian melody, which some may perceive as standing out of the grand romantic style of the oratorio, the borrowed melodies provide precisely the kind of archaizing atmosphere the composer longed for.[5] In fact, Liszt appears to have had more aesthetic, rather than philological, considerations in mind from the start. When he asked his son-in-law Émile Ollivier to have some melodies copied for him from old sources available in Paris, he added that they might as well be related to another St. Elisabeth, since it was only in the interest of authenticating the work through a Catholic cachet that "I would like to introduce and develop some of these liturgical into-nations that have no equivalent in our modern music."[6]

The composer's words thus betray a historical awareness that may help us better inter-pret a number of his own compositions. The wheel of history cannot be turned back, and no composer of Liszt's time could exactly reproduce relics of the past. Nevertheless, these relics—because they inextricably belong to a world left behind and "have no equivalent in our modern music"—could and indeed should be studied and used "as an indispensable stirrup for the present." Liszt's ongoing involvement with the music of the Middle Ages—in particular, Gregorian chant—can therefore best be understood as an effort to revive some of the values of a past long lost, but in constant awareness that such revivals can only be partial. His medievalism thus inevitably (and in Liszt's view probably optimally) resulted in something new, inseparably attached to the present.

In this way, we might speak of *medievalist modernism* as an essential part of Liszt's compositional style.

Liszt and Plainchant

Whereas most composers of his generation inevitably had personal experiences with liturgical music of some sort, Liszt appears to have been among the few who developed an almost scholarly interest in plainchant. Most important, the composer's library today kept at the Liszt Ferenc Memorial Museum and Research Center in Budapest features a number of chant-related publications, several of which include annotations in his own hand.[7] Louis Lambillotte's 1858 treatise entitled *Chants communs des messes* is a case in point: the chart Liszt drew up at the end of the volume neatly summarizes the basic information about each church mode, arguably as a memory aid for himself (see Figure 3.1).[8]

Liszt's correspondence suggests that the work of Louis Niedermeyer and Joseph d'Ortigue, as published in their *Dictionnaire liturgique, historique et théorique du plainchant* (1853) and *Traité théorique et pratique de l'accompagnement du plain-chant* (first published 1857), had an especially great influence on his views concerning Gregorian chant.[9] Additionally, Liszt sympathized with the work of the Benedictine monks of Solesmes, so much so that—in Nicolas Dufetel's view—his apparent interest in comparing different versions of the same plainsong could be seen as his quest for a reconstructed *Urfassung*, similar to that sought by the monks.[10] Be that as it may, Liszt remained first and foremost a composer, whose final judgments relied more on musical judgment and intuition than on the principles of philology.

Liszt showed an undeniable and detailed interest in plainchant in concrete terms. While his much-quoted 1835 essay *De la musique religieuse* outlined the idea of a *musique humanitaire* that should combine the apparently opposing values of theater and church music, by the 1850s he became strongly attracted to the simplicity of Gregorian chant

FIGURE 3.1 Liszt's notational summary of church mode finals and dominants.

and entertained ideas actively to participate in the reformation of liturgical music—a hope he had soon to give up because of the solid opposition of the higher clergy.[11] Admittedly, the composer's turning toward this field precisely in this period of his life may have been inspired by his new partner, the staunch Roman Catholic princess Carolyne zu Sayn-Wittgenstein, but one should recall that his strong attachment to Catholic faith originated with his parents, and his early relationship with Abbé Félicité de Lamennais already bore artistic fruit as well.

Liszt's early interest in plainchant is evidenced in the De profundis (1834), a "psaume instrumental" for piano and orchestra. This work uses one of Lamennais's favorite plain-songs, the words of Psalm 130 appearing against it in the score (this was later incorporated into Pensée des morts, no. 4 of the cycle Harmonies poétiques et religieuses of 1840–1853). Arguably under the influence of Berlioz's Symphonie fantastique, Liszt was inspired to improvise on the Dies irae melody on several occasions in the 1830s. In Totentanz—another work meant for piano and orchestra and sketched as early as 1838— he had already chosen the sequence as a starting point for an entire set of variations.[12] Even more important, Liszt's first piece of church music—a Paternoster for male chorus (published in 1846)—is also in essence a metric harmonization of the chant placed in the top voice. As its later arrangement for piano (no. 5 of Harmonies poétiques et religieuses) demonstrates, Liszt treats the chant with a certain freedom regarding chromatic inflections to allow for some harmonic diversity (see Example 3.2).[13] By the same token, Liszt's early Ave Maria setting (written in the early 1840s and usually identified by the Roman numeral I added to its title) also relies on the Gregorian melody. Like the Paternoster, this work was also arranged for piano and included as no. 2 in Harmonies poétiques et religieuses. All these compositions demonstrate the composer's avid interest in plainchant prior to his close contact with Princess Wittgenstein and his move to Weimar, which opened an altogether new phase in his compositional activities.

One of the ways in which Liszt used Gregorian melodies was as a symbol that encouraged identification with a religious sphere. The fifth motive that the composer describes in his appendix to the full score of Die Legende von der heiligen Elisabeth is a textbook example for this kind of semantic play between the present and the religious past. As he suggests, the three notes G–A–C (and, more generally, a rising major second followed by a rising minor third) function as a "tonisches Symbol des Kreuzes" in several of his works. Liszt mentions two traditional melodies that open with these intervals: the Magnificat he used in the final chorus of his Dante Symphony (1856–1857) and the hymn "Crux fidelis" (in fact strophe 8 of the well-known Pange lingua), which he quoted in his symphonic poem no. 11 Die Hunnenschlacht (1857).[14] Because this three-note motive, as Liszt himself points out, "is used in Gregorian chant very frequently," it therefore inevitably takes on a more general religious connotation, especially for a larger audience not closely familiar with Liszt's personal motivic vocabulary. This more general semantic function may be seen, for example, in the memorable Grandioso section of the Sonata in B minor (1852–1853), but also in lesser-known works like the "Invocation" that opens the cycle Harmonies poétiques et religieuses or the 1848 setting of Goethe's "Über allen Gipfeln ist Ruh" (in the latter case, the motive arguably suggests the redemption of

EXAMPLE 3.2 Liszt, Paternoster for male chorus (1846).

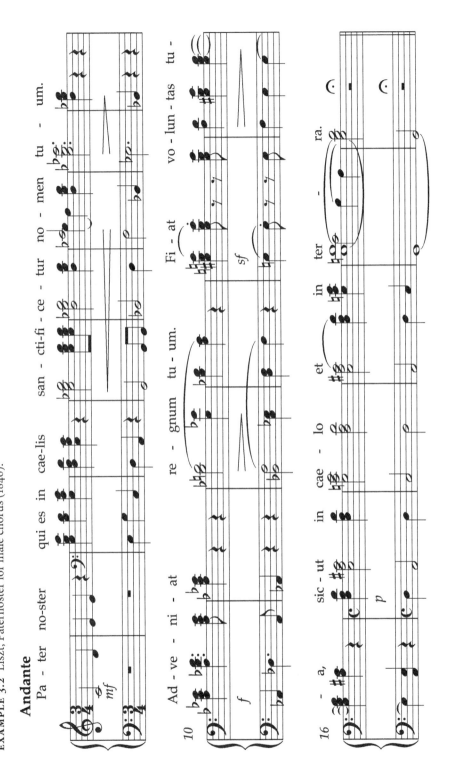

the wanderer). In short, the Gregorian-inspired motive invites different interpretations in every work.

To account for Liszt's ever more frequent uses of Gregorian material in his later compositions would require a monograph.[15] In this brief overview it should suffice to point out that his interest in medievalism reached a high point in the mid-1850s, the very years in which Liszt completed his *Dante Symphony* and *Die Hunnenschlacht* and prepared his first plans for *Die Legende von der heiligen Elisabeth*. The move to Rome in late 1861 brought an obvious change also in this respect: whereas the first *Episode from Lenau's Faust* (completed in 1861) still quotes "Pange lingua," Liszt's conscious turning away from secular orchestral works in favor of religious compositions inevitably resulted in a decline of such programmatic citations, but also in an increase in the number of Gregorian melodies used in their proper liturgical context. The year 1865, when Liszt took the holy orders from the Roman Catholic Church, represents a high point in this regard: The *Missa choralis* is arguably the composer's most concerted effort at a liturgical work based on plainchant melodies, among them that of *Sacerdos in aeternam* (an obvious reference to Liszt's new status). From this point on, however, the composer's interest in using Gregorian melodies—if not in writing religious music—began gradually to fade, suggesting that his earlier zeal could partly have been motivated by the great ambitions of his early Rome years to reform church music in general. That said, a number of lesser and greater works of his late years—including the monumental oratorio *Christus*—still include Gregorian melodies, which also had a clear influence on Liszt's own melodic writing. In fact, given the parallel existence of diverse versions of plainchant and Liszt's potential familiarity with the traditions of different geographic regions, it is often nearly impossible to establish with confidence whether he may have relied on a specific model or rather emulated the style of authentic plainchant melodies in any specific work.

Inventing Rhythms, Deriving Harmonies

Liszt's familiarity with contemporary treatises on Gregorian chant leaves little doubt that he was aware of the debates concerning the rhythmicization and the harmonization of plainchant melodies. Singing these without measured note values was eminently feasible for unaccompanied performance. But interpretation along the lines of some metrical scheme was another option, one better suited to—if not in fact required by—presentations of the chant with harmonic accompaniment. The Paternoster quoted above (see Example 3.3) clearly exemplifies the latter type: the $\frac{3}{4}$ meter, the turn to C at m. 17, and the different note values and rests are in essence arbitrary, even if they obviously take into account the inner accents and the phrase structure of the text. Nevertheless, most of Liszt's Gregorian citations exhibit a less angular approach—the "Crux fidelis" melody, for instance, when it unexpectedly surfaces in *Die Hunnenschlacht*, prompts a flexible alternation of diverse meters. Even more characteristic of Liszt, however, is the technique applied in the opening measures of *Die Legende von der heiligen Elisabeth*: the $\frac{6}{4}$ meter itself allows for a certain flexibility, and the antiphon melody (cf. Example 3.1) starts on an upbeat directly tied to the following downbeat—a rather refined rhythmic gesture that arguably seeks to make the listener experience a certain levitation before recognizing the actual pulsation with the arrival of further metric cues in mm. 2–3 (see Example 3.3).

By the same token, in the 1847 *Stabat Mater* Liszt has the plainsong enter on the second quarter of a C bar and essentially writes a series of half values consistently off the beat, producing a visual syncopation that should arguably inspire the performer to a "floating" interpretation (see Example 3.4).

More nuanced is the opening of *Via Crucis*, where the hymn "Vexilla regis" once again starts off the main beat and with syncopation—yet another levitating effect that, as the original manuscript kept in the National Széchényi Library reveals, Liszt struggled properly to bring to paper (cf. Example 3.5 and Figure 3.2). To what extent the metric and rhythmic freedom of plainchant may have informed Liszt's own works seems difficult to establish. Heinrich Sambeth, for one, suggested that the composer's polyrhythmic tendencies might go back to his efforts to notate such melodies—an idea

EXAMPLE 3.3 Liszt, *Die Legende von der heiligen Elisabeth*, mm. 1–4.

EXAMPLE 3.4 Liszt, *Stabat Mater* (1847), mm. 7–12.

EXAMPLE 3.5 Liszt, *Via crucis* (1876–1879), mm. 7–10.

FIGURE 3.2 Liszt's sketch for the "Vexilla regis" introduction to *Via crucis*.

that Peter Raabe found too daring, no doubt considering similar passages in nineteenth-century art music a more likely source of inspiration.[16]

In discussing the harmonic language of Liszt's works using plainchant, it seems crucial to realize that the harmonization of such historical melodies was au courant in the treatises of the day, several of which the composer possessed and studied in depth. Thus, when he sought to provide preexisting melodies with some sort of chordal accompaniment, he was less invested in emulating the Gregorian-based works of earlier generations of composers than in providing original solutions to a thoroughly contemporary artistic challenge. As we have seen, in his early Paternoster (see Example 3.2) Liszt experimented with a wide array of chords, going so far as to chromatically alter the notes of the original melody (see the E♭s in mm. 8–12 and the C♯s in mm. 16–19). His careful reading of the 1859 second edition of *Traité théorique et pratique de l'accompagnement du plain-chant* by Niedermeyer and Ortigue, however, must have raised his interest in a more "fundamentalist" approach, which strove to produce the accompaniment by applying the same "laws" one observed in the borrowed melody. In short, arrangers needed to take into consideration that (1) the accompaniment should restrict itself to the notes present in the scale used by the melody, and (2) the chords based on the *finale* and *dominante* should function the same way as the respective notes of the melody.[17]

Paul Merrick has suggested that Liszt came closest to realizing these principles in his 1860 set of *Responses and Antiphons*, but it is important to note that even these—by Liszt's standards—startlingly simple chord successions divert from the strict norms suggested by Ortigue.[18] Yet again, one suspects that the composer was conscious of his historical position and felt that faithfully deriving the entire accompaniment from these principles would prevent him from effectively communicating with nineteenth-century listeners. In this respect, the *Stabat Mater* cited earlier (see Example 3.4) also presents a fruitful compromise: Whereas the borrowed melody itself appears unchanged (i.e., without arbitrary alterations) in the top part, the chromatic touches in the lower parts provide the arrangement with an unmistakably up-to-date *neomodal* tint.

But Liszt's awareness of his historical embeddedness might in fact best be gathered from a curious insertion of a mere seven bars in the keyboard version of his *Ave maris stella* (written in 1868; see Example 3.6). The original version (for mixed chorus and

EXAMPLE 3.6 Liszt, keyboard version of *Ave maris stella*, mm. 1–12.

organ) opens with a plainchant intonation, in its brevity—and its emphatic use of the cross motive followed by simple scalar descent—potentially more a general stylistic hint for the listener than a quotation meant to be recognized by all.

However, while in the vocal version this intonation (corresponding to mm. 1–3 in Example 3.6) is directly followed by the main melody (cf. m. 11), the piano version offers us a real time-travel experience in between: In mm. 4–5 we hear simple modal progressions consisting exclusively of root-position triads, but m. 5 already touches on seventh and six-four chords, only to let us arrive in Liszt's own age with the emblematic alternation of third-related sonorities in mm. 7–8. Having gradually progressed from single-voice modal archaism to contemporary chromatic harmony, Liszt lets the somewhat commonplace accompaniment enter in m. 9 and, from m. 11 on, treats us with an enchanting melody that in fact—as regards both intervallic content and melodic gestures—hints at the opening intonation. In short, the composer carefully builds a bridge from "primitive" plainchant to the seductive and through-and-through harmonic melodiousness of his own time, eventually presenting the old wine in a new bottle for those who might otherwise have no tongues to taste or ears to listen.

Liszt and the Cecilian Movement

Liszt's ardent interest in Gregorian chant and its use in liturgical practice may remind one of the Cecilian movement—which also advocated the purification of church music through returning to earlier traditions. Yet, as we might imagine, given Liszt's acknowledgment of the inescapability of the modern in our revival of the past, the initial sympathy between the two sides started to wane in the longer run.[19] Indeed, the conflict was also unavoidable since both Franz Xaver Witt and Franz Xaver Haberl viewed Palestrina's style as the unsurpassable culmination of a tradition of church music based on Gregorian chant, implying that the work of the Renaissance master should also serve as models for contemporary musicians. By contrast, Liszt believed that the artistic achievements of the past were by necessity unrepeatable and felt little inclined to produce "copies" of the masterworks of the Renaissance or any other era. As Paul Merrick has cogently summarized, "Listening to Palestrina, Liszt marvelled not at the technique, but the state of mind that produced such music." If so, it is no wonder that he "did not study Palestrina's technique, but instead searched for harmonies that would evoke the world of enchantment conjured up in his imagination."[20] This differentiation is crucial not only for our understanding of the conflict between the Cecilian movement and Liszt, but also for reconstructing the intellectual background of much of the composer's late music with religious connotations. Whereas Witt and Haberl seemed hopeful that basing contemporary liturgical practice on plainchant and Palestrina-style vocal polyphony would somehow also restore the religious feelings of those earlier times, Liszt evidently believed that the revival of venerable musical relics that "have no equivalent in our modern music" should optimally serve as starting points and sources of inspiration for new works stylistically better suited to the sensitivities of contemporary audiences: "Art must strive to study the past and its masterpieces, rather than imitate in a servile manner the forms that are forever changing and vanishing as time itself forever changes and vanishes."[21]

Thus, not even Liszt's *Missa choralis*—a work written in the year of his taking the holy orders and occasionally described in the literature as his *messe grégorienne*—proved archaizing enough to fit Cecilian tastes.[22] Although the numerous chromatic passages may have rendered the musical rhetoric of the piece more accessible for contemporary listeners, they inevitably distanced the work from Palestrina's style, as well as from the Cecilian ideal of easy performability. It seems difficult to establish when Liszt realized that the gap between his approach and that of the Cecilians was unbridgeable; somewhat surprisingly, he submitted three of his works (including the rather radical *Via Crucis*) to the quasi-official Cecilian publishing house Pustet as late as 1884 and was severely hurt by their rejection.[23] From the perspective of Pustet, however, this rejection was eminently reasonable and was based on aesthetic considerations as well as on the limited marketability of such compositions (which Liszt also admitted). In the mid-1880s, *Via Crucis* was certainly "music for the future"—it is significant that its first performance did not take place until Good Friday 1929, some forty-five years later, in Budapest.

Medievalist Modernism?

In the preceding paragraphs, I have sought to demonstrate Liszt's thorough expertise in the field of Gregorian chant, as well as illuminate some of the ways in which he integrated this medieval repertory in his own compositions. In the remaining two sections, however, I should like to investigate a more sensitive question, namely, to what extent the composer's close familiarity with plainchant might be related to his much-discussed modernism and how this plausible connection might affect the discourse surrounding another oft-mentioned source of Liszt's modernism, namely the Hungarian-gypsy tradition.

As for the first of these questions, it is worth remembering that Liszt's consistent move away from conventional harmonic tonality was by no means restricted to its best known and most radical forms, his emblematic use of whole-tone patterns, gypsy scales spiced with augmented seconds, and the like. In his ever stronger avoidance of time-worn chord progressions, his experiences with modality undoubtedly played an equally crucial role—and in this regard the significance of his close familiarity with plainchant and its traditional church modes, as well as his extensive efforts to introduce such melodies in his own compositions, would be difficult to overestimate. Indeed, while reading Alix Tiron's *Études sur la musique grecque, le plain-chant et la tonalité modern*, published in Paris in 1866, Liszt added many remarks (in two different colors) on the margin, among others jotting a tick mark of agreement on page 153, next to the sentence that summarizes the basic agenda of the author: "By exposing to you the theory of ancient tonalities, I wanted to put you in a position to draw new ideas, new inspirations from it, through which you could enrich modern music."[24]

But Liszt's expertise in plainchant did not simply imply his familiarity with the "official" church modes; it must also have raised his awareness of another ancient

EXAMPLE 3.7   Liszt, *Via crucis* (1876–1879), mm. 1–6.

phenomenon: pentatonicism. Whereas the composer did not have the occasion to study old-style Hungarian folk songs, which would later call the attention of Bartók's generation to the importance of five-note structures, his analyses of Gregorian chant undoubtedly made him recognize the pentatonic skeleton behind many a traditional melody. After all, his own cross motive also exhibited a characteristically pentatonic kernel and appears in decisively pentatonic contexts in a great number of plainsongs. Furthermore, Liszt might easily have identified certain five-note skeletons lurking in the background of other, not strictly pentatonic plainsongs—a fact suggested by the very opening of his *Via Crucis*, which prepares the vocal entrance of the "Vexilla regis" melody (see Example 3.5) by a six-bar, characteristically pentatonic prelude (see Example 3.7) omitting a note from the borrowed melody.

The role of pentatonicism appears even more important if we look at one of Liszt's late religious works, the 1881 Ave Maria (traditionally numbered as IV; see Example 3.8).

In their *Traité*, as mentioned previously, Niedermeyer and Ortigue suggested that arrangers of plainsong should use the scale of the melody in the accompaniment as well—advice Liszt obviously found too strict to follow in the longer run. In this Ave Maria, nevertheless, the principle seems valid, even if it is used with a twist. The piece consists of three brief sections: Two iterations of "Ave, Ave Maria, Maria" frame a central statement, which opens with a decisive fourth gesture (mm. 12–13, varied repetition in mm. 14–15) using characteristic plainchant inflections and eventually descending an entire octave unaccompanied along the notes of a pentatonic scale (B–G♯–F♯–D♯–C♯–B). Especially in view of the *Traité's* suggestion, it is very likely no coincidence that the accompanimental figures used in the preceding bars (mm. 6–8 and 8–10, respectively) make use of the notes of this pentatonic set (first omitting C♯ and then G♯). Even more intriguing, the accompaniment features the same kind of four-note figuration from the start, using two different but equally "incomplete" sets (leaving E out in both mm. 1–2 and mm. 3–5). All of this produces a decidedly "natural" sound effect (as confirmed by Liszt's initial remark under the beginning of the keyboard part: "quasi Glockenläuten") and, in fact, also a curious type of "modulation" based on the gradual displacement of tones, which leads from the G-based tonality of mm. 1–2 to mm. 9–10, where the piano plays the exact same type of figuration, but a major third higher. Accordingly, the middle section could best be interpreted as being centered on B—even though the piano adds a mere two chords, both based on G♯, the very note omitted from the pentatonic set in mm. 9–10. Leaving behind this unusually pentatonic world, the final *Più lento* section (not shown

EXAMPLE 3.8 Liszt, Ave Maria (1881), mm. 1–21.

in Example 3.8) moves toward more familiar ground through a modally flavored succession of triads, until it reaches the G-major key one could only suspect at the beginning. In addition, this arrival is highlighted by a 9–8 suspension in the melody—a decidedly contemporary gesture very much like the one we saw in *Ave maris stella* (Example 3.6, mm. 11–12), which incidentally also had a touch of pentatonicism in its accompaniment. Having safely established the key, the voice part concludes its journey with plainsong-like simplicity, only to let the piano add a brief postlude "dying away" (*Smorzando*), which does not question the tonality, but nonetheless makes the conclusion slightly enigmatic.

While Liszt's Ave Maria does not explicitly quote plainchant, its voice part clearly relies on Gregorian models at several points, and much of the accompaniment is also

EXAMPLE 3.8 Continued

derived from this melodic material. Nonetheless, I would argue that the influence of Gregorian chant might reach even deeper, since the relative paucity of artistic means—in other words, the striking minimalism of the piece—could also be seen as an up-to-date realization of the austerity associated with plainchant in general. To be sure, some would argue that this feature has little to do with the composer's interest in the Gregorian repertoire, since austerity, introspectiveness, compression, fragmentariness, and retrospectivity are typical features of late works in general.[25] Even if similar features tend to appear with some frequency in the works of aged composers, however, there is no reason to question that, specifically with Liszt, the composer's ever increasing involvement with religion, his laying out plans to reform church music, and his thorough analysis of much of the relevant repertory might have been the prime mover behind his gradual change of style, catalyzing the radical austerity of several of his late works.

Half Gypsy, Half Franciscan

Having argued that Liszt's long and intensive involvement with Gregorian chant had an influence on several of his works and notably some of his radical late works, I would like to conclude by exploring how this notion may shed new light on the more traditional idea that much of Liszt's modernism derives from his contact with a rather different repertory, namely *verbunkos*-style music as performed by the Romani in Hungary.

In exploring this problem, it is worth remembering that, whereas modern analysts of Liszt's works tended to interpret the Otherness of gypsy music in a national and geographical context, the composer himself apparently appreciated the peculiarities of this musical idiom also from a chronological viewpoint, suggesting that this tradition was brought to Europe in the Middle Ages. His monograph *Des Bohémiens et de leur musique en Hongrie* returns to this point several times. We first learn that the Romani "arrived in Europe in the 14th century with little noise and with small steps, so imperceptibly as if they had emerged from under the earth."[26] Furthermore, "one possesses some data about the presence of Gypsies in Hungary as early as the 13th century; thus, two hundred years prior to their immigration to the rest of Europe."[27] But Liszt goes even further, pointing out that this date is still at best a *terminus post quem* since "there is no fact to prove that they had not been there previously."[28] Overall, the "gypsy book" leaves no doubt that Liszt viewed this music not only as national and exotic, but also as very old and connected to the Middle Ages in time. Liszt also goes on directly to connect this ancient past with his own time by citing Carl Spindler's 1827 novel *The Jew (Der Jude)* as a vivid description of gypsy camps "in the Middle Ages (which one could equally encounter today)."[29] To be sure, Liszt was aware that the culture of medieval gypsies would not have been transmitted unchanged over the centuries and, precisely therefore, found it a challenge to reconstruct their long-forgotten "epic" from the fragments that have survived. Nonetheless, it is safe to conclude that, for him, the attraction of gypsy music resided not only in its *transcultural*, but also in its *transtemporal* aspect—just as his interest in plainchant was not motivated exclusively by the religious connotations of this music, but also the fact of its representing an old age and, consequently, its having "no equivalent in our modern music."[30]

In this light it is little wonder that Liszt's famous description of his meeting with the celebrated Romani violinist János Bihari also associates the charm of the latter's playing with a medieval tradition:

> The emotions we then experienced should resemble the effect produced by one of those mysterious elixirs allegedly concocted by the bold alchemists, demonized magicians of the Middle Ages, in their secret laboratories: beverages full of virtue, which instilled into our veins a new principle of strength, virility, courage, pride, incorruptibility and invulnerability.[31]

This fascinating recollection is all the more remarkable since it does not merely connect Bihari's "magic" to the Middle Ages, the period Liszt associated with the appearance of Romani and their music in Europe, but also relates it specifically to alchemy, thereby emphasizing the pagan nature of Bihari's art. To be sure, some alchemists were eager to support their ideas through biblical exegesis, but the relationship between alchemy and Christianity was mostly strained, and Liszt might easily have had this association in mind as well when describing Bihari's influence on him.[32] Intriguingly, several passages of *Des Bohémiens et de leur musique en Hongrie* suggest that the composer viewed the rejection of intellectual dogmas and Christian moral principles as an inherent characteristic of gypsies in general. "Authority, law, rule, precept, principle, obligation, duty are insufferable notions and things for him, since their admission requires reflection with an application of the spirit that is antipathetic to him," Liszt insists, adding that the gypsies' life is "without purpose and result" and, "for them, nothing can equal the liberty of satisfying at all times the least of their caprices."[33] In other words, "veilless and undisguised egoism, without mitigation and delay; frank and absolute egoism is the only drive of the Gypsies' life," and so "these big children, preoccupied uniquely and exclusively with themselves, like the small ones, never identify with others, and are even less capable of associating themselves with an idea."[34] In view of this complete lack of fraternal love and idealism, it is little wonder that Liszt diagnoses a "complete absence of any religious inclination," even though he is quick to reject the usual accusation that the gypsy would in fact have repugnance for Christians: "They detest neither the Christian nor the Muslim nor the Buddhist; they only abhor civilization, which trails along all the stabilities of social life."[35] For this reason, gypsies in fact "never reject baptism, which they take for a mere ceremony," but nevertheless escape all definitions of social boundaries, and arguably rightly so: "Could we guarantee that this European world, which calls itself Christian, could give him more than the joys of nature and freedom, to which it might make him insensitive?"[36]

All this inevitably invites us to view the two potential sources of inspiration for Liszt's modernist tendencies as a pair complementing each other. While, as our analysis has shown, the composer viewed not only plainchant, but also gypsy music as a relic of the Middle Ages, the two stood in sharp contrast from an ideological point of view. Though closely connected with the Roman Catholic liturgy and thus the composer's own confession, for nineteenth-century Europeans plainchant also represented religious faith in general. By contrast, at least for Liszt, the music played by the gypsies came perforce to be associated with its performers' antibourgeois moral characteristics, among them irreligiosity. The composer seems to have been fully aware of the paradox inherent in his attraction to both these poles—his own ironic description of himself as "half Gypsy, half Franciscan" in a letter as early as 1856 leaves no doubt in this regard.[37] In the context of the present volume, however, it is less the moral differences than the chronological kinship that seems relevant: both Liszt's Franciscan and gypsy sides implied his investment in musical repertories he associated with the Middle Ages. That his experiences with these traditional styles eventually inspired him to write music "for the future" testifies to the outstanding inventiveness of Liszt's "secret laboratory," which allowed him to concoct new stylistic combinations that injected "a new principle of strength, virility, courage" into nineteenth-century music.

NOTES

1. Cf. *Franz Liszt's Briefe*, ed. La Mara (Leipzig: Breitkopf & Härtel, 1893–1905), 7:57–58.
2. Quoted from Liszt's 1855 essay entitled *Marx und sein Buch: Die Musik des neunzehnten Jahrhunderts und ihre Pflege*, in Cornelia Szabó-Knotik, "Tradition as a Source of Progress: Franz Liszt and Historicism," in *Liszt and the Birth of Modern Europe* (Franz Liszt Studies Series No. 9), eds. Michael Saffle and Rossana Dalmonte (Hillsdale, NY: Pendragon Press, 2003), 143–156, 150.

3. For Bach's comparison to Thomas Aquinas, see Liszt's letter to Franz Servais dated December 20, 1869, in *Franz Liszt's Briefe*, 2:153.

4. The term appears in Mihály Mosonyi's July 1858 letter to Liszt; see the thoughtful summary in Nicolas Dufetel, "Religious Workshop and Gregorian Chant: The Janus Liszt, or How to Make New with the Old," in *Liszt's Legacies. Based on Papers Presented at the International Liszt Conference Held at Carleton University, Ottawa, Canada, 28–31 July 2011*, eds. James Deaville and Michael Saffle (Hillsdale, NY: Pendragon Press, 2014), 43–71.

5. The rather modern style of the song "Nem ettem én ma egyebet" (proposed by Reményi) is highlighted by its conspicuous similarity to the chorus "Szép örömkönny ragyogása" from Ferenc Erkel's opera *Bánk bán*, first performed at the National Theater in Pest on March 9, 1861.

6. The original letter (in French) is quoted in Klára Hamburger, "Liszt and Émile Ollivier," *Studia Musicologica Academiae Scientiarum Hungaricae* 28, nos. 1–4 (1986): 65–77, 76.

7. A list of the surviving volumes with brief descriptions of Liszt's autograph notes is available in *Franz Liszt's Estate at the Budapest Academy of Music. I. Books*, ed. Mária Eckhardt (Budapest: Liszt Ferenc Zeneművészeti Főiskola, 1986).

8. The same memory aid appears in three other volumes of Liszt's library; see Eckhardt, *Franz Liszt's Estate I. Books*, 50, 76–77, 91–92, 125, 182.

9. See, in particular, Liszt's letters to Princess Wittgenstein (August 9, 1856) and Ortigue (November 28, 1862) in *Franz Liszt's Briefe*, 4:311 and 8:155–159, respectively.

10. See Liszt's remark at the end of his letter dated June 5, 1878, in *Franz Liszt's Briefe*, 7:220–222; as well as Dufetel, "Religious Workshop," 18.

11. *De la musique religieuse* is quoted in full in English in Lina Ramann, *Franz Liszt, Artist and Man, 1811–1840*, trans. E. Cowdery (London: Allen, 1882), 383–385.

12. While *Totentanz* owes much of its effect to the obstinate recurrence of the Dies irae melody, as Liszt's sketchbook reveals, the composer originally intended also to incorporate a four-part harmonization of Psalm 130 (the very De profundis he had used in his "psaume instrumental"), but gave up on this idea as late as 1859. See Adrienne Kaczmarczyk, "Liszt, Lamennais und der Totentanz," *Studia Musicologica Academiae Scientiarum Hungaricae* 43, nos. 1–2 (2002): 53–72.

13. In Example 3.2, I have placed the text for the original chant above the staves rather than between them, to clarify that this text is linked to the original chant and not to the keyboard arrangement. I have followed the same procedure with regard to Examples 3.5 and 3.6.

14. In the dramaturgy of the symphonic poem, the quotation plays such a central role that one tends to take at face value the words Liszt wrote to his cousin Eduard on January 23, 1876: "I wrote the 'Hunnenschlacht' absolutely for the sake of the hymn 'Crux Fidelis.'" (See *Franz Liszt's Briefe*, 2:235.) Paul Thissen has suggested that the work also quotes the antiphon *Quia vidisti me, Thoma, credidisti* from m. 314 on; see his *Zitattechniken in der Symphonik des 19. Jahrhundert* (Sinzig: Studio, 1998), 91.

15. Heinrich M. Sambeth's "Die gregorianischen Melodien in den Werken Franz Liszt's und ihre Bedeutung für die Entwicklung seiner Religiosität und Kunstanschauung" (PhD Diss., Kaiser-Wilhelms-Universität Münster, 1923) is still a useful point of reference.

16. See Sambeth, "Die gregorianischen Melodien," 157–158; and Peter Raabe, *Liszts Schaffen* (Stuttgart: Cottasche Buchhandlung Nachfolger, 1931), 231.

17. See Louis Niedermeyer and Joseph d'Ortigue, *Traité théorique et pratique de l'accompagnement du plain-chant* (Paris: Heugel, 1857), 15.

18. See Paul Merrick, *Revolution and Religion in the Music of Liszt* (Cambridge: Cambridge University Press, 1987), 92. On a similar note, Serge Gut has identified the Te Deum laudamus of 1859 as Liszt's first piece applying modality from beginning to end and attributed this innovation to the composer's interest in the *Traité*. See his "Die historische Position der Modalität bei Franz Liszt," in *Liszt Studien 1. Kongress-Bericht Eisenstadt 1975*, ed. Wolfgang Suppan (Graz: Akademische Druck- u. Verlagsanstalt, 1977), 97–103, 97–98.

19. For a useful overview of the composer's relationship to the movement, see Zsuzsanna Domokos, "Liszt's Connection with the Cecilian Movement in the Light of His Music Library in Budapest," in *Franz Liszt's Estate at the Budapest Academy of Music. II. Music*, ed. Mária Eckhardt (Budapest: Liszt Ferenc Zeneművészeti Főiskola, 1993), 76–84.

20. Merrick, *Revolution and Religion*, 213–214.

21. Quoted from Liszt's 1855 essay entitled *Marx und sein Buch: Die Musik des neunzehnten Jahrhunderts und ihre Pflege* in Szabó-Knotik, "Tradition as a Source of Progress," 152.

22. The expression appears in a letter the composer sent to Princess Wittgenstein on August 20, 1860—a date too early to make a direct connection with the 1865 *Missa choralis* convincing. Cf. *Franz Liszt's Briefe*, 5:41.

23. See Alan Walker, *Franz Liszt. Volume Three: The Final Years 1861–1886* (London: Faber & Faber, 1997), 383–384.

24. Intriguingly, Liszt also put a + sign next to Tiron's music example demonstrating the *gamme chromatique phrygienne*, a Phrygian scale in which scale degrees 3 and 7 are raised—a gypsy-type variant that Liszt used with some frequency. See the facsimile in Eckhardt, *Franz Liszt's Estate I. Books*, 197.

25. See Joseph N. Straus, "Disability and 'Late Style' in Music," *Journal of Musicology* 25, no. 1 (Winter 2008): 3–45, 8–12. Dolores Pesce has discussed Liszt's late style in this light in her *Liszt's Final Decade* (Rochester, NY: University of Rochester Press, 2014), 217–218.

26. Franz Liszt, *Des Bohémiens et de leur musique en Hongrie* (Paris: Bourdilliat, 1859), 19.

27. Liszt, *Des Bohémiens*, 258. Liszt provides more details about the increase in the gypsies' numbers in this century on p. 289.

28. Liszt, *Des Bohémiens*, 260.

29. Liszt, *Des Bohémiens*, 107–108.

30. Shay Loya's recent account of the composer's creative relationship with the *verbunkos* style describes the phenomenon as transcultural modernism; see his *Liszt's Transcultural Modernism and the Hungarian-Gypsy Tradition* (Rochester, NY: University of Rochester Press, 2011).

31. Liszt, *Des Bohémiens*, 295.

32. See Tara Nummedal, "Alchemy and Religion in Christian Europe," *Ambix* 60, no. 4 (November 2013): 311–322, 321.

33. Liszt, *Des Bohémiens*, 53–54.

34. Liszt, *Des Bohémiens*, 60–61, 99. The uncommon word *veilless* here means "unconcealed" or "overt."

35. Liszt, *Des Bohémiens*, 122–123, 98.

36. Liszt, *Des Bohémiens*, 145, 208.

37. See the composer's letter to Princess Wittgenstein dated August 13, 1856, in *Franz Liszt's Briefe*, 4:316. A useful recent overview of Liszt's close relationship with the Franciscans is Nicolas Dufetel's "Franz Liszt, franciscain 'du berceau jusqu'à la tombe,'" *Études franciscaines* 2, no. 2 (2009): 303–339.

CHAPTER 4

SOLDIERS AND CENSORS

Verdi's Medieval Imagination

LIANA PÜSCHEL

BETWEEN 1857 and 1858, Giuseppe Verdi undertook a long and difficult negotiation with the Neapolitan censors to obtain the authorization to perform his *Gustavo III* (soon to become *Un ballo in maschera*) at the San Carlo Theatre. Among the many changes the censors required was one that Verdi was completely unwilling to accept: to backdate the setting of the opera to a time when the witches' scene could be acceptable. Originally, *Gustavo III* was set in the Swedish court in the second half of the eighteenth century, but the censors insisted on setting the opera in fourteenth-century Florence, amid the battles between Guelphs and Ghibellines. The composer, commenting on the heavily revised libretto rechristened for the occasion *Adelia degli Adimari* (or "degli animali" as Verdi ironically used to call it), wrote,

> Even a blind man could see how much damage has been done to the action by chang-
> ing the character of Gustavo in this way: everything becomes false, uninteresting,
> and that indefinable element of brilliance and chivalry, that aura of gaiety that per-
> vaded the whole action and which made a fine contrast and was like light in the
> darkness surrounding the tragic moment, has vanished. With the leader of a faction,
> and a Guelph one, at a time of blood and iron, everything becomes gloomy, dark,
> heavy and boring.[1]

Do these words summarize the vision Verdi had of the Middle Ages, as a period colored in the shades of blood and darkness? The fact that a dozen of his operas (or even more, if we include works such as *Clara di Perth*, the Neapolitan censored version of *Rigoletto*) had medieval settings makes this a difficult question to answer (see Appendix 4.1). These works were created over a period of more than fifty years, a period in which the style and interests of the composer developed in new directions and in which his status within the profession changed significantly (increasing his success in negotiating with librettists, singers, and theater directors). The Italian social and political situation changed in many significant ways as well. Theaters acquired new technical capabilities, and interest in historical novels grew and decreased. My aim in this essay is to bring to the surface some of the associations and expectations that the medieval locale stimulated in the composer, his librettists, and his Italian public by taking a broad look at Verdi's works and the historical contexts of their composition. My focus will be on two examples: the failed refashioning of *Un ballo in maschera* as a medieval opera and the successful transformation of *Stiffelio* into *Aroldo*.

Patriots and Poets: Perception of the Middle Ages in Nineteenth-Century Italy

The considerable number of operas with medieval settings written by Verdi is not accidental. During the romantic age, enthusiasm for the Middle Ages spread all over Europe and found fertile ground in Italy, where it was often associated with patriotic issues both before and after the unification of the country. During most of Verdi's life, Italy was politically divided. The situation was not new, because since the fall of the Western Roman Empire, the Italian Peninsula, with its "destructive charms," had attracted many invaders and had lost its political unity.[2] Nevertheless, after the Congress of Vienna and the awakening of nationalisms in Europe, many in Italy looked forward to the constitution of a unitary state. During the Risorgimento, as Adrian Lyttelton explains, many Italians looked to their history to provide a focus for their national identity:

> Italy was handicapped by a lack of unifying political institutions in the past....Only ancient Rome was a possible point of reference. But the Roman tradition was both too local and too universal to serve as a satisfactory foundation for national identity....
>
> The Renaissance as a whole suffered from the stigma associated with political defeat, and its cultural glories were sometimes explained as the survival of an earlier and happier period. In the Middle Ages Italian liberty was at least vigorously defended.[3]

Given these premises, it is not surprising that in the first decades of the nineteenth century men and women turned to the Middle Ages as a source for the roots of their national identity. They individualized and promoted those episodes and characters from the Middle Ages that proved to be useful as exempla in the fight for freedom, at the expense of those that might convey messages adverse to the cause of independence.[4] Episodes like the creation of the Lombard League against Barbarossa, the Sicilian Vespers, or the challenge of Barletta became extremely popular as demonstrated by their quotation in patriotic hymns such as "Il canto degli italiani" (1847) by Goffredo Mameli, set to music by Michele Novaro. The fourth stanza of this hymn, now the Italian national anthem, references the Lombard League and the Vespers: "From the Alps to Sicily, / Legnano is everywhere; ... Every trumpet blast / sounds the Vespers."[5]

To Verdian listeners, *Legnano* and *Vespers* are familiar words: In fact, the historical events cherished by the supporters of the Risorgimento fueled the imagination of writers, painters, and, of course, composers of Verdi's age. The cross-pollination among the various artistic genres contributed to the dissemination of certain characters and stories: The long narrative poem *Le Fantasie* (1829) by Giovanni Berchet, which describes the fight of the Lombard communes against Barbarossa, inspired Francesco Hayez's painting *Battaglia di Legnano* (1831) and probably Massimo D'Azeglio's painting on the same subject (1832).[6] D'Azeglio's novel *Ettore Fieramosca* (1833), which narrates the challenge of Barletta, provided the subject for several operas and ballets; even Salvadore Cammarano was enthralled by the subject and offered it to Verdi in 1848.[7] These writers and painters (along with other members of the intelligentsia) were the main champions of the revival of the Middle Ages in the first half of the nineteenth century, when Italian professional historiography had not yet taken its first steps. They had a predilection for the age of the communes, fed by the monumental *Histoire des républiques italiennes du Moyen Âge* by the Swiss historiographer Simonde de Sismondi, but they also demonstrated a growing interest in the barbarian invasions of the early Middle Ages.[8] Poets, painters, and musicians transformed historical facts into long-lasting myths that remained unaltered even when, decades later, professional historians scaled them down or denied them, myths that penetrated deep into popular culture.[9]

With the constitution of the Kingdom of Italy in 1861, the interest in the medieval period did not diminish, but instead, perhaps, became even more widely disseminated. The flourishing of historical research in the Middle Ages and the restoration of medieval buildings (often undertaken with excessive imagination rather than attention to historical verisimilitude) testify to the continual hold that this period had on the Italian imagination. Not surprisingly, writers and artists of this period reinterpreted well-known episodes from the past (or selected new ones) to use as a bedrock for the construction of the national history and for the validation of the Savoy dynasty.[10] As demonstrated by the use of the icon of the Lega in many theater curtains after the unification, for example, the Lombard League and the Battle of Legnano were still much in vogue; the use of this symbol in theaters is significant, since theater-goers belonged to different classes.[11]

As previously stated, Verdi was also infatuated by those episodes of national medieval history that could be read as metaphors for the present state of Italy and that were part of the common patriotic discourse; *I Lombardi alla prima crociata* (1843), *Attila* (1846), *La battaglia di Legnano* (1849), and *Les vêpres siciliennes* (1855) are examples of this interest. We can also find patriotic statements in medievalist operas that do not refer to national myths, such as the Shakespearean *Macbeth* (1847): Here, the chorus "Patria oppressa" joins the discourse of national feeling and desire for justice. In recent years, Verdi's political involvement and the reception of his operas as patriotic symbols have been put into question: In this regard, Philip Gossett has perhaps expressed one of the most even-handed positions. Since Verdi participated as a passionate observer of the Italian efforts toward independence and unity, Gossett explains, his operas dealing with subjects associated with this fight cannot be casual; at the same time, the composer was able to make compromises, accepting the requests of the censors to facilitate the performance and circulation of his works and to avoid prison or exile.[12] *Compromise* is a key word for understanding the ways in which the subjects of Verdi's works were chosen, at least in the first years of his career. Indeed, as a man of theater Verdi must have known that in the complex world of opera there could not be success without the support of theater directors and other influential personalities. Even if the public was ready and able to decipher the potential patriotic messages of a work, moreover, this does not mean that Verdi was necessarily viewed as a leader of the Risorgimento.

In the cultural panorama in which Verdi's operas were situated, the Middle Ages were not only the source for national myths but also generally associated with the adventurous, the poetic, and even the bizarre, as witnessed by the success in Italy of historical novels such as *Ivanhoe* by Walter Scott (first Italian translation 1822), *Margherita Pusterla* (1838) by Cesare Cantù, and *Ildegonda* (1820) and *Marco Visconti* (1834) by Tommaso Grossi.[13] At the beginning of the century, the success of the medieval myths promoted by the Risorgimento was made possible thanks to a widespread vogue for that historical period, while later, the medieval taste was further sustained by patriotic propaganda.[14] In Italy, as in other European countries, the patriotic reading of the Middle Ages (and its role in the construction of a national identity) could sometimes intermingle with its decorative role as a backdrop for stories dealing with love, revenge, and supernatural forces.

Silk and Sicilianas: Verdi's Historical Accuracy

Verdi's operas bear testimony to the aforementioned double use of the Middle Ages in Italian culture: A medieval setting was favored for patriotic works but also for highly adventurous and passionate dramas. In *I lombardi alla prima crociata*, these two aspects are combined with a preponderance of the novelesque, while in *Il trovatore* there are no traces of Risorgimento political references. The source of inspiration for the latter opera, the Spanish chivalric drama *El trovador* (1836) by Antonio García Gutiérrez, reminds us that Verdi's interest in subjects set in the medieval period was not restrained to Italian history and that the vogue for that specific age was shared by all European nations. In general terms, the choice of medieval subjects by the composer was determined by the Italian interest for that specific period, by the suggestions coming from the cultural milieu Verdi frequented, and by the composer's involvement in a common European sensibility. *Attila*, for example, has its origins in a German drama by Zacharias Werner, which previously had inspired Giuseppe Persianis's *Attila in Aquileia* (1827) and Francesco Malipiero's *Attila* (1845, soon retitled *Ildegonda di Borgogna*); it seems that Verdi was introduced to this play in Madame de Staël's *De l'Allemagne*, but he nevertheless asked for advice from Andrea Maffei, a friend and intellectual intensely involved in Verdi's development during his early years.[15] The opera not only may have touched distinctly Italian sensibilities, but also, as Carlotta Sorba maintains, participated "in a common European discursive web surrounding the birth of nations, which Verdi's musical realization helped to grow and popularize."[16] Sorba has argued that Verdi was inspired to set Werner's drama to music by "the possibility of giving life to a powerful piece of national medieval history through a mixture of choruses and incisive characters— that interaction between chorus and the individual on which Mazzini had so insisted— and the possibility of representing the past with the visual and sonorous accuracy that romantic drama required." Indeed, in his *Filosofia della musica* (1836), Giuseppe Mazzini not only highlighted the important role of the chorus, but also urged musicians to reach a greater musical realism, looking for a proper local and historical color:

> Yet as there is an architectural, pictorial, and poetic art expressive of every epoch and every land, so might there be a musical expression of them. Why not study it? Why not disinter such fragments of it as exist hidden among archives and libraries, since it seems there are none who have sufficient earnestness and interest to trace in those national songs which popular tradition and the lips of mothers so long preserve, but which, alas! Are gradually passing away, lost to us forever, in the absence of any who care to study and collect them?[17]

Mazzini wrote *Filosofia della musica* during exile; the essay is imbued with the results of the French discussion on local color, which at those times was vigorous, even fashionable.[18] The research of authentic musical sources, to which the philosopher alludes in the quotation, was already to some degree taking place, since many grand opera composers were using national songs and characteristic instruments to achieve an accurate historical and/or geographical *couleur locale* in their musical scene setting.[19] These naive experiments, however, produced only superficial effects. The solutions adopted by Giacomo Meyerbeer in his historical dramas—which were very much admired by Mazzini—were more convincing (even if the author was not concerned about the exact origin of his characteristic tunes).[20] Insofar as it relates to the idea of "sonorous accuracy," therefore, the concept of *couleur locale* appears then to be ambiguous, since it deals not with what is authentic but with what was perceived as authentic.

Verdi was, perhaps, even less engaged with the rigorous research of musical sources than Meyerbeer was.[21] When composing *Les vêpres siciliennes* and *Otello*, he showed signs of participating Mazzini's call to "disinter" authentic popular music, but in the end, he dispensed with the supposedly genuine material he had found. In 1855 the composer asked his Neapolitan friend Cesare de Sanctis for stylistic details of the tarantella: Were they always in minor mode and in 6/8? Could he send some examples showing other characteristics?[22] Finally, de Sanctis proved to be of no help and Verdi wrote a tarantella following the standardized and idealized model of the learned composers for *Les vêpres siciliennes*. Verdi tried a second time to involve his friend in a quest for traditional music, since act 3 of *Les vêpres siciliennes* was to end with a divertissement full of southern Italian local color: "I would like you to send me a Sicilian song or air or whatever. But I want a real Siciliana, that's to say a folksong and not a song manufactured by your composers."[23] De Sanctis complied with the request, but the material was judged unsatisfactory and, in the meantime, the characteristic southern number had been replaced by the divertissement "Les quatre saisons." Verdi was no more fortunate in his search for authentic musical material in 1894, when he requested from the editor Ricordi some dances from the Renaissance, in addition to oriental and Greek melodies and "something Venetian" for *Otello*. Not one score sent by Ricordi's musicologists pleased the composer, who preferred the *Chant du muezzin* (1844) by Félicien David and melodies of his own to the more "authentic" materials that he received.[24]

This choice is also typical of Verdi's approach to popular music and local color. In his broad study on Verdi and Spain, Víctor Sánchez Sánchez demonstrated that the composer never tried to capture Spanish flavor through the borrowing of original songs and dances; he rather preferred to invent it using generic Spanish elements, such as dance rhythmic patterns.[25] An analogous observation could be made with regard to the medieval color in certain scenes of *La Battaglia di Legnano* and *Il trovatore*. Verdi wrote a complex musical scene for *La battaglia di Legnano*, act 4, scene 1, for instance, in which two different choruses (one of basses and one of mixed voices) interweave with the voice of Lida (the female leading role) to raise a prayer for the soldiers who are fighting for their freedom. Each vocal line has individual melodic contours and texts to portray the reactions of different characters and to contribute to the dramatic continuity.[26] The music for the basses, which is loosely inspired by plainchant, conveys the medieval color of the scene. This offstage choir represents a group of priests who, inside the Basilica of Sant'Ambrogio, intone a portion of a Latin version of Psalm 83. The use of the Latin language and the organ accompaniment contributes to the religious character of the chorus while other elements (a monodic style in which the rhythm is dictated by word declamation, the absence of modulations, and the limited vocal range) spread on the music a generic antique glaze.[27] *Il trovatore* offered Verdi another commonplace of medieval imagery: a troubadour singing a romance to his lover accompanied by his lute. In his study on the reception and the reinvention of troubadour music, John Haines comments on Manrico's romanza in these terms: "Giuseppe Verdi's *Il trovatore* may have been situated in 15th century Spain, but moments such as the troubadour's romance 'Deserto sulla terra' in the first act clearly ape the well-established French musical medievalism."[28] Haines's characterization of Verdi is rather harsh, but it confirms that Verdi was not concerned about writing a historically informed rendition of a troubadour's song. "Deserto sulla terra," in fact, follows the model of the French romances in medieval fashion: It is a strophic song in simple, regular style that begins in minor and finishes in major mode (E♭mi–E♭M), the accompaniment is elementary (a series of arpeggiated chords played by the harp) and the vocal range is limited.[29] Nevertheless, the composer tinged the romance with some Spanish color, as testified by the exotic turn in the third measure of the vocal line.

Documentary sources seem to have had a tighter grip on Verdi's visual rather than musical imagination, and this is of no little consequence since, among the composers of his generation, Verdi, together with Wagner, was the most attentive to the various aspects of the mise en scène.[30] In *Attila*, the composer became personally involved in the conception of the costumes and asked his friend in Rome, Vincenzo Luccardi, to make a sketch of Raphael's fresco in the Vatican portraying Attila and Leo the Great: "Make a quick sketch, then explain me with words and numbers the colors of clothing; I'm especially interested in the headgear."[31] In *I due Foscari*, there is a clear demand for a precise rendition of the Venetian locale, as proved by the stage direction for act 3, scene 1: "Old piazzetta of San Marco. The canal is full of gondolas passing to and fro.... In the distance is the Island of Cypresses, now called San Giorgio."[32] Mercedes Viale Ferrero acutely interprets these words as "a clear warning not to reproduce the Palladian church, built after the time in which the action takes place and, in short, to observe in the scenery the historical truth that Verdi felt was indispensable to achieve dramatic likelihood."[33] In *Macbeth*, the author asked for details on the scenographic solutions used in London to set Shakespeare's drama and forbade the use of silk and velvet costumes because the action was not set at the time of Ossian (!). Many years later, however, he was almost indifferent to the proposal of having models from London for the costumes of *Falstaff*. The attitude of Verdi toward the mise en scène was not uniform during his career; nevertheless, his interest in documentary sources is significant for his visual ideas, while it seems of little relevance for his musical inspiration.[34]

Tartan and Tarantellas: The Middle Ages as Harmless Setting

As I mentioned previously, Verdi's survey of southern Italian popular music at the time of the composition of *Les vêpres siciliennes* ultimately proved fruitless. Since the night of its first performance at the Parisian Académie Impérial de Musique in 1855, one of the most applauded numbers of the opera was the siciliana "Merci, jeunes amies," sung by Hélène in act 5. This siciliana is a bolero (even the first French reviewers perceived it as such) and the musical number that precedes it, the chorus "Célébrons ensemble," is seasoned with Spanish spices too, because it is accompanied by castanets.[35] The inclusion of these two Spanish numbers in the context of the celebration of Hélène and Henri's wedding at the beginning of the final act has nothing to do with the recreation of Sicilian or medieval local color: It aims instead to evoke the light-hearted atmosphere of a party before the tragic conclusion, so it evoked no negative comments from the public or the reviewers.[36] For modern ears, the Spanish flavor of those pages may seem more appropriate in the censored Italian version of *Les vêpres siciliennes*, *Giovanna de Guzman*, which transposed the action to Portugal in the year 1640 (the final year of Spanish rule). In Italy, after the revolutionary riots of 1848 and after the First War of Independence of 1848–1849 (which did not immediately lead to unification), censorship in the various states became even stricter, so Verdi accepted the refashioning of the libretto knowing that this compromise was the only way that his opera would be performed in Italy. If the

Spanish numbers may seem a little curious in an opera set in medieval Sicily, it is also rather puzzling to find some south Italian color in an opera set in baroque Portugal. The composer, in fact, made no effort to change such numbers as the tarantella of act 1 or the (real) siciliana in the summer episode of the divertissement "Les quatre saisons."

Neither *Les vêpres siciliennes* nor its Italian version (*Giovanna de Guzman*) seems to reflect Mazzini's words about musical realism, but it should be noted that among the Italian composers of Verdi's age, the use of local color was far less developed than it was, for example, in France.[37] The musician of Busseto, instead, embraced another more general idea expressed by Mazzini in his *Filosofia della musica*: "Individuality is sacred,"[38] which means that each opera should have an individual character. Verdi pursued the specificity of each one of his works not through local color, but through the *tinta* (mood color).[39] If the relationship between local color and setting is clear, that between Verdi's idea of *tinta* and setting is less univocal. Particularly during the decade before the Italian unification, he probably considered (or accepted for practical reasons) that more than one setting was suitable for an opera.

Knowing the unwritten rules of the production system of the Italian theaters, Verdi could accept the alterations in the setting of his operas imposed by censorship as long as they did not interfere with the *tinta* or the plot. From the composer's point of view, a backdrop depicting Sicily in the thirteenth century was interchangeable with one showing Portugal around 1640, and one portraying Milan in 1176 could be substituted with another representing Haarlem in the sixteenth century (as demonstrated by the conversion of *Les vêpres siciliennes* to *Giovanna de Guzman* or *La battaglia di Legnano* to *L'assedio di Arlem*).[40] In these two occasions, it was essential to remove all references to episodes of medieval Italian history cherished by Italian patriots, but the Middle Ages were not by themselves a historical setting to avoid: in this regard, *Clara di Perth*, the censored version of *Rigoletto*, is eloquent.

Clara di Perth was a "monstrosity" (as Verdi called it) generated in 1853 by the Neapolitan censorship, which, in those years, was among the most severe of the peninsula.[41] The plot is set in the Scottish city of Perth and the libretto announces that "the plot comes from Walter Scott's novel *The Fair Maid of Perth*. It is supposed to take place in the Carnival of 1349. The costumes are in the true Scottish fashion."[42] Mario Lavagetto demonstrated that *Clara di Perth* has very little in common with *The Fair Maid of Perth*: the cross-reference to the British writer aimed to erase the perilous derivation from Victor Hugo's *Le roi s'amuse*, a play banned even in Paris.[43] Changing the historical and geographical setting helped to neutralize the memory of the original libretto, but it may also have had a commercial purpose, since Scott's novels were very popular in Italy. Reading again the stage directions of the libretto, it is clear that the medieval setting was nothing but a fashionable and comfortably distant backdrop and that the profusion of tartan plaid in the costumes was a warranty for the tranquility of the censors.[44]

Verdi judged *Clara di Perth* a monstrosity because it was a completely distorted version of his opera, but the composer probably did not care much about the new setting since he himself, in an early stage of the opera's elaboration, took into account the possibility of moving the plot to the fourteenth century. In fact, even before the opera's debut at La Fenice, the milder Venetian censorship proposed radical changes in the plot and in the behavior of the characters. Verdi was uncompromising on many points, but he was open to the variation of the locale, as shown in a letter to the director of the theater, Carlo Marzari:

> If you needed to change the names, you should have changed the setting too, changing the character into a Duke, a Prince of another place, for example Luigi Farnese, otherwise you could backdate the action before Louis XI, when France was not a united kingdom, and make him a Duke of Burgundy or Normandy etc. etc., in any case an absolute master.[45]

As Lavagetto points out,

> Verdi does not object to the change of historical referentiality, which in fact corresponds to a conspicuous intensification of the device "once upon a time." Censorship, on the other hand, sought to disorient, to move the dramas to unspecified backgrounds that, without undoing the operation of the dramatic machine, minimized the historical connotation.[46]

From the point of view of the various censors, a libretto set in the Middle Ages needed a refashioning if the historical and geographical references were too precise, as in the cases of *Les vêpres siciliennes*, *La battaglia di Legnano*, or *Giovanna d'Arco*, but if those references were blurred, the Middle Ages could be reassuringly obscure and distant. With this criterion, *Giovanna d'Arco* became *Orietta di Lesbo*, *Rigoletto* became *Clara di Perth*, and *Un ballo in maschera* was to become *Adelia degli Adimari*. After the Italian unification, the repressive panorama changed and *Les vêpres siciliennes* could finally be published in Italy as *I vespri siciliani* in 1860 and performed as such in 1861.

For practical reasons, Verdi could tolerate an alteration of the locale, but he was not inclined to accept all changes. As I mentioned in the introduction of this essay, the musician of Busseto undertook a long negotiation with the Neapolitan censors regarding *Un ballo in maschera*: His deliberations over the more appropriate setting for this opera provide insight into his general idea of the Middle Ages as operatic setting. When Somma started to work on the libretto in October 1857, the drama was to unfold in the Enlightened court of Gustave III (1771–1792) of Sweden. After only a month of writing, the librettist received a memorandum from the censors asking for some changes in the plot and in the setting. Somma suggested moving the action to Pomerania in the twelfth century, but Verdi disapproved: "I really think that the 12th century is too distant for our Gustavo. It is such a rough and brutal time especially in those countries that I find it sheer nonsense to have characters sculpted in the French style like Gustavo and Oscar."[47] The plot of the opera is so full of irony and contrasting light effects that the composer needed a brilliant period in which to set it, so he chose the seventeenth century. For the censors, this compromise was not enough; they responded with *Adelia degli*

Adimari, a libretto very freely inspired by Somma's proposal and set in fourteenth-century Florence. In this occasion too, and in a more determined manner, Verdi refused the medieval locale. Perhaps because too many operas were set in those times, Verdi judged the period as "a time of blood and iron," gloom, darkness, heaviness, and even boredom. Finally, he gave up his contract with Naples and offered his opera to the Teatro Apollo in Rome, where it had its debut in 1859, with the action taking place "in and around Boston, Massachusetts" at a time toward the end of the seventeenth century.[48]

Sofas and Shepherds: *Stiffelio* Becomes *Aroldo*

In the case of *Un ballo in maschera*, Verdi already had a plot, a constellation of characters, and a *tinta*: He needed only a fitting locale, reassuring to the eyes of the censorship and consistent with the characteristics of the drama. He had found himself in a similar situation only a few years before, while working on the refashioning of another conjugal drama, *Stiffelio*: In that occasion he accepted to transfer the action to the Middle Ages. At first glance, it seems strange that Verdi could accept the idea of a divorce taking place in the Middle Ages, even while he rejected the idea of a masked ball taking place in the same epoch. To understand this apparent contradiction, we must step back to consider the reasons why *Stiffelio* provoked the grievances of censors in many Italian states.

The origins of *Stiffelio* date back to the beginning of 1850, when Piave, in his quest for new subjects to submit to Verdi's attention, came across *Stifellius!*, a new French mélo-drame recently translated into Italian. Although the play's subject was rather anomalous for the Italian operatic stage (or maybe because of this reason), he resolved to suggest it to the composer. The original play, *Le pasteur, ou L'évangile et le foyer* [The Minister, or The Gospel and the Hearth], was written by Émile Souvestre and Eugène Bourgeois and was based on Souvestre's 1838 novel *Le pasteur d'hommes*.[49] The play made its Parisian debut at the Théâtre de la Porte Saint-Martin in the winter of 1849, but it achieved a greater success in Italy than in France, being translated twice and performed several times.[50] *Le pasteur*, set in contemporary Austria, portrays the internal struggle of Stiffelio, an Evangelical minister belonging to the fictional sect of the Ahasuerians, who discovers that his beloved wife Lina has betrayed him with another man. At first, he offers her a divorce but, in the end, he understands that Lina loves him sincerely and he forgives her. The play, then, deals with sin, adultery, and divorce, posing uncomfortable questions: Is a young woman, who has had an extramarital relationship, inevitably dishonest? Does she deserve forgiveness? Can the sinful be reintegrated into society? Is a man of faith and, in particular, a religious minister able to put into practice the Gospel he preaches? In an unsuspecting way, the interest of Piave and Verdi in this play drew them near to such contemporary writers as Nathaniel Hawthorne and Elisabeth Gaskell, who were confronting these themes (respectively) in the novels *The Scarlet Letter* (1850) and *Ruth* (1853).

As Emilio Sala has clearly pointed out, *Le pasteur* is a sort of hybrid that stands halfway between the bourgeois drama and the *pièce à spectacle*. On the one hand, Souvestre overturned the adultery scheme typical of many romantic plots, where true love is found outside marriage and is never consummated: in the play, the female character, Lina, loves her husband, Stiffelio, and commits adultery out of a tragic physical and psychological fragility. On the other hand, Bourgeois stuffed the play with *coups de théâtre* and adapted his work to the aesthetics of the tableau, setting, for example, the final scene in a magnificent Gothic church.[51] Passing through Piave's quill, *Le pasteur* acquired more spectacular grandeur and, at the same time, lost many of its attractions and realistic elements, first and foremost the psychological survey of Lina's behavior.[52] The librettist preserved an almost contemporary setting but, to prevent the intervention of censorship, looked to distance the plot from the present time by changing many details of the stage directions, obscuring the allusions to adultery, which became a sort of fated mishap, and blurring some references to the religious ministry of Stiffelio. Piave was so skillful with scissors and eraser that he managed to retain what Verdi judged the most intriguing and original element of the play, the dual role of Stiffelio as husband and Evangelical minister. The substantial religious aspect, even if partially disguised, was precisely what the censors could not tolerate: Shortly before its debut, in November 1850 at the Teatro Grande of Trieste, the libretto underwent further revision, which—as the first reviews confirm—resulted in the loss of much of its original meaning and effect. The reviewer of *La favilla* commented explicitly on this point:

> We will not say anything about the finale of the third act since the maiming by the censors and the demands of the police regarding the staging were such as to falsify completely the musical concept and thus take away any effect.[53]

A few days later, the same reviewer further explained the absurdities created by the intervention of the censors:

> The Ahasuerians [in act 3] are gathered in a church, which is no longer a church, because the cross has been banned from it, the kneelers taken away from it, and the faithful are even prohibited from kneeling on the ground (!!) and must pray standing on their feet (!!!) and take care not to give the least clue that they are gathered there to listen to the word of God.[54]

If at Trieste, to make the performance possible, the religious aspects of the drama were considerably watered down, to permit the Roman debut it was necessary to erase them completely. In February 1851, when the opera reached the Papal States, the libretto was refashioned as *Guglielmo Wellingrode*: Under this disguise, the opera enjoyed a modest success for some years through the peninsula. *Guglielmo Wellingrode* moves the action back to fifteenth-century Germany and transforms the main character into the state minister of a German prince. This version of the opera was a new monstrosity to the eyes of Verdi and Piave, who began to discuss implementing some changes to the plot to make it suitable to most Italian theaters.

In the spring of 1856, after much consideration, the composer and the librettist finally started to work on a more acceptable version of *Stiffelio*. The librettist proposed to back-date the drama to the thirteenth century and to transform the Evangelical minister Stiffelio into the crusader Aroldo: Verdi was reluctant, but in the end, he surrendered.[55] The original idea was simply to change the setting, give a few strokes to the libretto and to the music (making it more fitting for the new verses), and write the troublesome last act anew. As the reshaping started to progress, Verdi understood that many more modifications were needed and finally wrote an almost new work. The two operas have in common (with some revisions) the overture and acts 2 and 3; act 1 of *Aroldo* contains some borrowings from the corresponding act from *Stiffelio* but the endings are completely different.[56]

Reworking act 1, Verdi could have had the opportunity to introduce some medieval color in scene 7, where a chorus of knights and ladies greet Aroldo, who has just come back from the Palestinian battlefields. The composer let this chance drop and preferred to reuse what Budden labeled the "waltz-like theme," a theme taken from the act 1, scene 3, chorus of *Stiffelio*: "A te Stiffelio un canto" and already heard, in a slightly different version, in the overture.[57] The waltz theme seems more befitting for the party at Flora's Parisian house than for celebrating a Saxon crusader, but here Verdi, as at the beginning of *Les vêpres siciliennes*, act 5, tried to convey an atmosphere of gaiety. The assignment of evoking the historical and geographical context was entrusted to the libretto and to the staging.

A closer look at the libretto reveals that the choice of the medieval locale was not dictated exclusively by the wish to create a safe distance between the public and the plot. It could have been determined by the realization that some elements predisposed the drama to be moved back to the Middle Ages. The main character, for example, is an uncommon religious minister, since there is a halo of violence around some of his declarations and behaviors. That this harshness, unusual for a religious man, was already recorded by Verdi's peers is confirmed by a review by the *Gazzetta ufficiale di Venezia* of a production of *Stiffelio* at La Fenice in 1852. In this review, Stiffelio's threat of physical violence to Lina ("Il mio piè ti schiaccerà!") is described as a rather strong expression for a man of the cloth.[58] By turning the minister of *Stiffelio* into the crusader of *Aroldo*, Piave and Verdi reinforced the natural vehemence of the character.[59]

Unlike *Un ballo in maschera*, whose plot had appealing spots of levity, brightness, and irony that Verdi feared could be overshadowed by the dimness of the medieval atmosphere, the general mood of *Stiffelio* was uniformly gloomy. Frivolity, sarcasm, and even wit are found in many dialogues of *Le pasteur*, but are completely absent from *Stiffelio*, which, in comparison, is darker. Abramo Basevi, the first commentator of Verdi's operas, remarked on this alteration as well: "Piave transformed to thickest darkness what little light the French authors had introduced into in their drama."[60] The "little light" of the French play went along with some concessions to the Gothic fashion so widespread in Europe at the beginning of the nineteenth century: Lina and her seducer Raffaele exchange letters through a book bound in the Gothic fashion, act 4 takes place in an old graveyard, and act 5 takes place in a Gothic church.[61] In his endeavor to make *Le pasteur* more spectacular, Piave intensified these Gothic elements, thus laying the foundations for the eventual transformation of *Stiffelio* into *Aroldo* (see Appendix 4.2).

What seems out of place in the twelfth-century ambience is the divorce, a *coup de théâtre* and a key turning point in the development of *Stiffelio*. Divorce was a delicate issue in Verdi's times, discussed in aristocratic circles and in novels like Anne Brönte's *The Tenant of Wildfell Hall* (1848) and Charles Dickens' *Hard Times* (1854). More unexpected, perhaps, it was also a recurrent subject in stories with a medieval backdrop like the aforementioned *The Fair Maid of Perth* (1828) and *The Betrothed* (1825), another novel by Scott, which, as Budden pointed out, could have been a source of inspiration for *Aroldo* since it deals with the marital problems of a crusader upon his return from Palestine.[62] To Piave, it could have seemed natural to relocate the action to those "hard and iron days" when annulments of marriage were so frequent.[63]

As already noted, the action of *Le pasteur* takes place in a contemporary setting interspersed with Gothic elements. The stage directions for its first three acts portray the interior of a bourgeois dwelling, simple and comfortable, where its inhabitants read, sew, and have frivolous conversations. Sofas and armchairs are the symbols of this familiar atmosphere: At the opening of the curtain in act 3, for example, the sober Ahasuerian minister Jorg is at his ease on a sofa reading the Bible. The three opening acts, with their homely frame, are thus closer to the bourgeois drama. Interested in the most melodramatic and eye-catching elements of the original play, Piave and Verdi consequently suppressed the first two of these acts, retaining only the third for plot issues. To add splendor to it and to ennoble the action, the house was transformed into a castle, its owner (Lina's father Stankar and originally a forester) became a count, and even the furniture changed, losing most of its plain comfort. In act 1, scene 1 (corresponding to act 3, scene 1, of the play), for example, Jorg found himself deprived of his sofa and is seated instead at a table. The ennoblement of the settings probably added some luster to the decor but was not unanimously welcomed: the reviewer of *La favilla*, for example, commented, "In the mise-en-scène we would have preferred more accuracy, both with the decor as well as with the wardrobes. The hall and the ballroom in act 1 in no way evoke the house of an Evangelical minister or the gathering place of a religious community."[64]

There is nothing more typical in a medieval landscape than a castle. When Piave transformed *Stiffelio* into *Aroldo*, therefore, he could simply cut and paste the stage directions of the original opera into the manuscript for the adaptation, making a few interesting adjustments. The retouches demonstrate that with *Aroldo* the librettist and the composer pursue a further ennoblement of the action: In *Stiffelio* act 1, scene 1, there is a window and in *Aroldo* act 1, scene 1, the window is "large"; in *Stiffelio* act 1, scene 9, there is a reception hall prepared for a celebration, while in *Aroldo* act 1, scene 7, there is a whole suite of rooms prepared for a "grand" celebration. In *Aroldo*, interior backdrops seem more magnificent and allow us to imagine a deeper perspective; in fact, the large window shows the battlements of the castle, which, as an element of defensive architecture, can allude to the continuous state of war usually associated with the medieval period. "Iron and blood" is insinuated into the scenery through the identity of the characters: the Evangelical minister Stiffelio was forced into the armor of the crusader Aroldo, and the aristocratic Raffaele (Lina's lover) took on the guise of the soldier of fortune Godvino; Stankar, already an old colonel in *Stiffelio*, preserved his martial character when—in *Aroldo*—he took on the clothes of the old knight Egberto.

The comparison between the stage directions for act 1 of both operas reveals something else. The "hearth with a fire alight," which warms the scene in *Stiffelio*, disappears in *Aroldo*, certainly not because the weather in the county of Kent is milder than in Austria. In *Stiffelio*, the hearth provided the visual materials for a *coup de théâtre*, which Verdi dropped from *Aroldo*; the hearth thus no longer had a dramatic function.[65] Yet, in *Stiffelio* the hearth had a metaphoric role as well, because it represented the domestic intimacy and, probably, alluded to the "foyer" (hearth) in the title of the French play. The hearth, along with the modern costumes adopted, was thus part of an effort to preserve some of the realistic contemporary atmosphere of the original play. It was a meager attempt indeed, but since it collided with the grandness of the mise en scène and the Italian audience's love for period costumes, it was even more remarkable. The removal of the hearth form *Aroldo* confirms its symbolic significance and its association with the more epic atmosphere of the medieval period, where traces of bourgeois comfort have no place.

Many reviewers complained about the modern costumes of *Stiffelio* and, looking at the frontispiece of the piano–vocal score of the work, printed in 1852, we can at least partially understand why (see Figure 4.1). In the drawing, which illustrates the final scene of act 2, the costumes in the fashion of the 1840s seem to be out of place in a medievalist setting marked by an ancient graveyard, a Gothic church, and an old castle; to the audience's taste it would probably have seemed more appropriate to see the scene crowded with *Aroldo*'s medieval knights and ladies. The location was already present in the French play, where it was described in very succinct terms, while in the libretto it is wrapped with Ossianic haziness (see Appendix 4.2). Piave's caption does not offer references for precise sound effects, such as wind blowing or tempest roaring. The visual images nevertheless suggest a Gothic scene; these poetic images seem to have inspired Verdi to write a short and evocative prelude in E♭ minor, which is preserved without modifications in *Aroldo*. The composer suggests the somber atmosphere through an austere orchestration dominated by low-pitched instruments, the preponderance of *piano* and *pianissimo* dynamics, the use of chromaticism (especially in the bass line), and the repetition of a mysterious two-bar theme at various pitch levels and with slight variations, a theme that is characterized by its rhythmic ambiguity.[66]

To opera-goers of Verdi's time, the setting of *Stiffelio*'s act 2 could recall the final scenes of *Lucia di Lammermoor*, Donizetti's opera on Scott's novel, which takes place in

FIGURE 4.1 Verdi, *Stiffelio*, frontispiece for piano-vocal score, 1852.

a graveyard showing a castle and a chapel. It is not certain whether Lucia, in her madness, ever entered into Piave's imagination, but Scott certainly did, leading him to the shores of Loch Lomond in Scotland, the homeland of Rob Roy, for the final act of *Aroldo*.[67] The closing scene of *Stiffelio*, which takes place in the impressive interior of a Gothic church, was magnificent and medieval enough to enter the new opera but, at the same time, it was too full of religious implications to be accepted by many theater censors. The entire act was therefore written completely anew by Piave and Verdi. An open-air setting in the faraway mountains of the Highlands was visually appealing and morally unobjectionable; besides, echoes of Scott's novels were very attractive to the public, since in the 1850s the novelist was still one of the favorite authors of Italian readers.[68] As Budden has noted, one of Piave's sources for *Aroldo* was *The Lady of the Lake* and its operatic version, Rossini's *La donna del lago*. Rossini's opera begins with a scene featuring choruses of shepherds and huntsmen, with a set design that shows the ridge of Ben Ledi, a wooded hillside, and Loch Katrine.[69] Composer and librettist could, as well, have found a lake, shepherds, and huntsmen, along with a church bell, horns, and bagpipes in Rossini's

Guillaume Tell, act 2. The storm that is featured in act 4 of Rossini's opera may also have provided inspiration for a similar scene in *Aroldo*. In these two operas, the characters move in an Alpine locale, which in Italian operas of the first half of the nineteenth century, as Emanuele Senici has proved, was usually associated with the sublime, the idyllic, and, most important, the virginal heroines.[70] All these associations slipped into *Aroldo's* last act along with the mountainous landscape, removing the medieval atmosphere and inspiring Verdi's delicate pastoral choruses and an impressive orchestral storm. In the peaceful mountain environment, Aroldo surrenders his sword and helmet to wear the simple clothes of the hermit. Yet he still has not found the calm that dominates the place because the remembrance of Mina haunts him; the sentimental storm that torments his soul has its physical counterpart in the storm that hits the lake and throws Mina and his father to the shore. Upset by the weather's harshness but partially purified by the balsamic air of the Alpine locale, the woman cannot recover her virginity (she is a married woman and has presumably been raped) but at least some of her primeval innocence has been restored. So, when the sky becomes clear again, Aroldo finds his wife and, pressed by his feelings, the words of his friends, Mina's prayer, and the sublimity of the landscape, he finally forgives her. Transferring the final scene to the shores of Loch Lomond made the action even more chronologically and geographically distant and made the reintegration of the adulterous woman into society more acceptable to the audience.

Aside from the works by Scott cited previously, on Piave's working desk we could have found the libretto *La sposa del crociato*, written by Giovanni Battista Canovai in 1852, which supplied the librettist with many elements useful to transform *Stiffelio* into a new opera. Canovai's work tells the story of a crusader who comes back from Palestine to find out that his beloved wife is about to marry a baron. The crusader keeps his identity hidden and, in act 1, scene 5, manages to have a nocturnal meeting with his wife by an old cemetery near an illuminated church, where a group of hermits sings the psalms; at her arrival, the woman prays to the Virgin Mary and confesses her true love for the baron. After she faints, the crusader tries to stab her, but an old servant stops him; finally, the crusader throws himself into the servant's arms and proclaims his love for the woman. At the wedding ceremony, the crusader reveals his identity and duels with his rival; during the fight, the woman is accidentally wounded and dies truly repentant in her husband's arms as he forgives her.

The return of a crusader after a long absence was a common premise for operatic and novel plots set in the Middle Ages, but, probably, Piave found *La sposa del crociato* a good source for borrowings because it had many interesting points of connection with *Stiffelio*.[71] The clearest similarities are between the setting and situations portrayed in *La sposa del crociato*, act 1, scene 5, and *Stiffelio*, act 2, and, most important, between the main characters of the two operas, since both are loving and hapless husbands. *La sposa del crociato* might very well have given Piave the idea to transform his Evangelic minister into a crusader and to adopt the name and identity of Canovai's hero, the Saxon knight Aroldo; he also considered it wise to move the action to the same English region previously chosen by his colleague, the county of Kent. Needing only to rewrite the last act, Piave found the *La sposa del crociato* prologue inspiring; here, in a traditional pastoral location (animated by shepherds and hunters heard along with horns and bagpipes), Aroldo presents himself disguised as a pilgrim and looks for shelter in a hermitage. Borrowing the pastoral locale and the hermitage, Piave found the right combination to bypass the censor's obstacles.

In *Aroldo*, while the main character loses his double role of religious minister and husband (a double role that provides the heart of the dramatic conflict in *Stiffelio*), the female character gains dramatic and vocal importance.[72] A comparison between Mina and Canovai's heroine allows us to appreciate the novelty of Verdi's opera despite the medieval disguise. Canovai's female character finds love outside marriage and dies accidentally, a divine punishment that restores the traditional order. The fact that Mina, as Lina before her, survives her act of adultery and manages to regain her status as a wife, however, places Verdi's opera in opposition to this social order. Transposing the setting of the opera to the geographically distant Highlands and the chronologically distant Middle Ages enabled Piave and Verdi to retain the potentially transgressive core of their story.

This change of historical setting had no great consequences for the score, since the newest music is found principally in the final act where the Alpine locale overlies the medieval one. Nevertheless, the cases of *Stiffelio* and *Un ballo in maschera* demonstrate that, to Verdi, the medieval period was not simply a neutral backdrop apt to be used for any drama. Interspersed as they were with Scottian references, the medieval plots of these revisions could evoke a period associated with blood and somberness. Mysterious, violent, and attractive, the Middle Ages could offer to librettists a shelter in times of strict censorship, shelter that allowed them—along with Verdi—the space to address essential themes and topics of nineteenth-century Italian society.

Appendix 4.1 Verdi's Operas with Medieval Settings

Title	Librettist	First performance	Time and place of the action[73]	Annotations
Oberto, conte di San Bonifacio	Solera, Temistocle	Milan (Kingdom of Lombardy-Venetia, crown land of the Austrian Empire), Teatro alla Scala, 1839	"The action takes place in Bassano, in and near the castle of Ezzelino. Epoch: the year 1228."	
I Lombardi alla prima crociata	Solera, Temistocle	Milan (Kingdom of Lombardy-Venetia, crown land of the Austrian Empire), Teatro alla Scala, 1843	"The scene of Act I is set in Milano, of Act II in and near Antique, of Act III and IV near Jerusalem." [1097–1099]	Based on Tommasso Grossi's poem I Lombardi alla prima crociata (1826)
I due Foscari	Piave, Francesco Maria	Rome (Papal States), Teatro Argentina, 1844	"The scene is set in Venice, the year 1457."	Based on Lord Byron's play The Two Foscari (1821)
Giovanna d'Arco	Solera, Temistocle	Milan (Kingdom of Lombardy-Venetia, crown land of the Austrian Empire), Teatro alla Scala, 1845	[France, 1429]	Based on Schiller's play Die Jungfrau von Orleans (1801)
Orietta di Lesbo	Solera, Temistocle	Rome (Papal States), Teatro Argentina, 1845	[Lesbo, thirteenth century]	Censored version of Giovanna d'Arco
Attila	Solera, Temistocle; Piave, Francesco Maria	Venice (Kingdom of Lombardy-Venetia, crown land of the Austrian Empire), Teatro La Fenice, 1846	"In the Prologue, the scene is set in Aquileia and the Adriatic lagoons; in the three acts, it is set near Rome. Epoch: the middle of the fifth century."	Based on Zacharias Werner's play Attila, König der Hunnen (1809)
Macbeth	Piave, Francesco Maria; Maffei, Andrea	Florence (Grand Duchy of Tuscany), Teatro della Pergola, 1847	"The scene is set in Scotland, mainly in the Castle of Macbeth. The beginning of Act IV takes place on the Anglo-Scottish border." (ninth century)	Based on Shakespeare's play Macbeth (1606?)

Title	Librettist	Place / Year	Setting	Notes
Jérusalem	Solera, Temistocle; Royer, Alphonse; Vaëz, Gustave	Paris (Kingdom of France), Théâtre de l'Opéra National, 1847	"Act I takes place in Toulouse in 1095, after the council of Clermont. The other acts take place four years later, in Palestine."	French version of I lombardi alla prima crociata
La battaglia di Legnano	Cammarano, Salvadore	Rome (Papal States), Teatro Argentina, 1849	"Parts I, III and IV take place in Milano. Part II takes place in Como. Epoch: 1176."	Based on Joseph Méry's play La battaille de Toulouse (1836)
Gerusalemme	Solera, Temistocle; Royer, Alphonse; Vaëz, Gustave; Bassi, Callisto	Milan (Kingdom of Lombardy-Venetia, crown land of the Austrian Empire), Teatro alla Scala, 1850	"Act I takes place in Toulouse in 1095, after the council of Clermont. The other acts take place four years later, in Palestine."	Italian version of Jérusalem
Guglielmo Wellingrode	Piave, Francesco Maria; ??	Rome (Papal States), Teatro Apollo, 1851	"Scene: the castle of the Count of Lohrstein in Germany by the river Sulzbach and its surroundings. Epoch: the beginning of the 15th century."	Censored version of Stiffelio
Il trovatore	Cammarano, Salvadore; Bardare, Leone Emanuele	Rome (Papal States), Teatro Apollo, 1853	"The action takes place partly in Biscay, partly in Aragon. The epoch of the action is the beginning of the fifteenth century."	Based on Antonio García Gutiérrez's play El trovador (1836)
Clara di Perth	Piave, Francesco Maria; Bardare, Leone Emanuele	Naples (Kingdom of the Two Sicilies), Teatro Nuovo, 1853	"The scene is set in and near Perth. The plot comes from Walter Scott's novel The Fair Maid of Perth. It is supposed to take place in the Carnival of 1349. The costumes are in the true Scottish fashion."	Censored version of Rigoletto

(continued)

Appendix 4.1 Continued

Title	Librettist	First performance	Time and place of the action	Annotations
Gli Unni e i Romani	Solera, Temistocle; Piave, Francesco Maria	Palermo (Kingdom of the Two Sicilies), Teatro Carolino, 1854	"The scene is set in Aquileia and the Adriatic lagoons during the Prologue; it is set near Rome during the three acts. Epoch: the middle of the fifth century."	Censored version of *Attila*
Les vêpres siciliennes	Scribe, Eugène; Duveyrier, Charles	Paris (French Empire), Théâtre de l'Académie Impériale de Musique, 1855	[Palermo, 1282]	Based on Augustin Eugène Scribe and Charles Duveyrier's libretto *Le duc d'Albe* (1838)
Batilde di Turenna	Scribe, Eugène; Duveyrier, Charles; Caimi, Ettore	Naples (Kingdom of the Two Sicilies), Teatro San Carlo, 1857	"The scene is set near Tours in Touraine by the river Loire, in the thirteenth century."	Censored version of *Les vêpres siciliennes*
Simon Boccanegra	Piave, Francesco Maria	Venice (Kingdom of Lombardy-Venetia, crown land of the Austrian Empire), Teatro La Fenice, 1857	"The action takes place in and near Genova, in the first half of the fourteenth century."	Based on Antonio García Gutiérrez's play *Simón Bocanegra* (1843)
Aroldo	Piave, Francesco Maria	Rimini (Papal States), Teatro Nuovo, 1857	"Epoch: around the year 1200. Scene: for the first three acts Egberto's dwelling in Kent, for the fourth act the rivers of Loch Lomond in Scotland."	Revised version of *Stiffelio*
I vespri siciliani	Scribe, Eugène; Duveyrier, Charles; Fusinato, Arnaldo	Paris (French Empire), Théâtre Lyrique, 1865	"The action takes place in Palermo. Epoch: 1282."	Italian version of *Les vêpres siciliennes*, published in 1860. The first performances took place after the creation of the Kingdom of Italy in 1861.
Macbeth	Piave, Francesco Maria; Alexandre Beaumont; Charles Nuitter	Paris (French Empire), Théâtre Lyrique, 1865	[Scotland, ninth century]	Revised version of *Macbeth*

Simon Boccanegra	Piave, Francesco Maria; Boito, Arrigo	Milan (Kingdom of Italy), Teatro alla Scala, 1881	"The action takes place in and near Genova, in the first half of the fourteenth century."	Revised version of *Simon Boccanegra*
Otello	Boito, Arrigo	Milan (Kingdom of Italy), Teatro alla Scala, 1887	"Scene: a seaside city in the island of Cyprus. Epoch: the end of the fifteenth century."	Based on Shakespeare's *Othello* (1603?)
Falstaff	Boito, Arrigo	Milan (Kingdom of Italy), Teatro alla Scala, 1893	"Scene: Windsor. Epoch: Kingdom of Henry IV of England [1399–1413]"	Based on Shakespeare's plays *The Merry Wives of Windsor* (1597?) and *Henry IV* (1597?)

Appendix 4.2 Medievalizing *Le pasteur*

Note. The appendix compares the main captions of the drama *Le pasteur* (*Stiffelius!* in the Italian translation) by Émile Souvestre and Eugène Bourgeois with the corresponding captions of the libretti *Stiffelio* and *Aroldo* by Francesco Maria Piave. In the transformation of *Le pasteur* into *Stiffelio* and of *Stiffelio* into *Aroldo*, there was a gradual intensification of the Gothic and spectacular aspects: The comparison of the captions shows the elimination of the elements that allude to contemporary and bourgeois life and, in parallel, the addition of "medievalizing" details that make the scene more imposing. Note, for example, the changes in the cemetery scene (*Le pasteur*, act 4; *Stiffelio* and *Aroldo*, act 2, scene 1).

Note on translation. Writing *Stiffelio*, Piave worked with the Italian translation of *Le pasteur*, *Stiffelius!*. There are some significant differences between the two versions of the drama, but the captions here quoted are identical. The translations of the captions of the French drama are my own. The translations of the captions for *Stiffelio* are taken from Julian Budden, *The Operas of Verdi*, 1:455–466; the translation of the captions for *Aroldo* are taken from Julian Budden, *The Operas of Verdi*, 2:336–350. In both cases, some changes were introduced to make the English translation adhere more closely to the Italian original.

(continued)

Appendix 4.2 Continued

Le pasteur/Stiffellius!	Stiffelio	Aroldo
General setting [Stankar's dwelling by the river Salzbach [sic] and its surroundings]	**General setting** The action takes place in Germany at Stankar's castle by the river Salzbach [sic] and its surroundings. Epoch: the beginning of the nineteenth century.	**General setting** The action takes place in Egberto's castle near Kent for the first three acts; by the shores of Loch Lomond in Scotland for the fourth. Epoch: ca. 1200.
Act 1: A hall: upstage two doors. On the left a door and a window, a stove and an armchair; on the right a sewing basket with some fabric on a small table: in the same side, backward, a piano, and back to the upstage flower vases on a dresser.	Act 1, scene 1: A hall on the ground floor of Stankar's castle in Salzburg: upstage center is a door; to the audience's far left a window; on the right a hearth with a fire alight. In front of the window toward the center of the stage is a large table with several books on it, among them a rather large one, expensively bound and fastened with a clasp. Writing materials to hand.	Act 1, scene 1: Drawing room in Egberto's dwelling. A large window in the center from which will be seen the battlements of the castle. Doors on either side and a table with writing materials, chairs, etc.
Act 2: A hall: upstage center a door, on the right a little door, on the left two doors;, on both sides little tables and armchairs, on the left a pendulum clock on a hearth; oil lamp and candlestick alight on the right-side table, another candlelight on the left-side table.		
Act 3: A hall: upstage center a door and a window, doors on either side. On the right a table with materials for writing and an armchair, on the right a sofa.	Act 1, scene 9: Reception hall in the castle, illuminated and prepared for a celebration.	Act 1, scene 7: A suite of rooms illuminated for a grand celebration. In the first there are some pieces of period furniture, on one of which rests a book locked by a clasp with a key.

Act 4: An ancient graveyard; on the right trees, tombs, and a big cross with steps; on the left the church lit up. Night

Act 5: Hall, doors in the upstage center and on both sides, on the right a table with materials for writing and a chair, on the left a chair.

Act 5, scene 6: Scenery change in view. The interior of a Gothic church with pillars. Many people on their knees. The organ plays. A pulpit mounted by a double stairway.

Act 2, scene 1: An ancient graveyard. In the center a cross with steps. On the left the door of a church lit up within, to which a grand stairway gives access. On the right, further back, Stankar's castle can be seen. The moon rains its light over the scattered tombs which are shadowed by thick cypresses. Among the tombs, there is one of recent construction.

Act 3, scene 1: An antechamber [in Stankar's castle] with doors leading into various other rooms. On the table are two pistols and writing materials.

Act 3, scene 9: The interior of a Gothic church with a large arcade. No altar is to be seen, only a pulpit placed up against one of the pillars and mounted by a double stairway.

Act 2, scene 1: An ancient graveyard of the castle of Kent. In the center is a cross with steps; on the right, the door of a chapel lit up within, to which a grand stairway access; on the left, further back, a castle can be seen; the moon lightens faintly the scattered tombs, which are shadowed here and there by age-old cypresses. Among the tombs, there is one of recent construction.

Act 3, scene 1: An antechamber in Egbert's dwelling that opens onto various apartments. On the table are writing materials.

Act 4, scene 1: A deep valley in Scotland. The shore of Loch Lomond is seen in the background. Mountains (practicable props) covered with woods to the right and left, where there is a small grove of pines and beside it a modest house. The sun is setting. Distant sounds of horns and bagpipes approaching. Voices of shepherds. Women and huntsmen who come down from the mountains and meet.

Act 4, scene 3: It is night: the moon, which has arisen during the prayer, is shadowed by big clouds. The wind, tempestuous, blows and upsets the lake.

NOTES

1. Simonetta Ricciardi, ed. *Carteggio Verdi—Somma*, Appendix 6 (Parma: Istituto Nazionale di Studi Verdiani, 2003), 353; translated in Julian Budden, *The Operas of Verdi*, 3 vols. (New York: Cassell, 1978), 2:370.

2. The expression *destructive charms* in reference to the interest raised by the Italian territories in foreign nations is used by George Gordon Byron in *Childe Harold's Pilgrimage*, canto IV, stanza XLIII (Cambridge: Cambridge University Press, 1913), 142.

3. Adrian Lyttelton, "Creating a National Past: History, Myth and Image in the Risorgimento," in *Making and Remaking Italy: The Cultivation of National Identity around the Risorgimento*, ed. Albert Russell Ascoli et al. (Oxford: Berg, 2001), 31, 60.

4. See Renato Bordone, "Il medioevo nell'immaginario dell'Ottocento italiano," *Bullettino dell'Istituto storico italiano per il Medioevo* 100 (1997): 111; see also Alberto Banti, *La nazione del Risorgimento: Parentela, santità e onore alle origini dell'Italia unita* (Milan: Einaudi, 2000), 73–78.

5. Goffredo Mameli, *Il canto degli italiani: poesie d'amore e di guerra*, ed. Guido Davico Bonino (Milan: Bur, 2013)no page number. "Dall'Alpe a Sicilia,/Dovunque è Legnano;.../ Il suon d'ogni squilla/I Vespri suonò." Unless otherwise noted, all translations are my own.

6. See Federico Cardini, "Federico Barbarossa e il romanticismo italiano," in *Italia e Germania. Immagini, modelli, miti fra due popoli nell'ottocento: il Medioevo*, ed. Reinhard Elze et al. (Bologna: Il Mulino, 1988), 98–99.

7. Letter to Verdi, November 4, 1848; Carlo Matteo Mozza, ed., *Carteggio Verdi—Cammarano* (Parma: Istituto Nazionale di Studi Verdiani, 2001), 81. Among the ballets inspired by D'Azeglio's novel, we can mention *Ettore Fieramosca* by Salvatore Taglioni (Naples, 1837) and *Ettore Fieramosca o La disfida di Barletta* by Giovanni Galzerani (Milan, 1837). Among the operas are *Ettore Fieramosca* by Antonio Laudamo (Messina, 1839, libretto by M. D'Azeglio); *Ettore Fieramosca* by Costantino Quaranta (Venice, 1839, libretto by G. Gallia); *Ettore Fieramosca* by Marcello Manzocchi (Naples, 1844, libretto by L. Tarantini); and *Ettore Fieramosca* by Bernardo Geraci (Palermo 1845, libretto by G. Sapio).

8. The first edition of the *Histoire des républiques italiennes du Moyen Âge* was published in four volumes between 1807 and 1808; the second edition was enlarged and consisted of sixteen volumes published between 1809 and 1818. A significant work inspired by Sismondi's volumes is the tragedy *Il conte di Carmagnola* (1820) by Alessandro Manzoni.

9. See Mauro Moretti and Ilaria Porciani, "Italy's Various Middle Ages," in *The Uses of the Middle Ages in Modern European States*, ed. R. J. W. Evans et al. (Basingstoke: Palgrave Macmillan, 2011), 188–189.

10. See Ilaria Porciani, "Il medioevo nella costruzione dell'Italia unita: la proposta di un mito," in *Italia e Germania. Immagini, modelli, miti fra due popoli nell'ottocento: il Medioevo*, 182–184; see also Bordone, "Il medioevo nell'immaginario dell'Ottocento italiano," 112–113.

11. See Moretti and Porciani, "Italy's Various Middle Ages," in *The Uses of the Middle Ages in Modern European States*, ed. R. J. W. Evans et al. (Basingstoke: Palgrave Macmillan, 2011), 190.

12. See Philip Gossett, "Giuseppe Verdi and the Italian Risorgimento," *Studia Musicologica* 52 (2011): 241–257.

13. See Mariarosa Bricchi, "Vera la storia, vera l'invenzione," in *Atlante della letteratura italiana*, ed. Domenico Scarpa (Milano: Einaudi, 2012), 3:40–46. Grossi was also the author of *I Lombardi alla prima crociata* (1826), which inspired Verdi's opera.

14. See Bordone, "Il medioevo nell'immaginario dell'Ottocento italiano," 116.

15. See Anselm Gerhard, "Verdi's Attila: A Study in Chiaroscuro," *Cambridge Opera Journal* 21 (November 2009): 279–280.

16. Carlotta Sorba, "Attila and Verdi's Historical Imagination," *Cambridge Opera Journal* 21 (November 2009): 248.

17. Giuseppe Mazzini, *Giuseppe Mazzini's "Philosophy of Music" (1836): Envisioning a Social Opera*, ed. Franco Sciannameo, trans. Emilie Ashurst Venturi (Lewiston, NY: Mellen, 2004), 52.

18. *Filosofia della musica* appeared for the first time in print in the Italian magazine *L'italiano*, published in Paris during the year 1836.

19. For a discussion on the concept of *couleur locale* in relation to Meyerbeer and other French grand opera composers, see Anselm Gerhard, *The Urbanization of Opera: Music Theater in Paris in the Nineteenth Century*, trans. Mary Whittall (Chicago: University of Chicago Press, 2000), 162–170.

20. In his introduction to Mazzini's *Filosofia della musica*, Sciannameo discusses Mazzini's interest on Meyerbeer's dramas (Sciannameo, *Giuseppe Mazzini's "Philosophy of Music,"* 18–24).

21. It is not certain whether Verdi knew *Filosofia della musica*: Gary Tomlinson hypothesizes that the composer read it and, inspired by it, wrote *I due Foscari* (Gary Tomlinson, "Italian Romanticism and Italian Opera: An Essay in Their Affinities," in *19th-Century Music* 10, no. 1 [Summer 1986]: 60). In any case, the composer most probably knew Victor Hugo's preface to *Cromwell* (1827), which expresses, in general terms, a concept of local color similar to Mazzini's, even if it does not deal with the problem from a musical point of view; see Giuseppe Mazzini, *Philosophie de la musique: vers un opéra social, 1835*, ed. and trans. Martin Kaltenecker (Paris: Van Dieren, 2001), 43.

22. Letter to de Sanctis, January 18, 1851. Alessandro Luzio, ed., *Carteggi Verdiani*, 4 vols. (Rome: Reale Accademia d'Italia, 1935), 1:22–23.

23. Letter to de Sanctis, April 10, 1855. *Carteggi Verdiani* I:30–1. For a comment on this request of authentic popular music and the analysis of the siciliana in the divertissement "Les quatre saisons," see Marcello Conati, "Ballabili nei 'Vespri.' Con alcune osservazioni su Verdi e la musica popolare," *Studi verdiani* 1 (1982): 39–46.

24. Letter to Giulio Ricordi, August 11, 1894. Marcello Conati, ed., *Carteggio Verdi—Boito* (Parma: Istituto Nazionale di Studi Verdiani, 2014), 456.

25. See Víctor Sánchez Sánchez, *Verdi y España* (Madrid: Akal, 2014) ch. 8 "España vista desde Francia": 198–231.

26. See Andreas Giger, "French Influences," in *The Cambridge Companion to Verdi*, ed. Scott L. Balthazar (Cambridge: Cambridge University Press, 2004), 118.

27. Verdi's use of the organ is generally associated with the evocation of liturgical atmospheres, not necessarily medieval ones (see *Luisa Miller* III, 2; and *Stiffelio* III, 9). The organ continues to be an instrument widely present in Roman Catholic churches.

28. John Haines, *Eight Centuries of Troubadours and Trouvères. The Changing Identity of Medieval Music* (New York: Cambridge University Press, 2004), 164.

29. Ibid., 127–164.

30. Mercedes Viale Ferrero, "'Servire il dramma.' Le idee di Verdi sulla scenografia," in *La realizzazione scenica dello spettacolo verdiano*, ed. Pierluigi Petrobelli et al. (Parma: Istituto Nazionale di Studi Verdiani, 1996), 25.

31. Letter to Luccardi, February 11, 1846. Gaetano Cesari and Alessandro Luzio, eds., *I Copialettere di Giuseppe Verdi* (Milan: Stucche Ceretti, 1913), 441. "Fammi dunque due

segni colla penna, poi spiegami colle parole ed i numeri i colori del vestiario; soprattutto ho bisogno dell'acconciatura della testa."

32. Translated in Budden, *The Operas of Verdi*, 1: 194.

33. Viale Ferrero, "'Servire il dramma.' Le idee di Verdi sulla scenografia" in *La realizzazione scenica dello spettacolo verdiano*, ed. Pierluigi Petrobelli et al. (Parma: Istituto Nazionale di Studi Verdiani, 1996), 26. "[. . .] chiaro monito a non riprodurre la chiesa palladiana, costruita successivamente al tempo in cui si svolge l'azione e insomma a rispettare nel quadro scenico la verità storica, che Verdi riteneva indispensabile per ottenere la vero-simiglianza drammatica."

34. For a discussion on the visual ideas of Verdi, their development, and, in particular, his interest in the historical rendition of the scenes, see Olga Jesurum, *Il personaggio muto: due secoli di scenografia verdiana* (Parma: Istituto Nazionale di Studi Verdiani, 2014), 7–18.

35. See Sánchez Sánchez, *Verdi y España*, 206–208.

36. See Andreas Giger, *Verdi and the French Aesthetic. Verse, Stanza, and Melody in Nineteenth-Century Opera* (Cambridge: Cambridge University Press, 2008), 122–123.

37. Budden, *The Operas of Verdi*, 2:8; see also Michele Girardi, "Esotismo e realismo nell'opera lirica francese del Romanticismo," *Quaderni del Teatro Regio* 18 (1986): 109.

38. Mazzini, *Giuseppe Mazzini's "Philosophy of Music,"* 53.

39. The concept of *tinta* has been amply discussed. See especially Julian Budden, "Problems of Analysis in Verdi's Works," in *Nuove prospettive nella ricerca verdiana: atti del Convegno Internazionale in occasione della prima del Rigoletto in edizione critica*, ed. Marisa di Gregorio Casati and Marcello Pavarani (Parma: Istituto di Studi Verdiani—Ricordi, 1987), 125–129; Gilles de Van, *Verdi's Theater: Creating Drama through Music*, trans. Gilda Roberts (Chicago: University of Chicago Press, 1998); David Rosen, "Meter, Character, and *Tinta* in Verdi's Operas," in *Verdi's Middle Period, 1849–1859: Sources, Studies, Analysis, and Performance Practice*, ed. Martin Chusid (Chicago: University of Chicago Press, 1997), 339–392.

40. In the 1850s, *L'Assedio di Arlem* had a very poor circulation. Having great esteem for *La Battaglia di Legnano*, Verdi attempted to revive it through a revision similar to the one made with *Stiffelio*, which implicated a change of the locale (see letter to de Sanctis, July 6, 1854, Luzio, *Carteggi Verdiani*, 1:25).

41. The expression "monstrosity" appears in a letter to Torelli, February 14, 1858. Cesari and Luzio, *I Copialettere*, 566.

42. Leone Emmanuele Bardare, *Clara di Perth* (Naples: Tipografia de' Gemelli, 1853), 4. "L'azione in parte è tratta dal romanzo di Walter Scot [sic]: La bella fanciulla di Perth. Si finge avvenire nel carnevale 1349. Il vestiario è nel costume pienamente scozzese."

43. See Mario Lavagetto, *Un caso di censura. Il Rigoletto* (Milan: Bruno Mondadori, 2010), 76–81.

44. In the most repressive states, censors controlled also the costumes and the stage designs. See David Kimbell, *Verdi in the Age of Italian Romanticism* (Cambridge: Cambridge University Press, 1981), 26.

45. Letter to Carlo Marzari, December 14, 1850. Cesari and Luzio, *I Copialettere*, 109–110. "S'era necessario cambiare i nomi, dovevasi cambiare anche la località, e farne un Duca, un Principe d'altro luogo, per esempio un Pier Luigi Farnese o altro, oppure portare l'azione indietro prima di Luigi XI quando la Francia non era regno unito, e farne un Duca di Borgogna o di Normandia etc. etc., in ogni modo un padrone assoluto."

46. Lavagetto, *Un caso di censura*, 58. "Verdi non si oppone per principio al cambiamento della referenzialità storica che equivaleva, nei fatti, a un'intensificazione molto forte del

dispositivo 'c'era una volta.' La censura cercava, dal canto suo, di spaesare gli spettacoli, di spostarli su sfondi indeterminate che, senza annullare il funzionamento della macchina drammatica, riducessero al minimo la connotazione storica."

47. Letter to Somma, November 26, 1857. Ricciardi, *Carteggi Verdi-Somma*, 243; translated in Budden, *The Operas of Verdi*, 2:369.

48. On the relation between Verdi and the Roman censorship, see Andreas Giger, "Social Control and the Censorship of Giuseppe Verdi's Operas in Rome (1844–1859)," *Cambridge Opera Journal* 11 (November 1999): 233–265.

49. Émile Souvestre and Eugène Bourgeois, *Le pasteur, ou L'évangile et le foyer* (Paris: Dondey-Dupré, 1849). Gaetano Vestri's Italian translation of the play, retitled *Stifellius!* (Milan: Borroni e Scotti, 1848), was published a year before the French original version.

50. See Hellmut Ludwig, "La fonte letteraria del libretto. Le pasteur, ou l'évangile et le foyer," in *Stiffelio, Quaderni dell'Istituto di Studi Verdiani*, 3 (1968): 10–11.

51. See Emilio Sala, "Tra mélodrame e dramma borghese: Dal Pasteur di Souvestre-Bourgeois allo Stiffelio di Verdi-Piave," in *Tornando a Stiffelio: popolarità, rifacimenti, messinscena, effettismo e altre "cure" nella drammaturgia del Verdi romantico. Atti del Convegno Internazionale di Studi, Venezia, 17-20 dicembre 1985*, ed. Giovanni Morelli, *Quaderni della Rivista italiana di musicologia* 14 (Florence: Olschki, 1987), 129–139.

52. Piave wrote his libretto keeping under his eyes Vestri's Italian translation of the drama, which was receptive to the public's and authorities' sensitivity over moral and religious issues; see Diana Dionisi Ascari, "Da Stiffelio a Guglielmo Wellingrode: gli interventi della Censura," in *Tornando a Stiffelio, popolarità, rifacimenti, messinscena, effettismo e altre "cure" nella drammaturgia del Verdi romantico. Atti del Convegno Internazionale di Studi, Venezia, 17-20 dicembre 1985*, ed. Giovanni Morelli, *Quaderni della Rivista italiana di musicologia* 14 (Florence: Olschki, 1987), 129–139. For a discussion of the faults of Lina as perceived by the Italian audience, see Susan Rutherford, *Verdi, Opera, Women* (New York: Cambridge University Press, 2013), 149–158.

53. *La favilla*, November 17, 1850, reprinted in *Stiffelio, Quaderni dell'Istituto di Studi Verdiani* 3 (1968): 101–103; translated in Kathleen Kuzmick Hansell, "Introduction to the Critical Edition of *Stiffelio*," *Works of Giuseppi Verdi* I, no. 16 (2003): xxvi.

54. *La favilla*, November 24, 1850; reprinted in ibid.; translated in ibid.

55. See Steven Shrader, "Verdi, Aroldo, and Music Drama," *Verdi Newsletter* 13 (1984): 11.

56. See Philip Gossett, "New Sources for *Stiffelio*: A Preliminary Report," in *Verdi's Middle Period, 1849–1859: Sources, Studies, Analysis, and Performance Practice*, ed. Martin Chusid (Chicago: University of Chicago Press, 1997), 19–43; and Julian Budden, "Differences in Musical Language between *Stiffelio* and *Aroldo*," in *Tornando a "Stiffelio": popolarità, rifacimenti, messinscena, effettismo e altre "cure" nella drammaturgia del Verdi romantico. Atti del Convegno Internazionale di Studi, Venezia, 17-20 dicembre 1985*, ed. Giovanni Morelli, *Quaderni della Rivista italiana di musicologia* 14 (Florence: Olschki, 1987), 273–280.

57. Budden, *The Operas of Verdi*, 1:463.

58. *Gazzetta musicale di Venezia*, January 25, 1852; reprinted in *Stiffelio, Quaderni dell'Istituto di Studi Verdiani* 3 (1968), 125.

59. Musically, the transformation has its most important consequences in act 1, in particular in the cavatina "Sotto il sol di Siria ardente" enlivened with martial echoes.

60. Abramo Basevi, *The Operas of Giuseppe Verdi*, ed. Stefano Castelvecchi, trans. Edward Schneider (Chicago: University of Chicago Press, 2014), *Stiffelio*, 150.

61. Souvestre and Bourgeois, *Stifellius!*, 22.

62. Budden, *The Operas of Verdi*, 2:337. Verdi himself got involved with divorce issues since he was the legal witness of the divorce of his friends Chiara and Andrea Maffei in 1846.

63. The expression "hard and iron days" (referring to the Middle Ages) comes from Walter Scott, *The Fair Maid of Perth, or St. Valentine's Day* (Adelaide, Australia: University of Adelaide Press, 2014) https://ebooks.adelaide.edu.au/s/scott/walter/fair/ Access date 10/06/2017

64. *La favilla*, November 17, 1850; reprinted in *Stiffelio, Quaderni dell'Istituto di Studi Verdiani*, 106. "Nella messa in scena avremmo desiderato maggior esattezza, sì nelle decorazioni che nel vestiario.—La sala del primo atto, quella del ballo, non indicano per niente la dimora d'un ministro evangelico, né il luogo di convegno di una comunità religiosa."

65. See Martin Chusid, "Apropos Aroldo, Stiffelio and Le pasteur," in *Tornando a "Stiffelio": popolarità, rifacimenti, messinscena, effettismo e altre "cure" nella drammaturgia del Verdi romantico. Atti del Convegno Internazionale di Studi, Venezia, 17–20 dicembre 1985*, ed. Giovanni Morelli, *Quaderni della Rivista italiana di musicologia* 14 (Florence: Olschki, 1987), 286.

66. On the rythmic ambiguity of the theme, see Tito Gotti, "L'opera appunti per un'analisi," in *Tornando a "Stiffelio": popolarità, rifacimenti, messinscena, effettismo e altre "cure" nella drammaturgia del Verdi romantico. Atti del Convegno Internazionale di Studi, Venezia, 17–20 dicembre 1985*, ed. Giovanni Morelli, *Quaderni della Rivista italiana di musicologia* 14 (Florence: Olschki, 1987), 65–66.

67. Rob Roy was the titular hero of Scott's novel *Rob Roy*, published in 1817.

68. See Erminia Irace and Gabriele Pedullà, "Walter Scott in Italia e il romanzo storico," in *Atlante della letteratura italiana*, ed. Domenico Scarpa 3: 47–50.

69. See Budden, *The Operas of Verdi*, 2: 337.

70. See Emanuele Senici, *Landscape and Gender in Italian Opera: The Alpine Virgin from Bellini to Puccini* (Cambridge: Cambridge University Press, 2005).

71. *La sposa del crociato* (libretto by Canovai, music by Antonio Buzzi) was first performed at Cremona, Teatro Concordia, in the season 1852–1853. Piave probably had a copy of the libretto in the version performed at La Fenice in March 1855 under the title *Editta*, since at those times he worked for the theater.

72. See Budden, *The Operas of Verdi*, 2: 339.

73. The references to time and place of the action are translated from the first edition of each libretto. Where not explicitly indicated, the references are inferred from the text.

CHAPTER 5

···

THE DISTANT PAST AS MIRROR AND METAPHOR

*Portraying the Medieval in Historical
French Grand Operas*

···

DIANA R. HALLMAN

OVER the decades of political turmoil and transformation in early nineteenth-century France, as the nation shifted from revolutionary and imperial regimes to the *néo-ancien* Restoration, images of the distant past flourished in a multitude of public forms. Inspired by nostalgia for seemingly simpler times; myths of a poetic, chivalrous era; or impulses to reclaim a disparaged history, French essayists, historians, novelists, dramatists, and composers became increasingly entranced by *le Moyen Âge*. The allure of the medieval became so prevalent in these early decades that it helped to define the romantic period, within France and beyond, as an age of medievalism. In the years traditionally understood as the beginning of French romanticism—typically viewed, at least with regard to music, as beginning either with the Restoration or with the 1830 July Revolution and outset of the July Monarchy—medievalism appeared in starkly contradictory and ambivalent guises. Although a "taste for the exotic in time and place" characterized much of French romantic medievalism, as Michael Glencross notes, political implications are also strongly sensed in early nineteenth-century representations of the medieval.[1] Within the July Monarchy of Louis-Philippe (1830–1848), established with a renewal of revolutionary zeal and promises to return to liberal, republican principles, Voltairean castigations of the medieval centuries as barbaric, superstitious, and backward coexisted with idealizations of medieval chivalry and religious morality that echoed the sympathies found in Chateaubriand's *Le Génie du christianisme* of 1802. In this master text, labeled an *apologie du Moyen Âge* by Christian Amalvi, Chateaubriand defended the Catholic religion and passionately opposed "the libertine and impious century of the Philosophes and the 'saturnales' of the Revolution."[2]

As France recovered from the trauma of the 1789 Revolution and the decades of political upheaval that followed, romantic historians and novelists sought to define a new national identity through narratives of origin that were rooted in medieval centuries. In an early passage of his multivolume *Histoire de France*, published from 1833 to 1867, French historian Jules Michelet wrote poetically of the Middle Ages as the legend-filled period of France's *enfance* and likened the medieval nation to a "sad child, torn from the very womb of Christianity, who was born in tears, who grew up in prayer and reverie and the anguishes of the Heart, who died without achieving anything."[3] Victor Hugo, in his 1831 epic novel *Notre-Dame de Paris* (set in 1482), attempted to reconstruct this forgotten past through the image of the grand, but deteriorating, Gothic cathedral of Paris, even as he articulated ideas on contemporary society and advocated for the restoration of France's heritage of architectural monuments, many of which had been demolished or left to ruin after the Revolution. Other presentations of medieval subjects, icons, and settings in the romantic period carried clear political overtones; some functioned as metaphorical markers of a national identity to be reclaimed from the "ruins" of tradition or, at times, as foils to new ideals of a modern France.

In the early to mid-nineteenth century, French medievalism was not precisely defined chronologically, and medieval centuries sometimes blurred with those of the Renaissance, which was not consistently regarded as a discrete period, as both Katharine Ellis and Sarah Hibberd have discussed.[4] Moreover, ideas of the "medieval" sometimes evaded boundaries of time, recurring diachronically within later periods, in some sense, existing anew as neomedieval expressions or practices. In Michelet's introduction to his later volume on the Renaissance in *Histoire de France*, published in 1855, he reflected more harshly on the Middle Ages and its "bizarre and monstrous, prodigiously artificial state" and the feudalism that continued beyond its time into the sixteenth century and even up to the Revolution, kept aloft by the nobility, but especially by the clergy.[5] Despite being buffeted by "time, criticism, and the progress of ideas," the clergy—and the medieval—persisted, as Michelet dramatically declared: "Thus the Middle Ages endures, all the more difficult to kill since it was dead long ago. [But] to be killed, it must live. How many times [has it been] finished!"[6]

The fascination for the medieval past and its exploitation as political metaphor converge in many works of French grand opera, or *grand opéra*—a genre closely associated with the era of the July Monarchy but also extending well beyond it. A large portion of French grand operas—these four- or five-act works characterized by dazzling, innovative visual spectacle, increasingly dramatic singing, complex choral and dance scenes, and rich orchestration—were set in centuries that were deemed medieval at the time, although some settings encompassed years now categorized as the early to late Renaissance. These medieval settings often featured actual historical events and historical figures, typically woven into fictionalized histories to accommodate newly created romances or ahistorical subplots. Of the first four French grand operas written for the Paris Opéra, medieval locales were featured in two: Gioachino Rossini's *Guillaume Tell* (1829), set in thirteenth-century Switzerland, and Giacomo Meyerbeer's *Robert le diable* (1831), set in Sicily in a nondefined century of the Middle Ages. In its adaptation of a play by Friedrich Schiller that was centered on the legendary tale of William Tell, *Guillaume Tell* anticipated a central theme of French grand opera of the July Monarchy, one that had already appeared in Daniel-François-Esprit's *La Muette de Portici* of 1828: the trope of an oppressed people struggling under and often fighting against their oppressors. In Auber's work, the Neapolitan revolt of 1647 against Spanish rule that served as the basis of its plot places it outside a medieval framing, though its past may have bordered on the medieval in the French mind. After the appearance of Auber's *Gustave III* of 1833, which retold the story of the 1792 assassination of the Swedish king, the theme of political oppression again merged with medieval symbols in two central Parisian works of the 1830s that soon made their way into the international nineteenth-century repertoire: *La Juive* of 1835 and *Les Huguenots* of 1836.

French grand operas written by leading composers of the genre, Fromental Halévy (1799–1862) and Giacomo Meyerbeer (1791–1864), are the topic of this chapter, and my particular focus will be the aforementioned works of 1835 and 1836, along with Halévy's grand operas of the early 1840s: *La Reine de Chypre* (1841) and *Charles VI* (1843). Visual displays of Gothic cathedrals, armor-plated soldiers, and ermine-ensconced royalty in the productions of *La Juive* and *Les Huguenots* captivated audiences, yet political import simmered beneath the surface texts and staged spectacles of these operas. The Council of Constance (1414–1418) and St. Bartholomew's Eve (1572), events of medieval or quasi-medieval history that became contentious topics in historical, religious, and philosophical discourse of the eighteenth and early nineteenth centuries, served as touchstones of social-political critique in these operas. Through staged re-enactments, these medieval emblems functioned as metaphors for an intolerant, absolutist past and as mirrors of national concerns, fears, and myths.

In contrast with the medievalism of *La Juive* and *Les Huguenots* (as well as that of Meyerbeer's *Le Prophète*, a work rooted in the 1830s in the early stages of its libretto), Halévy's *La Reine de Chypre* and *Charles VI* offered a more nostalgic, patriotic view of *le Moyen Âge*. Both operas incorporated medieval icons that were revered by Chateaubriand and other romantic writers and that were featured in historical plays and contemporary operas: the heroic peasant girl Jeanne d'Arc (Joan of Arc) and the chivalrous knight.[7] Though Odette, the young companion to the mad king in *Charles VI*, does not bear the name of Jeanne, she appears as an inspirational leader who urges Charles VI and VII into battle against the British. In *La Reine de Chypre*, a retelling of the fifteenth-century story of the Venetian-born queen of Cyprus, Catarina Cornaro carries Jeanne-like features as she, too, leads her people to resist the Venetian yoke.[8] The two men who love her, Gérard de Coucy and Jacques de Lusignan, are both cast as exiled French knights who fight for her and protect her honor. I will examine these medieval plot motifs—along with images of the Gothic cathedral and auto-da-fé, selected historical figures, and *ancien* musical symbols—in these operas to uncover their cultural and political resonances. Secondary references to medieval signifiers in other French grand operas and correspondences in contemporary literary and theatrical works will help to contextualize my argument.

La Juive and *Les Huguenots*: Medievalism as National Critique

The setting for *La Juive*, the early fifteenth-century Council of Constance, brought the weight of a problematic church history to the stage as it invoked Enlightenment critiques of the council's medieval barbarism and fanaticism.[9] In his *Essai sur les moeurs et l'esprit des nations*, Voltaire repudiated the council's Inquisition-like condemnation of Jan Hus (1372/1373–1415) and Jerome of Prague (1365–1416), Bohemian religious reformers who were burned at the stake at the council's command. Scribe's representation of the council was profoundly shaped by this Enlightenment-tinged perspective, as a perspective that was intimated in the earliest stages of Scribe's libretto. The term and the plot device of the auto-da-fé—signifying the Inquisition's burning of heretics at the stake—appears as a short-hand reference to the denouement of act 5 in Scribe's preliminary sketch, entitled "la belle juive."[10] In Scribe's more filled-out synopsis, which he would give to Fromental Halévy by the summer or early fall of 1833, the term reappears in his altered title, "Rachel, ou l'auto-da-fé."[11] Scribe clearly knew of the association of the term with the Inquisition and may have initially planned to locate this opera in Goa, a former Portuguese province of western India where the Inquisition was established in 1560.[12] A few years prior to Scribe's work on the libretto of *La Juive* and before he finalized its setting, Voltairean ideas about the Inquisition and the Inquisition-like Council of Constance as institutional forces of barbaric despotism reverberate more strongly in his personal writings, most emphatically in his travel journals (*carnets de voyage*) that relate his visit to Constance in 1826 and the papal palace in Avignon in 1827.[13] In Constance, he jotted down notes about the council's heresy trial of Jan Hus and Jerome of Prague, carefully describing everything connected with the trial that distressed him and his traveling companions: the *salle de concile*, the thrones of the emperor Sigismund and Pope Martin V (who endorsed the council's actions), the stone block on which Hus kneeled at his sentencing, the chair that bore him to the stake, and the site where his offending books were burned.[14] The librettist's focus on religious persecutions overseen by the church continued in his 1827 descriptions of the Inquisition tribunal in the Gothic Palais des Papes in Avignon, in which he described the *salle préparatoire*, where the Inquisitors summoned, as Scribe acerbically noted, "the Holy Spirit or, rather, the devil who inspires them," and the *salle des tortures*, where prisoners were bound in iron chains and tortured with "barbaric" instruments.[15]

As Scribe drafted his libretto, he shifted away from the auto-da-fé ending and back again. Although the method of execution—the hurling of Rachel into a vat of boiling liquid rather than the equally brutal method of burning her at the stake—may have been drawn from a plot detail in Christopher Marlowe's *The Jew of Malta*, Louis Véron gave Scribe the credit for originating the idea of the cauldron denouement.[16] With Scribe's decision to substitute both Rachel and her adoptive father Eléazar as victims of the council, rather than the historical Jean Hus and Jerome of Prague, he consciously evoked the victimization of Jews in the violent Inquisition history that was well known by his French audiences.[17] Moreover, in his modeling of Eléazar and Rachel on Shylock and Jessica in Shakespeare's *The Merchant of Venice*, as well as Isaac and Rebecca in Sir Walter Scott's *Ivanhoe*, Scribe engaged familiar literary tropes of the avaricious Jewish father and his exotic, beautiful daughter that may have galvanized social stereotypes accepted by some strands of the French public, as they touched on the contemporary "Jewish question" in the national discourse.[18] Were Jews to be fully part of the French nation, as their 1791 "emancipation" suggested, or were they to remain pariahs or "heretics" separate from the dominant Catholic populace? Scribe again addresses the fate of minorities, or Others, in the face of an oppressive Inquisition in his anticlerical libretto for Donizetti's French grand opera *Dom Sébastien* (1843), in which the Moorish Zayda is a victim of the sixteenth-century Portuguese Inquisition along with the dethroned Portuguese king, Dom Sébastien, who saves her from the stake, defies the grand inquisitor, and accuses him and his fellow inquisitors of treason.[19]

In *La Juive*, the brutal medievalism conveyed by the ultimate action of an intolerant council is enhanced by musical and visual symbols, elements of *couleur locale*, and paratexts of the first production at the Paris Opéra in 1835, although certain aspects of the dramaturgy may be viewed as audience-pleasing homages to medieval Catholicism that help to mitigate the opera's underlying critique. Although some journalists complained of historical distortions after the premiere, many effusively praised the opera for its effective recreation of the medieval world, including Théophile Gautier, who exclaimed, "The Middle Ages in all their entirety are unfolded before us.... It is the medieval period itself in all the infinite variety of its dress and its hierarchy."[20] The drama begins with the historical re-enactment of the opening of the council at a crossroads in the town of Constance. In the first set of act 1, designed by Charles Séchan (1803–1874), Léon Feuchère (1804–1857), Edouard Despléchin (1806–1870), and Jules Diéterle (1811–1889), an accurately rendered Gothic cathedral is seen at stage left as phrases of a Te Deum, a prominent musical symbol of the medieval church, are sung *a cappella* offstage by Catholic worshipers at the beginning and at key moments of the first scene.[21] Corresponding to visual cues, Halévy's music helps to set the medieval aura, although he alludes to rather than exactly replicates late medieval style.[22] When Halévy juxtaposes its phrases with verbal attacks of the Christian townspeople on the Jew Eléazar, this musical emblem of traditional Catholicism becomes deeply ironic. Its association with the council's opening, with further textual–visual representations of the church and council, particularly the council's leader Cardinal Brogni, deepens its significance in the whole of the drama.

The portrayal of the historical figure of Jean-François Brogni, or Jean Allarmet de Brogny (1342–1426), carried the aura of authenticity, heightened by well-researched costumes designed by Paul Lormier, which he modeled after iconography of early fifteenth-century southern German clerics.[23] In costume sketches, Lormier identifies the cardinal as "Jean françois de Brognye eveque de Vivian/archeveque d'Arles" and carefully renders his red-and-white robes and scarlet *galero*, or wide-brimmed hat, accompanied by a double-sided panel of fifteen tassels, that emulated details found in fifteenth-century historical paintings[24] (see Figure 5.1). The printed libretto for the February 23 premiere further communicates to audiences the historical realism of the cardinal's role as the council's leader; although the excerpted passage from *Biographie universelle* refers to the Hussites (followers of Jan Hus), no overt statement is made about executions or the cardinal's responsibility for them:

> The ending of the schism and the maintenance of the authority of the Church threatened in Germany by the new opinions of the Hussites were what affected the cardinal the most. Despite his advanced age, he went to Constance in August of 1414 to discuss with the imperial magistrates and officers the advent of the Council which was to bring peace to the Church. He presided during forty sessions and had meetings day and night with Emperor Sigismund, with princes and prelates, etc.[25]

Though Scribe and Halévy offer a balanced portrayal between the altruistic and malevolent sides of the medieval council and cardinal, the overruling image of Brogni is that of a man who willingly bends to vicious, "doctrinal" intolerance and pays a steep personal price for it. In the cardinal's first appearance in act 1, in his lilting cavatina, "Si la rigueur," he benevolently calls for reconciliation between the Catholic mobs and their Jewish victims, Eléazar and Rachel. Yet his benevolence is reversed in the finale to act 3, in which he delivers an implacable malediction, intensely depicted in his broad authoritative lines strengthened by low brass doublings that add force to his condemnations and command for the death of the Jews (and the offending lover of Rachel, Léopold, the Christian prince who had disguised himself as the Jewish painter Samuel, but who is ultimately pardoned). At the end of act 5, as Rachel is thrown into the boiling vat, Brogni shockingly discovers that she is his own biological daughter (raised as a Jewess), whom he and the council have executed.

The religiosity of the medieval past more fully permeates *La Juive* in the staging of ritual: in the Catholic processions of acts 1 and 4 and the depiction of a private Jewish seder in act 2. The act 1 cortège (see Figure 5.2) allowed for lavish visual spectacle, with brilliant, metallically armored soldiers, insignia-laden banner carriers, trumpeters, clerics, and council guards making way for the pompously dressed king and cardinal in an extended display before the residents of Constance and the Paris Opéra audience, as elaborately described by a reviewer for *Le Constitutionnel*:

> What a splendid medley of colors is this population of lords and priests arriving there from all countries, realms, abbeys, convents, and cathedrals: some mitred, others covered in crimson; some crowned in silver, others with a lavish shield and golden helmet sparkling in the sun! There the round, bare chin of the choirboys and the young priests, and the long and white beard of the old cardinals; foot soldiers and cavalry, cute pages, beautiful *châtelaines* and the black, filthy robes of mendicant friars; lances, military flags, crosses, candles, banners bearing the image of the Virgin and the saints, the gruff voices of soldiers handling their lances, and the clear and silvery voices [of the choristers] chanting litanies.[26]

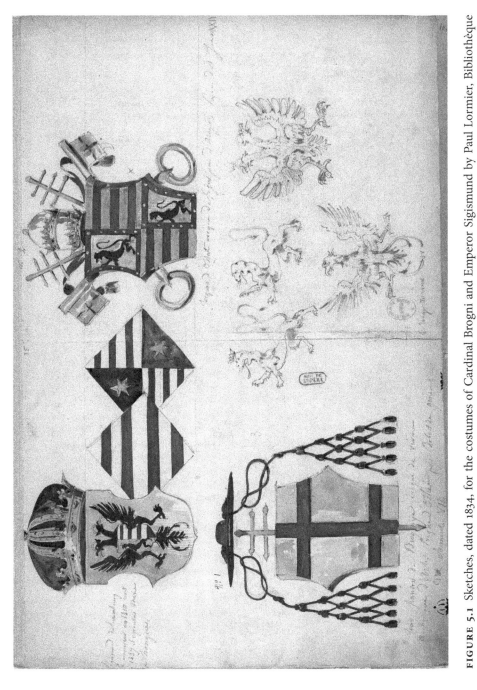

FIGURE 5.1 Sketches, dated 1834, for the costumes of Cardinal Brogni and Emperor Sigismund by Paul Lormier, Bibliothèque nationale, Bibliothèque-musée de l'Opéra.

FIGURE 5.2 Cortège at the end of act 1 of *La Juive*, Paris Opéra, 1835, engraving by "LB" in *L'Artiste* (1835), Bibliothèque nationale.

Again, the glories of the act 1 celebratory ritual are further tainted in act 5, offset by the funeral ceremony that reinforced the brutality of the medieval council in the final scenes. At the opening of the act, set within a "vast tent supported by Gothic columns," townspeople sadistically sing of pleasure and joy (Scribe's "Plaisir, ivresse et joie!" of the libretto was replaced by "Quel plaisir, quelle joie" in the score) at the realization that they will be avenged against the Jews, who await death.[27] They then watch as a *cortège* files past, which includes monks, pages, cardinals, penitents, and the Jew Eléazar, surrounded by soldiers.[28] To a haunting orchestral accompaniment, a barefooted Rachel, draped in white, is brought in by guards, followed by the town magistrate Ruggiero, the council secretaries dressed in black, and then the cardinal and principal members of the council. According to *mise en scène* documents and iconography, the mute figure of the emperor enters on horseback, signifying the united front of church and state in sealing the fate of the Jewish heretics.[29] Although the reviewer for *La Gazette de France* objected to what he viewed as outrageous distortions of church history, the critic for the anticlerical *Le Temps* found the act a convincing portrayal of the Dark Ages.[30]

Religious intolerance and violence, though of the late sixteenth century, are revisited in Meyerbeer's *Les Huguenots*, a work ideologically parallel to *La Juive* and one also created from a libretto by Eugène Scribe. In setting up the religious opposition of Catholics versus Huguenots/Protestants, rather than the Catholic-versus-Jewish conflict of *La Juive*, Scribe and Meyerbeer highlight the frivolity and decadence of Catholic lords, in contrast to the sincere, but somewhat fanatical piety of the old Huguenot soldier, Marcel (a character largely developed by the composer) and the humility of the young Raoul. Meyerbeer immediately symbolizes the minority Protestants with the overture's variations on "Ein feste Burg," the Lutheran chorale that serves throughout the work as a "pan-Protestant" emblem and a symbol of resistance to Catholic control and aggression. The chorale melody returns in phrases intoned by Marcel, characterized as a leader and an embodiment of the Protestant faith, in both its naiveté and its self-righteousness. Although suggestions of Marcel's own intolerance, like Eléazar's, point to a dual-sided focus, the primary critical targets in *Les Huguenots*, as in *La Juive*, are the religious hypocrisy of the Catholics and the absolutist power of a medieval church and state.

The historical event at the basis of Meyerbeer's opera sharpened the anticlerical, antiabsolutist critique by bringing it even closer to France's own history: that of the infamous massacre of "St. Barthélemy," or St. Bartholomew's Eve, in which over three thousand French Huguenots were killed in Paris on August 23, 1572. Just as Scribe's first title for *La Juive* ("Rachel, ou l'autodafé") laid bare his focus on the controversial event, so too does his original title for *Les Huguenots*—"Léonore, ou La Saint Barthélemy"—draw attention to the act of persecution. The well-read librettist and dramatist would likely have been aware of the subject's treatment in Voltaire's *La Henriade* and *Essai sur les guerres civiles de France*, as well as Marie-Joseph de Chénier's revolutionary tragedy, *Charles IX, ou l'École des rois* (republished in the 1820s), and plays of the July Monarchy, including Jean-Pierre-François Lesguillon's *Aoust 1572, ou Charles IX à Orléans* (1832) and Joseph-Bernard Rosier's *Charles IX* (1834). One historical adaptation, Prosper Mérimée's novel *Chronique du règne de Charles IX*

(1829), has been cited as a source for Scribe's libretto, though Steven Huebner emphasizes that there is "little evidence" for the connection.[31] Central to the event's contentiousness was the belief that both Charles IX and his mother Catherine de Medici, formerly the queen of France (r. 1547–1559) and regent (1560–1563), had ordered the massacre. Scribe adopted this interpretation by initially including Catherine in the libretto (though excluding Charles IX). When the government's theatrical censors forced him to omit the queen, the *metteur en scène* Edmond Duponchel fought with the interior minister, Camille Montalivet, to retain her appearance in the act 5 massacre.[32] Despite Montalivet's alleged retort that "the memory of Catherine de Medici was more precious than the reputation of a *décorateur*," according to *Le National* of January 11 and May 7, 1836, a compromise was reached to have Catherine's livery, in red velour, appear "as a point of light," with closed curtains hiding the identity of the occupant.

As told from the Voltairean perspective, the story of St. Bartholomew's Eve encircles the oppositional lovers, the Huguenot Raoul and the Catholic Valentine, from the moment the tocsin's signals for the massacre's commencement interrupts their expressions of love in the expansive duet that ends act 4. In the final act, Raoul and Valentine become the foregrounded victims of the savage massacre, which begins in the offstage imagination in scene 1 as Huguenots celebrate the marriage of Marguerite to Henry of Navarre (an alliance intended to bring peace among Catholics and Protestants). In scene 2, near a Protestant cemetery where Marcel is helping to construct barricades, Raoul sees his wounded friend and Valentine presses Raoul to surrender or adopt her Catholic faith, rather than fight the assassins; when he refuses, she, with increasing agitation, embraces his. "Ein feste Burg" can be heard from the church where fleeing Huguenots have found refuge, intoned by an offstage chorus as Marcel counters with intense leaps and admiring words of the "innocence and faith" in their prayers as they face death. Following a prolonged bass clarinet solo that poignantly introduces the trio, Marcel blesses the *noces funèbres* of Raoul and the now-converted Valentine; as they sing to God, a final phrase of "Ein feste Burg" sounds with them from a distance, but is cut short as gunshots explode and Catholic assassins burst into the church. In the final trio section marked "Vision," Marcel sees the heavens open as celestial harps resound and Valentine and Raoul look on, before all three defy the murderers with rising pitches and escalating lines of "Ein feste Burg." They escape to the street, with Raoul mortally wounded, before the Catholic leader St. Bris orders all three shot, recognizing too late (just as Brogni did in the final scene of *La Juive*) that it is his own daughter whom he has killed.

Although the St. Barthélemy massacre that Scribe and Meyerbeer portray so viscerally lies within the Renaissance period as defined by some nineteenth-century writers or as presently constructed, the arbitrary, intolerant power of the state as it is represented in *Les Huguenots* belongs very much to the idea of the medieval put forward by Voltaire, Michelet, and other liberal, anticlerical voices. In this sense, both *La Juive* and *Les Huguenots* might be understood as a critique of the conservative Restoration regime of Charles X (perhaps viewed as a proxy for his namesake, Charles IX) and the neomedieval system that was replaced, after the 1830 revolution, by the rule of the *citizen king*. Both works address questions that were actively debated within the July Monarchy concerning the meaning and extent of religious freedom and governmental protection of religions other than Catholicism—in sharp contrast to the repressive turns of Charles X, who had not only demanded press censorship and dissolved a newly elected chamber (actions that would bring down his government), but also tried to impose a "sacrilege law" in 1825 that called for death to those who committed blasphemy against the church and the Catholic faith. The medievalist metaphor of these operas also taps into the July Monarchy's new, or renewed, concept of nationhood and national identity in relation to its treatment of practitioners of minority religions, which it had expelled or persecuted in earlier centuries—corresponding with ideas that Michael Ragussis proposed in his contextualization of Scott's *Ivanhoe*.[33] The theme of medieval intolerance that Scribe developed and that Halévy and Meyerbeer enhanced in these operas strongly resonates with the admonition of Joseph Mérilhou, who had fought against Charles X's restrictive ordinances and who, as ministre de l'instruction publique et des cultes under the July Monarchy, proposed a law for extending governmental protection to "les ministres du culte Israelite" (Jewish rabbis) in 1831. As Mérilhou addressed his colleagues in the French governmental chambers, he reminded them of the indignity of retaining the "rust of the Middle Ages" in an "enlightened century," pleading, "Let us erase these last vestiges of an oppression that must never be reborn, and let us ensure that in France there are only French citizens, rather than *religionnaires* divided by religion."[34]

La Reine de Chypre and *Charles VI*: Medievalism as National Reclamation

In Halévy's works of the early 1840s, medieval metaphors serve primarily as emblems of national remembrance and reclamation, shifting away from the overt political critique of an intolerant church and state in *La Juive* and *Les Huguenots*. *La Reine de Chypre*, written to a libretto by J. H. Vernoy de Saint-Georges and first appearing at the Paris Opéra on December 22, 1841, retells the history of the Venetian queen Catarina Cornaro, ruler of the island of Cyprus from 1474 to 1489—in correspondence with a spate of Cornaro operas that appeared in European theaters.[35] With the dual locales of Venice and Cyprus, *La Reine* again thrilled Parisian audiences with rich, exotic local color, festive processionals, and extravagant costumes. The opera also returned to the idea of institutional oppression, but in this case linked to the politically infused, and seemingly outwardly directed, trope of Venetian despotism or *terreur*—a trope that was prominently represented in nineteenth-century plays such as Lord Byron's *Marino Faliero* (1821) and *The Two Foscari* (1821) and operas such as Gioachino Rossini's *Bianca e Falliero, o sia Il Consiglio dei Tre* (1819), Gaetano Donizetti's *Marina Faliero* (1835), and Giuseppe Verdi's *I due Foscari* (1844).[36] As reinterpreted in *La Reine de Chypre*, the opposition to Venetian *terreur* carried a special connection to French revolutionary ideology and the legacy of Napoléon, which permeated the late eighteenth-century

French play that was seminal in the trope's formation: *Blanche et Montcassin, ou Les Vénitiens* (1798) by Antoine-Vincent Arnault. According to historian James H. Johnson, Arnault's drama helped to establish the "myth" of Venetian tyranny and to solidify the author's role as a mouthpiece of revolutionary rhetoric and propaganda, particularly in relation to Napoléon's military actions to liberate Venice from the Council of Ten and State Inquisition during the Italian campaign of 1796–1797.[37] This association, along with the play's dedication to Napoléon (who requested that its original happy ending be changed to a tragic one), would lead to the banning of Arnault's work after the Hundred Days, the dismissal of the dramatist from the Académie française, and his exile from France until 1819.

The Napoleonic past and its remembrance of the former consul's liberation of Venice from its tyrannical rulers are made explicit and implicit in *La Reine de Chypre* through pointed and veiled references in the libretto, staging, and score that corresponded with important texts of Venetian history or myth.[38] The most discernible indication of a Napoleonic subtext is the inclusion of a historical excerpt in the preface to the libretto's first edition: a passage from *Histoire de Venise* by le comte Pierre-Antoine-Noël-Bruno Daru, a soldier and statesman who served as *commissaire* in Napoléon's Northern Italian campaign.[39] In correlation with Arnault's drama, Daru writes of Venice's power over the Cypriot king, a possible Venetian conspiracy behind his likely poisoning, and Catarina's courageous refusal to submit to Venetian control in the excerpt; in other passages of Daru's history, he underscores the malevolent authority of the Council of Ten, noting that "this monstrous tribunal" ("ce tribunal monstrueux") closely monitored the populace and authorized public and hidden deaths.[40]

In its plot, staging, and music, *La Reine de Chypre* conveys a similar interpretation to that of Daru; moreover, it echoes Arnault's dramatic choice of a broken engagement and politically forced marriage, strongly implying a source connection to the play, a possibility made more probable by the dramatist's renewed prominence during the July Monarchy. Both Arnault's and Daru's Napoleonic ideology strongly filter through the opera's portrayal of the sinister, conspiratorial Pietro Mocénigo, a council member who first threatens the patrician Andrea with death if he does not prevent the marriage of his niece Catarina with the chevalier Gérard de Coucy. As a signifier of Mocénigo and the council's menacing authority, Halévy creates a recurring motive (the "council motive"), built on an ominous repeated-pitch ostinato in quarter notes; it first sounds in C minor in the Mocénigo–Andrea duet of act 1 in the clarinet, then horns, underlying Mocénigo's unyielding order, and resounds throughout the tension-packed *parlante* of this duet (see Example 5.1). He also develops it beyond the scene, bringing it back overtly in act 2, no. 8, immediately before Andrea reinforces that "Venice has ordained" the breaking of Catarina's vows to Gérard, and again when he informs the resistant Catarina that the council would kill Gérard if she did not follow their command. In act 5, it returns in Catarina's heart-rending recitative, shortly before she questions Lusignan's succumbing to "un mal inconnu," thus musically confirming the council's guilt in poisoning the king. Halévy also subtly varies it to comment further on the council's control over the fate of

EXAMPLE 5.1 "Council motive" from *La Reine de Chypre*, act 1, no. 3, Mocénigo–Andrea duet.

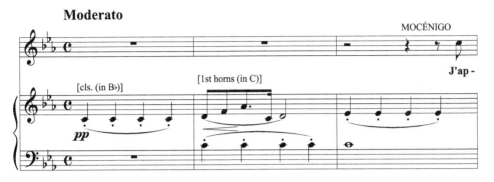

the three principal characters. As the drama unfolds, Catarina and her rival lovers, Gérard and Lusignan, are captured as sympathetic symbols of Venetian oppression and French heroism. As she leads the Cypriots to defy the despotic Venetians in act 5, Catarina emerges as a French heroine, if not inhabiting the spiritual zeal of Jeanne d'Arc, perhaps donning the "Phrygian cap" of Marianne, France's republican symbol of *liberté*.[41]

In quite visceral ways, the opera's portrayal of Catarina's story of the late Middle Ages functioned as a re-enactment of France's heroic past: not only mirrored by the Cypriot victory over the Venetians, but also evoked by the patriotic oaths of the exiled French chevaliers in act 3 and, most strikingly, by the spectacle of act 4. In the staging at the Paris Opéra, this grand public ritual, although part of a festival to celebrate the marriage of Catarina and Lusignan, purposefully integrated symbols from the real-life, multi-staged ceremony that had commemorated the return of Napoléon's remains from the island of his exile and death, St. Helena. This commemoration, commonly known as "Le retour des cendres," culminated in the procession of Napoléon's ornate funeral carriage through the streets of Paris to the Invalides on December 15, 1840, one year prior to the opera's premiere, a timing that has the opera's appearance nearly marking the anniversary of the ceremony.[42] In the opera's first staging, as Catarina disembarks from her ship (perhaps symbolizing the arrival at Corbevoie of La Dorade, the ship that carried Napoléon's remains up the Seine), participants in the *cortège*, including the archbishop of Cyprus, members of the clergy, children of the choir, soldiers, banner-carrying *hérauts d'armes*, heads of state, and the king, move through the "grand place" of Nicosia among celebrating Cypriots. Placed on the steps of the palace are at least twelve *grandes trompettes* of the thirty-one that had been used in Napoléon's ceremony, as reported in French newspapers.[43] In *La Presse*, a week after the opera's premiere, Théophile Gautier pointed out the significance of these instruments in his description of the extravagant act, set in Cyprus, with processions rivalling those of *La Juive*:

> This fourth act is almost all staging and spectacle. [...] Some batteries of long trumpets, known as "Roman trumpets," which you no doubt noticed in the convoy of the Emperor, sweep down on the balustrade of the terrace and start to sound brilliant fanfares to which the canon, and the Cypriot music in another corner, respond forcefully. Then a triumphal march begins [...]. The king, preceded by his pages, his heralds of arms, his grand officers head for the cathedral with the queen [...]. The leaders of the army and navy, the deputies of the Venetian senate, the grand dignitaries of State, high personnages of the court follow at slight intervals. [...] The army of the king of Cyprus brings up the rear of the march: *hallebadiers*, archers, *pertuisaniers* who advance beating drums, signs deployed; we can hardly believe that at least five hundred people were on the scene who cross, mingle, and move in a picturesque disorder, but without confusion.[44]

As embodied by military displays, the "natural" movement of hundreds of performers on stage, the soundscape of a double orchestra performing ceremonial music—compared by Berlioz to "le bruit solennel des grandes fêtes nationales"—and the emblematic use of *grandes trompettes* from Napoléon's funeral procession, this act could be viewed as a compressed "reprise" of Napoléon's "return" to Paris.[45] Halévy, along with two other leading French composers—Daniel Auber and Adolphe Adam—had contributed newly written marches for the commemoration, but of these, only Halévy's was scored for the trumpets in question.[46] Not only does Halévy use these special trumpets in both his *Marche funèbre* for the 1840 ceremony and the *Marche triomphale* of *La Reine*, but also he makes clear the intertextuality of these works by his replication of the same fanfare in the same key (A♭) from his 1840 march in the opera's act 4 procession.[47]

In this public ritual re-enacted within the public art form of grand opera, the medievalist "Marche triomphale" of *La Reine* epitomizes the July Monarchy's reclamation of a tarnished history, once again honoring the heroism of the defeated Napoléon shortly after his remains—his "ruins"—were returned to French soil. Enhancing the Napoleonic allegory, the romantic image of the medieval chevalier is embodied in the figures of the two exiled Frenchmen who are divided as love rivals but bonded as national brothers. Central to the first two acts set in Venice is Catarina's first betrothed, Gérard, who escapes to the island of Rhodes after Andrea's interruption of his wedding at the end of act 2, but returns in acts 3 and 4 in hopes of assassinating his rival; later in act 5, dressed as a chevalier of Rhodes and guided by "duty" (*le devoir*), Gérard reappears to join in the Cypriot fight against the Venetian oppressors. Portraying an even nobler chevalier is the French-born Cypriot king Lusignan, who saves Gérard's life, despite his attempts to kill· him, and gives his blessings to both Catarina and Gérard before dying by Venetian poisoning in the final act.[48] Images of the exiled hero are rife through the nineteenth century and certainly intersect with the archetype of the romantic Wanderer, but joined with act 4's ceremonial references, the exiled, chivalrous characters of *La Reine* (especially Lusignan) may also have operated as figurative triggers for recalling, and empathizing with, the fate of Napoléon, who was depicted staring out to sea during his imprisonment on St. Helena before his death in 1821.[49] As reflected in many reviews of the opera's premiere, the patriotic salute of these chevaliers in the duo finale of act 3 greatly moved Parisian audiences, particularly the *cantabile*, "Triste exilé," which expresses their shared melancholia as exiled Frenchmen "sur la terre étrangère." At the beginning of act 5, as Lusignan lies dying, he briefly recalls the opening phrase of *Triste exilé*, signaling his remembrance of their knightly, brotherly bond in a *chant désolé* that Berlioz described as "one of Halévy's most profoundly dramatic ideas."[50] Their solidarity holds to the end of the opera: in the quartet (which Wagner deeply admired), as Lusignan, Gérard, and Catarina resist Mocénigo's power, and in Lusignan's final blessing to Gérard and Catarina before his death.[51] Immediately after the knightly king takes his last breath, perhaps signaling a final allusion to Napoléon as revolutionary hero and liberator, Catarina calls out, "Au martyr de votre indépendance," and stirs the Cypriots to join in a "Marseillaise"-inspired chorus of defiance. Although writers rarely assessed the opera's historical import in early reviews of *La Reine*, other than briefly recounting Cornaro's history,[52] the work might be placed comfortably alongside Horace Vernet's historical paintings of Napoléon's victories commissioned by Louis-Philippe and presented in his newly constructed Musée de l'Histoire de France at Versailles from 1837 as visual displays of reconciliation with the Bonapartist past, in dedication "to all the glories of France" ("À toute les gloires de la France").[53]

Medievalist enactments of national remembrance continue in *Charles VI*, a fully patriotic work that appeared as a near *pièce de circonstance* in its direct response to a national crisis.[54] In July 1840, not long before the initial stages of the opera's genesis (and only a few months before "Le retour des cendres"), France was rocked by the Oriental (or Near Eastern) Crisis following the seizure of the Ottoman province of Syria by the

French ally, Egyptian pasha Muhammed Ali (1769–1849). When the British foreign minister Lord Palmerston, in opposition to Ali's territorial expansion and resistance to Ottoman control, negotiated the Convention of London with Prussia, Austria, and Russia, but excluding France (echoing the anti-French alliance of 1814), the French minister Adolphe Thiers immediately prepared for war against England. Although Louis-Philippe ultimately quelled Thiers's bellicosity, replacing his ministry with that of François Guizot and helping to resolve the Egyptian–Ottoman conflict by July 1841, Franco–British relations remained precarious by the time of the premiere of *Charles VI* on March 15, 1843. The opera's early fifteenth-century setting near the end of the reign of Charles VI and the Hundred Years' War, its portrayal of Isabelle de Bavière's treasonous attempts to cede the French throne to Henry V of England, and its reminiscences of the lost Battle of Agincourt captured the anti-British fervor of the moment, even leading to a censorial intrusion by the French minister Guizot.[55] As reported in the press leading up to its premiere and as documented in libretto sources, Guizot objected to the phrase "Guerre au anglais!" ("War on the English!") that recurred throughout the martially spirited *chant national*—first sung in act 1 and repeated in the call for war ending the opera—and requested a change in wording to the more universal expression, "Guerre aux tyrans!" ("War on the tyrants!").[56]

The dramatization of the story of the "mad king" Charles VI (1368–1422) was not unprecedented in the July Monarchy, because several plays about this historical figure had been written during the 1820s, including the five-act tragedies *Charles VI* (1826) by La Ville de Mirmon, *Isabelle de Bavière* (1829), and *La Démence de Charles VI* (1826) by Népomucène Lemercier. However, Lemercier's play, which provided the central model for Casimir and Germain Delavigne's libretto of *Charles VI*, did not make it to the stage, since its characterization of king and queen had been judged too offensive by Restoration censors. As Sarah Hibberd outlines, histories published in the Restoration and July Monarchy also centered portions of their narratives on the figures of Charles VI, Isabelle, and Henry, including Prosper de Barante's *Histoire des ducs de Bourgogne* (1826), Henri Martin's *Histoire de France* (1833–1836), and Michelet's *Histoire de France* (vol. 4, 1840), some of which built on earlier chronicles that were republished during these decades.[57]

Correlating with the arousal of national empathy for exiled chevaliers in *La Reine de Chypre* and the metaphorical references to the exile and death of a former hero of *liberté*, Halévy's *Charles VI* merges compassionate portrayals of the troubled, mentally unstable king and his son, Charles VII, with martially infused music and allusions to medieval battles and historical French patriots. At the outset of the drama, Halévy and his librettists highlight the importance of remembering heroes, and remembering them empathetically: in the opening chorus, young peasant girls sing plaintively of Charles VI, this "good old king" who has forgotten the boatman's songs, "but without forgetting us" ("mais sans nous oublier"). After Odette enters, she sings of "a recollection so dear" ("Une si chère souvenance") and "homesickness" ("le mal du pays"), followed by words of pity for the king and dauphin: "Poor son, poor father! / One is exiled, the other insane" ("Malheureux fils, malheureux père! / L'un est proscrit, l'autre insensé"). The soldier

Raymond remembers, too, as he sees a sword hanging on the wall: "My good sword of Azincourt, / When will I take you again?" (Ma bonne lame d'Azincourt, / Quand donc pourrai-je te reprendre?).

Memories of war permeate the depiction of the king's fluctuating sanity, in Odette's efforts to steady him, and in his act 4 visions. In act 2, when Charles VI's mind wavers between dreams and reality in the *Scène et romance*, he recalls the battle that led to his mental breakdown and foresees the king's death, momentarily forgetting he is the king. In the next number, the "Duo des Cartes", Charles's young *guardienne* Odette de Champdivers, the Burgundian peasant girl who is later transformed into a Jeanne-like leader, spurs him to recall the glorious battles and patriots of France in the form of a card game. Halévy sets up the game, in which Charles "fights" for the French and Odette for the English, with Odette's call of "bataille!" on a leaping sixth from E4 to a long-held C5, then echoed by Charles. In multiple sections of the duet, the composer creates a combative ambience through his use of military-style dotted rhythms, fanfares, march patterns, and the thrust and parry of the players' exchanges, "Sonnez clairons!" and "Battez tambours!" Alluded to or directly named in their game, as found in fifteenth-century cards of the French court, are the medieval knight Ogier, as the Jack of Spades, and La Hire, the military leader of the Hundred Years' War who fought with Jeanne d'Arc and the dauphin, as the Jack of Hearts, and, finally, Charlemagne, the French founding father and Charles's namesake, the King of Hearts—the name that Odette calls out immediately before the king cries victory over the English ("a moi j'ai gagné la bataille, j'ai vaincu les anglais").[58]

Reminders of dark times in late medieval French history and premonitions of Charles's death come in the supernatural scene of act 4, in which the hallucinating king hears "lugubrious murmurs" and sees "fearful" ghostly figures. In the dim light of a "lampe fantastique," with sounds of clanking armor and rattling chains, a spectral chorus, in A minor, sings of "pales fantômes" coming from an open tomb. Swept in with a voluminous, plunging, chromatic line in strings and winds, the first ghost, L'homme de la forêt de Mans, appears—he is the man who had warned Charles VI of betrayal in 1392, setting off the king's first mental breakdown. In the scene, as the orchestra chromatically rises from F minor, to F♯ minor, to G minor, L'homme sings in a sinister voice, taunting Charles: "You remember me from the forest of Mans, well, tell me, do you recognize me, King?" ("De la forêt du Mans te souviens tu, dis moi eh bien, me reconnais tu roi?"). As Charles's agitation intensifies, he authoritatively orders the ghost to flee before breaking into a diminished triad, E–C♯–A♯, as he questions his sanity. Joining L'homme in his foreboding are three soldiers in Charles's life who had been assassinated or nearly assassinated: the Breton soldier [Olivier de] Clisson, whose murder had been ordered by Duke John IV, whom he had formerly served; Le duc [Louis] d'Orléans, Charles's brother, who had been killed by their cousin, Jean-sans-peur (Duke of Burgundy) in 1407 (instigating the Armagnac–Burgundian civil war), and Jean-sans-peur himself, who was slain by the military leader Tanguy du Chastel in 1419. The four specters, singing *sotto voce* in homorhythmic unity, predict (incorrectly) that Charles, too, would be assassinated, by the hand of his son.

In the opera's final act, two national icons prominent in medievalist representation are brought together: the Basilica of Saint Denis, the palace and burial grounds of French kings, and the figure of Jeanne d'Arc. The setting of Saint Denis not only reminded Parisian audiences of their monarchical heritage, but also, by placing the treacherous Isabelle and Bedford within its hallowed walls, exploited national fears of British power that had recently threatened French stability. After Isabelle had stripped the Dauphin of his heritage by tricking the confused Charles VI into signing a treaty that would yield power to the young English noble, Lancashire, English soldiers had already arrived on the steps of the Hôtel Saint-Paul, the king's refuge, in act 3. As the theater changes at the end of act 5, scene 2, revealing the interior of the even more significant monument of Saint-Denis, adorned with banners of the Crusades and past wars of France and in view of royal tombs, the figure of Odette appears as Jeanne d'Arc beneath the *oriflamme* that is her national emblem. Although Odette had served as a humble protector of the king in previous acts, her destiny as redeemer of France had been foretold from the opera's beginning; as she grasps the *oriflamme* in the final scene, Charles VI, who regains his sanity before taking his last breath, compels the French to follow her into battle against the English; the Dauphin, and future king, takes up his sword and leads the chevaliers and people in a last refrain of the *chant national*, "Guerre aux tyrans."[59]

In its presentation of national calamities drawn from French medieval history—the remembered loss at Agincourt, the recurring British threat to France's throne, and the instability of a king—*Charles VI* indeed realizes Nicholas White's characterization of French grand opera as a genre that responded to and constructed history around "moments of inauguration and crisis."[60] Through its layers of metaphor, its card-game replication of battles once fought, its fantastical apparitions of dead warriors, and its culminating Jeanne-led victory, the opera's medievalism forged a national message centered on overcoming a troubled past and the reclamation of national glory. Although its themes aimed to recapture a sense of nation defined by territory, monarchical inheritance, and military courage, as they reflected very real fears of the British-led challenge to France's global power, the opera's relationship to national meanings and moods took different forms within shifting contexts and audiences. Its *chant national*, evoking French resistance to foreign rule as well as anti-British sentiments, despite the Guizot-directed text alteration of the "Guerre" refrain, would soon take on new functions outside the theater, becoming a song of opposition to Louis-Philippe's placating policies toward the British, according to Berlioz, who reported that "three-quarters of the audience gave tongue and joined in with the chorus" of "Guerre aux tyrans" as he conducted his 1844 concert in the Industrial Exposition building; it was also sung as a patriotic and oppositional chorus in gatherings around the time of the Revolution of 1848.[61]

Charles VI, along with Halévy's other French grand operas of the July Monarchy and Meyerbeer's *Les Huguenots*, exemplified the nineteenth century's fascination with the Middle Ages—"le goût du Moyen Âge," or "la manie du gothique" (as Michelet attributed to Chateaubriand and Hugo)—through the retelling of a "long" medieval history, the re-enactment of medieval ritual, and the appropriation of medieval icons. With stunning, audience-riveting mise en scène, intertextual amalgamations, and fictionalized stories of fated love against the backdrop of problematic political events and institutional histories, these works questioned the relevance of the distant past within the French present, the role of religion and diverse religious traditions within a modernizing state, and the relationships and conflicts between ideas of revolution, *liberté*, power, and tyranny. The political and cultural meanings that these operas embody, as the creations of multiple collaborators working under changing conditions of censorship from the early to mid–July Monarchy, invite multiple interpretations as they reflect a range of voices and stances within the French milieu, as I have argued more fully in my book on *La Juive*.[62] The critiques of "medieval" intolerance and abuses of Catholic Church and state against Jews and Huguenots, often cast as parallel minorities who had suffered institutional blows and restrictions as "heretics" and alien Others in France, mirrored contemporary views of liberal voices such as Joseph Mérilhou, while simultaneously attracting and offending traditionalists such as the reviewer for *La Gazette de France*, who accused Scribe, in *La Juive*, of "ly[ing] with impunity about the institution that is the most necessary to the social order."[63] The rejection of medieval abuses in these French grand operas vied with, and vacillated between, the worship of medieval "monuments": between Voltaire's and Michelet's reminders of the *terrorisme* and *bûchers* of the Middle Ages and Chateaubriand's and Hugo's romancing of medieval *chevalerie*, "ruines," and "temples que gardait l'oriflamme."[64] The exploitation of French medievalism in *La Reine de Chypre* and *Charles VI* swings away from the Enlightenment-inspired castigations in *La Juive* and *Les Huguenots* to a merging of romantic medieval remembrance with the reclamation of a national past. Yet the critiques embedded in the grand operas of the 1830s may not have been set aside in the early 1840s, but may lie submerged beneath nostalgic displays of patriotism and chivalrous salutes. Did Venetian despotism, as that of the Council of Constance and Catherine de Médici, shine a mirror on France's own past and present, on Louis-Philippe, and even on the restored Napoléon himself, the "liberator" of Venice and the *triste exilé* whose images reverberated through the libretto, music, and 1841 staging of *La Reine de Chypre*? Did the hallucinations of Charles VI bring forward another specter from his monarchical past that remains shrouded in the opera's text: that of his banning of Jews from France in 1394?

Within the explicit, implicit, and possibly hidden metaphors of medievalism, the cultural relevance and political power of these French grand operas can be sensed. Through them, the Middle Ages—or at least an imagined *Moyen Âge*—not only endured but also flourished at the Paris Opéra and in other lyric theaters that staged these influential works (particularly *La Juive* and *Les Huguenots*) throughout the nineteenth century. Indeed, in their spectacular productions, medieval or medievalist events functioned at least to some degree as in Voltaire's historical essays or Michelet's history: as representations of a barbarous past that must be overcome by the forces of enlightenment and modernity. And yet, these magnificent works also served to reclaim and re-envisage the medieval history that lay at the heart of the nation, combining homages to national spirit and courage with "liberating" remembrances of a problematic past.

The complex and multivalent images of the Middle Ages that these works present became a crucial part of French, as well as European, historical consciousness that continues to be reflected and refracted in the mirrors of our modern ages.

NOTES

1. Michael Glencross, *Reconstructing Camelot: French Romantic Medievalism and the Arthurian Tradition* (Cambridge: Brewer, 1995), ix.

2. Christian Amalvi, *Le gout du moyen âge* (Paris: Plon, 1996), 25: "au siècle libertin et impie des Philosophes et aux 'saturnales' de la Révolution." (Translations of passages in this chapter are mine, unless otherwise noted.)

3. As cited in Amalvi, *Le gout du moyen âge*, 21–22: "triste enfant, arraché des entrailles mêmes du christianisme, qui naquit dans les larmes, qui grandit dans la prière et la reverie, dans les angoisses du Coeur, qui mourut sans achiever rien." Amalvi cites the "première version" of Michelet's *Histoire de France*, p. 30.

4. The subsuming of the Renaissance within the medieval by French romantics also touched nineteenth-century categorizations of sixteenth-century music, particularly the music of Palestrina, as Katharine Ellis notes in *Interpreting the Musical Past: Early Music in Nineteenth-Century France* (Oxford: Oxford University Press, 2005). She writes that "Palestrinian music became a contested area," with romantics viewing the composer "as in some sense 'gothic' and, therefore, 'medieval'" and Ultramontane Catholics (in agreement with Chateaubriand's characterization of the late fifteenth and sixteenth centuries as "decadent" and secular) emphasizing "his 'newness' and antitraditionalism"(180). Sarah Hibberd writes, in *French Grand Opera and the Historical Imagination* (Cambridge: Cambridge University Press, 2009), 87, that "the Renaissance was not yet seen in its own right as a separate period" and, aligning with Ellis, recognizes the religious and political divides that affected views of the Middle Ages and Renaissance. For perspectives on the ways in which nineteenth-century German intellectuals understood the divide between the medieval and Renaissance periods, see Laura Stokes's contribution to this volume, "Medievalisms in Early Nineteenth-Century German Thought."

5. Jules Michelet, *Histoire de France au seizième siècle*, vol. 7, *Renaissance* (Paris: Chamerot, 1855), ["l'état bizarre et monstrueux, prodigieusment artificiel,"] iv.

6. Ibid.: "le temps, la critique et le progress des idées"; "Ainsi dure le moyen âge, d'autant plus difficile à tuer qu'il est mort depuis longtemps. Pour être tué, il faut vivre. Que de fois il a fini!"

7. Other heroes of French medievalism include Roland, the military leader under Charlemagne who defended Frankish borders, Étienne Marcel, protector of guildsmen in the early fourteenth century, and Bertrand du Guesclin, the Breton knight and military leader of the Hundred Years' War. See Amalvi, *Le gout du moyen âge*, 22.

8. The later representations of Jeanne d'Arc described by Donald Greig in his essay "Re-sounding Carl Dreyer's *La Passion de Jeanne d'Arc*" and by Elizabeth Dister in her essay "Tolling Bells and Otherworldly Voices: Joan of Arc's Sonic World in the Early Twentieth Century" on pp. 247–266 and pp. 422–448 of this volume, respectively, provide interesting counterpoints to these operatic examples.

9. For a fuller discussion of the political significance of the opera's portrayal of the Council of Constance, see Diana R. Hallman, "The Council of Constance and the Voltairean Critique," in

Opera, Liberalism, and Antisemitism in Nineteenth-Century France: The Politics of Halévy's La Juive, (Cambridge: Cambridge University Press, 2002), 108–149.

10. Eugène Scribe, "Quelques idées des pieces," F-Pn, Ms. (Paris: Bibliothèque Nationale de France, Département des Manuscrits), n.a.fr. 22584, vol. VIII, fol. 66r. Also see Hallman, *Politics of Halévy's* La Juive, 212–215.

11. Eugène Scribe, draft scenario, F-Pn, Ms., n.a.fr. 22502, I°:2°, 1.

12. Léon Halévy, in a biography of his brother, *F. Halévy: Sa Vie et ses oeuvres*, 2nd ed. (Paris: Heugel, 1863), writes that Goa was the setting in "le plan primitif" (p. 23). Léon's "hidden" role as reviser of Scribe's libretto, although known primarily through his own account and the corroboration of Edouard Monnais, strengthens the validity of his claim. A sketch of an abandoned act 5 set by Pierre-Luc-Charles Cicéri (1834?), which depicts hundreds of clerics seated in elevated galleries above an amphitheater, seemingly corresponds to the idea of a setting of the Inquisition at Goa; see F-Po (Paris: Bibliothèque Nationale de France, Musée-Bibliothèque de l'Opéra), [Esq. Cicéri 13–14].

13. Eugène Scribe, "Carnets de notes et de voyages en France, Suisse et Italie, 1826–1852," F-Pn, Ms., n.a.fr. 22584, vol. 1, fols. 14v–15v.

14. Ibid.

15. F-Pn, Ms., n.a.fr. 22584, vol. 2, "Voyage dans le Mydi de la France, Ier Avril-1827," fols. 19v–20r.

16. In his memoirs, Véron, who was *Directeur-Entrepreneur* of the Paris Opéra at the time of *La Juive's* premiere, commended Scribe for his "invention" and stated enthusiastically, "The Classicists would never have had this stroke of genius! This denouement [of boiling the Jewess], M. Scribe, will give you the greatest honor all your life." See *Mémoires d'un bourgeois de Paris comprenant la fin de l'empire, la restauration, la monarchie de juillet, la république, jusqu'au rétablissement de l'empire*, 6 vols. (Paris: Libraire Nouvelle, 1856–1857), 3:181.

17. Contemporary publications about the Inquisition included the history by É.-L. de Lamothe-Langon, *Histoire de l'Inquisition en France, depuis son établissement au XIIIe siècle, à la suite de la croisade contre les Albigeois, jusqu'en 1772, époque définitive de sa suppression* (Paris: Dentu, 1829), which speaks of the "dreadful history written in strokes of blood," even in France, and warns of a "return to the errors of our fathers" (x).

18. See the discussion of various literary precedents in Hallman, *Politics of Halévy's* La Juive, chap. 5, 210–252.

19. Verdi's five-act French grand opera *Don Carlos* (Paris Opéra, 1867), set in sixteenth-century Spain, would also feature an auto-da-fé (act 3, scene 2) and a confrontation of Crown and church, as the grand inquisitor forces King Philip to have the freedom-loving Rodrigue, Marquis Di Posa, put to death (act 4, scene 1), although both unite in condemning Philip's son Don Carlos, along with Carlos's beloved, the king's wife Elisabeth.

20. Cited and translated in Karin Pendle and Stephen Wilkins," "Paradise Found: The Salle le Peletier and French Grand Opera," in *Opera in Context: Essays on Historical Staging from the Late Renaissance to the Time of Puccini*, ed. Mark Radice (Portland, OR: Amadeus Press), 192.

21. The Te Deum often served as a processional chant in Catholic tradition, although it had variant liturgical uses and was even adapted within Lutheran and Anglican practices. Its medieval symbolism may also be challenged by the fact that later-period composers such as Lully and Haydn also created settings of the Te Deum.

22. Anselm Gerhard, *The Urbanization of Opera: Music Theater in Paris in the Nineteenth Century*, trans. Mary Whittall (Chicago: University of Chicago Press, 1998), 167–168, derides Halévy for his lack of "convincing coloration" in his "old-sounding Te Deum."

23. Nicole Wild, *Décors et costumes du XIXe siècle*, vol. 2, *Théâtres et décorateurs* (Paris: Bibliothèque Nationale, Département de la Musique, 1987), 328.

24. F-Po, [D. 216 (10)-II, fol. 105].

25. The "schism" refers to the Papal Schism, or Western Schism, of 1378–1417, in which two, and then three, popes claimed legitimacy. The passage, cited from "*Biographie Universelle*, tom. 6, pag. V," appears in libretti of *La Juive* published in Paris by Maurice Schlesinger, including a libretto dated February 18 (an earlier projected date for the premiere) that preceded the February 23 libretto, as well as later printed libretti: "L'extinction du schisme et le maintien de l'autorité de l'église menace en allemagne par les nouvelles opinions des hussites, étaient ce qui affectait le plus le cardinal. Malgré son grand âge il se rendit à Constance au mois d'août de l'année 1414 pour s'y concerter avec les magistrats et les commissaires impériaux sur la venue du concile qui devait rendre la paix à l'église. Il se présida pendant quarante sessions et eut jour et nuit des conférences avec l'empereur Sigismond, avec les princes et les prélats, etc."

26. *Le Constitutionnel*, February 25, 1835, in *Fromental Halévy, La Juive: Dossier de presse parisienne*, ed. Karl Leich-Galland (Saarbrücken: Musik-Edition Lucie Galland, 1987), 10. Also see the descriptions of the act 1 *cortège* in both the Duverger and the Palianti manuals (L. V. Duverger, *Mise en scène et decorations de* La Juive [...] ([Paris]: Bureau de Commission Théâtrale, n.d.); and L[ouis] Palianti, comp., *Collection de mises en scène*, "La juive": *Opéra en cinq actes de M. E. Scribe, musique de F. Halévy; Représenté pour la première fois à Paris, sur le Théâtre de l'Opéra, le 23 février 1835* ([Paris]: Palianti, n.d.; reprinted in H. Robert Cohen, *The Original Staging Manuals for Twelve Parisian Operatic Premières/ Douze livrets de mise en scène lyrique datant des creations parisiennes* (Stuyvesant, NY: Pendragon Press, 1991)). In his chapter "Analyzing Mise-en-Scène: Halévy's *La Juive* at the Salle le Peletier," in *Music, Theater, and Cultural Transfer*, ed. Annegret Fauser and Mark Everist (Chicago: University of Chicago Press, 2009) 176–194, Arnold Jacobshagen challenges Cohen's and other scholars' association of the Palianti manual with the 1835 premiere; he suggests that Palianti's manual instead reflects later productions of the 1860s and that Duverger's coordinates with the 1835 staging at the Salle le Pelletier.

27. See the printed libretto of *La Juive* published in Paris by Maurice Schlesinger in 1835, as well as the first orchestral score published by Schlesinger, most likely in 1835. (This score, which is reprinted in the series *Early Romantic Opera*, published by Garland in 1980, corresponds with the archival score reflective of the 1835 production at the Paris Opéra, F-Po, A. 509b, vols. 1–6.)

28. In Duverger's manual, the description of costumes for "Le peuple" in act 5 compares them to medieval costuming in other contemporary theatrical works: "Men and women of Constance, dressed in the Middle Ages, as in *le Comte Ory* [the 1828 opera by Rossini], *Jeanne d'Arc* [perhaps the five-act Schiller play], *Tour de Nesle* [Dumas's 1832 drama]" ("Hommes et femmes de Constance, vêtus au moyen-âge, ainsi que dans *le Comte Ory*, *Jeanne d'Arc, Tour de Nesle*.")

29. See, e.g., Duverger, *Mise en scène*.

30. *La Juive: Dossier de presse*, 50–54, 155–156.

31. Karin Pendle, *Eugène Scribe and French Opera of the Nineteenth Century* (Ann Arbor, MI: UMI Research Press, 1977), 472–473, discusses the novel as a possible source, but Steven Huebner casts doubt on this link in *The New Grove Dictionary of Opera*, 2:765).

32. As Milan Pospíšil notes in "Meyerbeer's *Les Huguenots* in Prague and Austrian Censorship," in *Meyerbeer and Grand Opéra from the July Monarchy to the Present*, ed. Mark Everist (Brepols: Turnhout, 2016), 110, Meyerbeer reported to his wife, in a letter of October 24, 1835, that censors determined "that Catherine [de' Medici] must definitely go, as must the ending and the title [i.e., *Léonore ou La Saint-Barthélémy*]" ("das Catherine bestimmt wegbleiben muss, eben so der Schluss, und auch der Titel") (his translation).

33. Michael Ragussis, in *Figures of Conversion: "The Jewish Question" and English National Identity* (Durham, NC: Duke University Press, 1995), 90, views this master text as an exploration of "the relationship between Jewish persecution and the incipient birth of English national unity in the twelfth century."

34. *Archives parlementaires de 1787 à 1860: Recueil complet des débats législatifs et politiques des chambres françaises, seconde série*, ed. J. Mavidal and M. E. Laurent (Paris: Société d'Imprimerie et librairie administrative/Paul Dupont, 1887), 65:317: "effaçons ces derniers vestiges d'une oppression qui ne doit plus renaître, et faisons qu'il n'y ait en France que des Français citoyens, et nullement des religionnaires divisés par leur culte."

35. Several works were based on Saint-Georges's libretto, including Franz Lachner's adaptation, the four-act opera *Catarina Cornaro, Königin von Cypern*, which premiered at the Munich Hofoper on December 3, 1841, a few weeks before the appearance of *La Reine de Chypre*. A few years later, Alfred Bunn reworked the Parisian libretto for Michael William Balfe's *The Daughter of St Mark*, presented in 1844 at Drury Lane Theatre in London. See Arnold Jacobshagen's comparison of five different operatic adaptations, including Halévy's, Lachner's, and Balfe's operas, in his chapter, "Staging the Queen—French *grand opéra* and Five Operatic Portraits of Catarina Cornaro," in *Catarina Cornaro, Last Queen of Cyprus and Daughter of Venice/Ultima regina di Cipro e figlia di Venezia*, ed. Candida Syndikus and Sabine Rogge (Münster: Waxmann, 2013), 367–384. (This publication developed out of an international conference in Venice in 2010 that explored Cornaro's historical significance.)

36. Rossini's opera, with a libretto by Felice Romano, was based on Arnault's work, although it downplays the portrayal of political despotism in the original work. Donizetti's librettist Giovanni Emauele Bidera adapted Casimir Delavigne's tragedy *Marino Faliero* (1838) rather than Byron's play and again obscured the trope of Venetian repressiveness, whereas it is overt in Verdi's *I due Foscari* (1844).

37. James H. Johnson, "The Myth of Venice in Nineteenth-Century Opera," *The Journal of Interdisciplinary History* 36, no. 3 (Winter 2006): 537–538.

38. Fromental Halévy, *La Reine de Chypre*, Ms. autograph, F-Pn, Musique, [Ms. 7332]; *La Reine de Chypre, Opéra en cinq actes, paroles de Mr de Saint Georges, musique de F. Halévy* (Paris: Maurice Schlesinger, 184[2]; La Reine de Chypre, Opéra en 5 actes, paroles de M. de St. Georges, musique de F. Halévy (Paris: Brandus, s.d.). The Palanti mise en scène manual, *Collection de Mises en Scène rédigées et publiées par M. L. Palianti de La Reine de Chypre, Opéra en cinq actes [...]*, appears to date close in time to the opera's premiere.

39. "Notice historique sur Catarina Cornaro, Reine de Chypre," in the libretto, La Reine de Chypre, *opéra en cinq actes, M. de Saint-Georges, musique de F. Halévy* [...] (Paris: Maurice Schlesinger, 1841).

40. Pierre Antoine Noël Bruno Daru, *Histoire de la République de Venise*, 3rd ed. (Paris: Firmin Didot, 1826), vol. 3, livre xvi, 144–147. A similar passage appears in a publication with the shortened title *Histoire de Venise* (as cited in the libretto of *La Reine*) (Brussels: Wahlen, 1838), vol. 1, livre xvi, 249–250.

41. See Mark Pottinger's interpretations of Catarina as French heroine in relation to the historical approaches of Jules Michelet in "The Staging of History in France: Characterizations

of Historical Figures in French Grand Opera during the July Monarchy" (PhD diss., City University of New York, Graduate Center, 2005). Regarding the iconic figure of Marianne, see Clair Rowden, "Massenet, Marianne and Mary: Republican Morality and Catholic Tradition at the Opera" (PhD diss., City University, London, 2001). For a discussion of Jeanne d'Arc in French theater, with secondary comparisons to Marianne, see Sarah Hibberd, "Marianne: Mystic or Madwoman? Representations of Jeanne d'Arc on the Parisian Stage in the 1820s," in *Medievalism and the Quest for the "Real" Middle Ages*, ed. Clare A. Simmons (London: Cass, 2001), 87–97.

42. There are many publications that assess the historical significance of this ceremony, including Gilbert Martineau, *Le Retour des cendres* (Paris: Éditions Tallandier, 1990), and Michael Paul Driskel, *As Befits a Legend: Building a Tomb for Napoleon, 1840–1861* (Kent, OH: Kent State University Press, 1993).

43. Hector Berlioz, for example, writes of "ces douze trompettes romaines sur la terrasse du palais, cette bande militaire sur le théâtre," in *Journal des Débats* (December 26, 1841), as transcribed in *Fromental Halevy, La Reine de Chypre: Dossier de presse parisienne (1841)*, ed. Anne-Sophie Métairie (Weinsberg: Musik-Edition Lucie Galland, 2005), 134.

44. Théophile Gautier, *Histoire de l'art dramatique en France depuis vingt-cinq ans*, 6 vols. (Paris: Hetzel, 1858–1859; repr., Geneva: Slatkine Reprints, 1978), 196–197. "Ce quatrième acte est presque tout de mise en scène et de spectacle. [...] Des batteries de ces longues trompettes, dites trompettes romaines, que vous avez sans doute remarquées au convoi de l'empereur, s'abbatent sur la balustrade de la terrasse et se mettent à sonner d'éclatantes fanfares auxquelles répond le canon des fortes et la musique cypriote d'un autre coin de la place. Alors commence une marche triomphale [...]. Le roi précédé de ses pages, de ses hérauts d'armes, de ses grands officiers se dirige vers la cathédrale avec la reine [...]. Les chefs de l'armée de terre et de mer, la deputation du sénat de Venise, les grands dignitaries de l'État, les hauts personnages de la cour se suivent à de légers intervalles. [...] Le marche est fermée par l'armée du roi de chypre: hallebadiers, archers, pertuisaniers qui s'avancent tambours battans, enseignes déployées; nous ne croyons pas qu'il y a au moins cinq cents personnes sur la scène qui se croisent, se mêlent et se meuvent dans un désordre pittoresque, mais sans confusion pourtant."

45. Berlioz, *Journal des Débats* (December 26, 1841), in La Reine de Chypre, *Dossier*, 134. In addition to Berlioz's descriptions of the formidable "pompe musical" created by dual orchestras in act 4, with many instruments *sur le théâtre*, he praised Halévy's nuanced orchestration throughout the score.

46. Berlioz was invited to contribute a march two weeks prior to the ceremony, but he declined to participate, likely offended by the "last-minute" request. In a letter to his sister, Adèle Suat, the composer spoke mockingly of the marches by the three theatrically successful composers, which he heard in a preliminary concert at the Conservatoire two days before the commemoration, suggesting that they compared miserably to his "apothéose de Juillet," the *Grande Symphonie Funèbre et Triomphale*, commissioned for the tenth anniversary of the July Revolution. See Frédéric Robert, "De Berlioz aux compositions de circonstance," in *Napoléon aux Invalides: 1840, Le Retour des Cendres*," edited by Jean-Marcel Humbert (Paris: Éditions de l'Albaron, 1990), 79.

47. Fromental Halévy, *Marche héroïque pour les funérailles de l'Empereur Napoléon*, F-Pn, Musique, Ms. 8676; La Reine de Chypre, *Opéra en cinq actes, paroles de Mr de Saint Georges, musique de F. Halévy* (Paris: Maurice Schlesinger, 184[2]).

48. Gérard, a tenor role, was first performed by Gilbert Duprez (1806–1896), the leading tenor at the Paris Opéra who displaced Adolphe Nourrit in 1837 with his "ut de poitrine" and more dramatic singing style; Lusignan, a baritone role, was performed by Paul-Bernard Barroilhet (1810–1871). The role of their mutual beloved, Catarina, was created by mezzo-soprano Rosine Stoltz (1815–1903). All three singers were consistently praised for their vocally and dramatically effective portrayals in the French press.

49. In Edgar Quinet's 1835 poem "Napoléon" and other contemporary writings, Napoléon is compared to Prometheus, who suffers for mankind and France's glory; in images and popular literature of the July Monarchy, he is also likened to Christ, with "the lonely rock at Saint Helena [...] compared with the hill at Calvary," as noted by Driskel, *As Befits a Legend*, 20–22.

50. Berlioz, *Journal des Débats* (December 26, 1841), in La Reine de Chypre: *Dossier*, 135.

51. Richard Wagner, *La Revue et gazette musicale* (May 1, 1842), in La Reine de Chypre: *Dossier*, 257, wrote that the act 5 quartet was "the most sublime piece in the score" (le morceau le plus sublime de la partition"), but he also lauded other numbers, including "Triste exilé," and spoke highly of Halévy's nuanced orchestration and the dramatic power of his music. Wagner knew the work intimately, having produced the opera's vocal score reduction and other arrangements for publisher Maurice Schlesinger during his early Paris years; he would praise Halévy's opera for its development of a richly diverse, path-breaking style in this and three other articles published in *La Revue et gazette musicale* of 1842. See Mark Pottinger's assessments of Wagner's articles, corresponding ideas of exile and redemption in *La Reine de Chypre* and *Der fliegende Holländer*, and possible Halévy influences on Wagner.

52. Many Parisian reviews of 1841–1842 were consulted, including those collected in Anne-Sophie Méttérie's *Fromental Halévy* La Reine de Chypre: *Dossier de presse parisienne* (1841) (Weinsberg, Germany: Musik-Edition Lucie Galland, 2005).

53. See my forthcoming article on *La Reine de Chypre* in the context of the July Monarchy's efforts to rehabilitate Napoléon's image and France's national identity. Historian Sudhir Hazareesingh writes of "the evolving representation of the Napoleonic heritage in France," which "decisively determined the ideological structure and orientations of French liberalism in *The Legend of Napoleon* (London: Granta, 2004); he has also published several articles on the same subject.

54. Nicholas White writes that French grand opera "often constructs history in terms of its moments of inauguration and crisis," in "Fictions and Librettos," *The Cambridge Companion to Grand Opera*, edited by David Charlton (Cambridge: Cambridge University Press, 2003), 57.

55. Drawing from my conference papers of 1999 (AMS) and 2000 (Royal Holloway), I discuss the topical connections between *Charles VI* and France's Near Eastern/Oriental Crisis and the use of national symbols briefly in my chapter, "The Grand Operas of Fromental Halévy," *The Cambridge Companion to Grand Opera*, ed. David Charlton (Cambridge: Cambridge University Press, 2003), 245–247. Sarah Hibberd offers further details and rich assessments of the political–historical significance of this work in "*Charles VI*: Creating the Future," in her book *French Grand Opera and the Historical Imagination* (Cambridge: Cambridge University Press, 2009), 114–152.

56. See Hallman, "Grand Operas," *Cambridge Companion to Grand Opera*, 246.

57. Hibberd, *French Grand Opera*, 115–117. She also explains the Delavignes' conflation of historical events in the opera, in which they "collapsed the interval between the signing of the

Treaty of Troyes in 1420 […] and Charles VII's accession in 1429 and the return of Paris to the French in 1435" (118).

58. Charles VI, *opéra en cinq actes, paroles de MM. Casimir Delavigne et Germain Delavigne, musique de F. Halévy […]* (Paris: Maurice Schlesinger, 1843) [libretto]; (Paris: Henri Lemoine, s.d.) [piano–vocal score]. Jules Michelet, in *Histoire de France*, 5:238, writes of Charles VI's love of playing cards "in his retreat in the Hôtel Saint-Paul." Also see Hibberd, *French Grand Opera*, 145–151, who offers a comprehensive description of the opera's card game, citing figures in fifteenth-century French court cards that are represented and discussing the form and key structure of the duet.

59. In addition to this *chant national*, Sarah Hibberd (*French Grand Opera*, 127–134) writes of other popular *chansons* in the opera that "promot[e] a collective (national) spirit, revealing the influence of history and politicising it," in light of Michelet's view that song engages "'the collective revelation of history'" and his comparison of medieval *chansons* and revolutionary songs. She discusses, for example, Isabelle's *villanelle*, Odette's *ballade*, and a soldier's *virelai*.

60. White, "Fictions and Librettos," *Cambridge Companion to Grand Opera*, 57.

61. Hector Berlioz, *The Memoirs of Hector Berlioz*, trans. and ed. David Cairns (New York: Knopf, 2002), 382. See Hallman, "Grand Operas," *Cambridge Companion to Grand Opera*, 246; "Guerre aux tyrans" also appeared in an anthology of French national songs published in 1848 by Brandus.

62. See, e.g., Hallman, *Politics of Halévy's* La Juive, 23–24, 296. See also Jane F. Fulcher's influential, but heavily critiqued, ideas about the political function of French grand opera, in relation to the ideals and agenda of the July Monarchy, in *The Nation's Image: French Grand Opera as Politics and Politicized Art* (Cambridge: Cambridge University Press, 1987), as well as Sarah Hibberd's discussion of the topicality, multivalency, and varied "conceptualisations of history" present in French grand opera in her book *French Grand Opera and the Historical Imagination* (see n54).

63. Review of *La Juive* in *La Gazette de France* (February 27, 1835), in *Dossier de presse:* La Juive, 58–59.

64. See the quoted text in Michelet, *Histoire de France au seizième siècle* (Paris: Chamerot, 1855), cxxxi, and Hugo, *La Bande noire*, cited in Roland Mortier, *La poétique des ruines en France: Ses origins, ses variations de la Renaissance à Victor Hugo* (Geneva: Librairie Droz, 1974), 213.

CHAPTER 6

MEDIEVALISM AND REGIONALIST IDENTITY IN LALO'S *LE ROI D'YS*

ELINOR OLIN

IN the wake of the inconceivable destruction left by World War I, writer Henry Malherbe contemplated the creative legacy of a composer who had also known the emotional and material desolation of bloody conflict. Yet Édouard Lalo, he recalled, was not diminished by the ravages of war; rather, he was an artist whose inspiration "sprang from defeat to revitalize modern French music."[1] Lalo's refusal to toe the line set by musical officialdom earned him the reputation during his life and afterward as admirably independent: a composer whose music was both "audaciously original, and enchanting."[2] This reputation for daring independence came partly from Lalo's ability to face and overcome adversity and partly from his pursuit of a less-than-traditional path to compositional success. Having first established his reputation among musicians who were familiar with his chamber music and orchestral works, Lalo was in many ways the poster child for the so-called *jeune école*, "young" composers whose prospects for realizing productions of their music—especially operas—were grim, at best.[3] Yet even as he faced an uphill battle to fame and fortune, Lalo seems to have kept to advice he received from his earliest composition teacher: "Avoid all that is common and conventional, . . . avoid the path to easy success; write only what you find within yourself, a single unique note is worth volumes of imitation."[4]

This essay examines Lalo's opera *Le Roi d'Ys* as an illustration of the shifting musical systems in France during the transitional years between the Second Empire and the firm establishment of the Third Republic.[5] A pivotal figure in the transformation of musical tastes during these years, Lalo established his reputation as a symphonist during a time when orchestral music was considered Germanic and not French. He found his way to success on the operatic stage via the composition of a ballet and had the courage to write an opera with clear references to a controversial political movement originating in the provinces of France. This work was *Le Roi d'Ys*. Lalo's only successful opera, it was originally subtitled *Legend of the Breton Wars of the 5th Century* and was one of the earliest manifestations of musical regionalism to achieve success on a major Parisian stage.[6] Set in medieval Brittany, the opera incorporates plainchant-style melodic constructions, Breton folk melodies of unnamed provenance or chronological specificity, and musical references to the emerging political movement of regionalism. Synthesizing these elements, Lalo developed an innovative form of regional medievalism alluding to a time-honored cultural heritage based in the antiquity of *la petite patrie*, which, at the same time, provided resistance to a centralized, Parisian determination of high culture in France.

One of the sources for the medieval legend of *Le Roi d'Ys* was the *Livaden Geris-Ies Kerne* in *Barzaz Breiz: Chants populaires de la Bretagne*, collected and translated by Théodore Hersart, vicomte de la Villemarqué.[7] The evocative medievalist tone of the text is established with its first lines:

> As-tu entendu, as-tu entendu, ce qu'à dit l'homme de Dieu au roi Gradlon qui est à Is?
>
> [Have you heard, have you heard, what the man of God said to King Gradlon of Is?]

King Gradlon was the fifth-century ruler of the coastal Breton city of Is, and in this early ethnography, La Villemarqué briefly outlines what was known about his history. Saint Gwenolé, the founding abbot of the first Christian monastery in Brittany, is credited with saving this good king but not his city, which disappeared beneath the waters of the invading sea. The Breton *chant populaire* transcribed by La Villemarqué adds a few sensational details: to please her lover, the wicked Princess Dahut steals the key to locks protecting the city from the ravages of the ocean. Things do not end well.

> Maudite soit la blanche jeune fille qui ouvrit, après le festin, la porte du puits de la ville d'Is, cette barrière de la mer![8]
>
> [Cursed be the blonde maiden who, after the feast, opened the floodgates of the wall protecting the city of Is from the sea!]
>
> As-tu vu, pêcheur, la fille de la mer, peignant ses cheveux blonds comme l'or, au soleil de midi, au bord de l'eau?
>
> J'ai vu la blanche fille de la mer, je l'ai même entendue chanter: ses chants étaient plaintifs comme les flots.[9]
>
> [Fisherman, have you seen the sea maiden combing her golden blond hair, in the sunlight of noon at the edge of the water?
>
> I have seen the pale sea maiden, and I have heard her sing. Her songs were as sorrowful as the waves.]

The legend of the city of Is (variously designated Keris, Ker-Is, or Ys) subsequently attracted the attention of other French ethnographer-writers, and the details of the story became progressively more vivid. Nearly contemporary with Le Villemarqué's *Barzaz Breiz*, Émile Souvestre's collection *Le Foyer breton: Contes et récits populaires* (1845) presents the tale as a local fisherman's narrative.[10] In this version, King Grallon is burdened with a daughter whose conduct does not conform to the mores of her station in life; "a princess of dissolute conduct."[11] The Princess Dahut, here a formidable sorceress, occupies her own castle, which is the site of continuous debauchery. Like Ariosto's Alcina, she grows tired of her lovers, who soon meet an untimely demise.[12] Dahut meets her match with a "bearded prince" (the Devil) who opens the locks of the seawall by stealing the princess's key. The city is flooded, and King Grallon chooses to save his daughter rather than throwing her to the waves, as Saint Corentin[13] demands: "Throw off the sin behind you (Dahut on the back of his horse) and God will save you." The king cannot forsake his daughter so Saint Corentin touches his cross to the shoulder of Dahut and she slides into the briny deep. The city of Keris is saved and King Grallon falls to his knees in thanks.

By 1886, Paul Sébillot reported in his two-volume survey of legends associated with meteors, storms, and the sea that "the submersion of the city of Ys is well known" and (quoting Le Villemarqué) that "in the 16th century, people dared to insist that while fishing during low tide, one often saw the ruins of ancient walls."[14] Some sailors reported to Sébillot that certain rocks along the coast bore the imprints of the Devil's hoof-prints; others maintained that they were those of King Grallon's horse. Still others claimed to have heard the bells of the submerged city's church towers, coming from below the waves.

Taking on this "well-known" legend as the basis for an opera, Édouard Blau and Édouard Lalo turned away from current trends on the principal operatic stages in Paris, sidestepping the conformist portfolio by French composers producing works on themes of Greek mythology, grand-operatic history, or farce, which had been the stalwarts of the Opéra and the Opéra-Comique.[15] For their new opera, begun sometime before December 1875, Blau and Lalo reworked the legend of the sunken city of Ys, combining elements of medieval history and regional culture to create characters and sounds representing issues of contemporary France. In a letter to the businessman and amateur composer Hector Colard (dated December 6 or 7, 1875), Lalo mourned the lack of opportunity for French composers exacerbated by the recent demise of the Théâtre-Lyrique. In the postscript of his letter, Lalo mentions that he had just finished a three-act grand opera: *Le Roi d'Ys*. Taking ownership of the subject, he writes that it

> is one of the most famous legends of Brittany; it is the destruction of the city of Ys
> by invasion of the sea. In the legend, it is Satan who breaks open the dykes; in my
> opera, it is a woman who orders this lovely little bit of devilry. My libretto is superb,
> very dramatic, and quite varied; I have finished it, but haven't yet written a note of
> orchestration.[16]

Le Roi d'Ys is among the earliest operas to highlight precepts of the emerging and controversial regionalist movement in France. Regionalism had begun in the 1850s with a literary revival of the ancient *langue d'oc* by activist Provençal poets bringing attention to the "beautiful language of the troubadours...preserved without corruption by shepherds and sailors."[17] Beyond its initial focus on publishing literature by contemporary poets and the *chansonniers* of their predecessors, the movement soon morphed into a political cause advocating for the "defense of a race fighting against the invading unitarism."[18] What had begun in Provence found resonance in other perceived cultural margins of France, especially Brittany. Not surprisingly, provincial voices speaking out for the legitimacy of their native traditions were viewed by some as a threat to Parisian hegemony and were labeled dangerous separatists.[19]

Charles Gounod's opera *Mireille*, after the poem *Miréio* by Provençal poet Frédéric Mistral, had been produced by the Théâtre-Lyrique in 1864 (revised for the Opéra-Comique in 1874 and 1889) and may have been a direct inspiration to Lalo.[20] At the time of *Le Roi d'Ys'* conception, however, *Mireille* had not yet found lasting success, although Gounod was a veteran stage composer with multiple operatic successes under his belt, including three productions staged by the venerable Opéra.[21] Lalo's *légende bretonne* was the third attempt by this as-yet-unsuccessful member of the *jeune école* still striving to achieve lasting recognition on a Parisian musical stage.[22] The odds were undeniably stacked against him. Even young composers who had followed a more common course found their compositional efforts barred from the stages of the Opéra and, to a lesser extent, the Opéra-Comique. In this context, the subject of the submerged Breton city seems to have been an unusual choice for an unproven composer aspiring to recognition by the directorship of the most prestigious musical institutions in France. Regionalist themes were extraordinarily rare in the operas performed in Parisian theaters, and basing a work on an archetypical Breton story was potentially inciting controversy.

Le Roi d'Ys and French Musical Politics

But Édouard Lalo had never pursued a risk-free approach either to musical advancement or to political activity. From his youthful enthusiasm for the republican cause in 1848 to his founding membership in the Société nationale de musique, Lalo was nothing if not an independent, even an activist voice. In July 1848, the twenty-five-year-old Lalo joined forces with his cousin, Auguste Wacquez, to form the Association des artistes musiciens, a "committee of artists, composers, performers, singers and amateurs from the *département du Nord*" with the explicit goals of "rigorously maintaining republican principles," reconciling "the progress of art with national dignity," and "educating the masses."[23] The provisional founding committee for the Association des artistes musiciens included other composers who would remain influential to Lalo, including Jules Armingaud, in whose string quartet Lalo would play viola, and Edmond Membrée, whose affiliation with Provençal regionalism will be explored later in this section.

According to biographer Georges Servières, Lalo received his initial musical training at the Conservatoire de Lille, under the tutelage of a violinist named Muller and a cellist "of German origins."[24] This latter detail is likely in explanation of Lalo's somewhat extraordinary inclination toward instrumental music, as a chamber music performer and composer of orchestral genres. After moving to Paris at the age of seventeen, Lalo studied at the Paris Conservatoire, although he seems not to have been officially enrolled. Servières, whose examination of the matriculation documents revealed no registration for Lalo, implies that this Parisian musical education was largely informal.[25] Lalo never sought to win the prestigious Prix de Rome, which was understood to have been an essential prequalification for composers seeking to access the boards of the Opéra.[26] Having published only a few *mélodies* and chamber music works for piano and strings, Lalo made his living during the 1850s and 1860s as violist in the Quatuor Armingaud and by giving music lessons.[27] In a letter to Jules Armingaud written in early 1865, Lalo shared his discouragement and reluctance to remain

> a poverty-level boarding school teacher [*professeur de pension*]. If I am ridiculously vain, too bad for me, but I believe that I am something other than just a grammar school teacher [*professeur de college*]; I want to try to succeed in the theater, this has become an obsession [*idée fixe*].... Up to this point it has been slow going, though constantly moving forward; I have encountered and will encounter many obstacles.[28]

Even aware of his uphill climb to recognition as a successful composer, Lalo's musical–political endeavors continued with his early participation in the Société nationale de musique. A member from at least December 1871, he was elected to the leadership committee of the society on which he served continuously from 1872–1873 to 1880–1881.[29] That the Société nationale was not simply a group of musicians who gathered to hear their works performed has been widely discussed. The activist nature of their goals, however, bears revisiting. The Société nationale was more than just a standard-bearer for French nationalism following the demise of the Second Empire and the subsequent Prussian occupation of Paris. It was nothing less than the platform for a resistance movement organized in clear defiance of the musical status quo, including challenges to a single definition of what might properly be defined as "French."[30] As part of the society's leadership, Lalo was among the first to hear proposed works for Société nationale concerts and participated as performer in his own premieres, in addition to those of his fellow *sociétaires*. Most important, however, Lalo established close working relationships with like-minded, activist composers, some more well established, some still working under the radar of widespread public recognition.

Among those in the latter category were Louis-Albert Bourgault-Ducoudray (1840–1910) and Edmond Membrée (1820–1882).[31] In addition to shared membership in the society, these composers shared a particular fascination with ancient music and the music of regional France. Bourgault-Ducoudray's collection of Breton airs, *Trente mélodies populaires de Basse-Bretagne* (collected from 1881), was published in 1885, and his unpublished opera *Bretagne* was begun in 1885.[32] Both of these works were more or less coincidental with Lalo's Breton legend *Le Roi d'Ys*, which was written during the mid-1870s and (finally) premiered in 1888. Significantly, Bourgault-Ducoudray's *mélodie* "Chant de ceux qui s'en vont sur la mer: Adieu patrie" was performed at one of the first Société nationale concerts (December 23, 1871) by its dedicatée, Madame Lalo.[33]

The text for Bourgault-Ducoudray's *mélodie* was Victor Hugo's poem of the same name (subtitled "Air breton") from his collection *Les Châtiments* (*The Punishments*, 1853; revised 1870) written in full protest voice against the "great bludgeoning" (*grands coups de bâton*) by Napoleon III with his coup d'état of 1851.[34] Madame Lalo also participated in the premiere of Bourgault-Ducoudray's *Noël* for two voices and chorus on the Société nationale concert of December 27, 1873. The title of this work alludes not only to the Christmas season, but also to a genre of *chansons* held in high esteem by regionalists as a living link to medieval music and literature.[35]

Another activist *sociétaire* was Edmond Membrée, who had been a comrade with Lalo in the 1848 Association des artists musiciens described previously, and who was the dedicatee of Lalo's String Trio, op. 7 (1849).[36] An early adherent to the cause of Provençal musical regionalism, Membrée was a featured composer at the regionalist festival Les Fêtes d'Orange from its inception in 1888 to 1904. Membrée's re-creation of Greek *mélopée* in the music for Sophocles' *Œdipe-Roi* was held up by the organizer of this festival as one of the most successful conduits of "the classic, Mediterranean spirit holding off the barbaric currents . . . for centuries."[37] The implication was that the revival of musico-dramatic works with physical origins in *la terre provençale* provided a living link between the two principal objectives of the regionalist Félibres: broadly, the restoration of pride for Provençal culture, and specifically, the renewal of the traditions of the troubadours. Lalo's close, long-term friendships with Membrée and Bourgault-Ducoudray certainly stimulated his serious investigation of both medieval and regionalist musical concerns.

Several accounts of the origins of *Le Roi d'Ys* have attributed the composer's interest in composing a Breton opera to the influence of his wife, Julie-Marie-Victoire Besniers de Marigny Lalo. Joël-Marie Fauquet has noted the coincidence of Lalo's marriage to Julie with his interest in composing for the theater (see the letter from Lalo to Jules Armingaud quoted previously) and states that Lalo composed the role of Margared in *Le Roi d'Ys* expressly for his wife.[38] The couple's son, Pierre Lalo, wrote in "La vie d'Édouard Lalo" that "frequent visits to Brittany after his marriage inspired in [Lalo] a vivid attachment to that region; from this fondness *Le Roi d'Ys* was born."[39] It is unfortunate that very little detailed biographical information can be found today about Julie Lalo, except that she was the daughter of a high-ranking military officer, born and raised in the Vendée region of Brittany, that she possessed a highly regarded contralto voice, and that she occasionally accompanied herself at the piano in performance.[40] At the celebration of Lalo's centenary, Henry Malherbe described Madame Lalo's influence on her husband's opera in appropriately flowery language:

> The young woman [was] of Breton origins. And, as the personification of sea breezes carrying the scent of seaweed, here are Margared and Rozenn, embodied in a single person. A love so deep and perceptive revealed to the composer all the mysteries of his companion's Armorican [Breton] soul which exploded in the proud music of *Le Roi d'Ys*, already in his ears. This marriage stimulated new ambitions.[41]

Beyond her personal relationship with the composer of *Le Roi d'Ys*, Julie Lalo was intimately associated with the creation of her husband's Breton opera. Although she did not perform on stage in the role that her husband composed for her, Julie Lalo created the contralto role of Margared at numerous performances, excerpting the work in concerts of the Société nationale. Mme Lalo was a regular performer from one of the earliest concerts of the organization (Concert 3 on December 23, 1871, cited previously), to April 12, 1880. Her final appearance on these concerts seems to have been April 14, 1888, just days before the official premier of *Le Roi d'Ys* at the Opéra-Comique. Performing works by Georges Bizet, Louis-Albert Bourgault-Ducoudray, Alexis de Castillon, Gabriel Fauré, Théodore Gouvy, Charles Lefebvre, and Franz Schubert, as well as those by her husband, Julie Lalo appeared on twenty Société nationale programs, performing with piano and with orchestra. Among these twenty concert programs were seven featuring excerpts from *Le Roi d'Ys*.[42]

The dates of Mme Lalo's performances at the Société nationale between April 1876 and April 1880 provide a useful companion outline to the compositional history of *Le Roi d'Ys* and its arduous route to production. As with many works by the so-called *jeune école*, the path of this opera to any of the mainstages of Paris was difficult at best, despite the advocacy and performances by Mme Lalo and others. There is little concrete evidence explaining why this was the case, although the work's Breton flavor alluding to a regionalist agenda may well have worked against it.

At the recommendation of Emmanuel de Vaucorbeil (then the commissioner of subsidized theaters in Paris), Lalo was promised a production of his opera as one of the *nouveautés* required of the newly reopened Théatre-Lyrique under the direction of Léon Escudier. Lalo hoped for an opening in September 1878, but Escudier's directorship came to an end in August 1878 and the production was not realized.[43] When Vaucorbeil became director of the Opéra, Lalo had renewed hopes for a staging but he was disappointed once again. Vaucorbeil, who had earlier given his highest recommendation of *Le Roi d'Ys* to his predecessor Olivier Halanzier, apparently refused Lalo's opera on the grounds that its "libretto was impossible."[44] In September 1886, Lalo reported to his librettist Édouard Blau that he was discouraged "by the lack of success of all our attempts to bring our work to the stage" and that he was in communication with Choudens to publish the piano score in a marketing strategy to stimulate future productions.[45] Finally, *Le Roi d'Ys* achieved its long-overdue premiere on May 7, 1888, at the Opéra-Comique under its new director, Louis Paravey.

The critics were ecstatic. In a lengthy review for the *Journal des Débats*, Ernest Reyer praised the "local color that M. Lalo has been able to convey, happily with the aid of several Breton themes, and without resorting to the inevitable bagpipes." Giving the work his highest personal endorsement, Reyer concluded his comments with the expression of extreme pleasure at the production of *le Roi d'Ys*, "a distinguished work, the work of a master; no one is more pleased than I at M. Lalo's success, his very great success."[46] An unsigned review for *Le Temps* on May 9, 1888, reported gleefully on the brilliant success of M. Édouard Lalo's *Roi d'Ys* last night at the Opéra-Comique. An elite audience warmly applauded the robust, powerful and colorful work. It was conceived twenty years ago, then massaged at length by the composer and completed two years ago; it has finally found the reception it deserves.[47]

While not entirely accurate, this anonymous review was on board with the congratulatory bandwagon. It had taken a very long time, indeed, for the work to gain acceptance by an official venue of the Parisian stage.

Le Roi d'Ys and the Regionalist Movement: Provence and Brittany

The years during which *Le Roi d'Ys* languished in its composer's folder of *œuvres inédites* coincided with the establishment and intensification of a regionalist movement in France. Organized in 1854 by poet Fréderic Mistral, the movement was formed to legitimize and preserve the language of one's *pays natal* through modern poetry and the honoring of its medieval origins. Among the early champions of regionalism was the Breton poet Auguste Brizeux: "As I have defended my language and my people [*ma race*]," he wrote in a letter to Mistral and his fellow Provençal poets on the occasion of their gathering on August 12, 1855, "you are defending yours. My heart is with all of you." In an ode accompanying his letter, Brizeux transmitted his hope that "the errant voice of Merlin / must ever breathe."[48]

By 1888, Mistral's Félibres were the most well-organized and publicized regionalist association. In his magnum opus *Lou tresor dóu Felibrige ou Dictionnaire Provençal-Français embrassant les divers dialects de la langue d'Oc moderne* (ca. 1887), Mistral defined the word *Félibre* as a noun signifying "a Provençal poet from the second half of the 19th century, a literary figure writing in the *langue d'Oc*. See *troubaire*." By extension, the *Félibrige* was "the association of Félibres, [the] order of the new troubadours, [and] the Provencal renaissance."[49] The overarching objective of the Félibres, and the broader regionalist movement they inspired, was to encourage deep, almost pious devotion to one's *terre natale*, encouraging reverence for the birthright of localized folklore and ancient cultural traditions, especially those of the medieval troubadours. In support of the education and outreach arm of the movement, Paul Mariéton (one of Mistral's closest disciples) established the Revue félibréene in 1885. Responding to a general misunderstanding of the organization, Mariéton declared that "*Félibrisme* is simply a *lyre*, a *sounding board*, . . . can it aspire to become the instrument of defense for a people fighting against an invading centralism?"[50]

Further in pursuit of the Félibrian cause, Mariéton founded and directed the Fêtes d'Orange, a long-running music/dramatic festival sponsored by the Félibres from 1888 to 1910, held at the restored first-century Roman theater in Orange, in the heart of

Provence. The festival focused on "the history and patriotism reborn among the Provençal people...reborn at its source": the roots of their civilization in the glory of classical Greece.[51] Providing an essential continuity between ancient Greece, medieval troubadours, and contemporary Provençal culture, a recurring element in the repertory of the festival was the Félibres' anthem, "La coupo santo" written by Frédéric Mistral to the melody of a historic Provençal *noël*. Although the term *noël* has become closely associated with Christmas music, it historically had a much broader application. The *Dictionnaire liturgique, historique et théorique de plain-chant et de musique d'église au moyen âge et dans les temps modernes* establishes the origins of the term *noël* as "around the year 1200" and defines it as "a joyful cry, celebrated in our history, uttered by the French people during certain religious ceremonies associated with political events."[52] Four types of *noëls* are outlined:

1. The *noël religieux*, devoted to the celebration of the Nativity of Our Lord Jesus Christ;
2. The *noël royal*, composed for monarchs either at the occasion of their coronation, marriage or celebration of victories; or for their banquet at the feast of Noël, or a[nother] significant event associated with their person or their reign;
3. The *noël politique*, having as its object the celebration of an important person, either an official of the State or of the Church;
4. The *noël badin*, concerning private individuals and a common subject [*sujet vulgaire*].[53]

Modern usage of the term noël recognizes only the first of these definitions, albeit with a certain inflection of antiquity. But in the late nineteenth century, especially through its use in the Fêtes d'Orange, the noël took on important regionalist associations.

Programs of this festival list the works of composers and the participation of a conductor, associated with Édouard Lalo in the Société nationale (and earlier): Georges Bizet, Édouard Colonne, Alexandre Luigini, Edmond Membrée, Charles Gounod, Jules Massenet, Ernest Reyer, and Camille Saint-Saëns.[54] Given the early and frequent participation by Membrée, Reyer, and Saint-Saëns at the Félibres' festival and their close personal and musical associations with Lalo, it is highly likely that a regionalist enthusiasm, including a strong interest in foundational medieval traditions, was at least discussed if not shared by these men.[55] The idea of the noël would become one of the most important ways in which this regionalist/medievalist interest would find expression in *Le Roi d'Ys*.

Another central initiative of the Félibres was a focus on the long and noble history of the Provençal language through the publication of historical literature. "From the troubadours to the Félibres," wrote Mariéton, "there is an uninterrupted chain of storytellers and poets who, for three centuries, have preserved this glorious, golden tongue from corruption."[56] Though not always historically accurate, collections of medieval poetry and songs were produced by Félibrian publishers in Avignon to document a literary tradition untainted by the modern assaults of Parisian cultural overreach. One such collection was the *Receuil des noëls composés en langue provençale par Nicolas Saboly, ancien bénéficier et maître de musique de l'Église de Saint-Pierre d'Avignon*, edited and published by François Seguin in 1856.[57] Nicolas Saboly (1614–1675) was elevated as a kind of "Félibrist avant la lettre," and his anthem "La coupo santo" (with words by Mistral) was collectively sung at every formal and informal gathering.[58] In the preface to his 1856 edition of Saboly's *noëls*, Seguin traced a direct lineage of troubadours from Guillaume IV ("the earliest troubadour whose works have survived") to Saboly, who "is justifiably recognized as the troubadour of the 17th century." Seguin's prefatory remarks also characterize Saboly as a *musicien-poète*, emphasizing his transmission of an "antique and civilizing influence": that is, the *langue d'oc* of the troubadours.[59] The collection includes sixty-seven *nouvés* [Provençal for *noël*], metered, strophic settings of vaguely Christian stories and moral parables.

Regionalist Music in *Le Roi d'Ys*

To articulate a Breton regionalist identity in *Le Roi d'Ys*, Lalo took on the mantle of modern troubadour, carrying forward the "brilliant genealogy" of Saboly, thereby reinforcing the regionalist agenda through a medieval perspective.[60] At significant points in the opera, Lalo transmitted both meaning and melody from Saboly's compositions, thus folding together elements of Provençal and Breton regionalism. Lalo's procedure in this regard is evident in the first scene of the opera. The opening of act 1 of *Le Roi d'Ys* is set on a terrace of the king's palace. The stage directions describe gardens to the left, a vast granite stairway to the right, and the vista of the ocean at the horizon. The opening chorus begins with five unison/octave statements of "Noël" by sopranos and tenors, offset at the rhythmic interval of a sixteenth note by the echoing basses. The festivities are in praise of Saint Corentin, patron saint of the city, celebrating the peace of a truce. Princess Margared (Dahut in earlier versions of the legend) has been betrothed as a ransom of war to Karnac, leader of a tribe previously in conflict with the people of Ys. There is no reference to Christmas. Instead, this is a *noël royal* as defined by Arnaud's *Dictionnaire liturgique*, "composed for monarchs either at the occasion of their coronation, . . . or significant event associated with their person or their reign"[61] (see Examples 6.1 and 6.2).

An even more definitive connection to Saboly's noëls occurs later in the opera, during another royal celebration. During the act 3 "Noce bretonne," the marriage of Margared's sister Princess Rozenn to the local hero Mylio, the chorus declaims reverently, "Hail to the bridegroom and the bride," with each voice part on a static pitch. In response, referring to the ancient custom of young girls defending the bride's door from the friends of the groom, Rozenn answers, "Do you think that I would leave the lover at the door, when Love has already entered here?"[62] Rozenn's melody is very similar in profile to that of Saboly's Nouvé no. 35, "Sant Jousé m'a dit"[63] (see Examples 6.3 and 6.4). Both melodies

EXAMPLE 6.1 Choral entrance at the opening of act 1.

EXAMPLE 6.2 Saboly, *Receuil des noëls*, nouvé 1.

open with a rising fourth to the tonic pitch and then move by ascending steps to the third scale degree before descending to end a four-bar phrase on an open cadence.

In each case, the same melodic phrase is repeated, again finishing with an open cadence, to accompany the next line of text. Lalo designates Rozenn's melody as a "Thème breton," although he declined to give any specifics regarding its origins, except that he had heard his wife sing the tune.[64] By side-stepping the particulars of source attribution, Lalo may have hoped to substantiate a connection between medieval customs, legend, and music. When the theme recurs shortly thereafter, the chorus is greeting the newlyweds as they leave the wedding chapel. This time, the Breton theme/*noël* melody is sung by the chorus in combination with the text from their earlier salutation: "Hail to the bridegroom and the bride! Heaven has blessed the young lovers."

EXAMPLE 6.3   "Thème breton," from *Noce bretonne*, act 3, premier tableau.

Pour - quoi lut-ter de la sor - te, pen-sez-vous que je vou - drai — Lais-

ser l'am-ant à la por - te, Quand l'a - mour est en - tré! —

EXAMPLE 6.4   Saboly, *Receuil des noëls*, nouvé 35.

Sant Jóu - sè m'a di: Pren - te gar - do, pren - te gar - do!

Sant Jóu - sè m'a di: Pren - te gar - do pèr ei - ci!

In a stroke of musical and dramatic genius, Lalo consolidates these regionalist and medievalist elements as the work builds to a climactic moment. In between the two iterations of this "Thème breton," the chorus sings "Te Deum laudamus/Te Dominum confitemur/Te Deum laudamus," accompanied by bells and an off-stage organ.[65] The melody here follows the parallel construction of a plainchant canticle, although at first it is set as a four-part chorale. Between subsequent choral phrases of the Latin prayer, Margared and Karnac burst onto the scene, revealing their plans to open the protective locks guarding the city from the constant threat of inundation. In a sarcastic parody of plainchant declamation, Karnac sings, "You must show me the way to the locks," threatening Margared as she shows reluctance to destroy her own city. The chorus' single-phrase restatements of "Te Deum laudamus" are now sung on static, repeated pitches, interspersed with Margared's uncertainty: "I no longer want to commit such a crime!" (see Example 6.5). At the point of highest dramatic tension, all three characters (Margared, Karnac, and the chorus) are singing a polyphonic superimposition of individual supplications. The chorus returns to a melodic presentation of "Te Deum confitemur" in complementary phrases. Karnac mocks Margared, who has earlier jilted him, in a bitter parody, singing a rhythmic variation of the chorus's Te Deum, in parallel octaves with the sopranos. At the same time, Margared sings "God almighty, save me!" in rhythmic imitation and to an inversion of Karnac's melody[66] (see Example 6.6).

EXAMPLE 6.5 Margared's regret and choral, Te Deum, act 3, scene 1.

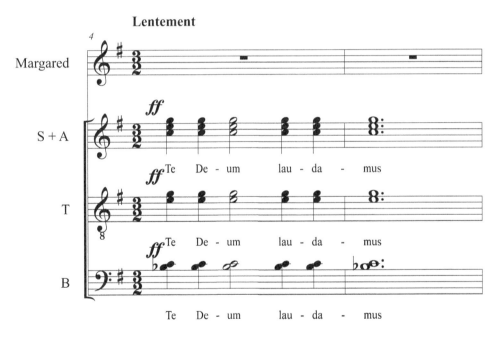

The final scene of the opera takes place at the top of a hill where the people have taken refuge from their flooded city. The curtain rises to reveal a stormy, dark sky and waters that continue to rise. The citizens of Ys are on their knees, declaiming a unison prayer on the same interval (a rising m3, here transposed a semitone higher) to which their jubilant *noëls* were sung at the opening of act 1. This time, however, there is more

EXAMPLE 6.6 Margared, Karnac, and chorus, act 3, scene 2.

repetition of each pitch, giving the impression of solemn plainchant. As the intensity of the orchestral timbres, harmonies, and rhythms increases, Margared suddenly appears. She announces that she will offer herself as sacrifice to the encroaching waters, cries out (singing B♭5, her highest pitch in the opera) "My judge calls me," and hurls herself off the cliffs into the waves. Saint Corentin appears suddenly, "enveloped in a shimmering radiance," and the waters recede. The curtain falls as the chorus declaims a final prayer, "Gloire à Dieu tout puissant."[67]

Through conflation of Breton and medieval themes both musical and dramatic, Lalo brought to fruition the fundamental objective of regionalism: communication of the profound cultural legacy of *la petite patrie* through the overlap of legend and verifiable history, in creation of an identifiable, vernacular mythology geographically and artistically independent from the culture of Paris. *Le Roi d'Ys* is neither a musicological re-creation of medieval music nor an ethnological study of Breton folk melodies. The composer's intention to blend these two influences, however, conveys an impulse to educate rather than simply to achieve personal success. Writing an opera on an "impossible" subject, as Vaucorbeil had called it in 1879, Lalo chose to celebrate local

EXAMPLE 6.6 Continued

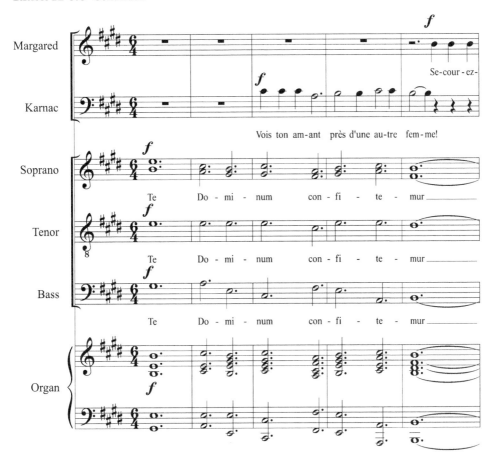

traditions from a specific, regional perspective, far exceeding his predecessors' more superficial staged depictions of *couleur locale*.

As if in commendation of Lalo's efforts to point up the ancient cultures underscoring the regionalist activism of both Bretons and Provençals, Ernest Renan, perhaps the most famous Breton of his time, addressed a gathering of Félibres in 1891. Renan extolled their mutual love for *la terre natale*, "in touch with its ancient genius [*antique génie*], rich in all its glories." Speaking as a self-identified "Félibre de l'Ouest" from a dais in Paris, Renan mentioned a book his mother had given him, *Les cantiques de Marseille*, noting especially that "the kingdom of Is is brother to the kingdom of Arles." Each one of the assembled enthusiasts, he continued, "gives voice to the poetry of his birthplace, sings of local glories . . . and curses centralization at his ease."[68]

Through musical, literary, and dramatic productions, the tenets of regionalism gradually became more acceptable, even to the conservative directors of the major Parisian stages. By 1923, the centenary of Lalo's birth, Georges Servières reported that Lalo's music was a significant influence, having provided an artistic lineage for later composers, "projecting a ray of sunlight" to free French music from the insipidity that had "engulfed it in fog" at the end of the nineteenth century.[69]

Lalo's landmark *Roi d'Ys* paved the way for productions of later regionalist/medieval works, including the following:

Vincent d'Indy's *Fervaal* (Opéra-Comique, 1898)

Paul Ladmirault's *Myrdhin* (composed 1899–1902; Saint-Hilaire-de-Chaléons, Nantes, 2015)

Charles Widor's *Les pêcheurs de Saint-Jean* (Opéra-Comique, 1905)

Déodat de Séverac's *Le cœur du Moulin* (Opéra-Comique, 1909)

Guy Ropartz's *Le pays* (Nancy, 1912; Opéra-Comique, 1913)

Each of these works assimilates regional musical themes into a libretto steeped in a specific locale in the provinces of France, an endeavor that prior to *Le Roi d'Ys* might well have been considered too radical for an official Parisian production, even on the relatively adventurous stage of the Opéra-Comique. Full appreciation of Lalo's opera and its influential position in the transformation of French dramatic music must take into account its political *and* musical content. Defining Frenchness from both contemporary and medieval perspectives, *Le Roi d'Ys* provided the double impetus to pull away from Parisian dictates on high culture and bring to Paris ancient voices of *la France profonde*.

NOTES

1. Henry Malherbe, *Édouard Lalo: Conférence prononcée aux Concerts-historiques Pasdeloup: Opéra 23 Décembre 1920* (Paris: Heugel, 1921), 4.

2. Malherbe, *Édouard Lalo*, 9. (d'une originalité audacieuse et enchantée.)

3. "*La jeune école française*" was a phrase employed by *Le Ménestrel* in 1876 in reference to "the pléiade of talented composers" whose works had not yet been proven on the stage of the Opéra. ("Semaine théatrale," *Le Ménestrel* [August 13, 1876], 292.) Elsewhere in the same journal, Lalo was included in a listing of "the entire *jeune école*" present at a private concert held on March 12, 1876. Lalo was then fifty-three years old. ("Concerts et soirees," *Le Ménestrel* [March 19, 1876], 127.)

4. Édouard Lalo, *Correspondance*, ed. Joël-Marie Fauquet (Paris: Aux Amateurs de Livres, 1989), 105. (Letter to Arthur Pougin, December 10, 1873.)

5. See David Grayson, "Finding a Stage for French Opera," in *Music, Theater, and Cultural Transfer*, ed. Annegret Fauser and Mark Everist (Chicago: University of Chicago Press, 2009), 127–153. Grayson cites an essay by composer Victorin Joncières addressing difficulties facing as-yet unproven composers: "La question du Théâtre-Lyrique," in *Les annals du théâtre et de la musique* 6 (1881):1–18.

6. Lalo, *Correspondance*, 271. In a letter to Agenor Bardoux, ministre de l'instruction publique, dated March 31, 1878, Lalo hoped to win high-level governmental support for his work.

7. Théodore Hersart, vicomte de La Villemarqué, "Submersion de la ville d'Is," in *Barzaz Breiz: Chants populaires de la Bretagne: Avec une traduction français, des Arguments, des Notes et les Mélodies originales* (Paris: A. Franck, 1846), 1:65–74. All translations are my own.

8. La Villemarqué, *Barzaz Breiz*, 1:67.

9. La Villemarqué, *Barzaz Breiz*, 1:69.

10. Émile Souvestre, "Récit du vieux pêcheur: Kéris," in *Le Foyer breton: Contes et récits populaires* (Paris: Lévy, 1845), 119–126.

11. Souvestre, "Récit du vieux pêcheur," 119.

12. Ludovico Ariosto, *Orlando Furioso*, trans. Guido Waldman (New York: Oxford University Press, 2008). Cantos 6 and 7 of this pseudomedieval epic are the basis for Handel's *Alcina*.

13. Saint Corentin, Bishop of Quimper (d. 486), replaces Saint Gwenolé in Souvestre's version.

14. Paul Sébillot, "Les envahissements de la mer et les villes englouties," in *Légendes, croyances et superstitions de la mer* (Paris: Charpentier, 1886), 2:299.

15. A representative sampling of these works includes *Les Huguenots* (Opéra, 1836), music by Giacomo Meyerbeer, libretto by Eugène Scribe, in production at the Opéra through 1914 (J.-G. Prod'homme, *L'Opéra (1669–1925)* [Paris: Delagrave, 1925], 110); *Maître Pathelin* (O-C, 1856), music by François Bazin, libretto by Adolphe de Leuven and Ferdinand Langlé, in repertory at the O-C from 1856 to 1869 (Loewenberg, 1:924, and Robert Ignatius Letellier, *Opéra-Comique: A Sourcebook* [Newcastle-upon-Tyne: Cambridge Scholars, 2010], 132); *La Sirène* (O-C, 1844–1852, 1861–1862, and 1887), music by Daniel Auber, libretto by Eugène Scribe, revived at the Théatre-Lyrique in 1865–1866 (Loewenberg, 1:839, and Letellier, 110); and *Jeanne d'Arc* (Opéra, 1876), music by Auguste Mermet, libretto by the composer. Mermet's opera was the first new work staged at the recently built Salle Garnier. The opening program at the new Opéra (January 5, 1875) featured scenes from *Les Huguenots* and the first two acts of Fromenthal Halévy's *La Juive* (1835) (Loewenberg, 1:1051).

16. Lalo, *Correspondance*, 207.

17. Paul Mariéton, "Rapport sur le concours des jeux floraux du Félibrige de Paris, Fête de Sainte-Estelle (Sceaux, 25 Mai 1884)" (Paris: Bloy, n.d.), 2.

18. Paul Mariéton, "Chronique," *Revue félibréenne* I, no. 10 (June 1, 1885): 197.

19. Mariéton, "Séparatisme et félibrige," *Revue félibréenne* II (juin/juillet 1886): 213.

20. The earliest correspondence between Lalo and Gounod dates sometime before February 1871 when the younger composer's letter addressed to "Mon cher Gounod" thanks the latter for his news of "nos horribles désastres." Lalo, *Correspondance*, 197. In addition to comparably tumultuous paths to production success, there are similar dramatic elements in *Mireille* and *Le Roi d'Ys*: specific regional settings in each libretto, as well as the convergence of magic and Christianity (the origin of Margared's character in *Roi d'Ys* is that of a sorceress, as is Taven in *Mireille*; both are contralto roles). See Steven Huebner, *The Operas of Charles Gounod* (Oxford: Clarendon Press, 1990), 133–154.

21. Loewenberg, 1:894, 916, 955. *Sapho* (1851), *La nonne sanglante* (1854), and *La reine de Saba* (1862).

22. Édouard Lalo, *Le Roi d'Ys: Légende bretonne. Opéra en trois actes et cinq tableaux. Partition chant et piano* (Paris: Heugel, n.d.), title page.

23. Letters from Lalo to fellow musician Jules Deneux and to Antoine Senard, citoyen ministre de l'intérieur, July 1848. Lalo, *Correspondance*, 41–43.

24. Georges Servières, *Édouard Lalo: Biographie critique* (Paris: Laurens, [1925]), 8.

25. Composition instruction was at the hands of the pianist Schulhoff and a certain Crévecœur, whose musical career ended when "he returned to his native city of Calais, as a manufacturer of lace." Servières, *Édouard Lalo*, 8.

26. In December 1873, Lalo wrote to music critic Arthur Pougin after inviting him to attend the next concert of the Société nationale. "I have never run after the Prix de Rome," he wrote, "the '*opéra-comique*' aspects of that contest were always detestable to me." Lalo, *Correspondance*, 11 and 105.

27. H. Malherbe, Conférence, 8. Malherbe is the only biographer to specify what kind of music Lalo taught: harmony lessons. This is an interesting detail informing the biography of his student, later his wife, singer Julie Bernier de Marigny.

28. Lalo, *Correspondance*, 83.

29. Michel Duchesneau, *L'Avant-garde musicale et ses sociétés à Paris de 1871 à 1939* (Paris: Mardaga, 1997), 235. The program for the December 23, 1871, concert of the Société nationale included several performances by "Marie" Lalo (Julie-Marie-Victoire Besniers de Marigny Lalo, a.k.a. Mme Édouard Lalo). According to the statutes of the organization, only active members might have their works performed; composers of these works would choose the performers for their music. That Lalo's wife was a performer on this concert, and that women were restricted to "honorary" or "adjunct" membership status, indicates that Édouard Lalo was the member; Mme Lalo was invited to participate as his adjunct. See also Michael Creasman Strasser, "*Ars Gallica*: The Société nationale de musique and Its Role in French Musical Life, 1871–1891" (PhD diss., University of Illinois at Urbana–Champaign, 1998), 591–596, ProQuest 9904597.

30. See Michael Strasser, "The Société nationale and Its Adversaries: The Musical Politics of *L'Invasion germanique* in the 1870s," *19th-Century Music* 24, no. 3 (Spring 2001): 226–227. Duchesneau goes so far as to label the Société nationale an organization with a "radical orientation." (Duchesneau, *L'Avant-garde musicale*, 17.)

31. Léon Mention, *Un compositeur valenciennois: Edmond Membrée* (Paris: Fischbacher, 1908), 66, https://archive.org/details/edmondmembre1800ment.

32. The introduction to this collection contains a lengthy discussion of the inseparability of words and music in these songs, as well as their connection to both Greek folk song and medieval music as they were based in "tous les modes diatoniques antiques." Louis-Albert Bourgault-Ducoudray, *Trente mélodies populaires de Basse-Bretagne* (Paris: Lemoine et fils, 1885), 10–12. For information about the unpublished opera, see Gringoire (first name unknown), *L'œuvre de L.-A. Bourgault-Ducoudray* (Nantes: Guist'hau, 1898), 27–28, http://gallica.bnf.fr/ark:/12148/bpt6k991466v/f1.image.r=Bourgault-Ducoudray,%20 Louis-Albert.

33. Bourgault-Ducoudray, "Chant de ceux qui s'en vont sur la mer: Adieu patrie" (Paris: Mackar, n.d.), https://imslp.org/wiki/Le_chant_de_ceux_qui_s%27en_vont_ sur_mer_(Bourgault-Ducoudray%2C_Louis-Albert.

34. Victor Hugo, *Les Châtiments* (Jersey?, n.d.), 165, 167–168, https://babel.hathitrust.org/cgi/ pt?id=uc1.$c182922;view=1up;seq=7.

35. Duchesneau, *L'Avant-garde musicale*, 228. The Société nationale concert no. 28 (December 27, 1873) included the premiere of Bourgault-Ducoudray, *Noël* (two voices and chorus) performed by de Caters and Marie Lalo. See also Jean-Baptiste Ripert, "Musique et Musiciens d'Avignon," in *Mémoires de l'Académie de Vaucluse*, ser. 2 (Avignon: Seguin, 1916), 16:91–105.

36. It is unfortunate that no correspondence between Lalo and either Bourgault-Ducoudray or Membrée discussing this mutual interest survives. Fauquet's edition of Lalo's correspondence includes reference to only one letter from Lalo to Bourgault-Ducoudray dated March 1873; only a brief summary of this letter's contents is given. Fauquet indicates that

letters from Lalo addressed to Membrée, among others, "have to a great extent been destroyed." Lalo, *Correspondance*, 202, 46.

37. Paul Mariéton, *Le Théâtre antique d'Orange et ses chorégies* (Paris: Editions de la Province, 1908), 9.

38. Lalo, *Correspondance*, 84fn1.

39. Pierre Lalo, "La vie d'Édouard Lalo," *La Revue musicale* (1923): 122.

40. In a review of the April 29, 1876, Société nationale concert, A. M. commented that "Madame Lalo sang with great verve, in a chest-voice contralto, accompanying herself at the piano; a pianist-singer of true talent." A. M., "Concerts et soirées," *Le Ménestrel*, May 7, 1876. Hugues Imbert offered little more. On p. 170 of his chapter on "Édouard Lalo." from his book *Nouveaux profils de musiciens. Avec six portraits graves à l'eau-forte par A. & E. Burney* (Paris: Fischbacher, 1892), Imbert focuses on her physical appearance, describing her as a "striking figure, an attractive though stern profile, with beautiful black hair and eyes full of fire! Has anyone been unmoved to hear her sing, with her slightly masculine contralto voice?"

41. Malherbe, *Conférence*, 8.

42. Duchesneau, "Annexe I: Programmes de la Société nationale (1871–1939)," in *L'Avant-garde musicale*, 225–304; and Michael Strasser, personal email communication, July 17, 2017.

43. See letter dated August 5, 1878, from Lalo to Léon Escudier. Lalo, *Correspondance*, 272.

44. See letter dated October 21, 1879, from Lalo to Mme Scheurer-Kestner (whose husband was the dedicatee for *Le Roi d'Ys*). Fauquet surmises that the intervention of M. and Mme Scheurer-Kestner was what finally tipped the scales in favor of an 1888 production at the Opéra-Comique. Lalo, *Correspondance*, 265, 274–275.

45. Lalo, *Correspondance*, 275.

46. Ernest Reyer, "Revue musicale," *Journal des débats: politique et littéraire* (May 13, 1888): 1–2, http://gallica.bnf.fr/ark:/12148/bpt6k464301n/f1.item.

47. Unsigned, "Spectacles et concerts," *Le Temps*, May 9, 1888, http://gallica.bnf.fr/ark:/12148/bpt6k231770z/f4.item.

48. Unsigned, "Brizeux et les Félibres," *La Revue félibréenne* VI (1890): 94.

49. Fréderic Mistral, "Félibre," in *Lou tresor dóu Felibrige ou Dictionnaire Provençal-Français embrassant les divers dialects de la langue d'Oc moderne…* Aix-en-Provence: Veuve Remondet-Aubin [n.d., 1878?], 1:1113 and 1114.

50. Paul Mariéton, "Chronique," *La Revue félibréenne* 10 (June 1885): 197.

51. Paul Mariéton, *La Terre provençal* (Paris: Lemerre, 1890), v.

52. Abbé A. Arnaud, "Noel," in *Dictionnaire liturgique, historique et théorique de plain-chant et de musique d'église au moyen âge et dans les temps modernes*, ed. J(oseph) d'Ortigue (Paris: Potier, 1854), 919, http://gallica.bnf.fr/ark:/12148/bpt6k6298607m?rk=21459;2.

53. Arnaud, *Dictionnaire liturgique*, 933.

54. Georges Bizet, *L'Arlésienne* (August 15, 1904; August 7, 1905); Charles Gounod, *Stances de Sapho* (August 13, 1899); Alexandre Luigini, *La voix des cloches* (August 12, 1888); Jules Massenet, *Les Erinnyes* (August 2, 1897; August 3, 1907), *Phèdre* (August 11, 1900; July 12, 1902); Edmond Membrée, *Œdipe-Roi* (August 11, 1888; August 11, 1894; August 9, 1902; August 7, 1905); Ernest Reyer, overture to *Sigurd* (August 11, 1888) excerpts from *Salambô* (August 11, 1900); and Camille Saint-Saëns, *Hymne à Pallas-Athéné* (August 11, 1888; August 14, 1899), *Antigone* (August 12, 1894; August 3, 1897; August 8, 1909), excerpts from *Déjanire* (August 11, 1900), *Samson et Dalila* (June 16, 1902), *Andromaque* (August 14, 1904). Edouard Colonne and "l'orchestre Colonne" were listed on programs of August 2–3,

1897; August 14–15, 1904; and August 5–7, 1907. Repertory lists collated from festival programs, Bibliothèque Ceccano d'Avignon Fol 6.435, 8° 30.195 et al., and Paul Mariéton, *Le Théâtre d'Orange et ses chorégies: Suivi d'une chronologie complète des spectacles depuis l'origine* (Paris: Éditions de *La Province*, 1908).

55. No surviving correspondence from Lalo to these men references the Fêtes d'Orange, nor have I yet found any letters between Lalo and Paul Mariéton in the uncatalogued "Lettres de divers correspondants à Paul Mariéton" (cartons from 1888 to 1910), Bibliothèque Ceccano d'Avignon, mss 4646–4667. Nonetheless, the informality and intimacy of language in Lalo's correspondence with Membrée and Reyer, in particular, suggest that topics other than those left in writing must have been part of their amicable discussions. See Lalo, *Correspondance*, 100, 109, 163. See also Arthur Pougin, "Edouard Lalo," *Le Ménestrel* 58, no. 18 (May 1, 1892): 140. Pougin includes excerpts from Massenet's eulogy for Lalo.

56. Paul Mariéton, *Rapport sur le concours des jeux floraux du Félibrige de Paris, Fête de Sainte-Estelle (Sceaux, 25 Mai 1884)* (Paris: Bloy, s.d.), 2.

57. Fr[ançois] Seguin, *Receuil des noëls composés en langue provençale par Nicolas Saboly, ancien bénéficier et maître de musiquede l'Église de Saint-Pierre d'Avignon: Nouvelle édition plus complète et plus correcte que les précédentes publiée pour la première fois avec les airs notés, receuillis, et arrangés pour le piano ou l'orgue par Fr. Seguin* (Avignon: Seguin ainé, 1856), http://gallica.bnf.fr/ark:/12148/bpt6k55461542?rk=21459;2. It is notable that Seguin wrote at length about standardizing the orthography in Saboly's collection, but did not speak to editorial changes he made to the music. The title of this collection, as well as Seguin's references to "les mélodies de Saboly," indicates that the original versions of this music were monophonic. Seguin, *Receuil des noëls*, ix–xii, xvii.

58. Critobule (pseud. Eugène Vial), *Paul Mariéton d'après sa correspondance* (Paris: Crès, 1920), 1:18.

59. Seguin, *Receuil des noëls*, vi–viii, ix–xi.

60. Seguin, *Receuil des noëls*, viii.

61. *Nouvé 1* in Seguin's edition of Saboly noëls is subtitled "Composed in the year 1660, after the marriage of Louis XIV." Seguin's notes give further details about the compositional circumstances of this air: "Louis made his entry to Avignon on 19 March 1658. The city council had decided to give the king *a beautiful and magnificent entrance.*" Seguin, *Receuil des noëls*, xxxvii.

62. Lalo, *Roi d'Ys: Légende Bretonne. Partition pour Chant & Piano*, 166–167.

63. Seguin, *Receuil des noëls*, 43.

64. Fauquet cites his discovery of an undated note in the collections of the New York Public Library from Lalo to an unidentified recipient declaring that "I made use of no collection [of Breton melodies] nor am I familiar with any. Mme Lalo's family is Breton, and the tunes I have used were sung to me by her. Lalo, *Correspondance*, 166.

65. Lalo, *Roi d'Ys*, 184, 171–180.

66. Lalo, *Roi d'Ys*, 179.

67. Lalo, *Roi d'Ys*, 227–231.

68. Paul Mariéton, "Discours de M. Ernest Renan, Président de la Société Celtique," in *La Revue félibréenne: publication littéraire* 7 (1891): 245–246.

69. Servières, *Édouard Lalo*, 123.

CHAPTER 7

....

ROMANTIC MEDIEVALIST
NATIONALISM IN
SCHUMANN'S *GENOVEVA*,
THEN AND NOW

....

MICHAEL S. RICHARDSON

Although little known today, Robert Schumann's only opera, *Genoveva* of 1850, represented a synthesis of important developments in German opera at the time of its premiere. Prior to Richard Wagner's dominance of the German operatic scene in the second half of the nineteenth century, a healthy competition to establish a distinctively Germanic tradition of grand opera occupied the minds and activities of several prominent composers. In seeking to establish their own operatic tradition, a number of German composers looked to the Middle Ages for their source material. The appeal of the Middle Ages in nineteenth-century art, literature, and music emerged as a result of romantic nostalgia and yearning for the past, along with a burgeoning demand for cultural and historical identity in the drive for a unified German nation. Schumann's *Genoveva* represents an important contribution to the quest for German grand opera as well as the height of the German romantic medievalist aesthetic in opera, which was a specific variety of German medievalism that would be quite different from that which Wagner would cultivate after mid-century.

Certain characteristic features of medievalist German opera in the first half of the nineteenth century are present in Schumann's opera, including church music as both a signifier of the distant past and an emblem of cultural identity, diegetic portrayals of medieval/folk song, and a "chivalric" or "masculine" brand of musical nationalism. Indeed, because of the time in which the work was produced, and because it does not carry Wagner's distinct artistic-ideological baggage, Schumann's *Genoveva* is perhaps the best case study for an understanding of the full development of the romantic-medievalist trend in early nineteenth-century German grand opera that began roughly with Carl Maria von Weber's *Euryanthe* of 1823 and culminated in Wagner's *Lohengrin* of 1850.

This essay will investigate the musical medievalism of Schumann's *Genoveva* and its nationalistic underpinnings, first by examining the historical interest in the Middle Ages present in Germany in the first half of the nineteenth century and then by tracing the influence of this societal fascination with medieval times on the development of German opera. I will then look at the genesis of Schumann's dramatic stage work, followed by three sections that will examine how medievalism was manifested in German opera, and more specifically in *Genoveva*, through on-stage allusions to church music, folk song, and a chivalric style, respectively. Within each of these three sections, I will also address the political and nationalistic significance of such signifiers for "medieval" music in tandem with my discussion of more specific aspects of musical style. A look at the reception of *Genoveva* at the time of its premiere (then) and the modern treatment of the work's medievalist/nationalist themes in a 2008 production by Martin Kušej (now) will follow. Comparing these two interpretations will allow us to investigate a radical departure in twenty-first century thought from the values of Schumann's time, a departure brought on in large part because of Germany's troubled twentieth-century history.

Historical Background

Fascination with the Middle Ages and with medieval lore has been a common theme throughout the postmedieval history of Western Europe. In Germany, during the preunification era of 1800 to 1870, the allure of a shared medieval past carried strong political implications. Following the devastation of the Thirty Years' War (1618–1648), a prevailing sense of economic and cultural inferiority to France throughout much of the eighteenth century, the Napoleonic Wars (1803 to 1815), and the onslaught of industrialization and a population boom from 1815 to 1848 that left many with inhumane working and living conditions, Germans in the first half of the nineteenth century desired to build their own sense of strength and unity as a people. In this period, however, Germany was not a single, unified cultural entity, but rather comprised an assortment of different states and principalities with their own unique cultures and dialects. As the Parisian Madame de Staël pointed out in 1810, "The Germans are Saxons, Prussians, Bavarians, Austrians; but the German character, on which the strength of them all must be based, is as fragmented as the land itself which has so many different rulers."[1] Indeed, regional interests persisted before and well after unification in 1871.[2]

Considering such fragmentation alongside the desire for a nation, the question as to what was German was perhaps most open to debate and definition in the first half of the nineteenth century than at any other time. To lay the foundation for a German state, many people looked toward an idealized medieval past as a source for national unity. The past provided a nostalgic escape from crude realities of the present day, and it also seemed to offer a path toward a brighter future. The Germans were more influenced by a growing awareness and rediscovery of the Middle Ages than any other country at that time, and their interest in medieval times formed a decisive motivational impetus to unite as a nation.[3] As Abigail Green indicates, a sense for the "statehood" of the Holy Roman Empire from the medieval past had in part facilitated and enabled a growing sense of nationalism that ran parallel with the overwhelming regional patriotism that dominated through much of nineteenth-century Germany.[4] A sense of continuity with the past and a shared common history among the different German-speaking cultures became an essential tool for furthering the nationalistic cause, while German national identity could also be mined from the common language that united the many diverse territories and regions.

Medievalism was one of the most important features of the romantic movement in Germany, and the very term *romantisch* in fact emerged in the eighteenth century to describe in a positive light the poetic style of medieval romances and epics.[5] Interest in history had indeed proliferated through all levels of German society from 1800 onward in a number of different ways, as nostalgia for the past had become commonplace throughout western Europe following the French Revolution.[6] Scholars and common citizens alike, for instance, searched through libraries and records for old tales and legends or for information on the beliefs and practices of their ancestors.[7] One of the most important works of medieval literature was the *Nibelungenlied*, or "Song of the Nibelungs," a thirteenth-century Middle High German epic poem that was rediscovered in the mid-eighteenth century and would eventually form part of the basis for Richard Wagner's operatic tetralogy *Der Ring des Nibelungen* (1876).[8] A number of national festivals that dealt with historical subject matter also emerged in the early nineteenth century as interest in both a united nation and a rediscovery of ancient ancestral roots took shape throughout German-speaking lands. Such festivals as the *Wartburgfest* of 1817—led by Protestant *Burschenschaften* (youth fraternities)—involved pilgrimages to the Wartburg Castle, famous for being the site where Martin Luther translated the Bible into German. At Wartburg, members of the *Burschenschaften* would dress up in what they thought was medieval German garb, and the festival came to represent a sort of connection or union with a common German past and heritage. Other festivals involved the staging of medieval tournaments and grandiloquent processions for the Prussian royalty.[9]

Coinciding with growing nationalism and interest in medieval history, the rise of German opera had a patchy start as various composers sought to forge a uniquely Germanic operatic repertory.[10] Prior to Richard Wagner's dominance of the operatic scene in the second half of the century, a strong desire for a national opera as distinct from the predominant French and Italian repertory arose. Opera is thus a ripe field for examining the rise of German nationalism in music at this time. In part because of their disjointed political state at the beginning of the century, the Germans did not have a single operatic voice that could compete with the inflow of French and Italian works. German operas in the first half of the century thus represent more a series of experimental starts and stops than a unified tradition. The majority of pieces performed in opera houses at the time continued to be French and Italian, although German dialogue operas were often performed as well.[11]

Ultimately, as Wagner's reputation grew, he began to outdo the collective intermittent attempts by various composers at establishing a national German opera, and by the second half of the century Wagnerian opera became practically synonymous with the genre. In the first half of the century, though, there remained a healthy competition to establish a national repertory, and it is no coincidence that in seeking to establish a national repertory, many German composers employed medieval themes and legends for their works. Ernst Theodor Amadeus (E. T. A.) Hoffmann's opera *Undine* of 1816 is one such example, which combines a fairy-tale atmosphere with medievalist imagery in a story of a mermaid who falls in love with a knight.[12] Apart from this type of fantastical *romantische Zauberoper* ("romantic magic opera"), however, it is evident that the first half of the nineteenth century—particularly starting in the 1820s with works like Carl Maria von Weber's 1823 *Euryanthe* and Heinrich Marschner's 1829 *Der Templer und die Jüdin*—witnessed a strong trend in the onstage portrayal of medieval history. Wagner, for his part, appears to have been more interested in the re-creation of history on stage in the first half of the century than in the second half, as evidenced by his operatic projects of this time being set in a fixed time and place rather than in a nebulous mythical past. Indeed, Wagner continued to be interested in history throughout the 1840s, and it was after *Lohengrin* that his focus—with the exception of *Die Meistersinger von Nürnberg* (1868)—switched more to myth.[13] The middle of the nineteenth century also more broadly witnessed an artistic and ideological shift from romanticism to realism, marking the 1850 premieres of *Genoveva* and *Lohengrin* as the final vestiges of German romantic operatic historicism in its fullest flowering.

Background of *Genoveva*

Ideas of creating some kind of stage work had circulated in Schumann's mind for some time prior to beginning work on *Genoveva*. As early as 1830, Schumann was inspired by seeing a grand opera based on Shakespeare's *Hamlet*, followed a decade later by a short-lived attempt at an opera based on E. T. A. Hoffmann's *Doge und Dogeressa*. The idea of composing an opera had occupied his mind throughout much of the early 1840s, particularly one that would help establish a sufficiently "Germanic" operatic repertory devoid of French or Italian influence. Prior to choosing the subject of Genoveva, he had been interested in a number of other possible subjects, many of them also medievalist. His interests included, among other topics, the *Nibelungenlied*, the Song Contest at Wartburg, Tristan and Isolde, Faust, Till Eulenspiegel, and Arthurian legend. The composer was indeed disappointed to discover that Wagner was busy on his text for his opera *Lohengrin* in 1845, writing, "I had been contemplating for about a year the same or at least a similar subject from the age of the Round Table—and now I must throw it in the fountain."[14]

After considering nearly fifty different possible subjects for an opera, Schumann eventually, in April 1847, decided on the legend of Saint Genevieve as told in Ludwig Tieck's poem of 1799 entitled *Leben und Tod der heiligen Genoveva* and Friedrich Hebbel's drama *Genoveva* of 1843. The narrative of a falsely accused innocent female who is ultimately redeemed had intrigued Schumann through his exposure to Weber's *Euryanthe*, which had a considerable influence on the composer and was likely a model for him in writing *Genoveva*.[15] The basic form of the Genevieve legend also appears in various ballads and sources of French, Scottish, Scandinavian, English, and German origin. Schumann had enlisted the help of his friend Robert Reinick to write the libretto, but feeling unsatisfied with Reinick's efforts, the composer opted to complete the libretto himself. Schumann finished the libretto by the end of 1847, and his inscription on the score states August 4, 1848, as the date of completion of the whole work. The opera premiered on June 25, 1850, at the Stadttheater in Leipzig, with the composer conducting.

Similar to Wagner's *Lohengrin*, which premiered in the same year, Schumann's opera also takes place in Brabant, although in the eighth century. The opera includes an overture and four acts. In act 1, Count Siegfried of the Palatinate heeds the call of Hidulfus, bishop of Trier, to go off to war in support of Carl Martel's campaign against the invading Moors. Siegfried leaves his wife Genoveva to the care of his friend Golo, who is secretly in love with her. In act 2, Genoveva longs for Siegfried's return. Golo makes advances toward her, but after being rebuffed by her, he plans for the steward Drago to be caught in her bedroom to frame her as an unfaithful wife. The plan works and Drago is killed, while Genoveva is thrown into a dungeon. Act 3 finds Siegfried in Strasbourg, where the sorceress Margaretha tells him a tale of a magic mirror that can reveal past events. After Golo arrives and informs Siegfried of Genoveva's alleged infidelity, Siegfried decides to use the mirror to see for himself. Believing the false visions that he sees in the mirror, Siegfried orders that Genoveva be executed. The spirit of Drago, however, forces Margaretha to follow Siegfried to reveal the truth. In act 4, Genoveva is being led to the forest to be put to death, and Golo tries to persuade her to flee. After Genoveva continues to reject him, Golo leaves her. Siegfried returns with the truth as revealed through Margaretha, and Genoveva's life is spared. The bishop of Trier then blesses the happily reunited couple amid festive jubilation.

Church Music and the Politics of Confession

To represent the faith-centered community in which the main story takes place, Schumann frames his work with musical numbers cast in a church music style, more specifically with a chorale.[16] In the opening of act 1, immediately following the overture, the scene opens with the townspeople singing a Bach-style chorale based on the church hymn "Ermuntre dich, mein schwacher Geist" ("Take courage, my weak spirit") (see Example 7.1). The chorale theme appears again in a double chorus at the end of act 4, following Siegfried and Genoveva's joyous reunion.

EXAMPLE 7.1 Chorale from act 1 of *Genoveva*.

It seems curious that the composer chooses to employ a Bach-style chorale for his representation of eighth-century church music, but when one examines the historical context surrounding the reception of Bach around Schumann's time, this gesture seems less unusual. The fact that a revival of Bach's music occurred in the nineteenth century is well known, and Schumann made no small contribution to those efforts. Not only was Schumann well acquainted with a wide range of Bach's music, but also he incorporated various elements of Bach's style into several of his compositions other than just his opera.[17] Like many of his contemporaries, Schumann also held Bach in the highest esteem. In a letter to Gustav Keferstein in 1840, the composer writes, "But the thoughtful combinations, the poetry and humor of modern music, originate chiefly in Bach...I myself make a daily confession of my sins to that mighty one, and endeavor to purify and strengthen myself through him...In fact, to my mind Bach is unapproachable—he is unfathomable."[18] Indeed, Schumann's idealization of Bach touches on his broader view of the composer as the origin or cornerstone of German music.[19] But an even more concrete and visible link between Bach and the Middle Ages occupied nineteenth-century thought—the association between Bach-style polyphony and medieval Gothic architecture.

A connection between Bach and Gothic architecture had indeed already developed by the late eighteenth century, as comparisons between Bach's fugal music and the Straßburger Münster appeared in Johann Friedrich Reichardt's *Musikalischem Kunstmagazin* of 1782. Annette Kreutziger-Herr points out that such comparisons were more of an "aesthetic rather than an art-historical nature," but that nevertheless the rediscoveries and resurgences of Gothic architecture and of Bach's music witnessed a strong convergence in the late eighteenth and early nineteenth centuries.[20] Carl Maria von Weber reinforces a connection between the two when he mentions how Bach built up a "veritable Gothic cathedral of the church of art" with his intricate rhythms, voice leading, and counterpoint.[21] Part of what triggered these connections was the idea of the multiple layers of Bach-style polyphony as filling a vertically oriented harmonic space, in the same way that Gothic cathedrals were believed to reach vertically upward toward the heavens.[22] An association between Bach and the Gothic Middle Ages also carried significant nationalistic impulses, as Germans sought out Bach instead of Palestrina, who represented Italian Catholicism, as the founder of their modern music.[23] Indeed, Franz Brendel in 1859 upholds Bach and Handel, both part of what he terms the *Old German school*, as pillars of German music history devoid of foreign influence.[24] Richard Wagner even equates Bach with the dusk of the Middle Ages in a statement recorded in the diaries of his wife Cosima, where she writes, "Then, regarding Bach, he [Richard Wagner] says to me, 'He was the culmination of the medieval world—Wolfram, the mystics, A. Dürer, Luther; after that a completely new world begins, the world of the sonata, the aria, which has also produced some fine things.'"[25]

Schumann likely had his own political motivations for employing a Bach-style chorale in his work. Given the strong nationalistic associations between Bach and the origins of German music history, the composer may have alluded to Bach as an idealistic portrayal of the origins of his culture's music in his desire to establish an ostensibly Germanic operatic tradition. Indeed, the opening chorale vividly portrays a homogenous German community singing with one voice as one people in a musical style inextricably connected to their own heritage and identity. The superimposition of an anachronistic chorale on people of the Middle Ages seems to serve as a means for reclaiming the German Middle Ages from the Latin church. The confessional divide between Protestants and Catholics in Germany was, after all, problematic for the building of a German national identity in the nineteenth century, because national identity was viewed to be closely tied to religion.[26] The early German nationalist movement was mostly Protestant in nature, expounded by Protestant philosophers like Johann Gottfried Herder. Catholic ties to Rome and the pope were viewed from the Protestant perspective as a threat to the nationalist cause, with tensions between the two factions escalating in the *Kulturkampf* of the 1870s following national unification.[27]

But attempts at interconfessional unity could also be found, for instance, in the project begun in the 1840s to complete the medieval Cologne Cathedral, which was at that time viewed as a "national church" that could reconcile Catholics and Protestants.[28] Moreover, German-language chorales were also sung in some Catholic churches in the nineteenth century, and the singing of hymns and other forms of liturgical music in the German language instead of in Latin was a means by which German Catholics could assert their inclusion in the national project.[29] But as a Protestant himself, Schumann may have felt personally invested in promoting a Protestant vision of a united German nation through his use of a Lutheran chorale in *Genoveva*. And patriotism was apparently at the forefront of Schumann's mind at the time that he was writing his opera, because he mentions his work on his "Patriotische Lieder" (*Drei Gesänge*, op. 62) next to work on *Genoveva* in his *Haushaltbücher*.[30] In addition, several of Schumann's compositions between the years 1848 and 1853 manifest an overtly political character in response to the revolutions of 1848 and 1849.[31]

But beyond the nationalistic significance and more surface historicity of Schumann's use of a Bach-style chorale, the composer employs modal harmonies to evoke in this opening scene a kind of music that sounds antiquated by its own nature. The tonal center shifts between F major and D minor in Schumann's chorale, with a hint of modal harmony in the frequent bass motions from C to D. The move of C to D is significant because it suggests a pretonal harmonic motion of a ♮VII subtonic chord to a minor i, which subverts the traditional function of the leading tone in establishing cadences and keys and hearkens to scales of the early church modes. Schumann drives this musical point home on the text "er ist der Quell der Gnaden" ("he is the fount of all graces")—the only portion of this opening chorale in which the voices break into four-part harmony—articulating a FM–B♭M–CM–Dmin harmonic progression

In the bar prior to the first FM chord in this chord progression, Schumann had secured the tonic in FM with a perfect authentic cadence, making this a curious harmonic moment. One can hear these chords either as a I–ii6–V–vi progression with a deceptive cadence in FM or as a III–iv6–♮VII–i modal progression in D minor. It is important to consider that the Dmin chord sounds like a tonic arrival in this moment, which Schumann reinforces with an A dominant at the start of the following phrase and a perfect authentic cadence in D with a Picardy third to conclude this section (see Example 7.2). Interestingly, in the original sketch of this chorale Schumann crosses out a final cadence in F major, with a bass motion from C to D at the start of the final phrase following "Quell der Gnaden" (see Figure 7.1).[32]

The composer was evidently then interested in reinforcing this modal-sounding bass motion as a prominent feature of this section from beginning to end. Indeed, the modal flavor of the chorale alone suggests an archaic, antique sound, which may have served to heighten the illusion of historical authenticity and perhaps make the audience more receptive to nationalistic or political themes in the work.[33]

EXAMPLE 7.2 Chorale from act 1 of *Genoveva* (final phrase).

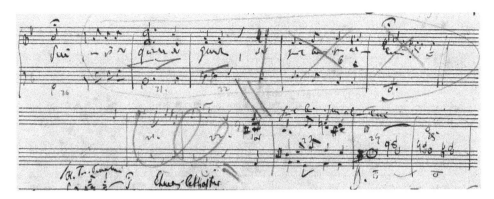

FIGURE 7.1 Schumann's sketch of the final cadence for the act 1 chorale of *Genoveva*.

Folk Song and the Lied

Like other German opera composers of his time, Schumann employs folklike Lied music that evokes the secular songs of medieval minstrels in his stage work. According to Annette Kreutziger-Herr, an association of medieval music with the secular songs of the troubadours, trouvères, and *Minnesingers* permeated nineteenth-century culture in Germany and France. She also describes the emergence of the medieval *Kunstlied* theory by historians like Hugo Riemann in connection to the composition of romanticized, medieval songs based on ancient texts by composers like Brahms, Schumann, and others.[34] In essence, invented medieval songs in the nineteenth century, and Lieder in particular, helped shape views and conceptions on how such songs may have sounded in their historical context. Such fabrications carried unique musical devices for evoking songs from an ancient, bygone era. John Haines, for instance, sees Hector Berlioz's *Chanson gothique* from his *Damnation de Faust* as embodying several features of such a medievalist song aesthetic. Haines states that the song's "prominent tritone evoked the mystery of a distant Middle Ages in the *romance* tradition, while its lilting $\frac{6}{8}$ rhythm tapped directly into the best tradition of naïve settings."[35] He sees these features as also predominating in Robert Schumann's *Blondels Lied* of 1840, op. 53, and Johannes Brahms's setting of Herder's Thibaut paraphrase of 1861.[36] A lilting $\frac{6}{8}$ meter also characterizes Schumann's Lied *Aus alten Märchen* from his *Dichertliebe*, which Jonathan Bellman discusses as a quintessential example of what he calls the *chivalric style* in the music of Schumann and Brahms.[37]

Schumann drew from a variety of influences for his folk-song moments in *Genoveva*. Joan Chissell, for instance, suggests that Schumann's use of folk song in his opera, including the strophic songs *Wenn ich ein Vöglein wär* (no. 9) of Genoveva and Golo and *Sie hatten Beid' sich herzlich lieb* of Caspar and Balthasar in act 4, was inspired by Weber.[38] The no. 9 duet is of particular significance for its text, which was quite popular in the German romantic movement. What Marjorie Hirsch calls the *Voglmotif* was a prominent

EXAMPLE 7.3 Reichardt's "Wenn ich ein Vöglein wär."

EXAMPLE 7.4 "Wenn ich ein Vöglein wär" duet from act 2 of *Genoveva*.

aesthetic that reflected the imagery embedded in the poem of the speaker taking flight to his beloved.[39] The earliest source for the anonymous text is from a 1756 *Flugblatt*, but it is most well known from the version contained within Herder's 1778 collection of *Volkslieder*. It subsequently made appearances in Arnim and Brentano's *Des knaben Wunderhorn* (vol. 1, 1806) and a number of other collections of *Volkslieder*. Although the original text did not contain an accompanying melody, Johann Friedrich Reichardt published a melody that he called a *Schweizervolkslied* in his Liederspiel *Lieb und Treue* of 1800, which became closely associated with the text (see Example 7.3).[40]

Although cast in the minor mode, Schumann's version of the song clearly resembles Reichardt's melody. In this sense, the Golo/Genoveva duet resembles countless other settings of this song that took Reichardt's music as a point of departure (see Example 7.4).[41]

The text carries a similar meaning for both characters, as Genoveva longs to be reunited with Siegfried, who has gone off to war, and Golo longs to be with Genoveva. After breaking off into recitative while Genoveva continues to sing, Golo then expresses his feelings for her. Hansjörg Ewert describes four layers to the song: the Herder–Goethe folk-song tradition, the naive "folk tone" and house music of the Biedermeier aesthetic, the dramatic need to justify the use of song in the *Singspiel* tradition of spoken dialogue, and the employment of a conventional duet type that functions as a cantabile.[42] Schumann moreover orders the strophes in an A B A B form, the B strophe of which moves to the dominant key of B major. As Ewert points out, "the sequencing of the melody over a major triad makes the middle [B] strophe sound closer to folk song," which in turn reinforces the overarching folklike character of the number.[43]

The medievalism of the duet can be traced in part to the zither accompaniment as portrayed by two violas, its lilting ⅜ meter, and in Schumann's use of folk poetry. Schumann frequently employed folk poetry in his song settings; in this he resembles Brahms much more than Schubert.[44] As Hirsch suggests, Schumann's choice of this particular text may also reflect a medievalist strain in the number because of associations between the text and an idealized, distant realm. "As one of the most popular songs in the cherished repertory of German *Volkslieder*," Hirsch writes, "['Wenn ich ein Vöglein wär'] quickly came to assume the character of a lost idyllic world, an object of yearning that acted like a polestar in guiding Lied poets and composers in their creative efforts."[45] It is precisely this yearning that simultaneously reflects the immediate desires of the two characters, Genoveva and Golo, within the context of the plot and the romantic longing for the lost beauty, innocence, and purity of medieval times that could stand as a model for the hoped-for German nation.

Chivalry, Masculinity, and Nation

Chivalry and its attendant constructions of masculinity are further key components of the medievalism in *Genoveva*, both in the text and in the music. Musically speaking, Bellman articulates his description of the chivalric style of Schumann and Brahms as comprising "fanfare figures, horn fifths, trumpet-call repeated notes, and in general clarion melodic lines that stress chord tones in a triumphant, heraldic manner," along with "a galloping ⁶⁄₈ meter, or continuous triplets in a brisk common time, suggestive of hoofbeats."[46] Alongside these musical features, general attributes of chivalric musical moments observable in early nineteenth-century medievalist German operas include but are not limited to a prominent timbral presence of brass and timpani, straightforward diatonic harmonies, and dotted rhythms that evoke images either of knights on horseback or of the stateliness and nobility of a medieval court. Textually speaking, depictions of chivalry in the medievalist genre also typically go hand in hand with nationalist rhetoric, mirroring the surging nationalism that developed throughout the majority of the nineteenth century in the German quest for statehood ultimately attained in the 1870s. Even in operas like *Euryanthe* and *Der Templer und die Jüdin*, neither of which is set in Germany, the appearance in the libretti of such nationalistic terms as *das Volk* and *das Vaterland* indicates a specifically Germanic context given the national excitement for the Fatherland following the Germans' liberation from France after the Napoleonic Wars.[47]

In Wagner's 1850 *Lohengrin* and in *Genoveva* in particular, however, the libretti in various spots exalt the military might of the medieval German Empire and create a strongly nationalistic dichotomy between insiders and outsiders. Both operas begin in act 1 with a figure rallying men to defend German lands from a foreign threat: in *Lohengrin* with King Heinrich and in *Genoveva* with Bishop Hidulfus. King Heinrich sings, "East and West, to all I say: / let every acre of German soil put forth troops of soldiers, / never again shall anyone abuse the German Empire!" ("ob Ost, ob West, das gelte allen gleich! / Was deutsches Land heisst, stelle Kampfesscharen, / dann schmäht wohl niemand mehr das Deutsche Reich!"). The Saxons proclaim, "Let us away! With God for the honor of the German Empire!" ("Wohlauf! Mit Gott für Deutschen Reiches Ehr!"). Later in the last act, the chorus repeats King Heinrich's nationalist call: "For German land the German sword / Thus be our country's might on guard!" ("Für deutsches Land das deutsche Schwert! / So sei des Reiches Kraft bewährt!").

Whereas Heinrich focuses on the might of the German Empire, Hidulfus in *Genoveva* focuses more on the perfidy and treachery of the enemy within the religious context of Christians versus Muslims. He describes the latter as the "arch-enemy of our faith" ("Erzfeind unsers Glaubens") and urges the soldiers to fight for the "glory and honor of Christendom" ("Christenheit zu Ruhm und Ehr"). The chorus interjects with "ruin him" ("Verderben ihm") and "we are prepared for struggle and combat, to go to our deaths for Christ our Lord" ("Wir sind bereit zu Kampf und Streit, für Christ den Herrn zum Tod zu geh'n"). Later in act 1, no. 5, the chorus sings "Carl Martel, Carl Martel, mighty hammer, bring the heathens to their knees!" ("Karl Martell, Karl Martell, tapf'rer Hammer, allem Heidenvolk zum Jammer!"). Although the militaristic tone and dramatic function of the "call to battle scenes" in these two operas are quite similar, the *Genoveva* scene takes on a more religious context than its analogue in *Lohengrin*. Religion in *Genoveva* thus becomes an essential element for the assertion of national and cultural identity. In both cases, however, the nation is in part defined through its opposition to a hostile foreign power.[48]

A martial, masculine, or chivalric character permeates the music in such moments, with vocal lines of the choruses outlining trumpet calls with abundant intervallic leaps of ascending and descending perfect fourths and fifths. The ascending fourth takes on a particularly masculinist and militaristic tone here as it suggests armies raising their courage figuratively and rising up literally to attack the enemy. It also suggests resoluteness in the outlining of a bass motion in a perfect authentic cadence. Indeed, Hidulfus opens his address to the soldiers with an ascending perfect fourth along with the score indication of "mit Kraft" ("with strength"), and he subsequently begins each new phrase of text prior to his statement of the chorale theme with either an ascending perfect fourth or a stepwise motion outlining the same interval. The no. 5 chorus leading to "allem Heidenvolk zum Jammer" also features many parallel thirds in the choral writing, which Barbara Eichner describes along with horn fifths and arpeggiated chords as "signifiers of rural simplicity, bygone ages and life 'in tune' with nature."[49] Interestingly, all three medievalist elements (church music, folk song, and chivalry) are summed up in the end of act 4 of *Genoveva* when in the no. 20 "Doppelchor" ("Double Chorus") Choir

I sings a folklike tune ("Bestreut den Weg mit grünen Mai'n") that is then juxtaposed by the return of the chorale theme from act 1, sung by Choir II. Both choirs eventually unite to declaim once again, "Er ist der Quell der Gnaden," before the reappearance of Bishop Hidulfus is proclaimed by a drumroll and trumpet fanfare. Brass and timpani also accompany the final chorus as the people sing the praises of the exalted male/female pair (Siegfried and Genoveva), and the curtain falls following a robust fourfold declamation of "Heil!" ("hail!") in a sunny E major.

Nineteenth-Century Reception of *Genoveva* (Then)

Much anticipation had built up for the opening performance of Schumann's first opera, and many prominent figures in music were present for the 1850 Leipzig premiere.[50] Although the work was subsequently staged in many different cities, however, the piece unfortunately never attained any kind of enduring success and fell out of the repertory fairly quickly. Nineteenth-century critics gave mixed reviews of the work, with some speaking of the piece as noble and of great merit and others describing it as too undramatic for the operatic stage.[51] Eduard Hanslick sees all four elements of the German romantic aesthetic as meeting in *Genoveva*, including a "German-medieval milieu, Christian piety, mystical wonders, and even reminiscences of folk song."[52] He concludes, however, that "innumerable good intentions are hidden in the score, but they do not come forth. Many French and Italian opera composers, although artistically beneath Schumann, write much better operas!"[53] In terms of the medieval content of the work specifically, an 1850 review in the *Signale für die musikalische Welt* mentions that "the source material chosen for the opera was a good one, for apart from the suitability of this material to dramatic rendering, the ancient legend of Genoveva, which emerged from German folk poetry, had from the outset earned the sympathy of the masses."[54]

In his 1850 review, however, Franz Brendel speaks ambivalently of the historical subject matter of the work:

> I demand from modern opera another interest from what this material can offer. People prefer anyhow to return to the past, the early sagas, our folk poetry, but especially to generate anew the great figures of old German poetry in the modern consciousness. I believe this path is not only the right one, but a necessary one before our opera may experience an upsurge. But there is lacking in our modern opera a new ideal concerning this too commonly-treated material, and this is the deeper reason why no opera in the last age has managed to penetrate the popular consciousness.[55]

Brendel goes on to describe the competing types of operatic material employed by Gluck, Mozart, the Italians, and the French, whereas in Germany the spirit of the romantic (or medieval) ideal as portrayed by Spohr, Weber, and Marschner had taken hold, stating,

> It certainly was a distinctive direction [the romantic ideal], which was the prevailing mood of the era. But now this kind of focus is lacking, for everywhere there are attempts and people groping about. Richard Wagner is surely the happiest in this choice of material, but the ideal that everyone is looking for and that would satisfy all has not yet been found. I would say it is thus that people always return to the past—I see in this material the unraveling of the mysteries of the present*)—but the story of Genoveva cannot satisfy in the present any longer.[56]

Brendel sees the return to the past as necessary before a revival in opera may occur, yet he also is suggesting that the treatment of medieval material has become too common-place and is lacking in true ideal or purpose.[57] It is interesting, though, that he nevertheless emphasizes the significance of returning to the past to help understand the present. The asterisk in the concluding sentence of the last quotation refers to a footnote that shows a clear link in Brendel's mind between the return to the legendary past and growing nationalism. He states in the footnote, "For example the subject of the Nibelungen, which would have been available as operatic material, certainly would have made an extraordinary impact in the last few years in the aspirations for German unity and con-siderations of an all-encompassing Fatherland."[58] Perhaps then for Brendel it is not the historical subject matter itself that is lacking, but rather the treatment of it.

Martin Kušej's Production of *Genoveva* (Now)

But if the medievalist-nationalistic themes in a work like *Genoveva* strongly attracted nineteenth-century audiences, these same themes—particularly given Germany's trou-bled history with nationalism in the twentieth century—almost certainly push most contemporary audience members in the opposite direction. In his 2008 production of the work with Opernhaus Zürich, however, Martin Kušej manages both to revive Schumann's all but forgotten opera and to comment on the medievalist nationalism in a way that presumably avoids alienating the modern viewer. Bishop Hidulfus, for instance, is portrayed as a wild-eyed religious zealot, while Siegfried is depicted as a hypocritical chauvinist for declaring Genoveva be put to death for infidelity after engaging in his own liaison with Margarethe (implied in the staging but not in Schumann's original). The pristine white room in which the staging takes place gradually becomes bloodied and dirty, and at the end of act 4, an overabundance of pristine white Virgin Mary statues on stage (the act 4 apparition of the Virgin Mary) seems a forced attempt at glossing over the transgressions that have occurred in the storyline up to that point. Genoveva and Siegfried, meanwhile, are solemn and gaze with traumatized stares as the chorus sings their jubilant praise, which appears to be Kušej's way of exposing the hollowness of the "happy ending."

The relationship between Siegfried and Genoveva, moreover, is depicted as contrived and inauthentic both in act 1 and once again in act 4, when in a repeating cycle Siegfried kisses Genoveva on the forehead and she faints and stumbles, suggesting that they are merely play-acting the role of the "noble pair." When Bishop Hidulfus appears for the last time in act 4, he is still as manic and wild-eyed, only now he childishly wields a sword, completely out of touch with the militaristic campaign against the foreign "enemy." Members of the on-stage chorus at the conclusion of act 4, likewise, can be seen wielding a variety of weapons including axes and bayonets, making them appear more as an angry mob than a jubilant throng. The medievalist-nationalist ideals expressed or implied in the original work—unreflective religious faith, fear of the foreign enemy, militaristic/chauvinistic chivalry, and the glorification of the noble male/female pair—are thus exposed through the staging as inherently flawed and embarrassingly naive. Kušej's production therefore appears to be both reviving the music and confronting what may be considered uncomfortably nationalistic content, even if veiled under a seemingly innocent medieval setting.

Schumann's *Genoveva*, ultimately, remains an important synthesis of the prevailing characteristics of the medievalist/historicist trend in German opera in the first half of the nineteenth century, as its themes of Christianity, folk/medieval song, and chivalry exemplify the stock features of medievalist German opera from Weber's *Euryanthe* to Wagner's *Lohengrin*. In the context of nineteenth-century Germany, medievalism not merely reflected romantic nostalgia, but also served as an important tool for both implicit and explicit expressions of nationalism and for the building of a common cultural identity thought to be rooted in the past. The then/now dichotomy moreover applies just as much to Schumann's appropriation of the Middle Ages as it does to Kušej's revival of the German composer's mostly forgotten opera. In both instances, the treatment of medieval subject matter says more about the current culture than it does about the past, as reflected in the nationalistic concerns of Schumann's time versus the antinationalistic stance of Kušej's generation. Future productions may yet add additional layers of meaning to the multitiered medievalism of a work like *Genoveva*.

NOTES

1. As quoted in John Warrack, *German Opera: From the Beginnings to Wagner* (Cambridge: Cambridge University Press, 2001), 210.
2. Abigail Green, *Fatherlands: State-Building and Nationhood in Nineteenth-Century Germany* (Cambridge: Cambridge University Press, 2001), 21.
3. Agnes Addison, *Romanticism and the Gothic Revival* (New York: Gordian Press, 1967), 10; Francis G. Gentry and Ulrich Müller, "The Reception of the Middle Ages in Germany: An Overview," *Studies in Medievalism* 3, no. 4 (Spring 1991): 403; Francis G. Gentry, "The Politicization of the Middle Ages: Nationalism and Festivals in Nineteenth-Century Germany," *Studies in Medievalism* 3, no. 4 (Spring 1991): 468. See also Laura K. T. Stokes's contribution to this volume, "Medievalisms in Early Nineteenth-Century German Musical Thought."
4. Green, *Fatherlands*, 4.
5. Addison, *Romanticism and the Gothic Revival*, 10; Gloria Flaherty, *Opera in the Development of German Critical Thought* (Princeton, NJ: Princeton University Press, 1978), 253, 294.

6. George S. Williamson, *The Longing for Myth in Germany: Religion and Aesthetic Culture from Romanticism to Nietzsche* (Chicago: University of Chicago Press, 2004), 2–3. Williamson adds that interest in the German Middle Ages was not a new phenomenon, with many scholars and civilians as early as the fifteenth century expressing great interest in ancient literature, heirlooms, artifacts, and the like (74).

7. Ibid., 2. Williamson indicates that generally no new medieval works of literature were being discovered in the nineteenth century, but interest in these works had increased considerably during this time (76).

8. Gentry, "The Reception of the Middle Ages in Germany," 404.

9. David E. Barclay, *Frederick William IV and the Prussian Monarchy: 1840–1861* (Oxford: Clarendon Press, 1995), 2.

10. Although genres like *Singspiel* and other light or comic forms of opera written in the German language were already well established in the early nineteenth century, the development of a uniquely Germanic operatic repertory here refers to the rise of more "serious" or "grand" opera written in the German language.

11. Warrack, *German Opera*, 341–342. French and Italian operas performed in Germany in the first half of the century were either translated to German or performed in their original languages. For further discussions of performance languages, see Warrack, *German Opera*, 210–211; and Stephen C. Meyer, *Carl Maria von Weber and the Search for a German Opera* (Bloomington: Indiana University Press, 2003), 25–26, 28–29.

12. The tale of Undine was popularized in Freidrich de la Motte Fouqué's 1811 novel of the same name, and as with Sir Walter Scott's 1820 *Ivanhoe*, the work had a marked influence on medievalist art and taste in the first half of the nineteenth century and beyond. See Eda Sagarra and Peter Skrine, *A Companion to German Literature: From 1500 to the Present* (Oxford: Blackwell, 1997), 97–98.

13. Stewart Spencer echoes this notion when he states that "history, rather than myth, continued to interest Wagner for much of the 1840s." See Stewart Spencer, "The 'Romantic Operas' and the Turn to Myth," in *The Cambridge Companion to Wagner*, ed. Thomas S. Grey (Cambridge: Cambridge University Press, 2008), 71; see also Mary A. Cicora, *Wagner's Ring and German Drama: Comparative Studies in Mythology and History in Drama* (Westport, CT: Greenwood Press, 1999), 9, in which the author discusses how many scholars have viewed Wagner's abandonment in 1848 of a plan to write an opera based on Friedrich Barbarossa and to instead write an opera on Siegfried as the crucial shift in Wagner's focus from history to myth. Cicora, however, argues that Wagner would not necessarily have made such a clear distinction between the two, because he viewed "history in relation to myth, and vice versa." With regard to *Lohengrin*, Carl Dahlhaus describes the work as occupying an "area midway between historical drama and fairy-tale opera," while Berthold Hoeckner sees the connection between the forbidden question and the Oedipus myth as marking a shift from historical to mythological meaning in the work. See Carl Dahlhaus, *Richard Wagner's Music Dramas*, trans. Mary Whittall (Cambridge: Cambridge University Press, 1979), 38; Berthold Hoeckner, "Elsa Screams, or The Birth of Music Drama," *Cambridge Opera Journal* 9, no. 2 (July 1997): 124.

14. Letter to Felix Mendelssohn from Dresden on November 18, 1845. In F. Gustav Jansen, ed., *Robert Schumanns Briefe. Neue Folge* (Leipzig, Germany: Breitkopf und Härtel, 1904), 255. Original German: "Wagner hat uns zu unserer Überraschung gestern seinen neuen Operntext vorgelegt, Lohengrin—zu meiner doppelten, denn ich trug mich schon seit einem Jahre mit demselben, oder wenigstens einem ähnlichen aus der Zeit der Tafelrunde herum—und muß ihn nun in den Brunnen werfen." Translation my own.

15. Peter Oswald, *Schumann: The Inner Voices of a Musical Genius* (Boston: Northeastern University Press, 1985), 215; Warrack, *German Opera*, 369.

16. For more information on Schumann's religious views and his composing of sacred works, see Laura Tunbridge, *Schumann's Late Style* (Cambridge: Cambridge University Press, 2007), 59–68.

17. For a more in-depth discussion of Schumann's relationship to Bach's music, see Georg von Dadelsen, "Robert Schumann und die Musik Bachs," *Archiv für Musikwissenschaft* 14. Jahrg., H.1. (1957): 46–59.

18. As translated in Robert Schumann, *On Music and Musicians*, ed. Konrad Wolff, trans. Paul Rosenfeld (Berkeley: University of California Press, 1946), 93. Original letter to Keferstein on January 31, 1840, from Leipzig in Jansen, 177–179.

19. Holly Watkins, *Metaphors of Depth in German Musical Thought: From E. T. A. Hoffmann to Arnold Schoenberg* (Cambridge: Cambridge University Press, 2011), 94.

20. Annette Kreutziger-Herr, *Ein Traum vom Mittelalter: Die Wiederentdeckung mittelalterlicher Musik in der Neuzeit* (Köln, Germany: Böhlau Verlag, 2003), 52–53. Translation my own.

21. Carl Maria von Weber, "Johann Sebastian Bach (Artikel über die Familie Bach)," *Allgemeine Enzyklopädie der Wissenschaften und Künste 7* (1821): 28–29, accessed September 24, 2013, http://www.weber-gesamtausgabe.de/en/A002068/Writings/A030809.

22. Kreutziger-Herr, *Ein Traum vom Mittelalter*, 53–54.

23. Ibid., 56.

24. Ibid., 57–58.

25. Cosima Wagner, *Cosima Wagner's Diaries: Volume II, 1878–1883*, ed. Martin Gregor-Dellin and Dietrich Mack, trans. Geoffrey Skelton (New York: Harcourt Brace Jovanovich, 1980), 276. Interestingly, the opening of act 1 of Wagner's *Meistersinger* also begins with a chorale in a church setting like in Schumann's opera. Giacomo Meyerbeer, moreover, famously incorporated into his 1836 opera *Les Huguenots* the Lutheran chorale "Ein feste Burg" to represent the Huguenots (Protestants), a move that did not curry favor with Schumann. Schumann writes, "I am no moralist, but it enrages a good Protestant to hear his most cherished hymn shouted upon the boards, it enrages him to see the bloodiest drama in the whole history of his religion degraded to the level of a farce at a fair for the purpose of raising money and applause; indeed the whole opera irks him, beginning with the overture, with its ridiculously cheap holiness, to the ending, where we are all condemned to be burnt at the stake." As translated by Paul Rosenfeld in Schumann, *On Music and Musicians*, 194.

26. Jennifer Bain, *Hildegard of Bingen and Musical Reception: The Modern Revival of a Medieval Composer* (Cambridge: Cambridge University Press, 2015), 123.

27. Christopher Clark, "Religion," in *The Short Oxford History of Germany: Germany 1800–1870*, ed. Jonathan Sperber (Oxford: Oxford University Press, 2004), 180; Bain, *Hildegard of Bingen*, 125. It should be noted too that it was in Prussia that the first seeds of German nationalism were planted and that the Prussian character dominated the nationalist movement. See Helmut Walser Smith, "Nation and Nationalism," in *The Short Oxford History of Germany: Germany 1800–1870*, ed. Jonathan Sperber (Oxford: Oxford University Press, 2004), 237.

28. Gentry, "The Politicization of the Middle Ages," 474.

29. Bain, *Hildegard of Bingen*, 118, 127.

30. Robert Schumann, *Tagebücher, Band III: Haushaltbücher, Teil 2, 1847–1856*, ed. Gerd Nauhaus (Basel: Stroemfeld/Roter Stern, 1982), 450. Schumann writes, "Started instrumentation of Genoveva—in the evening Liedertafel and my patriotic songs—much joy—." Original German: "An Genoveva zu instr.[umentieren] angefangen—Abends Liedertafel

u.m.[eine] patriotischen Lieder—Freude—." Translation my own. John Daverio moreover points to Schumann's statements in a letter to Friedrich Kistner on December 9, 1847, that the "patriotic songs," as Schumann termed them, "owed their existence to the November 1847 victory of the Swiss federalists." See John Daverio, *"Einheit—Freiheit—Vaterland*: Intimations of Utopia in Robert Schumann's Late Choral Music," in *Music and German National Identity*, ed. Celia Applegate and Pamela Potter (Chicago: University of Chicago Press, 2002), 62.

31. Daverio, *"Einheit—Freiheit—Vaterland,"* 62.

32. Schumann's original sketch of act 1 of *Genoveva* acquired at the Robert-Schumann-Haus in Zwickau, Germany, in October 2012. Reproduced with permission from the Robert-Schumann-Haus (127-A1).

33. Various scholars have discussed the natural-VII to the tonic motion, among other musical factors, as a signpost for musical archaism. See, for instance, Jonathan Bellman, *"Aus alten Märchen*: The Chivalric Style of Schumann and Brahms," *The Journal of Musicology* 13, no. 1 (Winter 1995): 119–120.

34. Annette Kreutziger-Herr, "Imagining Medieval Music: A Short History," *Studies in Medievalism: Correspondences: Medievalism in Scholarship and the Arts* 14 (2005): 89.

35. John Haines, *Eight Centuries of Troubadours and Trouvères: The Changing Identity of Medieval Music* (Cambridge: Cambridge University Press, 2004), 164.

36. Ibid.

37. Bellman, *"Aus alten Märchen,"* 119, 129.

38. Joan Chissell, *The Master Musicians: Schumann* (London: Dent, 1948), 194.

39. Marjorie W. Hirsch, *Romantic Lieder and the Search for Lost Paradise* (Cambridge: Cambridge University Press, 2007), 216.

40. Ibid., 217–218.

41. Ibid., 217.

42. Hansjörg Ewert, *Anspruch und Wirkung: Studien zur Entstehung der Oper Genoveva von Robert Schumann* (Tutzing, Germany: Schneider, 2003), 243–245.

43. Ibid., 246. Original German: "Durch die Sequenzierung über den Dur-Dreiklang klingt diese Mittelstrophe näher am Volkslied." Translation my own.

44. Rufus Hallmark, "Robert Schumann: The Poet Sings," in *German Lieder in the Nineteenth Century*, ed. Rufus Hallmark (New York: Schirmer, 1996), 81.

45. Hirsch, *Romantic Lieder*, 221.

46. Bellman, *"Aus alten Märchen,"* 119.

47. Kreutziger-Herr, *Ein Traum vom Mittelalter*, 39. Incidentally, the English equivalent term, *Fatherland*, does not appear in Scott's *Ivanhoe*, the novel on which Marschner's opera is based.

48. Barbara Eichner, *History in Mighty Sounds: Musical Constructions of German National Identity, 1848–1914* (Woodbridge, UK: Boydell Press, 2012), 7, writes that "from the start…the German nation was only thinkable vis-à-vis a hostile 'other,' and for the most part of the nineteenth century France fulfilled that role."

49. Ibid., 246.

50. Ewert, *Anspruch und Wirkung*, 13. Notable figures included Franz Liszt, Louis Spohr, Giacomo Meyerbeer, Niels W. Gade, Ignaz Moscheles, and Franz Brendel, among others.

51. See *Allgemeine Musikalische Zeitung* (*AMZ*) VIII, no. 49 (December 3, 1873): 780; *Dwight's Journal of Music* (*DJM*) XXXIII, no. 19 (December 27, 1873): 149; *La Revue et Gazette Musicale de Paris* 42, no. 11 (March 14, 1875): 87; *AMZ* X, no. 17 (April 28, 1875): 269–270; *DJM* XXXV, no. 19 (December 25, 1875): 145–146. Dietrich Fischer-Dieskau, *Robert*

Schumann: Words and Music—The Vocal Compositions, trans. Reinhard G. Pauly (Portland, OR: Amadeus Press, 1988), 176–177, indicates that Schumann was rather hurt by negative reviews of the work and blamed the failure of the opera on the "shallow taste of the public and the strangle hold of foreign operas on fashionable opinion." Ewert, *Anspruch und Wirkung*, 191, points out that the oratorio-like choruses that frame the work left the best impression on early critics.

52. Eduard Hanslick, "Robert Schumann als Operncomponist," in *Die moderne Oper* (Berlin: Hofmann, 1875), 256–257. Original German: "Das entsprach dem Romantiker in Schumann; deutsch-mittelalterliches Wesen, christliche Frömmigkeit, mystische Wunder, endlich sogar Anklänge an's Volkslied—alle vier Elemente der deutschen Romantik treffen hier zusammen." Translation my own.

53. Ibid., 261. Original German: "Unzählige feine Intentionen mögen in dieser Partitur stecken, aber sie kommen nicht heraus. Wie viele französische und italienische Operncomponisten, die künstlerisch tief unter Schumann stehen, schreiben bessere Opern!" Translation my own.

54. V., "Genoveva von Robert Schumann," *Signale für die Musikalische Welt* 8, no. 27 (July 1850): 265. Original German: "Was die Wahl des der Oper zum Grunde gelegten Stoffes betrifft, so darf dieselbe eine entschieden glückliche genannt werden; denn ganz abgesehen von der erfolgreichen Verwendbarkeit dieses Stoffes zu mannigfachen dramatischen Zwecken, hat derselbe in der uralten Legende von der Genoveva, die mit der deutschen Volkspoesie verwachsen ist, von vorne herein schon die Sympathien der Massen für sich." Translation my own.

55. Franz Brendel, "R. Schumann's Oper: Genoveva," *Neue Zeitschrift für Musik* 33, no. 1 (July 2, 1850): 2. Original German: "Ich fordere von der Oper der Gegenwart ein anderes Interesse, als was durch diesen Stoff geboten werden kann. Mag man immerhin in die Vorzeit zurückgehen, die frühere Sagengeschichte, unsere Volkspoesie, insbesondere aber die großen Gestalten der alten deutschen Poesie neu erzeugen in dem modernen Bewußtsein. Ich halte diesen Weg nicht blos für den richtigen, ich halte ihn für den durch die Zeit gebotenen, der zuerst unserer Oper einen neuen Aufschwung verleihen wird. Es mangelt in der Oper der Gegenwart ein neues Ideal hinsichtlich der zu behandelnden Stoffe, und dieß ist der, meines Wissens noch nicht ausgesprochene tiefer liegende Grund, weßhalb keine Oper der leßten Epoche in das Volksbewußtsein einzudringen vermochte." Translation my own.

56. Ibid. Original German: "Stets war es eine bestimmt ausgeprägte Richtung, welche in einer Zeitepoche die vorherrschende war. Jeßt fehlt ein solcher Mittelpunkt, überall werden Versuche gemacht, man tappt umher; Richard Wagner ist wohl der Glücklichste gewesen in der Wahl der Stoffe; aber das Ideal, welches von Allen gesucht wird, Alle befriedigt, ist noch nicht gefunden. Mag man demnach, sage ich, in die Vorzeit immerhin zurückgehen— ich erblicke in diesen Stoffen die Lösung des Räthsels der Gegenwart*)—die Geschichte der Genoveva vermag in der Gegenwart nicht mehr zu befriedigen." Translation my own.

57. In a similar vein, a concert review of the overture to *Genoveva* that appeared in the Boston-based *Dwight's Journal of Music* states that Schumann's opera failed "greatly owing, no doubt, to its ill-chosen romantic subject," *DJM* XXV, no. 26 (March 17, 1866): 207.

58. Brendel, "R. Schumann's Oper," 2. Original German: "z.B. die Nibelungen, die wären sie als Oper vorhanden gewesen, in den leßten Jahren bei dem Streben nach deutscher Einheit, bei der Besinnung auf das große Gesammtvaterland, gewiß von außerordentlicher Wirkung gewesen sein würden." Translation my own.

CHAPTER 8

··

RICHARD WAGNER'S
MEDIEVAL VISIONS

··

BARBARA EICHNER

WHEN Richard Wagner traveled from Paris to Dresden in April 1842, he caught a glimpse of the Wartburg castle "during the only sunlit hour of this journey. [...] Whereas I had already sensed the deep significance of the fact that I had crossed the legendary Rhine for the first time on my way home from Paris, it seemed a particularly prophetic indication that I should first sight the Wartburg, so rich in history and myth, at precisely this moment."[1] In Wagner's fertile retroactive imagination, the moment certainly became prophetic, since river and castle encapsulated the topics that would dominate his creative imagination for the rest of his life: the legends, stories, and myths from the (German) Middle Ages. No overview of Wagner's works fails to remark that every opera from *Tannhäuser* onward is based in some way on medieval material or set in the Middle Ages.[2] To these, the earlier opera *Rienzi* and the abandoned draft *Die Sarazenin* should also be added. While they build on existing medievalist fiction or historical scholarship rather than original sources, they are without doubt set in an unmistakably medieval milieu, just like *Die Meistersinger von Nürnberg*.[3] Or, to be precise, they are set in a world that Wagner (re-)created and that his contemporaries—and to some extent succeeding generations until today—recognized as a compelling invocation of the Middle Ages.

In his attempt to bring a lost past back to life—or rather, in Umberto Eco's acerbic remark, by fashioning the Middle Ages "as a sort of mythological stage on which to place contemporary characters"—Wagner was not alone.[4] When he began to immerse himself in medieval literature during his first Paris sojourn in the late 1830s, medievalism had already been prominent in both high art and popular culture for several decades, from Friedrich Schiller's historical dramas about Jeanne d'Arc and Wilhelm Tell, to Walter Scott's historical novels, to the paintings of the Nazarene brotherhood. Although it was part of the wider movement of historicism—that is, the discovery and creative appropriation of the past—the engagement with the Middle Ages in particular resonated strongly with the pan-European rise of nationalism around 1800 and its yearning for a golden age of (national) unity and glory. With regard to the representation of the Middle Ages on the operatic stage, Wagner was by no means a pioneer but could draw on—or distance himself from—medievalist models in repertoire works such as Carl Maria von Weber's *Euryanthe* (1823), Heinrich Marschner's *Der Templer und die Jüdin* (1829), Gaspare Spontini's *Agnes von Hohenstaufen* (1829), and Jacques Fromental Halévy's *La Juive* (1835). In Dresden, Wagner himself supervised the premieres of Marschner's *Kaiser Adolph von Nassau* (1845) and Ferdinand Hiller's *Konradin* (1847). A *Tanhäuser* by Carl Amand Mangold was premiered only months after Wagner's opera of the same name; Heinrich Dorn's *Die Nibelungen* (1854) pre-empted the completion of Wagner's *Ring* by two decades, and the medieval epic poem *Gudrun* inspired several operas between the 1850s and the 1880s.[5] What set Wagner apart from the majority of his predecessors and contemporaries—as well as epigones who continued writing medievalist operas into the twentieth century—was the intensity with which he read and researched medieval literature to craft his texts, a task that usually fell to the librettists.[6] Wagner's private library at Dresden would have been the envy of professional philologists, since it contained not only editions and translations of medieval texts but also up-to-date academic publications, and it was supplemented by the Dresden Royal Library.[7] Wagner the poet-composer thus unites two facets of the nineteenth-century medievalist endeavor, characterized by "a curious oscillation between fantastic neomedievalism and responsible philological examination."[8]

This aspect of Wagner's literary and musical output has elicited considerable scholarly interest. Specialists in German or Old Norse literatures as well as musicologists have meticulously traced Wagner's inspiration back to its medieval sources and their nineteenth-century editions, untangling in the process the many false leads the composer left in his autobiographical writings. Volker Mertens and more recently Danielle Buschinger offer comprehensive overviews of Wagner's entire output and its medieval sources. Joachim Heinzle prefaces his contribution to the anniversary *Wagner Handbuch*, which succinctly summarizes the relationship between operas and sources, with a thoughtful introduction to Wagner's understanding of myth and mythology.[9] Of the studies dedicated to individual operas, only some can be mentioned here, for example, Mary A. Cicora's investigations of *Tannhäuser* and *Parsifal* and their literary sources. The convoluted genesis of the *Ring* and its complicated relationship to German as well as Old Norse literature has attracted several in-depth studies, notably Elizabeth Magee's careful evaluation of the books that Wagner actually did possess and read; Árni Björnsson's scene-by-scene comparison, which claims the lion's share of Wagner's inspiration originated from the Icelandic tradition, and Deryck Cooke's sadly unfinished book *I Saw the World End*, which interweaves an in-depth interpretation of the music and meaning of the *Ring* with an account of the medieval models. Others have shown how medieval literature influenced not only plotlines but also the very fabric of the music dramas, for example, through the deployment of archaisms and archaizing neologisms or the transfer of the nonlinear interlace design of medieval romance into the text and music of the operas.[10] In retracing Wagner's steps, many authors not only comment on the thoroughness with which the composer engaged with the material, but also highlight the quality of his engagement. Mertens, on the one hand, contrasts Wagner's reception of medieval texts with that of other artists, who used medieval themes "less because of their mythic potential than because of their Romantic coloring." Wagner, on the other hand, seeks "a universal humanity (which is how he interpreted myth)."[11] This not only is somewhat patronizing toward Wagner's contemporaries, but also casts Wagner in the double role of the most painstaking philologist as well as the artist who transcended the "limitations" of his medieval materials. Such a reading is in thrall to Wagner's negative assessment of his source materials, which needed, in his view, the master's hand to be restored to their true meaning: the expression of the "purely human." Wagner's self-serving claims should always be taken with a grain of salt, particularly when no other nineteenth-century composer's—or for that matter librettist's—creative adaptation of medieval sources has been scrutinized with equal scholarly rigor.

In contrast to the bulk of past scholarship, the present chapter will not mainly be concerned with Wagner's relationship with and adaptation of his medieval sources. Rather than asking how he arrived at a particular vision of the Middle Ages, I will focus on the kind of Middle Ages he created. What was important for him about this era? Is there anything that sets his vision apart from medievalist operas by contemporary composers? Were they recognized as distinctly medieval or particularly successful with critics and audiences? It must be borne in mind, however, that we are missing a vital aspect for the successful evocation of the past: the mise en scène. Surviving stage models, newspaper illustrations, or costume figurines give important visual clues, but they cannot replace the immersive experience enjoyed by nineteenth-century audiences. The Paris Opéra led the way with stagings that became an "integral and unalterable [...] aspect of the finished work," and painstaking historical research was undertaken to "gratify audiences' demand for complete scenic illusion."[12] Wagner fully supported this aesthetic, which is attested not only by the fact that he drew on the expertise of Édouard Desplechin, stage designer for *Les Huguenots* and *La Juive*, for the first production of *Tannhäuser*. He also tried, well before he could direct model performances at Munich or Bayreuth, to control the visual element with the same attention to detail with which he crafted his scores. He strongly resisted suggestions to reuse the great hall of Charlemagne from Weber's *Oberon* for the premiere of *Tannhäuser*, since he "did not want a brilliant throne room but rather the particular scenic vision I had conceived, which could only be called forth according to my specifications."[13] When Franz Liszt prepared the first performance of *Lohengrin*, Wagner sent him detailed performance instructions, including sketches for the scenery and decoration (poking gentle fun at his inability to draw trees in perspective) and referred him to the stage directions for the *Personenführung*.[14] And when it became apparent that he would not be able to conduct any *Tannhäuser* performance in the 1850s, he published a treatise, "Über die Aufführung des Tannhäuser," and circulated stage designs based on the Dresden premiere, which at least smaller theaters were obliged to observe if they wanted to put Wagner's first nationwide operatic success on the stage (see Figure 8.1, an illustration of the Wartburg hall).[15]

Attention to detail does not, of course, automatically equal historical correctness. As Annette Kreutziger-Herr astutely remarks about Desplechin's designs for the Dresden *Tannhäuser*, every historically educated audience member must have been aware that

FIGURE 8.1 "*Szenarium* for Richard Wagner's *Tannhäuser* (ca. 1850), Universität- und Landesbibliothek Darmstadt, Hs. 3933, p. 16 (detail)." Used with permission.

the operatic Wartburg looked nothing like the real castle in the early thirteenth century. Historical correctness is subordinate to the stylization of an ideal past, an artificial medieval paradise designed to satisfy nineteenth-century desires.[16] This aspect of Wagner's magic is irretrievably lost today, not only because the medieval "look" that enthused audiences in the 1850s would seem dated today (in the same way that costume dramas start showing their age after a few decades), but also because opera has—at least in Europe—turned its back on stage realism and instead embraces *Regietheater*'s temporal and spatial displacements. Current medievalist visions are rarely an option for contemporary directors: stagings of *Lohengrin* with the aesthetic of a Ridley Scott movie or the *Ring* tetralogy with a nod to *Game of Thrones* are rare and would potentially be just as controversial as historicist pedantry.

   In another aspect, Wagner did not aim for historical veracity. He never tried very hard to capture the actual music of the Middle Ages.[17] The contrapuntal soundscape of *Die Meistersinger von Nürnberg* owes more to Wagner's studies with *Thomaskantor* Theodor Weinlich and the nineteenth-century enthusiasm for J. S. Bach as an exemplar of "true German art" than to late-medieval *Meistersinger* lore and melodies. When Wagner wrote the first prose draft of the opera in 1845, he had studied Georg Gottfried Gervinus's *Geschichte der poetischen National-Literatur der Deutschen* (1840–1844), which contained detailed information about the *Meistersingers* and Hans Sachs, but no melodies. Only when he revisited the sketch in 1861 did he study Johann Christoph Wagenseil's *Buch von der Meister-Singer holdseligen Kunst* (1697), which gave not only examples of original poems but also melodies or *Töne*, one of which inspired the so-called King David motif associated with the *Meistersinger* guild in the opera.[18] But even access to original material did not necessarily influence Wagner's artistic conception. While medieval *Minnesinger* melodies were available in Friedrich Heinrich von der Hagen's edition of 1838, Wagner decided that standard harp arpeggios would be sufficient to give his Wartburg song contest a medieval hue—if one does not want to follow Larry Bomback's cautious suggestion that the repeated-tone figure of Wolfram's and Walther's contributions owes something to the *Minnesingers'* recitation patterns.[19] In the 1840s, the rediscovery of medieval and early Renaissance music was only in its infancy, and since it was not yet a living, performed reality, nineteenth-century audiences would probably have failed to appreciate attempts at sonic archaeology. Wagner even castigates his French colleagues for seeking inspiration and national "color" in folk melodies as a "novel secret to galvanize the half-decomposed corpse of opera."[20] As his later operas move away from the set pieces that attracted local or temporal coloring, the question of incorporating authentic medieval music became less urgent. Even in those cases when the music is required to hint at temporal remoteness Wagner creates material that derives its authentic feel from what audiences imagined, rather than from what they knew about the Middle Ages. Hagen's call to the Gibichung vassals in act 2 of *Götterdämmerung* evokes a sense of the archaic not because it references specific early-medieval music, but because its limited range, repetitive simplicity, and the framing with the rude sounds of the *Stierhorn* contrast so strongly with the complexity of the rest of the score. Likewise, the unison melodies of the Grail Knights in acts 1 and 3 of *Parsifal* invoke liturgical-ritualistic chanting, but their shape and tonal centering is none too similar to genuine chant melodies. It should be remembered that Wagner probably had little experience of Gregorian chant as a living practice, because his duties at the Catholic court church in Dresden included the conducting of choral–orchestral masses on Sundays and feast days.[21] Throughout Germany, the rediscovery and liturgical revival of medieval chant only slowly got underway in the second half of the century. Any chant-like melodies might thus have been inspired by the medievalist inventions such as Franz Liszt's *Die Legende der heiligen Elisabeth* or other contemporary oratorios, Wagner's disdain for the art form notwithstanding.

Thus, while operatic medievalism did not depend on philological or historical correctness for its success, Wagner certainly popularized medieval plotlines and poetry for a wider audience and thus gave a boost to the fledgling academic discipline of medieval studies.[22] In turn, his adaptations gave rise to creative misunderstandings or interpretations that persist in contemporary scholarship thanks to the impact of the operas. For example, discussions of the medieval *Tristan* romance center on Gottfried von Strassburg's revolutionary conception of love rather than his rethinking of vassalage relationships because Wagner was interested in the former rather than the latter. Interpretations of the love poems of the historical Wolfram von Eschenbach have focused on the elevated rather than the bawdy or playful part of his output because of the chaste outpourings of his operatic alter ego in *Tannhäuser*.[23] Even more noticeable is the effect of Wagner's medieval imaginings on later writers and other artists, becoming "a kind of conduit through which medieval narratives pass on their way to later adapters and interpreters," channeling them toward a general public that might only dimly be aware that "their" Middle Ages are constructed from Wagnerian building blocks.[24] Wagner's influence on the development of medievalism and on the reception of the Middle Ages more generally has been enormous and cannot be elucidated here; the final section of this chapter will offer a few glimpses of this vast panorama. But even within the confines of his own oeuvre, Wagner created many different visions of the Middle Ages that coexisted with— and to some degree contradicted—one another. Instead of the customary chronological presentation of Wagner's development, the operas will therefore be grouped in three categories: the *chivalric*, the *civic*, and the *mythic* Middle Ages. This more systematic and diachronic reordering is intended to tease out some of the contradictions but also unexpected resonances of his medieval(ist) visions.

Chivalric Medievalism

The first group of Wagner's "mature" (i.e., Bayreuth-worthy) works is often subsumed under the rubric *romantic* operas and, in that configuration, usually comprises *Der fliegende Holländer* (1843), *Tannhäuser und der Sängerkrieg auf der Wartburg* (1845), and *Lohengrin* (1848/1850). For the present purpose of exploring medievalism in Wagner's operas, however, *Der fliegende Holländer* will not be considered, since its setting is essentially timeless and could take place at any time before the invention of the steamboat. Instead, the focus will be on *Tannhäuser* and *Lohengrin* as well as the draft of *Die Sarazenin*. At first, this may not seem like an obvious choice, because *Die Sarazenin* is loosely based on actual historical events as narrated in Friedrich von Raumer's six-volume *Geschichte der Hohenstaufen und ihrer Zeit* (1823–1825), rather than the mixture of medieval literature, folk tales, and legends that fed into *Tannhäuser* and *Lohengrin*. This aligns *Die Sarazenin* with Wagner's other historical opera *Rienzi*, and the composer himself pointed out the similarity when he characterized *Die Sarazenin* as a step back toward the five-act format of grand opera, which he had overcome when the Tannhäuser story gripped his imagination.[25] The differing source material aside, all three operas are set recognizably in an age of chivalry, with courts, battlefields, knights, and kings, and all three are explicitly anchored in historical time and space: *Die Sarazenin* telescopes events from Sicilian and South Italian history in 1254 to 1258, dramatizing the power struggle of Manfred, the illegitimate son of Emperor Friedrich II, with a fictional love interest added by a mysterious Saracen woman who turns out to be Manfred's half-sister. The score of *Tannhäuser* places the action in and near the Thuringian Wartburg Castle at the beginning of the thirteenth century, and *Lohengrin* is set in the first half of the tenth century, with educated listeners probably being aware that the historical King Heinrich I (the Fowler) defeated the Hungarians in 933. The creation of the three operas is also more closely intertwined than Wagner's memoirs have led us to suppose. While the first inspiration for *Die Sarazenin* can be dated back to the Paris years, Wagner fashioned the prose draft in Dresden in January to February 1843.[26] The prose draft of *Tannhäuser* actually dates to the preceding summer and was only versified in the spring of 1843 when Wagner had given up on the *Sarazenin* project; the text of *Lohengrin* followed two years later.

The latter opera is often seen as the culmination of Wagner's efforts to create a convincing vision of the Middle Ages. The composer himself claimed to have "provided a complete portrait of the Middle Ages" in *Lohengrin*, and Cosima Wagner concurred that *Lohengrin* "is the only monument that shows the *beauty* of the Middle Ages."[27] A critic of the 1850 premiere was particularly excited about the specific German qualities of Wagner's vision, greatly overestimating the historical fidelity of the opera: "Just like *Tannhäuser*," he asserts,

> *Lohengrin* is rooted in the rich, wondrous soil of patriotic legends, wherefrom the best, freshest flowers and fruits of medieval epic poetry have sprung forth.... Wagner's poem... transfers us straight into the sphere of courtly love, of heroes and warriors, of fights, of the public and domestic conditions of *our ancestors*, a time of devout, faithful enthusiasm, of naivety, simplicity, energy and strength.... This poem mirrors faithfully German customs of earlier centuries.[28]

Even Friedrich Nietzsche, who otherwise rejected the Middle Ages for being hidebound to religion, exclaimed in his fourth *Untimely Meditation*, "Where else has the courtly Middle Ages been transformed into a flesh-and-blood figure as it has in Lohengrin?"[29] Novelist Heinrich Mann, the elder brother of writer and Wagnerian Thomas Mann, memorably ridiculed the Wilhelminian fondness for the opera in his novel *Der Untertan* of 1918. Protagonist Diederich Heßling visits the opera with his fiancée, wallows in the spectacle of medieval glory and heroism, compares it with the mediocrity of contemporary politics, and finally exclaims, "A thousand performances of such an opera, and there would be nobody left who isn't a nationalist!"[30] Interestingly, the fictional Diederich responded mainly to the visual and nationalist clichés, stereotypes Wagner had already inherited from *Ivanhoe* or *Euryanthe* and that have proved remarkably resilient, especially in popular culture: "Undergraduates... when asked about the Middle Ages, rarely speak of the thousand years from the fall of the Roman Empire (476) to the fall of Constantinople (1453)," sighs literary scholar Elizabeth Emery. "Instead, they tend to identify stereotypes drawn from fairy tales: knights, princesses, magic."[31] Wagner provides all three in his chivalric operas. Lohengrin and Elsa are the prototypes of the knight in shining armor and damsel in distress, and if Tannhäuser and Manfred themselves owed more to the type of the irresolute and somewhat dissolute romantic hero than to his epic counterpart, belligerent Biterolf and the entourages of the main protagonists represented the knightly, heroic stereotype.[32] Another stock character of medievalist opera was, at least since André Ernest Modeste Grétry's opera comique *Richard Cœur de Lion* of 1784, the minstrel or the minnesinger. Walther von der Vogelweide and Wolfram von Eschinbach (sic) perfectly embody ideals of self-effacing courtly love in their contributions to the song contest, shaping nineteenth-century understanding of *Minnesang* to the extent that music historian Hugo Riemann used examples from *Tannhäuser* to demonstrate the ethos of medieval song and poetry.[33]

These recognizably medieval types act in a staged world that is carefully calculated to evoke a distant past in all its glory. There is an abundance of historicist detail, such as the trial by combat in *Lohengrin*.[34] Other medieval tropes attached themselves to staples of the grand opera tradition, such as processions and religious ceremonies, for example, the entry of the guests to the Wartburg in act 2 of *Tannhäuser* or the interrupted wedding (complete with off-stage organ music) in act 2 of *Lohengrin*. In nineteenth-century performances, horses and dogs on stage would have added to the realistic impression of the hunting party in act 1 of *Tannhäuser* or the arrival of the counts in act 3 of *Lohengrin*, where the generous provision of diegetic music—here fanfares—adds to the dramatic illusion. The second half of act 2 of *Lohengrin* opens with a quaint depiction of life in a medieval castle, with two watchmen blowing the reveille and various servants and retainers going about their duties—a perfect "dramatized history painting."[35] To these romantic images familiar to and beloved by German audiences *Die Sarazenin* would have added an interesting visual and aural dimension: Not only were the opera's sets intended to reflect the oriental splendor of medieval Sicily, *Die Sarazenin* would also have featured an abundance of exoticist diegetic music, including a "Saracen" dance for Manfred's delectation in act 1 or Fatima's and Nuredin's "Arabian" wedding procession in act 4, which—in true grand opera fashion—would have been skillfully intercut with Manfred's acclamation as king of Apulia.[36] Since Wagner's later operas eschew the straightforward deployment of exotic *couleur locale*—the flower maidens of *Parsifal* sound nothing if not squarely European—it is regrettable that this opera never developed beyond the prose draft. Interestingly, Wagner scholars praise the composer for the earnestness with which he researched medieval lore, but paradoxically then dismiss the medievalism as mere decoration or coloring.[37] In this they follow the lead of the composer, who, in letters as well as the autobiographical *Eine Mittheilung an meine Freunde* (*A Communication to my Friends*, 1851), stresses the mythical roots and true meaning of his historical-romantic operas, pointing out parallels between Tannhäuser's escape from the Venusberg with Ulysses' flight from Circe and Calypso or the doomed relationship of Lohengrin and Elsa with Zeus and Semele.[38] This is, however, a transparent attempt to bring his earlier works (after *Rienzi*) in line with the "mythological turn" of the late 1840s. He employed the same trope when he explained why he abandoned Friedrich Barbarossa for Siegfried several years later.

In the same essay, Wagner forcefully rejected the suggestion that *Lohengrin* was at its core a Christian legend, stressing repeatedly its "purely human" essence. He maintained that the medieval poem had presented the figure in a dubious mystical form that at first filled him with distrust and repugnance, like the carved and painted roadside saints in Catholic countries.[39] Contemporary audiences, however, could have been forgiven for reading the opera in this way, since it was Wagner who introduced the good-versus-evil conflict of Christian knight and pagan witch to the medieval story. In contrast, the idea that Elisabeth's prayers bring about Tannhäuser's salvation is congruent with medieval beliefs, although her motivation—sublimated erotic love—belongs to the nineteenth century.[40] Critics were of two minds about the Christian elements of the opera: while a writer for the *Dresdner Anzeiger* declared that those who sensed a "Roman-Catholic tendentiousness" were mistaken, since the religious element was part of the necessary historical color, his colleague from *Didascalia* found the Tannhäuser subject "too medieval, reeking too much of relics and clergy."[41] In *Mein Leben*, Wagner even claims that others used *Tannhäuser* for propagating the German Catholic reform movement, which sought to liberate German Catholicism from its allegiance to Rome and its ecclesiastical hierarchies.[42] It is interesting to note that, compared with other contemporary medievalist operas, *Tannhäuser* and *Lohengrin* did not put priests, nuns, or monks on stage as dramatic characters, perhaps because this could have caused conflicts with censorship in Catholic countries; Wagner had probably learned from his experiences with staging *Rienzi* in Dresden when all references to the pope had to be eliminated.[43]

Nevertheless, the church plays an important role in *Die Sarazenin* and *Tannhäuser* (and *Rienzi*) as a powerful antagonist to the main characters, whether it is motivated by secular interests (holding on to power in Southern Italy) or religious concerns (controlling the penitents). Wagner offers interesting alternatives to mundane organized religion: the grail community, the sublimated love of "Saint" Elisabeth, and, most intriguingly, the vision of a religiously tolerant, ethnically mixed society in *Die Sarazenin*. "I was delighted even in those days," Wagner writes in *Mein Leben*,

> to find in the German mind the capacity to transcend national barriers and appreciate purely human qualities.... Friedrich II embodied this quality at its highest;...a monarch who gathered at his court the poets and sages of Eastern countries and...who had been betrayed by the Roman clergy to the infidel on his crusade..., who, excommunicated by the same church, struggled in vain against the raging bigotry.[44]

In Wagner's mind, however, these admirable traits were a particular quality of the German spirit inspired by ancient Greece, not necessarily a genuinely medieval heritage. Despite developing such viable alternatives to conventional depictions of religion on stage, *Tristan und Isolde* and the *Ring* dispensed with organized religion altogether: Hagen's cynical exhortation (in *Götterdämmerung*) to sacrifice to Fricka for a blessed marriage ironically highlights that divine rule is truly dead. Although religiosity is a central dramatic agent in the chivalric operas, the transcendent or miraculous is even more important. Fairy-tale elements (such as the magic mountain, the enchanted swan, or the vision of Manfred's departed father, Friedrich II) abound, and—crucially—they are not challenged by the humans experiencing them, which makes the people on stage convincingly medieval in the eyes of nineteenth- and twenty-first-century audiences. It is ironic that such credulousness in the face of the miraculous would have been considered foolish naiveté in the high Middle Ages when the *Lohengrin* poem was written.[45] Whatever the historical accuracy of plot, characters or scenery in tenth-century Antwerp or thirteenth-century Thuringia, the chivalric operas owe much of their medieval flair and authenticity to the fact that they occupy the same imaginary space as the fairy tales of the Brothers Grimm, the folk poetry collection *Des Knaben Wunderhorn*, or Novalis's fragmentary medievalist novel *Heinrich von Ofterdingen*.

Civic Medievalism

In contrast to the romantic operas, which are set largely in the courtly environment from which their medieval literary sources emanated, two stage works play out in medieval cities. *Die Meistersinger von Nürnberg* (1868) is set in mid-sixteenth-century Nuremberg and revolves around the historical figure of Hans Sachs, while *Rienzi, der letzte der Tribunen* (1842) charts the rise and fall of historic popular leader Cola di Rienzo in Rome during the years 1347 and 1354.[46] Putting one of Wagner's early, "noncanonic" operas and a mature masterpiece side by side might at first appear somewhat forced, but in combination they reveal changes and continuities in Wagner's approach to the Middle Ages. *Die Meistersinger* was immediately welcomed as a truthful depiction of the Middle Ages, with even Eduard Hanslick praising Wagner because "he turned his back to his dwarfs, giants and Valkyries, stands squarely in the real world and offers us images from the lives of medieval German people and citizens full of vitality."[47] While the plot is not based on a medieval model, the composer thoroughly researched the traditions of the *Meistersingers* with the aid of Johann Christoph Wagenseil's *Buch von der Meister-Singer holdseligen Kunst*, which he mined not only for the names of historic Meistersingers, but also for David's enumeration of the Meistersinger tunes and even some near-literal quotations in the "Tabulatur" (rule book) expounded in act 1.[48] Linguistic archaisms and quaint folklore add to the impression that *Die Meistersinger* is "the most realistic and historically accurate of all Wagner operas—which, in the context of an oeuvre that includes flying Valkyries and knights who sail away on swans, does not mean that it is a realistic or historically accurate opera," as Stephen Brockmann wryly remarks.[49] But the very fact that it is possible to point out inaccuracies and anachronisms reveals how specific the *Meistersinger* setting in an identifiable place and time actually is.[50] That time is usually identified as Middle Ages, though modern historians consider the mid-sixteenth century, post-Reformation era early modern; however, as will be shown later in this section, Wagner employs several strategies to medievalize his Nuremberg. In contrast, *Rienzi* is usually excluded from surveys of Wagner's medieval operas, because it is not set in the German Middle Ages and thus is not part of the nostalgic–nationalist narrative; Mertens even classifies *Rienzi* as a Renaissance story, though without further explanation.[51] In addition, the opera is based not on medieval sources, but instead on the contemporary novel *Rienzi, the Last of the Roman Tribunes* (1835) by Edward Bulwer-Lytton and possibly on contemporary dramatizations such as Mary Russell Mitford's play *Rienzi*. However, *Die Meistersinger* likewise owes a great debt to Nuremberg literature from the romantic age, most notably E. T. A. Hoffmann's story *Meister Martin der Küfner und seine Gesellen* (1819) and Johann Ludwig Deinhardstein's play *Hans Sachs* (1827), which Albert Lortzing transformed into a successful comic opera (1840). Thus, both of Wagner's *city operas* draw heavily on material already refracted through the lens of nineteenth-century sensibilities.

Wagner's contemporaries would have thought of Nuremberg and Rome as major European tourist destinations, although their attraction worked in different ways. Thanks to economic stagnation and restrictive building regulations, Nuremberg's inner city remained fundamentally unchanged between the sixteenth and the mid-nineteenth centuries, making it *the* destination for nostalgic travelers who wanted to revel in the glories of the past.[52] Rome, however, was one of the highlights of the *grand tour* that brought north European visitors to Italy, although they usually prioritized the remains of classical antiquity to the exclusion of the substantial medieval buildings and artworks. Opera audiences would thus have expected to recognize the outline of the city (such as the vista of Nuremberg in act 3 of *Meistersinger*) or prominent landmarks (such as the capitol in acts 2 and 5 of *Rienzi*), whether from their own travels or the ubiquitous paintings and prints. This need for recognition went so far that, in the first performance of *Rienzi* in Dresden, the façade of San Giovanni in Laterano (act 4) shows a stylized version of the neoclassical eighteenth-century façade, not the unadorned brickwork of the medieval church. And in preparation for the Munich premiere of *Die Meistersinger*, set designers Angelo Quaglio the Younger and Heinrich Döll were sent on a field trip to Nuremberg "to study the local architecture and to create sets that were historically authentic" or at least "true to the spirit, if not the letter, of the original."[53]

These realistic urban spaces are populated by different social strata that are more complex than the feudal society of knights and servants in *Tannhäuser*, *Lohengrin*, or *Tristan*. Mertens stresses this by heading his survey of *Meistersinger* "The Middle Ages as Social Milieu."[54] The lists of characters from both *Meistersinger* and *Rienzi* introduce a new social group, "citizens and their wives," or even, in *Rienzi*, "male and female citizens" (Bürger und Bürgerinnen). Wagner must have consciously used this politically loaded term to indicate the prominent role the citizens should take in shaping the fate of their communities, which ties in with ideals of civic participation before the Revolution of 1848/1849. When acting together as the chorus, the citizens of Rome bring about both Rienzi's elevation to the office of tribune and his downfall after they accuse him of ignoring the will of the people. In Wagner's Nuremberg, the middle-class craftsmen derive their claim to civic leadership from their "devotion not to money but to art," making the city "a kind of bourgeois paradise, full of free citizens whose highest embodiment is the charismatic Hans Sachs himself."[55] This does not, however, equal a classless society. Rienzi's Rome is torn by a clash between the aristocracy and the rest, and in Sachs's Nuremburg, both Sachs and Veit Pogner criticize the aristocracy's lack of artistic and patriotic spirit, whereas Walther von Stoltzing initially rejects the *Meistersinger's* chain of office as a bourgeois symbol. With the exception of Sachs himself, the middle-class Meistersingers, for their part, have a low opinion of "the people." While such careful gradations of rank and power made the world of the operas realistic and relevant to nineteenth-century audiences, they are not accurate depictions of medieval societies. Medieval and early-modern Nuremberg was actually ruled by a small group of inter-married dynasties that, from the late fifteenth century onward, called themselves *patricians* in humanistic emulation of the ruling elite of classical Rome.[56] Guilds were banned after the craftsmen's rebellion of 1348–1349, which gave them less political leverage than in comparable cities such as Augsburg or Cologne. In contrast, sixteenth-century Nuremberg boasted a thriving banking sector and international trade connections, an aspect that Wagner had to suppress if he wanted to stay true to his anticapitalist convictions.[57] It could thus be argued that the composer medievalizes the early-modern city by stripping away trade and commerce, creating a small-town idyll in place of a cosmopolitan metropolis.

In addition to the historicist topography and society, the cities in both these operas boast a religious soundscape anchored in their specific time and place. The Rome of *Rienzi* belongs to the Catholic Middle Ages, characterized by the Latin chanting of priests and monks (replaced because of censorship considerations with friars) in act 4 when Rienzi, expecting a Te Deum to celebrate his victory, stops outside San Giovanni in Laterano and hears the male choir intone, "Vae, vae tibi maledicto!" The scene is a variant of the interrupted-wedding trope of grand opera, which Wagner would utilize again in *Lohengrin*. The actual "chanting" of the basses in homophonic chords, however, bears little resemblance to Gregorian chant (the text has no traceable liturgical source either), but its homophonic chords, which are juxtaposed with a disregard for functional relations (e.g., D♭ major–E♭ minor–B♭ minor for the first two phrases), are modeled on nineteenth-century ideas of "pure church music" as articulated by Thibaut or Hoffmann.[58] On the operatic stage, the five-part, chordal Te Deum opening Jacques Fromenthal Halévy's *La Juive*, which Wagner knew well, provides a direct precursor.[59] Hans Sachs's Nuremberg, in contrast, has adopted Protestantism, which Wagner characterizes musically through Protestant hymnody. In the opening scene in St. Katherine's Church it is not a group of sinister priests and monks who chant Latin (pseudo-) liturgy, but the people themselves— men and women—who sing the chorale "Da zu dir der Heiland kam," a transparent adaptation of Luther's hymn "Christ, unser Herr, zum Jordan kam."[60] The hymn provides the framework for Walther and Eva's flirtation, and it grounds the Nuremberg congregation firmly in the early years of a religious movement that the nineteenth century considered genuinely German. Egon Voss, however, has suggested that nineteenth-century audiences would have heard the *Meistersinger* chorales not as an echo from a distant past but as part of their own, living, musical and religious tradition, as hymn singing was cultivated in middle-class homes as well as in church.[61] And the "Wach auf" chorus on the festival meadow in act 3, which is based on the opening lines of a poem celebrating Martin Luther by the historical Hans Sachs, is directed not so much at the citizens of Nuremberg and their guests on the operatic stage, but at the audiences, sending a clear message to Germans to awake from the political stupor of the 1850s and 1860s. Interestingly, *Rienzi* also contains a "Wake up" chorus, sung by a double choir at the end of act 1 from within the Church of San Giovanni in Laterano and preceded by a diegetic organ prelude. It provides both an interruption to and an intensification of the frenetic on-stage acclamations of Rienzi. However, while the "Wach auf" chorus from *Meistersinger* clothes its political message in natural imagery and an implied allusion to Martin Luther only accessible to the educated, the "Erwacht" chorus from *Rienzi* leaves nothing to the imagination:

Erwacht! Erwacht! Ihr Schläfer nah und fern,	Awake! Awake! You sleepers near and far,
und hört die frohe Botschaft an:	and hear the glad tidings:
daß Romas schmacherloschner Stern	that Rome's star, expired in ignominy
vom Himmel neues Licht gewann.	has received new light from heaven.
Seht, wie er strahlt und sonnengleich	See, how it blazes and like a sun
in ferne Nachwelt siegend bricht!	victoriously shines on distant posterity!
Zur Nacht sinkt Schmach, so totenbleich,	Ignominy, deathly pale, sinks into night,
zum Wonnetag steigt Freiheitslicht!	the light of freedom rises to a joyful day!

In both operas, the "Wake up" choruses occupy parallel dramatic positions. They precede speeches by the charismatic leaders that contain the central message of the opera—Rienzi's follows immediately, Hans Sachs's admonition half an act later—and they capture the precise moment when the respective populations come together as true civic communities.[62] The scenes are, however, placed differently within the operas: while the apotheosis of Hans Sachs concludes *Die Meistersinger*, Rienzi's acclamation happens at the beginning of the work and marks the climax of the tribune's career before his downfall. As John Deathridge perceptively points out, *Rienzi* uses the revolutionary plotline of grand opera but turns it into "a didactic and somewhat pessimistic attempt to envisage the…aftermath of a bloodless revolution," which disintegrates because of the leader's errors of judgment.[63] Whereas in *Die Meistersinger* the popular outbreak of violence in the famous choral "fugue" at the end of act 2 precedes the "Wach auf" chorus and is resolved in the general jubilation on the festival meadow, in *Rienzi* the people wreak death and destruction at the very end of the opera.

Nevertheless, the parallels between the communities in *Meistersinger* and *Rienzi* can be extended further, beyond the shared violent undercurrents and their celebration of charismatic leadership figures. In both operas the civic communities look back on a past that is explicitly articulated within the works, a *two-storied medievalism* that sets them apart from the romantic operas where some characters but not the communities are conscious of their (pre-)history.[64] The *Meistersingers* are keenly aware that they are the only practitioners of an art that was formerly esteemed at princely courts, and this consciousness of their role as guardians of true, German art partly explains why they desperately cling to their rules until Hans Sachs and Walther von Stoltzing—himself nostalgic for the poetic age of his namesake Walther von der Vogelweide—carefully inject new enthusiasm into a fossilizing practice.

Whereas *Die Meistersinger* looks nostalgically back from the sixteenth to the thirteenth century (by no accident, the time when the literary works were created that formed the basis of Wagner's other operas), for *Rienzi* the point of reference is the Rome of classical antiquity, when Rome was peaceful and free. The spirit of the Roman Empire is hibernating in the medieval city (just as Nuremberg preserves the spirit of German art against the disintegration of the Holy Roman Empire), and the tension between the sordid present and a more glorious past motivates Rienzi to bring about a future that will make Rome great again. The conflict between and reconciliation of past and present finds its expression in the ballet of act 2: after the pantomime of Tarquinius and Lucretia (which was not included in the final orchestral score), knights in medieval costumes rush on stage, challenging the Roman warriors, who vanquish them. The allegory of peace appears accompanied by young women in classical and medieval dress. The unification of medieval present and classical past culminates in a dance where each medieval maiden partners with a classical warrior and each classical virgin with a medieval knight. However, the celebration is interrupted by the aristocrats' attempt to assassinate Rienzi. The reconciliation of past and present thus remains a transient vision, furthermore, one that was choreographed by Rienzi himself, not a part of the "life of the people" like the procession of the guilds in act 3 of *Die Meistersinger*. The possibility of a brighter future is only hinted at in Rienzi's final words, which, at least in the revision of 1847, promised (or maybe threatened?) the return of the tribune as long as Rome still stands. It could thus be argued that *Rienzi* is set in the Middle Ages not only because the era provided a colorful backdrop for a political parable; Wagner has located his opera in the very historiographic spot that nineteenth-century historians assigned to the actual Middle Ages: literally an uneasy middle age of discord and decay between the glorious past of classical antiquity and the promises of modernity.

Mythic Medievalism

Much has been made of Wagner's decisive turn away from history and toward myth as the foundation of his later music dramas. Scholarship and popular reception alike have followed, often unquestioningly, the leads the composer provided in *Eine Mittheilung an meine Freunde*, where he presents the turning point as a decision between an opera (or perhaps even a spoken drama) about the historical emperor Friedrich I "Barbarossa" (1122–1190) and the legendary hero Siegfried, the protagonist of the medieval *Nibelungenlied*.[65] In Wagner's historical construction, Barbarossa was "the historical rebirth of the ancient, pagan Siegfried," but the necessity to represent the social complexities (Verhältnisse) of the twelfth century on stage put him off the historical character and led him to "pure myth," as embodied in Siegfried.[66] This is once more a retrospective obfuscation, as the prose drafts for a five-act drama *Friedrich I* continue into December 1848, when the text of *Siegfrieds Tod* (the first version of what became *Götterdämmerung*) had already been completed. Nevertheless, it is correct that in his later operas, despite continued or even intensified engagement with medieval texts from a range of traditions, the Middle Ages retreat further and further into a mythical sphere that Wagner conceives as universal and timeless. The heroes continue wielding swords and lances, and horses and ships are the preferred mode of transportation between manorial halls, castles, and untamed nature, but none of the operas completed after 1848—with the exception of *Meistersinger*—is set in a recognizably historical time or, indeed, place. Again, Wagner antedates this shift in emphasis to the Dresden years, reminiscing that the architect (and later radical coactivist) Gottfried Semper "considered me the representative of a Catholic medievalism and fought against it with fury. It took me a lot of effort to convince him at length that my studies and inclinations were really concentrated on German antiquity and the discovery of the ideals inherent in the early Germanic myth."[67] This antagonism of medievalism and (German) antiquity begs the question of how medieval *Der Ring des Nibelungen* (1848–1876), *Tristan und Isolde* (1859/1865), *Parsifal* (1882), or other projects such as the prose scenario for *Wieland der Schmied* actually are, beyond their origins in medieval literature.

If Wagner's disdain for the somewhat obscure, anonymous thirteenth-century *Lohengrin* novel and the romantic reworkings of the *Tannhäuser* legend are to some extent comprehensible, his criticism of the *Nibelungenlied* went against the grain of contemporary reception. At its rediscovery in the mid-eighteenth century, the epic poem (probably written in today's border region between Germany and Austria around 1200) had at first aroused the interest of antiquarians and philologists only, but with the surge in patriotic feeling in the wake of the Napoleonic Wars, the demand for a national literature became more urgent. Poets, philologists, and philosophers such as Friedrich and August Wilhelm Schlegel, Friedrich Schelling, and von der Hagen saw the *Nibelungenlied* as "a collective creation that reflected the 'German national character.'"[68] Whether the medieval poem ever attained the status of a German national epos—as comparisons with Homer's *Iliad* insinuated—remains open to debate, but there were no lack of attempts to recreate the *Nibelungenlied* for the present.[69] Felix Mendelssohn Bartholdy, Giacomo Meyerbeer, and Robert Schumann are only the most well-known composers who at some point contemplated (and abandoned) the idea of a Nibelungen opera, and reproductions of the Nibelung cycles by painters such as Peter Cornelius and Julius Schnorr von Carolsfeld shaped the visual imagination of the educated middle classes. After the patriotic fervor of the Napoleonic Wars deflated in the reactionary era, the reception of the *Nibelungenlied* focused less on the heroic scenes (such as Siegfried's fight with the dragon or the final battle at the court of Attila the Hun) and more on the episodes of conjugal love and family feeling, which seemed to embody a host of bourgeois virtues that were construed as specifically German: keeping faith, youthful innocence, purity of spirit and body, and family values.[70] Up to the German unification of 1870/1871 and until the wider impact of the *Ring* made itself felt, the main character to exercise the national imagination was Kriemhild, who transforms from conventionally sweet princess to merciless avenger.

Wagner's decision to focus on *Siegfrieds Tod* as the nucleus of the story, which he later extended into the *Ring*, and to cast him as a revolutionary free spirit was thus somewhat unusual in the late 1840s. He was able to conceive an alternative hero by extending his immersion into medieval literature beyond the *Nibelungenlied*, at the same time downplaying the extent to which the medieval poem had shaped his creative imagination.[71] "My studies," Wagner emphasizes in *Eine Mittheilung an meine Freunde*,

> carried me from the medieval poetry through to the foundations of the old, ur-German myth.... Although the wonderful figure of Siegfried had long attracted me, he completely delighted me when I had successfully stripped away all later coating and saw him in his purest, human form. Only now I realized the possibility to make him the hero of a drama, which had never crossed my mind as long as I only knew him from the medieval *Nibelungenlied*.[72]

In contrast to *Tannhäuser* and *Lohengrin*, where Wagner had to reconstruct a putative mythical core of the medieval poems, for the *Ring* he found a ready-made literary tradition that seemed to have preserved the archaic stories that in the *Nibelungenlied* were overlaid by courtly tastes and fashions: the Old Norse *Poetic Edda* and *Prose Edda*, which transmit the lore of the Nordic Gods, and the *Völsunga Saga*, which tell the stories of Sigurd and his ancestors, Brynhildr, Gudrun, and their offspring. Wagner was not the only one who looked beyond the German medieval tradition. The philosopher Friedrich Theodor Vischer advocated in 1844 the Nibelungs as an ideal subject for a national opera and compared the respective suitability of the German and Eddic versions for specific scenes.[73] Likewise, when the poet Ludwig Rellstab suggested a Nibelung opera to Meyerbeer in 1847, he included Norns and Valkyries in the outline of the first two acts.[74] But while these Eddic inspirations might have been more ornamental than structural—Rellstab's draft and Meyerbeer's response are sadly lost—Wagner refashioned the Nibelung story by merging it with the fate of the Nordic gods, thus creating a "cosmological framework" for the Siegfried plot where the death of the free hero brings about the self-imposed downfall of the old rule.[75]

The reasons for this regression to a putatively more archaic and hence more mythical version of the story were artistic rather than philological. In Thomas Mann's succinct summary, "The saga was not enough for him: nothing less than the primal myth itself would do. Even the medieval *Nibelungenlied* signified modernity, distortion, theatricality, historicity—it was nowhere near primitive or musical enough for the sort of art he had in mind."[76] While Wagner certainly used his most advanced musical language to create an impression of archaic grandeur, the traces of the Old Norse sources are most apparent in the language of the *Ring* libretto. Not only did Wagner model his unrhymed verses on the alliterative short lines of the *fornyrðislag* meter (retaining *Stabreim* and the free stress pattern, while ignoring its stanzaic structure), which he had found in Ludwig Ettmüller's translation of the songs of the *Edda*, but also he invented Nordic-sounding names or revived archaisms based on an imaginative use of etymology.[77] This attempt to uncover an older and more authentic historical stratum of the story was mirrored in the costumes that Carl Emil Doepler designed for the 1876 Bayreuth premiere of *Der Ring des Nibelungen*. Rather than relying on the standard romantic imagery of the medieval knight or the classicizing attire for stage gods, Doepler extensively researched accessories and ornaments from the Scandinavian Bronze and Iron Age accessories and ornaments. However, it was this very attempt at historical accuracy and authenticity that displeased Richard and Cosima Wagner, who complained of the costumes' "ethnographic absurdity."[78] The difficulty of establishing a convincing iconography for the gods and heroes of the *Ring*, as well as the reception of the tetralogy, show that Wagner's conflation of Nordic and German aspects soon led to a "bewildering juxtaposition of ancient Germanic, Viking-age Scandinavian and [German] high-medieval elements."[79] This is most clearly seen in the spread of the horned helmet, today widely regarded as an authentic headgear of Viking warriors, but in fact an invention of Wagner's costume designer Doepler, which subsequently took on a life of its own.[80]

Wagner's attempt to demedievalize the Nibelungs by drawing on the *Eddas* and the *Völsunga Saga* ignores, however, that at least in their written form these texts emerged in the thirteenth century, that is, roughly contemporary with the *Nibelungenlied*, and as products of a post-Christianization literary culture. While the Old Norse sagas and mythological poems drew without doubt on older traditions—the exact extent to which they did so is hotly debated—their extant literary form responded to a specific need of high-medieval Icelandic elites to create an independent and venerable cultural tradition rooted in a shared pagan past. The interference of gods and other creatures of mythology in *Völsunga Saga* is thus not necessarily a sign of their greater age and closeness to an original myth, as Wagner understood it, but the Scandinavian poets interpolated the Nordic gods into heroic stories from continental Europe to give them a veneer of old age and authenticity.[81] The premedieval paganism of the *Ring* is thus a result of archaizing tendencies at play in the high-medieval Scandinavian literature itself, tendencies that Wagner used to escape the courtly medievalism of the *Nibelungenlied*. However, it had the desired effect to remove all traces of the Christian Middle Ages from the Nibelung story, thus setting it apart decisively from the romantic medievalism in *Tannhäuser* and *Lohengrin*. Again, Wagner was not alone in postulating that the Scandinavian tradition preserved ancient Germanic folklore and religion that had been lost in Germany as a result of the "Romanizing" influence of the church; Jacob Grimm's *Deutsche Mythologie* (1835) and Karl Simrock's edition of Eddic mythology (1851) tried to anchor this claim in solid academic evidence. However, from the late nineteenth century onward, the conflation of "Old Norse and Middle High German motifs [created] an impression, which has endured, that valkyries and norns, Valhalla and the twilight of the gods, were timelessly German."[82]

The nationalist discourse plays a lesser role in the reception of the two operas that interrupted or followed the completion of the *Ring*: *Tristan und Isolde* and *Parsifal*. While Wagner likewise assumed that the medieval models were reducible to a single-minded message and meaning, unlike the *Nibelungenlied* and *Völsunga Saga*, the medieval texts were not transmitted anonymously and could thus not be ascribed to the agency of the people. Gottfried von Strassburg's poem *Tristan* (written before 1210/1215) and Wolfram von Eschenbach's romance *Parzival* (ca. 1205–1210) were—and are— widely acknowledged as highlights of High Middle German literature, but unlike the *Nibelungenlied*, they were the preserve of specialists, not focal points of the national(ist) imagination. In both cases it was understood that the High Middle German poems in turn had been inspired by Old French models and pan-European Arthurian legends. Together with the risqué depiction of sexual desire and erotic danger in the second acts of *Tristan und Isolde* and *Parsifal*, respectively, the French-language romance heritage could lead to ambivalent reactions or outright rejection of the operas as un-German. The law specialist and poet Felix Dahn characterized *Tristan* as a "lying Celtic love affair" and contrasted it with the "Germanic" virtues demonstrated by the heroes and heroines of his spoken dramas.[83] And while *Parsifal* has been interpreted—and arguably intended—as the depiction of a racially pure (and purely masculine) mystic community, this was not a concept that lent itself to popular patriotism. In contrast to *Tannhäuser*, *Lohengrin*, and the *Ring*, the imagination of German audiences could not anchor itself in familiar landscapes and landmarks such as the Rhine or the Wartburg. Tristan's Cornwall is even less of a real place than the Flying Dutchman's Norway, and with the setting of *Parsifal* in the mountains of Gothic Spain (Montsalvat) and the hills of Arabic Spain (Klingsor's magic castle), Wagner revisits the Mediterranean landscapes of *Die Sarazenin*. For the first Bayreuth performance of 1882 and subsequent revivals until well into the twentieth century, the grail castle was modeled on the cathedral of Siena, a cupolaed hall shrouded in a mystical twilight that contrasted with the light-flooded spaces of transalpine Gothic churches. Although Wagner had equated the Holy Grail with a spiritual conception of the "Hoard of the Nibelungs" in his historiographical fantasy *Die Wibelungen* and thus connected the legendary treasures with world history seen through a German lens,[84] when he came to create *Parsifal*, "both time and space have disintegrated and metaphysically merged. Wagner's mythical world is new indeed."[85]

In part because the *Ring*, *Tristan*, and *Parsifal* share a tendency to move away from dramatic action toward epic reflection, Wagner's use of the medieval sources (especially for the latter two works) was radically different from that which he employed for his chivalric and his civic operas.[86] Rather than merging or conflating several traditions and sources, he radically reduced the action-rich plots of the medieval models to a sparse three-act structure that he considered the true core of the underlying "myth" that the medieval author had obscured. When he returned to the *Tristan* story in the autumn of 1854, he criticized the dramatic plans of his friend Karl Ritter because he "had confined himself to the adventurous incidents of the romance, while I had been immediately struck by its innate tragedy and was determined to cut away all the inessentials from this central theme."[87] Such incidentals included, for example, the episode where Brangäne substitutes herself for Isolde in King Marke's marital bed, a humorous touch at odds with Wagner's tragic conception of the story. Gottfried von Strassburg imagined the existential power of love as an adulterous relationship that has to founder on the conventions of society, but his lovers can grant "precisely through their love…absolute status to the highest of all courtly values and remain members of courtly society. In Wagner, by contrast, the lovers' end is one of mystic transfiguration." Whereas for the Middle Ages "love is transcendent only by analogy" to the divine, in Wagner's Schopenhauerian reading, "love is the *only* transcendental entity in a world that has become trivial."[88] A similar process is at work in *Parsifal*. Not only does Wagner strip down Wolfram von

Eschenbach's medieval "road movie" with its plethora of cast, locations, and subplots to a single-minded focus on rejection and redemption, but also he despaired over the poet's perceived inability to grasp the "actual content" of his story. As Wagner wrote in a famous letter to Mathilde Wesendonck from May 30, 1859,

> He [Wolfram] piles episode on episode, adventure on adventure, offers curious and strange images with the Grail motive and leaves the serious [reader] with the question, what did he actually want?...Wolfram is immature through and through, mainly due to his barbarian, completely confused age which hovered between the old Christianity and the new form of the state. In such an age nothing could ever be perfected; the profundity of the poet is immediately submerged in formless phantasm....Really, one only has to bring to life such a story from the true characteristics of the legend, as I did with the Grail legend, and then quickly compare, how a poet, like Wolfram, presented the same...in order to be repulsed by the incompetence of the poet. (I felt the same with Gottfried v. Strassburg in relation to Tristan.)[89]

In his attempts to distill the true meaning of the grail story, Wagner then practically inverts the central message of the medieval romance.[90] Whereas Wolfram's *Parzival* celebrates the many varieties of love, including physical and erotic love, Wagner reduces it in nineteenth-century fashion to an opposition of dangerous, destructive desire (activated in Amfortas and Klingsor by Kundry) and its negation in more or less enforced abstinence and celibacy.[91] While a figure like the seductress Kundry in act 2 does reflect medieval types such as Eve or Mary Magdalene, her despair over her fate betrays her modern, nineteenth-century consciousness. Nietzsche's criticism that *Parsifal* is a "Catholic revival" for once misses the mark.[92] While there is doubtless a "presence of important Christian relics, rituals, terminology, and phraseology," all these "borrowings" appear in quotation marks[93] and thus should not be understood as nostalgic re-enactments of medieval rites. Wagner's message of regeneration was intended to point contemporary audiences toward the future, not toward the past.

Aftermath

In his later operas Wagner reveals himself, as Edward R. Haymes perceptively observed, "as a reluctant medievalist, a medievalist who really did not like the Middle Ages," since he saw them "as a period his national myths had passed through on their way to [the] more nearly definitive form in his dramas."[94] Thus we return to the paradox observed earlier in this chapter: that Wagner's research into medieval literature, customs, and lore was unusually thorough, but that he freely adapted the sources because he was not satisfied that they could communicate his aesthetic and political visions. This, however, did not deter his contemporaries or successors from enthusiastically adopting Wagner's medievalisms for their own ends. Not only did Wagner's operas spark an interest for the original poems and romances outside a narrow circle of professional philologists, but also his storylines, stage designs, and to a lesser extent even his music had a pervasive impact on the medievalist fantasies of subsequent generations. A reception history of "Wagner's Middle Ages" would require a book of its own; thus, only a few pointers can be given here.

The first monuments to Wagner's medieval visions were built on a truly grandiose scale by his main benefactor, King Ludwig II of Bavaria. In 1868 he wrote to the composer about his project of building a new castle in the place of the ruined Hohenschwangau, which would become "a worthy temple for the divine friend, who alone brings salvation and true blessings to the world. You will likewise find reminiscences from *Tannhäuser* (the singers' hall with a vista of the castle in the background) and *Lohengrin* there (court-yard, open passage, the way to the chapel)."[95] Like at Hohenschwangau, the castle his father Maximilian II had built, murals with scenes from German medieval literature and legend adorned the walls, including those that formed the basis of Wagner's operas. However, the influence of the operas was even more pervasive. The architect Christian Jank had to integrate ideas from the performances at the Munich Court Opera, which is particularly apparent in the inner courtyard, closely modeled on the *Lohengrin* set designs by Angelo Quaglio the Younger.[96] While Neuschwanstein was still a construction site, Ludwig II focused his attention on a hunting lodge, which from 1869 onward was transformed in the bijou palace Linderhof. The palace itself is decorated in neo-Rococo style, but the extensive park features two "reconstructions" of sites from Wagner's operas: the grotto of Venus from *Tannhäuser* and Hunding's hut from act 1 of *Die Walküre*. Although these buildings were originally intended only as realizations of the monarch's escapist fantasies, they soon became major tourist attractions. Particularly the neo-Gothic Neuschwanstein encapsulates for many what a medieval castle *should* look like, a feeling that has been reinforced by serving as one of the inspirations for the Sleeping Beauty Castle at Disneyland, although the top of the Disney castle was turned sideways to minimize the resemblance to Neuschwanstein.[97] Since 1985, the silhouette of the castle has become a global icon through its adaptation for Walt Disney Pictures.

Wagner's operas certainly had an impact on the film music of movies, although the direct influence that is ritually invoked by ambitious screen composers and film critics is in itself something of a cliché and is not always borne out by musical analysis.[98] Wagnerian influences are most frequently observed—or invoked—for the epic fantasy genre, which usually rely heavily on underscoring as well as more or less developed leit-motivic allusions.[99] It seems that the epic-heroic plots and imagery, partly inspired by the grandeur of Wagner's *Ring*, and the Wagnerian soundscapes often travel together, the indebtedness to the composer being implicitly assumed rather than explicitly articulated. A special case in this genre is the score of Peter Jackson's Lord of the Rings trilogy, where this dual connection is very clearly articulated: On the one hand, Wagner's *Ring* (despite the protestations of the author to the contrary was one of the many sources that fed into J. R. R. Tolkien's novels, although some similarities stem from the fact that both authors drew on the same Old Norse material.[100] On the other hand, composer Howard Shore repeatedly acknowledged Wagner's inspiration in interviews, including a more complex approach to leitmotivic technique than usually heard in the cinema.[101] As

Stephen C. Meyer has shown, Shore—like Wagner—makes hardly any attempt to create a historical soundscape, and where there are medieval reminiscences, either they can be traced back to prior medievalisms (such as the music for the Ringwraiths inspired by Carl Orff's archaizing chorus "O Fortuna" from *Carmina Burana*) or the very attempt to create an authentic diegetic sound, as in Éowyn's pseudo-Anglo-Saxon lament, threatens to undermine "the full immersion by drawing attention to musical manipulation."[102] Thus, it could be argued that a loosely conceived "Wagnerian" score appears to be "correct" for the vaguely medieval, feudal-heroic worlds of epic fantasy, since Wagner himself had bridged over the chronological gap between prehistoric or medieval storylines and the music of advanced romanticism.

At this point, the discussion of Wagner's Middle Ages crosses over into the realm of the neomedieval. As Umberto Eco hinted as early as 1975 in his taxonomy of medievalisms, where Wagner's works feature both in the category of operatic pretext and in the Dark Ages,[103] the operas have become in themselves sources of medievalist inspiration, which his successors freely use instead of or in addition to engaging with the historic Middle Ages. Wagner's medieval visions are thus feeding into the "self-conscious, ahistorical, non-nostalgic imagining or reuse of the historical Middle Ages that selectively appropriates iconic images, often from other medievalisms."[104] An extreme example of the appropriation of such an iconic image that gestures toward the Middle Ages but has become iconic thanks to its prominent role in Wagner's *Lohengrin* is the swan knight, which has made a surprising reappearance in toy shops as "Peppa Pig Once upon a Time Fairytale Swan."

The reference to the opera is probably lost on the majority of parents or children (and was maybe already lost on the toy designers), because the Wagnerian image has been totally absorbed into the vaguely medievalist realm of fairy tales, where the "push-along swan" is marketed side by side with a dragon, a pumpkin carriage, and an "enchanting [!] tower." Instead of deploring this as an abuse of high art, we should remember that Wagner himself had not created "his" Middle Ages from a blank slate, but had already reused and reinterpreted the medieval visions of poets, painters, and philologists before him, making him a neomedievalist *avant le lettre* and one of the most powerful catalysts in the appropriation of the Middle Ages in the ongoing medievalist project.

Notes

1. Richard Wagner, *My Life*, trans. Andrew Gray, ed. Mary Whittall (Cambridge: Cambridge University Press, 1983), 219.
2. All of Wagner's stage works will be addressed as operas to avoid the hierarchy implicit in calling some operas and others music dramas or stage festival plays.
3. For the purposes of this chapter, the setting of *Meistersinger* will be considered medieval, although historians usually have the early-modern era begin with the Reformation. For more on the ways in which the division between the medieval and Renaissance (or early-modern) eras manifested itself in nineteenth-century music and music history in

Germany, see Laura K. T. Stokes's essay in this volume, "Medievalisms in Early Nineteenth Century Thought," pp. 17–37. For a discussion of the ways in which this division was understood in nineteenth-century France, see Diana Hallman's contribution to this volume, "The Distant Past as Mirror and Metaphor: Portraying Medievalism in Historical French Grand Operas," pp. 109–134.

4. Umberto Eco, "The Return of the Middle Ages," in *Faith in Fakes. Travels in Hyperreality*, ed. Umberto Eco, trans. William Weaver (London: Minerva, 1995), 61–85, here 68.

5. Wolfram Klante, "Carl Ludwig Amadeus Mangolds *Tanhäuser*-Oper," in *Tannhäuser in der Kunst*, ed. Heinrich Weigel, Wolfram Klante, and Ingrid Schulze (Bucha bei Jena: Quartus, 1999), 112–132, 251–268. Barbara Eichner, *History in Mighty Sounds: Musical Constructions of German National Identity, 1848–1914* (Woodbridge, Suffolk, UK: Boydell, 2012), especially chap. 1, "The Pure Mirror: National Epic as National Opera," 41–80.

6. This trend was first analyzed by Theodor Kroyer, "Die circumpolare Oper. Zur Wagnergeschichte," in *Jahrbuch der Musikbibliothek Peters für 1919*, vol. 26, ed. Rudolf Schwartz (Leipzig: Peters, 1920), 16–33. For a more recent overview see Jens Malte Fischer, "Singende Recken und blitzende Schwerter: Die Mittelalteroper neben und nach Wagner. Ein Überblick," in *Mittelalter-Rezeption: Ein Symposium*, ed. Peter Wapnewski (Stuttgart: Metzler, 1986), 511–530.

7. Elizabeth Magee, *Richard Wagner and the Nibelungs* (Oxford: Clarendon Press, 1990), chaps. 2 and 3.

8. Eco, "The Return of the Middle Ages," 63. The term *neomedievalism* has itself been the subject of a lively scholarly discourse. See, for example, the essays collected in *Studies in Medievalism XIX: Neomedievalism* and *Studies in Medievalism XX: Neomedievalism II* (both edited by Karl Fugelso). See also the introduction to this volume by Stephen Meyer and Kirsten Yri, pp. 1–13.

9. Volker Mertens, "Wagner's Middle Ages," in *Wagner Handbook*, ed. Ulrich Müller and Peter Wapnewski, trans. Stewart Spencer, translation ed. John Deathridge (Cambridge, MA: Harvard University Press, 1992), 236–268; a more substantial version is available in German by Volker Mertens, "Richard Wagner und das Mittelalter," in *Richard Wagner und sein Mittelalter*, ed. Ursula Müller and Ulrich Müller (Anif/Salzburg: Verlag Ursula Müller-Speiser, 1989), 9–84. Danielle Buschinger, *Le Moyen Age de Richard Wagner* (Amiens: Presses de l'Université de Picardie-Jules Verne, 2003). Joachim Heinzle, "Mythos, Mythen und Wagners Mittelalter," in *Wagner Handbuch*, ed. Laurenz Lütteken (Kassel: Bärenreiter; Stuttgart & Weimar: Metzler, 2012), 102–109.

10. Mary A. Cicora, *From History to Myth: Wagner's* Tannhäuser *and Its Literary Sources* (Bern: Lang, 1992); "Medievalism and Metaphysics: The Literary Background of Parsifal," in *A Companion to Wagner's* Parsifal, ed. William Kinderman and Katherine R. Syer (Rochester, NY: Camden House, 2005), 29–53. The relationship of Wagner's *Ring* with its sources is covered in Magee, *Richard Wagner and the Nibelungs*, 25–56; Árni Björnsson, *Wagner and the Volsungs: Icelandic Sources of* Der Ring des Nibelungen (London: Viking Society for Northern Research, 2003); Deryck Cooke, *I Saw the World End: A Study of Wagner's* Ring (London: Oxford University Press, 1989). To these studies, Ulrich Müller's and Oswald Panagl, eds., *Ring und Gral. Texte, Kommentare und Interpretationen zu Richard Wagners "Der Ring des Nibelungen," "Tristan und Isolde," "Die Meistersinger von Nürnberg" und "Parsifal"* (Würzburg: Königshausen und Neumann, 2002) should be added. For the influence of medieval language on Wagner see Nikolaus Henkel, "Wagners

Vorstellungen von den Nibelungen: Einblicke in das Mittelalter-Gedächtnis des 19. Jahrhunderts," in *Wagners Siegfried und die (post-)heroische Moderne*, ed. Tobias Janz (Würzburg: Königshausen & Neumann, 2011), 135–156. This article builds on Oswald Panagl, "'Vermählen wollte der Magen Sippe dem Mann ohne Minne die Maid': Archaisches und Archaisierendes in der Sprache von Wagners *Ring*," in *Richard Wagner und sein Mittelalter*, 157–170. In English, Stanley R. Hauer, "Wagner and the *Völospá*," in *19th-Century Music* 15, no. 1 (1991): 52–63, offers a good introduction to Old Norse poetry. J. P. E. Harper-Scott, "Medieval Romance and Wagner's Musical Narrative in the *Ring*," *19th-Century Music* 32, no. 3 (2009): 211–234.

11. Mertens, "Wagner's Middle Ages," 237.

12. Simon Williams, "The Spectacle of the Past in Grand Opera," in *The Cambridge Companion to Grand Opera*, ed. David Charlton (Cambridge: Cambridge University Press, 2003), 58–75, here 61. For the integral role of stage design and staging for nineteenth-century (French) opera, see also Rebecca S. Wilberg, "The Mise-en-Scène at the Paris Opera: Salle Le Peletier (1821–1872) and the Staging of the First French Grand Opéra—Meyerbeer's *Robert le Diable*" (PhD diss., Brigham Young University, 1990); Nicole Wild, "La question de la mise en scène à l'époque du grand opéra," in *Le répertoire de l'Opéra de Paris (1671–2009): Analyse et interprétation*, ed. Michel Noiray and Solveig Serre (Paris: École des Chartes, 2010), 313–320. Several national traditions are covered in *Opera in Context: Essays on Historical Staging from the Late Renaissance to the Time of Puccini*, ed. Mark A. Radice (Portland, OR: Amadeus, 1998), including Douglas E. Bomberger, "The Neues Schauspielhaus in Berlin and the Premiere of Carl Maria von Weber's *Der Freischütz*," 147–169; Karin S. Pendle and Stephen Wilkins, "Paradise Found: The Salle Le Peletier and French Grand Opera," 171–207; Evan Baker, "Richard Wagner and His Search for the Ideal Theatrical Space," 241–278. There is less research about the staging of grand opera in the German-speaking countries in particular, but *Meyerbeers Bühne im Gefüge der Künste*, ed. Sibylle Dahms, Manuela Jahrmärker, and Gunhild Oberzaucher-Schüller (Feldkirchen: Ricordi, 2002) covers several aspects of Meyerbeer stagings and reception.

13. Wagner, *My Life*, 302.

14. Letter to Franz Liszt, July 2, 1850, in *Richard Wagner: Sämtliche Briefe*, vol. 3, *Briefe der Jahre 1849–1851*, ed. Gertrud Strobel and Werner Wolf (Leipzig: VEB Deutscher Verlag für Musik, 1975), 344.

15. Richard Wagner, "Über die Aufführung des Tannhäuser," in Richard Wagner, *Gesammelte Schriften und Dichtungen*, 2nd ed., vol. 5 (Leipzig: Fritzsch, 1887), 123–159. For the "Scenarium," see Hartmut Säuberlich, "Die Dekorationspläne der frühen Tannhäuser-Aufführungen," *Maske und Kothurn: Vierteljahresschrift für Theaterwissenschaft* 8 (1962): 74–84; Dietrich Steinbeck, ed., *Richard Wagners* Tannhäuser-*Szenarium* (Berlin: Selbstverlag der Gesellschaft für Theatergeschichte, 1968). The influences of grand opera design on *Tannhäuser* and the historicity of the set designs are discussed in Sven Friedrich, " 'Mit diesem Werk schrieb ich mir mein Todesurteil': *Tannhäuser* und die 'Grand Opéra,' " in *"…der Welt noch den Tannhäuser schuldig": Richard Wagner: Tannhäuser und der Sängerkrieg auf der Wartburg*, ed. Irene Erfen (Regensburg: Schnell und Steiner, 1999), 47–73; and, in the same volume, Oswald Georg Bauer, "Nicht das Historische, sondern das Charakteristische: Bemerkungen zum Bühnenbild des Tannhäuser," 195–220.

16. Annette Kreutziger-Herr, *Ein Traum vom Mittelalter: Die Wiederentdeckung mittelalterlicher Musik in der Neuzeit* (Cologne: Böhlau, 2003), 82.

17. Michael Scott Richardson contends that Wagner did resurrect the medieval (?) bar form and incorporated stylistic elements of chant, Palestrinaesque harmonies, and baroque forms, thus striving for "antique" sounds that should be considered medievalist. This understanding of antiquarianism, however, would be problematic if applied to scenery or plot lines and seems to somewhat stretch the remit of medievalism. Michael Scott Richardson, "Evoking an Ancient Sound: Richard Wagner's Musical Medievalism" (MMus diss., Rice University, 2009), 61–62.

18. For a survey of Wagner's engagement with and knowledge of preclassical music, see Martin Geck, "Richard Wagner und die ältere Musik," in *Die Ausbreitung des Historismus über die Musik*, ed. Walter Wiora (Regensburg: Gustav Bosse, 1969), 123–146. Wagner's access to and use of nineteenth-century *Meistersinger* research is set out in John Warrack, *Richard Wagner* Die Meistersinger von Nürnberg (Cambridge: Cambridge University Press, 1994), chap. 1, "The Sources and Genesis of the Text," 1–37, and chap. 3, "Sachs, Beckmesser and Mastersong," 49–65.

19. Larry Bomback, "Wagner's Access to Minnesinger Melodies prior to Completing *Tannhäuser*," *The Musical Times* 147, no. 1896 (2006): 19–31.

20. Richard Wagner, "Oper und Drama," in *Gesammelte Schriften und Dichtungen*, 2nd ed. (Leipzig: Fritzsch, 1887), 3:266: "Ein neues Geheimniß, den halbverwesten Leib der Oper zu galvanisiren, war gefunden, und so lange konnte die Oper nun wieder leben, als man irgend noch nationale Besonderheiten zur Ausbeutung vorfand."

21. Claudia Heinze and Manfred Fensterer, "Die Messen von Carl Gottlieb Reissiger," and Martin Geck, "Richard Wagners Beschäftigung mit geistlicher Musik während seiner Dresdner Zeit," in *Die Dresdner Kirchenmusik im 19. und 20. Jahrhundert*, ed. Matthias Herrmann (Laaber: Laaber, 1998), 89–104 and 121–132, respectively.

22. Ulrich Müller, "Vom *Parzival* zum Liebesverbot: Richard Wagners Umgang mit dem Mittelalter—vier Thesen. Mit zwei Postscripta: Wagners ungeschriebene Oper von *Erec und Enide*, und: zur mittelalterlichen Musik on Wagners Mittelalter-Stoffen," in *Richard Wagner und sein Mittelalter*, ed. Ursula Müller and Ulrich Müller (Anif/Salzburg: Verlag Ursula Müller-Speiser, 1989), 85–102, here 85.

23. Müller, "Vom *Parzival* zum Liebesverbot," 80.

24. Ray M. Wakefield, "Middle Ages," in *The Cambridge Wagner Encyclopedia*, ed. Nicholas Vazsonyi (Cambridge: Cambridge University Press, 2013), 302–303, here 303.

25. Richard Wagner, "Eine Mittheilung an meine Freunde," in *Gesammelte Schriften und Dichtungen*, 2nd ed. (Leipzig: Fritzsch, 1888), 4:272: "Mit der "Sarazenin" war ich im Begriffe gewesen, mehr oder weniger in die Richtung meines "Rienzi" mich zurückzuwerfen, um eine große fünfaktige "historische" Oper zu verfertigen: erst der überwältigende, mein individuelles Wesen bei weitem energischer erfassende Stoff des Tannhäusers, erhielt mich im Festhalten der mit Notwendigkeit eingeschlagenen neuen Richtung."

26. Bernhard Zegowitz, *Richard Wagners unvertonte Opern* (Frankfurt am Main: Lang, 2000), 107–109.

27. Cosima Wagner, *Cosima Wagner's Diaries*, vol. 2, *1878–1883*, ed. Martin Gregor-Dellin and Dietrich Mack, trans. Geoffrey Skelton (London: Collins, 1980), 319 (June 6, 1879).

28. Fr. M., "Lohengrin: Andeutungen zu Richard Wagner's gleichnamiger Oper," in *Frankfurter Konversationsblatt* 1245 (November 25, 1850), col. 1122b, reprinted in *Situationsgeschichte der Musikkritik und des musikalischen Pressewesens in Deutschland, dargestellt vom Ausgange des 18. bis zum Beginn des 20. Jahrhunderts*, ed. Helmut Kirchmeyer, part 4, *Das zeitgenössische Wagner-Bild*, vol. 3, *Dokumente 1846–1850* (Regensburg: Gustav Bosse, 1968),

col. 779: "Wie der 'Tannhäuser,' so wurzelt auch 'Lohengrin' in jenem reichen, wundersamen Boden des vaterländischen Sagenkreises, aus welchem die mittelalterliche epische Poesie ihre besten, frischesten Blüten getrieben und Früchte gezeitigt hat.... Schon das Gedicht Wagner's...versetzt uns mitten hinein in den Kreis der Minne, des Helden- und Kriegertums, der Kämpfe, der öffentlichen und häuslichen Zustände unserer Vorvordern, in die Zeit hingebender, gläubiger Begeisterung, schlichten Sinnes, der Einfachheit, Thatkraft und Stärke... Es ist dies Gedicht... ein treuer Spiegel deutscher Sitte der früheren Jahrhunderte."

29. Volker Mertens, "Mittelalter und Renaissance," in *Wagner und Nietzsche. Kultur—Werk—Wirkung: Ein Handbuch*, ed. Stefan Lorenz Sorgner, H. James Birx, and Nikolaus Knoepffler (Reinbek bei Hamburg: Rowohlt, 2008), 79–105, here 79; Friedrich Nietzsche, *Untimely Meditations*, trans. R. J. Hollingdale (Cambridge: Cambridge University Press, 1983), 206.

30. Heinrich Mann, *Der Untertan* (Leipzig-Wien: Kurt Wolff Verlag, 1918), 379: "Tausend Aufführungen einer solchen Oper, und es gab niemand mehr, der nicht national war!"

31. Elizabeth Emery, "Medievalism and the Middle Ages," *Studies in Medievalism* 17 (2009): 77–85, here 79.

32. Simon Williams, *Wagner and the Romantic Hero* (Cambridge: Cambridge University Press, 2004), 8–16.

33. Kreutziger-Herr, *Ein Traum vom Mittelalter*, 87–88.

34. Volker Mertens, "Durch Gottes Sieg...Gottesurteile im *Lohengrin* und anderswo," in *Wagnerspectrum* 10, no. 1: *Schwerpunkt: Lohengrin* (2014): 61–80.

35. Mertens, "Richard Wagner und sein Mittelalter," 30.

36. Bernd Zegowitz suggests that the opening theme of *Die Sarazenin* inspired the Venusberg scenario in *Tannhäuser*. Zegowitz, *Richard Wagners unvertonte Opern*, 139–140; Richard Wagner, *Sämtliche Werke*, vol. 31, *Dokumente und Texte zu unvollendeten Bühnenwerken*, ed. Isolde Vetter and Egon Voss (Mainz: Schott, 2005), 207 and 218.

37. For example, Buschinger, *Le Moyen Age de Richard Wagner*, 150.

38. Wagner, "Eine Mittheilung an meine Freunde," 289–291.

39. Wagner, "Eine Mittheilung an meine Freunde," 288.

40. Mertens, "Richard Wagner und sein Mittelalter," 28 and 21.

41. Helmut Kirchmayer, *Situationsgeschichte der Musikkritik und des musikalischen Pressewesens in Deutschland, dargestellt vom Ausgange des 18. bis zum Beginn des 20. Jahrhunderts. Das zeitgenössische Wagner-Bild*, vol. 2, *Dokumente 1842–1845* (Regensburg: Gustav Bosse, 1967), cols. 637 and 643: "Das Sujet ist auch zu mittelalterlich, riecht zu sehr nach Reliquien und Klerus."

42. Wagner, *My Life*, 313.

43. See, for example, Wagner's letters to Theodor Winkler (February 23, 1841) and Ferdinand Heine (March 18, 1841). For a summary, see Eugen Mehler, "Rienzi und die Dresdener Theaterzensur," *Die Musik* 46, no. 10 (1913): 195–201.

44. Wagner, *My Life*, 210.

45. Lisa Feurzeig, "Don't Ask: Faith, Magic, Knowledge, and Sources in *Lohengrin*," in *Wagner outside the* Ring: *Essays on the Operas, Their Performance and Their Connections with Other Arts*, ed. John Louis DiGaetani (Jefferson, NC: McFarland, 2009), 80–104, here 83.

46. The historical Hans Sachs (1494–1576) was a widower only in 1560/1561, between his first and his second marriages.

47. Eduard Hanslick, *Die moderne Oper: Kritiken und Studien* (Berlin: Hofmann, 1875), 299: "Er wendet endlich seinen Zwergen, Riesen und Walkyren den Rücken, stellt sich mitten

in die reale Welt und gibt uns lebensvolle Bilder aus dem deutschen Volks- und Bürgerleben des Mittelalters."

48. Egon Voss, "Es klang so alt, —und war doch so neu, —Oder ist es umgekehrt? Zur Rolle des Überlieferten in den *Meistersingern von Nürnberg*," in Egon Voss, *"Wagner und kein Ende": Betrachtungen und Studien* (Zurich: Atlantis, 1996), 145–154, here 146.

49. Stephen Brockmann, *Nuremberg: The Imaginary Capital* (Rochester, NY: Camden House, 2000), 99.

50. Brockmann, *Nuremberg*, 100.

51. Mertens, "Mittelalter und Renaissance," 86–87.

52. Stewart Spencer calls this aspect of the cityscape *neomedieval*: Stewart Spencer, "Wagner's Nuremberg," in *Cambridge Opera Journal* 4, no. 1 (1992): 21–41, here 24.

53. Spencer, "Wagner's Nuremberg," 33.

54. Mertens, "Wagner's Middle Ages," 263.

55. Brockmann, *Nuremberg*, 103–104.

56. Peter Fleischmann, *Rat und Patriziat in Nürnberg: Die Herrschaft der Ratsgeschlechter vom 13. bis zum 18. Jahrhundert*, vol. 1, *Der kleinere Rat* (Neustadt an der Aisch: Schmidt, 2008), 227.

57. Brockmann, *Nuremberg*, 100.

58. See Stokes, "Medievalisms in Early Nineteenth-Century German Thought."

59. Diana Hallman discusses the Te Deum from *La Juive* on pp. 112–119 of her essay, "The Distant Past as Mirror and Metaphor."

60. Arthur Groos, "Constructing Nuremberg: Typological and Proleptic Communities in *Die Meistersinger*," *19th-Century Music* 16, no. 1 (1992): 18–34, here 20.

61. Egon Voss, "*Die Meistersinger von Nürnberg* als Oper des deutschen Bürgertums," in Voss, *"Wagner und kein Ende,"* 118–144, here 143–144.

62. It is no coincidence that studies of both operas stress the community-building aspect, although usually separately. For example, see Groos, "Constructing Nuremberg," and Rachel Nussbaum, "Wagner's *Rienzi* and the Creation of a People," *The Musical Quarterly* 84, no. 3 (2000): 417–425.

63. John Deathridge, *Wagner's* Rienzi: *A Reappraisal Based on a Study of the Sketches and Drafts* (Oxford: Clarendon Press, 1977), 21.

64. Edward R. Haymes, "Two-Storied Medievalism in Wagner's Die Meistersinger von Nürnberg," *Studies in Medievalism* 3 (1991): 505–513.

65. In his essay *Die Wibelungen: Weltgeschichte aus der Sage* (Leipzig: Otto Wigand, 1850), Wagner even connects the medieval Staufen dynasty with an archaic conception of kingship expressed in the myth of Siegfried and the treasure ("Hort") of the Nibelungs via the forced etymological equivalence of the Ghibellines (pro-emperor faction) with the "Wibelungen" and the "Nibelungen."

66. Wagner, "Eine Mittheilung an meine Freunde," 312–315. For the general myth making in this essay, see Barbara Eichner, "Eine Mittheilung an meine Freunde: Lebens- und Schaffensmythen in der letzten Zürcher Kunstschrift" in *Wagner—Gender—Mythen*, ed. Christine Fornoff and Melandie Unseld (Würzburg: Königshausen & Neumann, 2015), 89–105.

67. Wagner, *My Life*, 321.

68. Otfried Ehrismann, "Reception of the *Nibelungenlied* in Germany," in *The Nibelungen Tradition. An Encyclopedia*, ed. Francis G. Gentry, Winder McConnell, Ulrich Müller, and Werner Wunderlich (New York, London: Routledge, 2002), 219–224, here 220. Starting

with Ehrismann's work in 1975, *Das Nibelungenlied in Deutschland: Studien zur Rezeption des Nibelungenlieds von der Mitte des 18. Jahrhunderts bis zum Ersten Weltkrieg* (Munich: Fink, 1975), there is a plethora of studies about the *Nibelungenlied* reception, of which only a few can be named here. Joachim Heinzle and Anneliese Waldschmidt, eds., *Die Nibelungen. Ein deutscher Wahn, ein deutscher Alptraum: Studien und Dokumente zur Rezeption des Nibelungenstoffs im 19. und 20. Jahrhundert* (Frankfurt am Main: Suhrkamp, 1991), takes a critical view of the political appropriation. Ebba-Christina Hagenberg-Miliu, "…*Denn nur der Ruhm des Vaterlandes ist mein Ziel": Zu Erneuerungen des Nibelungen- und des Kudrunepos* (PhD diss., Bonn, 1988), and Annegret Pfalzgraf, *Eine deutsche Ilias? Homer und das 'Nibelungenlied' bei Johann Jakob Bodmer: Zu den Anfängen der nationalen Nibelungenrezeption im 18. Jahrhundert* (PhD diss., Marburg, 2003), explore the *Nibelungenlied* as a national epic. The musical reception is covered in Christa Jost, "Die Nibelungen auf dem Weg zur Oper," in *Nibelungenlied und Klage: Ursprung—Funktion—Bedeutung*, ed. Dietz-Rüdiger Moser and Marianne Sammer (Munich: Institut für Bayerischer Literaturgeschichte, 1998), 483–505, and Bernd Zegowitz, "Die Nibelungen vor dem *Ring*: Zur (Vor)Geschichte eines Opernstoffes," in *Getauft auf Musik: Festschrift für Dieter Borchmeyer*, ed. Udo Bermbach, Hans Rudolf Vaget, and Yvonne Nilges (Würzburg: Königshausen & Neumann, 2006), 257–274.

69. For a critical view, see Klaus von See, "Das Nibelungenlied—ein Nationalepos?," in *Die Nibelungen: Ein deutscher Wahn, ein deutscher Alptraum*, 43–110.

70. von See, "Das Nibelungenlied—ein Nationalepos?," 65; Eichner, *History in Mighty Sounds*, 55–63.

71. See Edward R. Haymes, "*Ring of the Nibelung* and the *Nibelungenlied*: Wagner's Ambiguous Relationship to a Source," *Studies in Medievalism* 17 (2009): 218–246.

72. Wagner, "Eine Mittheilung an meine Freunde," 312: "Meine Studien trugen mich so durch die Dichtungen des Mittelalters hindurch bis auf den Grund des alten urdeutschen Mythos…Hatte mich schon längst die herrliche Gestalt des *Siegfried* angezogen, so entzückte sie mich doch vollends erst, als es mir gelungen war, sie, von aller späteren Umkleidung befreit, in ihrer reinsten menschlichen Erscheinung vor mir zu sehen. Erst jetzt auch erkannte ich die Möglichkeit, ihn zum Helden eines Dramas zu machen, was mir nie eingefallen war, so lange ich ihn nur aus dem mittelalterlichen Nibelungenliede kannte."

73. Friedrich Theodor Vischer, "Vorschlag zu einer Oper," in *Kritische Gänge*, ed. Friedrich Theodor Vischer (Tübingen: Ludwig Friedrich Fues, 1844), 2:399–436, here 411–414.

74. Ehrismann, "Reception of the *Nibelungenlied* in Germany," 279–280.

75. Hauer, "Wagner and the *Völospá*," 53.

76. Thomas Mann, "Richard Wagner and *Der Ring des Nibelungen*: November 1937," in *Pro and Contra Wagner*, trans. Allan Blunden (London: Faber & Faber, 1985), 171–183, here 180.

77. Hauer, "Wagner and the *Völospá*," 54–57; Panagl, "'Vermählen wollte der Magen Sippe dem Mann ohne Minne die Maid.'" 157–170; Henkel, "Wagners Vorstellungen von den Nibelungen," 145–150.

78. Frederic Spotts, *Bayreuth: A History of the Wagner Festival* (New Haven, CT: Yale University Press, 1994), 57–61; Wagner, *Cosima Wagner's Diaries*, 1:917 (July 28, 1876).

79. von See, "Das Nibelungenlied—ein Nationalepos?," 95.

80. Roberta Frank, "The Invention of the Viking Horned Helmet," in *International Scandinavian and Medieval Studies in Memory of Gerd Wolfgang Weber*, ed. Michael Dallapiazza, Olaf Hansen, Preben Meulengracht Sørensen, and Yvonne S. Bonnetain (Trieste: Edizioni Parnaso, 2000), 199–208, here 199.

81. This has been argued most decidedly by Klaus von See in "Das Heidentum in der Sicht des christlichen Mittelalters" and "Die Nibelungen auf skandinavischen Bilddenkmälern," in *Europa und der Norden im Mittelalter* (Heidelberg: Winter, 1999), 99–108 and 182–192, respectively.

82. Frank, "The Invention of the Viking Horned Helmet," 199.

83. Felix Dahn, *Erinnerungen: Viertes Buch. Würzburg—Sedan—Königsberg (1863–1888). Zweite Abtheilung (1871–1888)* (Leipzig: Breitkopf & Härtel, 1895), 382: "keltische Lügenliebschaft."

84. Wagner, *Die Wibelungen*, section XI: "Aufgehen des idealen Inhaltes des Hortes in den 'heiligen Gral,'" 64–68.

85. Cicora, "The Literary Background of *Parsifal*," 40.

86. Müller, "Vom *Parzival* zum Liebesverbot," 91.

87. Wagner, *My Life*, 511.

88. Mertens, "Wagner's Middle Ages," 258–259.

89. Wagner, *Sämtliche Briefe*, ed. Martin Dürrer (Wiesbaden: Breitkopf & Härtel, 1999), 11:105–106: "Er hängt Begebniss an Begebniss, Abenteuer an Abenteuer, giebt mit dem Gralsmotiv curiose und seltsame Vorgänge und Bilder, tappt herum und lässt dem ernst gewordenen die Frage, was er denn eigentlich wollte?... Wolfram ist eine durchaus unreife Erscheinung, woran allerdings wohl grossentheils sein barbarisches, gänzlich confuses, zwischen dem alten Christenthum und der neueren Staatenwirthschaft schwebendes Zeitalter schuld. In dieser Zeit konnte nichts fertig werden; Tiefe des Dichters geht sogleich in wesenloser Phantasterei unter.... Wirklich, man muss nur einen solchen Stoff aus den ächten Zügen der Sage sich selbst so innig belebt haben, wie ich diess jetzt mit der Gralssage that, und dann einmal schnell übersehen, wie so ein Dichter, wie Wolfram, sich dasselbe darstellte... um sogleich von der Unfähigkeit des Dichters schroff abgestossen zu werden. (Schon mit dem Gottfried v. Strassburg ging mir's in Bezug auf Tristan so)."

90. Müller, "Vom *Parzival* zum Liebesverbot," 90.

91. Mertens, "Richard Wagner und das Mittelalter," 77–78.

92. Friedrich Nietzsche, *The Case of Wagner, Nietzsche contra Wagner, and Selected Aphorisms*, 3rd ed., trans. Anthony M. Ludivici (Gloucester: Dodo Press, 2008), 57.

93. Cicora, "The Literary Background of *Parsifal*," 51.

94. Haymes, "The *Ring of the Nibelung* and the *Nibelungenlied*," 240.

95. Letter May 13, 1868, quoted in Michael Petzet, *Gebaute Träume: Die Schlösser Ludwigs II. von Bayern* (Munich: Hirmer, 1995), 46: "...ein würdiger Tempel für den göttlichen Freund, durch den einzig Heil und wahrer Segen der Welt erblüht. Auch Reminiscenzen aus Tannhäuser (Sängersaal mit Aussicht auf die Burg im Hintergrund) und Lohengrin (Burghof, offener Gang, Weg zur Kapelle) werden Sie dort finden."

96. Petzet, *Gebaute Träume*, 58–61.

97. Beth Dunlop, *Building a Dream. The Art of Disney Architecture* (New York: Disney, 2011), 23. The reference to "Bavarian Black Forest castles" is nonsense, because the Black Forest was never part of Bavaria. For (Walt) Disney's medievalisms and antimedivalisms more generally, see Susan Aronstein and Nancy Coiner, "Twice Knightly: Democratizing the Middle Ages for Middle-Class America," *Studies in Medievalism* 6 (1994): 212–231, and the volume edited by Tison Pugh and Susan Lynn Aronstein, *The Disney Middle Ages: A Fairy-Tale and Fantasy Past* (New York: Palgrave Macmillan, 2012).

98. For a critique of the simple equation of Wagnerian style and symphonic film scores, see Christoph Henzel, "Wagner und die Filmmusik," *Acta Musicologica* 76, no. 1 (2004): 89–115.

99. Stephen C. Meyer, "Soundscapes of Middle Earth: The Question of Medievalist Music in Peter Jackson's *Lord of the Rings* Films," *Studies in Medievalism* 18 (2010): 165–187, here 168–169.

100. For a summary of Tolkien's complicated relationship with Wagner and a comparison of both *Rings*, see Jamie McGregor, "Two Rings to Rule Them All: A Comparative Study of Tolkien and Wagner," *Mythlore* 29, nos. 3/4: 133–153, accessed January 2, 2018, https://dc.swosu.edu/mythlore/vol29/iss3/10.

101. Judith Bernanke, "Howard Shore's Ring Cycle: The Film Score and Operatic Strategy," in *Studying the Event Film* The Lord of the Rings, ed. Harriet Margolis, Sean Cubitt, Barry King, and Thierry Jutel (Manchester: Manchester University Press, 2008), 176–184, here 176.

102. Meyer, "Soundscapes of Middle Earth," 174.

103. Eco, "The Return of the Middle Ages," 68–69.

104. David W. Marshall, "Neomedievalism, Identification, and the Haze of Medievalisms," *Studies in Medievalism* 20 (2011): 21–42, here 22.

SECTION 2

PERFORMING THE MIDDLE AGES

CHAPTER 9

"WHAT ENGLAND HAS DONE FOR A THOUSAND YEARS"

Medievalism in Christmas Lessons and Carols Services

JACOB SAGRANS

IN 1941, the British Ministry of Information released a short propaganda film titled *Christmas under Fire*.[1] Showing the devastation of the Blitz bombing of Britain during the Christmas season of 1940, the film was aimed at encouraging Americans to join the war effort. Toward the end of the film, the narrator mentions that, even during the Blitz, "on Christmas Eve, England does what England has done for a thousand years: she worships the prince of peace."[2] Immediately following this statement comes footage of the Choir of King's College, Cambridge singing "Adeste fideles" ("O Come, All Ye Faithful") in the Festival of Nine Lessons and Carols service held every Christmas Eve at King's College. At the start of the second verse, the camera cuts from the King's College chapel to a London Tube station during an air raid. The platform is packed with people who are in surprisingly good spirits, despite the circumstances: they are chatting, reading, knitting, decorating a Christmas tree, and (later) sleeping soundly (see a screenshot in Figure 9.1). The message conveyed is that long-standing national and religious traditions—represented here by the singing of the King's College Choir—give British people a sense of comfort that allows them to remain optimistic, even during war.

Although *Christmas under Fire* suggests that the King's College Lessons and Carols service and other British Christmas traditions have been practiced for "a thousand years," many of these traditions are modern. Modern Christmas carol and hymn-singing traditions came out of the nineteenth-century revival of carols.[3] "Adeste fideles"—one of the two choral works featured in *Christmas under Fire*—has a nineteenth-century text paired with music written no earlier than the seventeenth century.[4] Furthermore, while

FIGURE 9.1 Screenshot from *Christmas under Fire* (at 8′23″).

King's College and its choir were founded in the late Middle Ages (the mid-fifteenth century), the college's first Lessons and Carols service was held in 1918.[5]

Despite its modern genesis, the King's College Lessons and Carols service asserts a medieval image. There is a lengthy history of cultivating this image in British media. For instance, in an introduction for the service written for BBC radio broadcasts in 1939, it was claimed that the Lessons and Carols service had been held at King's College for almost five hundred years.[6] And in 1954, a *Radio Times* article asserted, "Christmas has always been a Festival at King's since the days of the Boy Bishop," referring to the medieval custom where boys would parody bishops.[7]

This chapter explores the significance of Lessons and Carols services for modern listeners, focusing especially on how these services evoke a vague medieval past that is ill-defined and yet still quite powerful.[8] I focus on the service at King's College because it is one of the best-known Lessons and Carols services and because its history has been extensively documented. I also briefly consider how medievalism in Lessons and Carols services extends beyond King's College. By making listeners feel that they are participating in Christmas traditions that date back to the Middle Ages, the services foster a sense of long-standing traditions and identities, particularly with regard to nationality, religion, gender, and race. These medievalist associations can appeal to listeners facing modern trends that seem to threaten valued traditions and identities, trends such as increasing secularity. Lessons and Carols services also hold a medievalist appeal by evoking historical "authenticity" and featuring newly composed carols that reference medieval musical styles or set medieval texts.

An Overview of the History of Christmas Lessons and Carols Services

The first Lessons and Carols service was held not at King's College, but in Truro, Cornwall, on Christmas Eve in 1880.[9] It included nine readings ("lessons") from the Bible progressing from Genesis to the Gospels. The lessons were read by churchmen in hierarchical order, starting with a boy chorister and ending with the bishop. In between, the choir sang six carols and three anthems with texts related to the lessons.[10] The service was the brainchild of Bishop Edward White Benson (1829–1896) who, according to his son, Arthur Benson, "arranged from ancient sources a little service for Christmas Eve—nine carols and nine tiny lessons."[11] It is unclear which specific ancient sources Bishop Benson was drawing on. Here *ancient* seems to mean medieval, much as the terms ancient and old were used to allude to the Middle Ages in the titles of nineteenth-century carol collections; in fact, some of the carols sung in this first Lessons and Carols service were from such collections.[12] The purportedly ancient nature of the service reflects a broad medievalist trend in nineteenth-century Europe, where medieval styles, history, and themes were referenced for nationalistic purposes.[13] In this context, the ancient nature of the Truro service made it an emblem of the achievements of medieval British culture.

The Truro service continues to this day and has served as a model for Lessons and Carols services elsewhere, both in England at places such as Addington Palace (from 1883) and King's College, Cambridge (from 1918), and abroad, including in the United States at places such as Harvard University (from 1910) and Brown University (from 1917).[14] The first King's College Lessons and Carols service was similar to the Truro service. Nine lessons progressing from Genesis to Galatians were read by college affiliates and Cambridge churchmen starting with a boy chorister and ending with the provost of the college. Nine carols were sung along with five hymns and a Magnificat. The hymns replaced the anthems sung at Truro, a change that allowed for more congregational singing.[15] In 1919, the King's College service was modified to a form it has followed every year since: the text of the ninth lesson was changed (taken from the Gospel of John instead of Galatians), and an arrangement of the hymn "Once in Royal David's City" by choir director Arthur Henry Mann (1850–1929) was placed at the start of the service.[16] While the number of carols and hymns and the specific ones used have varied, since 1919 the King's College service has begun with "Once in Royal David's City" and the same nine lessons have been read.[17] The service has also always been held on Christmas Eve.

Eric Milner-White (1884–1963) was responsible for starting the Lessons and Carols service at King's College. He had been the chaplain of the college from 1912 until 1914, when he left to work as an army chaplain in France. Serving in the First World War gave him the desire to make Anglican worship more relevant, accessible, and appealing to congregants facing the realities of war.[18] In 1916, while stationed in France, Milner-White wrote a letter to King's College provost Montague Rhodes James where he outlined his ideas for reforming Anglican worship:

> At the present moment of utter chaos...we have a chance which, boldly taken, might make King's one of the most important churches in the land....It is my passionate conviction that if we could catch and crystallize the wisest principles of liturgical reform in the worship of our Chapel, we should be doing a great work, not only for the college and university, but also for the Church and the Empire....Colour, warmth and delight can be added to our yearly round in many ways.[19]

Upon returning to King's College as dean of the chapel in 1918, one of Milner-White's first initiatives was to launch the Lessons and Carols service. With its focus on beloved Christmas carols, the service conveys the "colour, warmth and delight" that he and congregants desired directly following the devastating war. Held several weeks after the November 11th Armistice, the first service provided a powerful commemorative experience. This commemorative nature is especially apparent in the Bidding Prayer that Milner-White wrote to be read after the first hymn, which includes the following passage: "Let us remember before Him them who rejoice with us, but upon another shore and in a greater light, that multitude which no man can number."[20] In this respect, the inauguration of the Lessons and Carols service at King's College can be situated within a broader cultural impulse, through which the British people understood the soldiers of the First World War as modern versions of chivalrous medieval knights who were called on to protect their nation with honor.[21] Indeed, the music and images of the *Christmas under Fire* film that I referenced previously might be understood as an extension of this same impulse: extended from the soldiers of the First World War to the English people themselves, and "soldiering on" through the terrors of the Second.

The connections to the First World War may make the King's College Lessons and Carols service seem more modern and less medieval (or medievalist) than the service in Truro. Yet the fact that the King's College service came out of Milner-White's desire for liturgical reform does not obscure its medievalist nature. His wish to reinvigorate worship ultimately led to the use of medieval and medievalist texts and music in the service. Milner-White's later account of the origins of the Lessons and Carols service is highly telling in this regard: "As it stands," he wrote, "the service is a fruitful example of the use of ancient forms in a new combination to create a true Christmas devotion, with dignity of order, development, mood, colour, action and variety of parts, all concentrated upon the coming of our Lord Jesus Christ."[22] This reference to "ancient forms" resonates with the idea that the Truro service was based on "ancient sources" and is a reminder that both Benson and Milner-White were building on the nineteenth- and early twentieth-century English trend of creating new traditions inspired by medieval conventions. Among other examples, this trend can be seen in the nineteenth-century carol revival (mentioned previously), the Gothic revival in architecture, the Arts and Crafts movement, and the Oxford movement's push for the Church of England to draw on medieval Catholic practices.[23]

Milner-White's reference to ancient forms points to modern liturgical practices inspired by the Middle Ages rather than specific medieval musical works or sacred texts. In this respect, the medievalism of the Lessons and Carols service is markedly different from that which inspired the Cecilian movement in Germany and the revival of Gregorian chant at the Abbey of Solesmes in France.[24] With regard to the music of the Lessons and Carols services in Truro and at King's College, the so-called English musical renaissance—a late nineteenth- and early twentieth-century movement to create an English musical identity rooted in the country's musical history—is more directly relevant.[25] To craft this identity, musicians turned to early music and folk music from England, collecting, performing, studying, editing, and publishing these repertoires.[26] In addition, composers such as Ralph Vaughan Williams (1872–1958) drew on English early music and folk music when writing new compositions.[27]

Christmas carols held prominent positions in the English musical renaissance, likely because of the importance of carols in English musical history and because carols are part of both folk and early music traditions.[28] In addition to being sung in Lessons and Carols services, older English carol melodies and texts served as inspiration for new compositions, such as the *Fantasia on Christmas Carols* (1912) by Vaughan Williams and *A Ceremony of Carols* (op. 28, 1942) by Benjamin Britten.[29] Many of these carol-oriented compositions from the English musical renaissance are also medievalist in nature in that they reference medieval texts and medieval musical styles.[30]

Another important early and mid-twentieth-century trend connected to the history of Lessons and Carols services (and especially the service at King's College) was the rise of radio and television. The growing presence of the King's College Choir in mass media enabled the service to reach a large number of listeners. Annual live radio broadcasts of the King's College Lessons and Carols service began in England in 1928 and spread abroad in the 1930s. Television broadcasts of an abbreviated, prerecorded version of the service began in 1963.[31] The service is now broadcast live online and on the radio around the world, including on approximately one thousand stations in the United States alone.[32] The King's College Choir has also become one of the world's best-known vocal ensembles thanks to its large output of LP and CD recordings.[33] This fame has bolstered the popularity of the choir's Lessons and Carols service. By leveraging modern technologies, the King's College service became a widely recognized sonic representative of purportedly medieval sacred traditions.

Lessons and Carols services outside King's College have also helped spread medieval and medievalist music. The significance of these services is discussed in the conclusion to this chapter. The following sections focus in more depth on the medievalist aspects of the King's College service.

Traditions and Identities at King's College: Gender, Race, Timbre, and Authenticity

Medievalism is involved in the King's College Lessons and Carols service when it is viewed as embodying deep-rooted traditions and identities, particularly with regard to nationality, religion, gender, and race. The importance of identity and tradition is especially apparent in the context of the Second World War. The previously mentioned 1954 *Radio Times* article about the King's College service includes the following passage:

> During the war...the music and the prayers gave hope and comfort....In Caserta in Italy an Anglo-American choir of troops sang carols, and the lessons were read in a series starting with a private, ending with a general. In a Japanese prisoner-of-war camp the curtain rose on a scene representing a room at the BBC. An announcer said "We are taking you to King's"; then it rose again on two rows of prisoners, dressed in white costumes, meant to look like surplices, and singing carols.[34]

If troops and prisoners of war listened to and re-enacted the King's College service, it suggests that it held a strong appeal as an English national and religious tradition that was continuing despite the war and would continue after the war ended. This continuity provided listeners with a sense of stability and hope in a time of uncertainty. In *Britten's Unquiet Pasts: Sound and Memory in Postwar Reconstruction*, Heather Wiebe supports this idea and relates the appeal of the King's College Lessons and Carols service to modern medievalist and nationalistic impulses within the Church of England:

> The Festival [of Nine Lessons and Carols service at King's College, Cambridge] epitomized a larger effort to position the Church of England as an institution of national memory, one that connected twentieth-century British culture with the medieval past through the vehicle of ritual....In the course of the Second World War, the Festival began to accrue a powerful mythology....In part, it came to stand for tradition itself, continuing under the most difficult circumstances; not even King's College Chapel was a safe haven—the absence of the stained-glass windows, removed to Welsh caves, was a reminder of this—but faith, ritual, and art, the Festival declared, persisted nonetheless.[35]

Wiebe's claim that the Festival of Lessons and Carols connected twentieth-century British culture with the medieval past might seem questionable. Actual medieval music, after all, is not common in the service, and when it is present, it is typically in the form of a medieval carol melody with a more recent harmonization.[36] The service also features twentieth- and twenty-first-century compositions, some of which are atonal or employ other modern idioms. It is therefore hard to see the King's College service as an authentic re-creation of a medieval ceremony. However, the sense of a connection to the medieval past, I will argue, rests not on the idea that the service is an "actual" re-creation of a medieval event, but rather on more diffuse—albeit no less powerful—aspects of performance and context. The first of these is simply the status of the King's College Choir itself. The choir, chapel, and college were founded in the late Middle Ages and the choir appears as if it has not changed substantially since then.[37] As institutions founded in the late Middle Ages, King's College, its chapel, and its choir were well suited to participate in the mid-twentieth-century medievalist push to portray the Anglican faith as a central part of England's national identity. Because the college and choir have medieval lineages, it is easy to imagine that the Lessons and Carols service reflects long-standing English sacred traditions.

As with other liturgical choirs, a part of the medievalist aura of the King's College choir comes from the fact that it continues to perform sacred music in regular services and with only male singers. Indeed, for its entire history, the King's College Choir has consisted exclusively of boys and men. It has also never had a female music director or organ scholar, even though King's College has had women among its faculty since 1970 and in its student body since 1972. The college's chaplains and chapel deans have also all been men. Of course, the exclusion of girls and women at King's College is not unique: for most of the history of the Church of England, women were not permitted to become deacons, priests, or bishops and girls and women were not allowed in choirs, although since the late twentieth century women have been able to take on increasingly powerful leadership positions and an increasing number of Anglican choirs have admitted female singers.[38] The continued exclusion of women and girls at King's College has been justified on the basis that it seems more historically authentic for performing early sacred music (this topic is explored in more depth in the following paragraphs).

The gender of singers in the King's College Choir is also an important part of its image. The boys and men in the choir perform in formal menswear (Eton suits under their robes), have short hair, and are portrayed as behaving in stereotypically masculine ways. For example, a video released as part of a 2013 choir recruitment campaign shows the boys who sing treble engaging in a variety of activities traditionally associated with boys and men, including playing rugby and football, roughhousing, conducting science experiments, and tinkering with electronics.[39] A listener who sees the choir perform or who views images of the singers cannot ignore that they are all males and that they dress and behave in ways expected of boys and men. Thus, it is possible to imagine that the choir embodies a sense of masculinity that has not been altered by recent trends such as coeducation or accepting a greater range of gender identities and expressions.

The fact that the choir excludes women and girls is also linked to another aspect of its medievalist aura, namely, the assertion of authenticity in pursuit of its particular sound. Support for this idea can be found in a 1990 report on the status of women at King's College:

> [The choir] has an unbroken tradition and hard-won reputation for excellence in the authentic performance of early church music—authentic to the extent of being a men-and-boys choir based on the highly specialized training of boy trebles.... The performance of early church music could be continued with a mixed choir from a general musical background, as happens in other colleges, but the emphasis on authenticity necessitates a men-and-boys choir.... [To quote the (then) dean of King's College chapel John Drury:] "The authenticity movement in modern music is decidedly in favour of boy choristers."[40]

From the standpoint of 2019, claims about the authenticity of particular timbres and/or performance practices are somewhat suspect. As Richard Taruskin and others have discussed, the idea that specific performances and recordings can or should replicate how musical works were played and sung in the eras in which they were composed very much reflects twentieth-century sensibilities.[41] While there are primary sources such as music treatises that suggest how music was performed in various historical eras, the lack of sound recordings before the late nineteenth century makes it impossible to know precisely what earlier performances sounded like. Modern performers and listeners, however, have not been deterred by the lack of recordings. Even in cases where primary source evidence is unclear or fragmented, musicians have created seemingly plausible authentic or *historically informed* performance practices by piecing together limited evidence.[42] Since most listeners are not experts in performance practice, they are likely to take performers' and music scholars' claims of historical authenticity at face value. For this and other reasons, Taruskin suggests that the quest for authenticity primarily reflects the desires and values of modern music performers, scholars, and listeners.[43] In other words, it is more important for performances to *seem* authentic or historically informed than for them to actually re-create historical performance practices. Adapting this idea, Annette Kreutziger-Herr has argued that medievalism occurs when medieval music is performed in ways that are "*perceived* to be authentic" (my emphasis).[44]

The way the King's College Choir sings—what I call the *King's sound*—seems to reflect the gender-based authenticity of the choir, because the boys who sing soprano and the countertenors who sing alto create a light, bright, breathy, and vibrato-free sound that one is less likely to expect from adult women singing soprano or alto.[45] The choir also sings with precise intonation and text declamation and has highly coordinated rhythms and relatively slow and unvarying tempi.[46] The King's sound is essentially a variant of what I call the *English sound* for choral music, which is found among many other British choirs, particularly all-male Anglican church choirs. The English sound is bright, light, blended, limited in vibrato, nonnasal, and breathy, although some choirs that use this sound are more nasal and less breathy than the King's College Choir.[47] These kinds of timbres, it should be noted, are quite similar to those used in many recordings of early music from the late twentieth century, and it is in this respect hardly surprising that (in the passage quoted above) the dean of the King's College chapel should make a direct link between the use of boy choristers and the idea of historical authenticity.

If the sound of the King's College Choir evokes a sense of the past, so too, I will argue, does the fact that most current and past choir members appear to be white.[48] Melanie L. Marshall has discussed the mostly white racial composition of British sacred choirs that sing with the English sound.[49] She adapts the Italian phrase *voce bianca* to suggest that the way these choirs sing reflects the white identity of choristers. Literally, *voce bianca* translates to "white voice," although Italians use it in the plural form (*voci bianche*) to refer to children singing treble parts in choirs. *Voce bianca* also describes a singing technique that relies on the so-called head voice, resulting in a seemingly disembodied sound resonating primarily in the head rather than in the chest/body.[50] These two meanings of *voce bianca* are evident in the King's and English sounds, where the light and bright timbre suggests heavy use of head voice.[51] The limited use of vibrato (a natural vocal characteristic) also contributes to the sense of disembodiment in the King's and English sounds.[52]

Marshall's racialized view of the *voce bianca* hinges on the disembodied character as well as the high level of blend in the English sound. She argues that blend creates an "illusory…purified unity" where differences between individuals are minimized.[53] If nonwhite singers are present in a choir with the English sound, they sonically assimilate by blending their voices with white singers. To support this idea, Marshall notes that English singers are often valued for the "purity" of their sound, which may parallel a privileging of white racial purity in certain contexts in Britain.[54] This sonic and racial purity also may reflect a desire to rid British culture of seemingly foreign influences, a desire that gained firm footing during the rise of conservative political ideologies in the 1980s and still resonates in post-Brexit Britain.[55] The sense of disembodiment that comes from relying on head voice and from limiting vibrato also may reflect a belief that white people transcend bodily realities (such as sexual and racial markers) in ways that non-white people do not.[56]

The idea that singers within a single racial group, nationality, or gender produce a pure sound is extremely problematic. The sound of the Westminster Cathedral Choir— for example—which is also an all-male and mostly white English church choir, is quite different than that of the King's College Choir. Similarly, the idea that the King's College Choir somehow sounds like English choirs of the fifteenth or sixteenth centuries—in part because of its relatively static racial composition since its foundation—is impossible to demonstrate. Indeed, it is likely that the sound of white male English singers changed in response to shifts musical aesthetics in the past five and a half centuries. Ultimately, the dearth of sound recordings from any period before the twentieth century makes claims of authenticity highly speculative. However, historical evidence may be less important than contemporary social contexts. If the "whiteness" of the King's sound— that is, its high level of blend and its disembodied character—suggests a medievalist sense of historical authenticity, this whiteness might also evoke the more homogenous ethnic and racial composition of Britain before twentieth-century waves of immigration led to greater diversity.[57] Given the potential inclination to view the Middle Ages as a white era, the racial homogeneity of the King's College Choir may hold a kind of nostalgic appeal for certain groups of white listeners in England and elsewhere in the West who are facing racial, ethnic, and religious tensions in an increasingly diverse society.[58] At least for some members of its audience, then, the choir's mostly white composition can provide an escape from these tensions.

New Medieval Carols at King's College

If the timbre of the King's College Choir, alongside its mostly white and all-male composition, might invoke a kind of medievalist nostalgia, so too does this nostalgia inform the newly written carols that are performed during the Lessons and Carols service. Commissioning carols for the service has been an annual tradition since 1983.[59] The genre of the carol has significant roots in medieval England, so these new carol compositions are in many ways an assertion of historical continuity with the distant past.[60]

Much of this sense of historical continuity comes from the use of older forms of English and/or liturgical languages. An archaic sense of language, it should be noted, is central to the entire Lessons and Carols service. Many of the carols sung in the service set texts in Middle English or Latin (or both), creating an archaic feeling even if the music or text was written in the nineteenth century (or even more recently). In addition, the lessons are taken from the King James version of the Bible, which conveys a medievalist sensibility through its syntax and its liberal use of old-fashioned words such as "hast" and "thou."[61] Newly commissioned carols also tend to feature medieval texts or texts that evoke an archaic sensibility. Of the thirty-nine carols commissioned so far (through December 2018), six use Middle English texts or Middle English and Latin macaronic texts. One carol is an English translation of a medieval Latin text. Two additional carols use traditional liturgical texts, another uses a Latin text written in the twentieth century, and another uses a sacred Latin text of unknown origin, texts that are not necessarily medieval but nonetheless convey an archaic feeling. In sum, eleven of the thirty-nine commissioned carols, or slightly over a quarter of them, have medieval or medievalist texts. A list of these eleven carols is presented in Table 9.1.

In addition to these carols, the fifteenth-century macaronic Middle English and Latin text "Adam Lay Ybounden" is often sung in settings by former choir directors Boris Ord (1897–1961) and Philip Ledger (1937–2012).

Taken as a whole, then, the texts for these newly commissioned carols reinforce what we might call the *linguistic environment* of the Lessons and Carols service, in which language forms from many different eras comingle. This linguistic environment, I argue, helps to sustain the sense of historical continuity that (as I described previously) is also evoked by the gender and ethnic identity of the choir, as well as by its particular sound. More difficult to quantify, albeit equally important, is the extent to which the musical style of these newly commissioned carols might help to create this sense of historical continuity. Few, if any, of the newly commissioned carols could be regarded as a straightforward imitation of a particular musical work or musical genre from the Middle Ages. Instead, the newly commissioned works tend to incorporate musical markers of the medieval into a larger musical canvas. As shown in Table 9.2, commonly used medievalist markers in the commissioned carols include: passages resembling plainchant (medieval church music comprising one melody line only and not strictly metered); organum (a melody accompanied by another, note for note, in parallel fourths or fifths); or fauxbourdon (a melody harmonized note for note in parallel motion, at the sixth, fourth, and/or third). In addition, one of the carols employs the Phrygian mode (a significant medieval church mode) and another uses drone notes (a common improvised accompaniment for monophonic medieval music). Note that the five carols marked with asterisks are also included in Table 9.1—these carols both have medievalist texts and employ medievalist musical markers.[62]

To this list, we might also add the 1980 setting of "Adam Lay Ybounden" by Philip Ledger, the erstwhile director of music at King's College, Cambridge. Although this setting

Table 9.1 The Eleven Carols with Medieval or Medievalist Texts Commissioned for the King's College Lessons and Carols Service, Ordered by Composer Surname

Composer	Title	Year of commission	Period and language of text
Berkeley, Michael	"This Endernight"	2016	Fifteenth century, Middle English
Burrell, Diana	"Christo paremus cantica"	1993	Fifteenth century, Middle English and Latin
MacMillan, James	"Seinte Mari Moder Milde"	1995	Thirteenth century, Middle English and Latin
Maw, Nicholas	"Swetë Jesu"	1992	Thirteenth century, Middle English
Pärt, Arvo	"Bogoroditse dyevo"	1990	Church Slavonic, Orthodox liturgy
Paulus, Stephen	"Pilgrim Jesus"	1996	Twentieth century, Latin and English
Rutter, John	"Dormi, Jesu!"	1999	Sacred Latin text of unknown origin
Rütti, Carl	"In hoc anni circulo"	2014	English translation of twelfth-century Latin text
Swayne, Giles	"Winter Solstice Carol"	1998	Latin Magnificat antiphon (with newly written English text interpolated)
Turnage, Mark-Anthony	"Misere' nobis"	2006	Medieval, Middle English and Latin
Weir, Judith	"Illuminare, Jerusalem"	1985	Fifteenth century, Middle English and Latin

was written before the annual carol commissioning tradition began, it now forms part of the service's regular repertoire. Ledger's setting includes sections that evoke plainchant and fauxbourdon, helping to create a sense that the service (to paraphrase Milner-White) is firmly rooted in ancient forms.

Conclusion

Since the end of the Second World War, the King's College Lessons and Carols service has continued to foster a sense of stable English and Anglican traditions and identities that can appeal to listeners facing social changes that seem to threaten these traditions and identities, such as increasing ethnic and religious diversity and a rise in secularity. The service projects an image of how England "used to be" and conveys a sense that recent social changes have not affected the core elements of English and Anglican identity that are on display in the service. Despite—or perhaps precisely because of—its specifically English associations, the Lessons and Carols service has also been successfully exported to other countries. Brown University in Rhode Island, for example,

Table 9.2 The Eleven Carols Commissioned for the King's College Lessons and Carols Service That Employ Medievalist Musical Styles, Ordered by Composer Surname

Composer	Title	Year of commission	Medievalist musical characteristics
Bennett, Richard Rodney	"Nowel"	1986	Passages similar to organum
Burrell, Diana*	"Christo paremus cantica"	1993	Passages similar to organum, uses a cantus firmus
Causton, Richard	"The Flight"	2015	Passages similar to plainchant, modal passages (Phrygian)
Dove, Jonathan	"The Three Kings"	2000	Drones
MacMillan, James*	"Seinte Mari Moder Milde"	1995	Passages similar to plainchant, passages similar to organum
Muldowney, Dominic	"Mary"	2008	Passages similar to plainchant
Pärt, Arvo*	"Bogoroditse dyevo"	1990	Composer's unique tintinnabuli technique bears similarities to organum
Paulus, Stephen*	"Pilgrim Jesus"	1996	Drones, passages similar to plainchant
Sculthorpe, Peter	"The Birthday of Thy King"	1988	Passages similar to organum
Weir, Judith*	"Illuminare, Jerusalem"	1985	Passages similar to fauxbourdon
Woolrich, John	"Spring in Winter"	2001	Passages similar to organum

recently celebrated one hundred years of Lessons and Carols services. Like its counterparts in England, the services at Brown evoke long-standing traditions and identities and establish historical continuity with medievalist elements. The 2016 Brown University service, for instance, featured a carol with a medieval melody ("O Come, O Come, Emmanuel") and several other carols with medieval texts and texts in Middle English or Latin.[63] The fact that Brown was established in the eighteenth century and not during the Middle Ages, however, creates a very different context for these kinds of medievalist signifiers. In another corner of the world, the Lessons and Carols service at the Achimota School in Accra, Ghana, operates in a cultural context that is perhaps even more conflicted. For some listeners, at least, the "Englishness" of the Lessons and Carols could be linked to a pernicious legacy of British colonialism.[64] Detailed examinations of medievalism in Lessons and Carols services around the world would be prime topics for future research. It would be particularly interesting to explore how medievalism intersects with identities and traditions in Lessons and Carols services held in non-English and non-Anglican contexts. It will also be important to see how the medievalist appeal of Lessons and Carols services changes as England and other nations become increasingly diverse and as discriminatory practices such as excluding female singers are increasingly challenged. Changing religious sensibilities are also creating new contexts for Lessons and Carols services. Listeners are undoubtedly drawn to the services for different reasons, and many who enjoy the services (either in person or through radio or television broadcasts) are not Christian. How does the medievalism of Lessons and Carols services function in spiritual environment, in which its sacred dimension is to some degree displaced?[65]

Finally, it is worth noting that Lessons and Carols services are part of a much broader medievalist resonance of Christmas music and sacred choral music today. This can be seen in everything from the medievalist contemporary Christmas carols discussed in this chapter to the arrangements of Christmas carols played as background music in supermarkets and malls. How Lessons and Carols services are connected to broader medievalist trends in contemporary Christmas music and sacred choral traditions also merits exploration.

ACKNOWLEDGMENTS

I especially want to thank Kirsten Yri and Stephen Meyer for inviting me to contribute to this volume and for providing invaluable feedback on multiple drafts of my chapter. I also want to thank Patricia McGuire of King's College, Cambridge, Janet Cooper Nelson of Brown University, and staff of the BBC Written Archives Centre for fielding research questions and providing access to collections.

NOTES

1. Harry Watt, dir., *Christmas under Fire* (1941), Crown Film Unit, Ministry of Information (UK), available on the British Film Institute's official YouTube channel, accessed September 13, 2017, http://youtu.be/aGK5EsGzKIg. See the discussion of the film in Nicholas John Cull, *Selling the War: The British Propaganda Campaign against American "Neutrality" in World War II* (New York: Oxford University Press, 1995), 108.

2. This statement starts at 7′30″ in the YouTube video of the film.

3. Collections of carols published in the early nineteenth century attest to this revival. See, for example: Henry Ramsden Bramley and John Stainer, eds., *Christmas Carols, New and Old* (London: Novello, 1841); Davies Gilbert, *Some Ancient Christmas Carols* (London: Nichols, 1822); and William Sandys, *Christmas Carols Ancient and Modern* (London: Beckley, 1833).

4. Two choral works are featured in the film, both sung by the King's College Choir. For more information about the history of "Adeste fideles," see Dom John Stephan, *The 'Adeste fideles': A Study on Its Origin and Development*, originally published 1947, accessed September 14, 2017, http://www.hymnsandcarolsofchristmas.com/Hymns_and_Carols/Images/Stephan/adeste_fideles_a_study_on_its_or.htm. The other choral work is the carol "Ding Dong Merrily on High," which has a melody from the late sixteenth century ("Branle de l'official" from Thoinot Arbeau's *Orchésographie*, 1588).

5. The history of King's College, its choir, and its Lessons and Carols service is discussed in: Alexandra Coghlan, *Carols from King's: The Stories of Our Favourite Carols from King's College* (London: BBC Books, 2016), 107–158; Jean Michel Massing and Nicolette Zeeman, eds., *King's College Chapel 1515-2015: Art, Music and Religion in Cambridge* (London: Miller, 2014); and Jacob Sagrans, "Early Music and the Choir of King's College, Cambridge, 1958 to 2015"

(PhD diss., McGill University, 2016), 2–4, accessed September 15, 2017, http://digitool. Library.McGill.CA:80/R/-?func=dbin-jump-full&object_id=145396&silo_library=GEN01.

6. Internal circulating memo from J. Snagge to Overseas Ex., December 23, 1939, BBC Written Archives Centre, R30/233/1.

7. John Sheppard, "Carols from King's College Chapel," *Radio Times*, December 17, 1954, 5.

8. I use the term *listeners* instead of *congregants* or *audiences* because many people listen to Lessons and Carols services in broadcasts or recordings. *Medievalism* refers to the post-medieval cultural resonance of the Middle Ages, particularly since the early nineteenth century in literature and other artistic outputs that reference medieval themes or medieval history or reimagine or attempt to re-create medieval practices. See, especially, Umberto Eco, "The Return of the Middle Ages" (1973), in *Travels in Hyperreality*, trans. and ed. William Weaver (New York: Harcourt, 1986), 61–85. For overviews of medievalism in musical contexts, see the introduction to this book and Annette Kreutziger-Herr, "Medievalism," *Oxford Music Online*, July 1, 2014, accessed September 15, 2017, https://doi.org/10.1093/gmo/9781561592630.article.2261008

9. It was held in a temporary wooden church used for services while Truro Cathedral was being built. See Nicholas Nash, "'A Right Prelude to Christmas': A History of *A Festival of Nine Lessons and Carols*," in *King's College Chapel 1515-2015: Art, Music and Religion in Cambridge*, ed. Jean Michel Massing and Nicolette Zeeman (London: Miller, 2014), 323–327.

10. This general form of reading lessons in biblical order in alternation with carols and hymns became the defining characteristic of Christmas Lessons and Carols services. However, some congregations vary the number of lessons, carols, and hymns and some do not present the readers in hierarchical order. Some congregations hold Christmas Lessons and Carols services on a different day during Advent (not on Christmas Eve).

11. Arthur Christopher Benson, *The Life of Edward White Benson, Sometime Archbishop of Canterbury* (London: Macmillan, 1899), 1:484.

12. See, especially: Bramley and Stainer, *Christmas Carols, New and Old* (1841); Gilbert, *Some Ancient Christmas Carols* (1822); and Sandys, *Christmas Carols Ancient and Modern* (1833). A list of the carols sung in the 1880 Truro service is presented in Nash, "'A Right Prelude to Christmas,'" 325. Three of the six carols sung in the service are found in the "ancient" or "old" carol collections cited here: "The First Nowell" (Gilbert, 1823 edition); "Good Christian Men, Rejoice" (Bramley and Stainer, 1871 edition); and "The Lord at First Had Adam Made" (Sandys). Two of the six carols sung in the 1800 Truro service are arrangements of medieval texts and music: "O Come, All Ye Faithful" ("Adeste fideles") and "Good Christian Men, Rejoice." For information about the history and sources of these and other carols, consult "The Hymns and Carols of Christmas," accessed September 13, 2017, http://www.hymnsandcarolsofchristmas.com/.

13. See, for example: Kreutziger-Herr, "Medievalism"; and Michael S. Richardson, *Medievalism and Nationalism in German Opera, 1800–1850* (London: Routledge, 2018).

14. After 1918, Lessons and Carols services were typically modeled on the King's College service instead of the Truro service.

15. At King's College and other places that hold Lessons and Carols services, the distinction between carols and hymns is not always clear. For instance, in the 1918 King's College service, "Hark! The Herald Angels Sing" was designated as a hymn, but in 1919 it was designated as a carol. See Nash, "'A Right Prelude to Christmas,'" 335–336 and 337–339.

16. Nash, "'A Right Prelude to Christmas,'" 335–336 and 337–339. "Once in Royal David's City" was written in the mid-nineteenth century and has text by Cecil Frances Humphreys Alexander and a melody by Henry John Gauntlett.

17. A list of the carols and hymns sung in the King's College Lessons and Carols service between 1918 and 2009 is presented in *Christmas at King's College: Carols, Hymns and Seasonal Anthems for Mixed Voices from the Choir of King's College, Cambridge, Selected by Stephen Cleobury* (London: Novello, 2009), 250–252.

18. Eric Milner-White, "Worship and Services," in *The Church in the Furnace: Essays by Seventeen Temporary Church of England Chaplains on Active Service in France and Flanders*, ed. F. B. Macnutt (London: Macmillan, 1917), 175–210.

19. Eric Milner-White to Montague Rhodes James, July 13, 1916, held at the Archive Centre of King's College, Cambridge, King's/PP/MRJ/C/4, 3–4. The Provost and Scholars of King's College, Cambridge hold copyrights to the published and unpublished writings of Eric Milner-White. Quoted with permission.

20. Eric Milner-White, Bidding Prayer for the Festival of Nine Lessons and Carols at King's College, Cambridge, 1918, as cited in Nash, "A Right Prelude to Christmas,'" 334. The Provost and Scholars of King's College, Cambridge hold copyrights to the published and unpublished writings of Eric Milner-White. Quoted with permission. This prayer has been read after the first hymn in every King's College Lessons and Carols service. It has never been substantially modified.

21. Shannon Ty Bontrager, "The Imagined Crusade: The Church of England and the Mythology of Nationalism and Christianity during the Great War," *Church History* 71, no. 4 (2002): 774–798; Charles Brown, "The Modern Call to Knighthood," *Quiver*, May 1916, 653–654; Mark Girouard, *The Return to Camelot: Chivalry and the English Gentleman* (New Haven, CT: Yale University Press, 1981), 275–293; Stefan Goebel, *The Great War and Medieval Memory: War, Remembrance and Medievalism in Britain and Germany, 1914–1940* (Cambridge: Cambridge University Press, 2006), 1–27.

22. The Archive Centre of King's College, Cambridge, Coll. 21.1, accessed January 28, 2019, http://www.kings.cam.ac.uk/archive-centre/college-archives/tour/religion/nine-lessons2.html. The Provost and Scholars of King's College, Cambridge hold copyrights to the published and unpublished writings of Eric Milner-White. Quoted with permission

23. Megan Aldrich, *Gothic Revival* (London: Phaidon, 1994).

24. Elizabeth Cumming and Wendy Kaplan, *The Arts and Crafts Movement* (London: Thames & Hudson, 1991); Kenneth Hylson-Smith, *High Churchmanship in the Church of England: From the Sixteenth Century to the Late Twentieth Century* (Edinburgh: Clark, 1993). See Katherine Bergeron, *Decadent Enchantments: The Revival of Gregorian Chant at Solesmes* (Berkeley: University of California Press, 1998); and Hubert Unverricht, ed., *Der Caecilianismus: Anfänge—Grundlagen—Wirkungen* (Cecilianism: Beginnings, Foundations, Impact), in *Proceedings of the International Symposium on Nineteenth-Century Church Music, Catholic University of Eichstätt, 1985* (Tutzing: Schneider, 1988).

25. Frank Howes, *The English Musical Renaissance* (London: Secker & Warburg, 1966); Meirion Hughes and Robert Stradling, *The English Musical Renaissance, 1840–1940*, 2nd ed. (Manchester: Manchester University Press, 2001).

26. Arnold Dolmetsch (1858–1940) was a particularly influential figure in the English early music revival and Cecil Sharp (1859–1924) was especially influential in the English folk music revival. See Margaret Campbell, *Dolmetsch: The Man and His Work* (London:

Hamish Hamilton, 1975); and Frank Howes, "Sharp, Cecil (James)," *Oxford Music Online*, accessed September 13, 2017, http://doi.org/10.1093/gmo/9781561592630.article.25594.

27. Michael Kennedy, *A Catalogue of the Works of Ralph Vaughan Williams*, 2nd ed. (Oxford: Oxford University Press, 1996). In her contribution to this volume, "Hucbald's Fifths and Vaughan Williams's Mass: The New Medieval in Britain between the Wars," Deborah Heckert discusses medievalism in Vaughan Williams's music.

28. For more information on the history of carols in England, see: Coghlan, *Carols from King's*, 1–33; Hugh Keyte and Andrew Parrott, eds., *The New Oxford Book of Carols* (Oxford: Oxford University Press, 1992), xi–xxvi; and John Stevens and Dennis Libby, "Carol," *Oxford Music Online*, accessed September 13, 2017, https://doi.org/10.1093/gmo/9781561592630.article.04974.

29. See the discussion of carols in Hughes and Stradling, *English Musical Renaissance*, 81–83.

30. See, for example, the discussion of *A Ceremony of Carols* in Heather Wiebe, *Britten's Unquiet Pasts: Sound and Memory in Postwar Reconstruction* (Cambridge: Cambridge University Press, 2012), 50–56.

31. Documents pertaining to broadcasts of the King's College Lessons and Carols service can be found at the BBC Written Archives Centre, R30/233 and R30/3,938 (radio documents) and T14/621 and T14/2,428 (television documents).

32. The King's College Lessons and Carols service is broadcast on most of the nearly one thousand public radio stations in the United States. See "About Us," American Public Media, accessed September 15, 2017, http://www.americanpublicmedia.org/about/.

33. By the end of 2015, the King's College Choir had issued 168 LPs and CDs, not counting re-releases or compilations of previously issued recordings. For a list of these albums, see Sagrans, "Early Music," Appendix B, section B.

34. Sheppard, "Carols from King's, 5"

35. Wiebe, *Britten's Unquiet Pasts*, 50. This "larger effort to position the Church of England as an institution of national memory" that Wiebe mentions is also discussed in James Obelkevich, "Religion," in *The Cambridge Social History of Britain 1750–1950*, vol. 3, *Social Agencies and Institutions*, ed. F. M. L. Thompson (Cambridge: Cambridge University Press, 1990), 250–252.

36. See *Christmas at King's College*, 250–251, for a list of carols and hymns sung in King's College Lessons and Carols services. An example of a carol with a medieval melody and postmedieval harmonization that has been sung in the service is "Of the Father's Heart Begotten." A medieval carol with minimal postmedieval modifications that is often sung in the service is "There Is No Rose of Such Virtue" (from the fifteenth-century Trinity Carol Roll).

37. In fact, the composition of the choir changed significantly in the late nineteenth and early twentieth centuries, when young and relatively inexperienced undergraduate choral scholars began replacing the older professional lay clerks who had sung the alto, tenor, and bass parts. Since 1928, only choral scholars have sung these parts. The shift from lay clerks to choral scholars probably affected the sound of the King's College Choir; however, it is hard to know what the effects were since only the choir's first three recordings include lay clerks. These recordings were also produced at a time (the 1920s) when choral scholars had already replaced most of the lay clerks. See Timothy Day, "The Establishment of Choral Scholarships at King's College, Cambridge," *Journal of the Royal College of Organists* 2 (new series) (2008): 64–73; Timothy Day, *I Saw Eternity the Other Night: King's College*,

Cambridge, and an English Singing Style (London: Allen Lane, 2018), 93–127; and Sagrans, "Early Music," 2–4 and 56–58.

38. In the Church of England, female deacons were first permitted in 1985, female priests in 1992, and female bishops in 2014. Currently, about 80 percent of the Anglican college chapel choirs at the University of Cambridge and the University of Oxford include both male and female singers. See Sagrans, "Early Music," 87.

39. See the Choir of King's College, Cambridge, "Swing Low, Sweet Chariot: Give Your Child a Voice," uploaded December 15, 2013, accessed September 15, 2017, http://youtu.be/j3u9P-koQX-I. See also the discussion of this video and other ways in which the choir projects a masculine image in Sagrans, "Early Music," 89–96.

40. Andrea Spurling, *Report of the Women in Higher Education Research Project: 1988–90* (Cambridge: King's College Research Centre, 1990), 66.

41. Laurence Dreyfus, "Early Music Defended against Its Devotees: A Theory of Historical Performance in the Twentieth Century," *Musical Quarterly* 69, no. 3 (1983): 297–322; Dorottya Fabian, "The Meaning of Authenticity in the Early Music Movement: A Historical Review," *International Review of the Aesthetics and Sociology of Music* 32, no. 2 (2001): 153–167; Bruce Haynes, *The End of Early Music* (Oxford: Oxford University Press, 2007), esp. 119–162; Joseph Kerman et al., "The Early Music Debate: Ancients, Moderns, Postmoderns," *Journal of Musicology* 10, no. 1 (1992): 113–130; Peter Kivy, *Authenticities: Philosophical Reflections on Musical Performance* (Ithaca, NY: Cornell University Press, 1995); Richard Taruskin, *Text and Act: Essays on Music and Performance* (New York: Oxford University Press, 1995), esp. 90–154.

42. An example of suggesting that a modern performance practice is authentic or historically informed despite limited evidence can be found in Christopher Page's theory that the sound of many contemporary English choirs reflects how English choirs sang in the Renaissance, as the modern sound seems (in Page's opinion) to be particularly well suited for Renaissance music. Christopher Page, "The English *a cappella* Renaissance," *Early Music* 21, no. 3 (1993): 454. See the criticism of Page's theory in Donald Greig, "Sight-Readings: Notes on *a cappella* Performance Practice," *Early Music* 23, no. 1 (1995): 125–127.

43. Taruskin, *Text and Act*, 5.

44. Kreutziger-Herr, "Medievalism."

45. Similar claims of historical authenticity could be applied to other all-male choirs that sing with the English sound.

46. For an in-depth discussion of the King's sound, see Sagrans, "Early Music," 29–46.

47. For an in-depth discussion of the English sound, see Sagrans, "Early Music," 47–56.

48. Browsing through the annual choir photographs posted on the website of the King's College Choir Association, there are no more than a few choir members of approximately thirty per year who appear not to be white. See King's College Choir Association, "Annual Choir Photographs," accessed March 26, 2018, https://web.archive.org/web/20180326160614/http://www.kccaonline.org/choir_archive_annual_photos.html. It is possible that someone who appears to be white could identify as a different race or someone who appears to be of a different race could identify as white. There are no published statistics detailing the racial composition of the choir.

49. Marshall does not use the phrase "the English sound," but it is clear from her descriptions that the choirs she references sing with what I call the English sound. Melanie L. Marshall,

"Voce Bianca: Purity and Whiteness in British Early Music Vocality," *Women and Music* 19 (2015): 36–44. See also the discussion of Marshall's article and race in British choral contexts in Sagrans, "Early Music," 83–86.

50. Marshall, *"Voce bianca,"* 42; Kirsten Yri, "Remaking the Past: Feminist Spirituality in Anonymous 4 and Sequentia's Vox Feminae," *Women and Music* 12 (2008): 9.

51. It is intriguing that the phrase *voce bianca* comes from Italy when it seems most appropriate for describing choirs with the English sound (a sound that most Italian choirs do not have). *Voce bianca* could still connote that the children in Italian choirs (or other choirs that do not have the English sound) typically have lighter, brighter, and less vibrato-rich voices than adults. This is even the case in choirs that sing with sounds quite different from the English sound, such as the Sistine Chapel Choir.

52. For greater discussion of the disembodied sound of English choirs, see: Vincenzo Borghetti, "Purezza e trasgressione: il suono del Medioevo dagli anni Cinquanta ad oggi" [Purity and transgression: The sound of the Middle Ages from the 1950s to present], *Semicerchio* 44 (2011): 46–49; Greig, "Sight-Readings," 141; and Yri, "Remaking the Past," 3–4 and 9–11.

53. Marshall, *"Voce bianca,"* 37.

54. Marshall, *"Voce bianca,"* esp. 36–37 and 42–43. See also the discussion of British practices aimed at maintaining white racial purity in Hazel V. Carby, "Becoming Modern Racialized Subjects," *Cultural Studies* 23, no. 4 (2009): 624–657.

55. The relationship between the rise of conservatism in Britain in the 1980s and the sound of British vocal ensembles is discussed in Borghetti, "Purezza e trasgressione," 44; and Marshall, *"Voce bianca,"* 43.

56. Richard Dyer, *White* (London: Routledge, 1997), 1–40; Greig, "Sight-Readings," 141 and 143; Marshall, *"Voce bianca,"* 39 and 42; Yri, "Remaking the Past," 9 and 11. As Dyer notes, in the West, white has become the default race or even a non-race. This can be seen in the tendency to specify the races of non-white people but not those of white people. The supposed racial purity of white people is seen as a reflection of their supposed sexual purity, as white people must carefully select sexual partners to give birth to children who will maintain the white nature of their family line.

57. While immigration to Britain from non-Western nations became particularly pronounced in the twentieth century, especially from British colonies and former colonies such as India and Jamaica, the population of Britain was not exclusively white before then. For instance, in the eighteenth century, there were around fourteen thousand black people in Britain. See Gretchen Holbrook Gerzina, "Ignatius Sancho: A Renaissance Black Man in Eighteenth-Century England," *Journal of Blacks in Higher Education* 21 (1998): 106. On the topic of immigrants in England in the late Middle Ages and early Renaissance, see W. Mark Ormrod, Bart Lambert, and Jonathan Mackman, *Immigrant England, 1300–1550* (Manchester: Manchester University Press, 2018). For more information on immigration to Britain in the twentieth century, see Carby, "Becoming Modern Racialized Subjects."

58. This potential inclination is medievalist and anachronistic, as whiteness is a concept that first emerged in the eighteenth century. Furthermore, some medieval European societies were ethnically diverse, particularly on the Iberian Peninsula. See Dyer, *White*, 1–40; Dario Fernandez-Herrera, *The Myth of the Andalusian Paradise: Muslims, Christians, and Jews under Islamic Rule in Medieval Spain* (Wilmington, DE: Intercollegiate Studies Institute, 2016); and Helen Young, "Where Do the 'White Middle Ages' Come From?," *Public Medievalist*, March 21, 2017, accessed September 15, 2017, http://www.publicmedievalist.com/white-middle-ages-come/. For more on race in the Middle Ages as well as on modern

racist appropriations of medieval history, themes, etc., see: Andrew Albin et al., eds., *Whose Middle Ages?: Teachable Moments for an Ill-Used Past* (New York: Forham University Press, 2019); Geraldine Heng, *The Invention of Race in the European Middle Ages* (Cambridge: Cambridge University Press, 2018); the Public Medievalist's recent series on "Race, Racism, and the Middle Ages" (February 2017–present), accessed January 30, 2019, https://www.publicmedievalist.com/race-racism-middle-ages-toc/; Richard Utz, *Medievalism: A Manifesto* (Kalamazoo, MI: Arc Humanities Press, 2017), esp. 53–68; and Daniel Wollenberg, *Medieval Imagery in Today's Politics* (Kalamazoo, MI: Arc Humanities Press, 2018). In the past several years, the International Society for the Study of Medievalism (http://medievalism.net/) has devoted significant attention to race and racism in connection to the Middle Ages and medieval/medievalism studies, and there have also been regular sessions related to these topics at the annual International Congress on Medieval Studies at Western Michigan University (https://wmich.edu/medievalcongress).

59. Stephen Cleobury, "New Every Christmas," in *A Book of King's: Views of a Cambridge College*, ed. Karl Sabbagh (London: Third Millennium, 2010), 50–52. A list of the thirty-nine commissioned carols (up to December 2018) can be found in the 2018 order of service, p. 47, accessed October 17, 2019, https://www.kings.cam.ac.uk/sites/default/files/documents//9lc-order-service-2018.pdf.

60. Coghlan, *Carols from King's*, 1–33; Keyte and Parrott, *New Oxford Book of Carols*, xi–xxvi; Stevens and Libby, "Carol."

61. Of course, the Kings James version of the Bible was compiled after the Middle Ages, in the seventeenth century.

62. The King's College Choir has recorded many of these commissioned carols. Some of the recordings can be streamed online in the Naxos Music Library (http://www.naxosmusiclibrary.com). Scores of some of the commissioned carols are also published in the *Christmas at King's College* collection. The extent to which Pärt's tintinnabuli style might be understood as a direct evocation of medieval organum is open to debate. For more on Pärt's medievalism, see Laura Dolp's contribution to this volume, "Linear Practices in the Music of Arvo Pärt" pp. 367–396.

63. Order of service for Lessons and Carols, Sayles Hall, Brown University, Providence, Rhode Island, December 4, 2016. See also O'rya Hyde-Keller, "Brown Celebrates 100 Years of Lessons and Carols," December 5, 2016, accessed October 17, 2019, https://www.brown.edu/news/2016-12-05/carols; and "Brown's 100th Service of Lessons and Carols" (full video of the 2016 service), Brown University official YouTube channel, uploaded December 14, 2016, accessed September 15, 2017, http://youtu.be/RjdS689CcL4.

64. The Achimota service is discussed in Kofi Agawu, *Representing African Music: Postcolonial Notes, Queries, Positions* (New York: Routledge, 2003), 14. John MacBeth, "Living with the Colonial Legacy: The Ghana Story," CCE Report No. 3 (October 2010), Centre for Commonwealth Education, Faculty of Education, University of Cambridge, accessed September 15, 2017, http://www.educ.cam.ac.uk/centres/archive/cce/publications/CCE_Report_No3-Ghana_LivingTheColonialLegacy.pdf. Ghana gained its independence from the United Kingdom in 1957.

65. Evidence for the non-religious appeal of Lessons and Carols services can be found in "Nine Lessons and Carols for Godless People," a musical variety show that was performed at London's Bloomsbury Theatre during the Christmas seasons of 2009, 2010, 2011, and 2012.

CHAPTER 10

....

MEDIEVAL FOLK IN THE REVIVALS OF DAVID MUNROW

....

EDWARD BREEN

AT the height of his career, David Munrow (1942–1976) was simultaneously a prominent figure in British broadcasting, a university lecturer, and one of the most widely known performers of medieval music, both as a soloist and in his role as director of the Early Music Consort of London.[1] His regular presence on BBC Radio and television as both interviewer and interviewee offered him ample opportunity to outline to a nonspecialist audience his own approach to, and understanding of, medieval music. In 1976, together with BBC director Paul Kriwaczek, Munrow created the popular television series *Ancestral Voices*. This chapter suggests that Munrow and Kriwaczek's *Ancestral Voices* constructs a cultural allegiance to the popular medievalist genres prevalent in the mid-1970s through both its prominent position as a cultural BBC program and Munrow's high-profile musical personality.[2] Through Munrow, medieval music and medievalism in the mid-1970s reached a wider cultural sphere than might reasonably have been assumed. Throughout his career, as we will see, Munrow occupied an uneasy liminal space: between academic musicology and popular music, between the hegemonic culture and the countercultural movements of the 1960s and 1970s, and between historical determinism and a more fluid—and often anarchic—understanding of the past.

As Annette Kreutziger-Herr notes in her discussion of the revival of medieval music in modern times, "the reconstruction and performance of medieval music is situated between productive, reproductive, and scientific medievalism." The fluidity of these forms in practice produces indelible links between medievalism and medieval studies. Whatever the intentions of a performer may be, modern performance of medieval music will always be a form of medievalism.[3]

The reconstruction of medieval monophonic repertoire in particular was problematic for performers. In an interview, Munrow described the sparse notation of monophonic music suggesting (to the surprise of those steeped in the authenticity movement) that performers adopt a freer approach to the music:

> I think the most difficult to come to definite conclusions about performance is the music of the troubadour and trouvère and minnesingers period [. . .] generally speaking, the less that there is written down then the harder it is until you finally reach medieval dance music where there is hardly anything written down. I mean, there are just a handful of dances and what are we all to do when we have all played all the dances that there are? Well I think then perhaps we ought to start making up some of our own. As far as dance music is concerned I think it is rather absurd to try and treat it reverently as if it was a mass. And so we [the Early Music Consort of London] try to take the spirit rather than the letter.[4]

One way in which the Early Music Consort followed "the spirit" involved looking to folk cultures from around the world, especially those whose instruments exhibited similarities with surviving medieval and Renaissance specimens. Performance traditions of living folk cultures thus became a source of inspiration for the ensemble's development of new performance practices. Munrow was by no means alone in this reasoning; the idea had a lengthy history. Speaking of the unnotated secular music of the Middle Ages, "the songs that accompanied the life of the people themselves," Curt Sachs—one of the towering figures of early twentieth-century ethnomusicology and organology—suggested that modern folk instruments and music were useful to historians in many ways:

> Unable to reach this music directly, the historian is forced to retro-project late medieval styles upon this vacuum. Even modern folksong can step into the breach; and its study has indeed been helpful.[5]

Neither Munrow nor Sachs—as their explanations demonstrate—attempted to conceal his lack of objective knowledge. What is produced is better described as medievalism and not medieval performance; the latter, indeed, would be chronologically and historically impossible.

Faced with reconstructing medieval music practices from almost nonexistent sources, modern performers also looked beyond Europe to musical practices of non-Western cultures and borrowed their instrumental and, sometimes, vocal techniques. Modern performers of medieval music have turned particularly to Eastern practices not only for ideas about sound production, but also for information about the construction of instruments as well as improvisatory and accompaniment methods. Herein lies a key point: looking to Eastern music, to the so-called Orient, meant a consideration of instruments and practices that were sometimes also relegated to traditional or folk categories. A certain slippage thus occurs between the categories of *Eastern* and a geographically wider definition of *folk*. The fact that many of the instruments most important to the Western medieval tradition had their origins in the East, and the many examples of Eastern influence on the medieval West as shown by literary, iconographic, and scientific historical evidence, lend scholarly support to this Eastern connection.

This suggests that at the heart of such explorations, Western art music, and perhaps Western art more generally, has something of an early identity crisis, as literary historian John Ganim has explained:

> The idea of the Middle Ages as it developed from its earliest formations in the historical self-consciousness of Western Europe is part of what we used to call an identity crisis, a deeply uncertain sense of what the West is and where it came from.[6]

Such an identity crisis may also take the form of orientalism: Thomas Wharton makes the point in his *History of English Poetry* that the origin of medieval romance lies in the meeting of Saracens and crusaders. This idea resonates with another observation by Ganim concerning the possible blending of different regional traditions. When speaking of medieval literature, he notes the eighteenth-century obsession with its non-Western origins and reflects that "the metaphor of the earliest studies of medieval romance is one of miscegenation." This mixing of two different races, expressed through notions of "uncertain parentage" and embraced by scholars, has itself a long history; in particular, the continued investigation of Moorish influence on Spain generates an important vein of scholarship running through medieval studies. Such strands often come together to suggest a simple chain of causality: the medieval West accessed ideas and objects from the medieval East, which they developed into familiar forms known or remembered today. Ganim, again, summarizes this eloquently: "The connection between Romanticism, medievalism and orientalism is so much a given that we accept it as a matter of literary or architectural taste."[7]

In the case of the early music revival, particularly the growing interest during the 1960s and 1970s in the performance of works written before 1600, we see many of these ideas in operation, particularly in the field of organology, where several books by leading musicians discussed the Eastern origins of medieval instruments.[8] And, like the sister disciplines of literature, archaeology, and anthropology, the early music revival has its own growing body of scholarly literature exploring medievalism and orientalism.

Medievalism and Orientalism in the Early Music Revival

In 1978, David Fallows lamented the demise of "three of the world's most influential performing groups for medieval music": the New York Pro Musica, the Early Music Consort of London, and the Studio der Frühen Musik.[9] Only Musica Reservata, at his time of writing, remained active. Taking Fallows's lead in grouping these four ensembles together, we observe that a significant volume of scholarly work has been dedicated in recent decades to understanding their work in terms of medievalism and orientalism and the slippery connections folk traditions have to both, as alluded to previously.

In her work on the New York Pro Musica, Kirsten Yri has demonstrated how performances of liturgical drama in the late 1950s "necessarily implicate the creators and musicians in decision-making processes that shed light on the complex relationships among music making, ideology, and the cultural values that produce them."[10] Inspired by Safford Cape's Pro Musica Antiqua, director Noah Greenberg collapsed the performance practices from folk music onto medieval songs, performed with an array of unusual instruments from psaltery, rebec, and recorders to Arabian nakers, Turkish cymbals, Near Eastern finger cymbals, and Scottish bagpipes. This easy elision between folk and the Orient was not limited to Greenberg, but found in him an expression that produced a musical result that was popular and attractive to many audiences. The terms folk and Orient connoted an Otherness, or an alternative, to what Greenberg frequently called the "tyranny of the standard repertoire," and their deliberate use as inspiration for medieval performance practice stretches back at least as far as the 1920s.[11] As John Haines notes, the oriental percussion instruments and colorful costumes of the New York Pro Musica's *The Play of Daniel* ushered in a new approach to early music performance that found justification in the scholarship of H. G. Farmer and inspired Thomas Binkley's exploration of Indian, Turkish, and North African music in his 1964 album *Carmina Burana*. As Haines demonstrates, the classical Moroccan Andalusian suite— the *nûba*—led Binkley to develop the *Arabic style* of accompaniment for monophonic medieval music.[12] Contextualizing Binkley's orientalism within earlier Eastern explorations by Arnold Dolmetsch and Greenberg, Haines summarizes thus:

> Just as 19th-century Europe had gone to the Islamic Orient for its own roots, so did the European American studio turn to Arabic music after World War II for the renewal of early music performance practice.[13]

Examining Binkley's use of Arab–Andalusian instruments and traditions in medieval music by the Studio der Frühen Musik, Yri argues that orientalism is not necessarily a fruitful lens through which to examine the Arabic style. Although the studio's performances appear to reinscribe the discourse of orientalism defined by Edward Said as "a Western style for dominating, restructuring, and having authority over the Orient," Said's model of orientalism is unable to fully acknowledge Binkley's intentions within a 1960s cultural context and has been rejected by Arabic and Hispanic scholars arguing for a greater acknowledgment of the Arabic influence on medieval Spanish culture.[14] For Yri, the main issue arising with the application of orientalism to Binkley's performances is that it divides the world into Occident and Orient and erects a "myth of Westernness." It is this myth that Binkley's work challenged by "remaking European medieval music to include Arabic influence."[15] For this reason, as Yri suggests, "the Studio's performances are better viewed as anti-Eurocentric undertakings that complicate the West-versus-East paradigm."[16] This point is particularly pertinent to the present study as I explore Munrow's performance decisions in the context of the division between West and Other.

It would be wrong to suggest that mid-century early music ensembles were only looking to the East for inspiration. As we have already noted, Greenberg and others also used European folk music models (albeit from the remoter areas) in medieval music performance practice. It was the perceived Otherness of this folk music that was construed as historical by the musicologist Thurston Dart in 1953:

> Evidence may be found in the remoter regions of Europe and the Near East. The music and musical instruments heard in the mountains of Sardinia and Sicily, and the bands still used for Catalan dance music are medieval in flavour. The Arabian lute, rebec and shawm are still much the same as they were when they were introduced into Europe by the Moors. The singing of Spanish *canto jondo* and *flamenco* singers will give us some idea of how the long vocal roulades found in so much medieval music were probably sung originally; the traditional harp accompaniments to Irish songs noted down by zealous eighteenth-century antiquaries record for us the style of accompaniment favoured, perhaps, at the ducal courts of the fifteenth century.[17]

Dart's hypothesis clearly suggests that European folk music contains ossified remains of a medieval performance practice. His observation that various Arabic instruments are "still much the same" as their Moorish ancestors neatly segues into observations about European folk music. Taken together, the two observations suggest something of a fluid barrier between Dart's own separation of Eastern and folk. Dart was writing as a musicologist at Cambridge University and the authority that his research and opinion carried at this time should not be underestimated. These arguments are likely to have originated from his postwar studies with Charles van den Borren, who was musical advisor to *L'Anthologie sonore* recordings by Safford Cape and Pro Musica Antiqua de Bruxelles.[18] Dart's book, which was written within a year of the founding of Noah Greenberg's New York Pro Musica, was a catalyst for the collapsing of folk and oriental styles that continued to spread through the medium of recorded sound.

Dart's observations are also linked with the work of Michael Morrow and his ensemble, Musica Reservata. In particular, it should be noted that Morrow also studied "records of folk-singers on the borders of Europe."[19] Morrow's use of these field recordings to inform his performance practice, particularly their influence on the singing of mezzo-soprano Jantina Noorman with Musica Reservata, is a particularly interesting example of medievalism since Morrow hoped that the hard-edged alterity he heard in Balkan folk music might actually be the ossified remains of a medieval performance practice.[20]

Morrow's approach to Balkan folk music was perhaps an inspiration for the Early Music Consort, as Munrow combined aspects of Morrow's approach to Balkan folk music with Binkley's Arab–Andalusian models.[21] In particular, Munrow's use of folk instruments from South America, supported by his own multi-instrumental abilities, led to a more connected view of East and West reminiscent of Ganim's comments about uncertain parentage. Perhaps more important for our current discussion, Munrow's inclusion of South American folk instruments appears to echo Binkley's complication of the basic West-versus-East paradigm and the suggestion that Westernness was a myth. Munrow, like so many of his peers, was strongly influenced by personal experience of non-Western music. Jasper Parrott (Munrow's university friend and agent) has suggested that Munrow's Peruvian gap year convinced him that music from all over the world was related. Even before his scholarly experience of early Western instruments at Cambridge University, traveling through South America in the early 1960s may have helped the Otherness of non-Western music seem less remote to the young Munrow. This sudden broadening of Munrow's horizons beyond the public school system in which he grew up led to him experiencing, firsthand, the footnotes he would have read in the book he won for his school music prize: Anthony Baines's *Woodwind Instruments and Their History*.[22] As Parrott remembers, the trip gave Munrow a sense that "music was all joined up" and that "it didn't matter where it comes from":

> I remember he told me a wonderful story about travelling from São Paulo to Bolivia on the slow train—which unfortunately has been now withdrawn—but you could get on and off at any time you liked and any sort of person jumped on and jumped off and that was one of the highlights of his arrival in Bolivia and then in Peru.[23]

This anecdote indicates an experience of South America not merely confined to Peru. Like the slow train, Munrow collected influences from across the continent and, in doing so, realized that music too could absorb influences from different places. Parrott may also suggest that through this formative experience of travel, Munrow further realized that once a musical trait gets "into" the music, its origin is no longer relevant. Munrow may also have considered the Other a myth (in much the same way the West could be viewed as a myth). Through this South American journey Munrow seems to have realized that all music is hybrid, and this led him to reject the rigid East/West binary.

Munrow's Cultural Context: Understanding Popular Culture

What distinguished Munrow from the other directors mentioned previously was his level of popularity and commercial success as a performer on the recorder, bassoon, and a plethora of other early wind instruments. Not only was he director of the Early Music Consort, but also he was a regular broadcaster on British radio and television channels and created a strong public profile within the traditional classical music industry, foremost in Britain, but also overseas. Munrow was often viewed as a popularizer of early music, medieval music in particular, and the title of his radio program, *Pied Piper*, was sometimes conflated with the persona of the presenter himself lending a medieval sheen to his on-air persona. Like the legendary figure named in the program's title, Munrow could also lure people with his musical pipe, although without the suggestion of kidnapping that the medieval tale recounts!

Munrow was also active in other popular genres where medievalism and myth abound. In particular, he worked with elements of popular culture, supplying medieval music for film and radio. One particularly famous example is a 1969 BBC Radio adaptation of J. R. R. Tolkien's *The Hobbit*. The soundtrack was one of Munrow's first major recording projects and he appears playing crumhorn and Chinese shawm in tracks that were electronically altered by the BBC Radiophonic workshop.[24] The BBC adaptation of *The Hobbit* was a popular program that reached a wide audience and the music was featured on a special LP release. It had brought Munrow into contact with both the BBC Radiophonic workshop and the composer David Cain, with whom he was to later also record music for other radio dramas, including *The Jew of Malta*.[25] We should note that David Cain was particularly associated with quasi-historic projects and his music was once described in a liner note as having a special ability to "suggest other times and other places."[26] Indeed, one reviewer invoked links to the past as he described Cain's music as having "originated in the same real, believable mythology as the text."[27] Another reviewer focused on exoticism and the perceived strangeness of Munrow's instruments:

> David Cain's music was exotically atmospheric: extraordinary strains from strange mediaeval instruments which carried the listener into an imaginary world of sharp colours and misty contours.[28]

Film soundtracks also helped launch Munrow's career. In 1971, Munrow performed music on another popular quasi-medievalist project: Ken Russell's *The Devils* (score by Peter Maxwell Davies), a film heavily censored for its nudity, sexual content, and blasphemous language, a famously vibrant historical representation of religious orders in seventeenth-century France. The film opens with Munrow's Early Music Consort of London playing dances from Michael Praetorius's *Terpsichore* in a ballet sequence danced by Louis XIII of France (Graham Armitage) while audience members exchange slanderous gossip. The contrast of the bright, upbeat music and the dark tone of the dialogue is striking. In 1974, Munrow also worked with director John Boorman on *Zardoz*, a film that Boorman was inspired to write while preparing to adapt Tolkien's Lord of the Rings for film. Unlike *The Devils*, the soundscape for Zardoz contains no straightforward renditions of preexisting historical works, although it is peppered with recognizable quotations. Rather, it blends historical works with folk traditions and newly composed passages to make the familiar sound unfamiliar. For example, the credits for *Zardoz* list Beethoven's seventh symphony performed by the Concertgebouw Orchestra Amsterdam, conducted by Eugen Jochum, but as these credits roll, we only hear the theme from the second movement. This theme, however, is not a straightforward rendition: Jochum's recording has been overlaid with the countertenor voice of James Bowman—soloist for Munrow's Early Music Consort of London—multitracked in two parts. His vocals double

Beethoven's upper string parts on an open vowel sound and are further supported by low chords played on a church organ. Beethoven's familiar work is thus rendered unfamiliar, and the overall effect is slightly menacing. This feeling of impending danger comes from the visual footage of a slow camera zoom toward a large, flying stone head that hovers over a green landscape like a hot air balloon, but it is also largely a result of the horror-film associations of the church organ and the disembodied sound of a countertenor voice performing a vocalise. Together, these references simultaneously evoke several historical time periods, with the resulting multitemporality conjuring up unease. That same year, Munrow also created the soundtrack for Joel Santoni's documentary *La course en tête*, documenting the life of cyclist Eddie Mercx. Here, Munrow's striking use of medieval dances, each played incredibly quickly and on either a sopranino recorder or the shawm, add a vibrant medievalist quality. The frenetic nature of the loud and fast dances, especially played by the shawm with the throb of low drone instruments, invites us to equate the visual effort of Mercx's cycling triumphs to the striking aural effort of Munrow's impressive shawm technique. This effect is further enhanced as the medieval dances end on a sustained high note (and percussion flourish) that is synchronized with Mercx crossing the finish line with his arms high in the air.[29] Munrow's involvement in popular culture—especially in genres involving medievalism—suggests that he would have been keenly aware of the role of classical music in popular culture and especially the role of early and folk musics in setting historical scenes and signaling distance in time. Medieval music, in particular, provides historic distance, but there is also the important aspect of defamiliarization provoked by both the unusual rendering of familiar works and the use of lesser-known instruments: the countertenor voice and the shawm. Taken like this, Munrow would have likely followed the trajectory of the folk and medievalism in many types of films throughout the 1970s.

The power of medieval music when used this way is related to its own countercultural status within the established classical music scene of the 1960s and 1970s.[30] If the "tyranny of the standard repertoire" was not significantly threatened by Noah Greenberg and Thomas Binkley, the scale of Munrow's commercial success could hardly be ignored.[31] Medieval music's contemporary allegiance to the countercultural forms of folk and progressive rock increased its airtime and promoted early music to new, younger audiences. Munrow performed on historic instruments with established folk artists: He recorded with Shirley Collins, the Young Tradition, and the Roundtable.[32] He also collaborated with Pentangle for their single, "Wondrous Love." This strophic song sets alternate verses to Pentangle and the Early Music Consort and contrasts the soft, light voice of Jacqueline McShee accompanied with gentle guitars to the more strident tone of James Bowman with crumhorns.[33] Munrow's collaborative projects enable us to situate some of his work within a late 1960s, early 1970s countercultural context that includes hippies, the revival of folk music, and the birth of progressive rock.[34] Munrow also shares with such countercultural movements a revival of the *primitive*, which has been mapped onto folk in ways that appear to reject the norms of modern, bourgeois society. This rejection is manifest in a focus on primitive ritual, magic, and mythical themes, which offer a threatening counterpoint to the structures of modern society.

Munrow's Early Music Consort of London was founded the same year as the Beatles' *Sgt. Pepper* album, an album that celebrated "the fusion of rock, classical, jazz, folk, and Indian styles."[35]

During the 1970s, Munrow began a sequence of organology projects. Despite his specialization in wind instruments, Munrow was interested in the history of all types of instruments and he quickly became a public voice in the field of organology through speaking engagements for music clubs throughout Britain and frequent broadcasts on BBC Radio. In 1973, he began a joint project with Oxford University Press and EMI Records to produce a book and recordings to guide listeners through the world of old instruments.[36] Munrow's text amalgamated existing scholarship with his own knowledge of folk instruments and experience as a performer. What is interesting to modern-day readers is the introduction, in which he acknowledged the main sources for his research. He divided this introduction into eight sections. Under "Original Instruments," he drew particular attention to Frederick Crane's survey *Extant Medieval Instruments* and Anthony Baines's *European and American Musical Instruments*.[37] Yet in the introductory paragraph to "Folk Instruments," no references were listed, suggesting that much of this knowledge came from the author's own collection (as evidenced by the photograph captions throughout the book). From this book project grew two television series that survey long trajectories of music history across several cultures and, in doing so, perhaps best illustrate how Munrow considered music "all joined up."

Ancestral Voices

The first television series that involved Munrow—for Granada Television in 1976, called *Early Musical Instruments*—comprised six episodes exploring medieval and Renaissance instruments divided as follows: "Reed Instruments," "Flutes & Whistles," "Plucked Instruments," "Bowed Instruments," "Keyboard & Percussion," and "Brass Instruments." The first series was written and introduced by David Munrow and produced by Peter Potter. The second, also in 1976—the series for BBC Television entitled *Ancestral Voices*—included five episodes and was described in the *Radio Times* as a "recreat[ion of] the music and myth of early instruments before an invited audience."[38] Here, the five episodes were divided into "Origins & Flutes," "Horns & Trumpets," "Reeds," "Strings," and "Zithers & Keyboards." It was presented by David Munrow, produced by Victor Poole, and directed by Paul Kriwaczek. Whereas in the first series Munrow had led viewers from medieval instruments toward families of Renaissance instruments, in *Ancestral Voices* he took a much longer-range trajectory attempting to connect the earliest known instrument types to those used in the twentieth-century Western symphony orchestra. Since little documentary evidence survives, Munrow's initial vision for this program is unclear. The title seems not to have been intended to invoke literal voices—singing is almost entirely absent from the series—but rather to suggest a handing down of knowledge across generations and continents. The sense here is that echoes of the past can still be detected in modern musical practice. Indeed, the fascination with the past is particularly strong in Munrow's work, where it is often linked to a sense of discontent with the present. As he had explained in his earlier radio program, *Instrumental Music from Scotland and Ireland*,

> For me, and I suspect many other people, the lure of the past is stronger than that of the future. Collecting antique furniture, historical novels and films, the revival of interest in early music, these are symptomatic of a growing antiquarian interest on many levels. Unlike previous ages, we just do not seem to be content with what is contemporary: in many cases we reject the latest developments in art, music or literature, preferring the solid worth and proven attractions of the past.[39]

A transcription of the first episode of *Ancestral Voices* reveals that it is almost completely drawn from one source: a short span from the opening chapter of Curt Sachs's *The History of Musical Instruments*.[40] In itself, it is not surprising to find a major textbook by Sachs used for a television script. Curt Sachs was a towering figure in early twentieth-century musicology. He studied with Hugo Wolf in his home city of Berlin before completing a doctorate in art history. In 1914, he coauthored "Systematik der Musikinstrumente" (1914), proposing a classification system for both Western and non-Western instruments that was translated into English in the *Galpin Society Journal* in 1961.[41] By 1920 he was appointed director of the Staatliche Instrumentensammlung, where he oversaw the reorganization and restoration of one of Europe's most important instrument collections. Such was his standing that Sachs was even approached by the Egyptian government to act in an advisory capacity on oriental music.[42] Being a Jewish academic, he was forced to leave Germany in 1933, working first in Paris and then settling in America, where he became a consultant to the New York Public Library and an adjunct professor at Columbia University. He was president of the American Musicological Society from 1950 to 1952.

The extent to which Sachs's iconic musicological work was mined to create this script is particularly evident in the introduction. Like Sachs's monumental history, which investigates the development of instruments in primitive and ancient cultures, particularly their function in spiritual and fertility rituals, Munrow notes that he will focus on two themes in the evolution of instruments, the religious and erotic:

> The story of musical instruments is almost as old as that of mankind. Their beginnings lie shrouded in prehistory and the process of their evolution has been a gradual one amazingly slow in the early stages. Just as homo sapiens has retained some of the basic animal instincts of his forebears, so have musical instruments retained many of their primitive functions and associations. Two themes occur throughout their history: one religious, the other erotic.[43]

At times this takes on an orientalist hue, but Munrow finds notions of the folk and primitive in many Western sources as well as Eastern. If we pursue this primitivist line of argument for a moment, immediately apparent are two striking allegiances with

Ancestral Voices: besides highlighting religious and erotic themes, Munrow's *Radio Times* program indicates he heralded spiritual and ancient themes for this first episode:

> The flute has age-old magical associations. Aztec slaves played it before being sacrificed: in Africa it brought rain and was a giver of life. David Munrow recreates the music and myth of early instruments before an invited audience.[44]

Munrow's emphasis on the magical associations of the Western symphony orchestra's ancestors could display a deliberate resonance to the cluster of 1970s television/film works discussed previously. At the same time, the extent to which themes of spirituality, primitivism, and ritual were informed by Sachs can also be seen in the first sequence of *Ancestral Voices*, which considers the human body an instrument:

> What were the first musical instruments? Well I think the audience here can answer that question if you just stamp your feet and clap your hands a moment. Well that's the answer! The first musical instrument was the human body itself. From the earliest music, a simple rhythmic accompaniment like that which accompanied dancing. And that takes us back to pre-history, to the earliest days of mankind when clapping and stamping developed naturally as a part of the unique instinct for rhythm that separates man from the primates.[45]

This appears to come from the following passage by Sachs:

> Actually he [early man] was quite unaware, as he stamped the ground or slapped his body, that in his actions were the seeds of the earliest instruments. [...] But man alone, apparently, is [...] gifted with conscious rhythm.[46]

Other sequences from *Ancestral Voices* show clear allegiances and overlap with Sachs's content, maintaining the drama of mysticism and primitivism. A reading (voiced by Alan Lumsden) concerning the ritual of the Maidu Indians in Southern California is used to suggest development of rattling instruments to evoke a rattlesnake in an eerie ritual, directly quoting an anthropologist himself quoted by Sachs.[47] Similarly drawn from Sachs is the series' link of unexpected sounds such as a gourd rattle to introduce the bull-roarer and its use by Malayan boys to frighten the elephants away.[48] A further example concerns drums, which—as Munrow explains—occupy "a special place of honour in primitive societies." Here, too, the material, addressing the practicality of drum ceremonies for maintaining good condition of drum skins before taking up the phallic significance of drum sticks, is taken from an anthropologist's visit to the Banyankole, first published in 1923, and quoted in Sachs.[49] On the one hand, concordances may be specific, as in the shared use of a passage from Ernest Hemingway's *Farewell to Arms*, which, in the context of courtship, forbade the use of flute for serenading.[50] On the other hand, the script exhibits general beliefs of the time, found in Sachs, assumptions that place the modern, urban instruments of the orchestra and the timeless instruments of folk culture from the countryside on a continuum. It is the peasant nature of these folk instruments that indicates why we can still find them and use them as exemplars of olden times.

If the debt this first *Ancestral Voices* script pays to Sachs is clear, it is also understandable that the work of a distinguished academic should be used to script a factual television series. Yet, despite Sachs's formidable academic standing in the field of organology, we do not find Munrow relying on his book for repeated quotations elsewhere. In fact, *The History of Musical Instruments* appears just twenty times in the 813 footnotes to Munrow's own book, and it is therefore a surprise to see it used so heavily here. This may suggest that it was Kriwaczek who quoted so liberally from Sachs. This does not negate the possibility that Munrow suggested the entire project and, indeed, the use of Sachs as a foundation. Put simply, the evidence does not suggest that either writer significantly disagreed with the other's ideas.

If Munrow was not the only writer of *Ancestral Voices*, neither can his responsibility for specific passages be conclusively established. Indeed, the problematic authorship of *Ancestral Voices* is one of the keys to understanding the series. The scripts would have been commissioned and overseen by the BBC producer Paul Kriwaczek, who would have also been responsible for the final editing of the broadcast version of the program. Kriwaczek also had notable musical interests and a particular expertise in Asian current affairs, possibly as a result of his stint practicing as a doctor in central Asia, Southern Africa, and Afghanistan before joining the BBC in 1970 and working for Further Education Television and the Asian Service. He was a multilinguist and enthusiastic musician, at one point filing a patent for a "string organ" he had invented.[51] Later in life he wrote books on early civilizations and Jewish and Islamic history. His son, Rohan Kriwaczek, remembered his father's musical involvement in *Ancestral Voices* as being practical and hands-on:

> My father [...] was making a TV series on ancient music, with David Munrow, and for two weeks the front room of our Golders Green house was filled with copies of ancient instruments, working props for the show.... At weekends, when he was home, he would take me in there and demonstrate the instruments.... I particularly remember the ancient Egyptian harp, modelled on pictures found in tombs. [...] my obsession with ethnic instruments I am sure started there, together with the set of bagpipes my father made from an old car inner tube and some drilled metal piping.[52]

Kriwaczek is here remembered as not only able to demonstrate the instruments himself but also to have made his own set of bagpipes from modern materials, pointing toward a particular personal interest and involvement beyond commissioning David Munrow to write a script. In an email exchange with a prospective Munrow biographer in 2005, Kriwaczek recalled the difficult circumstances surrounding the script preparation and how that impacted on his own role as BBC producer:

> I wrote the draft scripts, which he [Munrow] was supposed to turn into his own words. We began in the studio at 10:00 each morning. Munrow insisted on delivering the finalised scripts at midnight the evening before, so that I had to work all night to prepare the camera script—and was myself not in the best shape to do the difficult job of directing the large assembly of craftspeople involved in any television production.[53]

This email suggests that it was Kriwaczek who designed the outline of the scripts and therefore he who quoted liberally from Sachs. Yet it does not negate the possibility that Munrow suggested the entire project or the use of Sachs as a foundation for the material. Put simply, the evidence does not suggest that either writer significantly disagreed with the other's ideas.

Furthermore, the *Radio Times* listing—despite only crediting Munrow as the writer—states, "series devised and directed by Paul Kriwaczek."[54] Evidence for Munrow personalizing the narrative rather than writing it completely can also be found in the scripts for Program 2 (brass instruments) and Program 4 (strings) preserved in the archives of the Royal Academy of Music, which both show annotations in Munrow's hand. However, there are important differences between these scripts: They are typed on different machines with different styles of layout and the strings script exhibits a higher volume of annotation, whereas the brass script is more colloquial in style, with many of Munrow's asides written out in full. Notably, this brass script contains demonstration sequences such as the following:

A bewildering variety of subtle rhythms are used in the droning which accompanies aboriginal ceremonies, and dijerdoo [sic] players display a virtuoso technique. There are the "spat" notes jumping from one octave to another:

Demonstrates

And players speak into the instruments whilst playing:

Demonstrates

And sing as well, usually in a high falsetto:

Demonstrates[55]

This suggests a script already adjusted by Munrow, since detailed demonstrations would likely have been plotted by the performer himself. Furthermore, the document itself shows signs of use in the television studio since it contains stage directions such as "get to drums" or "seated, on high stool," which could only have been worked out after the camera script was planned. Several of Munrow's stock phrases identifiable from other scripts also occur. One example may be found from the discussion of brass instruments in North Africa. "In Morocco and many other places in the near and far east," the script reads, "the trumpeter is still very much a one note man."[56] This is a phrase we also find in Munrow's book: "The Moroccan trumpeter is very much a one-note man, quite content with a supporting role in the ensemble."[57] We can, in fact, trace even further back to Anthony Baines's *Woodwind Instruments and Their History*, where he writes that "in the East a trumpeter is a one-note man, and bass at that."[58] This incorporation of a Munrow stock phrase furthers the suggestion that this particular script has already been altered by Munrow.

The other script, "Strings," is typed in the more usual BBC format with underlined title sequences and indented body text. The fact that the typed text contains no detailed demonstration sequences, only general indications for musical examples (e.g., "James plays

Arab lute piece"); that it has fewer colloquialisms; and that it instructs the performers to "end with suitable piece" suggests the typed script is Kriwaczek's.[59] Also on the script are many informal annotations in Munrow's hand. Consider this annotation from the bottom of page 4a:

> It's difficult to know quite how such a limited instrument could have such a devastating effect. The Greeks, after all, used the lyre mainly to accompany poetic recitation and singing. In the music contests—like those at Delphi—was a lyre section involving skilful Kithera accompaniment.[60]

These annotations are consistently informal in tone, making them identifiable as Munrow's style and enabling us in turn to look at the other script and detect passages potentially inserted by Munrow. If Kriwaczek's recollection that Munrow delivered finalized scripts at midnight is accurate, then there may not have been time to turn Munrow's annotations into typescript.

Another distinguishing feature of Munrow's annotations is his reference to Eastern music and instruments and the notable slippage between them and folk instruments. This is a point that resurfaces several times. Take, for instance, this likely example of Munrow's informal tone in the brass program that concerns Moroccan trumpets:

> It was eastern trumpets like that which first came to Europe in the time of the Crusades, and immediately became the prerogative of the aristocracy and nobility, as well as the herald of war, just as they had been for centuries in the East. Assyrian soldiers played them and in ancient Egypt two trumpets were buried with King Tutankamun [sic]; one of silver, one of copper both chased with intricate decoration. The story of what happened in 1939 when the BBC wanted to have one of them played in a live broadcast from the museum in Cairo is an object lesson in how not to treat very old and fragile instruments. The silver trumpet was to be played by a military bandsman from one of the units stationed in Egypt and he evidently had a bit of difficulty producing what he though[t] was a good sound on the instrument. At a rehearsal one day he decided to try using his own mouthpiece. At this moment the director of the Cairo Museum and King Farouk came in, only to see the poor bandsman giving the mouthpiece a firm tap with his hands, as brass players do to get them properly seated, whereupon the priceless silver trumpet of King Tutankamun fell to pieces at King Farouk's feet. It took some hours of explanation and quite a lot of glue, before the instrument finally and rather querously [sic] went on the air.
>
> Gramophone: Tutenkamun's trumpets 0′30″
>
> No wonder Plutarch described the Egyptian trumpet as sounding like an asses bray [sic]. I wonder what he would have said about the buccina played by Roman foot soldiers.[61]

This lost passage is typical of Munrow's style in that it addresses an Eastern lineage for many instruments. Two other features suggest this passage was penned by Munrow: first, the informal anecdotal nature of the passage and its use of a gramophone recording, consistent with Munrow's style for his radio program *Pied Piper*. Second, the abstruse word *querulous* is used by Munrow in his Granada television series to describe the sound from a 1684 regal made by Haase.[62] This anecdote was removed from the final edit, the broadcast linking directly from the Egyptian trumpets to Plutarch:

> Assyrian soldiers played them in ancient Egypt: two trumpets were buried with King Tutankhamen. We're not quite sure what sort of music they may have played but Plutarch described the Egyptian trumpet as sounding like an ass's bray.[63]

To continue this point we may consider the program on reed instruments where Munrow discusses the Crusades in the context of a regular anecdote about the history of the shawm:

> Well, the shawm according to tradition was a Mohammeden invention developed at the court of Harun Al Rashid in the 8th century in Baghdad. And judging from folk music survivals all over the world today it must have been a devastating success in terms of decibels if nothing else. This shawm [holding] comes from China and here are some others from India, where it is called the shanai, from Egypt, from Turkey, from Morocco and nearer at home from Spain and Brittany. And in all of these places it comes as no surprise to discover that the shawm is played out of doors.[64]

This particular story is told elsewhere by Munrow with an emphasis on crusaders capturing a shawm player and bringing him back to the West. For *Ancestral Voices*, this shawm segment has been shorn of Munrow's remarks found previously in concert notes about crusaders having their "ears assaulted" and "senses terrified" by the sound of shawms or by having "captured" and "tamed" by Eastern shawm players.[65] Again, the uncertain authorship of the script and, indeed, the editing process may have contributed to this change in the story of the shawm's history, but the point about its non-European parentage has been retained.

The above examples show us how passages in informal style, likely penned by Munrow, frequently refer to the Orient, folk, and/or the primitive. Certainly these alleged Munrow insertions negate cultural histories, and although they are evolutionist, they do not always hierarchize and dominate the way Said describes. For this reason some, but not all, may be considered orientalist.[66] With such insertions, Munrow appears to be offering a similar narrative to that which we observed from Thomas Binkley, a narrative that proposes Western medieval music is not purely Western at all. For instance, at another point in *Ancestral Voices*, we see Munrow introduce an anecdote that requires the use of one of his own folk instruments collected during his gap year in Peru. It concerns a South American recorder carved from an organ pipe:

> I suppose the most common type—and I must admit, the easiest to play—is the recorder prototype with its built-in whistle mouthpiece [demo].... Actually, does this instrument remind you of another one that you might see in church for instance? [audience: "organ"] An organ pipe! Well that's just what it is! In fact when the Spaniards conquered South America and set the Indians busy building their big

cathedral churches they set them to build the organs inside them too. And at some stage, one day, an Indian must have pinched an organ pipe, taken it home, bored holes down the front turned it into a recorder. And as a result in Peru today a renaissance organ has turned into a folk instrument.[67]

Drawing on Munrow's own experience, this anecdote suggests a West–East counterflow while still reporting Spanish domination. The fact that the program then goes on to recount the creation myth of the Navajo Indians of America strongly suggests that among the many theories regarding the origins of the Native American flute, Munrow was keen that viewers should be aware of some that privileged Native American agency. This suggests he did not want to privilege the "passive" view of the colonial enterprise and was keen to show that influence is not always in one direction only. Munrow therefore complicates the general narrative of the series, which otherwise tends to stress how Eastern instruments are developed by the West.

However, Munrow also suggested that in some parts of the world instruments were being made the same way for centuries. As Munrow put it for an interview on *Woman's Hour*, when he related his youthful traveling experiences,

> I made a marvellous journey down the Andes from Peru going down almost to the Tierra del Fuego in Chile and back again all by land and I came across instruments like the flute and the recorder and the harp, which had been brought over by the conquistadores and adopted by the Indians and they'd kept them, you know, in exactly the same way. You know they'd gone on making them in the same way that flutes and recorders and harps were made in the renaissance and that was really when I started collecting instruments.[68]

One can read here a tacit assumption that the society in question has remained unchanged while the West is viewed as a center of development. Munrow observed folk instruments in South America as a young man and from these observations he extrapolated a folk tradition that valued continuity. This idea of folk as a key to older musical traditions returns throughout Munrow's work and demonstrates how both folk and oriental influences can be used to offer a sort of living history, as well as an alternative to Western norms. These observations from his experience in South America also suggest that Munrow's folk instrument knowledge privileges personal experience over scholarly literature. He frequently chooses his own folk instrument collection over visual iconography to demonstrate earlier instrumental forms.

With its emphasis on the origins of familiar instruments through myth, magic, religion, and the exotic, *Ancestral Voices*, following the dictates of "drama" in television, tends to privilege the arcane and emphasize the "eerie." The series illustrates that such arcana can still be detected in the ancestry of our modern instruments and, in many cases, still exerts a significant influence.

Having explored the notion of slippage between Eastern and folk categories in these television scripts, we should note that there are also instances of Eastern references that are readily identifiable as orientalism in *Ancestral Voices*. Arguably the most obvious and consistent instance of orientalism is the performance of music from other cultures by Western musicians from staff-notation transcriptions, thus inserting the material into a Western European framework. Munrow's papers for *Ancestral Voices* include a Bhatiali transcribed for flute in common time, D major labeled "up 4th."[69] The fact that in this program Western musicians appear to "represent" Bengali music is itself a form orientalism. Viewers trust the song is performed with appropriate cultural understanding but are left unaware that it is an oral tradition, which is performed here from Western notation. In this respect, *Ancestral Voices* articulates a clear Western viewpoint on music, a viewpoint that Munrow unexpectedly admits in the last episode.

Munrow's Caveat

I have argued so far that Munrow softens the standard textbook musicology in Kriwaczek's scripts toward his own anecdote-based narrative focused on instrumental demonstration and performance. In doing so, he reveals a viewpoint of other musical cultures that could be understood as reinscribing orientalism. In fact, throughout the first four episodes Munrow portrays a confident Western viewpoint; wearing bright shirts with bold patterns and fashionably wide collars and cuffs, he is joined by other British musicians to play vibrant renditions of folk and early music from modern notation on a wide array of instruments: ethnic, antique, reconstructed, or modern, they play them all themselves. He also frequently invests the instruments with an "eeriness" and distance—which reflects back on the *Ancestral Voices* title—through sequences that involve colored lighting and performers in silhouette. The visual power of Munrow and his colleagues for dominating a variety of categories of Other, the folk and the primitive, is as inescapable as it is unquestioned. It comes as a surprise, therefore, to find a subtle caveat at the beginning of the last episode just after the opening musical sequence where Rudrani Balakrishnan (the only person of color to participate) plays the veena:

> With our story about the evolution of musical instruments we could be accused of a certain amount of bias. In the first four programmes in this series the story has been: primitive man invented it, and we developed it retaining some of the old myth and magic. And behind it all has been the underlying assumption that the western symphony orchestra represents the ultimate stage in the process of evolution: each instrument a testament to man's musical and scientific ingenuity. Yet, we have no instrument as exotic as the Indian *veena* you have just heard. We've got nothing as sensual as the Japanese *shakuhachi*, no violin as soft as the Chinese *huqin*, no instrument specifically designed to be played on horse-back like the Chinese *pipa*, nor one employed principally for seduction like the *shamisen* played by the Japanese Geisha girls. So, one way and another, we've missed out on quite a lot! What's more the civilizations outside Europe got going long before we did.[70]

The passage—with its unexpected candor—appears to be written by Munrow himself since the language closely follows his informal style.[71] Munrow's caveat suggests his unease with the evolutionary language of Curt Sachs and appears to question the very idea that "evolution" is always positive. Indeed, Munrow suggests that instruments have not always been improved as they have developed.

One possible reading for this caveat being placed in the last episode of the series rather than being up front in the first was suggested by Kriwaczek himself: Since Munrow returned personalized scripts the night before each filming date, he may not have formed an overall opinion of the series until production started. Furthermore, if we accept for the moment that the language of this caveat is Munrow's, then one possible reading of its placement late in the series is that Munrow is making a desperate, late attempt to modernize Kriwaczek's script and thus redeem the series from overt Western superiority. This is not to suggest that Kriwaczek was trying to peddle imperialist attitudes; indeed, he once referred to himself as "master of the tertiary source" and readily acknowledged his limitations.[72] However experienced he was as a researcher and writer, it is entirely possible that Kriwaczek did not follow the latest developments in musicology. This is not to imply that he was unquestioning in his use of material, but rather to suggest that he would likely be unaware of new developments in early music performance and the general tenor of unpublished scholarly debate at that time. Yet this reading is complicated by Munrow's own scripted orientalism, which we have already traced. Since these do not suggest that Munrow was aware of assuming Western superiority, it is more likely that this late inclusion suggests Munrow wanted to make viewers aware he was unfairly stressing the evolutionary nature for dramatic reasons and that he felt that he should safeguard against misunderstanding of that enthusiasm. Certainly, Munrow was painfully aware of critical judgment throughout his career and once remarked in an interview,

> Sometimes I just feel the arrows being sharpened by the specialists, so that you get to the stage that you write programme notes almost to pluck out the barbs in advance. I prefer those who come to try and enjoy the *performances*, rather than indulging in one-upmanship.[73]

With the reference to voices that the title *Ancestral Voices* carries, it is striking that the series almost entirely ignores singing. Munrow's thoughts on singing remained unpublished during his lifetime, despite the fact that two talks, with accompanying recordings, can be found among his papers.[74] It is also significant that the script of *Ancestral Voices* departs from Sachs's first chapter only when singing is mentioned. And when singing is alluded to during the demonstration of the didgeridoo, Munrow avoids further exploring this path. This further suggests that Munrow's agenda is fixed firmly on the evolution of musical instruments, inviting the question, what was the motivation for *Ancestral Voices*? Remembering Thomas Binkley's use of Arab–Andalusian instruments and Yri's suggestion that "the Studio's performances are better viewed as anti-Eurocentric undertakings that complicate the West-versus-East paradigm," we could view Munrow's tendency to look East for origins as part of the same 1960s iconoclastic concept that Yri points out.[75] It appears that Munrow shifts emphasis away from a purely Western lineage for Western music history and casts the net wider to include influences across cultural and geographic boundaries, potentially as a result of his engagement with popular culture.

Conclusions

The BBC television series *Ancestral Voices* presented the evolution of musical instruments with an emphasis on myth, magic, religious, and exotic associations. The series was presented by David Munrow, a high-profile BBC music presenter who was also one of the most famous performing musicians in early music, particularly notable as a specialist in rare woodwind instruments. Munrow was given scripts for *Ancestral Voices* by the producer Paul Kriwaczek that emphasized Curt Sachs's notion of instrumental evolution, which he then personalized to include anecdotes and musical sequences. Munrow's anecdotes laid emphasis on his own area of interest: the musical contact between Saracens and crusaders during the Middle Ages and other instances of contact between Eastern and Western musical cultures. Despite apparent unease with Curt Sachs's positivist narrative device centered on progress—instrumental evolution from primitive to modern Western forms—Munrow continued this theme until the final episode, when he drew attention to qualities not found in Western orchestral instruments and emphasized the early advancement of non-Western cultures. I suggest that this narrative device, with its emphasis on evolution, myth, and legend, was deliberately employed to align *Ancestral Voices* with countercultural music and film genres prevalent on the BBC in the 1960s and 1970s. Munrow's preoccupation with 'folk' as simultaneously an escape from modernity and his cultivation of all things 'eerie' resituates *Ancestral Voices* as an example of medievalism in popular culture.

NOTES

1. Initially known as the Early Music Consort.
2. For a survey of specific comments from Munrow's peers and reviewers about his popular appeal, see Edward Breen, "The Performance Practice of David Munrow and the Early Music Consort of London: Medieval Music in the 1960s and 1970s" (PhD diss., King's College London, 2014), 21–65.
3. Annette Kreutziger-Herr, "Medievalism," *Oxford Music Online*, accessed June 28, 2015, http://o-www.oxfordmusiconline.com.catalogue.libraries.london.ac.uk/subscriber/article/grove/music/2261008.
4. David Munrow speaking on *Talking about Music 161*, vol. 1, LP0200417, British Library Sound Archive, 1974.

5. Curt Sachs, "Primitive and Medieval Music: A Parallel," in "A Musicological Offering to Otto Kinkeldey upon the Occasion of His 80th Anniversary," supplement, *Journal of the American Musicological Society* 13, no. 1/3 (1960): 43.

6. John Ganim, *Medievalism and Orientalism: Three Essays on Literature, Architecture and Cultural Identity*, The New Middle Ages, ed. Bonnie Wheeler (New York: Palgrave, 2005), 3.

7. Ganim, *Medievalism and Orientalism*, 6.

8. Two notable examples, both explored later in this essay, are Anthony Baines, *Woodwind Instruments and Their History* (New York: Norton, 1957); and David Munrow, *Instruments of the Middle Ages and Renaissance* (Oxford: Oxford University Press, 1976).

9. David Fallows, "Performing Medieval Music," in *The Future of Early Music in Britain*, ed. J. M. Thomson (London: Oxford University Press, 1978), 1.

10. Kirsten Yri, "Noah Greenberg and the New York Pro Musica: Medievalism and the Cultural Front," *American Music* 24, no. 4 (Winter 2006): 422.

11. Ibid., 421–422.

12. John Haines, "The Arabic Style of Performing Medieval Music," *Early Music* 29, no. 3 (2001): 369–378.

13. Ibid., 374.

14. Edward Said, *Orientalism* (London: Penguin Modern Classics, 1978): 3, as quoted in Yri, "Thomas Binkley and the Studio der Frühen Musik: Challenging 'The Myth of Westernness,'" *Early Music* 38, no. 2 (2010): 274.

15. Ibid., 279.

16. Ibid., 274, 279.

17. Thurston Dart, *The Interpretation of Music* (New York: Harper Colophon, 1954; repr., 1963), 153–154.

18. Daniel Leech-Wilkinson, *The Modern Invention of Medieval Music: Scholarship, Ideology, Performance* (Cambridge: Cambridge University Press, 2002), 74–75. See also Edward Breen, *Thurston Dart and the New Faculty of Music at King's College, London: A Fiftieth Anniversary Biography*, 2015, accessed September 3, 2017, https://issuu.com/ahkcl/docs/thurston_dart_and_music_at_kcl/1?ff=true&e=16507444/12965715.

19. Fallows, "Performing Medieval Music in the Late-1960s: Michael Morrow and Thomas Binkley," in *Essays in Honor of Laszlo Somfai on His 70th Birthday: Studies in the Sources and the Interpretation of Music*, ed. Laszlo Vikarius and Vera Lampert (Lanham, MD: Scarecrow Press, 2005), 52.

20. Breen, "Travel in Space: Travel in Time; Michael Morrow's Approach to Performing Medieval Music in the 1960s," in *Studies in Medievalism* XXV, ed. Karl Fugelso (Woodbridge, UK: Boydell & Brewer, 2016), 89–115.

21. See Edward Breen, "David Munrow's 'Turkish Nightclub Piece,'" in *Representations of Early Music on Stage and Screen* (London: Routledge, 2018), 124–138; and Breen, "The Performance Practice of David Munrow and the Early Music Consort of London."

22. Anthony Baines, *Woodwind Instruments and Their History* (New York: Norton, 1957).

23. "Mr Munrow, His Study," presented by Jeremy Summerly, BBC Radio 4, January 7, 2006.

24. J. R. R. Tolkien, *The Hobbit*, music by David Cain, various artists with the Early Music Consort of London, dir. David Munrow, BBC Records, 1968. ISBN 0-563-38999-0 [CDx5] ZBBC1925.

25. *The Hobbit*, 09/JH/JB Radio 4 (DA355H), BBC Written Archives Caversham, M31/1491, August 15, 1968, misc. MUC-MZ David Munrow.

26. John Powell [liner notes] describing music by David Cain on *Four Radio Plays*, David Munrow and the Early Music Consort of London, BBC Records 1971, stereo REC 91S.

27. Paul Ferris, *The Observer*, October 27, 1968, quoted in John Powell [liner notes].

28. Gillian Reynolds, *The Guardian*, September 30, 1968, quoted in John Powell [liner notes].

29. See "Renaissance Suite," music composed and arranged for the soundtrack of the Joel Santoni film *La Course en Tete*, EMI Records HQS 1415, 1974.

30. See Laurence Dreyfus's discussion of resistance against the modern classical canon in "Early Music Defended against Its Devotees: A Theory of Historical Performance in the Twentieth Century," *Musical Quarterly* 69, no. 3 (1983): 297–322.

31. Greenberg, as cited in Yri, "The New York Pro Musica," 428.

32. For a discography of Munrow's work, readers are referred to "David Munrow (August 12th, 1942–May 15th, 1976)—A Discography," last updated November 30, 2012, accessed December 12, 2012, http://www.medieval.org/emfaq/performers/munrow.html.

33. Pentangle and the David Munrow Ensemble, "Wondrous Love" (London Weekend Television, *Journey into Love*, 1971), available on Pentangle, *The Time Has Come, 1967–1973*. Castle Music CMXBX664, 2007, CD.

34. For further evidence as to his influence on folk rock and progressive rock, see Section 5, "Echoes of the Middle Ages in Folk, Rock, and Metal," this volume, especially, Caitlin Carlos, "'Ramble On': Medievalism as Nostalgic Practice in Led Zeppelin's Use of J. R. R. Tolkien," and Scott Troyer, "Medievalism and Identity Construction in Pagan Folk Music."

35. Van der Graaf Generator's David Jackson, as quoted in Edward Macan, *Rocking the Classics: English Progressive Rock and the Counterculture* (Oxford: Oxford University Press, 1997), 1.

36. Munrow, *Instruments of the Middle Ages*.

37. Frederick Crane, *Extant Medieval Musical Instruments: A Provisional Catalogue by Types* (Iowa City: University of Iowa Press, 1972); and Anthony Baines, *European and American Musical Instruments* (London: Batsford, 1966).

38. "Listings," *Radio Times*, May 17, 1976, 29. All listings can be viewed at BBC Genome Project, accessed August 4, 2017, http://genome.ch.bbc.co.uk/search/0/20?order=asc&q=ancestral±voices#search.

39. David Munrow, "Instrumental Music from Scotland and Ireland, ca. 1970," DM/7/6, *Papers of David Munrow*, Royal Academy of Music Library, London.

40. Curt Sachs, *The History of Musical Instruments* (London: Dent, 1942), 26–47.

41. Curt Sachs and E. M. von Hornbostel, "Systematik der Musikinstrumente," *Zeitschrift für Ethnologie* xlvi (1914): 553–590, trans. *Galpin Society Journal*, xiv (1961): 3–29.

42. Howard Mayer Brown, "Sachs, Curt." *Oxford Music Online*, accessed October 1, 2017, http://o-www.oxfordmusiconline.com.catalogue.libraries.london.ac.uk/subscriber/article/grove/music/24256.

43. David Munrow, "Origins and Flutes," *Ancestral Voices*, prod. Paul Kriwaczek, BBC Television, May 1976.

44. BBC Genome Project.

45. We must allow for the possibility of Munrow misreading his own script on air, since humans are primates and it is not completely clear that other primates (and, indeed, some other animals) lack the instinct for rhythm. David Munrow, "Origins and Flutes," *Ancestral Voices*, prod. Paul Kriwaczek, BBC Television, May 1976.

46. Note how Sachs uses the word *apparently* to signal some inconclusivity over this: Sachs, *The History of Musical Instruments*, 25–26.

47. The anthropologist quoted is Stephen Powers, *Tribes of California* (Washington, DC: Government Printing Office, 1877): 306. Quoted in Sachs, *The History of Musical Instruments*, 27, and appearing in Munrow's series entitled "Origins and Flutes."

48. Sachs discusses this in *The History of Musical Instruments*, 42; Munrow's sequence follows the rattle sequence in "Origins and Flutes."

49. John Roscoe, *The Banyankole* (Cambridge: The University Press, 1923), 44, condensed and quoted in Sachs, *The History of Musical Instruments*, 35.

50. Ernest Hemmingway, *A Farewell to Arms* (New York: Scribner, 1929): 78, quoted in Sachs, *The History of Musical Instruments*, 45; used in Munrow, "Origins and Flutes."

51. Hugh Purcell, "Paul Kriwaczek Obituary," *The Guardian*, March 17, 2011.

52. "A Treasure Cave of Instruments," posted by Pied Piper (Robert Searle), DavidMunrow. org, April 8, 2009, accessed November 8, 2017, http://www.earlymusic.co/davidmunrow/index.php?topic=101.msg181#msg181.

53. "Contemporaries of David Munrow Remember," posted by Pied Piper (Robert Searle), DavidMunrow.org, August 21, 2008, accessed November 8, 2017, http://www.earlymusic.co/davidmunrow/index.php?topic=47.msg103#msg103.

54. BBC Genome Project, accessed August 11, 2017, http://genome.ch.bbc.co.uk/search/0/20?order=asc&q=ancestral+voices&svc=9371535#search.

55. Munrow, "Origins and Flutes."

56. Munrow, "Horns and trumpets," *Ancestral Voices*; also see "Kriwaczek—Music and Spare Scripts," ca. 1976, DM/6/4, *Papers of David Munrow*, Royal Academy of Music Library, London.

57. Munrow, *Instruments of the Middle Ages*, 19. For the importance of Baines's book on Munrow's early musical development, see Breen, *David Munrow's "Turkish Nightclub Piece."*

58. Anthony Baines, *Woodwind Instruments and Their History* (New York: Norton, 1957), 231.

59. See "Kriwaczek—Music and Spare Scripts," *Papers of David Munrow*.

60. "Kriwaczek—Music and Spare Scripts," *Papers of David Munrow*.

61. Ibid.

62. Munrow, "Keyboards and Percussion," in *Early Musical Instruments*, dir. Peter Plummer, Granada Television (UK), October 1976; produced for DVD by David Griffith, Viking New Media 2007; accessed May 12, 2009, http://www.DavidMunrow.org.

63. Munrow, "Horns and Trumpets," *Ancestral Voices*.

64. Munrow, "Reeds," *Ancestral Voices*.

65. For a detailed study of Munrow's shawm presentation, including these quotes and their relationship to Baines's *Woodwind Instruments and Their History*, see Breen, *David Munrow's "Turkish Nightclub Piece."*

66. Said, *Orientalism*, 3.

67. Munrow, "Origins and Flutes," *Ancestral Voices*.

68. Munrow interviewed on *Woman's Hour*, presented by Sue MacGregor, BBC Radio, September 3, 1975.

69. The surviving musical scripts in Munrow's hand are all in staff notation, including "Bhatiali" (Bengali Boatman's Song). See "Kriwaczek—Music and Spare Scripts."

70. Munrow, "Zithers and Keyboards," *Ancestral Voices*.

71. A written copy of this script is not preserved among Munrow's other papers. However, the language has direct parallels in Munrow, *Instruments of the Middle Ages and Renaissance*, 5. It also closely resembles a 1943 essay by a founding member of the Galpin Society who complains of modern instruments that "we are well content to let these sleek and efficient

prototypes stand token for the whole of their several ancestries": Eric Halfpenny, "The Influence of Timbre and Technique on Musical Aesthetics," *The Music Review* iv (1943): 250.

72. Daniel Snowman, "Obituary for Paul Kriwaczek," *The Independent*, April 11, 2011.

73. Alan Blyth, "David Munrow Talks to Alan Blyth," *Gramophone*, May 1974, 2010.

74. Munrow, "Vibrato," in *Papers of David Munrow*, DM 9/11, Royal Academy of Music Library, London, ca. 1970; and Munrow, "What Should It All Sound Like?," in *Papers of David Munrow: DM 9/14*, Royal Academy of Music Library, London, ca. 1970. A spool of audio tape (¼ inch) in its original box, which has written on it "title 'What should it all sound like?', duration '7½ mins.'" This spool has been transferred to CD and is available to listeners visiting the RAM archive. Both of these topics are covered in Breen, *The Performance Practice of David Munrow*.

75. Yri, "Thomas Binkley and the Studio der Frühen Musik," 274.

··

CHAPTER 11

RE-SOUNDING CARL THEODOR DREYER'S *LA PASSION DE JEANNE D'ARC*

··

DONALD GREIG

WRITING about using ancient Roman and Greek music in his score for *Quo Vadis*, Miklós Rósza worried that he might "produc[e] only musicological oddities instead of music with a universal, emotional appeal."[1] Rósza's concern about musical alienation will resonate with musicologists, and particularly with performers and concert promoters who seek new ways to bring medieval music to a modern audience. In that context, historical performance practice has occasionally been made to bear the blame for the failure of an esoteric repertoire to convince.

The following addresses some of these issues through a recent Orlando Consort project entitled *Voices Appeared*.[2] This is a live score of French, Burgundian, and English music performed or composed during the brief lifetime of Jeanne d'Arc (ca. 1412–1431), designed to accompany screenings of Carl Theodor Dreyer's acclaimed silent film, *La Passion de Jeanne d'Arc* (1928). The live score engages with the film's particularly fascinating history, which fluctuates between musical veneration and respectful silence. The original premise of the project was to amplify the historical period of the film's narrative while offering a historically *informed* "soundtrack" that was in keeping with Dreyer's own historical research. My purpose in this chapter is thus not to make claims for the project's historical accuracy, but to consider it an example of medievalism, based on the inescapably modern location of medieval music's performing subjects. At the same time, considerable efforts have been made to choose pieces that may have had a special meaning to Jeanne d'Arc or that may have comprised the musical background of her life. The performance of these medieval selections against the film's historical narrative offers a form of alterity, designing a soundscape that is medieval at the same time that it reflects back on the present.

Historical Background of Dreyer's *La Passion de Jeanne d'Arc*

We might approach this history by beginning with the response of the director to a postwar version of *La Passion de Jeanne d'Arc* to which baroque music had been added. "Why did he add music from an era considerably later than Jeanne's?" asked Dreyer.[3] The director's complaint about anachronism prompts several immediate thoughts. What violence does anachronistic music do to historical films? How does such historical incongruity shape our viewing experience? And, following from that, how might music from the early fifteenth century enhance or distort Dreyer's vision of his work?

In 1925, in the wake of the international success of *Master of the House* (*Du skal ære din hustru*), Dreyer was invited by the Société générale de films to make a film in France. Of the three subjects offered—Catherine de Medici, Marie Antoinette, and Jeanne d'Arc—it was the last on which he decided, apparently by drawing matchsticks, a somewhat ironic method given the role that fire played in Jeanne d'Arc's demise and the destruction of the original negatives of *La Passion de Jeanne d'Arc*. However the choice was made, it was certainly timely: in 1920, Jeanne had been canonized, and in the same year Pierre Champion published a new translation of the records of the condemnation trial of 1431. Furthermore, in 1925, Joseph Delteil's novel *Jeanne d'Arc* was awarded the Prix Femina.[4]

Though Dreyer acquired the rights to the novel, his approach was ultimately guided by research. Champion was employed as historical advisor and the screenplay drew explicitly on the 1431 trial, something echoed in the film by its introductory sequence that shows a hand turning the pages of the transcript held in the Bibliothèque de la Chambre des députés in Paris. Stretching the point somewhat, 48 of the 174 original Danish intertitles can confidently be traced back to records from the first trial, ranging from paraphrases to exact quotations. Dreyer also observes the chronology of the various settings—the chapel, Jeanne's cell, the cemetery of Saint Ouen, the Old Marketplace—condensing the three-month trial into a single day. But it is the other major historical source, the later nullification trial of 1455–1456, that furnishes most of the drama, including the profiles of key Jeanne sympathizers: Massieu, dean of Rouen; Martin Ladvenu; and Pierre Manchon, one of the notaries. This second trial is also the source for de Houppeville's banishment from the trial room and of the shadowy presence of Warwick, overseeing agent of the English crown. While episodes are dramatized by Dreyer, all the dialogue for those scenes is invented.

Historical research similarly informs the production design. The miniatures in *Le Livre des Merveilles*, a fifteenth-century compendium of travelogues by Marco Polo, John Mandeville, and others, are clearly the basis of Hermann Warm's set designs.[5] The book's suggestive history might also have appealed to the director. It was originally a gift from John the Fearless, Duke of Burgundy, to the Duc of Berry in January 1417, in recognition of his help in relieving the siege at Bourges. It thus contained uncanny echoes of the captured Jeanne being handed from the Burgundians to the English and her role in the famous siege of Orléans. Held in the Bibliothèque nationale in Paris (BN2810) and available in reproduction, the miniatures were painted by the Boucicaut Master and his collaborators, the images of foreign lands owing more to local Northern architecture than to firsthand experience.[6] This led to "a scenery style that was content to *suggest* the era without imposing itself."[7] Rooted in a form of painterly authenticity, it was the unsettling oneiric qualities that appealed, a channeling of fifteenth-century sensibility through expressionism and surrealism.[8]

The set fulfilled a further expression of authenticity, becoming a place where medieval life itself could be lived by the actors, an arena for Stanislavskyan gestures of emotional verisimilitude. Highly unusually for any film, it was shot in sequence, the actors employed for the full six months of the shoot, the priests tonsured, faces unadorned by makeup, their lines delivered exactly according to the script, in French.

Musical Accompaniments to Dreyer's Film

To address the reception of the film and the role that music of various kinds played in it, it is necessary first to trace the convoluted history of the print. The first negative was destroyed by fire in 1929 and the second, completed by Dreyer and his editor from alternate takes, suffered the same fate just one year later.[9] Released on the cusp of the sound era, receiving only lukewarm response and subject to various political censorships (the church in France demanded various cuts and it was banned in England for two years because of its negative portrayal of English soldiers), the film remained unseen for several years while its status as a classic grew. A butchered version of the film with a voiceover by radio star David Ross was released in America in 1933 and a more famous sonorized version was released in 1952 with baroque music (mentioned above). Then, in 1981, came a phoenix-from-the-ashes discovery of a pristine, 35mm positive print in the unlikely venue of the Dykemark Sykehus, a Norwegian psychiatric hospital, complete with the original Danish censor's stamp.[10]

Coming just one year after the 1980 restoration of Abel Gance's *Napoléon* (1927) (coincidentally made one year before *La Passion de Jeanne d'Arc*), the rerelease coincided with a renewed interest in silent film and its musical accompaniment.[11] In 1980 in Britain, a thirteen-episode series on silent film, *Hollywood*, had aired with music by Carl Davis, and it was he who was asked to provide a new score for *Napoléon*. In the United States, Carmine Coppola wrote his own score. Both offered the modern audience a parallel experience to that of some filmgoers of the late 1920s: watching a movie in a large space with a full orchestra.[12] In 1982, *La Passion de Jeanne d'Arc* was graced with a commissioned score by the Danish composer Ole Schmidt, and others followed. From the classical world, Richard Einhorn's 1994 *Voices of Light*, described as an oratorio, is probably the best known, one that gives the film a woman's voice and a nod to modern performance practice of medieval music by using the American female ensemble

Anonymous 4 to represent Jeanne.[13] From the pop world came scores by Cat Power, Nick Cave, and the Dirty Three and, more recently, a score by Adrian Utley of Portishead and Will Gregory of Goldfrapp.[14] *Voices Appeared* thus takes its place as one in a long line of live soundtracks that have been created since 1981, though it differs in being a combinative score, collated from various musical sources, thereby harkening back to the cue-sheet system of the silent film era.[15]

As a journalist, practitioner, and, later in life, manager of the Dagmar cinema in Copenhagen, Dreyer knew that the exhibition of early film (including the nature of its musical accompaniment) was determined by each individual movie house and its musical resources, not by the film's director.[16] This was the case even for the premieres: the April 21, 1928, premiere of *La Passion de Jeanne d'Arc* in Copenhagen was accompanied by an amalgam of music compiled from cue sheets and arranged by Jakob Garde (best known today for his tango *Jalousie*), at the time the musical director of the Palads Teatret; and the Paris premiere of October 25, 1928, received a commissioned score for small orchestra and singers by Victor Alix and Léo Pouget, which bears the hopeful inscription "L'exécution de cette partition est OBLIGATOIRE pendant la passation du film."[17]

That Dreyer even considered a soundtrack for screenings of *La Passion de Jeanne d'Arc* might seem surprising; many scholars and critics have implied and sometimes insisted that Dreyer wanted his film to be exhibited in silence.[18] Although directors of silent film often used music on the set to prompt appropriate emotional responses in actors, a 1927 article by the critic Jean Arroy reported that Dreyer eschewed this practice, deeming it an artificial device, contrary to his search for emotional truth. More than this, according to Arroy, Dreyer was "a believer in film projected without musical accompaniment," though the context of the interview in a special issue of *Cinémagazine* renders his comments less doctrinal, the preference of one who was spending a good deal of time constructing the movie in silence in an editing suite.[19]

When first approached by Lo Duca in 1949 with the idea of adding J. S. Bach's music to his film, Dreyer deemed it "an excellent idea."[20] His reservations about the project concerned what he rightly divined was a wholesale ontological transformation of a silent film into a sound one.[21] The gala repremiere of February 9, 1952, at the Cinéma d'Essai in Paris (of which Lo Duca was the director), being essentially a silent film with musical accompaniment, might thus have met with Dreyer's approval if, as was probably the case, Lo Duca had made no changes to the discovered print. Music came from a separate sound source—a wire recorder—and was a confection of music by not only J. S. Bach but also Beethoven, Palestrina, and César Franck.[22] The sonorized version was created a few months later in time for a screening in the Venice Biennale on September 12, 1952, the music assembled from extant baroque recordings of concerti by Tomaso Albinoni, Antonio Vivaldi, Francesco Geminiani, Giuseppi Torelli, and Giovanni Sammartini. Further musical material came from a recording made in a church in Paris in the summer of 1952, this of Alessandro Scarlatti's *Passio Secundum Ioannem* and three very short linking organ improvisations.[23]

Dreyer finally saw the completed version in 1956 and discovered the full extent of Lo Duca's intervention. He had added not only a soundtrack but also, where he could, subtitles. What intertitles remained were pasted over facile backgrounds—flames, stained-glass windows, and medieval cityscapes. Lo Duca had also cropped the image to accommodate the soundtrack, thereby compromising the original startling framings. A credit sequence and stentorian voice-over provided the referential contexts that Dreyer had deliberately eschewed in favor of the film's intense intimacy, a portrait of "the real Joan, not in armour but simple and human, a young woman who died for her country," as the original rolling intertitles have it.

The use of baroque music with film was not a new idea. Bach chorales were common-place in film-music anthologies as signifiers of solemnity, and church-trained organists were not afraid to use the Toccata and Fugue in D minor, a recurrent motif in horror films in the 1930s, to inspire terror.[24] Indeed, a more obviously historicist precedent for Lo Duca's purely baroque approach existed in a combinative score for Ernst Lubitsch's *Anna Boleyn* (1920: released as *Deception* in the United States) by the New York–based arranger/conductor Hugo Riesenfeld. It featured music by J. S. Bach, Jean-Philippe Rameau, Vivaldi, Handel, and Arcangelo Corelli, among many others, with harpsi-chord, oboe da caccia, and viola d'amore thrown in for good measure. That Anne Boleyn was executed in 1536 and J. S. Bach was not born until 1685 did not for a moment prevent a breathless enthusiasm for what was taken as musical authenticity by commentators of the time.[25] Preromantic music seems to be the point here: baroque music, by virtue of difference, invokes a broad historical Otherness, its stately formality deemed appropri-ate for a drama set in a royal court.

There is nothing to suggest that Lo Duca was familiar with Riesenfeld's score, but it is not only anachronism that makes Lo Duca's musical choices seem so odd; it is the lack of attention to the narrative and to emotional tone. The repeated baroque patterns relent-lessly churn beneath the more varied rhythms of the film, and the fact that the sound designers present entire movements with no editing means that music crashes over scene or mood changes as if blind to the images that it accompanies. The scene where the English soldiers taunt Jeanne, for example, is underscored by the mournful Albinoni Adagio in G minor, presumably meant to invoke sympathy for Jeanne, yet the visual tone here is obscenely comic (the cue for the Alix/Pouget score, by contrast, is entitled "Grotesque" and features a solo, farting bassoon *très détaché*). Later, when the crowd riots, Lo Duca cuts and pastes various recitatives and baying choral interjections from the Scarlatti Passion whose textual specificity entirely contradicts the crowd's support for Jeanne. The overall impression is of individual movements from a limited set of concerti grossi laid end to end to fill the time of the movie, an organization of baroque music by the yard.

Today the Lo Duca version stands as something of a curio, of interest only to film scholars as a version of the second print, but between 1952 and 1981, when the Oslo print came to light, it was the most readily available version of Dreyer's film, together with the silent print held by the Department of Film at the Museum of Modern Art. A more nuanced solution to the with/without music binarism comes from curator Eileen Bowser. Having staged a major retrospective of his work in 1964 at the Museum of Modern Art, where *La Passion de Jeanne d'Arc* received no musical accompaniment, she met Dreyer the following year, when he came to New York for the US premiere of *Gertrud*:

I think that it was one of the others, who quickly joined us, not me, who asked about music for Jeanne d'Arc. And my impression is that he did not exactly mean that he wanted it shown silent but rather, he did not like any of the musical solutions so far that had been used and had not found the music he thought was right for it. And until he did, he preferred it without music. That is a little different.[26]

Writing in 1973, the film scholar David Bordwell advised readers to rent either the Museum of Modern Art print or the Lo Duca version and switch the sound off for the latter: "*La Passion de Jeanne d'Arc* is one silent film that doesn't suffer by being shown without music."[27] But retrospectives in museums and academic study bring with them a certain responsibility to screen the movie without musical intervention, even if music was an authentic part of cinema exhibition during the so-called silent era. The negotiation of meaning between music and image, after all, potentially distorts the authorial image, which goes some way to explaining the contempt heaped on the Lo Duca version by Dreyer-loving film critics.

Medieval Music in Films about Jeanne d'Arc

Sound films about Jeanne d'Arc have not had to contend with questions of silence and have invoked medievalism in a variety of ways. Hugo Friedhofer's score for Victor Fleming's 1948 film *Joan of Arc* starring Ingrid Bergman, perhaps surprising for a Hollywood film of this era, demonstrates distinct historic-musical knowledge. The coronation scene includes an *alternatim* (plainchant alternating with polyphony) arrangement of *Veni creator spiritus* by Guillaume Dufay (ca. 1397–1474). Though the setting had not been written by 1429, the plainchant hymn on which it was based was part of the ordained service, as was the plainchant Te Deum that follows it in the film.[28] Even more surprising for a Hollywood film of this era, the same scene includes a late-thirteenth/early-fourteenth century motet from the Montpellier Codex, a piece written over a hundred years before the event it illustrates.[29] These musicologically informed performances are figured diegetically. Nondiegetically, the music functions more formulaically, making use of the fifteenth-century secular song *L'homme armé* in strident brass as Jeanne, monks, and her army march toward Orléans. Elsewhere, a theme reminiscent of the Dies irae plainchant is furnished with a panoply of familiar Hollywood tropes—parallel fourths and fifths, brash brass, tubular bells, and menacing pedal points—frequently used to suggest anything from ancient Rome to the Middle Ages.

Since the 1960s and concomitant with the growth of the early music movement, there have been more concerted efforts to provide films about Jeanne d'Arc with medieval music. One example is Robert Bresson's *Procès de Jeanne d'Arc* (1962), which, like Dreyer's film, concentrates on the trial and execution, modeling some of its dialogue on the court records and alluding to Dreyer's film in various ways. There is very little music other than the occasional interjection from a side drum and fanfare, sparseness consistent with the director's ascetic approach to film and suggestive at most of an underdeveloped musical culture.[30] Jordi Savall, following his work on *Tous les matins du monde* (1991), a film set in the late seventeenth century, was the musical director for Jacques Rivette's two-part biopic, *Jeanne la Pucelle I—Les batailles* (1994) and *Jeanne la Pucelle II—Les prisons* (1994). He arranged several fifteenth-century compositions for voices and instruments, including chansons by Dufay and Antoine Busnois (ca. 1430–1492), sections from Dufay's Missa *L'homme armé*, and settings of the *L'homme armé* tune itself.[31] Though the music was not all written in the early part of the fifteenth century, only those with intimate knowledge of music of the period would confidently accuse it of anachronism. More recently, Éric Serra's score for Luc Besson's *The Messenger* (1999) channels medieval sources through Carl Orff, the cue *Angelus in Medio Ignis* being almost a rewrite of "O Fortuna" from *Carmina Burana*.

Savall's score was only thinkable when medieval music was part of the currency of recording and concert-giving, which was not the case in 1928 or even in 1956 when Dreyer pondered the possibility of a musical accompaniment drawn entirely from the early fifteenth century.[32] And it is difficult to say quite how Dreyer would have wanted such repertoire used; his later sound films belong to an entirely different aesthetic and offer few clues. The closest we come to Dreyer using music as he might have done for a silent film is *Vampyr* (1932), his first sound film and one that harks back to the earlier era with its intertitles, minimal dialogue, and a virtually through-composed score by Wolfgang Zeller.[33] But given the historical basis of screenplay and design, the addition of medieval music in *Voices Appeared* would seem to be an appropriate gesture, deepening the film's engagement with the period it represents and amplifying a commitment to historical research. The Orlando Consort's sustained commitment to historically informed performance and its profile as an exponent of the "English *a cappella* heresy" with its advocacy of all-vocal performance offered meaningful associations.[34] The role of voices, after all, is already apparent in *La Passion de Jeanne d'Arc* in a number of ways: as a courtroom drama it stages a mise en scène of dialogue and makes it an exceptional generic choice for a silent film; images of vocality and aurality abound, consistently begging the question of sound—priests cup their hands to hear answers, Beaulieu casually clears his ear with an index finger and examines the wax, priests whisper messages down the line, and d'Estivet delivers a gob of spittle close to Jeanne's ear, a detail that James Allan Schamus convincingly relates to images of *conceptio per aurem* in the medieval era.[35]

Voices Appeared and the Constraints of Repertoire

The selection of repertoire followed a self-imposed series of guidelines, similar in some ways to the Dogma 95 manifesto of Dreyer's later famous compatriots, Lars von Trier and Thomas Vinterberg.[36] Repertoire was to be limited to compositions or musical practices of French, Burgundian, or English origin, that is, the three national forces that shaped Jeanne's trial, and had to have been written or performed in the twenty years or so in which Jeanne lived. Such historical and geographical specificity constantly implied that Jeanne might have heard some of this music and rested on the few specific known instances of her contact with fifteenth-century musical culture. The condemnation trial informs us that she knew her Credo, Ave Maria, and Paternoster, and if she learned them initially in spoken form, then the nullification trial informs us that she subsequently heard the sung texts.[37] That same source describes how she was accompanied on her travels from Blois to Orléans by monks singing the plainchant hymn *Veni creator spiritus* (this the scene to which Friedhofer set the *L'homme armé* tune in *Joan of Arc*), and on other occasions she sang Marian texts at dawn and dusk.[38] Whether Jeanne, a devout Christian who attended Mass daily, encountered any of the rich polyphony by named composers is considerably more conjectural. That presupposes the maintenance of choirs at a time when the financial impact of the Hundred Years' War encouraged many French composers to the relatively safer and certainly more lucrative courts and chapels of Southern Europe, notably Italy. Nevertheless, Jeanne's various travels through France would have afforded her some opportunity. After raising the siege at Orléans, there were celebrations in the streets and services in the cathedral, an obvious opportunity for an ad hoc group of singers to assemble and perform, if only "singing upon the book" (*cantare super librum*).[39] The later journey with Charles VII to Reims for the coronation took Jeanne to Auxerre, where the Cathédrale Saint-Pierre et Saint-Paul had its own choir.[40] The party subsequently laid siege to Troyes for four days and was finally admitted within its walls on the fifth, another opportunity for some kind of sacred celebration.

We can be fairly sure that Charles VII, the Dauphin, disparagingly referred to as the King of Bourges for his residency in that town, was unable to maintain a royal chapel. However, the coronation of Charles VII on July 17, 1429, in Reims, even if it did not live up to that of his grandfather Charles V on May 19, 1364, for which Machaut almost certainly wrote his *Hoquetus David*, might not have been such an austere occasion. There was a proud tradition of highly trained soloists at Reims Cathedral that dated back to the 1350s.[41] The *dernier ordo capétien* that Patrick Demouy claims was the basis for the ceremony certainly called for several musical contributions, including processional chants (*Ecce mitto angelorum* and Psalm 20: *Domine in virtute tua laetabitur rex*), a Te Deum, and several plainchant hymns specifically allocated to a choir, though whether any polyphonic settings, improvised or otherwise, were heard remains conjectural.[42] Jeanne may not have been familiar with any of that music or that of the Mass proper to the day (Ninth Sunday after Pentecost), which followed the coronation service, but she would surely have been heartened to hear the plainchant hymn *Veni creator spiritus* again.[43] One might wonder if, when captured by the Duke of Burgundy's forces and before being handed over to the English, Jeanne was deliberately taunted by the wealth and symbolic power of the Burgundian court in the form of the famed Burgundian chapel choir. Again, the exact details of the state of that institution are unclear; Philip the Good disbanded the Burgundian Chapel choir in 1419 and only began reassembling a permanent membership late in the 1420s or possibly in the 1430s.[44] More speculative still, the scenes in *La Passion de Jeanne d'Arc* of the eucharist might echo a real encounter with the musical forces of Rouen, where some 150 *chapelains* were resident.[45]

The nationality of composers is more certain, though we know next to nothing of their political or nationalistic loyalties. Dufay, for example, may have maintained his ties with Cambrai throughout his life and counted himself French when he came to write his will, but he was active in Italy in the 1420s, leaving Laon for Bologna in 1425. Some stayed close to home in the 1420s: Franchois Lebertoul and Reginaldus Libert remained in Cambrai, the latter as magister puerorum; Estienne Grossin worked in Paris, under English occupation at the time. Others traveled—Beltrame Feragut was active in Milan and Johannes de Lymburgia most likely in Padua and Vicenza in the 1420s. And the paucity of manuscripts and archival records from the first part of the fifteenth century renders Salinis, Gautier Libert, and Billart virtually anonymous. As essentially self-employed singers, we may surmise that expediency was probably the chosen course for most; still, nationalistic identity served as a useful guideline for choosing the music for *Voices Appeared*.[46]

Medievalism and the Realization of *Voices Appeared*

The *Voices Appeared* score manifests a distinctly French orientation and a strong inclination toward the sacred. The latter is entirely consistent with the drama's ecclesiastical setting, and specific episodes invited direct liturgical illustration. Jeanne's Latin recitation of the Paternoster is lip-synced by the countertenor voice and two separate stagings of the Eucharist received distinctly diegetic engagements. Both services begin with processions, accompanied in *Voices Appeared* by plainchant introits, the traditional "entrance" portion of the mass or liturgy. During the first Mass, in Jeanne's cell, an Agnus Dei is heard while the host is held temptingly before her as a reward if she signs the abjuration. When she refuses, Mass is abruptly ended with a Deo Gracias, the response to *Ite, missa est* ("Go, the dismissal is made"). When, later, Jeanne is finally granted communion after relenting, a priest blesses the congregation and again elevates the host, both standard parts of the drama of Eucharist, here illustrated by solemn communion tones and responses. A different Agnus Dei is now heard, the repeated liturgical form underlining the narrative rhyme.

Elsewhere, sacred music amplifies the emotional tone of the scene while its text acts as an ironic commentary: a vigorously polyrhythmic Sanctus by Richard Loqueville (d. 1418) metaphorizes a montage of ever-threatening torture instruments with Pythagorean-tuned leading notes and "crude" parallel fifths and octaves used to grating effect (see Figure 11.1 and Example 11.1).[47]

In contrast, fauxbourdon—the late medieval technique creating a series of parallel thirds and sixths—elsewhere expresses the cloying machinations of Jeanne's inquisitors (see Figure 11.2 and Example 11.2).

And Johannes Lymburgia's setting of the Song of Songs text, *Descendi in ortum meum*, is about an altogether darker garden than the one of which he speaks: the cemetery of St. Ouen, where flowers wither and maggots crawl from skulls.

FIGURE 11.1 Still from *La Passion de Jeanne d'Arc* showing instruments of torture. Used with permission from Eureka Entertainment.

Textual allusions also offered apposite metaphorical meanings. The French title of the film expressly parallels the passion of Christ with that of Jeanne, as does the Danish title—*Jeanne d'Arcs lidelse og død*—Jeanne d'Arc's suffering and death. An Ave Verum Corpus by Johannes Reson (fl. ca. 1425–1435), the text of which references the physical examination and bleeding of Christ's body, accompanies the scene where the doctors bleed Jeanne, the word *sanguinis* coinciding exactly with the moment when blood spurts from her arm. Similar overt textual correspondences are used in Dufay's *Vexilla regis* when the word *crux* aligns with the shadow of a cross on the cell floor and the word *rex* echoes a reference in an intertitle to Jeanne's king.

Such foregrounded textual correspondence mitigated against the use of chansons; the word *amour* and derivations of it, so common in that repertoire, would be entirely anomalous. However, Dufay's chanson *Je me complains* proved the perfect vehicle for verses from Christine de Pizan's *Ditié de Jehanne d'Arc*, written in 1429, *contrafacta* that became prologue and epilogue for the film. Gautier Libert's simple, haunting *De tristesse*, whose opaque text expresses sadness, suffering, and sacrifice, functioned as a leitmotif, appearing during the most pained and profound moments of Jeanne's suffering and thus becoming, in film-music terms, "Jeanne's theme."

The score thus advances its obeisance to musical, liturgical, and textual authenticity and freely exploits the liminal spaces between narration and illustration, as well as those between the diegetic and nondiegetic. The particular ontology of silent film and live music played on an ongoing re-presentation of medieval sound for the audience by the ever-present performers, while also suggesting Jeanne's auditory hallucination. For example, when Jeanne is led to the stake, a solo countertenor voice sings the *Veni creator spiritus*,

EXAMPLE 11.1 Loqueville, *Sanctus.*

the hymn that heralded her greatest achievement at Orléans and that now presages her martyrdom, functioning as both commentary and an implied personal memory.

Essential to the success of such a strategy was the exact synchronization between music and image that is made possible by digital technology; visual cues were provided on a laptop synced to the film, a flick track rather than a click track.[48] Paradoxically, this was both constraining and liberating, enabling a considerably more overt performance style than that of the concert stage.[49]

Performance knowingly enacted an English subjugation of the female voice, something implicit in the fact that the performers of *Voices Appeared* are five British men. Something of the ambiguity of Jeanne's cross-dressing is recovered in the countertenor voice, a female-register sound emanating from a male body. At the other extreme of the vocal compass, the addition of a low bass voice to the standard four-voice lineup of the Orlando Consort further actualizes patriarchal prohibition. Medieval music here,

FIGURE 11.2 Still from *La Passion* showing Jeanne's inquisitors. Used with permission from Eureka Entertainment.

that "especially convincing dream of the Middle Ages," stands in service to a film, engaging and amplifying its histories, filtering them through a calibrated musicohistorical prism if ineluctably informed by modern performance styles.[50] Music and performance are thus caught in a new matrix of meaning, shaping and revising our perception of a historical era and, in turn, shaped and revised by the material it illumines.

This nexus recalls various issues of medievalism in music over the past fifty years, a path that has led us toward the notion of invention.[51] Invention is a word that echoes and reinforces notions of historical alterity that medievalism addresses and ultimately embraces. It also announces an abandonment of faith in us ever comprehending a world that exists so far away, a potential nihilism that emerges from the precariousness of modern performance and historical performance practice. Invoking Eco's distinction and returning us to the very issues raised in a different context by Rósza at the beginning of this essay, perhaps it is, then, correct to describe all modern performance of such repertoire as *fantastic neomedievalism* and contrast it with academic study as *responsible philological examination*.[52]

The search for connections between Jeanne and the music of her life, the account of Dreyer's historical research, the parsing of Dreyer's few comments about music, and even the "honest" admission of nationalistic musical traditions to which I have held up my hand ultimately seek to justify a project that wears medievalisms on its sleeve, celebrating the interactions of modern performance and medieval history. Like the Baucicaut miniatures, where medieval Otherness is filtered through comforting images of the familiar, national musical traditions confirm an acceptable image of medieval music.[53]

EXAMPLE 11.2 Binchois, *Salve Sancta parens.*

In this case there is a double amplification of medievalisms: the film's representation of medieval history and the representation of medieval musical history in modern sound. Considerable doubt has been cast particularly on the latter, its refashioning in modern dress deemed inescapable, but the engagement of such music with a representation of medieval history offers something of a postmodernist critique, an interrogation not unlike the hectoring priests questioning Jeanne, who in turn rounds on her captors to accuse them of hypocrisy.

Silence may have been the only option for Dreyer in 1956 when the performance of medieval music was rare, but, suspect as the sound of medieval music will always be, we at least now have something more provocative to ponder.

ACKNOWLEDGMENTS

My thanks to Birgit Granhøj and all at the Dreyer Archive in the Danish Film Institute in Copenhagen for their gracious help and guidance. Thanks also to Mervyn Cooke, Nick Baragwanath, Joshua Rifkin, and the editors for their helpful comments on earlier drafts.

NOTES

1. Miklós Rósza, "*Quo Vadis*," *Film/TV Music* 11, no. 4 (November/December 1951), repr. James L. Limbacher, *Film Music from Violins to Video* (Metuchen, NJ: Scarecrow Press, 1974), 147–153, further repr., *The Hollywood Film Music Reader*, ed. Mervyn Cooke (Oxford: Oxford University Press, 2010), 165–171. Quotation from Cooke, 169.
2. I designed the soundtrack and the project was developed with the financial support of the Arts Council of England in 2015. There have thus far been some sixty performances in the United Kingdom, the United States, Canada, Germany, Italy, France, Denmark, Sweden, Slovenia, Italy, and Spain. For more details, accessed July 29, 2019, see http://www.orlando-consort.com/voicesappeared.htm.
3. Letter of March 16, 1956, written in French to Jean Jay, directeur générale of Gaumont Actualités. Dreyer Archive D (Dreyer Archive) II, A:1243.
4. The subject was also explored by Maurice Jaubert and Arthur Honegger; see Elizabeth Dister, "Tolling Bells and Otherworldly Voices: Joan of Arc's Sonic World in the Early Twentieth Century," this volume, pp. 423–448. See also Diana Hallman, "The Distant Past as Mirror and Metaphor: Portraying Medievalism in Historical French Grand Operas," this volume, pp. 109–134.
5. Britta Martensen-Larsen wrongly suggests that the entire manuscript consists only of Mandeville's *Le Livre des merveilles du monde*. See Britta Martensen-Larsen, "Inspirationen fra middelalderens miniaturer." *Kosmorama* 39, no. 204 (1993): 26–31. On Polo's and Mandeville's texts, see Simon Gaunt, "Travel and Orientalism," in *The Cambridge History of French Literature*, ed. W. Burgwinkle, N. Hammond, and E. Wilson (Cambridge: Cambridge University Press, 2011), 121–130. Warm is best known today for the expressionist sets of *Das Cabinet des Dr. Caligari* (1919).
6. The reproduction Dreyer might have consulted was H. Omont, *Le Livre des merveilles: Marco Polo, Odoric de Pordenone, Mandeville etc. Reproduction des 265 miniatures du manuscrit français 2810 de la Bibliothèque nationale* (Paris: Berthaud, 1907). For more detail on the history of the manuscript, see Millard Meiss, *French Paintings in the Time of Jean de Berry (2)* (London: Phaidon, 1967), 49.
7. Carl Theodor Dreyer, "My Only Great Passion," from a radio interview in 1950: Skoller, *Dreyer in Double Reflection*, ed. Donald Skoller (New York: Da Capo, 1973), 144.
8. Warm's recollection is that he discovered the miniatures independently: "I found a history of Jeanne d'Arc illustrated with medieval miniatures in a Parisian bookstore. The simple renderings of buildings, landscapes and people, the naïve lines and distorted perspective,

were the basis for the film's design. A combination of surrealistic elements provided the uncanny style that Dreyer endorsed." (Herman Warm, "Dreyer brugte sandfærdigheden som stilmiddel," *Kosmorama* no. 90: 147). However, Jean Hugo, husband of Valentine Hugo, the costume designer for the film, who worked alongside Warm as art director, recalls Dreyer handing him a folder that contained copies of the miniatures. See Martensen-Larsen, "Inspirationen," 27.

9. For more detail, see Casper Tybjerg, "La Passione di Giovanna d'Arco: Molte versioni, un solo film?," in *Per Dreyer: Incarnazione del cinema*, ed. Sergio Grmek Germani and Giorgio Placereani (Milan: Il Castoro, 2004); and Tony Pipolo, "The Spectre of Joan of Arc: Textual Variations in the Key Prints of Carl Dreyer's Film," *Film History* 2 (1988): 301–324.

10. See Nicholas De Jongh, "Dreyer's La Passion Found in Cellar," *Manchester Guardian Weekly*, May 5, 1985, 20.

11. Dreyer visited the set of *Napoléon* in 1926 when he was preparing the screenplay for *La Passion de Jeanne d'Arc*.

12. The first performance of *Napoléon* with the score by Davis in the United Kingdom was in November 1980, followed in January 1981 by a performance with music by Carmine Coppola in New York. For details on the use of symphonic orchestras in silent-film exhibition in the United States, see Gillian B. Anderson, "The Presentation of Silent Films, or, Music as Anaesthesia," *The Journal of Musicology* 5, no. 2 (Spring 1987): 257–295, esp. 264–265.

13. For a lengthy analysis of *Voices of Light* and Dreyer's film, see Rachel May Golden, "Polyphonies of Sound and Space: Motet, Montage, *Voices of Light*, and *La Passion de Jeanne d'Arc*," *Musical Quarterly* 96, no. 2 (2013): 296–330.

14. *Voices of Light* is an option in the Criterion Collection DVD version of *La Passion de Jeanne d'Arc*, no. 62. This edition plays at the equivalent of 24 frames per second (fps), the industry standard of the sound era, producing a running time of 82 minutes. The Blu-Ray restoration of the film by Eureka Entertainment (EKA70267) plays at 20fps and therefore lasts longer, some 96 minutes. In October 2017 a new version was released by Gaumont in France, which plays at 20fps, with a new musical accompaniment on organ by Karol Mossakowski first heard at Le Festival Lumière in Lyon in October 2015. The Criterion Collection edition (no. 62), released in North America in March 2018, includes the Einhorn score, the Gregory/Utley score, and a further piano score composed and performed by Mie Yanashita. The edition also includes a version at 20fps with Danish intertitles.

15. The cue-sheet system created scores by combining preexistent compositions. See Rick Altman, *Silent Film Sound* (New York: Columbia University Press, 2004), 345–365.

16. A brief exchange with a Monsieur G. Carré of the Ciné-Club de Chartres, who is seeking information about the music used for the premiere of *La Passion de Jeanne d'Arc*, elicits a perfectly polite expression of ignorance on Dreyer's part: He knows nothing about the music used. See D II, A:299 and 300.

17. La Passion de Jeanne d'Arc. *Choeurs de Serge Plaute. Musique d'écran de Léo Pouget et Victor Alix, pour le film de Carl Dreyer, (Alliance cinématographique). Instrumentation de E. Météhen. Partition du piano conducteur* (Paris: Éditions musicales Sam Fox, 1928); Gillian B. Anderson recreated the score and performed it with the film in Washington, DC, in 1995: https://www.washingtonpost.com/archive/local/1996/07/25/orchestra-and-singers-bring-silent-film-to-life/97e4c00e-e7ef-4b55-aeaa-e520c12290f8/?utm_term=.72b5ed174e84. Anderson suggests that the score might have been part of a broader strategy to temper the anticlerical sentiments of the film. See Gillian B. Anderson, "The Shock of the Old: The Restoration,

Reconstruction, or Creation of 'Mute' Film Accompaniments," in *The Routledge Companion to Screen Music and Sound*, ed. Miguel Mera, Ronald Sadoff, and Ben Winters (New York: Routledge, 2017), 201–212, esp. 204–205.

18. A qualified version of this appears in the accompanying booklet to the Eureka Entertainment edition: "As far as is known, Dreyer's preference was for *La Passion de Jeanne d'Arc* to be shown in silence, with no musical accompaniment," Eureka Entertainment booklet, 2.

19. Jean Arroy, "Carl Dreyer," in *Cinémagazine*, special edition (1927): 29–39. This edition falls somewhere between a magazine and trade promotion, with pictures of its stars and extensive space devoted to information on how to order the film.

20. D II, A:1649.

21. "I wish to be sincere to you and for this reason I must say that it in my opinion artistically [it] is a great, great mistake to try to transform 'Joan of Arc' in [*sic*] a talkie." From a letter of May 21, 1946, to Lo Duca, retrieved from a bookseller, accessed June 6, 2019, https://www.royalbooks.com/pages/books/139112/carl-theodore-dreyer-joseph-marie-lo-duca/archive-of-four-letters-discussing-a-sound-version-of-the-passion-of-joan-of-arc. Some ten years later, after watching Lo Duca's version, Dreyer wrote to Jean Jay as follows: "An old film 'classic' is a museum piece that should be restored to its original form. In my opinion to modernize such a film is an absurdity." D II, A:1649.

22. Dreyer learned about the music from various press clippings sent to him by Helge Wamberg, at the time working in Paris as the Danish Press and Cultural Attaché: D, I, A; Jeanne d'Arc, 2. The actual program supplied by the Cinéma d'Essai cites music by Bach, Albinoni, Vivaldi, Beethoven, Palestrina, and César Franck, though different reviews do not mention all of the composers. Though he never saw this early version, such knowledge explains Dreyer's reference to Beethoven in an interview with Lotte Eisner in 1955: "I knew that my rhythm would be destroyed, it is not the rhythm of Bach's music, or Beethoven's." Lotte Eisner, "Rencontre avec Carl Th. Dreyer," *Cahiers du Cinéma* 7, no. 48 (June 1955): 5.

23. A letter from Lo Duca to Dreyer in July 1952 refers briefly to a recording made in Saint Eustache in Paris: D II, A:1663. This must have been for the Scarlatti, as no recording of the work existed at the time. Nearly all the other music cues came from two extant recordings on the Éditions phonographiques parisiennes label: EPP SLP 1 and EPP SLP 2. My thanks go to Nick Morgan for his considerable help. There is an interesting subplot here with the use of the Albinoni Adagio in G minor, a cue that appears twice in Lo Duca's version. This was the first occasion that the music had been used in the film, the piece itself a spurious reconstruction by the Italian musicologist Remo Giazotto (still co-credited with the composition), this based on two fragments discovered in a Leipzig library that he was never able to produce when challenged, This has not, though, prevented the music being used in countless films, usually as a signifier of loss and suffering, notably in *Rollerball* (1975), *Gallipoli* (1981), *Flashdance* (1983), and, more recently, *Manchester by the Sea* (2016).

24. "The immortal chorales of J. S. Bach became an 'Adagio Lamentoso for sad scenes,' " writes Max Winkler in "The Origins of Film Music," *Films in Review* 2, no. 34 (December 1951), repr. *Film Music: From Violins to Video*, 22, quoted in Altman, *Silent*, 2004, 361. *Dr Jekyll and Mr Hyde* (1931) and *The Black Cat* (1934) both used the Toccata and Fugue in D minor and, less obviously horrifying, though sharing some of the genre's fascination with body horror, *Rollerball* (1975) used it in its opening title sequence. Like the Albinoni Adagio in G minor, the Bach has been questioned on grounds of musicological authenticity. See Peter F. Williams, "BWV 565: A Toccata in D Minor for Organ by J. S. Bach?," *Early Music* 9, no. 3 (July 1981): 330–337.

25. See Altman, *Silent*, 315–316.

26. Private correspondence, email of November 12, 2014.

27. David Bordwell, *Filmguide to* La passion de Jeanne d'Arc (Bloomington: Indiana University Press, 1973), 79.

28. The three-part polyphony is transposed up and sung by high female voices, which gives it a celebratory feel. For more on the order of service, see Patrick Demouy, "La liturgie du sacre de Charles VII," *Annales de l'Est* no. 2 (2015): 111–121.

29. This is the three-part *Alle psallite cum luya*, F-MO H 196, fol. 392, a suitably exultant motet, though it seems very unlikely that it would have had any place in the Coronation of 1429. It was published in modern notation in *Polyphonies du XIIIe siècle: Tome III*, ed. Yvonne Rokseth (Paris: Editions de l'Oiseau Lyre, 1936), 256–257. Friedhofer implicitly claims a role as supervisor of the Coronation scene, citing "a lot of plain-chant (*sic*) and one thing of Guillaume Dufay's," but makes no mention of any other music. See *Hugo Friedhofer: The Best Years of His Life: A Hollywood Master of Music for the Movies*, ed. Linda Danly (Lanham, MD, Scarecrow Press, 2002), 123. It seems unlikely, though, that Friedhofer would have had such detailed knowledge of the early medieval repertoire, and though Roger Wagner, a conductor at the University of California–Los Angeles at this time, whose chorale performed the music for the Coronation, would have had access to an edition, I am inclined to think that Walter Rubsamen, then a professor at the university, may have played a part. He regularly contributed articles on film music to *Arts and Architecture* between 1945 and 1947 and organized a symposium on film music in 1945 to which he invited Hugo Friedhofer. Note also that the *L'homme armé* tune and *Alle psallite cum luya* were published in Historical Anthology of Music, Vol. 1: Oriental, Medieval, and Renaissance Music, eds. Archibald T. Davison and Willi Apel (Cambridge, MA: Harvard University Press, 1947).

30. Bresson was critical of the actors' "horrible tomfoolery, the frightful grimaces" ("les horrible pitreries, des grimaces épouvantables") in *La Passion de Jeanne d'Arc*, very different from his own preferred unemotional acting style. However, it is difficult not to take details such as Warwick's spying on Jeanne through a crack in the wall, the fluttering of birds away from the scene of execution, the cross held up and visible through smoke, and the final shot of the charred stake as anything other than homages to Dreyer's film. The quotation is from a transcript of a press conference, published as "Propos de Robert Bresson," *Cahiers du cinéma* no. 75 (October 1957): 9.

31. See Isabelle Ragnard, "Le thème de *L'homme armé* dans le film *Jeanne La Pucelle* de Jacques Rivette," *Le Paon d'Héra* 8 (2012): 27. The chansons are Dufay's "Ce jour de l'an" and "Ce jour le doibt," which from their place in the original manuscript (GB-Ob MS. Canon. Misc. 213, Bodleian Library, Oxford, England) and on stylistic grounds seem likely to have been written no later than 1430. David Fallows suggests that the Missa *L'homme armé* was written in the 1450s and the earliest date for the tune itself, according to Alejandro Planchart, is 1434. See David Fallows, *Dufay* (London: Dent, 1982), 70; and Alejandro Enrique Planchart, "The Origins and Early History of L'homme armé," *The Journal of Musicology* 20, no. 3 (Summer 2003): 305–357. *Resjois toi terre de France* is unconvincingly credited to anonymous in the liner notes to the soundtrack of the film. Certainly the motet-chanson was not confidently attributed to Busnois until the 1970s, but the alternative composer was Johannes Ockeghem, and by 1992 the debate was all but settled. See Andreas Lindmayr-Brandel, "'Resjois toi terre de France/Rex Pacificus'": An 'Ockeghem' Work Reattributed to Busnoys," in *Antoine Busnoys: Method, Meaning, and Context in Late Medieval Music*, ed. Paula Higgins (Oxford: Oxford University Press, 1999), 277–294.

32. The first of the eventual seven volumes of Gilbert Reaney's *Corpus Mensurabilis Musicae Early Fifteenth Century Music* series was only published in 1955. Until then, the main sources for editions in modern notation were John Stainer, *Dufay and His Contemporaries: Fifty Compositions… Transcribed from MS Canonici misc. 213 in the Bodleian Library, Oxford* (London: Novello, 1898); Charles van den Borren, *Polyphonia Sacra: A Continental Miscellany of the Fifteenth Century* (London: Plainsong and Medieval Music Society, 1932); and Jeanne Marix, *Les musiciens de la cour de Bourgogne au xve siécle (1420–1467) Gilles de Binche (Binchois), Pierre Fontaine, Jacques Vide, Nicole Grenon, Gilles Joye, Hayne de Ghizeghem, Robert Morton. Messes, motets, chansons* (Paris: Editions de l'Oiseau-lyre, 1937). The performance of this repertoire was considerably less developed and mainly confined to the academy. See Daniel Leech-Wilkinson, *The Modern Invention of Medieval Music* (Cambridge: Cambridge University Press, 2002), 77–87; and Annette Kreutziger-Herr, "Imagining Medieval Music: a Short History," in *Studies in Medievalism XIV: Correspondences: Medievalism in Scholarship and the Arts*, ed. Tom Shippey with Martin Arnold (Cambridge: Brewer, 2005), 81–109, esp. 93–99.

33. Dreyer made three sound films after *Vampyr*: *Vredens Dag* (1943), *Ordet* (1955), and *Gertrud* (1964). All are based on stage plays, use music very sparingly, and seem to be working toward "spoken films that do not have the need for music, film in which the words do not come out short." Carl Theodor Dreyer, "A Little on Film Style" (1943), in Skoller, *Dreyer*, 141.

34. Such points were suggested in press materials, program notes, and interviews and echoed in reviews. The specific history of the group and its close association with musicologists, for example, is hinted at in the biography of the group ("fresh scholarly insight"—http://www.orlandoconsort.com/materials.htm) and the limitation of music to the specific era of Jeanne's life was praised for its "compelling sense of authenticity," accessed June 6, 2019, http://www.musicaltoronto.org/2016/04/04/scrutiny-orlando-consort-reimagines-the-passion-of-joan-of-arc/. On the "English *a cappella* heresy," see Leech-Wilkinson, *Modern Invention*, esp. 147–153.

35. This moment forms the basis for the third chapter of James Allan Schamus's thesis on Dreyer: Schamus traces the "rhetorical history" of immaculate conception through the ear, "a forced entry of language into the woman's body." "*The Moving Word*" (PhD diss., University of California, Berkeley, 2003), 2. See also James Schamus, *Carl Theodor Dreyer's Gertrud: The Moving Word* (Seattle: University of Washington Press, 2008), esp. 64–90.

36. For an account of Dogma 95 and its place in film history, see Scott MacKenzie, "Manifest Destinies: Dogma 95 and the Future of the Film Manifesto," in *Purity and Provocation: Dogma 95*, ed. Mette Hjort and Scott MacKenzie (London: British Film Institute, 2003), 48–57.

37. The testimony of Frère Jean Pasquerel is that he sang Mass to her: "Le lendemain, il l'entendit en confession et chanta la messe en sa présence," accessed June 6, 2019, http://www.stejeannedarc.net/rehabilitation/dep_jean_pasquerel.php.

38. See the testimony of Frère Jean Pasquerel, accessed June 6, 2019, http://www.stejeannedarc.net/rehabilitation/dep_jean_pasquerel.php. Jean d'Orléans, comte de Dunois, formerly the Bastard of Orléans, cites other occasions where Jeanne surrounded herself with singing, http://www.stejeannedarc.net/rehabilitation/dep_dunois.php.

39. "Cantare super librum" continues to be a contentious issue. See Margaret Bent, "'Resfacta' and 'Cantare Super Librum,'" *Journal of the American Musicological Society* 36, no. 3 (Autumn 1983): 371–391; and Rob C. Wegman, "From Maker to Composer: Improvisation

and Musical Authorship in the Low Countries, 1450–1500," *Journal of the American Musicological Society* 49, no. 3 (Autumn 1996): 409–479.

40. We have the tantalizing glimpse of a singer called Michel Dart, or d'Arc—no relation—who had connections with the Royal Chapel choir, having sung at the funeral of Charles VI in Paris on October 21, 1422. He was a canon at Auxerre. See David Fiala, "Michel d'Arc [Darc]," in *Prosopographie des Chantres* (Tours: CESR/Ricercar), http://92.154.49.37/CESR_CHANTRES/ and http://92.154.49.37/CESR_CHANTRES/items/show/1022, accessed July 29, 2019. Fiala offers a not dissimilarly teasing prospect with the case of an English singer praising Jeanne in the Rehabilitation trial, though it turns out to have been a case of mistaken identity, see David Fiala, "La musique à la cour de Bourgogne," *Annales de l'Est* no. 2 (2015): 59–60.

41. In 1285, the chapter founded what was effectively its choir, consisting of twelve clerics, all of whom were required to sing. See Pierre Desportes, *Fasti Ecclesiae Gallicanae 3 Diocèse de Reims: Répertoire prosopographique des évêques, dignitaires et chanoines des diocèses de France de 1200 à 1500* (Brepols: Turnhout, 1998), 20. A bull of 1352 led to an expansion of performing forces in the 1350s and 1360s that went hand in hand with the development of complexity and technical demands in Machaut's compositions. See Anne Walters Robertson, *Guillaume de Machaut and Reims: Context and Meaning in His Musical Works* (Cambridge: Cambridge University Press, 2007), 48–52 passim.

42. Demouy suggests that the Mass setting may have been Machaut's *Messe de Nostre Dame*, a not-inconceivable idea given its obvious connection with Reims Cathedral, see Demouy, "La liturgie," 119.

43. Ibid.

44. Like his father, John the Fearless, before him, Philip the Good cut the size of his chapel when he became duke, but descriptions of his wedding to Isabel of Portugal in January 1430 and the commission of the motet *Nove cantum melodie* in January 1431 suggest a healthy chapel choir, earlier than the date for which archival evidence exists. See Craig Wright, *Music at the Court of Burgundy, 1364–1419: A Documentary History* (Henryville: Institute of Medieval Music, 1974), 106; and Fiala, "La musique à la cour de Bourgogne."

45. Not all these chapelains would have been singers, but the cathedral's commitment to choral polyphony is demonstrated in the expansion of its numbers from four to six in 1413 and six to eight in 1471. See Vincent Tabbagh, *Fasti Ecclesiae Gallicanae 2 Diocèse de Rouen: Répertoire prosopographique des évêques, dignitaires et chanoines des diocèses de France de 1200 à 1500* (Brepols: Turnhout, 1998), 14–15.

46. A complete list of compositions and composers and a cross-referenced scene breakdown can be found at http://www.orlandoconsort.com/scenebreakdown.htm. For more on the history of the Orlando Consort, see Donald Greig, "Sightlines and Tramlines: The Orlando Consort at 25," *Early Music* 43, no. 1 (2015): 129–144.

47. Pythagorean tuning is premised on exact mathematical ratios and produces significantly different tunings to the modern equal-tempered scale.

48. The click track, whereby regular clicks helped a conductor create an orchestral performance that could by precisely synchronized with particular onscreen gestures, was commonly used in the predigital era of film production.

49. In this context, see Christopher Page, "The English *a cappella* Renaissance," *Early Music* 21, no. 2 (1993): 453–472, and my response: Donald Greig, "Sight Readings: Notes on *a cappella* Performance Practice," *Early Music* 23, no. 1 (1995): 125–148; repr. *Renaissance Music*, ed. Kenneth Kreitner (Farnham, UK: Ashgate, 2011). For a more recent consideration, see

Greig, "Sightlines," 2015, this partially in response to justifiable criticism of a straight-jacketed performance style among (mainly) British groups by Bonnie J. Blackburn, "Tramline Music," *Early Music* 41, no. 1 (2013): 52–53.

50. Kreutziger-Herr, "Imagining," 84.
51. The obvious reference here is Leech-Wilkinson, *Modern Invention*.
52. See Umberto Eco, "Dreaming of the Middle Ages," in *Travels in Hyperreality: Essays*, trans. William Weaver (San Diego: Harcourt Brace Jovanovich, 1986), 63.
53. See Page, "The English."

MEDIEVALISM AND COMPOSITIONAL PRACTICE IN THE TWENTIETH CENTURY

....

CHAPTER 12

MEDIEVALISM AND ANTIROMANTICISM IN CARL ORFF'S *CARMINA BURANA*

....

KIRSTEN YRI

WITH its twenty-five poems drawn from a medieval manuscript found in 1803 in the Benedictine Monastery in Bavaria and a musical accompaniment that makes use of unison choral settings, simple rhythms, and archaic sounding harmonies, Carl Orff's *Carmina Burana* would seem to offer a clear example of medievalism for its time.[1] The most famous selection—"O Fortuna"—has frequently been used in films set in the Middle Ages; its plainchant-inspired melody and largely "primitive" driving rhythms have come to signal the medieval in popular culture. In and of itself, this placement of "O Fortuna" at the forefront of musical medievalism is significant for the ways that it appears to conjure up a dark, threatening Middle Ages very much in line with the notion of the Gothic.[2] The allusions to medieval chant in "O Fortuna" might suggest Orff imitated medieval music as an attempt to authentically accompany the medieval poetry. After all, Orff could have reconstructed the sounds of medieval music based on the scholarly work on medieval music theory and history that had exploded at the end of the nineteenth and beginning of the twentieth centuries. And surface details of some of the songs support the notion that Orff was interested in authenticity, in presenting medieval music "as it really was," to quote from Ranke's prescription for historical writing.[3] Moreover, even Michel Hofmann, with whom Orff worked closely, asserted that he "awakened" the "original" melodies.[4] The curious fact remains, however, that despite setting poems from the Codex Buranus, as the medieval manuscript is now called, only a handful of selections in *Carmina Burana* appear to be closely aligned with medieval music. The view of "O Fortuna" as a synecdoche for medievalism in *Carmina Burana* thus fails to account for a range of selections that, indeed, share little of its archaic, plainchant-inspired sound.

Any exploration of medievalism in *Carmina Burana* must also contend with the Nazi taint that, as Michael Kater and Richard Taruskin noted, has shaped the work's reception history almost since its premiere in 1937.[5] The work generated some negative press for its risqué subject matter and use of primitive rhythms associated with the "degenerate" composer Stravinsky, but as is well known, it soon became a success, and during the 1940s it garnered praise that used the language of Nazi slogans.[6] The semidramatized format replete with mass choruses, a large orchestra heavy in brass, and percussion, helped align it with the state-sponsored national festivals.[7] Moreover, some of the musical settings appeared to resemble the popular songs that came to be associated with National Socialist music.[8] The success of the work under the National Socialists may also speak to the essential role that the Middle Ages played in the regime's agenda. The Nazis were known to employ medieval themes and symbols to authorize a host of concepts for propagandistic purposes. It would not, therefore, be unwarranted to ask how a work that uses medieval poetry and appears to evoke medieval music relates to the dominant ideology. In what ways could Orff's use of the medieval poems be complicit with the recovery of the Middle Ages for nationalist purposes? Did Orff share with some contemporary musicologists and historians of the Middle Ages support for the recovery of German art, music, and literature to justify the nation's racist self-aggrandizement?[9]

This chapter examines medievalism in the *Carmina Burana* cycle in the context of a political program that saw the Middle Ages as a tool for propaganda. Although *Carmina Burana* was used by the National Socialists and has since been described as model music for mass rallies, this is largely, I would suggest, because the plainchant-inspired choruses, archaic modes, and simple rhythms of "O Fortuna" have eclipsed close readings of the remainder of the cycle.[10] Indeed, the failure to examine the role of the poetry and interpret it in the context of Orff's remaining musical settings has led to a skewed understanding of the work. The poems in the Codex Buranus were collected and/or written by the wandering goliards who offered satires of the clerics and parodies of religious practices, but the fact that at least some of these poems mock religion and authority and critique clichéd images of courtly love in ways that paralleled modern disillusionment with society and antiromantic sentiment is infrequently discussed. And yet, as attested to in the letters between Orff and Hofmann on the subject of *Carmina Burana*, these parodies are a significant component of the work, perhaps even its raison d'être.[11]

Drawing on these letters, archival material, and letters between Orff and the medievalist Rudolf von Ficker, I propose to follow Orff's musical medievalism along a number of trajectories. It is generally believed that Orff's compositional language was influenced by medieval music and that he sought to represent medieval music in his settings. This has produced a muddled understanding of *Carmina Burana* and Orff's compositional idiom that collapses all Orff's engagement with the Middle Ages into a singular medievalism. As I will illustrate, it is more productive to distinguish between three levels of engagement. The first is the influence of medieval music that can be described as architectural and that plays out in Orff's compositional idiom by informing not only *Carmina*

Burana, but also other works. For simplicity's sake, I have avoided the term *medievalism* to connote this compositional influence. The second engagement with medieval music, and one that we can call medievalism, is better considered on the level of *style*, wherein sacred medieval musical forms are imitated for their associative meanings and gestic interplay with the poems.[12] Though these styles are altered somewhat to fit Orff's compositional purpose, they are by and large recognizable as pastiche. As my analysis of *Carmina Burana* demonstrates, pastiche is also apparent in Orff's use of familiar musical styles and topics common to the popular choral repertoire of the nineteenth century. These familiar styles derive from medievalism as it was musically constituted in state-sponsored oratorios and *Liedertafel*, as well as choruses described with the motto "wine, women and song." Following Edward Haymes, I define these allusions to nineteenth-century styles as *two-storied medievalism*, in which the primary reference is not to medieval materials per se, but rather to an intermediary form of medievalism.[13] Examining Orff's allusions to various medieval musical styles against an interpretation of the poetry, I suggest that *Carmina Burana* voices a parody of the romantic, imperial, and idealistic medievalism of his youth in the last decade of the nineteenth century and first decade of the twentieth.

Medievalism under Kaiser Wilhelm II and National Socialism

By the time Orff and the archivist and philologist Michel Hoffmann began work on *Carmina Burana* in April 1934, one year after Hitler became chancellor, the Nazi regime was already exploiting medievalism as a nationalist, self-aggrandizing tool for the purposes of propaganda. It is not that the Nazis invented the interest in the Middle Ages or that they were the first to litter medieval history with their own vainglories and nationalist images. As other essays in this handbook have detailed, Germany's fascination with the Middle Ages extends well back into the nineteenth century, where it served a variety of different social, historical, and political purposes. In a time defined by the Napoleonic Wars, the 1848 Revolution, the Franco-Prussian War, and the establishment of the Second Reich, the medieval model of the Holy Roman Empire of the German nation offered Germany an idealized image of religious and national unity.[14] A fascination with the Middle Ages had already seeped into the musical fabric of the romantic movement as background settings for operas, as chivalrous heroes idealized in the revival of the *Minnesang*, or as a nostalgia or longing for a better time, for many, "a Golden Age of (national) unity and glory."[15] As David Barclay describes, especially after 1871, it was this latter image of the Middle Ages that became the "official" medievalism of Imperial Germany, masking other competing medievalisms that served nostalgic or escapist purposes, as well as those that had cosmopolitan, religious, or democratic agendas.[16]

Spending their first twenty-five years under the Hohenzollern Empire, or Second Reich, Orff and Hofmann had observed the official medievalism espoused by Kaiser Wilhelm II. They were educated under the curriculum that viewed Wilhelmine Germany as the second incarnation of the Holy Roman Empire, one that returned Germany to its allegedly united, medieval glory. They were also well aware of Kaiser Wilhelm II's penchant for pomp, patriotism, and aggressive foreign policy, all of which resonated with the medieval chivalric codes that colored so much of the artistic output of German romantics. German citizens—particularly those from Orff and Hofmann's generation— rejected "the aesthetic values, authoritarian rituals and 'hurrah patriotism' of the *Kaiserreich*'s official culture."[17] They witnessed the political and social disillusionment that encouraged numerous youth groups (*Wandervögel*) and life reform (*Lebensreform*) groups' pursuit of "alternative" values, namely "freedom" from the meddling forces of bureaucracy and the desire to live a balanced and simple life, eschewing "vulgar display and ostentation."[18]

Of course, the notion that Germany's social problems were products of industrialization—and the realization that the world could not be managed through Enlightenment thought—was already a feature of medievalism in the romantic era. The concept of disillusionment had been a steady source of inspiration for writers and composers, whether they turned back to the Middle Ages or simply rejected values inherent in the modern condition. But under Kaiser Wilhelm's bureaucracy, his pursuit of order and rules, and the ostentatiousness with which he reigned, discontentedness reached new heights. Wilhelm II's policies and governing style drew even more criticism in Orff and Hofmann's Bavaria, a region with a contingent that was critical of German unification under Bismarck and certainly resented the installment of a Prussian king as German emperor (Wilhelm I) in 1871.[19]

Given the disdain that Kaiser Wilhelm II had earned as head of state and the fact that the National Socialists held him responsible for Germany's defeat in World War II, it is perhaps surprising that the components of official medievalism would become such an important part of the Nazis' political program.[20] Even the conflicted position that the idea of *empire* aroused among many Germans was not enough to thwart the Nazis adoption and abuse of Wilhelmine Germany's glorification of the Middle Ages and imperialism. The mythologies both of late nineteenth- and early twentieth-century Imperial Germany and of the Third Reich were modeled on the spirit and "divine right" of figures such as emperor Barbarossa to support the authority of Kaiser Wilhelm I and II and, ultimately, that of Hitler himself.[21] Besides the parallel that was drawn between the medieval Holy Roman Empire and the Third Reich, the National Socialists projected virtues they considered intrinsic to the functioning of this medieval empire into the present. The medieval chivalric codes of order, loyalty, and military virtue were revived from the official medievalism of the nineteenth century. Honor and loyalty to Hitler and the National Socialist *Gemeinschaft* was frequently described with the Wagnerian term *Nibelungentreue*, referencing not only Wagner's music drama *The Ring of the Nibelung*, but also the medieval epic that Wagner used for some of his source material.[22]

Medievalism as Critique

So, when the Nazis adopted the well-worn codes of Wagner's mythical medievalism and began to espouse the ideals of romanticism, some of the public discredited these ideals as old-fashioned. And when the regime began to endorse the pomp and patriotism of Kaiser Wilhelm's official medievalism and to make proclamations regarding the "glories of the Holy Roman Empire," citizens familiar with this rhetoric dismissed it with an eyeroll.[23] It is into this context that I would like to place Orff and Hofmann, for as we will see, they, too, shared with some of their generation a growing suspicion of this use of medieval symbols for "historical justification and sentimentalized glorification."[24]

It was, in fact, this association between medievalism and imperialism that Hofmann drew attention to in a letter to Orff in late 1933. At this point, Orff had asked Hofmann for recommendations of medieval texts, having expressed an interest in medieval music that juxtaposed sacred texts in Latin over secular texts in the vernacular. Significantly, Hofmann cautioned Orff against using medieval texts in general, writing,

> All medieval material, which I had considered in Munich, on closer inspection, is unsuitable, because it is almost entirely dominated by the "imperial ideal" [Kaisergedanke] of the Holy Roman Empire of the German Nation and more generally, by the whole imperial idea of the Middle Ages. The stories are simply unusable. There are Latin texts, but they are too dynastic for the most part, and contain allusions that virtually nobody can understand.[25]

In suggesting that medieval material would be unsuitable because of its associations with the imperial ideal of the Holy Roman Empire of the German nation, Hofmann appears to want to disassociate himself from texts that supported such values. Although he does not specifically reference the recently dismantled Hohenzollern Empire of Kaiser Wilhelm II, the fact that the hierarchical social structures and jingoistic patriotism of the Second Reich were so closely associated with the *Kaisergedanke* suggests that—at least for Hofmann—medieval texts were inextricably and negatively associated with imperialism and the Wilhelmine regime.

If medievalism was largely associated with imperialism and dismissed for these reasons, what attraction could it hold? And why, when Orff came across Johann Andreas Schmeller's 1847 edition of the Codex Buranus, did he select the medieval poetry as the source for his next work? One possible answer to this question rests in the interpretation of the wandering scholars' poetry as an attractive alternative to the official view of the Middle Ages. Some of the poems appeared to reject the stereotype of the positive, religious, and imperial "model" of the Middle Ages. The poets' disillusionment with the church and the Holy Roman Empire as well as the cynical view of the romantic ideals epitomized in the courtly love literature offered a version of the Middle Ages that could not be wielded to glorify the religious, political, and social framework.

Surprisingly, perhaps, the Benediktbeueren manuscript's discord with official late nineteenth-century views of the Middle Ages had, in fact, already become part of its reception history. One famous description of the poetry, for example (written in 1884 at the height of Kaiser Wilhelm I's reign) announces,

> They [the poems] are almost wholly destitute of domestic piety, of patriotism, of virtuous impulse, of heroic resolve. The greatness of an epoch which throbbed with the enthusiasms of the Crusades, which gave birth to a Francis and a Dominic, which witnessed the manly resistance offered by the Lombard burghs to the Teutonic Emperor, the formation of Northern France into a solid monarchy, and the victorious struggle of the papacy against the Empire, finds but rare expression in this poetry.[26]

If the lack of "virtuous impulse" and "heroic resolve" in the Codex Buranus could be interpreted to counter the official medievalism of Wilhelmine Germany—the glorious image of the Holy Roman Empire that had previously been resurrected—it also spoke to a disillusionment that found parallel among the reform movements, the *Wandervögel* and *Lebensreform*. The order or fraternity developed by the medieval wandering scholars was emulated by the youth group, the *Wandervogel*, and became its "most powerful image and ideal."[27] The notion that medieval citizens would voice their disapproval of the empire and church seemed particularly surprising to modern historians given the role and power of the Holy Roman Empire for the period. The poets' focus on the false ideals rampant in the social constructs of love also paralleled the growing resistance to bourgeois values among the *Lebensreform*. The absence of heroism, honor, and virtue and the notion that the poems voiced distaste for their social, political, and religious norms countered both versions of medievalism—the official medievalism of Wilhelmine Germany that had extended its reach well beyond the demise of the Second Reich and the medievalism that it inspired for the Third Reich, under the National Socialists.

Given the status of the Codex Buranus in late-nineteenth and early twentieth-century German culture, Hofmann's initial rejection of medieval texts for a new Orff work is somewhat curious.[28] Quite possibly, Hofmann had forgotten about the codex's existence when Orff sought advice on medieval texts, for he certainly seemed knowledgeable about the codex when Orff later proposed to set them. Although the extent to which the duo was familiar with this reception history is unclear, their use of the codex is consistent with the status of this text in the Wilhelmine and Weimar period. My argument, then, is that Orff and Hofmann's turn to the medieval codex functioned as a corrective to the status of official medievalism and its concomitant ties to glorifying bureaucracy and imperialism. In place of the Middle Ages used by Kaiser Wilhelm II, Orff and Hofmann suggested a more honest, even unvarnished image of the period. In his history of medievalism in the early twentieth century, Bruce Holsinger argues that critical theorists' preoccupations with the Middle Ages, as medievalists or not, served to negate the social formations and systems of thought in the modern condition. In their own processes of discovery, these theorists found philosophies, social and cultural models, and "systems of thought" that, in their premodern condition, could be wielded to counter the modern beliefs in evolutionary progress, universalism, and structuralism. The acknowledgment that the conditions of humankind had not progressed through "heroic resolve" from the Middle Ages to the present was substantiated in the poems of the Codex Buranus. The themes that characterized the medieval world of the Codex Buranus—greed, corruption, deceit, excess, and tyranny—could easily function as a critique of the spoils of modernity under Germany's industrialization. Borrowing from Holsinger, we may understand Orff's alternative medievalism along the same lines: "In its variegated assault on the legacy of the Enlightenment, the critical generation of this era turned to the Middle Ages not in a fit of nostalgic retrospection, but in a spirit of both interpretive and ideological resistance to the relentless inevitability of modernity."[29] *Carmina Burana*'s alternative medievalism would fashion an antiromantic, and ultimately anti-Enlightenment, sentiment. However, as we will see, although Orff may have wanted a more accurate representation of the Middle Ages to replace the well-worn romanticized and idealized medievalism, he acknowledged the problematic representation of the Middle Ages, or any period, as singular, or monolithic. If *Carmina Burana* suggested that official medievalism was false, it also acknowledged, with a healthy dose of humor, that the representation of life's experiences would always be conflicting and paradoxical and attempts to capture them would necessarily fall short. Orff's channeling of an alternative Middle Ages comes closer, then, to social critique and philosophical inquiry.

Certainly the poems in the Codex Buranus offered Orff the opportunity to explore disillusionment along the lines suggested above. But besides the antiromantic and anticlerical nature of some of the poems, many of them relied on techniques of parody, satire, and irony, techniques that Orff admired and developed in the 1920s alongside other German artists in the Weimar Republic.[30] In 1930, Orff had completed *Catulli Carmina I* and *II* on texts by Gaius Valerius Catullus (ca. 84–54 BCE), a Roman poet with a penchant for dualism, the simultaneous expression of two opposing sentiments that Orff valued in parody and satire and that, by its very nature, thwarted any attempt at expressing a singular view.[31] Orff's Catullus settings also channeled the poet's social commentary and its invective, critiques clothed in sexual rhetoric for which Catullus was famous and that Orff could recognize in some of the poems from the codex that were critical of sentimentality and the idealized values in courtly love literature. Taking cues from many of the satires and parodies in the medieval texts, Orff's musical setting would thus use familiar musical tropes to convey various levels of meaning following the techniques of gestic commentary developed during his association with Brecht. In particular, Orff composed a musical setting that would convey the dualism that was necessarily part of parody, satire, and irony by drawing on the cultural capital of particular musical styles and setting them in tension with the text. The organization can be seen in Table 12.1.

Table 12.1 Structure and organization of *Carmina Burana*

FORTUNA IMPERATRIX MUNDI	
1. O Fortuna	(CB 17)
2. Fortune plango vulnera	(CB 16)
I	
PRIMO VERE	
3. Veris leta facies	(CB 138)
4. Omnia sol temperat	(CB 136)
5. Ecce gratum	(CB 143)
UF DEM ANGER	
6. Tanz	
7. Floret Silva	(CB 149)
8. Chramer, gip die varwe mir	(CB 16*, CB 136)
9. Reie	
Swaz hie gat umbe	(CB 167a)
Chume, chum, geselle min	(CB 174a)
Swaz hi gat umbe	(Rep)
10. Were diu werlt alle min	(CB 145a)
II	
IN TABERNA	
11. Estuans interius	(CB 191, v. 1-5)
12. Olim lacus colueram	(CB 130, v. 1, 2, & 5)
13. Ego sum abbas	(CB 222)
14. In taberna quando sumus	(CB 196)
III	
COUR D'AMOURS	
15. Amor volat undique	(CB 87 'Amor tenet omnia', v. 4)
16. Dies, nox et omnia	(CB 118 'Doleo quod nimium', v. 4, 5, &7)
17. Stetit Puella	(CB 17, v. 1 & 2)
18. Circa mea pectora	(CB 180 'O mi dilectissima', v. 5, 6, &7)
19. Si puer cum puellula	(CB 183)
20. Veni, veni, venias	(CB 174)
21. In trutina	(CB 70 'Aestatis florigero tempore', v. 12a & 12b)
22. Tempus est iocundum	(CB 179, v.1, 4, 7, 5, 8)
23. Dulcissime	(CB 70 'Aestatis florigero tempore', v. 15)
BLANZIFLOR ET HELENA	
24. Ave formosissima	(CB 77 'Si linguis angelicis', v. 8)
FORTUNA IMPERATRIX MUNDI	
25. O Fortuna	(Rep)

Engaging with Medieval Music

The corrective to official medievalism that is discernible in *Carmina Burana* took different musical paths that are best contextualized in terms of Orff's knowledge of medieval music and the medieval music revival. As mentioned at the outset, the first decades of the twentieth century witnessed an explosion in the awareness of early music as seemingly infinite numbers of manuscripts from the twelfth to fifteenth centuries were discovered, studied, transcribed, and examined in tandem with the theoretical treatises that had been interpreted into the eighteenth and nineteenth centuries.[32] Orff had been exposed to medieval music theory and history at the Munich Academy and continued his study of early music in the 1920s and early 1930s. His library had an enviable collection of books on medieval and Renaissance history and performance; books on folklore; books on drama, including the mystery and passion plays; editions and histories by Johannes Wolf; editions and histories by Heinrich Besseler; and books by Riemann on medieval music.[33] At the academy, Orff had also been in the composition studio of Walter Courvoisier with Rudolf von Ficker, a Munich native who studied composition there until 1912, when he left for Vienna to work on his doctorate on the sixteenth-century Italian madrigal with Guido Adler. The explosion in medieval scholarship encouraged the development of *collegia musicum* at numerous centers around Germany, with Hugo Riemann, Arnold Schering, and Riemann's student Willibald Gurlitt leading the way. These *collegia* brought the exciting sounds of medieval music to the public, and even music organizations with completely different mandates supported medieval performance. Ficker, a well-known medievalist in the later 1920s, organized a concert of Gothic polyphony under the banner of the Beethoven Centennial, March 26–31, 1927, in Vienna, which Orff attended.[34] Then, in March 1930, Orff also heard the "highly suggestive organum quadruplum *Sederunt principes*," which Ficker had just presented in a revised, new edition in the context of the Society for Contemporary Music and the Munich Bachverein.[35]

As scholars have already shown, engagement with medieval music in Germany at this time could generate questions regarding nationalist agendas. Pamela Potter has discussed ways in which some medieval scholars were praised and supported for an attention to "old German" masterpieces, which, following the stated aims of German musicology, would help "preserve Germany's national treasures."[36] Annette Kreutziger-Herr and Daniel Leech-Wilkinson have illustrated the musicological drive to define a Nordic sound, in some cases, with clear national-political purpose. Some of the early German medievalists of the twentieth century were prone to include Italian or French composers in a German lineage that would secure the development of harmony and polyphony as specifically German.[37] It is unclear to what extent Orff was impacted, if at all, by the nationalist tension in this scholarship. He had read Ficker's scholarship on medieval music (which Ficker designated Gothic on the basis of its era, not its aesthetic) and corresponded with him before Ficker moved back to Munich, at which point the two presumably were able to meet in person.[38] Since Orff had read his scholarship, he may have noted that Ficker's work shared with other medievalists the discussion of a Nordic sound. But Orff's description of Ficker's concert of Gothic polyphony and his exposure to medieval music reveal another layer of understanding. In his *Dokumentation*, Orff cites Ficker using language that offers a corrective to the outmoded view of medieval music. Specifically, Ficker notes that the re-evaluation of the "basic laws" of music has contributed to the realization that music of the Gothic age is not "primitive and aesthetically worthless"; the compositional technique can now be heard as a meaningful expression of life's sounds.[39] The idea, not explicitly stated here, is that earlier medieval scholars' derision of parallel voices and doubled leading tones led to the marginalization of medieval polyphony. Contemporary developments had established a "bridge back 700 years" allowing for a new appreciation of medieval song. The fact that this could be construed as a recovery for nationalist purposes was not noted, though it could be interpreted this way. The complex context of the nineteenth-century medieval revival borne of a rejection of the Gothic aesthetic was also not discussed. More important to Orff, and seemingly in support of his corrective to medievalism, was the conversion of a marginalized music into a privileged and appreciated form. For Orff, as for Ficker, music of the Gothic era was a valuable expression of the past that should not be disparaged as primitive or barbaric.

Regarding Orff's compositional language, Werner Thomas has argued that it shows the influence of Gothic polyphony and primary sound forms (*klangformen*) as they were described in Ficker's scholarly work.[40] According to Thomas, these put Orff's language into "close affinity with monophony, paraphony, and the ostinato scaffolding techniques of world music, as well as the sonic tectonics of Cathedral art of the European Middle Ages."[41] It is this affinity to medieval monophony and paraphony—the German term for organum at a fourth or fifth—that has caused confusion about Orff's medievalism. It is necessary, though, to read the whole passage to understand Thomas's statement of influence: "sound," he suggests, "is no longer raw material, but becomes a primary factor of composition. The repetition of sound montages or sound blocks which are organized in the same fashion does not mean monotony, but, rather, the specific construction of form."[42] We can perhaps interpret Thomas's description to mean that blocks of sound that are constructed and repeated form the essence of the piece, in much the same way as later minimalist composers. This kind of connection speaks to an architectural form. Though recognizable as "Orffian," this component of his compositional language does not always signal medievalism. That is to say, the use of and repetition of sound blocks may suggest the language of romanticism, as it does in "Floret Silva" or "Stetit puella," to name just two examples. If the short motives contain harmonic dissonances, appoggiatura gestures, and arch-shaped melodies and are set following the more complex rhythmic patterns of an aria or madrigal, medievalism is unlikely to be communicated. But when these consist of the accretion of voices, in parallel, and in largely undifferentiated rhythms, they may conjure up the sounds of Gothic polyphony.

That said, the first two selections of *Carmina Burana* draw on both primary sound forms as described previously and a medieval musical style derived from the examples of organum that Ficker discussed. "O Fortuna" and "Fortune plango vulnera" present the repetition of short sound blocks, as well as voices moving in parallel octaves, fifths or thirds, presumably derived from Ficker's discussion of paraphony.[43] Although the idea of using strict metrical proportion for different sections of text is a common feature of many liturgical forms, the fact that the opening tempo of "O Fortuna," $\quartnote = 60$, is half that of the remaining sections, $\quartnote = 120–132$, may well be a nod to Ficker's opening of *Sederunt principes*, which transcribes the opening "Sed," as a series of dotted half notes tied over four bars before moving on to the faster-moving melody defined by the quarter note.

Orff's interest in building intensity from short rhythmic motives that collect and accumulate over the longer form may also stem from his exposure to Ficker's work on *Sederunt principes*. Praising medieval music, Ficker noted "the stupendous effect in wide spaces of powerful massed tones and chords, simultaneously combined with the overpowering sweep of rhythmical energies."[44] These were composed of "comparatively short choral phrases" that "renounce[d] the treatment of melodic motives or themes" but still managed to produce an "unheard of homogeneity of form."[45] Perotin's organa, according to Ficker, "is the music of grand rhythmic intensifications, whose equal is not found elsewhere in musical history. The periods are shaped by a symmetrical, exactly balanced enchainment of short metrical members."[46] With their short choral phrases and rhythmic ostinatos, "O Fortuna" and "Fortune Plango Vulnera" appear to approximate the aesthetic—at least as this aesthetic was understood by Ficker—of Perotin's organa.

In this connection, Ficker's discussion of clausula seems particularly apt:

> Out of these excerpts [melismata] from the cantus firmus he constructed independent compositions in a novel style—the above-noted clausulae. In the example given above, the single tones of the regnat-melisma are gathered together one after the other into short, metrically scanned four-tone groups separated by pauses. To this "Tenor" is then added a higher part in like metre; and this clausula becomes a motet by providing said higher part, the Motetus, with a complete text. For fuller effect a third part, the Triplum, is set to the other two; in the earliest form of the motet, now under consideration, it has the same text as the Motetus.

It would be hard to miss the similarity to "O Fortuna," a piece defined by "short, metrically scanned" four-note (two-tone) groups set apart by rests. Ficker's description of clausula can also be applied to the form of the piece; its material resembles an extended melisma redefined as note-against-note discant and is ostensibly an extended ornamentation or peroration that finally closes on D. The architectural scaffolding of higher parts mimics the motet's structure, though here it unfolds in real time. As Kreutziger-Herr remarks, the sound world of Ficker's *Sederunt principes* is suggested in Orff's opening for *Carmina Burana*, which manifests "something of an elementary force, a down to earth sensuality that sees the 'ideal image of a religiously motivated folk culture' in the Middle Ages, and which relies less on differentiation than on massive sound, surging sound masses, expressive dynamics, great melodic arcs and terraced, or increased effects."[47]

And yet in comparing the settings devoted to Fortune/Fate with Ficker's writings on medieval music and his edition and performance of *Sederunt principes*, it is also striking how very different they are in melodic treatment, form, and tone. First, conspicuously absent in Orff's selections is a melismatic treatment of upper voices as presented in Ficker's organum. Second, the structure of a *cantus firmus*, a medieval technique discussed at length by Ficker, does not appear in Orff's compositional language or in his borrowing of musical forms. Besides the architecture of paraphony, the allusion to more complex medieval polyphony—a development esteemed to be "Germanic" and "Nordic"—is also absent in Orff's musical language. Finally, the rhythmic differentiation present in Ficker's discant and organum is lacking, with "O Fortuna" composed only of half and whole notes. It would seem, then, that Orff's engagement with medieval music ignored some of the medieval properties he knew to be present because he chose only those that best suited his aesthetic and the text.

We see his careful union of style with poetic meaning in his treatment of "O Fortuna" and "Fortune plango vulnera," which imitate characteristics of the litany and the *Geisslerlieder*—or medieval chants of the flagellants. Orff knew the generic properties of liturgical recitations since he suggested this format to Hofmann for "Ego sum abbas" in *In Taberna*.[48] Musicologist Peter Wagner had described these recitations as syllabic with little pitch movement and suggested that some forms showed the interesting pattern of a longer melodic line divided into two parts, the first closing on the mediant and the second on the final. The litany, Wagner suggested, derived from a liturgical recitation and consisted of a versicle—the priest's invocations of saints, or other deities, followed by the congregation answering with a set melodic and textual pattern: *Déus misérere nóbis, libera nos Dómine*, or even *Kyrie eleison*.[49] The simple melodic patterns lent themselves to procession, while the melodic repetitions provided exigency to the supplicants' imploring message. In their invocations to the goddess Fortuna and the formal structure of a versicle, the first two selections do indeed suggest a litany. This form is clearest in "Fortune plango vulnera" (see Example 12.1), which features a baritone solo as the priest twice singing a melodic line broken up by open and closed cadences (Part A), followed by a unison chorus singing their response to a new melodic pattern (Part B).

However, there are also textual and musical reasons to align the first two settings with the tradition of *Geisslerlieder*, a musical form that had experienced significant scholarly attention between 1930 and 1935, satisfying—because a group of these songs survived in German—the musicologists' search for "German" medieval forms.[50] As Paul Runge had pointed out in his 1900 book on Hugo Spechtshart of Reutlingen's 1349 account of the penitents (*Chronicon Hugonis sacerdotis de Rutelinga*), these *Geisslerlieder* were chanted during the processions into the city and the public displays of penance.[51] It is perhaps this nod to the idea of the flagellants' procession that Orff heard in the poem "O Fortuna," in the lines "I bear my back to Fortune's blows," and that encouraged him to articulate a gradual increase in volume to suggest the penitents procession, after the initial cry of lament. *Geisslerlieder* exhibited some of the same characteristics of the litany, as it was thought to have influenced the formal pattern.[52] However, different from the litanies, the *Geisslerlieder* had longer melodic lines sung to verses, instead of a

EXAMPLE 12.1 "Fortune plango vulnera," mm. 1–16.

refrain. Figure 12.1, taken from Runge, shows the development of longer lines from the alternation of shorter patterns.

Moreover, *Geisslerlieder* were said to resemble religious "folk" songs in so far as they were strophic, syllabic, and used simple melodic lines composed of short, memorable motives sung in the vernacular and uniform in meter and rhyme. Runge's account also describes the form of the practice: a leader would sing the text with two (possibly three) repetitions of the melody, after which the flagellants would respond in unison with a chorus composed of repetitions of two melodic lines sung in alternation to make a longer one composed of "open" and "closed" endings.

The resemblance of the choruses of both "Fortune plango vulnera" and "O Fortuna" to Song 4 of Hugo's *Chronicon* (Figure 12.1), and included in Runge's book, is striking. But to a certain extent, whether Orff was thinking about *Geisslerlieder* is not important; the point, rather, is that the generic properties—syllabic setting, narrow range, circular motion, and repetition of short motives—construct a formulaic structure that continually hovers between tension and resolution and helps conjure up the aesthetic of litany or penitent song.

A judicious mixture of medieval characteristics with modern features affirms Orff's desire to compose a structure that would best convey the lament of the poet—that he is at Fate's mercy, her wheel of fortune, and bears his back to her blows, before finally pleading for all to join him in lament. Amplifying the march-like status of the procession with strident rhythms secured an aesthetic that best matched the zeal of the poet's lament. The accompaniment pattern signifies the giant wheel of Fortune circling through a D–A pedal with an added seventh. The tension in the opening cluster's DEF is matched by the regular clashes of the E in the melody against the *perpetuum mobile* of the D pedal point, the clashes being aural reminders of repeated flagellation. The cadence at "mecum omnes plangite"—in which the text moves to direct address—uses, for the first time, the leading tone (C♯) and moves, thus, from d (Dorian) to D major with a Picardy third peroration extended for eight measures. This peroration is set with a fanfare in brass and glockenspiel that, as we will later see, provides an element of irony that is supported by the "irrational" move from Dorian to Mixolydian.[53]

Though it more accurately only describes the musical settings of the first two selections in *Carmina Burana*, it is this aforementioned aesthetic that has long defined Orff's medievalism *tout court*. Yet medievalism in "O Fortuna" and "Fortune plango vulnera" is heard mainly through an imitation of medieval style, not technique. The mere existence of Thomas's sound blocks and an architectural structure that owes to paraphony are but small aspects of the settings, whose archaic harmonies, simple melodies, and largely uniform durations conjure up significantly more of a medieval aesthetic. Most of the remaining songs of the cycle avoid the style of plainchant and use different medieval and two-storied medieval musical styles and symbols for their specific connotative purposes. Importantly, as we will see, when plainchant forms are imitated, they do not connote the aesthetic of the first two selections.

FIGURE 12.1 Runge, transcript of Song 4, *Geisslerlied*.

Medievalism as Dualism

Armed with the knowledge that Orff's medieval allusions could be specifically employed to serve semantic purposes, I turn now to a discussion of the relationship between texts and the medievally-inflected music that sets them. If the opening two pieces conjure up a litany, or flagellants united in a lament against the vagaries of the Goddess of Fortune the first piece in the next section, "Veris leta facies," uses natural imagery to describe the advent of spring, an arrival that is accompanied by the freedom to "love" and sing of "a thousand joys." This selection imitates the gentle sounds of plainchant from the Mass. The melody opens with rising thirds in unison before moving into a narrower ornamented line. Each strophe follows an aabb' form, in which the altos and basses alternate with the tenors and sopranos, accompanied by an open fifth and octave drone. Each line of text is followed by a response that mimics a congregational Amen in the form of a fifth and octave (G D G), moving up in parallel motion to A E A (see Example 12.2). The flexible accents of plainchant are reflected by the shift between the triple meter vocal melody and the duple meter of the organ's "response." The end of each section includes a comic reference to the "amen," but here the melisma is only on "a," denying the final, and expected, "men." Alluding to sacred music in a context of profane texts provides a kind of dialogical juxtaposition that takes on the characteristics of a humorous parody. We might interpret the dualism suggested in this tension as follows: instead of worshipping God and obeying his laws, we are exhorted to worship spring and obey the laws of nature and "to run in the race of love."

An interpretation of the poems against the musical setting and in the context of gestic techniques demonstrates how Orff's corrective to official medievalism might function. Musical associations with sacred medieval music are also made in the next two selections of *Primo vere* and provide tension with the secular text, highlighting its effect of parody. Orff knew that the traditions of sacred and secular music and texts overlapped

EXAMPLE 12.2 "Veris leta facies," mm. 1–3.

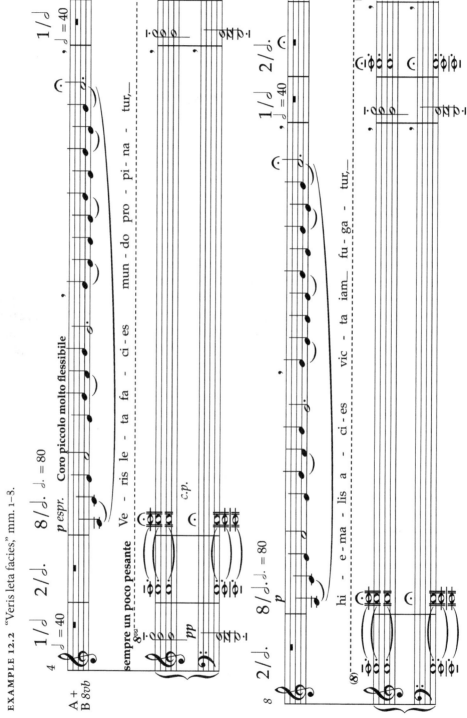

and influenced one another during the Middle Ages because he was familiar with thirteenth-century motets that juxtaposed springtime imagery in the vernacular with praise to the Virgin Mary in Latin. But he also recognized the pervasive use of satire in the poems of the *Carmina Burana* and seemed poised to make it speak to his contemporaries. "Omnia sol temperat" continues the associations with Catholic ritual with its reference to a liturgical recitative, intoned by a priest with the free declamation of *rubato* over a drone periodically shifting up and back from its semitone neighbor. Against this, the poem positions the sun, not God, as the commander of all things, while the poet pleads, in language that reveals the overlapping of sacred prayers and secular love poetry with its reference to "heart, soul, and body" and "faithful love," that his lover will not reject him. The third song of the section, "Ecce Gratum," another poem that demands the pursuit of love, begins with a soloist declaiming the "incipit" in a slow, deliberate fashion that gestures toward a reciting tone, answered by a buoyant, homorhythmic hymn characterized by leaps of fourths and thirds. A contrasting middle section features a rising melodic line that weaves around its consonant triadic chord tones in a fashion alluding to second-species counterpoint highlighted by the two notes per syllable setting, while the third section plays with echoes and voice exchange in the manner of a motet. In these kinds of selections, Orff's medievalism can be characterized as style: medieval musical allusions to sacred music draw on the cultural capital of prayer and reverence to advance the ironic connection of love (Venus) with Christian worship and might be interpreted as an attempt to position this love as chaste, a contrived forecast since it is revealed to be false at the end of *Carmina Burana*.

Two-Storied Medievalism

The notion that medievalism for Orff was not an end in itself, but a mode of gestus, or a double-voiced parody, becomes even more pronounced in the third way Orff engages with the Middle Ages, namely, the two-storied medievalism that I introduced previously. In what approximates a *historicizing* practice, Orff drew on the familiar topics, symbols, and musical styles of official medievalism—state-sponsored oratorios, national festivals, and mass-produced settings for choruses that informed so much of Kaiser Wilhelm II's hurrah patriotism of nineteenth-century Germany. These particular forms, as Barbara Eichner discussed, exhibited a "brazenly cheerful style" of brassy fanfares, clear forms, strict march-like material and an attention to percussion to best capture the glory and patriotic fervor of the Kaiser.[54] As with the presence of allusions to medieval sacred music, two-storied medieval references force the listener to consider the text from a dualistic perspective. However, while the references to sacred medieval musical forms may speak in a more timeless language, the musical styles of two-storied medievalism allude to medieval styles as seen through a nineteenth-century lens. And as we may predict, because two-storied medievalism includes some musical styles that had already taken on the status of clichés, it is more prevalent in the poems that have satire or parody at their core.[55]

Perhaps it is unsurprising that some of the subjects of the poems overlap in topic, shape, and form with the oratorio, a genre that was at least to some extent an *ipso facto* force of official medievalism in nineteenth-century Germany. Orff, who owned Arnold Schering's 1911 *Geschichte des Oratorium* and was active as a conductor and director for the Munich Bachverein, referred to the oratorio's structure and format in his letters to Hofmann. Though no direct comparison to specific oratorios or themes is recorded, *Carmina Burana* repeats many of the topics Schering discussed in his overview of secular German oratorios, which gained in prominence after 1870. These explored medieval German historical heroes or emperors—Barbarossa, Arminius, Alaric, Otto der Große—and told the patriotic story of Germany's birth. They provided a program designed to bolster historical pride in the nation, allegiance, and an adherence to the religious and social mores of "contemporary" Germany. Schering described the content as follows: "Some beautiful freedom choruses, sumptuous drinking choruses, and some battle scenes illustrated in great detail are what surface here, some gloomy tragic choral works of compelling force, some haunting prayers, some songs of sacrifice."[56] The oratorio's ethical mission, as Eichner notes, was assumed, as was its position on instilling values of honor and obedience. The introduction of "exotic rituals and sensual love scenes" would make bourgeois morality clear; themes were constructed in "stark binary oppositions, contrasting 'freedom and oppression, decadence and morality, tyranny and love of peace.'"[57] Also striking is Schering's apparent scorn for the secular oratorio with its mass appeal and "stimulating effects": "wherever world history offered events whose poetic-musical treatment promised strong, stimulating effects on the masses, [composers and librettists] snatched at the offer."[58] That this Adornian type of dismissal was attached to the secular oratorio may have been a sentiment shared by Orff since he too made it a subject of ridicule.

In this sense, *Carmina Burana* occupied an ironic position with regard to the nineteenth-century oratorio: adopting much of its formal structure even while rejecting—or mocking—its moralistic imperatives. If oratorios from the nineteenth century presented "great events and heroes of the past," *Carmina Burana*, as we will see, told the tale of the antihero and his demise; if the earlier oratorios negotiated "national and religious identities," Orff's presented the nation and religion through clear kitsch and satire; and if the oratorio idealized love as chaste, or only sanctioned by the church, Orff's suggested that desire and sex were always "noble" pursuits.[59] Carmina Burana thus imitated the format of the eighteenth and nineteenth-century oratorio even as it partially subverted the latter's ideological substructure.

This relationship is clear in the first number of *Carmina Burana*, "O Fortuna." In the typical nineteenth-century oratorio, the purpose of the first chorus is to praise a benevolent God or leader or to make heroic pronouncements.[60] Positioning the goddess Fortune as the omnipotent ruler, the opening chorus of *Carmina Burana* inverts this ideological alignment. Instead of the traditional call to "cease to be fearful, forget lamentation," "O Fortuna" presents the opposite: the truth that all live in fear and that all are subject to Fortune/Fate's whims. The audience is called not to set aside anxiety, but rather to "join in lamentation," which, as we have seen, is couched in the language of a litany or penitent song. The traditional message of the oratorio—that goodness, loyalty, and morality are rewarded—is replaced by the image of an authoritarian goddess figure who looks on humanity's struggles with absolute indifference. These kinds of inversions occur frequently throughout the work, communicated textually, through the poems themselves or through amusing juxtaposition. For example, "the happy face of spring" ("Veris leta facies"), a theme that signals jubilation and is used as such in the oratorio format, is positioned incongruously after the opening lament of *Fortuna Imperatrix Mundi* and is given not a jubilant setting but, as we saw, a serene, prayer-like setting.

The other popular soundtrack in *Carmina Burana*'s two-storied medievalism involves the mass-produced songs described as *Liedertafel* as well as choral settings accompanied with brass and played by the many regiments for ceremonies and state-sponsored national festivals.[61] This choral repertoire's dedication to the well-worn themes of "wine, women, and song, nature, spring, and fatherland *ad nauseam*" and its lack of creativity would make it an object of debasement.[62] The repertoire was also associated with "the worst" of Wilhelmine culture, in part through Kaiser Wilhelm II's commission of a series of song books (*Kaiserbücherlieder*) on these themes in an effort to inject patriotism into the musical life of nineteenth-century Germany.[63] Inspired by the revival of medieval Minnesang, *Liedertafel* also played a role in aligning women with love of nature and love of fatherland. Many of the songs also drew on the chivalric codes of honor, loyalty, and faithfulness that spoke to the medieval courtly love tradition. The clichés of such patriotic and valiant codes were already the subject of ridicule for many by Orff's adulthood. Carl Zuckmayer's hugely successful 1925 comedy, *Der fröhliche Weinberg* [*The Happy Vineyard*], lampooned these themes, from the benign (drinking and free love), to the grim (the "patriotism" of a *Freikorps* student and the right-wing nationalism of a politician).[64]

On the surface, the poems in *Primo vere* and *Uf dem Anger* confirm themes of nature, spring, and love that made up a significant portion of the wine, women, and song topics of the *Kaiserliederbücher* and *Liedertafelstil* of Orff and Hofmann's youth. But, contrary to the religious morality of the secular oratorio's choral selections, the duo drew poems from the codex that expressed the topic of love through religious imagery. The poems in *Primo vere* offer a light parody that was perhaps more meaningful in the wandering scholars' religious context. As already noted, the sacred musical settings suggest that rather than observe the "laws of religion" and interpret God as "worthy of worship," these poems suggest the "laws of nature" should be pursued, and Venus (desire) is "worthy of worship." The poems in *Uf dem Anger* present something quite different—a characterization of love united by the sentimental, ostentatious, and false flattery of courtship that in the original poems seem poised to critique the values espoused in the troubadour poetry or *Minnesinger*. A kind of maudlin desperation is palpable in the poem, "Who will love me? Now that my lover has ridden away?," while vanity colors

"Merchant give me rouge; let me please you young men." But we can also understand a satire of the nineteenth-century chivalric conventions of faithfulness and loyalty that surfaced in the patriotic images of Germania in the oratorio traditions, some of the *Volkslieder*, and *Liedertafel*. The poem, "Swaz hie gat umbe," deceives us with sarcasm in the ironic statement, "The girls who dance around here wish to be without men." The final text in this section states the desire for love in the most hyperbolic of terms: "I would yield all of my lands from the Rhine to the sea to embrace England's Queen." The latter's ostentatious and exaggerated claims were already familiar to audiences as the expressions of a chivalric style of the nineteenth-century popular collections.

The image of courtship is perhaps most powerfully expressed in the music of *Uf dem Anger* where the sentimental and ostentatious expressions of the poetry appear to be caricatured with a nod to the "formulaic, folksy, sentimental or brazenly cheerful style" that was the object of ridicule for trained composers and musicians.[65] Sentimentality and flirtation are conveyed in the musical settings of "Floret Silva" and "Chume, Chum, geselle min." The overly saccharine sounds created by thirds and sixths in "Floret Silva," the clear harmonic register and folklike rhythm, together with the kitsch yodel on *"meus amicus,"* conjure up the nineteenth-century revival of the *Volkslied*, while the timpani rhythm that closes the selection suggests the lover's departure on horseback and places the narrative in a natural setting. The sensuous, alluring "Chume, Chum, geselle min" also connects this section to the well-worn tradition of *Volkslieder* with its clear harmonies and repeated dance rhythm with pronounced appoggiatura gestures.

In key places, Orff's musical treatment also alludes to the chivalric style with its trumpet calls, fanfare motives, exuberant use of percussion, and clear tonality directed to the strong beats of the form.[66] Orff's framing of choral parts by instrumental introductions, interludes, or postludes as witnessed in *Uf dem Anger* could potentially derive from Ficker's discussion of slightly later fifteenth-century repertoire. Ficker isolates a "Trumpetta Introitus," a double canon played by four trumpets as an introduction to an Ave Virgo by Johannes Franchois.[67] We see this kind of "introitus" in "Swaz hie gat umbe" (see Example 12.3). The melody is introduced with a "horn call"—a seven-measure tutti announcement in perfect fifths that is played on strings and filled out in bar 5 with a driving "oom pah" treatment. After delivery of the text, the brass and horns take over the fanfare with the marking *ff*.

It is more likely, however, that Orff is alluding to the baroque oratorio tradition. The similarity to the Credo in the Mass in B minor where the string fanfare is taken over by trumpets at the words "Et resurrexit" is striking. Moreover, in its stripped-down style, Orff's fanfare alludes to Mendelssohn's reworking of the Mass with its "compact fortissimo reinforcement" and decidedly "nonvirtuosic" treatment.[68] In its simplicity and "brazenly cheerful" style, Orff's fanfares and allusions to the chivalric style speak better to the "trivial" nature of the patriotic music under Kaiser Wilhelm.

An interpretation of the chivalric style also appears in the final song of *Uf dem Anger*, "Were diu werlt alle min." Orff described this as "truly like folk song" and "a really gaudy piece."[69] Four measures of brass fanfare in C major open the work, aptly conveying the

EXAMPLE 12.3 "Swaz hie gat umbe," mm. 1–12.

status of the queen, before moving into a peroration on the dominant that prepares us for the entry of the text. Orff captures the folklike setting with its unison treatment and clear diatonic melody with brash accent and imitation. The poet's boastful statement, "I would willingly forego, all the lands from the sea to the Rhine to have the Queen of England," is epitomized in the final musical phrase with its *poco ritenuto* and upwardly marching melody, which turns to accented and then slurred eighths in a move that elaborates the overly "precious" claim of a pedantic lover. The climax is underscored by the return of the exaggerated fanfare repeated *ad nauseum*, a fitting parallel not only to the queen's status, but also to the hyperbole of the statement. The jingoistic sounds of patriotic song are clearly captured with "the blaring trumpets" and here, as in the settings they mock, appear to underline "the heroic and belligerent attitude of the patriotic repertoire."[70]

The poems and their musical treatment in *In Taberna* also counter the official views of the Middle Ages and could be read as capitalizing on the idea of the antihero, negating the heroic figure in patriotic imagery of repertoire under Kaiser Wilhelm and questioning the sacred authority that governed the nineteenth-century secular oratorio. The subject is now utterly disgraced and lies, in Orff and Hofmann's descriptions, "at the bottom of the wheel of fortune."

As I have discussed elsewhere, *In Taberna* incorporates music that apes the stylistic idioms of Verdi and Rossini's medievalist operas.[71] Not wishing to repeat my arguments here, I will limit my discussion to two instances where Orff employs idioms of sacred chant to amplify the satire present in the original poem. "Ego sum Abbas," a liturgical parody in its poetic form, which follows the abbot of Cockaigne as he makes a mockery of his sacred vows through greed and gambling, is fittingly set with an *a cappella* recitation in liturgical style that mimics the rhythmic freedom and exaggerates the ornate melodic character of an antiphon with its interminable oscillation between pitches A and C. But the medieval traits stop there, as Orff interrupts the oration with a dissonant "laughing chorus" that behaves like the response to the Abbot's anguished exclamations and regret. Reference to the ethos of a litany is conspicuous in the next selection, "In taberna quando sumus," a drinking song that parodies the form of a prayer for "the whole state of Christ's Church" in the Catholic Mass, with a musical setting in Phrygian mode that alludes to the character of chant through its unison singing of simple descending melodic motives above a harmonically static, but rhythmically active pedal. Here, the chant's status as a "community" ritual is leveraged to parallel the poems' thirteen toasts to all the members of the drinking community. Besides the sheer humor invoked in these selections, the buffoonery of the abbot and "communion" in the tavern neither glorify the image of Germany in the Middle Ages nor uphold a model view of the church and its authorities, although this anticlerical sentiment was also one shared by supporters of National Socialists.

The associations that medieval music in its sacred and nineteenth-century reimagined forms provide a deeper layer of interpretation for *Carmina Burana*'s text. A final example that illustrates the complex interplay between two-storied musical references and the possible meanings evoked in their juxtaposition can be seen in the ordering of the final three selections of the work: "Dulcissime," "Ave Formosissima," and "O Fortuna." *Cour d'amours* largely articulates the expression of desire by both men and women and spells out the "real" drama of love, that is, one in which love is openly expressed and consummated. The soprano's "Dulcissime" promises she will yield, with "I give myself to you" set in a rhapsodic, Delibesian expression. The next selection, "Ave Formosissima," is set as a hymn of praise and, with its chorale-like setting, is particularly poised to gesture at the laudatory songs of the oratorio finale. The title suggests the "Ave" of an *Ave Maria*, but only after the attributes of beauty, preciousness, and virginity are acclaimed does it become clear that Venus is the object of glory, thereby affirming the praise of sexual love over chaste love. Hofmann a suggested he compose a parody of a medieval feast, the feast of Corpus Christi, whose celebration of the body of Christ would take on the scintillating effects of celebrating Venus, instead of Mary, as the "Ave" in the poem's title suggests.[72] This celebration of Venus would be a veiled joke that reinterpreted "redemption through love," a marked feature of the courtly love tradition and its nineteenth-century revival as "redemption through sex."

The subsequent nod to the German patriotism of the popular oratorio is implied in Hofmann's advice for Orff to borrow elements from the "Mussinan March," written by Karl Andreas von Bernbrunn and named after a famous Bavarian cavalry officer in the Franco-Prussian War.[73] Orff chose a majestic chorale style with clarion tones, in which each stately motive of the melody is sung twice and interpolated with brass and string fanfare amplifications (see Example 12.4). That this apotheosis is followed by the return of "O Fortuna," with its musical references to medieval forms of penance, in a poem lamenting the whims of Fate/Fortune seems all the more powerful, if humorous, in its statement.

Indeed, the denial of the tenets of official medievalism conveyed in *Carmina Burana* is perhaps best exemplified in the return of "O Fortuna" at this point. The utter lack of heroism is apparent in the failure to overcome the "struggles" with nature, love, and fleshly vices that one reading of the cycle may imply. By returning to the Goddess of Fate/Fortune as the omnipotent ruler against which the "hero" or poet must "lament," Orff turns the idea of the hero's quest on its head, suggesting a cycle that eschews progress, change, and, of course, victory, a narrative readily apparent in the state-sponsored secular oratorios.[74] Irony functions not only in the lack of victory for the hero, but also in the claiming of victory for Fortune herself. The musical setting's introduction of the Picardy third that moves the focus to D major launches a brassy fanfare that thrashes between D major and C major chords in a bid to draw on the archaicism of parallel chords. The continued return to the lowered seventh in this climactic section is a feature of the song's medievalism, and the archaic aesthetic appears incongruous with the references to the nineteenth-century chivalric style's fanfare. Finally, the hyperbole of this repeated gesture and heavy use of percussion amplify the climax on "plangite," suggesting, perhaps, Fate's arrogance in her victory over the poet.

EXAMPLE 12.4 "Ave Formossissima," mm. 1–6.

Conclusion

I have argued here that one of the ways to interpret *Carmina Burana* is as a droll and critical indictment of the values inherent in the official medievalism of Orff and Hofmann's youth. The chosen poems from the Codex Buranus and the medieval-inspired content of the musical setting betray an allegiance to an alternative medievalism that can be understood along the same lines as Holsinger describes in the premodern condition: they embody a general disillusionment with the modern beliefs in progress, universalism, and even structuralism cast here through attention to the antiheroic, antiromantic, and downright nihilistic images that had been witnessed in expressionism and the new sobriety [*die neue Sachlichkeit*]. By pastiching well-known musical topics and styles associated with "the worst of Wilhelmine culture," *Carmina Burana* both invoked and parodied the musical and social values associated with all that was wrong with nineteenth-century Germany.

Some citizens in Germany, seeing the similarities between official medievalism and medievalism espoused by the Nazis, would elide the two, raising significant questions regarding the intentions and the reception of medievalism-inspired works. There is no evidence to suggest that Orff and Hofmann considered the National Socialists specifically as a target of their alternative medievalism. Indeed, this seems unlikely for several reasons. As Andrew Kohler has discussed in detail, Orff avoided discussing politics or making political statements of any kind and, as his friends and family noted, lived in fear of the regime. Moreover, his works both before and after the Third Reich betray a lifelong fascination with philosophy and humanism. Kohler also notes that in answer to a question posing whether *Carmina Burana* could be interpreted as "resistant" to the Nazis, Orff replied simply that he "would not make such a grand interpretation."[75] Orff's desire to dismiss and offer a vague response to this question is significant, but so too is the very fact that it is even raised. For a public that viewed Nazi medievalism as an extension of official medievalism's emphasis on pomp, patriotism (read nationalism), and romanticism, any rejection of official medievalism could be understood as a rejection of the Nazi discourse. Thus, critiques of these values could be read as critiques of society under National Socialism, despite Orff's intentions. But any critique of values is complicated by the historicity and authority of the texts that sanctioned their meanings. In this way, *Carmina Burana* could offer, but need not take responsibility for, an indictment of contemporary Germany as channeled through the social and religious disillusionment of the wandering goliards.

Some of the songs in *Carmina Burana* could also be heard as complicit with National Socialist musical idioms, even though, as Potter has argued, the view of Nazi Germany as a monolithic dictatorship that functioned according to rigid cultural policies, that is, that prescribed the style and type of music composed, is not entirely accurate. More often, decisions were made on a makeshift level and often resulted from monitoring public opinion. Leaders like Hitler began to see that they could garner support from the populace by simply endorsing cultural products that were popular regardless of whether they could be viewed as complicit.[76] It became the job of the propaganda office, then, to make these products "fit" by focusing on particular details at the expense of the whole. Orff's *Carmina Burana* offered itself as an easy target for manipulation for numerous reasons, not the least of which was its attention to the Middle Ages. Orff's medievalism did not need to be consistent or coherent or, indeed, ideologically complicit to be directed to reiterate propaganda. Yet, the work did contain themes that could easily support ideologies of the regime. The narrative of struggle in *In Taberna* conjured up the *kampfzeit* of the Nazi "threshold periods" even when it did not produce a "superior" condition.[77] And *In Taberna's* anticlerical status would support the official rejection of the church by the regime (even though many members were Catholic). But there were other clearer ways that *Carmina Burana's* music explicitly resembled Nazi music and appeared to be aligned with it. Large choruses and characteristics pastiched from the chivalric style—clear marching rhythms, folk song-like structure, brass fanfares, and horn calls—were also revived and used by the Nazis. For this reason, some of the selections in *Carmina Burana* could even be interpreted as "good" examples of Nazi music or as "redolent of the songs sung in the thirties by Nazi groups."[78]

As a weapon of propaganda for the Third Reich and a discourse that dictated the ideological interpretation and "knowledge" of medieval material, Nazi medievalism exerted an enormous pressure that is borne out in numerous reviews of *Carmina Burana* in the 1940s. Perhaps it is not surprising given the power of the regime, and the fear instilled by its arbitrary extension of rules, to find an article written by Hofmann for the premiere of the work that expounds on the work's nationalist elements. Published under the guise of a "letter" to Orff from Hofmann in the *Frankfurter Zeitung* (June, 6, 1937), it extolled the poetic and musical elements of *Carmina Burana* with the language of Nazi propaganda, highlighting Orff's "folklike rhythms," the "clarity of form," and the relationship of the poems to the "youth" of the German nation. Hofmann recounts his "baptism" of the work in language that conjures up the baptism of Walther's prize song in Wagner's *Die Meistersinger*. And finally, describing "O Fortuna," he asserts, "the music reflects the unbending, static nature of the eternity of fate's superior strength, but also the unbroken will of existence of those who do not turn silent to her, but who invoke, captivate, and overcome."[79] Unmistakeable here is the "will to power" that has been read into the work's reception and that certainly seems calculated to secure the work's popularity with the regime.

Building on a lengthy tradition of parody and satire in Germany and directing it at the Second Reich, a regime that had already been caricatured and mocked by members of Orff's generation as sentimental, ungenuine, and imperialist, *Carmina Burana* was guaranteed to succeed. Orff's two-storied medievalism worked to simultaneously distance it from the 1930s and historicize it in the nineteenth century through the mechanism of medievalism's first revival. The elements of the chivalric style, the patriotic songs associated with *Liedertafelstil*, the parodies of medievalist operas, and the nod to forms in the secular oratorios were all associated with Wilhelmine culture and spoke the language of contemporary parody. However, given what has been described by Kohler as Orff's lifelong fascination with destiny and liberty, it is worth remarking that Orff reserved his most authentic musical medievalism for the flagellant-inspired songs of "Fortuna Imperatrix Mundi."[80] Against the dualistic, satirical, and playful nature of two-storied medievalism, the poet's afflictions appear more "earnest," railing against the hateful impulses of Fate and the brutality of Hecuba. But as I hope to have shown, Orff's *Carmina Burana* is much more than "O Fortuna." Rather, the medieval sacred forms and popular themes of official medievalism become conveyors of gestus and parody that are self-reflexive, questioning both the idealistic and the romantic outlook of the Middle Ages and the contemporary German value system contained within it.

NOTES

1. There is some discrepancy in the way that the poems are counted: "Swaz hie gat umbe" and "Chume min geselle" are two separate poems and bring the count to twenty-five.
2. It is this style that James Deaville refers to in his article 'Evil Medieval: Chant and the New Dark Spirituality of Vietnam-Era Film in America,' this volume, pp. 709–728.
3. Leopold von Ranke, as cited in Nicholas Kenyon, *Authenticity and Early Music* (Oxford: Oxford University Press, 1988), 201.
4. Frohmut Dangel-Hofmann, ed., *Carl Orff-Michel Hofmann: Briefe zur Entstehung der Carmina Burana* (Tutzing: Hans Schneider, 1990), 128; Hofmann to Orff, April 11, 1937. Hofmann also alerted Orff to concordances in other manuscripts and in notation that was readily decipherable (or that had already been transcribed into modern notation). There is no evidence that Orff did this. He later stated that he had no interest in the original melodies and did not pursue them.
5. Richard Taruskin, "Can We Give Poor Orff a Pass at Last?," in *The Danger of Music and Other Anti-Utopian Essays* (Berkeley: University of California Press, 2008), 162; Pamela Potter, *Most German of the Arts, Musicology and Society from the Weimar Republic to the End of Hitler's Reich* (New Haven, CT: Yale University Press, 1998), 7. The debates regarding Orff's conduct during the Nazi regime have also encouraged controversy. Taruskin notes that "the worst Orff can be accused of is opportunism," but notes the work's successful reception under the Nazis. Michael Kater describes Orff's moral failings (*Composers of the Nazi Era, Eight Portraits* [New York: Oxford University Press, 2000]), arguing that Orff was essentially apolitical, but he was complicit with the regime for agreeing to supply music for *A Midsummer Night's Dream*, essentially replacing Mendelssohn's work, since he was a Jew. He also suggests that Orff lied during the denazification process and claimed he had been a member of the resistance. Andrew S. Kohler unpacks the controversy in detail, paying particular attention to Orff's relationship with Huber. Kohler notes that Orff did not support the Nazi regime, but found ways to successfully maneuver through its highly bureaucratic and authoritarian structure, in some cases cutting ties with particular people and in others writing glowing letters to those who held the purse strings, see " ' "Grey C," Acceptable': Carl Orff's Professional and Artistic Responses to the Third Reich" (PhD diss., University of Michigan, 2015), 88–101.

6. Taruskin, "Can We Give Poor Orff a Pass at Last?," mentions "the radiant, strength-filled life-joy" (Horst Büttner) that aligns it with Nazi propaganda, 163.

7. Gwendolyn Morgan, "Medievalism, Authority, and the Academy," *Studies in Medievalism* XVII (2009): 55–67, here 65.

8. Taruskin notes that songs "were redolent (according to German acquaintance of mine) of the songs sung in the thirties by Nazi youth groups," "Can We Give Poor Orff a Pass," 164.

9. Potter, *Most German of the Arts*, 7.

10. Kater, Taruskin, and Karen Painter (*Symphonic Aspirations: German Music and Politics, 1900–1945* [Cambridge, MA: Harvard University Press, 2007]) all remark that *Carmina Burana* was an attractive work for mass propaganda.

11. These letters are published as Dangel-Hofmann, ed., *Carl Orff-Michel Hofmann: Briefe*.

12. Bertolt Brecht's *epic theater* and *gestus* provided a model for Orff's development of social commentary and religious critiques, models he explored in the setting of six poems (*Werkbuch II*) from Brecht's 1927 *A Manual of Piety*, a bitter attack on Germany's bourgeois values following the format of prayers and readings from the Catholic Mass. For a discussion of Orff's gestic techniques, see Kim H. Kowalke, "Burying the Past: Carl Orff and His Brecht Connection," *The Musical Quarterly* 84, no. 1 (Spring 2000): 58–83.

13. Edward R. Haymes, "Two-Storied Medievalism in Wagner's *Die Meistersinger von Nürnberg*," *Studies in Medievalism* 3 (1991): 505–513. The fact that many forms of medievalism reference intermediary, oftentimes fantastical, images of the Middle Ages is key to the idea of neomedievalism that is central to the work of many scholars in this field.

14. See especially Laura Stokes's essay, "Medievalisms in Early Nineteenth-Century German Musical Thought," this volume, pp. 17–37.

15. Barbara Eichner, "Richard Wagner's Medieval Visions," in this volume, pp. 174–204; see also Michael S. Richardson, "Romantic Medievalist Nationalism in Schumann's *Genoveva*, Then and Now," this volume, pp. 155–173, and Annette Kreutziger-Herr, "Imagining Medieval Music: A Short History," *Studies in Medievalism* XIV (2005): 81–109.

16. David Barclay, "Medievalism and Nationalism in Nineteenth Century Germany," *Studies in Medievalism* V (1994): 5–22.

17. Matthew Jefferies, "Lebensreform, A Middle-Class Antidote to Wilhelminism," in *Wilhelminism and Its Legacies, German Modernities, Imperialism, and the Meanings of Reform, 1890–1930*, ed. Geoff Eley and James Retallack (New York: Berghahn Books, 2003), 93; see also Potter, *Most German of the Arts*, 7.

18. Jefferies, "Lebensreform, A Middle-Class Antidote to Wilhelminism," 95. I have discussed this context in Yri, "*Lebensreform* and *Wandervögel* Ideologies in Carl Orff's *Carmina Burana*," *Musical Quarterly* 100 (2017): 1–30.

19. Barclay, "Medievalism and Nationalism," 12; see also Barclay, "Medievalism and Monarchy in Nineteenth Century Germany: Ludwig I and Frederick William IV," in *Selected Papers on Medievalism*, ed. Janet Goebel and Rebecca Cochran (Indiana, PA: Indiana University of Pennsylvania Press, 1988).

20. Kreutziger-Herr also discusses this point in "Imagining Medieval Music: A Short History."

21. Moreover, as Barclay argues, the power of leaders to use the Middle Ages for political purposes had limited success because of their reliance on such worn out clichés; "Medievalism and Nationalism," 18.

22. The relationship between the music dramas and Nazi ideology has garnered considerable scholarly attention. See especially William Niven, "The Birth of Nazi Drama?, *Thing* Plays," in *Theatre under the Nazis*, ed. John London (Manchester: Manchester University Press, 2000).

23. Robert Carl Schmid, "German Youth Movements: A Typological Study" (PhD diss., University of Wisconsin, 1941), 50–58.

24. Ingo R. Stoehr, "(Post)Modern Rewritings of the Nibelungenlied—Der Nibelungen Roman and Armin Ayren as Meister Konrad," in *Medieval German Voices in the 21st Century, The Paradigmatic Function of Medieval German Studies for German Studies*, ed. Albrecht Classen, (Leiden, Netherlands: Brill, 2000), 167.

25. Dangel-Hofmann, *Carl Orff-Michel Hofmann: Briefe*, 14, Hofmann to Orff, December 8, 1933. Hofmann then goes on to suggest texts by Hoffman von Fallersleben, whose national liberal views colored his collection of "Unpolitical Songs," causing him to lose his university post and be exiled from Prussia until 1848.

26. John Addington Symonds, *Wine, Women, Song, Mediaeval Latin Students' Songs First Translated into English Verse with an Essay by John Addington Symonds*, 1884 (repr., New York: Cooper Square, 1966), 190.

27. Schmid, "German Youth Movements," 53–65.

28. Bernhard Joseph Docen, *Miszellaneen zur Geschichte der deutschen Literatur* V. 2 (Münich: Scherer, 1807): 189–208; Hans Spanke, "Der Codex Buranus als Liederbuch," *Zeitschrift für Musikwissenschaft* 16 (February 1931): 242–251.

29. Bruce Holsinger, *The Premodern Condition, Medievalism and the Making of Theory* (Chicago: University of Chicago Press, 2005), 5.

30. The revival of the classics from ancient Rome and Greece, in particular, the Menippean satires of Petronius's *Satyricon* and Apuleius's *Metamorphoses* or *The Golden Ass*, had prepared the way and influenced writers from Nietzsche to Ibsen.

31. Orff, *Dokumentation* 4, 7. For more on Brecht's dualism, see Frederic Jameson, *Brecht and Method* (New York: Verso, 1998), especially 58–61.

32. A few of the familiar names include Peter Wagner, Friedrich Ludwig, Heinrich Besseler, Willibald Gurlitt, Wilhelm Mayer, Jacque Handschin, Johannes Wolf, and Guido Adler, who all collected, transcribed, edited, interpreted, and published collections of medieval music.

33. These include *Aufführungspraxis alter Musik*, 1931; *Geschichte des Oratoriums*, 1911; *Geschichte des Instrumentalkonzerts bis auf die Gegenwart*, 1905; and *Studien zur Musikgeschichte der Frührenaissance*, 1914.

34. Annette Kreutziger-Herr, *Ein Traum vom Mittelalter: Die Wiederentdeckung mittelalterlicher Musik in der Neuzeit* (Cologne: Böhlau Verlag, 2003), 408.

35. Daniel Leech-Wilkinson mentions this in "Yearning for the Sound of the Middle Ages," in *Mittelalter-Sehnsucht? Texte des interdisziplinären Symposions zur musikalischen Mittelalterrezeption an der Universität Heidelberg. April 1998* (Kiel: Wissenschaftsverlat, 2000); see also Kreutziger-Herr, "Imagining Medieval Music."

36. Potter, *Most German of the Arts*, 93–95.

37. See Kreutziger-Herr, "Imagining Medieval Music"; Daniel Leech-Wilkinson, *The Modern Invention of Medieval Music* (Cambridge: Cambridge University Press, 2002), 167–172.

38. Orff acknowledges reading Ficker's work in his *Dokumentation*, and in a letter to Ficker, Orff alludes to his scholarly writing.

39. Ficker's program for the concert cited by Orff in *Dokumentation* II, 141–142.

40. Thomas cites the Ficker article "Primäre Klangformen" (in *Jahrbuch der Musikbibliothek Peters für 1927* [Leipzig: Verlag von C. F. Peters, 1928]) in *Das Rad der Fortuna, Ausgewählte Aufsätze zu Werk und Wirkung Carl Orffs* (Mainz: Schott Musikwissenschaft, 1990), 152–154; and in *Dokumentation* I, 208.

41. Ibid. Thomas also notes that Orff's settings of Franz Werfel and, to a lesser extent, Brecht poems also experimented with undifferentiated rhythm and parallel voices in the style of paraphony.

42. Ibid.

43. Werner Thomas, "Der Weg zum Werk," in *Dokumentation* I, 208.

44. Ficker, "Polyphonic Music of the Gothic Period," trans. Theodore Baker, *The Musical Quarterly* 15, no. 4 (1929): 491.

45. Ibid.

46. Ibid.

47. Kreutziger-Herr, *Imagining Medieval Music*, 194.

48. Orff to Hofmann, May 31, 1934; ibid., 39–40.

49. Peter Wagner, *Gregorianische Formenlehre; eine choralische Stilkunde*, vol. 3 of *Einführung in die gregorianischen Melodien: ein Handbuch der Choralwissenschaft* (Leipzig: Druck und Verlag von Breitkopf & Härtel, 1911).

50. See, for example, Arthur Hübner, *Die deutschen Geisslerlieder* (Berlin: de Gruyter, 1931); Hans Joachim Moser, *Tönende Volksaltertümer*, 1935; Hans Joachim Moser, *Geschichte der deutschen Musik*, 1930; Josef Müller-Blattau, "Zu Form und Überlieferung der ältesten deutschen gestlichen Lieder," *Zeitschrift für Musikswissenschaft* 17 (1935): 129.

51. Paul Runge, *Die Lieder und Melodien der Geissler des Jahres 1349, nach der Aufzeichnung Hugo's von Reutlingen* (Leipzig: Druck und Verlag von Breithopf & Härtel, 1900), 16. See also Joseph Müller-Blattau, "Die deutschen Geißlerlieder," *Zeitschrift für Musikswissenschaft* 17 (January–December 1935): 6–18.

52. See, for example, Gustave Reese, *Music in the Middle Ages* (New York: Norton, 1940); and Peter Wagner, *Gregorianische Formenlehre*, T. 3, *Einführung in die gregorianischen Melodien* (Leipzig: Breitkopf & Härtel, 1921).

53. It may be worth pointing out that this is a modal move that the final line of Hugo's Song 4 also exhibits, though this kind of technique is common in baroque and romantic oratorios (among other repertoire).

54. Although trumpet calls were considered part of the performance practice of some medieval secular repertoire, associations with the nineteenth-century chivalric style are more immediate.

55. Orff and Hofmann thought about parody in many specific instances. For example, Orff described the section *In Taberna* as follows: "Estuans (Verdi- thriller); swan solo for falsetto; chorus Ego sum abbas (spicy parody); and In taberna, Rossini, opera finale, the worst style." He also labeled the *In Taberna* section *Farce, Satire, Irony, and Deeper Meaning* [*Scherz, Satire, Ironie, und tiefere Bedeutung*], quoting the 1822 German play by Christian Grabbe, a social satire of literary pretensions, philistine values, and vacuous social trends. Dangel-Hofmann, *Carl Orff-Michel Hofmann, Briefe*, 90, Orff to Hofmann, March 15, 1935. The operas by Verdi and Rossini that Orff pastiches (*Il trovatore* and *Guillaume Tell*) also have medieval settings.

56. Arnold Schering, *Geschichtes des Oratoriums, Kleine Handbücher der Musikgeschichte nach Gattungen*, Hermann Kretzschmar, ed. Bd III (Leipzig: Breitkopf & Härtel, 1911), 495.

57. Schering, *Geschichtes des Oratoriums*, 495, as cited in Barbara Eichner, *History in Mighty Sounds, Musical Constructions of German National Identity 1848–1914* (Woodbridge, Suffolk: Boydell Press, 2012), 164–196.

58. Eichner, *History in Mighty Sounds*, quoting Schering, 165.

59. Quotations are from ibid.,164.

60. Compare with Max Bruch's secular oratorio *Arminius*, which opens, "We are the sons of Mars the mighty, from Gods and heroes have we sprung! Before our arms unconquer'd the tribes of earth lie prostrate, they break asunder, like to moulds of clay, we crush them, they break asunder," or with Mendelssohn's *Elijah*, "Help Lord, Help Lord, wilt thou quite destroy us?"

61. See Eichner's discussion, *History in Mighty Sounds*, 206–207.

62. Ibid., 206.

63. Ibid., 208.

64. Connections between German patriotism and themes of wine, women, and song were also reinscribed in 1922 in the declaration of A. H. Hoffmann von Fallersleben's 1841 text, *Das Lied der Deutschen* (commonly known as "Deutschland über alles") as the German national anthem, where "German women, German loyalty, German wine and German song" are positioned as the inspiration for Germany's noble deeds.

65. Eichner, *History in Mighty Sounds*, 206.

66. Jonathan Bellman, "*Aus alten Märchen*: The Chivalric Style of Schumann and Brahms," *The Journal of Musicology* 13, no. 1 (1995): 119. I do not wish to imply that Orff's chivalric style was similar to that of Schumann or Brahms; Orff uses a simpler treatment.

67. Rudolf von Ficker, "Agwillare, a Piece of Late Gothic Minstrelsy," *Musical Quarterly* 22, no. 2 (April 1936): 131–139.

68. For more on the Mass in B minor and Mendelssohn's reworking, see Yo Tomita, Robin A. Leaver, and Jan Smaczny, eds., *Exploring Bach's B minor Mass* (Cambridge: Cambridge University Press, 2013), 263.

69. Dangel-Hofmann, *Carl Orff-Michel Hofmann, Briefe*, 40; Orff to Hofmann, May 31, 1934.

70. Eichner, *History in Mighty Sounds*, 209.

71. Yri, "*Lebensreform* and *Wandervögel* Ideologies," 14–22.

72. Dangel-Hofmann, *Carl Orff-Michel Hofmann, Briefe*, 59; Hofmann to Orff, June 22, 1934.

73. Ibid., 94.

74. Compare, for example, Franz Abt's "Siegegsang der Deutschen nach der Hermannsschlacht" (1864) or Heinrich Zöllner's "Jung Siegfried," in Eichner, *History in Mighty Sounds*, 209, 218.

75. Orff in conversation with Martin Konz. The German reads, "Ich möchte daß nicht gar so groß interpretiert sehen." I thank Andrew S. Kohler for alerting me to this source, "Auf den Mond zu fliegen ist elementar. Rückbesinnung auf die Ursprünge: Interview mit dem Komponisten Carl Orff," in *Neue Musikzeitung* 24, heft 2 (April/May 1975): 3.

76. Potter, *Art of Suppression, Confronting the Nazi Past in Histories of the Visual and Performing Arts* (Oakland: University of California Press, 2016), 1, 6. Hitler was averse to "associating his name with unpopular measures that would dilute his demagogic powers of persuasion," thus the most popular artists of the time saw greater success even if their art did not support the Reich's "nazification."

77. Nazi ideologues characterized the Middle Ages as "*Schwellenzeiten*" or "threshold periods," periods of struggle (*Kampfzeit*) that were instrumental in the evolution of Germany's superiority, Niven, "The Birth of Nazi Drama?, *Thing* Plays," 137.
78. Taruskin, "Can We Give Poor Orff a Pass at Last?," 164.
79. The letter is reprinted in Dangel-Hofmann, *Carl Orff-Michel Hofmann, Briefe*, 196–199.
80. Kohler discusses Orff's fascination with destiny and antiauthoritarianism in "'Grey C,' Acceptable," see especially 44–55 and 108–146.

CHAPTER 13

....

PAST TENSE

Creative Medievalism in the
Music of Margaret Lucy Wilkins

....

LISA COLTON

A fundamental aspect of late twentieth-century music is its stylistic plurality: its combination of features that reject neat notions of historical transition or progress. If medievalism can be found in the music of the past seventy years, then, it is unlikely to present as a stable tradition, a coherent set of strategies, or a coordinated response to the past. Rather, musical medievalism challenges the musicologist to look beyond the notes to aspects of motivation, significance, and meaning in pieces that, while engaging with history, are realized in diverse and contradictory ways. British composer Margaret Lucy Wilkins's experience as a performer of medieval music allowed her to express her own interest in medievalism through a body of works that range from chamber music to music for large ensembles and from theatrical vocal music to electroacoustic repertoire. This chapter will analyze two pieces by Wilkins, *Musica Angelorum* (1991) and *Revelations of the Seven Angels* (1977), confronting the tensions found in music that is inspired by the medieval past but that is nonetheless part of an emphatically modern aesthetic. The aspect of medievalism that is most pertinent to the discussion here is the Gothic, as defined in architectural history by John Ruskin (1819–1900), since it provides an ideal frame for the examination of structural and stylistic characteristics within Wilkins's music.

Composers working during the second half of the twentieth century could not help but encounter two mutually informing, ostensibly opposed, musical traditions: the early music revival and the modernist avant-garde.[1] A composer associated with a British academic institution in the 1970s—whether music college or university music department—frequently had on hand performers immersed in the exploration of extended techniques for their instrument, but who also took the opportunity to use early instruments, new performing editions, and the latest historical research. Academic curricula after World War II had been redrawn to include more medieval topics, such as Gregorian chant and isorhythmic motets, which in turn helped to inform and inspire the original work of composers.[2] Similarly, a new wave of performers was created, equally at home on the baroque violin as the modern one or on the harpsichord as the piano, performers excited by the distinctive colors of different instruments and playing styles.

Much has been written about the disjointed relationship between musicologist and performer within the early music movement, one characterized as either antagonistic or a two-part process in which a researcher discovered facts about the past that were, in turn, recreated by performers.[3] This conceptual segregation is exemplified in the writing of Manfred Bukofzer (1910–1955), whose views were captured in a posthumous publication:

> Like the scientist and the historian, the musicologist is bent on research, on the discovery and explanation of new material that will enlarge the fund of human knowledge and open up new vistas and new conceptions.... but the good musicologist must be aware of the fine line of demarcation that separates the investigation from the interpretation of his material.[4]

Essentially, Bukofzer and others argued that the musicologist should not dirty their hands with the practical implications of what they had discovered. Composers, by contrast, have always quite happily straddled the two worlds of research and creative interpretation, drawing from previous models as inspiration while realizing their ideas imaginatively. Composers of the later twentieth century had access to an unprecedented range of historical materials and cutting-edge techniques, whether in the library, practice room, concert hall, or studio. Since many composers were also accomplished performers, it is unsurprising that some of the most dynamic work of the period 1960–2000 drew on influences from early and new musics and was designed to exploit diverse technologies, from reproduction viols to computer software.

Twentieth-century interest in medieval ideals and craftsmanship reflected not only an awareness of the actual historic past, but also an understanding of that history filtered through the lens of the Gothic revival. This movement had been initiated in the mid-eighteenth century, but was most influential during the nineteenth. Fundamental to modern appreciation of the Gothic, a key part of medievalism, were the writings of John Ruskin and his contemporaries, many of whom were motivated by their Catholicism.[5] These writers and artists reveled in the romanticism of the medieval past, reimagining it as a time of innocence.[6] The concept of the Gothic lay at the heart of Ruskin's academic understanding of medievalism, but the term has since been employed more broadly, moving toward its employment as "an omnibus label for counter-cultural phenomena imbued with mysticism and a vague historicism."[7]

When, in 1854, Ruskin divided history into classical (ancient), medieval, and modern, he placed three vast periods of time in opposition to each other, not only chronologically but also aesthetically.[8] For Ruskin, the structural and distinctive stylistic gestures within medieval architecture were what made it Gothic. Contrasting medieval architectural features with the tightly uniform shapes of ancient Egyptian monuments (made in slavery) and industrial-age products with a perfect finish (made by machines and by workers in servitude), Ruskin argued that Gothic buildings reflected the freedom of expression of their masons and that the effect was morally informed and spiritually uplifting.[9] Such liberty was visually apparent in the quirky, freehand lines and decorations found in medieval churches and cathedrals, from the individually recognizable features of particular buildings to the inclusion of ugly and obscene sculptural details in tracery.

The sheer variety of forms found in medieval architecture was an important part of Ruskin's notion of Gothic and can be likened to twentieth-century attitudes toward medievalism in otherwise modern musical language. For Ruskin, the Gothic character in architecture was a flexible set of elements, the majority of which needed to be present for the style to be apparent, namely, savageness, changefulness, naturalism, grotesqueness, rigidity, and redundancy.[10] These qualities were not simply objective descriptors, but also closely related to the perceived personality of the Gothic mind, that of the builder engaged in creative projects, who might himself be savage or rude, enjoy change and nature, possess a disturbed imagination, and be stubborn but also kind and giving. Similarly, analytical work on medievalism in music can identify markers of the Gothic in sonic language that is potentially diverse, and medievalism can be inferred from music across a wide stylistic range, even within the output of a single composer. The humanity of the medieval past, something admired by Ruskin and his contemporaries and most easily recognized in examples of Gothic architecture that are highly colorful or humorous, acts as an almost magical connective between the artistry of the two periods.

Medievalism and Gothic as Style in Twentieth-Century Music

The twentieth century has generated and maintained diverse stylistic approaches in art music. Plurality of style and response to underlying principles sit well with Ruskin's view of what the term "Gothic" meant:

> The principal difficulty [in measuring Venetian architecture against a perfect type of Gothic] arises from the fact that every building of the Gothic period differs in some important respect from every other; and many include features which, if they occurred in other buildings, would not be considered Gothic at all.[11]

One can easily transfer this passage to a discussion of twentieth-century music, in which defining, for example, the avant-garde or modernism is equally problematic.[12] The tension between the smaller-scale features of a Gothic building and their appreciation within the overall style of each construction is immediately apparent in the visual arts. Within music, the connection between short, expressive gestures and the broader stylistic language in which they are situated can be more difficult to conceptualize. Put simply, the presence of musical medievalism can be harder to determine than in the visual arts because its appreciation relies on both small-scale or surface sonic cues (melodic gestures from plainchant, use of Middle English text) and more broad aural signifiers such as harmonic context and timbral palette; all these factors require an audience to have some knowledge of the cultural history of music and its language for them fully to perceive creative medievalism at work. As I will demonstrate in my analyses, Wilkins's success in capturing and expressing medievalism lies in her combination of numerous medieval signifiers, some of which (such as bells or the use of a Gothic space in performance) cannot be missed.

Pugh and Weisl argued that in musical expressions of medievalism since 1900, "the ideologies and views of the Middle Ages often stem more from Victorian medievalism than from the Middle Ages."[13] Such an analysis can be applied to a wide range of music. One must acknowledge that even the most historically aware composer of the twentieth century was incapable of seeing and hearing medieval music entirely without the influence of Victorian medievalism or early twentieth-century nostalgia or through the goggles of "faux Catholicism" that peeked at the dramatic idea of the liturgical past, without having to get involved in detailed musicological survey.[14] Yet, many examples are sufficiently informed by knowledge of preexistent materials and their context to support a level of analysis that draws out some of the dialogue between ancient past and present music more fully. When new music written by composers with direct knowledge and understanding of early repertory borrow explicitly from medieval song, they engage with the musical past at a deeper level.

Creative Medievalism in Late Twentieth-Century British Music

Medievalism as a subject has taken some time to catch on in musicology, a discipline that, as Susan McClary famously noted, has typically lagged behind the other humanities in engaging with critical, cultural perspectives in relation to its central musical questions.[15] Berns and Johnston have remarked that as result of engaging with what might be seen as popular rather than academic perspectives, medievalism has been seen to "lack scholarly credentials."[16] For musicians working on pretonal repertoire, long tainted with an associative brush of costumed performances of "Greensleeves" at weddings, there has been much at stake in fully engaging in the subject of medievalism in relation to creative practice. Yet, there is little doubt that medievalism was highly prevalent within British new music in the later twentieth century. Indeed, if one takes into consideration music by any composer who takes the distant past as their central "subject matter or inspiration," one could reasonably assert that medievalism was one of the most dominant forces of those decades.[17]

It would be possible to see the incorporation of medieval reference points in contemporary music as merely a superficial or commercially driven device for making abstract or challenging musical style more appealing to audiences and commissioning bodies. However, the approach of many composers was typically a blend of personal academic interest, practical experience of early repertoire during higher-level study, and theoretical engagement with ideas that could be used as the basis for radical new sounds. This perspective chimes most fully with Annette Kreutziger-Herr's first category of medievalism, a "productive, *creative medievalism*, in which topics, themes, forms, works of art, and individuals of the Middle Ages are formed into a new work of art" [my emphasis].[18] It is important to state at this point that few, if any, composers at this time would have identified their work as part of a discourse of medievalism per se. For the purpose of making sense of sonic practices and musical meaning from the 1960s to the 1990s, it can be helpful to use Kreutziger-Herr's phrase creative medievalism as a catch-all for diverse compositional approaches. At its most basic, creative medievalism might encompass work in which new music draws on early monophony, regardless of how audible the original might be in the final product. One can place in this category such contrasting works as Sir Peter Maxwell Davies's *Worldes blis* (1969), which disguises its foundational material almost beyond recognition, and James MacMillan's concerto for percussion and orchestra, *Veni, Veni, Emmanuel* (1992), which relishes in twisting the medieval song within inventive melodic, rhythmic, and textural gestures.[19] Further types of creative medievalism can be detected in works that were inspired by medieval culture at a deeper level, by architecture or poetry, or by pieces intended for performance in Gothic spaces such as castles, private chapels, or cathedral churches.

Margaret Lucy Wilkins

My focus in this chapter is on a composer whose music embodies the contrasts and conflicts of many of the areas of creative medievalism outlined above. Margaret Lucy Wilkins (b. 1939) was a founding member of the Scottish Early Music Consort between 1969 and 1976. She performed on various instruments, but is best known as an acoustic and electroacoustic composer and as a lecturer in composition at Huddersfield Polytechnic, later the University of Huddersfield (1976–2003).[20] She has been described as a composer "with a distinctive voice and personality"[21] and as "a composer who has things to say, and who says them in the best possible way, in vivid, arresting and often gripping terms."[22] The intellectual basis of Wilkins's music has been a significant part of her creative voice. Wilkins has positioned herself as an advocate for women composers, as well as archiving her work jointly through the Scottish Music Information Centre and the British Music Collection (formerly the British Music Information Centre), testimony to her personal ties north and south of the border.[23] Before 1960, Wilkins developed her creative work through studies at Trinity College of Music, London, and the University of Nottingham, but her work came to most prominence after 1970 with a series of prizes, high-profile commissions, and her educational endeavors. Sophie Fuller observed that "a fascination with medieval culture has inspired much of her music."[24]

Examination of Wilkins's oeuvre illustrates the control of the composer of a startling variety of genres, forms, and media.[25] Her works include pieces for solo or chamber ensemble, chamber and large choir, orchestra and other large ensembles, pieces with electronics, and music embracing performance art and installation. The large-scale works are highly ambitious; *KANAŁ* (1990), for example, is an "environmental event," setting texts by Pablo Neruda, Jorge Luis Borges, Bertolt Brecht, William Blake, and John Milton, complete with choreographed oboist, four ensembles (in different locations), up to a dozen actors, voices, a variety of orchestral instruments, actors, fixed media, dancers, percussion, and two conductors.

Wilkins's style occupies an avant-garde space that also embraces aspects of the historical past, drawing on dramatic poetry in particular. Her textual choices are often female centered, or dark, and her musical language sometimes draws on preexistent repertoire for intertextual or humorous reasons. Wilkins was first drawn to early texts when studying French and English at school; Geoffrey Chaucer's *Canterbury Tales* was one of the set texts during her A-levels.[26] While there is little evidence in her output of Wilkins's engagement with female-authored literature, she has frequently set lyrics that reflect on female experiences, especially unconventional ones: *Witch Music* (1971), for instance, sets eight sixteenth-century witches' spells. An example of all these aspects— dark humor, female outsiders, intertextuality—can be heard in Wilkins's setting of Heinrich Hoffman's poetry in Wilkins's *Struwwelpeter* (1972), which incorporates quotations from the famous "Barcarolle" from Offenbach's *Tales of Hoffman*. The third movement of *Struwwelpeter* sets the cautionary tale of "Harriet and the Matches." Wilkins transforms Offenbach's lilting melody into disturbing, almost comical material, prominent in the clarinets, piano, and the rhythmic vocal line. As the instruments whine, the singer's phrases "You'll burn to death! You'll burn to death!" are accompanied by timbres suggestive of the alarmed and judgmental cats who look on as Harriet brings about her own demise.[27]

The medieval and Renaissance influences on Wilkins's music can be understood as more firmly rooted in practical experience of ancient repertoire than for many other composers. Wilkins's professional performances on vielle, for example, go significantly further than Britten's sustaining of the "one note" in performances of Purcell's viol consort known as the *Fantasia upon One Note*, not least since Britten played on the viola as part of an enhanced string quartet.[28] Wilkins's allusion to early music in terms of stylistic traits, evocations, and aesthetic approach might thus be considered rooted in a more "authentic" medievalism than for composers without such direct engagement. For

Wilkins, engagement with early music is not a matter of pastiche. In her own textbook aimed at aspiring composers, she cites Antonio Canova's advice to student sculptors: "Study nature, consult the works of great masters of Antiquity, and, after careful comparisons, arrive at your own original style."[29] A central purpose of this chapter is to examine the manner in which Wilkins's creative output is informed by her own masters of antiquity, as well as to illustrate that this synthesis allowed her to establish a flexible, personal style that goes beyond imitation: a medievalism that paradoxically facilitates a distinctive personal expression in her music.

Heavenly Image, Heavenly Song in *Musica Angelorum*

The Gothic spirit of Wilkins's music is both structural and gestural, creating spaces and colors that are informed by historical buildings, materials, and preexistent music. In several cases, the visual aspect of a piece's inspiration is also conjured sonically through particular scoring or through theater. In some works, such as *Witch Music* and *Revelations of the Seven Angels*, the overall impression of a piece can only be fully gained through witnessing a live performance: the suspension of percussion in a cruciform shape to imply occult ritual in *Witch Music*, for instance, would be lost on a recording. In others, like *Musica Angelorum*, the listener is encouraged to meditate on a visual idea through musical forms and the handling of motivic ideas that create quasi-programmatic spatial effects.

It would be tempting to assume a correlation between the colorful nature of performances of medieval repertoire in the mid-twentieth century and Wilkins's own aesthetic choices for orchestration and compositional technique. Wilkins's performance of medieval instrumental music during the 1960s and 1970s were no doubt informed by the prevailing sound worlds conjured by leading groups of the time and in recent memory. Performers like Noah Greenberg and David Munrow created dazzling spectacles in the repertoire through orchestrational contrasts, supported by scholarship that foregrounded richness of color in instrumental accompaniments.[30] Arguing against this otherwise tempting association, Wilkins has spoken of her preference for scorings that emphasize blend over more unusual combinations in her original music. In *Witch Music*, for example, Wilkins has commented that the instrumentation fixed by the funders of the time (the Society for the Promotion of New Music) was "a terrible ensemble, because you've got a singer, pitched against a trumpet, a clarinet, and a double bass.... I like ensembles which *blend* within themselves; well these don't blend with each other, they stick out like a sore thumb!"[31] As such, the coherence of the string ensemble scoring in *Musica Angelorum* is colorful in a more delicate manner, not in the way one might find in mid-twentieth-century performances of early music. Wilkins's attitude to excessive contrast in orchestration is strikingly similar to Ruskin's disapproval of color in the painted glass of the nineteenth century, which he argued robbed the glass of its principal properties:

> Next in the case of windows, the points which we have to insist upon are, the transparency of the glass and its susceptibility of the most brilliant colors; and therefore the attempt to turn painted windows into pretty pictures is one of the most gross and ridiculous barbarisms of this pre-eminently barbarous century.... In the second place, this modern barbarism destroys the true appreciation of the qualities of glass. It denies, and endeavors as far as possible to conceal, the transparency, which is not only its great virtue in a merely utilitarian point of view, but its great spiritual character.... The true perfection of a painted window is to be serene, intense, brilliant, like flaming jewelry; full of easily legible and quaint subjects, and exquisitely subtle, yet simple, in its harmonies.[32]

Musica Angelorum was commissioned by the Goldberg Ensemble, and its expressive character is likewise legible, subtle, simple in its harmonies. The piece is written for twelve solo strings (four first violins, three second violins, two violas, two cellos, double bass). The composer's seating plan indicates that players should be distributed in an arc, with a single line of violins on the left and a cluster of lower strings to the right, closest to the conductor. The explanatory note indicates the central importance of imagery, both as stimulus and in the mind of the listener:

> Mediaeval paintings portray multitudes of angels playing instruments. How does this angelic music sound? In this moment of enraptured ethereal art, we hear the swish and flutter of angels' wings as they descend earthwards, cherubic whistles and laughter, and heavenly harps much larger than earthly ones. All this, and more, alternates with a melody, half-heard at first, which becomes more distinct with each repetition. The angelic orchestra passes right beside us, then continues on its celestial journey, disappearing from human hearing in a cloud of harmonics.[33]

The use of a carefully specified location for each musician adds to the impression of spatial movement in concert performance. *Musica Angelorum* is thus not merely evocative, but also descriptive, an exercise in figurative sound painting. The stimuli for the work were stained glass images of angel instrumentalists from Winchester Cathedral, and the contemporary performers stand in for these historically imagined players. Such images appear in both Gothic and neo-Gothic church settings, as can be seen in Figure 13.1, which shows an example of medieval glass from Norwich.

The music language of *Musica Angelorum* does not offer a pastiche of either the sonic qualities of vielles or the instrumental music of the Middle Ages. Instead, expressive textures built from a range of string techniques conjure the ethereal landscape imagined in the program notes. The opening section (and its mirror at the end of the eleven-minute work) serves as a representative illustration of the quasi-programmatic nature of the whole piece. In this section, tremolandi, glissandi, *sul ponticello* bowing, and harmonics are used to depict fluttering wings (see Example 13.1).[34]

FIGURE 13.1 Angel playing a bowed string instrument, depicted in the fifteenth-century glass of the Church of St. Peter, Hungate, Norwich, in Norfolk. Photographer: Mike Dixon. Reproduced with permission.

The ubiquity of Es and As, sometimes approached as if in a dominant–tonic relationship, but with ambiguity from the use of both C♯ and C♮, flirts with the Aeolian mode commonly associated with the harp. Even within textures built from other pitches, the strength of natural harmonics on notes such as A and E ensures that the drone-like open fifth underpins the first section, leading to a powerful unison E–A cadential gesture (mm. 15–16) that opens somewhat unexpectedly to an arpeggiated melody, again based on A (see Example 13.2).

The luminescence of this opening expresses both the numinous subject and the medieval architecture that stimulated the work. Here and throughout, notably toward the close, *Musica Angelorum* suggests the heavenly/mystical imagined angels of Winchester Cathedral through a palette that infuses the avant-garde with recognizable modern signifiers of a primitive past, such as resonant fifths and semimodality. The curved seating arrangement of the players helps visually and performatively to underline the staggered entries and small points of imitation that also evoke the echoes of medieval religious architectural spaces.

EXAMPLE 13.1 Margaret Lucy Wilkins, *Musica Angelorum* (mm. 1–8). Reproduced with permission.

EXAMPLE 13.2 Margaret Lucy Wilkins, *Musica Angelorum* (mm. 14–17).

Structuring Sound in Revelations of the Seven Angels

In her own advice to developing composers, Wilkins noted that a conceptual inspiration for new work could determine musical elements such as overarching structure, tempo, or mood and that imaginative stimulus might be found across the arts and sciences, including art history, mathematics, or architecture.[35] Structure and form are of paramount importance to Wilkins, not only in a sonic dimension but also—as a painter herself—as a fundamental element of the visual and plastic arts and in relation to physical movement. For Wilkins, structure is something that can develop naturally and creatively from ideas or materials beyond the musical per se. The medievalism in *Revelations of the Seven Angels* is likewise a blend of Gothic symbolism and current stylistic language.[36] Given the imposing scale of the piece in terms of both its forces and its duration, space will not permit a comprehensive exploration of all the aspects of medievalism found in *Revelations*, so I will focus most fully on the selection, manipulation, and significance of borrowed materials.

Revelations embraces creative medievalism in more diverse and provocative ways than *Musica Angelorum*, including direct borrowing of early chant and polyphony, in its conceptual design for performance within a Gothic cathedral, and more subtly in its dramatic structure, its concern with numerology and symmetry, its incorporation of movement and procession resonant of liturgical ritual—not least in the audience's placement at the heart of the ensemble—and through the importance of bells.[37] In these references, *Revelations* sits within a frame that includes the spiritual or mystical works by John Tavener and Arvo Pärt, who have often been inspired by the liturgies of the Russian and Greek Orthodox churches. The use of bell has religious connotations in Pärt's *Canticum in Memoriam Benjamin Britten* (1977), for example, with the striking of a bell (pitched on C) against descending scales in the strings evoking a memorial ritual in church. As has been argued by Martin Thomas with regard to composers like Tavener, Weir, MacMillan, and others, the function of such pieces is not typically to accompany worship, but to create music with a "non-dogmatic but quasi-religious feel to it."[38] The same can be argued for *Revelations*, as well as other works by Wilkins, but I would refute in all cases the underlying disparagement inherent in some of Thomas's critiques.

Revelations lasts approximately an hour in performance and incorporates a large ensemble of instrumentalists and singers. The spatial elements of *Revelations* allow the audience to engage with the passage of sound around the cathedral, from the West Door, through side chapels, and in different combinations, in a manner found in performances of Thomas Tallis's iconic work *Spem in Alium*.[39] Wilkins reflected on the dual heritage of this aspect of the music as lying in electroacoustic music (frequently engaging with spatial concerns in design or performance) and in the *chori spezzati* repertoire and performance context of the Italian renaissance church in particular.[40] Wilkins's work was also inspired by the book of Revelation, but the composer recast the pessimism of "plagues and pestilences heralding the demise of the World" with "other metaphysical states characteristic of the human experience"; her musical landscape is suggestive of "an imaginary spiritual and aural journey by the Seven Angels to Seven Stations," a progression corresponding to the Stations of the Cross:

Alpha: The Beginning
The Angel of Universality
Station 1:   The Firmament (Universality)
The Angel of Love
Station 2:   Seraphim (Love) [men's voices]
The Angel of Visions
Station 3:   The Stars (Visions)
The Angel of Security
Station 4:   Earth Mother (Security) [solo soprano]
The Angel of Compassion
Station 5:   The Lamb of God (Compassion)
The Angel of Wickedness
Station 6:   Gargoyles (Wickedness)
The Angel of Innocence
Station 7:   Cherubim (Innocence) (forty-nine Alleluias) [boys' voices]
Omega: Eternity

Revelations references the Middle Ages in various ways, most notably through allusion to medieval construction and composition. The composer gathers material from a range of medieval sources, creating a dramatic texture that makes audible the visual, acoustic, musical, and philosophical heritage of the distant past. In *Revelations*, these aspects are suggested by performers' movement through space, the ritual placement of musicians, texts drawing on fifteenth-century Christian spirituality, the borrowing of historical materials, a series of near-symmetrical pitch centers, and numerological significance (especially the number 7), all of which might be understood as engaging with ideas that resonate conceptually with Gothic cathedrals.[41] A comparative work is Peter Maxwell Davies's musical-theater piece *Vesalii Icones* (1969), which explores ritual space (notably through the presence of a dancer), historical quotation (e.g., plainsong associated with Good Friday, Maxwell Davies's own motet *Ecce manus tradentis*, and Mass setting *Missa super L'homme armé*), and Stations of the Cross; an underlying interest in sacred and sacrilegious rituals can be detected in several works by both composers. Wilkins's focus on mysticism and numerological significance also aligns her creative practice with that of contemporary Sophia Gubaidulina; the Russian composer's concerto for violin and orchestra, *Offertorium* (1980), draws on preexistent music by J. S. Bach, transforming the melody from *Das musikalische Opfer* (BWV 1079) through a series of thematic variations and more freely composed sections that are intended to evoke liturgical ritual.

The borrowed material in *Revelations* is largely derived from pieces found in the first volume of the *Historical Anthology of Music*, "Oriental, Medieval and Renaissance

Music," a rich repository for researchers working in the later twentieth century and one that had a direct impact on the selection of preexistent materials for many other composers, notably Maxwell Davies.[42] Wilkins's borrowing comprises texted music from the Middle Ages, dispersed through the overall fifty-minute structure: the plainchant "Benedicamus Domino" and a motet found in thirteenth-century sources, *Candida virginitas/T. Flos filius*, performed by men's voices (Station 2); a fifteenth-century Marian lyric sung by the solo soprano (Station 4); and the Alleluia plainchant sung by boys (Station 7).

The first striking use of preexistent material occurs in Station 2: Seraphim, in which the plainchant "Benedicamus Domino" and the two-part Latin motet are introduced, ancient songs "representing timeless-ness."[43] The scoring of this station gives an impression of a church organ, using two B♭ clarinets, bass clarinet, and bassoon, to support the male voices. The two-part motet *Candida virginatas ut lilium* is based on the tenor *Flos filius eius*, whose text is the final words of the tenor responsory *Stirps Jesse*, originally part of the liturgy for the Nativity and for the Assumption of the Blessed Virgin Mary. The plainchant melody of *Flos filius eius* is identical with that of the "Benedicamus Domino," creating a strong bond between the two pieces of borrowed material (see Example 13.3). The motet survives in sources of Notre Dame polyphony, which is associated with the virtuosic choral music copied and performed in thirteenth-century Paris and elsewhere (Example 13.3).[44]

Benedicamus Domino. Response. *Deo gratias.*
[Let us bless the Lord. Thanks be to God.]

Stirps Jesse produxit virgam: virgaque florem. Et super hunc florem requiescit spiritus almus. Verse. *Virgo dei genetrix virga est,* flos filius eius.
[The stalk of Jesse produced a brand: and the branch, a flower. Verse. The Virgin mother of God is the rod] the flower is her son.

EXAMPLE 13.3 Similarity of borrowed *Benedicamus Domino* plainchant melody and borrowed motet tenor *Flos filius eius*. Ellipses in square brackets indicate that the pitches above do not appear in the *Flos filius eius* chant or motet tenor. [NB: this does not reproduce any of Margaret Lucy Wilkins's music].

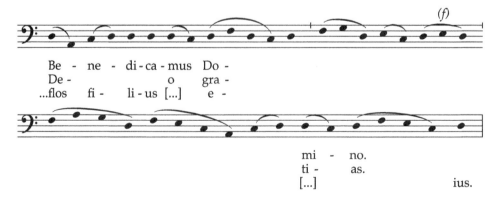

The use of medieval music as a structural component in building a more expansive texture is in itself redolent of theoretical writings on counterpoint from thirteenth- and fourteenth-century France and England. One of the primary methods available to musicians for the creation of polyphonic music was the employment of a preexistent tune as a structural base, typically placing it in the tenor voice; other voices would be superimposed in relation to it rather than in relation to each other, essentially in two-part counterpoint.[45] It is therefore not surprising that architectural metaphors permeated not only medieval treatises but also twentieth-century explanations for compositional practice in motets. For example, Christopher Page has drawn attention to a fourteenth-century theorist who advised singers to lay their counterpoint over the stability of a strong, foundational tenor.[46] Furthermore, motets of the same period commonly used architectural metaphors in relation to music and the body.[47]

The first presentation of the "Benedicamus Domino" is unaccompanied and in free rhythm, a character that the chant quotation retains for the whole section. The original chant is barely changed from its source notation except for a basic transposition down a whole tone to fit the composer's pitch center design (m. 131). Although for the most part the chant is heard monophonically, in m. 136 the tenors state "*Deo*," dividing from unison to a two-note tone cluster, with pitches a tone apart, held as a drone against the bass presentation of the phrase "*Deo gratias*," and the pitches are strengthened by instrumental accompaniment (see Example 13.4). The four-measure phrase at mm. 136–139 builds harmonic density as new pitches are supported by the addition of held notes in the clarinets and bassoon. Here, the effect is one of holding down successive keys on an organ, perhaps with the addition of pedal effects to make the sound swell and fade (Example 13.4).

With the abrupt introduction of the motet material (m. 149), the mood shifts to one of contrasts in which the stability of the medieval chant is interrupted and threatened by the unpredictable motet text, whose melody has been discarded in favor of pitch material drawing freely from the plainchant. Rhythmically unmeasured statements of "*Deo gratias*," separated by long-held tones, are rudely interrupted by the motet text with which it is interlaid. The woodwinds maintain stillness, droning on held notes until the voices have completed their phrase, after which they become active. Typically, modal melodic gestures based on seconds and minor thirds are repeated in all lines. In particular, the second word of the plainchant, "*Do[mino]*"—with its rising and falling minor third followed by a dip to a tone below and a return to the first pitch—provides the basis for the new texted material in Wilkins's tenor lines from m. 172. It happens more subtly in the instrumental parts, which sometimes treat tones as semitones or present the reference in retrograde or inversion (see Example 13.5). The vocal lines draw freely on melodic properties found in the plainchant or motet tenor, and the rising fourth at words like "*caput*" (head, mm. 172–173) mirrors the falling fourth in the chant incipit "*Be-[nedicamus]*" (Example 13.5).

Station 2 includes numerous examples of stylistic features that Ruskin found in his appreciation of Gothic nature, perhaps most strikingly the notion of musical savagery. Wilkins raises the leading tone of the melody when it is paired with the lyrics. The effect is aurally transformative, recalling elements of Carl Orff's *Carmina Burana* (written

EXAMPLE 13.4 Margaret Lucy Wilkins, *Revelations of the Seven Angels* (mm. 136–139). Reproduced with permission.

*N.B. the score is notated at sounding pitch

EXAMPLE 13.5 Margaret Lucy Wilkins, *Revelations of the Seven Angels* (mm. 172–178). (a) "*Hastis conferit*" (retrograde treatment) (Tenor 1, mm.172–174), (b) "atrium" (inversion) (Tenor 1, mm. 175–176), (c) "filium" (minor third but semitone) (Tenor 2, mm. 176–177). Reproduced with permission.

1935–1936), also an exercise in exploring medieval musicopoetic heritage within a large-scale framework, a piece that focused on perceptions of the simultaneously beautiful, rough, spiritual, and primitive world of twelfth-century monasticism.[48] Perhaps significantly, Wilkins's focus on exploiting the potential of smaller intervals recalls the use of liturgical chant—or newly composed liturgical chant—in horror film, a genre whose musical signifiers stem from Gothic and film noir examples in the early to mid-twentieth century.[49] Van Elferen notes that these include such notable examples as the semitone shifts of John Williams's score for *Jaws*, the use of the Dies irae in *The Shining* (Stanley Kubrick, 1980), and the quasi-liturgical music composed for vampire movies, such as *Interview with a Vampire* and *Dracula* (Francis Ford Coppola, music by Wojciech Kilar, 1992).[50]

The presentation of borrowed material helps to evoke some of the properties of Gothic architecture, not least the resonance of stone cathedrals and their interlocking visual and sonic spaces. At m. 171, the "Benedicamus Domino" incipit is split between basses as an imitative texture, now referencing the motet tenor *Flos filius eius*. The use of canon here suggests echo; this can be understood in relation to both the architecture of buildings and the use of imitative, repeating textures in thirteenth-century English (and to a lesser extent French) song.[51] From m. 172, the motet upper text is combined with the motet tenor in a manner that disrupts their normal sympathetic relationship. The tenor, in compound time, reflects the rhythmic shape of the modal rhythm used in the thirteenth-century archetype. Its melody retains fidelity to the plainchant, in transposed form. Over this, the divided tenors state fragmented lines of the poetry, in duple time, above the clarinets and bassoon, whose instrumental lines are locked with them rhythmically, as if declaiming Latin poetry themselves. With both bass voices scored at the upper end of their range, it is the plainchant material that stands out here: they are melodically, rhythmically, and texturally contained, perhaps even suspended, in a musical space and time (see Example 13.6).

EXAMPLE 13.6 Margaret Lucy Wilkins, *Revelations of the Seven Angels* (mm. 171–174). Reproduced with permission.

*N.B. the score is notated at sounding pitch

Later in *Revelations*, Wilkins draws on other signifiers of the past and on elements of numerology, itself a fascination for medieval artists and craftsmen. The final section of the work, for example, comprises forty-nine Alleluias, a sounding out of seven multiplied by seven. But arguably, the resonances of old and new are most dramatically audible in sections that include texted material, such as Station 4: Earth Mother, which sets fifteenth-century words to a lyrical melody. This station takes words that represent Mary's sadness as she contrasts the "laughing, kissing and merry cheer" of a mother bouncing a child on her knee with her sadness at seeing her son's body taken down from the cross following his crucifixion. In this part of the work, Wilkins places the humanity and suffering of Mary at the forefront of her dramatic language. The evocative text, "But ever, alas, I make my moan, to see my son's head as it is here. I prick out thorns by one and one, for now lieth dead my dear son dear," is set to an original melody with sensitivity that might well have resonated with late medieval listeners for whom contemplation of the Virgin's personal suffering was also a powerful meditation. Although the overall effect, especially with the rocking instrumental accompaniment, is not tonal, the triadic and arpeggio movement of the soprano line is comforting, like a lullaby, except for darker sections in which the suffering of Christ is emphasized (see Example 13.7).

Conclusions

Ruskin was one of the first English writers to employ the term medievalism, using it as early as 1854.[52] His definition of the word, in which the nature of Gothic held a central place, is closely analogous to the medievalism expressed in Wilkins's music. Ruskin's view was that the shapes and styles that could be perceived in the plastic arts were filled with an essence of a particular attitude, prioritizing freedom in expression, and his interpretations mixed observation with moral message.[53] Ruskin's ideas, not atypical of his age and certainly influential, led to Gothic designs being imitated in new churches and secular buildings of the nineteenth century. Similarly, the apparently moralizing force of devotional music is an attractive stimulus for the contemporary composer, who blends skilful technical craft with contemporary wit, as did the medieval stonemason. The result in the music of composers interested in medievalism is more spiritual than it is specifically Christian; this is pre-Reformation religion made secular for public entertainment by the historical distance lent by borrowed plainchant and motets placed outside their devotional context, even as their approach seeks to imbue some of that Gothic style in the new work created.

One element of Gothic that Ruskin treated swiftly but considered essential to its character was "the sense of the grotesque"; on this point, he remarked that "the tendency to delight in the fantastic and ludicrous, as well as in sublime, images, is a universal instinct of the Gothic imagination."[54] The same could easily be said of many works of twentieth-century music, and it is certainly a pervasive feature of Wilkins's output, if not in every piece, then in some of her most arresting, characterful, and imposing works. Interest in

EXAMPLE 13.7 Margaret Lucy Wilkins, *Revelations of the Seven Angels* (mm. 360–368). Reproduced with permission.

EXAMPLE 13.7 Continued

medieval culture and society impinged on a significant proportion of twentieth-century theoretical writing outside the strictly musical and lay at the heart of those helping to define and theorize the avant-garde. It comes as little surprise, then, that in invoking medievalism in their music, composers such as Wilkins experienced not incongruity, but sympathy and inspiration. Likewise, Holsinger has argued that theorists and literary critics have turned to the medieval era "not in a fit of nostalgic retrospection, but in a spirit of both interpretive and ideological resistance to the relentless inevitability of modernity."[55]

The production of medievalist contemporary music after 1950 was discernibly differ-ent to some of the incorporation, arrangement, or evocation of early music found in the oeuvre of British composers of earlier decades. The aesthetic had shifted away from one engaged in acts of nostalgia and pastoralism (what composer Elisabeth Lutyens infamously criticized as "cow-pat music, folky-wolky melodies on the cor anglais").[56] Holsinger identifies, for example, that "idiosyncratic medievalist historicism—promot-ing neither an unbroken continuity with the medieval past nor the epistemic ruptures implied in modernity's disavowal of the Middle Ages—provides in turn a powerful mechanism for questioning traditional schemes of periodization and temporality in the Western tradition."[57] Such an attitude can likewise be perceived in music, in which medievalism, even when loosely defined to include everything from inspiration from the distant past to the incorporation of plainchant within otherwise serial works, pro-duced music that was experimental, expressive, energetic, and current. Musical medie-valism functioned less as a single overarching style per se than as stimulus that could be communicated flexibly. In this way, it was closely connected to Ruskin's flexible defini-tion of Gothic style in art and architecture.

As performer and composer, Wilkins has engaged with two main aspects of medie-valism as identified by Alexander: "the recovery of materials…for the study of the Middle Ages" and "the imaginative adoption of medieval ideals and forms."[58] Indeed, it is clear that the second category, in Wilkins's music, was inflected by her involvement with the first and that even though the firsthand recovery in question was done via the publications of scholars such as Davison and Apel, such a dual appreciation of the medi-eval lends her work greater credibility. Creative medievalism requires a level of fantasy that sometimes sits uneasily with scholarship. Kreutziger-Herr reminds us that nostal-gia and idealism have been fundamental pillars of creative practice across the arts engaging with the historical past.[59] Weisl and Pugh offer the critical view that "the medi-evalism present in music—as performance, form, or subject matter—is a fantasy of authenticity, of the blending of the contemporary poetic soul with the (imagined) poetic soul of the past."[60] Certainly, the fictional narrative within *Musica Angelorum* that has been stimulated by an image from medieval glass—the sort of vignette of the Middle Ages that one finds on Christmas cards—is more fantasy than history. The use of bor-rowed materials in *Revelations of the Seven Angels* is not recreating a performance of the "Benedicamus Domino" for the audience, nor does its appearance require any deep knowledge of liturgy to be effective.

By focusing on the signifying elements of medieval music, such as its rhythmic, melodic, and modal qualities, Wilkins conjures the Gothic within a distinctly modern palette. All creative activity engages with reality only as far as it allows critical understanding of new artistic expression. In sum, to associate the work of Wilkins and similar composers with mere fantasy or nostalgia—on account of their embrace of medievalism—risks failing to engage with the middle ground, the connective tissue between old and new that enables modern expressions to be meaningful in the present.

NOTES

1. On early music as movement and revival, see especially John Haines, "Antiquarian Nostalgia and the Institutionalization of Early Music," *The Oxford Handbook of Music Revival* (New York: Oxford University Press, 2014), 73–93; and Bruce Haynes, *The End of Early Music: A Period Performer's History of Music for the Twenty-First Century* (New York: Oxford University Press, 2007). On the influence of early music on British composers, see Lisa Colton, "The Female Exotic: Tradition, Innovation and Authenticity in the Reception of Music by Judith Weir," *Contemporary Music Review*, 29, no. 3 (2010): 277–289.

2. Annette Kreutziger-Herr, "Medievalism," *Oxford Music Online*, accessed February 6, 2015, http://www.oxfordmusiconline.com.libproxy.wlu.ca/grovemusic/view/10.1093/gmo/9781561592630.001.0001/omo-9781561592630-e-0002261008?rskey=petrOY&result=1.

3. See Daniel Leech-Wilkinson, *The Modern Invention of Medieval Music: Scholarship, Ideology, Performance* (Cambridge: Cambridge University Press, 2002).

4. Manfred Bukofzer, *The Place of Musicology in American Institutions of Higher Learning* (New York: Liberal Arts Press, 1957), 27.

5. For another discussion of Ruskin, medievalism, and music, see Deborah Heckert," Hucbald's Fifths and Vaughan Williams's Mass: The New Medieval in Britain between the Wars," this volume, pp. 327–339.

6. The relationship between Catholicism and Gothic music is explored in Isabella van Elferen, "Music That Sucks and Bloody Liturgy: Catholicism in Vampire Movies," in *Roman Catholicism in Fantastic Film*, ed. Regina Hansen (Jefferson, NC: McFarland, 2011), 97–13; and Isabella van Elferen, *Gothic Music: The Sounds of the Uncanny* (Cardiff: University of Wales Press, 2012).

7. Kevin Murphy and Lisa Reilly, "Gothic," in *Medievalism: Key Critical Terms*, ed. Elizabeth Emery and Richard Utz (Woodbridge: Boydell & Brewer, 2014), 179–197.

8. John Ruskin, "Lectures on Architecture"; discussed in Michael Alexander, *Medievalism: The Middle Ages in Modern England* (New Haven, CT: Yale University Press, 2007), xvi–xxvii.

9. These points are raised and treated most fully in John Ruskin, "The Nature of Gothic," in *The Stones of Venice, Volume the Second. The Sea-Stories* (London: Smith, Elder, 1853), 151–230. See also Alexander, *Medievalism*, 90.

10. Ruskin, "The Nature of Gothic," 155.

11. Ruskin, "The Nature of Gothic," 151–152.

12. See Laura Tunbridge, ed., "Round Table: Modernism and Its Others," *Journal of the Royal Musical Association* 139, no. 1 (2014): 177–204, in which seven authors respond to the challenge of defining modernism in relation to stylistically diverse repertoire.

13. Tison Pugh and Angela Jane Weisl, *Medievalisms: Making the Past in the Present* (Oxford: Routledge, 2013), 103.

14. Victoria Nelson, "Faux Catholic: A Gothic Subgenre from Monk Lewis to Dan Brown," *Boundary 2* 134, no. 3 (2007): 87–107.

15. Susan McClary, *Feminine Endings: Music, Gender and Sexuality* (Minneapolis: University of Minnesota Press, 1991), 6. On the origins of medievalism as a discipline, see Ute Berns and Andrew James Johnston, "Medievalism: A Very Short Introduction," *European Journal of English Studies* 15, no. 2 (2011): 97–100.

16. Berns and Johnston, "Medievalism: A Very Short Introduction," 97.

17. Pugh and Weisl, *Medievalisms: Making the Past in the Present*, 1.

18. Kreutziger-Herr, "Medievalism."

19. See Peter Owens, "*Worldes Blis* and Its Satellites," in *Perspectives on Peter Maxwell Davies*, ed. Richard McGregor (Aldershot, UK: Ashgate, 2000), 23–50; and Peter Lawson, "Maxwell Davies's *Worldes Blis*," *Tempo* 90 (1969): 23–27.

20. I am grateful to Margaret Lucy Wilkins for enabling me to interview her about her music in relation to this research and for sharing her published and unpublished materials with me in 2013. My thanks also go to the University of Huddersfield Archives at Heritage Quay, which facilitated access to materials held in the British Music Collection.

21. Gwyn Parry-Jones, review of *Free Spirit*, http://www.musicweb-international.com/classrev/2003/Apr03/Margaret_Lucy_Wilkins.htm, April 2003, accessed July 28, 2017.

22. Herbert Culot, review of *Free Spirit*, http://www.musicweb-international.com/classRev/2003/Oct03/wilkins1.htm, October 2003, accessed July 28, 2017.

23. For a discussion of the relationship between the avant-garde and broader questions of value as pertain to cultural factors such as gender and ethnicity, see Susan McClary, "Terminal Prestige: The Case of Avant-Garde Music Composition," *Cultural Critique* 12 (1989): 57–81.

24. Sophie Fuller, *The Pandora Guide to Women Composers: Britain and the United States, 1629–Present* (London: Pandora Press, 1994), 335.

25. The most complete published works list for Wilkins is that compiled by the Living Composers Project, http://composers21.com/compdocs/wilkinsm.htm, accessed August 31, 2017.

26. Interview with the composer.

27. A recording of *Struwwelpeter* can be found on *Free Spirit* (Vienna Modern Masters, 2003, VMM 3055) performed by Alison Wells and the Firebird Ensemble.

28. Britten played the note as a second viola part in a performance with the Zorian Quartet, recorded on November 4, 1946; *Purcell: Fantasia upon One Note*, the Zorian String Quartet with Benjamin Britten, recorded in EMI's Studio No. 3, Abbey Road, London, on Gramophone Company 78-rpm matrix 2EA 11334, issued as HMV C 3539 (1947). On Britten's use of medieval source materials, see Heather Wiebe, *Britten's Unquiet Pasts: Sound and Memory in Postwar Reconstruction* (Cambridge: Cambridge University Press, 2012).

29. Margaret Lucy Wilkins, *Creative Music Composition: The Young Composer's Voice* (New York: Routledge, 2006), 7–8.

30. On the scholarly debates surrounding instrumentals in the performance of medieval song, see Leech-Wilkinson, *The Modern Invention of Medieval Music*, especially 69–70 and 93–95.

31. Interview with the composer.

32. Ruskin, *The Stones of Venice*, 396–397.

33. Program note by the composer.

34. I am grateful to Solomiya Moroz for her assistance in preparing music examples for publication, and to the composer for giving her permission for us to do so.

35. Margaret Lucy Wilkins, *Creative Music Composition: The Young Composer's Voice* (London: Routledge, 2006), 15–16, 24–26.

36. A DVD of the full work was released as Margaret Lucy Wilkins, *Revelations of the Seven Angels*, conducted by Barrie Webb, Corul Filarmonicii Banatul, Filarmonica Banatul, Vienna Modern Masters: VMM 1055, 2004.

37. The work is briefly described in Geoff Smith and Nicola Walker Smith, "Sonic Architecture in the Music of Margaret Lucy Wilkins," *Contemporary Music Review* 11, no. 1 (1994): 319–324.

38. Martin Thomas, *English Cathedral Music and Liturgy in the Twentieth Century* (Farnham, UK: Ashgate: 2015), 193–195.

39. Tallis's motet was likely performed at Nonsuch Palace during the sixteenth century, where the octagonal banqueting hall (including four balcony spaces) would have provided an ideal architectural setting for the eight, five-voice choirs that form the ensemble. Modern performances have often placed singers in the round, sometimes surrounding their audience, to make the spatial properties of *Spem in Alium* more audible to the listener. This feature of the work was famously presented in Janet Cardiff's multichannel installation of the piece, entitled *The Forty Part Motet* (2001).

40. Interview with the composer.

41. It is important to distinguish here between the use of numerological proportion in *Revelations* and the interpretative musicological readings of medieval works that themselves may have been structured to reflect particular devotional spaces, such as Guillaume Du Fay's *Nuper rosarum flores*. See Craig Wright, "Dufay's 'Nuper Rosarum Flores,' King Solomon's Temple, and the Veneration of the Virgin," *Journal of the American Musicological Society* 47, no. 3 (1994): 395–441.

42. Archibald T. Davison and Willi Apel, eds. *Historical Anthology of Music. Oriental, Medieval and Renaissance Music* (Cambridge, MA: Harvard University Press, 1946). On Maxwell Davies's use of the *Historical Anthology of Music*, see Owens, "*Worldes Blis* and Its Satellites."

43. Wilkins, *Revelations of the Seven Angels* score, 3.

44. Sources are Wolfenbüttel, Herzog August Bibliothek, Guelf.1099 Helmst., no. 114, ff.145v–146r and GB-Lbl Additional MS 30091, no. 2, ff.1–1v. The vernacular text is also found in W2, item 211, as the duplum of a three-part motet, *Quant revient et foille et flors contre la doucour/L'autre jor m'en alai par un destor/Flos filius eius*, on ff.206v–207r. The melody of *Candida virginitas ut lilium* also appears in manuscripts with the secular lyric "L'autrier jor m'en alai par un destor", a pastorelle. See discussions of these songs in Sylvia Huot, *Allegorical Play in the Old French Motet* (Stanford, CA: Stanford University Press, 1997), 90–99; and David Rothenberg, *The Flower of Paradise: Marian Devotion and Secular Song in Medieval and Renaissance Music* (Oxford: Oxford University Press, 2011), 24–57.

45. The dyadic nature of medieval polyphony is outlined in Margaret Bent, "The Grammar of Early Music: Preconditions for Analysis," *Tonal Structures in Early Music*, ed. Cristle Collins Judd (New York: Garland, 1998), 15–59.

46. Christopher Page, "The Performance of Ars Antiqua Motets," *Early Music* 16 (1988), 147–164, at 162.

47. Lisa Colton, "The Articulation of Virginity in the Medieval *Chanson de nonne*," *Journal of the Royal Musical Association* 133, no. 2 (2008): 159–188.

48. For more on this topic, see Kirsten Yri's contribution to this volume: "Medievalism and Antiromanticism in Carl Orff's *Carmina Burana* pp. 269–300.

49. James Deaville, "The Topos of 'Evil Medieval' in American Horror Film Music," in *Music, Meaning and Media*, ed. Erkki Pekillä, David Neumeyer, and Richard Littlefield (Helsinki: Semiotic Society of Finland, University of Helsinki and International Semiotics Institute at Imatra, 2006), 26–44; See also James Deaville's contribution to this volume: "Evil Medieval: Chant and the New Dark Spirituality of Vietnam-Era Film in America," pp. 709–728

50. Van Elferen, *Gothic Music*, 58–59. Beyond Gothic, horror soundtracks also commonly employ music that draws on liturgical monody or sacred genres, such as hymns and chorales, to signify religion or the occult. See Philip Hayward, *Terror Tracks: Music, Sound and Horror Cinema* (London: Equinox, 2009).

51. Repetition and canon techniques are ubiquitous in medieval English song; the most well-known example remains *Sumer is icumen in*, copied at Reading Abbey in the 1260s.

52. Ruskin used the term in his *Lectures on Architecture and Painting* (1854); see Emery and Reilly, *Medievalism: Key Critical Terms*, 197.

53. Murphy and Reilly, "Gothic," 188.

54. Ruskin, "The Nature of Gothic," 105.

55. Holsinger, *The Premodern Condition*, 5.

56. The remark is thought to have occurred as part of a lecture given at Dartington College of Arts in the 1950s.

57. Holsinger, *The Premodern Condition*, 6.

58. Alexander, *Medievalism*, xxii.

59. Kreutziger-Herr, "Medievalism."

60. Weisl and Pugh, *Medievalisms: Making the Past in the Present*, 111.

CHAPTER 14

HUCBALD'S FIFTHS AND VAUGHAN WILLIAMS'S MASS

The New Medieval in Britain between the Wars

DEBORAH HECKERT

WE begin at a specific moment...the critic Henry Cope Colles attends a performance by the City of Birmingham Choir under Joseph Lewis in Birmingham Town Hall on December 6, 1922, and the next day he writes a review of the performance—six paragraphs long—that is published in the issue of the *Musical Times* dated January 1, 1923.[1] The work he heard that night was Ralph Vaughan Williams's new unaccompanied choral piece, Mass in G minor. If one was looking for controversy or invective, one would not find it in this review. Colles clearly liked the piece, and it would be easy to move on.

So what incites interest in Colles's review? Why look again? Because buried in the fifth paragraph of his review appears a "throwaway" line included, one would imagine, with a wry smile: "Have there since Hucbald been so many consecutive fifths in a Mass?" For those conversant in the history of medieval music, this reads like a mistake and, as such, is surprising to see in the work of a musically educated man like Colles. A closer look into British early twentieth-century references to Hucbald, however, finds that Colles is not alone in perpetuating a mistake nearly 150 years old, that of attributing to the medieval theorist Hucbald a description of early polyphonic practice that for many marked the beginnings of Western polyphony. For example, in the July 1921 issue of *Musical Times*, Herbert Antcliffe wrote, "Imagine a singer of today with the resources only of his predecessor in the time of Guido D'Arezzo or the composer with only the resources of even, say, Bach and Handel, much more with those of Hucbald or John of Reading!" In 1926, Walford Davies published a series of four essays in the *Musical Times* called "The Perfect Fourth: From Hucbald to Holst."[2] And Hucbald is mentioned twice in

Constant Lambert's *Music, Ho!* published as late as 1934. The first comes in his discussion of Debussy:

> But Debussy takes a certain chord and, by leaving it unresolved, or by putting it under every note of a phrase (in a manner that dates back to Hucbald in the eleventh century), he draws our attention to this harmony as an entity in itself, with its own powers of evocation.[3]

The second forms part of the introduction to the fascinating chapter "The Age of Pastiche":

> The idea that music of an earlier age can be better than the music of one's own is an essentially modern attitude. The Elizabethans did not tire of their conceits and harken back to the sweet simplicity of Hucbald, any more than the late Caroline composers deserted the new and airy Italian style for the grave fantasias of Dowland.[4]

In these passages—as well as in early twentieth-century British writings about music history more generally—Hucbald functions as a simplified metonym for medieval music.

These mistaken understandings of Hucbald and his role in the development of polyphony call to mind the famous Ernest Renan quote repeated by Eric Hobsbawm (among many others): "Getting its history wrong is part of being a nation."[5] This particular mistake involves the authorship of a Carolingian music treatise most often called the *Musica enchiriadis*, which is now dated to the late ninth or very early tenth century. The treatise is part of a group of writings that have come to us from the late Carolingian period that includes, among others, Aurelian's *Musica disciplina*, Hucbald's *De harmonica institutione*, the anonymous *Alia musica and Scolica enchiriadis* and which culminates in Guido of Arezzo's *Micrologus* treatise. This group of treatises is central in defining and perpetuating the advances in music theory during the period from the second half of the ninth century to the early eleventh century that laid the foundations for the instruction and performance of liturgical music for the next several centuries. The *Musica enchiriadis* treatise is probably, after Guido's treatise, the most important of the group, widely disseminated, and from which several of the other treatises of the period, including Guido's, draw. What makes *ME* (as I will abbreviate it henceforth) noteworthy is that it is the first treatise in the Western tradition to include chant examples "notated" using fixed-pitch notation and chants written in such a notation rather than just cited by their text incipits.[6] For historians of modal theory, it is also one of the first treatises to discuss melodies in terms of their finals. Most important for the narrative of Western music history, the *ME*'s second part—Chapters 10–18—contains the earliest description of improvised harmonic practices found in surviving medieval European manuscripts. The treatise offers an elucidation of the rules of two-part organum (called diaphony in *ME*) based on the consonances of the fourth, fifth, and octave and pushes the improvised practice further with a chapter justifying the departure from purely parallel-part singing to contrary and oblique motion between voices. This independence of vocal lines has traditionally been seen to give European music its unique harmonic character, and this treatise served the musical historical narrative as a beginning point for that trajectory well into the twentieth century.

Obviously a popular and frequently copied treatise, there are several surviving manuscripts containing *ME* in whole or in part, including one in the Arundel collection, British library Arundel MS77, dating from the late eleventh century. Many of these manuscripts have been known about and have received scholarly attention since at least the eighteenth century. In 1784, Martin Gerbert included an edition of *ME* in his *Scriptores ecclesiastici de music sacra potissimum*, in which he posited that *ME* had been written by Hucbald, whose complementary *De harmonica institutione* was from approximately the same period. In England, Charles Burney continued this misattribution in his 1789 *A General History of Music from the Earliest Ages to the Present Period*. Burney claims to have been able to peruse one of the *ME* manuscripts, which was then part of the French royal collection, probably the one now in the Bibliothèque nationale, and his account goes into considerable detail, offering examples copied from the treatise of its explication of organum among other things, and noting how odd to modern ears would be its reliance on consonances of the octave, fourth, and fifth.[7] Burney's misattribution of *ME* solidified Hucbald's reputation as the progenitor of Western polyphonic music for English readers, and as the musical historical narrative continued to be replicated and added to, Hucbald remained a placeholder for the point of *the* beginning, and a necessary name for historical accounts of the development of music in premodern Europe. As late as 1905, the new edition of *Grove's Dictionary of Music and Musicians* still included Rockstro's earlier Hucbald entry for the first edition that cites Hucbald as the author of *ME* and posits him as the first Western polyphonic composer.[8] Hucbald serves this purpose as well in the 1905 edition's extended article on harmony written by F. G. Shinn. Time and again in English histories of music, the name is connected with concepts of earliness, of evolutionary beginnings, or of primitive awakenings.

However, by the turn of the twentieth century, the theory that Hucbald was the writer of *ME* had been discounted. In 1884, the German music historian Hans Müller argued in his *Hucbalds echte und unechte Schriften über Musik*—an edition of Hucbald's extant works—that Hucbald had not written *ME* after all, and this was soon after confirmed by the work of other German scholars in the emerging field of *Musikwissenshaft*: musical scholarship in the way we might think of it today. Drawing on new methods coming from philology and paleography, Müller and others compared vocabulary usage between treatises in descriptive passages elucidating common concepts, and these investigations showed significant differences between *De harmonica institutione* and *ME* in how the authors used key terminology. Furthermore, in the ninth century the writings of the much earlier philosopher Boethius were rediscovered and incorporated into treatises such as Hucbald's *De institutione musica*, and Boethius's work treatise became the primary authority for Carolingian music theory. As the Carolingian treatises were exhaustively compared, Müller and other German scholars realized that a crude dating/ordering for the treatises could be reached by focusing on the analytical grasp of Boethius displayed by the treatises. Earlier treatises show less knowledge of Boethius, while later ones have a firmer, deeper grasp. Hucbald's *De harmonica institutione* and *ME*'s understanding did not match up in their utilization of Boethius. Hence, by 1890, on the continent it was evident; Hucbald clearly did not write *ME*.

Importantly, the milieu for this new scholarship was mostly German, though some French scholars were also working on medieval manuscripts in an attempt to chronicle a continuous music history for France-the *archaeologie nationale*-as well as the seminal work being done with chant manuscripts at Solesmes.[9] There was a general rivalry between the German and French camps, but the emerging methodologies were shared between the two groups, as was a fundamental impetus that was essentially nationalistic, creating images of the nation through increased understandings of captured moments from the medieval past. The discourse was scientific and geared toward specialists. From it emerged, as Nancy van Deusen has argued,

> the interpretative constructs of clear dialectical distinctions between "sacred" and "secular" medieval music, monophony and polyphony, liturgical and paraliturgical, or liturgical music versus "accretions," the concepts of "composers" belonging to "schools" of "form," and of "compositional style."[10]

These determining agents within, and descriptive mechanisms for, medieval music were in place by 1930.

In England, however, most music (and art) historical accounts were targeted toward a general reading public and were written not by medievalists, but by generalists. Rather than aspiring to the scientific, most were descriptive, critically amorphous and, if they were specific in nature, continued antiquarian traditions that treated the items at hand as documents rather than acting as components within a critically complex "history" in the way they did on the continent. While continental, particularly German, scholars argued for an impersonal search for knowledge using new approaches of *Stilkritik*, periodicization, and formalism, the English were much more likely to pursue a cultural historical method aimed at reading the work of music, art, or literature as an index of the mentality and collective psyche of the period.[11] John Ruskin, one of, if not the, preeminent essayists on art and aesthetics of the Victorian period, formulated this approach in his 1853 *Stones of Venice*, which essentially argues the inseparable link between art and the society that produces it. *Stones of Venice* includes the seminal essay "The Nature of the Gothic," in which Ruskin uses the Venetian medieval architecture he describes as a means to lambast the ills of contemporary English society and the Industrial Revolution, as he traces Venice's decline against the backdrop of the shift from medieval to Renaissance artistic and architecture aesthetic styles.

An important medievalist example of this particular English bias toward broad, cultural history writing is H. O. Taylor's 1911 book *The Medieval Mind*.[12] A product of the early twentieth century in first two, and then later four, volumes, Taylor's treatment of the medieval period offers an enormous panoramic historical account of the entire thousand-year period that is radically different from specific, focused studies of particular medieval moments or texts emerging from the new styles of scholarship on the continent. Massive in its scope, Taylor's goal is not to increase particular knowledge through analysis or other methods, but to use the canvas of the medieval period as a basis for broad, painterly sweeps of generalization and synthesis. The "medieval mind" is fantastical, alien, and distant; yet Taylor's account of the otherness of the medieval is completely complicit in the strands of pre-twentieth-century British history writing that use the remoteness of the past to address the present. As Taylor writes in his introduction,

> The Middle Ages! They seem so far away; intellectually so preposterous, spiritually so strange. Bits of them may touch our sympathy, please our taste; their window-glass, their sculpture, certain of their stories, their romances,—as if those straitened ages really were the time of romance, which they were not, God knows, in the sense commonly taken. Yet perhaps they were such intellectually, or at least spiritually. Their *terra*—not for them *incognita*, though full of mystery and pall and vaguer glory—was not the earth. It was the land of metaphysical construction and the land of spiritual passion. There lay their romance, thither pointed their verriest thinking, thither drew their utter yearning.
>
> Is it possible that the Middle Ages should speak to us, as through a common humanity? Their mask is by no means dumb: in full voice speaks the noble beauty of Chartres Cathedral. Such medieval product, we hope, is of the universal human, and therefore of us as well as of the bygone craftsmen. Why it moves us, we are not certain, being ignorant, perhaps, of the building's formative and earnestly intended meaning. Do we care to get at that? There is no way save by entering the medieval depths, penetrating to the *rationale* of the Middle Ages, learning the *doctrinale*, or *emotionale*, of the modes in which they still present themselves so persuasively.
>
> But if the pageant of those centuries charm our eyes with forms that seem so full of meaning, why should we stand indifferent to the harnessed processes of medieval thinking and the passion surging through the thought? Thought marshalled the great medieval procession, which moved to measures of pulsating and glorifying emotion. Shall we not press on, through knowledge, and search out its efficient causes, so that we too may feel the reality.... This would be to reach human comradeship with medieval motives, no longer found too remote for our sympathy, or too fantastic or shallow for our understanding.[13]

Taylor swiftly lays out his methodology, which seems a sharp contrast to new, pseudo-scientific research coming from the continent:

> Obviously, if we would attain, perhaps, no unified, but at least an orderly presentation of medieval intellectual and emotional development, we must avoid entanglements with manifold and not always relevant detail.... Let the student be mindful of his purpose (which is my purpose in this book) to follow through the Middle Ages the development of intellectual energy and the growth of emotion. We shall not stray from our quest after those human qualities which impelled the strivings of medieval men and women, informed their imagination, and moved them to love and tears and pity.[14]

This approach remained prevalent well into the 1920s, a holdover from Victorian attitudes for whom, as the literary historian Robichaud has put it, "the Middle Ages served as a kind of screen onto which fantasies and anxieties about contemporary society could be projected. The Victorians invoked the Middle Ages to articulate their desire for social harmony and cultural tradition, imagining the medieval world as a time of meaningful social relations and authentic feeling, though one, like Camelot, threatened with disintegration, compensating for the class tension and social upheavals of the industrial present."[15] This accurately describes the uses of the medieval made by such figures as Ruskin and William Morris, who found in the communalism of medieval society and the idealized figure of the medieval worker/craftsman an antidote to the ills of the Victorian present brought on by industrialization and the diminished value, artistic and social, of the worker and his work.[16] Ruskin's Gothic is a period and a style that allowed the worker to act in freedom and individuality and, because of this, acts as a golden age on which to look back with nostalgia. From Ruskin's assertion of the value of the medieval craftsperson, Morris built his own utopian, Socialist theories on the importance of reviving medieval arts and crafts as a way of transforming contemporary English society.[17] Ruskin and Morris were only one direction in which ideological appropriations of the medieval were taken; the perceived social stability, communalism, and intense religiosity of the period led to a multitude of appropriations as a way of countering modern malaise.

Some scholars in England did read Müller, and their work displays a general cognizance of new German advances in the understanding of this nexus of medieval treatises. For instance, also in the 1905 edition of the *Grove Dictionary*, both John Stainer's and Walter Frere's articles on Odo and Hoger respectively, mention Müller's work and argue the case for new attribution using comparative methodologies that had become part and parcel of how German and French scholars were approaching questions pertaining to medieval works and issues of authorship and transmission.[18] That they also misattributed the work is beside the point—they were using new methodologies to argue possibilities rather than merely replicating misinformation that had attained the weight of truth.

The example of a figure like Walter Frere demonstrates the adoption of both German and French paleographic techniques and the use of these techniques to create a new, contemporary vision of an English medieval that is scientific in technique but nationalistic in its ideology. Born in 1863, Frere was educated at Charterhouse and Trinity College, Cambridge, and then took Anglican religious orders. Frere was above all a liturgist—until the 1920s he was part of the Community of the Resurrection, which sought to create a space for the Benedictine monastic tradition within the liturgy of the Anglican church. Sarum chant and the manuscripts in which it survives became Frere's scholastic obsession in the years between the mid-1880s and the first decades of the twentieth century, not just to provide music for his brothers to chant but also in a fierce, abstract drive for knowledge. Ultimately, he created complete editions of the medieval Sarum service books, including the gradual, the antiphoner, and the Winchester troper, thereby, as Mary Berry puts it in Frere's *Grove Music Online* entry, "becoming the first modern scholar to disentangle successfully the complex web of English medieval church services and to present a complete and coherent picture of the Sarum chant dialect."[19] He was completely wedded to the emerging paleographical approaches in medieval scholarship that were quite new in Britain in the late nineteenth century, but that were more and more present in German and French work on medieval liturgical sources. Frere obviously knew of the German medieval *Musikwissenschaft* being produced at the same time he was exhaustively editing manuscript sources for English music—for instance, he mentions Müller's questioning of the attribution of *ME* to Hucbald in his entry on Odo. And the editions and attendant scholarship emerging from the manuscript workshop at Solesmes had a profound effect on Frere, both in the idea of the facsimile that Frere developed further in his editions, and, equally important, in their mission to produce a "sounding" liturgical music for the present day. In fact, Peter Allan points out that Frere falls clearly into Katherine Bergeron's second stage in the revival of chant, in his scholarship's forensic character, tenacious precision, and conviction that "the technical arguments, if correctly applied, led to the elucidation of an accurate musical text."[20]

Frere serves well as representative of the first British wave of "music history": what we might define as an active process of research and scholarship. This is quite opposed to the "history of music": the spinning of a chronological narrative with an aim to support a grander thesis beyond the specifics at hand, whether those are evolutionary-developmental, sociocultural, political-nationalistic, or one of any number of others. This is just the distinction Roger Fry made between art history and the history of art in a 1928 lecture often pointed to as the first to use the term *art history* in England and celebrating the foundation of the first academic art history department in England at the Courtauld Institute.[21] Frere was not alone. One might also mention William Barclay Squire, H. J. W. Tilyard, Henry Briggs, and others, all of whom worked within a community of writers who shared ideas, a mindset of the times, and (like Frere and other early scholar-liturgists) a desire to influence sounding music through analysis and speculation. The last point here is to say that even by 1920, this kind of work had no institutional, university, or other academic standing in Britain the way it had in Germany, Switzerland, and France. The dominant discourse still was the *history of music*, not *music history*. So, for most British writers on music in 1920 including Colles, continental scholarship had not permeated into a general consciousness and had not attained a sufficient authority that would replace habitual paths trodden again and again in British historical narratives.

It makes sense, therefore, that Colles's review would tap into understandings of the medieval that fall into the tropes and conventions created through a perspective informed by the history of music and would see in the Mass in G minor a work that used its medievalist inspiration to speak to the present, rather than as an artifact of emerging knowledge about the period. The work's effect on himself and the other listeners is at the center of the experience, much as Taylor's inflated rhetoric in the introduction of *The Medieval Mind* explicates a desire to know the medieval from the effects it has on the contemporary person.

In his review, Colles struggles to come up with appropriate descriptive language to communicate the effect the piece had on him, and he falls back on the metaphor at the heart of the medievalist experience for many in England: the cathedral. Cathedralism, as

Christopher Page explains it, is a major trope within musical medievalism since the eighteenth century, gaining descriptive energy by associating medieval music—particularly liturgical music—with the space of the medieval cathedral.[22] It feels like a natural move to make, though Page warns of the inconsistencies and misreadings inherent in projecting our understanding of the cathedral as a trustworthy way to understand medieval music. Colles turns to this tried-and-true descriptive trope as symbolic short-hand to communicate meaning without the use of specific words, extended analysis, and concrete experiential description. It is an image and analogy that had enormous power during the years surrounding the turn of the twentieth century, particularly in England, where the fascination of the antiquarian and the romantic alike for the English cathedral had spawned a scholarly, artistic, and tourist industry for over a century.

Colles's cathedralist approach to a vocal piece by Vaughan Williams was strengthened by the cathedralist interpretations of an earlier Vaughan Williams piece that is easy to link to the Mass: *Fantasia on a Theme by Thomas Tallis*.[23] Percy Young, for example, commented that "the atmosphere for the cathedral is surely felt within the music," and Ursula Vaughan Williams (the wife of the composer) wrote that Vaughan Williams had "the Norman grandeurs of Gloucester Cathedral in mind and the strange quality of the resonance of stone" when composing the work. These comments reflect a vein of writing on the *Tallis Fantasy* that began early in the work's performance history and continue to this day and that are extended to the Mass in G minor.[24] Add to this the known connections of the piece to Westminster Cathedral's director of music Richard Runciman Terry, who played a crucial part in the revival of the performance of liturgical polyphonic music from the Renaissance in England, and it becomes clear that this potent symbol of the medievalist mindset is a facile but evocative ploy in Colles's review.

What the Mass is *not* is even more revealing. For Colles, it is not excessive, neither is it an overblown statement of personal subjectivity using the ancient mass ordinary as a springboard for a host of subjective associations. "The texture," he writes, "is intensely personal, however the personal expressiveness is subjugated.... It comes not, on the one hand from a Regerish itch for note-spinning, or, on the other, from a romantic, egoistic impatience with foregoing methods and styles in the musical treatment of the text, or for the sake of a crude breaking-down of known limits of expressions."[25] The German composer Max Reger (who died in 1916) is the one person, apart from Hucbald, who is mentioned in this review, and we may ask why he is the particular figure against which Vaughan Williams and his new mass are placed. Reger was a composer who also wrote music blending historical techniques—fugues, counterpoint, continuo—with a musical language firmly connected to post-Wagnerian harmonic idioms. In constructing Reger as a foil to Vaughan Williams, Colles was probably reacting to Reger's known nationalist sentiments and the preferred historicist sources of his borrowing from within the Germanic tradition. For English composers in the 1920s such as Vaughan Williams and others associated with what came to be called the English Musical Renaissance, the creation of an English musical national identity had as its perhaps most important tenet a reliance on the models of English musical history derived from both folk and art music in a complex combination. But this history was limited, marked by a borderline created by the works of Henry Purcell, and fixed much more firmly on the English golden age of the sixteenth and early seventeenth centuries. For Colles, therefore, Reger was problematic both because of his use of a "foreign" set of historical sources and also because of his alignment with other, "nasty" tendencies. Colles thus uses Reger as an embodiment of twentieth-century stereotypes about romantic, excessive Victorian predecessors and their messy, subjective annexations of the distant past.[26]

In this review, then, Colles wants to disconnect the Mass from an older, nineteenth-century form of historicism by characterizing the piece as "reactionary towards the nineteenth century." "There was some haste here to make it out to be 'Tudor' or even 'Palestrinian,'" Colles writes, "but while Dr. Vaughan Williams has not lived his life in obliviousness of the sixteenth century, the music is of course his own."[27] Brought together here are a historicist and a modernist aesthetic, but Colles dismisses categorically the nineteenth century and the types of historical appropriation that figured in the late romantic style. We hear this echoed again in something R. R. Terry wrote to the composer soon after getting his first copy of the Mass, which he would then perform in Westminster Cathedral. Terry was the man whose program to resurrect the polyphonic heritage of the past through the live performance of the music with the Westminster Cathedral choir within the appropriate frame of the cathedral's liturgical services was the inspiration for Vaughan Williams's composition of his Mass. He complemented Vaughan Williams, saying, "In your individual and modern idiom you have really captured the old liturgical spirit and atmosphere."[28] Colles and Terry both seem to advocate for new compositions that position the past as a reference point, creating bridges between the distant past and present that bring the past alive within a contemporary frame. This historicist bridge noticeably avoids the nineteenth century and, in doing so, aligns Colles's reading of the Mass in G minor with continental neoclassicism, but using a very different set of sources that draw on historical periods that have the ability to resonate with a particularly English narrative of music history.

Colles's comments demonstrate a profound ambivalence regarding the recent past. But the mention of "Tudor" and "Palestrinian" in this passage also displays a confusion regarding the medieval that is more indicative of conflicting attitudes toward the Middle Ages that were not helped by the ideological appropriation of the period in the late nineteenth and early twentieth centuries in England by Morris and others. For if the "medieval mind" was communal and collective, it was also viewed as cosmopolitan and hence, to some extent, antinationalistic. As part of the historical narrative being created by critics and writers on music like Colles, English musical nationalism in the early decades of the twentieth century was firmly rooted in the renaissance of the Tudor, Elizabethan, and Jacobethan periods. Vaughan Williams and other English composers were upheld as the creators of this new national musical style; therefore, how to combine a Renaissance-centric historicity with medieval sources rather than Tudor, Elizabethan, or Stuart ones caused problems both in how composers gestured toward medieval influences and in how those works then were placed critically within the nationalist agenda. This is especially a problem when an academic, research-oriented knowledge of English medieval sources was barely emerging, and hence there was little sense of an "English" medieval corpus of works, let alone a sense of distinctive characteristics.

R. R. Terry's involvement in the commission for the Mass further complicates a picture of medieval–Renaissance ambiguity surrounding this work. Much has been written about Terry's importance in reviving the tradition of performing Renaissance sacred vocal music, both within the liturgy and in concert settings through his work with the Westminster Cathedral choir.[29] He was involved in "Englishing" the Renaissance— he brought to public attention English Renaissance vocal polyphony by Tye, Tallis, Byrd, Phillips, and others, thereby contributing to the centrality of these figures for emerging narratives of English musical history. But, as befitting a Roman Catholic institution, Terry's choir also performed sixteenth-century sacred works by continental composers such as Allegri, Palestrina, and de Victoria, works that are decidedly not English and not part of the Anglican tradition. Terry was deeply influenced as well by the chant revival instigated by Solesmes and integrated these continental chant sources into the liturgy at the cathedral.

There is no way of definitively knowing whether the range of music sung by Terry's choir in its Roman Catholic setting muddied a clear perception of the work's English identity with Renaissance polyphony and steered critical reception of this piece toward alignment with the medieval. Vaughan Williams's Mass was written during the period following the First World War as part of a group of works that include *The Lark Ascending*, *The Pastoral Symphony*, and *The Shepherds of the Delectable Mountains*. These works are often seen as tied to the "pastoral" within Vaughan Williams's works, though recent work by Eric Saylor and others has complicated this simplistic pastoral label.[30] They may just as easily be linked by an impetus to create contrasting identities across many levels by returning to bedrock values that are connected in a very general sense to an English experience, including those expressions of identities that were carried by shared history, literature, landscape, and, of course, religion. For Vaughan Williams as an agnostic, this was not a personal belief, but a sensitivity to the communal values that were embodied in a traditional religious expression that was a part of English identity through a series of words, texts, and actions and that carried great power through their repetition over the centuries. As more was known about the texts—musical and otherwise—of the English Middle Ages, the more drawn to these texts were the generation of English composers from the 1920s on.

Gustav Holst, Vaughan Williams's close friend and musical confidante, was a central figure in the composition of the Mass. Vaughan Williams's debt is confirmed by the piece's dedication to Holst, who had written several works in the years before 1921 that reflect an emerging interest in the medieval period that sought to combine both historiographic and modernist aesthetics. The most important model was probably Holst's *Hymn to Jesus*, in turn dedicated to Vaughan Williams, with its divisi choruses and use of plainsong melodies. His 1915 *Nunc dimittis*, also written for R. R. Terry, is another predecessor that can be directly linked to Vaughan Williams's subsequent Mass. These two Holst works may have suggested a means of using an invocation of the medievalist aesthetic as a way of negotiating the twin claims of national identity and preromantic stylistic sources.

The Mass in G minor hints that some early twentieth-century English composers like Vaughan Williams were still searching for definition on the appropriate historical sources for a new compositional style connected to ideas of English identity. Clearly the Tudor period of the sixteenth and early seventeenth centuries was well on its way to being one important source, secured by the status this period had attained over the previous decades as a nostalgic golden age of English culture and society. The medievalist reception of the Mass shows that, as a new methodology and scholarly attitudes slowly made their way across the channel and were applied to English sources, the medieval could be renovated away from nineteenth-century communal and cosmopolitan understandings toward one that could also be "nationalized" as part of an English history of music. Vaughan Williams and other English composers of the period were ultimately modernists, albeit modernists attempting to create an English version of modernism, and needed to walk a tight line between a conservative backward glance to history and the forward-looking demands of contemporary music in ways that marked them as different from their nineteenth-century forbears. When source material overlapped, the rhetoric applied to the appropriations needed to be updated.

For all that Colles seems to commend Vaughan Williams's allusions to the distant past at Reger's expense, Walter Frisch's concept of historical modernism developed in a 2004 *Musical Quarterly* article on Reger offers a partial theorization of some characteristics of the new, early twentieth-century British medievalism.[31] I and others have argued elsewhere that British modernists were not at ease with continental neoclassicism—an unease that often created strange disjunctions between philosophy and praxis—and Frisch's concept offers another direction for thinking about twentieth-century music written before World War II composed with an eye backward toward the historical. In his Reger article, Frisch describes historical modernism as involving works that were intended and received as modern, but that derived their compositional energy primarily from techniques of a more remote past, in a way that does not involve aspects of irony and pastiche that are central to twentieth-century neoclassicism. A focus on a slightly earlier time period of the late nineteenth century and on Austro-Germanic works complicates a simple transference of Frisch's definition of historical modernism to the British works from the period surrounding Vaughan Williams's Mass. But what we see in the Mass in G minor, in Terry's comments to Vaughan Williams, and in Colles's review is something I feel falls between historical modernism and neoclassicism, pointing to a pivotal moment in Britain's absorption and transformation of continental modernism in light of British historicist leanings.

The connections Colles makes between medievalism, antiromanticism, and the Mass are intriguing ones that rest on contemporary understandings of medieval music and music theory in the scholarly and compositional environment during the decades immediately before and after World War I. Much has been written about eighteenth- and nineteenth-century medievalism in Britain. Scholars have explored antiquarianism, literature and the visual arts, the ways in which the Middle Ages functioned as fantasy space for social reformers of all types, and other topics as well. Less work has been done on the ways in which British medievalism changed in light of modernist trends across society and the arts from 1890 to 1935, as new manuscripts were discovered, new methodologies were brought to bear, and findings were interpreted in new ways. Perhaps we can speak of a *historicist modernism* in Britain comparable to the one Walter Frisch argues for with regard to Austro-German music in the years surrounding the turn of the twentieth century? And, if so, how is this different from the neoclassicism on the continent in the years around 1920? More work is needed on this topic before we can truly understand the complexities of the historical impulse in English music of the period.

Notes

1. Henry Cope Colles, "Dr. Vaughan Williams's Mass," *The Musical Times* 64, no. 959 (January 1, 1923): 36–37.

2. Herbert Antcliffe, "Facts in Science and Art," *The Musical Times* Vol. 62, No. 941 (Jul. 1, 1921), pp. 482-483; Walford Davies, "The Perfect Fourth: From Hucbald to Holst," *The Musical Times* Vol. 67, No. 996 (Feb. 1, 1926), pp. 113–119.

3. Constant Lambert, *Music, Ho!* (London: Penguin Books, 1934), 26.

4. Ibid., 64.

5. The translation is Eric Hobsbawm's and is found on page 12 of *Nations and Nationalism Since 1780: Programme, Myth, Reality* (Cambridge University Press, 1992). The original comes from Ernest Renan's 1882 Sorbonne lecture, *Qu'est-ce qu'une nation?* ("L'oubli et je dirai même l'erreur historique, sont un facteur essentiel de la formation d'une nation et c'est ainsi que le progrès des études historiques est souvent pour la nationalité un danger").

6. Raymond Erickson, "Introduction," in *Musica Enchiriadis* and *Scolica Enchiriadis*, trans., with introduction and notes, Raymond Erickson, ed. Claude V. Palisca (New Haven, CT: Yale University Press, 1995).

7. Charles Burney, *A General History of Music: From the Earliest Ages to the Present Period,* Vol. 2 (Cambridge: Cambridge University Press, 2010), 116.

8. *Grove's Dictionary of Music and Musicians*, 2nd ed., ed. John Fuller-Maitland et al. (London: Macmillan, 1905), 438–439.

9. For more on the process carried out at Solesmes to revive the chant sung tradition and the accompanying production of chant publications, see Katherine Bergeron, *Decadent Enchantments: The Revival of Gregorian Chant at Solesmes* (Berkeley: University of California Press, 1998). Of particular interest is the Solesmes idea of publishing photographic facsimiles of medieval chant manuscripts.

10. Nancy Van Deusen, "Introduction to Part II: Music," *Medieval Scholarship: Philosophy and the Arts*, ed. Helen Damico et al. (Abingdon, UK: Taylor & Francis, 1995), 147.

11. For a broader look at the bibliography examining this issue, see Marc Baer's essay review, "The Memory of the Middle Ages: From History of Culture to Cultural History," *Studies in Medievalism* IV (1992): 290–308.

12. Henry Osborn Taylor, "Preface," in *The Medieval Mind: A History of the Development of Thought and Emotion in the Middle Ages* (London: Macmillan, 1911), 1. This book was enormously successful and significant well into the twentieth century, going through several editions.

13. Ibid.

14. Ibid.

15. Paul Robichaud, *Making the Past Present* (Washington, DC: Catholic University Press, 2007), 5.

16. For more on Ruskin's medievalism, see Dwight Culler's "Ruskin and Victorian Medievalism," in *The Victorian Mirror of History* (New Haven, CT: Yale University Press, 1985), 152–184. See also Lisa Colton's discussion of Ruskin in "Past Tense: Creative Medievalism in the Music of Margaret Lucy Wilkins," in this volume, pp. 301–326.

17. It is important to note that Vaughan Williams was very much influenced by William Morris's ideas, and his good friend Gustav Holst was a member of the Hammersmith Socialist League, which was based on Morris's political ideas. See Paul Harrington, "Holst and Vaughan Williams: Radical Pastoral," in *Music and the Politics of Culture*, ed. Christopher Norris (New York: St. Martin's Press, 1989), 106–127.

18. John Stainer, "Odo," and Walter Frere, "Otger," in *Grove's Dictionary of Music and Musicians* 2nd ed., ed. John Fuller-Maitland et al. (London: Macmillan, 1905), 426–427 and 573, respectively.

19. Mary Berry, "Walter Frere," *Oxford Music Online*, accessed May 5, 2018, http://www.oxfordmusiconline.com/grovemusic/view/10.1093/gmo/9781561592630.001.0001/omo-9781561592630-e-0000010217.

20. Peter Allen, "Like an Elephant Waltzing," in *Walter Frere: Scholar, Monk, Bishop*, ed. Nicholas Stebbing and Benjamin Gordon-Tayler (Norwich: Hymns Ancient and Modern, 2011), 201.

21. Roger Fry, "Art History as an Academic Study," from *Last Lectures* (London: Macmillan, 1939) discussed in Garrett Caples's *Retrievals* (Seattle: Wave Books, 2014), 17.

22. Christopher Page, "Cathedralism," *Discarding Images* (Oxford: Clarendon Press, 1993), 10–42.

23. Anthony Pople, "Vaughan Williams, *Tallis*, and the Phantasy Principle," in *Vaughan Williams Studies*, ed. Alain Frogley (Cambridge: Cambridge University Press, 1996), 47–80.

24. Percy Young, *Vaughan Williams* (London: Dobson, 1953), 45; and Ursula Vaughan Williams, *R. V. W.: A Biography of Ralph Vaughan Williams* (Oxford: Oxford University Press, 1964), 88. More recent evocations of the cathedral include Allan Atlas's "On the Structure and Proportions of Vaughan Williams's 'Fantasia on a Theme by Thomas Tallis,'" *Journal of the Royal Musical Association* 135, no. 1 (2010): 115–144.

25. Colles, "Dr. Vaughan Williams's Mass," 37.

26. We are only a few years after World War I, of course, and attitudes toward German music shifted back and forth during the years just before, during, and immediately after. For an opinionated treatment of the topic, see Meirion Hughes and Robert Stradling's "Being Beastly to the Hun," in their *The English Musical Renaissance: 1840–1940* (Manchester: Manchester University Press, 2001), 115–162.

27. Colles, "Dr. Vaughan Williams's Mass," 37.

28. Quoted in Michael Kennedy's *The Works of Ralph Vaughan Williams* (Oxford: Oxford University Press, 1966), 159.

29. See, for instance, Timothy Day's "Sir Richard Terry and 16th-Century Polyphony," *Early Music* 22, no. 2 (May 1994): 296; and Thomas Muir's "'Old Wine in New Bottles': Renaissance Polyphony in the English Catholic Church during the Nineteenth and Early Twentieth Centuries," *Nineteenth-Century Music Review* 4, no. 1 (2007), 81.

30. Eric Saylor, *English Pastoral Music: From Arcadia to Utopia, 1900–1955* (Urbana: University of Illinois Press, 2017).

31. Walter Frisch, "Reger's Historicist Modernism," *Musical Quarterly* 87, no. 4 (Winter 2004): 732–748.

....

CHAPTER 15

THE RETURN OF
ARS SUBTILIOR?

*Rhythmic Complexity in the Chantilly Codex
and in Selected Twentieth-Century Works*

....

ALEKSANDRA VOJČIĆ

"The idea of canon or round, for instance, has influenced motets, fugues,
and then, among others, the music of Anton Webern and my own phase
pieces.... Good new ideas generally turn out to be old."[1]

—Steve Reich

THE Chantilly Codex is undoubtedly one of the most important collections of late
fourteenth-century music, nowadays referred to as *Ars subtilior*.[2] Among the most distinguishing features of *Ars subtilior*, besides rhythmic and melodic sequences, canonic
instructions, and chromatic inflections, is its richly varied notation primarily used to
represent rhythmically complex relations that include syncopation and proportion on
various levels of rhythmic structure. Similar to much twentieth-century modernist
music, music of the *Ars subtilior* has in the recent past been viewed as a hyperintellectual
experiment in complex rhythmic notation.[3] Characterized by Willi Apel as nothing
more than a demonstration of technical prowess, *Ars subtilior* compositions were thus
deemed unsuitable, if intended, for performance. In discussing the notational intricacy
in fourteenth-century madrigals, James Haar suggested that the written notation
approximated fluidity and projected "a fully developed rhetoric of the song."[4] Anne
Stone applied this observation of notation as descriptive, rather than prescriptive to the
Ars subtilior repertory and suggested that the notation aimed to capture "habitual rhythmic gestures that were either performed or heard by whoever notated the music."[5] As we
shall see, the notation appears complex because it aims to capture in some detail the
thriving practice of virtuoso (vocal) improvisation. However, as Donald Greig illustrates,

performing *music* transcends performing its notation.[6] Analysts and performers (including this author) of rhythmically complex music written six hundred years after the songs of *Ars subtilior* face similar challenges, both in deciphering the notation and in understanding its message.

This chapter explores and classifies different types of medievalism in twentieth-century Western concert hall music. It illustrates the medieval ancestry of many compositional techniques developed for and popularized in numerous posttonal works, beyond the small selection included in this chapter. The process of defining this far-reaching ancestry unfolds in the context of a broad range of contemporary repertory that is often distinct in sound from its medieval antecedents but exhibits tangible conceptual connections. The types of medievalism under scrutiny process medieval ideas and patterns in a fairly functional and nonsentimental way. As Stephen Meyer articulates it, "Instead of emulating easily recognizable medievalist markers (e.g., drones or chant-like melodies harmonized in parallel fifths), these composers focus on the deeper rhythmic and structural elements of their conceptual antecedents."[7] This chapter aims to underscore the conceptual connection in complex rhythmic organization between late medieval music (exemplified by *Ars subtilior*) and twentieth-century modern and postmodern music utilizing what I refer to as structural medievalism.[8] Lawrence Earp draws a similar parallel between medieval and twentieth-century practices by positioning isorhythmic motets of Machaut as a "realization that comes closer to the most progressive music of our time than any music of the common practice period."[9]

I contend that the medieval ancestry is not a simple matter of direct influence, appropriation, or emulation. Rather, I wish to show how both eras experienced a dramatic increase in compositional and performative interest in the rhythmic domain and that this exploration took a similar path in both centuries. My examples from the Chantilly Codex illustrate a progression from the relative proportional simplicity in Suzoy's ballade *Pictagoras*, to an increase in foreground rhythmic dissonance (e.g., cross rhythms) and syncopation in Senleches's *En attendant*, and finally to the emergence of the quixotic, particolored note values of Uciredor's *Angelorum Psalat*. In the twentieth-century repertoire, proportional tempi and simultaneous use of related meters are illustrated with examples by Carter, Ligeti, and Lutosławski, progressing to the structurally more complex use of 2:3 proportion in Maxwell Davies and concluding with time value notation in Adès, which parallels explorations of Uciredor.

Leslie Workman defines medievalism as a continuous (and continuing) process of recreating, re-enacting, and reinventing medieval culture.[10] In recent years, the concept of neomedievalism has gained prominence, defined by Elizabeth Emery and Richard Utz as ahistorical "medievalism of popular culture."[11] But the idea of neomedievalism can also be extended beyond the realm of popular culture. Robinson and Clements discuss neomedievalism as a "post-modern ideology of medievalism," in that it is an independent, detached, conscious, and purposeful alternative to medievalism.[12] My view is closest to that of Nils Holger Petersen, who attributes a "lack of interest in building up a historical authenticity" to the medievalism of the twentieth-century avant-garde.[13] Whereas certain domains of medievalism may attempt to reconstruct and (re)present facets of the European Middle Ages or examine the epistemological status of the concept of medieval in general and medieval objects in particular, musical medievalism has often defined itself by "exceptional presentism."[14] In the discussion that follows, three different types of medievalism (with their categories) are seen as possible influences on the creative process of any individual artist looking back to the musical heritage preceding the common practice period. However, I argue that it is not the source material, but the composer's attitude toward the medieval ancestry that separates the nostalgic (or even "regressive") sentiments from the more utilitarian approaches. I outline various twentieth-century approaches to medieval concepts and forms based on the three primary types of structural medievalism. While pre–common practice influences on modernist composers cover a broad period of early Western art music (including the Renaissance and the Middle Ages), this chapter primarily contextualizes those influences deriving from the rhythmic intricacy of *Ars subtilior* (ca. 1380–1415), as exemplified by the polyphonic songs transmitted in the Chantilly Codex.[15]

The three categories of medievalism I propose are evocation, adaptation, and assimilation.[16] Considering the breadth of twentieth-century repertoire and the ideas these categories encompass, full consideration of each type and category exceeds the scope of the current essay. This is especially true of evocation, which primarily relies on coding. Since evocation properly falls under the auspices of semiotics, I only offer a few musical examples of this category in the current essay. My analytical examples include comparative discussion of adaptation and two analyses that demonstrate assimilation.

Evocation

Evocation (or cursory resemblance) includes those aspects of a musical work that allude to certain unique elements common to an earlier era, such as the use of Latin language, novel or rudimentary notation, and *Augenmusik*, or eye music. These categories deal with the properties of musical works outside the primary compositional domains (like pitch and rhythm) and parameters (dynamics, timbre, etc.). The use of Latin text is clearly not confined to the medieval period, but it is frequently associated with the sacred and liturgical themes, whose setting of other musical attributes in the twentieth-century repertoire differs from those in the earlier eras. This category is crowded with musical examples, including Stravinsky's *Oedipus Rex* and *Symphony of Psalms*, among others; Prokofiev's "The Crusaders in Pskov" from *Alexander Nevsky*; Jung-sun Park's *Inchon Mass*; many works by Arvo Pärt, including *Passio*; as well as numerous works by Messiaen, Duruflé, Poulenc, Villa-Lobos, Britten, Milhaud, and many more.[17]

Orthography or pitch notation that appears novel or in some sense rudimentary includes staff and nonstaff notation that is indicative of a search for a new nomenclature, largely absent from the common practice period. In a way, the twentieth-century search for new nomenclature parallels early (and late) medieval periods when new and competing musical notations were emerging to disseminate complex musical constructions and sounds that could be and were already being produced in performance. During the course of the twentieth century, novel notations were developed for electronic, microtonal, and experimental and extended instrumental techniques. Well-known musical works illustrating this paradigm include Karlheinz Stockhausen's *Gesang der Jünglinge*, Krzysztof Penderecki's *Threnody for the Victims of Hiroshima*, and Henry Cowell's *The Banshee*. *Augenmusik* comprises pictorial scores that use staff notation, but evokes visual codes with extramusical connotations.[18] These types of musical scores are not necessarily reflective of the way the music sounds, but are notated with visual symbolism in mind and communicating primarily with the performer. Like Baude Cordier's rondeau *Tout par compas suy composés*, notated in a circle to symbolize the perpetual chase of two canonic voices, twentieth-century music abounds in examples of *Augenmusik*: George Crumb's Agnus Dei from *Makrokosmos* is written on a circular musical staff, with interpolated staff fragments in the shape of a peace sign, and *Crucifixus* is given the shape of the cross, while Stockhausen's *Die zehn wistigen Wörter* (Christmas, 1991) features a green musical staff in the shape of an evergreen tree engraved with a Christmas hymn. Often referred to as *visual* scores, these symbolic representations were common enough in the period following World War II that John Cage (along with Alicia Knowles) assembled a sizable collection titled *Notations*, published in 1969.[19]

Metric Structuring in Medievalist Music

Before discussing the musical examples that illustrate the second and third categories of medievalism (adaptation and assimilation), I offer a brief primer on the terminology used in the comparative analyses that follow. Since the structuring elements of each work under scrutiny prominently derive from the rhythmic domain, I discuss elements of rhythmic and formal hierarchy as they unfold on three levels: (a) background; (b) middleground; and (c) foreground.[20] The structural *background* encompasses an entire work or a movement and may be formally summarized in relation to tempo changes or other structural markers that conceptually or aurally delineate longer formal sections. The rhythmic *middleground* correlates with (multi-)phrase-level events that may be driven by prosody in works with text or rhythmic and metric patterns with self-defined boundaries in the music without text. Clearly, these two aspects of phrase boundary delineation can, and often do, interact in interesting ways. Finally, the rhythmic *foreground* comprises pulses, *tactus* beats, and beat groups, and its potential complexity includes cross rhythms, tempo changes on the level of *tactus*, and irrational or time-value notation.

One way of understanding the beat hierarchy in posttonal repertoire is in relation to the medieval concept of mensuration where *tempus* and *prolatio* stand for a top-down approach to time-span subdivision into two of three equal durations. With either *tempus* or *prolatio*, a higher-level beat is divided by duple or triple subdivisions, although not both duple and triple on the same level of beat or in the same voice—at least not without further notational indications for the divergence from the mensuration.[21] However, conflicting subdivisions of the breve or semibreve into two or three lower-level beats do occur in earlier music: (a) between polyphonic voices, as in Ockeghem's *Missa Prolationem* with four different *mensurae*, one for each vocal part; (b) as means of sectional, middleground, contrast (tempo modulation), using the signs for augmentation or diminution, and changes in mensuration from duple to triple meter; and (c) through the use of hallowed, colored, or particolored notation in the foreground to subdivide semibreves or even minims (common in *Ars subtilior* scores).

Figure 15.1 summarizes my approach to beat hierarchy in metric music. This approach recognizes five levels of beat extending from the foreground into the middleground.[22] The main counting unit is called *tactus*, thus avoiding the more general and imprecisely used term *the beat*. The grouping of counting units into a higher-level beat gives rise to *supratactus*, which can, but does not have to correspond to a notated bar (if there are any). The subdivision of the counting beat is *pulse*, while the pulse level subdivides into *subpulse* units. In the presence of multiple beat levels, either pulse or subpulse can represent the *chronos protos* level—the smallest common denominator between various metric units.[23] *Tactus* beats are primarily defined by our cognitive restraints on the perception of tempo. French psychologist Paul Fraisse defines a generous range of *tactus* speeds as 40–200 beats per minute (bpm). If the tempo falls outside of this range, it represents time spans on a different level of beat (*supratactus* or pulse).[24]

The highest level of the beat hierarchy is indicated as a metameasure. This level pertains to the repertoire based on composite meters, since metameasures organize beats and beat groups into middleground periodicities that avoid traditional metric interpretations. I define metameasures as recursive composite metric patterns that can be represented with a composite time signature. While metameasures are not essential to the discussion of twentieth-century medievalism, they do feature prominently in the Ligeti and Maxwell Davies works I examine later in the essay.

5. Metameasure

4. Supratactus

3. Tactus (counting beat)

2. Pulse (can also be chronos protos)

1. Subpulse (chronos protos)

FIGURE 15.1 Five levels of beat hierarchy. [inline]

Adaptation: Structural Medievalism in Works by Ligeti, Carter, and Lutosławski

The second category of medievalism, adaptation, comprises a wide variety of different practices, including:

1. quotation, parody, pastiche, and/or collage;
2. new settings of liturgical texts intended for liturgical purposes;
3. the use of just intonation and the contemporary construction and use of the monochord; and, most significant to the current essay,
4. the engagement with and the modification of those concepts that were prevalent in the precompositional stages of writing medieval music, such as the frequent use of proportion on various levels of musical structure.[25]

This type of adaptation of medieval ideas and structures is frequently audible, but is, even more significantly, formative and irreducible, thus representing a type of structural medievalism.[26] In twentieth-century music, structural proportions are regularly adapted so as to include more complex ratios, although the musical examples by Ligeti, Carter, and Lutosławski still rely on simple proportion common in *Ars subtilior* works. Adaptation is a broad category of medievalism that spans extremes such as the use of the monochord for teaching purposes on one end of the spectrum and composing a postmodern work utilizing collage techniques on the other. However, with our current understanding of medieval music and its stylistic limitations, a twentieth-century *a capella* work could aurally evoke potential medieval ancestry, whereas a string quartet by Elliott Carter would most certainly not.

As previously noted, musical examples in this essay demonstrate only a few categories of medievalism introduced above and do so by focusing on the temporal domain. To illustrate medieval adaptation, we can compare the proportional relations of simultaneous speeds as they appear in a late fourteenth-century ballade *Pictagoras, Jarbol et Orpheus* by Suzoy, from the Chantilly Codex and twentieth-century works by Ligeti, Carter, and Lutosławski. Suzoy's ballade is an early example of rhythmic emancipation in *Ars subtilior*, while György Ligeti's piano etudes and Elliott Carter's string quartet heralds an era of true rhythmic polyphony in more recent times. Whereas Suzoy's music explored the Pythagorean ratios contextualizing the text, which lamented the loss of true mastery gone with the ancients, Ligeti, Carter, and Lutosławski gleefully looked toward the future.

Suzoy's ballade (see Example 15.1) is marked with three different, although related time signatures, allowing the music to flow with wonderful elasticity as a result of the perceptible independence of its constituent voices.[27] The transcription of Suzoy's ballade

EXAMPLE 15.1 Suzoy, *Pictagoras, Jarbol et Orpehus*: three simultaneous, but proportionally related mensuration signs.

in Example 15.1 features modern time signatures and added barlines, but the bars are individual to each of the three parts.[28] Even though the time signatures for both cantus and tenor indicate the same number of pulse units (six) and possible convergences on each breve (the modern downbeat), the arrows in Example 15.1 show that the composer sought to minimize these possible convergences with frequent rests and syncopation. Yolanda Plumley views tenor and countertenor as a single compositional unit because they consistently exchange the lowest note between them.[29] However, from the standpoint of its foreground rhythmic profile, the countertenor appears less bound to the tenor part than Plumley's statement would suggest. In addition, while the range and the melodic leaps appear quite traditional for the setting of the third voice, the sense of continuous falling of quick melodic fragments in the contra distinguishes it from the other voices.

Suzoy primarily utilizes some of the most perfect of Pythagorean ratios. The 3:2 ratio—that of the perfect fifth—is symbolized by the duple versus triple subdivision of the breve in cantus and tenor, respectively ($\frac{6}{8}$ versus $\frac{3}{4}$ meter in the transcription), as well as a brief tempo modulation to imperfect *tempus*, minor *prolatio* in the cantus part leading up to the cadence (bars 25–27 of the transcription, not included in Example 15.1). While the Chantilly Codex abounds in proportional indications of a great variety, whether through note shapes, changes in mensuration, or the use of numerals, Suzoy's ballade stands as a rather simple representation of simultaneous proportion. A comparable example from the Chantilly Codex is Matheus de Sancto Johannes's *Inclite flos orti Gebenesis*, whose proportional mensuration signs at the onset of the B section can be transcribed as $\frac{2}{4}$, $\frac{9}{8}$, and $\frac{3}{4}$. Incidentally, these three time signatures are precisely the ones chosen by Peter Maxwell Davies in the example I discuss in Example 15.4. The difference is that in lieu of assigning three time signatures to three independent parts (polyphonic voices), as is the case in *Inclite flos*, Maxwell Davies uses the three time signatures in recurring concatenation, thus giving rise to larger middleground periodicities or metameasures.

Examples of proportion in twentieth-century music on multiple levels of structure are too numerous to account for in this brief chapter. As a result, very simple interactions are illustrated by my examples, drawing on the conceptual purity of simultaneous proportional tempi in Suzoy or de Sancto Johannes (rather than cross rhythms at the level of *tactus*). This approach is also taken by György Ligeti in the piano etude *En suspens* (1998), his setting of swing (see Example 15.2). Ligeti closely studied mensural notation of the fourteenth and fifteenth centuries earlier in his career.[30] Speaking of Ockeghem, Ligeti admired the "constant stream, a continual flow: there are no climaxes, only an unchanging tension. And it's stasis! It is always flowing, yet remains like an expanse of water which preserves its shape."[31] This description of Ockeghem's music describes a number of works by Ligeti in different styles and compositional periods, including the etude *En suspens*. While Ligeti signs the etude with $\frac{6}{4}$ ($\frac{12}{8}$), these meters do not alternate (either *x* or *y*), but are, like in Suzoy's ballade, juxtaposed from the very first sound onset (*x* and *y*). As shown in Example 15.2, rhythmic reduction, the pianist's left hand outlines a syncopated compound meter of $^{12}_8$. At the notated tempo of 98bpm per quarter note, the dotted quarter (presumed *tactus* in $^{12}_8$) is slower at ca. 65bpm, relating to the quarter notes of the right hand in a simple 2:3 proportion. The presumed *tactus* in the $^6_4$ meter of the right hand, the dotted half note (ca. 33bpm), is far too slow to carry the counting beat, suggesting a *tactus* shift down to the level of the quarter note at 98bpm. However, the juxtaposition of halves and dotted half values is implicit considering Ligeti's notated accents for the foreground groups that indicate asymmetrical aksak meters (e.g., $^3_4$, $^2_4$, $^2_4$, $^2_4$ for the first phrasing slur), thus even more deeply embedding the 2:3 proportion into the temporal flow associated with the right-hand pulse stream.

The first movement of Elliott Carter's String Quartet no. 1 (1950–1951) features similar juxtapositions of different meter and tempi among four voices; see Example 15.3 (measures 22–27).[32] The cello part corresponds to the indicated *tactus* speed of 120bpm in the notated $^4_4$ meter, rendered by the cello in persistent quarter notes. The viola enters in triplet quarters, producing a 2:3 cross rhythm with the cello. Triplet quarters are on the faster end of *tactus* speeds at 180bpm, so that the cello and the viola parts might both be simply heard as duple or triple subdivisions of a half-note *tactus* at 60bpm. In contrast, isochronous entries in the second violin part are five-sixteenths long, corresponding to the tempo of 96bpm, whereas the uppermost part (Violin I) is the slowest, with long durations at 36bpm outlined by durations corresponding to ten notated triplet eighths.

The speed of 36bpm in Violin I is too slow to be heard as a viable *tactus* speed and relates to the initial tempo of the movement (originally, ♩ = 72bpm). The first violin's isochronous entries are thus best interpreted as *supratactus* of the initial *tactus* speed. Notice in the reduction how Carter introduces the 72bpm tempo into the violin part by including one shorter duration (the fifth note) in the series, as if initiating a syncopation. The original tempo of the movement (tempo A at 72bpm) is thus transferred from the

EXAMPLE 15.2 Proportional *tactus* and tempi in Ligeti's *En suspens*.

EXAMPLE 15.3 Carter, String Quartet no. 1: multiple tempi in mm. 22–27.

EXAMPLE 15.3 Reduction.

cello to the violin part in m. 22, while tempo B, introduced by the second violin in bar 12 as counterpoint to tempo A, remains at the same speed in the same instrument (mm. 22–27), even though its notation changes from a three-sixteenth duration to a five-sixteenth duration.[33] Despite the more complex ratios in Carter's string quartet, the four textural voices are perceived as independent, not syncopated, in part because of the persistence of isochronous sound articulations within each layer. The proportional tempi in Carter's string quartet (Tempo A-C) focus on the less perfect ratios than Suzoy, but they are still relatively simple:[34]

Tempo A (72bpm/36bpm) + Tempo B (96bpm) = 3:4
Tempo A (72bpm) + Tempo C (60bpm) = 6:5
Tempo B (96bpm) + Tempo C (60bpm) = 8:5

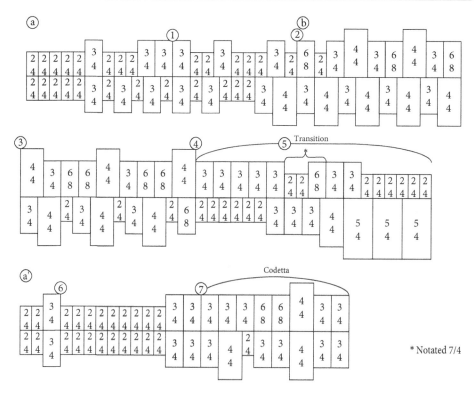

FIGURE 15.2 Time signature map for Lutosławski's Dance Prelude no. 3.

Of the five dance preludes for clarinet and piano by Witold Lutosławski (1955), four are based on metameasures that alternate duple and triple meters. The two parts diverge and converge, shaping the musical narrative in traditional ways, but its motivic transformation is reflected in the metrical structure. Figure 15.2 presents a time signature map of Dance Prelude no. 3 and illustrates how, using only duple (simple and compound) and triple (simple) meter, Lutosławski projects stability of the thematic section a, metric divergence in transition to the formal Section b, and use of b material (namely the ⁶⁄₈ meter) in the transition back to Section a. Since this is a small form, it is extended though a sizeable coda and a cadenza-like transition between rehearsals 4 and 5.

Assimilation in Peter Maxwell Davies's Piano Sonata

The third category of medievalism, assimilation, represents transformative advances and changes that may or may not be visually or aurally apparent. Assimilation thus includes:

(1) music written without allusions to specific liturgical texts or works of an earlier repertoire, but still transformative in its reliance on compositional features, themes, and techniques of the early polyphony and sacred drama;

(2) polyphonic layering drawn from the isorhythmic principles that generate polycyclic compositions, conceptually reaching back to Machaut, but with a distinctly new sound and in a variety of genres and styles;[35] or

(3) principles of mensuration and long-range syncopation that are extended to include multiple and simultaneous divisions on different levels of beat hierarchy. This type of simultaneous subdivision of any beat level into duple and triple can generate significant density of cross rhythms and even foreground tempo modulation (e.g., examples 15.4, 15.6, and 15.7). It is evident that categories 2 and 3 of medieval assimilation derive mostly from the temporal, rather than the pitch domain.[36]

As my first example of assimilation, I have singled out for closer scrutiny Peter Maxwell Davies's Scherzo from the 1980 Piano Sonata because it highlights some of the medieval antecedents previously mentioned and illustrates new ones. Maxwell Davies has openly drawn from medieval sources throughout his career, most notably from plainchant and, in this regard, his Piano Sonata is no exception.[37] According to Richard McGregor, Piano Sonata is related to Symphony no. 2 in that both draw on the plainchant melodies *Nativitas Tua* and *Panem de Caelo* from *Liber Usualis*.[38] As a fantastically prolific composer whose final work reached op. 338, Maxwell Davies has drawn on and, in particular, parodied numerous medieval and Renaissance sources. The influences are more overt earlier in his career.[39] Michael Hall claims that Maxwell Davies's primary "means of dealing with betrayal . . . is through the use of parody." To borrow is to transform and, when the transformation is "mocking the original," parody becomes "travesty."[40] In *Antechrist* (1967), Maxwell Davies dissolves a thirteenth-century motet into a mockery of the tritone (*diabolus in musica*), whereas in *L'homme armè* (1968, rev. 1971) he takes Agnus Dei from an unfinished fifteenth-century mass and transforms it into a foxtrot. However, unlike his use of plainchant melodies and more substantial parody, the foreground interactions between duple and triple subdivisions on various beat levels in the Scherzo movement are more similar to the features of later *Ars subtilior* works, such as Senleches's ballade *En attendant*. I will compare several aspects of rhythmic organization in Senleches's ballade with that of Maxwell Davies's Scherzo, including the performance-challenging phasing or delay in one of the textural pulse streams.

Common to the fourteenth- and fifteenth-century repertoire is the use of proportional speeds for sectional variation or even as means of frequent contrast in the formal middleground. Rather than employing simultaneous presentation of different meters and tempi (like Suzoy and Carter) or contrasting proportionally related *tactus* speeds between large sections, Maxwell Davies combines three different meters into one composite and recurring pattern. In essence, Maxwell Davies forgoes simultaneous hemiolic patterns on the level of *tactus* and creates a new middleground entity from the proportional *tactus* speeds of different triple and duple meters. Example 15.4 reproduces the opening of the second movement notated with a composite time signature pattern $\frac{9}{8}, \frac{9}{8}, \frac{3}{4}, \frac{2}{4}, \frac{2}{4}$—a metameasure—comprising two steps of acceleration with respect to the speed of the *tactus* and *supratactus*. The three longer beats, corresponding to dotted quarters in $\frac{9}{8}$, become three shorter beats in $\frac{3}{4}$, with further contraction of the third metric group from three (dotted half *supratactus*) to two beats in $\frac{2}{4}$ (half-note *supratactus*). It is worth noting that an alternative interpretation of *tactus* durations in $\frac{2}{4}$ is suggested by the motivic grouping in m. 4 and could represent a further acceleration of the *tactus* speed in a 3:2 proportion, contracting the quarter-note beat to a sixth-note beat (equivalent to two triplet eighths). The speed of the sixth note would equal 252bpm in the notated tempo, thus exceeding our perceptual threshold for *tactus* speeds. I do not adopt this reading of complete proportional acceleration in part because of the resulting tempo, but also because Maxwell Davies provides a traditional subdivision of the quarter note on the last beat of m. 5 as a performance aid that leads the pianist to relate the duple subdivisions of the quarter note to the duple subdivisions of the dotted quarter in the ensuing repetition of the metameasure (see Example 15.4).[41]

With either reading of the metric pattern, and on a return to $\frac{9}{8}$, the tempo is reduced because *tactus* is again a longer duration.[42] The ensuing metameasure repeats the progression of *tactus* beats just heard.[43] Most of this movement is marked by foreground tempo modulation with *supratactus* alternating between duple and triple, as well as simple and compound meter, but the clearest presentation of the foreground tempo

EXAMPLE 15.4 Composite meter and tempo modulation in Maxwell Davies's Scherzo, mm. 1–9.

modulation is in the opening measures that are monophonic and stable.[44] The issue of net difference in tempo is undoubtedly on the composer's mind, as he indicates a double tempo for the movement (simple meter = 112bpm/compound meter = 168bpm), one for each proportionally related *tactus* beat. The duple subdivision of the $\frac{2}{4}$ bar arches back to the opening figure of the $\frac{9}{8}$, allowing us to hear the change between the two tempi in comparative foreground at the onset of the second metameasure. This 2:3 tempo ratio is audible in the middleground, at the level phrase. A foreground preoccupation with beat subdivision into two and three is also clearly heard, with the final outcome of a constant and flexibly elusive shift between the duple and triple groupings on the levels of *tactus* and pulse.

A portion of the transcription of Senleches' *En attendant esperance* is enclosed in Example 15.5.[45] The ballade, originally without mensuration signs, is transcribed in $\frac{6}{8}$ reflecting the metric organization of the tenor part.[46] Syncopated segments appear as predominantly red notes in the facsimile, with a few black notes that anchor them with respect to the tenor. The flagged black and hollowed notes indicate triplets on a lower

EXAMPLE 15.5 Senleches, *En attendant*: alternate beat subdivisions in cantus and phasing in countertenor.

level of beat, whereas the hollow and flagged red notation denotes duplets. Additionally, the direction of stems, as well as stem ornaments, indicates faster or slower duplets in relation to the underlying perfections. The notation is very elaborate. The uppermost part (cantus) features rich ornamentation, with frequent displacement of three notes by two or four. Cantus also infrequently corresponds to the $\frac{6}{8}$ meter of the transcription; rather, there are syncopated segments of duple meter ($\frac{2}{4}$) in mm. 4–6 and 10–12, as well as a possible $\frac{3}{4}$ meter in mm .7–8 of the transcription.[47] I have omitted all barlines that obscure syncopation from Example 15.5, thus illustrating a process of end-accented-phrase shaping that is diametrically opposed to that of Lutosławski—here phrases open up with metric instabilities and aim toward metric consonance and confluence at cadence points.[48]

The layering of duple and triple cross rhythms in *En attendant* resembles Maxwell Davies's polyphonic setting of the two pulse streams in the Scherzo. Example 15.6 shows the polyphonic layering (mm. 11–16) where 2:3 and 3:4 cross rhythms occur in both duple and triple meters and conflict with the expected subdivision of the *tactus*. These cross rhythms between the hands are indicated with boxes in Example 15.6. Some of the notational intricacy in Maxwell Davies's work arises as a result of the phasing or delay of both pulse streams and their conflict with the notated barline. Among the several challenges I experienced playing this work was the issue of polyphonic independence, exemplified by the right-hand pulse stream in mm. 15–16. The right hand is delayed by a sixteenth rest and playing this hand separately shows that, without the delay, the right-hand stream would simply articulate isochronous eighth notes (the third eighth in a group is habitually a rest) in perfect time.[49] As it is, the right-hand pulse stream is still isochronous, but delayed—out of phase—in relation to the barline and the left-hand pulse stream. The last sixteenth in the right hand of m. 16 returns this pulse stream and its syncopation in phase with the barline—it completes the "perfection" (see Example 15.6).

This out-of-phase example parallels Senleches's treatment of the middle voice in *En attendant*. In m. 11 of the transcription (Example 15.5), contra similarly diverges from the "notated" meter. The notated eighth-note rest effectively causes the displacement—twice on line 2 of the transcription. In the first instance, contra is out of phase with the tenor but outlining the same *tactus* beats (transcribed as dotted eights). In the second instance, contra's isochronous pitches outline longer durations (transcribed as half notes) in a slower tempo and in 3:4 proportion with the earlier syncopation. Even the pitch contour is similar (high, low, middle).

The performance challenge in Maxwell Davies's work resembles the challenge of performing a song from the Chantilly Codex. As in any polyphonic setting, each voice should avoid sounding precisely mechanical and syncopated and aim instead to be flowing and independent. Producing and listening to a midi playback of the Senleches's ballade yields quite a bit of harshness because of all the notated clashes between the voices. However, a recording of this song by ensemble XASAX (three saxophones) projects lilting smoothness, taking a slow tempo and producing music that sounds very different than reproduced notation in the midi playback.[50] Similarly, a commercially available

EXAMPLE 15.6 Maxwell Davies, Scherzo: cross rhythms and phasing in mm. 11–16.

recording of Maxwell Davies's Sonata by David Holzman closely approaches the notated speed of the Scherzo movement (ca. 110bpm) in blithe, exciting performance that remains perceptually challenging even on second hearing. Another performance, by Maxwell Davies's colleague Stephen Pruslin, to whom this work is dedicated, takes a substantially slower tempo than notated in the score (ca. 83bpm).[51] The perceptual discernment of the surface detail thus increases dramatically, even though Pruslin's frequent leaning onto the front end of the beat suppresses some potentially Giocoso moments. As is often the case, we are left to ponder how much liberty a performer is entitled to with respect to the interpretation of and improvisation on the notated score.[52]

In both epochs, performers and listeners face perceptual challenges despite the analytically simple conceptual framework. The juxtaposition of duple and triple beat subdivision on more than one level of beat, together with asynchronous polyphony, yields challenges in perception and kinetic delivery of individually simple sound streams. Whereas the Senleches's ballade might entail a performance by three people, Maxwell Davies places the burden of demonstrating the polyphony and smooth interaction between the constituent compositional voices on a single performer. The improvisatory nature of individual lines challenges the clear principle of common temporal organization through mensuration.

It is likely that Senleches, like Maxwell Davies, wrote down what he heard or could perform and did not invent hypercomplex notation for its own sake. Any notation is more likely to be approximate when greater improvisatory flow is sought, an important relation to highlight between score notation and interpretive readings. As mentioned previously, the interest here also lies in the apparent dichotomy between the complexity of notation in the works of *Ars subtilior* and many contemporary scores, and a rather simpler notion of aiming to achieve emancipated polyphonic lines that can readily stand in contrast and juxtaposition to one another when rhythmically distinct. To understand a score as an imperfect record of an idea or an improvised performance is helpful to the performer, who can then approach the written record with some degree of liberty, striving to bring the music to life rather than perform its "notation."[53]

Modern Proportion and Time-Value Notation as Assimilation of Medieval Practice

Complex notation becomes even more abstruse when partial *tactus* or *supratactus* units are involved. C. Uciredor's *Angelorum Psalat*, one of Chantilly's two ballades in Latin, illustrates one additional manner of duple/triple superimposition in *Ars subtilior*.[54] The half-black and half-red figures on line four of the facsimile may: (a) correlate to the value of the initial note in the figure further augmented or imperfected by *one half* of the value of the fully colored note (true to the ancient Greek definition of hemiola as one and a half); or (b) represent a durational sum of one half value of one red and one half value of one black note.[55] Line four of the facsimile shows particolored figures comprising perfect and imperfect beat subdivisions and likely indicates a durational value of two and a half minims. The particolored values in *Angelorum Psalat* correspond to the beginning of the fourth verse and one of its more colorful words, "Pestifera."[56]

An alternative to the traditional rhythmic nomenclature of the common practice era, Henry Cowell suggested alternative orthography reminiscent of C. Uciredor's particolored notation more than a century ago. Cowell lamented that "our system of notation is incapable of representing any except the most primary division of the whole note."[57] He posited that any progress in the accuracy of rhythmic notation would require consistent treatment of time-value durations.[58] The time-value notation he proposed would entail different-shape noteheads for each category of the whole note subdivision. In this manner, a "third" note represents a division of the whole note into three equal durations, supplanting the customary practice of notating it as a triplet half note. By extension, a fifth note would represent a division of the whole note into five equal durations, and Henry Cowell provided a table that included the division of the whole note by other (prime) numbers. Significantly, after the initial division of the whole note into two, five, or nine parts, further subdivision is always a power of two, so that the third note generates sixth and twelfth values and a fifth note generates tenth (and twentieth) notes. Cowell's time-value orthography corresponds to type 2 evocation in my proposed framework for structural medievalisms.

In twentieth-century scores, partial *tactus* beats frequently yield alternative measures that reflect the notational inadequacy in the customary notation of partial *tactus* or *supratactus* beats. This type of notation appears, among other composers, in the music of Maxwell Davies's younger compatriot Thomas Adès. Adès's *Aetheria* for solo piano (from *Traced Overhead*, 1995–1996) prominently features temporal shaping based on frequent shifts between pulses of different speed. Notated quarter notes at 148bpm, as indicated by the composer, are already on the fast end of the tempo spectrum for *tactus* speeds. A half-note *tactus* beat at 74bpm is also quite plausible and, depending on the performer and the speed chosen for the movement, possibly more likely as a referential speed. In this instance, any note values faster than the quarter note, including the "sixth" note at 222bpm, represent pulses, not *tactus* beats.

Adès's use of time signatures such as $\frac{2}{6}, \frac{5}{12},$ or $\frac{9}{20}$ is explained by the composer in a prefatory note: "The lower number of the time signature denotes the number of equal divisions of the semibreve. For example: [on] page 7 m. 4, $\frac{5}{12}$ = 5 triplet quavers in the prevailing tempo; [on] page 10 bar 2, $\frac{9}{14}$ = 9 septuplet quavers."[59] Unlike Brian Ferneyhough's concern with actual changes in tempo or middleground changes in "event density," the primary concern in *Aetheria* is the delineation of phrase segments via local temporal dissonances or proportional time values.[60] In addition to the emerging melodic line in the inner voice (marked tenuto in Example 15.7, there are two additional layers in the overall texture. In Example 15.7, I boxed recurring chord pairs in $\frac{2}{6}$ meter. Note that a recurring set of paired triadic sonorities recurs notated with either eighth notes or sixth notes. In the $\frac{2}{6}$ meter, the sequence of chords is repetitive: the first and the third occurrence (mm. 8 and 14) feature <C7, E>, whereas the second and the fourth occurrence shift to B, C♯min⁷. The tentative ascent of the tenuto-marked melody (F5, G5) eventually changes direction and descends to E5 and then continues along its downward curve, proceeding to D and C, outlining a descending fifth over the course of the section (mm. 1–32). The <D, C> motive appears in counterpoint in mm. 12–13 (circled in the example) and is repeated in mm. 17–18. In both instances, the <D, C> fragment follows the $\frac{2}{6}$ meter set to the same pair of chords (<B, C♯m7>). Each of the chord pairs in *Aetheria* articulates varied beat durations. For instance, in addition to the setting in sixth notes, the <B, C♯m7> chord pair is also notated in eighth notes and various chord pairs also appear as quarters. However, the position of the $\frac{2}{6}$ meter in relation to the chordal repetition and the unfolding of the melodic line is strategic and aurally distinctive. The $\frac{2}{6}$ meter participates in the delineation of motivic boundaries in an otherwise "ethereal" setting, where frequent iteration of familiar elements (e.g., chord pairs) in an alternate durational profile engenders structural fluidity. There is parallelism to Adès's phrase construction with temporal and pitch elements contributing to suggested boundaries: the chord pairs that follow the iterations of the primary melodic line delineate phrase segments in *Aetheria* using the same ordered progressions of time signatures and chords. Note how the B♭

EXAMPLE 15.7 Proportionally related beats as phrase-defining elements in *Aetheria* by Thomas Adès, mm. 1–18.

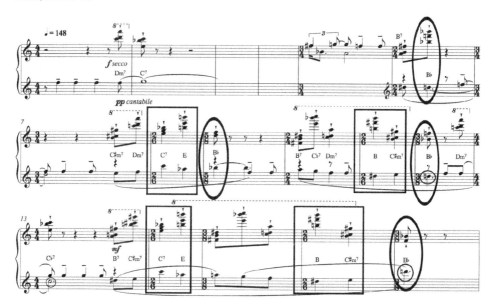

triad, circled in Example 15.7 assumes a cadential function in association with the ordering and function of dyad pairs.

The level of complexity in *Aetheria* is once again reduced from what the complex notation may suggest at a glance: The different exotic time signatures all indicate different groupings (and representative beat levels) of only two categories of time values: Suzoy's 3:2 proportion in meters of $\frac{2}{6}, \frac{5}{12}, \frac{9}{24}$, and $\frac{11}{24}$ (Cowell's third-note series) and Carter's 5:4 proportion in meters of $\frac{2}{5}, \frac{3}{10}$, and $\frac{9}{20}$ (the fifth-note series). Figure 15.3 summarizes the time value notation in these alternative time signatures alongside their traditional and arguably more cumbersome notational counterparts.[61] This succession of proportionally related speeds is related to those in the foreground of Maxwell Davies's Scherzo, but taken a step further. Maxwell Davies does not encounter the same notational problems as Adès, since his metrical structure is more stable—he retains the consistent upper-level beat succession in at least one of the two textural voices. In essence, Maxwell Davies creates an asymmetrical form of modus, or metameasures, as a primary level of containing rhythmic complexity of the lower levels of beat.

Without wishing to diverge from the topic, I offer one final example of foreground rhythmic complexity in *Aetheria*. This is the passage with the greatest density of juxtapositions (mm. 24–30) between two alternating speeds and resembles frequent changes (foreground proportion) in many *Ars subtilior* songs such as Goscalch's ballade *En nul estat*.[62] In essence, the passage employs two beat speeds, regular quarters and triplet quarters, the latter notated in $\frac{1}{6}$ and $\frac{2}{6}$ bars. Three versions of this passage in Example 15.8 resemble transcriptions of late medieval music including a facsimile, a modern

Third-note Series		Fifth-note Series	
in 2/6	in 2/4 or 1/2	in 2/5 or 4/10	in 2/4 or 4/8
in 5/12	in 4/8	in 3/10	in 3/8
in 11/24	in 4/4	in 9/20	in 2/4

FIGURE 15.3 Alternate meters in Adès's *Aetheria* in comparison with traditional notation of the same time values.

transcription (which is often unwieldy and challenging to performers), and an "alternate" notation that tries to mediate between the two other versions.

The top staff of Example 15.8 reproduces Adès's seemingly chaotic metric schema, which contrasts time values in $\frac{1}{4}$ and $\frac{1}{8}$ meters with alternate time values in $\frac{1}{6}$ and $\frac{2}{6}$ meters. Clearly, none of these metric designations correlates with a full measure or a *supratactus*. In this example, each brief metric unit corresponds to a single *tactus* or pulse (the latter is the case in $\frac{1}{8}$ and $\frac{1}{6}$ meters). The second line of Example 15.8 gives an alternate hearing of beat proportions, from the standpoint of the performer who must rapidly shift between different time values. As previously surveyed, *Aetheria* begins with a conventional quarter-note bar division (i.e., $\frac{4}{4}$, $\frac{3}{4}$) at 148bpm. Instead of hearing the $\frac{1}{6}$ metric unit in m. 25 as a shorter value (two thirds of the earlier quarter-note *tactus*), one can also shift to hearing the sixth note as the organizing pulse in this passage and relate $\frac{1}{4}$ and $\frac{1}{8}$ values to the sixth note as proportionally longer.[63] Observing the tempo Adès indicates in the score precludes the sixth note from being heard as *tactus* because of its speed (222bpm). However, if a performer decides on a slower tempo to begin with (ca. 132bpm instead of 148bpm, for a quarter note), the speed of the sixth note would be less than 200bpm. The fluidity in hearing and notation exemplified by reduction 1 underscores the proportional relation between two different kinds of time values and affords an option to the performer, who may be more accustomed to proportionally lengthening the beats, rather than shortening them (and perhaps playing at a tempo slower than indicated by the composer). Reduction 2 on the bottom staff of Example 15.8 notates the passage in the most conventional manner, representing the sixth note as a triplet quarter. This notation is not conducive to traditional time signature notation since one or two sixth notes (tied triplet eighths in the reduction) do not sum up to a higher-level beat, such as *tactus* or *supratactus*. What this rhythmic reduction does clarify is the manner in which Adès disturbs the proportional progression of beats in this passage. Namely, the

EXAMPLE 15.8 Three different notations of the same passage in *Aetheria*.

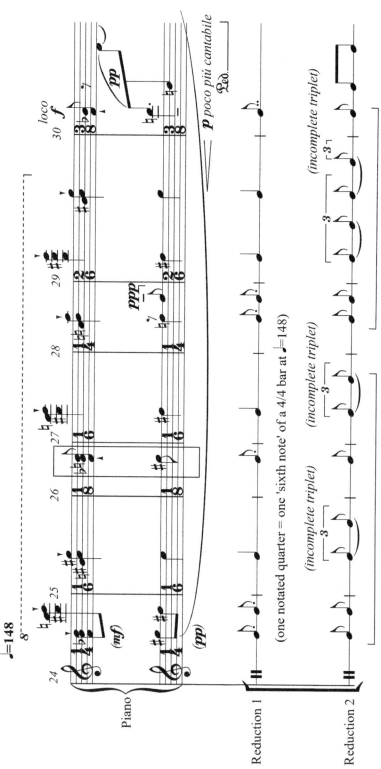

(one notated quarter = one 'sixth note' of a 4/4 bar at ♩=148)

The first two incomplete triplets 'lack' an eighth note. The final incomplete triplet 'lacks' two eighth notes.

eighth notes of m. 24 represent pulses (296bpm) and subdivide the quarter-note *tactus* into two. Subsequent foray into triplet quarters represents an equivalent subdivision of the third note into two sixth note pulses in a slower tempo than the eighth notes. The <Low, High> profile of the right hand suggests that the sixth note in m. 25 might be followed by the sixth note in bar 27. However, the two sixth notes are separated by a single eighth note, throwing the tempo modulation off kilter. The second sequence of two eighth notes, followed by two sixth notes, is sequential (see the brackets in Example 15.8) and without a metric "hiccup" the single eighth in m. 26 appears to engender. The interpolated eighth note resembles other long-range syncopation onsets, as seen in the Suzoy and Maxwell Davies, Examples 15.1 and 15.6.

As the musical illustrations in this essay indicate, the works by Ligeti, Carter, Lutosławski, Maxwell Davies, and Adès do not look or sound medieval, but their works exhibit marked similarity to the rhythmic issues found in medieval polyphony and *Ars subtilior* songs in particular. While Ligeti, Carter, and Maxwell Davies have studied early music and might have consciously emulated certain aspects of late medieval rhythmic organization, Adès's compositional process is even more abstractly removed from its medieval ancestry. However consciously or serendipitously worked out, the adaptation and assimilation principles demonstrated by these composers illustrate a nonsentimental and utilitarian approach to irreducible (medieval) rhythmic techniques and represent what I term structural medievalism. While the scholars working with posttonal music might analyze rhythmic structures in posttonal works, they usually have little access to the repertoire or scholarship pertaining to *Ars subtilior* repertory. Similarly, the scholars specializing in *Ars subtilior* music usually have little contact with their colleagues working on posttonal music. I hope that more comparative analyses of these repertoires will take place in the future and that the conversation will broaden for the benefit of all.

Notes

1. See Steve Reich, "Postscript to a Brief Study of Balinese and African Music," in *Writings on Music 1965–2000*, edited by Paul Hillier. (New York: Oxford University Press, 2002), 70; and "It's Gonna Rain," ibid., 20. "Postscript" was originally published in different form as "A Composer Looks East" in the *New York Times*, September 2, 1973.

2. Other representative *Ars subtilior* collections include Modena, Biblioteca Estense, MS Alpha.M.5.24, and Torino, Biblioteca Nazionale Universitaria J.II.9. The term *Ars subtilior* was coined by Ursula Günther in "Das Ende der Ars Nova," *Die Musikforschung* 16 (1963): 105–120. Willi Apel referred to this body of work as *mannerism* and Besseler simply identified it as *late Ars nova*. See Wili Apel, "Mannered Notation," in *The Notation of Polyphonic Music 900–1600* (Cambridge, MA: Mediaeval Academy of America, 1950), 403–426; and Heinrich Besseler, "Studien zur Musik des Mittelalters. I. Neue Quellen des 14. und beginnen den 15. Jahrhunderts," *Archiv für Musikwissenschaft* 7 (1925): 167–252.

3. This infamous criticism was offered by Apel, "Mannered Notation," 10–13.

4. See James Haar, "The Trecento," in *Essays on Italian Poetry and Music on the Renaissance, 1350–1600* (Berkley: University of California Press, 1986), 15.

5. Stone evokes Charles Seeger's concepts from "Prescriptive and Descriptive Music Writing," *Musical Quarterly* 44/2 (1958): 184–195. See Anne Stone, "Glimpses of the Unwritten Tradition," *Musica Disciplina* 50 (1998): 84.

6. In this connection, see Donald Greig, "*Ars subtilior* Repertory as Performance Palimpsest," *Early Music* 31, no. 2 (2003): 196–198, 200–202, and 205–209.

7. Private communication with the author.

8. The music of our new century (the twenty-first) seems turned toward the concepts of overt mixing and intra- and interdomain layering centrally explored in electroacoustic and multimedia works, regardless of other stylistic cues.

9. Lawrence Earp, *Guillaume de Machaut: A Guide to Research* (New York: Garland, 1995), 282.

10. Kathleen Verduin, "The Founding and the Founder: Medievalism and the Legacy of Leslie J. Workman," *Studies in Medievalism* 17 (2009): 1–27.

11. Neomedievalism thus embraces a plurality of approaches that incorporate philosophical and technological progress and change and resemble an "alternate universe." See Elizabeth Emery and Richard Utz, eds., *Medievalism: Key Critical Terms* (Suffolk: Boydell & Brewer, 2014).

12. Carol L. Robinson and Pamela Clements, "Living with Medievalism," *Studies in Medievalism* 18 (2008): 61–62.

13. Nils Holger Petersen, "Medieval Resurfacing, Old and New," in *Studies in Medievalism* XX, ed. Karl Fugelso (Rochester, NY: Boydell & Brewer, 2011), 39.

14. See Leslie Coote, "A Short Essay about Neo-Medievalism," in *Studies in Medievalism* XIX, ed. Karl Fugelso (Rochester, NY: Boydell & Brewer, 2010), 25; and Amy S. Kaufman, "Medieval Unmoored," *Studies in Medievalism* XIX, 5.

15. The primary source for this collection is a recent publication of complete facsimiles in color. See Yolanda Plumley and Ann Stone, *Chantilly Codex, MS 564: Critical Study and Facsimile Edition* (Turnhaut: Brepols, 2008).

16. This tripartite organization echoes Walter Frisch's approach to defining Brahms's influence on later composers. He distinguishes among the concepts of quotation, allusion, and absorption. Frisch, however, makes a qualitative distinction between these three types of *neo-Brahmsianism* by positing that "truly" absorbing the fundamentals of the compositional craft is unequivocally superior to appropriating stylistic traits or even underlying compositional principles. See Walter Frisch, *Brahms and the Principle of Developing Variation* (Berkeley: University of California Press, 1994): 95.

17. For a discussion of medievalism and Pärt, see Laura Dolp, "Linear Practices in the Music of Arvo Pärt," this volume, pp. 367–396.

18. The dictionary entry on *Augenmusik* is translated into English and titled "Eye Music." See Dart Thurston, "Eye Music," in *Oxford Music Online*, accessed June 10, 2015, http://www.oxfordmusiconline.com.proxy.lib.umich.edu/subscriber/article/grove/music/0915.

19. Because it was a general collection of visual scores, Cage's *Notations* included the symbolic, *Augenmusik* scores as well as nonsymbolic but novel orthography. See John Cage and Alicia Knowles, *Notations* (New York: Something Else Press, 1969).

20. The concept of structural levels with the same English names (originally *Schichten*) originates with Heinrich Schenker, for whom they represent hierarchical organization of tonal events and the elaboration of a fundamental structure. Schenker likewise considered structural levels as flexible categories, whose number would vary from one work to another. In this manner, a work may have one or several "shallow" and "deep" middleground levels. In Schenker's theory the lower levels of hierarchy are intrinsically connected with the

structural background as each represents further "composing out" or "prolonging" of events in the background. My use of structural levels pertains to rhythmic and formal events without the implication of interconnectedness. In short, no component of pitch-structure theories is implied in my use of structural-level terminology for posttonal works. See Heinrich Schenker, *Free Composition,* ed. and trans. Ernst Oster (New York: Longman, 1979), 26.

21. The alternative understanding of beat hierarchy, bottom-up approach, organizes fast *chronos protos* (subpulse or pulse) units into duple and triple groupings. In twentieth-century scores we often encounter a mixture of duple and triple elements on one beat level, thus generating a lack of uniformity on a higher level of beat, prompting metric analyses based on the common fast pulse (*chronos protos*). In this connection, see Aleksandra Vojčić, "Beat Patterns and Beat Hierarchy: From Aksak to Composite Meter," *Current Musicology* 98 (2014): 41–70.

22. While beat levels 1–4 in Figure 15.1 apply to any instance of metric hierarchy, level 5 (metameasure) is applicable only to composite metric patterns that cohere into formal units at or above the level of phrase.

23. The term *chronos protos*, used here to identify the level of beat that is the smallest common denominator between various metric units, was used by Aristoxenus in *Elements of Rhythm* and *Elements of Harmony*, fourth century BCE. The surviving work has been translated and edited by Andrew Barker in *Greek Musical Writings*, Vol. 2, *Harmonic and Acoustic Theory* (New York: Cambridge University Press, 1990), 119–208.

24. See Paul Fraisse, "Rhythm and Tempo," in *The Psychology of Music*, ed. Diana Deutsch (New York: Academic Press, 1982), 149–180.

25. In this connection, see David Metzer, *Quotation and Cultural Meaning in Twentieth-Century Music* (Cambridge: Cambridge University Press, 2003); Linda Hutcheon, *A Theory of Parody: The Techniques of Twentieth-Century Art Forms* (Champaign: University of Illinois Press, 2000); see Catherine Losada, "Between Modernism and Postmodernism: Strands of Continuity in Collage Compositions by Rochberg, Berio, and Zimmermann," *Music Theory Spectrum* 31 (2009): 57–100; J. Peter Burkholder, "Collage," *Oxford Music Online*; the Roman Catholic liturgical music written in the twentieth century follows the reforms of the Second Vatican Council (1962–1965), accessed March 30, 2015. doi:10.1093/gmo/9781561592630.article.53083; David B. Doty, *The Just Intonation Primer: An Introduction to the Theory and Practice of Just Intonation* (San Francisco: Just Intonation Network, 2002); Harry Partch: *Genesis of Music: An Account of a Creative Work, Its Roots and Its Fulfillments* (New York: Da Capo, 1974); Kathryn Buehler-McWilliams and Russell E. Murray, "The Monochord in the Medieval and Modern Classroom," *Journal of Music History Pedagogy* 3, no. 2 (2013): 151–172.

26. Certain categories of the third type of medievalism, assimilation, such as the isorhythmic principles and polycycles discussed below, also represent structural medievalism.

27. The three signatures are a dotted C for the cantus (transcribed as $\frac{6}{8}$); a C for the counter-tenor (transcribed as $\frac{2}{4}$); an O for the tenor (transcribed as $\frac{3}{4}$).

28. The facsimile of this ballade also illustrates a middleground contrast of different mensurae—the type 2 contrast of duple versus triple on the level of *tactus*.

29. See Yolanda Plumley, "The Grammar of 14th-Century Melody: Tonal Organization and Compositional Process in the Chansons of Guillaume de Machaut and the *Ars subtilior*," in *Outstanding Dissertations in Music from British Universities*, ed. John Caldwell (New York: Garland, 1996), 259–261.

30. Ligeti's fascination with the study of Renaissance and medieval music is well documented. He admitted to a strong influence of Ockeghem when writing *Requiem* (1963–1965). He also discussed medieval and Renaissance cadence formulae at length, starting with Perotinus and de Vitry, followed by Dufay, Josquin, Lassus, and Palestrina. See Marina Lobanova, *György Ligeti: Style, Ideas, Poetics* (Berlin: Verlag Ernst Kuhn, 2002), 360–365.

31. Lobanova, *György Ligeti*, 365.

32. As a result of cello and viola potentially outlining the same *tactus* speed, there may be three rather than four viable *tactus* tempi in this section. Discussion follows.

33. The viola is notated in isochronous dotted eights in mm. 12–15 and isochronous quarter-plus-sixteenth durations in mm. 22–27, indicated in Example 15.3 below the rhythmic reduction.

34. Literally speaking, the speeds of 36bpm (Violin 1) and 96bpm (Violin 2) are in a 3:8 proportion. However, that relation does not account for comparable beat levels (i.e., *tactus* vs. *tactus*). This is an apparent rather than real proportion.

35. Well-known musical works in this category range from polycycles in Stravinsky's "Procession of the Sage" from *The Rite of Spring* to multiple *taleae* in Messiaen's 'Liturgie' from the *Quartet for the End of Time*. More abstractly, Carter's works like *90+* for solo piano, or any number of études by Ligeti, are based on polycyclic forms, a conceptual extension of formal interactions in isorhythmic motets. Indeed, a full-length essay, or even a monograph, could be devoted to the principles and polyphonic parameters of type 2 assimilation.

36. Granted, the medieval concept of *color*—an ordered progression of pitches used as a fundamental structuring device in a musical composition—remains fantastically popular in many musical practices of the twentieth century, inclusive of the pitch series fundamental to dodecaphony.

37. Maxwell Davies's fascination with medieval (Latin) culture extends to literature, *Summa Theologica* by St. Thomas Aquinas being his favorite book. See Ivan Hewett, "Harrison Birtwistle and Peter Maxwell Davies: The Twin Titans of Modern Music at 80," *The Telegraph*, July 9, 2014, accessed May 23, 2015, http://www.telegraph.co.uk/culture/music/classicalmusic/10953884/Harrison-Birtwistle-and-Peter-Maxwell-Davies-the-twin-titans-of-modern-music-at-80.html.

38. See Richard McGregor, "Compositional Processes in Some Works of the 1980s," in *Perspectives on Peter Maxwell Davies*, ed. Richard McGregor (Aldershot, UK: Ashgate, 2001). My analysis associates the Scherzo movement more closely with the latter chant with its F *finalis*, opening with an upper neighbor <S, L> figure and extensively based on (024) melodic outlines. This aspect of the Maxwell Davies movement falls into the second category of adaptation.

39. Some of the early works include the opera *Taverner* (1956), wind sextet *Alma Redemtoris Mater* (1957), and *O Magnum Mysterium* (1960).

40. See Michael Hall, *Musical Theatre in Britain, 1960–1975* (Woodbridge, UK: Boydell & Brewer, 2015), 74.

41. Namely, the suggested *tactus*, equivalent to triplet quarters, represents the time value of one sixth of a whole note, or a sixth note, as suggested by Henry Cowell. I will return to the sixth note later in the discussion and reference it further in relation to particolored notes in *Angelorum Psalat* and time-value meters in Thomas Adès's *Aetheria*.

42. Note that (as with mensuration) the eighth note is of the same duration in all meters, even though *tactus* speed varies.

43. There are two five-bar-long metameasures summarized in the reduction.

44. With the introduction of the second voice in m. 11, the polyphonic layering along with cross rhythms in both voices significantly complicates the foreground rhythm.

45. Senleches's *En attendant* appears in both Chantilly and Modena collections. Stoessel provides an exhaustive account of notation principles and a transcription of *En attendant* that, with respect to certain surface detail in the cantus part, differs from mine. See Jason Stoessel, "Symbolic Innovation: The Notation of Jacob de Senleches," *Acta Musicologica* 71, no. 2 (1999): 136–164.

46. The breve is divided into two semibreves and the semibreve is divided into three minims.

47. Measures correspond to a dotted half *supratactus*.

48. The alternate notation with limited barlines (in Example 15.5) attempts to capture the original notation that contains no barlines to coordinate the vocal parts.

49. This series of isochronous eighths is marked with a curved bracket above the staff and joins F5's in mm. 15 and 16.

50. XASAX, "*Saxophone—Ars Subtilior*," Hat Art "Now" 107, 1997.

51. Stephen Pruslin's performance was issued on an LP. See Stephen Pruslin, "Peter Maxwell Davies, Piano Sonata/Alexander Goehr, Capriccio/Nonmiya," Auracle Records, 1983.

52. David Holzman, "Music for a Dancer," Centaur B0000057UD, 1993.

53. See Greig, "Ars Subtilior Repertory as Performance Palimpsest."

54. For a facsimile, see Plumley and Stone, *Chantilly Codex*, 2008. C. Uciredor appears to be an anagram for Rodericus, but the precise name of the author is still under dispute. Josephson speculates that the respelling of Redericus as C. Uciredor is related to the textual canon *Retro mordens ut fera pessima*. A full transcription, still a primary source, is included. See Nors S. Josephson, "Rodericus, *Angelorum Psalat*," *Musica Disciplina* 25 (1971): 113fn2.

55. For a discussion of numerous notational intricacies in the Chantilly Codex, see Stoessel, "Symbolic Innovation," and Crawford Young, "Antiphon of the Angels: *Angelorum psalat tripudium*," *Recercare* 20, nos. 1/2 (2008): 5–23. Stoessel transcribes the particolored notation in other Chantilly songs (he does not transcribe *Angelorum Psalat*) as the sum of one half values (e.g., a quarter note tied to a dotted quarter).

56. *Pestifera* (a feminine form of the adjective) can be translated as foul, pestilential, or even wicked. For possible interpretations of this ballade's text, see Uri Smilansky, "Rethinking Ars Subtilior: Context, Language, Study and Performance" (PhD diss., University of Exeter, 2010). The first instance of particolored notes in the facsimile appears to be assigned an erroneously copied syllable "ri" that duplicates the last syllable from the previous word *inferi*.

57. See Henry Cowell, *New Musical Resources*, 3rd ed., ed. David Nicholls (Cambridge: Cambridge University Press, 1996), 56.

58. As is the case in many *Ars subtilior* scores, time-value duration (or foreground proportions) could be represented in different ways through the use of mensuration signs, note shapes, coloration, etc.

59. See Thomas Adès, *Traced Overhead* (London: Faber Music, 1997).

60. This is comparable with Maxwell Davies's reliance on composite meters and metameasures as agents of phrase structure in Scherzo.

61. The rests in the right-most column of Figure 15.3, notated in simple meters, illustrate *missing* sound articulations, which, were they present, would complete the larger beat

(perfection) and render time-value notation unnecessary. As it stands, the time-value signatures indicate partial *tactus* or *supratactus* beats.

62. The entire work is beautifully flowing in the performance with the composer at the piano. See Thomas Adès, *Life Story*, EMI Classics 272022, 2002.

63. Perceptually, this hearing of the sixth note as a referential beat works better at slower speeds, a necessity in preparation for a performance.

CHAPTER 16

MISERERE

Arvo Pärt and the Medieval Present

LAURA DOLP

As the camera for the 2015 documentary *The Lost Paradise* trains itself on the Estonian composer Arvo Pärt, he raises his right hand to his lips, searching for the right words. He speaks plainly, pausing now and then: "Every one of us has his own destiny and his own relationship with his creator based on his own experiences. This pain…This pain can be found in the works of all great artists. Although it doesn't always have to be pain. It can also be light. Think of Fra Angelico. I can think of no better example."[1] The cultural tangle, and crystalline directness, of Pärt's fifteenth-century reference, as seen in Figure 16.1, serves here as a meaningful entry point to consider his relationship to the past, which is rich in personal connection and self-professed indebtedness to older interpretive models.

As it happens, Pärt's connections to the premodern past are both deep and wide ranging. This chapter utilizes his *Miserere* (1989, revised 1992)—a work for soloists, chorus, and instrumental ensemble that sets Psalm 50/51 and the thirteenth-century Dies irae hymn—as a case study to illustrate these connections. In relation to this work, I engage in formal analysis and issues of aesthetics, theology, and reception, which, when considered collectively, create a portrait of Pärt's compositional output and, by extension, the broader mechanisms at work in his oeuvre. Over a period of three decades, as readers can readily imagine, *Miserere* has been subject to numerous interpretations and has been absorbed into the labor of culture and commerce. This study braids together three areas of consideration: first, the origin story of Pärt's tintinnabuli technique, which emphasizes creative rebirth through early music, and how this story relates to the composition of *Miserere* in particular (grouped here under the heading *Liber Usualis*); second, how the relationship of his music to the medieval has been immortalized in recording and debated by the academy (*charta*); and finally, how his music has been popularly received and drawn into other media, including its evocations of virtual liturgy (*coaevus*).

FIGURE 16.1 Fra Angelico, *Il giudizio universale*, ca. 1431 (tempura on wood, 105 × 210 cm, Museo Nazionale di San Marco).

That Pärt has been labeled a *neomedievalist* on several occasions registers a general acknowledgment of his link to the past.[2] But the nebulous quality of this term in relation to Pärt's musical practice and industry necessitates that we engage from the onset with Umberto Eco's question of which past we are considering.[3] For Pärt, as for other contemporary composers, the medieval has never been simply a chronological concept that is fixed in the past; it has been an ideological state of being, a referential state of historical development that, as David Matthews suggests, might return and in fact could be re-entered much more easily than it could be left behind.[4] Moreover, the reception of his works has been characterized by a wide range of political and philosophical responses. As Louise D'Arcens has observed, the "elasticity" of a discourse about medievalism often includes both "regret and relief" for a "vanished past." In Pärt's case, this dynamic has made his music and ethos equally amenable to progressive and conservative ideological positions; its "valency" has shifted as it moved across contemporary political terrains.[5]

I should say as a matter of clarification that I employ the terms *early music* and *early practice* to refer to the repertories and practices from antiquity through the beginning of the seventeenth century. Pärt's creative field of reference certainly extends beyond this period—his *Passio* from 1989 draws on the genre of the German passion and more specifically on the music of J. S. Bach—but to retain reasonable parameters for this study, I have included only those musical models produced before the baroque.[6] Likewise, I refer to other elements of Pärt's medievalism—involving reception, interpretation, or re-creation—as referring to this early period. I make these references with the understanding that it clearly extends beyond the epoch that is commonly understood as the Middle Ages and even though he would not refer to his own inspiration or influences explicitly in those terms.

Pärt's relationship to the past cannot be summarized easily. Some writers have focused on the goals of creative process (more specifically on the types of problems Pärt has tried solve), while others have viewed them as the product of a postwar psychology (antihumanism breeding a turn to "ancient prehumanism").[7] Recently, more nuanced ways of understanding Pärt's tintinnabuli style have come to light. These include fuller assessments of the origins of the composer's compositional process, which not only evidences creative originality, but which also bears the marks of the creative and political exile that resulted from Pärt's forced immigration in the 1980s. For example, Kevin Karnes has argued that the ontologies of tintinnabulation blossom when viewed as practices set in contradistinction to social realism since they are more broadly reflective of Estonian musical experience in the 1970s, which included early music.[8] This issue of contradistinction has arisen in other assessments regarding Pärt's place among postwar composers who turned to the musical traditions of the Middle Ages for inspiration.[9]

Pärt's affinities for premodern music have also drawn him unwittingly into a critical debate about minimalism. In 1996, Robert Schwartz included Pärt in his book entitled *Minimalists*, which grouped similarly minded composers, many of whom shared inspiration from pre-Enlightenment models.[10] That same year, in a widely read biography of the composer, Paul Hillier cautiously acknowledged the practice of associating Pärt with minimalism, noting that he shared, along with many of his contemporaries, an "ancient attitude towards sound."[11] Pärt's minimalist classification, and its muddy conceptual overlap with medievalism, has been repeated ad infinitum in the popular press, while being concurrently rejected by his academic commentators and dismissed by the composer himself.[12]

Suffice to say, medievalism has been omnipresent in the way Pärt has been singly interpreted and discussed, but what if there was a more fluid and inclusive way of understanding its composition and dynamics? Would it not be useful to consider its complexities in a "third space" that was informed by the composer's personal accounts but could also encompass the other meanings of medievalism as it relates to his output, its forms of collective remembrance and broader musical culture? Two aspects of Homi Bhabha's work seem particularly useful here; the first is that such a space could be *productive*, not merely discursive. It would enable other positions to emerge. The second is that it could harness the impulse to live beyond the borders of our times. It could develop a space of intervention for the purposes of the here and now.[13] My argument employs both aspects of Bhabha's theory. Along the way, I weave some of the broader rhetorical patterns about medievalism—its claim to Christian origins, its appeal to ancient authority, introspection, purity, and asynchrony—with tropes characteristic of Pärt's personal history and his reception.[14] These tropes include:

- the interrelationships of sacred and secular;
- East/Orthodox–West/Christian dichotomies, in the context of a post-ideological Christian Europe;
- historiography of the Baltic region, Germany, and the legacy of Soviet occupation; and
- themes of exile and return and issues of alterity.

First, I will suggest that Pärt's *third-space medievalism* records an ambivalence toward framing his music as either exclusively sacred or secular. This relates to the composer's assertion of its universality, describing it as "many dialects...blended together."[15] This trope also includes the notion that the integrity and power of tintinnabulation originates in the sacred, but it ultimately transcends its context. It also includes the values of authority and purity.

Second, Pärt's third space is Christian in its cultural orientation and it encompasses both the western European sacred musical tradition and a theological alignment with the Byzantine East. Here I turn to Jeffers Engelhart, who has proposed that Pärt's music mediates representations of Estonia and Estonianness that are poised between a stereotyped East and West. In this manner, it serves an "ecumenical, post-ideological, non-essentialized Christian cultural memory" that appeals to traditional but also marginalized Christian groups.[16]

Third, the role and significance of the Middle Ages in the construction of national pasts and national identities play a role when considering Pärt's place of origin and return. Estonia, and particularly the city of Tallin, has had a long-standing reputation as an authoritative and nostalgic medieval environment as well as an invigorated landscape for contemporary music.[17] Pärt's role as a cultural ambassador during the period of Tallin's status as a European capital of culture underscored the eagerness of Estonia to reclaim him. That said, Pärt's third space is also strongly colored by a German culture with its own claims to medievalism (including his crucial relationship with Manfred Eicher and ECM Records), as well as the Soviet influences that sought to define it.[18]

Finally, Pärt's third space incorporates several narratives of exile and return and the conditions of alterity that arise from these journeys. These tropes have been formal as well as experiential. For example, Hermann Conen's 1991 commentary on Pärt's Passion music points to its ancient Christian authority and its description of great upheavals and of flight, exile, and inner emigration.[19] But they have also informed Pärt's biography, literally and metaphorically. I turn now to the many tangled stories of *Miserere*, which illustrate Pärt's myriad connections to the past.

Liber Usualis: Origin Stories, Compositional Style, and Early Music Praxis

Of the many stories about Pärt's creative process, perhaps the most moving, seminal, and oft-repeated is the account of his creative crisis in the early 1970s and his turn inward to reinvent his compositional voice.[20] The centerpiece of this story has been the role of plainchant and early polyphony in Pärt's study and as an agent in the creation of his new compositional technique. Two accounts have provided the most complete sense of Pärt's working methods with this repertory. The first account was a

1997 analysis by his first biographer, the conductor Paul Hillier. The second was related by the composer himself, during a 2004 interview conducted by the musicologist Enzo Restagno.

As an early music specialist, Hillier was uniquely suited to understand the potential that this repertory held for Pärt's compositional practice. Hillier's account contains many markers of Pärt's third-space medievalism, including his emphasis that the composer's reconstitution of art was both productive and visionary for the purposes of the present. For example, he writes that the composer within a "sense of past and future time" led to the forces of a "new life." Moreover, this act of reconstituting the past was synonymous with "rejuvenating" the present. Several tropes of Pärt's creative history also came to light in Hillier's account: the centrality of Western Christian sources, his tendency toward introspection, the purifying of his technical vocabulary and his relationship to the sensory world, and finally the reliance on the old to synthesize temporal worlds.[21] Similarly, in Restagno's later interview with the composer, third-space markers come strongly to the fore. These include Pärt's deference to authority (his characterization of music as "the source of everything"), his inward contemplation (the individual search for music that "breathed inwardly," for an understanding "down to its very roots"), his newfound purity (equating new understanding with new blood), and his awareness of asynchrony (his frequent reference to the rebirth of contemporary creative experience based on "distant epochs" and "ancient polyphony").[22]

What is less explicit in the early origin stories of Pärt's compositional practice is the effect of the considerable social and creative pressures of which he was a part. There was an official Russian skepticism toward baroque and early music.[23] But as Karnes has demonstrated, there was also a vibrant new and early music scene, whose "alternative" claims were aligned with the tropes that I have described as Pärt's third space. These included the philosophical positions introduced by composers like Vladimir Martynov and Valentin Silvestrov, who were interested in "effacing" the creative self, or turning away from the fetishizing of the composer.[24] These stances were related to Orthodoxy, as well as the political subcultures of resistance to the Soviet occupation. Additionally, there is reason to re-evaluate the conventional story of Pärt's dramatic compositional break since the preliminary results of his study of early music—which led to his tintinnabuli technique—did not immediately solidify its technical parameters (what would later become the juxtaposition of melodic and harmonic voices), nor did it significantly depart from Pärt's earlier compositional concerns.[25]

At a formal level, the tintinnabuli process is generally described as the relationship between two types of musical parts that move simultaneously: one that arpeggiates a triadic structure (T voice) and the other that moves diatonically in stepwise motion (M voice). The often narrow ambitus and conservative movement of the M voice has often been compared to the movements of plainchant. Likewise, the overlap that can happen between the T voice and the M voice is sometimes likened to organum.[26]

Hillier's biography draws an explicit relationship between plainchant and Pärt's developing sense of musical topography and proportion.

With Gregorian chant as his source, he [Pärt] studied how to write a single line of music. Writing semi-automatically, page after page, filling book after book, he sought to enter a different sense of time, to fully assimilate all that might be meant by the idea of "monody." Sometimes he would draw a shape, such as the outline of wings or a landscape, and then create a melodic line that would fill that shape.[27]

But plainchant and organum were not the only reference points for Pärt's new technique. He has repeatedly mentioned early repertories that inspired him, including the Notre Dame school, the troubadours, Machaut, Dufay, Josquin, Palestrina, and Victoria. Following his authoritative lead, many commentaries have sought parallels between this repertory and Pärt's compositional approach.[28] Pärt describes the influence of these composers as both rigorous and transformative: "They all pushed me forward and at the same time taught me a lot about what a 'millimeter' means in terms of a musical score. And what a powerful instrument this can become when one has total control over it."[29] He identifies the center of early music or what he terms *Old Music* as the *Ars nova*, particularly the music of Machaut, although he views composers from the later sixteenth century such as Palestrina and Victoria as having strong allegiances to earlier periods; in his terms, not only does their thinking have a common "root" with their predecessors, but also their music has similar "goals."[30]

Two additional aspects of his compositional process figure heavily in Pärt's affinities with early music. The first is his privileging of pitch and rhythm over instrumentation. This flexibility with regard to tone color has often been characterized as an aesthetic connection to earlier periods, in which the essence of music lay in the pitches and not in the variety of possible instrumental timbres.[31] Second is Pärt's logocentric approach, which relies heavily on text as not only generative of compositional structures but is also rooted in his belief in the intrinsic divinity of the Word. As he encapsulates simply, "the words write my music." In this sense, sacred texts are best treated not as literature or works of art but as points of reference, or as models.[32] Leopold Brauneiss has been careful to point out that Pärt's manner of "reference" to the text does not follow medieval compositional rules, but that it does indicate Pärt's personal strategy of reliance on the text to determine musical duration; thus, his compositions follow the syntax of sacred text.[33] This approach, which carries its own historical, spiritual, and liturgical implications, sets Pärt apart from other composers who set religious texts but do not work outward with the same methodology.[34]

In addition to these factors, his oeuvre is marked by the relative frequency and diversity of other references to early music in his compositional process.[35] Besides allusions to plainchant and organum, these references also include hocket, Landini cadences, Franco-Flemish polyphony, use of ison, mensuration canons, and extramusical references such as idiomatic notation, historical instrumentation, and quotation of plainsong (summarized in Table 16.1).

Like so many of his other works, *Miserere* is marked by Pärt's allegiances to the past, but it does not duplicate older processes.[36] Pärt sets Psalm 50:3–21 from the Latin Vulgate while interpolating the first seven verses of the thirteenth-century Latin hymn,

Table 16.1 Early musical materials and their occurrences in Pärt's works

Early musical materials or process	Explicit occurrences, Pärt's works
conspicuous evocations of plainchant lines	Symphony No. 3 (1971)
organum [generally defined as a plainchant melody with an added voice(s) to enrich the horizontal texture]	*Annum per Annum* (1980) – in its juxtaposition of duplum and melismatic organum *Te Deum* (1984/85, 98, 07) – two-part organum
hocket [where a melody is shared between two or more voices so that alternately one voice sounds while the other rests]	*I am the True Vine* (1996)
parallel 6/3 progressions (fauxbourdon), doubled raised leading-notes at cadences ("Landini" cadences)	Symphony No. 3 (1971) *Littlemore Tractus* (2001) *Da Pacem Domine* (2004)
polyphony reminiscent of Franco-Flemish repertory	*Da Pacem Domine* (2004)
ison [sustained pitches in the Orthodox tradition], close-harmony and other Orthodox elements	*Te Deum* (1984) *Kanon Pokajanen* (1997) *Triodion* (1998) *Alleluia-Tropus* (2008)
mensuration canons	*Calix* (1976) *Arbos* (1977) *Cantus in Memory of Benjamin Britten* (1977) *Festina lente* *Stabat Mater*
Extra-musical references	
notation [durations indicated through horizontal lines above the notes, reminiscent of St. Gall notation]	*Cantate Domino Canticum Novum* (1977/1996)
instrumentation [quinterne, or "gittern"—a short-necked lute]	*Sei globt, du Baum* (2007)
literal quotation of plainsong	*Statuit ei Dominus* (1990)

Dies irae, between its verses. Scored for soloists (SATTB), SATB choir, ensemble and organ, its alternating instrumentation, and form can be summarized as in Table 16.2.[37]

The work exhibits the global tendency of tintinnabuli processes to carry traces of plainchant and thus carries a ubiquitous trace of early music, but in its deployment, the work contains a harmonic intensity and powerful sense of direction not contained in earlier works.[38] Likewise, Pärt's innovation extends to the logogenetic devices guiding the intonations and structure of its text.[39] Unlike earlier works where Pärt uses the text as strict structural model according to syllabic count, in *Miserere* he alters the pitch level according to stressed syllables near the ends of phrases. These modifications to the earlier process render the work closer to psalmody.[40]

Table 16.2 *Miserere* structure

Section	Text	Scoring	Bars	Early music references
1. Psalm	vv. 3–5	soloists, woodwinds and timpani	Rehearsal 1–9	hocket technique (at v. 4)
2. Dies irae	vv. 1–7	choir and ensemble	Rehearsal 10–17	mensuration canon on A, 1:2:4:8:16
3. Psalm	vv. 6–8 Interlude I vv. 9–11 Interlude II vv. 12–14 Interlude III vv. 15–19 Interlude IV vv. 20–21	Soloists and ensemble without strings	Rehearsal 18–49	
4. Dies irae	verse 8	choir, SA soloists, organ and percussion	Rehearsal 50	mensuration canon

Miserere is third in a group of Pärt's works (including *Passio* and *Stabat Mater*) that explores the passion of Christ. Psalm 50 is penitential in nature, because the narrator acknowledges the sins of humankind. Pärt has stated that he views the Psalm as an exploration of human imperfection and causal events: When man recognizes and admits his own insignificance, this makes possible his inner liberation.[41] Andrew Shenton's 2017 study of the vocal works suggests that Pärt's placement of the Dies irae after its third verse represents an increasing maturity and deepening of the composer's theological stance, at least in his longer works.[42]

In *Miserere*, Pärt also employs thirteenth- and fourteenth-century techniques—hocket and mensuration canons—while other techniques are more impressions than traceable devices. The work can be described as having aspects of hocket, particularly when the voices are brought increasingly closer together.[43] Likewise, mensuration canons are deployed at rehearsal 10, where the Dies irae is introduced.[44] In both cases, Pärt borrows the principles of these compositional techniques but modifies them for his own purposes. For example, in fourteenth-century mensuration canons, a melody typically serves as the repeating structure and layers of this melody are prepared and resolved within the conventions of polyphonic writing. In Pärt's case, the canons are constructed according to empirical formulae.[45]

That said, the story of *Miserere* and its early music allegiances extends well beyond its compositional origins to include its realization in the concert hall and its later dissemination through recording, film, and theater. Two music ensembles have been seminal in supporting and shaping Pärt's exploration of early music: the Estonian group Hortus Musicus, directed by Andres Mustonen, and the British-born Hilliard Ensemble, directed by Paul Hillier. Mustonen was the first of these alliances and one that proved to be deeply important both creatively and personally.[46]

FIGURE 16.2 Pärt and Mustonen in 1978.

In the period before the Pärts left Estonia, Mustonen and Pärt studied early repertories together, exploring the music of Machaut, Dufay, Obrecht, Ockeghem, and
Victoria (see Figure 16.2).[47] Mustonen also had his group play Pärt's compositional
sketches so that he could hear them realized. Because of Mustonen's encouragement,
Pärt heard music that would have otherwise been consigned to the drawer.[48] The
instrumentation of the ensemble did not always satisfy Pärt's expectations for his
scores, but he has often expressed appreciation for the opportunity to have heard
something new.

Mustonen and Hortus Musicus were also the driving force behind the concert that
introduced audiences in Tallin to the word tintinnabuli for the first time (October 27,
1976). Mustonen's idiosyncratic and countercultural personality is evident in several
accounts of this period, with his performances sometimes described as having the "zeal
and energy of a rock band."[49] The concert program drew an explicit relationship between
Pärt's music and its compatibilities with late fifteenth-century sacred music. The first
half featured Pärt's works, including *Calix*. The program then turned to Dufay's mid
fifteenth-century *Missa L'homme armé*. Although Hortus Musicus was most closely
associated with Pärt's early life in Estonia, their professional ties resurfaced in a 2011
compilation recording organized by Mustonen and entitled *Early Music of 3rd
Millennium*. Pärt contributed a short piece to the project: *Palgest palgesse* (Face to Face,
2005), a work for soprano, baritone, clarinet, viola, and double bass, that sets a Russian

text of 1 Corinthians 13:12, "For now we see through a glass darkly; but then face to face: now I know in part; but then shall I know even as also I am known." In the liner notes, Pärt recapitulates his conviction, forty years hence, that "schools" (or styles) of music such as those represented by Dufay or Josquin can also function in the metaphysical sense as a means of "sculpting the soul."[50]

By contrast, Pärt's long-term engagement with Paul Hillier's ensemble—which has generated its own force field in his exposure to early music—began after the composer's move to the West in the 1980s. Pärt was overjoyed by their sound.[51] Under Hillier's direction, the ensemble recorded nine of Pärt's works (*Passio* twice) and performed his music worldwide.[52] Hilliard interpretations, which now carry Pärt's imprimatur, exert both authority and considerable influence for interpreters.[53]

Miserere is at the center of this circle of valuation. It was commissioned by the Festival d'Eté de Seine-Maritime in Rouen, France, and that summer, Hillier led the premiere on June 17, 1989. On more than one occasion, Pärt has emphasized the precision and collaborative process necessary between composer and performer to produce concerts and record works. He has stated outright that *Miserere* would not have come about without the help of Hilliard Ensemble and their patient participation in the recording process.[54]

Hillier drew on his considerable experience with early music to interpret Pärt's compositions. During his first encounter with a Pärt score, he writes that "the notation had the appearance of having been refracted through medieval music"; there was "nothing there...but from my experiences with medieval music, I knew that therefore *everything* might be there."[55] This experience was helpful interpreting scores like *Tabula rasa*, where necessary information was missing. Hillier has also written about the direct linkages between the spiritual posture and technical organization of Ockeghem and Josquin and Pärt's creative process.[56] This understanding fueled his advocacy for appropriate acoustic spaces in performance, even suggesting at one point that the physical idealization—the space, liturgy, action, movement, odor, and sound—of an Orthodox Church "conspire to create the right conditions" for Pärt's music.[57]

Hillier and Mustonen are not the only early music interpreters of Pärt's music to ascribe the qualities of directness, transparency, and austerity to these historical orientations. The fact that they have arrived at these judgments through a combination of study, experience, and mutual reinforcement through vibrant twentieth-century performance, however, raises crucial aesthetic issues. As Kay Shelemay reminds us, judgments regarding beauty and Otherness are intimately tied to assumptions about instrumentation and material culture and notions of the West. For example, describing Pärt's attraction to plainsong and its expressive potential as one of a "general feeling of prayerfulness" as well as "the kind of phrasing it engenders, beginning quietly, intensifying towards the centre, then falling away," is the product of late twentieth- and twenty-first-century, not medieval, musical values.[58] Moreover, the performance practices that were considered edgy in Tallin in the 1970s are now standard to the conventions of the contemporary stage, which often pair contemporary music with these musical aesthetics and early music.[59]

Charta: Imprinting the Medieval Pärt, through Recording and Debate

The presence of the medieval in the dissemination of Pärt's music through recording, and the concurrent debate about its meanings, has been an ongoing part of a third space. In the early years, the characteristics of this dissemination were carefully controlled by ECM Records, who immortalized interpretations of Pärt's music through the recording process while shaping his public image. The tropes ECM introduced—both in its visual marketing and in its accompanying commentary—emphasized Pärt's reliance on medieval Christian authority, his consistent sense of introspection, and the purity and other-worldliness of his compositions. At the same time, these strategies became fodder for the academy, whose cultural theorists were invested in the meanings of Pärt's third-space medievalism and its ideological place in the constructions of modernism and postmodernism. ECM's framing of Pärt as both East and West, and beyond the boundaries of sacred or secular and the uncertainties produced by his own cultural alterity, fueled the theoretical debate that has tried to articulate his position not only compositionally but also culturally in the sphere of contemporary music.

In 1991, *Miserere* was the recipient of ECM's meticulous attention to recording, packaging, and marketing of their artists, a practice that forms the backbone of their reputation in the recording industry. Manfred Eicher's working methods are exceptionally precise. When *Miserere* was recorded that year in London, the sound engineers (in consultation with the composer) spent two days resetting microphones to achieve the optimum sound (see Figure 16.3).[60] The album, which was named after *Miserere*, also contained *Festina Lente* (1988/1990) and *Sarah Was Ninety Years Old* (1976/1990). For the cover, ECM designers evoked the mystery of judgment (see Figure 16.4). The title, in blood red calligraphy rising across a dark gray background, relays the work of a medieval hand, at times dripping elegantly but ominously below its characters. With its implication of a medieval text inside, the booklet opens to textual translations, brief essays, and images of the composer and conductor in rehearsal. Like so many of Pärt's ECM images, these images contain the visual cues of familiar ritualistic gestures.[61]

By the time the *Miserere* recording had been issued, Sandner's liner notes to *Tabula rasa*, from six years earlier, had already established the main lines of journalistic discourse about Pärt.[62] After rehearsing the period of the composer's silence, Sandner mentions his study of French and Franco-Flemish choral part music, including Machaut, Ockeghem, Obrecht, and Josquin, and then observes that Pärt himself wrote a few compositions in the spirit of early European polyphony.[63] Three years later, Wilfred Mellers writes in conjunction with another of Pärt's ECM recordings that in "medieval plainsong and organum, Pärt found musics which were, of their nature, in the Western sense non-harmonic. Such monody and heterophony imply a different notion of what music is 'about' and 'for.' His music not only has affinities with medieval

FIGURE 16.3 Manfred Eicher and Pärt at the recording session of *Miserere* in Rouen, 1989. Photo: Jean-Pierre Larcher, ECM Records.

liturgical cantillation, but also with sundry ritualistic concepts typical of folk and ethnic cultures."[64]

ECM enlisted two liner-note authors for the *Miserere* recording with different texts, one in German by Peter Hamm and the other in English by Hermann Conen. In the first essay, Hamm reimagines Pärt's music into mythical, historical spaces and wonders if Pärt's kind of music had not already been experienced in the Gothic and Roman cathedrals.[65] In Conen's account, Pärt is framed as a "poet of the Middle Ages," whose musical gestures are coded by human deficiency on the one hand and indicators of the original music on the other. He also characterizes the use of the hocket technique as parallel to that employed by the "medieval masters" to separate the instrumental from the vocal lines.[66]

After the completion of the ECM imprinting of *Miserere*, a broad and inclusive third space for Pärt's works continued to expand. For example, in the commentary for the 2006 recording *Misterioso*, Jurg Stenzl relates the processes of Pärt's *Spiegel im Spiegel*— a process that provides "constantly changing views of a single musical object"—to the formal principles used in fifteenth-century Franco-Flemish polyphony and in the great sets of variations from Frescobaldi via Bach and Beethoven to Webern. Stenzl draws a parallel between this formal process and a unifying spiritual principle, identified as "ideal polyphony" that functions as "unceasing prayer." Stenzl also revisits the analogy of early sacred architecture, stating that "music and its fabric are not sufficient

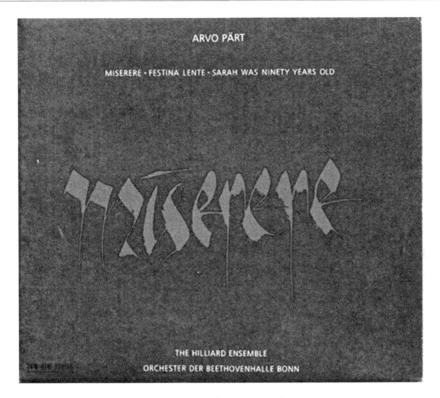

FIGURE 16.4 ECM *Miserere* (1991).

unto themselves, but are meant to redirect listeners to something else: an idea from the 'age of cathedrals.' "[67]

Pärt's long-time publisher, Universal Edition, also emphasizes these allusions to the past. On ECM's website, a review of *Miserere* by Tyan Grillo from 2010 describes the passage between the third and fourth interludes (beginning "Docebo iniquos vias tuas") as a ritualistic embodiment of the liturgy. He characterizes it as "an *a cappella* passage that is transfiguration incarnate, each soloist pawing the air like a sleeping lion. The winds slog through the valleys, heavy sins in tow, while voices linger in the firmament."[68] In a commentary designed to be an introduction to the composer's work, Andreas Peer Kähler likewise suggests that Pärt's music reconstitutes the basic materials of music. In this music, Kähler writes, "The faded supermarket and pop triad suddenly becomes a dome of sound, in which three individual notes completely abandon their individuality in favor of a higher order. The medieval or Renaissance musician may have harbored a natural awe for these phenomena—for the listener today, it is nothing less than the rediscovery of them."[69]

Liner notes were not the only place that Pärt's third-space medievalism was positioned as a rediscovery of a "higher order." From the early 1990s on, his music became drawn into the ongoing debate about modernism and its discontents in the academy. For some commentators, coming to terms with modernist and postmodernist discourse in relation to Pärt meant addressing issues of asynchrony, the interrelationships between sacred and secular, and the origins of tintinnabuli as a form of political and aesthetic resistance. In a 1993 analysis by David Clarke, excerpts from *Miserere* were used to highlight the ideological ramifications of the tintinnabuli style. Arguing that the tintinnabuli style was symptomatic of a deepening crisis in the future of concert music, Clarke argued that Pärt's compositional approach was more than just a set of musical features, that it amounted "to a rhetoric, a contradictory strategy which seeks on the one hand to meet modernism on its own terms, and on the other to deny modernism's own denial of certain aesthetic possibilities." For Clarke, Pärt's strategy employed two main tactics; the first one implemented "critical processes from within the music itself" and the second invoked "a significant extra-musical discourse which urges the primacy of the music's spirituality over and above the concerns of modernity." Clarke's bold critique ran counter to much of the commentary that had made its way to academic and popular press, and it sought to articulate why Pärt's explanations, as well as the music that he produced, were so hard to pin down. In one instance, Clarke explained this critical "inoculation" as the result of a consciously formed paradox, in which this same critical stance (above) was applied to the treatment of tintinnabuli's own historically retrieved materials.[70]

The issue of Pärt's position in a modernist discourse was taken up again a decade later by Benjamin Skipp, who argued for Pärt's resistances to postmodernist plurality via his allegiances to the past. In Skipp's view, the composer's works exhibited three elements that opposed a "fetishism" of the means. These elements included "the absence of subject-matter drawn from living memory" (traditional, even ascetic, materials), an eschewal of contemporary technology, and his adoption of a form of orthodoxy within his material (as a form of self-discipline). These factors, Skipp proposed, functioned collectively as a personal stand against the "turmoil" of multiplicity.[71] In this view, Pärt's medievalism was positioned as a response to something missing in the modern condition. Since his response reflected a unified set of values, his creative output was ready-made for canonic status based on something new. A new "aesthetic conversion" to unity, which could under other circumstances be considered aligned with the modernist project, was instead symptomatic of a break with it, rather than a realignment. Additionally, the narrative of Pärt's religious conviction surfaced once again in Skipp's assessment, which he used to emphasize the relationship between Pärt's attraction to plainsong and his valuation of self-erasure. In Skipp's formal parallel, the model of two-part organum—from which tintinnabuli draws powerful structural analogies—capitalizes on an effective dynamic between "freedom and fixity," on the one hand with the principal voices (fixed) and, on the other, with the organal (extemporized) voices.[72]

More recently, Shenton retheorizes this philosophical basis of Pärt's output as synthesis of the modern and the postmodern, in what he calls a condition of *metamodernism*. In his view, the techniques of medieval music are more effectively interpreted as a postmodern response, while Pärt's new compositional techniques are reflective of a modernist stance. Shenton's analysis focuses on the oscillation between these two dynamics, effectively casting Pärt's third space as another kind of discourse: different, but inextricably bound to the content of both practices.[73]

In 2005, the first full-scale study to directly address the issue of Pärt and medievalism, as such, reassessed many of the formalist arguments and observations that had been a default of Pärt's third-space discourse since the late 1980s.[74] Its author, Leopold Brauneiss, a theorist and long-time advocate for Pärt's work, identified three parallel features of the tintinnabuli style with the Middle Ages: first, its lack of "egotism" and the ramifications of this lack for performance; second, its evocations of the "everlasting musical harmony" and Boethius' *musica mundana*; and third, the parallels between the lack of specific instrumentation in medieval music and the intentional flexibility of Pärt's music with regard to tone color. Brauneiss's project sidesteps the fallacy of equivalencies, on the one hand by arguing that Pärt does not imitate but rather blends historic layers into a *postmodern* construction, and on the other by describing medieval music in the form of plainchant as a kind of catalyst.[75] Almost as an afterthought, but with arresting insight, the essay ends with the suggestion that perhaps it is even the other way round, that "this music makes us understand the Middle Ages in a new way."[76] In a 2005 article entitled "The Unification of Opposites," Brauneiss returned to his larger philosophical point concerning the question of Pärt's rootedness, this time comparing his philosophical stance and the work of the fifteenth-century religious philosopher Nicolaus Cusanus. He compares Pärt's metaphoric idea of the single note—which combines relative and absolute unity while serving as a coincidence of opposites—with Cusanus's idea of the *primum principium* (the unified fundament and origin of the world) and the *coincidentia oppositorum* (opposites coincide at the greatest and smallest point where they can no longer be conceived).[77]

In a sense, Brauneiss's stance more specifically realizes older statements made by writers such as Paul Griffiths who choose to emphasize Pärt's relationship to the "primordial." In a commentary that appears in a 2010 ECM special edition of *Tabula rasa*, Griffiths expounds on notions first offered by Wolfgang Sandner in the original release (1984). Griffiths writes of Pärt's mystical connections to the past:

> Pärt's connections with the past are clear: connections with chant, with the choral traditions of his native Estonia (his instruments are wordless voices) and even with specific episodes in music history. All such echoes are perfectly integrated, as if they were waiting to be found, by a composer continuing along what is his own path. An idiosyncratic and highly artificial technique turns up objects of memory. This, though, is only scratching the surface. The palimpsest of allusion is just part of the story.... Reaching far beyond the limits of a human lifespan, extending back to long before the limits of a human lifespan, extending back to long before the whirlwinds of music since 1945, this music situates us in a deep present, a now that is centuries old and an ancientness that is still alive.[78]

Here Sandner's leitmotifs of the unknowable—the mystical connections (in the form of a "palimpsest") and the primeval recollections of a prophet (an "ancientness that still is alive")—are reworked with Griffith's appeal to the "deep present."[79]

Finally, the medievalism of Pärt's third space has also been invigorated with comparisons between Russian Orthodox icons and the spirit of regard that Pärt holds for chant and early music. Hillier formalized this comparison, arguing that like the Byzantine icon—whose presence negates the question of contemporaneity—the "timelessness" of Pärt's music incorporates a similar manner of operation. This approach to sound has an expression of "all-encompassing purpose," and while Pärt's music is not created for liturgical use, it exhibits the same criteria that direct composers of sacred music away from exclusively aesthetic or subjective goals, toward the continuation and preservation of a tradition. This can only be achieved, Hillier writes, "by an existential entry into the living texture of that tradition, not simply treating it as a subject of external study."[80] Likewise, in his discussion of hesychasm, the mystical practice of the Russian Orthodox Church, Hillier emphasizes that Pärt's inspiration comes from the church's "contemplative core."[81] The imprints from Byzantine models are also acknowledged in Shenton's later monograph, which attributes the composer's principal aesthetic, in the form of a "radical simplicity that embodies a sort of 'voluntary poverty,' a detachment from self and from things, and a desire to compose that effaces his own subjectivity," to his discovery of Orthodoxy.[82]

Coaevus: Receiving the Medieval Pärt in Film, in Theater, and on the Web

The productivity of third-space medievalism is particularly evident in the ways that Pärt's music has been incorporated into other art forms like film, as well as with its appropriation in the creative industry of the web. In film, Pärt's music has repeatedly infused narratives with states of introspection and stillness; it has accompanied stories of liminal political and cultural spaces and has been deployed to transform the secular into the sacred. The use of *Miserere* also serves to highlight the ways that Pärt's medievalism has become more broadly popularized on the Web and in the visual arts more generally.

The extensive record of Pärt's music in film is proof of the uncanny flexibility and power of his music in association with the moving image. To date, his precomposed music has been used in over one hundred films. This total does not include sixty earlier films for which he composed original scores. *Miserere* has been used twice; once in Nanni Moretti's *Habemus Papem* (We Have a Pope) from 2011 and also in Terrence Malick's *Knight of Cups* (2015). Other works such as *Spiegel im Spiegel, Cantus in Memory of Benjamin Britten, Fratres*, and *Für Alina*, have been employed, some would say exploited, so frequently as to have spawned a kind of soundscape all their own.[83]

Film directors have often capitalized on Pärt's music as a mechanism for stillness in film. Moretti's later film *Mia Madre* quotes several of Pärt's works for this purpose, but *Habemus Papem*, an otherwise quiet film, utilizes the dramatic Dies irae from *Miserere* (rehearsal 10) at the film's surprising conclusion to illustrate the Papacy momentarily shaken to its roots.[84] Set in the present day, the film tells the story of a reluctant participant in the thousand-year-old institution of the papal conclave. Cardinal Melville (Michel

Piccoli) is chosen by the college to be Pope, but he experiences a psychological crisis before his introduction to the crowds in St. Peter's Square and suddenly retreats, to the bewilderment of the church and his new faithful. Moretti, playing a savvy, sweet, and respectful Roman psychologist, is brought in to counsel Melville. At one point during his "rehabilitation," Melville escapes his security detail and wanders the streets in civilian clothing in a state of confused bewilderment. As Melville encounters ordinary people, even joining a theater troupe (Chekhov is on the bill), Moretti entertains the cardinals back at the Vatican to take their minds off their predicament. Inevitably, Melville returns home and finally emerges onto the balcony to greet his flock. Amassed together on the balconies to either side of the new pope, in front of the waiting crowd and the media, the cardinals' faces reflect their relief and joy at the prospect of security renewed.

To this point, the soundtrack of the film features an understated score by Moretti's long-time collaborator Franco Piersanti, excerpts of diegetic liturgical chant, and a popular song.[85] But as Melville begins to speak over the bustle of the crowd and the cardinals realize that he has more doubts than certitude, their expressions change from confusion to disbelief (see Figure 16.5).

At the moment that Melville's intentions are fully clear ("In this moment, I can only say, pray for me / The guide that you need, is not me / I can't be the one"), Pärt's setting of the last line of Psalm 51 in *Miserere*, " et peccatum contra me est semper" (and my sin is ever before me), with its tritone dissonances between vocal soloists, overtakes the soundtrack (rehearsal 9, m. 3). In the pregnant pause after Melville's last words, the timpani makes a dramatic crescendo (rehearsal 9, m. 4) and as Melville turns and retreats a final time into the darkened room, Pärt's terrifying Dies irae erupts, erasing the diegetic sound completely and cutting to the black screen of the film credits.

FIGURE 16.5 Film still from Nanni Moretti, *Habemus Papem* (2011): The cardinals respond to Melville's statement, "I can't be the one."

In effect, Pärt's setting of the quintessential moment of judgment in the Christian liturgy accompanies Melville's confession of fragility and shortcomings in front of the Christian world. Its impact is made more startling by the overriding quiet of the film to this point, which plays on the intimate, humorous, and sometime absurd predicaments of clergy and brethren alike. The meanings of Pärt's third-space medievalism reside here: in the utility of his music to catapult Melville and by association, all those watching, toward their consequences. The entrance of the Dies irae illustrates the rootedness of Pärt's music and his ethos in the Christian context, its appeal to ancient authority, and its close-knit relationship to introspection, within the uneasy dislocations of medieval and contemporary life.

In 2013, the Hilliard Ensemble celebrated its fortieth anniversary. It was a landmark for early music performance in general, and for Pärt in particular, since the group had been singularly influential in creating the pervasive "Pärtian" sound in the West. The magnitude of their musical presence was reiterated in several anniversary reviews, which summarized their characteristic sound as "riveting, chastely beautiful" and "exceptionally pure."[86] Unsurprisingly after forty years of concerts and recordings, the Hilliard has a substantial presence on the Web. Through the labor of its community of users, Pärt's music has become inextricably bound with the sound of the Hilliard as well as the visual branding of ECM. The Hilliard is not the only group to have been honored with official sanction from the Pärts; the Estonian Philharmonic Chamber Choir with Tõnu Kaljuste has been crucial through their numerous performances, their partnership with ECM, and their ongoing stature as a premiere ensemble in an already rich Baltic choral tradition.[87]

Pärt's virtual third space has also been defined by the popular discourse around early music and the residual legacies of his association with "holy minimalism." A user-generated video of the Hilliard's ECM recording of *Miserere* on YouTube is typical of this communal discourse, featuring the fetishized detail of Michelangelo's panel from the Sistine Chapel depicting the Creation of Adam as its visual backdrop and its Papyrus font announcing Pärt and the Hilliard Ensemble, with its markers of medieval calligraphy (see Figure 16.6).[88]

The term holy minimalist, which has caused prolonged consternation for some of Pärt's advocates and a profitable rhetorical loop for others, also remains an active part of the third space.[89] In online blogs, in YouTube commentary, and in print, commentators continue to announce concerts by describing Pärt's "seductive vision of modern spiritual music, one that seeks to escape our world—into a monastic-style pseudo-medievalism— rather than to embrace it" or in other cases as a form of "religio-minimalist earnestness."[90] Rehearsing commentary about the composer's early compositional models and its parallels in expressive qualities, Pärt's music is commonly described as "spare," "slow-moving," "contemplative," "mystical," and cyclical in its returns to the "same root."[91]

The tropes of authority, introspection, purity, and asynchrony figure heavily in these statements and are reminiscent of the rhetoric that accompanied the commercial revivals of plainchant recordings and the music of Hildegard of Bingen that occurred in

FIGURE 16.6 Screenshot from Arvo Pärt—*Miserere*—The Hilliard Ensemble. Guy-Louis Morel, published on YouTube, October 12, 2013, accessed May 16, 2017.

the early 1990s. In her analysis of Hildegard's contemporary reception, Jennifer Bain notes that in Richard Souther's *Vision* CD (1994), which she identifies as targeting New Age audiences, historically verifiable accounts are supplanted with positioning Hildegard as a universal, spiritual figure.[92] Likewise, Katherine Bergeron's perceptive comparison of two chant recordings from 1994 and 1999 proposes that while both performances reflect diverse ideologies, they share the positioning of chant as something that "offers something more, a truth beyond the venal world of the music industry, because this mysterious music transcends the circulation of capital. The meaning of chant, we are to believe, is born of a holy lack." In both cases, Bergeron concludes that the allusions to an exotic life of ritual contribute to the desires for an asynchronous condition, where music displaces time. At the same time, the capacity for chant to be performed in a virtual space of "neither/nor" (neither sacred music, nor not sacred music) proposes the ways that the "authentic" might be reimagined.[93]

In the throes of the ironic and sometimes humorous echo chamber of modern identity, an unidentified monk from the Santo Domingo de Silos retorted at one point, "We are monks, not rock stars!"[94] It is difficult not to hear, echoing back, Pärt's own retort to the dramatic escalation of his commercial pigeonholing: "I am not a prophet,

not a cardinal, not a monk. I am not even a vegetarian."[95] Nora Pärt recounts the
personal difficulties engendered by the early stages of this attention:

> When we came to the West, Arvo was a real gift for the media. It was such a gratifying
> topic to report about: an exotic being, mystic, monk, beard, medieval vocabulary,
> detached from the world, etc. It wasn't all meant in a bad way (though some was bad
> enough) and the more well-meaning it was the more the distorted picture upset us
> and did us harm. The idea that within the field of spirituality there can also exist a
> normality and naturalness that doesn't land immediately in the realms of mysticism
> was obviously quite foreign to the general public.

In that same interview, Pärt responds to her story by interjecting, "Some people even
thought I wore a false-beard!"[96]

As if to answer the cosmic question at hand, in 2002, the Milanese portrait painter
Marco Ventura pushed the "iconic" status of Pärt to its literal end (see Figure 16.7),
capitalizing materially on what Engelhart has characterized as the semiotic power of
the icon: its "musical quotation, mimesis, structural articulation, vocal timbre, sound
and style, and the felt correspondence of musical affect to an authentic self."[97]

FIGURE 16.7 Marco Ventura, *Arvo Pärt* (2002, oil on wood).

In 2015, the inexhaustible drive of Pärt's interest in ancient authority was demonstrated in a large-scale staged collaboration, *Adam's Passion*, between Pärt and the American theater director Robert Wilson, premiered in Estonia and later released on DVD.[98] Pärt chose *Miserere* and positioned it last in a sequence of four of his works that comprise the music for the *Passion*, including *Sequentia* (2015, a new work dedicated to Robert Wilson), *Adam's Lament* (2009), and *Tabula rasa* (1977). Pärt and Wilson met in 2009 at a Vatican convention, and *Adam's Lament* was the result of their decision to make a piece that would address human history on a cosmic scale, from the beginning to the apocalyptic end. Pärt's earlier thought processes about the story of Adam, addressed through the text of Silouan the Athonite in *Adam's Lament* for choir and orchestra, are the clear instigator of the later work. Across the production, Adam is the embodiment of human grief, in the words of one commentator, the "Biblical figure of mourning par excellence."[99] In its placement at the end *Miserere*, it adds further commentary to Adam's fall and is prepared with a period of grace in the form of *Tabula rasa*. The impulse to view *Adam's Passion* as a kind of *Gesamtkunstwerk* is evident in many of the responses to the work, as well as framing it as a summation of Pärt's creative output using the tintinnabuli technique.[100]

Wilson's visual language is renowned for its slow painterly effects and the evocation of classical Greek sculpture and has strong affinities with the deliberate and crystalline structures of Pärt's music and its appeal to the themes that have informed this theoretical space. That said, Pärt's theological focus and fidelity to the text are not shared by Wilson, who seems at times oblivious to the word, or at least not interested in acknowledging its dramatic meanings on stage. After the introduction of *Sequentia*, Wilson focuses almost exclusively on the figure of Adam (Michalis Theophanous), identified in the production credits as a "Man," during *Adam's Lament*. His glacially slow motion along the thrust of the stage culminates when he places a felled tree branch on his head and then begins to revolve slowly, ushering in *Tabula rasa* and the figure of a "Woman" (Lucinda Childs). It is not until the end of *Tabula rasa* that the visual world of the stage becomes more complicated, through the introduction of other figures (with the younger girls and boys acting as mirrors of their older versions) and the descent of an upside-down tree of life from the ceiling.

Wilson marks the beginning of *Miserere* with the Boy, who places a book on his head in a mirror gesture of the Man at the end of *Adam's Lament*. Although the choreography and visual effects are the most involved throughout *Miserere*, characters rarely respond directly to the musical cues. When they do, they seem to have woken from a parallel dream, momentarily jarred by a change in timbre or shift in register, but not enough to pull them away from their own.[101] Pärt's setting invites shifts in visual dramaturgy as he moves the pitch orientation between psalm verses or changes textural relationships. Wilson addresses them through the introduction of characters on or off the stage or through lighting shifts, but with rigorous control and pacing. In a manner of speaking, Wilson has taken the topography of Pärt's interjections of the Dies irae, or the interludes between Psalm verses, and flattened it. Its energetic high points are absorbed and averaged over the course of the entire *Passion*, rather than responsive to Pärt's logocentric approach.

Of Adam's story, Pärt writes, "You see, this story is your story, one that questions me. And this story is my story, that responds to you. This is our common story. The story of Adam is the story of all mankind. And it is one of tragedy." This quote is prominently featured on the DVD of *Adam's Passion*, as well as several of his other aphoristic statements, each of which reinforces the universality, unity, and timelessness of the project and, by extension, the visionary work of Pärt and Wilson individually. In tandem, the dynamics of Pärt's third space are strongly reinforced and broadened, reaching back to a prelapsarian world and expanding outward past the boundaries of ideological religion.[102]

Coda

While *Miserere* makes a useful red thread in the constellation of meanings of Pärt's third-space medievalism, so many of the features of this complex crossroad—the ontologies of tintinnabuli and its claims regarding the authority of early music, the alignment of Pärt's music with medieval music praxis, the commercial immortalization of Pärt as both belonging to a premodern past and anticipating the postmodern future, the work of some commentators to reconcile Pärt between modernism and postmodernism, the utility of Pärt's music in the evocation of asynchrony in the moving image, and finally the equation of Pärt's music as a text encoded with a pre-Enlightenment world—can be mapped onto his work as a whole. In the end, this constellation speaks to the pervasive and variegated nature of the past in his music. But it is also a profound tribute to tenacious relevancy of that past, in the present.

NOTES

1. Arvo Pärt, in Günter Atteln, *The Lost Paradise* (Accentus Music, 2015), film.
2. UniGregoriana, "Il Suono Del Verbo (Prof. Giorgio Monari—P. Ramón Saiz-Pardo Hurtado)," Lecture: Convegno Internazionale «L'esperienza religiosa cristiana del vedere e dell'udire: per un'arte contemporanea» (Roma, 17–18 marzo 2015) https://youtu.be/ MUjkUdHZktw (2015); Benjamin Skipp, "Review: Symphony No. 4; Fragments from Kanon Pokajanen by Arvo Pärt; *Tabula rasa*, Universal Edition, Containing "Fratres"; "Cantus in Memory of Benjamin Britten"; *Tabula rasa* by Arvo Pärt, Guido Gorna," *Tempo* 65, no. 256 (2011); Robert Schwartz describes Pärt's music as *quasimedieval*. K. Robert Schwarz, *Minimalists* (London: Phaidon, 1996), 216.
3. Tison Pugh and Angela Jane Weisl, *Medievalisms: Making the Past in the Present* (London: Routledge, 2013), 3. "Every time one speaks of a dream of the Middle Ages, one should first ask which Middle Ages one is dreaming of," Umberto Eco, "The Return of the Middle Ages," *Travels in Hyperreality* (San Diego: Harcourt, 1986), 68, 71.
4. David Matthews, *Medievalism: A Critical History* (Cambridge: Brewer, 2015), Loc 1403/6301.

5. David Matthews, *Medievalism: A Critical History* (Cambridge: Brewer, 2015), Loc 1403/6301. (Cambridge: Cambridge University Press, 2016), 2–5; Laura Dolp, "Arvo Pärt in the Marketplace," in *The Cambridge Companion to Arvo Pärt*, ed. Andrew Shenton (Cambridge: Cambridge University Press, 2012), 177–192.

6. Beate Kowalski and Michaela Christine Hastetter, *Die Johannespassion von Arvo Pärt* (Stuttgart: Verlag Katholisches Bibelwerk, 2015); Oliver Kautny, "Arvo Pärts 'Passio' und Johann Sebastian Bachs 'Johannespassion'—Rezeptionsästhetische Perspektiven," in *Arvo Pärt: Rezeption und Wirkung seiner Musik: Vorträge des Wuppertaler Symposiums 1999*, ed. Oliver Kautny (Osnabrück: Electronic Publishing [EPos Music], 2001), 198–222; Enzo Restagno, Leopold Brauneiss, and Kaale Karela, *Pärt, Arvo. Arvo Pärt in Conversation* (Champaign, IL: Dalkey Archive Press, 2012), 14. The first edition was published in 2004 in Italian.

7. Paul Hillier, *Arvo Pärt* (Oxford: Oxford University Press, 1997), 65; Richard Taruskin, *Oxford History of Western Music*, Vol. 5 (Oxford: Oxford University Press), 43–44.

8. Kevin Karnes, *Arvo Pärt's Tabula rasa*, ed. Kevin Karnes (Oxford: Oxford University Press, 2017), 36; Michel Rigoni, "Musique De Postmodernité: Pour Un État Des Lieux," *Musurgia, Dossiers d'analyse (1998)* 5, no. 3/4 (1998):109–122.

9. In one study, Pärt is grouped with those who have responded to music of the 1100s–1300s, including Sofia Gubaidulina, Alfred Schnittke, Cary Boyce, Richard Einhorn, Patricia van Ness, and Sid Corbett. Annette Kreutziger-Herr, *Ein Traum Vom Mittelalter, Die Wiederentdeckung mittelalterlicher Musik in der Neuzeit* (Köln: Böhlau Verlag, 2003), 214. Other comparisons have included Tarik O'Regan's references to Machaut. Rick Anderson, "Review: Tarik O'Regan: Guillaume De Machaut: Gavin Bryars," *MLA* 66, no. 2 (2009): 393.

10. Ironically, in the course of his commentary Schwartz expresses his skepticism about the viability of classifying Pärt in this manner. Schwartz, *Minimalists*, 217; Josiah Fisk, "The New Simplicity: The Music of Gorecki, Tavener and Pärt," *Hudson Review* 47 (1994): 394–412.

11. Hillier, *Arvo Pärt*, 13.

12. In a catty article from 2009, for example, Toronyi-Lalic from the *Sunday Telegraph* writes, "Ask a twenty something to name a classical composer and they will give you Arvo Pärt, Glass or Ludovico Einaudi…minimalists were asking their Western listeners to ignore the fundamental acoustical premise of the past 500 years. The medieval idea of stasis was to supplant the renaissance aim of direction and purpose." In 2012, Benjamin Skipp sets out to demonstrate how Pärt's minimalism does, or does not, correspond with received notions of modernism and postmodernism. Igor Toronyi-Lalic, " 'Outcasts' Come in from the Cold; Minimalists Finally Take Centre Stage at the Proms," *The Sunday Telegraph*, August 9, 2009; Benjamin Skipp, "The Minimalism of Arvo Pärt: An 'Antidote' to Modernism and Multiplicity," in *The Cambridge Companion to Arvo Pärt*, ed. Andrew Shenton (Cambridge: Cambridge University Press, 2012). In his interview with Restagno, Pärt states, "I cannot believe, as some of the critics do however, that I belong to a category of "sacred minimalism." This subject is really not worth talking about," in *Arvo Pärt in Conversation*, Enzo Restagno, Saale Kareda, Leopold Brauneiss & Arvo Pärt, eds., (Champaign, IL: Dalkey Archive Press, 2012), 57.

13. Homi Bhabha, *The Location of Culture* (London: Routledge, 1994), 4, 7; "The Third Space: Interview with Homi Babha," in *Identity, Community, Culture, Difference*, ed. J. Rutherford (London: Lawrence & Wishart, 1990), 209, 11.

14. For issues of asynchrony, see Erin Felicia Labbie on pop medievalism and the issue of temporality in the history of Christianity, *Studies in Medievalism XXIV, Medievalism on the Margins*, ed. Karl Fugelso. New York and London: Boydell & Brewer (2015): 21–30; see also William C. Calin, "Christianity," in *Medievalism: Key Critical Terms*, ed. Elizabeth Emery and Richard Utz (Rochester, NY: Brewer, 2014) 35–42; Gwendolyn Morgan, "Authority," ibid., 27–34; Nils Holger Peterson, "Resonance," ibid., 215–222; Stephanie Trigg, "Medievalism and Theories of Temporality," in *The Cambridge Companion to Medievalism*, ed. Louise D'Arcens (Cambridge: Cambridge University Press, 2016), 196–209; Helen Dell, "Musical Medievalism and the Harmony of the Spheres," ibid., 60–74; Carolyn Dinshaw, *How Soon Is Now?: Medieval Texts, Amateur Readers, and the Queerness of Time* (Durham, NC: Duke University Press, 2012).

15. Pärt's wife Nora has gone one step further and noted that from the perspective of the liturgical music tradition, his music should be viewed as secular. Restagno and Pärt, "Arvo Pärt in Conversation," 57–58.

16. Jeffers Engelhardt, *Singing the Right Way: Orthodox Christians and Secular Enchantment in Estonia* (New York: Oxford University Press, 2014), 4–5.

17. For example, the British novelist Adam Thorpe uses Pärt as a cultural protagonist in his 2007 novel, *Between Each Breath*. The young composer draws a parallel between Pärt's ingenuity at setting the text of *Miserere* and the marvels of engineering a medieval wall in the old city. Peter Reynolds, "Tallin: Estonian Music Days," *Tempo* 62, no. 246 (2008) 53–54; Adam Thorpe, *Between Each Breath* (London: Vintage 2007), 11.

18. Adrian Bridge, "A Town of Many Talents; Adrian Bridge Watches Tallin Pick Up the Baton as a European Capital of Culture and, Right, Previews the Year Ahead in Turku," *The Daily Telegraph*, January 8, 2011; Guy P. Marchal, "Introduction," in *The Uses of the Middle Ages in Modern European States*, ed. R. J. W. Evans and Guy P. Marchal (Basingstoke: Palgrave Macmillan, 2011), 2.

19. Hermann Conen, "The Lenten Time of Music: On the Music of Arvo Pärt," *Miserere*, ECM Records 1430, 1991.

20. Andrew Shenton, *Arvo Pärt's Resonant Texts: Choral and Organ Music 1956–2015* (Cambridge: Cambridge University Press, 2017), 33, 35.

21. Hillier, *Arvo Pärt*, 74.

22. Restagno confirms Pärt's recollection of Jeppesen's *Kontrapunkt: Lehrbuch der klassischen Vokalpolyphonie* (Leipzig: Breitkopf & Härtel, 1935) as well as his counterpoint book entitled *Der Palestrinastil und die Dissonanz* (Lipzig [sic]: Breitkopf & Härtel, 1925). Restagno and Pärt, "Arvo Pärt in Conversation," 12n6, 28–29. Pärt also recalls his first exposure to plainchant in the 2002 Supin film. Dorian Supin, *Arvo Pärt: 24 Preludes for a Fugue* (Estonia, 2002), film. Pärt also discusses this in the 2016 Dorian Supin documentary *Even If I Lose Everything*.

23. Pärt has confirmed Restagno's explanation, adding that "teachers of music history—were more vulnerable to the system and had to suffer a great deal for their convictions." Restagno and Pärt, "Arvo Pärt in Conversation," 11, 13.

24. Kevin Karnes, "Forgotten Sounds, Unheard Sound: Tintinnabuli and the 1970s Soviet Underground," (unpublished manuscript, 2017).

25. The name *tintinnabuli* itself has symbolic resonance, since the term refers to the sound of small bells, with its associations to early Christian Europe. Hillier locates its onomatopoeic origin in the seventh-century writings of St. Isidore of Seville. He also notes that the word is to be distinguished from *campana*, which refers to larger and deeper sounding bells originating from the Italian peninsula. See Hillier, *Arvo Pärt*, 19.

26. Despite the simplicity of Pärt's technique, it yields remarkable potential for permutation diversity and compositional control. See Thomas Robinson, "Analyzing Pärt," in *The Cambridge Companion to Arvo Pärt*, ed. Andrew Shenton (Cambridge: Cambridge University Press, 2012), 93–100.

27. Hillier, *Arvo Pärt*, 74.

28. Shenton, *Arvo Pärt's Resonant Texts*, 32; Jamie McCarthy, "An Interview with Arvo Pärt," *Musical Times* 130, no. 1753 (1989): 59; Hillier, 78ff; Enzo Restagno, ed. *Arvo Pärt in Conversation* (Champaign, IL: Dalkey Archive Press, 2012), 33.

29. Pärt also mentions Mozart and Schubert. This is an echo of his statement printed in the liner notes of the 2011 Hortus Musicus recording. Jordi Savall, "A Conversation with Arvo Pärt," in *Music & Literature No. 1: Pärt, Selby, Marcom*, ed. Taylor Davis-Van Atta (Music & Literature, 2012), 8.

30. In contrast to his musical judgments, Pärt draws a strong differentiation in the visual arts between the Renaissance and the Middle Ages, saying that in contrast to the earlier period, the Renaissance was "imbued with a strong sense of day to day realism." Pärt mentions that Mustonen shared his views in this regard. Restagno and Pärt, "Arvo Pärt in Conversation," 35–36.

31. Alexander Lingas proposes four areas of congruence between Pärt's music and early Christian chant: tonal systems and modality (a preference for minor modes, use of Phrygian scales with or without augmented seconds), the T voice and its functional role as an ison, its logogenic strategies, and his "eschewing" of large-scale goal-directed tonal structures. Leopold Brauneiss, "Arvo Pärt's Tintinnabuli Style: Contemporary Music towards a New Middle Ages?," *Postmodern Medievalisms* XIII (2005): 31; Paul Hillier and Tõnu Tormis, "On Pärt," in *On Pärt* (Copenhagen: Theatre of Voices Edition, 2005), 51; Alexander Lingas, "Christian Liturgical Chant and the Musical Reorientation of Arvo Pärt" (unpublished manuscript, 2017); Restagno and Pärt, "Arvo Pärt in Conversation," 33.

32. Peter C. Bouteneff, *Arvo Pärt: Out of Silence* (Yonkers, NY: St. Vladimer's Seminary, 2015), 70–84.

33. In this context, Brauneiss also mentions another controlling parameter: that all voices of a tintinnabuli work are derived from a basic melodic line. Brauneiss, "Arvo Pärt's Tintinnabuli Style," 31–32.

34. Hillier, *Arvo Pärt*, x; Bouteneff, *Arvo Pärt: Out of Silence*, 57.

35. Shenton creates a dividing line at 1997 between music before that employs pre-Bach musical models and music afterward that turns more thoroughly toward Bach and other influences. Shenton, *Arvo Pärt's Resonant Texts*, 201. For a fuller analysis of these works, see ibid.; Hillier and Tormis, *On Pärt*, 60.

36. Jonathan Cross, "Review: Beatus Petronius, for Two Choirs & Two Organs: Statuit Ei Dominus, for Two Choirs & Two Organs by Arvo Pärt," *Music & Letters* 73, no. 2 (1992): 343; Alex Ross, "Consolations: The Uncanny Voice of Arvo Pärt," *The New Yorker*, December 2, 2002.

37. The ensemble is scored for oboe, C clarinet, bass clarinet, C trumpet, trombone, electric guitar, electric bass, percussion, and organ (revised in 1992).

38. These include features such as semitone and augmented-second dissonances, rhythmic embellishments, and echo effects. For complete analyses, see David Clarke, "Parting Glances: Aesthetic Solace or Act of Complicity? David Clarke Reassesses the Music of Arvo Part," *The Musical Times* (1993): 680–682; Hillier, *Arvo Pärt*, 151–162; Shenton, *Arvo Pärt's Resonant Texts*, 145–151; Thomas Holm, "Analysis and Comparison of Three

Major Vocal/Instrumental Works of Arvo Pärt" (DMA thesis, University of Illinois at Urbana–Champaign, 1998), 24–46.

39. Karnes makes this important distinction in his analysis of the temporal distinctions between parts in *Tabula rasa* (1977). Enzo Restago draws a parallel between the ambiguity in the instrumentation at the beginning of Verse 5 ("Quondiam")—he notes that it is difficult to determine whether the soloist really is a human voice—and the ambiguities created by medieval tenor lines given over to instruments. Jeffers Engelhardt, "Perspectives on Arvo Pärt after 1980," in *The Cambridge Companion to Arvo Pärt*, ed. Andrew Shenton (Cambridge: Cambridge University Press, 2012), 39; Hedi Rosma, Kristina Kõrver, and Kai Kutman, eds., *In Principio: The Word in Arvo Pärt's Music* (Laulasmaa: Arvo Pärt Centre, 2014); Restagno and Pärt, "Arvo Pärt in Conversation," 73.

40. Hillier, *Arvo Pärt*, 154.

41. Restagno and Pärt, "Arvo Pärt in Conversation," 72.

42. Shenton, *Arvo Pärt's Resonant Texts*, 151.

43. Restagno and Pärt, "Arvo Pärt in Conversation," 73.

44. This passage is modeled after one in *Calix*, from 1976, which was subsequently removed from Pärt's authorized works. Pärt recalls that originally he wanted to call the earlier work *Dies irae*, but religious titles were forbidden during that period by the Soviet authorities. Ibid., 70.

45. Additionally, Karnes takes issue with Benjamin Skipp's proposal that Pärt is strongly resistant to technology in the creative process. Karnes proposes instead that the mensuration canons (and for that matter the rest of the tintinnabuli strategy) reflect a predisposition toward additive processes, one that often accompanies the working methods via electronic means of composers such as Steve Reich. Benjamin Skipp, "Out of Place in the 20th Century: Thoughts on Arvo Pärt's Tintinnabuli Style," *Tempo* 63, no. 249 (2009): 4; Karnes, *Arvo Pärt's Tabula rasa*.

46. Although the group was founded in the 1970s to explore the music of the European Christian tradition, Mustonen's interests have broadened significantly and now include Indian, Arab, and Jewish traditional music. Mustonen was an important presence in Pärt's Estonian circle. Nora relates the moment that they left for the West: "There was no time for nostalgia or emotions, we had to leave. All our friends came to us in the flat and Andres Mustonen came with his whole orchestra. Then we opened all the doors and the whole stairwell was full of music and tears." Restagno and Pärt, "Arvo Pärt in Conversation," 46.

47. Pärt remembers that they did not have the musicians to perform Perotin. Ibid., 34. See also Immo Mihkelson, "A Narrow Path to the Truth: Arvo Pärt and the 1960s and 1970s in Soviet Estonia," in *The Cambridge Companion to Arvo Pärt*, ed. Andrew Shenton (Cambridge: Cambridge University Press, 2012), 27; Karnes, *Arvo Pärt's Tabula rasa*, 46–47.

48. Restagno and Pärt, "Arvo Pärt in Conversation," 32.

49. The Centre downplays the fact that Hortus Musicus performed nearly the same program two days before at the University of Tartu on October 25, because the composer was not present. Immo Mihkelsen, "The Cradle of Tintinnabuli—40 Years since a Historic Concert," Arvo Pärt Centre.

50. The recording was designed for and dedicated to the memory of Helle Mustonen, founding member of the group, soprano, and Andres's wife, who had died in 2005. It contains works by Alexander Knaifel, Erkki-Sven Tüür, Peeter Vähl, Valentin Silverstrov, and Giya

Kancheli. Hortus Musicus, *Early Music of the 3rd Millenium (Erp 4611)* (Tallin, Estonia: Estonian Record Productions, 2011).

51. Restagno, *Arvo Pärt in Conversation*, 49, 51.

52. This includes *An den Wassern zu Babel, De Profundis, Summa, Stabat Mater* (ECM 1325), *Passio* (Arthaus Musik 100 248; ECM 1370), *Da pacem Domine* (ECM 1930) *Miserere*, *Sarah Was Ninety Years Old* (ECM 1430), and *Litany* (ECM 1592).

53. Andrew Shenton, "Performing Pärt," in *Arvo Pärt's White Light: Media, Culture, Politics*, ed. Laura Dolp (Cambridge: Cambridge University Press, 2017), 236–240.

54. Restagno and Pärt, "Arvo Pärt in Conversation," 67, 77, 52.

55. Hillier, *Arvo Pärt*, vii.

56. Ibid., ix, 2.

57. Hillier and Tormis, *On Pärt*, 57–59.

58. Paul Hillier, "Observations on the Performance of Arvo Pärt's Choral Music," in *Arvo Pärt Collected Choral Works* (Universal Edition, 1999), 7, 55; Kay Kaufman Shelemay, "Toward an Ethnomusicology of the Early Music Movement: Thoughts on Bridging Disciplines and Musical Worlds," *Ethnomusicology* 45, no. 1 (2001).

59. Peter Burkholder and Andrew Burke in particular have written about the natural alignments between early and contemporary music in this regard. See also Mark Gotham, "Coherence in Concert Programming: A View from the U.K.," *International Review of the Aesthetics and Sociology of Music* 45, no. 2 (2014): 299–300.

60. Restagno and Pärt, "Arvo Pärt in Conversation," 52.

61. Dolp, "Arvo Pärt in the Marketplace," 184–186; Yri also examines the visual aspects of the CD packaging of Pärt's music in "Medieval Uncloistered," 220–223.

62. This precedence extends also to the musical interpretation. The importance of authorized recordings as influential texts is taken up by Andrew Shenton, who argues that is also necessary to trace the impact full circle, with the recording as a text that reflectively shapes live music making. Shenton, *Arvo Pärt's Resonant Texts: Choral and Organ Music 1956–2015*, 184–187.

63. Wolfgang Sandner, "[Liner Notes]," *Tabula rasa*, ECM New Series 1275, 1984.

64. Wilfred Mellers, "Longing for Home," *Arbos*, ECM Records 1325, 1987.

65. Christopher Page describes this as "cathedralism." Peter Hamm, "Ablganz Der Ewigkeit: Notizen Zu Kompositionen Von Arvo Pärt," *Arbos*, 1987; Christopher Page, *Discarding Images* (Oxford: Clarendon Press, 1993), 1–42.

66. Conen, "The Lenten Time of Music."

67. "Ideal" counterpoint is capable of creating ideal relations in every place and every thing," and it does so "in voluntary poverty." Jurg Stenzl, "Misterioso—Near and Far Away," *Misterioso*, ECM Records 1959, 2006, 19.

68. Tyran Grillo, review, "Arvo Pärt: *Miserere* (ECM New Series 1430)," ECM Records, https:// ecmreviews.com/2010/07/23/miserere/.

69. "A scale is suddenly no longer something to be taken for granted, it becomes a conscious experience of climbing and falling," Andreas Peer Kähler, "Arvo Pärt: About the Music," Universal Edition, http://www.universaledition.com/composers-and-works/Arvo-Paert/composer/534/aboutmusic.

70. Clarke, "Parting Glances," 680–683.

71. Skipp reminds us that these values are tautological with music; identifying unity in a work legitimates it, because only estimable works within the canon validate the notion of unity. Skipp, "Out of Place in the 20th Century," 4, 6.

72. Pärt speaks of this impulse to regain a sense of sacredness from a previous age with Restagno: "With Andrew Mustonen we tried to win back this part that has been lost in modern music, and that is exactly why we dedicated ourselves to old music, getting to know it, playing it," Restagno and Pärt, "Arvo Pärt in Conversation," 36.

73. Shenton borrows this term from the work of Timotheus Vermeulen and Robin van den Akker. Shenton, *Arvo Pärt's Resonant Texts*, 280–284.

74. Brauneiss, "Arvo Pärt's Tintinnabuli Style." See also Oliver Kautny, *Arvo Pärt Zwischen Ost Und West: Rezeptionsgeschichte* (Stuttgart: Metzler, 2002); "'Dem Himmel Ein Stück Näher…' Der Neoromantische Mythos 'Arvo Pärt,'" *Neue Zeitschrift für Musik* 5 (2002); and Kirsten Yri, "Medieval Uncloistered: Uses of Medieval Music in Late Twentieth Century Culture" (PhD diss., Stony Brook University, 2004), whose fifth chapter analyzes Pärt's medievalism and modernism.

75. Brauneiss, "Arvo Pärt's Tintinnabuli Style," 27, 28, 33.

76. Ibid., 34.

77. Brauneiss examines three aspects of Pärt's music that run parallel to these formulations: first, how scales form both melodic minimum and maximum; second, the way that sound and line form fundamental musical opposites in the tintinnabuli style; and third, how elementary opposites like stasis and movement, silence and sound, and time and timelessness, coincide. "The Unification of Opposites: The Tintinnabuli Style in the Light of the Philosophy of Nicolaus Cusanus," in *Music & Literature No. 1: Pärt, Selby, Marcom*, ed. Taylor Davis-Van Atta (Music & Literature, 2012), 55–56.

78. The rereleased CD is accompanied by a facsimile, study scores, and other materials. Paul Griffiths, "Now, and Then," *Tabula rasa*, ECM Records/Universal Edition AG, ECM Records, 2010.

79. See Sandner, "[Liner Notes]," *Tabula rasa*; Dolp, "Arvo Pärt in the Marketplace."

80. Hillier, *Arvo Pärt*, 3–5.

81. Ibid., 6–10.

82. Shenton, *Arvo Pärt's Resonant Texts*, 93–94, 100.

83. For a recent analysis of its varied associations with empathy and an analysis of an increasing number of film composers task with writing "Pärtian" music, see Maria Cizmic, "Empathy and Tintinnabuli Music in Film," in *Arvo Pärt's White Light: Media, Culture, Politics*, ed. Laura Dolp (Cambridge: Cambridge University Press, 2017), 20–46; and Robert Sholl, "Pärt and the Sound of One-Hand Clapping," ibid, 47–73.

84. The soundtrack for *Mia Madre* includes *Tabula rasa*, *Sarah Was Ninety Years Old*, *Für Alina*, *Pari Intervallo*, *Cantus in Memoriam Benjamin Britten*, *Festina Lente*, and *Silouans Song*.

85. "Todo Cambia" by Julio Numhauser.

86. Ivan Hewett, "Why the Hilliards Are Going Out with a Bang," *The Daily Telegraph*, May 23, 2013; Michael Church, "The Long Goodbye; after 40 Years Together, the Hilliard Ensemble Are About to Sing Their Last," *The Independent*, November 2, 2014.

87. The central place of Pärt in the life of the ensemble is reinforced in the 2017 video introducing Kaljuste's predecessor, Kaspars Putniņš, which features him conducting Pärt's music.

88. Chris Costello, the creator of the Papyrus typeface in 1982, has said that he was thinking about the Middle East and "biblical" times while he was developing it and that he thinks it works "just fine for yoga studios, stores selling craft arts, New Age stores, and in Christian contexts." John Brownlee, "Meet the Man Who Created Papyrus, the

World's (Other) Most Hated Font," http://www.fastcodesign.com/3055865/meet-the-man-who-created-papyrus-the-worlds-other-most-hated-font.

89. The term holy minimalism came into its own in the English-speaking press in the context of a review of Gorecki's Third Symphony, which had enjoyed record-breaking success after its 1992 release on the Elektra imprint of Nonesuch Records featuring Dawn Upshaw and London Sinfonietta, David Zinman conducting. "Is there a useful pigeon hole to hand? Holy Minimalism. Who else writes Holy Minimalist music?: John Tavener, the Greek orthodox British composer; Arvo Part [sic], the Estonian composer; and Giya Kancheli, the Georgian symphonist." This was repeated little over a month later in the *Times* in the same context. "Pass Notes No 52: Henryk Gorecki," *The Guardian*, December 22, 1992; Nicolas Soames, "Man from Katowice Heads Up the Charts," *The Times*, February 12, 1993. More recently, see Larry Rohter, "The Musical Diplomat; Recalling the Composer Who Brought Sounds of East to Music of West," *The International Herald Tribune*, November 8, 2011.

90. Zachary Woolfe, "'Classical Music' the Listings: [Schedules]," *The New York Times*, November 8, 2013; Paul Driver, "Estonian Rhapsody," *The Sunday Times*, May 6, 2013. Other overt medieval references have included comment by a Massachusetts journalist that the "repeated figurations in *Summa* described as suggesting 'a dirge in a cathedral.'" Andrew L. Pincus, "Performing Artists in Residence: Fine Music for a Sunday Afternoon," *The Berkshire Eagle*, November 18, 2013.

91. David Hawley, "Orchestra Taking Religious Composers to Church," *St. Paul Pioneer Press*, November 8, 2007; Martin Adams, "Pieces of Pärt," *The Irish Times*, February 9, 2008; Kevin Bazzana, "Sacred Music by Mozart for Finale," *Times Colonist*, June 2, 2011; Tom Budlong, "Arvo Pärt St. John Passion," *Library Journal*, October 1, 2011; Kevin Bazzana, "Festival Features Two Masterpieces," *Times Colonist*, May 15, 2014; Peter Jacobi, "Pro Arte Nails Score That Calms and Stuns the Listener," *Herald-Times*, April 26, 2011; Valerie Hill, "Choirs Unite for a Weekend of Music; Estonia Composer Arvo Pärt's 80 Birthday Celebrated with a Pair of Concerts," *Waterloo Region Record*, November 19, 2015; Andy Cronshaw, "Arvo Pärt: Manchester Camerata and Vox Clamantis at the Bridgewater Hall for Mif15 Review," *Manchester Evening News*, July 17, 2015; David Kettle, "Classical Review: Rsno/Kristjan Järvi/Anoushka Shankar, Edinburgh," *The Scotsman*, April 14, 2014; Adam Sweeting, "Sax in the Middle Ages," *The Daily Telegraph*, May 19, 2011.

92. Bain argues that New Agers make the monistic assumption that the self itself is sacred…and these assumptions of self-spirituality ensure that the New Age Movement is far from being a mish-mash, significantly eclectic, or fundamentally incoherent. Jennifer Bain, *Hildegard of Bingen and Musical Reception: The Modern Revival of a Medieval Composer* (Cambridge: Cambridge University Press, 2015), 12, 15.

93. These include "Chant" (Angel Records, 1994) by the Benedictine monks of Santo Domingo de Silos and "Chant Cistercien" (Harmonia Mundi, 1999) by Ensemble Organum and Marcel Pérès, Katherine Bergeron, "The Virtual Sacred," *The New Republic* (1995): 29–30, 33–34. Bergeron traces these contemporary allusions to the activity of the monks at Solesmes that developed the current conventions of chant performance practice.

94. *Chicago Tribune*, "Next Perhaps: 'The Best of Gregorian Rappers,'" news release, January 11, 1994.

95. Quoted in Bouteneff, *Arvo Pärt: Out of Silence*, 47.

96. Restagno and Pärt, "Arvo Pärt in Conversation," 62.

97. Engelhardt, "Arvo Pärt and the Idea of a Christian Europe," 224–225.

98. Robert Wilson, stage direction, set design, and lighting concept; Tõnu Kaljuste, music director and conductor; Estonian Philharmonic Chamber Choir and Tallin Chamber Orchestra; Andy Sommer, director; Paul Smaczny, producer. The premiere took place in the Noblessner Foundry in Tallin in May and was released afterward as a DVD, produced by Accentus Music.

99. Joseph Cermatori, "Short Reviews: Arvo Pärt & Robert Wilson: Adam's Passion (DVD)," *Performing Arts Journal* 115 (2017): 119.

100. Toomas Siitan, "The Silence of Adam," in *Adam's Passion: Music by Arvo Pärt; Stage Direction, Set Design and Lighting Concept by Robert Wilson* (Leipzig: Accentus Music, 2015).

101. For example, the Woman registers the shift to the winds at rehearsal 21.16, between verses VII and VIII; or again at rehearsal 31.7 in reaction to the tutti entrance during the second interlude.

102. For more on this topic, see Engelhardt, "Arvo Pärt and the Idea of a Christian Europe."

....

CHAPTER 17

THE POSTMODERN
TROUBADOUR

....

ANNE STONE

Two Troubadour Operas

....

THE scene (Figure 17.1): a nocturnal encounter in a garden between a man and a woman. They are observed by another woman who rests her hand on the foliage that hides her from their sight. The emotion of the scene is communicated both in gestures (his raised arm pointing toward a castle in the background, her hands clutching his) and in words; the caption reads "The dawn! the dawn! its brightness augurs ill, Its roseate gleam is death, for we must part."

The print abounds in visual cues of Pre-Raphaelite medievalist style. The earnest emotionalism of the faces and the gestural positions of the bodies are clearly of the nineteenth century. But a massive medievalish castle dominates the background, and the clothing is exotic, flowing, vaguely medieval though not philologically correct. The man's breeches seem to date to the eighteenth century and his coat's puffy sleeves recall the sixteenth-century Florentine aristocracy. His low-heeled shoes are tied with ribbons. The woman's sleeveless, flowing, floor-length gown seems timeless. Thus it is unsurprising that this print, which appeared in the July 19, 1886, issue of the weekly London magazine *The Graphic*, represents a scene from an opera called *The Troubadour* by Alexander Mackenzie, which premiered on June 8 of that year, and the scene depicted is the parting at dawn of the troubadour from his love, the lady of the castle.[1] The trope of lovers parting at dawn of course evokes the *alba*, a staple genre of troubadour lyric.

The fanciful depiction of the troubadour in the print is curiously at odds with the scholarly credentials of the opera's librettist, Francis Hueffer (1845–1889), a German-born romance philologist whose PhD thesis from Göttingen was a biography and critical edition of the works of the troubadour Guillem de Cabestaing.[2] Hueffer moved to London in 1869 and worked as a musicologist and music critic, served as editor of the Master Musician series, and wrote several books in English, including a biography of Wagner

Act III. *Guillem and Margarida.* GUILLEM:—"The dawn! the dawn! its brightness augurs ill,
Its roseate gleam is death, for we must part."

SCENE FROM MR. MACKENZIE'S NEW OPERA, "THE TROUBADOUR"

FIGURE 17.1 Print depiction of *The Troubadour* by MacKenzie and Hueffer, *The Graphic*, July 19, 1886, © Illustrated London News Ltd/Mary Evans.

and a book about the troubadours. He moved in Pre-Raphaelite social circles: His wife, Catherine Madox Brown, was an artist and model, the daughter of Ford Madox Brown, and their son was the novelist Ford Madox Ford, whose lifelong love of Provence often worked its way into his writing.

In the preface to his English-language book on the troubadours published in 1878, Hueffer firmly established his scholarly credentials in contradistinction to other approaches to the troubadours:

> [The book] claims to be the first continuous and at all adequate account in the English language of the literary epoch which forms its subject. For I cannot concede that name to a book on "The Troubadours, their Loves and Lyrics," published some years ago.[3]

The book from which the concession was withheld, published only five years prior by John Rutherford, indulged in too much romanticizing for the philologist Hueffer, and his critique pointed to a tension in the nineteenth-century medievalist world that Richard Utz has recently described as the "philologization" of medieval studies.[4] According to Utz, interest in premodern texts and artifacts began as a largely amateur activity in the eighteenth century, but slowly professionalized so that by the 1880s there was a "demand for trained full-time specialists" in philology. Thus the figure of the troubadour meant different things to different people, caught between the romanticizing gaze of the amateur and the scientific dissection of the scholar. Hueffer's book on the troubadours, clearly in the latter category, was both encyclopedic and technical, providing a history of the Occitan language, an assessment of the social context of the troubadours, a chapter on each of the lyric forms, and a chapter on the narrative poetry, biographies of the most important troubadours, and an extended study of the technical aspects of their poetic structures. Word-for-word translations of selected texts in an appendix attempted to offer a scientific rather than poetic approach toward rendering the texts in English.

Yet despite Hueffer's supercilious attitude toward Rutherford, he did not apply the same standards of scholarly rigor to his own operatic libretto, based on the grisly story of Guillem de Cabestaing. This was the subject of his thesis and therefore a story to which he had the privileged access of a scholar, but which in his hands conformed more to expectations of nineteenth-century romantic medievalist nostalgia than to philological accuracy. Like that of many troubadours, Guillem's music circulated in some manuscripts with a short prose biography, a *razo*, purporting to describe the circumstances that prompted the composition of a given song.[5] According to his *razo*, Guillem was seduced by the wife of his patron, Raimon de Roussillion. When Raimon discovered the affair, he killed the troubadour, cut out his heart, and served it to his wife for dinner. Upon learning what she had eaten, she jumped off a balcony to her death.

Hueffer's libretto is structured around tableau-like pseudomedieval events, none of which is present in the original story and, that gesture toward a variety of historical pastimes: "The Vintage" and "The Masque" organize the first act, "The Hunt" takes up the second act, and "The Feast" the third. Hueffer takes liberties with the story to heighten its romantic appeal. In the *razo*, the wife of count Raimon of Roussillion seduces the troubadour, while in *The Troubadour*, the wife follows Victorian decorum and has already known and been in love with the troubadour Guillem before her marriage to Raimon, so that her infidelity is less morally problematic. Hueffer also invents the scene representing the alba depicted in the print in Figure 17.1, in an act of what might be called philological fiction, drawing on his knowledge of troubadour poetic forms. Its text bears a passing resemblance to the anonymous alba that Hueffer uses as an example in his book, *En un vergier sotz fuelha d'albespi* (PC 461, 13), whose refrain he translates as "Ah God, ah God, the dawn! It comes too soon!"[6]

While what we might call the philological and fictional approaches to the troubadour were in tension with one another, they nevertheless were both founded on a shared certainty: that troubadours and their medieval society existed long ago, but were recoverable through philology and/or reimagination. The narrative presented in *The Troubadour* is straightforward and unproblematic, a seamless juxtaposition between contemporary mores and medievalish trappings. The opera does not worry about temporal distance, but confidently assumes that the characters' feelings and actions can be empathized with. The narrative foundation provided by the thirteenth-century *razo* is burnished by nineteenth-century sensibilities, not unlike the contemporaneous Pre-Raphaelite paintings of Dante Gabriel Rosetti and others in Hueffer's circle.

Troubadours have been part of Western literary and musical consciousness for eight centuries (according to the title of a recent book by John Haines), and Mackenzie and Hueffer's opera came at the end of a long run of operatic representations of troubadours in the long nineteenth century.[7] Whether these troubadours were entirely fictional (as in Verdi's *Il trovatore*) or adapted from medieval sources in a pseudophilological manner (like Weber's *Euryanthe* or Wagner's various neomedieval libretti, as well as Hueffer's adaptation), operatic troubadours played a central role in the nineteenth-century construction of the Middle Ages.[8] But the troubadour largely disappeared from the twentieth-century operatic stage, seemingly swept away with the antiromantic sentiment that dominated musical thought of most of the twentieth century.

Thus, it is intriguing that two of the most celebrated operas to have been composed since the beginning of the twenty-first century have turned again to troubadours to be their lead characters. Since its premiere in 2000, *L'amour de loin*, composed by Kaija Saariaho to a libretto by Amin Maalouf, has been performed at major opera houses across Europe, in Canada, and in the United States and won the composer the prestigious Grawemayer award. George Benjamin's *Written on Skin* premiered in 2012 in Aix-en-Provence and has since had runs at the Paris Opéra and Covent Garden, tours of Europe, and several performances in the United States. Both operas have received critical assessments verging on the hyperbolic ("one of the first operatic masterworks of our young century"[9]) and they seem likely to remain in the repertory.

Written on Skin is based on the same troubadour *razo* as that of Mackenzie and Hueffer, that of Guillem de Cabestaing, a coincidence that offers us the opportunity to ask what the figure of the operatic troubadour might tell us about our relationship with the Middle Ages at the present moment. That the relationship is no longer characterized by nostalgia for a lost age is apparent immediately on viewing the original set designed by Katie Mitchell for the premiere (see Figure 17.2). In contrast to *The Graphic*'s harmonious visual spectacle of the Pre-Raphaelite Middle Ages shown in Figure 17.1, *Written on Skin*'s stage is starkly divided into two realms differentiated by lighting and props to evoke two different temporalities, one seemingly modern and clinical, with stainless steel, glass, and bright artificial light, and the other vaguely medieval, with simple wood furniture, muted natural tones, and soft natural light. This vertiginous visual juxtaposition underscores an equally vertiginous atemporality that pervades the opera.

The opera's text by the modernist playwright Martin Crimp follows the contour of the original *razo* with striking precision, but makes a few crucial changes, not so much to the details of the story but rather to the way it is presented. In particular, Crimp's text thematizes mediality by calling on two tropes of representation—ekphrasis and palimpsest—whose pedigrees show that they are medievalist concepts themselves. That is, both palimpsest as a figure of history and ekphrasis as a figure of mediated representation are terms that gained currency since the nineteenth century precisely because of the authority lent them by their apparent links to the distant past.

Palimpsest originated as a technical term of philology, where it referred to a parchment whose writing has been erased and overwritten with new writing.[10] Because of the chemical nature of the inks used, however, the erased text is not entirely removed and it is possible, sometimes only with the aid of certain kinds of technology, to recover at least partially the erased text. Thus the palimpsest can be a crucial site of information, containing texts that are otherwise lost to history, like the famous Archimedes Palimpsest.[11] The palimpsest also offers a suggestive alternative metaphor of history to that of the line of time; it is layered, and the layers peek through, disrupting our sense of secure temporal orientation. The metaphor of the palimpsest has also become central to postmodern criticism with Gerard Genette's labeling of all textual relations palimpsests—that is, every text has some kind of relationship with prior texts, even just by virtue of using words that have been used previously.[12]

That the figure of the palimpsest is central to the opera can be surmised from its title, but the relation of the term to the opera goes considerably beyond this. Both the opera's language and its music, I suggest, encourage the reader and hearer to read and hear relationally, in Genette's term, so that the opera itself is not self-contained but radiates outward palimpsestuously to make connections to other artworks.[13] And often, as we shall see, those connections themselves wend their way to the Middle Ages through some route or other. Thus we understand the opera's narrative simultaneously as a story and as a story about how we make stories. The music is likewise permeated with gestures and moments that point elsewhere. Benjamin does not use overt quotation or pastiche of styles; nevertheless, his music's heterogeneity invites the listener to hear musical palimpsests.

Table 17.1 offers a summary of the opera's structure,[14] which is closely modeled on the longest of the surviving versions of Guillem de Cabestaing's story.[15]

FIGURE 17.2 Set by Katie Mitchell for *Written on Skin* by Benjamin and Crimp.

Table 17.1 Overview of opera *Written on Skin* by Benjamin and Crimp

Part 1

1 Chorus of Angels	2 Protector, Agnes, Boy	3 Chorus of Angels	4 Agnes and Boy	5 Protector and visitors	6 Agnes and Boy
	MINIATURE 1: An Act of Mercy				MINIATURE 2: A House in Winter
Scene setting: "cancel the flights at the international airports"	Protector commissions boy to write a book; he shows example of his work	"Stone the Jew…invent the world in seven days"	Woman's primary attraction to the boy: she commissions an illumina- tion that represents her	Woman's sister and her husband complain about the book's expense and the Boy's presence	Boy shows Woman the page she requested; love affair begins; Woman reveals her name: Agnes

Part 2

7 Angels	8 Protector, Agnes	9 Protector, Boy, Agnes, Angels	10 Agnes, Boy
Angels act as scandal- mongers, gossiping about affair in Protector's dream	Protector rebuffs sexual advances of Agnes; she tells him to "ask the Boy what I am"	Protector confronts Boy in the forest; Boy lies; Protector reports lie to Agnes	Agnes confronts Boy and tells him to "make me a new page" that documents their love

Part 3

11 Protector, Agnes, Boy	12 Protector, Agnes	13 Angels, Protector	14 Protector, Agnes	15 Boy
				MINIATURE 3: A Woman Falling
Boy shows completed book to Protector and Agnes; the page he prepared for Agnes is in words, not pictures	Protector reads the words of the secret page to Agnes	Angels create human emotions ("create a man…make him jealous") and urge Protector variously to be merciful and violent	Dinner scene; Agnes eats the heart and says "nothing will ever take the taste of that Boy's heart out of this body"	Boy describes how he has drawn the Woman's death

The story recounts a love triangle between a powerful lord, his wife, and a man who is invited by the lord to live in his household (scene 2). In the original *razo* the troubadour is identified by toponym, Guillem de Cabestaing, and by class, "the son of a poor knight," and his patron was Raimon de Roussillon, a name that exists in the historical record; both Capestang and Roussillion are towns that survive in modern-day France. In *Written on Skin*, though, the characters are all anonymized and become everyman-like: Lord Raimon is (ominously) the Protector, Guillem is the Boy (and is sung by a counter-tenor), and the wife is the Woman (until a dramatic moment where she reveals her name, Agnes, in scene 6). This is important to our consideration of the opera, because while thirteenth-century *razos* were full of historical names and places that gave the texts a kind of truth claim, an authority rooted in their purported reality, the opera seeks the opposite: to compromise the story's claim to specific historical truth by effacing the names of the characters. This substitution removes the historical truth value so central to the original and replaces it with a feeling of universality: the Woman is every woman or oppressed person; the Protector is every ruler or institution that wields absolute power. The universality of the characters, I argue, invites the reader to read them palimpsestuously, to connect them to other operatic and historical characters.

According to the *razo*, Raimon's wife becomes attracted to and initiates a love affair with Guillem (opera scenes 4 and 6) and, as a proper troubadour, he is inspired by his love for her to write songs whose texts are so suggestive that people start gossiping and Raimon becomes suspicious (opera scene 7). He confronts Guillem one day when they are out hunting alone, but Guillem lies, telling him that he is in love with his wife's sister (opera scene 8). When Raimon gleefully tells his wife that Guillem is having an affair with her sister, she "feels a heavy sorrow" and confronts the troubadour, who assures her that this was a lie for her benefit (scene 10). She commands him, however, "to compose a song in which he would show that he loved no other lady but her," which the *razo* identifies as "Lo douse cossire"); in the opera, Agnes commands the Boy to make an illuminated manuscript page.[16] When Raimon hears the song (sees the page), he realizes the truth (scene 12), summons the troubadour outside, cuts off his head, cuts his heart out of his body (scene 13), and has the heart roasted and served to his wife. Informed afterward of what she had eaten, she declares that it "had been so good and tasty that never again would anything eaten or drunk remove from her mouth the taste that Sir Guillem's heart had left there" (scene 14).[17] Raimon then tries to kill her with his sword but she jumps off a balcony first (scene 15). There follows in the *razo*—but not, significantly, in the opera—a lengthy description of retribution: The wife's kinsmen protest and Raimon is shunned and eventually imprisoned by the king of Aragon. The erasure of this last part of the story once again prevents us from locating the story in a fixed historical place and time.

Having dispensed with the kinsmen, barons, and king of Aragon, *Written on Skin* adds a framing world inhabited by angels, of whom three have singing roles, leaving the frame and entering the main story of the opera to sing the roles of the Boy, the Woman's sister, and the sister's husband. The angels are aware of historical time but they live in a world apart, entering the historical world by changing clothes and becoming characters. They reel off orders at a dizzying rate and with no sense of temporal order or, indeed, continuity. In the opera's opening, they bark out commands, seeming to prepare to go back in time to tell the story of the opera:

Scene 1 (entire)
Angels:
Strip the cities of brick, dismantle them. Strip out the wires, cover the land with grass. Force chrome and aluminum back into the earth. Cancel all flights from the international airport and people the sky with angels. **Erase** the Saturday car-park from the marketplace, **rub out** the white lines. Make each book, each new book a precious object written on skin. Make way for the wild primrose and slow torture of criminals. **Fade out** the living, snap back the dead to life. (my emphasis)

But "back in time" is not quite accurate; in this case the directions seem to have more to do with place than with time. The idea seems to be that if we remove the objects of modern life (brick, chrome, and aluminum) and put grass back, the distant past will appear. Some of the verbs, bolded in the example, reinforce a nontemporal relationship between present and past—"erase" and "rub out" conjure writing, suggesting that the present is a palimpsest written over the past, while "fade out" is a cinematic term, allowing the past to appear on the same screen as the present. The location of the opera's premiere, Aix-en-Provence, located in the territory of medieval Occitania, is here seemingly brought into the fabric of the opera, and in fact its authors have said that they chose the troubadour story for the commission because of the location of the premiere.[18] Thus, at its premiere the opera was not an "absolute" work, but a site-specific installation, a kind of art that Alexander Nagel has recently explored as having both medieval and modern resonances.[19] A self-conscious knowledge of its location permeates the opera, in repeated references to the natural world outside the confines of the stage house where the action takes place; "eglantine," "wild primroses," and also burning villages are described out the windows of the Protector's house.[20] When the angels order that the asphalt be stripped away and chrome and aluminum be forced back into the earth, and the parking lot be erased, we can understand them to mean right there, at the location of the opera house.[21]

But by the third scene the angels are on to more challenging tasks than tearing up parking lots, and on a larger temporal scale:

Angel 2: Stone the Jew, make him wear yellow.
Angel 3: Crusade against the Muslim: map out new territory with blood.
Angel 2: Invent the world. . .
Angel 3: . . . in seven days invent the whole world.
Angel 2: invent. . .
Angel 3: . . . in a single day. . .
Angel 2: . . . sun. . .
Angel 3: . . . moon, man. . .
Angel 2: Invent man and drown him.

Angel 3: Good.
Angel 2: Burn him alive.
Angel 3: Good.
Angel 2: Bulldoze him screaming into a pit.
Angel 3: Good.

"Stone the Jew / Make him wear yellow / crusade against the Muslim" are instructions that apply equally to the Middle Ages and today, as well as every moment in between. "Invent the world in seven days…invent a man..drown him…burn him…bulldoze him screaming into a pit" is a cheerily merciless instruction that covers the entire Christian history of mankind from Genesis to the Apocalypse. God seems at this moment like a chief executive officer too busy offstage to make an appearance; the angels are carrying out his instructions. Thus the hasty paraphrase of the beginning of Genesis ("And God saw that it was good") is shortened to a single "good" muttered in a distracted way by an overworked angel, a cog in the bureaucratic order. The ability of these angels to think about all time periods at once, and at myriad scales at once, makes us understand that the events of the story they happen to be telling at the moment are not located in historical time, even if it is rooted to a place.

Ekphrasis and Palimpsest

In one of the opera's most notable departures from the vida, the Guillem character, the Boy, is transformed from a troubadour (maker of songs) to a manuscript illuminator, a maker of books.[22] The song that reveals the wife's infidelity in the *razo* becomes in the opera a revelatory manuscript page. This change drives a central preoccupation of the opera: its thematizing of the book both as a material object and as a metaphor for narrative and for history. The title, *Written on Skin*, invokes the book's violence and its materiality: Books are the vehicles through which knowledge is transmitted, and ownership of books is ownership of attendant knowledge and power. But they are also sources of bodily violence, not just because they are written on the skin of a once-living animal, but because those who control history do so violently. The opera does not merely point to these ideas but embodies them: the opera is understood as having become the book that it is describing.

The book makes its first appearance in the second scene, in which the Protector hires the Boy to make a book about his life and his possessions. The Protector is a swaggering brute ("addicted to purity and to violence") who boasts about owning everything in sight (oak trees and peaches out the window, as well as "his wife's body"). The book is to show him and his family in paradise, but also should depict the end of the world: He requests a picture of the damned being "shoveled into ovens." Here is a textual moment that invites a palimpsestuous reading. Its rank brutality gives us pause, as does its transtemporality: Images of people being shoveled into ovens are common in medieval depictions of the Apocalypse, so the medieval character, the Protector, can be imagined to be thinking of one of those. But the twenty-first-century listener is more likely to imagine the widely reproduced image of the Apocalypse of Hieronymous Bosch from the fifteenth century, and almost certainly to think of the ovens of that twentieth-century Apocalypse, the Holocaust. Thus, the medieval character's words generate a rich series of palimpsests that are, paradoxically, temporally posterior to the medieval world that this character inhabits: It is future texts that are partially erased beneath the surface of "the damned shoveled into ovens." Moments like these once again confuse the temporal order and position the narrative as being in an atemporal zone.

In this second scene we are also introduced to the curious habit the opera's characters have of narrating their own speech and action, as when the Protector says, "And by day, says the Protector, fruit trees, blue heads of iris," and the Boy responds, "The book costs money, says the Boy." As others have noted, this gives the characters a mediated quality, preventing the audience from sliding into an easy "suspension of disbelief" relationship with them. But this device also mimics the way direct speech is handled in a book, and it invites us to imagine that instead of seeing the story in an opera, we are reading it in a book and the action on the stage is a projection of our imagined vision of the written text.

The original stage design as depicted in Figure 17.2 also participates in the opera's positioning itself as a book; the main story takes place in a middle rectangle, flanked by the modernist space of the angels, visually replicating an illuminated book, whose central writing block is generally ringed by a margin of paratextual material, whether illumination or commentary. The relationship to the book goes beyond the merely visual: Both margins (book and opera) are populated by inhabitants that are supernatural as well as paratextual, and both margins serve as commentaries on their central texts.

The substitutions of writing for song, and opera for book, draw our attention toward the role of mediation in storytelling and further resonate with other gestures that pervade the opera. Chief among these is the device of ekphrasis, for which the *Oxford English Dictionary* offers a double definition: originally "an explanation or a description of something, esp. as a rhetorical device;" now "a literary device in which a painting, sculpture, or other work of visual art is described in detail."[23] Ekphrasis is by definition intermedial—text describing art, words standing in for pictures. And as Valentine Cunningham explains, ekphrasis is also by nature intertextual: Famous descriptions such as Homer's shield of Achilles, revisited by Vergil and then again by W. H. Auden in "The Shield of Achilles," show that "from early to late, from the beginning to now . . . this kind of encounter, stories of this kind of encounter, keep happening, keep returning, keep being textually renewed."[24] Ekphrasis, in other words, calls attention both to intermediality and to intertextuality, or palimpsestuousness.

The use of ekphrasis and the thematizing of the palimpsest culminate in a dramatic reveal in the opera's last scene, in which the Woman, Agnes, kills herself by jumping off a balcony. Up to this point the story has been presented as drama: Characters sing their lines and move naturalistically on the stage. The last scene, however, during which Agnes jumps to her death, is not acted, but narrated by the Boy in his incarnation as Angel 1. It is narrated, moreover, at one remove, as the description of a painting of the action, or ekphrasis, rather than as the action itself. The Boy/Angel, talking directly to the audience, describes how he has rendered the woman's death as a manuscript illumination:

> This, says the boy, shows the Woman Falling: here, look, the man takes a knife but the woman's quicker, and jumps. See how her body has dropped from the balcony, how I pause her mid-fall at the exact centre of the page.[25]

The Boy's description of how he has depicted her death "on the page" has been set up by two earlier scenes in the opera, both of which, like this last scene, are identified in the score as "miniatures" and treated as ekphrastic asides in the narrative. In the first, in scene 2, the Boy shows the Protector a sample of his work, marked in the score as "Miniature 1: A Work of Mercy," describing both the material and the emotional content in detail:

> This, says the boy, shows a Work of Mercy: here look, three men all starving, two wheeling on this cart the third. And here's a rich man—see him?—in a red satin coat lined with green. In his face round his eyes see his expression as he offers the three sick men wine and bread: not just kind—explains the Boy—kind is too easy—but merciful. (scene 2, bars 151–188)

In the second, labeled "Miniature 2: A Woman in Winter," the Boy shows Agnes the page she has commissioned from him, describing how he has drawn a woman according to her specifications, again focusing both on details of color and form and on the emotion of the portrayed woman:

> This, says the Boy, shows a house in winter: here look white stars—Orion—and in this wide blank space, the moon. See how I've lifted the roof like a jewel-box lid. Inside's the woman—see her?—unable to sleep: buried in the hot white pillow her head feels heavy like stone. Round her legs round her arms I've buried a lead-white sheet like a living person and tightened her skin, darkened her veins with blood. (scene 6, bars 605–643)

When we arrive at the last scene, we thus are made to realize that the entire opera has been a product of the Boy's labors: He has depicted the story (including the parts where he describes the illuminated pages to the other characters) for another patron, outside the fiction of the opera, to whom he is talking in the last scene. At the very end of the scene, furthermore, he metafictionally refers to himself and the two other angels:

> As she drops from the house, three small angels—look—are watching her calmly from the margin. (scene 15, mm. 590–594)

He is describing, of course, the operatic stage on which the story has taken place, complete with "margin" that represents the Angels' realm. This final scene is crafted as a jarring interruption of the grisly dinner in which the Protector has compelled the Woman to eat the heart of her dead lover (mm. 478–end):

SCENE 14, mm. 478–end
Agnes: What has my husband. . .
Protector: His. . .
Agnes: . . . my Protector. . .
Protector: heart. . .
Agnes: given me to eat?
Protector: . . . Agnes.
Agnes: What heart?
Protector: His heart the Boy
Agnes: No.
Protector: His heart the Boy
Agnes: No. No nothing. . .
Protector: His heart his heart
Agnes: Nothing. . .
Protector: the Boy
Agnes: . . . you can do. . .
Protector: his heart
Agnes: Nothing I ever eat nothing I drink will ever, ever, ever take the taste of that boy's heart out of this body. No force you use nothing you forbid can take away the pictures that Boy's hands draw on thins skin. He can unfold the tight green bud, unwrap the tree, darken the wood, lighten the sky, blacken the dust with rain each mark he makes on me is good, each colour clear. Crush. Burn. Break. Tear. Put out my eyes. Hang. Drown Stone. Stab. Cut out my tongue. Nothing, nothing, not if you strip me to the bone with acid, will ever take the taste of that Boy's heart out of this mouth.
(SCENE 15)
Angel 1/Boy: This says the Boy shows the Woman Falling, here, look, the man takes a knife but the woman's quicker, and jumps . . .

In the join between these last two scenes we are wrenched, roller-coaster-like, from the middle of an operatic climax of cruelty, defiance, and cannibalism to the distanced position of listening to a description of the representation of its denouement—from drastic to gnostic on the turn of a dime. This enactment of the move from action to narration, or from event to its representation, reminds us of our role as receivers of the narration and reminds us that our empathy with the characters, encouraged in the dinner scene and denied in the ekphrasis of the final scene, is a manipulation of that narration. Furthermore, as Maria Ryan has pointed out, the move replicates within the opera the original troubadour story, the moment in the Middle Ages when they were written into manuscripts and became nostalgic "troubadour-figures."[26] Rather than relegate the troubadour to an irrecoverable historical moment and nostalgically invoke it, the opera exposes the fictionality of that sense of loss. It reminds us that history exists only in mediated forms and that media are palimpsestuous by nature, always referring to other representations, never fixed in meaning or temporality.

If the Boy/Angel 1 is narrating the illumination of Agnes's death to us, the audience of the opera, then the opera until that point must be retroactively understood to have been the book that he was writing and the other two miniatures as books within the book. If we think about this more closely, we find ourselves confronting a *mise en abyme*. What space is the angel occupying during this scene, whose voice do we understand his to be, and who is his addressee? In the piano–vocal score of the opera his character is named "Boy" in this final scene, while in the full score he is identified as "Angel 1;" in his soliloquy he identifies himself as "the Boy." Since the Boy is dead, one imagines that it is the Angel 1 character speaking. Yet he is Angel 1 still performing the Boy's character, describing a page that he has just painted (complete with three angels, one of which is presumably him), to a new client, a new Protector figure that the audience understands to be itself. Is the Angel at this moment an as-yet unnamed character in another opera, for which the opera we have just seen serves as a book within a book?

Martin Crimp has acknowledged that a source for his angel is Walter Benjamin's famous essay "Angelus Novus," the ninth of his "Theses on History" (1940).[27] Significantly, the text of this ninth thesis is itself an ekphrastic description, admittedly of a very particular sort, of the monoprint "Angelus Novus" by Paul Klee that Benjamin had purchased in 1922:

> A Klee painting named *Angelus Novus* shows an angel looking as though he is about to move away from something he is fixedly contemplating. His eyes are staring, his mouth is open, his wings are spread. This is how one pictures the angel of history. His face is turned toward the past. Where we perceive a chain of events, he sees one single catastrophe which keeps piling wreckage upon wreckage and hurls it in front of his feet. The angel would like to stay, awaken the dead, and make whole what has been smashed. But a storm is blowing from Paradise; it has got caught in his wings with such violence that the angel can no longer close them. The storm irresistibly propels him into the future to which his back is turned, while the pile of debris before him grows skyward. This storm is what we call progress.[28]

This has become one of the most cited of Benjamin's writings, in part because of the tragic circumstances it compels us to remember, its extraordinary provenance, and partly, perhaps, because these circumstances caused him to read the print in a very particular way, a kind of shocking, yet profoundly apt, misreading.[29] Benjamin's reading of the angel has another resonance for the opera beyond the character of the angel and the use of ekphrasis: His reading of "Angelus novus" presents an emblem of temporal confusion, with the angel facing backward as he is blown forward; the past, particularly its horrors, continues to generate the present.

By a coincidence that bears on this discussion, it has recently been discovered that Klee's print itself is a palimpsest. The artist R. H. Quaytman, who was commissioned to do an installation at the Tel Aviv Museum that now owns the Klee print, made this remarkable discovery as she was preparing to incorporate the print into her installation. She noticed, seemingly for the first time, that *Angelus Novus* was mounted onto another print, whose outline could just be seen in the margins. Two years of work allowed her to identify the image: It was a nineteenth-century print of a 1522 Cranach engraving depicting Martin Luther. This seems to be an example of almost magical replication, of life imitating art: The opera draws on Klee's *Angelus Novus*, as interpreted by Walter Benjamin, as the model for its angel character and twins it with the idea of history as palimpsest; unbeknownst to Benjamin, or to Crimp, the Klee model itself is a palimpsest, originating a web of associations between Klee's angel and the print of Martin Luther (itself, of course, a copy of an original centuries older) that have yet to be disentangled.

Musical Palimpsests

It is hard to talk about George Benjamin's music beyond using metaphors—"music of a miraculous liquid ease and brilliant sheen"—that describe his innovative orchestration.[30] I am struck by the allusive nature of his music for *Written on Skin*, by which I mean that his style allows itself to be heard referentially, and thus palimpsestuously. Benjamin himself described the heterogeneous nature of his music for opera: "it is theatre music, so you have to come up with different kinds of material for different situations, rather than trying always to have everything emerge as a smooth logical progression."[31] Perhaps the medieval topic of the opera's story encourages a hearing of this "different kinds of material" as allusive to the Middle Ages; to my ears, various twentieth-century understandings of what medieval sound was like seem to be refracted through his imagination. It is not always clear whether a certain sound one hears is a medieval sound that has been filtered through a modern lens or a modern sound that seems to refer back to the Middle Ages. For example, the prominent use of drones in the opera is potentially multivalent. Are these drones to be understood as referencing medieval music? Or do they reference the myriad other potential meanings of drones, which can signify the exotic, or the ecstatic, or the meditative? Or do they signify an allegiance to minimalist musical styles of the later twentieth century?

Furthermore, his music has the ability to change its relationship to the text it is setting depending on the context. At times, he employs what sound like traditional text-painting devices, setting the word "merciful" in scene 2 with a long Handelian melisma, for example.[32] At other times, the vocal lines are articulated with chant-like flatness, and at still others his singers are singing enormous leaping atonal melodies with passion.

Benjamin's pitch language is extremely heterogeneous and can contain triadic sonorities, prominent uses of the octatonic collection, fifths and fourths foregrounded, and chromatic saturation at various moments. I would like to focus on one striking use of triadicism that to my ears acts as a palimpsest. The moment occurs in a short passage in scene 2, just after the Boy has sung his description of the miniature "A Work of Mercy." The Woman is suspicious and asks a series of questions: "What does this Boy want? What does this thing this picture mean?" The Protector silences her with a peremptory statement: "His talent's clear. I'm satisfied. You will welcome him into our house," a passage set strikingly to a series of triadic sonorities played by the brass. These triads pop out of the surrounding atonal musical context and invite a reading of them as mimetic: brass triads sound authoritative, historic, and connected to masculine importance. But to my ears they invoke something more specific: Hunding's theme from act 1, scene 2, of *Die Walküre*, though without the martial rhythm (see Examples 17.1a and 17.1b).

Hunding's theme juxtaposes F minor with G major, a progression that contains a chromatic shift from Ab to G and C to B natural. Benjamin's progression starts and ends on the same harmonies, though with their modes swapped (F major to G minor), extending the progression into a six-chord triadic passage connected by parsimonious voice-leading. The musical connection is strengthened by a seeming reference to the beginning of *Die Walküre* in the text of the opening of *Written on Skin*'s scene 2. The Protector is describing his lands to the Boy in his opening soliloquy:

> Stand here. Look. My house is perfect. . . . I own the fields: I own everyone in them. Every beech, each visible oak is as much my property as my dog my millstream or my wife's body—her still and obedient body—is my property. (mm. 83–114)

This bears a notable resemblance to *Die Walküre*'s opening scene, when Siegmund, wounded and newly arrived at Sieglinde's house, asks Sieglinde who she is:

> Erfrischt ist der Mut, das Aug'erfreut des Sehens selige Lust
> Wer ist's, der so mir es labt?
>
> Refreshed is my heart, my eyes rejoice over the blessed joy of sight/
> Who is it that gladdens them so?

Sieglinde's reply is,

> Dies Haus und dies Weib sind Hunding's Eigen.
> This house and this wife are Hunding's property. (*Die Walküre*, scene 1)

Thus, rather than revealing her name, she refers to herself in the third person as a wife, a function, and equates her status as property with that of Hunding's house, all features of the presentation of the Woman in *Written on Skin*'s opening.[33]

This is not to suggest that this intertext is deliberate or to assert Wagner as the most significant intertext for Benjamin and Crimp, but rather to attempt to describe the easy way allusions enter the fabric of the composition. The brass chords universalize the figure of the brutish husband, uniting the Protector with Hunding and potentially many more threatening masculine figures, as well as the subservient wife. The palimpsest does not stop at Wagner, however, since Wagner's sources for the *Ring* were medieval; rather,

EXAMPLE 17.1A *Written on Skin*, scene 2, mm. 214–220.

EXAMPLE 17.1B Hunding's theme, *Die Walküre*, act 1, scene 2.

we glimpse beyond through the Wagnerian underlay a further partially effaced text, that of his medieval sources.[34]

Not all the palimpsestuous musical moments have specific sources; sometimes the music seems to allude to a soundscape rather than a composition. One striking example of this kind of allusion occurs in the last scene of the opera (scene 15, Third Miniature: The Woman Falling). This scene begins, as mentioned already, with the disembodied sound of the glass harmonica and viol, sustaining soft sonorities with little rhythmic articulation. As the Boy/Angel 1 sings his final descriptive monologue, an arresting sound begins to emerge from the orchestral texture (see Examples 17.2a and 17.2b): a discordant sonority played at first hesitantly, then more consistently in a kind of jagged ostinato, by a heterogeneous constellation of instruments (violin, viola, mandolin, brass, bass viol, three maracas, bongo, oboe).

This gives the effect of a very old and tired gear works suddenly coming to the fore—was it always there? It suggests, perhaps, the "strict mechanism of the world" (scene 2, m. 92) alluded to earlier in the text—the inexorable workings of nature. The transformation of the music's foreground from the languid and disarticulate sounds of the sustained glass harmonica to the metallic ostinato enacts a kind of change of consciousness, as if the listener is pulled away from the story by the incursion of reality or perhaps pulled away from rumination by the intrusion of present-day life. The repetition of the ostinato figure after the end of the Boy/Angel 1's speech is driven forward by a steady increase in dynamics so that its final iteration is marked *sffff*—a gesture that threatens to overwhelm the hearer, invoking, perhaps, Walter Benjamin's storm that "irresistibly propels [us] into the future."

I suggest that the sonority's particular timbre and its jagged repetition is a familiar sound from the British modernist tradition, specifically from that tradition's direct engagement with the Middle Ages. We hear something similar, for example, in Birtwistle's *O livoris feritas*, a setting of Machaut's Motet 9, the first movement of his *Machaut a ma maniere* (1988). In this setting, fragmentary quotations of the motet are juxtaposed with ostinato-like repetitions of syncopated rhythmic gestures in a heterogeneous instrumentation that juxtaposes strings, trumpets, and piccolos, a texture and timbre that recall the mechanical, creaky ostinato of *Written on Skin*'s end. This piece is only the most recent of Birtwistle's engagements with the music of Machaut; in 1982, he

EXAMPLE 17.2A *Written on Skin*, scene 15, mm. 596–563.

EXAMPLE 17.2B *Written on Skin*, final measures.

organized a Machaut-themed event at the BBC Proms, and still earlier, in 1969, he orchestrated Machaut's *Hoquetus David* for another heterogeneous ensemble including flute, clarinet, violin, cello, glockenspiel, and bells. Mark Delaere has noted a "striking coincidence" between Birtwistle's orchestration and the version of *Hoquetus David* recorded by the early music pioneer David Munrow on his epoch-making double album *Music of the Gothic Era*, released in 1974 but based on several years of earlier concert performances. Munrow founded the Medieval Ensemble of London in 1967, the same year that Birtwistle and Peter Maxwell Davies founded their contemporary ensemble, the Pierrot Players. According to Delaere, the Pierrot Players routinely inserted medieval motets into their performances of contemporary music.[35] Thus the sound of British modernism in the late 1960s was conditioned by the imagined medieval, and the sound of the medieval was inflected with 1960s modernity. A heavily layered palimpsest thereby emerges: Machaut, refracted via Munrow and Birtwistle, repurposed by Benjamin for the sound of time grinding on like a celestial gearworks.

Conclusion

While Birtwistle directly engages with specific works of the Middle Ages, staging a dialogue of sorts between the original sounds of Machaut and his modernist idiom, *Written on Skin*'s relationship with the medieval past is indirect and attenuated. Attenuation, refraction, palimpsest, ekphrasis—these words capture the sense that *Written on Skin* is a work about mediation as much as it is about the story of the troubadour's eaten heart. And certainly the manner in which *Written on Skin* recounts the troubadour's story does not conjure a distant Middle Ages. Rather, its engagement with Guillem de Cabestaing underscores that the Middle Ages never really left us; it is not located far back in the recesses of time, but right below us, under the asphalt, and spectrally, or palimpsestuously, within our language and our music, kaleidoscopically able to shift positions of temporal ordering with us, depending on where our perspective is or who is telling the story. Perhaps this perception of immediacy is why the attention to mediation in the opera, the postmodern gestures of distancing and metafiction, does not deprive us of feeling genuine emotion at the terrible story. Paradoxically, the angel figure, while presented as having no emotion toward the story he is telling, conveys its horror to that much greater effect in that final scene. And as is fitting for an opera that thematizes palimpsest and ekphrasis to such a degree, the power of the final scene relates palimpsestuously to one more ekphrastic intertext: In the matter-of-fact tone of Angel 1's description of "The Woman Falling" I hear the conversational voice of Auden's narrator in the poem "Musée des Beaux Arts" strolling through the museum, idly noting that "About suffering they were never wrong / The old Masters: how well they understood / Its human position." That narrator famously continues to a description of the painting *Landscape with The Fall of Icarus* by Pieter Breughel the Elder, noting "how everything turns away / Quite leisurely from the disaster; the ploughman may / Have heard the splash, the forsaken cry, / But for him it was not an important failure." The direct point of contact between this poem and Crimp's text are only two non-contiguous words, "turn" and "fall." When Angel 1 reports that

> three small angels—look—are watching her calmly from the margin. In their face in their eyes, see their cold fascination with human disaster as they turn from the falling woman to where the white lines of the Saturday car park cover the heaped up dead

we hear the same staging of disinterest that we heard from Auden's art-loving narrator, a disinterest that is removed because it is attributed to a figure in the painting under discussion. And paradoxically the very coolness of tone and the multiple distancing of the falling figure in both cases achieve the opposite effect in the reader, an empathetic rush of feeling for the tragedy. Thus, while the return of the troubadour to the operatic stage at the dawn of the twenty-first century does not herald a return to romantic nostalgia about the distant Middle Ages, the postmodern operatic troubadour is still able to rouse deep emotion in his audience.

Acknowledgments

An earlier version of this essay was delivered at the conference "Postmodernity's Musical Pasts" at the Barry Brook Center of the CUNY Graduate Center in March 2015. I am grateful to the students in two seminars at the CUNY Graduate Center for their insightful comments on *Written on Skin* and to Emma Dillon, who invited me to participate in a one-day workshop on *Written on Skin* at King's College London in May 2016.

Notes

1. *The Graphic: An Illustrated Weekly Newspaper*, vol. 32 (1886). For background on Hueffer's career in Britain, including the goal for *The Troubadour* to "create a ground breaking English opera in the Wagnerian tradition," see Meirion Hughes, *The English Musical Renaissance and the Press 1850–1914: Watchmen of Music* (London: Routledge, R/2016), 20–23. Although the opera has all but disappeared from view, its premiere was a substantial enough event that the *Musical Times* of June 1, 1886, contains a lengthy preview of the opera complete with music-notated examples.
2. Published as Franz Hüffer, *Der Trobador Guillem de Cabestainh. Sein Leben und Werk* (Berlin: Heimann, 1869).
3. Francis Hueffer, *The Troubadours: A History of Provençal Life and Literature in the Middle Ages* (London: Chatto & Windus, 1878), v. The book he sneers at, *The Troubadours, Their Loves and Lyrics, with Remarks on their Influence, Social and Literary*, by John Rutherford, had been published only five years earlier, in 1873.
4. Richard Utz, "Academic Medievalism and Nationalism," in *The Cambridge Companion to Medievalism*, ed. Louise D'Arcens (Cambridge: Cambridge University Press, 2016), 123.
5. The troubadour *vidas* and *razos* were edited in 1849 by Jean Boutière and A-H. Schutz as *Biographies des Troubadours: Textes provençaux des XIIIe et XIVe siècles* (Paris: Didier;

Toulouse: Privat, 1950), 154–172; they published four different versions of the *razo*. English translations are found in William Burgwinkle, trans., *Razos and Troubadour Songs* (New York: Garland, 1990), 310–315. As Burgwinkle and others have noted, the story of the eaten heart traveled throughout the Middle Ages. For the theory that the story originated in India, see "The Legend of the Eaten Heart," John E. Matzke, *MLA Notes* 26 (1911): 1–8.

6. Hueffer, *The Troubadours*, 91.

7. John Haines, *Eight Centuries of Troubadours and Trouvères: The Changing Identity of Medieval Music* (Cambridge: Cambridge University Press, 2009).

8. A quick search of operatic treatments of troubadours in Franz Stieger's *Opernlexicon* (1975) turned up eighteen between Gretry's *Richard Coeur de Lion* (1784) and the Vaudeville-Opera *Madame Troubadour* by Felix Albini (1907). See also Marie Sumner Lott, "From Knight Errant to Family Man: Romantic Medievalism in Brahms's *Romanzen aus L. Tiecks Magelone*, op. 33 (1865, 1869)," Liana Püschel, "Soldiers and Censors: Verdi's Medieval Imagination," and Michael S. Richardson, "Romantic Medievalist Nationalism in Schumann's *Genoveva*, Then and Now," this volume, pp. 38–62; 81–108, and 155–173, respectively.

9. Jean-Pascal Vachon, notes to Tanglewood performance of *Written on Skin*, August 12, 2013.

10. On the history of the term palimpsest, see Sarah Dillon, *The Palimpsest: Literature, Criticism, Theory* (London: Continuum, 2007).

11. For a history and discussion of the significance of the Archimedes Palimpsest, now at the Walters Art Museum in Baltimore, see http://www.archimedespalimpsest.org.

12. Gerard Genette, *Palimpsests: Literature in the Second Degree*, trans. Channa Newman and Claude Doubinsky (Lincoln: University of Nebraska Press, 1997).

13. Genette, *Palimpsests*, 399, attributes the neologism "palimpsestuous" to Philippe Lejeune without citing its bibliographic source.

14. I note an almost match with the structure of Alban Berg's *Wozzeck*, organized into three acts of five scenes each.

15. Translated in Burgwinkle, *Razos and Troubadour Songs*, 307–318.

16. Indexed in A. Pillet and H. Carstens, *Bibliographie der Troubadours* (R/Milan: Ledizioni, 2013) (PC) as 213, 5.

17. Burgwinkle, *Razos and Troubadour Songs*, 314.

18. George Benjamin interview with Adam Wasserman, *Opera News*, July 2012, https://www.operanews.com/Opera_News_Magazine/2012/7/Departments/The_Skin_He_s_In.html, accessed January 22, 2018.

19. Alexander Nagel, *Medieval/Modern* (London: Thames & Hudson, 2012).

20. Eglantine, scene 2, bar 101; wild primrose, scene 1, bars 47–48; burning villages, scene 8, bar 45.

21. By a happy coincidence, this essay was first delivered as a conference paper on the day the remains of King Richard III of England, who died in the Battle of Bosworth Field in 1485 and whose body was found under a parking lot in September 2012, was reburied in Westminster Cathedral. "The ceremonies," according to the *New York Times*, "drew hours of live television coverage and days of newspaper headlines, almost as if Britain had lost a 21st-century monarch" (John F. Burns, "Richard III Gets a Kingly Burial, on a Second Try," *New York Times*, March 26, 2015, https://www.nytimes.com/2015/03/27/world/europe/king-richard-iii-burial-leicester.html, accessed March 26, 2015).

22. This transformation is explored in Emma Dillon, "Vocal Philologies: *Written on Skin* and the Troubadours," *Opera Quarterly* 33 (2018): 207–248. According to Benjamin, the authors decided to make the change because they had already written an opera with a singer as its central character and they did not want to repeat themselves (*Opera News* interview).

23. "Ekphrasis, n," *Oxford English Dictionary Online*, March 2018, accessed March 25, 2018, http://www.oed.com/view/Entry/59412?redirectedFrom=ekphrasis.

24. Valentine Cunningham, "Why Ekphrasis?," *Classical Philology* 102 (2007): 57–58.

25. *Written on Skin*, mm. 564–580.

26. Maria Ryan, "Angels in the Archive: Animating the Past in *Written on Skin*, in *Recomposing the Past: Representations of Early Music on Stage and Screen*, ed. James Cook, Alexander Kolassa, and Adam Whittaker (Abington: Routledge, 2018), 174–187.

27. Martin Crimp, interview with Alain Perroux, translated by Kenneth Chalmers for the program book of the 2013 production of *Written on Skin* at Covent Garden, at p. 18. For more on the relationship between Walter Benjamin's Angel of History and Martin Crimp's libretto, see Ryan, "Angels in the Archive," 185-186. See also the situating of Walter Benjamin's Angel in the context of the complex temporality of the opera in Emma Dillon, "Vocal Philologies: *Written on Skin* and the Troubadours," 210.

28. Walter Benjamin, *Illuminations*, ed. Hannah Arendt, trans. Henry Zohn (New York: Schocken Books, 1969), 249.

29. Benjamin bought the print in 1921 in Munich and owned it until 1940 when, escaping Paris the Nazis, he entrusted it to George Bataille, the medievalist and intellectual. Its "extraordinary provenance" includes "passing through the hands of four important modern philosophers before entering the collection of the Israel Museum in Jerusalem" (Jason Farago, "How Klee's Angle of History Took Flight," BBC Culture, April 6, 2016, accessed March 10, 2018, http://www.bbc.com/culture/story/20160401-how-klees-angel-of-history-took-flight). Benjamin wrote the moving description of the print in the spring of 1940, just a few months before he fled Paris and eventually committed suicide while waiting to cross the border into Spain. See also R. H. Quaytman, *Chapter 29* (New York: Sequence Press, 2015), accessed March 10, 2018, http://miguelabreugallery.com/exhibitions/%D7%97%D7%A7%D7%A7-chapter-29/: "This struck Quaytman as highly relevant, not only to what Klee intended with this gesture of defacement, but also to Walter Benjamin's well known essay, "On the Concept of History," which situates the temporal past in front, not behind the Angel."

30. *The Telegraph*, June 2, 2010, accessed April 3, 2018.

31. George Benjamin, discussing the music of "To the Little Hill," quoted in *The Telegraph*, June 2, 2010.

32. *Written on Skin*, scene 2, bars 195–197.

33. Richard Wagner, *Die Walküre* (New York: Dover, 1978), 21.

34. A recent consideration of Wagner's relationship to his medieval sources, with further bibliography, is J. P. E. Harper-Scott, "Medieval Romance and Wagner's Musical Narrative in the *Ring*," *19th-Century Music* 32 (2009): 211–234. See also Barbara Eichner's contribution to this handbook, "Richard Wagner's Medieval Visions," pp. 174–202.

35. Mark Delaere, "Self-Portrait with Boulez and Machaut (Ligeti Is There as Well): Harrison Birtwistle's *Hoquetus Petrus*," in *The Modernist Legacy: Essays on New Music*, ed. Björn Heile (Farnham: Ashgate, 2009), 193fn4.

SECTION 4

REIMAGINING THE MEDIEVAL WOMAN

....

CHAPTER 18

TOLLING BELLS AND OTHERWORLDLY VOICES

Joan of Arc's Sonic World in the Early Twentieth Century

....

ELIZABETH DISTER

ON May 9, 1939, French music critic Paul Le Flem gave one of his regularly scheduled broadcasts on the radio program *La Vie musicale*. Le Flem's broadcast focused on the French premiere of Paul Claudel and Arthur Honegger's oratorio *Jeanne d'Arc au bûcher* (*Joan of Arc at the Stake*), and he drew attention to the recent French vogue for musical compositions about the saint:

> It is not the first time that Jeanne d'Arc has inspired poets, artists, and composers. Since the war, they have frequently been attracted by her heroic destiny. They have sung the praises of the little French girl who, faithful to her "voices," traversed a region of France overrun by bands of soldiers in order to inspire confidence among those who had lost it and who no longer believed in their country. More than just a single inspired work has come out of this mystical contact between the twentieth-century artist and she who, on the stake in Rouen, suffered for her faith in the future of a vanquished but indomitable France.[1]

Composers of the interwar period indeed showed renewed interest in Jeanne d'Arc as a musical subject, although compositions about the saint had already proliferated in the nineteenth century.[2] This large body of so-called "johannique" music encompasses nearly every genre: operas, oratorios, masses, orchestral works, choral works, piano repertoire, incidental music, solo vocal music, national hymns, radio dramas, and even music to accompany large-scale re-enactments of Jeanne's story. By the time Le Flem gave his radio review, composers' interest in Jeanne's tale had been heightened by the traumas of the Great War, her canonization as a Catholic saint in 1920, the five-hundred-year anniversary of her martyrdom in 1931, and mounting international tensions immediately preceding the Second World War. Her story remained flexible enough to support a multiplicity of partisan readings in this era of rapid political change.[3] But even before this period, the romantic era's fascination with all things medieval, combined with the rediscovery of early music in France during the nineteenth century, stimulated interest in the time during which Jeanne lived (ca. 1412–1431).[4] This fascination with the Middle Ages helped to pave the way for the twentieth-century outpouring of artistic tributes to the saint.

Those tributes were frequently caught up in a dialogue about how France's musical past—especially its medieval past—should inform current musical practices. Often, composers drew on Jeanne's story as a way of articulating the primacy of French culture, folding in actual medieval music and the sounds of the medieval world to assert the richness of the French tradition. In her study on the nineteenth-century French revival of early music, Katherine Bergeron finds that "historiographical myths of French primacy and superiority are as pervasive as expressions of national self-doubt."[5] Responses to johannique music in the early twentieth century navigated this tension between these opposing characterizations of French history. Artists and audiences used such compositions to assert France's central place in the modern artistic world, while piloting their way through national doubts and their inferiority complex vis-à-vis Germany.

Le Flem's comments reflect this same tension. Drawing a connection between Jeanne's powers of inspiration on the medieval battlefield and her current powers of artistic inspiration, Le Flem suggests that Jeanne offers succor for flagging artistic and national morale: As Jeanne "inspired confidence among those who had lost it and who no longer believed in their country," so she forged a "mystical contact" with "the twentieth-century artist" to create "inspired" works. Jeanne's story, therefore, offered an especially potent narrative around which French listeners could concentrate their hopes for their country during periods of national doubt, all while negotiating what the French past meant in modern times.

Music representing Jeanne d'Arc's story can also tell us much about how listeners of the nineteenth and twentieth centuries imagined the medieval world and its mysterious soundscape. As nineteenth-century composers such as Charles Gounod, Auguste Mermet, Verdi, and Tchaikovsky turned increased attention to the saint, compositions about her began to take on a defined character. By the end of the nineteenth century, a coherent musical soundscape of Jeanne's world had emerged, defined by tolling bells, otherworldly timbres, and disembodied voices. Ethereal timbres such as bells, celesta, harp, and ondes Martenot were favorite choices to portray Jeanne's connection with the divine, and these colors were frequently layered with various combinations of speaking and singing voices. Indeed, many of these works featured prominent speaking components, and many relied heavily on *mélodrame*, or capitalized on a contrast between speaking and singing voices to portray earthly versus heavenly realms. In addition, these works often referenced medieval genres—especially French folk songs, plainchant, and sacred polyphony—or even made direct borrowings. The johannique repertoire also featured a rich pastiche of sacred and secular elements, much like the medieval mystery plays that served as the inspiration for many of these works and like the national festivals for which they were created.

These yearly celebratory fêtes across France were the primary venue for much of this music, shaping both composers' musical choices and audiences' reception of these works. This essay begins by contextualizing works about Jeanne within such national fêtes, highlighting how these celebrations fashioned diverse forms of medievalism around the figure of Jeanne. It then traces the emergence of the johannique soundscape and its reliance on bells, mystical timbres, and references to medieval musical genres, while also considering how the medievalisms of such works reflected larger nationalist concerns in France.

Tracing Jeanne's Footsteps through the Remnants of the Medieval City

Many nineteenth- and twentieth-century compositions dedicated to Jeanne were created for the lavish yearly festivals held in her honor across France each May, elaborate mashups of religion, nationalism, medievalism, and civic pride. In Orléans, the anniversary of Jeanne's liberation of the city from an English siege has supposedly been celebrated every May since 1429. These fêtes continue today, and for almost six hundred years, they have included three important elements: music, parades, and a mass. These elements recall the very first of these fêtes, when Jeanne triumphantly entered the city on May 8, 1429, and led a procession of thanksgiving, decreeing that all the inhabitants and all of her soldiers should go to Mass.[6] This triumphant entry into the city and her movement across the medieval urban landscape are re-enacted every year by the town's inhabitants, with parades that retrace her path through the city and with cultural events, religious services, memorials, and entertainments at important sites where she fought, walked, slept, and prayed.

By the early twentieth century, these fêtes had burgeoned into a weeks-long affair that included re-enactments with actors playing Jeanne and other historical characters, political speeches, historical lectures, religious services, musical events throughout the town, and other diversions.[7] Today, they still include the traditional masses, memorials, and parades, but add on various pseudomedieval amusements and popular entertainments: jousting tournaments, encampments of medieval re-enactors, marketplaces selling chainmail and costumes, petting zoos, choreographed duels, medieval food, early music performances, and DJ-ed concerts accompanied by exhilarating light displays where tens of thousands dance until the wee hours of the morning.[8]

While the celebrations in Orléans are typically celebratory in nature, reflecting the city's festive place in Jeanne's narrative, the yearly events at Rouen, the site of her execution on May 30, 1431, are more somber. Here, participants' movements across the medieval landscape of the city trace not a triumphant entry of liberation, but rather a *via dolorosa* toward the site of Jeanne's martyrdom. The sites in this path of sorrows include the tower where Jeanne was supposedly imprisoned, the dungeon where she was threatened with torture, the Saint-Ouen Church where she was tried and then publicly admonished, the Vieux-Marché (Old Market Square) where she was burned alive, and the banks of the Seine, where her ashes were dumped (along with her heart, which, according to legend, refused to burn).

In the early twentieth century, music accompanied nearly every step of this path, with concerts at many of the important locations in Jeanne's narrative, folk songs sung by school and scouting groups, patriotic tunes sung by veterans' groups, municipal ensembles playing in town squares, marches played by military bands, performances by early music ensembles, and religious services accompanied by soloists, choirs, and organs. Many of these musical performances took place on or along the path toward Jeanne's execution or simply at important historical sites where Jeanne had actually been present.[9]

Despite the somber trajectory of Rouen's festivities, in the late nineteenth and early twentieth centuries, the Rouen festivals also incorporated a fair amount of pomp. The fêtes of 1920 (the year of Jeanne's canonization) and 1931 (the five-hundred-year anniversary of her martyrdom) proved to be especially grand occasions. The 1920 Rouen fête served as a collective processing of the traumas of the Great War, with massive groups of wounded veterans embodying Jeanne's martyrdom by walking her path, and featured music that celebrated the recent reintegration of Alsace-Lorraine into France (with performances of the "Marche lorraine" by the Rouen Municipal Band and by local schoolchildren) and the newly strengthened alliance between France, Britain, and Belgium (the "Marseillaise," "God Save the King," and the "Brabançonne" all featured prominently).[10]

The 1931 fête was even grander, reaching new heights of pageantry with thousands of re-enactors and two different young women playing the role of Jeanne. Indeed, looking at the program of events for this fête, we see that the organizers and participants used Jeanne's story as a point of departure for diverse medievalisms of all kinds.[11] Here, we not only see how the categories of medievalism proposed by Annette Kreutziger-Herr bleed together, but also how each one nourishes the others, providing fodder for further elaboration and development.[12]

For instance, the fête boasted a great deal of "scientific medievalism," including exhibitions on Jeanne d'Arc iconography, books, manuscripts, and art, an exhibition of medieval religious art, a conference on Jeanne d'Arc in history and literature, and lectures by famed historians. City monuments, especially those places where Jeanne had set foot, were given pride of place in the programming, and in a sort of "reproductive medievalism," the newly restored Hôtel de Ville was afforded a special dedication ceremony and many of the town's historic buildings were specially illuminated in the evenings. Group tours were organized to these city monuments and excursions arranged to visit the Normandy abbeys whose abbots had participated in Jeanne's trial. Meanwhile, many of these historic sites played host to the "productive, creative medievalisms" of new works of art inspired by Jeanne and the Middle Ages, including performances of the winning compositions of a Jeanne d'Arc cantata competition, a gala performance of *Jeanne de France* (a mystery play with music by Jean Nouguès), and a concert mass dedicated to Jeanne by composer Paul Paray composed specially for the occasion (Paray had spent much of his childhood and early career in Rouen).[13] Such creative medievalisms often asserted a connection to the scientific category, since dramatic and lyric works relied on histories of Jeanne and her time. And even music that had no ostensible connection to the Middle Ages or to Jeanne could be reimagined and medievalized by its proximity to other medievalisms, since historical lectures, re-enactments, and musical performances often took place side by side or synchronously.

"Political and ideological medievalism" was also omnipresent, as speakers used Jeanne's story to highlight the importance of the sacrifices made by soldiers during World War I, the necessity for continued peace and defensive action against Germany, and (a bit ironically) the value of English–French cooperation.[14] Large re-enactments and spectacles were arranged, some featuring casts of over a thousand: Roman chariot races, an equestrian obstacle course, parades of French soldiers throughout the ages, appearances by Jeanne and her army, Charles VII's triumphant entry into Rouen in 1449, dramatizations of Jeanne's recantation and sentencing, and funeral vigils for Jeanne. Music for all of this was provided by schoolchildren, military bands, local ensembles, church choirs, celebrated soloists, and early music ensembles playing period instruments, collapsing the boundaries between styles of medievalism and generating creative reimaginings that explored and performed the medieval world in new ways.[15]

Hearing Voices: Bells, Angels, and Demons

Much of the music at Jeanne's fêtes was borrowed from other contexts, performed simply because it was convenient or because it had an appropriate national or religious tone. But much of it was written specifically about Jeanne d'Arc. In works about the saint and in works composed expressly for her festivals, a coherent soundscape of Jeanne's world began to emerge, detailed here through a brief discussion of several johannique works. The medieval world composers sought to portray in these works was bathed in the sonorous vibrations of bells and drenched with the mysterious sounds of angelic realms, as if those who lived in Jeanne's time had special access to the divine.

Charles Gounod's incidental music for the stage play *Jeanne d'Arc* by Jules Barbier appears to have influenced many later French works about the saint, as this work solidified the standard Jeanne soundscape that had begun to emerge over the course of the nineteenth century. The work premiered in 1873 and was made famous in an 1890 revival starring Sarah Bernhardt.[16] For this play, Gounod supplied instrumental music for entrances and exits, large choruses, solos and duets, marches, and a few scenes of melodrama. Melodrama typically involves declaimed spoken text on top of instrumental accompaniment, but some of Gounod's melodrama scenes for this work went a step further, layering and juxtaposing a profusion of sonic elements. For instance, the melodrama scene in the first act includes a mixture of declaimed speech (Jeanne), choral singing (angelic choirs), solo and duet singing (for the mystical "voices" Jeanne hears: Saint Catherine and Saint Margaret), and orchestral accompaniment.[17] This combination of disparate sonic elements would appear again and again in works about Jeanne.

Gounod's score also included prominent tolling bells, a ubiquitous feature in johannique music. The act 1 melodrama scene begins with repetitive tolling bells, which then seamlessly give way to the singing voices of a hidden choir and Saints Catherine and Margaret, as if the bells were calling up these sonic apparitions. This use of bells, and their connection to saintly voices, was inspired by Jeanne's own testimony during her trial of condemnation, in which she claimed that her saintly visions often materialized after hearing tolling bells, oftentimes the bells for Vespers, Compline, or Matins (see Example 18.1).[18]

Further evidence suggests that Jeanne had a fascination with bells and that she went out of her way to immerse herself in their sound. During the trial of her rehabilitation, which occurred twenty years after her death and reversed the first trial's findings, several witnesses mentioned Jeanne's fascination with bells in the course of testifying about her extreme piety and conscientious devotional habits. Two witnesses who had grown up with Jeanne in Domrémy mentioned that Jeanne would drop to her knees and pray when she heard the village church bells sound.[19] The person in charge of ringing those bells to announce masses and offices—Perrin Le Drapier, the Domrémy church warden—also provided his own testimony. Le Drapier claimed that Jeanne would get upset if he neglected to ring the bells for Compline and that she would bring him wool from her family's sheep or little cakes she made to ensure that he rang the bells properly.[20] Yet another witness, Dunois, the "bâtard d'Orléans" (one of Jeanne's military companions), testified that Jeanne made it a daily habit to go to church at nightfall and to have the bells rung for half an hour prior to further devotions.[21]

These details in Jeanne's story may help explain why composers so consistently relied on bells in their musical portraits of Jeanne's world. The texts of her two trials became widely available to French readers upon the publication of Joseph Fabre's 1884 and 1888 translations.[22] But even if composers and audiences did not know of these details, the connection between bells and angels, and that between bells and the medieval world, may have appeared obvious to nineteenth- and twentieth-century French listeners. Victor Hugo's *Hunchback of Notre Dame*, after all, portrayed the soundscape of medieval Paris as a vast sea of tolling bells.[23] Eighteenth- and nineteenth-century writers and church theorists claimed that bells had the power to drive out demons from the air and to summon angels to pray alongside the faithful.[24] Even today, bells still hold deep meaning for the French, as they represent an idealized French countryside removed from modern concerns, as well as the passing of time and seasons (in particular liturgical seasons, because church bells do not ring during Lent and peal with renewed vigor at Easter). As historian Alain Corbin explains, by the nineteenth century, writers used bells "to impart a feeling of time passing, foster remembrance, recover things forgotten, and to consolidate an individual's identification with a primordial auditory site."[25] There are also many moments within Joan's standard narrative in which it simply makes sense to include bells: her pastoral upbringing in a small town, her triumphant entry into Orléans, the coronation of Charles VII in Reims, and her death by execution. By the

EXAMPLE 18.1 Gounod, *Jeanne d'Arc*, act 1, no. 3, mm. 17–38.

EXAMPLE 18.1 Continued

lâ - che!   cœur sans foi___   d'av - oir tant att - en - du!

JEANNE: Non! Non! grâce! pitié! pour moi! pour mon vieux père! Il m'aime! voulez-vous que je le desespère!...

time Gounod composed his incidental music, the connection between bells, angels, remembering the past, and the presumed mysticism of the imagined medieval world were well established.

The manner in which Gounod marshaled his diverse sonic forces—bells, speaking voices, solo vocalists, orchestra, choir—provided a template for other composers to emulate: He chose to divide the sonic landscape into an earthly realm populated by speaking voices (Jeanne and the other characters) and an angelic realm populated by singing voices (Saints Catherine and Margaret and angelic choirs). And the way that Gounod overlapped the bells with angelic singing—the seamless transition between the tolling bells and the voices of Saints Catherine and Margaret—suggested that the point of connection between those two worlds actually occurred through sound itself, more particularly, through bells.[26] Most important, however, Gounod's score provided a precedent for creating music that supported Jeanne in a speaking role, rather than a singing role, which would become a hallmark of the johannique repertoire, as in Claudel and Honegger's *Jeanne d'Arc au bûcher*.

In contrast to Barbier and Gounod's speaking Jeanne, there were a number of nineteenth-century operas that afforded Jeanne a singing role, most notably Verdi's *Giovanna d'Arco* (premiered at La Scala in 1845), Auguste Mermet's *Jeanne d'Arc* (premiered at the Palais Garnier in 1876), and Tchaikovsky's *The Maid of Orléans* (premiered at the Mariinsky Theatre in 1881). Although Jeanne's story may have been politically flexible, it did not prove to be as easily moldable to the musical and dramatic conventions of nineteenth-century opera. All three of these works had to take large liberties with Jeanne's story to make it work for the operatic stage—for instance, by clumsily shoehorning Jeanne into a romantic pairing. In Tchaikovsky's version, Jeanne is in love with a Burgundian knight, Lionel, and in Mermet's, she receives the attentions of a French knight named Gaston de Metz. In Verdi's version, which was heavily indebted to the 1801 stage play *Die Jungfrau von Orleans* by Friedrich Schiller, her romantic partner is the very king of France himself, and the improbable pair warble their way through several soprano–tenor duets. Large-scale changes to Jeanne's story that defied what was understood as the historical record did not tend to go over well in the late nineteenth century in France.[27] Furthermore, histories of the time tended to portray Jeanne as plainspoken and pure, so the idea of her producing coloratura fireworks while cavorting with the king of France (or any romantic partner) may have seemed ill-fitting.

Composers also seemed to like the effect of juxtaposing speaking voices with singing voices to amplify the supernatural atmosphere of scenes involving divine beings, and they enriched the mysticism of these scenes by relying on eerie timbres and unusual combinations of voices. Such techniques were tried-and-true methods for portraying the otherwordly, used in chilling melodrama scenes in opera (in Weber's *Der Freischütz* and Beethoven's *Fidelio*, for instance) as well as in more low-brow, sensationalist entertainments such as phantasmagoria light shows and boulevard theater.[28] Within Jeanne's story, these sort of effects painted a portrait of a medieval world that was haunted by mystical beings and their otherworldly vibrations, a world where the fabric between heaven and earth was worn thin.

Instruments that had acquired otherworldly associations in nineteenth-century opera were popular choices to represent such scenes, recalling moments such as the famous mad scene in *Lucia di Lammermoor*, which was originally scored for the eerie timbre of the glass harmonica. Many works therefore included prominent harp strumming, tinkling celesta, and other supernatural colorings. For instance, composer Henri Tomasi's incidental music for *Jeanne et la vie des autres* included repeated tolling bells and otherworldly timbres meant to sound ethereal and angelic at the moment Jeanne first hears her voices: celesta, harp, flute, cymbal, and violin harmonics.[29] Composers also turned to more unusual instruments that would produce curious and disquieting sounds. Gounod apparently wanted to heighten the effect of the saints' appearance in his score by using the eerie sounds of the pyrophone, a sort of organ in which sound is produced through combustion. Lacking the time to install the instrument, however, he abandoned the idea.[30] With the advent of electronic music, composers of the early twentieth century struck on a similar idea. The ondes Martenot, an electronic instrument with a sound similar to the theremin, proved to be a favorite among composers writing for Jeanne d'Arc. The instrument's otherworldly tone added a mystical sheen to scenes involving Jeanne's angelic voices, such as in Honegger and Claudel's *Jeanne au bûcher* and in several other Jeanne works from the late 1930s and early 1940s.[31]

Many works about Jeanne from this time period were composed for the radio, which offered an added layer of meaning in the scenes involving Jeanne's sonic apparitions: Listeners could essentially become Jeanne, since these angelic, disembodied voices were magically piped into their homes. Several compositions capitalized on this effect, and one work in particular was especially attuned to the sonic and spatial effects made possible through the radio: *Jeanne d'Arc*, a radio drama commissioned by the French government in 1941 and written by seven pairs of writers and composers, each of which contributed a chapter to the drama.[32] Many of the composers who contributed to this collaborative work seemed sensible to the sonic possibilities radio afforded and nearly all used angelic timbres and unusual combinations of voices. Raymond Loucheur's movement included tubular bells and celesta; Tony Aubin's called for celesta, harp, and ondes Martenot; and Louis Beydts's contained harp, celesta, vibraphone, and tubular bells, plus wordless "ahs" from a female chorus.

Angelic female choirs were a standard part of Jeanne's soundscape, and several movements in this radio work also pitted groups of voices against one another in a showdown between good and evil, with angelic voices facing off against demonic voices. In Pierre Capdevielle's contribution, a small, beatific female choir represents the voices of angels and saints, singing reassurances to Jeanne. Below them, the tenors and basses first adopt the perspective of Jeanne's male jury, urging her to recant, and then take on a demonic role, chanting in measured spoken recitation, "Fear, Death, and Fear of the Fire," over and over. André Jolivet's contribution to this radio drama also included a showdown between angelic singing voices and demonic speaking voices. Here, a diabolical chorus of female speaking voices attempts to masquerade as Jeanne's saintly voices, telling her to recant her testimony and save herself from the fire, but Jeanne's "true" saintly voices prevail, and Jeanne stands firm and accepts her death by fire. The technique of using spoken voice to represent evil and singing voice to represent good recalls one medieval liturgical drama in particular: Hildegard von Bingen's *Ordo virtutum*, where the saintly Virtues are portrayed by female singing voices, while the male Devil only speaks, having no access to music's divinity.[33] Honegger also used this technique in *Jeanne au bûcher*, in which several passages include a contrast between spoken male voices chanting demonically and angelic female soloists and choirs.

All these techniques—tolling bells, eerie vibrations, otherworldly chimes and tinklings, and face-offs between angelic and demonic voices—portrayed the strangeness and mysticism of Jeanne's medieval world. But Jeanne's world also included actual music, and composers were keen to reference musical styles of the past to help plunge listeners into Jeanne's story. They saw such references not as backward-looking atavism but as a way of enlivening Jeanne's tale and enriching modern music.

What Music Belongs in Jeanne's Medieval World?

Composers and listeners seemed to agree that certain kinds of music belonged in stories about Jeanne d'Arc and that the music should somehow "authentically" represent Jeanne's time. This did not mean that audiences required accuracy—both Gounod and Honegger both referenced baroque genres as much as medieval ones—but simply that they expected the music portrayed in Jeanne's world to feel archaic. Sometimes, composers relied on borrowings from repertoires easily identified as medieval, as in Gounod's *Jeanne d'Arc*, which uses insertions and adaptations of actual plainchant (*Vexilla regis*, *Veni creator spiritus*, and *Orate pro ea*). Composers also sought to enliven their own contemporary approaches—which French interwar artists and critics complained were long overdue for a rejuvenation—with references to French musics of the past. Works about Jeanne d'Arc frequently found themselves caught up in a discourse of national artistic renewal, and critics often asserted that the most effective form of cultural resurgence occurred when composers went back to their roots.

For instance, composer Paul Paray's *Messe du cinquième centenaire de la mort de Jeanne d'Arc*, composed for Jeanne's 1931 fête in Rouen, was lauded specifically for the way that Paray incorporated references to medieval genres, and critics presented this work and its author as the long-awaited retort to perceived deficiencies in the modern French repertoire.[34] The *Messe* is a traditional work in Latin scored for SATB soloists, SATB choir, organ, and orchestra, and its premiere took place at a pontifical mass during the 1931 Jeanne fête in Rouen, so it was situated within the medievalist trappings of this festival.[35]

Reviews of the *Messe* during this period tended to praise Paray's traditional style—described with words such as *classic*, *precise*, *clear*, and *ordered*—and to hold Paray up as a model of Frenchness that other young composers should emulate, an answer to those who would doubt the primacy of French art.[36] Part of this Frenchness involved references to French musical styles of the past, in particular, to plainchant and Renaissance polyphony. For instance, the opening of the Gloria features an unmeasured, modal passage sung by three of the soloists in turn. Although this passage did not actually feature borrowings from plainchant, its free rhythm and unaccompanied, modal melody had enough of a Gregorian character for several reviewers to point it out: one called it a *Gregorian vocalise*, while another said that it was "comparable to the neumes of Gregorian chant" (see Example 18.2).[37]

Reviewers also drew attention to Paray's choral writing, particularly his use of imitation and learned counterpoint.[38] One passage in the Gloria served as an homage to the great Franco-Flemish masters of polyphony of the fifteenth and sixteenth centuries, complete with a deliberately studied contrapuntal texture and self-consciously archaic white-note notation of the *stile antico* (see Example 18.3). These two traditions, Gregorian chant and Renaissance polyphony, had been emphasized by Pope Pius X in his *moto proprio* of 1903, which established guidelines for the composition of new Catholic church music and advised that modern composers emulate these two traditions.[39] The positive response specifically to Paray's "traditional" style and to his references to plainchant and Renaissance polyphony shows that audiences found it fitting that Jeanne's story was accompanied by medievalish music.

It also seemed appropriate to listeners that the medieval sonic world would include French folk songs and popular tunes. In the late nineteenth and early twentieth centuries, well-known folk songs and more obscure French chansons unearthed by musicologists featured prominently during Jeanne's fêtes, sung by scouting and school groups

EXAMPLE 18.2 Paray, *Messe*, Gloria, mm. 1–11.

EXAMPLE 18.3 Paray, *Messe*, Gloria, mm. 159–164.

and played by local bands and period ensembles.[40] Many johannique compositions incorporated such melodies into their scores. A favorite technique was to introduce wandering minstrel or court troubadour characters into the story to provide this sort of medieval color. Gounod, for instance, used some pseudomedieval minstrel singing in his incidental music for Barbier's play. Others opted for actual borrowings from widely available nineteenth-century anthologies of French *chansons*, often with the aim of increasing the authenticity of their work. For instance, the 1938 performance of composer René Bruyez's play *Jeanne et la vie des autres* featured incidental music composed of arrangements of *chansons populaires* (French folk songs), and the printed program touted the work as "a prologue, ten tableaux and interludes intermixed with authentic fifteenth-century sacred and secular songs and the ringing of bells."[41]

In addition to using troubadour characters, composers sometimes used the chorus to sing folk songs or occasionally asked Jeanne herself to sing an old tune. While grand operatic expressions might have seemed unfitting (as discussed previously), *chansons populaires* seemed more appropriate for a country girl from Domrémy. In works where Jeanne had a singing role, folk songs lent her voice a certain truthfulness, a pure simplicity that seemed to suit her character. In addition to highlighting Jeanne's simplicity and humble origins, using invented folk songs or actual *chansons populaires* afforded composers extra pathos during a standard scene in many Jeanne narratives: when Jeanne, facing her death, reflected back on her life and recalled her childhood.

One piece that used such a technique was composer Maurice Jaubert's *Symphonie concertante, Jeanne d'Arc* (1937), scored for solo soprano and orchestra.[42] Set to a text by the famed Catholic poet Charles Péguy, the work's three movements chronicle three crucial moments of Jeanne's life and are told from her perspective: leaving her hometown, her military exploits, and her death.[43] As Jeanne says farewell to her hometown in the first movement, Jaubert includes two pseudo–folk songs, one about Jeanne's family home and one about the river that winds through her village. Set apart from the rest of the movement by recitative-like passages and featuring repetitive rhythms, lilting meters, and simple melodies, the impression is that Jeanne is singing folk songs that she learned in childhood. Jeanne reprises these two folk songs in the final movement as she remembers her life and prepares for her execution.

At a high-profile gala performance of this work in 1942, one review focused on the pathos of this moment in the final movement, when Jeanne faces her death and remembers her past through imagined folk songs.[44] For wartime audiences, this moment was heightened by the heroic status of both the poet who wrote the text and the composer himself. As another reviewer discussed, Charles Péguy died on a battlefield near the Marne in 1914, and Maurice Jaubert died during the German invasion of France in 1940.[45] Jaubert's pseudo–folk songs, with their pastoral depictions of small-town France, celebrated the very homeland this trio of martyrs—Jeanne, Péguy, and Jaubert—had given their lives for.

For French audiences, part of the appeal of Paray's and Jaubert's works was that they presented a staunchly traditional portrait of Jeanne. That traditionalism involved calling up a sonic landscape that listeners perceived as an appropriate backdrop for a historical subject from the Middle Ages. For such listeners, folk songs, plainchant, and sacred polyphony all belonged in their imagination of the medieval world, even when those elements were emulations, not really the genuine articles.

Most music dedicated to Jeanne relied on such conventional musical elements and often looked to traditional texts by respected Catholic authors. Composers who chose different directions faced confusion and reproach from audiences. One such work was Manuel Rosenthal's symphonic suite for orchestra and speaker, *Jeanne d'Arc* (1936).[46] Rosenthal based his work on an infamous novel, Joseph Delteil's *Jeanne d'Arc* (1925).[47] Delteil's unorthodox portrayal of the saint had caused a literary ruckus in the 1920s, with conservative Catholic detractors decrying the work as scandalous and trashy. Critics complained that Delteil's portrayal of Jeanne was too erotic (which some readers found demeaning), too intimate (much hagiography relies on a certain distance from the subject), and too anachronistic (Jeanne's crude speech was littered with modern slang).[48]

Rosenthal's orchestral suite featured a narrator who set the scene for each of the five movements, reciting passages of Delteil's novel before each movement began.[49] Although the sections of Delteil's text that Rosenthal chose to include were not the most objectionable passages, Rosenthal made a great effort to portray the style and spirit of Delteil's writing through his musical choices. And, like Delteil, Rosenthal faced disapproval for his unorthodox approach. At issue was Rosenthal's disruption of Jeanne's standard sonic landscape. Rosenthal's Jeanne did not live in the idealized medieval world that audiences were so familiar with, dominated by sober references to French musics of the past. One reviewer complained of "painful clashes, a disagreeable profanity, immoderate poor taste, immature or scandalous effects," and "harsh crudeness."[50] Most significant, Rosenthal adopted Delteil's anachronisms, choosing to insert the sounds of the French Revolution into the fourth movement, which was meant to portray the apogee of the standard Jeanne narrative, when Charles VII is finally crowned at Reims Cathedral. Here, Rosenthal includes a passage where the opening sol-do motive of the "Marseillaise" ripples across the orchestra, pervading the sonic landscape and disrupting the standard portrayal of Jeanne's medieval world.

Rosenthal's inclusion of the "Marseillaise" was directly inspired by Delteil's text, and the passage of the novel that mentions the "Marseillaise" would have been recited by the speaker immediately prior to the movement. Some, however, found this effect ill-fitting and even shocking.[51] In terms of sounds that audiences believed "belonged" in Jeanne's world, accuracy seemed to matter little, but the illusion of authenticity was paramount. The "Marseillaise" was such a clear sonic marker of the Revolution, which came three centuries after Jeanne, and some could not tolerate this rupture.

The Medieval and the National: Honegger's *Jeanne d'Arc au bûcher*

Although the early twentieth century saw great enthusiasm for music dedicated to Jeanne d'Arc, Paul Claudel and Arthur Honegger's "dramatic oratorio" *Jeanne d'Arc au bûcher* is the sole johannique work to have found a secure place in the modern repertoire. The work's perceived quality, the depth of its libretto, the appeal of its compositional style (which manages to combine traditional ingredients, "popular" elements, and modernist techniques), and the distinguished reputation of its creators have ensured that this piece remains remembered as one of the most significant contributions to French music of this era. Nevertheless, the work features many of the same compositional elements as other pieces dedicated to Jeanne: bells, combinations of speaking and singing voices, otherworldly timbres, folk songs (real and imagined), actual plainchant borrowings, and allusions to musics of the past (including grand opera, baroque dances, Gregorian chant, and Bachian choral writing).[52] *Jeanne au bûcher* is thus the inheritor of the johannique music tradition crystalized by Gounod and the generation that followed.

The person who commissioned *Jeanne au bûcher* was the iconic Ida Rubinstein, a Russian dancer-turned-actress. Rubinstein had become a crucial figure of the interwar period in France, commissioning and performing dozens of new works, and she had studied with Sarah Bernhardt, the famed interpreter of the Barbier–Gounod *Jeanne d'Arc*. Since Claudel and Honegger's *Jeanne* was created for Rubinstein herself to perform, Jeanne is a speaking role.[53] The work calls for an army of performers, including speaking characters, singing characters, SATB chorus, children's chorus, and orchestra, augmented by two pianos and the electronic ondes Martenot. *Jeanne au bûcher* can be performed as an unstaged concert work, a fully staged opera, or, as is most common, something in between, with minimal costumes, a simple set design, and basic blocking. Although Claudel and Honegger had completed *Jeanne au bûcher* by 1935, it did not receive its French premiere until several years later, during the 1939 fête for Jeanne in Orléans.[54] The work unfolds as a series of flashbacks that proceed roughly backward in chronology. Waiting for her execution, Jeanne remembers the pivotal moments of her short life, from the recent torment of her trial to the triumph of Charles VII's coronation to hearing her angelic voices as a child in Domrémy.

Rubinstein's idea for the work had been inspired by newfound interest in medieval theater in the early twentieth century.[55] Many were particularly fascinated with mystery plays, medieval liturgical dramas that treated sacred subjects but often incorporated secular elements and that were often staged outdoors in front of churches or in town squares. In France, the movement to revive this repertoire was led by Gustave Cohen and the Groupe de Théâtre médiéval de la Sorbonne (also called Les Théophiliens), who staged outdoor performances of medieval mystery plays in the 1930s and 1940s, sometimes accompanied by medieval music.[56] Both Rubinstein and Honegger were familiar with the Théophiliens' performances, and Claudel and Honegger aimed to infuse their oratorio with the "popular" flair of a medieval mystery play.[57] Indeed, Honegger had participated in a performance of the medieval mystery play *Le Jeu de Robin et de Marion* in 1917.[58]

Part of French artists' and audiences' interest in medieval theater had to do with their desire to restore the social purpose of theater, because they believed that modern theater had been corrupted and deprived of its proper function, which was to bring people together in mass communion.[59] Propelled by avant-garde directors such as Jacques Copeau and Vsevolod Meyerhold, this movement reflected a growing international interest in opening up theater to people of all stations and enlivening performances by looking to the traditions of the past, such as *commedia dell'arte*.[60] Medieval mystery plays, as communal celebrations aimed at the masses, offered a template for this modern theater revival. In the 1930s and through World War II, French youth and scouting theater groups often staged such mystery plays (or pieces they viewed as inspired by the medieval *mystère*), regularly using Jeanne d'Arc as a subject and often staging the works outdoors in amphitheaters, in town squares, or on the steps of cathedrals.[61] Such youth spectacles formed a crucial part of local Jeanne d'Arc fêtes in many towns each May.

Audiences recognized that *Jeanne au bûcher* came out of this popular medievalist movement and remarked on the work's similarities to *mystères* from the Middle Ages. For instance, one critic at the 1939 performance of *Jeanne au bûcher* at Jeanne's fête in Orléans proclaimed, "The work has the features of a medieval mystery play to which the people, first and foremost, are invited.... The clear intent of these two masters is to mediate their art and to make compromises in order for it to more directly engage everyone."[62] In other words, this reviewer saw the work's connection to medieval theater as a way for the authors to appeal to a wider audience and to recenter the social aspect of theater. By speculating that the authors' intent was to "mediate their art" and "make compromises," the reviewer linked the work's appeal to some of Claudel and Honegger's stylistic choices, which he thought held wide appeal.

Reviews of performances throughout the late 1930s and 1940s show that the work did indeed hold wide appeal. Its success was largely a result of the way it directly engaged audiences and how Claudel and Honegger spoke to audiences' collective memories of the imagined French past and the sounds of an idealized, provincial France.[63] Much of the discussion in reviews centered on scene 8, "Le Roi qui va-t-à Rheims," which Honegger and Claudel referred to as the "kermesse" (village fête). The scene depicts a group of French villagers—the choir and the children's choir—engaged in an outdoor village festival on Christmas Eve, waiting for Charles VII and Jeanne d'Arc to pass through the town on the way to the king's coronation in Reims.

The scene includes both real and invented folk songs and features two characters who are meant to represent the two halves of France. Costumed as a windmill, the character Heurtebise stands in for the grain-producing northern part of the country, while the character La Mère aux tonneaux (the Mother of Barrels) represents the wine-producing east and south. The libretto indicates that the two should speak with exaggerated accents from Picardy and Burgundy.[64] Combined with the rustic speech of the villagers and the real and pseudo–folk songs, the scene buzzes with regional accent and "popular" zest. After some carousing with Heurtebise and La Mère aux tonneaux, the villagers are interrupted by the local priest, who reminds his congregation to remember the spirit of the season and leads them in singing the plainchant "Aspiciens a longe," a responsory for the first Sunday of Advent. Soon, though, the *cortège* with Charles VII begins to approach, and the rest of the scene depicts a parade sweeping through the town, accompanied by a triumphant march.

In their depiction of this village festival, Honegger and Claudel chose to include many of the standard elements of local French fêtes that audiences would have experienced themselves. Indeed, the scene features some of the same elements that would have been present at the Orléans fête for Jeanne d'Arc at the French premiere in 1939 and at many of the other Jeanne d'Arc fêtes during which this work was performed in subsequent years.

EXAMPLE 18.4 Honegger, *Jeanne d'Arc au bûcher*, scene 8, mm. 179–193.

The fetishizing of regionalism (as with the characters Heurtebise and La Mère aux Tonneaux) was a standard aspect of Jeanne's fêtes, as was the inclusion of folk songs, with throngs parading dressed in traditional French regional costumes and school groups singing regional folk songs. Likewise, the scene includes a purposeful intermixture of sacred and secular elements, as the plainchant "Aspiciens a longe" overlaps with the triumphant march music accompanying the king's *cortège*, the two mingling together in a jumble of sacred and profane (see Example 18.4). This sort of muddle was a hallmark of Jeanne's fêtes, with the dividing line between secular entertainment and religious ceremony continually smudged.

Perhaps most important, Honegger carefully constructed the sonic composition of the scene so that it would echo the actual experience of witnessing a parade at Jeanne's fête. This involved marshalling diverse sonic forces to increase and decrease in intensity several times over the course of the scene, each element dissolving into the next, giving listeners the embodied experience of being a parade onlooker. Honegger created this effect by layering a profusion of sounding elements and spatial effects. Speaking voices and singing voices combine as the crowd anticipates the king's arrival, and the SATB choir and children's choir are meant to fade in from the distance at different parts of the

EXAMPLE 18.4 Continued

scene. A small wind ensemble with percussion represents a passing village band, and later we hear an approaching drum corps that announces the king's arrival, later made complete with a full orchestra (the brass fanfares muffled with mutes in their initial approach and final retreat). Two pianos, a celesta, and the electronic ondes Martenot represent pealing village bells celebrating the king's arrival. Together with the folk songs, the shouts of villagers, regional accents, and the noise of the celebrating throng, the overall effect plunged listeners into the soundscape of provincial France and its celebratory fêtes, and the audience themselves became participants in this *mystère*.

Part of this work's success had to do with the fact that it achieved what many had hoped for in terms of artistic renewal in early twentieth-century France: it was a popular yet serious, high-quality work, inspired by and written for "the people," based on a subject of national fascination, and inspired by medieval theater. Many reviewers linked the work, and this scene in particular, to the popular, to artistic "renewal" and "revival," and especially to a heightened sense of collective national communion. Reviewing the 1943 recording of *Jeanne d'Arc au bûcher*, critic Robert Desnos wrote,

EXAMPLE 18.4 Continued

Paul Claudel's work is a national work and I defy whoever has the sound of our towns and our countryside in his ear, the color of our sky in his eye, the flavor of our air in his mouth, not to be deeply moved by Scene VIII…where the harmony between the poet and the composer achieves such a vibrant richness that the listener is compelled to participate in it.[65]

This "vibrant richness" was achieved through Claudel and Honegger's construction of a soundscape of Jeanne's medieval world, a soundscape that sounded intimately familiar to listeners who participated in festivals dedicated to Jeanne. Desnos's assertion that *Jeanne au bûcher* is a "national work" echoes what many reviewers claimed about the oratorio, especially during the German occupation of France. In the wake of the embarrassing defeat by Germany in 1940, Jeanne's story offered inspiration and solace to the demoralized French populace. Even if France had been defeated on the battlefield, the success of *Jeanne au bûcher* showed that French art was alive and well and that the French spirit was indomitable.

This sort of rhetoric surrounding Jeanne d'Arc and the French spirit persists in France today, caught up in the pomp and medievalisms peddled at the current fêtes in Orléans. In May 2016, the festivities were presided over by a rising star on the French political scene: Emmanuel Macron. Macron had yet to confirm his bid for the presidency, but journalists searched his speech for hints that might reveal his presidential aspirations.[66] His speech argued that today's France remains divided by uncertainty and doubt, and he proclaimed that the solution was to unite behind Jeanne to strengthen the nation's ties to its rich history:

> Ultimately, Jeanne invites us to consider a doubting France, the France of the little kingdom of Bourges of 1429 [that Jeanne fought for], the France of London in 1940 [the Resistance during the Occupation], and maybe even our France today, that wants to renew the threads of its long history.[67]

Jeanne d'Arc, therefore, serves much the same function today as she did in the early twentieth century. Her story—and the medievalisms her story fashions and replicates— offers France a path forward, a path that cleaves to the past as a way of pushing ahead.

NOTES

1. "Ce n'est pas la première fois que Jeanne d'Arc inspire poètes, artistes, musiciens. Depuis la guerre, ceux-ci se sont souvent penchés sur cette destinée héroïque. Ils ont chanté la petite Française qui fidèle a ses 'voix', traversait une partie de France infestée de bandes armées, pour créer la confiance chez ceux qui l'avaient perdue et ne croyaient plus à leur pays. Plus d'une œuvre inspirée est sortie de ce contact mystique entre l'artiste du XXe siècle et celle qui expia sur le bûcher de Rouen sa foi en l'avenir d'une France vaincue mais indomptée." Paul Le Flem, "Jeanne au bûcher (Honegger)," transcript for the radio broadcast *La Vie musicale*, May 9, 1939, Fonds Paul Le Flem, Médiathèque Musicale Mahler.

2. For a discussion of Dreyer's treatment of the subject, see Donald Greig, "Re-sounding Carl Dreyer's *La Passion de Jeanne d'Arc*," this volume, pp. 247–266.

3. For an overview of Jeanne d'Arc in French history, politics, and culture, see Michel Winock, "Joan of Arc," in *Realms of Memory: Rethinking the French Past*, Vol. 3, *Symbols*, trans. Arthur Goldhammer, ed. Lawrence D. Kritzman (New York: Columbia University Press, 1998), 432–480.

4. On the French fascination with the Middle Ages, see especially Elizabeth Emery and Laura Morowitz, *Consuming the Past: The Medieval Revival in Fin-de-siècle France* (Burlington, VT: Ashgate, 2003). On the revival of medieval music in France, see Katherine Bergeron, *Interpreting the Musical Past: Early Music in Nineteenth-Century France* (New York: Oxford University Press, 2005).

5. Bergeron, *Interpreting the Musical Past*, xxii.

6. On the 1429 establishment of Jeanne's fête in Orléans, see "Chronique de l'établissement de la fête," an eyewitness account of the Battle of Orléans and the celebration that took place afterward, reprinted from a manuscript held at the Bibliothèque de l'École des chartes, Jules Quicherat, *Procès de condemnation et de réhabilitation de Jeanne d'Arc*, vol. 5 (Paris: Renouard, 1849).

7. The Centre Jeanne d'Arc in Orléans conserves much of the archival material related to these fêtes, in Orléans and elsewhere: Centre Jeanne d'Arc, Littérature et célébrations, Fêtes johanniques.

8. This description is based on the author's participation in these fêtes in 2013 and research conducted at the Centre Jeanne d'Arc in Orléans.

9. These activities are chronicled in programs and commemorative albums printed for the fêtes, Centre Jeanne d'Arc, Littérature et célébrations, Fêtes johanniques, Rouen.

10. Commemorative booklet by Louis Boucher, *La Première Fête nationale de Jeanne d'Arc à Rouen* (Rouen: Defontaine, 1922).

11. See commemorative albums, booklets, and programs, Centre Jeanne d'Arc.

12. Annette Kreutziger-Herr, "Imagining Medieval Music: A Short History," *Studies in Medievalism* XIV (2005): 84.

13. For a complete outline of the musical activities that took place at the 1931 Rouen fête, see Elizabeth Dister, "Inspiring the Nation: French Music about Jeanne d'Arc in the 1930s and 1940s" (PhD diss., Washington University–St. Louis, 2015), 83–86.

14. Edmond Spalikowski, ed., "Le V⁰ Centenaire de Jeanne d'Arc à Rouen, 1431–1931," Commemorative album (Rouen: Imprimerie Maugard, 1931), Centre Jeanne d'Arc, Littérature et célébrations, Fêtes johanniques, Rouen.

15. Spalikowski commemorative booklet and "Jeanne d'Arc 5e Centenaire, Rouen, Mai 1931," official program booklet (Rouen: L'Imprimerie Le Cerf, 1931), Centre Jeanne d'Arc, Littérature et célébrations, Fêtes johanniques, Rouen.

16. This was first performed in 1873 at the Théâtre de la Gaîté, and the revival with Sarah Bernhardt was staged at the Théâtre de la Porte-Saint-Martin in 1890. For a study of both the Barbier–Gounod play and Gustave Mermet's opera on Barbier's text, see Thérèse Hurley, "Jeanne d'Arc on the 1870s Musical Stage: Jules Barbier and Charles Gounod's Melodrama and Auguste Mermet's Opera" (PhD diss., University of Oregon, 2013).

17. Charles Gounod, *Jeanne d'Arc*, drame en 5 actes et en vers, de Jules Barbier, piano–vocal score (Paris: Choudens, 1885).

18. At different points, she explained that her voices rang out from the direction of the church and that she had heard them at the hour of Vespers and when the Ave Maria was rung in

the evening. Joseph Fabre, *Procès de condemnation de Jeanne d'Arc, d'après les textes authentiques des procès-verbaux officiels, traduction avec éclaircissements* (Paris: Delagrave, 1884), 56, 67. After Jeanne's execution, a number of witnesses and individuals involved in her execution gave depositions about the event and about their interactions and observations of Jeanne in her last days. Several individuals involved in the trial, including Maître Pierre Morice and Frère Jeane Toutmouillé, claimed that Jeanne said that she was still hearing her voices on the day of her sentencing and that she said that she had heard the voices when the bells sounded for Compline and when they rang in the morning for Matins. Fabre, *Procès de condemnation*, 394–395.

19. See the testimonies of Simonin Musnier and Dominique Jacob, who both knew Jeanne as children, in Joseph Fabre, *Procès de réhabilitation de Jeanne d'Arc, raconté et traduit d'après les textes latins officiels* (Paris: Delagrave, 1888), 1:99, 110.

20. Fabre, *Procès de réhabilitation*, 1:106. Here, Fabre notes that the two Latin sources differ, so it is not entirely clear whether Jeanne gave Le Drapier wool, "lanas," or cake shaped like a moon, called *lunas*.

21. Fabre, *Procès de réhabilitation*, 1:201.

22. Fabre, *Procès de condemnation*; Fabre, *Procès de réhabilitation*.

23. See Annette Kreutziger-Herr's discussion of Hugo in "Imagining Medieval Music," 81.

24. Alain Corbin, *Village Bells: Sound and Meaning in the 19th-Century French Countryside*, trans. Martin Thom (New York, Columbia University Press, 1998), 187–188.

25. Corbin, *Village Bells*, x.

26. Bells are also featured prominently as a marker for this kind of liminality in Margarethe von Trotta's 2009 film, *Vision—Aus dem Leben der Hildegard von Bingen*. See Jennifer Bain's contribution to this volume, "Nature as Enlightenment in *Vision—Aus dem Leben der Hildegard von Bingen*," pp. 468–483.

27. Hurley, "Jeanne d'Arc on the 1870s Musical Stage," 5–6.

28. On phantasmagoria, boulevard theater, and melodrama, see Laurent Mannoni and Ben Brewster, "The Phantasmagoria," *Film History* 8, no. 4 (1996): 390–415; and James R. Lehning, *The Melodramatic Thread: Spectacle and Political Culture in Modern France* (Bloomington: Indiana University Press, 2007).

29. Tomasi's score is unpublished but the manuscript is conserved in the Archives of Radio France, Documentation musicale. The original version of this play, written by René Bruyez, was first performed in Orléans in 1938, and it was later broadcast on the radio with incidental music by Tomasi in 1941 and 1943. "La Radio," *Le Jour: L'Écho de Paris* (May 11, 1941): 2; "Les galas de la Radio nationale," *Comœdia* (May 8, 1943): 4; announcement of radio programming on Radio nationale for May 8, 1943, *Radio nationale* (May 2–8, 1943): 12.

30. Hurley, "Jeanne d'Arc on the 1870s Musical Stage," 11.

31. The ondes Martenot were used in a number of works about Jeanne by youth theater ensembles and Jeune France, such as Léon Chancérel, Raoul Serène, and G. Croses-Planes, *Mission de Jeanne d'Arc*, Répertoire des Comédiens Routiers, vol. 12 (Paris: La Hutte, 1938), Fonds Léon Chancerel, Bibliothèque nationale, Arts du spectacle. The instrument was also used in eight performances of *Jeanne et la vie des autres* at Vichy and Lyon in 1942. Outline of programs planned for the Casino de Vichy, Archives de Louis Hautecoeur, F/21/8096, Archives nationales; *Jeanne et la vie des autres* poster from 1942, Archives of the Ministère de l'Information, F/41/308, Archives nationales.

32. The full scores and parts for most of the movements are available for consultation at the Archives of Radio France, Documentation musicale.

33. The idea of casting the devil as a speaking part in a sung drama also appears in later works, most notably in Carl Maria von Weber's *Der Freischütz*.

34. For details on Paray's career, see W. L. Landowski, *Paul Paray: Musicien de France et du monde* (Lyon: Éditions et Imprimeries de Sud-est, 1956); and Jean-Philippe Mousnier, *Les Grands Chefs d'orchestre: Paul Paray* (Paris: L'Harmattan, 1998). Although Paul Paray was perhaps better known as a conductor than a composer and although this work rarely receives performances today, in the 1930s and 1940s, it was performed so frequently that it was perhaps the most oft-performed and well-known johannique work of the period. In Rouen, Paris, and Marseille alone, this work was performed at least a dozen times between 1931 and 1943. See chart of performances in Dister, "Inspiring the Nation," 98–99.

35. It includes four movements: Kyrie, Gloria, Sanctus, and Agnus Dei. Only the piano–vocal score is readily available: Paul Paray, *Messe du cinquième centenaire de la mort de Jeanne d'Arc, pour soli, chœur et orchestre, partition réduite par l'auteur* (Paris: Lemoine, 1934).

36. See, for instance, the following reviews and commentaries: Jacques Janin, "La 'Messe du V. centenaire de Jeanne d'Arc' de M. Paul Paray," *L'Ami du peuple du soir* (November 11, 1931), *Articles de presse sur "Messe de Jeanne d'Arc," musique de Paul Paray*, Bibliothèque nationale, Arts du specacle; M. B., "Orchestre Symphonique de Paris," *Le Ménestrel* (November 13, 1931); Paul Le Flem, "Les Concerts symphoniques," *Comœdia* (November 9, 1931); R. F., "Concerts-Colonne," *Le Ménestrel* (November 4, 1938); Paul Le Flem, "Causerie: Messe du 5e Centenaire de la Mort de Jeanne d'Arc," transcript for the radio program *Causerie Musicale*, May 9,1940, Fonds Paul le Flem, Médiathèque Musicale Mahler.

37. Le Flem, "Les Concerts symphoniques"; Critic Henri Hie quoted in Spalikowski commemorative album, Centre Jeanne d'Arc.

38. See M. B., "Orchestre Symphonique de Paris"; Le Flem, "Les Concerts symphoniques."

39. For the *moto proprio*'s influence on French music of the interwar period, see Sylvain Caron and Michel Duchesneau, eds., *Musique, art et religion dans l'entre-deux-guerres* (Lyon: Symétrie, 2009).

40. See commemorative albums, booklets, and programs, Centre Jeanne d'Arc.

41. "Un prologue, dix tableaux et interludes mêlés de vers, de chants profanes et sacrés et de sonneries authentiques du XVe siècle." René Bruyez, *Jeanne et la vie des autres*, program for performances on May 5, 7, and 8, 1938, at Orléans (Orléans: Impr. de "La France du Centre," 1938), Dossiers de presse, Bibliothèque nationale, Arts du spectacle.

42. The score remains unpublished, but the orchestral and piano–vocal scores are in the Fonds Maurice Jaubert, Bibliothèque nationale, Arts du spectacle. On Jaubert's life and works, see François Porcile, *Maurice Jaubert: Musicien populaire ou maudit?* (Paris: Les Éditeurs Français Réunis, 1971).

43. The text is drawn from Charles Péguy, *Jeanne d'Arc: Drame en trois pièces* (Paris: Cahiers de la quinzaine, 1897).

44. F. I. "Critique des Concerts: Hommage à Jeanne d'Arc (9 mai)," *L'Information musicale* (May 22, 1942): 948.

45. Serge Moreaux, "La Musique: Musique pour Jeanne au Gala de 'La Gerbe,' " *La Gerbe* (May 14, 1942): 7.

46. Manuel Rosenthal, *Jeanne d'Arc* (Paris: Jobert, 1936).

47. Joseph Delteil, *Jeanne d'Arc* (Paris: Grasset, 1925). The novel also played a role in the conception of Dreyer's famous film *La Passion de Jeanne d'Arc*. For more on the relationship between film and novel, see Donald Greig's contribution to this volume, "Re-sounding Dreyer's *La Passion de Jeanne d'Arc*," pp. 247–266.

48. See the reviews in *Recueil factice d'articles de presse sur* Jeanne d'Arc *de Joseph Delteil*, Fonds Rondel, Bibliothèque nationale, Arts du spectacle. See also Rim Taga Gabsi, "Delteil tel qu'on ignore, chantre de Jeanne d'Arc," in *Delteil en détail*, ed. Anne-Lise Blanc (Perpignan: Presses universitaires de Perpignan, 2011), 103–118.

49. Although the published score includes no text, in Rosenthal's manuscript score the composer copied short passages from the sections of Delteil's novel that corresponded to each movement, and reviews from the 1930s show that the work was performed with a speaker. The manuscript is held in Fonds Manuel Rosenthal, Médiathèque Musicale Mahler.

50. "La plupart de mes confrères ont été emballés sur cette *Jeanne d'Arc* turbulente, mais ont remarqué ça et là des heurts pénibles, une impiété désobligeante, un mauvais goût excessif, des effets naïfs ou scandaleux, des crudités acides." Durand, "Promenade musicale: Colonne, Lamoureux, O. S. P., Pasdeloup, Poulet-Siohan, Société des Concerts," *La Page musicale* (October 30, 1936): 2.

51. According to Rosenthal's biographer, the premiere was a debacle. Dominique Saudinos, *Manuel Rosenthal: Une Vie* (Paris: Mercure de France, 1992), 88. One critic was particularly shocked by this effect and wanted the *récitante* to provide some reason for the inclusion of the "Marseillaise." Durand, "Promenade musicale," 2.

52. Arthur Honegger and Paul Claudel, *Jeanne d'Arc au bûcher* (Paris: Éditions Maurice Senart, 1947).

53. The most complete study of the oratorio is Huguette Calmel and Pascal Lécroart, *Jeanne d'Arc au bûcher de Paul Claudel et Arthur Honegger* (Geneva: Éditions Papillon, 2004).

54. Prior to the 1939 performance in Orléans, the work premiered in 1938 in Basel under the direction of Paul Sacher, although Rubinstein, Claudel, and Honegger had always hoped it would premiere at the Paris Opéra.

55. Calmel and Lécroart, *Jeanne d'Arc au bûcher*, 12.

56. On Gustave Cohen and the Théophiliens, see Helen Solterer, *Medieval Roles for Modern Times: Theater and the Battle for the French Republic* (University Park: Pennsylvania State University, 2010). The public's fascination with medieval dramas even led to a medieval theater exhibit at the International Exposition in 1937. See Fonds Théophiliens, Bibliothèque nationale, Arts du spectacle.

57. On Rubinstein's familiarity with the Théophiliens, see Calmel and Lécroart, *Jeanne d'Arc au bûcher*, 12.

58. Honegger's friend Fernand Ochsé was directing this play and convinced him to play the part of a musician within the drama. Later, Honegger collaborated with Ochsé to provide music for a libretto Ochsé had written for a medieval *mystère* called *Mystère de Pâques*, which was intended to be produced at the Théâtre du Vieux-Colombier but never materialized. See letters in Arthur Honegger and Harry Halbreich, ed., *Lettres à ses parents: 1914–1922* (Geneva: Éditions Papillon, 2005), 147, 178.

59. Serge Added, *Le Théâtre dans les années Vichy* (Paris: Éditions Ramsay, 1992), 231–234. See director Jacques Copeau's writings, especially *Le Théâtre populaire* (Paris: Presses universitaires de France, 1941).

60. On the connections between Meyerhold and Copeau, see Jane Milling and Graham Ley, *Modern Theories of Performance: From Stanslavski to Boal* (London: Palgrave, 2001), 55–86.

61. Perhaps the most important such group was the Comédiens routiers, led by Léon Chancerel. Much of the group's documents are conserved in the Beaux-arts Archives, Archives nationales, F/21/8373, and the Fonds Léon Chancerel, Bibliothèque nationale, Arts du spectacle. See also Hubert Gignoux, *Histoire d'une famille théâtrale: Jacques*

Copeau, Léon Chancerel, les Comédiens-routiers, la décentralisation dramatique (Lausanne: Éditions de l'Aire, 1984); Véronique Chabrol, "Jeune France: Une Expérience de recherche et de décentralisation culturelle, novembre 1940–mars 1942" (PhD diss., University of Paris–Sorbonne, 1974), 142, 197.

62. "Elle [l'œuvre] a les traits d'un mystère médiéval où le peuple, d'abord, est convié.... L'évident intention de ces deux maîtres est précisement d'arbitrer leur art de toute concession pour qu'il s'adresse plus directement à tous." André George, "Jeanne au bûcher," *Les Nouvelles littéraires* (June 17, 1939), *Jeanne au bûcher: Dossier d'œuvre*, Bibliothèque nationale, Opéra.

63. For a reception history that explains this in full, see Dister, "Inspiring the Nation," chap. 4.

64. Paul Claudel, *Jeanne d'Arc au bûcher* (Paris: Gallimard, 1939), 57–58.

65. "A ce titre, l'œuvre de Paul Claudel est une œuvre nationale et je défie quiconque a dans l'oreille le bruit de nos villes et de nos compagnes, dans l'œil la couleur de notre ciel, dans la bouche la saveur de notre air, de ne pas être bouleversé pas la scène VIII...où l'accord entre le poète et le musicien atteint une telle plentitude vibrante que l'auditeur est obligé d'y participer." Robert Desnos, "Disques: Jeanne d'Arc au bûcher," *Aujourd'hui* (July 21, 1943); *Recueil "Jeanne au bûcher": Auditions diverses et enregistrement intégral, 1940–1943*, Bibliothèque nationale, Arts du spectacle.

66. The French political magazine *Le Nouvelle observateur* published the entire text of Macron's speech, annotated with humorous interpolations communicating the unspoken meaning of each part: Pascal Riché, "Emmanuel Macron et Jeanne d'Arc: Le Discours intégral (et ses messages subliminaux)," *Le Nouvel Observateur* (May 9, 2016).

67. Riché, "Emmanuel Macron et Jeanne d'Arc," *L'Obs*.

CHAPTER 19

MEDIEVALISM AND RUED LANGGAARD'S ROMANTIC IMAGE OF QUEEN DAGMAR

NILS HOLGER PETERSEN

THIS chapter discusses the Danish composer Rued Langgaard's (1893–1952) interest in medieval imagery in his Ninth Symphony (1942), namely, the use of traditional Danish ballads featuring Queen Dagmar of Denmark (ca. 1186–1212) that tell the story of her tragic early death in childbirth. Conspicuously, Langgaard borrowed the melody of the most famous of these ballads and used the ballads' narrative material in mottos for three of the four movements. The medieval queen was also reflected in the title for the symphony, *From Queen Dagmar's Town*. Generally, Langgaard's compositions do not focus on medieval topics, nor do they employ or appropriate medieval music to any marked extent. One might well wonder, then, what purpose this medievalism served. I suggest that the medieval figure and musical material found in Langgaard's symphony is not a nostalgic retrospective of the past, but a desire to integrate elements of a (purported) saintly past into his own music and that this saintly past functioned as a source of inspiration for his individual development. Medievalism here is related to his undogmatic religious Christian beliefs and his fascination with musical romanticism. Langgaard's medievalism will be discussed partly in contrast to the medievalism of Thomas Laub (1852–1927), a scholar, an influential Danish composer of church music, and a church music reformer, whose Cecilianism-inspired ideas Langgaard fought, but whose (idiosyncratic) version of the aforementioned medieval melody was used by Langgaard in his symphony.

At first glance, the symphony seems to have been inspired by a particular occasion—the reopening of the Danish national site Riberhus Slotsbanke on June 14, 1942. In 1940–1941, the National Museum in Copenhagen had carried out the excavation of the Palace Hill for the medieval royal residence *Riberhus*, just outside of Ribe, some three hundred kilometers from Copenhagen. Though only the moat and a few stone remnants were preserved at this site, it had been a well-known *lieu de mémoire* for Queen Dagmar, and a statue carved by the well-known Danish sculptor, Anne Marie Carl-Nielsen, wife of composer Carl Nielsen, had been erected there in 1913. In 1942, when the site was reopened to the public after restoration work, the event was marked with a festal service in Ribe Cathedral, where Langgaard had been appointed organist in 1940. For this occasion, Langgaard composed his organ work, *Fantasy on the Folktune "Queen Dagmar lies ill in Ribe,"* based on the most well-known melody for the ballad *Dronning Dagmar ligger i Ribe syg,* "Queen Dagmar lies ill in Ribe."[1] Since 1933, this melody had sounded daily from the carillons in the tower of the cathedral. Following the premiere of his *Fantasy*, Langgaard then composed the Ninth Symphony, orchestrating the organ *Fantasy* for its third movement and including it as a voice in the orchestra, ad libitum. He drew on similar, Dagmar-related narrative material for the first two movements.[2] However, the symphony is much more than simply an expansion of the organ work. It may take its point of departure from the Dagmar narrative and the town of Ribe, but it ends with a much broader musical representation of how to relate to the past. It is the aim of this chapter to characterize Langgaard's medievalism in this work, through an interpretation of the finale and its relation to the Dagmar material in the previous movements.

At the time of Langgaard's writing, the Danish *folkeviser*, or traditional ballads, were believed to date from the Middle Ages, though documentation for the ballad texts dates back only as far as the sixteenth century, and collections and transcriptions of the melodies date only from the beginning of the nineteenth century.[3] Four ballads with variants about Queen Dagmar are preserved, but there is comparatively little historical and biographical information about her.[4] She is known to have been the daughter of the Bohemian king, Ottokar I. Around 1205, she traveled to Denmark to marry King Valdemar II (king from 1202 to 1241). The Dagmar ballads connect her to two localities in Denmark. All the ballads situate her in the town of Ribe in the far southwest of the country. There, according to the ballad about her death, she fell ill during childbirth and died at the age of twenty-six. The refrain of one ballad states that her body was moved to St. Bendt's (St. Benedict's) Church in Ringsted, in the center of the island of Zealand, to be buried with the other Danish royalty. Her grave is marked by a ledger stone in the church floor in front of the high altar next to the grave of King Valdemar II with the inscription *regina Dagmar prima vxor Waldemari secvndi* ("Queen Dagmar, first wife of Valdemar II").[5]

The Danish traditional ballads seem to have been cultivated privately, possibly in noble houses in the Renaissance. As already stated, there is little knowledge about such songs before the sixteenth century. However, as I will touch on further, some scholars, such as Thomas Laub, believed that the melodies were written in a style similar to medieval chant and were therefore much older. The ballad about Queen Dagmar's death may have originated before the Reformation since it contained references to Catholic notions of purgatory in its oldest preserved (manuscript) version. These references are expurgated in the first printed edition based on this manuscript and published by a Danish humanist and Lutheran pastor.[6] As in many other parts of Europe, however, around 1800, romanticism inspired a general interest in the Middle Ages, which produced scholarly endeavors, among them a philological interest in poetry and traditional ballads. These were systematically collected and a large body of ballad texts were published in a scholarly edition, beginning in the mid-nineteenth century, with the first volume appearing in 1853.[7] Some melodies were also collected and published during the nineteenth century, but a scholarly edition of melodies was only established in the second half of the twentieth century. The melody for *Queen Dagmar lies ill in Ribe* had been printed in a collection of old ballad melodies arranged by the naturalized Danish composer C. E. F. Weyse (1774–1842) and later by another romantic composer, A. P. Berggreen. However, it was the edition by Thomas Laub (first published in 1899) that came into general use, and it was his version that was used by Langgaard in his *Fantasy* and Ninth Symphony.[8]

At the same time that the ballads began to attract interest, attention turned to revitalizing and elaborating the image of Queen Dagmar as a mild and saintly person. During the nineteenth century, scholars and artists pursued a mixture of historical speculation and fantasy about the saintly Dagmar. The novelist and poet Bernhard Severin Ingemann drew attention to Danish royal medieval history through his medievalist novels beginning in 1824.[9] His novel *Valdemar Sejr* (1826), which was translated into English as *Waldemar Surnamed Seir, or the Victorious*, in 1841, was largely responsible for the later reception of Queen Dagmar as saintly and beautiful. This image of Dagmar as a saint was also affirmed by the American folklorist Tracey R. Sands's work. Studying the reception of Queen Dagmar, Sands noted the presence of a painting of a young woman in prayer on the wall in the nave of St. Bendt's church in Ringsted where Queen Dagmar is buried. Although this has been a Lutheran church since the Danish Reformation in 1536, the painting has an inscription that speaks to the Catholic image of Dagmar as a saint and includes the expression, "God's angel, Dagmar, pray to Our Savior to heal what is broken in the land of Denmark," dated 1916.[10] The establishing of a statue of Queen Dagmar in 1913, the restoration of the Palace Hill outside Ribe, and the celebration in Ribe Cathedral in 1942 should all be seen as part of a reception history that sought to connect Queen Dagmar to the Danish nation. Undoubtedly, the interest in Danish medieval history, not least as it came to the fore in Ingemann's novels, was important for the construction of a Danish national identity in the nineteenth century. This national identity became even more important after Denmark lost the southern part of Jutland in the Danish–Prussian War in 1864. Ribe, situated in the northern part of Schleswig, was preserved as a Danish territory, but after 1864, the town was situated extremely close to the new Danish–German border. The strength of Danish nationalism won out in 1920 after World War I, when inhabitants of northern Schleswig (Germany) chose by referendum to be part of Denmark, which thereby won back territory that had been lost in 1864.

However significant national identity was to the Danes at this time, it does not seem to have played a meaningful role for Rued Langgaard's treatment of Queen Dagmar. Rather, Langgaard appears to have been drawn to the Catholic vision of Dagmar as a saint and leveraged this image for his own artistic aesthetic. Langgaard was drawn to the Catholic Church more than to Danish Lutheranism, although he formally remained

Lutheran and did not convert. Altogether, his faith can be characterized by an undogmatic Christian outlook based on personal experience and inspired by theosophy. His views were fundamentally biblical with a focus on the integration of music, theater, and religion, inspired by Wagner's *Parsifal*. In the first part of the 1920s, he expressed a vision of a new kind of religious music far exceeding traditional Lutheran church music and not confined to performance in the church. Musically, this came to the fullest expression in his allegorical opera *Antichrist* (1921–1923, with later revisions), now considered one of his most important works. Only fragments of it were performed during his life.[11]

The Ninth Symphony, and the organ *Fantasy* based on the same Dagmar ballad, may be seen as a product of the opening of Riberhus, a historical site of Danish national identity, but Langgaard appears to have been most interested in the broader musical and religious inspiration shaped by the reception of Queen Dagmar and the vision of her as a medieval Catholic saint. Langgaard usually gave poetic titles to his works and used musical mottos to invoke ideas he wanted to express. This is also the case for the Ninth Symphony, wherein the titles for the first three movements use the name Ribe, the location of the castle Riberhus where Dagmar is reputed to have lived with King Valdemar. Langgaard quoted traditional Dagmar ballads as mottos for the first three movements, the titles of which are "Queen Dagmar Sails to Ribe" (first movement), "The Dance at Ribe Palace" (second movement), and "Ribe Cathedral" (third movement). The fourth movement, "Finale: The Turbulent Life of the Past," does not use a musical motto, nor does it refer to Ribe.[12] The lack of a motto from the ballads and the intriguing title for the finale of the symphony in conjunction with an interpretation of its music reveal something of Langgaard's relationship to the Middle Ages and to the past as such.

Although today Langgaard is one of the most esteemed Danish composers of the early twentieth century, he was far from well established as a composer or musician during his lifetime. Langgaard has been described as having been born at the wrong time, living and working in the shadow of his older contemporary, Carl Nielsen, who dominated Danish music throughout Langgaard's life and, because of dedicated followers, even more after his death in 1931. The Langgaard scholar, Bendt Viinholdt Nielsen, maintains that this only partly explains the poor reception of Langgaard's music during his life.[13] Langgaard was a romanticist at a time when romanticism was no longer in vogue in Denmark. Moreover, Langgaard's musical aesthetic occasionally included modernist visionary musical elements before Denmark was introduced to continental modernism. His sometimes very unusual blend of musical styles is reminiscent of Charles Ives. In contemporary Germany and internationally, many different styles were present simultaneously, though rarely within the same composer's oeuvre. Richard Strauss had huge success internationally while new musical movements were appearing in many places, for instance, in France (not least in the music of Stravinsky but also that of "Les Six"), Austria (Schoenberg and his school), and Hungary (Bartók). As a small country, Denmark may have been particularly prone to single influences and was indeed dominated by Carl Nielsen's musical tastes and style(s) for decades after his death. Thus, romantic music (especially Wagner and the late romantics) was generally dismissed and new modernistic trends were not heeded, although in limited ways they were reflected in some of Nielsen's own later works.

Langgaard was not oriented toward Danish music or toward Danish nationalism. Indeed, he was extremely critical and, it seems, jealous of Carl Nielsen despite certain of his works bearing something of Nielsen's musical style.[14] Most spectacularly, his jealousy and anger came to the fore in June 1948, when he wrote a sarcastic piece for chorus and organ with the title *Carl Nielsen Our Great Composer*, which he sent as a proposal to the Danish Radio.[15] The text of the composition is identical to the title; the piece comprises thirty-two bars and indicates it should be repeated "eternally."[16] Instead, Langgaard found his musical inspiration in two rather incompatible romantic composers, the Danish Mendelssohn-inspired Niels Wilhelm Gade (1817–1890) and Richard Wagner (1813–1883). In 1932 he wrote, "If Wagner and Gade constitute the *end* of Romanticism, they are also a *beginning*" (Langgaard's emphasis).[17] Richard Strauss also seems to have been an important inspiration behind his music, although Langgaard's deeply rooted religious outlook separates him and his music significantly from Strauss; in his childhood home there was a particularly critical attitude toward the secularity of Strauss and other contemporary composers.[18]

As discussed, Langgaard was not highly valued as a composer in his lifetime, although he was recognized as a great musical talent and a child prodigy. Occasionally, some of his music was performed, but he did not achieve a prominent position as a composer until he was rediscovered in the late 1960s. While the Ninth Symphony was not performed in concert before 1993, it was broadcast live by the Danish Radio from a studio and performed by the Danish Radio Symphony Orchestra (as it was named at the time) in May 1943, and individual movements were also performed occasionally during the following years.[19] Only eight of his sixteen symphonies were performed before his death. Bendt Viinholdt Nielsen argues that because Langgaard was an autodidact composer and musician (whose parents mostly taught him at home and kept him from school), he became an outsider, not only as a musician and composer, but also more generally.[20] In his youth, he had an early success in Germany, where his First Symphony was praised by Arthur Nikisch. Max Fiedler and the Berlin Philharmonic Orchestra performed the symphony at a sponsored concert in Berlin in 1913, for which the Danish queen Alexandrine acted as patron. The concert also included two other Langgaard compositions and was well received in Germany as well as by Danish critics. In the early 1920s, some of his works continued to be performed with success in Germany, but these individual successes did not help to establish a secure reputation for Langgaard in Denmark during his lifetime. Indeed, with some exceptions, his works were heavily criticized in Denmark if they were performed at all. Despite the occasional recognition, Langgaard was not understood in Denmark and was viewed as a pathetic and burdensome figure.[21] It was therefore a singular event when, in 1949, he was invited to a concert in Ribe by the Aarhus Symphony Orchestra, who performed the third movement of his Ninth Symphony outside the program, and Langgaard, for once, received enormous applause.[22] It is difficult not to associate this latter success with a nationalist reception of this particular work.

As already stated, Langgaard's composition of the *Fantasy* and symphony owed much to a recent post as organist at Ribe Cathedral. Musicians who heard his performances in their youth testified to Langgaard's great talent as a performing organist and pianist. The composer and director for the Music Conservatory in Odense, Tage Nielsen, described Langgaard as an accomplished musician who was able to render the most complicated scores on the piano without any hesitation. Music critics also agreed that his organ playing was outstanding. It is striking, then, that Langgaard did not attain a permanent post as church organist until 1939, although he had applied for organist positions earlier. Ironically, since it played into his later compositional success, he viewed the post of organist at Ribe Cathedral as a kind of exile, feeling that he had been banned from Copenhagen, the musical center of Denmark. Indeed, he was not the only person who understood his position in Ribe in such terms. The influential Danish conductor and church musician, Mogens Wöldike, who apparently in practice if not formally seems to have helped him secure the position, is remarked to have said in a private statement, "We put a stamp on his back and sent him out of our midst."[23] Part of Langgaard's problem in obtaining a permanent position as a church organist, despite his acknowledged qualifications, was that he was known to be in strong opposition to the church music reforms, initiated by the aforementioned Thomas Laub.

Laub's reform ideas were inspired by German Cecilianism, not least by Carl von Winterfeld's (1784–1852) idea that "Lutheran music from the Reformation should constitute the primary paradigm for Protestant church music."[24] Like Winterfeld, Laub was even critical of J. S. Bach as a composer of church music.[25] While not always popular with congregations and certainly not supported by Langgaard, Laub's ideas of church music reform became influential among church musicians and some theologians. Wöldike, who was a staunch Laubian and acted as a consultant for the Danish Ministry for Church Affairs in connection with organist posts in Danish churches, could thus not recommend Langgaard as a church organist, that is, until it seemed opportune to send him away from Copenhagen.[26] These seemingly personal animosities however, did not lead Langgaard to reject every aspect of Laub's legacy. Laub was one of the most influential editors of the traditional ballad melodies at the beginning of the twentieth century, and this work was useful for Langgaard's purposes. Langgaard's rejection of Laub's ideas for reforming church music therefore, did not extend to a dismissal of his editorial work.

As I have pointed out, the interest of Laub and other contemporary composers such as Carl Nielsen in medieval modal song belonged in an entirely different context than one defined by romanticism and its interest in Danish medieval history and narrative. Like his Catholic and Protestant German counterparts, Laub sought to reconstruct and appropriate medieval and reformation melodies to purge the contemporary style of church hymns but also popular song of its romantic subjectivity. The modal character of these melodies would match Laub's desire to erase what he thought of as musically suspicious elements and thus supported his reform of Danish church music.[27] He edited and published the melody of the Dagmar ballad, *Queen Dagmar lies ill in Ribe*, according to his ideas of medieval melody around the turn of the twentieth century.[28] Laub's version of this melody impacted performance traditions in Denmark throughout the twentieth century, not least through its inclusion in the so-called *Højskolesangbogen* (a widely used songbook used in Danish folk high schools and in many private homes) and its accompanying music book (*melodibog*). First published in 1922 and edited by Laub and Carl Nielsen with numerous subsequent editions, Laub's version would become known to generations of Danes. Langgaard's interest in the medieval melody, however, was quite different from Laub's. To characterize Langgaard's medievalism, it will thus be important to compare Langgaard's setting and treatment of the ballad melody to Laub's version and to contextualize them against the differences between Laub's and Langgaard's attitudes to church music.

Langgaard, Laub and the Melody for *Queen Dagmar lies ill in Ribe*

In 1899, Laub and Axel Olrik published twenty-eight melodies of old ballads in an edition that set all stanzas so the melodies' individual adaptions to each stanza were predetermined and obvious. The ballad, *Queen Dagmar lies ill in Ribe*, appears as no. 22 with twenty-two stanzas.[29] The songs were set without harmonization or accompaniment, but Laub added an appendix with a few chords for each ballad, clearly meant to give a minimum of support for *a cappella* or solo singing.[30] Although the first edition provided no introduction, an introduction was included in later editions. Laub wrote a similar introduction about the performance of the old ballads for the first edition of the *Højskolesangbogen*, a songbook for Danish high schools published in 1922 and reprinted in the fourth edition in 1940. The version from the *Højskolesangbogen* (1922/1940) is the closest in chronology to Langgaard's setting (of 1942) and the most likely source for Langgaard. A comparison of Laub's musical setting of the Dagmar ballad from the 1940 edition with Langgaard's setting reveals that they are identical. Laub's original setting of 1899 provides a single melodic line for a soloist to sing, whereas in the *Højskolesangbogen*, Laub set the refrain for four voices, probably for use as a piano accompaniment for the community's singing of the refrain and to provide musical support for each voice. Laub's 1940 version of the ballad can be seen in Figure 19.1. Only variants for melodies of two stanzas are included in that version, whereas in the 1899 version all stanzas were set with the necessary slight melodic variations and the chords for the accompaniment only partly covered the refrain, directives that spoke to Laub's idea of performance. In his introduction to the old ballads in this songbook, Laub first makes it clear that the ballads are narrative songs:

> They are only shown to full advantage, the values of their poetic and musical beauty can only be in evidence, when they are sung by an individual, a lead singer, who is able to bring alive the content, the narrative. Then the refrain, the constantly repeated answer of the audience to the address of the singer, can really express how they (the audience) are moved by the cause of events.[31]

Referring to the scholarly editions published by Svend Grundtvig, Laub maintains that since we now know more about the ballads, there is no reason to perform them as

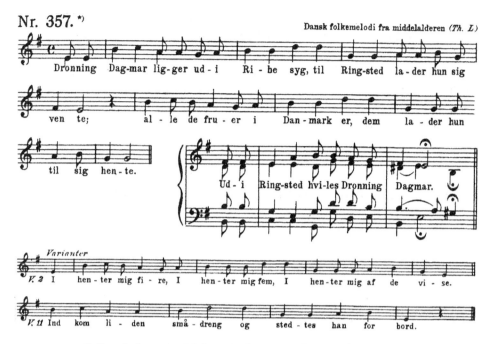

FIGURE 19.1 Folk melody no. 357, Nielsen, Laub, Ring, and Aagaard, 1940, 155.

community songs, which necessitated unfavorable metric and melodic modifications. He then continues,

> One treats the ballads in an even worse way when they are made into art achievements for professional singers, and the melodies are transformed into modern romanzas with modern piano accompaniment, that is they are moved into a style, which is entirely opposite to their own. If in addition they are embellished with all kinds of refined theatre gimmicks, the audience will cheer, but where have the ballads gone?[32]

A straightforward comparison between Laub's setting and the setting of the melody in Langgaard's organ *Fantasy* (identical, except for the instrumentation, with the third movement of the symphony) does not make sense. Langgaard's setting is not for singing, but uses the melodic material for a purely instrumental composition, a work of art music, an organ prelude, intended for a church service. Despite Laub's statements, he would not necessarily have been against such an artistic appropriation. In his *Musik og kirke* (Music and church) from 1920, his second and most comprehensive presentation of his view of music history and of what is required for music in the church, he makes a fundamental distinction between church music and art music:

> Let us imagine that one of David's Psalms, a psalm of praise or a penitential psalm is to be set in music. This can be done in two ways. The composer can identify with David's mental state, identify with him, and thereby be capable of expressing all the

emotions that pass through his mind. He can make his musical expression for these emotions so beautiful and moving that we are all engaged.... Such a music can have a great artistic value, it can also have a religious value, but it is not music for the church service. The churchgoers do not assemble at the service to feel emotions about the emotions of another person, even if they are ever so beautifully expressed; they assemble to state the words of the liturgy and thereby their own praises and prayers, stating them in the common tone that expresses the mental position of the whole congregation, not of the individual, in relation to the words.[33]

For Laub, this basic theological view of the purpose of music for church services was combined with a view on music history, which, briefly summarized, made "modern" tonality (in the major and minor modes) inappropriate for the task of writing music for church services. In Laub's view, modern tonality had developed to be able to express individual feelings, as opposed to the music before ca. 1600. Thus, medieval chant and music in the old church modes were better equipped for the needs of church services, and Laub accordingly based his church music reforms on inconsistent attempts at composing new hymns in a style that was at least inspired by Lutheran hymn melodies and Gregorian chant. At the same time, he heavily criticized what he felt were romantic hymn melodies. The main point for him was to avoid what he called *modern chords*, by which he seems especially to have meant modulations within a hymn (although he did occasionally employ modulations, albeit in a limited way, in his own hymn melodies).[34] Laub required liturgical music to take its cue from a supposed lack of individual emotionality in medieval melody, and his own hymns attempt to follow this ideal, however historically dubious this may be.[35]

Even though Laub might not have objected to a different setting in a performance context outside the church service, he would probably not have approved of such art music as the organ prelude *Fantasy* being part of the festal service on June 14, 1942. Bendt Viinholdt Nielsen pointed out that for Laub, the only music that belonged in the church service was what supported and kept together the congregational song. For Laub, the service was not about listening to music.[36]

It is instructive to look at Langgaard's criticism of Laub's reform ideology, which, as pointed out by Bendt Viinholdt Nielsen, primarily regards what he perceived as a narrowness in Laub's idea of a "pure church style": "Here he was in total disagreement with Laub and the adherents of 'the pure church style' who wanted to eliminate all emotionality, pathos and subjective artistic display from the church service."[37] In an article published in the journal *Kirken* ("The Church") in 1933 with the (translated) title "Art and the Singing of Hymns," Langgaard presents his view on church music as church art. He does so partly through positive inspiration from the parables of Jesus, Wagner (citing Wagner's 1880 *Art and Religion*), and the great early modern church painters and partly in criticism of, and in fierce opposition to, Laub's ideas. For the purpose of this chapter, one important statement from this article should be quoted:

And even though "the old artistic style of singing," Palestrina, was, as Laub maintains, "an expression of what the congregation felt in their hearts," in contrast to the later style, which according to Laub "seduces" people to put themselves forward in a *vain and conceited* manner, how is it possible to draw the line between "the heart of the congregation" and "vanity"?[38]

Langgaard thus questions a fundamental assumption in Laub's thought, the idea that one may find a "pure" or "true" church music by avoiding certain styles that, in Laub's opinion, are conceited or serve individual emotional purposes and are not completely subordinate to the widespread notion of "the Word" (of God) as possible only to express in words. Langgaard claims the opposite: that Christ is poetic, that the church service, to be Christian, must be poetic, and that music is essential in that context. To him, Laub's distinction between acceptable and unacceptable stylistic traits is impossible, or rather based on completely subjective (or idiosyncratic) value judgments. He points out the analogy between visual embellishment of churches through "great art" and the use of art music and asserts that if one claims that art music does not belong in church services, then it follows that neither do art works.

What emerges from Langgaard's article is an attitude that understands individual emotionality as an important expression of Christianity and thus must include music as a fundamental Christian means of expression. What matters, it seems, is not the style, but true emotion—the atmosphere. Music should, indeed, support the Gospel, but "there is nothing to support the view that congregational singing, as Laub maintains with reference to the oldest church music, 'must *only* be a profoundly simple Yes and Amen to the Word.'"[39]

In the context of Langgaard's *Fantasy* on the Dagmar ballad, the consequence of Langgaard's attitude must be that there are no preconceived stylistic norms. The piece is neither *against* Laub's style nor *for* it. It is also neither against nor for medieval music. It rather integrates the music of the past, as well as different music styles, into an overall musical form that Langgaard felt was poetically and musically relevant. The same is true, in a broader context and larger musical form for the full symphony, a work and a genre, which for Langgaard was not distinct from church music. Though it is a different genre, with different practical performance conditions, in terms of theology and aesthetics, it is not separate from the world of church music:

> In its best moments, the so-called "secular" development of music did not lead to the demise of church music—on the contrary. Laub's position, which he attempts to impose in a dictatorial fashion, is moreover self-contradictory, for how can any opponent of art in the church tolerate Palestrina's artistic singing as ecclesiastical at all?[40]

Langgaard's *Fantasy* is a composition in the European art music tradition of the nineteenth century, a tradition Laub respected for nonliturgical purposes, but did not consider relevant for church music. For Laub, a symphony and music for a church service belonged in two different worlds. But considering a symphony from the perspective of church functionality was, as we have seen, not only irrelevant, but also wrong in Langgaard's eyes. The differences in Langgaard and Laub's approaches to the ballad melody are

FIGURE 19.2 Langgaard, *Fantasy*, mm. 6–10.

conspicuous even though, as previously stated, Langgaard used Laub's version of the ballad melody. Indeed, it is possible this was the only version available to him.

The *Fantasy* does not set the full melody. Only the first phrase is quoted and repeated toward the end of the short piece. The *Fantasy* thus seems to contextualize the ballad rather than set it. As Langgaard's ideas about church music and art music demonstrate, it was not problematic for Langgaard to use Laub's version of the ballad melody or to respect its modal characteristics, since he contextualized it in a musical style of a different kind. It is, as already mentioned, typical for Langgaard to integrate what appear to be different musical styles, sometimes in quite unusual ways. In the organ *Fantasy*, the mix of tonalities and musical styles is not drastic, at least not in comparison with many other of Langgaard's works or from a present vantage point. Figure 19.2 shows Langgaard's setting of the first melodic line of *Queen Dagmar lies ill in Ribe* in the organ piece.

The Laub version of the ballad melody, used by Langgaard, differs markedly from the version of the tune that appears as No. 1 (the melody for the Dagmar's death ballad) in the scholarly edition of preserved melodies from 1976. When compared to Laub's version of the melody, it is apparent that Laub modified what must have been his material in accordance with his "conclusion that as regards their melodic and tonal characteristics the Danish ballad melodies derived from the church music of the medieval and Reformation periods."[41] The originally collected melodies were first published in preliminary additions to the volumes of *Danmarks gamle Folkeviser* ("Old popular ballads of Denmark") in 1959 and later integrated into vol. 11 cited here. Laub may well have been right in at least some of his general assumptions, but his version of the melody cannot be verified historically, nor did he himself claim that it could be.[42] In his 1899 edition (and his later editions), Laub notated the melody in D, apparently replacing an original C♯–D with the C–C. In the version in Figure 19.1, notated in E, this corresponds to the D–D replacing an original D♯–E.[43] Laub clearly regarded the leading tone to tonic melodic motion as an indicator of modern tonality; by eliminating it, he felt that he was restoring the modal character of the original.

The melodies arranged in the nineteenth century by Weyse and Berggreen correspond almost completely to the melodies of scholarly editions published much later.[44] Although Laub would have regarded their tonal arrangements as anachronistic, they actually fit the collected versions, which were all assembled in the nineteenth century.

A closer look at Langgaard's organ piece shows that while the tonal arrangement made by Langgaard in his setting of the first line of the ballad does not go beyond what Laub did in his harmonization of the refrain, the musical context, into which the setting of the melody fragment has been inserted, is strongly marked by major/minor tonality. The first six bars, before the ballad melody begins, assert a D minor tonality, set in motion with repeated upbeats in the pedal of a rising or falling fifth against changing tonic and dominant chords, before a cadence on the dominant. Then follows the quotation of the first sentence of the ballad melody set so that the modal character of Laub's version is respected except for a regular cadence on the tonic (D minor), indeed, similar to how Laub himself ended his setting of the refrain, except that Laub used the major tonic. In Langgaard's piece there follows a melodic development of fragments of the ballad melody modulating over F major back to D minor with a surprising chromatic turn to the secondary dominant. From there, the music goes back to D minor with the opening figure of the second clause of the ballad melody. This figure is imitated by the pedal and leads to a cadence on the dominant. Then follows the middle section of the piece in triple time over D minor, which is developed in a fugue-like manner with chromatic modulations over A minor to E minor and back to D minor ending this section calmly on the dominant. Finally, the ballad melody from the opening returns in approximately the same setting as in the beginning, bringing the piece to a monumental closure with six bars corresponding to the opening bars of the *Fantasy*, now with a chromatic cadence in D minor.

Langgaard's *Fantasy* contextualizes the Laubian version of the ballad melody in a larger music historical framework with its shift from modal to tonal voice leading, chromaticism, and fugal development. Langgaard's setting of the opening line of the ballad respects the modal character of the melody, but subjects it to modern minor tonality, concluding with that framework. In Langgaard's piece, however, the melody is further inserted in an overall context of traditional organ music, which at the very least suggests associations with Mendelssohn's Bach-inspired corpus of works for the instrument.

Titles and Mottos in Langgaard's *Dagmar Symphony*

As mentioned earlier, Langgaard employed titles and mottos from old ballads connected to the figure of Dagmar for the first three movements of the symphony. The titles for all four movements were written directly into the score, whereas the mottos for the first three movements are quotations from three ballads about Queen Dagmar and Ribe Palace.[45] The first movement, "Queen Dagmar Sails to Ribe," a *molto allegro* in triple meter, can be experienced as expressive of a dream world of hope and anticipation. It is possible to interpret it as a sonata form, but the movement does not fall into sharply delimited sections. It develops organically with an exuberant opening and is, on the whole, joyful music in one of Langgaard's favorite keys, F major, although small, more shadowy, and reflective passages are also included. In an interview before the first performance of the symphony, Langgaard stated (about the whole symphony) that, with the exception of his use of the Dagmar ballad in the third movement, "there is nothing medieval about the music. This is the Romantic orchestra describing Ribe."[46] The music in the first movement definitely corroborates this. Still, it is easy to understand why, as a motto, Langgaard used three stanzas from the old ballad *Dronning Dagmar i Danmark* ("Queen Dagmar in Denmark"), which describe her arrival on a ship, her reception by King Valdemar, and her procession to the royal palace, *Riberhus*.[47] The music lends itself to the idea of joyful anticipation, which, at least in a fantasy of the Middle Ages, could be connected to images of the future queen of Denmark on her way to meet her new country and husband. This hopeful and joyful dream world was quite in opposition to Langgaard's own life experiences (especially in Ribe) and differed significantly from the historical situation in Denmark, which had been under Nazi occupation since April 1940.[48]

The second movement, again in triple time, is a dance, which, for the only time in the symphony, briefly invokes traditional nineteenth-century musical medievalism. For its title, "The Dance at Ribe Palace," Langgaard referred to the motto "They dance in the streets of Ribe / The palace has been captured," from the ballad *Indtagelsen af Riberhus* ("The Capture of Ribe Palace").[49] This ballad is not about Dagmar, but in the context of the romantic dream world of Langgaard's symphony it becomes associated with Dagmar and Valdemar II in Ribe. Musically, the movement is shaped as an elegant dance, more reminiscent of Tchaikovsky and ballet music than of the Middle Ages. A section of eight bars, beginning at rehearsal 2 (measure 31 in Example 19.1), however, hints at nineteenth-century musical medievalism, based on the romantic musical style of setting ballad tunes (similar to the arrangements of such tunes by, for instance, Weyse and Berggreen). It is repeated again shortly after rehearsal 4 (bars 67–74). Its musical style was employed in Danish medieval operas, for instance, by J. P. E. Hartmann in his *Little Kirsten* (1848) and Peter Heise in his *King and Marshall* (1878). This section is not medieval in any musicohistorical sense, but would have been heard as invoking "olden days" for a contemporary audience.

The third movement, "Ribe Cathedral," an orchestration of the earlier organ *Fantasy*, has already been discussed in terms of its musical content—the romantic, Mendelssohn-like contextualization of Laub's modal version of the ballad melody of *Queen Dagmar lies ill in Ribe*. This movement also used one stanza from the ballad as a motto:

> Queen Dagmar raised herself from her bed,
> Her eyes were red as blood:
> "Alas, alas, my noble lord!
> Why did you do this harm to me?"[50]

This motto seems surprising in its symphonic context. According to an interview with Langgaard, the third movement is intended to describe "the monumentality of the church, an episcopal seat for a thousand years."[51] In the context of the ballad, the quoted stanza describes how Queen Dagmar was awakened from death through the intervention of the king, who arrived after she had died. Unhappy about the king disturbing her in death, she takes the opportunity to ask him for favors, primarily to help the people.[52]

EXAMPLE 19.1 Langgaard, Symphony no. 9, *From Queen Dagmar's Town*, second movement, mm. 27–38; see especially mm. 31–38.

This strange episode in the concluding part of the ballad narrative emphasizes the saintliness of Queen Dagmar and has little to do with the monumentality of the cathedral, highlighted by Langgaard in the interview. It might make more sense to consider the motto as referring to Langgaard's own symphony movement awakening Queen Dagmar, or maybe the past, in this movement. Perhaps such an understanding would also fit in well with the title for the finale (without motto), "The Turbulent Life of the Past," which was characterized by Langgaard as an *apotheosis* by "reference to Ribe's glorious history."[53]

EXAMPLE 19.1 Continued

The finale takes up the thread, as it were, from the first movement. It is, on the whole, an exuberant F major with no medieval or other historicizing allusions. Forward momentum drives the symphony onward to its conclusion. The instrumentation is transparent and lucid and comparable to the two first movements. This differs somewhat from the sound of the third movement, which is characterized by bells and the organ (the latter, however, ad libitum) to double the melodic line of the ballad melody, giving it a heavier sound (more or less, according to the performance choice). There is, however, a brief episode, which slows somewhat, just before rehearsal 4 in the score (bars approximately 58 to 72), repeated again just before rehearsal 8. In the context of the whole symphony, and in view of its title "The Turbulent Life of the Past," it might be interpreted as a thoughtful reminder of the past, since the musical flow comes close to a halt. The overall atmosphere of the finale offers the feeling that life goes on and the past is over, no longer here. It is revived momentarily, mainly in the third movement; but also in these brief episodes in the finale, the past gives rise to a fleeting halt in the ongoing musical oscillations. Such an understanding is, of course, a reading, not an analysis of the movement. The English translation of the Danish title for the finale, "Fortids brusende Livsløb," may not capture the Danish meaning completely. "Brusende" can be translated as "turbulent" or "effervescent"—the latter may better fit the generally joyously forward-moving character of the movement.

Understood from such a perspective, the attitude that the finale brings to the symphony as a whole is one of integrating the past within the ever-ongoing pulsations of life and music. The music does not want to stay in the past or to make the past dominate the present, but it wants to reflect the past as something that moves continuously onward into the present and further into the future.

As pointed out by Bendt Viinholdt Nielsen, the symphony was appreciated by the public in a Danish nationalist context during the German occupation of Denmark, but little can support the view that a nationalist agenda was part of Langgaard's own intentions with this work.[54] Rather, it is in a historically based musical construction that Rued Langgaard's medievalism should be seen. Based on historiographical conceptualizations found in the work of Hayden White and Leslie Workman, medievalism is not necessarily to be understood as creating specific medieval "images," whether in academic writing, in creative artistic work, in paintings, in music, or in film. Medievalism may also comprise creative academic or nonacademic activity integrating medieval artifacts or imagery into a historically conscious conception allowing for a bridge between the medieval and the present.[55] The symphony may have been instigated by the incidental task of writing music for the celebration of the reopening of the *Riberhus Slotsbanke* in 1942, but this task also made Langgaard reflect on his relationship to the past. The result included his acceptance of Laub's focused and idiosyncratic medievalism as but one element in a much broader historiographical construction of his own compositional relationship to the past, even the distant past of the Middle Ages.

Notes

1. This is translated as *Queen Dagmar's Death* in E. M. Smith-Dampier, *Danish Ballads, Primary Source Edition* (Charleston, SC: Nabu Press, 2013), 28–31.
2. Bendt Viinholdt Nielsen, "About Symphony no. 9," *Rued Langgaard Edition Symphony no. 9,* (Copenhagen: Edition S, 2012), 7.
3. Pil Dahlerup, *Dansk Litteratur Middelalder* (Copenhagen: Gyldendal, 1998), 1:191–94; Nils Schiørring, "Transmission and Study of the Melodies," trans. John Bergsagel, *Danmarks gamle Folkeviser*, vol. XI, *The Tunes*, ed. Thorkild Knudsen, Svend Nielsen, and Nils Schiørring, (København: Universitets-Jubilæets Danske Samfund, 1966) 10; DUDS (Danish under Digital Study), "The Oldest Danish Ballad Tradition," *Digital text archives*, maintained by the Department of Nordic Studies and Linguistics, University of Copenhagen, accessed July 23, 2017, http://duds.nordisk.ku.dk/english/digital-text-archives/oldest_danish_ballad-tradition/viseboegerne/.
4. Dahlerup, *Dansk Litteratur Middelalder*, 1:215–216.
5. An image of the grave is found in Ane Bysted, *Ringsted Kloster og Skt. Bendts Kirke* (Ringsted: Historiens Hus, 2010), 54.
6. The oldest version of this ballad is found in the so-called *Svanings Haandskrift* (The Svaning ms), Part Two, now in the Royal Library, Copenhagen, under the shelf mark Nks. 815b,4°

and dated to the 1580s, see the DUDS website (n.d.), "The Oldest Danish Ballad Tradition;" Dahlerup, *Dansk Litteratur Middelalder*, 1:193. The first printed edition of the ballad, originally published in 1591, has been republished in recent years; see Anders Sørensen Vedel, *Hundredvisebog*, facsimile edition, ed. Karen Thuesen (Copenhagen: Reitzel, 1993).

7. Svend Grundtvig, *Historiske viser, Danmarks gamle Folkeviser*, vol. 3, ed. Svend Grundtvig et al. (Copenhagen: Universitetsjubilæets Danske Samfund, 1966–1976).

8. C. E. F Weyse, *Halvtredsindstyve gamle kæmpevise Melodier harmonisk bearbeidede* (Copenhagen: Lose & Olsen, 1840), 17, no. 35; A. P. Berggreen, *Danske Folke-Sange og Melodier, samlede og udsatte for Pianoforte*, 2nd ed. (Copenhagen: Gyldendal, 1860), 102, no. 48b; Thomas Laub and Olrik Axel, *Danske Folkeviser med gamle melodier. Musikken lagt til rette ved Thomas Laub, teksten ved Axel Olrik*, Folkeudgave (Copenhagen: Gyldendalske Boghandels Forlag, 1899), 36–41 and 78.

9. Nils Holger Petersen, "B. S. Ingemann (1789–1862): Danish Medievalism of the Early Nineteenth Century," *Makers of the Middle Ages: Essays in Honor of William Calin*, ed. Richard Utz and Elizabeth Emery (Kalamazoo, MI: Studies in Medievalism, 2011).

10. I would like to thank Tracey Sands for drawing my attention to the image and inscription. The original Danish reads, "Guds engel Dagmar, bed vor frelser om at hele hvad i Danmarks land er søndret."

11. Bendt Viinholdt Nielsen, *Rued Langgaards Kompositioner: Annoteret værkfortegnelse. With an English Introduction* (Odense: Odense Universitetsforlag, 1991), 232–236; Bendt Viinholdt Nielsen, *Rued Langgaard: Biografi* (Copenhagen: Engstrøm & Sødring, 1993), 102–108 and 150–156. Later his visions became less radical, ibid., pp 116–22 and 183–85.

12. Rued Langgaard, *Symphony no. 9, From Queen Dagmar's Town* (1942), score, critical edition by Bendt Viinholdt Nielsen (Copenhagen: *Rued Langgaard Edition*, Edition S, 2012).

13. Nielsen, *Rued Langgaard: Biografi*, 7.

14. Ibid., 141–143.

15. Nielsen, *Rued Langgaard: Biografi*, 375–376, 251. Langgaard wrote a new version of the piece two months later.

16. Nielsen, *Rued Langgaards Kompositioner*, 376.

17. "Er Wagner og Gade *Afslutningen* paa 'Romantiken,' saa er de tillige en *Begyndelse*," as quoted in Nielsen, *Rued Langgaard: Biografi*, 137.

18. Ibid., 49, 106.

19. Bendt Viinholdt Nielsen, "About Symphony no. 9," *Rued Langgaard Edition, Symphony no. 9*, (Copenhagen: *Rued Langgaard Edition*, Edition S, 2012), 8.

20. Nielsen, *Rued Langgaard: Biografi*, 23–25.

21. Ibid, 54.

22. Ibid., 223–224; Nielsen, "About Symphony no. 9," 8.

23. Nielsen, *Rued Langgaard: Biografi*, 222–223, 213, 219.

24. In its striving for going back to a "true" origin, Laub's reform thought is also analogous to the Benedictine ideas of chant revival; see Katherine Bergeron, *Decadent Enchantments: The Revival of Gregorian Chant at Solesmes* (Berkeley: University of California Press, 1998); James Garratt, *Palestrina and the German Romantic Imagination* (Cambridge: Cambridge University Press, 2002), 97–98; Thomas Laub, *Musik og Kirke*, with an introduction by Peter Thyssen (Herning: Poul Kristensens forlag, 1997; 1920).

25. Bernhard Stockmann, "Winterfeld, Carl Georg Vivigens von," *Oxford Music Online*, accessed July 23, 2017, doi:10.1093/gmo/9781561592630.article.30422. http://www.oxfordmusiconline.com.

26. Bendt Viinholdt Nielson, *Rued Langgaard: Langgaard versus Laub* (Copenhagen: Taarnborg, 2013), 6–7.

27. Nils Holger Petersen, "Resonance," in *Medievalism: Key Critical Terms*, ed. Elizabeth Emery and Richard Utz (Cambridge: Brewer, 2014), 216–220.

28. Laub and Olrik, *Danske Folkeviser*.

29. Ibid., 36–41.

30. Ibid., 77–79.

31. "De kommer kun til deres ret, deres poetiske og musikalske skønheds-værdier kan kun gøre sig gældende, når de foredrages af en enkelt, en *forsanger*, der formår at gøre indholdet, fortællingen, levende, sådan at omkvædet, tilhørernes stadigt gentagne svar på forsangerens tiltale, virkelig kan blive udtryk for, hvordan de (tilhørerne) er grebet af begivenhedernes gang [...]" Laub, "Om udførelsen af de gamle folkeviser" [About the Performance of the Old Ballads] (1922), *Folkehøjskolens Melodibog* (Copenhagen: Hansen, 1940), preface.

32. "Værre endnu handler man med viserne, når man gør dem til kunstpræstationer for professionelle sangere, forvandler melodierne til moderne romancer med moderne klaverakkompagnementer, d.v.s. flytter dem over i en stil der er ganske modsat deres egen. Pyntes de så ud med allehånde raffinerede teater-triks, ja så jubler publikum, men hvor er viserne blevet af?" Ibid.

33. "Lad os tænke os at en af Davids salmer, en lovsang eller en bodssalme, skal sættes I musik. Det kan gøres på to måder. Komponisten kan leve sig ind i Davids sjæleliv, gøre sig til ét med ham, herudfra ævne at udtrykke alle de rørelser der går gennem hans sind, gøre sit musikudtryk for disse rørelser så skønt og gribende at vi alle bliver revet med.... En sådan musik kan have stor kunstnerisk værdi, kan også have religiøs værdi, men gudstjænestemusik er det ikke. Kirkefolket kommer jo ikke sammen ved gudstjænesten for at føle rørelse over andres følelser, selv om de er nok så smukt udtrykt, det samles for selv at frembære dem I den fællestone der udtrykker, ikke den enkeltes, men hele menighedens sjælelige stilling overfor ordene," Laub, *Musik og Kirke*, 91–92.

34. Nils Holger Petersen, "Resonance," in *Medievalism: Key Critical Terms*, ed. Elizabeth Emery and Richard Utz (Cambridge: Brewer, 2014), 216–220; Niels Martin Jensen, "Laub, Thomas," *Oxford Music Online*, s.v., accessed April 22, 2017, http://www.oxfordmusiconline.com, doi:10.1093/gmo/9781561592630.article.16089.

35. Nils Holger Petersen, "Resonance," in *Medievalism: Key Critical Terms*, ed. Elizabeth Emery and Richard Utz (Cambridge: Brewer, 2014), 218–219.

36. Nielsen, *Rued Langgaard: Biografi*, 188.

37. Ibid., *Langgaard versus Laub*, 13.

38. Rued Langgaard, "Kunst og Salmesang," *Kirken V* (1933): 68–72, available with English translation, *Rued Langgaard: A Danish Composer Presented in Text, Pictures, Music, and Speech*, Langgaard Foundation, accessed April 24, 2017, http://www.langgaard.dk/litt/af/kunstog.htm and http://www.langgaard.dk/litt/af/kunstoge.htm.

39. Bendt Viinholdt Nielson, *Langgaard versus Laub*, 15–16; Langgaard, "Kunst og Salmesang," 70.

40. Ibid.

41. Nils Schiørring, "Transmission and Study of the Melodies," 26.

42. Ibid., 26–27.

43. Compare Laub and Olrik, *Danske Folkeviser*, 36, to Knudsen, Nielsen, and Schiørring, eds., *Danmarks gamle Folkeviser*, vol. 11, *The Tunes* (Copenhagen: Akademisk Forlag, 1976), appendix B, 147.

44. Weyse, *Halvtredsindstyve gamle kæmpevise Melodier*, 17; A. P. Berggreen, *Danske Folke-Sange og Melodier*, 102.

45. Nielsen, "About Symphony no. 9," 8.

46. Ibid.

47. Grundtvig, *Historiske viser*, 20–25, no. 133B; Rued Langgaard, Symphony no. 9, *From Queen Dagmar's Town* (1942), critical edition by Bendt Viinholdt Nielsen (Copenhagen: *Rued Langgaard* Edition, Edition S, 2012), 9.

48. Nielsen, *Rued Langgaard: Biografi*, 219–261.

49. Langgaard, Symphony no. 9, 9; Grundtvig, *Historiske viser*, 407–408.

50. Nielsen, "About Symphony no. 9," 9, with correction of the erroneously translated last line.

51. Ibid., 8.

52. Grundtvig, *Historiske viser*, 213–214.

53. Nielsen, "About Symphony no. 9," 8.

54. Nielsen, "About Symphony no. 9," 8.

55. Nils Holger Petersen, "Medieval Resurfacings, Old and New," *Studies in Medievalism XX: Defining Neomedievalism(s) II* (2011): 39–41; cf. the discussion of medievalism in Petersen's "Medievalism and Medieval Reception: A Terminological Question," *Studies in Medievalism XVII: Defining Medievalism(s)* (2009), and Leslie Workman, "Preface," *Studies in Medievalism* VIII (1996), ii–iii.

....

CHAPTER 20

NATURE, REASON, AND LIGHT IN *VISION—AUS DEM LEBEN DER HILDEGARD VON BINGEN*

....

JENNIFER BAIN

As Bettina Bildhauer suggested recently, the genre of medieval film is "one big medieval muddle."[1] A medieval film can be set in the Middle Ages with fictional characters (*The Seventh Seal*) or feature a medieval historical figure (Joan of Arc or Eleanor of Aquitaine) or explore medieval events (the Crusades, the plague, the Hundred Years' War), or draw on medieval themes in some way through magic and fantasy (Harry Potter), or through futuristic quests in science-fiction (Star Wars).[2] Medieval films can use live action or animation, and they can follow other genre characteristics linking them with any number of genres or subgenres, such as the romantic comedy (*The Princess Bride*), the thriller (*DaVinci Code*), or the epic (*Braveheart*). Their film scores can draw on musical styles ranging from Gregorian chant to minstrel music to romantic orchestral music to folk or rock music.[3]

Despite the sprawling nature of the genre, medieval films do share many visual and aural features and often present standard ways of viewing the Middle Ages. These standard views have been theorized by various authors, with Umberto Eco outlining "Ten Little Middle Ages" and John Haines proposing six medieval "moods."[4] Most recently, David Matthews has argued that there are only two popular versions of the Middle Ages: the *grotesque* and the *romantic*.[5] The grotesque involves "darkness, obscurity, the hidden and repressed" and aligns with Eco's "barbaric" Middle Ages and Haines's primitive mood of barbarism, simplicity, and irrationality.[6] By contrast, the *romantic* is that which "powerfully and positively revalu[es] an aspect of the medieval past"; it construes the medieval period as a time of "simple communitarian living and humanely organised labour, a pastoral time," resonating with Haines's pastoral mood of nature, forests, streams, and animals.[7] While reducing the representation of the Middle Ages into only two groupings may seem an oversimplification, these conflicting categories of the grotesque and the romantic are useful for thinking about Margarethe von Trotta's 2009 film, *Vision—Aus dem Leben der Hildegard von Bingen*. As Matthews describes, the two often exist side by side, or the romantic emerges from the grotesque.[8] Von Trotta draws heavily on these oppositional views of the Middle Ages, portraying Hildegard of Bingen as a member of the romantic realm, an enlightened and forward-looking thinker grounded in the natural world, emerging against the backdrop of darkness and ignorance in the barbaric and grotesque Middle Ages. Throughout the film, Hildegard's intellectual, spiritual, and creative life is associated with the natural environment, with light, and with reason. The lives of the community of women she leads are progressive and stand in sharp contrast to the regressive, dark, male authoritarian church. While the narrative, the cinematography, and the visual elements all contribute to this characterization of Hildegard, music and sound are critically important as well to the way in which she is presented.

The Grotesque in *Vision*

The apocalyptic opening of the film provides the backdrop for the grotesque before Hildegard is even introduced. Narrative, visual, and aural cues work together to establish the medieval populace as ignorant and irrational. As Peter Dendle states, the medieval era has been "stigmatized as one of closed-minded credulity—a period of unquestioned superstitions, entrenched religiosity, and a childlike acceptance of received doctrines."[9] The opening scene of the film sets out this perception. The film begins with a black screen and a low, reedy anticipatory drone, designed to produce a physiological response of fear. A superimposed text in German tells the audience that it is the last night of the first millennium and is followed immediately by an establishing shot of a night sky with a large full moon overlooking an ice- and snow-covered field or lake. The sense of bleakness is reinforced by the sound mix, which includes only a strong wind and occasional tinkling chimes above the drone. The scene cuts to a dark interior, lit with the yellow flickering of hundreds of candles, exposing the bloodied back of a man whipping himself, evidence of extreme (and misguided) religious piety. Families huddle together on their knees praying in a small, crumbling stone church, while monks engage in self-flagellation. The rich array of diegetic sound includes the murmurings of prayer, the voice of a priest preaching about the end of times, the torturous snap of the whips and accompanying grunts of the monks as the whips strike, and the dull metallic clanging of a censer. A gust of wind, underlining the draftiness and primitiveness of the church, suddenly extinguishes the candles, ushering in, supposedly, the end of the world.

The very next scene continues to emphasize the grotesque by exposing the gullibility, ignorance, and filth of those expecting the end of times, again through narrative, visual, and aural cues. The camera pans over the stone floor of the church, filled with people sleeping, dressed in scraps of fur and ragged brown and gray clothing: the garments of an impoverished people. While their snores and snuffles echo in the stone interior, a young man with limp, greasy hair opens his eyes and looks startled at the patch of light coming into the church through a high unseen window. As he opens the large wooden doors, they creak loudly, to establish their ancientness and the chronological distance of the Middle Ages from our own time. The darkness of the grotesque interior scenes opens onto a bright morning with a crisp blue sky and the cawing of crows. Amazed that the world has not ended with the millennium, the young man declares in disbelief and hope, "Das ist die Sonne!" ["That is the sun!"].

Everything about the cinematography and the sound design for this opening sequence portrays the Middle Ages as grotesque as a foil for the appearance of Hildegard, who represents the romantic Middle Ages. Indeed, Hildegard is cast throughout the film as an enlightened and rational thinker. Cinematically, through visual and aural means, she is associated with light and above all with nature. While the association of the feminine with nature and the masculine with reason has a long history, von Trotta shifts the focus of these tropes by using the natural world (the preindustrial world of Matthews's romantic Middle Ages) to emphasize Hildegard's rationality in opposition to the irrationality of the grotesque Middle Ages. The feminine is mapped onto nature, and in Von Trotta's representation nature is mapped onto reason.

The Middle Ages and the Sound of Nature

The carefully constructed sound design for the opening scene of *Vision* exemplifies the ways in which cinematic sounds can serve as aural cues to elicit expectation or emotion or to set a scene in the manner of an establishing shot. Many sounds have been used so frequently in so many different films that they operate as icons, as a shorthand for reinforcing genres. As Laurie Finke and Martin Schichtman argue, an icon refers to something that has been used in more than one film to represent a particular idea, while a symbol is something specific established as a recurring sign within a single film.[10] The sound design for the grotesque opening scene of *Vision* is a veritable catalog of these aural icons, which also appear in other kinds of cinematic contexts. The ritualization and omnipresence of the medieval church, for example, is established by whispered praying and clanking censers, as well as by the sounds of bells. The low drone and the whistling wind in the opening scene of *Vision*, to take another example, references similar kinds of acoustic gestures in horror film. The sound of the whip on flesh is yet another aural icon, the sound of self-flagellation functioning here as a symbol of the "close-minded credulity" of people in the Middle Ages and—by extension—of the menacing ideological power of the medieval church. There is a somewhat grisly scene of this kind in *The Seventh Seal* that involves laymen as well as monks who are whipping each other as they process through a village singing the Dies irae sequence and invoking the fear of damnation in the villagers.[11] The self-flagellation scene in *Monty Python and the Holy*

Grail pokes fun at this very scene in *The Seventh Seal* by including a group of processing monks each hitting themselves in the head with a block of wood as they sing the last two lines of text from the Dies irae: "Pie Jesu Domine, dona eis requiem." (The singing also, incidentally, pokes fun at Gregorian chant, by first repeating the same two lines over and over again and changing the melody into a repetitious drone on a single pitch, dropping a minor third only at the end.) The scene is only funny if the audience recognizes the aural and visual icons of the self-flagellating monk.

As I have suggested, the creaking door in the opening sequence of *Vision* helps to establish chronological distance and acts as another icon, the aural equivalent of the visual icon of crumbling buildings or ruins to suggest an earlier time period.[12] Squeaking doors are nearly ubiquitous in films or television series that are set in the medieval era. The famous "Red Wedding" sequence from *Game of Thrones* (2011–), for instance, begins with an exaggerated instantiation of this aural icon, as Lothar Frey enters a banquet hall and closes massive creaking wooden doors behind him. Introducing a gruesome and graphic massacre, the sound of the doors establishes both the sense of chronological distance and the idea of the grotesque Middle Ages, just as it does in *Vision*.[13] In Season 3 of the much more light-hearted *Blackadder* (1983), to cite another example, Edmund's chamber door creaks loudly as he lets his mother in after the ghost of his Uncle Richard (who Edmund accidentally killed) leaves him; the old door again emphasizes a distant past that in this case is filled with superstition and apparitions.[14]

The cawing of the crows when morning arrives at the end of the opening sequence of *Vision* also functions as an aural icon, but one that evokes a very different characterization of the Middle Ages. Sounds of nature are prominent in films set in the medieval period, where they evoke the romantic Middle Ages, a predominantly pastoral, agrarian life associated not only with hearty peasants, but also with the secular and religious landowners of a benevolent feudalism. Visual scenes of green or rocky landscapes, sometimes wild and sometimes cultivated, often devoid of buildings or dotted only with solitary castles or monasteries or tiny villages, are numerous, including at the beginning and end of *The Seventh Seal*.[15] The aural equivalent of these visual scenes comes from the sound of domesticated and wild animals and the sound of the elements. Aural icons of this type include the snorting and neighing of horses; the mooing of cows; the clopping of horses on hard tracks (mocked in *Monty Python and the Holy Grail* by a squire clapping coconut shells as his knight mimes riding a horse beside him); the chirping, calling, and squawking of birds; the sound of rushing rivers and burbling creeks; the rustling of leaves in lighter winds; and the whooshing of high winds.

This association of the Middle Ages with nature is prominent in Alfred, Lord Tennyson's poetry about the court of King Arthur, most notably in his epic *Idylls of the King* (1859–1885). Two poems from the *Idylls—Elaine and Lancelot* and Tennyson's shorter poem *The Lady of Shalott* (1832 and 1842), are especially relevant here because they also associate nature with the feminine, a concept embraced by a number of nineteenth-century writers as the *eternal feminine*, most notably Johann Wolfgang von Goethe.[16] Tennyson's conflation of nature and the medieval with the feminine is worth exploring because of von Trotta's similar approach to the representation of

Hildegard. Both *Elaine and Lancelot* and *The Lady of Shalott* tell stories of maidens in towers, who fall in love with Lancelot and die with their love unrequited. Elaine—the lily maid of Astolat—dies of a broken heart, and at her request her body is sent by barge along the river to King Arthur, with a letter in one hand and a lily in the other. The Lady of Shalott accidentally breaks a spell and so lays herself out in a boat, also on a river, and sings herself to death on her way to Camelot. These well-known poems have inspired numerous artists, musicians, and writers in the nineteenth, twentieth, and twenty-first centuries, including Lucy Maud Montgomery, who devotes a chapter of *Anne of Green Gables* to Anne's acting out of the role of Elaine in the first poem.[17] In the 1934 and 1985 film adaptations of the novel, this storyline is included, but both films rewrite the episode to feature instead Tennyson's poem *The Lady of Shalott*. Rather than the wild landscape featured at the beginning of *The Seventh Seal*, Tennyson's poem begins with a cultivated natural world, with a river running through fields:

> On either side the river lie
> Long fields of barley and of rye,
> That clothe the wold and meet the sky;
> And thro' the field the road runs by
>   To many-tower'd Camelot;
> And up and down the people go,
> Gazing where the lilies blow
> Round an island there below,
>   The island of Shalott.

In the 1985 film, although nondiegetic romantic string music features prominently in this scene, the diegetic sounds of birds chirping and of the lapping of the water reinforce the iconic medieval setting of nature, of a river surrounded by forest with only a primitive wooden bridge in sight as Anne recites several stanzas of the poem that suggest a parallel setting to the Lady of Shalott's "last song."[18] In the 1934 film, although wind is visible in the trees and the river is moving rapidly, the only diegetic sound we hear beyond Anne's recitation is the splashing of water as Anne tries to bail out the sinking boat. Visually, however, nature is emphasized even more in the 1934 adaptation than in the 1985 version, when there is no bridge at all in sight and Anne has to grab hold of a dead tree branch above the water rather than jump onto the piling of a bridge.

Nature as Symbol of Reason

In *Vision*, nature takes on an even deeper meaning as it moves beyond an intertextual icon of the romantic Middle Ages to become a symbol of Hildegard's progressive thinking and philosophy. The use of daylight and the sound of birds chirping are used repeatedly in connection with Hildegard and set off against the dim lighting and interior spaces that characterize the dark and oppressive monastic buildings. English-speaking audiences are likely to expect music to be important in a film about the life of Hildegard of Bingen and perhaps even be its focus, yet in *Vision*, she is not introduced as a composer until three quarters of the way through the film.[19] Instead, the German film foregrounds Hildegard's romantic rationality through her deep knowledge of and connection to nature, wild and cultivated, as well as her deep understanding of the medicinal properties of plants and stones.[20] The rest of this paper will demonstrate how the use of sound and image, and even Hildegard's own music, promotes a romantic representation of Hildegard connecting her to nature and to reason.

In this film about the life of Hildegard, the importance of the natural environment is accentuated by its placement at crucial moments in the narrative. Nature is used, for example, as a framing device. The film both begins and ends with the natural world, with no evidence of human impact: no buildings or structures and no agricultural fields. This focus on nature immediately has a distancing effect, placing the time of the film out of the realm of the modern era. The film opens with a nighttime view of black forest and dark sky with a full, luminescent moon shining and the ominous sound of the wind whistling. The film ends again with forest and sky, but this time with the sun low on the horizon, giving a muted, more welcoming, light. Hildegard and her supporter and scribe Volmar are riding horses, drawing on the iconic image of cowboys riding off into the sunset, although probably in this case they are riding off into the sun*rise* since they are beginning Hildegard's preaching tour.

In addition to highlighting the natural world, the opening and closing of the film also present a duality of night and day, or of dark and light, appearing as well in the film in the contrast between Hildegard's monastic childhood and adulthood.[21] The scenes of her childhood are almost all interior shots, in dark, cramped quarters with either dim natural light coming from unseen windows or candles or torches providing light, while many of the scenes of Hildegard as leader of her community are shot outside during daylight. A notable exception comes at the beginning of the film just before Hildegard is left as a child at Disibodenberg to begin her monastic life (in the dark and grotesque Middle Ages, where young children are given away to religious institutions).

As an immediate contrast to the millennial opening of the film, the credits begin with green-filtered light and movement, accompanied by a nondiegetic, modal melody, a strong differentiation from the darkness and the aural diegetic icons of the opening scene. The melody of this theme music conveys the "medieval" (the distance of the past) by its modal (Dorian) rather than tonal construction and by its solo performance on a stringed instrument, suggesting an intimate environment rather than the large concert hall of later periods that a full orchestra would convey. As demonstrated in Example 20.1, it is rhythmically straightforward, but it does not follow a regular metric (or mensural) organization, which distances the music and the era of the film from the strong metrical associations of the common practice period and contemporary pop music. The theme has two phrases, the first with an open ending on the fifth of the mode and the second

EXAMPLE 20.1 The opening theme of *Vision—Aus dem Leben der Hildegard von Bingen*.

phrase a repetition, but with a closed ending on the final, following the ouvert/clos organization of medieval song.

The green light and movement together with the modal music sets up the romantic medieval natural world that will introduce Hildegard. Just before the image comes into focus, a horse whinnies and leather harnesses and saddles creak, emphasizing the agrarian. Hildegard as a child sits in front of her father on a chestnut horse, while her mother rides a white horse and three servants accompany them, one also on a horse and the other two on foot; unlike in the opening sequence, even the servants here are dressed in clean and luxurious clothing. The forest is intensely green, and all the adults are wearing dark clothes, so that Hildegard, with pale skin, long golden hair, and light-colored dress and cloak, emerges as the focal point of the family group. A voice-over describes this girl, Hildegard, as the "light of the world" (normally a phrase reserved for Jesus), who "will understand the language of plants, stones, and animals" and will see signs revealed to few people.[22] The group comes to the edge of the woods and looks out toward the hill beyond where a cluster of buildings, the monastery at Disibodenberg where Hildegard will live, sits surrounded by nothing but forest. The string melody comes to an end with a long-held note, and just before the image cuts to the next scene, the horses snort and some distant birds caw. Visually and aurally, Hildegard is thus associated with a pristine natural world and with light, both literally and figuratively.

From Darkness to Light

The film's contrast of dark interior shots for Hildegard's childhood, representing the grotesque, with light exterior shots in her adulthood, representing the romantic, begins as soon as Hildegard enters the monastery of Disibodenberg as a child. The open vista and sound of the natural world are left behind in the following scene in what looks like a small but high-ceilinged receiving room, in the dark interior of Disibodenberg [4:49].[23] (Later in the film, when Hildegard meets the young Richardis, who is an able Latin scholar and who becomes a favorite of hers, the camera will show a much longer view of the room and light streaming through midlevel windows, creating a much different image of the room and the monastery as a place of learning and illumination). In this scene—which is presented starkly without musical accompaniment—the abbot smiles at a document in his hands and we hear the loud crinkling of its thick parchment being folded before he places it in a cabinet. The abbot closes the cabinet loudly; its echo and finality are strongly reminiscent of the iconic film sound of a jail cell door closing, cementing the gravity of Hildegard's institutionalization and the grotesqueness of a society that would send a child to an enclosed life. The father and abbot kiss to confirm the gift of the child and her dowry to the monastery, and the parents leave quickly.

While other monastic childhood scenes involving the elder Jutta are also in darkened settings, one exception is a scene in the cloister. With a roof and wall on one side and columns on the other side, the cloister is a liminal environment: Enclosed and yet suffused with daylight that is seeping from the garden, it is both dark and light, interior and exterior. The cloister scene unfolds on the day of Hildegard's arrival and a group of silent monks walks by the elder Jutta and Hildegard, keeping their eyes averted. The child asks why the monks did not look at them, and Jutta explains that it is a rule that the men may not look at the women, establishing their separateness in the monastery. Bells are ringing as the two enter the cloister, aurally and iconically setting the monastic scene, but also affirming the cloister's liminality. Monastic church bells are themselves liminal, located on the exterior of the church but sending out signals to the outer buildings and fields in the monastic complex and to the community for events that will happen or are happening in the building's interior. Ringing bells call people to services or toll when someone has died, and in a monastic community they also beckon monks or nuns to the bedside of a dying monastic.[24] The liminality of the cloister at this critical moment of Hildegard's entry at Disibodenberg represents the contradictions of the monastic oppressiveness that nevertheless will ultimately offer her access to learning.

While the childhood scenes in the film are important for establishing who Hildegard is, most of the film takes place after the elder Jutta dies and Hildegard assumes leadership of the now larger women's community at Disibodenberg. The film portrays this event—which took place when Hildegard was in her late thirties—as a new beginning and as a passage from darkness to light. The scenes surrounding this event in the film are crucial for establishing this narrative. Cutting from a childhood scene, a superimposed text tells the audience that it is thirty years later. A large group of nuns is walking hurriedly through the liminal cloister, called by the sound of bells ringing to Jutta's side as she nears the end of her life. Jutta is in a dark corner of a room in a candlelit setting, the kind associated with Hildegard's monastic childhood. She speaks to the group of nuns and then asks Hildegard to remain behind for a few private words. Hildegard sits with Jutta and, on Jutta's request, kisses her farewell. The door creaks open iconically and a priest enters. As we learn later, this is Volmar, Hildegard's faithful friend and scribe. He is carrying a jar of oil to anoint Jutta, and without speaking he begins to pour the oil, which acts as a sound bridge as it becomes the sound of water that the younger Jutta pours from a jug in an even darker room where the elder Jutta's body is now laid out. The bridging of the scenes suggests that even though the elder Jutta has died, Hildegard is still in darkness. She will not embrace her enlightened state until she becomes the leader of the community and can accept her visions and pursue learning without inhibitions, transitioning from the grotesque to the romantic.

The next scene emphasizes the repression of their monastic childhood, as Hildegard and the younger Jutta prepare the elder Jutta's body for burial in a very dark room, lit only with muted light coming from off-screen windows. The dark interior is enhanced by complete silence, with no infiltration of sound from the rest of the monastic complex or from outside. Hildegard uses scissors to cut away Jutta's cloak to wash her body, and the two gasp as they discover that she has been wearing a wide metal chain, pulled so tightly around her waist that it has become embedded in her flesh, which is oozing with infection. The only sound is their breath, as they gape in horror and tears at the damage their beloved Jutta has inflicted on herself. In the film, the audience knows that Hildegard had been aware that Jutta subscribed to other forms of mortification of the flesh. One night, when Hildegard was still a child, she awoke and wanted to see Jutta, but found that she was not in her bed. Startled and puzzled by the sound of a whip in the otherwise silent night, she followed the sound and was disturbed and saddened to find Jutta in a small room whipping her bare and bleeding back. These two experiences already establish Hildegard's disapproval of this kind of religious behavior, a behavior that is associated with the credulous and grotesque Dark Ages invoked in the opening millennial scene.

The use of interior light in the film starts to shift with the election of Hildegard as *Magistra* by her sister nuns.[25] This scene takes place in the dormitory, capturing the moment of transition from community member to community leader and, in broader terms, from ignorance to enlightenment. The only sound is diegetic: the voice of the nun calling each member forward to vote, their hurried footsteps on the stone floor, and the dropping of their individual marbles in the voting box. Although the room is not bright, the sister handling the box is standing by a window, so that her face is brightly lit as she rejoices in Hildegard's election. Scenes following the election that show Hildegard in her role as leader and teacher of the nuns take place outside in the daylight or indoors in brighter settings with windows in view, while those that depict her encountering resistance from the male authority of the church are once again set in dark, interior scenes.[26]

Hildegard's care of the flesh, which stands in marked contrast to the attitude of her teacher Jutta, becomes central to the film's representation of her as a progressive thinker, and again, aural cues contribute to this representation. From the first moments of Hildegard's appearance as a child in the film, she is presented as having a special affinity with nature, and after she assumes leadership of the community, her respect for nature is associated directly with her respect for the body. Shortly after the election scene, the film cuts to the monastery's infirmary, where the nuns are caring for sick people from the broader community, including an older possessed woman and a young man who had been overzealous in his self-flagellation. The first sound we hear is the lifting of a sticking cloth from the wounds on the back of a man and his cries of pain. We hear the footsteps of the nuns and occasional coughing of patients as Hildegard leads the way through the room, training the nuns as she works, quizzing them on what appropriate treatments would be. Both she and the younger Jutta demonstrate a deep knowledge about the medicinal properties of plants while they work and correct the nuns.

This infirmary scene emphasizes Hildegard's connection to nature and her belief in the connection between body and soul in her medical philosophy. As Hildegard applies a preparation to the knee of a woman, for example, she says to her, "Humans are created from the earth, and the earth will help you."[27] When she hears the cries of the possessed woman, she reaches into her cloak and pulls out a little sack with clinking stones and prescribes the use of a Chrysopras, instructing the woman to hold it at her neck "until it becomes warm. Afterwards you will feel no more anger."[28] She does not hesitate as well to offer her own thoughts on the mortification of the flesh. She asks the young man if he has been whipping himself, and when he says he has, she replies that "whoever kills the flesh, kills its inhabitant, the soul. God wants mercy, not sacrifice."[29] Having brought elements of the natural world into the infirmary, from the infirmary the nuns and Hildegard move into the garden for medicinal training and immediately the scene is suffused with the sound of birds chirping.

Even Hildegard's establishment of her own monastery at Rupertsberg is associated with her rootedness in nature and commitment to healthy living and acquisition of medicinal knowledge. The colorful outdoor procession from Disibodenberg of the nuns, some family members, villagers, and servants, with horses, carts, and caravans (accompanied by nondiegetic modal, rhythmic, string music) contrasts starkly with the silent and glum monks in the interior gray refectory, stewing over the departure of the nuns and their dowries [59:34]. As the outdoor procession continues, agrarian diegetic sounds—the jangling of bridles, horses snorting and walking, and caravan wheels rolling—fill the soundscape. Once construction is underway at Rupertsberg, no one is exempt from engagement in heavy manual labor, as the nuns themselves become involved in the actual building of their new facilities (with the sound of hammers accompanying their work), some of them rather ungraciously.

Hildegard has a conversation outside in the daylight that demonstrates her learnedness and interest in medical knowledge. She tells the master builder that she would like running water in all of the workrooms. When he responds that her request is "unusual and not so simple," her reply is that "water not only cleans the body, but also calms the soul" and she declares that the Romans already knew how to bring in running water.[30] She tells the builder that the location of the new building is important because of its proximity to Bingen and to the rivers Rhine and Nahe, giving the nuns more access to travelers bringing knowledge of the world. She has heard that Arabic medicine is much further advanced, and in response to the builder's statement that the Arabs are heathens, she answers, "Yes, but they understand something about the art of healing."[31] Her progressiveness is articulated in this scene through an ecumenical view of scientific knowledge that crosses "ethnic" divides; she is open to all knowledge from whatever source, not just from the teaching of the church.

It is significant that this discussion takes place outdoors, because important conversations for Hildegard—particularly those with her two most ardent supporters, Volmar and Richardis—tend to happen outside in a natural setting in the film.[32] Both Volmar and Richardis are portrayed as intellectuals, fully aligned with Hildegard's world view. When Hildegard has a major confrontation with Richardis about her leaving to become an abbess herself, the conversation takes place outside, beside the wall of the new convent at Rupertsberg [1:23:01].[33] Similarly, when Hildegard first tells Volmar about her visions, shortly after she becomes *Magistra* [24:00], they are in the garden accompanied by the sound of birds and crickets as Hildegard discloses this secret held since childhood. Her visions align with nature and also enlighten her and contribute to wisdom, knowledge, and her leadership. The only time that music enters during the two and a half–minute conversation is when Hildegard describes how she receives her visions. The music is extremely quiet and comprises a gentle layering of long-held pitches rising slowly, the pairing of lines creating occasional suspensions. The timbre is important, through these lines performed on acoustic string instruments with some use of whistling harmonics, providing an ethereal, otherworldly quality. The sound of nature, of birds and crickets, however, is more audible than the music. The visions may come from heaven, but Hildegard is rooted in the earth.

Even when Hildegard and Volmar or Hildegard and Richardis are interacting indoors, nature is as close as it could possibly be, particularly if the exchanges are intellectual. When Volmar encourages Hildegard to take on the role of *Magistra* as the abbot wishes, they are speaking in front of a bright window with light streaming in [15:14].[34] Later, Volmar enters Hildegard's study through an internal door with a stack of books borrowed from Bishop Siward, who was visiting the abbot and had with him his traveling library [17:21]. We hear the sound of birds singing before we see that Hildegard has the external door open and is tending to plants in the garden. Even the kind of books that Volmar has with him emphasizes the representation of Hildegard as a healer and a thinker; he explains that there are four books on medicine, one on precious stones, and two on works by classical authors. Much later in the film, Hildegard and Richardis are reading by a window with sunlight pouring in, and again an outside door is open just behind them, with chirping birds emphasizing the proximity of the natural world [1:07:24]. The same setting and soundscape are used again a few minutes later in the film as Hildegard recounts her visions for Richardis to write down [1:11:19].

Hildegard's visions are also presented as being connected to the natural world. The first time we see Hildegard receiving a vision, she is sitting at a table in an open gazebo in the garden. She is fully awake but becomes motionless, with her eyes wide open. A large eye shape appears in the sun with rays of light casting out [22:52], and we are to understand that her visions are heavenly, coming from God. Although she is in the garden, there is also an otherworldliness conveyed through the overpowering of all diegetic sound with an underscore of high-pitched harsh metallic sound alongside layered drones of electronically produced choral timbres on open vowels ("ooh" and "aah"). The layered drones are somewhat dissonant, but begin with a rising scalar major mode melody from D to A. The major quality of the melody becomes distorted with a gesture from F♯ to F to G♯. Another time in the film that Hildegard receives a vision she is in the liminal cloister, the space that is both inside and outside [55:22], and once again the same otherworldly music accompanies the scene.

Music, Nature, and Reason

When the audience is first introduced to Hildegard's own music, it is connected both to nature and to the practice of medicine. In the scene discussed earlier, where Hildegard lectures a young man on the ungodliness of self-flagellation, she next determines the best course of action for cleaning and treating his physical wounds (cleaning them with wine and applying yarrow [*Scharfgabe*]). She then leans in toward him [19:42] and says, "Music can also heal your wounds. And your soul."[35] She calls out, "Sieglinde?," and a seated nun begins to sing Hildegard's responsory for the Virgin, *O quam pretiosa* (without any indication that this is Hildegard's composition), accompanying herself on a viol. The responsory here is presented not as liturgical music, but as having an extraliturgical healing function. Sieglinde's performance of this music is reprised nondiegetically later in the film, where it is again very strongly associated with nature. Just after Hildegard has been criticized heavily by the nuns working on the Rupertsberg construction site, she wanders off into the forest and, in a voice-over, thinks about the difficulties faced by Moses when he had to lead the sons of Israel out of Egypt and over the Red Sea [1:05:08]. Being immersed in the forest, perhaps with the sound of the responsory in her head, Hildegard's equilibrium is restored, so that when Richardis finds her in the forest she is no longer unhappy and has worked out again how to lead the women and restore their faith in her plan for them. Here again it is music—in conjunction with the natural world—that effects healing.

These scenes where a female solo voice is associated with nature and healing are distinct from the first diegetic singing in the film. In an early scene, Jutta the child climbs up several steps to watch the monks in the monastic church through an opening from the hermitage occupied by the elder Jutta and the two children [8:09]. The men are at a remove from the woman and girls and are singing chant in unison in alternating groups of (overlapping) melody as part of a liturgical service in an institutionalized ritual, confined to the inside of the church. The group singing of the monks is aligned with darkness and obedience, in contrast to the music of Hildegard and her nuns, which is aligned with nature, healing, and learning.

There are also liturgical scenes in the film involving Hildegard and the women, but they all in some way express individuality aligning with Hildegard's progressiveness, rather than with group conformity. Once, the strong-willed Richardis is late for a service and races in to take her place among the nuns while they are chanting a psalm, with Hildegard leading the singing and the nuns responding [39:01]. Similarly, at the service in which Richardis formally takes her vows, a pair of nuns lead the singing with the monks, the other nuns, and the congregation responding in the litany sung over Richardis's prostrate body [44:54]. One of Hildegard's works, another responsory, *O vis aeternitatis*, appears liturgically, sung during the funeral service for the younger Jutta, but as a solo performance rather than as a group effort [1:31:35], again representing individuality rather than group compliance. Moreover, all the nuns, including the singer, have their eyes closed, and although presented in a liturgical setting, the music thus takes on a healing role, functioning here as consolation.

When Hildegard is finally introduced as a composer, over seventy minutes into the film [1:12:45], once again her music is associated in some way with the natural world. Through her music, she is also represented as having an independent, original, nonconformist streak. In this scene, Hildegard and the nuns are once again working in the garden. The nuns are all seated and Hildegard stands in front of them and tells them that she has an idea for a music drama. She uses her hoe to draw staff lines in the dirt and to draw neumes (note shapes) on the staff. The music drama is Hildegard's *Ordo virtutum* (The order of the virtues), which tells the story of a soul who is tempted by the devil and leaves the protection of the virtues to venture out into the world. The soul finally realizes her error and returns to the protection of the virtues to triumph with them over the devil. The performance of the *Ordo virtutum* in the film dramatizes another episode in Hildegard's life, documented in a letter, in which Hildegard is criticized by the superior of a foundation of canonesses.[36] The film shows an excerpt of the *Ordo virtutum* with all the nuns in costumes, wearing jewels, and with their hair exposed, while an elderly Magistra Tengswich watches the performance with visible disgust. For the visiting Magistra it is a disgrace to have nuns—whatever the occasion—dressed as aristocratic laywomen rather than in their religious habits. Hildegard's musical work, which came first from the garden, is thus equated with her renegade, forward-thinking ideas.[37]

This representation of Hildegard as a progressive thinker is rooted in the focus on her relationship to nature and her practice of medicine in the film. Even the cover lining on the German DVD release confirms this interpretation. Normally cover linings will include information about the film, with stills or biographical notes about the director and/or the actors and actresses. In this liner booklet, the only information about the film appears on the front and the back of the booklet: The front includes the film title, the name of the director, and three of the actors in the film, along with a photograph of Barbara Sukowa as Hildegard, while the back has another photograph of Sukowa as Hildegard, along with the chapter titles from the film. The inside front and back covers are advertisements, but not for the film; the inside back cover is an advertisement for a book about the medicinal knowledge of convent women, while the advertisement on the inside front cover is for the organic food producer, Allos, and features their Hildegard spelt cookies, spelt muesli, and granola bars. Finally, the inner twelve pages provide some background about Hildegard's medicinal philosophy and then provide detailed notes on ten plants and their medicinal uses according to Hildegard's writings. In this way, the accompanying material to the DVD release of the film strongly reinforces its representation of Hildegard as the feminized embodiment of natural healing, grounded in scientific observation.

For Margarethe von Trotta, Hildegard's relationship to the natural world is the lens through which we can understand her entire life, as a light of the world, bringing knowledge and reason to a bleak, ignorant, and oppressed Middle Ages. Using iconic sounds and musical references, the sound design for von Trotta's film strongly supports this image. In acoustic, as well as in visual and narrative terms, the film epitomizes the contrast between the grotesque and the romantic that is so important to our reception of the Middle Ages.

ACKNOWLEDGMENTS

I would like to thank my seminar on medievalism from the fall of 2014 for their many thoughtful insights, examples, and discussion in class, much of which has contributed to my own thoughts about medievalism and particularly to the effect of sound (quite apart from music) in film and television on conveying ideas about the Middle Ages: Robyn Chan, Joan Chandler, Julie Cuming, Sheila Meadley Dunphy, Katharine Harrison, John Hesler, Quincy Hiscott, Clare Neil, Elizabeth Rouget, and Patrick Salah.

NOTES

1. Bettina Bildhauer, "Medievalism and Cinema," in *The Cambridge Companion to Medievalism*, ed. Louise D'Arcens (Cambridge: Cambridge University Press, 2016), 46.
2. For a more in-depth overview of the genre issue, see Bildhauer, "Medievalism and Cinema," 46–49.
3. John Haines has done an extensive survey of musical genres in films set in the Middle Ages: *Music in Films on the Middle Ages: Authenticity vs. Fantasy* (New York: Routledge, 2013).
4. Umberto Eco, "Dreaming the Middle Ages," in *Travels in Hyperreality: Essays*, trans. William Weaver (San Diego: Harcourt Brace Jovanovich, 1986), 68–72.
5. David Matthews, "How Many Middle Ages?," in *Medievalism, a Critical History*, Medievalism VI, ed. Karl Fugelso and Chris Jones (Cambridge: Brewer, 2015), 13–41.
6. Ibid., 20; Haines, *Music in Films on the Middle Ages*, 7; and Eco, "Dreaming the Middle Ages," 69.
7. Matthews, "How Many Middle Ages?," 27; and Haines, *Music in Films on the Middle Ages*, 7.
8. Matthews, "How Many Middle Ages?," 30 and 35.
9. See Peter Dendle's essay, "'The Age of Faith': Everyone in the Middle Ages Believed in God," 49, in a collection that marvelously debunks the many stereotypes that prevail about the medieval period: Stephen J. Harris and Bryon L. Grigsby, eds., *Misconceptions about the Middle Ages*, Routledge Studies in Medieval Religion and Culture 7, ed. George Ferzoco and Carolyn Muessig (New York: Routledge, 2008).
10. See Laurie Finke and Martin Schichtman, "Signs of the Medieval: A Sociological Stylistics of Film," *Cinematic Illuminations, The Middle Ages on Film* (Baltimore: John Hopkins University Press, 2010), 47–48.
11. For more on this famous scene, see Alexis Luko's contribution to this volume, "Faith, Fear, Silence, and Music in Ingmar Bergman's Medieval Vision of *The Virgin Spring* and *The Seventh Seal*," pp. 636–661.
12. As Bildhauer notes, there is a certain irony about this iconic usage in particular, since many buildings in the Middle Ages—as in every era—were new, not old. Our experience of medieval structures today, however, is frequently of dirty and decaying buildings that are cold and smell of damp stone, so ruins and old buildings are a visual cue for a setting from a much earlier time period. Bildhauer, "Medievalism and Cinema," 50.
13. The episode appears in Season 3, "The Rains of Castamere [episode 9]," which aired on June 2, 2013. For more on the sound design for *Game of Thrones*, see James Cook's contribution to this volume: "Fantasy Medievalism and Screen Media (*Game of Thrones*)," pp. 729–749.

14. From the episode "The Ghost of Uncle Richard III."

15. For a discussion of the opening scene of *The Seventh Seal*, see Luko, "Faith, Fear, Silence, and Music in Ingmar Bergman's Medieval Vision of *The Virgin Spring* and *The Seventh Seal*."

16. For a consideration of the relationship of the eternal feminine with female spirituality and vocality in both sound and image, see Kirsten Yri, "Remaking the Past: Feminist Spirituality in Anonymous 4 and Sequentia's Vox Feminae," *Women and Music: A Journal of Gender and Culture* 12 (2008): 1–21.

17. L. M. Montgomery, "An Unfortunate Lily Maid," in *Anne of Green Gables* (London: Page, 1908; Seal Books, 1986), chap. 28.

18. "And at the closing of the day . . .
    The broad stream bore her far away . . .
    And as the boat-head wound along . . .
    They heard her singing her last song,
    The Lady of Shalott."

19. In North America and in the United Kingdom, Hildegard rose to public prominence through a major dissemination of her music from the 1980s onward. See Jennifer Bain, "Hildegard on 34th Street: Chant in the Marketplace," *Echo: A Music-Centered Journal* 6, no. 1 (2004), http://www.echo.ucla.edu.

20. In Germany, she is much more widely known for her medicinal knowledge than for her music, largely because of a mid-twentieth-century surge of reputation as a healer through the efforts of Dr. Gottfried Hertzka, a clinician who used Hildegard's medical theories in practical applications. Knowledge of Hildegard's contributions to medicine spread further through Hertzka's successor, Dr. Wighard Strehlow, as well as through the modern Hildegard Abbey in Eibingen, which produces and sells Hildegardian medicinal preparations. For further information, see Jennifer Bain, *Hildegard of Bingen and Musical Reception: The Modern Revival of a Medieval Composer* (New York: Cambridge, 2015), 12–13.

21. In the film, Hildegard looks like a girl of eight or nine when she arrives at Disibodenberg, when in fact she entered the monastery at the age of fourteen on November 1, 1112.

22. The whole voice-over states, "Am Ende dieses ersten Jahrhunderts einer neuen Zeit erblickt ein Mädchen, Hildegard, das Licht der Welt. Sie wird die Sprache der Pflanzen, Steine und Tiere verstehen. Und in ihrem Herzen die Zeichen erkennen, die nur wenigen Menschen offenbart werden." [At the end of this first century of a new era, a girl appeared: Hildegard, the Light of the World. She would come to understand the speech of plants, stones and animals. And in her heart she would recognize signs, that were made known to only a few others.]

23. All references to timing in the film correspond to the original German-language DVD release: *Vision—aus dem Leben der Hildegard von Bingen*, by Margarethe von Trotta, Home Edition Nr. 2746 (Concorde Home Entertainment, 2010).

24. For a longer discussion of bells in medieval film, see Haines, "The Bell," in *Music in Films on the Middle Ages*, 26–44.

25. Although the leader of the women's community at Disibodenberg, Hildegard was not their abbess since they all came under the rule of Abbot Kuno, who was ultimately responsible for both the men and the women. *Magistra* really means teacher, but in this context, it also takes on the meaning of leader and spiritual mother.

26. Scenes involving clashes with male authorities include one with clerics in Mainz at 28:42, in which no windows are visible, and several clashes with Abbot Kuno [51:59, 54:58, and

1:07:52]. In the first two scenes, Hildegard stands by the window in Kuno's receiving room, while the abbot sits at his desk half in shadow [51:59 and 54:58]. At 51:59 the first camera angle really emphasizes this association of light with Hildegard in an otherwise dark scene by showing her from above, windows to her right, with streaming light coming through. In the last scene, no windows are visible, but the abbot and some monks stand with arms crossed in a patch of muted light, while Hildegard stands in the shadow. When Hildegard has a victorious meeting with the bishop in Mainz, the interior room is light filled and colorful [1:09:58].

27. "Der Mensch ist aus Erde geschaffen, und die Erde wird dir helfen."

28. "Halt ihn an deine Kehle, bis er warm wird. Danach wirst du keinen Zorn mehr verspüren."

29. "Wer das Fleisch abtötet, tötet dessen Bewohner, die Seele. Gott will Barmherzigkeit, nicht Opfer."

30. The German in this passage is "ungewöhnlich und nicht ganz einfach"; "Wasser reinigt nicht nur den Körper, sondern besänftigt auch die Seele."

31. "Ja, aber sie verstehen etwas von der Heilkunst."

32. Hildegard also has an important conversation with the younger Jutta in the garden at Disibodenberg, when she tries to get Jutta's support for establishing a convent at Rupertsberg [53:51].

33. Hildegard and Richardis have another important conversation in the garden much earlier in the film about Richardis's vocation [40:23]. In the long shot of the garden before Richardis runs out to see Hildegard, the audience sees all the nuns outside, many of them reading in the sunlight.

34. Hildegard and Volmar have another important conversation at this window, when Hildegard wants to write to Bernard of Clairvaux and Volmar is worried that Bernard will destroy her [32:31].

35. "Auch die Musik kann deine Wunden heilen. Und deine Seele."

36. Letter 52, Mistress Tengswich to Hildegard, *The Letters of Hildegard of Bingen*, Vol. 1, trans. Joseph L. Baird and Radd K. Ehrman (New York: Oxford University Press, 1994), 127–128.

37. The interior space in this scene looks old and crumbling, when in fact we have just seen the buildings at Rupertsberg being constructed.

CHAPTER 21

DISCIPLINING GUINEVERE

Courtly Love and the Arthurian Tradition from Henry Purcell to Donovan Leitch

GILLIAN L. GOWER

IT is a commonplace among medievalists that the term *courtly love* is not original to the Middle Ages and was a neologism first coined by French scholar Gaston Paris in the early 1880s in reference to Chrétien de Troyes's twelfth-century Arthurian romance *Le chevalier de la charette*. Once a solely academic abstraction, the notion of courtly love has since become entrenched in Western popular culture and thought, where it remains a powerful romantic *topos*. Courtly love, therefore, can be said to be a form of medievalism in and of itself—one whose effects can be felt throughout a wide range of media in the West.[1]

Courtly love is distinguishable from other forms of fictionalized love by its characteristic narrative structure, which centers on a heterosexual romantic relationship between two parties of unequal social status: a subservient male character, often a knight, who pursues an aloof upper-class female character, frequently a princess or queen. The narrative is often realized in the form of the classic love triangle in which two men pursue the same woman, usually with tragic results. Typically, these male characters are fully realized subjects with complex backstories and motivations, while in contrast, the female characters are objectified: Devoid of agency, female courtly lovers are docile of temperament, physically beautiful, and unfailingly moral. Perhaps the most recognizable aspect of courtly love is that it is seldom requited and just as rarely consummated. Ironically, the most (in)famous pair of courtly lovers are Lancelot and Guinevere from the Arthurian tradition, who in every version of their story consummate their adulterous relationship, resulting in their ultimate downfall.[2]

In addition to its position as a fixture of contemporary scholarship and university curricula—including music history—the theme of courtly love remains present in other media, from popular history to literary fiction, poetry, video games, television, theater, and even journalism.[3] Courtly love is similarly prevalent in postmedieval music, where it finds a place in a wide variety of genres, including but by no means limited to folk songs, musicals, film scores, jazz, rock, and even hip-hop.[4] As is the case with other medievalist *topoi*, postmedieval musicians repurposed the idea of courtly love to address contemporary cultural contexts. In their operetta *Princess Ida, or Castle Adamant* (1884), for example, Gilbert and Sullivan used courtly love to satirize both the burgeoning women's movement and the medieval romance itself by lampooning both the studious title character and her buffoonish suitors. In *Princess Ida*—as well as in the examples that I will examine in more detail—the standard narrative dynamic between male and female courtly lovers embodies cultural anxiety about women's roles in society. In each of these iterations, the female figure in the dynamic of courtly love is depicted as weaker than her male counterpart and an object of a relentlessly male gaze, whether that of other characters or of the narrative itself. As I will explain, postmedieval discourses of courtly love position women as interlopers within—or even the destroyers of—homosocial spaces.[5]

This essay considers the role of gender in the music of this postmedieval courtly love tradition. My focus will be on the figure of Guinevere, who—as I will explain—served both as an idealized feminine consort and as a subversive figure of sexual agency. I begin by locating the origins of courtly love discourse and tracing its evolution from the troubadours to Gaston Paris and into the present day. I then turn to Guinevere as an iteration of what Helen Fulton terms the archetypal "faithless queen," once a trope of medieval fiction that I contend persists throughout the entirety of the courtly love tradition.[6] Fulton argues that "as a stock character, the faithless queen both supports and is produced by male fears of sexually independent women who act outside the roles determined for them by patriarchal cultures."[7] In other words, the faithless queen character acts out male anxieties, that she may be punished under the watchful eye of the male gaze. I then attempt to sketch an archeology of the discourse of courtly love vis-à-vis Guinevere, tracing the different uses to which the character has been put and the cultural nuances that transmuted the stereotypical faithless queen into a fully realized cultural icon. In the process, I consider two representative samples of staged Arthuriana—Henry Purcell's dramatick opera *King Arthur* (1691) and Alan J. Lerner and Frederick Lowe's musical *Camelot* (1960)—before turning to my primary case study, the song "Guinevere," written and recorded in 1966 by Scottish singer-songwriter Donovan.[8] Despite the seemingly disparate nature of these examples, I will show that while both courtly love and Guinevere are framed by the male gaze, they also offer ample opportunities for subversive musical play.

Gender and Courtly Love

Because of the superficial power dynamic of the courtly love relationship, some scholars have interpreted courtly love as protofeminist. Such readings, however, tend to ignore the problematic features of courtly love poetry: Not only does it focus solely on an elite group of privileged women, but also it is also highly restrictive because of its outsized glorification of women who exemplify physical and ethical beauty. To reduce woman to physical beauty, for example, is to objectify her. Similarly, valuing woman based on her adherence to the ethics of medieval Christianity and chivalry—that is, chastity—is to rid her of bodily autonomy.

Another problematic aspect of courtly love is its emphasis on female physical appearance as a metric of desirability. Female courtly lovers are held to Western beauty standards, evaluated through a gaze that is decidedly male. As much as the lady of courtly love may appear to be in control of the dynamic she shares with her male lover, the superiority is illusory. Courtly love may discipline the female lover's body in a number of ways: by making her invisible, by introducing a physical restriction such as a disability, by incorporating self-policing into her story, or simply by the fact of description, an act of violence that renders the lady adherent to compulsory heterosexuality and normative beauty standards. Courtly women who do not follow the rules, such as Guinevere, are threatened with corporal punishment: kidnapping, rape, burning, drowning. Guinevere's body is only at her own disposal within the context of her relationship with Lancelot. In exercising her bodily autonomy, Guinevere violates the conventions of courtly love; by making her love for Lancelot physical, she renders it neither courtly nor properly spiritual.

Given its origin in the mind of a male scholar of the late nineteenth century, some feminist scholars have argued that male–female relations in the courtly love mode do not reflect twelfth-century gender norms, but instead are constructed like other forms of medievalism.[9] Indeed, courtly love's attitude toward women seems to reflect the nineteenth century's increasingly conservative attitudes toward gender and sexuality. Because courtly love itself remains a disputed term, however, it may be more useful to think of it not as a static idea with a single definition but instead as a discourse in the Foucauldian sense. As the discourse unfolds over time, the meaning of "courtly love" alters to accommodate the shifting norms of its host culture, centering around anxiety over gender.

Such anxiety can be witnessed in the "writing out" of strong female characters in literary traditions. Following the work of Joseph Campbell, Maureen Fries has identified three categories of women in the Arthurian tradition: heroines, female heroes, and counterheroes. Women in the latter category include the tradition's archetypal female villain, Morgan le Fay, whose rejection of patriarchal norms is expressed through her adherence to magic, quest for power, and sexual freedom. Whereas the actions of female counterheroes mark them as immoral, female heroes are allowed to act. These heroes fall into two categories: the chaste virgin-hero (Lynette, Elaine) and the wife-hero (Enid). Medieval Arthurian heroines are perhaps best understood as foils not only for male heroes but also for female counterheroes—in other words, they are most prominent in the sources as models of normative, "good" femininity against whom counterheroes may be measured. Although prominently featured in the French romances of Chrétien de Troyes, few of these female heroes survived the later Middle Ages, a loss Fries attributes to an uptick in misogyny during the latter Middle Ages.[10] Fries has also argued that medieval writers were as concerned with gender as their modern counterparts, if not more so.[11] As this recent research demonstrates, courtly narratives have always problematized gender, offering a wide variety of gendered behaviors (and genders) to its audience to play with. As the Middle Ages wore on, however, courtly love reduced its scope to heterosexual relations between a lady and knight. Heteronormativity, then, is an essential aspect of courtly love as it is perceived and formulated in the postmedieval or medievalist contexts yet does not necessarily reflect actual gender relations and roles during the medieval period.

The Invention of Courtly Love

Although courtly love is commonly connected with Arthurian legend, it is also linked to the music of the troubadours, despite the demonstrable fact that no medieval troubadour would have used that term to describe his work.[12] Modern popular culture typically conflates the troubadours with their later northern counterparts, the trouvères. (Their female counterparts, the trobairitz, remain largely unknown to today's audiences.) Imagined as low-ranking knights, these pop culture troubadours are depicted solely as the authors of love songs. Yet this, too, is a misconception: Of the 460 known and named troubadours and their approximately 2,500 surviving songs, relatively few are about love at all.[13] Medieval troubadours wrote mostly about politics and religion; many of their *cansos* and *tensos* have been interpreted as political screeds or propaganda, while others deal with religious themes. These songs complicate our view of medieval music, suggesting a more porous barrier between secular and sacred song than we usually think of as native to the Middle Ages. Recent scholarship in court culture further lays bare the complex interactions between entertainment, religion, ethics, and aesthetics that shaped the landscape of medieval courtly music. As David Rothenberg has shown, for example, the language of courtly love pervaded even devotional music: As late as the fifteenth century, composers were setting poetry that used the floral imagery popularized in chivalric texts to praise the Virgin Mary.[14] It seems that so long as a woman's body was involved, a courtly affect was deemed appropriate.

The nature of medieval courtly love is further complicated by an ongoing debate over the physical origin point of troubadour song. Whether located in Occitan contact with the Arabic-speaking world or in the influence of pre-Christian European matriarchal cultures,[15] the identification of a precise origin for courtly love has long been hampered not only by the vagaries of time, place, borders, and manuscript sources, but also by an inability on the part of scholars (and the general public) to agree on what exactly it is that courtly love constitutes.

Further complicating the issue is the thorny history of courtly love and men who created it. Not only has the music of the troubadours been in and out of fashion repeatedly in the years between the thirteenth century and the present, but also our information about the troubadours themselves is spotty.[16] Additionally, there are issues with the transmission history of troubadour song because of the involvement not only of the composers, but also listeners, performers, and scribes.[17] As with many medieval repertoires, the manuscript tradition is itself incomplete—of the only four manuscripts in which troubadour song is transmitted, none can truly be described as complete.[18] Even within the extant sources, we cannot assume that individual troubadours shared precisely the same cultural perspective either on gender or on feudal society, writ large, particularly given that not all troubadours or trouvères were of noble or aristocratic origin.[19] We might also ask to what degree the antiquarian movement of the late nineteenth century informed translations of the primary sources, not only of the romances and troubadour lyrics, but also of texts by authors taken to be theorists, such as Andreas Capellanus, the author of the three-part treatise *De Amore* or *De arte honesti amandi*, now commonly known in English by the title given to it in 1941 by translator John Jay Parry: *The Art of Courtly Love*.[20]

Capellanus's ideology of love has roots in the medieval fascination with late antique culture. Specifically, it appears he patterned his work on Ovid's influential *Ars amatoria*, a work that received substantial attention during the twelfth century and that may have inspired the erotic poetry of one Leoninus, arguably the same person known as the father of Notre Dame organum.[21] As a cleric, however, Capellanus was equally influenced by a monastic program of misogyny intended to promote chastity by demonizing women and thereby sexuality. As Howard Bloch argues, "the medieval obsession with virginity, [lay] at the heart of medieval antifeminism."[22] While the first two volumes of Capellanus' text delineate the criteria for how and why to fall in love, the third focuses on the rejection of love. In this third volume, Capellanus backtracks, excusing the excesses of books 1–2 on the grounds that they taught one how to fall in love for the purpose of avoiding it.[23] As in the first volume, wherein Capellanus asserts that "character alone [...] is worthy of the crown of love,"[24] here the author is at his most overtly moralistic. Capellanus outlines at minimum sixteen reasons to reject love, many of them repetitive or indistinct from one another. Among these are complaints as ordinarily moralistic as the fear of lust and bodily pleasure, as pathetic as a concern for heartbreak, and as earth-shattering as war.[25] According to Capellanus, love leads to the dissolution of marriage, loss of one's good health, perjury, and even murder. Love violates Christian doctrine and the Second Commandment to "love thy neighbor as thyself" (Mark 12:31), because by falling in love, one automatically prizes the object of one's affection over and above oneself. Leaving aside the unhealthy relationships to which Capellanus appears to have been privy, either as observer or as participant, his exhortations tip into misogyny in his enumeration of the many reasons why loving women is pointless, for he argues that women are not only unworthy of love, but also fundamentally incapable of loving. Women, writes Capellanus, are unable to love because of their essential characteristics. In brief, these include greed, envy, gluttony, disobedience, pride, arrogance, faithlessness, lying, gossiping, poor rhetoric, untrustworthiness with respect to keeping secrets, licentiousness with regard to the body, and a propensity toward witchcraft.[26] For Capellanus, however, the greatest reason to reject love is that it makes men desire women they cannot have.

Capellanus's theories notwithstanding, scholars have long endeavored to make sense of the women addressed by the troubadour lyric. Evidence of scholarly debates over chivalric literature can be traced to the sixteenth and seventeenth centuries. The early modern period saw renewed enthusiasm for the texts, themes, and plots of medieval romances, sparked in Italy by a renewed interest in the works of Dante and Petrarch. While scholars in this period had little interest in these poems, by the late seventeenth century, interest in the topic began to stir.[27] By the nineteenth century, scholars were in agreement that the troubadour *canso* comprised a love story between aristocrats that was autobiographical in the strictest sense, positing that the *domna*'s true identity was deliberately obscured through the use of a *senhal*, or pseudonym assigned by the poet.[28] By disguising the *domna*, it was believed, troubadours were able to hide their affairs with married woman in plain sight while still managing to maintain her reputation.

As noted, it was Gaston Paris who first coined the term courtly love (*l'amour courtois*) in the context of Chrétien de Troyes's Arthurian romance *Le chevalier de la charette*. (Intriguingly, Paris used the term *l'amour courtois* interchangeably with the term *l'amour chevalresque*.) Based on his reading of Chrétien's work and his reading of Andreas Capellanus's *Art of Courtly Love*, Paris developed the intellectual framework that would come to underlie the ongoing courtly love discourse. Paris described a systematized dynamic between courtly men and women that relied on structural inequities in both social class and heterosexual relationships. But he was also clear that the type of love in *Le chevalier de la charette* was unique to this single source and not to be found elsewhere in the twelfth-century lyric.[29] In 1934, the French medievalist Alfred Jeanroy published his own version of a courtly love theory, which was followed two years later by C. S. Lewis's *Allegory of Love* (1936).[30] Neither theory differed extensively from Paris's own, although perhaps unsurprisingly, given his interest in Christianity, Lewis conceived of courtly love as a "rival religion."[31]

By the 1960s, however, this line of thought fell out of fashion and was replaced by a radical new reading of courtly love that centered neither on religion nor on romance, but instead on homosocial power relations in the medieval court. For example, in 1964, Erich Köhler argued that rather than being aristocrats, the troubadours were low-ranking knights who sought to develop social capital by espousing the ethics of courtly love through songs that exemplified relations not between single men and married women, but between vassals and their lords. Köhler interpreted the *domna* not as a literal woman whose affection might be won, but instead as a personification of the social status these knights wished to acquire. The commodification of prestige may seem mercenary, but as Köhler argued, it was not out of place within the troubadours' own descriptions of court dynamics as dominated by an economy not strictly of finances but rather of the lord's largesse.[32] In Köhler's reading, the attention these singers sought was now understood as a desire for parity with their social superiors, an interpretation the influential scholar Georges Duby would later affirm. In *The Mirror of Narcissus and the Courtly Love Lyric* (1967), Frederick Goldin sought to integrate the new idea that courtly love reflected the male poet's interiority with preexisting interpretations. Goldin suggested two coexisting readings of courtly love, each represented by a figure from Greek mythology. Goldin theorized that the male lover might be understood as either a Pygmalion obsessed with a generic construct of idealized femininity or a Narcissus preoccupied by the personification of his own vanity. Notably, neither of Goldin's allegorical figures gives voice to the lady herself; whether the lover acted as Pygmalion or Narcissus, his lady remained either the object of male attention or an extension of the male lover's own subjectivity, never a subject in her own right.[33]

During the 1980s, however, aristocratic women returned to the center of the discourse. In 1986, Ingrid Kasten proposed a new theory that the larger discourse of courtly love represented a kind of "fashionable game" for the intellectual and social elites of medieval court. Kasten reasserted that the *domnas* were indeed "real" women, arguing that the troubadours used *domnas* as ciphers not for their paramours, but rather for their female patrons, such as Eleanor of Aquitaine and Ermengarde of Norbonne. These patrons, Kasten argued, encouraged the troubadours to write even more songs, experiencing their adulation as a kind of prestige marker.[34] Kasten read the discourse of courtly love as fundamentally flattering to both the *domna* at its center and the medieval woman as a whole, but other scholars were not convinced. In 1987, Julia Kristeva argued that Western culture exhibits a "postromantic nostalgia" not merely for courtly love but also for romanticism itself.[35] For Kristeva, once courtly love was no longer an "utterance act"— that is, no longer a purely oral tradition—it lost any nuance and was reduced to unidimensional misogyny, as in the *Roman de la Rose*.[36] In the 1990s, with the rise of the third wave of feminism, more scholars challenged the fashionable game theory. For example, in 1991, Bloch argued that the "poetics of [female] virginity" underlying medieval theology and the role of woman in courtly love were closely linked. To Bloch, the very themes of courtly love that had long been read even by feminists as romantic were markers of misogyny. The "perpetually unsatisfied desire" expressed by the troubadour lyric was not merely an ache for an unavailable lover but also a desire for a lover who cannot him- or herself experience desire, for to experience desire was to violate the terms of the virginity expressly fetishized by both the laity and the clergy.[37] Despite these extensive debates, no further consensus on the identity of the *domna*—whether allegorical or real—has been reached.

Not only is the identity of the *domna* still up for debate, but also, in recent years, so has her sexual identity emerged as a point of contention.[38] Since Foucault (among others) traced the emergence of sexuality construed as an *identity* rather than a *behavior* to the nineteenth century, scholars have continued to problematize and historicize sexual identity as a nominative category.[39] Why, then, should courtly love continue to be construed as a solely heterosexual phenomenon? Perhaps because accepting courtly love as the dominant narrative around romantic relationships serves to further inscribe the power relations inherent in a patriarchal, homophobic culture. Compulsory heterosexuality is both implied and reified by the conventions of courtly love. Yet medieval love, then as now, was complicated by many factors, from gender roles to the identity of authors, leaving medieval gender relations unclear and open to misinterpretation. The traditions are inconsistent on this point. For example, according to Schultz, with the notable exception of the works of Wolfram von Eschenbach, most German courtly love songs obscure the beloved's primary and secondary sex characteristics, dealing in metaphor, color, and impression rather than genitalia.[40] And while Schultz argues that "women's bodies are more elaborately figured than men's and they provoke *more* intense reactions in those who see them,"[41] it is these reactions to the courtly lover's body rather than the body itself that reflect existing gender hierarchies.[42]

Put into this context, it is perhaps unsurprising that early troubadours were also misogynist. Although medieval gender and gender roles were complicated and demonstrably inconsistent across time, space, and class, it is important to acknowledge that sexism marks many of these lyrics. Some courtly lovers were downright misogynist. For all its contemporary association with romanticism, the troubadour lyric had a dark side. For the so-called first troubadour Guilhem (William) VII of Poitiers and IX of Aquitaine (1071–1127), refusing a knight's affections was grounds for brutal capital punishment, which he describes far more vividly than the women he deems wanting:

> If a woman commits the mortal sin
> of not loving a faithful knight
> or errs to the point of loving
>   a monk or priest,
> it is only right she should be burned
>   with a live coal.[43]
>
> (2.7–12)

The explicit violence Guilhem desires does more than discipline the body of the unfaithful *domna*—it suggests another kind of penetration, one that burns through the skin and leaves a scar. (We are left to wonder where, precisely, the burning coal should enter the woman's body.) It is tempting to dismiss Guilhem's threats of domestic violence as the ravings of an outlier or the machismo of a braggart. Yet Guilhem is by no means alone in his distrust of women and his desire to visit harm on them. In light of this evidence, we might conclude that "authentic" courtly "love" constitutes violence against female-identified bodies.

Guinevere: Gender, Heritage, and the "Matter of Britain"

That the archetypical *domna* is so ill-defined would seem an impediment to the persistence of courtly love in Western culture. Yet it is this very indeterminacy that contributes to the flourishing of heritage discourses such as courtly love and Arthurian legend. As David Lowenthal argues, "Ignorance, like distance, protects heritage from harsh scrutiny."[44] In other words, vagueness is essential to the propagation of heritage narratives. The female figure in the courtly love tradition often acts as a cipher rather than a real person, and not always an exemplary one. As a cipher, she can be anyone, at any time, sometimes more than one person at once. She may be an object of desire, but she is also available as a scapegoat, as in the case of Guinevere and the fall of Arthur.

Although Guinevere is one of the most recognizable characters among the standard Arthurian cast of characters and her illicit romance with Lancelot is one of the "matter of Britain's" most distinguishing features, both the individuals involved and the storyline have changed over the centuries. The Welsh Triads of the early Middle Ages make no real mention of Guinevere at all. It was not until the Welsh monk Geoffrey of Monmouth's *Historia regum Britanniae* (ca. 1136) that "Guanhamara" emerged as a prominent character. Within the Arthurian episode of this pseudohistory of Britain, Geoffrey envisioned Guinevere as the crown jewel of the Britons: the most beautiful and the highest-born woman on the whole island. As Fries argues, Guinevere's status makes her an essential "get" for Arthur; he must possess her through marriage to legitimize not only his rule, but also, and perhaps more important, his own self-image as rightful monarch.[45]

Unfortunately for Arthur, Guinevere's actions shatter both aspects of his legitimacy. Infidelity has always been part of Guinevere's character arc, but initially her affair was even more scandalous than the modern version. Geoffrey's *Historia* depicts Guinevere betraying her husband not with his best friend, but with his nephew, Modred, whom she goes on to marry. Geoffrey's narrative makes Arthur's queen's behavior triply taboo: Guanhamara is guilty not merely of adultery, but also of bigamy and incest.

Guinevere's affair with Modred is preserved in further medieval versions of Geoffrey's tale. The story was next taken up by the Anglo-Norman Wace's *Brut* (1155) and Middle English Layamon's *Brut* (ca. 1200), the latter of which relied primary on the former for its source material. Neither author would alter the narrative significantly, but both exacerbate Guinevere's guilt. Layamon goes so far as to suggest that Guinevere might face legal retribution for her crimes against the crown in the form of burning, a form of punishment reserved for women according to twelfth-century English law.[46]

Fulton defines the later Welsh Gwenhwyfar and the French Guinevere as two different characters with distinct roles in the literature. Gwenhwyfar's role as the chaste, childless wife leaves her "virtually absent" from the Welsh stories. Similarly, prior to the introduction of Lancelot, the French Guinevere is a nonactor because, "in a male-dominated society, Guinevere's potential range of social actions is more limited and of less interest to medieval audiences than her participation in a passionate courtly love relationship, the main topic of medieval secular literature."[47]

Both versions of Guinevere are "marginalized within patriarchal discourse. They are less foregrounded than the male characters, they have very limited autonomy, and they function as a reflection of what men want them to be or are afraid they might be. They do not speak for themselves."[48] Fulton argues that because of the different social systems and class systems found in the Welsh texts, in which Arthur is effectively a "local chieftain," versus in the French romances, in which Arthur is a "great king whose status is enhanced by that of his wife, entitled to be a great queen in her own right," Guinevere's role is entirely dependent on her husband's status.[49] The differences in her role also reflect different cultural needs and anxieties, derived from variant discourses on lordship, nobility, and power.

Wace, Layamon, and their fourteenth- and fifteenth-century successors preserve the identity of Guinevere's lover as Modred, retaining also the nature of her crimes as not only amoral but also unnatural. Indeed, Modred would not be replaced in the English tradition by Lancelot until Thomas Malory's *Morte d'Arthur*, first published by William Caxton in 1485.

As noted earlier, Lancelot first appears in Chrétien's *Le Chevalier de la charette* (ca. 1170–1180). That Lancelot originates in French rather than Welsh or English sources and that it apparently took some two hundred years for the character to make inroads across the Channel arguably speaks to French disinterest in English dynastic politics. Guinevere's relationship with Lancelot is unsurprisingly more romantic by modern standards. Lancelot's debut sees him rescue Guinevere from the evil king Meleagant, who has abducted and imprisoned her.[50] Although the kidnapping episode appears in earlier Arthurian literature, notably Caradoc of Llancarfan's *The Life of St. Gilda* (ca. 1130), this is the first known connection between Guinevere and Lancelot. Although Guinevere here fulfills the damsel in distress archetype, she is not entirely passive: Having been saved from probable sexual assault by Meleagant, she instead "surrenders her body" (to borrow Fries's expression) to her rescuer, a decision that demonstrates her bodily autonomy.[51] True, this is not a wholly unproblematic action on Guinevere's part, nor could we really call it protofeminist; to "reward" Lancelot for rescuing Guinevere from rape with consensual sex still treats her body as currency. Yet it is a startling moment of agency on Guinevere's part, especially in light of how passive the character becomes over time. In the thirteenth-century French Vulgate cycle and post-Vulgate cycle, which introduce the Holy Grail into the discourse, Guinevere's sexuality is treated not as a reward but as a despoiler, not only of her virtue but also of the homosocial dynamic of Arthur's court. It is Guinevere who disrupts the feudal order by bestowing a sword on Lancelot and Guinevere who causes Lancelot to fail his quest for the Grail.[52] Rather than allowing Lancelot to accept full responsibility for his own actions, these narratives reinforce late medieval beliefs about women and sin.

By the time Caxton published Malory's *Morte d'Arthur* in 1485, then, Guinevere's reputation was so thoroughly damaged that rather than alter the dynamic between Arthur's queen and Lancelot, the author instead introduced a new love interest for the knight.[53] This was Elaine of Astolat, better known in Tennyson as the Lady of Shalott, and the future mother of Lancelot's son, Galahad. The introduction of this secondary love triangle between Guinevere, Lancelot, and Elaine allowed Malory to dramatize Lancelot's moral struggle by personifying temptation (Guinevere). Without centuries worth of sexual baggage, Elaine was better equipped to play the part of an innocent damsel in distress. Like Guinevere, however, Elaine makes an imperfect foil for the courtly lover— unlike Guinevere, Elaine cannot sustain Lancelot's attention or affection. Unrequited love on the part of the female lover does not fit the courtly love paradigm, so despite Guinevere's moral failings, she remains the Arthurian lady most closely associated with courtliness.

From *King Arthur* to *Camelot*

The potential awkwardness of infidelity and adultery helps to explain certain key elements of the plot in Dryden and Purcell's 1691 semi-opera *King Arthur*. *King Arthur* is typically understood to be an allegory praising the newly anointed joint British sovereigns

William III (1650–1702) and Mary II (1662–1694). While the savior figure of Arthur made a good stand-in for William, Dryden would not have wished to compare his new queen to Guinevere. A cheating Guinevere would hardly be a flattering allegory for the Prince of Orange's co-ruler, the English Queen Mary II whose royal bloodline had granted the new king access to the throne. Although as the eldest child of her predecessor, James II, Mary's claim to the throne was strong, her reign represented a coup, because she was also replacing her father as sovereign on the grounds of his Catholic faith (which she did not share). Marrying Mary put the Prince of Orange in a strong position to legitimize his rule, but much as Geoffrey describes Arthur's reign as legitimized by his marriage to Guanhamara, William could not occupy the throne without his wife. To imply even vaguely that the queen might abandon her husband for a new one who happened to be his nephew would have been insulting in the extreme.[54]

In part to avoid this potential embarrassment, Dryden and Purcell based their *King Arthur* not on the romances but on the entirely more serious pseudohistory *Historia regum Britanniae* written by Geoffrey of Monmouth ca. 1136. In place of Guinevere, Dryden introduced a new character, Emmeline, as Arthur's love interest. Emmeline is a literal babe in the woods: chaste, innocent, and blinded through magic; she is lost in the forest, while Arthur battles the Saxons. Emmeline's blindness represents not disability but virtue; if, as many medieval theologians believed, desire enters through the eyes, then blindness might ensure a woman's chastity.[55] Emmeline's blindness, therefore, simultaneously protects and reifies her virginity; once she can see, she is able to love Arthur in the spiritual sense as well as in the physical.

Unlike the chaste Emmeline, Guinevere subverts the gender hierarchy by "troubl[ing] its] conventions while also exemplifying them," as Jane Burns observes.[56] Accusing a medieval woman of adultery was an easy yet effective way to smear her reputation—one that was particularly potent when directed at queens. Because of the requirements posed by dynastic succession, the queen's sexual faithfulness to her husband was considered paramount among her responsibilities. In the context of a feudal, majority Christian society deeply bound up with concerns of inheritance, it might seem peculiar that courtly love song should seemingly glorify adultery. In fact, it is precisely this frisson of adultery that made and continues to make courtly love titillating to its audiences. Just as the fictional lovers long for a physical relationship that is never realized, so does the audience long for a love so intense as to provoke transgressive sexual behavior. In other words, the more the relationship is forbidden, the more exciting it becomes—that is, as long as the relationship is never consummated. In the case of Guinevere and Lancelot, however, both lovers violate courtly convention by forming and sustaining an adulterous relationship. Through her dalliance with Lancelot, Guinevere subverts the ethical restrictions and concomitant behavioral expectations imposed on female courtly lovers. Recall that the Arthur–Guinevere–Lancelot love triangle is not an original feature of troubadour song: It was an addition made around the time of Chrétien de Troyes, in whose romances it first appears.

The most influential postmedieval instantiation of this love triangle comes in the work of Alfred, Lord Tennyson (1809–1892). Tennyson's interest in Arthurian romance spanned half a century and most of his career, ranging from his first stand-alone poem on the topic, "Sir Launcelot and Queen Guinevere" (begun in 1830 and first published in 1842), to the multipart epic *Idylls of the King* (published serially between 1859 and 1889).[57] By the time of Tennyson's *Idylls*, the position of Guinevere in the courtly love *topos* had been transformed. Once the strongest among female characters, the archetypal counter-hero was now reduced to a weak stereotype, as in the case of Vivien/Nimüe, Tennyson's Lady of the Lake. The female heroes Elaine of Astolat, Lynette, and Enid now existed solely as paragons of chastity countering the infidelities of Guinevere and Isolde. Indeed, Guinevere herself, Fries argues, no longer occupied the position of heroine; rather, with a renewed emphasis on her guilty affect in play, Tennyson's Guinevere had "become so distorted a heroine as to be an anti-heroine," minimizing Arthur's sins (jealousy, incest, and murder among them) in favor of foregrounding and amplifying those of his wife.[58]

Tennyson's *Idylls* were wildly popular, enjoying a wide readership into the twentieth century, where they would be reinterpreted by T. H. White in the novels published collectively as *The Once and Future King* (1958). Although Arthurian legend was hardly unknown in Britain before the publication of White's novels, the popularity of his work made the author almost single-handedly responsible for the wave of Arthuriana that swept through British and American popular culture in the 1960, when a series of films, television programs, radio plays, music, comic books, and other ephemera marched through the English-speaking world's popular consciousness. Whereas the previous decade had seen the release of only a single English-language film about Arthur (the 1954 *Knights of the Round Table*, directed by Richard Thorpe), at least four were released during the 1960s, three of them in 1963 alone.[59] Also in 1963, Dell published a movie tie-in comic book entitled *Lancelot and Guinevere*. And finally, in 1964, Mattel released "King Arthur Ken" and "Guinevere Barbie (or Midge)" outfits for its line of Little Theatre doll costumes, having prudently (or prudishly) opted to forego a design for perennial third-wheel Lancelot.

This new wave of Arthuriana might be said to have begun with the musical *Camelot* (with book and lyrics by Alan Jay Lerner and music by Frederick Lowe). Based on *The Once and Future King*, *Camelot* premiered on Broadway on December 3, 1960, just a few weeks before the inauguration of American president John F. Kennedy, whose short-lived administration would come to be so defined by the term "Camelot" as to make the musical's closing lines famous.[60] The leading roles of Arthur and Guenevere were originated by film stars Richard Burton and Julie Andrews, respectively, while Robert Goulet played Lancelot as a Francophone lothario. Many of the show's numbers wink at the Middle Ages, borrowing superficial features of early music without pretending to authentically recreate them. Instead, these sonic markers of what musicologists would recognize as Renaissance part-songs add to the scenery, creating an impression of "the past" that the audience would have recognized as premodern. For example, the score describes Lancelot's brief French serenade ("Toujours j'ai eu le même voeux"—which he sings to Guenevere immediately preceding the ballad "If Ever I Should Leave You" (2.1)—as a "madrigal" that concludes with a "lute solo."[61] Lancelot's madrigal and ballad convey his (stereotypically French) inability to control his emotions and the gravity of his feelings for Guenevere.

Following her initial reluctance to bond with Arthur during a chance meeting in the woods (1.1), as the first act unfolds, we see Guenevere's budding enthusiasm for her role as queen come to fruition in perhaps the most uplifting moment of the musical: the song and dance number "The Lusty Month of May" (1.5). The scene opens in a park near the castle, where an instrumental interlude allows time for a lively choreographed dance sequence. Guenevere then takes over, her rapturous solo recounting the joys of springtime buttressed by a chorus of her attendants. The scene is pure golden age Broadway— but it also hints at authentic musical medievalism by borrowing from the English tradition of May Day caroling.

May songs date from at least the thirteenth century, when the trouvère Moniot d'Arras composed his canso *Ce fut en Mai*. Similar undated examples include the Cambridgeshire and Bedfordshire May Carols as well as the Middle English "Maiden in the Moor Lay", a contrafact of the hymn *Peperit virgo*. Several vernacular works from the English Renaissance also refer to May as a joyous month, including Thomas Weelkes's madrigal "In Pride of May" and Thomas Morley's ballett or fa-la "Now Is the Month of Maying." These songs are still traditionally sung on the morning of May Day, as, for example, at Oxford University, following a night of carousing. Lerner, educated at Oxford, would have been unlikely to forget the May festivities.[62]

These pastoral songs celebrate the May Day feast and the transition from spring into summer—the seasons traditionally associated with fertility and increased sexual activity. Guenevere's "Lusty Month" is appropriately bawdy and embodied; the queen dances and flirts and generally enjoys herself, regaling her courtiers with the pleasures of the body:

> Tra la! It's here!
> That shocking time of year!
> When tons of wicked little thoughts
> Merrily appear.
>
> It's May! It's May!
> That gorgeous holiday;
> When ev'ry maiden prays that her lad
> Will be a cad!
>
> It's mad! It's gay!
> A libellous display.
> Those dreary vows that ev'ry one takes,
> Ev'ryone breaks.
> Ev'ryone makes divine mistakes
> The lusty month of May!

Despite the primness of Guenevere's language, her intent is clear: She is looking forward to a time of year when the rules of chastity and fidelity are temporarily suspended. To see—and hear—a woman celebrating such possibilities is frankly unusual, even, as she says, "shocking."

Lerner and Loewe's Guenevere, beholden as her fantasies are to the gender roles of the late 1950s ("Ev'ry maiden hopes her lad / Will be a cad"), cannot quite be called subversive. Yet arguably, by asserting her bodily autonomy, she subverts the gender hierarchy to which the Arthur–Guinevere–Lancelot love triangle is wedded. This Guinevere, however, like the rest of her name, cannot avoid a gruesome fate without male assistance. Here, she is sentenced to the corporal punishment considered by English medieval law to be most appropriate for women: burning.[63] Accompanied by an incongruously jaunty chorus of courtiers ("Guenevere," 2.7), Lancelot rescues the erstwhile queen—with Arthur's approval.

Donovan's Guinevere

Although the Arthur–Guinevere–Lancelot love triangle in *Camelot* is ultimately derived from medieval romances, Lerner and Lowe depart from the medieval archetype in at least one very important way. Noble birth notwithstanding, courtly love's heroines are passive figures who lack true agency. One of the features that distinguishes the lady from the shepherdess of the pastoral mode is sexual availability; her virginity or chastity (if she is married) is part and parcel of her nobility. Because of their subject position, these female characters also tend to lack a voice, in both the figurative and the literal sense. The consequence for medievalist music is that these women tend not to participate in musical discourse. They are sung to or about; they do not sing themselves.

If the "singing Guinevere" of *Camelot* represents a significant departure from the *topos* of the courtly love tradition, it was still atypical, even in the 1960s. The British folk rocker Donovan (Philips Leitch, b. 1946) offers a strikingly different version of Arthur's queen. In the eponymously titled "Guinevere" (*Sunshine Superman*, United States 1966; recorded 1965), Donovan depicts his subject from the perspective of a third-party observer who does not interact with Guinevere, only observes her. Like the "Hurdy Gurdy Man" he sings of in another track, he positions himself as a nameless itinerant musician, "singing songs of love." Unlike the troubadours and trouvères who were "moved" to song by their passions, Donovan does not moralize at Guinevere. Still, his is a fetishistic portrayal that places the focus on Guinevere's physicality via descriptive language and musical exoticism.

Donovan's "Guinevere" (1966) is but one of a large number of popular songs from this period that prominently feature thwarted medieval lovers (Crosby, Stills & Nash's 1969 "Guinnevere," which I will discuss briefly, provides another example of this phenomenon). Many of these recordings are indebted to the mid-century folk revival; for example, Deep Purple's hastily released second album *The Book of Taliesyn* (1968), despite featuring multiple cover songs by other artists, was at least superficially inspired by the Middle Welsh *Llyfr Taliesin* (Aberystwyth, Llyfrgell Genedlaethol Cymru/New Library of Wales MS Peniarth 2), a manuscript of fifty-six poems compiled in the early fourteenth century.[64] Derek and the Dominos' "Layla" (1970) cites the twelfth-century Persian poet Nezami Ganjavi's *Layla and Majnun* as an allegory for lead guitarist and songwriter Eric Clapton's infatuation with Pattie Boyd. This interest in medievalist romance pervaded multiple genres of British and American popular music beyond folk and rock: Miles Davis recorded an eighteen-minute cover version of Crosby, Stills & Nash's "Guinnevere" during the Bitches Brew sessions of 1970. And in 1975, Rick Wakeman of the prog-rock band Yes released a concept album entitled *The Myths and Legends of King Arthur and the Knights of the Round Table*, which features, unsurprisingly, a track entitled "Guinevere."

In Donovan's "Guinevere," the songwriter's lyrics present us with a description of the queen that conforms to the many of the stereotypical images from the courtly love tradition: she has indigo (sung as "in-DEE-go") eyes, light skin, and slim fingers that she adorns with bejeweled rings. She is richly dressed in a white gown made of expensive, luxurious fabrics ("velvet, silk, and lace") that "rustles" as she glides down one of Camelot's undoubtedly numerous marble staircases. The suggestion of refinement in the description of a medieval floor as made of marble speaks to a not wholly medieval sense of the past that is characteristic of Donovan's bricolage of references.

Donovan's notion of Guinevere also manifests an aristocratic or monarchical heritage. Each repetition of the refrain describes the ominous cries of the raven, a signifier of British royalty, situating us in a demonstrably English castle setting. The bird itself acts as medieval-style portent of "foreboding," also captured by the lyric: "dark [...] skies of the royal domain." Donovan here may be making an oblique reference to a superstition regarding the Tower of London, the medieval fortress-cum-tourist trap whose earliest structure was commissioned by William the Conqueror in the 1070s. Since the reign of Charles II, six ravens have occupied the grounds at all times, attended to by a member of the Tower guards, the Yeomen Warden Ravenmaster. Legend has it that should the ravens flee the Tower grounds, their departure will herald the fall of the British monarchy (as well as that of the building itself).[65] The ravens are so iconic that visitors to the Tower may even purchase a children's costume in their likeness.[66]

Much of Donovan's work exemplifies this quasi-medievalist character. Indeed, his oeuvre is rife with reference to myth, legend, and British heritage. For example, his mock folk song "Isle of Islay" pays homage to the southernmost of the Inner Hebrides with a melancholy melody accompanied by solo acoustic guitar played in finger-picked guitar arpeggios. His song "Atlantis" begins with a spoken bard-like invocation, in which Donovan imagines the legendary landmass as the universal origin point for seemingly every ancient culture: Egypt, Greece, Rome, the Celts, and so on. Among Donovan's works are a setting of Shakespeare's "Under the Greenwood Tree" (*As You Like It*, 2.5), the pastoral lyric Amiens and Jaques sing while in the Forest of Arden. These songs gesture at the same romanticism and vaguely nationalist fascination with an imagined Celtic-qua-British past that may have drawn Donovan to the Arthurian legend.

Given the context of "The Legend of the Girl Child Linda," a song that refers to Donovan's burgeoning relationship with future wife Linda Lawrence, we might conclude that "Guinevere" refers to Lawrence herself. But Donovan has offered inconsistent testimony about such an allusion. By contrast, the songwriter was quite clear about the interest in British heritage that led him to the so-called matter of Britain. On the one hand, as early as the liner notes for the album *Sunshine Superman*, Donovan wrote that when he wrote the song, he felt transported to "400 AD," a rough approximation of the time period in which some believe the "real" Arthur lived.[67] In a conversation around 1992 with Derek Taylor, on the other hand, Donovan reportedly said, "[*Sunshine Superman*] and the album of the same name were totally influenced by my unique relationship with Linda Lawrence."[68] In his 2005 autobiography, however, he writes,

> My ancestors arose out of their caves to attend me on this one. The lyric spoke of magical ways of seeing, and I was not surprised when girls at my concerts gave me gifts of crystals, flowers, and velvet pouches sewn by themselves. To many I was the embodiment of the New Age movement, Mystic Studies, Alternative Healing, Self-development, and Yoga.
>
> "Guinevere" in the story is "The Lady of the Land of Faery," the Celtic otherworld, an aspect of the Triple Goddess. My fascination with all things Celtic would help bring many to its mysteries.[69]

Donovan's characterization of Guinevere as part of the "Celtic otherworld" may help explain some of the more idiosyncratic aspects of the song's arrangement. The *Sunshine Superman* recording features an eclectic miscellany of instrumentation: acoustic guitar, sitar, and bongos. The use of a sitar—evocatively, if inexpertly, played by Shawn Phillips—not only effects a connection to British pop stars' affinity for Indian culture but also materially associates Guinevere with alterity. By associating the queen with the "exotic" sound of the Indian subcontinent, Donovan's arrangement makes her that much more alluring. Yet the instrumentation also illustrates Donovan's physical and psychological distance from the "Celtic" past, in addition to exemplifying his belief in a universal prehistoric culture, as described in the lyrics to "Atlantis":

> The great Egyptian age is but a remnant of the Atlantean culture;
> The Antediluvian kings colonized the world [sic];
> All the gods who play in the mythological dramas
> In all legends from all lands were from fair Atlantis.

Given his vision of Guinevere as a goddess of the Celts, perhaps Shawn Phillips's approach to the sitar on "Guinevere" is worth contextualizing not as a poorly executed appropriation of another culture's music, but rather as an earnest attempt to reproduce the arpeggios one might hear from a Celtic harp. In the same vein, Donovan may not have minded that "Candy" John Carr's bongos sounded neither like the Indian *tabla* nor like the Irish *bodhrán*, so long as the percussionist conveyed the *feeling* of timelessness and alterity central to his exoticized "Guinevere."[70]

Just as medieval writers exorcized their fears of female sexuality by first reveling in and then punishing Guinevere's adultery, so Donovan fixates on her physical characteristics, of which only the sexualized eyes, mouth, and fingers emerge with any clarity.

Like many medieval troubadours before him, Donovan is preoccupied by the shape of his lady's body—to mention that "Guinevere's" fingers are "slender" suggests that her build is equally so. He tells us that she drinks, but does not say if she eats. The unspoken question leaves us uncertain of the queen's desire. Does this Guinevere desire Lancelot? The song is full of "foreboding," yet even though we know how the story ends, we are not certain when she will take action. We might interpret Guinevere's slenderness as a signifier of lack of hunger—a lack of physical desire, not only for the pleasure of food but also for that of sexual gratification. Susan Bordo has argued that cultural norms, particularly those relating to physical appearance, act the same way as Foucault's state-sponsored punishments to discipline the female body, creating a prison that is culturally constituted, a crime that is culturally imposed, and a sentence that is self-enforced.[71] Bordo suggests that pathologizing disordered eating gives Western culture an easy out from confronting cultural pressures on women's bodies. That slenderness should figure prominently, along with skin color, in descriptions of courtly lovers' appearance is indicative of the extent to which the female lover's external appearance is a representation of her moral purity.

To be clear, I am not suggesting that courtly love is responsible for anorexia or for eating disorders more broadly. But it is worth considering what role courtly love plays in reifying standards of beauty that appear matched in Guineveres frequently being slender, blonde, and white. Moreover, self-discipline to beauty standards often manifests as disordered eating, which connects to the self-discipline exercised by Guinevere at the end of her story, when she gives up the pleasures of the flesh and surrenders herself to a convent, where she takes on the ascetic—that is, extremely physically disciplined—life of a nun. Yet Donovan's musical setting of "Guinevere" only serves to fetishize the queen, foregrounding her physicality and sensuality.

If we accept Donovan's Guinevere as at least to some extent a fantasy built around Linda Lawrence, transposing the object of desire into an exoticized and distant past, a similar process is at work in the eponymous song by Crosby, Stills & Nash. Their "Guinnevere" begins with the announcement that "Guinevere had green eyes / Like yours, my lady, like yours." By comparing his/their lover to Guinevere, the singer appears to pay her a great compliment, when in fact he only celebrates her physical appearance. Here, as elsewhere, Guinevere is not an individual but rather a cipher—or to use the troubadour parlance, a *senhal*, standing in for a real woman whose name cannot be sung.

But the connection with Linda Lawrence also exemplifies another important way in which the Guinevere figure intersected with music history, namely, through the phenomenon of the rock-band girlfriend. When not dismissed as groupies, these women are often viewed as interlopers in the all-male rock band's homosocial community. For example, Yoko Ono continues to bear the brunt of blame in the minds of many for the demise of the Beatles. In addition to Linda Lawrence (who married Donovan Leitch after Brian Jones left her for Anita Pallenberg), well-known examples of groupie girlfriends include Pattie Boyd, who left George Harrison for Eric Clapton, and Pallenberg herself, who famously dated Keith Richards after parting ways with Brian Jones. (Pallenberg reportedly had an encounter with Mick Jagger as well). This kind of partner swapping seems to have been relatively unremarkable in rock enclaves of the 1960s and 1970s and is often chalked up to the new relationship norms supplied by the era of "free love." What is important here is the tradition that Guinevere's adulterous liaison with Lancelot ultimately led to the end of her marriage to Arthur and, by extension, to the end of Arthur's reign. Although Lancelot also betrayed Arthur's trust, it is Guinevere who has often been assigned blame for the fall of the Round Table. In the musical instantiations of the courtly love tradition (especially those of the late twentieth century), she thus emerges as the archetypal interloper. It is perhaps not surprising, then, that the Arthurian love triangle between Guinevere, Arthur, and Lancelot might appeal to male songwriters of the late 1960s as a metaphor for their own relationships with other men's female partners. Such songs implicitly cast the singer in the role of a pining yet manly Lancelot, never the cuckolded, emasculated Arthur. In this way, the courtly love tradition could be repurposed to buttress the sexualized, counterculture persona of the male singer-songwriter.

Conclusion

In subsequent decades, the figure of Guinevere and her position within the courtly love tradition has taken on still other dimensions. Recent screen adaptations of Arthurian legend, for example, have taken on the mantle of what feminist media critic Andi Zeisler terms *marketplace feminism*.[72] Defined in part by the commodification of female empowerment, that is, "Girl Power," marketplace feminism's mascot is the so-called Strong Female Character, so ubiquitous in twenty-first-century popular culture that she merits her own Netflix genre. The modern Guinevere depicted on screen in the 2000s falls squarely into this category. In Antoine Fuqua's *King Arthur* (2004), for example, Guinevere (Keira Knightley) is a complex character positioned as both heroine and female hero. A fierce woman warrior in the mold of Boudicca, Fuqua's Guinevere is also pressed into service as consoler of male characters. The film's cinematography, which lingers on Knightley's body, and the digital enhancement of the actress's breasts in the promotional materials combine with the emotional labor Guinevere performs to emphasize her femininity and undermine the perceived masculinity of her physical strength. The film vacillates between objectifying Guinevere and positioning her as a protofeminist warrior maiden, culminating in a wedding scene more appropriate for the finale to a romantic comedy.[73] The muddle of male fantasy and marketplace feminism that resulted failed to land with audiences; the film received a lukewarm reception.

Similar issues surround the versions of Guinevere depicted in both the BBC's family-friendly *Merlin* (2008–2012) and STARZ's risqué fantasy *Camelot* (2011). Both series depict Guinevere (and her nemesis Morgan le Fay) as capable, complex characters, yet in-universe, other characters seem consistently taken aback by the notion that women could possibly be competent.[74] Moreover, although both series emphasize the importance of female community to the resilience of its women, these communities inevitably disintegrate, revealing the shows' claims to feminism to be superficial at best.[75] Most recently, Guy Ritchie's film *King Arthur, Legend of the Sword* (2017) side-stepped the issue of Guinevere entirely by substituting a mysterious female character known only as "the Mage" (Astrid Bergès-Frisbey), who has more in common with the Lady of the Lake or Merlin than Arthur's sometime queen. As Gwilym Mumford of *The Guardian* observed, both the plot and the tone of the *Legend of the Sword* suffered from an "overly male focus," to which he attributed the film's embarrassing failure at the box office.[76] If Mumford is correct, then while contemporary audiences are not yet entirely comfortable with Guinevere, neither are they willing to forgo her presence in episodes of the Arthurian tradition.

As Helen Fulton demonstrates, the character of Guinevere has always been responsive to the discourse(s) within which she finds herself. For example, the Guinevere of Welsh romance (Gwenhwyfar) is marginalized in a way that the Guinevere of French chivalric romance is not. While both the Welsh and the French narratives are part of the larger discourse of Arthurian legend and, in an even broader cultural sense, that of patriarchy, Guinevere is in many ways the ultimate female cipher: always available as an exemplar, whether she is needed to be beautiful and distant or dangerously available.

The mistake that courtly love makes lies in positioning itself as universally aspirational. Leaving aside the compulsory heterosexuality angle, in the twenty-first century, the role of the *domna* looks less and less appealing to many women. It is one thing to be the longed-for object of someone's affection, but quite another to be considered property. To a generation of women raised on choice feminism and girl power, the female courtly lover is unappetizing. In a world where rock *senhals* are seldom needed and men like Guy Ritchie no longer know what to do with Guinevere, perhaps we must ask, as Jane Burns once did, "Courtly love—who needs it?"[77]

NOTES

1. For a discussion of courtly love topics in the nineteenth century, see Section 1: "Romanticizing the Medieval: The Longing for the Middle Ages in the Nineteenth Century," this volume, pp. 17–202.

2. The spelling of this character's name differs significantly among the various sources in which she figures. "Guinevere," "Guanhamara," "Gwenhwyfar," "Guenevere," and "Guinnevere" (the forms of her name that I will reference in this essay) all refer to the same character.

3. Notions of courtly love have also infiltrated the way that the public encounters history, particularly through the genre of televised historical fiction. For example, in STARZ's adaptation of Philippa Gregory's novel *The White Queen* (2013), the relationship between Edward IV of England and his wife Elizabeth Woodville is framed as that of star-crossed lovers. Similarly, the teen drama *Reign* (The CW, 2013–2017) depicts the central struggles in the life of Mary Queen of Scots not as derived from religious or political strife but instead as a series of love affairs. Recent episodes in Arthuriana have received the same treatment.

4. See also Ross Hagen's discussion of courtly love in medieval metal, "A Gothic Romance: Neomedieval Echoes of *Fin'amor* in Gothic and Doom Metal," this volume, pp. 547–563.

5. Female courtly lovers appear to disrupt even academic homosocial spaces. On this point, see David F. Hult, "Gaston Paris and the Invention of Courtly Love," in *Medievalism and the Modernist Temper*, ed. R. Howard Bloch and Stephen G. Nichols (Baltimore: Johns Hopkins University Press, 1996), 211–215; Jane E. Burns, "Courtly Love: Who Needs It? Recent Feminist Work in the Medieval French Tradition," *Signs* 27, no. 1 (2001): 39–42.

6. Helen Fulton, "A Woman's Place: Guinevere in the Welsh and French Romances," *Quondam et Futurus* 3, no. 2 (1993): 1.

7. Ibid., 1.

8. For more on the terms used to describe Purcell's dramatic works, see Amanda Eubanks Winkler, "The Intermedial Dramaturgy of Dramatick Opera" Restoration 42-2 (Fall, 2018): 13–38.

9. See, for example, Burns, "Courtly Love: Who Needs It?"

10. Maureen Fries, "What Tennyson Really Did to Malory's Women," *Quondam et Futurus* 1, no. 1 (1991): 44–47.

11. See Maureen Fries, "Gender and the Grail," *Arthuriana* 8, no. 1 (1998): 67–79.

12. For example, this claim still appears in print. See, for example, Ffiona Swabey, *Eleanor of Aquitaine, Courtly Love, and the Troubadours*, Greenwood Guides to Historic Events of the Medieval World (Westport, CT: Greenwood Press, 2004), 76. The Occitan term *fin'amors* (usually translated as "refined love") is also widely in use as a synonym for courtly love.

13. Simon Gaunt and Sarah Kay Gaunt, ed. *The Troubadours: An Introduction* (Cambridge: Cambridge University Press, 1999), 1.

14. David J. Rothenberg, *The Flower of Paradise: Marian Devotion and Secular Song in Medieval and Renaissance Music* (New York: Oxford University Press, 2011), 127–144. See also R. Howard Bloch, *Medieval Misogyny and the Invention of Western Romantic Love* (Chicago: University of Chicago Press, 1991), 152–156.

15. Roger Boase, *The Origin and Meaning of Courtly Love: A Critical Study of European Scholarship* (Manchester: Manchester University Press, 1977), 62–99.

16. John Haines, *Eight Centuries of Troubadours and Trouvères: The Changing Identity of Medieval Music* (Cambridge: Cambridge University Press, 2004), 38; Boase, *The Origin and Meaning of Courtly Love*, 6–53.

17. Elizabeth Aubrey, *The Music of the Troubadours* (Bloomington, IN: Indiana University Press, 1996), 34.

18. Ibid., 34.

19. Catherine Léglu, "Moral and Satirical Poetry," in *The Troubadours: An Introduction*, ed. Simon Gaunt and Sarah Kay Gaunt (Cambridge: Cambridge University Press, 1999), 49.

20. Andreas Capellanus, "The Art of Courtly Love," ed. John Jay Parry (New York: Columbia University Press, 1941).

21. On Leoninus's poetry, see Craig Wright , "Leoninus, Poet and Musician," *Journal of the American Musicological Society* 39, no. 1 (1986): 1–35, and Bruce W. Holsinger, *Music, Body, and Desire in Medieval Culture: Hildegard of Bingen to Chaucer* (Stanford, CA: Stanford University Press, 2001), 137–175.

22. Bloch, *Medieval Misogyny and the Invention of Western Romantic Love*, 143.

23. Capellanus, "The Art of Courtly Love," 187.

24. Ibid., 35.

25. Ibid., 189–190.

26. Ibid., 200–211.

27. Boase, *The Origin and Meaning of Courtly Love*, 6–18.

28. Ruth Harvey, "Courtly Culture in Medieval Occitania," in *The Troubadours: An Introduction*, ed. Simon Gaunt and Sarah Kay Gaunt (Cambridge: Cambridge University Press, 1999), 18.

29. Gaston Paris, "Le Conte De La Charrette," *Romania* 48 (1883): 459–534; John C. Moore, "'Courtly Love': A Problem of Terminology," *Journal of the History of Ideas* 40, no. 4 (1979): 622.

30. Alfred Jeanroy, *La Poésie Lyrique Des Troubadours*, 2 vols. (Paris: Didier, 1934); C. S. Lewis, *The Allegory of Love: A Study in Medieval Tradition* (Oxford: Clarendon Press, 1936).

31. Moore, "'Courtly Love': A Problem of Terminology," 623.

32. Indeed, Köhler describes lordly give and take as not only a "principle function" of the medieval court, but also a moral imperative: "La cour d'un grand seigneur a pour fonction principale d'être le lieu où l'on donne et où l'on reçoit; sinon, comme le dit Sordel, ce n'est plus une cour, mais un rendez-vous de mauvaises gens." Erich Köhler, "Observations Historiques et Sociologiques sur la Poésie des Troubadours," *Cahiers de civilisation medievale* 7, no. 25 (1964): 29.

33. Frederick Goldin, *The Mirror of Narcissus in the Courtly Love Lyric* (Ithaca, NY: Cornell University Press, 1967).

34. Ingrid Kasten, *Frauendienst bei Trobadors und Minnesängern im 12. Jahrhundert: Zur Entwicklung und Adaption eines literarischen Konzepts. Germanisch-romanische Monatsschrift*, Beiheft 5 (Heidelberg: Winter1986): 53–75; Harvey, "Courtly Culture in Medieval Occitania," 18–19.

35. Julia Kristeva, *Tales of Love*, trans. Leon S. Roudiez (New York: Columbia University Press, 1987), 280.

36. Ibid., 281.

37. Bloch, *Medieval Misogyny and the Invention of Western Romantic Love*, 152.

38. Burns, "Courtly Love: Who Needs It?," 45–48.

39. On sexuality as a construct, see Michel Foucault, *The History of Sexuality*, trans. Robert Hurley, vol. 1 (New York: Vintage Books, 1990); Eve Kosofsky Sedgwick, *Between Men: English Literature and Male Homosocial Desire* (New York: Columbia University Press, 1985). On medieval sexuality, see also James A. Schultz, *Courtly Love, the Love of Courtliness, and the History of Sexuality* (Chicago: University of Chicago Press, 2006), 57; Carolyn Dinshaw, *Getting Medieval: Sexualities and Communities, Pre- and Postmodern* (Durham, NC: Duke University Press, 1999); Bruce Holsinger, *Music, Body, and Desire in Medieval Culture: Hildegard of Bingen to Chaucer*, Stanford, CA: Stanford University Press, 2001.

40. Schultz, *Courtly Love, the Love of Courtliness, and the History of Sexuality*, 35.

41. Ibid., 37.

42. The male subject position of the *Minnesinger*, for example, gives him license to observe and imagine the female body of his lover and his courtly audience permission to stare, precisely because looking at women was considered an accepted court pleasure. Schultz, *Courtly Love, the Love of Courtliness, and the History of Sexuality*, 38.

43. Andrew Bonner, ed. *Songs of the Troubadours* (New York: Schocken Press, 1972).

44. David Lowenthal, *The Heritage Crusade and the Spoils of History* (Cambridge: Cambridge University Press, 1998), 135.

45. Fries, "Gender and the Grail," 69.

46. Ibid., 69–70. Ironically, Layamon's Guinevere accidentally drowns following her flight to Caerleon.

47. Fulton, "A Woman's Place: Guinevere in the Welsh and French Romances," 3.

48. Ibid.

49. Ibid., 4.

50. The titular "*charette*" or cart refers to Lancelot's decision to use lower-class transportation to effect the rescue rather than his knightly steed.

51. Fries, "Gender and the Grail," 71.

52. Ibid., 71–72.

53. Ibid., 72.

54. Curtis A. Price, *Henry Purcell and the London Stage* (Cambridge: Cambridge University Press, 1983); Robert Shay, "Dryden and Purcell's King Arthur: Legend and Politics on the Restoration Stage," in *King Arthur in Music*, ed. Richard W. Barber (Cambridge: Brewer, 2002): 9–22.

55. Bloch, *Medieval Misogyny and the Invention of Western Romantic Love*, 143–164.

56. Burns, "Courtly Love: Who Needs It?," 24n23.

57. Alan Lupack, "Popular Images Derived from Tennyson's Arthurian Poems," *Arthuriana* 21, no. 2 (2011): 90–91.

58. Fries, "What Tennyson Really Did to Malory's Women," 47–53; quotation from 53.

59. These are *Siege of the Saxons*, directed by Nathan H. Juran; *Lancelot and Guinevere* (directed by and starring Cornel Wilde as Lancelot; and Disney's animated musical comedy *The Sword in the Stone*. The 1960s releases also included the 1967 film version of Lerner and Lowe's *Camelot*, starring Richard Burton and Vanessa Redgrave.

60. See Bruce A. Rosenberg, "Kennedy in Camelot: The Arthurian Legend in America," *Western Folkore* 35, no. 1 (1976): 52–59.

61. Frederick and Alan Jay Lerner Loewe, *Camelot (Vocal Score)* (New York: Chappell Music, 1962), 142–143.

62. Thomas S. Hischak, "Lerner, Alan Jay," *Oxford Music Online*, accessed March 9, 2018, doi:10.1093/gmo/9781561592630.article.16459.

63. Fries, "Gender and the Grail," 70.

64. Marged Haycock, "Llyfr Taliesin," *National Library of Wales Journal/Cylchgrawn Llyfrgell Genedlaethol Cymru* 25, no. 4 (1988): 357–386.

65. On the mythos of the Tower Ravens, see Boria Sax, *City of Ravens* (London: Duckworth Overlook, 2011).

66. Historic Royal Palaces, "Tower of London Raven Children's Cape," accessed February 12, 2018, https://www.historicroyalpalaces.com/giftcollections/britishgifts-souvenirs/raven-towerlondongifts/towerlondon-raven-dressup-cape.html.

67. Incidentally, Arthur predates Charlemagne, to whom the second verse anachronistically refers ("wine from the vineyards of Charlemagne").

68. Donovan Leitch, quoted in Derek Taylor, "Donovan Notes," liner notes to *Troubadour: The Definitive Collection, 1964–1976*. Epic/Legacy CD E2K 46986, 1992.

69. Donovan Leitch, *The Autobiography of Donovan: The Hurdy Gurdy Man* (New York: St. Martin's Griffin, 2005), 134.

70. In 2005, Donovan would describe Phillips and Carr as central to his 1966 touring band's status as "a truly 'world music' line-up." Leitch, *The Autobiography of Donovan*, 133.

71. Susan Bordo, *Unbearable Weight: Feminism, Western Culture, and the Body*, 10th anniversary ed. (Berkeley: University of California Press, 2003).

72. Andi Zeisler, *We Were Feminists Once: From Riot Grrrl to Covergirl, the Buying and Selling of a Political Movement* (New York: PublicAffairs, 2016).

73. Virginia Blanton, "'Don't Worry, I Won't Let Them Rape You': Guinevere's Agency in Jerry Bruckheimer's *King Arthur*," *Arthuriana* 15, no. 3 (2005): 91–111.

74. Jennifer C. Edwards, "Casting, Plotting, and Enchanting: Arthurian Women in Starz's *Camelot* and the Bbc's *Merlin*," *Arthuriana* 25, no. 1 (2015): 65.

75. Ibid., 72–73.

76. Gwilym Mumford, "Epic Fail: Why Has *King Arthur* Flopped So Badly?," *The Guardian*, May 16, 2017.

77. Burns concludes that courtly love is useful as a means by which to illustrate, explain, and ultimately deconstruct contemporary perspectives on gender. I concur. Burns, "Courtly Love: Who Needs It?," 48–50.

ECHOES OF THE MIDDLE AGES IN FOLK, ROCK, AND METAL

CHAPTER 22

··

EARLY MUSIC AND POPULAR MUSIC

Medievalism, Nostalgia, and the Beatles

··

ELIZABETH RANDELL UPTON

In the late 1960s and early 1970s there flourished a small trend for medievalist-flavored pop music. Combining folk music, electric guitars, and early music instruments, British performers and groups such as Fairport Convention, Shirley Collins, Pentangle, Jethro Tull, and Steeleye Span built on the mid-1960s hybrids of Bob Dylan's "going electric" and the Byrds' folk-rock amalgam of Dylan songs with Beatles instrumentation by adding older musical material to the mix.[1] These additions were chiefly modal or otherwise archaic-sounding folk songs with a random historical piece thrown in; two notable examples are the Young Tradition's performance of the fifteenth-century Agincourt carol, recorded for their album *Galleries* (1968), and "Gaudete, Christus est natus," a Christmas carol first published in 1582 that provided an unexpected hit single for Steeleye Span in 1973. Perhaps the most enduring recording from this repertoire is Led Zeppelin's hit "Stairway to Heaven" (1971), released on their fourth, untitled, album. Original songs such as "Stairway" convey their medievalness primarily through their lyrics, sometimes combined with modal melodic details and sometimes with the addition of historical instruments known from various early music revivals.[2] The emotional qualities of mystery, wistfulness, fantasy, and a sense of longing for other places and times that this music evokes are reinforced by the use of particular sounds. "Stairway" famously begins with acoustic guitar and low recorders, overdubbed—to produce an ensemble that, while technically dating from later periods in music history, came to signal the medieval in popular music of the 1970s. Clearly, this music is not medieval, in the sense of having its origin in any historical European culture of the past. Instead, its medievalism is built on a mix of musical elements, derived promiscuously from the different periods called *early music* (with slippage occurring among the details of any number of "premodern" musical styles and material), along with lyrical content derived from nineteenth- and twentieth-century medievalist literature.

Medievalism is generally defined as the study as well as the use of medieval material in later eras, so the fact that these songs only rarely build on genuinely historical material, be it poetry, musical compositions, or music, or the use of what specialists know about premodern instruments, may seem to exclude them from the category. Despite their distance from actual medieval materials, however, it is important to note that musicians and listeners in the 1970s and later used the word *medieval* in describing the style of these works.[3] If twentieth-century medievalism could make a place for fantasy elves, it can also encompass fantasy troubadours and minstrels. But it is worth exploring on what basis 1970s musicians and listeners made the claim of medieval inspiration. Perhaps instead of seeing the question as an ontological one, asking: what is medieval or, what counts (or should count) as medieval, the issue can better be examined epistemologically to ask how it is that different groups of musicians and listeners came to construct and understand their own definitions of medieval.

Specialists in music history logically base their definition of medieval as applied to music on what has been discovered by scholars about genuinely historical music. But the nonspecialist audience, as well as nonspecialist performers, constructed their sense of the medieval in music out of a particular mixture of more modern musical elements. In this essay I want to focus on how musical elements deriving from the eighteenth-century music generally labeled *baroque* became associated with an emotional sense of nostalgia, a notable element of the medievalist popular music of the late 1960s and early 1970s. I will argue that the emotional linkage between musical sounds that could be heard as "historical" and a personal sense of nostalgia was first made by the Beatles, in two of their songs: "In My Life" (1965) and "Penny Lane" (1967). The Beatles were arguably the most influential popular recording artists of their time, and their music was not only heard but also analyzed and discussed by a wide range of listeners.[4] Once created, this semiotic link between sound and idea became available to other artists who heard these songs. This combination of sound and emotion, heard through the kind of historical imprecision that merges musical elements from many centuries under the umbrella term early music into a single premodern, pre–classical music musical sound world, contributed to the sonic mixture that would later feel medieval, in the sense of premodern, rather than the musicological style period label, to popular music audiences in the 1970s.

Defining Early Music

As a term, early music implies a direct comparison: there is something called *music*, and then, by extension, *early music* is music that is older than that. In this formulation, the unmarked music is identifiable as *classical music*, the European concert repertories from the eighteenth and nineteenth centuries that formed the standard repertory primarily for orchestras in the mid- to late nineteenth century.[5] Classical music is anchored by the institutions of the symphony orchestra and the opera, supported on the one side by conservatories that train composers, singers, and instrumentalists and on the other side by concert-goers and philanthropists (with governmental support in different places and times) whose financial support pays for the performances and, since the twentieth century, recordings. In contrast, most of the compositions of early music did not stay in a performing repertoire. Instead, having been written down in manuscripts or published in print, these compositions outlived their own time by surviving in libraries and collections, waiting to be rediscovered and deciphered by scholars as the newly founded field of musicology got underway as an academic discipline in the nineteenth and twentieth centuries.

Defining the term early music more precisely is complicated, in part because the term's meaning conflates the overlapping, but not identical, viewpoints of musicologists, performers, and listeners. For musicologists who have long defined style periods using terms borrowed from the discipline of art history, early music is strictly a label for the music from a particular (if large) time span in European music history. It is used as an umbrella term covering the medieval, Renaissance, and baroque periods or, using the more current century designations, the time span from the earliest notated chant through the mid-eighteenth century. For nonpop performers, early music designates the music written before the later eighteenth- and early nineteenth-century classical period for which standard classical-music performance styles and techniques, especially vibrato, have been deemed inappropriate. For listeners, early music can be distinguished from later classical music not only by the specific, older, historical compositions performed, but also by a distinctive sonic signature. Early music performances can be characterized by their use of much smaller ensembles, with one- (or few-) on-a-part scoring instead of massed groups of identical voices or instruments, instrumental and vocal sounds distinct from the sounds of standard classical music in their timbre, and a "folkier," more informal atmosphere deriving from an almost countercultural set of institutions parallel to those of the established classical music world.[6]

Sorting out how different sounds become associated with particular meanings in music is complicated by the variety of listeners and the variety of their opinions, especially as commercial music recordings allow all kinds of music to reach larger and more varied audiences beyond its initial audiences. Sounds and musical works that have particular meaning for one group of listeners can be heard, reused, and reinterpreted simultaneously by other kinds of listeners, resulting in a multiplicity of possible meanings associated with the same sounds for different listeners. This is precisely what happened with baroque music in the 1960s. At the same time that the standard audience for classical music had begun exploring baroque music, chiefly in the form of Italian and Italianate concertos by such composers as Vivaldi and Bach, as a previously unheard extension of classical music, popular music producers and performers were able to adopt particular instrumental sounds and stylistic elements into popular music as novelties of a different sort. The distinctive sound of the harpsichord and baroque musical gestures lent sonic interest to what has been called baroque rock.[7]

Robert Fink outlines how postwar record companies, eager to issue recorded music in the new LP format, expanded the range of classical music for listeners by releasing recordings of eighteenth-century Italian instrumental music, especially the concertos of

Vivaldi.[8] The sound of these recordings was lighter and faster than earlier arrangements of Bach's music, for instance, as played by larger symphony orchestras. In reviewing a 1981 recording of Monteverdi's *Il ritorno d'Ulisse in patria*, John Rockwell characterizes the sound of 1950s baroque recordings compared to the older sound of baroque arrangements:

> Mr. Leppard seems to work with an updated version of the same philosophy that used to govern orchestral transcriptions of Bach organ music and full-scale symphonic inflations of Handel's "Water Music."...Mr. Leppard does not translate the Baroque into the Victorian, as Sir Thomas Beecham used to do. Instead, he conforms to the stylistic traits made familiar by the Baroque revival of the 1950's. There is usually a harpsichord, the playing is brisk and direct, and forces are held to a string ensemble plus needed winds and brass. But the instruments are modern and the sound fat and full, with the string players unashamed to exploit modern vibrato.[9]

Large-scale orchestrations of baroque music, like the giant choirs used for oratorios, represent a nineteenth-century romantic, classical music approach to eighteenth-century music.[10] Because of the music's transmission via notated scores, it was possible for eighteenth-century compositions to be adopted into newer performance and sound worlds. The advent of commercial sound recordings in the twentieth century allowed audiences to encounter baroque musical sounds at will, directly through hearing. Once heard on classical music recordings, these particular musical sounds and their characteristic figurations became available for use by producers and performers of popular music as well.

The Harpsichord as Signifier

The baroque element most extensively adopted in popular music was, as noted by John Rockwell, the sound of the harpsichord. First used in popular recordings in a jazz setting in the late 1930s and 1940s, the harpsichord was later used as an exotic sound flavoring 1950s and 1960s pop music.[11] Even though the harpsichord is distinctly different from the younger piano in its mechanism of sound production, the similarity of the keyboard meant harpsichords could be played by pianists without requiring a complete change in technique or training. The plucked-string sound of the harpsichord would be heard by listeners as distinct from the sound of a piano, experienced as something exciting and new, while at the same time understood as taking the same place in an instrumental texture as that normally occupied by a piano.

An analysis of the use of harpsichord in popular music for another project allows me to identify several different categories of meanings produced by the use of harpsichord in this genre.[12] While the sound of the harpsichord is similar in all recordings, the reasons why a producer or the musicians themselves added this sound to a particular recording seem to vary. In semiotic terms, the sound of the harpsichord is a signifier that can be and has been used to allude to a range of different signifieds. The categories I have identified are humorous juxtaposition, novelty sound, representation of the eighteenth century or the historical past in general, and representation of aristocracy or an upper class, either in the past or in the present. To these four, the Beatles added a fifth category, associating the sound of the harpsichord, and indeed baroque musical style in general, with a personal sense of nostalgia.

Humor

An important element of the earliest popular music recordings that feature harpsichords seems to be the humor inherent in combining an antique instrument, associated with the "old-fashioned" eighteenth century, with jazz and then-current popular music. This use is evident in what seems to be the first popular music recordings to use harpsichord: two 78s released by Columbia in 1938, containing four songs in a style best described as eccentric chamber jazz, recorded by the Alec Wilder Octet.[13] The first piece, titled "Concerning Etchings," introduces a solo harpsichord playing a line, in octaves, that quickly juxtaposes a straight rhythm with syncopation, hinting at the mixture of classical style and jazz at play in this side. The word *etchings* in the title connects the idea of antique artworks—of a type first produced in the late fifteenth century—with the sound of the harpsichord, while at the same time, the racy connotations of the word are matched with the genre-crossing popular style of the music. The innuendo of "viewing etchings" as an invitation to seduction seems to have its origin in a Horatio Alger novel from 1891, but it was still current in 1938.[14] In the titles of the first four sides, we see the whimsical mixture of social and musical registers: Besides "Concerning Etchings," they are "A Little Girl Grows Up," perhaps another title featuring innuendo; "A Debutante's Diary," referencing the upper class; and "Neurotic Goldfish," referencing then-fashionable and progressive ideas about psychology. The Alec Wilder Octet released two more discs, four songs, in 1939, and four discs, eight works, in 1940.

Boogie woogie pianist Meade "Lux" Lewis was the second artist to use harpsichord for popular music, releasing his four-part *Variations on a Theme* for Blue Note Records in 1939. The collection's title directs the listener to expect classical music, but the recordings instead present boogie woogie keyboard. The first part, "19 Ways of Playing a Chorus," alludes to classical music, here, romantic opera, in its quotation of the "Figaro, Figaro" motif from Rossini's "Largo al factotum." Classical harpsichordist Sylvia Marlowe returns the compliment in her *From Bach to Boogie-Woogie* (General Records) of 1939, playing Lewis's famous piece, "Honky Tonk Train," first recorded in 1927. The individual works "Bach Goes to Town" and "Boogie Woogie Rhapsody" directly reference the humorous juxtaposition, while "In an 18th Century Drawing Room" draws attention to the historical character of the instrument and its sound.

Humorous juxtapositions of the "antique" harpsichord and contemporary popular music continued to be made into the 1960s. Notable examples include the Epic Records

1958 doo-wop single "Summertime, Summertime," by the Boston vocal group the Jamies,[15] and the use of harpsichord in the theme song, written and sung by composer Vic Mizzy (1916–2009), and score of the ABC television show *The Addams Family*, aired from 1964 to 1966.[16] Joshua Rifkin's 1965 album *The Baroque Beatles Book* (Electra/Nonesuch, 1965) is more elegantly witty, using Beatles tunes as the themes for an orchestral suite, a set of variations on "Hold Me Tight," the cantata "Last Night I Said," and a trio sonata.[17] Rifkin's pastiche is more straightforward than his Juilliard classmate Peter Schickele's overtly comedic turns as the fictional P. D. Q. Bach; Schickele's first album, *Peter Schickele Presents An Evening with P. D. Q. Bach (1807–1742?)* (Vanguard, 1965) was recorded live at New York's Town Hall on April 24, 1965.[18]

Novelty Records

Let us return briefly to the first popular music recordings to include harpsichord in a jazz context. Composer Alec Wilder (1907–1980) had grown up in Rochester, New York, and studied privately with teachers from the Eastman School in the 1920s; he maintained his association with the school. The Alec Wilder Octet recordings were made at the instigation of oboist Mitch Miller (1911–2010), another Rochester native and Eastman graduate, then a member of the CBS symphony orchestra.[19] Miller later became a music producer and head of artists and repertoires (A&R), first for Mercury Records and then, from 1950, at Columbia Records in New York. At Columbia, Mitch Miller became famous for what were called *novelty* records, popular songs arranged with unusual instruments that catch the ear. Miller himself and his novelty singles were discussed in a 1957 sociological article on fads:

> A good example in the popular-music industry is the success of the current artist and repertoire director (the "A&R Man") at Columbia Records, Mitch Miller. A concert oboist himself, he was thoroughly trained as a serious musician. With an established reputation and a semibohemian personality which manifests itself in harmless ways, such as the wearing of a beard and keeping odd hours, he has been able to utilize good judgment in the popular-music world not only by being better educated but by having a far broader range of minorities [sic] to draw on for inspiration. Thus he is familiar with the attributes of French horns and harpsichords, with echo chambers and goat bells, and has been able to use all to full advantage.... The gimmicks have given Columbia Records a unique reputation.[20]

An early hit at Columbia for Miller was the 1951 recording "Come On-a My House," written by Ross Bagdasarian with lyrics by his cousin, William Saroyan, sung by Rosemary Clooney. Despite her initial reservations, the song became the title song of her album, released on June 6, 1951.[21] On the recording, Clooney is backed by a small ensemble: a harpsichord, played by Stan Freeman (1920–2001), plus guitar, bass, and drums. Nothing in the song or its lyrics connects with harpsichord; instead, the sound is included as an ear-catching and humorous novelty. "Come On-a My House" became a hit, spending eight weeks at number one. Miller was to include the harpsichord on twenty other recordings with Rosemary Clooney in the 1950s, as well as thirteen instrumental pop recordings released under his own name.[22] As with "Come On-a My House," none of the titles of these recordings suggests any meaning for the harpsichord sound beyond its use as a sonic novelty.

History, Wealth, and Social Status

The final two categories of pop songs employing harpsichords draw on the instrument's association with history and with the upper class. These two meanings are related: Songs that play with representation of the eighteenth century in their titles or musical style can also characterize that period as the natural environment of historical aristocrats. Henry Mancini's jazzy 1960 album *Combo!* featured harpsichord, played by "Johnny" Williams on five numbers, including one called "Powdered Wig" that humorously alternates baroque flourishes and more typical jazz.[23] The prominent harpsichord featured in Vic Mizzy's 1964 theme music for *The Addams Family*, mentioned earlier as an example of humorous juxtaposition, alludes both to the Addams's fabulous wealth and to the mixture of historical elements that characterized their home's peculiar furnishings. In the Rolling Stones' song "Play with Fire," the B-side of their 1965 single "The Last Time," Mick Jagger warns a rich girl of her danger in dating him; the ominous harpsichord, played by session musician and arranger Jack Nitzsche, is meant to indicate the girl's society status that would be threatened by association with a lower-class boy.[24] The Beatles later used harpsichord, played by producer Chris Thomas, to indicate social status in George Harrison's sharp, satirical "Piggies," released on the 1968 album *The Beatles* (aka "The White Album").[25]

The Beatles and Baroque Sound

In the 1940s and 1950s, the use of harpsichord in popular music was amusing and unexpected, but overall not very meaningful. This changed in the 1960s with the use of baroque sound by the most widely heard artists of the time, the Beatles. Not only did the Beatles use a harpsichord-like sound playing a baroque-style musical passage, but also the song in which this passage occurred, John Lennon's "In My Life" (1965), linked the sound with the feeling of nostalgia in a way that became intensely meaningful to listeners.

The Beatles had become Britain's top recording artists with the massive success of their second single, "Please Please Me," recorded in November 1962 and released in the United Kingdom in January 1963. By 1965, they were famous worldwide, with three international tours, four albums of mostly original music, and the critically acclaimed film *A Hard Day's Night* (1964) to their credit. For their first four albums, the Beatles' sound had been created by the four band members singing, playing their instruments, and clapping their hands; occasionally, their producer, George Martin, added keyboard parts, usually piano. John Lennon and Paul McCartney began playing keyboard themselves in 1964, while still relying on Martin for more elaborate keyboard parts. Starting with their fifth album, *Help!*, in 1965, the Beatles began to expand the instrumental timbre range of their recordings.[26] Two tracks on *Help!* feature, for the first time, instrumental parts played by non-Beatle session musicians. The first of these tracks, John Lennon's "You've Got to Hide Yourself Away," was performed in the film and appears on side A of the album. Here, flutist Johnnie Scott recorded two solo jazz-style flute parts, an octave apart, for alto and tenor flute to end the song; in the film, the gardener seen earlier clipping the lawn with plastic chattering teeth in George's section of the Beatles' shared home mimes playing a single flute. The nonfilm songs of side B ends with the Beatles' cover of a 1958 rocker "Dizzy Miss Lizzy," but the penultimate, contrasting item was the wistful ballad "Yesterday." For this track, the song's composer, Paul McCartney, sings solo and plays acoustic guitar, backed by a string quartet. This quartet marks the first use of classical musicians in a Beatles track. George Martin wrote the strings' arrangement, in consultation with McCartney:

> Paul worked with me on the score, putting the cello here and the violin there. There is one particular bit which is very much his—and I wish I'd thought of it!—where the cello groans onto the seventh the second time around. He also liked the idea of holding the very high note on the first [upper] violin in the last section. To be honest, I thought that was a bit boring, but I acceded to his request. The rest of the arrangement was pretty much mine.[27]

McCartney himself insisted on a "pure," nonvibrato style of playing for the strings:

> "We agreed that it needed something more than an acoustic guitar, but that drums would make it too heavy," says Martin. "The only thing I could think of was strings but Paul was unsure. He hated syrup or anything that was even a suggestion of MOR [Middle of the Road]. So I suggested a classical string quartet. That appealed to him but he insisted 'No vibrato, I don't want any vibrato!' . . . If you're a good violin player it's very difficult to play without vibrato. Paul told the musicians he wanted it pure. But although they did cut down the vibrato they couldn't do it pure because they would have sounded like schoolboys. I think Paul realised in later years that what he got was right."[28]

The Beatles' exploration of new timbres and instruments, from jazz, classical music, and world music, begun with two tracks on *Help!*, continued for the rest of their career. Their next album, *Rubber Soul* (1965), used a new instrument for only one track—George Harrison on sitar for "Norwegian Wood"—but the following release, *Revolver* (1966), included new instruments on five tracks, many played by outside musicians: sitar, again played by Harrison, on "Love You To" and "Tomorrow Never Knows," a brass section (three trumpets, two tenor saxes, and George Martin on organ) on "Got To Get You into My Life," a double string quartet for "Eleanor Rigby," and clavichord (played by Paul McCartney) and French horn on "For No One." John Lennon played harmonium on "Doctor Robert" and Hammond organ on "She Said She Said," while "Yellow Submarine" included taped and acoustic sound effects, and "Tomorrow Never Knows" incorporated multiple tape loops, inspired by *musique concrète* compositions. The Beatles' decision to quit touring after the summer of 1966 removed the need to record only songs the group could play live in concert and also freed up more time in their schedules for musical experimentation in the studio, a freedom reflected in the increased use of new sounds on *Revolver*.

At the same time that the Beatles were expanding the instrumental and timbral range of their recordings, they had also begun to explore a wider range of poetic possibilities in new songs, an exploration that would eventually take them to considerations of memory and the past. John Lennon started the move away from the love songs with which the Beatles had first achieved prominence. In contrast to the straightforwardly direct lyrics of earlier songs like "Please Please Me" (released on January 11, 1963, in the United Kingdom) and "She Loves You" (released July 1, 1963, in the United Kingdom), the lyrics of "I'm a Loser" (1964) and "You've Got to Hide Your Love Away" (1965) begin to include internal thoughts and feelings, a deliberate shift that Lennon himself claimed was inspired by the emotionally introspective nature of some of Bob Dylan's songs.[29] While Lennon stated in 1980 that his song "Help!" reflected his unconscious thought, the first Beatles song Lennon wrote that was explicitly personal in its inspiration was "In My Life," recorded in October 1965 and released in December on the Beatles' sixth album, *Rubber Soul*.[30] With "In My Life," the Beatles were to join the microfad for including baroque musical elements in popular music, while also creating a new meaning for the stylistic trope by connecting the sound of the harpsichord to the experience of reminiscence.

John Lennon began writing what would become the lyrics for "In My Life" as a longer poem of reminiscence, describing riding the bus from his childhood home to the center of Liverpool as it passed various landmarks and sites of significance to him. A single sheet of handwritten verses now in the British library shows how after beginning "there are places I'll remember," a draft line close to the final version, Lennon went on to list some of the places he was remembering.[31] Hunter Davies published a transcription of the rejected verses in 2014; the full sheet reads as follows:

> There are places I'll remember.
> All my life, tho' some have changed
> ~~Some forgotten~~
> Some forever but not for better
> Some have gone and some remain.
> ----------------
>
> Penny Lane is one I'm missing
> Up Church R[oa]d to the clock tower

In the circle of the Abbey
I have seen some happy hours
~~And the 5 bus into town.~~
~~Past the tram sheds with no trams~~
~~Past the Dutch and St Columbus~~
Past the tram sheds with no trams
On the 5 'bus into town
Past the Dutch and St Columbus
To the Dockers umbrella that they pulled down.
~~In the parks I spent some good times~~
~~Calderstones was good for jumping~~[32]
~~But if you want to really find me~~
        ~~Really want to find me~~
All these places have [unclear, crossed out] their memories
~~Some with loves~~[33] ~~forgotten now~~
~~Some with~~[34] [illegible] ~~to be with~~
~~some are dead and some are living.~~

Ian MacDonald quotes Paul McCartney from *The New Musical Express* on November 12, 1965: "It was, he said, 'a number about the places in Liverpool where we were born.... Places like Penny Lane and the Dockers' Umbrella [the Liverpool Overhead Railway, now demolished] have a nice sound, but when we strung them together in a composition they sounded contrived, so we gave up.'"[35] Having scrapped the idea of listing the meaningful places, Lennon instead summarized what he had learned from his initial exercise: "There are places I remember, all my life, though some have changed. Some forever, not for better; some have gone, and some remain."[36] The finished lyric consists of two eight-line stanzas: The first stanza speaks about how his memories of places, changed or not, remind him of the different people who shared his life, while the second stanza shifts its attention from the past to the present, valuing memory but ending with a focus on the one person he loves now:

> There are places I remember / All my life, though some have changed
> Some forever, not for better / Some have gone, and some remain
> All these places have their moments / With lovers and friends I still can recall
> Some are dead and some are living / In my life, I've loved them all.
>
> But of all these friends and lovers / There is no one compares to you
> And these memories lose their meaning / When I think of love as something new
> Though I know I'll never lose affection / For people and things that went before,
> I know I'll often stop and think about them / In my life I love you more.

Melodically, the setting of each stanza splits the eight lines into two halves, each setting four lines of verse. The melodic structure is tight: The first two couplets are set to the same melody; while the next two couplets are also sung to a (different) repeating melody, that melody changes for the second line of each couplet: a a b b.[37] The Beatles use vocal harmonies to complicate the simple melodic structure. For the first quatrain, John

Lennon and Paul McCartney sing the first line of each "a" couplet in harmony, while Lennon (double tracked) sings the second and fourth line alone, backed up by McCartney and George Harrison singing "ooh" in harmony. For the second quatrain, after John Lennon sings the first two syllables alone, all three singers sing the first line of each couplet in parallel harmonies; Lennon, double tracked, again sings the second line alone, now unaccompanied by the other singers.

The song begins with a four-measure instrumental introduction, two repetitions of a melodic motif played on electric guitar with electric bass, without percussion, and that same motif is repeated between the two stanzas: four-measure introduction; first stanza; two-measure interlude; second stanza. The second stanza is followed by an instrumental verse, written in baroque style—John Lennon described it as Elizabethan in his 1970 *Rolling Stone* interview—and played on piano by George Martin.[38] After a repetition of the second quatrain of the second stanza, the song ends with a coda: the two-measure guitar motif, John Lennon singing the final line of the second stanza, half in falsetto, half at normal pitch, as a refrain, and a final, modified, repetition of the guitar motif. Overall, the mixture of repetition and variation in vocal texture helps to create the mood of familiarity while maintaining listener interest through variation.

According to Mark Lewisohn, the song, excluding George Martin's instrumental stanza, was recorded on Monday, October 18, 1965: "After a period of rehearsal, three takes were put down, two of which were complete.... At this point the middle eight of the song was left open since the Beatles had yet to decide how best to use it. The hole was plugged with an imaginative overdub recorded on 22 October."[39] George Martin said, "There's a bit where John couldn't decide what to do in the middle and, while they were having their tea-break, I put down a Baroque piano solo which John didn't hear until he came back. What I wanted was too intricate for me to do live, so I did it with a half-speed piano, then sped it up, and he liked it."[40] Mark Lewisohn notes that the master tape box indicates that Martin first tried playing the solo on Hammond organ, but rejected that take in favor of piano.[41]

George Martin does not seem to have ever explained why he thought a "baroque" piano solo would fit in a song that otherwise does not reference baroque style, but the association between John Lennon's lyrical reflections on his personal past and the "past" of music history, newly popular with urban sophisticates through the LP, was a likely inspiration. George Martin had greater familiarity with baroque music than might have been expected for a popular music record producer: after World War II, Martin had studied composition, piano, and oboe at the Guildhall School of Music, and the first recordings he was asked to supervise when hired at EMI in 1950 were of baroque music—including "a lot of Bach"—played by an ensemble of top soloists, conducted by Dr. Karl Haas (1900–1970) and called the London Baroque Ensemble. About Dr. Haas, Martin wrote, "The good doctor was a musicologist rather than a great conductor, and he had a tremendous knowledge of baroque music, at a time when it was still very unfashionable."[42]

The solo Martin wrote for "In My Life" is eight measures of a simple texture of two independent voices each played by one hand, imitative but not aggressively so, reminiscent of a two-part invention by Bach and ending with both hands playing a descending scale in thirty-second notes. The eighteenth-century style of the solo directly references the historical past in music-historical terms, a feature that reinforces the lyrics' reflection on memories of the past recalled in the present. Martin's recording trick produced a solo at the correct pitch, but it also altered the piano's sound, shortening each note's decay with the result that the solo sounds like it was played on harpsichord. Alan W. Pollack feels this effect was intended: "George Martin's much celebrated solo on electric piano was played for the recording an octave lower, and half as slow as it sounds on the finished track. I would bet that the motivation for this was as much to distort the attack/decay timbre of the instrument to make it sound more like a harpsichord as it was to help project a sensation of almost un-natural speed in the performance." Intended or not, many listeners heard the solo as indeed played on harpsichord, a sonic effect reinforced by the antique musical style, complete with straightforward tonal harmony, as well as the lyrics that referred to the past in such open terms that every listener could imagine his or her own specific memories and the changes one begins to notice in young adulthood.[43] Released on December 3, 1965, in both the United Kingdom and the United States, the faux-harpsichord sound of "In My Life" also echoed for listeners the use of harpsichord in two hit singles earlier that same year: the Rolling Stones' "Play With Fire" (released on February 26, 1965, in the United Kingdom and March 3, 1965, in the United States) and the Yardbirds' "For Your Love" (released on March 5, 1965, in the United Kingdom and April 9, 1965, in the United States).[44]

"In My Life" turned out to be a strongly significant song for its listeners. John Lennon's nonspecific lyrics allowed listeners to fill in their own details, thinking about their own lives. Alan Pollack describes the song as "so ultra special if not sacred to the collective consciousness" and writes of hearing the song as a teenager and using it as a guide to judging the significance of any future love: "I have it on good authority that I'm not alone in my personal experience of, having heard it for the first time as an [sic] romantically earnest if yet adenoidally awkward teen, walking around for many years thereafter 'searching'…for the significant other to whom I could in all sincerity and good conscience dedicate this song." "In My Life" has been a favorite song for playing at weddings for decades. The deep emotional associations the song has for listeners combined with the harpsichord sound and baroque style of the instrumental break to produce a new emotional resonance and meaning for baroque sound.

The Beatles returned to the combination of baroque sounds with the theme of personal memory a year later. "Penny Lane," written by Paul McCartney, was recorded from December 29, 1966, to January 17, 1967, and released as a double-A-side single, along with John Lennon's "Strawberry Fields Forever," on February 13, 1967.[45] After their final international tour in the summer of 1966, the individual Beatles worked on separate projects in the fall, reconvening to begin work on their new album project on November 29, 1966. That album, their eighth studio album, would be released in May and June of 1967 as *Sgt. Pepper's Lonely Hearts Club Band*. The double-A single presented the first finished works to appear from the new project. Both songs return to the theme of childhood memory begun with John Lennon's draft of the lyrics for "In My Life." Paul McCartney describes working on the songs: "We were writing childhood memories: recently faded memories from eight or ten years before, so it was a recent nostalgia, pleasant memories for both of us. All the places were still there, and because we remembered it so clearly we could have gone on."[46]

In contrast to John Lennon's dreamy song about thoughts and emotions in the past set in a beautiful "secret garden" where he could "live in his dreams a little," Paul McCartney chose to portray his memories in crisp, surrealist details. He followed up on Lennon's initial draft for "In My Life," written the previous year, which used place as a key to exploring one's memories, by naming specific sights and places in Liverpool, beginning with Penny Lane itself, both a street and the name of a neighborhood. McCartney explains: "Penny Lane was the depot I had to change buses at to get from my house to John's and to a lot of my friends. It was a big bus terminal which we all knew very well. I sang in the choir at St. Barnabas Church opposite.... It's part fact, part nostalgia for a great place—blue suburban skies, as we remember it, and it's still there."[47]

The song has two sections of music, a four-line verse and a three-line chorus ("Penny Lane is in my ears and in my eyes"), arranged as follows:

Verse • Verse • Chorus | Verse • [Instrumental Verse] • Chorus |
Verse • Verse • Chorus | Chorus[48]

The first four verses each introduce someone who young Paul could have seen while walking in Penny Lane—a barber, a banker, a fireman, and a nurse—like a child's picture book of life in the city. The descriptions of these people seem written from a child's perspective, making sense of puzzling details of the adult world: The barber is showing photographs of people he knows, rather than displaying different hairstyles; the banker does not wear a raincoat like other adults (perhaps he carries an umbrella instead?), while the fireman carries a portrait of the queen in his pocket (is it on coins or notes?) and cleans his fire engine because he prefers it that way, not because it is his job. Only with the nurse selling poppies for Armistice Day do we get a more adult perspective: "though she feels as if she's in a play / She is anyway," a portrayal of consciousness informed by modernity. The fifth verse returns to the men from the earlier verses, one line for each as they finally inhabit the same space: The banker is waiting for a haircut from the barber, when the fireman rushes in. In contrast to the references to raincoats, pouring rain, and a holiday in November, the choruses speak of "blue suburban skies" in summer and the treats of adolescence, snacks and amorous experimentation, that reveal the whole lyric to be a set of memories over time rather than the portrayal of a single visit to Penny Lane.

As with "In My Life," "Penny Lane" was rehearsed and recorded by the Beatles, leaving a section of the form for non-Beatle instrumentals. The recording procedure was surprisingly complex for what would seem in its final version to be a straightforward song. Paul McCartney began alone, playing and overdubbing several rhythm parts on piano by himself, on Thursday, December 29, 1966. He and John Lennon first recorded vocals on Friday, December 30—Lennon sings harmony on the words "there beneath the blue suburban skies"—using a somewhat slower tape speed (47 ½ cycles per second as opposed to the normal 50) to be sped up on replay; "VariSpeed" recording technique changes pitch, but was primarily used to change vocal timbre. The Beatles resumed work after the New Year, on Wednesday, January 4, with John Lennon recording an additional piano part, George Harrison playing lead guitar, and Paul McCartney recording another vocal track; McCartney rerecorded his vocal the next day. Further work on Friday, January 6, added McCartney's bass guitar, Lennon's rhythm guitar, and Ringo Starr on drums. These new parts were also recorded at the slightly slower speed, to match the pitch of the vocals. Lennon overdubbed conga drums, and finally he and George Martin recorded more piano parts, handclaps, and all three singers scat singing in the place of the still-unrecorded brass instruments. The Beatles final overdubs for "Penny Lane" were made on Tuesday, January 10, adding sound effects, including a hand bell rung when the fireman and his engine were mentioned.[49]

There were two sessions for classical instruments to record music arranged by George Martin; the first, recorded on Monday, January 9, 1967, featured four flutists and two trumpet players, with three of the musicians overdubbing second parts, for two piccolos and a flügelhorn.[50] These instruments can be heard in the single as released, particularly the flute that punctuates the ends of lines in the verses and the brass heard primarily in the chorus. A second set of overdubs, featuring two trumpets, two oboes, two *cor anglais* (played by the oboists), and a double bass, was recorded to fill the "instrumental verse" on January 12. This first attempt can be heard on the *Beatles Anthology* recordings, volume 2, disc 2, track 4, remixed with other recorded elements by Martin and Geoff Emerick for that release in 1996. The nasal *cor anglais* and brassy trumpet arrangement sounds something like a 1940s dance band mixed with "swinging" 1960s jazz, an appropriate sound for a song about McCartney's memories of childhood (he was born in 1942), but he was not satisfied with the results.

The previous evening, Wednesday, January 11, Paul McCartney had been watching a music program on BBC2 television, *Masterworks*, and he heard and saw a performance of Bach's Brandenburg Concerto no. 2 by the English Chamber Orchestra broadcast from Guildford Cathedral. McCartney was particularly taken with the sound of the piccolo trumpet, and he asked George Martin about it.[51] Martin knew the player, David Mason, and hired him to record the following week, on Tuesday, January 17. Mason recalled, "We spent three hours working it out. . . . Paul sang the parts he wanted, George Martin wrote them out, I tried them. But the actual recording was done quite quickly. They were jolly high notes, quite taxing, but with the tapes rolling we did two takes as overdubs on top of the existing song."[52] The baroque-style trumpet obbligato became a memorable highlight of the finished song. Combined with McCartney's stepwise descending bass line in the verses, the virtuosic high trumpet line, opening with a melodic sequence of ascending triplets, adds a baroque music flavor to the song, with the well-placed sixteenth notes in the otherwise eighth-note triplets echoing the rhythmic start of the second Brandenburg's ritornello. These musical gestures to the distant past help the song's evocation of memory and history to seem more timeless, more universal, and more elevated. The high trumpet part adds a regal, ceremonial, historic tone to what might otherwise have seemed a mundane recital of ordinary details in the lyrics. *Childhood memories are important*, says the historical-sounding trumpet, *and you are important too, listener.*

The Beatles' use of baroque instruments, sounds, and musical style in these and other songs in 1967 cemented an association between "old" music and one's personal memories. This music came to be called *psychedelic*, referring directly to the influence of LSD on its creation (and its listeners' reception) but also indirectly to the non-drug-related voyages of imagination and self-reflection this music enhanced. The association between sound and memory also was understood as an association between sound and the feeling of nostalgia. Svetlana Boym details how the term first was used in the nineteenth century to describe a debilitating type of homesickness; she eventually defines nostalgia as a longing for a home one has never seen.[53] This kind of longing can be seen to drive interest in particular romanticized historical pasts, as well as, I would argue, interest in historical musics.[54] But one can also experience personal nostalgia, a longing for the past as represented by one's own childhood, a time remembered by many people as having been simpler and more positive, before one became aware of the complications of adult life. It is this kind of personal nostalgia that "In My Life" and "Penny Lane" both represent (for their creators) and inspire (for their audiences).

Allusions to baroque and older musical style in popular music continued in the 1970s, in the primarily British genres of "electric folk" and progressive rock. Electric folk, as noted previously, was an English take on American folk rock that emphasized the antiquity of folk music by the use of early instruments and historic pieces and original lyrics evoking magic and the past and comparing the musicians to minstrels (for example, Fairport Convention's song "Come All Ye" [*Liege and Lief*, 1969] and Steeleye Span's "A Calling-On Song" [*Hark! The Village Wait*, 1970], both written by Ashley Hutchings), aided by the paratextual medieval fantasies of their cover art. Some progressive rock albums were based explicitly on ideas of the past, both historic and legendary, such as keyboardist Rick Wakeman's albums *The Six Wives of Henry VIII* (A&M, 1973) and *The Myths and Legends of King Arthur and the Knights of the Round Table* (A&M, 1975). Edward Macan notes the use of old instruments in progressive rock:

> Certain premodern instruments were drawn on consistently enough that they should also be considered a minor part of the progressive rock soundscape. By far the most important instrument in this respect is the harpsichord.... Other archaic instruments that are occasionally used by these groups include the flute-like recorder (featured quite prominently at the beginning of Led Zeppelin's "Stairway to Heaven" and throughout Yes's "Your Move")' the lute, a more complex ancestor of the modern acoustic guitar that was championed by Focus's Jan Akkerman; the krummhorn, a buzzing kazoo-like wind instrument featured prominently on Gryphon's *Red Queen to Gryphon Three* LP; and the regal, a nasal, honking keyboard instrument whose strident sounds can be heard to good effect on Gentle Giant's "It's a Dog's Life." Like

the Mellotron, these instruments are often used in conjunction with acoustic guitars to introduce a bittersweet or pastoral ambience in more overtly "feminine" sections.[55]

The Beatles' combination of baroque musical sounds and nostalgia was successful because it is coherent—both elements belong to the past—and it is powerful because it encourages listeners to feel connected, personally, to their imagination of the past. In addition, through this combination of sound and meaning, the baroque sounds could become recoded as generically *old*, rather than referencing some particular historical time, such as the eighteenth century or the different associations otherwise possible with that time period. Further slippage in meaning, especially for nonhistorians, allows one element of the past to stand in for other historical times, through the common element of "oldness." This kind of slippage explains how baroque musical references in 1960s pop, originally by the Beatles and reinforced by other artists such as Simon and Garfunkel's otherworldly harpsichord in "Scarborough Fair/Canticle" (1966), come to represent the past in general in 1970s medievalist folk rock. The recorders in Led Zeppelin's "Stairway to Heaven" (1971) call up associations not with J. S. Bach, or colonial America, or Marie Antoinette, but with memory, magic, and nostalgia. The Beatles' mixing the novel sound of newly popular baroque music with a personal sense of nostalgia captivated listeners, inspiring other musicians to play with the mixture themselves; it may even have encouraged listeners to bring a sense of warmth and personal connection to early music itself.

NOTES

1. On British folk-rock performers and groups in this period, see Britta Sweers, *Electric Folk: The Changing Face of English Traditional Music* (New York: Oxford University Press, 2005), especially chap. 3, "The Performers and Groups," 69–110; and Rob Young, *Electric Eden: Unearthing Britain's Visionary Music* (New York: Faber & Faber, 2010). On Bob Dylan, see Elijah Wald, *Dylan Goes Electric! Newport, Seeger, Dylan, and the Night That Split the Sixties* (New York: Dey Street Books, 2015).

2. For discussion of medievalism and Led Zeppelin, see the next chapter in this volume, "'Ramble On': Medievalism as Nostalgic Practice in Led Zeppelin's Use of J. R. R. Tolkien," pp. 530–546.

3. Some writers include these 1970s medievalist-flavored works in the category of *neomedieval*, but I prefer to reserve that term for the subgenre of medievalist popular music of the late 1980s and later, the music for which the term was first used. There is to my ears a difference in performance style that probably derives from differences in sound and style in the 1960s versus 1980s early music performances that informs the different performances. See Alana Bennett, "Reinventing the Past in European Neo-Medieval Music," in *The Middle Ages in Popular Culture: Medievalism and Genre*, chap. 5, ed. Helen Young (Amherst, NY: Cambria Press, 2015), 91–112.

4. The Beatles bibliography is enormous. In my opinion, the best single-volume study of their life and works, and their influence on contemporary culture, is Jonathan Gould, *Can't Buy*

Me Love: The Beatles, Britain, and America (New York: Three Rivers Press, 2007). For lively discussion of every Beatles recording, including information about individual musicians on each track, see Ian MacDonald, *Revolution in the Head: The Beatles' Records and the Sixties*, 3rd ed. (Chicago: Chicago Review Press, 2007). For an exhaustive guide to the Beatles' career as performers and recording artists, see Mark Lewisohn, *The Complete Beatles Chronicle: The Definitive Day-by-Day Guide to the Beatles' Entire Career* (Chicago: Chicago Review Press, 2010).

5. Currently, the standard view of early music sees it as encompassing the first three style periods of a six-period schema: medieval, Renaissance, and baroque, as separate from classical, romantic, and modern (or twentieth century). For example, Thomas Forrest Kelly begins his *Very Short Introduction* by asking, "What does 'early music' mean?" (an epistemological formulation), and answering it, "This is a book about the music of the past. Medieval, Renaissance, and Baroque music have been repeatedly discarded and rediscovered since they were new." The ontological equation of early music with the first three style periods is given. Thomas Forrest Kelly, *Early Music: A Very Short Introduction* (Oxford: Oxford University Press, 2011), 1. Jessica Wood sees the disjunction between music and early music as incorporating a temporal break between performance traditions: "To its practitioners, 'Early Music' is often distinguished from 'music' more generally by the presence of an 'interruption' in performing traditions; it is music for which performance practices must be reconstructed"; "Keys to the Past: Building Harpsichords and Feeling History in the Postwar United States" (PhD diss., Duke University, 2010), 6. This is already a specialist explanation, informed by further knowledge of music history.

6. Lawrence Dreyfus makes this point in his unsympathetic "Early Music Defended Against Its Devotees: A Theory of Historical Performance in the Twentieth Century," *The Musical Quarterly* 69, no. 3 (Summer 1983): 297–322; see in particular the chart on p. 317, directly contrasting performance aspects of early music and musical mainstream.

7. See Bernard Gendron, *Between Montmartre and the Mudd Club: Popular Music and the Avant-Garde* (Chicago: University of Chicago Press, 2002), 172–174, 343. Gendron ascribes the classical music elements in the Beatles' music, appropriately enough, to the influence of their producer, George Martin, without also crediting the enormous curiosity and cultural appetite of the Beatles, remarkably quick studies themselves.

8. Robert Fink, "Prelude: I Solisti Di Hoople," in *Repeating Ourselves: American Minimal Music as Cultural Practice* (Berkeley: University of California Press, 2005), 209–212. Fink's fourth chapter, "'A Pox on Manfredini': The Long-Playing Record, the Baroque Revival, and the Birth of Ambient Music" (pp. 169–207), discusses classical music critics' negative response to the sudden popularity, via the new LP format, of baroque music among young sophisticates.

9. John Rockwell, "The Baroque Opera Battleground," *The New York Times*, January 11, 1981, http://www.nytimes.com/1981/01/11/arts/the-baroque-opera-battleground.html. The work of orchestrated Bach most familiar nowadays may be Leopold Stokowski's arrangement of Bach's organ Toccata and Fugue in D minor, BWV 565, which opens Walt Disney's concert film *Fantasia* (1940) with abstract as opposed to narrative images.

10. On nineteenth-century choirs performing eighteenth-century oratorios, see Howard Smither, *A History of the Oratorio*, vol. 4, *The Oratorio in the Nineteenth and Twentieth Centuries* (Chapel Hill: University of North Carolina Press, 2000).

11. For a short overview of the use of harpsichord in 1960s pop, see Marc Meyers, "Bach & Roll: How the Unsexy Harpsichord Got Hip," *The Wall Street Journal*, October 30, 2013.

12. I am basing my survey of harpsichord in popular music recordings on two big listings of pop harpsichord recordings. The first is provided by Jessica Wood as Appendix 1, "Selected Discography of Popular and Jazz Recordings Featuring Acoustic Harpsichord or Harpsipiano, 1939–1979," of her dissertation "Keys to the Past: Building Harpsichords," 211–224. The second was the collection of videos collected by harpsichordist Christopher D. Lewis, once hosted on his personal website, now removed.

13. The harpsichord on these recordings was played by Walter Gross (1909–1967), a New York pianist and later composer. On the Alec Wilder Quartet, see Philip Lambert, *Alec Wilder* (Champaign: University of Illinois Press, 2013), 18–22.

14. "'Etchings' euphemism," in "Etching," Wikipedia, accessed October 23, 2017, https://en.wikipedia.org/wiki/Etching#%22Etchings%22_euphemism. James Thurber played with the trope in a 1929 cartoon, and Dashiell Hammett included it in his 1934 novel *The Thin Man*. In 1937, the year before the Alec Wilder Octet's recording, the phrase was cited in a breach-of-promise lawsuit against violinist David Rubinoff, leading to "come up and see my etchings" becoming a catchphrase.

15. The Jamies, "Summertime, Summertime," b/w "Searching for You" (Epic Records, 1958 single 9281 mono). See Andrew Hamilton, "The Jamies," http://www.allmusic.com/artist/the-jamies-mn0000074213, accessed October 23, 2017. For an obituary of Tom Jamison, the single's composer, see Todd Batista, "RIP Tom Jamison of the Jamies," *The TopShelf Times*, August 10, 2009, http://topshelf.posterous.com/rip-tom-jameson-of-the-jamies.

16. For more on "Summertime, Summertime" and the *Addams Family* theme song, see Elizabeth Upton, "Concepts of Authenticity in Early Music and Popular Music Communities," *Ethnomusicology Review* 17 (November 2012), http://ethnomusicologyreview.ucla.edu/journal/volume/17/piece/591. In 2012, the earliest pop recordings to include harpsichord that I knew dated from 1940. Vic Mizzy's obituary in the *Los Angeles Times* was published on October 20, 2009: Dennis McLellan, "Vic Mizzy Dies at 93; Film and TV Composer Wrote '*Addams Family*' Theme Song," http://articles.latimes.com/2009/oct/20/local/me-vic-mizzy20.

17. Gendron, *Between Montmartre and the Mudd Club*, 172.

18. Information on P. D. Q. Bach can be found on Peter Schickele's webpage, http://www.schickele.com.

19. For a short biographical survey, see Albin Zak, "Miller, Mitch(ell)," *Oxford Music Online*, accessed December 9, 2017, http://www.oxfordmusiconline.com/grovemusic/view/10.1093/gmo/9781561592630.001.0001/omo-9781561592630-e-1002250251. The *New Yorker* published a profile of Miller in its June 6, 1953, issue. Elijah Wald discusses Miller's influence as a producer in chap. 12, "Selling the American Ballad" of his *How the Beatles Destroyed Rock 'N' Roll: An Alternative History of American Popular Music* (New York: Oxford University Press, 2009), 150–165.

20. Rolf Meyersohn and Elihu Katz, "Notes on a Natural History of Fads," *American Journal of Sociology* 62, no. 6 (May 1957), 598–599.

21. Wald, *How the Beatles Destroyed Rock 'N' Roll*, 160–161. Wald footnotes Rosemary Clooney's memoir, *Girl Singer* (New York: Doubleday, 1999), 74.

22. Jessica Wood, Appendix 1, "Selected Discography," in "Keys to the Past: Building Harpsichords," 212–213, 215.

23. John Williams, as he is better known, was later to become much more famous as an award-winning film composer, with his scores for *Star Wars* (1977), *Raiders of the Lost Ark* (1981), and many others.

24. "Play with Fire" was recorded in Los Angeles on January 11, 1965, with Mick Jagger on vocals and tambourine, Keith Richards on acoustic guitar, Jack Nitzsche on harpsichord and tam-tam, and Phil Spector playing the bass part on a retuned electric guitar. The single "The Last Time," b/w "Play with Fire," was released in the United Kingdom by Decca on February 26, 1965, and in the United States by London on March 13, 1965. Personnel from the *Time Is on Our Side* website, accessed December 3, 2017, http://timeisonourside.com/SOPlayWith. html. Recording dates from Wikipedia, "Play with Fire (The Rolling Stones song)," accessed December 3, 2017, https://en.wikipedia.org/wiki/Play_with_Fire_(The_Rolling_Stones_song).

25. Personnel from Ian MacDonald, *Revolution in the Head: The Beatles' Records and the Sixties*, 3rd ed. (Chicago: Chicago Review Press, 2005), 317.

26. Before their contract with EMI was renegotiated in 1967, the Beatles' albums as released in the United States by Capital Records presented different material than the corresponding UK releases. The UK album *Help!* contained seven songs from the film on side A, with seven nonfilm songs completing the album on side B. The US version of the album *Help!* presented the film's songs on side A, but included selections from the film's orchestral score, composed and conducted by British film composer Ken Thorne, on side B. The nonfilm songs from side B of the UK album were included on three later US albums, *Beatles VI* and *Rubber Soul* (both 1965) and *Yesterday and Today* (1966).

27. Mark Lewisohn, *The Complete Beatles Recording Sessions*, 59. "Yesterday" was recorded on June 14, 1965, between seven o'clock and ten o'clock at night.

28. Lewisohn, *The Complete Beatles Recording Sessions*, 59. I strongly suspect that the straight string tone in "Yesterday" and later Beatles recordings, such as the double string quartet in "Eleanor Rigby" (1966), influenced the predilection, among both performers and listeners, for straight-tone, vibratoless playing on British early music recordings in the 1980s. But that is an argument for another paper.

29. "Shortly after the release of *Beatles for Sale*, John Lennon told *Melody Maker* that both "I'm a Loser" and "I Don't Want to Spoil the Party" reflected the growing influence of Bob Dylan on the Beatles' songwriting. At this point, John was presumably referring more to the general tone of Dylan's music than to his words, since neither the content nor the style of the lyrics to either song, apart from their vaguely introspective cast, bears much resemblance to anything specific in Dylan's work." Jonathan Gould, *Can't Buy Me Love*, 259. Songs written entirely or primarily by John Lennon or Paul McCartney were all credited "Lennon–McCartney," and the details as to which composer wrote which song were eventually revealed in interviews, biographies, and memoirs.

30. "When 'Help' came out in '65, I was actually crying out for help. Most people think it's just a fast rock 'n roll song. I didn't realize it at the time; I just wrote the song because I was commissioned to write it for the movie. But later, I knew I really was crying out for help. It was my fat Elvis period. You see the movie: He—I—is very fat, very insecure, and he's completely lost himself. And I am singing about when I was so much younger and all the rest, looking back at how easy it was." Interview by David Sheff, September 1980; published in *Playboy*, January 1981.

31. Hunter Davies wrote the first authorized biography of the group, *The Beatles*, published in 1968. In the course of spending time with the group, he was given nine handwritten copies of lyrics, including the first version of "In My Life." Davies donated three of his handwritten Lennon lyrics, "In My Life," "Strawberry Fields Forever," and "She Said She Said," as well as two of John's letters and a postcard, to the British Library in 2013, in exchange for

a tax credit of £319,500. The lyrics were cataloged as British Library, Add MS 89019/1. A press release detailing the gift can be found on the British Library's webpage, https:// www.bl.uk/press-releases/2013/may/john-lennon-letters-and-lyrics-donated-to-the- nation—british-library-first-institution-to-benefit-f. The manuscript of the "In My Life" lyrics was reproduced in Hunter Davies, ed., *The Beatles Lyrics: The Stories behind the Music, Including the Handwritten Drafts of More Than 100 Classic Beatles Songs* (New York: Little, Brown, 2014), 131.

32. Davies puts the word "jumping" in square brackets. To my eye, "Jum" is clear, the next letter is unclear, then it looks like "ay."

33. Davies adds [or lives] but the vowel, compared with others on the page, is clearly "o."

34. Davies reads this as "Some its…" but the word "with" matches the same word in the line above it.

35. MacDonald, *Revolution in the Head*, 170.

36. John Lennon and Paul McCartney, "In My Life," ©1965 Northern Songs Ltd.

37. Alan W. Pollack and Walter Everett both label each stanza as *Verse* and *Bridge*, with Everett also using A and B for the two halves of each section. John Lennon himself referred to the second part of the stanza as the *middle eight*, the Beatles' standard term for referring to a contrasting musical section, no matter the song structure. Alan W. Pollack, *Notes on "In My Life,"* Notes on…Series #86 (IML), 1993, http://www.icce.rug.nl/~soundscapes/ DATABASES/AWP/iml.shtml. Walter Everett, *The Beatles as Musicians: The Quarry Men through Rubber Soul* (Oxford: Oxford University Press, 2001), 319–321.

38. John Lennon's interview with Jann Wenner was recorded in December 1970 and published in two parts, on January 21, 1971, and February 4, 1971. "Lennon Remembers: Part One," *Rolling Stone*, January 21, 1971.

39. Lewisohn, *The Complete Beatles Recording Sessions*, 64. Here, Lewisohn is echoing the Beatles' idiosyncratic use of the term middle eight to refer to any kind of contrasting section.

40. The Beatles, ed. Brian Roylance, Julian Quance, Oliver Craske, and Roman Milisic, *The Beatles Anthology* (San Francisco: Chronicle Books, 2000), 197.

41. Lewisohn, *The Complete Beatles Recording Sessions*, 65.

42. George Martin, with Jeremy Hornsby, *All You Need Is Ears* (New York: St. Martin's Press, 1979), 38–39.

43. Alan Pollack points out that the melody is "almost rigidly pentatonic," not touching the fourth scale degree (D) until the second half of the verse, on the first appearance of the word "lovers," while the seventh scale degree, G♯, appears only as the final pitch of the introductory guitar solo riff. Alan W. Pollack, *Notes on "In My Life,"* Notes on…Series #86 (IML), 1993.

44. Jessica Wood lists only two recordings featuring harpsichord released in 1964, both jazz LPs, by saxophonist Ben Webster and bandleader Lawrence Welk, aimed at older listeners. The year 1965 sees a generational split: six LPs—four jazz (Albert Ayler; Walt Dickerson, with Sun Ra on harpsichord; the George Shearing Quintet; and Martial Solal) plus two crossover novelties, Glen Campbell's unclassifiable instrumental album *Country Shindig*, featuring Leon Russell on harpsichord, and Joshua Rifkin's *Baroque Beatles Book* (Elektra)—plus the two pop hit singles. The year 1966 saw an explosion of albums, twenty of them, including harpsichord, by younger folk artists such as Judy Collins, Donovan, the Mamas and the Papas, and Simon and Garfunkel. The trend continued in 1967, with thirty-two albums listed by Wood.

45. Lewisohn, *The Complete Beatles Recording Sessions*, 91–93. The Beatles worked on the song on December 29–30 and January 4–6, 9–10, 12, and 17. After *Rubber Soul* (December 1965), the Beatles' seventh studio album, *Revolver*, was released in August 1966. The Beatles had been recording and releasing two albums a year, summer and winter, since 1963, but they did not release an album in winter 1966.

46. Barry Miles, *Paul McCartney: Many Years from Now* (New York: Holt, 1997), 308. Paul's description of "Strawberry Fields" as John's "secret garden" is from p. 307.

47. *The Beatles Anthology*, 237.

48. In McCartney's handwritten lyrics draft, he has labeled the verse sections "A" and the chorus "B" in the left margin in different ink. The instrumental verse was already part of his conception, represented by the words "(Ah Ah etc)," as was the plan to repeat the chorus up a step at the end: "B (then B in C)." Davies, *The Beatles Lyrics*, 186.

49. Lewisohn, *The Complete Beatles Recording Sessions*, 91–93.

50. Ibid., 93.

51. See also Martin, *All You Need Is Ears*, 201–202.

52. Lewisohn, *The Beatles Recording Sessions*, 93. David Mason was to play on four more Beatles songs in 1967: "A Day in the Life," "It's All Too Much," "Magical Mystery Tour," and "All You Need Is Love," where he can be heard as one of two trumpeters playing a Bach two-part invention at the end of the song.

53. Svetlana Boym, *The Future of Nostalgia* (New York: Basic Books, 2001).

54. Compare, for instance, with the discussion of nostalgia for medieval rural Britain housed in Tolkien's fantasy works, in Led Zeppelin, in Gothic metal, and in a premodern pagan world as discussed by Caitlin Carlos, Ross Hagen, and Scott Troyer in this volume, pp. 530–546, 547–563, and 586–610, respectively.

55. Edward Macan, *Rocking the Classics: English Progressive Rock and the Counterculture* (New York: Oxford University Press, 1997), 37. The Mellotron was a keyboard instrument that played a variety of tape loops with recorded instrumental sounds; a notable use of Mellotron is the flute-like chords at the beginning of the Beatles' "Strawberry Fields Forever" (1967).

CHAPTER 23

....

"RAMBLE ON"

Medievalism as a Nostalgic Practice in Led Zeppelin's Use of J. R. R. Tolkien

....

CAITLIN VAUGHN CARLOS

ALTHOUGH J. R. R. Tolkien completed *The Lord of the Rings* in 1954, his influence on popular culture did not begin in earnest until the late 1960s and early 1970s. Appealing to a new generation of readers, Tolkien's work seemed to resonate with the values of the counterculture. The editor for Warner Book's "Writers for the Seventies" series, Terrence Malley, explained in 1972 that Tolkien's writings seemed "particularly relevant in our own age of anti-heroes, in this time when we can readily identify with the small and the apparently powerless."[1] British youth faced a grim reality of economic decline and limited opportunity at the start of the new decade. Rejecting the cold, functional urban developments of the postwar period, but doubtful of the pure optimism found in the hippie movement of the late 1960s, a new generation of teenagers and young adults turned to romanticized images of rural Britain and embraced nostalgic expressions of fantasy and medievalism. The Middle Ages became a playground for championing the individual "antihero" as the rest of the world seemingly marched toward environmental, economic, and social destruction.[2] Rock musicians of the time also participated in this trend, searching for meaning and identity in idealized visions of Britain's past. One of these groups was the blues-based rock band Led Zeppelin. In many ways, the idealized British pastoral heritage imagined by Led Zeppelin and their contemporaries in the late 1960s and early 1970s was far more similar to Tolkien's medieval fantasy of Middle-earth than the industrial, late twentieth-century reality in which they lived.

The link between Middle-earth and the idealized pastoralism evoked in so much of Led Zeppelin's music was in some ways ironic. In terms of their background and social position, Tolkien had little in common with the members of the blues-rock band. Tolkien was a respected philologist, the Rawlinson and Bosworth professor of Anglo-Saxon at Oxford, best known for his work on the medieval romance *Sir Gawain and the Green Knight* and the Old English epic poem *Beowulf.* During his lifetime, he was sharply criticized by his colleagues for his turn to fantasy fiction. Public criticism of *The Lord of the Rings* was just as harsh. A review in the *Times Literary Supplement* forecasted, "This is not a work that many adults will read right through more than once."[3] Six years later (1961), Philip Toynbee expressed relief in the *Observer* that "today these books have passed into a merciful oblivion," an observation that could not have been more wrong. In 1965, Ace Publishing released an unauthorized paperback version of the novels that sparked renewed interest (an authorized version by Ballantine Books followed in 1965).[4] A decade later, Warner Books declared Tolkien a "Writer for the 70s"; in 2000, Oxford professor and well-known medievalist Tom Shippey declared Tolkien "Author of the Century."[5] While critical reception for Tolkien's work at the time of publication cast doubt on its relevance for the contemporary world, the legendarium of Middle-earth proved to be a powerful avenue for later generations to articulate values and even protest against their own environments.

This chapter will consider the role of *The Lord of the Rings* in the music of Led Zeppelin between 1969 and 1971. It will examine three songs that directly reference Tolkien's works: "The Battle of Evermore," "Misty Mountain Hop," and "Ramble On." Viewing the medievalism in these songs as a nostalgic practice, I will draw on nostalgia theory to explore how these songs embrace a fictional, medieval-inspired past that is both spatial and temporal. These songs offer an avenue for understanding how individuals and communities construct meaning and identity in periods of fragmentation and upheaval. Furthermore, by considering previous incarnations of medievalism and romanticism in British history as well as Tolkien's own participation in antiquarianism and constructions of Britishness, this chapter suggests that Led Zeppelin's allusions to Tolkien's literature rely on cultural memory to actively participate in a dialogue of urban criticism and a romanticized vision of rural Britain.

Medievalism as a Nostalgic Practice

To understand how creative uses of medieval tropes and fantasies, such as those of Tolkien and Led Zeppelin, make meaning in their contemporary environments, I propose to view medievalism as a nostalgic practice.[6] Like other nostalgic expressions, medievalism employs the past for present-day needs. Annette Kreutziger-Herr observes that expressions of medievalism "have nothing to do with the Middle Ages and everything to do with *our* era."[7] Often, these expressions are entwined with heritage and cultural memory, which, as David Lowenthal argues, "align us with forebears whose virtues we share and whose vices we shun."[8] The past becomes most useable when it seems to clearly articulate some value(s), which relate to the present. Medievalism, especially in creative and artistic works, relies on cultural memory and ideas of a historically distant past rooted in notions of authenticity and purity and viewed as a foil to the contemporary world: an imaginary past to which the nostalgic longs to return or from which he or she longs to learn. Nostalgic practices and medievalisms, then, use the past to imagine a future founded in those values.

Finding ways to access the past provides another challenge in articulating its relevance to a present world. In her groundbreaking study, *The Future of Nostalgia*, Svetlana Boym explores the etymological roots of the word *nostalgia* to distinguish between what she views as two types of nostalgias. Boym's nostalgias center around accessing the past through its recreation (restorative) or its emotive space (reflective): "Restorative nostalgia puts the emphasis on *nostos* and proposes to rebuild the lost home and patch up the memory gaps. Reflective nostalgia dwells in *algia*, in longing and loss, the imperfect process of remembrance."[9] Medievalism, also, can be delineated into practices that attempt to recreate some element of the past (whether historically or creatively) or to reflect on the emotional space, the feeling of longing. These two distinctions help us to navigate the ambiguity of that longing—is nostalgia yearning for a time or for a space? If we look back to the original context for the word nostalgia (coined by a seventeenth-century Swiss doctor, Johannes Hofer, to describe soldiers at war who longed for their homeland), we find that a sense of place was a defining element of this nostalgia—deemed a curable, medical illness—in which the displaced soldier yearned for a connection to a physical home that had been emotionally lost by distance or even physically lost to the damages of war.[10] However, the longing is not only for the place, but also for the perceived time of peace and calm associated with that home before the war. So, too, do more recent representations of nostalgia navigate the ambiguity of time and space. Boym writes, "Nostalgia tantalizes us with its fundamental ambivalence; it is about the repetition of the unrepeatable, materialization of the immaterial.... Nostalgia charts space on time and time on space and hinders the distinction between subject and object."[11] Nostalgia can be both spatialized and temporal. Through restorative and reflective efforts, through recreation and emotional attachments, individual creative expressions and medievalisms explore the past as time and as space. Tolkien's Middle-earth, then, is both a restorative practice of recreating a past world as a physical space and a reflection on what the past world would feel like and how that world feels different than the time and place of the author's contemporary environment.

Led Zeppelin's appropriation of Tolkien's Middle-earth further complicates these distinctions. Medievalism is a primary tool for Led Zeppelin's creation of mythic, fantasy worlds. As Susan Fast explains in her groundbreaking monograph, *In the Houses of the Holy: Led Zeppelin and the Power of Rock Music*,

> [the] idea that myth unites us is particularly important, for it is one reason that the mythology of Led Zeppelin is so powerful to many fans. When fans say that Led Zeppelin's music is "timeless" or that it "epitomizes humanity," this is, I think, what they mean. The feeling of connectedness to other people, to history, and to a supernatural world is profound, especially for those who feel alienated in their daily lives.[12]

Led Zeppelin's creation of a mythic world is not limited to their appropriation of Tolkien's legendarium. However, this particular fantasy space, as explored through the band's music, provides an interesting avenue for understanding how creative medievalisms work as nostalgic practices to make meaning in their contemporary environment. Each of the three Tolkien-inspired songs employs the medieval fantasy of *The Lord of the Rings* through different means and purposes. "The Battle of Evermore" attempts to recreate a scene from the stories and to create a sonic landscape for that recreation. "Misty Mountain Hop," decidedly contemporary in setting and sound, uses Tolkien references to allude to a longing for a different time and place and the values that the band associates with those spaces. "Ramble On" is perhaps the most ambiguous in its textual and sonic narratives, increasingly blurring the lines between past and present. The expression of medievalism in all three songs navigates the space between the object of nostalgic longing as both time and space. In examining the medievalism in these songs as a nostalgic practice, we can begin to understand the values that both Tolkien and Led Zeppelin attribute to the past and use to make meaning in the present.

"The Battle of Evermore"

The Edenic fantasy of rural Britain is one intimately tied with medieval imaginings. Even fictional depictions of the past, such as Tolkien's Middle-earth, rely on cultural memory of a romanticized British past that was both medieval and pastoral. This vision has been prominent in British culture since at least the nineteenth century, when, as Meredith Feldman asserts, "the impulse to conserve flora, fauna, and habitat" began along the same time that many scholars attribute the rise of medievalism.[13] Both ecoconservation and medievalism rely on a nostalgic impulse to retain a sense of Britishness and heritage that is viewed as innate to the British countryside. Lowenthal confidently argues that "landscape is Britain's archetypal legacy; two centuries of city celebrants made country life a metaphor for the national soul."[14] This romanticized image paints the landscape as a recoverable piece of Britain's past and cultural heritage— seemingly recoverable, both through an ecoconservative urge and as a fantasy space characterized by pastoral imagery. And yet this imagined space, the archaic British countryside, is ultimately intangible. Raymond Williams explores the problem of perspective in this British nostalgia, elucidating that "when we move back in time, consistently directed to an earlier and happier rural England, we could find no place, no period, in which we could seriously rest."[15] Tolkien's ventures into the imagined world of Middle-earth participate in this ecomedieval lineage.[16] As a philologist, Tolkien was fascinated by medieval words, but his fiction writings translate language into a new physical realm. He attempted to recreate the past in a fantastical exploration of the world in which the medieval tongue (even an imaginary medieval tongue) would have been spoken.[17] In doing so, Tolkien actively participated in shaping Britain's cultural memory for a rural, British past, associated with the medieval world.[18] Ann M. Martinez explains: "As a fantasy author, Tolkien wrote of an epic journey; as a medievalist, he situated this journey on a medieval landscape."[19] A continuation of this pastoral nostalgic impulse can then be seen when Led Zeppelin appropriates Tolkien's world for their own nostalgic fantasies.

Led Zeppelin's evocation of an ecomedieval play space was in full force by the issue of their fourth, untitled album in 1971.[20] This album's cover artwork juxtaposes a dilapidated cityscape against a fantasy image of a preindustrial, natural world (embodied by the painted image of an old man carrying a bundle of sticks on his back). Songs on the album, including "Stairway to Heaven" and "The Battle of Evermore," explore a sonic soundscape in which the band and their fans can visit a past world: even if that world may have never existed. Acoustic guitars, mandolins, and recorders work with other sonic effects to recreate what a past musical soundscape is imagined to have sounded like. Guitarist Jimmy Page acknowledges as much when he describes "Stairway to Heaven," saying, "It's…incredibly English. It sounds almost medieval. At times it sounds like, you know, you want to have swirling mists."[21]

"The Battle of Evermore" is, perhaps, Led Zeppelin's clearest example of a Tolkien-inspired, nostalgic soundscape that attempts to situate the listener in a spatialized fantasy world. Lyrical references to the outdoors and lighting ("dark of night," "morning light," "eastern glow," "sunlight," "clouds") not only depict a visual setting for the imagined space, but also find their sonic equivalent in timbral effects. Led Zeppelin's signature alternation between acoustic and electrified instruments, bright and dark timbres, and sparse and dense textures sets the scene. These sonic effects also carry semiotic connotations. The mandolins and acoustic instrumentation, for instance, signify the pastoral through their associations with folk music settings. The drone chords in the mandolin also evoke a more specific reference to a medieval folk past. They offer a sense of the archaic and blur the sense of tonality in the piece. In this same contemporary moment, Britain's folk-rock movement was appealing to many of the same audiences, exploring folk songs and traditions through a similar mix of electrified and acoustic instrumentation. Bands such as Fairport Convention and Steeleye Span drew on many of the same fantasy tropes of a romanticized, pastoral, medieval British world.

The lyrics to "The Battle of Evermore" are rich with seasonal references to a time of harvest, adding more specificity to the setting that the song constructs. When Plant sings, "The apples of the valley hold, the seas of happiness, the ground is rich from tender care," the lyrics evoke both a season of bounty and a pastoral setting in which humans are living in harmony with nature. The song takes place in an outdoor space that has been tenderly cultivated and is ripe with food. As the war begins, the symbols of this fertility (the apples) "turn to brown and black," a process that deepens the nostalgic tone implied by the rich, pastoral imagery described previously in the song. The images of decay and loss relate directly to the battle-scarred world of Tolkien's Middle-earth. Tolkien relates environmental degradation to Sauron's power:

> Upon its outer marches under the westward mountains Mordor was a dying land, but it was not yet dead. And here things still grew: harsh, twisted, bitter, struggling for life. In the glens of the Morgai on the other side of the valley low scrubby trees lurked and clung, coarse grey grass-tussocks fought with the stones, and withered mosses crawled on them; and everywhere great writhing, tangled brambles sprawled.[22]

Further, the effects of war are not limited to the realm of Mordor. As becomes clear in the "The Scouring of the Shire" at the end of the novels, even the idyllic Shire has suffered during Frodo's quest to return the Ring. Upon seeing their industrialized and corrupted homeland, Sam exclaims "This is worse than Mordor!... It comes home to you, they say; because it is home, and you remember it before it was ruined."[23] Here, Sam captures the heart of the nostalgic impulse in his longing for the home that he remembers, rather than the one that currently exists. As Salman Rushdie strikingly reveals in his discussion of homecomings in *The Wizard of Oz*, "the real secret of the ruby slippers is not that there is no place like home, but rather that there is no longer such a place as home; except of course, for the home we make, or the homes that are made for us, in Oz: which is anywhere and everywhere, except the place from which we began."[24]

The song's depiction of a war-torn state is made even more concrete through its lyric references to a battle scene inspired by *The Lord of the Rings*, which specifically alludes to the Queen of Light (possibly Galadriel—the queen of the elves) as well as the dark Lord and the Ringwraiths. The battle, which has often been identified by fans as the Battle of the Pelennor Fields from *The Return of the King*, provides a rich setting for nostalgic urges by contrasting times of war and conflict to the time of perceived peace that existed before.[25] This contrast looks both to nostalgia's history as a medical term for homesick soldiers and to the original meaning of *nostos*, which references Odysseus's homecoming and is inextricably bound up with ideas of war and homesickness. Led Zeppelin's sonic recreation of a Middle-earth battle captures a nostalgic tone of longing. Plant's vocal cries articulate strain and desperation, lying clearly above his comfortable tessitura. The continual downward motion of the melodic lines further evokes a sense of yearning. The haunting, pastoral soundscape layers a melancholy longing on top of the evocation of a rural, outdoor environment depicted through the lyrics and the acoustic instrumentation. In the song, Led Zeppelin sets up the destructive world of war in opposition to an idealized and Arcadian peaceful home.

At the same time, the battle scene also participates in a popular medievalism characterized by nostalgic longing for a romanticized image of medieval wartime. "The Battle of Evermore," as we have seen, situates itself in the imaginative space of Middle-earth. This setting is not only a place, but also, equally important, a time. This is the medievalism of Umberto Eco's third "little Middle Ages"—a vision that sees the Middle Ages as a "barbaric age." *The Lord of the Rings* is not just a tale of Frodo's quest, but also includes a series of battles. While the battles are barbaric, there is a constant return to goodness. Norman Cantor writes, "Here is the medieval world at its most bellicose, destructive and terrible moments: the Age of the Barbarian Invasions in the fifth and sixth centuries; the Hundred Years' War in the fourteenth and fifteenth centuries.... What is surprising and original in *The Lord of the Rings* is not the power of darkness but the force of good led by Frodo."[26] A key element of medieval fantasy, recreated musically by Led Zeppelin, is a popular vision of the Middle Ages as a time of noble actions amid barbaric wars. These actions are rooted in the common man—represented by Frodo and Sam—and their bravery in standing up against the forces of darkness. The hippies, standing up in opposition to the darkness and war of their own time, saw in themselves something of this bravery.

Further, the song's battle scene is simultaneously historical (albeit fabricated) and unrealistically fantastic. The song offers a nostalgic vision of the past in which war was fought with swords and archery, instead of fighter jets and bombs. At the same time, while these wars of the past seem more noble and romantic than those of the present, they were still destructive and chaotic events—events that may offer insight into the contemporary world. In both its original form and its future appropriations (such as those of Led Zeppelin), Tolkien's fantasy exemplifies Samuel Taylor Coleridge's view that literature creates "'Secondary Worlds,' which illumine, rather than simply reflect reality."[27] Middle-earth becomes a fantasy play space in which the contemporary world can be seen through the lens of a past one.[28] Sonically, the creation of a fantastical world, set in the past, is achieved through several methods, prominently the lead role of the mandolin and the inclusion of a female voice (Sandy Denny, lead vocalist of the folk-rock band Fairport Convention). Denny's folk-styled singing contributes to the ethereal aesthetic created for the song. Page explains: "[The song] sounded like an old English instrumental first off. Then it became a vocal and Robert did his bit. Finally, we figured we'd bring Sandy by and do a question-and-answer-type thing." For some listeners, the call and response may evoke older conceptions of singing, especially as found in liturgical church traditions including antiphonal psalm singing. Edward Macan draws specific connections between the Anglican church and the English progressive rock "sound" in "modal harmony, the emphasis on 'pipe organish' sonorities and quasi-choral vocal arrangements, the fondness for pure head tones and tempered singing."[29] The religious and archaic associations with these sounds offer a sense of timelessness. Further, Denny's voice also brings several layers of meaning to the exoticism of the soundscape. The fact that she is female and is clearly not a member of the core band (whether or not listeners recognize her identity) works to transport the listener someplace new. If listeners are aware of her place in the British folk-rock movement, then that too brings in specific meanings of folk, heritage, and Britishness. However, her gendered voice alone may have signified these folk connections. As Macan points out, while female singers were relatively more active participants in the folk-rock revivals of the sixties, they are largely absent from most rock of this era.[30] Thus, even outside her identity in Fairport Convention, her voice may have signified folk associations to listeners of this era. Ultimately, the song sounds like Led Zeppelin (Plant's voice is still recognizable and includes acoustic/folk soundscapes that have been explored by the band before), but the addition of an obvious outside vocalist differentiates this song's sound world from that of their other works. The historical-fantasy setting allows the band to create a world that operates in a completely different sense of time than the contemporary reality in which they lived.

"Misty Mountain Hop"

Spaces directly taken from *The Lord of the Rings* are also referenced in another song from the band's fourth album. "Misty Mountain Hop" uses the physical setting of the

Misty Mountain as an idealized space of adventure to which the singer longs to return. The Misty Mountains are a great mountain range in Middle-earth and represent the liminal space between fantasy and reality. In being situated to the east of the Shire, movement toward the mountains—the direction of the rising sun—can be used to allude to new beginnings or origins. For Zeppelin, this eastern setting contrasts with references to the West in other mythical songs from the same album. "Stairway to Heaven" is perhaps the most overt of these references in which the lyrics state, "there's a feeling I get, when I look to the West and my spirit in crying for leaving." Further, in medieval thinking, the East also had associations with Eden, which was imagined to be located in the farthest east of the world.[31]

For the hobbits, the Misty Mountains are the distant border that separates their safe haven of the Shire from the rest of Middle-earth. For both Bilbo Baggins in *The Hobbit*, and Frodo in *The Lord of the Rings*, the mountains are the gateway to a more magical realm. Indeed, the first land that is visited by the journeying hobbits in the novels, after passing through the Misty Mountains, is the most magical realm of all—the elven land of Lothlórien. The Misty Mountains, then, represent a place of longing and fascination for readers of the novels. Within the novels, they represent the future—the entrance to an adventurous and magical world beyond the Shire. For readers of the novel, they operate as a place of both fantasy longing and nostalgic remembrance. For the band and their listeners, the mountains represent a world of childhood play and fantasy from their own individual experiences of reading the novels.[32] The nostalgia in this case is a longing for the freedom of imagination and play that is associated with youth and childhood. Ultimately, however, it is a romanticized vision of the mountain range and all its fantastical possibilities, which allows them to work as the most idealized space for finding freedom of spirit and authenticity.

Led Zeppelin uses the image of mountains to contrast with the central scene of the contemporary psychedelic movement described in the song. The song highlights the peaceful idyllic lifestyle sought by the hippies, and yet there is a sense of apathy, of disillusionment with the idealism of the movement. Plant sings of "walkin' in the park," when he finds "crowds of people sittin' in the grass with flowers in their hair." The hippies "with flowers in their hair," smoking in the park, seek to live a peaceful existence, not unlike that of Tolkien's hobbits in the Shire. Indeed, many hippies of the era associated their experience with that of the hobbits and Middle-earth. In their 1968 article, "The Hobbit and the Hippie," William E. Ratliff and Charles G. Flinn write that "one hippie told the authors, 'I think Tolkien has come very close (not perfect) to a groovy way for human beings to get along better in this world.' "[33] Further, in his study of Tolkien's environmental vision, Matthew Dickerson argues, "the Shire represents an idyllic agrarian, preindustrial society where people can live comfortably at home in the natural world."[34] Led Zeppelin's hippies look to find something of that idyllic pastoral state in their own contemporary environment.

At the same time, both the hippies of the late sixties and the hobbits of the Shire face a constant pressure to "get in line."[35] This pressure can be both internal and external. The connection between the Shire and the contemporary hippie movements can then be viewed in two lights: the first, in which even the peaceful Shire cannot avoid the darkness of the outside world, or another in which the Shire itself, with its limitations and traditions, can be oppressive for a hobbit like Bilbo Baggins—one who longs to explore the world outside his safe, everyday existence. If the Shire is a quotidian space of limited imaginative possibilities, the Misty Mountains provide a fantastical foil for the insulated world described in Plant's lyrics. While contextually the lyrics express a longing to escape from the contemporary environment into a fantasy world, the chorus just as easily seems as if it could be the words of Bilbo Baggins himself, in his own exodus to explore the world outside the Shire:

> So I'm packing my bags for the Misty Mountains
> Where the spirits go now,
> Over the hills where the spirits fly, ooh.
> I really don't know.[36]

The mountains represent escape. Even with their uncertainty and danger, they are idealized as a place of freedom for the spirit.

While "The Battle of Evermore" creates a musical setting that seems to reside in a past fantasy realm, "Misty Mountain Hop" sets itself, both lyrically and in its electrified instrumentation, decidedly in the contemporary world. However, it also offers a dialogue between an imagined medieval past and 1970s British youth culture, through its connection to Tolkien's fantasy world. If the hippies represent a Shire-like existence, it is one that is predicated on time as much as place. When Led Zeppelin depicts a contemporary hippie scene, surrounded by the external pressure of the outside world, they romanticize a past time, finding "something about the imaginary land of the Shire that people want to imitate in the real world and incorporate into their own lives."[37] The nostalgic impulse of timelessness is one of these characteristics of the Shire, which is reflected in the song. Plant's lyrics depict a longing for a less rigorous devotion to time and commitment ("I really don't know what time it was, so I asked if I could stay a while"). This ambiguous grasp on time is also capture through the sky growing dark ("I didn't notice but it had got very dark") while on a drug trip. In addition to the loss of time to the influences of some drug, Plant also draws on social conventions of an older, "traditional" lifestyle ("they asked us to stay for tea and have some fun") and metaphors of "sitting spare, like a book on a shelf rustin.'"[38] The medievalisms of life in the Shire are juxtaposed against the experiences of a contemporary, psychedelic environment as a way of articulated shared values and a nostalgic pull toward a slower-paced way of life.

Further, in this slower-paced world, there is leisure time for social interaction and recreation. Even the drug references in the song find a connection to the lifestyle of the Shire.[39] Tolkien devotes the second section of his prologue to *The Fellowship of the Rings* to the hobbits' practice of smoking pipe-weed. Smoking in the Shire was a cultural activity, shared by the entire community: "When Hobbits first began to smoke is not known, all of the legends and family histories take it for granted; for ages folks in the Shire smoked various herbs, some fouler, some sweeter."[40] Although predating the psychedelic movement's embracing of marijuana and other drugs, Tolkien's description of a serene, pastoral existence, united by community smoking, appealed to the sensibilities of this movement. Only a few short years after the psychedelic revolutions in London and San Francisco, visions of a slower-paced, communal environment, infused with drug culture and pastoral fantasies, appealed to a generation of nostalgic young adults. And yet this psychedelic culture, in 1971, had lost some of its idealism. The peaceful, Shire-like lifestyle was now viewed as limiting and artificial, more a symbol of conformity than freedom. Plant sings, "You really don't care if they're coming, / I know that it's all a state of mind / If you go down in the streets today, Baby, you better / You better open your eyes / Folk down there really don't care, really don't care / Don't care, really don't / Which, which way the pressure lies." The psychedelic experience may seem transcending, but true freedom of the spirit is found with a return to the wildness of nature in the Misty Mountains.

"Ramble On"

While "The Battle of Evermore" and "Misty Mountain Hop" operate in specifically articulated settings, the situation of "Ramble On," from Led Zeppelin's second album (1969), is less clear. The opening lyrics paint an ambiguous, misty outdoor locale:

> Leaves are falling all around, it's time I was on my way.
> Thanks to you, I'm much obliged for such a pleasant stay.
> But now it's time for me to go. The autumn moon lights my way.
> For now I smell the rain, and with it pain, and it's headed my way.
> Sometimes I grow so tired, but I know I've got one thing I got to do.

There is some indication of a connection to nature with the text "leaves...falling all around" and the "autumn moon" lighting the way. However, it is unclear whether that setting refers to the reality of a contemporary environment (with metaphorical references to figures from *The Lord of the Rings*) or to the fantastical world of Middle-earth. Part of the confusion comes from overt references to Tolkien's characters and Middle-earth:

> Mine's a tale that can't be told, my freedom I hold dear.
> How years ago in days of old, when magic filled the air.
> T'was in the darkest depths of Mordor, I met a girl so fair.
> But Gollum, and the evil one crept up and slipped away with her, her, her...yeah.

The allusions to Gollum and Mordor seem to indicate a setting from Tolkien's works, and yet the rest of the lyrics—relating to meeting and losing a "girl so fair"—do not recount any particular scene from the novels and, further, do not actually make sense in the context of Middle-earth. In the novels, Gollum is depicted as an ancient, asexual being with his only desire being the Ring, and Mordor is a ruined land full of orcs, not a setting in which one would expect to find fair maidens. Lyrically, then, it appears that the references to figures from Tolkien's novels are used to depict a more contemporary narrative of journeying, desire, and struggle. Gollum's desire for the ring is, perhaps, akin to the singer's quest to "find the Queen of all my dreams." Mordor, then, represents the darkness of being alone and losing love. Ultimately, the singer constantly returns to a life of travel, in which he is journeying toward, even searching for, that love, but is never able to settle down ("got no time for spreading roots").

Without a specific Middle-earth setting, the spatialized nostalgia in "Ramble On" draws on other common English medievalisms of the pastoral mode and nature walks ("rambles"). These rambles are central to the song's nostalgic impulses, relying on cultural memory for outdoor walks as a popular English pastime. Historian Frank Trentmann has shown in his writing on "ramble" culture in early twentieth-century England that by this time "the countryside was already invested with the Arcadian aura of a 'Golden Age.'"[41] The Victorian romanticism rooted in pastoral imagery and medievalism carried into the later twentieth century. The sense of longing expressed in the song looks to rambles as a mode of accessing a spiritual connection to the outdoors. As Trentmann explains, "Ramblers approached nature as a teacher of the principles of simplicity, peace and a life of harmony with the natural elements."[42] Further, in the late sixties, when Zeppelin released "Ramble On," the song's title appealed to another shared value between ramble and hippie culture: that of the antimodern. Ramblers rejected the hyperprogressive attitudes of the contemporary world, and "rambling became an antidote to the quickening speed of the modern machine age, providing the psyche with silence and peace from the urban chaos."[43] Plant's lyrics build on these associations; motion is offered as a response to the feeling of being tired and trapped ("ah, sometimes I grow so tired, but I know I've got one thing I got to do . . . Ramble on"). The lyrics constantly reference time ("now's the time, the time is now") and the need to keep moving. Modernity is viewed as providing a stifling sense of time and a hyperprogressive pace of life. "Ramble On," instead, looks to a nostalgic view of motion as timeless and freeing.[44] Further, the interweaving of Tolkien figures into the song provides additional layers of meaning. The need for constant motion ("ain't no time for growing roots") is depicted as a timeless tradition of travel, going back even to the medieval world: "Mine's a tale that can't be told, my freedom I hold dear. How years ago in days of old when magic filled the air." The following references to Mordor and Gollum—even if they do not make narrative sense—provide meaning by connecting the song's own epic journey to that of *The Lord of the Rings*.

The legendarium of *The Lord of the Rings* centers around movement; from Bilbo's adventures in *The Hobbit* to the quest to return the Ring to Mordor, the novels rely on a constant state of motion. Further, within the novels, Tolkien offers several "walking songs" that accompany these journeys. Bilbo's "The Road Goes Ever, Ever On" songs first appear in *The Hobbit* and continue as "The Road Goes Ever On and On" in *The Fellowship of the Ring*. The versions in the first novel of the trilogy, both as song by Bilbo in Chapter 1 and later, as recounted by Frodo in Chapter 3, parallel the necessity of the movement that is captured in Plant's lyrics to "Ramble On." While the hobbits sing "The

Road goes ever on and on / Down from the door where it began. / Now far ahead the Road has gone, / And I must follow, if I can," Plant too must continue onward: "sometimes I grow so tired, but I know I've got one thing I got to do."[45] The repetition of "on and on" found in Tolkien's walking songs is sonically reimagined as "ramble on," which appears seven times within the Zeppelin song. "Ramble On" is not the only song from Led Zeppelin's repertoire to explore motion and walking songs in critique of the contemporary world. "Out on the Tiles," from the band's third album (released in 1970, a year after "Ramble On" and *Led Zeppelin II*), begins with the line, "As I walk down the highway, all I do is sing my song" and later characterizes the fast pace of his surroundings, as Plant sings, "People go and people come, see my rider right by my side / It's a total disgrace, they set the pace, it must be a race / And the best thing I can do is run."[46] Both songs look to motion as a constant pull—an unyielding force that compels the singer onward—similar to the perpetual wanderings of the heroic hobbits of Tolkien's legendarium.

While the lyrics relate to Tolkien's world through references to motions and rambles, they primarily operate in a contemporary, rather than fantasy, mode. Sonically, however, "Ramble On" works similarly to "The Battle of Evermore," relying mainly on semiotic associations with the acoustic mode and folk aesthetics to imply a timeless, mystical, pastoral world. The folk quality of the music implies timelessness because folk music is often viewed to have an indefinite past—a past that derives from a "general consensus that the song" (or in this case, the traditional as a whole) "was known in an earlier generation... and that it is probably much older than that."[47] The song begins with an acoustic guitar—a far cry from much of the heavy, electric blues rock of their previous work. Drummer Jon Bonham taps out a steady sixteenth-note "pitter-patter" that biographers Chris Welsh and Geoff Nicholls claim was played by Bonham tapping his fingers on the outside of an empty guitar case. Both the acoustic guitar and the tapping effect (regardless of how it was created) nod to the aesthetics of folk rock in the form of acoustic instrumentation and nonvirtuosic musicianship. To me, Bonham's sixteenth notes evoke the fast-paced rhythms of Celtic bodhrán—a frame drum played with both ends of a stubby stick. Even when the electric bass and vocals are added to the mix, they are soft and sweet. Robert Plant's vocal line alternates throughout the song between a breathy, limited-range melody and his iconic higher-pitched wails.

In many ways, the song seems to operate in the past. The folk and acoustic aesthetics evoke a timeless quality, while the lyrics look to past traditions of open-air walks or rambles in the English countryside. While the song's narrative may rest in a contemporary world, the nostalgic impulse of the song resides in a romanticized view of the past as an era more in communion with nature and the essential needs of humanity.

Conclusion

Grounding their romanticized vision of the past in the works of J. R. R. Tolkien, Led Zeppelin offers an avenue for understanding how medievalism acts as a nostalgic practice, recreating and reflecting on a fictional past as a monument of shared, contemporary values. The imaginative space was not only physical, but also rooted in temporal understandings of a slower-paced existence and timeless (albeit undefinable) values of authenticity and freedom. The unreality of this vision is irrelevant to the sense of continuity and cohesion provided by nostalgic, medieval-inspired expression. As Boym explains, the cultural myths of collective memory and nostalgia "are not lies but rather shared assumptions that help to naturalize history and make it livable, providing the daily glue of common intelligibility."[48] Creative works that employ nostalgic and heritage-based visions of the past thus reveal key insights into their own historical moments and into the needs, desires, thoughts, and emotions of people who have created them. "History," as Lowenthal writes, "is not just what happened at the time but the thoughts and feelings, hunches and hypotheses about that time generated by later hindsight."[49] Further, in examining what these creative practices meant in historical moments, we are forced to consider how our own contemporary understandings of ourselves are shaped by our presentist uses of these works.

Viewing the past as a green, pastoral space, Tolkien medievalism in Zeppelin articulates an ecoconservative urge against the destructive progress of modernity. Zeppelin's appropriation of Tolkien's characters and imagery aligns, historically, with a rise in conservationist attitudes and interest in medieval-inspired fantasies at the time. Meredith Veldman highlights the connection between conservationism and fantasy in her monograph *Fantasy, the Bomb and the Greening of Britain: Romantic Protest 1945–1980*, where she explains that the 1960s and 1970s in England brought an increased presence of "Greens or eco-activists" whose "vision of a better Britain blended elements of the fantasy world of Lewis and Tolkien—its medievalism, fear of science and technology, conservatism and religiosity."[50] For Led Zeppelin, Middle-earth offers a fantasy play space in which they can musically slip into an alternative reality.

Just as Led Zeppelin and Tolkien find values of freedom and authenticity in past spaces, they also articulate values of the past that are connected to understandings of time and progress. This form of nostalgia is founded on the idea that the past operated at a different pace, one that is more centered in its present than concerns of the future. Boym explains:

> Nostalgia appears to be a longing for a place, but it is actually a yearning for a different time—the time of our childhood, the slower rhythms of our dreams. In a broader sense, nostalgia is a rebellion against the modern idea of time, the time of history and progress. The nostalgic desires to turn history into private or collective mythology, to revisit time like space, refusing to surrender to the irreversibility of time that plagues the human condition.[51]

The nostalgic attitude toward time in these songs draws on an idealized vision of the perceived lifestyles and pace of a fictional past. Looking to notions of travel and quests, life in the Shire, and even a romanticized vision of past (and fictional) wartime, all three songs turn to Tolkien's works to ground their fantasy time travel. In doing so, the songs express antimodern, slower-paced values that they attribute to the past and long for in the present.

The three songs discussed in this chapter evoke the past through disparate sonic and lyrical tools, but offer shared critiques of their present space and gather shared values from the past to envision a better world. In viewing the medievalism in these works as nostalgic practice, we can see how the songs create cohesion in times perceived to be fragmentary and uncertain and how they find in the past and offer to the present shared values for their contemporary world. As creative works invoke the past for contemporary purposes, they often move from the attempted objectivity of history and into a realm of fantasy, myth, and play.[52] Creative uses of the past rely more heavily, then, on ideas of nostalgia and heritage. Both employ past visions and understandings for present-day concerns, for shaping understandings of self and other, and for infusing contemporary values and meaning with a larger sense of purpose. Lowenthal contends that, "to vilify heritage as biased is thus futile: bias is the main point of heritage.... Heritage thereby attests our identity and affirms our worth."[53] Tolkien's own use of the past in his fantasy works was a way of rejecting the contemporary world in which he lived. Reflecting on the relevance of Tolkien's writings for readers during mid-century, Veldman writes that "what fantasy offered twentieth-century readers was not only relief from the sheer ugliness of so much of modern life but also a means of combating the ugliness."[54] Led Zeppelin's appropriation of Tolkien's fictional, medieval world participates in this act of cultural memory building and heritage preservation to make sense of the contemporary time in which they lived.

NOTES

1. Robley Evans, *J. R. R. Tolkien* (New York: Warner, 1972), 15.
2. Ibid., 15.
3. Thomas A. Shippey, *The Road to Middle Earth: How J. R. R. Tolkien Created a New Mythology*, 3rd ed. (Boston: Houghton Mifflin, 2003), 1. The first edition was published in 1982.
4. Thomas A. Shippey, *J. R. R. Tolkien: Author of the Century*, (Boston: Houghton Mifflin, 2001), 306.
5. Ibid.
6. For further discussion on nostalgia, alterity, and medievalism, see the contributions of Elizabeth Randell Upton, Ross Hagen, and Scott Troyer, this volume, pp. 509–529, 547–563, and 586–608, respectively. Susan Fast equates medievalism in rock, especially progressive rock, as an evocation of the Other. In her reading of this music, the sense of longing is not for a homeland or a past, so much as it is for the Other "as a source of power alternative to that possessed by the dominant culture." See Susan Fast, "Days of Future Past: Rock, Pop, and the Yearning for the Middle Ages," in *Mittelaltersehnsuch*, ed. Dorothea Redepenning and Annette Kreutiger-Herr (Kiel: Wissenschaftsverlag Vauk, 2000), 35.
7. Annette Kreutziger-Herr, "Postmodern Middle Ages: Medieval Music at the Dawn of the Twenty-First Century," *Florilegium* 15 (1998): 188.

8. David Lowenthal, *The Heritage Crusade and the Spoils of History* (Cambridge: Cambridge University Press, 1998), xv.

9. Svetlana Boym, *The Future of Nostalgia* (New York: Basic Books, 2001), 41.

10. Boym, *The Future of Nostalgia*, 3–18.

11. Boym, *The Future of Nostalgia*, xvii–xviii.

12. Susan Fast, *In the Houses of the Holy: Led Zeppelin and the Power of Rock Music* (Oxford: Oxford University Press, 2001), 53.

13. Meredith Veldman, *Fantasy, the Bomb, and the Greening of Britain: Romantic Protest, 1945–1980* (Cambridge: Cambridge University Press, 1994), 208. For nineteenth-century roots of British medievalism, see Clare A. Simmons, *Popular Medievalism in Romantic-Era Britain* (New York: Palgrave Macmillan, 2011).

14. Lowenthal, *The Heritage Crusade and the Spoils of History*, 7.

15. Raymond Williams, *The Country and the City* (New York: Oxford University Press, 1975), 35.

16. For connections to medievalism, nature and ecology, and Paganism, see Scott Troyer, "Medievalism and Identity Construction in Pagan Folk Music," this volume, pp. 586–608.

17. Shippey quotes Tolkien's letter to a publisher: "The invention of languages is the foundation. The 'stories' were made rather to provide a world for the languages than the reverse. To me a name comes first and the story follows." Shippey, *Author of the Century*, xiii.

18. Boym defines the cultural myths of collective memory as "the common landmarks of everyday life" that "constitute shared social frameworks of individual recollections." Cultural memory relies on symbolic, rather than narrative, meaning. See Boym, *The Future of Nostalgia*, 53.

19. Ann M. Martinez, "Elvencentrism: The Green Medievalism of Tolkien's Elven Realms," *Studies in Medievalism* XXVI (2017): 32.

20. Taking video game designer Brian Upton's definition of play as "free movement within a system of constraints," we can examine creative nostalgic expressions (including medievalisms) as play. Upton's definition comes from a consideration of the work of Johan Huizinga's *Homo Ludens* (1938), in which Huizinga coins the term *magic circle* as a liminal space in which play occurs. Upton and others have since provided nuance to the definition of play, which considers the many different forms it takes in a twentieth/twenty-first-century world. See Brian Upton, *The Aesthetic of Play* (Cambridge: MIT Press, 2015).

21. Barney Hoskyns, *Led Zeppelin IV* (New York: Rodale, 2006), 97.

22. J. R. R. Tolkien, *The Return of the King* (New York: Ballantine Books, 1965), 243.

23. Ibid., 367.

24. Salman Rushdie, *The Wizard of Oz* (New York: Vintage International, 1996), 57.

25. For an example of fan interpretations, see "Led Zeppelin and Lord of the Rings—Rockers and Tolkien Fans," The One Ring, accessed February 22, 2018, http://www.theonering.com/reading-room/critical-viewpoints/led-zeppelin-and-lord-of-the-rings-rockers-and-tolkien-fans.

26. Norman F. Cantor, *Inventing the Middle Ages* (New York: Harper Perennial, 1991), 228.

27. Veldman, *Fantasy, the Bomb, and the Greening of Britain*, 46; Tolkien, himself, expresses a similar idea to Coleridge's "Secondary Worlds" when he writes about the concept of "Subcreation." See J. R. R. Tolkien, "On Fairy Stories," in *The Monsters and the Critics and Other Essays*, ed. Christopher Tolkien (London: Allen & Unwin, 1983), 109–61.

28. Middle-earth, even if it is an imaginary world, operates as an imaginary history—one that is applicable to the present. In the preface to the second edition of *The Lord of the Rings*, Tolkien himself would explain: "I much prefer history, true or feigned, with its varied applicability to the thought and experience of readers. I think that many confuse

'applicability' with 'allegory'; but the one resides in the freedom of the reader, and the other in the purposed domination of the author," J. R. R. Tolkien, *The Fellowship of the Ring* (New York: Ballantine Books, 1965), xi.

29. Edward Macan, *Rocking the Classics: English Progressive Rock and the Counterculture* (Oxford: Oxford University Press, 1997), 150.

30. Ibid., 135.

31. I wish to thank Elizabeth Randell Upton for her insight regarding the East in medieval thinking and its connection to the location of the Misty Mountains in Middle-earth.

32. Sociologist Barbara Stern distinguishes between two types of nostalgia—personal (a past experienced by the individual) and historical (a past never experienced by the individual)—in her work with advertising texts. Although it may sometimes be useful to analyze these nostalgias as distinct phenomena, they are rarely truly separate. In this case, the nostalgia for a historical fantasy that was never experienced by the individual is still connected to the personal, through childhood play. Barbara B. Stern, "Historical and Personal Nostalgia in Advertising Text: The Fin de Siècle Effect," *Journal of Advertising* 21, no. 4 (1992): 11–22.

33. William E. Ratliff and Charles G. Flinn, "The Hobbit and the Hippie," *Modern Age* 12 (Spring 1968), 142–146.

34. Matthew T. Dickerson and Jonathan D. Evans, *Ents, Elves and Eriador: The Environmental Vision of J. R. R. Tolkien* (Lexington: University Press of Kentucky, 2006), 92.

35. Led Zeppelin, "Misty Mountain Hop," recorded 1971, track 5 on Untitled (known as *Zoso*, Four Symbols, or the fourth album), Atlantic, 1971.

36. Ibid.

37. Dickerson and Evans, *Ents, Elves, and Eriador*, 92.

38. Led Zeppelin, "Misty Mountain Hop."

39. Ratliff and Flinn contend that many hippies looked to the novels as a "psychedelic manual," in which "passages from *The Lord of the Rings* are read before or during an LSD 'trip,' for instance, may greatly stimulate the individual's mind and make his 'trip' seem much more meaningful." Ratliff and Flinn, "Hobbit and the Hippie," 144.

40. J. R. R. Tolkien, *Fellowship of the Ring*, 8.

41. Frank Trentmann, "Civilization and Its Discontents: English Neo-Romanticism and the Transformation of Anti-Modernism in Twentieth-Century Western Culture," *Journal of Contemporary History* 29, no. 4 (October 1, 1994): 584.

42. Ibid., 588.

43. Ibid.

44. A trope of unending motion can be found across art forms. For instance, Alison Murray connects the ideas of "circular narrative motion" and "unspecified time frame" to a sense of timelessness that one finds in nostalgic films. See Alison Murray, "Women, Nostalgia, Memory: Chocolat, Outremer, and Indochine," *Research in African Literatures* 33, no. 2 (2002), 240.

45. The song appears in several forms in *The Lord of the Rings*, including in Chapter 1 of *The Fellowship of the Ring*. Led Zeppelin, "Ramble On," recorded 1969, *Led Zeppelin II*, track 7, Atlantic, 1969.

46. Led Zeppelin, "Out on the Tiles," recorded 1970, *Led Zeppelin III*, Atlantic, 1970.

47. Philip V. Bohlman, *The Study of Folk Music in the Modern World* (Bloomington: Indiana University Press, 1988), 130.

48. Boym, *The Future of Nostalgia*, 5.

49. Lowenthal, *The Heritage Crusade*, 115.

50. Meredith Veldman, *Fantasy, the Bomb, and the Greening of Britain: Romantic Protest, 1945–1980* (Cambridge: Cambridge University Press, 1994), 207.

51. Svetlana Boym, "Nostalgia and Its Discontents," *Hedgehog Review* 9, no. 2 (2007): 7–18.

52. For Lowenthal's discussion of history's "noble aim" of objectivity, see Lowenthal, *The Heritage Crusade and the Spoils of History*, 106.

53. Ibid., 122.

54. Veldman, *Fantasy, the Bomb, and the Greening of Britain*, 48.

CHAPTER 24

A GOTHIC ROMANCE

Neomedieval Echoes of Fin'amor *in Gothic and Doom Metal*

ROSS HAGEN

SINCE its inception, heavy metal music culture has had a lasting fascination with the medieval, albeit one often filtered through other medievalist media products like Tolkienesque "sword and sorcery" fantasy and the dark romanticism of Gothic horror movies. In the genre's formative years in the late 1960s and early 1970s, episodes or characters from *The Lord of the Rings* and *The Hobbit* were the subject of songs by Black Sabbath ("The Wizard") and Led Zeppelin ("The Battle of Evermore"), evincing listeners' and musicians' interest in medievalist fantasies continuing into the twenty-first century.[1] Beyond fantasy, metal bands of many different stripes have approached the idea of the medieval and the Middle Ages from a variety of angles, providing a productive illustration of the multivalent notions and interpretations of the Middle Ages, as the modern use of the medieval takes on a diverse and paradoxical array of forms. Tales of kings, knights, and battles, both historical and imagined, have proliferated globally across metal's soundscape for decades, and it would likely be impossible to provide a full accounting of heavy metal album covers that feature castles, dragons, warriors, or wizards. Some metal musicians even regularly don medieval armor and weaponry for photoshoots and performances, a practice also taken up by fans. Death metal and black metal bands often envision the Middle Ages as a period of brutality, omnipresent death, and religious violence, taking particular interest in medieval plagues and inquisitorial tortures. Vikings are likewise a popular subject, variously positioned as hypermasculine warriors in the mold of Conan the Barbarian, noble defenders of traditional Norse religious practices, or as subjects for creative coplay.[2] Folk metal bands frequently augment their standard electric guitars and drums with bagpipes, citterns, and shawms and, in some instances, adapt medieval texts and melodies to heavy metal contexts. Nationalist and white supremacist metal bands and their fellow travelers often go further, envisioning the Middle Ages as a time of monocultural ethnic and religious purity, using medievalism to authenticate their own identity politics.

A common thread across these diverse examples is the use of medievalism as a refuge from or alternative to modernity. This imagined dichotomy between modernity and "traditional" medieval society is a powerful organizing force, often creating an ideal of medieval society as conservative, rural, religious, and static, in opposition to modernity's secularism, cultural dynamism, and urban cosmopolitanism.[3] However, this binary conception becomes somewhat complicated and conflicted when applied specifically to performative and aesthetic recreations of the Middle Ages. As I have noted, metal bands can conceive of the Middle Ages as ordered, comfortably hierarchical, and enchantingly spiritual while simultaneously celebrating its supposed wildness, violent barbarism, and irrational superstitiousness. As Helen Dell argues, in this case the premodern represents what modern citizens must reject to be modern, which results in a perception of the past that is deeply nostalgic but also highly fluid.[4] For metal musicians and metalheads, the choice becomes less "now" versus "then," as it is "here" vs "somewhere else." Susan Fast notes that the medievalist aspects of this music become an evocation of Otherness, inviting alternative cultural expressions that offer a sense of integrity and substance in a fictional world beyond mundane lived experience.[5]

This chapter explores a particular manifestation of heavy metal medievalism through the echoes of *fin'amor* and courtly love poetry in the music of doom metal and Gothic metal bands like My Dying Bride and Cradle of Filth. As with other uses of the Middle Ages by metal musicians, those of Gothic and doom metal are usually filtered through the previous medievalisms of Gothic literature and horror films, weaving a complex web of significations in the process. *Fin'amor* poetry and literature, developed primarily by French troubadours in the eleventh to thirteenth centuries, typically involves the objectification of a married aristocratic or royal lady as a quasi-deified figure before which the male troubadour performs a kind of worshipful self-debasement. She ignores or rejects his affection and he suffers the pangs of melancholic lovesickness as a result. Eventually, the poet's love leads him to perform acts of valor in the name of the lady, which may ultimately win her affections and lead the couple to embark on a secret affair. However, rather than simply duplicate the medieval *fin'amor* aesthetic, these metal bands often playfully subvert the *fin'amor* dynamic through black humor, explicit eroticism, and scenarios in which the deified woman is characterized as malevolent or evil. Her malice may manifest itself simply through her scorn and indifference to the lyricist's lovesick sufferings, but in some cases she is also endowed with supernatural or vampiric powers of enchantment that render the male lyricist helpless to resist her charms.

The *fin'amor* dynamic is also considered from the opposite side, through female-fronted Gothic metal bands like Within Temptation, Nightwish, and Theatre of Tragedy. Bands of this nature often present the female singer as an ethereal and spiritually powerful force, effectively embodying the deified aristocratic lady of the *fin'amor* tradition. These singers typically employ a powerful operatic vocal style and are often juxtaposed with male death metal singers in a twin lead vocal pairing referred to as *beauty and the beast*, a term that not only describes the vocal tones but also hints at the gendered roles these singers enact. In instances without a male "beast" vocalist, the female lead singer still cuts a transcendent sonic profile against the metal instrumentation behind her voice.

Gothic and Doom Styles, *Fin'amor,* and Neomedievalism

The bands and musicians referenced here can all be situated within a constellation of Gothic-inflected extreme metal subgenres understood variously as *doom metal, death-doom metal,* or simply *Gothic metal.* As with all musical genres, the boundaries between these classifications are nebulous, and the hyphenation of death-doom especially makes such liminality explicit.[6] What these genres share is a tendency to avoid the fast tempos and displays of ensemble and individual virtuosity that other extreme metal genres like death metal, black metal, and grindcore have cultivated. In doom metal particularly, the tempos may be incredibly slow, with almost minimalistic drumming and guitar parts emphasizing long and drawn-out melodies and sustained power chords. The guitars are typically down-tuned, as in many other extreme metal genres. The death-doom variant indulges in sections with faster tempos and more active drumming, utilizing double-kick drum parts and rhythmic palm-muting techniques in the guitar. Doom metal singers often perform with the deep growl that is characteristic of death metal, but sung vocals by both male and female singers are also regularly included in lead vocal parts, background vocals, and beauty and the beast pairs. Piano and orchestral or choral keyboard parts reminiscent of film scores or Wagnerian opera are also prevalent in the music of many Gothic and doom metal bands, and more commercially successful acts occasionally record and perform with orchestras and choirs. Gothic metal tends to function as an umbrella term implying a musical and visual aesthetic indebted to the Goth music scenes of the 1980s, including neo-Victorian costumes, but with metal musical idioms like distorted guitars playing power chords.[7] In the interest of clarity, I am going to use the term Gothic metal in its broadest sense and reserve doom metal specifically for the slower and more languid death metal style. The Gothic and doom metal genres found their initial expression in the early 1990s, largely in a coterie of bands from Northern England, most notably My Dying Bride and Paradise Lost from West Yorkshire and Anathema from Liverpool. These bands were all on the early roster of the record label Peaceville, which was centered in West Yorkshire. As of 2019 all three of these bands remain active, although Paradise Lost and Anathema in particular have moved away from doom metal in favor of music that more closely resembles modern alternative rock or electronica. My Dying Bride, in contrast, has continued to cultivate a dramatic and magniloquent doom metal style, often including a violinist and melodramatic spoken word passages. The Suffolk band Cradle of Filth also became prominent in the late 1990s by combining a Gothic and vampiric visual and lyrical aesthetic with the musical idioms of black metal, including fast tempos and relentless double-picked guitar parts and drum "blast-beats."

The lyrics of Gothic and doom metal bands lean toward depictions of grief, death, depression, religion, and (often unrequited) romantic love, with frequent references to nature, mythology, and biblical imagery. As a result, the metaphors and tropes of lovesick melancholia permeate the music of these bands, even if explicitly medieval themes are not in play. It is also common for these bands to use pronouns from early modern English (thee, thou, thy/thine) as a way to imbue their lyrics with a sense of aristocratic archaism. For doom metal fans, this melancholic emotionality is one of the style's most privileged aspects, providing both a sense of personal attachment and individual catharsis while helping to foster a sense of community.[8] Fans also argue that the impassioned quality of doom metal distinguishes it from other genres of extreme metal, all of which tend to avoid depictions of emotional vulnerability in favor of expressions of power.

Even though the conceptions of romantic love found in Gothic and doom metal echo the medieval courtly love tradition, the genres often rely more directly on nineteenth-century romantic models for much of their lyricism. Indeed, the term *courtly love* itself is a romantic-era conceit, because it does not appear in medieval sources and was first coined as *amour courtois* by the French medievalist Gaston Paris in 1883. Its original use was as a description of the ardor uniting Lancelot and Guinevere in the twelfth-century romance *Lancelot or the Knight of the Cart* by Chrétien de Troyes.[9] For Paris, courtly love was defined principally as a secret extramarital affair that places the male lover at the mercy of a fickle and at times indifferent lady, inspiring feats of courage and also a code of behavior analogous to other chivalric codes. Yet defining courtly love is a thorny endeavor, particularly because the use of the term proliferated following Paris's article and became subject to numerous slippages, and it is not entirely clear whether the literary tropes ever extended into real life.[10] The corpus of literary sources for courtly love spans two centuries and multiple cultures and languages and potentially includes related traditions of love poetry from Germany and the Iberian Peninsula. Naturally, this wide repertoire holds significant variety, ranging from the often erotically charged Occitan tradition of the twelfth century to the later trouvère tradition of northern France, which ultimately spiritualized the female subject and adopted the vocabulary of *fin'amor* for devotional songs to the Virgin Mary.[11] This trajectory continued in Dante's writings, as his depiction of Beatrice in *The Divine Comedy* is so idealized and transcendent that she almost loses her humanity (and femininity) because of her proximity to the divine.[12] The interpretations of courtly love and its meanings can vary immensely depending on which of these texts are examined, and the perspective can shift even further if the courtly canon is widened to include works by women or other female-centric texts.[13] Sarah Kay has argued that courtly love is perhaps better understood less as a sort of codified system of rules and more as a purely literary expression of the social tensions inherent in royal and aristocratic court life.[14]

Despite (or maybe because of) its protean nature, *fin'amor* and its variants have become a lasting source of artistic and literary inspiration. Indeed, the medieval courtly love tradition has ultimately informed many prevailing Western cultural traditions and attitudes around romance, seduction, and normative gender roles.[15] With this in mind, it is not particularly surprising to find *fin'amor* echoed in emotive musical styles like Gothic metal simply because of the pervasiveness of its influence. Even then, this influence has been filtered and reflected from Paris's initial formulation through later works like C. S. Lewis's 1936 *Allegory of Love: A Study in Medieval Tradition* and numerous works of medievalistic fiction.

Given the clear influence of romanticism and nineteenth-century Gothic fiction on Gothic metal lyricists, the medievalisms of Gothic and doom metal are better described as neomedievalisms, in that they build on the medievalisms of the past rather than directly engaging with medieval source material. Indeed, there are few, if any, examples of these Gothic or doom metal bands utilizing medieval sources, although related musical genres like the German *Mittelalter* metal scene do adapt medieval melodies and texts to metal and rock music idioms. For these English bands, however, the lords and ladies of their musical and lyrical worlds are generally echoes of the medievalistic imaginations of the nineteenth century. The boundaries between medievalism and neomedievalism have been a source of significant debate over the past decade, inspiring several volumes of the *Studies in Medievalism* series in 2009–2011. For the purposes of this chapter, the main evidence driving my decision to consider Gothic and doom metal neomedievalistic is the bands' engagement with eighteenth- and nineteenth-century medievalism and the anachronistic and dehistoricized mixture of these earlier medievalisms within twentieth-century metal styles designed for mass consumption.[16] Past medievalisms fuse with the present, rejecting the distances of history and cultural difference, although Amy Kaufman argues that such denials of history may ultimately be expressing a latent desire for history instead.[17] Even though it is tempting (and arguably more accurate in some cases) to consider the refashioning of nineteenth-century medievalism as specifically *neoromantic*, in this case that impulse can be situated within the larger context of neomedievalism. In Gothic metal, the romantic nostalgia for the Middle Ages is rearticulated in an almost "hauntological" fashion, consolidating disparate centuries of history into a single pastoral, mythological, and antique alterity. It could be argued further that Gothic metal and related genres are not merely nineteenth-century musical practices influenced by romanticism, but are instead a connected part of an expressive continuum spanning multiple centuries.[18] Yet the pastiches of Gothic and doom metal and many other neomedievalisms (possibly including conceptions of *fin'amor* itself) remain fully immersed in the pluralistic and polyglot aesthetic of postmodern art, which, as evocatively put by James Currie, evades stasis, permanence, and hierarchy through fragmentary reflections and re-reflections. As he states, "images caught in mirrors are images that can never be caught."[19] In any case, this emptying of specific historical meaning allows the Middle Ages to become a reflection of the *modern* self, a simulacrum of the medieval that, like Baudrillard's Disneyland, seems all the more real in the absence of an original.[20]

Gothic literature and its various musical expressions have likewise been especially invested in similar destabilizations of time. Transgressions between the borders of life and death, fantasy and reality, and the past and the present are linchpins of these artistic and literary practices.[21] The specters and ghosts of Gothic literature, music, and film bring the past into the present, with their haunting working to effectively undermine the continuity of linear temporality and the integrity of the present, as famously noted by Jacques Derrida.[22] But even as Gothic music, literature, and film collapse the past (and future) into the present, their intent is not nostalgic but a purposeful rewriting of the past that engenders this collision and perpetuates a sense of liminality. Ultimately, the pastiches and anachronisms of Gothic media and similar neomedievalisms are not undertaken with deconstruction as the goal, but rather the creative reconstruction of a new Middle Ages out of these fragments.[23] As with myriad other medievalisms, the uncanny specters of Gothic media offer a cultural critique, unveiling the repressed anxieties and desires beneath seemingly well-ordered selves and societies.[24] In Gothic and doom metal, *fin'amor*'s interrogations of feudal norms around love and marriage echo within the nineteenth-century romanticists' supernatural breaches of Enlightenment rationality to ultimately inform twentieth-century musical genres that often revel in unfettered emotionality. This sense of emotional authenticity can then provide a respite from both the assumed inauthenticities of modern life and the supposed conformity of other metal music scenes.[25]

Medievalistic Melancholia and Lovesickness

Gothic metal's focus on topics of grief and depression results in a pervasive melancholia running throughout its lyrics and music, interfacing with medieval conceptions of pathological lovesickness resulting from the indifference or rejection of the poet's chosen lady. This emotional and physical distress is a key element of *fin'amor* that echoes into Gothic metal. In particular, lovesickness was associated with desires and passions that remained unfulfilled, resulting in symptoms such as sleeplessness, sighing, and loss of appetite, all of which were considered manifestations of the mind's efforts to restrain its passions.[26] Perhaps its most famous literary manifestation is in the "loveris maladye" suffered by Chaucer's knight Arcite in *The Knight's Tale*, but this concept of melancholy lovesickness as a physical ailment echoed through early modern literature. Indeed, melancholy has been a lasting spring of inspiration for writers, artists, and musicians and arguably forms one of the pillars of early concepts of subjectivity and interiority.[27] Even as the lyrics may express feelings of devotion, there is often a palpable undercurrent of resentment that the poet's love is not returned and his sufferings are not acknowledged. Melancholy has also typically been gendered as a male affliction, in part because of the well-documented privilege given to male artists and writers across the centuries. Indeed, being afflicted with melancholy became arguably a sign of a man's creative genius, both proof of his inspiration and a fortunate curse that granted him measures of cultural and literary legitimacy.[28] The romantic poets' engagement with their own imaginations can be considered a reclamation of the melancholy of medieval and early modern love poetry.[29] For the romantics, this was at least in part a reactionary stance in response to the focus on reason within the Enlightenment and the dawn of the Industrial Revolution. Just as the romantics sought refuge in the sense of greater integrity and emotional depth offered by nostalgic melancholy, so too does Gothic metal fire the imaginations of modern listeners with emotional medievalistic fantasy, gloomy atmosphere, and magic.

The melancholic nature of Gothic metal is often filtered through archetypes of the moody romantic hero as found in eighteenth- and nineteenth-century literary works like Goethe's *Sorrows of Young Werther* (1774), Emily Brontë's *Wuthering Heights*, and many works by Lord Byron. Indeed, Byron is so closely associated with this type of character that it is often referred to as a *Byronic hero*. The Byronic hero is often socially isolated and scornful of his fellow men, yet is capable of deep affection even as he holds his loneliness and misery close to his heart. The use of these literary tropes by English metal bands also has a nationalistic function in that it connects their music to specifically English literary traditions and authors. Further, several Gothic metal bands, most notably Cradle of Filth, regularly employ poetic meters in a manner reminiscent of these English poets, although metal music's predilection for dramatic shifts in meter and tempo generally preclude sustaining a single poetic meter for the duration of a song.

The opening and ending songs from My Dying Bride's 1993 album *Turn Loose the Swans*, "Sear Me MCMXCIII" and "Black God," are provocative examples of the melodramatic side of doom metal and its connection to English romantic poetry.[30] Neither song features the full band, instead relying on piano, synthesizer, and violin for musical backing, and singer Aaron Stainthorpe mostly recites the songs' lyrics rather than singing or growling as he does on the rest of the album. Although extended introductory and closing tracks are fairly common in heavy metal recordings, these function as bookends to the album because of their similarities and their marked difference from the rest of the music on the album. "Black God" also features a female singer, Zena Choi, who sings the text along with Stainthorpe's recitation, although her performance is synchronized more with the violin and synthesizer than with his vocals. The lyrics of "Black God" consist of two stanzas in English ballad meter, although the recitation in the recording is so languid that this aspect only becomes apparent when the lyrics are presented as text.

The lyrics of "Black God" are in fact the final stanza of an untitled poem by William Hamilton of Bangour, published in Allan Ramsey's 1724 collection *The Tea-Table Miscellany*, in which it was set to the melody of the Scottish air "Sour Plums of Galashiels."

> Ah the shepherd's mournful fate
>   When doom'd to live and doom'd to languish
> To bear the scornful fair one's hate
>   Nor dare disclose his anguish
> Yet eager looks and dying sighs
>   My secret soul discover
> While rapture trembling thro mine eyes
>   Reveals how much I love her
>
> The tender glance the redd'ning cheek
>   O'erspread with rising blushes
> A thousand various ways they speak

A thousand various wishes
For oh that form so heavenly fair
   Those languid eyes so sweetly smiling
That artless blush and modest air
   So fatally beguiling

Thy every look and every grace
   So charm where'er I view thee
Till death o'ertake me in the chase
   Still will my hopes pursue thee
Then when my tedious hours are past
   Be this last blessing given
Low at thy feet to breathe my last
   And die in sight of heaven.[31]

Even if the last stanza is excerpted from the earlier ones, it provides an illustration of the echoes of *fin'amor* in the traditions of romantic English poetry and those of twentieth-century Gothic metal. The amorous object of the poem possesses unparalleled beauty and refinement that haunts the narrator up to his death, although it is unclear whether this obsession actually hastens the narrator's demise. The poet's passing "in sight of heaven" at the feet of the beloved serves as a suitably "courtly" depiction of the lady as a transcendent and spiritualized figure, but also harbors an erotic subtext. When this stanza is considered in context with its preceding verses, the connections with the courtly love tradition deepen through its pastoral setting and its depiction of the female object as "scornful" and oblivious to the poet's secret anguish and torment. Although My Dying Bride's decision to perform this text with both male and female voices could be considered a device allowing the beloved of the poem to be voiced within the song, it ultimately seems that the female voice is used to underline and emphasize the emotions of the male subject.

Along with the literal recycling of romantic poetry and lyrical conceits, My Dying Bride's music occasionally indulges in musical tropes associated with medievalism, although they avoid the sprightly dance tunes and medieval instrumentation found in folk metal or *Mittelalter* metal. The lachrymose violin parts in My Dying Bride's music tend to mimic the legato phrasings of nineteenth-century art music as opposed to folk-style fiddling, which lends the music a certain aristocratic aura. For a more specific example of musical neomedievalism, the song "The Crown of Sympathy" (also from *Turn Loose the Swans*) contains a lengthy section in which Stainthorpe's vocals are accompanied only by minimal drums, synthesized strings and bells, and briefly by synthesized horn fanfares under the line "no sad adieus on a balcony." This line in particular conjures a host of medieval images, from *Romeo and Juliet* to the Occitan *alba* and related genres of medieval love poetry that expressed the longings of lovers who must part at dawn. These associations are underlined by the horn fanfare's evocation of chivalrous militarism.

Supplication, Domination, and Monstrous Women

Hamilton's poem of pastoral longing brings more to bear to My Dying Bride's music than just the appropriate measure of unrequited melancholic desire. The final verse of the poem especially adopts a worshipful tone toward its love object, endowing the poet's death with the aura of religious martyrdom. Similar conceits are found throughout the repertoires of medieval courtly love poetry, and love often functions as a simulacrum of religion in these repertoires.[32] Religious language is frequently deployed by troubadours and trouvères, and the ladies to which they are addressed have the ability to grant "mercy," which in this context comes laden with both religious and potentially erotic meanings.[33] Indeed, the division between the secular and sacred taken for granted in modern society may not have existed in the medieval period, so there was likely no sense of impropriety in such language.[34] The language of courtly love was ultimately also adopted for devotional texts, and courts in Europe cultivated the use of divine appellations for royalty as a form of reverent homage well into the early modern period.

Within this courtly love context, the absolute submission of the lover to his lady is interpreted as laudable, an act that brings honor to him. Further, the lady is impossible to possess, and she remains a distant destination that is forever unreachable for the lover poet.[35] In this conception the lady essentially becomes a divine object or idol rather than a fully realized person. As Marc de Kesel notes in his examination of Lacan's *Seminar VII*, the lady is rendered as an empty vessel; her substance is emptied out for her to provide sense to the words, gestures, and feelings of the poet. In his words, "the elevated 'object' in whose light everything else acquires sense is itself empty and senseless."[36] For all of its purported focus on the lady, this poetry is also often profoundly narcissistic, sometimes giving the impression that the true object of the poets' desire is desire itself. However, this conceit existed within a feudal culture that viewed even aristocratic and royal women as objects for matrimonial exchange within an entrenched and powerful system of patriarchal dominance. The notion of the lady as an object that dominates men offered a new position apart from the marriage economy, ultimately leading to significant changes in the conventions of romance and marriage.[37]

Yet, there is an inherent contradiction within a system of masculine dominance that also cultivates conventions of service and idealization toward women, even if the figure of the lady remains firmly objectified. There is an evident strain between two standards for upper-class masculinity, with men acting on the one hand as the dominant holders of cultural power and on the other as subservient fawns. This tension was also underscored by an increase in antifeminist treatises and invectives against secular love poetry over the course of the thirteenth century.[38] Mary Frances Wack argues further that the idea of lovesickness itself was a way to deal with the destabilizing potentials of *fin'amor* by displacing it and pathologizing it as a disease.[39]

These tensions underline the tendency toward misogyny in some medieval love poetry, particularly the genres of the *maldit* and *comiat*, both of which portray the idealized lady as cruel and spiteful because of her coldness toward the poet. Although the *maldit* especially is often a bluntly defamatory attack on its subject's character, such sentiments pervaded other genres as well, even if the invective is less acrimonious. Perhaps the most famous example of this is Bernart de Ventadorn's oft-anthologized mid-twelfth-century canso 'Can vei la lauzeta mover,' in which the poet renounces love and women, declaring himself destroyed by his lady's neglect. The fourteenth-century French composer and poet Guillaume de Machaut goes further in several of his ballades, in which he makes use of a number of animalistic metaphors to describe the wounds inflicted by his beloved's disdain, noting that she harbors inner rottenness and monstrosity despite her beauty and charm.[40]

This theme of self-debasement and its responding echo of misogynistic vitriol has been a well of inspiration for metal musicians and lyricists, inspiring both musical fantasies of sexual domination and the "torch song" power balladry of 1980s glam metal bands. For Gothic and doom metal bands, self-debasement before a powerful and near-deified female lover is a regular theme, as seen in the earlier example from My Dying Bride. In some cases, however, the lady also harbors sadistic inner cruelties and corruptions, often of a monstrous, demonic, or vampiric nature. For example, in Cradle of Filth's "A Gothic Romance (Red Roses for the Devil's Whore)" from their 1996 album *Dusk and Her Embrace*, the (presumably) male protagonist recounts being enchanted by a woman described as a "jewel more radiant than the moon."[41] She ultimately turns out to be a vampire, although knowledge of this fact does little to diminish his obsession with her. Cradle of Filth's entire oeuvre is populated with alluring yet demonic women, including mythological figures like Lilith, Lamia, and Hecate, along with a persistent fascination with the legendary aristocratic Hungarian murderess Elizabeth Báthory (1560–1614). These characters are also often voiced within the songs by female singers and actors, providing clearly enunciated and sung lines in contrast to the growls and screams of the band's main singer, Dani Filth. There is an uncanniness in the fact that the voices of demonic female characters in Cradle of Filth's music use "normal" singing and speaking voices, an extension of the Gothic conceit in which the unfamiliar and monstrous is endowed with uncomfortably human qualities.[42] The juxtaposition of Dani Filth's growled vocals with these female singers is an example of the beauty and the beast vocal pairing, although in many of Cradle of Filth's songs the gendered roles implied by beauty and the beast are subverted, with beauty becoming a mask for beastliness.

Cradle of Filth is tapping into well-trodden and widespread cultural and mythological tropes of beautiful yet ultimately monstrous women, nymphs, and demons, but their choices of subjects also indicate a particular fascination with English literature and horror films, especially those produced by London's Hammer Film Productions from the 1950s to the 1970s. "A Gothic Romance" also bears a striking resemblance to John Keats's famous poem *La belle dame sans merci* (1819), a medievalist ballad in which a knight is seduced and fatally enchanted by a beautiful "faery's child." Cradle of Filth's lyrics also regularly include explicitly erotic and sexual language, simultaneously describing these women and their actions in terms both lofty and vulgar, and the scenarios in their songs sometimes include intense bloody violence as well as sadistic sexual deviance. Although such Bataillean transgressions are a hallmark of many extreme metal styles, Cradle of Filth wraps it in a lyrical aesthetic that often mirrors nineteenth-century romantic poetry in its metrical construction, evocative imagery, and linguistic affectations drawn from early modern English. The sometimes jarring fusion of these elements, along with the band's predilection for intricate wordplay, dry puns, and creative portmanteaus, creates a pastiche in which Cradle of Filth has taken the Gothic horror of Hammer Films, added in direct references to medievalist Gothic literature of the nineteenth century, and then amplified the gore and depravity.

The religious simulacrum that characterizes much courtly love poetry is here inverted into something that retains some of its devotional character even as it emphasizes carnality and supernatural necromancy. In "A Gothic Romance," the protagonist is no less dominated and in thrall to his lover, who asks if he doesn't want to "worship [her] with crimson sacrifice," but the gift of his blood brings him no honor. His submission is ultimately caused by enchantment rather than any courtly code of behavior. Even though the protagonist does take this lady as his lover, her vampiric nature renders her impossible for him to possess, and he is left bereft in the end. However, unlike the deified ladies of *fin'amor*, her powers of domination are supernatural in nature, as opposed to being ascribed to her supposedly irresistible beauty and charm. In the figure of the female vampire, the inner monstrosity of the aristocratic lady is embodied in such a way that it manifests the contradictions of her power over the poet. As with many other powerful women throughout Western history, the sovereignty of both the lady-as-courtly-love-object and the fictional female vampire render them unnatural and potentially monstrous.[43] If courtly love is considered as a sublimation of the tensions between the feudal traditions of matrimonial exchange and the demands of erotic love, resulting in a poetic creation of a depersonalized or inhuman lover, the vampire continues this work in the Victorian era and beyond, giving metaphorical form to cultural anxieties over sex, gender roles, ethnicity, and religion in the guise of a shape-shifting, sexually amorphous, ravenous, and deadly creature.[44]

Beauty and the Beast

Not all evocations of romantic medievalistic love in Gothic metal involve a *fin'amor*-style dynamic of supplication and domination as seen in the examples from My Dying Bride and Cradle of Filth. The songs of the Norwegian Gothic metal band Theatre of Tragedy, for example, often enact dialogues in which the lady is given a voice and opinions of her own. Theatre of Tragedy employ a musical aesthetic that came to be called beauty and the beast, in which the female singer adopts an operatic vocal style while the male singer performs with the deep growls of death metal. Although other metal bands might occasionally feature female singers, beauty and the beast implies that the vocal duo essentially act as twin lead singers. My Dying Bride's "Black God," for example, might not fit because the inclusion of a female singer is a marked departure from their musical aesthetic and the male singer is using a "clean" vocal tone. Cradle of Filth comes closer to the beauty and the beast ideal because female vocals are an integral part of their musical aesthetic, but the female vocalists are used relatively sparingly and are often hired session musicians rather than full members of the band. In Theatre of Tragedy, however, the singers Raymond Rohonyi and Liv Kristine share the lead vocal role in the band.

Theatre of Tragedy's "A Hamlet for a Slothful Vassal" and "Cheerful Dirge" from the bands' self-titled 1995 album provide examples of this beauty and the beast vocal style that take place within a particularly neomedievalist context.[45] Most of Theatre of Tragedy's music from the late 1990s is written in early modern English; these particular songs are set as dialogues between lovers, and in many of their lyric booklets the words of the songs are described as "plays". "A Hamlet for a Slothful Vassal" finds an older man accusing his younger bride of being happy because she is unfaithful, which she denies. The argument plays out in the song's chorus section, with the growled and sung vocals overlapping one another as if in a dramatic conversation:

Female vocals (Liv Kristine)	Male vocals (Raymond Rohonyi)
That is a lie!	Ye beholdest but the shadow
Lief I am not!	Mayhap a tithe of trothplight
My words are but a twist.	I deem—e'er and anon!
'Tis a feignéd lie through loathing, I say!	To and fro, save hither, is thy love.
A dotard gaffer, I daresay...	Not a loth!—But vying for my kinsmen!
...a sapling not!	

The male voice in the song goes on to curse her as a "fiend angelical" and a "dove-feathered raven," which she protests, even as she accuses her husband of having gone senile. The song ends with her rueful departure in the face of his anger. "Cheerful Dirge," in contrast, is a scenario in which a knight proposes marriage to a lady. Her response is in some ways a counter to the "empty vessel" of the objectified lady of *fin'amor*, in that she asks him why he does not pay court to a fairer maiden, implying that she has a checkered past and telling him that he desires to "harvest roses" without counting thorns. The song ends with the knight's assurance of his honesty and good faith.

Theatre of Tragedy's musical plays take on a different tone than either My Dying Bride's melancholic odes or Cradle of Filth's vampiric horrors in that they attempt to provide some sense of balance to their narratives by extending the lyrical perspective beyond that of the lovesick male poet. The lady is no longer an objectified quasi deity but a more fully realized character who brings her own opinions to the scenario. Although this sort of call-and-response duet has several famous examples in the worlds of popular music and opera, such as Frank Loesser's "Baby It's Cold Outside" or Mozart's "La ci darem la mano" from *Don Giovanni*, it is a comparatively rare song format in both metal and medieval music and poetry. The most famous example of such a piece in the *fin'amor* repertoire is almost certainly the *tenso* by Provençal troubadour Raimbaut de Vaqueiras (1165–1207), "Domna, tant vos ai preiada" (Lady, so much have I endeared you), in which the troubadour poet expresses his love and devotion to an aristocratic Genoese lady who responds to him with insults and threats. Although Vaqueiras's *tenso* follows the *fin'amor* tradition in depicting the Genoese lady as cold and spiteful, she is at least able to voice her hostility in the face of the poet's repeated entreaties instead of being a mute and passive object. Additionally, the repertoire of medieval women's love songs also often sees the female poet as an active and desiring subject, although this aspect has perhaps been minimized or reinterpreted to better adhere to the heteronormative gender roles of modern society.[46]

The beauty and the beast pairing featured in Theatre of Tragedy's music is also employed by several other Scandinavian Gothic metal bands, including the Finnish band Nightwish, the Norwegian bands Tristania, Sirenia, and The Sins of Thy Beloved, the Norwegian/German band Leaves' Eyes, and the Dutch bands Within Temptation and Epica. These bands have all seen significant commercial success in the first decades of the twenty-first century. The division of vocal "labor" between the growling male singer and the female soprano varies in each group. In some cases, the female vocalists are utilized mostly for backing vocals resembling Carl Orff's "O Fortuna," often buttressed by synthesized orchestral parts or overdubbed choral-style vocals, but in others the soprano vocalist takes on the lead role to the near exclusion of the growling vocals.[47] The latter trajectory is particularly evident in the more commercially successful groups of this type and was put to its most profitable use by the American band Evanescence in their 2003 platinum-selling single "Bring Me to Life." Taken together, the paired disparate vocal styles present a dynamic in which each vocal type seems to lay claim to a particular gendered power. Death metal growls tend to evoke animals, demons, or other nonhuman monsters, and the timbral effects of the technique can often overwhelm attempts to understand the words while also burying vocal signifiers of age and nationality.[48] While in some contexts these vocal styles can seem to be a manneristic choice or even an attempt to mute normative emotional expression, in Gothic and doom metal the growling vocals evoke emotional excess. The heteronormative gender dynamic of beauty and the beast also reinforces reading these growled vocals as expressions of aggressive masculinity in this context and perhaps also as a strategy for countering the emotional vulnerability evident in many of the lyrics, which might otherwise be unseemly for a death metal singer.[49] The sung vocals of the lead female vocalist, in contrast, evoke control, restraint, and artistic cultivation. The vocal style's dramatic intensity mirrors that of the death growls, but the singers employ a variety of tones ranging from the airy lightness associated with New Age groups like Celtic Woman to powerful climaxes reminiscent of Céline Dion or operatic sopranos.

There is also an element of performed sonic "purity" involved, as the female vocalists rarely employ the growling or screaming techniques of extreme metal or even the overdriven sounds of hard rock singers. The singing style is powerful, but also contains as little grain or earthiness to the voice as possible, often rendering it an ethereal presence relatively devoid of corporeality. This choice of timbre creates a stark juxtaposition with death metal growling, and it remains common regardless of whether the band's aesthetic focus is explicitly medievalistic. The inclusion of an operatic soprano within a metal context is also a logical extension of the adoption of orchestral and choral instrumentations within various metal genres over the past few decades. Wagnerian opera and fantasy film scores have been dominant influences on this musical practice, which is appropriate since they provide both the musicians and the listeners with a readily understood set of musical codes that signify magic, fantasy, and "epicness."[50] Operatic female vocals slot neatly into this musical field. Album art and photoshoots can likewise present the lead singer as a quasi-angelic presence, as in the art for the 2008 reissue of Within Temptation's 2000 album *Mother Earth*.[51] The cover features singer Sharon den Adel in a flowing white dress with her arms outstretched in a gesture somewhat reminiscent of statues of the Virgin Mary, an impression heightened by the outlines of Gothic windows in the cover's computer-generated background. The title track of the album is a celebration of the Nature goddess, with den Adel's soaring vocals seeming to embody her power.[52] While the normal speech and singing of the female vampires in Cradle of Filth's music suggests their power by heightening the effect of supernatural uncanniness, here the operatic singing works to convey the impression of divinity. Although the musical depiction of female power practiced by den Adel and other Gothic metal singers often lacks other key elements of *fin'amor*, especially the supplicant male adorer and the aloofness of the female object, the aesthetic endows the female singer with powers of musical transcendence. In keeping with the operatic style, the singers' melodies are typically long *legato* melodies that seem to float above the densely rhythmic metal accompaniment. While growling vocals can often become part of the overall timbral palette of distorted guitars and heavy drums, the soaring melodies of these female singers are exercises in contrast; they remain apart from and "above" the metal maelstrom. They may not be scornful, monstrous, or "fatal" like the ladies of troubadour poetry, but they are similarly beyond reach.

Conclusion

These various approaches to neomedievalism not only demonstrate the diversity of its practice within just a narrow segment of heavy metal music, but also provide examples of the extent to which the medieval has continued to permeate artistic products and everyday attitudes into the twenty-first century. Rather than a linear trajectory connecting these bands to the distant past, their medieval influences are instead articulated through echoes and reflections from Gothic literature, horror films, and other media products.

Attempting to trace a path through these halls of mirrors continually brings to mind Helen Dell's assertion that in the modern imagination nearly anything can pass for medieval, especially such lasting concepts as melancholy and *fin'amor*.[53] This becomes apparent within neomedievalism's penchant for collapsing pasts into the present by minimizing the distances of history and cultural difference.

Further, studies of heavy metal music have often approached it as the product of isolated subcultures that attempt to stand proudly outside mainstream cultural life. Certainly some of this fixation is a result of the fact that studies of heavy metal music in the first decades of the twenty-first century have often focused on extreme metal genres and local metal scenes, many of which cultivate a certain insularity and hermeticism. In many cases, the medievalisms of these scenes, including everything from wearing armor or face paint onstage to entire metal festivals designed around Viking historical re-enactment, attempt to erect an imagined boundary between the fantasies and camaraderies of metal experience and the mundane experiences of everyday life. The creative anachronisms of neomedievalism provide another way to signal that those spaces and experiences are special while simultaneously reflecting not the past, but the participants' modern selves.

Yet the frame of *fin'amor* and its refractions challenges these boundaries, because even as doom and Gothic metal bands like My Dying Bride and Theatre of Tragedy look to the past for artistic inspirations, the cultural currents they explore remain pervasive in modern Western attitudes around heteronormative romance. Cradle of Filth's Gothic odes to erotic vampirism owe as much to Anne Rice as they do to Bram Stoker, and the band was clearly on the avant-garde of cultural trends regarding vampires in the first decades of the twenty-first century. In short, metal's enduring fascination with the Middle Ages is no longer something that separates it from the rest of Western popular culture (if indeed it ever was), but instead an illustration of metal's deep connections to its cultural environment.

NOTES

1. See Caitlin Carlos's contribution to this volume, "'Ramble On': Medievalism as Nostalgic Practice in Led Zeppelin's use of J. R. R. Tolkien," pp. 530–546.
2. Karl Spracklen, "'To Holmgard...and Beyond:' Folk Metal Fantasies and Hegemonic White Masculinities," *Metal Music Studies* 1, no. 3 (2015): 359–377. For more on the hypermasculine topic in Viking metal, see the next chapter in this volume by Simon Trafford, "Viking Metal," pp. 564–585.
3. Pertti. J. Anttonen, *Tradition through Modernity: Postmodernism and the Nation-State in Folklore Scholarship* (Helsinki: Finnish Literature Society, 2005), 12.
4. Helen Dell, "Musical Medievalism and the Harmony of the Spheres," in *The Cambridge Companion to Medievalism*, ed. Louise D'Arcens (Cambridge: Cambridge University Press, 2016), 60–74, here 61.
5. As discussed by Caitlin Carlos in her contribution to this volume, we see a preoccupation with nostalgia in the medievalism of Led Zeppelin. See also Susan Fast, "Days of Future Passed: Rock, Pop, and the Yearning for the Middle Ages," in *KulturReihe Aktuell*, ed. Dorothea Redepening (Kiel: Wissenschaftsverlag Vauk, 2000), 35–56.

6. M. Selim Yavuz, "'Delightfully Depressing:' Death/Doom Metal Music World and the Emotional Responses of the Fan," *Metal Music Studies* 3, no. 2 (2017): 201–218.

7. Isabella van Elferen, *Gothic Music: The Sounds of the Uncanny* (Cardiff: University of Wales Press, 2012), 152–153.

8. Yavuz, "Delightfully Depressing," 208–210.

9. Gaston Paris, "Etudes sur les romans de la table ronde: Lancelot du Lac," *Romania* 12 (1883): 459–534.

10. Lazar, "Fin'amor," 64; John C. Moore, "'Courtly Love:' A Problem of Terminology," *Journal of the History of Ideas* 40, no. 4 (October–December 1979): 621–632.

11. Moshe Lazar, "Fin'amor," in *A Handbook of the Troubadours*, ed. F. R. P. Akehurst and Judith M. Davis (Berkeley: University of California Press, 1995), 92.

12. Jacques Lacan, *The Seminar of Jacques Lacan, Book VII: The Ethics of Psychoanalysis, 1959–1960*, trans. Dennis Porter (New York: Norton, 1997), 149; Henry Staten, *Eros in Mourning: Homer to Lacan* (Baltimore: Johns Hopkins University Press, 1995), 77.

13. E. Jane Burns, "Courtly Love: Who Needs It? Recent Feminist Work in the Medieval French Tradition," *Signs* 27, no.1 (Autumn 2001): 31–32.

14. Sarah Kay, "Courts, Clerks and Courtly Love," in *The Cambridge Companion to Medieval Romance*, ed. R. L. Krueger (Cambridge: Cambridge University Press, 2000), 81–96.

15. Lacan, *Seminar VII*, 151.

16. Harry Brown, "Baphomet Incorporated: A Case Study in Neomedievalism," in *Studies in Medievalism XX: Defining Neomedievalism(s) II*, ed. Karl Fugelso (Suffolk: Boydell & Brewer, 2011), 1–10.

17. Amy S. Kaufman, "Medieval Unmoored," in *Studies in Medievalism XIX: Defining Neomedievalism(s)*, ed. Karl Fugelso (Suffolk: Boydell & Brewer, 2010), 2–4.

18. James Rovira, *Rock and Romanticism: Post-punk, Goth, and Metal as Dark Romanticisms* (New York: Palgrave-MacMillan, 2018).

19. James Currie, *Music and the Politics of Negation* (Bloomington: Indiana University Press, 2012), 7–8.

20. Jean Baudrillard, *Simulacra and Simulation*, trans. Sheila Faria Glaser (Ann Arbor: University of Michigan Press, 1994), 12.

21. Isabella van Elferen, "Spectral Liturgy: Transgression, Ritual, and Music in Gothic," in *The Gothic in Contemporary Literature and Popular Culture: Pop Goth*, ed. Justin D. Edwards and Agnieszka Soltysik Monnet (New York: Routledge, 2012).

22. Jacques Derrida, *Specters of Marx: The State of the Debt, the Work of Mourning and the New International*, trans. Peggy Kamuf (New York: Routledge, 1994), 10.

23. Lesley Coote, "A Short Essay about Neomedievalism," in *Studies in Medievalism XX: Defining Neomedievalism(s)*, ed. Karl Fugelso (Suffolk: Boydell & Brewer, 2010), 26–27; David W. Marshall, "Neomedievalism, Identification, and the Haze of Medievalisms," in *Studies in Medievalism XX: Neomedievalism(s) II*, ed. Karl Fugelso (Suffolk: Boydell & Brewer, 2011), 23.

24. Isabella van Elferen, *Gothic Music*, 14.

25. Yavuz, "Delightfully Depressing," 210.

26. Mary Frances Wack, *Lovesickness in the Middle Ages: The "Viaticum" and Its Commentaries* (Philadelphia: University of Pennsylvania Press, 1990), 5.

27. Josiah Blackmore, "Melancholy, Passionate Love, and the Coita d'Amor," *PMLA* 124, no. 2 (March 2009): 640–646.

28. Juliana Schiesari, *The Gendering of Melancholia: Feminism, Psychoanalysis, and the Symbolics of Loss in Renaissance Literature* (Cornell, NY: Cornell University Press, 1992), 7–8.

29. Marion A. Wells, *The Secret Wound: Love-Melancholy and Early Modern Romance* (Stanford, CA: Stanford University Press, 2007), 261–262.

30. My Dying Bride, *Turn Loose the Swans*, Peaceville VILE39CD, 1993.

31. Allan Ramsay, ed., *The Tea-Table Miscellany: Or a Collection of Choice Songs, Scots and English*, vol. 1, 10th ed. (London: printed for Millar and by Hodges, 1740), 89, Archive.org: National Library of Scotland.

32. Simon Gaunt, *Love and Death in Medieval French and Occitan Courtly Literature: Martyrs to Love* (Oxford: Oxford University Press, 2006), 3.

33. Lacan, *Seminar VII*, 152.

34. Gaunt, *Love and Death*, 17.

35. Helen Dell, "Dying for Love in Trouvère Song," in *Singing Death: Reflections on Music and Mortality*, ed. Helen Dell and Helen M Hickey (New York: Routledge, 2017), 121–122.

36. Marc de Kesel, *Eros and Ethics: Reading Jacques Lacan's Seminar VII* (Albany: State University of New York Press, 2009), 180.

37. Kesel, *Eros and Ethics*, 176.

38. Lazar, "Fin'amor," 94–95; Wack, *Lovesickness in the Middle Ages*, 167.

39. Wack, *Lovesickness in the Middle Ages*, 171.

40. Karen Desmond, "Refusal, The Look of Love, and the Beastly Woman of Machaut's Ballades 27 and 38," *Early Music History* 32 (2013): 71–118.

41. Cradle of Filth, *Dusk and Her Embrace*, Music for Nations CDMFN 208, 1996.

42. Isabella van Elferen, "Sonic Monstrosity," in *Monstrologi. Frygtens manifestationer*, ed. Jørgen Riber Christensen and Steen Ledet Christiansen (Aalborg: Aalborg Universitetsforlag, 2013), 127–146.

43. Ross Hagen, "A Warning to England: Monstrous Births, Teratology, and Feminine Power in Elizabethan Broadside Ballads," *Horror Studies* 4, no. 2 (2013): 21–41.

44. Lacan, *Seminar VII*, 150; Nina Auerbach, *Our Vampires, Ourselves* (Chicago: University of Chicago Press, 1995).

45. Theatre of Tragedy, *Theatre of Tragedy*, Massacre Records MASS CD 063, 1995.

46. Ria Lemaire, "Explaining Away the Female Subject: The Case of Medieval Lyric," *Poetics Today* 7, no. 4 (1986): 729–743.

47. For a discussion of medievalism in "O Fortuna," see Kirsten Yri, "Medievalism and Anti-Romanticism in Carl Orff's *Carmina Burana*," this volume, pp. 269–300.

48. Marcus Erbe, "By Demons Be Driven? Scanning 'Monstrous' Voices," in *Hardcore, Punk, and Other Junk: Aggressive Sounds in Contemporary Music*, ed. Eric James Abbey and Colin Helb (Lanham, MD: Lexington Books, 2014), 51–71.

49. The gender codings of growled or screamed metal vocals are often complex and contradictory, even if the context here reinforces hearing these vocals as masculine coded. See Rosemary Overell, "'[I] hate Girls and [Emo]tions:' Negotiating Masculinity in Grindcore Music," in *Heavy Metal: Controversies and Countercultures*, ed. Titus Hjelm, Keith Kahn-Harris, and Mark LeVine (Sheffield: Equinox, 2013), 201–227.

50. Berenger Hainaut, "'Fear and Wonder:' Le fantastique sombre et l'harmonie des médiantes, de Hollywood au black metal," *Volume!* 9, no. 2 (2012): 179–197.

51. Within Temptation, *Mother Earth*, Roadrunner Records 1686–179662, 2008.

52. Van Elferen, *Gothic Music*, 153.

53. Dell, "Musical Medievalism," 60.

CHAPTER 25

....

VIKING METAL

....

SIMON TRAFFORD

UNLIKE some of the other examples of musical medievalism explored in this handbook, Viking metal owes virtually nothing to the music of the era it celebrates, nor could it ever do so, because scarcely any usable trace of that survives. Written music from the Viking Age is uncommon everywhere in Europe, but from Scandinavia and the other centers of Viking activity in the north, it is entirely absent. Those very few early manuscript sources that do survive, such as the earliest, twelfth-century text of the Use of Nidaros (the rite of the Catholic Mass employed in Norway before the Reformation) are later and from contexts that are emphatically and remorselessly Christian, the very opposite of what, at least in the eyes of proponents of Viking metal, the Vikings were all about. Of Scandinavian secular music, there is no surviving evidence until the song "Drømde mik en drøm i nat" recorded in the Danish Codex Runicus in the early fourteenth century; nor, in an essentially oral culture, is it likely that very much music predating that piece had ever been written down in the first place.[1] Even without the direct evidence of transcribed melodies, something of the nature of the music of early medieval Scandinavia may be surmised from other sources: from archaeological finds of musical instruments or from descriptions of musical performance in narrative texts.[2] The sagas abound with references to music-making and singing, providing a vision of early medieval Scandinavian musical culture as very rich. Although it should never be forgotten that saga literature is not a primary source but produced retrospectively and nostalgically after the close of the Viking Age, there is no reason to doubt this general picture, especially as it seems to be borne out by contemporary outsiders, such as the account of the Spanish Arab Ibrahim al-Tartushi in 970 that the inhabitants of Haithabu in Slesvig were extremely partial to singing, although admittedly he said it was the worst he had ever heard, comparing their efforts unfavorably with the barking of dogs.[3] There is, furthermore, another factor to consider, because it has been argued that the poetry of the Viking Age, which survives in fair abundance and which quite clearly saw oral performance in some fashion, may in fact have been sung. Less convincingly, it is sometimes alleged that something of this—conceivably including "authentic" melodies—may have been preserved into the eighteenth century or later—late enough to have been recorded by collectors—in the folk-song traditions of Iceland or the Faroe Islands. However, it is exceptionally hard to prove any of this with the evidence available, especially in view of the demonstrable influence of external ballad traditions on the islands of the north Atlantic from the late medieval period onward.[4]

Undoubtedly, all this is suggestive, but the evidence we possess nevertheless amounts to not much more than a collection of hints and glimpses: the music of the Vikings is therefore effectively a blank space onto which succeeding ages can project what they choose, creating the sonic accompaniment that they deem appropriate for their image of the Vikings. That, of course, is a claim also routinely made *mutatis mutandis* of modern interpretations of many other kinds of medieval music, but in those cases there are at least some materials from the period on which to base interpretation; for the Vikings, there are virtually none.[5] As a result, Viking metal does not find exact counterparts in the attempts to *re-create* medieval music that form the subject of other chapters in this handbook: namely, in the efforts of the early music scene since the start of the twentieth century to find, recover, and authentically perform the music of the Middle Ages or, equally, in the reappropriation of the early music canon as pop music by groups like Dead Can Dance or the Mediaeval Baebes from the 1980s onward. Instead, Viking metal has rather more in common with the nineteenth-century romantic tradition across northern Europe that sought to construct—from whatever sources were available, regardless of whether they were authentically medieval—a suitably dramatic and primal-sounding music that could stand as a backdrop to the dramatization of stories from saga or *Edda*: examples include the Danish composer J. P. E. Hartmann's settings of *Þrymskviða* and *Völuspá*, Edvard Grieg's unfinished opera *Olav Tryggvason*, Edward Elgar's cantata *King Olaf*, which used Longfellow's *Saga of King Olaf* (in turn based on *Heimskringla*) as its text, and, most famous of all, Richard Wagner's *Ring of the Nibelung*.[6]

Despite this contrast, there are many points of comparison between Viking metal and other musical medievalisms. The important body of scholarship built up in recent years on modern-period interest in medieval music contains several insights and principles that will inform and structure what follows. Central to this body of thought has been the notion of yearning: that the Middle Ages are an object of desire for people of the present, serving as what Annette Kreutziger-Herr calls "a reservoir for emotions and feelings."[7] The medieval, however, is dead and gone and cannot be revived, so instead it is a category that must be constructed, Kreutziger-Herr says, "as a desired beyond or Other," and furthermore, one that, in the words of Susan Fast, is "a source of power alternative to that possessed by the dominant culture."[8] Responding to a perceived absence of authenticity and of harmony with the universe under capitalist economic structures, the medieval is among a number of *fictive domains*—others include the pastoral and the exotic—that are able to serve as sites of authentic experience. Popular music production that is concerned with invoking the Otherness of these fictive domains is concerned "with distancing itself from the hegemony of bourgeois capitalist culture by looking *both back and forward in time* and also horizontally, if you will, to living non-western cultures, to the archaic as well as the futuristic...[to] outer space...and to ethnic Others."[9] On a more concrete level, Daniel Leech-Wilkinson has noted that those who have sought early music have generally been looking for three not necessarily compatible things: for music that is new (to them), for "the product of an exotic culture far removed from our own," and for roots, that is to say, for music of their own culture with which they wish to connect.[10] Last, in her discussion of "Medievalism and Exoticism in the Music of Dead Can Dance," Kirsten Yri has concentrated attention on the ideals of authenticity and purity in alternative music scenes "rooted in an opposition to mainstream, commercial music industries"; these principles, Yri suggests, underpin Dead Can Dance's critique of the modern and interest in an idealized Middle Ages.[11] Although this complex of ideas is common currency among scholars of medievalist music, it has seldom been explicitly applied to Viking metal.[12] In part, what follows is an attempt to address that task.

It is useful to outline at this early stage some of the characteristics of Viking metal as I shall be using the term here. Viking metal is a widely recognized subgenre of heavy metal that shares most of the characteristic sonic qualities of its parent genre, namely, heavily amplified and distorted electric guitars combined with emphatic drum beats and overall loudness; equally, its lyrics, like those of heavy metal in general, are devoted to chaos, the lurid, and the extreme.[13] Viking metal arose in a specific subcultural context—the emergent extreme metal scene in Scandinavia in the late 1980s and early 1990s—and it has a number of qualities best explained and understood with close reference to the peculiarities of that subculture. The particular appeal of the Vikings for extreme metal fans and musicians was very strongly related to existing predilections within heavy metal culture, namely, a valorization of macho masculinity, a revulsion for genteel social norms, and a taste for themes of war and chaos.[14] Having said that, it is crucial that Viking metal also be understood as the product of an interest in the Vikings that extends far beyond the relatively narrow confines of extreme metal and that has been a feature of many parts of popular culture since at least the nineteenth century.[15] It was because the popular image of the Vikings as exciting and adventurous mavericks had achieved such common currency across literature, films, television programs, popular history, and the whole range of popular cultural production that they were so readily available to be appropriated for the purposes of heavy metal. Throughout the entirety of Viking metal's existence, it has been nourished by an abiding popular enthusiasm for the Vikings and for barbarian Others in general that has manifested not just in books, films, and television programs, but also in burgeoning interest in revived Norse "heathenism," Viking/medieval festivals around the world and—significantly—in other popular music that was not at first related to Viking metal. As will be explored here, the impulses and aspirations that in Scandinavia nourished the emergence of Viking metal encouraged in Germany the birth of *Mittelalter* music, a rather different type of modern medieval popular music.[16]

A further distinctive characteristic of Viking metal is its relative longevity. After the initial burst of enthusiasm for Viking metal in the early 1990s, it might easily have slipped quietly back into obscurity. This is what happened on the previous occasions that pop music experienced spasms of interest in the Middle Ages: for all the excitement poured into Arthurianism and medievalism by an impressive array of folk-rock and progressive-rock bands in the early 1970s, by the end of the decade most traces of it had been erased.[17] Equally, the popularity of Gregorian chant—either in a relatively pure form or mixed with dance beats—that sold huge numbers of records in the 1990s proved to be a short-lived phenomenon.[18] Viking metal, by contrast—while admittedly seldom troubling the mainstream charts—has persisted, developed, and diversified, cross-fertilizing with other types of music and establishing itself as a broad subgenre in its own right, complete with its own dedicated fan base and—in Scandinavia and continental Europe—its own festival circuit. The principal online listing of heavy metal bands, *Encyclopaedia Metallum*, recognizes "Folk/Viking/Pagan metal" as a genre comprising—at the time of writing—2,807 bands worldwide (although that bare figure needs further context to avoid exaggerating the popularity of the phenomenon; there are, for example, 39,434 entries in the "Death metal" category).[19] More than a quarter of a century after the first emergence of Viking metal as such, it is clear that it continues to exert an appeal and inspire both bands and audiences. Or perhaps—given that Viking metal has changed and diversified over the years, as indeed have its adherents—it is more accurate to say that the shifting bricolage of emotional, intellectual, spiritual, and nationalist ideas that constitute the discourse of Viking metal remains able to attract listeners—and participants in the subculture—who are enthused by some part or other of its various appeals.

Bringing together the substantial body of recent sociological and musicological research into Viking metal, this paper is an attempt to trace the origins and continuing development of the genre as a manifestation of medievalism, one that is comparable to, but frequently contrasts with, the other examples of modern musical usage of ideas of the Middle Ages considered in this handbook. First, the basic history and trajectory of the genre from the 1980s to the present will be sketched out; subsequent sections will examine, in turn, the musical character of Viking metal, its lyrical content and thematic preoccupations, its particular appeal to its practitioners and audiences, and, last, the way in which competing pressures of globalism and nationalism have been articulated within it. Throughout, the emphasis will be on how ideas of the Vikings have been appropriated, created, and manipulated to service modern needs and negotiate present-day anxieties.

A Very Short History of Viking Metal

Many years before the emergence of anything that might legitimately be acknowledged as Viking metal, the Vikings had already started to colonize the imagination of heavy rock. In the early 1970s, Led Zeppelin made the first and most famous pop references to the Vikings, but over the course of the following decades, a host of others, including many of what were then the biggest bands in rock and metal, produced songs that took the Vikings as their subject matter.[20] A very few performers, such as Manowar or

Jon Mikl Thor (otherwise famous mostly for his admittedly impressive onstage party trick of blowing up a hot water bottle until it burst), adopted a barbarian (or, in Thor's case, overtly Viking) image and appropriate fancy dress on a semipermanent basis; in most cases, though, artists' interest in the Vikings tended only to be sustained for the space of one or two songs. As well-defined and familiar figures from films, literature, and school history that an audience could be relied on to recognize, they were easily appropriated to lend an air of menace, romance, or adventure (not to mention a touch of historicizing class) but were then just as easily put down again when the band turned to other matters and other sources of lyrical inspiration.[21]

A turning point came, however, in the very late 1980s and early 1990s with the activities of Bathory, a Swedish band from Stockholm who have the strongest claim to be regarded as the founders of Viking metal proper. Formed in 1983 and dominated by the guitarist, songwriter, and composer/lyricist Tomas Forsberg (aka Quorthon), Bathory were instrumental in the creation of the Scandinavian extreme metal scene, establishing with their early albums a blueprint both for the harsh, aggressive sound of what was to become known as black metal and for its typical lyrical subject matter, in particular its almost fanatical loathing for Christianity. Earlier, Forsberg expressed this mostly in the form of Satanism, but the fourth album, *Blood, Fire, Death* (1988) signposted a new direction, with its cover art taken from *Åsgårdsreien*, an epic depiction of bristling Nordic deities painted in the full flood of nineteenth-century romantic enthusiasm for the old North by the Norwegian artist Peter Nicolai Arbo.[22] Subsequently, the Vikings were to be both the shock troops in Bathory's ongoing campaign against Christianity and lionized in their own right as strong, exciting, and adventurous figures to whom Forsberg himself, as a Swede, could claim links of blood and tradition. The next two Bathory albums, *Hammerheart* (1990) and *Twilight of the Gods* (1991), were both concept albums, entirely devoted to the Vikings.[23] *Hammerheart*, with a cover taken from Sir Frank Dicksee's *The Funeral of a Viking* (1893), is the most successful of Bathory's Viking albums and should be regarded as the foundational work of Viking metal.[24] Unlike Bathory's previous material, which had been typified by short, fast pieces notable for their extreme aggression and for vocals that were screamed or roared and generally incomprehensible, the songs are longer and slower, with an epic sound that is much closer to the more melodic approach of traditional heavy metal. The vocals are "clean"— that is, sung as opposed to screeched—and the words (in English) can fairly readily be understood; they celebrate the traditional Viking behaviors of sailing, raiding, and fighting, with a particular concentration on Norse gods and mythology. The lyrics also display an awe and respect for the natural world and in particular for the seas and the weather; this is reinforced by the atmospheric sounds of lapping waves, of fire and bird-song and thunder that are used as introductions or play-outs for several songs. Crucially, *Hammerheart*'s celebration of a thrilling, exciting Viking world ends on a melancholy note with the song "One Rode to Asa Bay," a story of more or less forcible Scandinavian conversion to Christianity. The moral is clear: Because of the intervention of Christianity, the life of the Vikings that Bathory and their audience revere so much is dead, gone, and unattainable. The traditional hostility of extreme metal toward Christianity is thus recast in a far more emotionally potent form, because the religion is stigmatized as an alien force that shuts down the desired Viking Age and, with it, all the untrammeled opportunities for youthful male uproar and excitement that its audience craves; what it installs instead is the dull, everyday, respectable world, which is precisely what Bathory's listeners are attempting to escape. The image also resonates in other ways: Clearly, Christianity stands here as a symbol of aging and for the inevitable choking off of care-free adolescent fun by responsibility, dull day jobs, and the adult world. Moreover, it also surely hints at anxieties in Scandinavian societies concerned about the erosion of their distinctiveness and cultural and racial integrity being challenged by impulses emanating from the European Union and the south.[25]

Bathory were one among a number of bands that established Scandinavia in the 1980s and early 1990s as one of the principal sites for the development of *extreme metal*, a new and fundamentalist form of heavy metal that rejected what it saw as the compromised commercialism of radio-friendly glam and pop metal that had dominated in the 1980s and instead espoused a far more aggressive sonic onslaught calculated to be less appealing to the mainstream.[26] Extreme metal is an umbrella term covering a variety of different scenes that, in their early stages, were highly localized and associated with small numbers of committed devotees in specific countries or cities. Of these, it was a scene that developed in Norway that started to make the running in Viking metal from the early 1990s onward. This was the consequence, first, of the emergence there of new bands such as Enslaved or Einherjer, who would adopt a wholeheartedly Viking identity. Enslaved's first full album, *Vikingligr Veldi* (1994), is another landmark release in the development of Viking metal, not least because it was the first to include any attempt at singing in Old Norse, thus introducing another highly characteristic element of the classic formula. The other important way in which the Norwegian scene contributed to the exposure and expansion of Viking metal was through the spectacular worldwide notoriety attracted by a number of murders and church burnings, including the destruction in 1992 of the eleventh-century Fantoft stave church, outside Bergen.[27] Previously, the extreme metal audience had been restricted to a small number of hard-core devotees concentrated in a few cities, but the huge publicity garnered by sensationalist coverage of the criminal activities of the Norwegian black metal scene rapidly propelled extreme metal to global infamy and positioned it in the minds of countless teenagers as the best and most extreme means available of outraging their parents. At the same time, links between the Nordic primordialist enthusiasms of the metal scene and extreme right-wing politics were made far more explicit by the pronouncements of Kristian "Varg" Vikernes, the leader and sole member of the band Burzum, who was jailed in 1994 for involvement in the church burnings and for the murder of Øystein "Euronymous" Aarseth, the leader of the band Mayhem.[28] In interviews from prison and in writings released through his website, Vikernes portrayed the burning of churches as an act of vengeance against Christianity for the supposed forcible conversion of Scandinavia. To Vikernes—and many others in the black metal scene—Christianity, with its foreign and Middle Eastern origins, had brought to an end a golden age of the north, a golden age defined explicitly in terms of national and racial purity.[29] The eye-catching antics of the Norwegian black metalers were, to be sure, short-lived: by the mid-1990s, as Ross Hagen has written, "the sociopathic element was either incarcerated or had simply outgrown such criminal activities." But even after acts of outright violence faded away, the association with racism, ultranationalism, and other extreme right-wing ideologies has never entirely left the scene, despite the best efforts of many members to distance themselves from them.[30]

After Viking metal achieved worldwide fame and an unwonted (and, for some, unwanted) commercial success, the later 1990s and early years of the twenty-first century saw both a steady stream of albums from established performers and the emergence of several new acts. It was during this time that bands such as Amon Amarth and Týr, later to become stalwarts of Viking metal, began to release their first records and develop fan followings. Alongside this basic continuity, though, were several developments that would eventually wreak considerable change in Viking metal. Most notably, the period saw the emergence and rapid growth of *folk metal* and *Pagan metal*, at first across northern Europe, but later worldwide.[31] In some ways, the development of folk metal was inspired by and a response to Viking metal. But the movement also had roots that were both entirely separate and radically different from those of Viking metal. In Germany, one of the heartlands of folk metal, for instance, bands such as Corvus Corax, Subway to Sally, or In Extremo sprang from a tradition of *Mittelaltermusik* or medieval-influenced folk music, performed in numerous *Mittelaltermärkte* (medieval markets) around Germany and Austria and heavily influenced by the medievalist folk group Ougenweide of the 1970s and 1980s (Ougenweide, in turn, were inspired by the medievalism of the early 1970s British folk-rock scene, so this constitutes, albeit at some remove, a link between rock's two principal medievalist episodes).[32] Elsewhere, emerging folk metal scenes followed a common formula, with bands adopting acoustic "folk" or traditional instruments into their sound and borrowing tunes and compositional effects that—at least ostensibly—derived from local folk-song traditions. Virtually all folk metal bands in addition are avowed Pagans or heathens, hence the other name frequently used for the genre, Pagan metal.[33] A standard set of themes dominate the songs: the power of nature; the beauties of the mountains, forests, rivers, hills, or lakes of the homeland; the hearty, manly, and frequently alcoholic lives lived by the ancestors and their heroic struggles in battle against outsiders. In common with Viking metal, most folk metal bands frequently lament what they regard as the imposition of Christianity on their homelands, which has severed the link between modern populations and their ancestral cultures, closing off the heroic primordial life, with its authenticity, its fierce passions, and its simple virtues. The past is, indeed, the central focus of folk metal, a place, in Deena Weinstein's words, "where you can walk in the same footsteps as the ancestors and pay homage to them so that the dead, in a sense, return to life."[34]

The marked similarity of philosophical and religious outlooks has promoted, despite their differing origins, a growing convergence in the twenty-first century of the Viking metal, Pagan metal, folk metal, neofolk, and ethereal Gothic scenes into a sprawling metagenre encompassing considerable variety in musical styles, but increasingly united in their heathen ethos, their festival circuit, their audience, and their shared longing for an exotic medieval Other.[35] Correspondences between Viking metal and folk/Pagan metal in particular are so many and so frequent that some—not least *Encyclopaedia Metallum*—see them as essentially the same phenomenon or even think of Viking metal as a subcategory of folk metal, with the Vikings being merely the Scandinavian entrants in a Eurovision Song Contest of primordial barbarians.[36] The terminology is used so loosely and the scenes are so heavily intermingled that attempting to unravel them completely is impossible and pointless, and yet Viking metal does remain to some degree distinct from folk/Pagan metal. This is partly discernible in the music. As is explored in the next section, some Viking metal bands have, indeed, adopted acoustic folk instruments, but many more stick to the conventional metal sound. More important, the long-held and enduring status of the Vikings as popular culture's barbarians of choice ensures that among all the ancient peoples of Europe, they remain very firmly *primi inter pares*, wielding an attraction that cannot be matched by any others.[37] It is notable, for instance, that while folk metal bands from outside Scandinavia or even outside Europe are perfectly willing to sing about Vikings, few bands have ever sung about any *other* ancient peoples from a country not their own.[38] Interestingly, as Imke von Helden has noted, the emergence of folk metal seems to have pushed some of the early Viking metal bands away from what they see as the cliché, crass nationalism and glorification of the past that is endemic in folk metal. Enslaved's albums since *Monumension* (2001) have played down Norse mythology in favor of more philosophical concerns and have included lyrics in English rather than Norwegian or Old Norse.[39] As Grutle Kjellson, Enslaved's singer, said in 2010,

> We came with a silly name—"Viking metal'"—we should never have done that, we regret that of course. We didn't know what we were talking about and the initial idea was not to make people play silly folk music and wear fur.[40]

Alongside changes to the character of the music were changes to the constitution of the scene. The rise of the Internet has been fundamental. The early days of Viking metal developed before the widespread availability of the Internet. The emergent extreme metal scene was characterized by small, close-knit groups, localized to particular countries or cities; it was relatively hard to find new bands and new recordings from around the world. It has grown up, however, alongside the Internet amid the process that Deena Weinstein has called "metal's second globalization"; barriers to contact have been removed, allowing potential fans—spread relatively thinly around the world—to find bands, videos, information, and one another and thus to achieve the critical mass to create a worldwide scene.[41] Going hand in hand with this has been the development of a large and very active festival circuit throughout the world, although concentrated especially in Germany and middle Europe. The diversity and variety of festivals are extraordinary. There are dedicated folk metal/Viking metal festivals, such as Ragnarök in Germany or Midgardsblot in Norway, but Viking metal bands can also very easily be accommodated at a mainstream and extremely large metal festival such as Wacken in Germany (which attracts crowds in excess of eighty thousand; Amon Amarth are regular performers). Viking metal performers can be equally at home outside the conventional metal circuit, for instance, at Castle Fest, the medieval/fantasy festival held since 2005 at Castle Keukenhof in the Netherlands, or in the Heidnisches Dorf, one of the venues at Wave Gotik Treffen in Leipzig, the world's biggest Goth festival.

As Viking metal approaches its thirtieth year, it remains a living and active scene. Bathory came to an end with the death of Tomas Forsberg in 2004, but Enslaved are still prolifically productive and regarded as elder statesmen of the genre (however much they may now regret inspiring fur-clad folk metalers); indeed, to some extent they have even been embraced by mainstream Norwegian society.[42] If "likes" on Facebook are any guide, though, the biggest Viking metal band of all is Amon Amarth (although they continually deny that they play Viking metal).[43] They have produced eleven albums since 1998 and are a major live act throughout the world; some indication of the distance traveled from the militant anticommercialism of the early extreme metal scene may be gathered from the fact that their lead vocalist, Johann Hegg, is co-owner of an online shop providing "authentic Viking products from Sweden," including Thor's hammer pendants, drinking horns, and beard-care products, as well as saga and *Edda* translations and books on the history and archaeology of the Vikings.[44] As well as these bigger bands from the 1990s, new groups are still emerging at a grass-roots level that call themselves Viking metal. Although they do not use that term of themselves, the most interesting of the bands to emerge in the past ten years is Wardruna—from Norway—who have attracted considerable attention both with their *Runaljod* trilogy of albums based around ideas of evoking Norse spirituality and through the appearance of their music in the History Channel television series *Vikings*, which has helped to make them effectively the sound of the Vikings for millions of viewers around the world.[45] Wardruna's music is created with acoustic instruments and electronics and has no similarity whatsoever to the sound of heavy metal, but their impeccable extreme metal credentials—their founder and artistic driving force, Einar Selvik, was formerly the drummer of the black metal band Gorgoroth—combine with their position as rising stars of the broader Viking scene to ensure that they can find both a place and a highly enthusiastic audience at metal festivals around the world.

Thus, over the course of the past three decades, from its origins in an extremely specific subcultural context, Viking metal has seen considerable changes in its character, its audiences, and its attributed meanings; yet throughout there have been strands of continuity in what performers and audiences have desired of their Viking past. The rest of this essay will now explore in more detail how the music, lyrics, and visual identity of Viking metal have been used to create and express a Viking Age that is meaningful and valuable to bands, fans, and all participants in the Viking metal discourse. At the same time, this will be compared and contrasted with other, more mainstream, musical medievalisms. From what we have seen so far, it is clear that Viking metal serves many of the same purposes and fulfills the same functions as other examples of music employing a medieval image. It is first and foremost about a desired Other: a more or less invented medieval that has characteristics felt to be absent in the modern world and that are therefore the object of yearning. Of course, what is actually desired is very different: in mainstream musical medievalism, the goal has been an imagined harmony, whereas in Viking metal, the emphasis has been far more on excitement and fighting.

The Sound of Viking Metal

The goal of many other musical medievalisms has been to bring forward and interpret surviving medieval compositions for a modern audience, whereas that is something Viking metal—as we have seen—does not and cannot do. On the contrary, its founders and early practitioners were immersed in the characteristically and emphatically late twentieth-century sound of heavy metal. The music that they wrote to accompany their Viking-themed lyrics was full square in that tradition. Bathory's first Viking metal albums sound like traditional heavy metal but achieve a far more epic quality than their non-Viking-themed predecessors. The songs are often longer, slower, and structurally more complex; the vocals are mostly clear and comprehensible rather than the harsh screams previously preferred; and there is notably greater dynamic variation, with quieter passages allowing a wider range of moods than the erstwhile all-out aggression. The orchestration enhances the grandeur, with multitracked choral backing harmonies and long, sustained synthesizer notes creating atmospheric ambience; a distinctly cinematic sensibility is added by sounds of drumming hooves, lapping waves, and roaring flames that accompany the beginnings and endings of many songs. The effect is to signal the historical subject matter in the sound in a way that is unmissable but avoids alienating the potential audience by departing unacceptably far from metal's sonic template as it was then constituted.

Since Viking metal has become established as a genre, though, and especially since it began to cross over and merge with folk metal, the most distinctive characteristic of the music has been its startling diversity. Perhaps the single most important cause of this diversity is the wildly varying extents to which performers have chosen to make their music sound Viking and the many ways in which, in the Baudrillardian absence of an original to emulate, they have set about that task. In this respect, all Viking metal bands can be seen to fall somewhere along a spectrum. At one extreme are bands that make little or no effort to make their sound correspond to their ancient subject matter, playing heavy metal (in one or another of its various forms) that could not—on the strength of the music alone—be distinguished from mundane, non-Viking metal. This camp includes some of the biggest and most influential Viking metal bands: Enslaved's early albums, for instance, sound essentially similar to any other black metal of their time.[46] Equally, Amon Amarth play straightforward melodic death metal that offers no indication whatsoever of their Norse interests. The very high status of these bands within the Viking metal scene strongly suggests that no particular penalty or sense of inauthenticity attaches to bands that do not attempt to sound Viking; instead, adherence to the aural code of metal guarantees their basic acceptability to fans, while their "Vikingness" is conveyed by the lyrics, stage sets, or the appearance of band members.

Other Viking metal performers, though, have endeavored to make their sound Viking or, at least, appropriately evocative of the remote past. Not surprisingly, bands have taken many different approaches to this task. Sometimes it can be through instrumentation, namely, the deployment—alongside the standard metal kit—of distinctive acoustic folk instruments. No attempt is made to restrict the folk and acoustic instruments employed to those which might have been heard by the Vikings or even to those particularly associated with Scandinavia. Rather, instruments are appropriated from modern folk music, such as the violin used by the Swedish band Månegarm throughout most of their career. This leads to some perverse outcomes: The very popular Finnish bands Ensiferum and Turisas both make accordions an important part of their sound, although that instrument was invented in Germany in 1822. Yet there is no perceived incongruity in attempting to impart an appropriately "historical" air to these bands' songs about Vikings using instruments that are emphatically postmedieval and derived from continental Europe. Accordions and fiddles sound folksy and are familiar from contemporary folk music, evoking a generalized traditional society of times past that cannot—and actively should not—be pinned down to a specific historical context if it is to have its effect.

Folk instruments can emphasize the temporal Otherness of the Vikings by associating them with the timeless once-upon-a-time land that most folk music occupies, but other elements of the Viking identity can also be brought forward by careful use and appropriation of sonic tropes. In particular, Aaron Mulvany has drawn attention to the way in which the Vikings' sea-going has been drawn into their musical representation in Viking metal through the use of various features of sea shanties such as stepwise progressions and singing in unison. Mulvany argues that these devices were originally appropriated for the aural depiction of early modern sailors and pirates in films and television, but were then borrowed as a signature sound of the Vikings in such films as the Kirk Douglas classic *The Vikings* (1958). With the benefit of such a popular and influential authority, the association stuck and music in the style of sea shanties could eventually be borrowed once again—into Viking metal—as an accepted sound that meant Viking.[47]

A rather different approach to the challenge of incorporating the sound of the Vikings into heavy metal is taken by the band Týr, who make extensive use of the corpus of traditional Faroese folk songs, *kvæði*, collected in the eighteenth and nineteenth centuries. Týr's music is a blend of traditional (nonextreme) metal with melodies drawn from traditional material and generally in unusual time signatures, but normally played on the standard metal instruments: guitars and drums. All of their albums include at least one (and often more) song where the melody and words are directly based on *kvæði*, and these songs form some of the most popular parts of their repertoire, including fan favorites such as "Sinklars Visa" or "Regin Smiður." Týr are able to parade their *kvæði* as guarantees of their authenticity, placing them, they say, in a closer relationship with the Vikings than any other Viking metal band and claiming—dubiously—a direct continuity in the transmission of *kvæði* from the Viking Age itself to the present.[48]

Last, and to complete the picture, we must consider a handful of performers for whom—in the sound, at least—the heavy metal element has been virtually or entirely removed: electric guitars are absent and the burden of producing sound is taken entirely by acoustic instruments or by instruments that would not normally be seen as canonically "metal." Much the most successful of these is the Norwegian band Wardruna. Although, as noted previously, they have strong extreme metal credentials, their sound is based on chant, complex percussion, swelling atmospheric electronic drones, and acoustic instruments based either on those from the Norwegian folk tradition (the Hardanger fiddle, for instance) or on those from archaeological finds (an array of lurs and the Kravik lyre). The music produced has nothing to do with heavy metal, finding its closest parallels in world music and even incorporating such exotic elements as throat singing; however, despite the prominence of folk instruments, Einar Selvik—Wardruna's driving force—insists that the intention is not to re-create Viking music, which is dead and gone, but to create something different and new using elements from the past:

> Wardruna is not about re-enactment, romantic ideas about the past or about neces- sarily being authentic. It is about taking some ideas, techniques and tools from the past and mak[ing] something new—that resonates with and is relevant to the present. That being said, a lot of it is quite authentic. Some of the instruments are quite limited in what you can and cannot do on them so to a certain degree almost anything played on them would be authentic.[49]

That said, the strong presence of Wardruna's music in the soundtrack to the History Channel's *Vikings* television series has lent their sound considerable weight as *the* aural signifier of Scandinavian prehistory: tellingly, a similar style has now been adopted by new bands such as Heilung (from Denmark/Germany) and Forndom (from Sweden).

In sum, then, the absence of proper traces of Viking music around which to constitute an aural practice has never been any sort of impediment to Viking metal, nor, despite the central importance placed by the extreme metal scene on authenticity in all things, has it ever been felt to detract from the experience of the listener. As a development or refinement of a preexisting musical style—heavy metal—with a set of characteristics that were already exceptionally strongly defined, Viking metal has not needed to estab- lish its validity with reference to the accuracy with which it reproduces a Viking sound. If the music seems to be suitably evocative of primitive society by virtue of its folkish instrumentation, then that may be a bonus, but many ways of implementing the sonic difference from the mainstream desired by Viking metal are permissible. The primary burden of creating the Viking identity of Viking metal falls more often to other elements, namely, to lyrics or to visual identity; it is to these that we shall now turn.

Lyrics, Themes, and Language

For medievalist music outside Viking metal, as has been noted already, it is primarily in the character and instrumentation of the music itself that its medieval qualities are displayed; however, the classical early music scene has always been surrounded by a paraphernalia and culture of its own that marks its difference from the standard classical concert repertoire. It tends to be encountered in different venues—in churches rather than concert halls—and is likely to see rather more flamboyant performances, marked by theatricality of dress, setting, or presentation.[50] The same is true, and to a greater extent, in medievalist pop music, where album artwork, costumes, and venues are fundamental to constructing the Other that it offers.[51] With Viking metal, though, this tendency is taken to an extreme, because it has always been in song lyrics and in the visual imagery adopted by artists that the major work of medievalizing is done.

Since the very first references to Vikings in rock music, their appeal has lain above all in the role of exciting, uproarious, hypermasculine supermen that popular culture has defined for them.[52] Stories about Viking seafaring, raids, and fighting told by song lyrics are the central and defining characteristic of Viking metal.[53] Examples are far too numerous to mention, but an example picked literally at random—Amon Amarth's "With Oden on Our Side" from the album of the same name (2006)—runs through much of the standard formula:

> Finally the storm arrives
> Our wait is at an end
> Under dark winter skies
> We make our final stand
>
> For each of us, there are four of them
> It matters not to us
> We won't leave this field in shame
> We are here to crush!
>
> Futile to resist
> You know why we have come
> Futile to resist
> The battle is already won!
>
> Our hearts are full of pounding rage
> Our mind hard as steel
> Right before the dying day
> We will have you kneel
>
> The snow turns red from all the blood
> Severed limbs and heads
> A sacrifice to one-eyed God
> He will claim the dead!
>
> Under the winter skies
> We stand glorious!
> And with Oden on our side
> We are victorious!

Violence, death, honor, and a stern unflinching (anti-)heroic ethos are to the fore: Vikingness is, among other things, a system of values and ethics in Viking metal.

Alongside these more philosophical and abstract ideas, though, are an abundance of more concrete items: references to snow, winter skies, and sacrifices to the one-eyed god situate the action firmly in the familiar Norse milieu. A standard Viking paraphernalia that includes, but is by no means limited to, axes, swords, stripe-sailed longships, dragon prows, stormy seas, thunder, ravens, wolves, burning villages, and an array of named places and people—Odin, Thor, Niflheim, Bifrost, and Hel—litters the lyrical imaginary of Viking metal, providing constant clues and reminders that the violent barbarian action described is not just *any* violent barbarian action but specifically that of the Vikings and is thus embedded in a rich complex of culture and associations that massively enhances its emotional and intellectual appeal.

Although many songs are simply tales of the deeds of warriors and sailors living their lives, the supernatural world of the Norse gods is always present as a backdrop or, more actively, in the form of prayers and invocations offered by the heroes.[54] For a number of bands, though, religion is actually the principal focus: Their songs revolve around stories from Norse mythology.[55] A small but very influential minority of performers (including Enslaved, Einherjer, and Wardruna, to name but a few) go so far as to appropriate sections of the *Edda* (the main source for Norse religion) in their original Old Norse for use as song lyrics.

This question of language is an important one and deserves further consideration, because language has rich emotional and national significance and Viking metal bands have used it extensively as a token of identification with the ancient European past. English was and is the traditional language of mainstream heavy metal, and up to the 1980s it was a part of the ubiquitous template of commercialized and globalized heavy rock, used even by bands for whom it was not native.[56] From the late eighties, though, one of the ways in which the emergent extreme metal scene distanced itself from this prevailing globalized culture and asserted values that were different, more localized, and more authentic was in its usage of local languages.[57] The Norwegian black metal scene was very active in this respect, with many of the early bands using one or other of the (many) Norwegian dialects for their songs. Enslaved, however, took a significantly more extreme step on their first album, *Vikingligr Veldi* (1994), becoming the first Viking metal band to use antiquated language to foster their image.[58] One song in particular, "Heimdallr," directly quotes Snorri Sturluson's Old Norse (from the description of the god Heimdall in Chapter 27 of Gylfaginning, the second part of the *Prose Edda* of ca. 1220). This was a bold move: Old Norse is a hard language and—with the exception of the Icelanders and Faroese—is incomprehensible to all but a tiny minority of Europeans, even in Scandinavia.[59] Nevertheless, other bands soon followed Enslaved's lead, and the use both of Old Norse and of ancient texts—translated or in the original—became a familiar part, if not a cliché, of Viking metal. One indication of the ubiquity of the habit—but also of the self-aware reading of this sort of linguistic signaling within the scene—is the coining of the word *kvlt*, used mockingly within extreme metal circles to refer to anyone or anything perceived to be absurdly or willfully obscure, elitist, and exclusive (in other words, meeting the ideals of extreme metal in an exaggerated way); the joke, of course, lies in the use of "v" for "u," in imitation of premodern orthography.

Using a well-nigh incomprehensible language breaks a cardinal unwritten rule of most commercial pop music: that the audience should be provided with words that are memorable, tell a vivid story, and stick in the mind. By the logic of extreme metal, however, such a radical departure from previous norms—not to mention apparent commercial imperatives—endowed Enslaved with considerable amounts of what Keith Kahn-Harris calls "transgressive subcultural capital," that is, respect within the scene for the ability to think radically, to reject those ways of doing things that are widely seen as normal, and altogether to stay true to oneself and one's artistic muse.[60] Precisely because singing in Old Norse was a wildly impractical gesture that made no sense within the terms of traditional metal, it became a valuable indication of authenticity and commitment both to the Vikings and to the principles of extreme metal. Viking metal bands were, though, by no means the first or only pop performers to exploit linguistic obscurantism, because the ploy goes back at least as far as Steeleye Span's "Gaudete," which charted in the United Kingdom in December 1972. Performers such as Enya, Dead Can Dance, and Enigma, alongside many other folk and pop groups quite outside extreme metal, have sung in dead languages (most often Latin). For these, as for the Viking metal bands who use Old Norse, dead languages establish their subcultural identity in opposition to mainstream values, but also have a further purpose, because the very strangeness and difficulty of the language is able to impart a sense of the numinous that is felt to be wanting in mundane modern life.[61] Rather than the language they use in the office or to buy their socks, the audience are presented instead with an alien and occulted tongue, imbuing whatever it is used for with a sense of grandeur, mystery, and the intriguing unknown. In this respect, though, it is interesting to note a minor, but perhaps significant, point of difference between Viking metal and other medievalizing users of dead language, because they show rather different attitudes toward provision of translations. Susan Fast has pointed out that the "translation" provided by Steeleye Span in the liner notes to their hit "Gaudete" is in fact anything but, and it largely conceals the Christian message of its sixteenth-century Latin text in favor of a more generalized idealized past Other unencumbered by association with the dominant religion of "respectable" society.[62] Yri notes a similar reticence in Dead Can Dance's failure to provide any translation to the stern Catalan warning about the Day of Judgment that forms the lyrics of their "Song of the Sybil," an act that, she says, "shift[s] the emphasis from a specific religious prayer for spiritual salvation to a vaguely mystical statement."[63] For Viking metal, by contrast, it is exactly the very specific, non-Christian culture of the Vikings that is a primary constituent of their appeal: translations are often made available in album notes or online. The point is generally not to hide the meaning, but, by making the listener work a little harder, to increase the value and significance of the words and to emphasize the importance of the band as intercessors between the audience and their chosen divine.

To conclude this section, it remains to say that Viking metal today remains linguistically varied and complex and subject to conflicting impulses. On the one hand, there is a natural desire to maximize the potential audience by using English, but on the other hand, for the reasons we have explored, it remains extremely important to some to maintain authenticity by deploying an ancient—or at least a local—language. Many bands—including Amon Amarth, the most successful—use English almost exclusively.

Others, such as Týr, generally use English, but will deploy a more distinctive, local language for effect on occasion; Týr use Faroese or Gotudanskt (Faroese-influenced Danish) for their *kvæði*; as their singer Heri Joensen remarked (not without candor), "To use Faeroese sets us apart from other bands and tells in itself that we come from elsewhere and makes us seem more true to our nationality. On the other hand if we only sang in Faeroese I think we would have much less fans abroad."[64] Plenty of bands use their own native (generally Scandinavian) languages in their modern forms; this no longer seems such a departure as once it did. For a significant minority, however, including Wardruna, ancient languages continue to hold their appeal.

Viking Metal and National Identity

Particular attention has been focused recently on the relationship between Viking metal and discourses of race and nation. Viking metal had its origins in Sweden and Norway and the majority of Viking metal bands—certainly of those that are successful—are Scandinavian; most of them display a strong sense of national pride, claiming direct descent from the Vikings and, by virtue of that shared blood, a particularly strong relationship with them. Viking metal, however, is a phenomenon that has spread to a global audience, recruiting both fans and bands from around the world: to take a not especially scientific but nevertheless convenient sample—the alphabetically first hundred bands on *Encyclopaedia Metallum* who list their sound as Viking—provides an indication of the numbers of bands hailing from various countries: Germany (fourteen); Norway (eleven); United States (ten); Canada, Italy, and Sweden (six); France (five); Brazil, Mexico, and the Netherlands (four); Australia, Austria, Spain, and Switzerland (three); Argentina, Finland, and the United Kingdom (two), and Belarus, Denmark, Georgia, Japan, Malta, New Zealand, Portugal, Russia, and Slovakia (one each).[65] Not too much stock should necessarily be placed in the exact figures, but some of the general trends that emerge are probably correct, especially if relative population sizes are borne in mind: The core of Viking metal's popularity is in Germany and Scandinavia, and—to a lesser extent—the English-speaking world, but there are appreciable numbers of bands throughout the rest of Europe and in Latin America and at least some representation in Asia. The globalization of Viking metal has activated and made far more pressing a tension between global appeal and ethnic identity that was implicit in the genre since its origins. Are the Vikings—and the enjoyment to be derived from the evocation of their world—equally available to everyone, regardless of origins? Or does the special link with the Vikings, or Norse myths, that so many of the Scandinavian bands have been so eager to proclaim mean that only Scandinavians (together with the inhabitants of those northern European countries that saw Scandinavian settlement in the Viking Age) are able to claim full rights to Vikingness and membership of the scene?[66] Such exclusive practices may be redoubled where those wishing to engage in the scene are not European or white. In a fascinating article, Hoad notes how the Brazilian Viking metal band Viking Throne use various devices to confront the derision frequently directed at non-Scandinavian members of the scene: by citing supposed Nordic explorations of South America, by stressing the European component in the peopling of Brazil, and by extending their thematic range to include historical narratives of liberation and glory—such as Germanic and Gaulish resistance to the Romans—that, while undeniably European, are not Scandinavian.[67] Such tactics are a playing out of "the friction that underpins the scene": between "the notion of 'Viking' as an identity borne from a specific attitude" and "a Viking identity that is explicitly and unavoidably ethnicized."[68]

Conclusions

Although, as was observed at the beginning, Viking metal is unusual by the standards of other music that evokes the medieval past in that the possibility of recovering the actual music of northern Europe in the Viking Age does not exist, in most other respects it is broadly comparable. It focuses on a desired Other, created in opposition to modernity, onto which a set of characteristics have been projected, although the exact nature of what is required of the Vikings is varied, contested, and has been subject to considerable revision over the decades of the genre's existence. A core set of standard pop culture Viking behaviors and attributes—violence, stripe-sailed longships, axes, beards, excitement, taciturn masculinity, and so on—are common to all, but from within this broad menu particular performers have placed greater emphasis on whichever elements have suited their aims and interests. For many, the simple transgressive and uproarious joy of Viking swashbuckling has been all they wanted, but others have chosen to place more weight on spirituality or on nationalist and racist considerations. The actual sound and musical qualities of Viking metal are not unimportant, because they have helped to define its audience, positioning it within the globally successful heavy metal subculture, but they have not borne the principal burden of historicizing, which has tended to be taken instead by lyrics, language, and visual identities. These are themselves extensions of a much older—and continuing—preoccupation with the Vikings that is manifest in novels, popular history, television, film, and the whole range of popular cultural forms; that popular music would be added to the mixture was, in the end, only a matter of time.

Notes

1. Ingrid de Geer, "Music," in *The Cambridge History of Scandinavia 1: Prehistory to 1520*, ed. Knut Helle (Cambridge: Cambridge University Press, 2003), 550–556.
2. Chihiro Tsukamoto, "What Did They Sound Like? Reconstructing the Music of the Viking Age" (MA thesis, University of Iceland, 2017). Musical instruments of Viking-age Scandinavia are among the targets of the large and ongoing European Union–funded European Music Archaeology Project. Accessed December 19, 2017, http://www.emaproject.eu/.
3. Haithabu (known in German as Hedeby) in present-day Slesvig/Schleswig was one of the principal trading centers of the Viking age. The most recent English translation of the relevant passage is that by Rawia Azzahrawi in Noël Braucher, "Throat Singing in Old

Norse Culture?" (Undergraduate essay, University of Manitoba, 2016), accessed December 19, 2017, https://www.academia.edu/22666429/Throat_Singing_in_Old_Norse_Culture.

4. Useful summaries of these debates are available in Joseph Harris, "The Performance of Old Norse Eddic Poetry: A Retrospective," in *The Oral Epic: Performance and Music*, Intercultural Music Studies 12, ed. Karl Reichl (Berlin: VWB, 2000), 225–232, and Joseph Harris, "'Ethnopaleography' and Recovered Performance: The Problematic Witnesses to 'Eddic Song,'" in *Western Folklore* 62, no. 1/2 (2003): 97–117.

5. See, for instance, Daniel Leech-Wilkinson, "Yearning for the Sound of Medieval Music," in *Mittelalter-Sehnsucht? Texte des interdisziplinären Symposions zur musikalischen Mittelalterrezpetion an der Universität Heidelberg, April 1998*, ed. Annette Kreutziger-Herr and Dorothea Redepenning (Kiel: Wissenschaftsverlag Vauk, 2000), 295–317, 307–309.

6. Jöran Mjöberg, "Romanticism and Revival," in *The Northern World: The History and Heritage of Northern Europe AD 400–1100*, ed. D. M. Wilson (London: Thames & Hudson, 1980), 207–238, 236. The distinction between these two approaches seems to be what Annette Kreutziger-Herr has characterized as the difference between "reproductive" and "creative" medievalism: "Imagining Medieval Music: A Short History," in *Correspondences: Medievalism in Scholarship and the Arts*, Studies in Medievalism 14, ed. Tom Shippey with Martin Arnold (Cambridge: Brewer, 2005), 81–109, 84. See Barbara Eichner, "Richard Wagner's Medieval Visions," this volume, pp. 174–202, for a discussion of Wagner's medievalism.

7. Leech-Wilkinson, "Yearning"; Annette Kreutziger-Herr, "Postmodern Middle Ages: Medieval Music at the Dawn of the Twenty-First Century," in *Florilegium* 15 (1998): 187–205; Kreutziger-Herr, "Imagining Medieval Music"; Susan Fast, "Days of Future Passed: Rock, Pop and the Yearning for the Middle Ages," in *Mittelalter-Sehnsucht? Texte des interdisziplinären Symposions zur musikalischen Mittelalterrezeption an der Universität Heidelberg, April 1998*, ed. Annette Kreutziger-Herr and Dorothea Redepenning (Kiel: Wissenschaftsverlag Vauk, 2000), 35–56.

8. Kreutziger-Herr, "Postmodern Middle Ages," 200; Fast, "Days of Future Passed," 35; see also Tison Pugh and Angela Jane Weisl, *Medievalisms: Making the Past in the Present* (London: Routledge, 2013), 102.

9. Fast, "Days of Future Passed," 36-37; compare with Pugh and Weisl, *Medievalisms*, 101.

10. Leech-Wilkinson, "Yearning," 295; c.f. Fast, "Days of Future Passed," 39–40.

11. Kirsten Yri, "Medievalism and Exoticism in the Music of Dead Can Dance," in *Current Musicology* 85 (2008): 53–72, 56.

12. Viking metal has a robust body of scholarship of its own, but it exists largely in isolation from academic discussion of what are perceived as more mainstream and legitimate musics. Note, though, the short but useful discussions in Pugh and Weisl, *Medievalisms*, 108–110; and Helen Dell, "Musical Medievalism and the Harmony of the Spheres," in *The Cambridge Companion to Medievalism*, ed. Louise D'Arcens (Cambridge: Cambridge University Press, 2016), 60–74, 70–72.

13. Deena Weinstein, *Heavy Metal: The Music and Its Culture*, revised ed. (Boston: Da Capo Press, 2000).

14. See Simon Trafford and Aleks Pluskowski, "Antichrist Superstars: The Vikings in Hard Rock and Heavy Metal," in *Mass Market Medievalism*, ed. David W. Marshall (Jefferson, NC: McFarland, 2007), 57–73, 59.

15. The literature on modern enthusiasm for the Vikings is far too large to list here; note, however, that high culture is better covered than popular culture. See, for example, Lars Lönnroth, "The Vikings in History and Legend," in *The Oxford Illustrated History of the*

Vikings, ed. P. H. Sawyer (Oxford: Oxford University Press, 1997), 225–249; Andrew Wawn, *The Vikings and the Victorians: Inventing the Old North in 19th-Century Britain* (Cambridge: Brewer, 2000). On popular interest in the Vikings, see Alexandra Service, "Popular Vikings: Constructions of Viking Identity in Twentieth Century Britain" (DPhil thesis, University of York, 1998). Imke von Helden, *Norwegian Native Art: Cultural Identity in Norwegian Metal Music* (Zürich: Lit Verlag, 2017) is a fascinating analysis of the way in which Viking metal responds to attitudes to the Vikings within wider Scandinavian society, but arrived too late to influence this essay.

16. On the Vikings in cinematographic and televisual culture, see the various essays gathered in *The Vikings on Film: Essays on Depictions of the Nordic Middle Ages*, ed. Kevin Harty (Jefferson, NC: McFarland, 2011).

17. See especially Fast, "Days of Future Passed," but also Edward Macan, *Rocking the Classics: English Progressive Rock and the Counterculture* (Oxford: Oxford University Press, 1997).

18. Kreutziger-Herr, "Postmodern Middle Ages," 192–197; Fast, "Days of Future Passed," 47–54.

19. http://www.metal-archives.com/browse/genre, accessed April 10, 2017. Precise enumeration of the relative popularity of bands and scenes presents considerable difficulties: record sales might once have been a metric, but figures are frequently unavailable and are in any case increasingly meaningless in scenes where file sharing is an abundant means of distribution. Counting the bands active in a genre, as used here (and previously in Deena Weinstein, "Pagan Metal," in *Pop Pagans: Paganism and Popular Music*, Studies in Contemporary and Historical Paganism, ed. Donna Weston and Andy Bennett [Routledge: London, 2013], 58–75) carries its own difficulties, because both the names of subgenres and the criteria for inclusion in a given subgenre are alarmingly flexible and inconsistently applied: A strong argument could be advanced that Amon Amarth be regarded as the leading current Viking metal band, but for *Encycylopaedia Metallum*'s purposes they are classified as "Melodic death metal." Another possible approach is to count the number of "likes" on bands' Facebook pages—an ad hoc expedient proposed (in full knowledge of its weaknesses) by Karl Spracklen, "'To Holmgard…and Beyond': Folk Metal Fantasies and Hegemonic White Masculinites," in *Metal Music Studies* 1, no. 3 (2015): 359–378, but this privileges a social network that is not necessarily that most favored by the typical Viking metal demographic. Nevertheless, see below, n42.

20. See Caitlin Vaughn Carlos, "'Ramble On': Medievalism as Nostalgic Practice in Led Zeppelin's Use of J. R. R. Tolkien," this volume, pp. 530–546.

21. Trafford and Pluskowski, "Antichrist Superstars," especially 60–62.

22. http://samling.nasjonalmuseet.no/en/object/NG.M.00258, accessed December 19, 2017.

23. Although Forsberg turned away from the subject of Vikings in his mid-1990s work, he returned to it for his later albums before his death in 2004.

24. https://artuk.org/discover/artworks/the-funeral-of-a-viking-204862, accessed December 19, 2017.

25. This argument is made in greater detail in Simon Trafford, "Blood, Fire, Death: Bathory and the Birth of Viking Metal," in *Gathering of the Tribe: Music and Heavy Conscious Creation*, ed. M. Goodall (London: Headpress, 2013), 302–308, 305–307.

26. Imke Von Helden, "Scandinavian Metal Attack"; on extreme metal in general, Keith Kahn-Harris, *Extreme Metal* is indispensable.

27. The activities of the Norwegian black metal scene centered on the Helvete record shop in Oslo attracted the attention not just of the pop music press, but also of the mainstream

media. They are famously charted in Michael Moynihan and Didrik Søderlind, *Lords of Chaos: The Bloody Rise of the Satanic Metal Underground*, 2nd ed. (Venice, CA: Feral House, 2003; 1st ed. 1998), a book that, in itself, considerably contributed to the mythologizing of the early scene. It requires careful and critical reading. See Ross Hagen, "Musical Style, Ideology and Mythology in Norwegian Black Metal," in *Metal Rules the Globe: Heavy Metal Music around the World*, ed. Jeremy Wallach, Harris M. Berger, and Paul D. Greene (Durham, NC: Duke University Press, 2011), 180–199, 181. On church burning, see Gry Mørk, "Why Didn't the Churches Begin to Burn a Thousand Years Earlier?," in *Religion and Popular Music in Europe: New Expressions of Sacred and Secular Identity*, ed. Thomas Bossius, Andreas Häger, and Keith Kahn-Harris (London: Tauris, 2011), 124–144.

28. Moynihan and Søderlind, *Lords of Chaos*; Dell, "Musical Medievalisms," 70–72, but see also Laura Wiebe Taylor, "Nordic Nationalisms: Black Metal Takes Norway's Everyday Racisms to the Extreme," in *The Metal Void: First Gatherings*, ed. Niall Scott and Imke von Helden (Oxford: Inter-Disciplinary Press, 2010), 161–173, which argues that the roots of black metal's Nazi tendencies lie at least as much in everyday Norwegian nationalist discourse as in black metal.

29. Mørk, "Why Didn't the Churches Begin to Burn a Thousand Years Earlier?"; Hagen, "Musical Style, Ideology and Mythology in Norwegian Black Metal," 190–194.

30. Hagen, "Musical Style, Ideology and Mythology in Norwegian Black Metal," 183. Important arguments on the depoliticizing strategies that have led black metal to avoid outright fascism are put forward in Keith Kahn-Harris, "The 'Failure' of Youth Culture: Reflexivity, Music and Politics in the Black Metal Scene," in *European Journal of Cultural Studies* 7, no. 1 (2004): 95–111.

31. Strictly, folk metal begins with the 1991 release of the first album by the English band Skyclad, followed up by the formation of Cruachan in Ireland in 1992 (see Wikipedia, "Folk metal," accessed December 19, 2017, https://en.wikipedia.org/wiki/Folk_metal; Spracklen, "To Holmgard…and Beyond"; Aaron Patrick Mulvany, "'Reawakening Pride Once Lost': Indigeneity and European Folk Metal" [MA thesis, Wesleyan University, 2000], 45–95), but the scene did not begin to proliferate until the late 1990s and only took off in the twenty-first century. See also Scott Troyer's chapter on Pagan music, this volume, "Medievalism and Identity Construction in Pagan Folk Music," pp. 586–610.

32. Steve Winick, "Eine kleine mittelalterliche Music: German Folk-Rock Gets Medieval," in *Dirty Linen* 123 (2006): 40–43; "A Medieval Bestiary: More Folk-Rock from the Middle Ages," in *Dirty Linen* 128 (2007): 24–27; "Old Songs for New Folks: Early Music and Folk-Rock," in *Dirty Linen* 139 (2009): 18–19; see also Kirsten Yri, "Corvus Corax: Medieval Rock, the Minstrel, and Cosmopolitanism as Anti-Nationalism," *Popular Music* 38, no. 3 (2019). On *Mittelaltermärkte* and their associated music, see Katharina Zeppezauer-Wachauer, *Kurzwîl als Entertainment: Das Mittelalterfest als populärkulturelle Mittelalterrezeption: Historisch-ethnografische Betrachtungen zum Event als Spiel* (Marburg: Tectum Verlag, 2012); Iwen Schmees, *Musik in der Mittelalter-Szene. Stilrichtungen, Repertoire und Interpretation* (Hamburg: Diplomica-Verlag, 2008).

33. Weinstein, "Pagan Metal," 59. See also Scott Troyer's contribution to this volume, "Medievalism and Identity Construction in Pagan Folk Music," pp. 586–610.

34. Weinstein, "Pagan Metal," 71.

35. Kennet Granholm, "'Sons of Northern Darkness': Heathen Influences in Black Metal and Neofolk Music," in *Numen* 58 (2011): 514–544.

36. Mulvany, "Reawakening Pride Once Lost," 46.

37. Von Helden, "Scandinavian Metal Attack."

38. Catherine Hoad, "'Hold the Heathen Hammer High': Viking Metal from the Local to the Global," paper presented at the International Association for the Study of Popular Music Australia–New Zealand Conference, Hobart, December, 5–7, 2012, 1–2, https://www. academia.edu/5768762/Hold_the_Heathen_Hammer_High_-_Viking_Metal_from_ the_Local_to_the_Global.

39. Von Helden, "Scandinavian Metal Attack," 35–36.

40. Grutle Kjellson and Ivar Bjørnson, "Enslaved—Grutle Kjellson & Ivar Bjørnson on Axioma Ethica Odini," *Thrash Hits*, September 22, 2010, accessed December 19, 2017, http://www.thrashhits.com/2010/09/interview-enslaved-grutle-kjellson-ivar-bj%C3%B8rnson-on-axioma-ethica-odini/.

41. Deena Weinstein, "The Globalization of Metal," in *Metal Rules the Globe: Heavy Metal Music around the World*, ed. J. Wallach, Harris M. Berger, and Paul D. Greene (Durham, NC: Duke University Press, 2011), 34–59.

42. Imke von Helden, "Barbarians and Literature: Viking Metal and Its Links to Old Norse Mythology," in *The Metal Void: First Gatherings*, ed. N. W. R. Scott and I. von Helden (Oxford: Inter-disciplinary Press, 2010), 5.

43. See above, n19. As of April 18, 2017, Amon Amarth had 1,334,836 likes, Enslaved 264,496, Týr 252,631, and Bathory 63,644. For comparison, Eluveitie, the most popular non–Viking folk metal band, had 823,775; Metallica, the world's biggest heavy metal band, had 37,635,278, and Shakira, the most popular pop star on Facebook, had 104,436,175.

44. Grimfrost, accessed 6 August 2019, http://www.grimfrost.com.

45. The drama series *Vikings* (History Channel: 2013–) has been a popular hit around the world, consistently maintaining a place in the top five most popular television series as listed by IMDB: http://www.imdb.com/title/tt2306299/.

46. Their later music has taken a different direction, borrowing in particular from progressive metal, but it remains generally free of folk influences or devices that their audience might interpret as characteristically Viking.

47. Mulvany, "Reawakening Pride Once Lost," 36–42.

48. Steven P. Ashby and John Schofield, "'Hold the Heathen Hammer High': Representation, Re-enactment and the Construction of 'Pagan' Heritage," *International Journal of Heritage Studies* 21, no. 5 (2015): 493–511, 501; Spracklen, "To Holmgard…and Beyond"; Hoad, "'Hold the Heathen Hammer High.'"

49. Einar Selvik, interview with the author, January 27, 2016. I would like to extend my thanks to Einar Selvik for his help.

50. See, for instance, Katherine Bergeron, "The Virtual Sacred: Finding God at Tower Records," *The New Republic*, February 27, 1995, 29–34.

51. John Haines, "Living Troubadours and Other Recent Uses for Medieval Music," *Popular Music* 23, no. 2 (2004): 133–153; Yri, "Medievalism and Exoticism," 59.

52. Trafford and Pluskowski, "Antichrist Superstars"; Service, "Popular Vikings."

53. Compare with von Helden, "Scandinavian Metal Attack," 34.

54. Bathory's lyrics are primarily about ordinary Viking warriors rather than the gods (Anna G. Piotrowska, "Scandinavian Heavy Metal as an Intertextual Play with Norse Myths", in Scott A. Wilson (ed.), Music at the Extremes: Essays on Sounds Outside the Mainstream (Jefferson, NC: McFarland, 2015), 101–114, 104–105), as are the majority of Amon Amarth's.

55. Mulvany, "Reawakening Pride Once Lost," 34; Trafford & Pluskowski, "Antichrist Superstars," 63; Kahn-Harris, *Extreme Metal*, 40–41; Weinstein, "Pagan Metal," 61.

56. Weinstein, "Pagan Metal," 45.

57. Keith Kahn-Harris, "'Roots'?: The Relationship between the Global and the Local within the Extreme Metal Scene," *Popular Music* 19, no. 1 (2000): 13–30, 20; Weinstein, "Pagan Metal," 65–68.

58. The ploy is strangely executed, perhaps indicating the difficulty that the then-teenaged band had in putting their aspirations into effect: Rather than using Old Norse as such, most of the songs are in (modern) Icelandic, presumably on the grounds that the language resembles Old Norse much more closely than any of the continental Scandinavian tongues and was an acceptable substitute.

59. To be fair, the potential drawbacks for Enslaved were minimized by the fact that the shrieked style of their singing in this period rendered many of their words virtually unintelligible even to someone fluent in the language in question. See Weinstein, "Pagan Metal," 67.

60. The idea of subcultural capital was developed by Sarah Thornton in *Club Cultures: Music, Media and Subcultural Capital* (Cambridge, MA: Polity Press, 1995) as an adaptation of Pierre Bourdieu's original concept of cultural capital (*The Field of Cultural Production* [Oxford: Polity Press, 1993]). On subcultural capital in the extreme metal scene, see Kahn-Harris, *Extreme Metal*, 121–131.

61. Fast, "Days of Future Passed," 46; Yri, "Medievalism and Exoticism."

62. Fast, "Days of Future Passed," 46–47.

63. Yri, "Medievalism and Exoticism," 59.

64. Heri Joensen, "Tyr," *Lords of Metal e-zine* 34, February 2004, accessed December 19, 2017, http://www.lordsofmetal.nl/en/interviews/view/id/757.

65. http://www.metal-archives.com, accessed April 15, 2017.

66. Spracklen, "To Holmgard…and Beyond," 376.

67. Hoad, "Hold the Heathen Hammer High," 5.

68. Ibid., 6.

CHAPTER 26

MEDIEVALISM AND IDENTITY CONSTRUCTION IN PAGAN FOLK MUSIC

SCOTT R. TROYER

PICTURE the scene: two women ride on horseback through a forest of deciduous trees and conifers, led by men dressed in black. The women wear modestly decorated black corset dresses with red accents. The men wear black trousers, shirts, and jackets; one has added a dark leather vest to his ensemble, another is shirtless in a floor-length coat fringed with animal fur. Everyone is wearing large leather belts and a few pieces of rustic jewelry. The group emerges from the tree line into a sandy clearing, where more women draped in loose white cloth pick up ribbons around a maypole and begin dancing, while the group in black begins singing and playing music on the hurdy-gurdy, nyckelharpa, and bass drum. The music is augmented by instruments and electronic sounds outside the diegesis. What time period are we witnessing? The visuals and the choice of instruments seem to suggest something archaic, perhaps medieval, while the rest of the soundscape places us, the listeners, in the twenty-first century.

This is the scene that opens Faun's "Walpurgisnacht" music video. Faun is a German Pagan folk band that describes itself as specializing in music of the Middle Ages and Renaissance.[1] Although one would be sorely disappointed if he or she expected to hear a reconstruction of medieval music at the band's concerts, the band is clearly engaging in a form of medievalism: referencing an imagined Middle Ages in the twenty-first century. This medievalist bent is instrumental in the construction of Faun's identity as a Pagan folk band; medieval and folk instruments define the band's sound, and medievalist clothing defines their appearance. Such constructions are common, or perhaps even essential characteristics that distinguish Pagan groups in the twentieth and twenty-first centuries.

First, it would be beneficial to explore exactly what I mean by "medievalism." This collection highlights the great variety of ways in which the postmedieval Western world has expressed its fascination with the Middle Ages. However, what, exactly, medievalism is remains slippery and difficult to define. From Wagner, to Orff, to the historically informed performance movement and the chant craze of the 1990s, medieval references have taken many and varied forms. The kind of medievalism that arises within Pagan folk music can be defined more by its function than by its signs. Medieval-inspired clothing, texts, melodies, and instruments help convey a medievalism that is defined as living harmoniously with nature in a pre- or non-Christian past free from the restrictions of modern society.

Paganism is often used as an umbrella term for individuals and religious communities who identify with pre-Christian European religions and religious practices.[2] While modern Pagans firmly claim pre-Christian religious traditions as their heritage, there are very few concrete, continuous ties to this older pagan culture.[3] Despite this, identification with pre-Christian Europe is one of the most essential elements for those concerned with defining the movement, both inside and out. It is here that the use of medieval references might seem somewhat counterproductive, because the period was dominated by the expansion of Christendom and the power of the church. Extant musical sources from which modern Pagan musicians might draw all come from a context in which the Christian church has completely subsumed older local religious practices. To square the historical record with constructed Pagan identities, musicians and audiences use medievalism as a tool with which they can craft an imagined past that is really rooted in an idealized Dark Ages. This invocation conjures up both the early medieval period and the connotations of the name "Dark Ages," but I will continue to use the term Middle Ages rather than Dark Ages in an effort to remain consistent with the Pagan music community.[4] The return to an idealized past populated by what are now religious and cultural Others also carries with it a strong environmentalist undercurrent and intersects with a focus on the body as a site of liberation.[5]

Medievalism, then, works to establish the ideological authenticity of Pagan groups and individuals, while also being formed, shaped, and presented by those same groups as authentic. It is at this intersection that Pagan music and Pagan identity engage in a reciprocal relationship, wherein authenticity is constructed in music through its adoption of a Pagan identity and Pagan identity is created and maintained through music. The content produced by Pagan folk artists embodies Pagan identity and influences Paganism through three primary, interrelated means: the aural, the textual, and the visual.

Paganism has been a growing area of scholarly study since its first international scholarly conference was held in 1993.[6] The practice of Paganism itself also saw a surge in the 1980s and 1990s and has exhibited continual growth since then. This growth is indebted to several cultural and economic factors, foremost among them the advent of the Internet.[7] With the growth of modern Pagan religions also comes a growth in Pagan music. Again, the role of the Internet, along with the reduced cost of production and availability of new technology, in the creation of new Pagan popular music cannot be overstated. Pagan music is not only created by practicing Pagans, but also includes music that has been used by or marketed to them. Thus, the world of Pagan music extends far beyond those bands that claim Paganism as a primary identity and is complicated by the issues of intent, interpretation, and appropriation.[8]

Pagan music and the Pagan scene, more generally, construct a sense of community or of religious–ideological solidarity. Participating in events like religious ceremonies or even popular music concerts is a vital part of constructing and maintaining a Pagan identity.[9] For music intended to be read as Pagan, either by the musician or by another party promoting or receiving it as such, this logically necessitates that said music be established as authentically or authoritatively Pagan, as the community has broad interpretive power. Damh the Bard, a popular Pagan artist and the pendragon of the Order of Bards, Ovates and Druids, emphasizes the role of intent and interpretation in the production of authentically Pagan music: "I guess to me Pagan music isn't a genre, it's a theme, an attitude, and a way of expressing our love for our Gods, myths, traditions, and the natural world."[10]

The Roots of Modern Paganism

The popular trends of the twentieth century produced an environment within which recently resurrected Paganism could thrive and become a significant cultural phenomenon. The eighteenth-century philosopher Jean-Jacques Rousseau planted the seeds of modern Pagan growth when he theorized an ancient, polytheistic religion that was based in nature, one that promised solutions to contemporary woes.[11] Rousseau's conception of an ancient nature religion in need of rediscovery is at the root of current Pagan beliefs. Much of the defining work of Pagan scholars in the 1990s substituted "nature religion" for Paganism.[12] One would be hard-pressed to find a significant number of Pagan groups that do not express in some way a feeling of connection to the natural world.[13]

While Rousseau expressed a practical interest in an ancient pagan nature religion as a latent presence in Europe that held solutions to contemporary woes, nineteenth-century romantics celebrated nature, the past, and the peasantry with a religious fervor of their own. The idea of an ancient, pre-Christian nature religion was predictably popular in a European society where the ideology of Rousseau's imagined paganism—that is, a religious reverence for nature preserved from the ancient or medieval past and practiced by the peasantry (or folk/*Volk*)—was essentially worshipped.[14] This also helps lay the foundation for a phenomenon one might call the "medieval-folk slippage" that characterizes many modern manifestations of medievalism.

The legacy of romanticism and of Rousseau's vegetation cult was also carried into the twentieth century by the Scottish anthropologist Sir James Frazer. Looking specifically at music, Frazer developed the idea that folk songs and traditions are the subdued remnants of pre-Christian paganism based on the work of the Grimm brothers and their student, Wilhelm Mannhardt.[15] Thus, in Frazerian terms, folk music and traditions developed during the Middle Ages as a way to covertly practice paganism under the noses of Christian oppressors—a hypothesis supported, again, by the medieval-folk slippage.

The growing skepticism of Christianity in the twentieth century, coupled with the mid-late-century counterculture, created an environment wherein anthropocentric Christianity could be abandoned for ecocentric Paganism. In particular, the romanticism of the mid-century counterculture, which rejected the "rational-scientific basis of progress and development in Western society" and embraced a "back-to-the-land" mentality, created the environment in which the Paganism of the late twentieth and early twenty-first century initially manifested in a recognizable form.[16] While most of the musicians who inhabited the mid-century countercultural scene did not explicitly identify as Pagan, the themes these musicians explored resonated with Pagan audiences and were adopted by explicitly Pagan musicians in the late twentieth and early twenty-first centuries.[17]

Columnist Nathan Hall identifies Gwydion Pendderwen as the earliest musician to popularize "music that he clearly branded as Pagan" in the 1970s.[18] Not only did many values of the countercultural moment align with what would become Pagan values, but also, perhaps just as important, the counterculture "brought with it an openness to alternative ideologies, spiritualties and aesthetic beliefs."[19] This openness was essential to the growth and popularity of Paganism in the Western world after centuries of normative Christian domination.

The first major parallel between the counterculture and Paganism is the oppositional approach to "mainstream societal values," which is clearly also represented by the opposition to Western society mentioned previously.[20] Second, the counterculture drew on premodern imagery and themes, as well as skepticism of a rational-scientific concept of progress, to counter twentieth-century technocracy.[21] The result was an emphasis on an idyllic, premodern past, a renewed interest in spirituality, and a connection to the natural world.[22]

These emphases arise in the 1973 film *The Wicker Man*, a twentieth-century countercultural film that illustrates the connections between nineteenth-century romanticism and Frazerian paganism. *The Wicker Man* follows the staunchly Christian police officer Sergeant Howie's investigation of the disappearance of a young girl on the Scottish island Summerisle, where residents have abandoned Christianity and embraced Paganism, or, as the island's leader Lord Summerisle puts it, worship "the old gods." Howie meets with Lord Summerisle, and the latter explains how the islanders came to once again embrace these gods: Summerisle's grandfather was a Victorian scientist who came to the island in search of cheap labor and the proper growing conditions for new strains of plants that he had developed. To inspire the islanders to work for him, he allowed them to resume worshipping the old gods, presumably because the people desired to do so, but were forbidden by the island's authorities. Summerisle explains that while his grandfather looked to paganism as a practical means of convincing the islanders to work for him, Summerisle and his father had grown to embrace the old gods genuinely.

The Victorian grandfather is analogous to Rousseau and his practical approach to localized, nature-based religions, while the father and Lord Summerisle could be interpreted as representatives of nineteenth-century romanticism and the twentieth-century counterculture in which the film is set. Summerisle is not ignorant or regressive, but rather is fully aware of the relationship between Pagan worship and Christianity on the island and has actively chosen to reject the mainstream societal values represented by Christian society, as well as the technocracy that had suppressed pagan practices for centuries and prevented the islanders from prospering. When he is accused by Howie of being a Pagan, Summerisle responds, "A heathen, conceivably, but not, I hope, an unenlightened one." The back-to-the-land mentality and its opposition to mainstream society as expressed by the return to an ancient religion not practiced since the Middle Ages is eloquently summed up by Summerisle near the close of that scene: "What my grandfather started out of expediency, my father continued out of love. He brought me up the same way: to reverence [sic] the music and the drama and the rituals of the old gods. To love nature, and to fear it, and to rely on it, and to appease it when necessary."

Pagan Music in the Late Twentieth Century

While the roots of modern Paganism lie in the lead-up to the middle of the twentieth century, modern Pagan music has been more directly and heavily influenced by popular music in the second half of the twentieth century. *The Wild Hunt*, a spin-off website from the religious blog hub *Patheos*, recently began hosting a column about Pagan music (March 26, 2017), and Nathan Hall's inaugural post seeks to define what exactly Pagan music is, partly by tracing its history back to the mid-century folk revival and Gwydion Pendderwen.[23]

In terms of musical style, Pendderwen very clearly resembles other singers of the 1960s folk music revival. Nevertheless, it would be a mistake to assume that Pagan music is simply a subgenre of this broader category. As mentioned previously, Pagan music is that which is intended to be or is understood as authentically Pagan; modern Pagan music conveys to its audience a reverence for pagan gods, myths, traditions, and the natural world.[24] The classification of music as Pagan is separate from generic classifications, even as certain genres intersect with Pagan themes and have had greater influence on Pagan musicians.

Pendderwen's 1975 *Songs for the Old Religion* stands as the first example of Pagan popular music in the second half of the twentieth century. The album establishes its authenticity musically through its adoption of the style of the folk music revival, resembling musicians like the Incredible String Band, whose 1968 album *The Hangman's Beautiful Daughter* also contains a variety of pagan references, textually through its focus on specifically Pagan practice and ideology and visually through album art, which features an image of Pendderwen adorned with Pagan symbols, such as a pentagram pendant.[25]

The British folk revival also played a significant role in shaping Pagan music in the late twentieth century. The band Traffic's hit song "John Barleycorn" personifies the grain that is used in whiskey and beer, its sardonic effect captured by the grim actions of sowing, harrowing, and harvesting "Barleycorn" until he is "dead."[26] This allegorical narrative inspired a significantly sympathetic reaction among Pagans. While clearly a drinking song (traceable to 1568 and potentially older still), the personification of plants and the narrative of ritualistic barbarous torture and rebirth inspired some, like the Watersons, to attribute the song to an ancient mythology.[27] This interpretation has persisted and extends beyond the British folk-rock scene, and subsequent versions of the song have frequently played into this idea, including a number of renditions by amateur and semiprofessional musicians.[28] These pagan references were initially points of interest to British folk-rock musicians, but they were never intended to be central to the interpretation of folk music, and many British folk musicians and audiences consider folk's reliance on pagan "superstition," at best, a necessary evil with regard to the preservation of the folk tradition.[29]

Folk rock was not the only genre to embrace pagan or Pagan themes: Metal also gravitated toward these ideas and heavily influenced subsequent Pagan musicians. Metal has its origins in the music of Black Sabbath and Led Zeppelin and has always included Pagan elements, specifically those dealing with the occult or Viking warriors, as a means of rejecting mainstream society and religion.[30] Deena Weinstein recognizes a handful of bands in the early 1990s that brought Pagan themes to the fore of their music, including Skyclad, Bathory, and Enslaved.[31] All of these bands are also recognized as Viking metal bands by Simon Trafford and Aleks Pluskowski.[32]

The choice of Vikings as subject matter resonates with both metal and Pagan music: for metal, Vikings are violent, romantic antiheroes that represent a hypermasculinity, while for Paganism, Vikings represent medieval warriors who resisted Christian conversion and serve as an attractive alterity to normative Western or Christian society, as well as a connection to ancient paganism.[33] These connections allow Pagan metal music to draw on the cultural capital contained within references to the Dark Ages as represented by more general medievalism and build a distinctly non-Christian identity out of them. The attraction to an identity that is "bad" to Christianity's "good" is evidenced throughout Paganism, such as in Damh the Bard's imagining of Lucifer as a benevolent god of the earth in his song "Green and Grey," or in Omnia's choice to associate themselves with J. R. R. Tolkein's villains from *The Lord of the Rings* in their song "Get the Halfling" and in a question-and-answer YouTube video.[34] Such references, transgressive in dominant Western culture, enhance the credibility of Pagan artists seeking to differentiate themselves from a Christian society often seen as equivalent to said culture.

Metal bands often use Pagan as a secondary or tertiary descriptor, and all place their primary emphasis on the characteristics of metal: loud sounds, amplified guitars, massive drum kits, and electronic keyboards.[35] However, bands that identify explicitly with Paganism also often include folk or premodern instruments, like tin whistles or the hurdy-gurdy.[36] This is a trait they share with more folk-oriented expressions of Pagan music. The metal band In Extremo, as an example, includes bagpipes as one of their primary instruments. In Extremo also draws from folk or medieval music, like in their rendition of the thirteenth-century *Minnesang* "Palästinalied." Pagan metal groups also use linguistic signifiers of pre-Christian European identity by singing in regional or ancient languages, following the broader move away from English lyrics in the early 1990s. The lyrical content of Pagan metal bands is as important as the language in which they are sung. Pagan metal lyrics often identify with pre-Christian Europe by expressing anti-Christian sentiments (not uncommon in metal generally), referring to specific premodern or pre-Christian practices, or, less often, voicing national socialist or racist sentiments. Visually, these bands often utilize pagan or anti-Christian symbols in their album art and perform in medievalist attire or in clothing meant to invoke a sense of the barbaric.

The third late twentieth-century genre to provoke a positive reaction from Pagan audiences is Goth, although many Goth musicians did not consider themselves Pagan, nor did they intend to market their music to a specifically Pagan audience.[37] The traits of Goth music that attracted Pagan audiences are very similar to those that gave birth to modern Paganism in the 1960s counterculture: "a romantic, decadent and inward-looking alternative to anger and nihilism."[38] Goth culture also appropriated a variety of religious symbols without committing to any one tradition, similar, again, to the openness of the counterculture mentioned previously.[39] Within Goth, a subset of musicians have made consistent use of medieval and occult elements, themes, and general references in service to Goth's broader obsession with an idyllic temporal space apart from the present moment.[40] Members of this "neofolk" subgroup not only directly influence Pagan musicians, but also, in many cases, move seamlessly between both worlds.[41]

Dead Can Dance is one of the clearest examples of a Goth band that never aligned itself with modern Paganism, but was consumed enthusiastically by Pagan audiences. This owes much to Dead Can Dance's alterity, representation of the Other through the incorporation of medievalist elements, exploration of pre-Christian themes, and highlighting of non-Western instruments.[42] Additionally, this style of "ethno-Gothic" music bears the strongest resemblance to the musical stylings of Omnia and Faun, particularly in their efforts to relate to the past as Other.[43] These bands harness the alterity of Dead Can Dance's conception of the past to create a Pagan identity that is also Other to the modern, Western world. This musical and lyrical content is what most strongly resonates with Pagan consumers.

Pagan Folk Music in the Twenty-First Century

Since Pagan music is characterized more strongly by ideology and specific associations than by strictly generic elements, it seems most productive to identify a subset of the Pagan music scene and explore the ways musicians within that subset negotiate their identity as Pagan musicians. "Pagan folk" musicians offer a particularly poignant window into the world of modern Pagan music, in part because of the historical connection between Paganism and folk music. As a genre, Pagan folk is loosely defined and is frequently applied to a variety of popular music groups that incorporate folk instruments and Pagan themes into their work. These bands stylistically draw not only from folk music, but also from metal and Goth. The music streaming service last.fm lists its top two artists labeled "Pagan folk" as Omnia and Faun. Both have distinct sounds, but they share a preference for European folk instruments and Pagan textual themes. Omnia is listed as the more popular artist, coming in at 172,787 "listeners," while Faun is listed as having 149,516.[44] The streaming service Spotify similarly rates the two very highly, and a search of the service for "Pagan folk" pulls up almost exclusively songs by Faun. Additionally, Omnia and Faun both self-identify as Pagan folk.[45] These two bands are also two of the first to identify with the Pagan folk genre, and both were formed and released albums within a few years of each other in the late 1990s.[46]

Omnia is a northern European quintet featuring Steve "Sic" Evans-van der Harten, his wife, Jenny Evans-van der Harten, Daphyd "Crow" Sens, Rob "Raido" van Barschot, and Satria Karsono. They play in a variety of musical styles, using a wide assortment of instruments, including drums, guitars, didgeridoo, hurdy-gurdy, harp, and several types of flutes.

Faun is a German band whose membership includes Oliver S. Tyr, Fiona Rüggeberg, Rüdiger Maul, Niel Mitra, Stephen Groth, and Laura Fella. The group also plays medievalist instruments, including the bagpipes, hurdy-gurdy, cittern, recorder, harp, numerous percussion instruments, and many others combined with electronic sounds mixed by Mitra.[47] Faun also performs some concerts without the use of "modern" instruments or electronic sounds.

Omnia and Faun offer two excellent examples of the ways in which musicians navigate Pagan identity in the twenty-first century, sometimes converging and sometimes diverging in their approach. Both draw on the legacies of Rousseau, romanticism, Frazer, and the twentieth-century counterculture to construct this specifically Pagan identity that stands in opposition to a Christianity represented by dominant Western culture. The bands draw on familiar textual, aural, and visual cues of medievalism for three reasons. The first function of medievalism is to create a connection to a pre-Christian past. Second, medievalism houses nostalgia for an idyllic, premodern world in which humans lived harmoniously with nature or were perhaps even subservient to it. The third function depends on the second insofar as it reinforces an embodied liberation of the self from the restrictions of Western society.

Omnia

Omnia engage in a form of medievalism that is focused on the alterity of the Middle Ages; they rely largely on signals of Otherness to indicate an imagined connection to the past. The Other is communicated through what Pitzl-Waters calls the "'ethno-Gothic' formula" or template established by Dead Can Dance, wherein the Middle Ages is represented as an "internal Other."[48] By extension, Otherness is also partially signified through the aforementioned medievalism and medieval-folk slippage; according to Andy Letcher, "part of folk's appeal is that it confers *alterity* through identification with tradition and the past."[49] For a Pagan identity that derives a significant portion of its distinctiveness through a pre-Christian or un-Christian affiliation, that which is normative in the modern Western world is equated to Christianity, and it is through alterity, or Otherness, that said identity is expressed; to be Pagan is to reject the Christian society that has dominated since the end of the Middle Ages and thus to reject that which is normative. This alterity is also sometimes drawn from sources other than the medieval or the folk to much the same effect. Understanding that medieval references, folk elements, and alterity function synonymously in this music is essential to deciphering the construction of an un-Christian connection.

One of the most visible and audible expressions of medievalist Otherness in Omnia's music is the instrumentation. The hurdy-gurdy presents one of the strongest connections to the medieval and takes full advantage of the medieval-folk slippage. The cranked chordophone is not part of the modern classical tradition and evokes a sense of the archaic and the simple through its use of drone strings. In recent years, the hurdy-gurdy has often appeared in medieval, folk, and metal bands. Considering the importance of medieval, folk, and metal music to modern Pagan music—and the phenomenon of medieval-folk slippage—it is hardly surprising to see Pagan folk bands also pick up the instrument.

Omnia foreground the hurdy-gurdy when they use it, often making it a primary melodic instrument. In their song "I Don't Speak Human" on the *Musick and Poëtree* album, as an example, the hurdy-gurdy provides a countermelody to the vocals; in "Alive" from the *World of Omnia* album, the hurdy-gurdy is featured during instrumental interludes. Part of Omnia's style, however, is the variety of instruments they play. While the hurdy-gurdy is a popular choice, in live performance it can be freely interchanged with other instruments. As an example, in Omnia's 2008 DVD recording of a live performance, Jenny plays her instrumental interludes on the hurdy-gurdy, while performances at Castelfest in 2015 feature Jenny performing on the harp instead. The two instruments can be easily exchanged in performance because both communicate alterity through the medieval-folk slippage.

Another instrumental choice that communicates a sense of alterity is the didgeridoo. At first glance, the indigenous wind instrument from Australia has very little to do with the medieval past Omnia draws on, yet the instrument has become an integral part of the band's sound and has been picked up by other groups that utilize medievalism as a means of connecting to an idealized European past.[50] The didgeridoo likely evokes a medieval sound for these groups because of its capacity as a drone instrument, its rhythmic potential, and its alterity to Western classical and popular music traditions.

The didgeridoo has been a part of Omnia since their 2003 album 3, often functioning as a bass instrument. The performer often switches between several didgeridoos during a performance; the slide didgeridoo offers the greatest flexibility to the musicians, because its telescopic capacity transforms it from the drone instrument mentioned previously into a melodic bass instrument. The alterity of the instrument not only helps position the band outside modern Western society, but also aids the medieval-as-Other construction. Additionally, the association with indigenous Australians also reinforces the pre-Christian aspect of Pagan identity, because the native peoples of Australia were also colonized by Christian invaders.

Many of Omnia's songs are new compositions and rarely refer explicitly to the Middle Ages. Rather, several of the band's songs strongly imply a Celtic-influenced music. Celtic music and culture are often interpreted as medieval, or at least distinct from modern Western society—specifically the Celtic world is often seen as a "pastoral world populated by Noble Savages."[51] This conception of the Celtic meshes perfectly with the Pagan medievalist nostalgia for an imagined past where humans lived harmoniously with nature. The incorporation of Celtic instruments, like the bodhrán and Celtic harp, thus suggests a complex medievalist connection to the past, as do Celtic songs and references, like their rendition of the Irish song made popular by the band Clannad, "Dúlamán," or their original song "Entrezamp-ni Kelted," the text of which may be translated as "Between us, the Alliance of Celts."[52] Additionally, Sic has praised the *Mittelalter* scene, specifically, in a 2014 interview, stating that he was drawn to it by its promotion of "real" music—that is, music that can be made without electronic equipment.[53]

In addition to the reciprocal alterity–medievalist relationship, Omnia employ medievalism in support of their environmentalist message. The medieval period serves ecocentric messaging well, being situated just before the modern era and calling to mind an idyllic, pastoral history within the context of pop culture.[54] The ethno-Gothic model formed by Dead Can Dance is a clear instance of the intersection between ecocentrism, late twentieth-century Goth music, and medievalism. The model, according to Yri, envisions "an idealized Middle Ages untouched by industrialization and other 'modern' practices."[55] In a 2014 interview, Sic implored viewers to do little things to save the environment.[56] Moments later, when asked why the band uses ancient or odd instruments, he responded by recounting his interest in "ancient" instruments as a child (referring to wooden flutes) and lamenting that "real music is dying," "real music" being that which can be produced without electronics; Omnia's music is "pure" because they use "ancient instruments."[57] Environmentalism, the pastoral premodern past, and medievalism go hand in hand for Omnia, down to their choice of instrumentation.

Omnia's visual representations of themselves also help to construct their environmentalist identity. One example is their 2008 *Pagan Folk Lore* DVD, which consists of a live performance interspersed with commentary by Sic. All of the sound equipment on stage for the performance is wrapped in ivy, which offers the odd visual pairing of the amplification technology that the band needs to be heard by the audience and symbols of the natural world.[58] The footage of the audience also reveals that many of them are dressed in the style of medieval clothing, including corset dresses and Ghillie shirts made of natural-looking fabrics, further emphasizing the band's medievalism.

Omnia's songs "I Don't Speak Human" and "Earth Warrior" and their accompanying music videos are the clearest and most strongly worded statements of the band's environmentalism. The first two stanzas of "I Don't Speak Human" are told from the perspectives of a wolf and a raven, respectively. Each laments the evil of humanity, the first stating, "You're the only evil creature here," and the second, "You people like a cancer grow, destroying all you see."[59] The song switches to the band's perspective in the third verse, where they distance themselves from the rest of humanity, "I won't run this human race, your war is not for me…It's us who are the strangers here and we don't own the land." This sentiment aligns Omnia with the animals invoked in the first two verses, and the chorus of "I don't speak human, I can't understand a word you're saying" applies just as much to the human members of the band as it does to the wolf and the raven.

The "I Don't Speak Human" music video does a lot of work to reinforce the sentiments expressed in the text. It is set in a snowy, wooded area; at the beginning, Sic creeps out from behind a fallen tree while singing the first verse, and his image is juxtaposed with that of a wolf, emphasizing the animal-like appearance created by his faux (presumably) fur mantle and feathered jewelry. Jenny joins in on the second half of the verse and is depicted behind her own fallen tree in a similar position and with similar dress. When the chorus starts, the entire band is shown in a clearing, dancing and playing their instruments in the snow. The costuming for the entire band is consistent with that of Sic and Jenny in the opening verse. The clothing and face paint that Sic and Jenny wear in several of the scenes also calls to mind Native American imagery, offering another connection to nature through cultural appropriation.[60] Last, images of ethically questionable animal breeding practices and animal abuse are used throughout the video to emphasize the evils of humanity. The video images alone, even without the music, clearly communicate that the members of Omnia are at one with nature and are set apart from the rest of humanity.

"Earth Warrior" is just as strong in its promotion of environmentalism. The song is a condemnation of industrialization, deforestation, and people who participate in practices that are harmful for the environment. The text speaks of protecting the earth and encourages listeners to take part. The chorus sums up the general message of the song quite well: "I'm a warrior, Earth Warrior / True born Pagan, yeah / I'm a Warrior, nature's soldier / Fighting for the earth."[61]

The music video makes more explicit exactly who the enemies of the earth are. The video starts with a "warning" and "disclaimer" that satirize copyright laws and prepare the viewer to expect large corporations and governments to be villainized:

Warning
It is permitted to watch this video in whatever way you like, there are no penalties or prison sentences if you watch this outside of your home, in a tent on an oil platform or in a spaceship, whatever. You may copy it on to any kind of medium, you may even stick it up your nose if you like. This is 100% Free Art containing a very important message wrapped up in beautiful musick [sic] and it's meant to be shared and enjoyed as much as possible. FBI, GEMA or similar organisations can go and f*ck themselves.

Disclaimer

The views and opinions expressed by the PaganFolk [sic] band OMNIA in this EarthMusick [sic] video are wholly and completely shared by PaganScum records, it's [sic] affiliates and it's [sic] parent company.

PaganScum (et al) completely agree with everything that OMNIA says or does because OMNIA is not a band of corporate enslaved pussies prostituting themselves for money. OMNIA is a self-managed band of actual Artists and Free-thinking musicians who do and say exactly what they want, where they want and however they want... every day!
HokaHey![62]

The video commences with images of an unnamed woman with face paint and feathers in her hair dancing in the woods, Sic's mouth as he sings the intro, and several scenes of people killing or mistreating animals along with cement logos of large companies with satirized names like "Hell" (Shell), "McDeath" (McDonalds), "Mitsushi," (Mitsubishi), and "Monsatan" (Monsanto). These cement blocks are crushed with a sledgehammer later in the video. While the music is reggae-influenced and does not feature any of Omnia's medieval instruments, the video does depict the band in clothing similar to that which they wear in "I Don't Speak Human," and the included footage of fans dancing to and singing the song features many of them dressed in medievalist garb, wielding swords, axes, and bows.[63] The choice to use reggae-style music may appear incongruous with Paganism and Pagan music, but here it works to ramp up the activist status of this message of environmentalism where medieval imagery might fail.

Finally, Omnia's Paganism is marked by a conception of the body that has been liberated from the strictures of the modern era and of Christianity. This aspect of Paganism has for the most part been ignored by existing scholarship, but it is a significant part of much of Pagan music.

Omnia's appearance in music videos and live performances often features the partially unclothed bodies of band members. The exposure of the body also displays Sic's and Jenny's tattoos and piercings for the audience to see. Not only does this liberate the body from standards of modesty promoted by Christian society, but also the presence of tattoos and piercings calls to mind both bodily markings associated with religious rituals outside the Western world and the tradition of cultural transgression through piercings and tattoos, specifically in the West.[64]

One of the simplest expressions of the liberation of the body within the world of Omnia is found in Jenny's 2015 solo album, *Naked Harp*, released under the band's name, rather than hers (see Figure 26.1). The very title calls to mind the laying bare of a body, which is reinforced in the cover art by Spanish artist Victoria Frances. On the album cover, Jenny is drawn in profile, nude, embracing her harp amid the woods in late autumn as the final leaves fall from the trees. Her hair is in its signature dreadlocks, adorned with feathers, and two petite horns rise gracefully from the top of her head, as if she were a mythical creature. Her harp is likewise intertwined with nature as a vine climbs gently up the front of it and drapes its tendrils over the top. Jenny's nudity is not sexual; rather, she has been caught in her natural state, liberated from the confines of the

FIGURE 26.1 Omnia, *Naked Harp*, detail.

modern world. She is turned away from the viewer, as if she is unaware that she has been observed, and thus she is not exhibiting herself or her music. She plays for herself and for nature, marrying her liberated body with Pagan ecocentrism. *Naked Harp* also refers to the album's musical content, which features the sound of the harp laid bare, unaccompanied by electronic sounds or covered by other instruments. As with Jenny on the cover, the harp is presented in its natural state.[65]

Omnia's music videos also showcase the casual freedom of the Pagan body, both in scripted scenes and in live performance. The "Fee Ra Huri" video features Sic performing live without a shirt. Not only does this symbolically rescue him from the restrictions of modern society, but also it prominently displays the tattoos on his arms and chest, which mirror those on Jenny's arms. Sic's tattoos are also exposed on his scalp where his hair has been shaved. Jenny's tattoos are also prominent, a display achieved by a halter top, rather than a totally exposed upper body. The exposed male torso also makes an appearance in the "I Don't Speak Human" music video, where Sens plays his digeridoo with only a small fur mantle to cover his shoulders. "Earth Warrior" also features scenes in which male members of the band appear without shirts, along with one of Jenny shooting a bow topless and an unnamed woman ripping open her shirt to reveal leaves covering her breasts. This final video is unique in its inclusion of fans who frequently present their bodies clothed (or not clothed) in a manner consistent with the band.

Faun

Faun's medievalism relies more heavily on recalling or signaling medieval sounds and melodies than Omnia's does. While alterity plays a significant role in the band's identity, Faun leans more heavily on concrete connections to the Middle Ages, rather than relying primarily on Otherness, to construct its own medievalism. In a 2010 interview, Tyr stated that the band originally played just medieval music, but started to branch out further in search of more emotional approaches to their songs, while also incorporating electronic sounds to expand their soundscape.[66] Their earlier albums, starting with the inaugural *Zaubersprüche*, have a much more acoustic medievalist style. This first album showcases the variety of instruments that members of Faun play, including the cittern, mouth harp, nyckelharpa, hurdy-gurdy, and recorder, to name just a few. The second album, *Licht*, also introduced the bagpipe to their music. Faun's instrumental choices aid them significantly in forging concrete connections to the Middle Ages.

The use of the hurdy-gurdy illustrates the different approaches to medievalism taken by Faun and Omnia. Unlike Omnia, Faun includes the hurdy-gurdy as part of their regular instrumental lineup; rarely, if ever, do they exchange the hurdy gurdy for another instrument. The cranked chordophone is an essential and indispensable part of Faun's sound. However, it does not do the same kind of heavy lifting for Faun that it does for Omnia, since it is one of the very few explicitly medieval instruments employed by the latter. Faun is able to rely on their range of period instruments to construct a medievalist identity, and thus the hurdy-gurdy blends with the other instruments, often doubling melodic lines presented by other players, and provides added rhythmic interest through the use of the trompette string. The treatment of the hurdy-gurdy also suggests a hierarchy of musicians typical of popular music groups. When Faun produces music videos, this hierarchy is reinforced visually by the foregrounding of the lead singers against the backdrop the other musicians. Groth, the hurdy-gurdist, is often placed toward the rear or on the periphery of the group, as exemplified by "Diese kalte Nacht," "Walpurgisnacht," "Federkleid," and many other videos.[67]

Faun's medievalism is not restricted solely to medieval instruments. The content of their songs comes from a variety of sources, and many pieces are also newly composed. The title of their 2005 album, *Renaissance (Pagan Medieval Folk)*, reveals the breadth of Faun's medievalism, which concerns itself not only explicitly with the Middle Ages, but also with a broadly imagined distant past. The album includes several references to German medieval and Renaissance music, such as "Tagelied," a tribute to the German medieval-Renaissance genre of songs about the departure of lovers at daybreak. Later albums occasionally depict medieval scenes as well, like "Tanz mit mir" from the *Von den Elben* (2013) album, which is set in a medieval tavern. Like Omnia, Faun also mixes the Celtic with the medieval, as in the sixth track on the same album, "Wilde Rose," which features a German text set to the Celtic tune "Siúil a Rún."

Faun also places significant emphasis on ecocentrism, though they rarely delve into environmental activism in the way that Omnia does. "Wind und Geige," featured on both the *Licht* (2003) and the *Luna* (2014) albums, is an example of a song about the interaction between humans and nature. The text itself is short and has no refrain. The song's subject is a violinist playing passionately and "singing" about love.[68] The wind hears the violin and asks what the violinist wants, to which he or she responds that they want luck. The song ends as the sound of the violin fades away, its music carried on by the wind.

Other examples include "Hörst du die Trommeln," "Frau Erde," and "Mit dem Wind." "Hörst du die Trommeln," from the *Luna* album, locates Pagan rituals in nature, emphasizing the tension between the modern world and the natural world that Pagans feel: "Two souls are in your body / and during the day you cannot deny / what drives you in the night."[69] The solution is to move, because the drums of nocturnal pagan rituals move the very earth.[70] "Frau Erde," also from the *Luna* album, is a quiet, gentle song about the sleeping earth that personifies the earth, the moon, and the wind. "Mit dem Wind," from the *Von den Elben* album, takes a slightly different tack, celebrating the coming of summer and the freedom of the season, rather than contemplating the inner struggles of Pagans or personifying elements of nature. Such references are present throughout the majority of Faun's repertoire.

There is one song in which Faun takes more of an activist stance with regard to environmentalism: "Zeitgeist." The song is on the aptly titled album *Eden* (2011). The *Eden* album itself is rather curious; though the group members are German and usually sing in German or Latin, several songs on *Eden* are in English. Many of them are also about nature or about the biblical Garden of Eden, such as their rendition of the fifteenth-century text "Adam lay ybounden." Eden is also situated in a transitional position in Faun's output. It is Faun's final album with tracks in a more strictly acoustic medieval style; the following albums, beginning with *Von den Elben*, are more heavily influenced by modern popular music. "Zeitgeist" is the second track on the album and it laments the loss of "die alte Welt," which has drowned in a sea of ideas.[71] While lamenting the loss of the idyllic, pastoral past is not so far afield from other ecocentric ideas present in most of Faun's music and promoted by associations with medievalism and Paganism more generally, "Zeitgeist" plays the part of an environmental activist song through a spoken English reflection sampled from an unidentified recording that separates the first two stanzas from the final two:

> You cannot employ non-hostile, non-destructive technical skill, unless you realize, basically, that you yourself are this whole domain of nature. That's the real you. You are not in a fight against nature, you are not here to conquer nature, because there's nothing to conquer. It's all you! So when you use technology to bulldoze everything into submission, you're fighting yourself.

Just as Faun's ecocentricism takes a more subtle tack than Omnia's, so, too, does their approach to the Pagan liberation of the body. While members of Faun do occasionally sport tattoos and dreadlocks, these features are less prevalent among the German group, and there is no analog to Sic's selectively shaved head that reveals his tattooed scalp. Faun's alternative to Christian bodily oppression is nuanced and shapes multiple elements of their repertoire, music videos, and live performances. The German band appears to advance egalitarian gendered relationships and a sex-positive message that counters traditional Christian gendered hierarchy and restrictions on sexual activity by drawing on an idyllic medieval past.

"Tanz mit mir," a collaboration with the hypermasculine German folk-rock band Santiano, demonstrates this approach. The song evokes the character of a drinking song with its repetitive lyrics and simple rhyme scheme and depicts an interaction in a medievalist tavern through its simple rhyme scheme, strophic form, and memorably repetitive melody. The text is a dialogue between two speakers, presumably patrons in a medieval tavern. The male patron initiates the conversation between the two by asking for a drink from the woman. They then engage in flirtatious banter, as each escalates their request of the other; he asks for a drink, she for a dance, he to dance on top of the table, she for a kiss, until eventually the two agree sleep together and not proposition anyone else.[72] The melody itself evokes a flirtatious exchange in its opening leap followed by a descending patter reminiscent of playful banter. The verses thus depict an imagined atmosphere of egalitarian sexual relationships within Faun's idyllic Middle Ages. The chorus underscores the transgressive nature of this exchange within Christian society by evoking religious ideas of "sin" and the "devil": "The sin is alluring / and the flesh is weak / so it will always be. / The night is young / and the devil laughs / come we will pour for ourselves."[73]

Beyond the content of the song lyrics, the very act of collaborating with Santiano, along with the music video, further enhances the idyllic and egalitarian medievalism of "Tanz mit mir." Santiano cultivates a hypermasculine image: the group is all male, emphasizes their identity as men on their website, and sing in rough, baritone voices.[74] This image strongly contrasts with Faun's, which can easily be interpreted as more feminine based on the prominence of their female vocalists and Tyr's long hair, use of heavy eyeliner, and smooth tenor voice. Thus, the collaboration itself is an egalitarian relationship between relatively gendered groups. The music video is set in a medievalist tavern, complete with jesters, musicians, and candles. The opening image is of Santiano's bassist, Björn Both, toasting some unnamed extras while the camera pans the room to reveal that Both is sitting with Faun's now former singer Katja Moslehner. The two eat, drink, and laugh together during the instrumental introduction. Both begins his part by holding up his tankard and gesturing to it, though the pitcher of wine is clearly closer to him than it is to Moslehner; Both's intention is clearly to get Moslehner to come closer to him. The two listen to each other with interest, flirting freely as indicated by the song's lyrics. During the instrumental interlude, the two knock back several drinks before Moslehner stands up to sing the final two verses, having agreed to dance "body on body" with Both.[75]

Faun also foregrounds Pagan liberation more subtly in music videos for songs that do not deal directly with gendered relationships. The "Walpurgisnacht" video highlights the importance of an embodied experience of Pagan rituals that is free from the restrictions of the modern world in a manner that presents Pagan bodies in nature that recalls Omnia's "I Don't Speak Human" and "Earth Warrior" videos. The settings of all the videos are in wooded areas devoid of signs of modern life (with the exception of the frequent cutaways to the environmental impact of modern life contained in "Earth

FIGURE 26.2 Faun, still of "Walpurgis Nacht."

Warrior"). The exposed torso is also an essential part of embodied Pagan liberation in each video: most of Omnia appears shirtless at least momentarily in "Earth Warrior," while Tyr plays the nyckelharpa wearing a jacket without a shirt and the female dancers appear draped in loose, open robes made of sheer material or completely topless in "Walpurgisnacht."

The loose clothing worn by the women dancing around the maypole and performing Pagan rituals in the "Walpurgisnacht" video communicates the freedom of Paganism found in its connection to nature, echoing the sentiments expressed in "Hörst du die Trommeln." As the first scene, centered around the maypole dance, transitions to the second, a nighttime ritual performed around a bonfire, the dancers cover their bodies with ashes in preparation (see Figure 26.2). In the final scene, which takes place the next morning, the women gather dew from the surrounding foliage and use it to wash the ashes from their bodies. This intense focus on the body highlights it as the site of the *Walpurgisnacht* ritual just as much as the sandy clearing in which they dance. It also vests Pagan religious authority in specifically female bodies, which contrasts markedly with the long tradition of patriarchal leadership in the Christian world.

Conclusion

Faun and Omnia represent two methods by which Pagan musicians operating in the popular music world can use medievalism to construct and project a Pagan identity through their music. Omnia's approach emphasizes the Otherness of Paganism as a way to connect it to the past, specifically using the medieval Other to create the connection to pre-Christian pagans that defines modern Paganism. Omnia is also heavily involved in environmental activism, in their lives and in their music, which plays to the ecological aspect of Paganism. Finally, Omnia presents a liberated image of the Pagan body in their music that intersects intensely with the alterity and ecocentrism of their medievalist Paganism. Faun also uses medievalism to create a connection to the pagan past, although they focus less on the Otherness of the past than they do on utilizing more explicit historical elements in their music. Like Omnia, Faun weaves an image of ecocentrism throughout their songs, though they rarely take the same sorts of activist stances that Omnia does; rather, ecocentrism helps to place the band in an idyllic, pagan past. Finally, Faun presents a broad conception of embodied Pagan liberation that conceives of egalitarian sexual encounters free from the oppression of Christian sexual mores. The band highlights the Pagan body, specifically the female body, and places her at the center of sacred rituals that subvert patriarchal Christian authority. These two bands offer but small windows into the complex and varied world of Paganism's intersections with medievalism.

Notes

1. A note on capitalization: It is common practice among the scholarly Pagan community and in Britain to use "Pagan" to refer to modern religious movements and "pagan" in reference to religions and groups that predate Christian dominance. See Jason Pitzl-Waters, "The Darker Shade of Pagan: The Emergence of Goth," in *Pop Pagans: Paganism and Popular Music*, ed. Donna Weston and Andy Bennett (Durham, UK: Acumen, 2013), 90n1; and Andy Letcher, "Paganism and the British Folk Revival," in *Pop Pagans*, 109n2.

2. Paganism is also very much defined by multiplicity, rendering the articulation of a single, universal definition that is broad enough to encompass relevant groups and individuals, yet narrow enough to be useful as a category nearly impossible. Of particular interest is the complex interaction of popular culture and religious life and the equally hard-to-define popular religion. Donna Weston and Andy Bennett highlight the significance of this complexity in the opening chapter, "Towards a Definition of Pagan Music," in *Pop Pagans*, 2. This essay articulates an expression of Pagansim that is particular to the bands being considered, springing from a basic definition that links modern and ancient practices.

3. Andy Letcher, "Paganism and the British Folk Revival," in *Pop Pagans*, 94–95.

4. Isabella van Elferen also notes how Pagan bands, as a subset of neofolk gothic musicians, use the medieval to forge a connection with the Dark Ages: "Lyrically, the link with the yearned-for Dark Ages is established through medieval, pagan, or occult texts. Neofolk's romantic nostalgia is musically expressed through the citation of original medieval melodies, the implementation of modal harmonies and bourdon drones, and the use of medievally connoted instrumental timbres," *Gothic Music* (Cardiff: University of Wales Press, 2012).

5. It should not be overlooked that the religious and cultural Others that populate the idealized past(s) most Pagan groups construct are almost entirely white, as are the liberated bodies on which Pagans focus, both past and present. The pervasive whiteness of Paganism has made it quite popular among the European radical right, though not all Pagan groups would relish this connection. As far as the specific bands that are the subject of this study are concerned, they appear lean more left than right. For a more detailed study of the connection between Paganism and the radical right, see Stéphane François, "The Euro-Pagan Scene: Between Paganism and the Radical Right," *Journal for the Study of Radicalism* 1, no. 2 (2008): 35–54.

6. Graham Harvey and Charlotte Hardman organized this conference at the University of Newcastle upon Tyne. In the same year, Dennis Carpenter and Selena Fox organized a Pagan Academic Network that met as an adjunct to the annual meeting of the American Academy of Religion. A more sizable international scholarly summit took place in 1996 at Lancaster University, entitled "Nature Religion Today." The Pagan academic journal *The Pomegranate: The International Journal of Pagan Studies* was also founded in 1996. For further reading on the history of Pagan studies, see James R. Lewis, "Pagan Academic Networking," in *Witchcraft Today: An Encyclopedia of Wiccan and Neopagan Traditions* (Santa Barbara, CA: ABC-CLIO, 1999); and Chas S. Clifton, "The Pomegranate Returns from the Underworld: A Letter from the Editor," *The Pomegranate* 6, no. 1 (May 2004): 5–10.

7. Weston and Bennett, *Pop Pagans*, 6; the growth of Pagansim also parallels the rising New Age movement of the last quarter of the twentieth century. The popularity of all things New Age did much to bolster sales of various kinds of medievalist music, focusing as it did on Hildegard von Bingen, Enya, and Celtic artists generally. New Age websites also tend to emphasize Pagan practices. Richard Witts, "How to Make a Saint: On Interpreting Hildegard of Bingen," *Early Music* 26, no. 3 (August 1998): 480; Narelle McCoy, "The Rise

of the Celtic Cyber-diaspora: The Influence of the 'New Age' on Internet Pagan Communities and the Dissemination of 'Celtic' Music," in *Pop Pagans*,179–180.

8. Weston and Bennett, *Pop Pagans*, 2; Lewis, "Pagan Academic Networking," 194.

9. Donna Weston, "Rememberings of a Pagan Past: Popular Music and Sacred Place," in *Pop Pagans*, 45–46.

10. Damh the Bard, quoted in Hall. "Damh" is the Welsh spelling of "Dave."

11. Weston and Bennett, *Pop Pagans*, 3.

12. See Catherine Albanese, *Nature Religion in America: From the Algonkian Indians to the New Age* (Chicago: University of Chicago Press, 1991); the 1996 conference at Lancaster University "Nature Religion Today" and the anthology it produced, Joanne Pearson, Richard H. Roberts, and Geoffrey Samuel, eds., *Nature Religion Today: Paganism in the Modern World* (Edinburgh: Edinburgh University Press, 1998); etc.

13. Another factor that may also draw Paganism toward nature connections is the etymology of the word Pagan. Ancient Romans used the term *paganus* to refer to rural peoples whose cultures and religious practices were tied to a particular locality and to the land, paganus meaning "people of place." Weston and Bennett, *Pop Pagans*, 3.

14. Ibid.; Pagansim was further bolstered prior to the twentieth century by the concept of the "noble savage" and by Edwardian scholarship's understanding of Darwinism; Letcher, "Paganism and the British Folk Revival," 92.

15. Letcher, "Paganism and the British Folk Revival," 94–96.

16. Bennett defines the countercultural moment as "a global youth cultural phenomenon that casts itself in opposition to the technocracy of Western capitalist society." It is this broad and generally pluralistic definition of the counterculture that will be used here. Andy Bennett, "Paganism and the Counter-Culture," in *Pop Pagans*, 13, 14, 16.

17. Ibid., 15.

18. Nathan Hall, "What Is Pagan Music?" The Wild Hunt: Modern Pagan News and Commentary, accessed October 10, 2017, http://wildhunt.org/2017/03/column-what-is-pagan-music.html.

19. Bennett, "Paganism and the Counter-Culture," 13.

20. Ibid.

21. Ibid., 14.

22. Ibid.

23. Hall. Pendderwen was a native of Berkeley, California, and became interested in Celtic mythology as a child. He attended California State University for theater, joined the Reformed Druids of North America, was active in the Society for Creative Anachronism, became an influential contributor to the Feri tradition, and founded Annwfn, a five-acre sanctuary for the Church of All Worlds Pagan religion. "Gwydion Pennderwen," http://CAW.org: Home of Church of All Worlds, accessed April 25, 2017, http://caw.org/content/?q=gwydion.

24. Damh the Bard, quoted in Hall.

25. *Songs for the Old Religion* contains songs that praise Pagan gods and goddesses in the broader style of popular music lyrics that explored nature and spiritualism beginning in the 1960s. "The Lord of the Dance," for instance, is Pendderwen's pagan creation myth and a contrafact of the Christian hymn by Sydney Carter. It highlights the presence of Pendderwen's god throughout all of human history and his importance in Pagan rituals as well as the connection between the natural cycle of birth, life, death, and resurrection found in the passing of the seasons while undercutting the macabre description of Jesus's death in Carter's original. "Song of Mari" is a hymn of praise to the goddess of twilight, who gives comfort to those experiencing hardship. This lyrical emphasis is also in part a

product of the lyrical shift toward political, mystical, and esoteric themes inspired by Bob Dylan and the Beatles. See Bennett, "Paganism and the Counter-Culture," 15.

26. Incidentally, this depiction of the birth-to-rebirth cycle also draws on some of the same imagery present in both Carter's and Pendderwen's "Lord of the Dance" and illustrates the power of the interpretive lens in appropriating imagery also common to Christianity while presenting it as particularly non-Christian.

27. Letcher, "Paganism and the British Folk Revival," 99.

28. The YouTube user savageminstrel introduces his version of "John Barleycorn" by talking about the spirituality of the song, exchanging "Pagan" for "Celtic," which is not uncommon, "John Barleycorn," YouTube, accessed April 1, 2017, https://www.youtube.com/watch?v=74sdEm4gSjY; the band Willow's Drum produced a music video of their rendition that takes an even more serious approach: set in an empty, bleak field, the duo sings with serious faces, and the cinematography emphasizes images of death, like a hangman's noose, a dagger, and farm implements (the scythe and the pitchfork) wielded as weapons. This interpretation contrasts sharply with Traffic's live performances of the song, which feature a significant amount of laughter and forgotten lyrics. "Willow's Drum—John Barleycorn," YouTube, accessed April 1, 2017, https://www.youtube.com/watch?v=zGGHmhBqj3o; Damh the Bard also has his own version of the song, and John Barleycorn features as one of several Pagan figures referenced in his song "The Wicker Man," on the 2015 album *Sabbat*, which is a musical prayer for the burning of the effigy named in the title.

29. Letcher, "Paganism and the British Folk Revival," 102–103.

30. Weinstein, "Pagan Metal," in *Pop Pagans*, 59.

31. Ibid., 60.

32. Simon Trafford and Aleks Pluskowski, "Antichrist Superstars: The Vikings in Hard Rock and Heavy Metal," in *Mass Market Medieval: Essays on the Middle Ages in Popular Culture* (Jefferson, NC: McFarland, 2007), 57–73. See also Simon Trafford's "Viking Metal," this volume, pp. 564–585.

33. Trafford and Pluskowski, "Antichrist Superstars," 58; Weinstein, "Pagan Metal," 60. Faun's latest album, *Midgard*, also has a specifically Norse focus: "*Midgard* is a journey into the myths and sounds of the ancient north." "Faun—*Midgard* (Tour Edition)," faun-shop.com, accessed December 11, 2017, http://faun-shop.com/index.php?main_page=product_info&cPath=2&products_id=2.

34. "Questiontime 5 'Nicknames,'" YouTube, accessed April 20, 2017, https://www.youtube.com/watch?v=vVqsRiE4IJI.

35. Weinstein, "Pagan Metal," 64–65.

36. Ibid., 65.

37. Pitzl-Waters, "The Darker Shade of Pagan," 78.

38. Ibid., 76. For more discussion on Gothic imagery and metal, see Ross Hagen, "A Gothic Romance: Neomedieval Echoes of *Fin'amor* in Gothic and Doom Metal," this volume, pp. 547–563.

39. Pitzl-Waters, "The Darker Shade of Pagan."

40. See Isabella van Elferen, *Gothic Music: The Sounds of the Uncanny* (Cardiff: University of Wales Press, 2012), 154–160.

41. Van Elferen lists both Omnia and Faun as part of this group of Goth musicians. Ibid., 155.

42. Kirsten Yri, "Medievalism and Exoticism in the Music of Dead Can Dance," *Current Musicology* 85 (Spring 2008): 53; Pitzl-Waters, "The Darker Shade of Pagan," 82.

43. Oliver S. Tyr of Faun explicitly names Dead Can Dance as one of his top two musical influences on the band's website. Faun, accessed December 18, 2017, http://www.faune.de/faun/pages/portrait_oliver_en.html.

44. "Pagan Folk," last.fm, accessed October 10, 2017, https://www.last.fm.

45. "FAUN–Interview with Band Member Oliver S. Tyr," YouTube, accessed April 20, 2017, https://www.youtube.com/watch?v=yP49k7ko8l8; "The Musick," World of OMNIA, accessed April 20, 2017, http://www.worldofomnia.com/band/about-music.

46. In discussing the ethno-Gothic template created by Dead Can Dance and adopted by many subsequent Pagan musicians, Pitzl-Waters also turns specifically to Faun and Omnia as examples of the Pagan folk subgenre, "The Darker Shade of Pagan," 82–83.

47. Mitra is the individual who often appears in the background of music videos hunched over a prop that hides his computer.

48. Pitzl-Waters, "The Darker Shade of Pagan," 83; Yri, "Medievalism and Exoticism," 54.

49. Letcher, "Paganism and the British Folk Revival," 91. Emphasis mine.

50. The Scottish nationalist band Albannach is a notable example of this. The group forms its entire identity around being authentically Scottish and sharing "Scottish heritage" with the rest of the world. Albannach identifies as a "pipes and drums" band and is composed of a core of three drummers, two of whom are also vocalists, and a bagpiper. They added a didgeridoo player after touring with him as a guest artist (year not mentioned). The band's website is careful to identify him as an "American born *Scotsman*" (emphasis mine) and highlights his attraction to bagpipe music, while never mentioning the provenance of the didgeridoo as an instrument. The didgeridoo was attractive to Albannach because of its "tribal" sound, which matches the "tribal style bass drumming" of the band. The entire ensemble works together to create a hyperaggressive, hypermasculine sound that is "aggressive, like a Celtic punch to the face." http://www.albannachmusic.com.

51. Narelle McCoy, "The Rise of the Celtic Cyber-Diaspora: The Influence of the 'New Age' on Internet Pagan Communities and the Dissemination of 'Celtic' Music," in *Pop Pagans: Paganism and Popular Music* (Durham, UK: Acumen, 2013), 179.

52. "Dúlamán" was popularized by the Irish band Clannad on their 1974 album of the same name. It began appearing on albums by Irish and Celtic musicians with more frequency beginning in the 1990s, with several choral groups picking up Irish composer Michael McGlynn's arrangement. The text appears as early as 1937–1938, when it was transcribed by the Irish Folklore Commission as part of their efforts to collect folklore from schoolchildren. The Breton lyrics of "Entrezomp-ni Kelted" are "Pa reomp ul liamm etrezomp-ni Kelted" in alternation with lilting.

53. "Interview with Omnia 2014 at Schlosshof Festival," YouTube, accessed April 10, 2017, https://www.youtube.com/watch?v=9dIuHNtXCok.

54. Compare with the discussion of ecomedieval nostalgia in Caitlin Carlos, "'Ramble On': Medievalism as Nostalgic Practice in Led Zeppelin's Use of J. R. R. Tolkien," this volume, pp. 530–546.

55. Yri, "Medievalism and Exoticism," 56.

56. As an example of the seriousness of environmentalism in the minds of band members, Sic goes so far as to jokingly suggest that fans kill some other humans to reduce their carbon footprint.

57. "Interview with Omnia 2014 at Schlosshof Festival." Ironically, Omnia relies heavily on amplification in their performances, recording equipment and audio engineering in the production of their content and the Internet in interacting with their fan base and spreading their message.

58. "Omnia—*Pagan Folk Lore*."

59. "Deep within the shadows, I'm the hungry wolf you fear / But I can see that you are the only evil creature here / Before you came we lived in peace but you have brought us death / I sing my pain up to the moon but it's a waste of breath.... Upon a wing, a flying thing,

to you I seem so small / But I look down on what you've done, my raven's eye sees all / You people like a cancer grow, destroying all you see / and seven billion mutant monkeys won't listen to me."

60. Cultural appropriation by mostly white European Pagans that draws on cultural objects associated with people of color is a common phenomenon, despite—or perhaps because of—the significant under-representation of people of color in Paganism and among the membership of popular Pagan bands. See also Omnia's reggae-inspired song "Earth Warrior," discussed below, and Afghan-inspired song "Dil Gaya," etc.

61. The chorus is immediately repeated each time it appears, swapping "dreadlocked soldier" for "nature's soldier" on the second statement.

62. "OMNIA (official)—'Earth Warrior,'" YouTube, accessed April 20, 2017, https://www.youtube.com/watch?v=71swxdSzY1w.

63. It should be noted that while the reggae sound does not reinforce Omnia's medievalist identity, it does draw on a history of political activism that rejects Eurocentric culture and mainstream society, is used in service of other environmentalist messages, and raises awareness of various political issues among listeners.

64. Marianna Torgovnick highlights that piercings and tattoos frequently act as functions of religious ritual outside the Western world and as protest against the commodification of modern life among committed piercers in the West. Even for casual piercers, these bodily ornaments serve to mark the individual as part of an outside group and register their protest of modern society, much like long hair or beards in the 1960s, but with more permanence. *Primitive Passions: Men, Women, and the Quest for Ecstasy* (New York: Knopf, 1997), 191, 196, 203.

65. Ironically, the production of the album relies heavily on modern recording technology, sound engineering, and printing technology.

66. "Faun—Interview with Band Member Oliver S. Tyr," YouTube, accessed April 20, 2017, https://www.youtube.com/watch?v=yP49k7ko8l8.

67. "Faun 'Diese kalte Nacht' [Official Video | HD]," YouTube, accessed April 1, 2017, https://www.youtube.com/watch?v=zr8d9sXioj4; "Faun—'Walpurgisnacht' (Official Video)," YouTube, accessed April 1, 2017, https://www.youtube.com/watch?v=nLgM1QJ3S_I; "Faun 'Federklied' (Official Video)," YouTube, accessed April 1, 2017, https://www.youtube.com/watch?v=zOvsyamoEDg.

68. "Sie sang von Liebe, so wild, so lind."

69. "Zwei Seelen sind in deinem Leib/Und am Tag kannst du nicht leugnen / Was dich in die Nächte treibt."

70. "Wer einmal im Mondlicht tanzte/Folgt den Trommeln / Wenn die Nacht anbricht. Darum bleib nicht einfach steh'n / Damit die Schatten keener sieht! / Es gilt, zu gehen/ Damit die Erde sich bewegt."

71. "Die alte Welt versinkt / In einem Meer / Aus ideen."

72. "Und später schöne teil das Bett mit mir ... Doch nur wenn du heut' keine andre küsst."

73. "Die Sünde lockt / und das Fleisch ist schwach / so wird e simmer sein. / Die Nacht ist jung / und der Teufel lacht / komm wir schenken uns jetzt ein."

74. https://www.universal-music.de/santiano/biografie; see also the music video for the song "Leinen los, volle Fahrt Santiano," https://www.youtube.com/watch?v=w3PFqqH15Po.

75. "Leib an Leib." The music video skips the verse where Both asks Moslehner to share his bed. However, the video clearly implies this request.

SECTION 6

MEDIEVALISM OF THE SCREEN

CHAPTER 27

FROM THE MUSIC OF THE AINUR TO THE MUSIC OF THE VOICE-OVER

Music and Medievalism in The Lord of the Rings

STEPHEN C. MEYER

AMONG the many important essays published in the 1992 *Wagner Handbook* is a wide-ranging exploration of medievalism in Wagner's life and works by Volker Mertens.[1] To cover this expansive topic in a single essay was, no doubt, a daunting task: depending on how one defines the topic, nearly every one of Wagner's works could be regarded as medievalist. Few composers were so deeply immersed in medieval literature, and in the music dramas themselves, the idea of the Middle Ages takes a wide variety of different forms. To write an effective essay on this topic, therefore, Mertens needed to provide his readers with a robust framing device: a clarifying lens through which to view this disparate and complex material. It is hardly surprising, then, to find the following sentence in the first paragraph of the essay:

> Wagner believed that he himself was the first person to have extracted the essential mythical meaning of these medieval narratives, and to have portrayed that meaning onstage, whereas what he actually staged, with the help of characters and episodes from these older accounts, were the problems of his own age, even of his own life.[2]

The idea that Wagner's music dramas—despite their medievalist settings—are thinly veiled autobiographies and/or dramatizations of nineteenth-century social dynamics is not original. Wagner himself articulated just this thought, for example, in the famous passage from *Eine Mittheilung an meine Freunde*, in which he describes the ways in which his opera *Lohengrin* dramatized the essential artistic problem of his own age.[3] In *The Perfect Wagnerite*, George Bernard Shaw famously interpreted the *Ring* cycle in terms of bourgeois-capitalist power dynamics, an idea that formed the basis of Patrice

Chéreau's now-classic centenary staging of the cycle at Bayreuth. Additional examples could be reproduced practically ad infinitum. Indeed, the effectiveness of Mertens's framing device rests to a large degree on the ways that it elegantly brings together various strands in the voluminous reception history of Wagner's works.

By setting up a contrast between "the essential mythical meaning of these medieval narratives" on the one hand and "the problems of his own age" on the other, Mertens implies a certain degree of self-delusion on Wagner's part. Here it is important to remember that Mertens was writing in the waning years of the authenticity wars that were such a prominent part of musicology during the 1970s and 1980s. Indeed, Mertens's framing concept might be understood as an analogue of Richard Taruskin's well-known critique of what he calls the "authenticist" approach to early music. In articles such as "The Pastness of the Present and the Presence of the Past," Taruskin famously uncovered the modernist aesthetics at work in the historically informed performance renditions of early music by conductors such as Christopher Hogwood and pointed to ways in which these performances reflected particularly late twentieth-century problems and concerns.[4] Using the syntax of Mertens's framing device to rephrase this argument, we could say (in the voice of Taruskin) that Hogwood believed himself to be realizing the authentic performance practice of the baroque period, while what he really performed and recorded were interpretations informed by his own personal aesthetics (or those of his own age).

What engages me here, however, is not the ways that Mertens's framing device might embody musicological trends of the 1980s and early 1990s or even its usefulness as a point of entry into Wagner's medievalism. Instead, I am interested in the structure of Mertens's argument, especially in the interlocking pairs of oppositions that it implies. The first of these, and the most obvious, is that between the present and the past—that is, between the medieval and the "problems of [Wagner's] own age." Connected to this opposition between the present and the past is one between superficial medievalism— "characters and episodes from older accounts"—and the "essential mythical meaning" of medieval narratives. Wagner's delusion—if we follow Mertens—was to believe that this essential mythical meaning could be brought to life, or perhaps could *only* be brought to life, through contemporary means. To stage the essential meaning of medieval works, Mertens might say, Wagner did not believe that he had to forego the phantasmagoric technologies of the nineteenth-century opera stage; on the contrary, the "extraction of the medieval" depended precisely on the "technology of the modern." In this sense, Mertens's framing device suggests a third opposition, namely, one between form and content.

The oppositions implied in Mertens's framing device provide a useful point of entry into the question of music and medievalism in *The Lord of the Rings*, not least because of the many affinities between the Tolkien/Jackson narrative and the story of Wagner's *Ring*.[5] Using Mertens in this way, however, is complicated by the twofold nature of my topic, that is, by my intention to discuss *both* the films of Peter Jackson and the novel on which the films are based. Although we might regard some aspects of the films as unmediated allusions to medieval narratives, Jackson's primary point of reference is Tolkien, not (for example) narratives such as *Beowulf* or the *Nibelungenlied*. Indeed, we might almost say that Jackson's relationship to Tolkien mirrors Tolkien's own relationship to these medieval sources. In this sense, Jackson's films might be described as examples of neomedievalism. In contrast to medievalism, Carol L. Robinson and Pamela Clements argue in their essay, "Living with Neomedievalism," "neomedievalism is further independent, further detached [from medieval sources], and thus consciously, purposefully, and perhaps even laughingly reshaping itself into an alternate universe of medievalisms, a fantasy of medievalisms, a meta-medievalism."[6] Tracing the oppositions of Mertens's framing device through the world of the Lord of the Rings, then, will inevitably compel us to think historiographically. As we move through history and among different genres, our frames of reference will be continually changing.

The idea that Tolkien's *Lord of the Rings* is essentially about either World War I or World War II, or that it allegorizes the postindustrial ecological crisis, is very widely distributed; in this sense, the novel, like Wagner's operas, can be understood to "stage the problems of [its] own age."[7] To interpret the Peter Jackson films in light of early twenty-first-century culture and politics is perhaps an even easier task. More interesting, however, are ideas that emerge when we apply the contrast between superficial and deep medievalism to the world of the Lord of the Rings. That this world incorporates many plot elements, names, and descriptive motifs from a wide range of medieval narratives hardly needs explication here, and in this sense, the superficial medievalism of both films and novel is easy to show. The question of deep medievalism is far more challenging to answer. It would be difficult to imagine someone more deeply versed in the languages and literatures of medieval Europe than J. R. R. Tolkien, and his medievalism could never be dismissed as easily as Mertens dismisses Wagner's appropriation of the Middle Ages. Tolkien may not have thought that he was extracting the "essential mythical meaning" of medieval narratives, but he was very interested in capturing the spirit of medieval culture and expressing it in his legendarium. In a similar manner (and one that exemplifies the idea of neomedievalism that I referenced previously), the Lord of the Rings films were often described as "bringing Tolkien's Middle-earth to life" or, in exactly the opposite manner, as a betrayal of "the aesthetic and philosophical impact of [Tolkien's] creation."[8] The question, then, concerns not merely the deep or structural medievalism of Tolkien's legendarium, but also the ways in which this deep medievalism finds—or fails to find—its way into the Lord of the Rings films. My focus will be on the role that music plays in this medievalist/neomedievalist matrix.

Interpreting *Beowulf*

Any discussion of medievalism in *The Lord of the Rings* leads us inevitably into the complex interchange between Tolkien's work as a philologist and his work as a novelist, poet, and myth-maker. More has been written on this topic, perhaps, than on any other aspect of Tolkien's creativity. The relationship between what Tolkien called subcreation— his own imagined world of Middle-earth—and the medieval texts that he studied so deeply takes many forms. The topic is a vast one, and it will be enough here to focus on a small but very significant corner of it—namely, the relationship between *The Lord of the Rings* and *Beowulf.*

Tolkien's well-known suggestion that "the invention of languages is the foundation [of his fictional world]" and that "the 'stories' were made rather to provide a world for the languages than the reverse" points to what is perhaps the most direct relationship between *Beowulf* and Tolkien's novel.[9] Tolkien based his invented languages on various European tongues, and as Tom Shippey and other scholars have pointed out, the language of the Mark in *The Lord of the Rings* is a hypothetical dialectical variant of the Old English in which *Beowulf* was written.[10] Tolkien also drew many concrete plot elements for his novel directly from *Beowulf.* The most direct borrowing comes in "The King of the Golden Hall" chapter from *The Two Towers.* In this section of the novel, Gandalf, Aragorn, Legolas, and Gimli come to Edoras, the political center of Rohan and the seat of its king, Théoden. As many scholars have pointed out, the arrival of Gandalf and his friends at the king's hall is modeled closely on the scene from *Beowulf* in which the eponymous hero and his followers are challenged by the coast guard of King Hrothgar (*Beowulf*, 229–300).[11] Meduseld—the name of King Théoden's hall—is also drawn directly from the Anglo-Saxon poem. In this sense, "The King of the Golden Hall" chapter—and other sections of *The Lord of the Rings* as well—exemplify a process that Tom Shippey calls *calqueing*, whereby a story or a motif is not only translated into a new language, but also reshaped to fit a new genre.[12] "It is obvious," writes Clive Tolley in his overview of this influence, "that [Tolkien's *The Lord of the Rings*] could not have been written, [nor] the films made, without the great Old English poem named *Beowulf.*"[13]

In this sense, then, Tolkien's appropriation of *Beowulf* would seem to be an example of surface-level medievalism. Tolkien, we might say, repurposed *Beowulf* to suit his own literary and philosophical ends just as—according to Mertens—Wagner repurposed "characters and episodes from . . . older accounts" to stage "the problems of his own age." But the influence of *Beowulf* on *The Lord of the Rings* can also be felt on a more abstract and general level. Tolkien's appropriation of the poem—to put this in terms of the dichotomy that I laid out above—is an example of both surface-level and deep medievalism. This deep medievalism has to do not with calqueing, but rather with Tolkien's understanding of the poem's worldview. Setting aside for the moment the ways in which *The Lord of the Rings* itself—and especially those parts of the novel that concern the Riders of Rohan—functions as a commentary or interpretation of the Anglo-Saxon poem, Tolkien's most explicit discussion of this worldview comes in his famous essay "*Beowulf*: The Monsters and the Critics" (1936).[14]

Scholars have long recognized many ways in which the topics that Tolkien articulates in his *Beowulf* essay find expression in *The Lord of the Rings.* A particularly potent example of the link between the *Beowulf* essay and the later novel can be found in the idea of "northern courage," which Tolkien identifies as the "great contribution of early Northern literature."[15] Northern courage might be defined as steadfastness and bravery in the face of seemingly inevitable defeat; it is a quality shared by many of the heroic characters in *The Lord of the Rings.* Many examples might be adduced here, but it is enough to reference a passage from Chapter 6 of *The Return of the King*, "The Battle of the Pelennor

Fields." At this point in the novel, King Théoden has died, and the leadership of Rohan has passed to his nephew, Éomer. The Riders of the Mark are surrounded by enemies, and Éomer fully expects that he and all of his warriors will perish:

> Stern now was Éomer's mood, and his mind clear again. He let blow the horns to rally all men to his banner that could come thither; for he thought to make a great shield-wall at the last, and stand, and fight there on foot till all fell, and do deeds of song on the fields of Pelennor, though no man should be left in the West to remember the last King of the Mark.[16]

What is significant here is not the idea of northern courage per se, but rather Éomer's determination to do "deeds of song," or—if I may expand slightly on Tolkien—to do deeds worthy of being remembered in song. The Mark—in contrast to its more "civilized" neighbor to the south, is essentially an oral society, in which, we assume, the most prestigious cultural form is the heroic lay. In geographical and perhaps chronological terms as well, then, Rohan is on the borders of literacy. The play between literature and orature (a word that Tolkien himself would surely have balked at) informs not only the contrast between Rohan and Gondor, but also many other aspects of the novel. *The Lord of the Rings* is extraordinarily rich in interpolated songs, and while some of these—such as the paean to hot water that the hobbits sing in Book 1 of *The Fellowship of the Ring*— are very different in tone than the kind of lyric commemoration for which Éomer wishes in the passage that I quoted above, they nevertheless represent a mode of creativity distinct from the written accounts that Gondor consults in Minas Tirith, or indeed from the quasi-autobiographical text that Bilbo will leave unfinished at his death ("There and Back Again").[17] In addition to their other attributes, characters such as Frodo and Aragorn are themselves storytellers, who inhabit a world suffused with song.

The care and attention that Tolkien lavishes on his depictions of Middle-earth's oral traditions is indeed extraordinary and is surely one of the most distinctive characteristics of *The Lord of the Rings*. But if Tolkien's work in this regard was profoundly original, it was also deeply informed by his immersion in medieval texts. Insofar as we might regard the orality of Middle-earth as an example of Tolkien's medievalism, however, it lies on a deep or structural level. While some of the songs and poems in *The Lord of the Rings* can be traced to early medieval (especially Old English) antecedents, the orality of Middle-earth is not a calque but rather a reflection—or better, a fantastic elaboration—of a medieval worldview. Here, too, *Beowulf* is a principal point of reference, not by virtue of any plot elements or motifs, but rather because of the way that it embodies a particular cultural position at the intersection of literature and orature.

If the imaginary societies of Middle-earth to some extent occupy this same cultural position, a second strand of Tolkien's deep medievalism—or, more particularly, a second way in which the structure of *Beowulf* influences *The Lord of the Rings*—concerns the relationship between what we might call the center and the periphery of the Old English poem. The central plot of *Beowulf*—the hero's arrival at the court of King Hrothgar, his defeat first of Grendel and then of Grendel's mother, his return to his own homeland and his final encounter with the dragon—is continually interrupted by digressions. In these, the *Beowulf* author tells other stories—of Ingeld son of Froda or of Sigurd the Dragon-Slayer—that might seem tangential to his main story. It is precisely this attitude that Tolkien targets in his essay. As an example of a larger trend in *Beowulf* criticism, he cites the following passage from Raymond Williams Chambers's preface to the 1925 Archibald Strong translation of the poem. "The folk-tale is a good servant," writes Chambers, "but a bad master: it has been allowed in *Beowulf* to usurp the place of honour, and to drive into episodes and digressions the things which should be the main stuff of a well-conducted epic."[18] In the sections that follow, Tolkien defends the "episodes and digressions" as central to the meaning of *Beowulf*. Referencing some of these supposedly tangential elements of the poem, Tolkien acknowledges that "*Beowulf* was not designed to tell the tale of Hygelac's fall, or for that matter to give the whole biography of Beowulf, still less to write the history of the Geatish kingdom and its downfall." Nevertheless, Tolkien continues, "it used knowledge of these things for its own purpose— to give that sense of perspective, of antiquity with a greater and yet darker antiquity behind. These things are mainly on the outer edges or in the background because they belong there, if they are to function in this way."[19]

If Chambers had been able to review *The Lord of the Rings*, he might have looked on these poems and fragmentary stories much as he viewed the "folk-tale elements" in *Beowulf*. The genealogy of hobbits and the tale of Beren and Luthien, after all, are not exactly "the main stuff of a well-conducted epic." But these digressions/insertions are a central part of Tolkien's aesthetic. Like the tangential stories in *Beowulf*, they serve "to give that sense of perspective—of antiquity with a greater and yet darker antiquity behind." They are crucial to what is surely the most distinctive quality of Middle-earth, namely, its extraordinary depth and density.

For enthusiasts of *The Lord of the Rings*, these "digressions"—the chapter "Concerning Hobbits," the episodes at the House of Tom Bombadil, the encounter with the Woses of Drúadan Forest in *The Return of the King*—are a large part of the appeal of the novel. Perhaps inevitably, however, it is precisely these parts of the *Lord of the Rings* plot that were cut from the screenplay.[20] But if Peter Jackson and his production team felt a "Chambers-like" urge to streamline the plot—or to focus more on the center and less on the periphery—they seemed also to recognize that the story demanded a sense of "antiquity with a greater and yet darker antiquity behind." Tom Bombadil and the Woses could be left on the cutting room floor, but something, at least, of Tolkien's epic sense of time needed to be preserved.

At a later point in this essay, I will turn to one of the most important ways in which Peter Jackson and Howard Shore worked to create this epic sense of time in the voice-overs to *The Fellowship of the Ring*. Before leaving "*Beowulf*: The Monsters and the Critics," however, I wish to introduce another topic that will be relevant for a discussion of deep medievalism in the Lord of the Rings films. This concerns the reception history of the poem, or better, the ways in which it reflects the historiography of the Middle Ages. Since *Beowulf* is the foremost example of literature in Old English, there is a kind of metonymical slippage between the poem and the language in which it was written.

For a contemporary speaker of English, the language of *Beowulf* lies at—or, more likely, just beyond—the horizon of comprehensibility. Grappling with its vocabulary and syntax feels like trying to remember a half-forgotten dream, and the strangeness of the poem is a constant reminder of the chronological gap that separates the world of *Beowulf* from our own. The joy of reading *Beowulf* is—in part—the pleasure of reaching over this gap. Something of this quality of joy is captured in the final stanza of Borges's "Embarking on the Study of Anglo-Saxon Grammar," a poem that, incidentally, is nearly contemporaneous with the publication of Tolkien's novel:

> All praise to the inexhaustible
> labyrinth of cause and effect
> which, before unveiling to me the mirror
> where I shall see no one or some other self,
> has granted me this perfect contemplation
> of a language at its dawn.[21]

The idea that *Beowulf* represents the dawn of the English language is very firmly established, and the poem is far more likely to appear near the beginning of an anthology than at the end of it. In this context, *Beowulf* seems like the golden treasure that rewards the historian's or philologist's quest for the roots of English.

The metonymical slippage between the poem and the language in which it was written, moreover, effects not merely the form of *Beowulf*, but also its content. If the language of *Beowulf* represents the dawn of the English language, so too does its content narrate events from the dawn of the Germanic peoples. It is a document, we might say, from the "childhood" of medieval history, before tribes had crystallized into nations, before Christianity had extended its influence into the north, before the contours of the modern world had begun to take shape.

Tolkien provocatively inverts this implied taxonomy. "*Beowulf*," he writes,

> is not a "primitive" poem; it is a late one, using the materials (then still plentiful) preserved from a day already changing and passing, a time that has now forever vanished, swallowed in oblivion; using them for a new purpose, with a wider sweep of imagination, if with a less bitter and concentrated force. When new *Beowulf* was already antiquarian, in a good sense, and it now produces a singular effect. For it is now to us itself ancient; and yet its maker was telling of things already old and weighted with regret, and he expended his art in making keen that touch upon the heart which sorrows have that are both poignant and remote. If the funeral of Beowulf moved once like the echo of an ancient dirge, far-off and hopeless, it is to us as a memory brought over the hills, an echo of an echo.[22]

The quality of lateness that Tolkien identifies in *Beowulf* is also central to *The Lord of the Rings*. Tolkien achieved this effect in part by placing the events of his novel at the very end of the Third Age of Middle-earth. The Fourth Age, inaugurated by the ascension of Aragorn to the throne of Gondor, will be the age of Men and not of the Elves. In this sense, the turn between the Third and Fourth Ages of Middle-earth parallels events in the "real world" (or what Tolkien might call the primary world) of early medieval England: namely, the conversion of the Germanic peoples of that land from paganism to Christianity. Tolkien thus places himself—or perhaps it is better to say "the narrative persona of *The Lord of the Rings*"—at a cusp that is at once historical and ideological. The age of the Elves is "already old and weighted with regret"; the age of Men is still in the process of emerging.

Disenchantment, Myth, History

The quality of lateness that Tolkien finds in *Beowulf* is closely related to what Christine Chism identifies as one of the most salient aspects of Tolkien's novel, namely, the pervasive sense that the magical fantasy world in which the plot unfolds is destined to slip away. "*The Lord of the Rings*," she writes,

> is a tale of the renunciation of mythology and the willed return to history. . . . Middle-earth unfolds, grows more intricate, more peopled, more culturally diverse, more deep as we wander through it, but it blooms forth only in the shadow of its own immanent destruction. The loss of the Ring consigns Middle-earth to the joys and depredations of history—and this consignment to history is costly. It is no accident that the loss of the Ring maims Frodo forever and disenchants Middle-earth.[23]

The idea that Tolkien's novel narrates a kind of fall from myth into history is obviously linked to the idea of a historical or ideological "cusp" and—albeit more distantly—to the relationship between literature and orature and that between "center" and "periphery" that I outlined previously. In this light, the "consignment to history" represents the movement from the fantastic preliterate narratives that we encounter in the songs and poems that are distributed so profusely in *The Lord of the Rings* to the objective or "fact-based" chronology included as Appendix B to *The Return of the King*. Similarly, it is the "intricacy" and diversity of Middle-earth, or—to use again the words with which Tolkien described *Beowulf*, the "sense of perspective" conveyed by those things that lie "on the outer edges or in the background"—that is threatened by the loss of the Ring. Seen through the lens of deep medievalism, then, we might say that the "renunciation of mythology" and the "willed return to history" that Chism finds in *The Lord of the Rings* is analogous to the historical transition so eloquently expressed in *Beowulf*. Like the monsters and dragons of the old pagan Germanic world depicted by the *Beowulf* poet, the Ents and Elves and other magical creatures of Middle-earth are passing away.

   Although Chism's focus is on the plot of *The Lord of the Rings*, her observations about the relationship between myth and history could therefore also be applied to the *Beowulf* story. Tolkien understood that the *Beowulf* poet was writing from a Christian perspective and that the mythological world of his poem was haunted by the "shadow of its immanent destruction." Yet in the *Beowulf* essay, Tolkien describes the relationship between myth and history in very different terms. "The significance of a myth," he writes, "is not easily to be pinned on paper by analytical reasoning. It is at its best when it is presented by a poet who feels rather than makes explicit what his theme portends; who presents it incarnate in the world of history and geography, as our poet has done."[24] Unlike Chism, Tolkien's focus here is not on the emplotment of myth and history, but rather on their interpenetration. History—to speak metaphorically—functions as an elaborate cloak, concealing the explicit meanings of the myth even as it gives it color, shape, form, and beauty.

Although the artistry of *Beowulf* may deserve special praise in this regard, the interpenetration of history and myth is a prominent feature of many other medieval texts as well. The plot of the *Nibelungenlied*—to choose a prominent example—contains many supernatural or mythical features, but it is nevertheless built around actual historical events, namely, the struggles of the Burgundian kings and queens during the fifth century. Theodoric was a historical Ostrogothic king, but he is also the hero of a group of sagas and legends that are freely populated with dwarves, dragons, and other mythical creatures. *King Harold's Saga* describes the superhuman exploits of its eponymous hero, but it also ends with a specific historical event: the defeat of the king at the battle of Stamford Bridge in 1066. In *The Lord of the Rings*, Tolkien expands the interweaving of myth and history to epic proportions. At the center of Tolkien's novel is a Ring with a host of magical properties; there are also seeing stones (the *palantir*), wizard staffs, and a pool that functions as a magical mirror. Yet all these objects—and the mythical encounters that the characters have with them—are framed by an extremely (some might say excessively) detailed chronology: a chronology that is laid out in timetable form as Appendix B to *The Return of the King*. That this chronology is imaginary does not affect the central aesthetic that is at work, an aesthetic that in a crucial way Tolkien derived from his close reading of medieval texts. In this light, we may understand the coexistence of hyperrealistic detail and supernatural elements in *The Lord of the Rings* as another manifestation of Tolkien's medievalism: an attempt to replicate the aesthetic principles and patterns of thought articulated in medieval works and not simply their surface detail. To put this in concrete terms, it is not just the calques of *Beowulf* in "The King of the Golden Hall" chapter that mark *The Lord of the Rings* as a medievalist work, but also the ways in which Tolkien passes seamlessly from the prosaic genealogies of the "Concerning Hobbits" chapter into a description of the Ring of Power glowing with the incantatory letters of the Black Speech and remaining cool to the touch even after it has been placed in the hottest part of the fire. Like the *Beowulf* poet, Tolkien is incarnating the magical elements of his story in a concrete history and geography.

This interpenetration of the magical and the mundane stands in what we might call an oblique relationship to the interplay between history and myth that Chism outlines. The plot of the novel may narrate a process of disenchantment: a fall from myth into history. Yet the novel—at least ideally—also manifests an act of incarnation: an intuitive presentation of myth in a concrete historical world. Both themes—disenchantment and incarnation—are very much rooted in Tolkien's reception of medieval texts (especially

Beowulf) and exemplify the deep medievalism that I have adumbrated. What we must now ask is how—or indeed if—this deep medievalism may be made manifest in music.

The Music of the Ainur

To respond to this question, we must turn to a text in which Tolkien expresses the idea of myth becoming incarnate in the world of history and geography in a much more direct sense. I am speaking of *Ainulindalë*, the early manuscript that describes the creation of Middle-earth and the imaginary cosmos of which it is a part.[25] Subtitled "The Music of the Ainur," *Ainulindalë* forms the first part of *The Silmarillion*, and (like so many other aspects of Tolkien's fiction) it draws freely from European oral and literary traditions. As many fans have pointed out, the characteristics of the individual Ainur (the gods of Middle-earth) find specific analogues in the members of the Norse pantheon. Both Manwë (the chief of the Ainur) and Odin, for example, are "all-seeing," and each is associated with ravens. The clearest connections, however, are between *Ainulindalë* and the Bible. In a general sense, Tolkien's text evokes the stately and measured prose style of the King James version, and some of the same gnomic quality of the biblical text also finds its way into *Ainulindalë*. More specific references are also at work. The musical instruments that Tolkien lists in *Ainulindalë*, for example, are similar to those that appear in Psalm 137, while his description of the Ainur singing around the throne of Ilúvatar evokes the image from the book of Revelation of the seraphim and cherubim singing continually around the throne of God.

But the most significant resonances between *Ainulindalë* and scripture have to do with the biblical account of creation, first as it is recounted in the opening of the book of Genesis and second as it appears in the first chapter of the gospel of John. The idea of an omnipotent creator god (Ilúvatar in Tolkien's legendarium) creating the cosmos out of nothingness reads to some extent like a recapitulation or calque of the biblical text. But the metaphysics of *Ainulindalë*, and the rhythm of the prose, more closely resemble the opening of John. Here is how Tolkien begins:

> There was Eru, the One, who in Arda is called Ilúvatar; and he made the Ainur, the Holy Ones, that were the offspring of his thought, and they were with him before aught else was made. And he spoke to them, propounding to them themes of music; and they sang before him, and he was glad.[26]

Tolkien has made a vital change to his creation story, one that is most significant for my argument here. In the opening passages of Genesis, it is light that is the primal vehicle for God's creative agency, while in John it is the Word. In Tolkien's text, however, the primal vehicle is music.

Subsequent passages in *Ainulindalë* describe the ways in which this primal music takes on corporeality and gives shape to the physical world, much as the primal *logos* in

John is the vehicle "through which all things were made." Here, the reference seems to be the Neoplatonic idea of the "music of the spheres" that finds its most succinct articulation in Boethius's *Consolation of Philosophy*. The opening passages of *Ainulindalë*, then, bring into dialogue the ideas of "incarnation" and "disenchantment" that are so important to the aesthetics of the *Beowulf* essay. Taking these points in reverse order, we may understand the story of the "Music of the Ainur" as a kind of fall from the timeless, transcendental world of myth into the mutable and contingent space of history. And yet this fall—at least initially—is figured as expansion and development, not as loss. After Ilúvatar declares his mighty musical theme to the Ainur, he invites or compels them to expand and develop his creation. "Of the theme that I have declared to you," he says,

> I will now that ye make in harmony together a Great Music. And since I have kindled you with the Flame Imperishable, ye shall show forth your powers in adorning this theme, each with his own thoughts and devices, if he will. But I will sit and hearken, and be glad that through you great beauty has been wakened into song.[27]

Evil enters the world through the will of Melkor, the greatest of the Ainur, who desires to enlarge his part in this great music and to act independent of Ilúvatar's intentions. Melkor is clearly a Satan figure, and just as Satan convinces many of the angels to follow him, so too does Melkor lead many of his fellow Ainur astray. Adopting Shippey's terminology, we might then regard this section of *Ainulindalë* as a calque of Milton's *Paradise Lost*. What differentiates Tolkien's text from its model, significantly, is the role of music. In *Ainulindalë*, Tolkien figures Melkor as a kind of errant chorister (or perhaps as a rebellious composer). "Some of these [rebellious] thoughts," Tolkien writes,

> he now wove into his music, and straightway discord arose about him, and many that sang nigh him grew despondent, and their thought was disturbed and their music faltered; but some began to attune their music to his rather than to the thought which they had at first. Then the discord of Melkor spread ever wider, and the melodies which had been heard before foundered in a sea of turbulent sound.[28]

Melkor's wilful disruption of initial harmony will mean that the subsequent history of Middle-earth will be informed by the need for recovery. The Ainur, the Elves, Dwarves, and Men will all—to adopt the primal metaphor of *Ainulindalë*—be listening for the dim echoes of that ancient harmony. They are all haunted by what we might call an existential nostalgia, a nostalgia that is central to the aesthetic of *The Lord of the Rings*. To paraphrase Tolkien once more, we can say that it is precisely the remoteness of this ancient harmony that makes keen its touch on the heart.

Ainulindalë lies outside the borders of Tolkien's novel, and there is nothing in *The Lord of the Rings* that references this creation myth in a direct sense. And yet the idea of a creation myth does appear in the Lord of the Rings films: specifically, in the expansive voice-over prologue at the beginning of Jackson's *The Fellowship of the Ring*. This voice-over prologue, to be sure, does not reproduce the narrative content of *Ainulindalë*;

Melkor and Manwe and the rest of the Holy Ones will play no part in the film. And yet, the voice-over prologue and *Ainulindalë* narrate—or perhaps we should say *embody*—the same essential intersection between history and myth. What makes the parallel between *Ainulindalë* and the voice-over prologue important for my argument here is the role that music plays in each. In *Ainulindalë*, we could say, music is the creative vehicle through which the will of the Holy Ones becomes incarnate in history. In the voice-over prologue, it is music that articulates this passage and leaves open the possibility that it might be reversed.

Mythological Voice-over

I am certainly not the first scholar to find connections between the sound design of this opening voice-over and Tolkien's account of music in *Ainulindalë*. James Buhler articulates precisely this connection in his essay "Enchantments of *Lord of the Rings*: Soundtrack, Myth, Language, and Modernity." "Very much in keeping with Tolkien's mythology," Buhler writes,

> the soundtrack renders the modern world as a fall to earth, as a lamentable descent from enchantment to disenchantment, from the sung but wholly disembodied heavenly Music of the Ainur to the unsung instrumental or earthly embodied music of Men.... This antimodern vision, filled with a characteristically modern nostalgia for a past that never was, twines the corporate origin of myth with the mythologized origin of international corporate capital, obscuring the historicity of the market in order to weave a veil of enchantment about the actual locus of modern power, that is, global capital.[29]

I will take Buhler's fundamental insight—that the soundtrack represents a mythological descent from enchantment to disenchantment—as a starting point for my own analysis of the opening voice-over. My purpose, however, is not to explore the "corporate origin of myth," but rather to investigate the ways in which the soundtrack articulates the twin dialectics—between enchantment and disenchantment and between history and myth—that are so central to the deep medievalism of Tolkien's imaginary world. A detailed examination of the opening voice-over, then, will allow us to understand the ways in which this deep medievalism passes over into the more contemporary cinematic instantiation of Middle-earth.

We should begin by acknowledging that there is nothing inherently medievalist about the *structure* of this cinematic introduction. Like so many other big-budget films from the late twentieth and twenty-first centuries, *The Fellowship of the Ring* begins with elaborate framing material. Cinematic logos identify distribution and production companies and a title card introduces not the title of the film, but rather the name of the franchise of which it is a part. Far from being a uniquely medievalist gesture, the framing

EXAMPLE 27.1 "Lothlòrien" theme.

materials that precede *The Fellowship of the Ring*—as Buhler points out in a later essay—exemplify a widely distributed cinematic practice.[30] Nor is there anything particularly unusual about the presence of the voice-over prologue that follows this framing material. Although such prologues are especially important for epic films, they can be found in a wide variety of genres from a wide variety of periods. The prologue to *The Fellowship of the Ring* is admittedly quite long, but this length in itself is hardly evidence of deep medievalism. Insofar as we may find such evidence, then, it lies in the *content* of the prologue and not in its existence per se.

In light of my discussion of *Ainulindalë*, it is significant that the prologue emerges out of strange, metadiegetic sounds, effects that accompany some of the corporate logos that precede the cinematic narrative. The sound engineer uses an uncanny effect that I have described elsewhere as sonic elision, whereby the pitch level of the metadiegetic sounds temporarily aligns with those of the underscore, so that the perceptual border between "noise" and "music" is elided. The melody that emerges from this elision is the "Lothlórien" theme that will become associated with the Elves and with their queen, Galadriel (see Example 27.1).

Emerging out of undefined sound, the "Lothlórien" theme appears here without any clearly defined rhythmic pulse. In terms of mode, the theme is best understood in F (harmonic) minor. But the leading tone to tonic motion that would secure this modal context is absent; indeed, the suggested tonic of F is never articulated. In terms of both rhythm and melody, then, the theme embodies a sense of mystery. The first words of the voice-over—which this theme introduces—reinforce this mood. Spoken in Quenya—the language that Tolkien invented for the High Elves of Middle-earth—and delivered in a half-whispered voice, they seem more like an incantation than the beginning of a narrative. Adopting Chism's framework, we could say that this opening gesture articulates the idea of enchantment: the starting point for the inevitable fall from myth into history that will constitute the main trajectory of the plot. The sense of enchantment in the voice-over will be retrospectively strengthened by the fact that it is spoken by Cate Blanchett—the actress who will portray Galadriel. In both a literal and a figurative sense, she is the voice of enchantment: the character who, more than any other, will embody the mystery of the fantasy world.

In the text of the voice-over, the Elvish phrase is followed by one in English that we take to be its translation. Philippa Boyens and Peter Jackson (who receive joint credit for the screenplay) maintain this alternating pattern for four more phrases, up to the text "Much that once was, is lost." The fact that the text speaks so clearly of loss encourages us, I believe, to understand translation itself—more specifically, the passage from Elvish to English—in the same terms: as what Buhler calls a "lamentable descent from enchantment

EXAMPLE 27.2 "History of the Ring" theme.

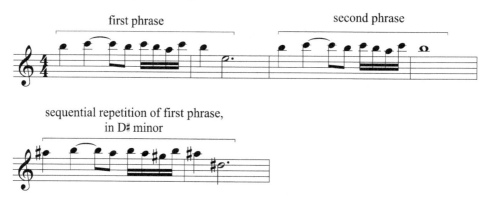

to disenchantment." Indeed, by placing the title card for the franchise immediately after this articulation of loss (at 0:56), Jackson to some extent imbues the entire cinematic trilogy with the aura of nostalgia.

The appearance of the title card is accompanied by a melody that will become one of the most important components of the soundtrack, the distinctive theme that scholars have labelled the "History of the Ring" motive (see Example 27.2). Played on the solo violin, the theme seems to balance between two expressive affects: a sense of yearning embodied by the opening upward semitonal motion and a sense of mourning or descent implied by the fall of the fifth at the end of the first phrase. In tonal terms, we almost certainly understand this descent as a fall from the dominant to the tonic (here in the key of E minor), although our attention is probably more focused on the curling nature of the melody than on its harmonic implications. After a second phrase—in which this descent is absent—Shore repeats the opening phrase a semitone lower: a gesture that seems on a macro level to reference both the semitonal melodic motion with which the motive begins and the sense of fall or descent with which the first phrase of the motive ends.

The presentation of the title card and this new theme articulate a structural break in the voice-over, initiating what we might call its second narrative arc. In this section of the voice-over, text and music are directly aligned. Although Boyens and Jackson abandon the Elvish/English "translation conceit," the script still retains some of the mythic aura of the first section of the voice-over. Clearly derived from the epigrammatic poem that prefaces Tolkien's novel, the script describes the forging of the great rings of power. The description of each of the three groups of rings (for the Elves, Dwarves, and Men respectively) is accompanied by a phrase of the "History of the Ring" motive, clearly establishing the leitmotivic associations of this melody. The motive comes to rest with an image of the map of Middle-earth, drawn directly from the one that prefaces Tolkien's novel (1:38). Here, it would seem, is a cinematic expression of the idea of myth becoming incarnate in the world of history and geography.

Just as the title card of the film was accompanied by the appearance of a new motive in the soundtrack, so too is the map associated with new musical materials. The new theme that Shore introduces at this point of the voice-over is a rhythmic pulse that will become associated with the Ringwraiths and—more generally—with images of war and conflict. Along with the image of the map, then, this new theme initiates the third narrative arc of the voice-over. This narrative arc is far longer and more complex than the preceding sections of the voice-over. It tells a crucial part of the prehistory of the plot: Sauron's rise to power and his battle against the Last Alliance of Elves and Men; it tells of how Sauron was defeated and how Isildur claimed the Ring; of how Isildur was ambushed by Orcs by the River Anduin and of how the Ring betrayed him. The soundscape of this section is quite complex. Shore's underscoring features various iterations and elaborations of the Ringwraiths' motive, along with an ostinato march theme (associated with the armies of Elves and Men), as well as adumbrations of the four-note theme that will become associated with the Land of Mordor and with Sauron's power more generally. Battle cries and diegetic sounds of war are combined with metadiegetic sounds and hyperamplified effects, imbuing the events narrated in the voice-over with a mythic and fantastic aura. The climax of this section comes when Isildur uses the haft of his father's sword to cut the Ring from Sauron's hand. As Isildur reaches out to take the Ring for himself, we hear the "History of the Ring" motive in the underscore. The melody appears to have "migrated" from its initial iteration in conjunction with the title card of the franchise, for it is now cast in D♯ minor (the "second key" of its initial statement) and played by a mid-range group of mixed strings. The final section of this third narrative arc tells of how Isildur was ambushed by Orcs on the shores of the River Anduin. Attempting to escape, Isildur puts the Ring onto his finger (rendering him invisible) and dives into the river. But the Ring slips from his hand, and as it does so, we hear the "History of the Ring" motive once again. Although it is shorn of its first phrase, the motive here begins in its home key of E minor and in its "home texture" of the solo violin. Taking on structural significance, the motive thus brackets the preceding section, providing a sense that this section of the "prehistory" of the main narrative is coming to a close.

In its earlier iteration (initiating what I have called the third narrative arc of the voice-over), the sequential descent comes to rest on a map of Middle-earth, suggesting— as I intimated previously—a "descent" from the world of myth into that of history and geography. In this light, the voice-over text that this latter iteration of the "History of the Ring" motive accompanies seems especially significant:

> The hearts of men are easily corrupted, and the Ring of Power has a will of its own. It betrayed Isildur to his death. And some things that should not have been forgotten were lost. History became legend, legend became myth. And for two and a half thousand years the Ring passed out of all knowledge.

What the voice-over is describing, of course, is the process of forgetting: Myth in this sense simply suggests an imperfect (or partially fictionalized) version of history. In this sense, the idea of myth referenced here carries a very different meaning than it does in Tolkien's *Beowulf* essay or, for that matter, in the passage from Chism's article that I quoted previously. It might be easy to dismiss this bit of text as a throwaway line: a meaningless interpolation whose only purpose is to make the voice-over seem more portentous. I would nevertheless like to take this passage seriously, as a reference not only to the two and a half millennia that follow Isildur's loss of the Ring, but also to a more fundamental process of mythologization that is at work in the films. If—as Chism claims—*The Lord of the Rings* is a story about the renunciation of mythology and the willed return to history, so too—at least in its cinematic iteration—does it suggest a renunciation of history and a willed return to mythology. History and mythology thus circulate in a kind of endless dialectic: a dialectic—we might add—for which the Ring is a perfect metaphor.

The temporal compression implied in the voice-over text about history and myth that I quoted previously ("for two and a half thousand years the Ring passed out of all knowledge") finds its visual expression in a simple fade-out: a gesture that articulates the juncture between the third and fourth narrative arcs of the voice-over. This new section begins with an arresting image: a dirty hand closing over the Ring. This image is accompanied by a croaking, half-whispered voice uttering the first genuine dialogue of the film: "My Precious."[31] The voice, of course, belongs to Gollum, who will be the primary subject of the next section of the voice-over. In this narrative arc, the camera follows Gollum deep into the Misty Mountains. The underscoring is nearly continuous, but it does not articulate a specific theme. Instead, Shore accompanies this arc with a thickening tone cluster (a technique that he uses for many other scenes in the Lord of the Rings films). The climax comes with yet another cinematic descent: a slow-motion image of the Ring bouncing down a rocky slope. Hyperamplified sound effects take the place of underscoring at this point, bringing the Ring to a point of rest just as the "History of the Ring" motive accompanied the descent of the Ring to the bottom of the River Anduin.

The next image that we see (7:08) is that of another hand closing around the Ring, forming a "visual rhyme" with the hand of Gollum that appeared at the beginning of the narrative arc. Here, however, the hand belongs to Bilbo Baggins. We hear the "History of the Ring" motive again, but although it appears in its home key of E minor, it now sounds in the oboe and not the solo violin; its ethereal essence is thereby attenuated: its mythological character is somehow made more prosaic. As in earlier iterations, the motive slips down into D♯ minor. Revoiced into the mid-range strings, it comes to rest on a sustained tone, and as it does, the camera fades into a close-up of the same map of Middle-earth that we saw at the cusp between the second and third narrative arcs of the voice-over. Here is another music-cinematic "rhyme," one that brings the fourth narrative arc—and the introductory voiceover as a whole—to a fitting conclusion.

Historical Voice-over

If the appearance of the map marked the cusp between what I have called the second and third narrative arcs of the opening voice-over, here it marks an even more important structural division, namely, that between the introductory section and what amounts to

EXAMPLE 27.3 "Shire" theme.

a second voice-over. In this voice-over, however, the *acousmetre* is not an Elven queen, but rather Bilbo Baggins, the character who—perhaps more than any other—represents the prosaic world of comfort and domesticity. The first acoustic marker for this domesticity is one of the most prosaic of all imaginable sounds, namely, Bilbo clearing his throat. In a structural sense, this throat clearing parallels the metadiegetic sounds with which the first voice-over begins. But there is no sense of uncanny sonic elision here—quite the opposite, in fact.

The opposition between these two acoustic gestures is just one of many ways in which the filmmakers set up an inversional relationship between the first and second voice-overs. Another has to do with the text of the screenplay. While the first voice-over begins with the intuition of change, this second voice-over begins by announcing a specific time and a specific place: "The 22nd day of September, in the year 1400, by Shire reckoning. Bag End, Bagshot Row, Hobbiton, Westfarthing, The Shire, Middle-earth." As Bilbo recounts this rather exaggerated address, the camera first leads us across the map from the Misty Mountains (where Bilbo discovered the Ring) to the Shire and then pans out to reveal greater and greater parts of the map. At the end of the address, the camera takes in the map's borders, so that we understand it for the first time as a sheet of parchment in Bilbo's study. The map, we might say, is diegeticized: transformed from a cinematic device into a prop.

As in the first voice-over, Shore's underscoring works to articulate the structural sectionalization of the film. The underscore for Bilbo's exaggerated address is a new melody, whose clear major-mode tonality contrasts sharply with so much of the thematic material that underscores the first voice-over (see Example 27.3). If Bilbo's voice-over locates the diegesis firmly in the Shire, so too will this theme function throughout the films as a leitmotivic marker for the hobbits and their homeland. With its (perhaps unconscious) reference to the hymn tune "Terra Beata" ("This Is My Father's World"), this music resonates powerfully with the mood of hyperdomestic Englishness that is such an important feature of Tolkien's descriptions of the Shire.[32] Significantly, this is the first moment in the film in which we have the unambiguous presentation of the major mode. Although I can make no claim to understand the composer's intentions, it seems as if Shore has held this harmonic gesture "in reserve" precisely to accentuate a sense of homecoming or arrival.

As the camera pans out from the parchment map, we hear the final words of the exaggerated address: "The Third Age of this world." With this, the "Shire" theme breaks off, and a new melody appears: the theme that will become associated with the ties that bind the members of the "fellowship of the Ring" together (see Example 27.4). As the new

EXAMPLE 27.4 "Fellowship" theme.

"Fellowship" theme sounds in the underscore, the title card for the film (that is, *The Fellowship of the Ring*) appears. This gesture echoes the cusp between the first and second narrative arcs of the first voice-over, when the appearance of the "History of the Ring" motive synchronized with the title card for the franchise (the Lord of the Rings). As the film title fades, the camera tracks through a cluttered study to come to rest on Bilbo, seated at a desk with his back to us. It continues to move and pivot until we see Bilbo's hand holding a pen, writing the first words of what promises to be an extensive manuscript. Just as the camera diegeticized the image of the map during the exaggerated address, so too does this image diegeticize the acousmatic words, so that we understand them as part of the internal drama of writing—or better, of history-making. Indeed, we may retrospectively interpret the words of the second voice-over as the introduction to this text.

The image of Bilbo's hand holding a pen might—at least subliminally—recall the other cinematic hands in the first voice-over, namely, those that clutched the Ring. In a similar manner, the paper of Bilbo's manuscript recalls the parchment of the map. And if the appearance of these cinematic hands and maps tended to mark structural moments in the first voice-over, so in the second voice-over does the image of the pen and the text mark similar kinds of structural divisions. As the "Fellowship" theme comes to a close, Bilbo asks himself "where to begin" and dips his pen in the inkwell. The camera then shows him writing the words "Concerning Hobbits" on the next sheet of his manuscript, and as it does so, a new, somewhat comical variation of the Shire theme begins in the underscore. This musicodramatic gesture exactly parallels the procedure of the first voice-over, in which the image of the hand grasping the Ring or the image of the map was articulated either by new thematic material or by a prominent reiteration of the "History of the Ring" motive. What emerges, then, is a cluster of parallel oppositions—between metadiegetic sounds and throat clearing, between the Ring and Bilbo's pen, between map and manuscript, between the Elven queen and the hobbit, that work together to intensify the inversional relationship between the two voice-overs.

Although many members of Peter Jackson's production team were deeply immersed in Tolkien's oeuvre (and not simply in *The Lord of the Rings*), it would be difficult to claim that this inversional relationship was an intentional realization of some of the ideas articulated in the *Beowulf* essay. We can nevertheless interpret the voice-overs in

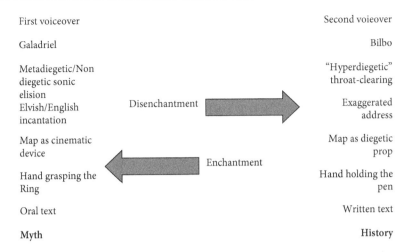

First voiceover   Second voieover

Galadriel   Bilbo

Metadiegetic/Non   "Hyperdiegetic"
diegetic sonic   throat-clearing
elision
Elvish/English   *Disenchantment*   Exaggerated
incantation   address

Map as cinematic   Map as diegetic
device   prop
                              Enchantment
Hand grasping the   Hand holding the
Ring   pen

Oral text   Written text

Myth   **History**

FIGURE 27.1 The structure of the voice-over prologues to *The Fellowship of the Ring.*

precisely these terms. The incantatory beginning of the first voice-over projects what we might call its fundamental orality, while the images of pen and paper link the second voice-over with written text. The "Concerning Hobbits" section of the second voice-over that is launched by Bilbo's titular inscription sounds—one is tempted to say "reads"— like a comic exaggeration of historical prose, designed to accentuate the contrast with mythic speech of the first voice-over. In this sense, the film lays out the passage from orature to literature that is such an important part of the world of *Beowulf.* Similarly, the elaborate cinematography of the map—and, more obliquely, the overdetermined nature of Bilbo's preamble—might be understood in terms of center and periphery. And if the funeral of Beowulf comes to modern readers (to quote again the passage from the *Beowulf* essay that I cited previously) "like…a memory brought over the hills, an echo of an echo," so too do the metadiegetic sounds and fantastic cinematography of the first voice-over invest its narrative with a "far-off" quality of lateness, a quality that Tolkien identifies as a central quality of *Beowulf.*

In this sense, then, the inversional relationship (see Figure 27.1) between the two voice-overs articulates the opposition between myth and history that is so central to what I have called Tolkien's deep medievalism, and the processes of disenchantment and enchantment are figured as the movement between these two inversionally related parallel structures.

Phantasmagoric (Dis)enchantment

With all this in mind, we might return to the framing idea in the essay on Wagner's medievalism with which I began my chapter. Rephrasing and recycling Volker Mertens's argument, we might wish to claim that—in the voice-over narratives to *The Fellowship of the Ring*—Peter Jackson and Howard Shore have "extracted the essential mythical meaning" of Tolkien's narrative and that they "have portrayed that meaning" in cinematic terms. The underscoring for the voice-overs—with an admittedly large amount of leeway—could even be described as a realization of Tolkien's creation narrative: with either the "Lothlórien" theme or the "History of the Ring" theme standing in for the original music propounded by Ilúvatar. But if we follow the trajectory of Mertens's argument, we must recognize this claim as a delusion. Just as Wagner's works (at least as they are described in the Mertens essay) inevitably staged not the Middle Ages but rather the "problems of his own time," so too do the Lord of the Rings films inevitably reproduce the cultural logic of late capitalism—the problems of our own *mal de siècle*—and not the "essential meaning" of Tolkien's novel.

Although James Buhler makes no reference to the Mertens essay, his observations about the music for the opening voice-over to *The Fellowship of the Ring* might be understood very much in these terms. Developing Buhler's thesis, we could say that the "veil of enchantment" woven by the music of the voice-over conceals not only global capital per se, but also the status of the film itself as simply another product in the hegemonic network of late capitalism. Following in the footsteps of Adorno, it is therefore easy to understand these films—and the entire cinematic genre that they represent—as an elaborate phantasmagoria, a simulacrum of the genuine artwork in which special effects are offered up as a grotesque compensation for the magic of an aura that is irretrievably lost. Like the Wagnerian operas that were the initial focus of Adorno's critique—and whose structures and aspirations they sometimes seem to emulate—epic fantasy films must continually mask the conditions of their own production. Indeed, their exchange value depends specifically on this masking ability. Adopting Buhler's metaphor once more, we could say that the primarily rule for epic fantasy film is that the veil of enchantment should not have any holes.

Following this idea prompts us to understand the opening voice-over to *The Fellowship of the Ring* as a kind of spell that Galadriel is casting—not over Frodo or Sam or any of the other characters in the film—but over the audience. The words of the voice-over serve as an introduction to the plot material of the film, but they are also a kind of promise to the viewer: a promise that *here*—that is to say, within this fictional cinematic world that you are about to enter—history will become myth; a promise that—at least during the viewing experience—the disenchantment that characterizes quotidian life in postindustrial society may itself be reversed. But the promise of the opening voice-over is false. It deludes us into thinking that the hypercapitalized cinematic apparatus responsible for the film is somehow a part of Middle-earth even while its true purpose is exactly the opposite, namely, to make Middle-earth a part of the hypercapitalized world of contemporary cinema.

The absorption of Middle-earth into the domain of late capitalist popular culture has been regarded by many Tolkien readers as a betrayal of the literary works. According to this line of thought, the transformation of *The Lord of the Rings* from novel into film was a kind of fall, whereby the magical, evocative beauty of Tolkien's original text was set aside in favor of the stereotypical banalities of epic fantasy movies. Indeed, this sense of loss is perhaps the dominant theme in negative criticism of the films. It may find its most poignant expression in a passage from a 2012 interview with Christopher Tolkien, J. R. R. Tolkien's son and literary executor:

> Tolkien has become a monster, devoured by his own popularity and absorbed into the absurdity of our time.... The chasm between the beauty and seriousness of the work, and what it has become, has overwhelmed me. The commercialization has reduced the aesthetic and philosophical impact of the creation to nothing. There is only one solution for me: to turn my head away.[33]

Although Christopher Tolkien is speaking generally about the entire corpus of works—or, should we say, the entire group of products—that were derived from his father's novel, the primary targets of his critique are Peter Jackson's films. In light of our discussion here, this critique takes on an additional level of meaning. What emerges is a kind of fractal structure in which the interlocking paradigms of fall and disenchantment appear simultaneously at many different levels of discourse. We find it, perhaps, in Tolkien's admiration for the ways in which the *Beowulf* poet evokes a legendary past that is in the process of dissolution. Following Chism, we might find these paradigms in the central aesthetic of Tolkien's novel and (with important qualifications) in other sections of his legendarium. The oppositions between the "mythical" first voice-over and the "historical" preamble that follows—as I have tried to show—are yet another manifestation of this paradigm. The quasi-Adornian understanding of the opening voice-over as a kind of phantasmagoria—and Christopher Tolkien's idea that his father's work has been "absorbed into the absurdity of our time"—transposes these paradigms of fall and disenchantment from the plot of the film into the critique of a genre (see Figure 27.2).

This latter critique would cast the music of the Lord of the Rings films into a particularly ironic light. Apart from any other functions that music might have, it certainly serves to suture the viewer into the cinematic fantasy or—to use Buhler's metaphor—to stitch up any holes that might appear in the veil of enchantment. And yet insofar as it succeeds in these tasks, it participates in the process whereby the Lord of the Rings story

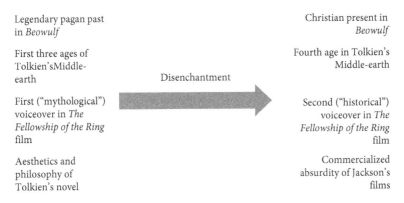

Legendary pagan past in *Beowulf* — Christian present in *Beowulf*

First three ages of Tolkien's Middle-earth — Fourth age in Tolkien's Middle-earth

Disenchantment

First ("mythological") voiceover in *The Fellowship of the Ring* film — Second ("historical") voiceover in *The Fellowship of the Ring* film

Aesthetics and philosophy of Tolkien's novel — Commercialized absurdity of Jackson's films

FIGURE 27.2 Inversional relationships between the first and second voice-overs in *The Fellowship of the Ring*.

is robbed of its "aesthetic and philosophical impact" and transformed into a mere product. In this sense, music is the channel for the "cathexis of the phantasmagoric": the field in which the paradoxical exchange between enchantment and disenchantment reaches its greatest intensity. Music, to put this another way, is precisely the aspect of the films in which their essential modernity is most clearly revealed. If this is true, then how might the music of the Lord of the Rings films—and specifically that which accompanies the opening voice-overs to *The Fellowship of the Ring*—be regarded as medievalist?

The answer to this question depends on the way that we understand the role of music in the circulation between myth and history, a circulation that is key to what I have called deep medievalism. Because if music is the channel for the cathexis of the phantasmagoric, so too is it a primary agent of this circulation. In terms of the cinematic diegesis, the music for the voice-overs to *The Fellowship of the Ring* articulates the fall from myth into history. But the music also continually offers the viewer a way back: from history into some kind of mythological substratum, perhaps from reality back into fantasy. Viewed negatively, this latter function makes music complicit in the essentially escapist (or, to use a favorite Adornian term, "regressive") nature of the films. But there is also another argument, namely, that fantasy—or better, the act of fantasizing—offers a way to resist modernity. Many authors have used such an argument to defend fantasy, but in the context of this essay, it is perhaps best to leave this task to Tolkien himself and his discussion of this topic in his famous essay "On Fairy Stories." "Fantasy," Tolkien writes, "remains a human right: we make in our measure and in our derivative mode, because we are made: and not only made, but made in the image and likeness of a Maker."[34] Later in the essay, Tolkien turns the idea of escapism from one of opprobrium into one of praise:

> Why should a man be scorned if, finding himself in prison, he tries to get out and go home, or if, when he cannot do so, he thinks and talks about other topics than jailers and prison walls? The world outside has not become less real because the prisoner cannot see it.[35]

Is music, then, a powerful tool for prying open the bars of this modernist prison? Or, on the contrary, is it a part of the prison itself: a false passageway that offers escape even as it leads the prisoner ever deeper into its depths? Perhaps the medievalism of the Lord of the Rings music resides precisely in the way that it articulates this paradoxical state, in which the yearning for escape combines with the lack of confidence that escape is truly possible.

NOTES

1. Volker Mertens, "Wagner's Middle Ages," in *Wagner Handbook*, ed. Ulrich Müller and Peter Wapnewski, trans. ed. John Deathridge (Cambridge, MA: Harvard University Press, 1992), 236–268. Barbara Eichner provides a new and somewhat different perspective on this topic in her excellent essay in this volume, "Richard Wagner's Medieval Visions," pp. 174–202.

2. Mertens, "Wagner's Middle Ages," 236.

3. "Eine Mittheliung an meine Freunde" appears in the Richard Ashton Ellis translation as "A Communication to my Friends." The relevant passage reads as follows: "The most natural and urgent longing of such an artist [i.e., the character of Lohengrin, in which Wagner sees himself reflected] is, to be taken up without reserve into the Feeling, and by in understood; and the *impossibility*—under the modern conditions of our art-life—of meeting with this Feeling in such a state of freedom and undoubting sureness as he needs for being fully understood," Richard Ashton Ellis, *Richard Wagner's Prose Works*, 1:344.

4. Richard Taruskin, "The Pastness of the Present and the Presence of the Past," in *Authenticity and Early Music: A Symposium*, ed. Nicholas Kenyon (Oxford: Oxford University Press, 1988), 137–207.

5. The connections (and the points of divergence) between Wagner's *Ring* cycle and *The Lord of the Rings* have been the subject of countless essays, articles, and blog posts, and space does not permit me to reference this extensive bibliography. A useful point of entry into the topic is Alex Ross, "The Ring and the Rings: Wagner vs. Tolkien," first published in the December 22, 2003, issue of *The New Yorker*, accessed March 17, 2018, https://www.newyorker.com/magazine/2003/12/22/the-ring-and-the-rings.

6. *Studies in Medievalism* 17 (2009): 55–75, here 59.

7. A particularly interesting development of this line of thought may be found in Verlyn Flieger, "A Postmodern Medievalist," in *Tolkien's Modern Middle Ages*, ed. Jane Chance and Alfred K. Siewers (New York: Palgrave MacMillan, 2005), 17–28.

8. The words are from the interview with Christopher Tolkien. For an insightful comparison between Tolkien's novel and Jackson's films (and one that is largely sympathetic to Jackson's project), see Tom Shippey, "Another Road to Middle-earth: Jackson's Movie Trilogy," in *Understanding the Lord of the Rings: The Best of Tolkien Criticism*, ed. Rose A. Zimbardo and Neil D. Isaacs (Boston: Houghton Mifflin, 2004), 233–254.

9. J. R. R. Tolkien, *The Letters of J. R. R. Tolkien*, ed. Humphrey Carpenter (Boston: Houghton Mifflin, 1981), 219.

10. Tom Shippey makes this point in the note to p. 123 in *The Road to Middle-Earth*, rev. and expanded ed. (Boston: Houghton Mifflin, 2003). Subsequent citations to *The Road to Middle-Earth* are also to this revised and expanded edition. While the language of the Mark is quite closely related to its model (that is, to Old English), Tolkien's other invented languages have a more oblique relationship to their models. Quenya—the language that Tolkien invented for the High Elves—is most strongly influenced by Finnish, while Sindarin—the language of the Grey Elves—is more directly modeled on Welsh. For an overview of Tolkien's invented languages, see Arden Smith, "Invented Languages and Writing Systems," in *A Tolkien Companion*, ed. Stuart Lee (Hoboken, NJ: Wiley–Blackwell, 2014), 202–213.

11. Tom Shippey discusses the connection between these two scenes in *The Road to Middle Earth*, 124–125. For a critique of Shippey's analysis, see Michael R. Kightley, "Heorot or Meduseld?: Tolkien's Use of Beowulf in 'The King of the Golden Hall,'" *Mythlore* 24, no. 3–4 (Spring 2006): 119–134. See also Clive Tolley, "Old English Influence on the Lord of the Rings," in *Beowulf and Other Stories: A New Introduction to Old English, Old Icelandic and Anglo-Norman Literatures*, ed. Richard North and Joe Allard (Harlow, UK: Pearson Longman, 2007), 38–62, especially 42–44.

12. Shippey discusses this term on pp. 101–102 of *The Road to Middle Earth*. *Calque*, as Shippey points out, is technically a linguistic term (sometimes described as "loan translation"). Shippey uses the term in a broader sense.

13. Tolley, "Old English Influence," 39.

14. This essay was read on November 25, 1936, and then published in the *Proceedings of the British Academy*, 22 (1936), 245–295. It has been frequently reprinted. The most authoritative and readily available edition (which I will cite here) is J. R. R. Tolkien, *The Monsters and the Critics and Other Essays*, ed. Christopher Tolkien (Boston: Houghton Mifflin, 1984), 5–48.

15. Tolkien, "*Beowulf*: The Monsters and the Critics," 20. Tolkien was deeply engaged with *Beowulf* throughout his long career. Readers may also wish to consult his essay "On Translating *Beowulf*," reprinted in the same collection *The Monsters and the Critics and Other Essays*, 49–71, as well as Tolkien's own translation of the poem: *Beowulf: A Translation and Commentary, Together with Sellic Spell*, ed. Christopher Tolkien (Boston: Houghton Mifflin Harcourt, 2014).

16. James Moffett, "A Tolkienist's Perspective," accessed October 16, 2016, https://atolkienist-perspective.wordpress.com/2016/09/16/northern-courage-ofermode-and-thorin-oakenshields-last-stand/.

17. The hobbits sing what they describe as "one of Bilbo's favourite bath songs" ("Sing hey! For the bath at close of day") in Chapter 5 of *The Fellowship of the Ring*, "A Conspiracy Unmasked."

18. Tolkien, "*Beowulf*: The Monsters and the Critics," 12–13. Tolkien is quoting from p. xxvi of the Strong translation.

19. Tolkien, "*Beowulf*: The Monsters and the Critics," 33.

20. "Concerning Hobbits" is a part of the extended edition of *The Fellowship of the Ring*, but not the theatrical version.

21. "Embarking on the Study of Anglo-Saxon Grammar," by Jorge Luis Borges from a collection called "The Maker" ("El Hacedor") that was published in 1960. Jorge Luis Borges, *Selected Poems*, ed. Alexander Coleman (New York: Viking, 1999), 129. This particular poem was translated by Alastair Reed.

22. Tolkien, "*Beowulf*: The Monsters and the Critics," 33.

23. Christine Chism, "Middle-earth, the Middle Ages, and the Aryan Nation: Myth and History in World War II," in *Tolkien the Medievalist*, ed. Jane Chance (London: Routledge, 2003), 63–92, p. 64.

24. Tolkien, "*Beowulf*: The Monsters and the Critics," 15.

25. J. R. R. Tolkien, *The Silmarillion*, compiled and ed. Christopher Tolkien (London: Allen & Unwin, 1977; first American edition, Boston: Houghton Company, 1977). *Ainulindalë* may be found on pp. 15–22 of this edition.

26. *Ainulindalë*, 15.

27. *Ainulindalë*, 15.

28. *Ainulindalë*, 16.

29. James Buhler, "Enchantments of Lord of the Rings: Soundtrack, Myth, Language, and Modernity," in *From Hobbits to Hollywood: Essays on Peter Jackson's Lord of the Rings*, ed. Ernest Mathijs and Murray Pomerance (Amsterdam: Rudopi), 231–248, here 234.

30. In his essay "Branding the Franchise," in *Music in Epic Film: Listening to Spectacle*, ed. Stephen C. Meyer (New York: Routledge, 2016), pp. 3–26 Buhler develops the ideas that he laid out in his "Enchantments of Lord of the Rings" essay and applies them to analogous sections from other cinematic franchises such as Marvel comics and the Harry Potter films.

31. In the third narrative arc, Elrond utters a few battle cries (in Elvish), but these are completely subsumed into the diegetic sounds of the film.

32. The opening lines of this hymn connect directly to our discussion of music in *Ainulindalë*: "This is my Father's world / and to my listening ears / All nature sings, and round me rings / The music of the spheres."

33. Accessed August 27, 2016, http://www.worldcrunch.com/culture-society/my-father-039-s-quot-eviscerated-quot-work-son-of-hobbit-scribe-j.r.r.-tolkien-finally-speaks-out/hobbit-silmarillion-lord-of-rings/c3s10299/#.UMCVFpPjnfY.

34. "On Fairy Stories" was delivered as a lecture at the University of St. Andrews on March 8, 1939, and then published in 1947 in the *Essays Presented to Charles Williams*. Like "*Beowulf*: The Monsters and the Critics," it has been frequently republished. I will cite the authoritative edition prepared by Christopher Tolkien in J. R. R. Tolkien, *The Monsters and the Critics and Other Essays*, ed. Christopher Tolkien (Boston: Houghton Mifflin, 1984), 109–161. This quotation appears on p. 145.

35. Tolkien, "On Fairy Stories," 148.

CHAPTER 28

FAITH, FEAR, SILENCE, AND MUSIC IN INGMAR BERGMAN'S MEDIEVAL VISION OF *THE SEVENTH SEAL* AND *THE VIRGIN SPRING*

ALEXIS LUKO

IN a program note that accompanied the release of *The Seventh Seal* (*Det sjunde inseglet*) in 1957, Swedish film director Ingmar Bergman explained that he sought to "paint in the same way as a medieval church painter."[1] With his "paintbrush" he conjured up the Middle Ages again a few years later in the cinematic world he created for *The Virgin Spring* (*Jungfrukällan*, 1960). While both films employ detailed sets and costumes that evoke medieval times, they also incorporate into the cinematic context a number of stock "medievalisms" derived from other genres.[2] In *The Seventh Seal* these include a failed holy crusade, plague-infested villages, a knight and his squire, an accused witch who dies at the stake, a traveling troupe of entertainers, and a holy procession of flagellants. Ultimately and inexorably, the film draws us into the medievalistic *danse macabre*, with an iconic image that has since been burned into the collective consciousness. In *The Virgin Spring* the focus is on the medievalism reflected in rituals of paganism and Christianity that collide against the backdrop of day-to-day goings-on in a typical medieval household: dressing, praying, food preparation, sleeping, eating, and tending to animals. It culminates in a series of brutal murders, which set an early cinematic benchmark for our modern perception of "going medieval."[3]

Both films, in fact, present a medieval worldview where violence takes center stage.[4] This is violence that is multivalent: from the grand-scale war machine of the Crusades to the rape of a young girl by bandits; from flagellation and bodily mutilation to murder in the name of medieval law; from spiteful magic cast in a prayer to Odin to the creeping internal violence of the plague reflected in the terror inspired by the appearance of the Grim Reaper. On the one hand, both films are considered paragons of the horror genre.[5] On the other hand, within their medieval contexts, violence can be viewed as legitimized and symptomatic of the gruesomeness of an era in which, according to French medievalist Marc Bloch, "terror...was...deep-rooted in the social structure and in the mentality of the age."[6]

In his writings, Bergman makes clear that much of the inspiration for his imagination of the medieval is personalized and cobbled together from childhood memories:

> As a child I was sometimes allowed to accompany my father when he travelled about to preach in the small country churches in the vicinity of Stockholm....For a small boy the sermon itself of course is a matter purely for grown-ups. While Father preached away in the pulpit and the congregation prayed, sang or listened, I devoted my interest to the church's mysterious world of low arches, thick walls, the smell of eternity, the coloured sunlight quivering above the strangest vegetation of medieval paintings and carved figures on ceiling and walls. There was everything that one's imagination could desire: angels, saints, dragons, prophets, devils, humans. There were very frightening animals: serpents in paradise, Balaam's ass, Jonah's whale, the eagle of the Revelation. All this surrounded by a heavenly, earthly and subterranean landscape of a strange yet familiar beauty. In a wood sat Death, playing chess with the Crusader. Clutching the branch of a tree was a naked man with staring eyes, while down below stood Death, sawing away to his heart's content. Across gentle hills Death led the final dance towards the dark lands. But in the other arch the Holy Virgin was walking in a rose-garden, supporting the Child's faltering steps, and her hands were those of a peasant woman....On the other hand, I defended myself against the dimly sensed drama that was enacted in the crucifixion picture in the chancel. My mind was stunned by the extreme cruelty and the extreme suffering. Not until much later were faith and doubt to become my constant companions. It has been self-evident and profitable to give shape to the experiences of my childhood.[7]

Here, the links between Bergman's childhood and the narrative of *The Seventh Seal* are striking. Peeling away the layers of the medievalist clichés of Bergman's memories and imaginings (both of which typically meld into one another), one might say that his medieval films permitted him to live vicariously through the existential crises of his protagonists—crises that authorized him to pose his own personal questions about the influence of his Lutheran minister father, Erik Bergman, and the significance of religion in his life. It was, after all, shortly after directing these films that he went on to make *Through a Glass Darkly*, *Winter Light*, and *The Silence*—his so-called Trilogy of Faith that symbolizes his break with the church.[8]

It is no wonder, then, that Bergman's brand of medievalism *questions*, seeking light in an otherwise "dark age."[9] *The Virgin Spring* and *The Seventh Seal* may feature their fair share of medieval religious zealots, but where there are zealots, there are also characters internally haunted by their own profound spiritual doubts. Antonius Block, the knight in *The Seventh Seal*, and Töre, the father of *The Virgin Spring*, for example (played by Max von Sydow in both cases), are destabilized by the extreme and needless violence in their worlds and the fear that God may not exist. Both appear willing to battle supernatural powers, with Antonius Block taking on Death through a game of chess and Töre combatting an unseen and unknowable power (is it God, guilt, nature, faith, or fear?) in the form of a tree.

Bergman is often justly lauded for his psychologically engaging narratives and beautiful images, including his stunning use of light and shadow. The images in *The Virgin Spring* and *The Seventh Seal* must certainly be accounted among his best. But as I have argued elsewhere, Bergman was no less masterful in how he crafted his soundtracks.[10] Indeed, it is with sound and music that he takes risks, departs from convention, and establishes a unique style.

As with his later work, Bergman uses music and sound in *The Virgin Spring* and *The Seventh Seal* in powerfully unsettling ways. He and Swedish composer Erik Nordgren (1913–1992) aimed for stylized medieval tunes alongside more modern and even jarringly anachronistic scoring.[11] At times, the soundtrack relies on a type of Brechtian alienation effect, one that destabilizes and leads viewers to question the film and the filmmaker, just as the characters in Bergman's narratives question their beliefs in higher powers such as love and faith. In terms of scoring for *The Seventh Seal* and *The Virgin Spring*, I would argue that, in these early films, we can already hear a distinctive Bergmanian sonic style beginning to congeal. It is this auteurist perspective of sonic medievalism that serves as the focus of this chapter.

Below, I will set out to explore how the soundtracks of *The Seventh Seal* and *The Virgin Spring* draw on musical inspiration from the Middle Ages and how they play a role in underlining medievalism's oft-cited tropes of Christianity versus paganism, nature, death, brotherhood, and violence. I argue that music and sound effects in these films play key roles in fetishizing medieval violence, establishing sonic horror tropes, underscoring beautiful moments of brotherly communion, and highlighting, simultaneously, both faith and doubt in God. For *The Seventh Seal*, my discussion of Bergman's approach to musical medievalism will focus on how music is mapped onto medieval ritual to forge bonds of brotherhood. Bergman also employs music to create a sense of medieval atemporality, ultimately supporting the dichotomy between religious fervor and doubt in the existence of God. This opposition between Christianity and its "lack," whether represented by doubt or paganism, is also taken up in my discussion of *The Virgin Spring*, where musical medievalism is invoked to fetishize medieval violence and establish sonic horror tropes. Further, a musical theme is woven through different semantic spaces of the film's narrative, heard first as an innocent medieval tune and later as a terrorizing acoustic presence from offscreen. Bergman's narratives and music might indeed hearken back to medieval times, but medievalism for Bergman becomes an alternative lens through which to not only question his own notions about faith but also to present his own distinctive cinematic vision of the world.

The Seventh Seal

The *Seventh Seal* begins and ends with a quote from Revelation:

> And when the Lamb opened the seventh seal, there was silence in heaven about the space of half an hour....And the seven angels, which had the seven trumpets, prepared themselves to sound.[12]

It is, seemingly, within this silence that *The Seventh Seal* unfolds—an in-between space as time stands still for a metaphorical half hour.[13] This is the calm before the fire and brimstone of Judgment Day. It is within this liminal space that the Knight encounters Death and attempts to outwit him during a chess match while contemplating love, faith, and the existence of God. Though silence plays an important role in *The Seventh Seal* and is a part of Bergman's signature sonic style (discussed below in the section "Karin's Song: Balladic Transformations"), the film is also rich in music and sound. In fact, as was often the case with Bergman, music served as inspiration in the film's conception.[14]

> I had acquired a huge record player, and I bought Carl Ferenc Fricsay's recording of Carl Orff's *Carmina burana*. I used to let Orff thunder forth in the morning before I set off for rehearsal....One day when I was listening to the final choral [sic] in *Carmina burana*, it suddenly struck me that I had the theme for my next film![15]

Orff's *Carmina Burana* is based on a manuscript of the same name containing over 250 eleventh-, twelfth-, and thirteenth-century texts and songs.[16] Though Orff's music is not featured in the film, the medieval inspiration that incited its creation is certainly embedded in the narrative.[17] And, whether Bergman was aware of it or not, miniatures from the manuscript underline topical themes from the film: the *Rota Fortunae* (Wheel of Fortune), a forest, a pair of lovers, a drinking scene—and even a game of chess.

Music and Downfall

According to Bergman's memoirs, what particularly inspired him about *Carmina Burana* was "the whole idea of people traveling through the downfall of civilization and culture, giving birth to new songs." In the *Seventh Seal*, there are two such characters: Jöns (a squire traveling with a crusader) and Jof (a roving musician, acrobat, and juggler), both of whom sing along their routes while pestilence, rape, murder, and violence become symptomatic of the medieval world order. As the trusty squire of Antonius Block, Jöns has voyaged for ten years through the Holy Land and witnessed the atrocities of war on a crusade that he claims is "so stupid that only an idealist could have thought it up." With his down-to-earth, jovial outlook on life and his bodily preoccupations, Jöns is a good foil to the spiritual, intellectual, and brooding knight. He proudly describes himself as a man who "grins at death, scoffs at the Lord, laughs at himself, and leers at the girls.... Absurd to all. Even to himself. Meaningless to heaven and of no interest to hell." His style of music exposes his lower social class and his irreverent but simultaneously honest approach toward life. He seems like a modern agnostic, comfortable with the idea that there may be no God and that it is up to humanity to chart its own course. He has an uneducated working-class common-sense attitude, which was often admired and held up as an example by educated socialists in the 1960s.[18]

From this perspective, a character like Jöns diverges from the tortured artists, actors, dancers, and musicians of the educated elite who populate Bergman's films. Anyone who has watched more than a couple Bergman films would appreciate the fact that it is typical to encounter miserable self-loathing artists, who attempt to escape the bleakness of their reality by seeking out glimmers of artistic beauty. When Bergman depicts musicians, overly rehearsed music is often associated with characters who are psychologically detached from reality and/or devoid of the ability to make meaningful human connections.[19] As an unrehearsed musician who sings out of personal enjoyment, Jöns is clearly not part of this group.[20] The tune by which we are introduced to him is perhaps not so far off in tone from some of the more risqué *Carmina Burana* texts and tells us much about the differences between the knight and squire.

> Between a strumpet's legs I lie
> That's the place for such as I
> The Lord is aloft you know
> But Satan finds us here below.

As he sings, he has a look of mischief in his eyes, clearly attempting to provoke (albeit playfully) the noble knight he serves. The songs of Jöns are spontaneously created, exhibiting unrehearsed purity and musical honesty.

The Seventh Seal's other traveling musician is Jof. He and his wife, Mia, comprise two members of a three-person traveling theater troupe. Along with their infant son Mikael, Jof (re: Joseph) and Mia (re: Mary) are akin to a holy family. Spared from death, they represent the only hope for the future amid a bleak backdrop of plague, death, and barbarity. Unlike Block and Jöns, Jof has unwavering faith in God. He is not searching for escape from his bleak reality. Even when faced with death and forcibly coerced to dance like a bear in the bar, his faith is unshaken because he already lives in a blessed state.

His obliviousness to the suffering of the era and his cheery outlook serve as a refreshing (if not comedic) counterpoint to the doom and gloom around him. Jof is consistently featured in beautiful family shots, in lush natural settings, incessantly smiling with a look of blissful contentment plastered on his face and bathed in a soundscape of birdsong. This obliviousness has much to do with his immersion in art and family life—preoccupations that permit him a seemingly atemporal existence, allowing him to somehow escape the bitter realities of the medieval period.

When we first meet Jof, he is waking up in the theatre troupe's traveling wagon. He humorously swats at a fly, playfully interacts with his horse, and starts to practice his juggling. Then, in the morning light, he suddenly sees an apparition of the Virgin Mary and Child. The scene is accompanied by nondiegetic angelic choral singing. The same music repeats when Mia tells Jof she loves him, thus creating a link with the holy family that is not only thematic but also musical. Later in the film, Jof has a second vision when he sees Death and the knight playing chess (he is the only individual other than Block who can see Death) and a third and final vision—perhaps the most poignant image of any Bergman film—of a *danse macabre* involving a human chain composed of the

FIGURE 28.1 *Danse macabre* from *The Seventh Seal*. © AB Svensk Filmindustri.

knight, the smith Plog, and Lisa, his wife, Raval, Jöns, Skat on his lute, and Death with his scythe victoriously leading the way (see Figure 28.1).

Besides the birdsong and angelic choral singing, Jof is also associated with a tune that he claims he wrote while lying awake the previous night. He sings it *a cappella* to the lovely Mia as she naps in his arms under the shade of a tree:

> A dove is perched on a branch
> At Midsummer time
> He sings so sweetly of Jesus Christ
> And in heaven there's great rejoicing.

Jof's song is later repeated when it becomes the accompanying music to what is apparently the most poignant moment of Antonius Block's life. It is a scene of serene beauty in which Block, Jöns, the mute girl, Jof, and Mia share in a communal meal of wild strawberries and milk. When Jof asks the group if they would care to listen to his song about springtime, Jöns brags that he too writes songs—particularly one about a "wanton fish," that they would probably not want to hear anyway, as some among them "don't appreciate art." It is Jof who ultimately performs his spring song for the group, but he opts to forego the lyrics in favor of humming. While fingering the strings of his lute, he is quite

FIGURE 28.2   "Jof's Song" from *The Seventh Seal*. © AB Svensk Filmindustri.

unaware of the ominous death mask poised over his right shoulder, an almost comedic example of Bergman's preoccupation with the topic of art's obliviousness as medieval civilization crumbles (see Figure 28.2).

Music and Medieval Ritual: Forging Bonds

During the scene in which Jof performs his tune about springtime, Bergman employs an effect akin to a visual close-up, but this is an *aural* close-up.[21] Jof stops humming but continues to strum the strings of his lute, thus permitting Bergman to focus on Block's voice:

> I shall remember this hour of peace, these strawberries, this bowl of milk, your faces in the dusk, Mikael asleep, Jof with his lyre. I'll try to remember what we spoke of. And I'll hold this memory between my hands as carefully as a bowl brimming with fresh milk.

This is a technique that Bergman used later in his career in countless films that is typically reserved for intimate moments in which characters express profound thoughts. In more extreme cases, Bergman departs from one of the most basic conventions of cinematic realism by breaking the rules of ambience in sound design and dispensing entirely with "room tone"—the background added postproduction that lends a sense of depth and verisimilitude to the setting of a scene. In films such as *Sawdust and Tinsel, Hour of the Wolf, Winter Light,* and *From the Life of the Marionettes,* Bergman employs something Michel Chion would call *suspension*—the menacing and mysterious effect of interrupting ambient sounds—by muting most sounds so as to single out the dialogue and permit (according to Bergman) "the voices to ring freely" or by muting dialogue (*verbal chiaroscuro*) and ambient sound so as to highlight one lone sound effect.[22] This latter device, known as a *hyperbolized sound effect,* is most famously expressed through the ticking clocks, the dripping water, the tolling bells, and the tweeting birds (examined in the section "Medievalisms in *The Virgin Spring*" below) of the Bergmanian soundscape.[23]

In the case of Block's speech, *suspension* aids in generating a sensation that is otherworldly, adding to the layered religious connotation(s) of the scene. Indeed, juxtaposed with Jof's Christian tune, there is a pagan and ritualistic sense to how Block makes his pronouncement and to how he anoints the moment by cupping both hands around the bowl and taking a sip of the milk. Akin to a holy communion, this is truly one of the only times in the film that Block smiles contentedly, indicating that he has found a sense of inner peace. After years of searching and crusading in the Holy Land, is this finally his answer to the meaning of life? Jof's humming resumes as Block breaks away from the beautiful moment to rejoin Death, who is eager to resume their chess match. Though unspoken, it becomes clear, nonetheless, that Block's fresh gusto is driven by his new-found desire to save Mia, Jof, and Mikael from Death's clutches.

What can we make of Bergman's use of music in this scene? As in many Bergman films, some moments of diegetic music-making resonate with magic, with seducing, healing, and affecting moments that shape and transform the characters of his narratives. In his later films, Bergman often relied on the music of Bach to express narrative "moments of perfection" in which characters experience a sense of intense communion.[24] In earlier films such as *The Seventh Seal* and *The Virgin Spring*, however, Bergman uses a wide variety of different music for these kinds of moments. This wide variety allows for a correspondingly wide range of semantic possibilities. Jof's tune about springtime, for example, is open to different interpretations. Is it possible that it was divinely inspired? Does it reflect his connections to nature or of his visions of the Virgin and Child? Is he attempting to create a pseudochurchlike setting by providing musical accompaniment to the "holy" communion that unfolds? Whatever we are to believe, it is a tune that certainly gives Jof and Block's lives meaning and, through performance, helps to weave a spell on one of the most memorable scenes of *The Seventh Seal*. Jof's music, combined with wild strawberries and milk, stimulates the senses of Antonius Block, creating an at once sensual and pseudoreligious experience that is more powerful than what any crusade or institutionalized religious experience has offered him to date. The music forces time to stand still, generating a Bergmanian prolonged moment of "silence" and creating a sense of spiritual community that is felt so strongly that it acts as a salve, healing and purifying Antonius Block, ultimately making him feel so connected to Jof, Mia, and Mikael that he changes the course of the narrative and decides to dedicate himself to saving Jof's family from the clutches of Death.

Observation and Atemporality

To contrast with the above example, where music is responsible for bringing community together and individuals are brought to a deeper understanding of themselves, we turn now to a scene in which music is employed to underscore conflict. In Bergman's films, the violent acts he depicts often involve perpetrators, victims, and also observers. The cinematic "gaze," therefore, is perceptible not only at the level of the film viewer, but also at the level of the on-screen observer. Bergman's observers are sometimes horrified and at other times complicit—demonstrating a sort of abject pleasure in the violence they witness.

One of the most poignant moments in *The Seventh Seal* that focuses on violence and observers and happens to also involve music, is the procession of the flagellants.[25] Before investigating this scene, I would like to reflect on the main protagonist, Antonius Block, and his role as observer. Though he seems to embody the stereotypical figure of a medieval paladin, Bergman's knight in shining armor wears a look of weariness and despair on his face. Having just fought for ten years in the Crusades, Block returns to his homeland, wondering about the point of his efforts. Now home, he wages new fights against fate and faith. Rather than bravely rescuing a damsel in distress, he half-heartedly attempts to save an accused witch from burning at the stake. When she gives a sign of being possessed by some form of disturbing spirit, he finds himself unable to act, other than to question her in hope of finding some kind of proof of the existence of God or the Devil. Unsatisfied, he then "adopts" a family of traveling performers and makes it his new goal to save them from Death. And, while questioning the existence of God, he comes to terms with his place in the world. He is a decidedly modern man—questioning, philosophizing, and grappling with his faith. His experience in an iconic medieval role, as a crusader, has made him an outsider and observer of his own medieval world. In these ways, one might say that Block works outside the *medieval imaginary*.[26]

How does Bergman's soundtrack reflect Block's status as outsider? When we first see him, he is praying on a beach. The scene is white and washed out, the lack of cinematic focus and clarity perhaps reflective of his own self-doubt. Rather than a great revelation through prayer and rather than God communicating something poignant to the knight (his most fervent wish throughout the film), it is, instead, Death that answers his prayers.[27] The appearance of Death on the beach (which has, by now, become one of the most commonly referenced Bergman scenes on film) coincides with a sudden sounding of a melodramatic stinger for bass voice and orchestra and the muting of the crashing waves, evoking a distilled quality and ethereal silence that is perhaps the underlying stillness of that apocalyptic half hour referred to in the book of Revelation. Is this the imagination? Is it a reflection of memory? Is it the end of time?[28] Whatever the answer, the deathly stillness is linked to Block and to Death, thus situating both figures on the same plane—an in-between place beyond reality. Following the silence, the knight and Death begin their chess game, meant essentially to delay the inevitable and buy the knight time as he contemplates his beliefs. As they begin, the "Death stinger" expands slightly to include a three-note descending motive. Along with the frightful modernist crashes of the "Dies irae, Dies illa" shrieked by voice and orchestra during the opening credits, these stingers (which are admittedly reminiscent of unsophisticated Hollywoodisms) do seem like peculiar musical choices in a film about the Middle Ages, but through their jarring quality, they aid in enhancing Block's outsider status.

Bergman does indeed allow for quite a musical potpourri in *The Seventh Seal* (folk song, dramatic stingers, modernist scoring, medieval/modal-styled interludes), but I would argue that much can be said for a technique that manages to destabilize the listener or viewer and set temporality off-balance.[29] Such an atemporal approach does much, in fact, to demonstrate what Bettina Bildhauer has defined as something that typifies medieval films' "conception of time as non-linear" and to feature past and future "as co-present."[30] The jarring musical juxtapositions also aid in creating a distancing effect that underline key thematic conflicts in the film: paganism/Christianity, blind faith/questioning, life/death. These effects alienate the audience from the film and cause them to question the filmmaker, just as his characters question their God. In the soundscapes created for *The Seventh Seal*—and, as I will discuss below in the section

"Medievalisms in *The Virgin Spring*," for this latter film as well—Bergman musically underlines thematic oppositions of paganism and Christianity in medieval religious society as Odin and the Grim Reaper clash with an invisible and mute God.

The Procession of the Flagellants: Expressing Religious Faith and Doubt through Music

Similar alienation and distancing effects return in the procession of the flagellants— arguably the most remarkable musical event of *The Seventh Seal*.[31] In this scene, there are two principal musical techniques that aid in amplifying a sense of disorientation, thus highlighting those narrative moments where religious faith and doubt collide: *aural counterpoint* (when musical juxtapositions occur) and *aural disjuncture* (for sudden unexpected shifts from one sonic event to another).

Immediately before the flagellant scene begins, a theatrical performance unfolds with Mia dressed as a jester, Jof donning horns, and Skat in a feather headdress. Though the troop seems to rely on their art for their livelihood, they appear naive and untalented. The camera pans for reactions of audience members, who are less than impressed with the performers' poor entertainment skills. Snide comments can be heard and, to great peals of laughter, a tomato is even thrown at Skat's face, thus prompting him to depart from the stage to have a tryst with the smith's wife. The two have a comical encounter in the forested area behind the theater stage, an example of life imitating art, as it echoes the earlier on-stage action in which Jof played a cuckolded husband. As the absurd romantic tryst carries on in the background, Jof and Mia sing a particularly relevant song about Death with a refrain that warns, "The Black One is on the shore." The song has lyrics about a world turned upside down and is replete with animal sounds (hilariously sounded by Mia and Jof and actual animals nearby). The joy on the performers' faces and their sense of play demonstrate naivety and complete obliviousness to the prescience of their song and the actual reality that Death *is* indeed waiting for them on the beach. As Mia beats harder on her hand drum and Jof strums more convincingly on his lute, chanting "The Black one stays and stays on the shore," their tune is suddenly cut short through aural counterpoint, with the overlap of new music—the Dies irae (Day of Wrath)—a chant from the Mass for the Dead.

Bursting on the theatrical scene, a competing and much more commanding type of theater unfolds, this time involving a group of flagellants. Jof and Mia's tune is obliterated as a powerful beat, with a timbre akin to a war drum, accompanies the procession, and we hear the authoritative chanting of a choir of synchronized voices.[32] A close-up of Jof and Mia's faces reveals fear.

The camera is positioned at a low angle as the flagellants enter the scene. The swinging incense holders held by monks pour forth billows of smoke and, besides the drum, we hear the screaming of the flagellants who (as reflected in the script) "whip themselves and each other, howling ecstatically…in violent, almost rhythmic outbursts." As is the case in countless other Bergman films, the observers are as important in this scene as the flagellating "performers." Bergman cuts back and forth among flagellants, village folk, close-ups of the effigy of Christ, the horrified reactions of onlookers, pained faces of believers, crying women reaching their hands into the sky, kneeling penitents, and the stoic nonreactions of Squire Jöns and Block.[33]

The next prominent acoustic disruption comes through a technique that I will call *aural disjuncture*.[34] Suddenly, the Dies irae stops and Bergman focuses only on the sound effects of the wailing. There is the simultaneous murmur of at least fifty voices reciting prayers and executing pained cries. Once again, this is a trademark Bergman technique, where screaming and/or crying is the focus of a scene (e.g., *Hour of the Wolf*, *Saraband*, *Fanny and Alexander*).[35] Another moment of aural disjuncture arrives (as screams are interrupted with dialogue) when a man angrily begins shouting at the crowds. His harangue emphasizes how the Black Death has made all their earthly concerns pointless. Bergman places him in a shot with the proscenium of the traveling troupe behind him, thus making links between his speech and theater, reminding us of the intricate layers of illusion that Bergman generates in this scene. Though he speaks directly and powerfully to the crowd, his speech seems rehearsed and smacks of theatricality:

> God is punishing us. We shall all perish from the Black Death. You there gaping like cattle, and you bloated with complacency, don't you know this could be your final hour? Death is at your back. I see his crown gleaming in the sun. His scythe flashes above your heads. Which of you will he strike first?…don't you know you fools are all going to die? You're all doomed. Do you hear me? Do you hear me? Doomed! Doomed! Doomed!

Another moment of aural disjuncture occurs as a deep bass voice leads a recapitulation of the Dies irae. The flagellants take up their whips and crucifixes as they continue their parade to the next town. After the camera shifts to a top-down angle (perhaps signifying Block's increased detachment from organized religion), a visual fade of the flagellants occurs and the singing is suddenly muted.[36] Complete silence accompanies a shot of an open field for a few seconds. But this is only to be disrupted one final time with a dismissive, quite humorously timed comment from Squire Jöns: "All this ranting about doom. Do they really expect modern people to take that drivel seriously?" Cue the laughter in the cinema.

Bergman's stark juxtaposition of Jof and Mia's ditty about "Death on the Beach" with the flagellant procession makes it almost impossible to refrain from comparing and contrasting both musical experiences. The constant sonic shifts create a sense of destabilization that emulates a Brechtian alienation effect, thus forcing the viewer to actively question what exactly has transpired. Bergman suggests that there is a similar level of artifice in both displays, thus blurring the line between theater and religion. Those like the townspeople can see through the laughable amateur play and song performed by Jof, Skat, and Mia, while those like Block and Squire Jöns can see through both the theatrical troupe's performance and the religious procession. By constantly tearing the rug from under our feet—moving swiftly from medieval song, to religious chant and violent procession, to scream, to rhetorical harangue, to religious procession, to irreverent commentary—and by focusing on performers *and* observers, Bergman therefore drains the intensity of the theatricality and ensures that we, as viewers, have little chance to get overly caught up in the illusion of the religious procession. Here, music and sound (in terms of substance and competition) underscore the conflict between different groups of observers and participants in Bergman's medieval universe, thus emulating a struggle that transpires within Block's own psyche.

Medievalisms in *The Virgin Spring*

Of all Bergman's films, perhaps none so blatantly fetishizes violence as much as *The Virgin Spring*. Its plot is adapted from "Pehr Tyrsons (or Töres) döttrar i Wänge"/*Töres' Daughters in Vänge*, a medieval ballad that shocked Bergman and his screenwriter, Ulla Isaksson, in how it "censored nothing...report[ing] its tale harshly and ruthlessly."[37] The harshness of the ballad translates into a film so violent that it was censored in the United States upon its release. Vernon Young of the *Film Quarterly* wrote that it was "unbearably fraught with potency and terror."[38] Paul V. Beckley for *The New York Herald Tribune* called the rape scene "the most uncompromising thing of its kind on film," while Alton Cook for *The New York World Telegram* wrote about Bergman's "shock treatment" of the story and the narrative's "explosive" impact, wreaking havoc on "queasy stomachs," with a "rape scene explicit enough to shock sophisticated European audiences."[39] *The Virgin Spring* is now heralded by horror aficionados as the first rape-revenge horror film and was even remade by Wes Craven as *The Last House on the Left* (1972).

The *Virgin Spring* folk tale is found in a large number of Scandinavian, English, and Germanic sources, among which Bergman was most familiar with that relayed in an anthology of Swedish folk songs edited by Erik Gustaf Geijer and Arvid August Afzelius: *Svenska folk-visor från forntiden* (Ancient Swedish Folk Songs, published 1814–1816).[40] Once again, as with so many of Bergman's films, the inspiration is music. In this folk version, the three daughters of Töre dress in luxurious clothing and set out for church to attend Mass. En route, three bandit brothers approach them, asking, "Will ye be our wives or lose your lives?" When the three girls opt for the latter, the bandits murder them and steal their fine clothing. By coincidence, the bandits happen on the home of the unsuspecting Töre family, who feed them and put them up for the night. The parents reach the sickening realization that their daughters are dead when, in thanks for the hospitality, the bandits offer the silk dresses the daughters wore the morning of their disappearance. In revenge, Töre kills two of the men before asking the third his father's name. In a bitter twist of fate, he answers "Töre," indicating (impossible as it may seem) that the bandit brothers are long-lost sons. Devastated at the realization that so many of his children are dead, Töre vows to build a church to compensate for his sins.[41]

In Bergman's version, rather than three daughters, there are the two disparate personalities of Karin (Birgitta Pettersson) and her stepsister Ingeri (Gunnel Lindblom), who represent the clash of medieval Christianity and paganism. Bergman and his screenwriter invented the new character of Ingeri, undoubtedly to heighten a sense of psychological violence in the narrative. In this film version of the story, Ingeri's hatred of Karin becomes the center of a prototypical Bergmanian family-drama subplot that aids in ratcheting up tension in the film.

Our first glimpse at the family dynamic immediately suggests that, on the one hand, the Christian, fair-haired, and virginal Karin is spoiled. She has both mother (Birgitta Valberg) and father (Max von Sydow) wrapped around her little finger and seeks any means she can to manipulate them. Ingeri, on the other hand, with her wild hair and filthy clothing, has a questionable position in the family, assuming the status of both a stepsister and a servant girl, leaving many unanswered questions as to how she came to join them in the first place (Is she the product of infidelity? Is she an orphan?). While Karin represents Christianity and all that is virtuous, virginal, and pure, Ingeri occupies a Pagan, supernatural world. She is connected to nature in such a powerful way that she seems to blend quite literally and figuratively into the forest, where she hides when she acts as voyeur to her stepsister's rape and murder. She is also connected to the man in the woods, to fertility (with her pregnant belly), and to all that is bodily and earthy.

Karin's Song: Balladic Transformations

As is the case with *The Seventh Seal*, *The Virgin Spring* features diegetic music-making that plays a central role in the narrative. In fact, the entire film is enveloped in music. Besides the direct musical inspiration offered up by the ballad on which it is based, another folk-style ballad serves as a recurrent theme throughout, with music composed by Erik Nordgren and text by Ingmar Bergman: *Tigarrens och Karins visa*. The ballad "travels" throughout the film, acting as a vehicle of semantic meaning, aiding to guide the viewer as different "medievalisms" play out. First, it is presented as "whole" and pure and is eventually abstracted and transformed into something more ominous and predatory. An instrumental version of the ballad is introduced for the first time during the opening credits (see Figure 28.3).[42]

As shown in Figure 28.3, there is nothing authentically medieval about the tune. It features two modern flutes accompanied by a drum. It is in E natural minor and loosely follows baroque fugal practice with a fugue subject (mm. 1–2) borrowed from the monophonic folk tune introduced later in the film. The subject is introduced in Flute I

FIGURE 28.3   Nordgren, ballade, *Tigarrens och Karins visa.*

and repeated by Flute II (mm. 8–12) in counterpoint with a countersubject. Further re-entries of the subject are heard, creating counterpoint reminiscent of baroque textures.

The ballad is heard a second time, as Karin sets off for the church with Ingeri (see Figure 28.4). This is a condensed version that is quite different from the fugal style of the opening credits. Marked as cue *M 31 A "Början"* ("at the beginning") in Nordgren's score,

FIGURE 28.4 Nordgren, ballade, *Tigarrens och Karins visa*, condensed, with the sounds of birds overlaid.

it features a simple melody on Flute I accompanied by Flute II.[43] The sound effects of songbirds are heard for the first phrase with cuckoo birds joining for phrase 2.

Here, Karin sets off with Ingeri on horseback. As resident virgin, Karin is designated the duty of bringing candles to the church in the name of the Virgin Mary. After insisting on wearing her finest silk dress, Karin (demonstrating her childish nature) begs her family to make believe she is a rich woman. They feed her vanity, permitting her to wear her finest clothes; they bend to her wishes, going against their better judgment to keep her home for the day; and they grant her desire to bring along her half-sister Ingeri. It is important to set this up, because it helps establish a network of guilt concerning Karin's eventual demise.

After the instrumental introduction, the tune takes on a new permutation (see Figure 28.5), this time as a monophonic ballad sung by a male voice—a beggar (*tiggarens* in Swedish) played by Allan Edwall.

> So lovely an apple orchard I know
> A maiden with virtues so dear
> Her hair like spun gold does flow
> Her eyes like the heavens so clear
> The streams flow so merrily
> All under the verdant trees
> In Springtime's breeze.

In this abbreviated version, the tune becomes more medieval by virtue of its reduced range and its monophonic texture.[44] After the first stanza about a maiden with golden

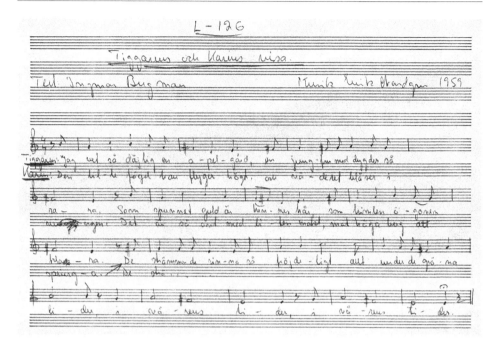

FIGURE 28.5 Nordgren, ballade, *Tigarrens och Karins visa*, monophonic setting.

hair—an obvious reference to Karin—the refrain text mentioning streams that "flow so merrily under the verdant trees" seems particularly poignant given the spring that suddenly appears at the site of Karin's murder. Here, the carefree nature of the text adds a level of bitter irony. As was the case with *The Seventh Seal*, the music here is oblivious to the terror about to unfold.

An instrumental interlude follows featuring yet a further condensed version of the ballad for only Flute I and the accompaniment of songbirds and cuckoo sounds. The music of the instrumental interlude (marked in Nordgren's score as cue M31 A "Slutet," meaning "End" in Swedish) fades in near the conclusion of a phrase, as if we are stumbling on a scene in which the music had previously started.[45]

For the second stanza, in a meta-moment, Karin takes over singing her own ballad as she and Ingeri continue their voyage on horseback by a lake and through a forest. As Karin sings, she refers to a bird soaring above mountains. But this is not an effortless flight path for the little bird. The poem suggests that it is, in fact, a laborious journey. Again, there is the accompaniment of birdsong and cuckoo birds.

> The little bird he soars so high
> And rides the wind on his wing
> It is such work, such work to fly
> And over high mountains to spring.

Though the text of the ballad has a folklike simplicity, the modal quality of the tune, the haunting timbre of the flutes, and the innocent voice of the childish girl create a sense of melancholy creepiness that evokes the supernatural. In this way, the song *establishes* (rather than draws on) a classic device in horror film—the children's song—found in *A Nightmare on Elmstreet* ("Freddy's Coming for You"), *The Birds* ("Risselty-Rosselty"), *Dark Water* ("Itsy Bitsy Spider"), and the lullabies in *The Ring* and *Rosemary's Baby*. The filming of the ballad montage is also rather unnerving, as many shots are from a distance, suggestive of an off-screen voyeur—perhaps a nod to Akira Kurosawa. His medieval-era masterpiece, *Rashomon*, is a film that Bergman admitted studying before making *The Virgin Spring* and one that, incidentally, also involves a rape in a forest viewed by a hidden observer.[46]

Besides the inherent creepiness in the tune, there is evidence to suggest that the supernatural also infiltrates the music through the accompanying sound effects. As mentioned previously, Bergman was very particular about the Foley effects that he introduced into his soundscapes and, as with everything in his films, he was meticulous about the quality and placement of every sound.[47] It is therefore important to question his use of birdcalls in *The Virgin Spring*. In an interview with Reuters near the end of his career in 2002, Bergman admitted, "I am normally afraid of birds." He also revealed how he linked birds to the otherworldly, stating that he believed that the ghost of his late wife Ingrid came to him in a dream as a "large, shimmering green bird."[48] We see evidence of Bergman's fears in many of his films. In *A Passion*, for example, a bird flies into a window pane as part of a chain reaction of escalating violence in the lives of Anna Fromm and Andreas Winkelman; as the words from the book of Revelation are spoken in *The Seventh Seal*, there is a shot of a lone bird flying through the air accompanied by one of Nordgren's clashing dissonant stingers[49] and there is a dead bird in *The Prison*, anticipating Birgitta-Carolina's suicide. Birds also figure prominently in *Hour of the Wolf* in a scene reminiscent (according to Robin Wood) of Hitchcock's *The Birds*, wherein Max Von Sydow moves through a corridor with sparrows and wild robins chasing him.[50] Later, in the same film, Sydow is attacked by birds and during *The Magic Flute* puppet presentation, Papageno's birds turn into ravens.

Besides those of the cuckoo and songbirds, other bird sounds figure prominently in *The Virgin Spring*. In the first frame we hear the crow of a rooster as Ingeri calls to her pagan God through a type of magical incantation: "Odin come, Odin come." The crowing continues through the cut to a new scene in which Christian ritual is the focus. Töre and his wife Märeta demonstrate religious fervor in front of a crucifix. As they pray, Sydow's ascetic wife pours hot wax on her wrist to honor "Jesus' day of agony." Here, the fact that the crowing can be heard throughout the pagan and Christian scenes suggests that that two types of religious prayers are occurring simultaneously in different rooms of the same household. This is how Bergman sets up the soundscape for the two main themes that will drive the narrative of the film—binaries that also accord with medievalist stereotypes. A similar style of juxtaposition occurs while the Töre family eats breakfast. There is an uncanny "Last Supper" style to how Bergman visually sets the scene. The rooster continues to crow, reminiscent of Peter's disloyalty in the Bible, and a foreshadowing, perhaps, of Ingeri's impending betrayal of her own stepsister. The sounds of a little chick are featured moments later with the servant woman:

"I nearly stepped on them out there in the dark," she exclaims, "You poor thing. Live out your wretched little life the way God allows all of us to live." Here, the bird is met-aphorically linked to Karin herself, who, unfortunately, will not manage to avoid being "stepped on" in the dark forest. Later, in what is arguably the most powerful scene of *The Virgin Spring* and one of the more formidable moments in Western art cinema, as Töre fells a tree with his bare hands, there is the accompanying sound of birdsong. The birdsong returns at the end with the nondiegetic accompaniment of an *a cappella* chorale as he gives his final speech at the site of the gurgling spring, where he swears to God that he will build a church in memory of his daughter and the murders he has committed.

The cuckoo is traditionally associated with cuckoldry, but it also has a range of other meanings that may be less familiar to international audiences. In Baltic cultures, the cuckoo is a symbol of pain, an announcer of important events such as birth and death, and is even related to the devil. According to Swedish folklore it was once customary to ask the cuckoo, "How many years shall I live?"[51] Along with the crowing rooster and the sound of an owl later in the film (discussed below), these bird sounds are associated with the supernatural, with paganism, and—by extension—with Ingeri, whereas the songbirds seem to underline narrative moments where Christianity is highlighted at the fore. Therefore, the sound effects themselves provide a key to reading the Christianity/paganism binaries that play out throughout the film.

Sound effects play an important role again with the old hermit soothsayer in the cottage, who claims to be able to hear and see things. He is a figure who may actually be Odin, given that both have one dead eye and that the latter was said to travel the world in a humble disguise. There is also an unmistakable sound of a raven (yet another birdcall) heard as Ingeri scrambles away from his cottage, a reference to Odin's trusty feathered companions, Huginn and Muninn who, according to the *Edda*, watch and listen to everything in the world and serve as his messengers. As he says to Ingeri, "I hear what I want to hear and see what I want to see. I hear what men whisper in secret, and see what they think no one sees. You can hear it yourself if you wish." Then, challenging Ingeri herself to open her ears and listen, she hears the pounding of horses' hooves that the old man prophesizes is the sound of "three dead men riding north."

Returning to the text of the ballad itself, the song accurately reflects Karin with her golden hair and clear blue eyes. After all, her beauty is noted by her proud parents, by jealous stepsister Ingeri, and, indeed, by all men who pass by. She has the onscreen attention of everyone. Even the soundtrack positions her as the subject of the ballad. The song may therefore be considered another musical permutation of Laura Mulvey's gaze, fusing both the visual and the aural spectrums.[52] Here, Bergman uses the ballad to fixate on Karin as subject of the film and the object of men's fantasies.

But the dynamics of the gaze in *The Virgin Spring* are more complex than what Mulvey's model allows. Karin is certainly objectified—but only until her death. After her murder, in the spirit of a true rape-revenge horror film, Karin's manifestation through the vestiges of the tune serves as a spooky reminder of her omnipresence and of her off-screen power as supernatural watcher, "gazing" from without in the shadows.

After the rape and murder of Karin, the tune transforms, shifting from a diegetic to a nondiegetic cinematic presence. Through death, Karin becomes what Michel Chion would identify as an *acousmêtre* (acoustical being): a powerful unseen/bodiless being with a voice that haunts from off screen.[53] The first transformation of Karin's tune/voice can be heard as the boy keeps watch over her dead body. Two phrases of the tune for solo flute are heard at a slowed-down tempo with altered pitches. Here, it is hardly surprising that it is the innocent young boy, a witness to Karin's murder, who is haunted by the tune as he seems to be the only one plagued with guilt. He vomits shortly following her murder and is too sick to eat while at the Töre family dinner table. The excruciating close-ups on his face make his moral terror all the more palpable. Later, as the boy attempts to fall asleep, he is wide-eyed, fearfully studying the shadows and the funnel of smoke as it escapes through the roof. Two phrases of Karin's tune return to haunt the boy. This time, the soundscape also includes the hoot of an owl and the bleat of goats, the latter further underscoring the boy's deep feelings of guilt because these animals were stolen by his bandit brothers, an appropriate biblical symbol of betrayal and blame thus highlighting themes of guilt in the film (of the boy, the parents, Ingeri, the bandits, and perhaps even the guilt of the transfixed cinematic viewer who is complicit in Karin's objectification, rape, and murder as the violence unfolds).[54]

The type of musical repetition featured in *The Virgin Spring* reflects what later becomes idiomatic of Bergman's sonic style, as illustrated in films such as *All These Women*, *Through a Glass Darkly*, *Cries and Whispers*, *Fanny and Alexander*, *Saraband*, and *In the Presence of a Clown*.[55] At times, through repetition, Bergman's musical excerpts take on a leitmotivic quality, representing a character or thematic idea. In other cases, repetition highlights relationships between characters. At other times, as in this instance, Bergman begins a film with a piece of music in its fullest form (usually during the opening credits) and subsequently varies and/or abstracts it on each repetition, allowing it to acquire new meaning on each repetition. "Tigarrens Visa," which begins its life as a full-fledged instrumental baroque-style fugue in the opening credits, eventually becomes abstracted as an innocent folk tune for voice and flutes and finally haunts and terrorizes from off screen as an abbreviated solo flute tune with altered pitches.[56]

In several films, from *Autumn Sonata* to *Saraband* to *Life of the Marionettes*, Bergman asks the question: What happens when musical magic falls into the wrong hands? This is because music in Bergman's films is often used as a weapon for competition, humiliation, seduction, and manipulation. A case in point in *The Virgin Spring* is the little ditty played by the bandits on the mouth harp, ostensibly what the bandits use to help attract the attention of Karin and ensnare her. The simplicity of the music cons her into making her believe in their innocent motivations. Enchanted and entertained, she reacts to their music like an enthralled child. Their music provides an illusion of safety, inspiring her to share her lunch with the bandits.

As for Karin's ballad, it becomes part of a magical sonic brew. She sings her own musical incantation through the first part of the film: a mix of music and sound effects that suggest the infiltration of Ingeri's pagan spell. Eventually, music of the original ballad is cinematized as art imitates art. Later in the film, through "Tigarrens Visa's" afterlife as nondiegetic music, a new spell is cast as it is increasingly associated with Karin's powers to exact revenge, by inciting terror in the young boy after her death.

Perhaps most haunting, however, is the terrible silence that marks the second half of *The Virgin Spring*. Without the happy chatter of Karin and without the diegetic singing, all sound effects (of birds, of eating with the bandits at the dinner table, of the brutal murders, of the chortled grief of the parents) resound with haunting potency. In this way, Bergman's sculpted soundscape of revenge and guilt is comparable to the in-between space quoted in Revelation—a "deafening" silence before the storm that terrorizes from an off-screen locale where Bergman, the sonic auteur, pulls the strings.

Conclusion

In *The Seventh Seal* and *The Virgin Spring*, we are witness to juxtapositions that have come to typify medieval films: Christianity versus paganism, brotherhood versus alienation, rich versus poor, extreme violence versus compassion, and faith versus superstition. For these two early films, Bergman might have found inspiration in medieval music, but where he strays from medievalist tropes is in the way his own auteurist visions infiltrate his narratives and soundscapes. As I mentioned previously in reference to *The Seventh Seal*, many of the most enduring images spring from Bergman's childhood memories. In this way, like so much of Bergman's art, autobiography and imagination meld and coexist.

I have shown how Bergman's brand of sonic medievalism fits more generally into his sonic style. Though the soundtracks themselves merely make modest attempts at authenticity in terms of musical instrumentation, medieval styles, or genre, they do manage, nonetheless, to establish Bergman's sonic thumbprint while simultaneously highlighting the overriding medievalist juxtapositions mentioned previously. Musical techniques for *The Seventh Seal* include: (1) a sense of atemporality through diverse musical choices that cover a range of styles, (2) diegetic compositional spontaneity to suggest unrehearsed honesty and communion with nature, God, and other individuals, (3) the use of modern nondiegetic music to represent the sense of alienation of the knight as he finds himself outside the medieval imaginary, and (4) jarring musical shifts (aural counterpoint and aural disjuncture) to create an alienation effect, underlining key thematic conflicts. For *The Virgin Spring*, musical techniques include: (1) sound effects that symbolize the juxtaposition of paganism and Christianity, (2) the use/invention of sonic horror tropes such as the haunting ballad sung by Karin that ends up serving as the main leitmotivic material for the film, (3) musical repetition, abbreviation, and transformation to signal a change in how music is used/perceived, and (4) an *acousmêtre* that takes the form of the tune, which ultimately represents Karin's spirit, haunting from off screen. Finally, perhaps the greatest indicator that we are indeed in the "Dark Ages" is Bergman's copious use of silence in both films to create a sense of discomfort, terror, ignorance, and fear of the unknown. Evoking the silence described in the book of

Revelation, this cinematic silence suggests that time itself is standing still, transporting us to an in-between off-screen space where imagination, art, and dream intersect in a typically Bergmanian universe.

Bergman believed in the magical powers of music and that it had the ability to act as salve (as Jof's tune in *The Seventh Seal*). But he also highlights it as a medium for more dangerous acts—to brainwash desperate villagers (Dies irae), to seduce unsuspecting and naive young girls (the mouth harp), to disrupt cinematic illusion and force viewers to question what they are viewing (aural counterpoint and disjuncture), and to haunt from off screen (Karin's ballad).[57] But, more often than not, the true "demon" was beyond the screen, behind the camera lens, assuming the form of Bergman himself, using diegetic and nondiegetic music to destabilize and torture characters and audience members alike.[58]

Bergman's struggle with his faith can be read through the soundscapes of *The Seventh Seal* and *The Virgin Spring*. They alienate, disrupt, confuse, frighten, induce guilt, and, at times, for precious moments, succeed in bringing individuals together in beautiful communion. Bergman's identity as a filmmaker was shaped fundamentally by *The Virgin Spring* and *The Seventh Seal*, meaning that from early on, medievalisms fused with his instinctive cinematic tendencies so as to create a decidedly Bergmanian aesthetic that endured for the remainder of his career.[59]

NOTES

My thanks to Stephen Meyer, Kirsten Yri, and Campion Carruthers, who provided invaluable critiques on earlier drafts of this chapter.

1. "My intention has been to paint in the same way as the medieval church painter, with the same objective interest, with the same tenderness and joy. My beings laugh, weep, howl, fear, speak, answer, play, suffer, ask, ask. Their terror is the plague, Judgment Day, the star whose name is Wormwood. Our fear is of another kind but our words are the same. Our question remains." From a program note issued by Svensk Filmindustri, coinciding with the film's release in 1957. See Birgitta Steene, ed. "A Program Note to *The Seventh Seal* by Ingmar Bergman," in *Focus on the Seventh Seal* (Englewood Cliffs, NJ: Prentice Hall, 1972), 71. Translator unknown.
2. Though these stock medievalisms may not yet have been established in film, they are certainly encountered in plays, poetry, and songs from the Middle Ages and beyond.
3. Quentin Tarantino's *Pulp Fiction* (1994) most famously popularized the phrase "get medieval on your ass."
4. As put by Bettina Bildhauer, "*Medieval* is often used as a by-word for brutality, torture and violence…and medieval films abound with battles, brawls, dungeons and death." See *Filming the Middle Ages* (London: Reaktion Books, 2011), 51.
5. Many writers have acknowledged Bergman's influence on the horror genre. Emily Brick identifies *The Virgin Spring* as a prototypical rape-revenge horror film in "Baise-moi and the French Rape-Revenge Films," in *European Nightmares: Horror Cinema in Europe since 1945*, ed. Patricia Allmer, Emily Brick, and David Huxley (London: Wallflower Press, 2012), 94. Also see Samuel J. Umland, "World of Blood and Fire: Lang, Mabuse, and Bergman's

The Serpent's Egg," in *European Nightmares*, 195–206. Bergman's interest in horror is also discussed by Roger Ebert, who links Bergman's *Cries and Whispers* and William Friedkin's *The Exorcist*, http://www.rogerebert.com/reviews/the-exorcist-1973, accessed January 26, 2017. As I note in Chapter 6 of *Sonatas, Screams, and Silence*, Bergman's films explore horror-genre topics such as cannibalism, vampirism, psychological torture, mutilation, murder, sexual taboos, madness, and the supernatural.

6. Marc Bloch, *Feudal Society*, vol. 2, *Social Classes and Political Organization*, trans. L. A. Manyon (London: Routledge, 1961), 411. Translation of *La société féodale* (Paris: Michel, 1939–1940).

7. Steene, *Focus on The Seventh Seal*, 70–71.

8. Bergman's break with religion is perhaps best represented by the frightful "spider god" that terrorizes Karin in *Through a Glass Darkly*.

9. In *Filming the Middle Ages*, Bildhauer writes, "Such images [of plague-stricken worlds and death] have shaped (and been shaped by) our rather biased view of the Middle Ages as a dark time of barbarism and ignorance, brutality and superstition, dungeons, disease and dirt," 8.

10. Alexis Luko, *Sonatas, Screams, and Silence: Music and Sound in the Films of Ingmar Bergman* (New York: Routledge, 2016).

11. Nordgren was a Swedish composer who scored thirteen films for Bergman between the years 1949 and 1967. Bergman's consistent collaboration with Nordgren was convenient because of the latter's role as the in-house composer at Svensk Filmindustri.

12. Revelation 8:1 and 8:6.

13. In Bergman's *Wood Painting*, the knight speaks of "silent music" in a speech before the final *danse macabre*: "Across a spiritual desert, I feel God's nearness like the vibrations of a mighty bell. Suddenly my emptiness is filled with music of no tone, as if in waves of innumerable voices." Translated in Steen, *Focus on the Seventh Seal*, 172.

14. Bergman often compared his films to musical genres. He described *The Seventh Seal* as an oratorio. Steene, "*The Seventh Seal*: An Existential Vision," in *Focus on The Seventh Seal*, 97.

15. Ingmar Bergman, *Images: My Life in Film*, trans. Marianne Ruuth (New York: Arcade, 2007), 232. The same day (January 1956) is described by Frank Gado:

> The phonograph, turned to full volume to drown out the noise of the electric razor, was playing...*Carmina Burana*. Suddenly, mental pictures, inspired by Orff's opera, became associated with earlier impressions from Picasso's *Les Saltimbanques* and Dürer's copper engraving, "Knight, Death, and Devil," invading the morality and fusing themselves to its scenes. See Frank Gado, *The Passion of Ingmar Bergman* (Durham, NC: Duke University Press, 1986), 197.

16. Much of the content of the Codex Buranus satirizes and critiques the Catholic Church, covering topics of rape, death, fate, drinking, and gambling. For a discussion of medievalism and Orff's *Carmina Burana*, see Yri, "Medievalism and Anti-Romanticism in Carl Orff's *Carmina Burana*," this volume, pp. 269–300. *The Seventh Seal* is also strongly influenced by *The Phantom Carriage* (1921) by Victor Sjöström.

17. *The Seventh Seal* is based on a play penned by Bergman called *Wood Painting*, first performed on Swedish radio in 1954 and then on stage in 1955 at the Malmö City Theatre and the Royal Dramatic Theater in Stockholm.

18. Jöns is so modern that a contemporaneous review from 1957 by Jurgen Schildt complains about actor Gunnar Björnstrand's "Stockholm lingo" and "modern slang." I would argue that this only adds to the alienation and atemporal aesthetic that Bergman generates in the

film. *Veckojournalen*, no. 9 (1957). Translated by Steene in *Focus on The Seventh Seal*, 46–48.

19. Examples of such characters inhabit many music-themed films such as *To Joy*, which features Stig, a failed concert violinist, *Autumn Sonata*, with Charlotte, the concert-pianist mother to Eva whose overly practiced Chopin Prelude is as harsh and devoid of a soul as she, and *Saraband*, with the cellist Henrik, who forces his daughter to practice under his tutelage in a manner that enslaves her to such a degree that he makes her a victim of incest. For discussions of *To Joy*, *Autumn Sonata*, and *Saraband*, see Luko, *Sonatas, Screams, and Silence*.

20. He also demonstrates strong abilities to make human connections (through his discussion with the painter in the church and through his relationship with the girl he saves from rape). When Jöns tells the girl he could have raped her too, we discover that rather than being restrained by any fear of divine punishment, he *chooses* to be good.

21. On the *aural close-up* see Luko, *Sonatas, Screams, and Silence*, 72–76.

22. Michel Chion, *Film: A Sound Art*, trans. Claudia Gorman (New York: Columbia Press, 2009), 492; Bergman uses the *aurally hermetic effect* in *Winter Light* and *From the Life of the Marionettes*. See Chion, *Film: A Sound Art*, 204, 211, 221, 266.

23. This technique is discussed by Russian film director Andrey Tarkovsky (1932–1986) in *Sculpting in Time: Reflections on the Cinema*, trans. Kitty Hunter-Blair (Austin: University of Texas, 1987), 159. See Luko, *Sonatas, Screams, and Silence*, 205, 207, 221.

24. Ibid., 59–67, 119–129. In *The Silence*, for example, Bach is heard played on a radio where music is the only means of communication between a woman and the concierge of a hotel in a foreign country. In *Cries and Whispers*, a Bach cello suite accompanies a scene of reconciliation between estranged sisters and accompanies a Pietà-like embrace between a dying woman and her nurse.

25. Observers of violence in *The Virgin Spring* include Ingeri and the young boy (watching the rape and murder of Karin) and the mother watching the murder of the young bandit-child. For observers in *The Seventh Seal*, we have Block watching the burning of the alleged witch accused of causing the Black Death, the throng of village inhabitants observing the flagellants, and the barfolk watching Jof dance like a bear.

26. Medieval imaginary is a term I borrow from Nickolas Haydock, *Movie Medievalism: The Imaginary Middle Ages* (Jefferson, NC: McFarland, 2008).

27. As stated by Bildhauer, it is typical of medieval film to see "representation of the dead as…reanimated and encroaching upon the living" (*Filming the Middle Ages*, 51).

28. Bergman's continued use of these techniques throughout his cinematic output could almost lead one to surmise that all his films take place in this same in-between place.

29. Lisa Colton discusses the destabilization of temporality in Paul Giovanni's score for *The Wicker Man* in "Medievalism, Music, and Agency in the Wicker Man (1973)," in *Recomposing the Past: Early Music on Stage and Screen*, ed. James Cook, Alexander Kolassa, and Adam Whittaker (Abingdon, UK: Routledge, 2017).

30. Bildhauer, *Filming the Middle Ages*, 51.

31. For more on contrapuntal sounds and/or aural counterpoint in Bergman's films, see Luko, *Sonatas, Screams, and Silence*, 187–195. *Aural counterpoint*, *contrapuntal sound effects*, and *aural disjuncture* are encountered in Bergman's later films: in *Fanny and Alexander* during the climactic scene in which the children ritualistically chant, "Die you Devil!" in counterpoint with Vergerus's flute music and the pounding sound effects of a thunderstorm; in *Shame* when the clock chimes along with the Meisen music box;

and in the *Dream Play*, which features a scene in which "Ugly Edith" practices a Bach toccata so as to engage in a cacophonic Ivesian battle with the waltz music emanating from the nearby dance hall.

32. The crowd's overwhelming focus on the flagellants (as compared to Jof and Mia's theatrical presentation) proves the point that the artist (in defense of his morbid Dance of Death painting) makes to Jöns about the selling-power of fear: "Why make them happy? Why not scare them? A skull is more interesting than a naked woman!"

33. The same crucified Christ in the flagellants' procession is featured in *Winter Light*. Fixing the camera on listeners/viewers and audience members is a typical Bergmanian technique, found in *Face to Face*, *Hour of the Wolf*, *Autumn Sonata*, and *The Magic Flute*. On listening in Bergman films, see Luko, *Sonatas, Screams, and Silence*, 73–75.

34. My thanks to Stephen Meyer for suggesting this term.

35. Luko, *Sonatas, Screams, and Silence*, 90–91, 187–191, 195–196.

36. James F. Scott, "Ingmar Bergman in the 1950s," in *Focus on the Seventh Seal*, 32.

37. Jerry Vermilye, *Ingmar Bergman: His Life and Films* (Jefferson, NC: McFarland, 2002), 105. In 1960, *The Virgin Spring* received the Academy Award for Best Foreign Film and the 1960 Cannes Film Festival International Critics Prize. This was Bergman's first time using Sven Nyqvist as cinematographer.

38. Vernon Young, Review: *Jungfrukällan* (The Well of the Virgin) by Ingmar Bergman, *Film Quarterly* 13, no. 4 (Summer 1960): 43–47.

39. Paul V. Beckley, *The New York Herald Tribune*, November 15, 1960, 17. Alton Cook, *The New York World Telegram*, quoted in Vermilye, *Ingmar Bergman*, 107.

40. As noted by Francis James Child, the ballad exists in Swedish, Scottish, English, Danish, Norwegian, and Icelandic versions. See Francis James Child, ed., *The English and Scottish Popular Ballads*: vol. 1 (Cambridge: Cambridge University Press, 2015), 170–177. For the Swedish versions of this ballad, see Erik Gustaf Geijer and Arvid August Afzelius, *Svenska folk-visor från forntiden*, vol. 3 (Hæggström, 1816). Version 1: pp. 193–197, version 2: pp. 197–202, version 3: pp. 202–205; http://www.archive.org/details/svenskafolkvi-soo2afzegoog, accessed February 8, 2017. Also see Arwidsson, vol. 2, 413, no. 166. E. C. J. Wessén, "De paroecia Kärna" (PhD diss., Uppsala, 1836).

41. In other versions of the story, the girls are beheaded, three springs burst forth upon their murder, and the father has an iron band fastened around his waist by the blacksmith to purge his sins.

42. Thanks to Håkan Lundberg at Svensk Musik for providing me with the scores. All scores are reproduced with kind permission of the Nordgren estate.

43. Note that according to scores I located in the archives, Erik Nordgren originally intended the intro and interlude to include both flutes throughout. I have crossed out the second flute part to accurately reflect what we hear in the final version.

44. Though the melody outlines a hexachord from E to C (EF♯GABC), it has an aeolian quality that does not align with medieval practice.

45. This is a technique called *continuation* that Bergman would later use in *Cries and Whispers* and *Saraband*. It is an unsettling device that usually involves a fade-in that does not coincide with the beginning of a musical work. On continuation in *The Shining*, see Kate McQuiston, *We'll Meet Again: Musical Design in the Films of Stanley Kubrick* (Oxford: Oxford University Press, 2013), 70–71.

46. On the links between *The Virgin Spring* and *Rashomon*, Bergman famously admitted, "I want to make it quite plain that *The Virgin Spring* must be regarded as an aberration. It's

touristic, a lousy imitation of Kurosawa. At the time, my admiration for the Japanese cinema was at its height. I was almost a samurai myself!"

47. On Bergman's use of sound effects in his films, see Luko, *Sonatas, Screams, and Silence*, chaps. 7 and 8.

48. Xan Brooks, "Bergman Talks of His Dreams and Demons in Rare Interview," *The Guardian*, December 12, 2001, https://www.theguardian.com/film/2001/dec/12/news.xanbrooks.

49. Though Bergman's script identifies the bird as a seagull, it has been identified in different sources as a hawk and eagle. Steene, *Focus on the Seventh Seal*, 9fn10.

50. Robin Wood, *Ingmar Bergman* (Detroit, MI: Wayne State University Press, 2012), 208. Perhaps an argument can be made here that the eagle from Bergman's childhood apocalyptic memories was also linked for him to disruptive, disturbing sounds.

51. Benjamin Thorpe, *Northern Mythology, Comprising the Principal Popular Traditions and Superstitions of Scandinavia, North Germany, and The Netherlands*, vol. 2, *Scandinavian Popular Traditions and Superstitions* (London: Lumley, 1851), 107–108, 271.

52. Laura Mulvey, "Visual Pleasure and Narrative Cinema," *Screen* 16, no. 3 (1975): 6–18.

53. See Luko, *Sonatas, Screams, and Silence*, chap. 6. Michel Chion, *The Voice in Cinema*, trans. Claudia Gorbman (New York: Columbia University Press, 1999), 9.

54. Goats are associated with betrayal and blame, as in a *scapegoat*. Goats are also associated with Judas Iscariot, who betrayed Christ, and in the Old Testament, on the Day of Atonement, a priest would confess the sins of the Israelites over the head of a goat and then drive it into the wilderness, bearing their sins away.

55. On repetition in Bergman's films, see Luko, *Sonatas, Screams, and Silence*, chap. 5.

56. Bergman uses similar abstracting techniques in several films, including (but not limited to) *Through a Glass Darkly, In the Presence of a Clown, From the Life of the Marionettes*, and *Fanny and Alexander*. See Luko, *Sonatas, Screams, and Silence*, chaps. 4, 5, and 8.

57. For Bergman, in the wrong hands, music can be misused and misappropriated. Many of his characters in films such as *Autumn Sonata, Shame, Hour of the Wolf, To Joy*, and *Saraband* attempt to find beauty in art and music while surrounded by misery and violence (whether psychological, domestic, or wartime). But at times, when suffering is too profound, music is revealed as a means of escapism—sometimes pure and beautiful, at other times artificial and insincere, and at still other times oblivious to world events. When misery is accompanied by feelings of vengefulness, music can be used to hurt or haunt.

58. Bergman was nicknamed the "Demon Director," an epithet to which he was so attached that he compulsively drew pitchfork-wielding demonic figures on scripts, on video tapes (his copy of *Orfeo*), and on the walls of his home, and he particularly enjoyed using them as a pseudo signature. In his interview with Xan Brooks in *The Guardian*, he admitted that "the demons are innumerable… [they] arrive at the most inappropriate times and create panic and terror." But he also credited these demons for inspiring his most famous films. Bergman's belief in demons and the supernatural exposes a medieval imagination, indicating that there was likely personal resonance for him in these early films.

59. Though Bergman abandoned medievalist themes after making these two early films, he never let go of many of these sonic tricks: his love for silence, fetishized musical violence, the use of music to terrorize, the repetition and transformation of musical themes and related semantic meaning, and the use of techniques of aural counterpoint and disjuncture. What might have started, therefore, as the cultivation of a medieval aesthetic was later assimilated into his style as a cinematic auteur.

CHAPTER 29

HOPE AGAINST FATE OR FATA MORGANA? MUSIC AND MYTHOPOIESIS IN BOORMAN'S *EXCALIBUR*

DAVID CLEM

As an exercise in cultural medievalism, John Boorman's *Excalibur* (1981) has primarily been understood in two contexts. It has been studied as an adaptation of Arthurian legend, with attention paid to how it interacts with its various filmic and literary predecessors. Studies in this vein focus on various elements within *Excalibur*, such as style of armor, symbolism, treatment of characters, and treatment of sources.[1] It has also been analyzed within the broader context of cinematic medievalism, appearing in studies that focus on the cultural and ethical implications of the construction of nostalgia and invocation of "authenticity" in films that engage with the Middle Ages.[2] Examined in the context of Cinema Arthuriana, *Excalibur* often ends up fragmented into its component parts at the expense of a holistic analysis of the film. Examined in the context of cinematic medievalism, it is grouped with other films to help support a larger theory, often in ways that understandably fail to account for the rich complexity of *Excalibur* itself. While these approaches provide valuable insight into the ways in which *Excalibur* interacts with various genre conventions, they typically lead to interpretations of *Excalibur* in which John Boorman's poetics are overshadowed by broader debates about authenticity and nostalgia.

Scholarship focused on the music tends toward a similar fate. Boorman's *Excalibur* makes extensive use of four preexisting pieces of music. In consultation with composer Trevor Jones, who supplied original cues for the film, Boorman elected to use three Wagnerian pieces, billed as "Prelude" to *Parsifal*, "Prelude" to *Tristan und Isolde*, and "Siegfried's Funeral March" from the *Ring* [sic], each specially recorded by Norman Del Mar and the London Philharmonic Orchestra, as well as "O Fortuna" from *Carmina Burana* by Carl Orff, dubbed from a recording of Herbert Kegel conducting the Leipzig

Radio Symphony Orchestra and Chorus.[3] While much notice has been taken of the preexisting music, particularly the excerpts from Wagner, this scholarship fails to place the borrowed music within the context of the entire score. Apart from John Aberth's reference to the Kyrie sung during the wedding of Arthur (Nigel Terry) and Guenevere (Cherie Lunghi) and references to the scenes that exemplify the tropes explored by John Haines in *Music in Films on the Middle Ages*, very little has been written about the music Trevor Jones supplied for the film.[4] Without a more comprehensive consideration of the role music plays in Boorman's film, it becomes too easy to construct a reading of *Excalibur* that reflects only fragmented aspects of a larger whole. Such interpretations reinforce existing theoretical constructs that perceive medievalism in *Excalibur* as creating nostalgia for the good old days: mythologizing and reifying democratic idealism, reactionary politics, and conservative gender identities. While such views place *Excalibur* squarely within genre conventions of many Arthurian films, they ignore John Boorman's own political views.

This disjuncture has left several scholars wondering if Boorman made poor artistic choices that prevented *Excalibur* from being interpreted as he intended. "Though the documentation on the film's genesis and development reveals no overtly political agenda on Boorman's part," Roy Wakefield asserts,

> the way he prepared Arthurian material for his filmic text, including a deliberate decision to depict Arthur as charismatic leader *par excellence*, a Jungian focus on the masculinity in Malory's *Morte D'Arthur*, and a penchant for undisguised borrowing from other films, literature, and the visual arts, had repercussions for German audiences and film critics which were unique among film audiences in the West.[5]

Among the borrowings discussed in his text, Wakefield includes the music of Orff and Wagner and visual reminders of Riefenstahl's *Triumph des Willens* (1935), arguing that they come together in a way that, perhaps unintentionally, brings Nazi aesthetics and masculine identity politics into *Excalibur*.[6] Jonathan Bignell similarly makes the case that the music of Wagner and Orff brings a hard-edged masculinity to the film that does not seem completely consistent with Boorman's politics.[7] Although they take more positive approaches to *Excalibur*, Susan Aronstein and Brian Hoyle still puzzle over the decision to use images and music that carry fascist overtones into the film.[8] Aronstein argues, however, that even though certain elements have lent themselves to a "neo-fascist reading of [Boorman's] Arthurian epic…such a reading can only be supported by ignoring the film's critique of the very cultural myths such a reading would authenticate."[9] She goes on to elucidate how shifting the focus to Boorman's desacralization of the Grail myth generates a reading that downplays a utopian vision of Camelot and realigns the film with the politics found in other parts of Boorman's oeuvre. Yet even this interpretation comes in the midst of a book on the politics of Arthurian cinema and does not address the entirety of the film or synthesize the seemingly disparate musical elements with her claims. In this essay, I offer a close reading of *Excalibur* examining how the music operates as part of Boorman's mythopoiesis. Building on Aronstein's argument,

I contend that Boorman's *Excalibur* mythologizes Arthurian legend, in essence creating what Barthes referred to as a second-order myth.[10] Boorman accomplishes this by drawing attention to fatalistic elements of the plot, which in combination with his desacralization of the Grail create a mythic world that requires more than a charismatic Arthur and a naive sense of democracy to thrive. Boorman draws on a wealth of preexisting material to create his myth, and as many scholars have pointed out, *Excalibur* is necessarily in intertextual dialogue with the traditions it draws from. By examining in more detail how Boorman uses these traditions, we can better understand *Excalibur*'s unique contribution to an ongoing cultural discourse on the medieval. Finally, while the focus of this essay is on Boorman's unique contribution to a broader cultural discourse on the Middle Ages, I wish to propose the concept of the mythic medieval as a specific register that can function as a metaconceptual space in which this discourse can be analyzed.

Situating *Excalibur*: Authenticity and Nostalgia in Boorman's Myth

It is well established that Boorman draws from a wealth of sources in *Excalibur*. Norris Lacy, Kevin Harty, Brian Hoyle, and others, including Boorman himself, have discussed the film's reliance on White's *Once and Future King*, Tennyson's *Idylls of the King*, Eliot's *The Waste Land*, Jessie Weston's *The Grail in Myth and Romance*, images from Burne-Jones and the Pre-Raphaelites, and Wagnerian opera, as well as what Boorman considers the original texts by Malory, Chrétien de Troyes, and Wolfram von Eschenbach.[11] It is also well established that Boorman diverges from these sources in expected ways, trimming plot episodes and eliding characters to condense centuries of legend into a 140-minute movie. Yet the film's credits claim it is "adapted from Malory's 'Le Morte d'Arthur.'"[12] As Hoyle and others have pointed out, this might function simply as an appeal to authority to give credence to the film's literary standing. As Hoyle also suggests, given the wealth of influences that Boorman publicly acknowledges, crediting Malory might also be the result of Boorman's conceit that Malory is the chief English source for the myth and therefore is essential to rekindling a shared national origin.[13] This is, arguably, borne out by Boorman's own testimony that he was constructing an imaginary world of myth in the same manner of Tolkien's *Lord of the Rings*. But his insistence that "the film has to do with *mythical* truth, not historical truth" offers a third reason for crediting Malory, which offers a glimpse into Boorman's thinking on mythopoiesis.[14] In the director's commentary, Boorman explains that he sees himself as "belonging to a long line of storytellers" who, as Malory did before him, can draw on any number of passed down sources to create the myth anew.[15] He tells interviewer Harlan Kennedy that "the retelling of these stories is like the rediscovery of them—it 'catharizes' and then gives solace."[16] As Kennedy points out, Boorman sees myths as "both a close-knit and an open body" of works that can be "rearranged" without altering their essential "resonances."[17] Boorman conceived of *Excalibur* as his own construction of the legend, regenerating the mythic truth of Malory for modern audiences and freely drawing from other sources to aid in the adaptation process, as Malory did himself when he created his written record of the life and death of Arthur. Crediting Malory, then, might be Boorman's way of escaping what Lacy calls the *tyranny of tradition* by authorizing Boorman himself as a mythopoet of Arthurian lore.[18]

Referencing Malory in this way also helped Boorman distance himself from the idea of the historical Arthur. As he tells Kennedy,

> The first trap to avoid is to start worrying about when or whether Arthur existed. The stories that inspire us were really fifteenth-century works, by Thomas Malory and the rest, looking back nostalgically on the twelfth.[19]

That many historians suspect the real Arthur, if there was one, more likely existed in the fifth or sixth century (rather than the twelfth) is beside the point. Boorman is interested in the mythical Arthur and has expressed in interviews with Michel Ciment and Gavin Smith that Arthurian legend provides the mythic impulse behind all his films—a fact borne out by the detailed analysis of Brian Hoyle.[20] In the interview with Dan Yakir, Boorman states, "I'm interested in films that are dream-like, mythic, poetic, or stylized. Realism is limited and boring—and fundamentally dishonest. It doesn't tell the truth."[21] Boorman seems less interested in promoting the past as a location for nostalgia and more intent on using myth and fantasy as a means to speak truths that he perceives humanity needs to grapple with. In this sense, Boorman is engaging in what Barthes referred to as *mythology*. Barthes states that "the best weapon against myth is perhaps to mythify it in its turn. . . . All that is needed is to use it as the departure point for a third semiological chain."[22] If Boorman, as mythopoet, is engaged in crafting a myth from what is already the mythic medieval, then analysis of *Excalibur* can only benefit from treating it accordingly. In this case, not only do all the filmic components, including the preexisting music, point outward to an intertextual network of other versions of Arthurian myth, but also they might be interpreted as Boorman's commentary on Arthurian myth. If we treat *Excalibur* as a type of Barthesian speech act, it is important still to acknowledge that Boorman does not speak into a void with *Excalibur*, but necessarily engages discursively with the traditions of medieval film and Cinema Arthuriana.

In light of this, a re-evaluation of the preexisting music used in *Excalibur* is in order. If Boorman is constructing an Arthurian myth that critiques Arthurian myth, then perhaps the music of Wagner and Orff does not just bring unwanted fascist elements into the story that muddy the clarity of his critique. I contend that this music contributes to Boorman's construction of a mythic Middle Ages in which characters trapped by their fate need to participate in a nostalgic *"bon vieux temps"* themselves. As they seek out their destiny, resolution only comes when they give in to fate and fulfill their mythic, archetypal roles, which are to create and perpetuate a story that reminds humanity of its need for a lost union with a natural order.

Going in Circles: Destiny and Fate

In his interview with Michel Ciment, Boorman says,

> The story of the Grail deals with people who are trying not to discover themselves, but their place in the world, a much more humble attitude. What they strive to learn is their destiny, the universe to which they belong, and their relations with their fellow men. That's really what generates the narrative, and it strikes me as far healthier than an endless quest for self.[23]

The idea of destiny, then, is of central importance to Boorman's realization of Arthurian legend. Framed this way, Arthur's quest is not one of self-discovery or personal glory, but one in which he must discover the role he has to play. The moments when he steps off the path are the moments that bring despair, as when Excalibur is broken by his pride or when his anger and pain at the affair between Lancelot (Nicholas Clay) and Guenevere cause him to give up his role, symbolized by his leaving Excalibur in the ground between the lovers, which begins the Wasteland episode. When the lovers awaken to discover the sword between them, Lancelot exclaims in horror (supported by appropriately placed dissonant stinger chords), "The King without his sword, the land without a King!"[24] While the physical injury to Arthur comes when he is struck by lightning at the moment of Mordred's birth, it is his act of abdication that plunges the realm into desolation as he assumes the role of Fisher King. This is why the secret of the Grail, that the king and the land are one, is the key to his restoration—redemption comes by re-embracing his destined path. That path, however, leads ultimately to his death at the battle of Camlann. Much of the preexisting music used in *Excalibur* helps to foreground this concept of destiny.

The idea of destiny intersects powerfully with what is perhaps the most prominent example of borrowed music in the film, "Siegfried's Funeral March" from Wagner's *Götterdämmerung*. Excerpts from the funeral march are heard twelve times throughout *Excalibur*, and it notably begins and ends the soundscape of the film. It accompanies the opening three minutes, sounding with the Orion logo, before the narrative begins, and it accompanies the final seven minutes and is the only music heard during the end credits. Alexandra Sterling-Hellenbrand argues that by bookending the film with extended quotations of Wagner, "Boorman employs the funeral march to create a guiding concept for his film."[25] In her estimation, the extensive use of "Siegfried's Funeral March" invites us to read Arthur as a type of Siegfried and *Excalibur* as an Arthurian *Götterdämmerung*.[26] While the decision to use the funeral march so prominently does beg the comparison, I think it is more likely that Boorman, who often describes things in Jungian terms, would consider Siegfried and Arthur two manifestations of the same archetype. His interview with Michel Ciment seems to support this notion:

> But I'd never studied the original texts. It was later I came to them and I was extraordinarily impressed by them: Malory's *Morte d'Arthur*, the works of Chrétien de

Troyes, and especially, the most fascinating and modern of them all, Wolfram von Eschenbach's *Parsifal*. There are the three great books, English, French and German, in which our respective national cultures are inscribed. Malory leads to T. H. White, Chrétien de Troyes to Bresson and Rohmer, von Eschenbach to Wagner.[27]

He later writes, when discussing *Excalibur* in his autobiography, "As part of my preparations for the great endeavor, I went...to Bayreuth to see Patrice Chereau's production of the *Ring* cycle, whose Germanic myth has many elements in common with the Grail legend."[28] Boorman clearly considered Wagner's late works part of the extensive network of sources he was interested in drawing from for the creation of his own myth. He goes on to explain that Wagner's music inspired some of the early stages of his work on the script, and he decided to use it in the movie after consulting with Trevor Jones, who helped him select the excerpts.[29] While I think Sterling-Hellenbrand takes the comparison too far, she makes some interesting points in her essay. In fact, her idea that the film is Arthur's funeral march might offer another reason for Boorman's citation of Malory's *Morte d'Arthur* in the credits. Further, I agree with her assessment that Siegfried and Arthur have similar fates. Where I differ from her most is that rather than claiming that *Excalibur* reinscribes nationalist values onto a mythic Middle Ages, I believe the use of the funeral march to emphasize Arthur's fate is one of the elements that points to *Excalibur* as a second-order myth. That is, Boorman appropriates Wagner's music and uses it for his own mythopoetic purposes, as the following analysis will demonstrate.

The chthonic tones of the funeral procession set the mood for the film, beginning with the Orion logo, as mentioned previously, and preceding any narrative imagery. The excerpt synced with the opening logo begins nine measures after Siegfried's last words in act 3, scene 2, of Wagner's *Götterdämmerung*. As the Orion logo fades, we hear tympani strikes that are synced with the opening lines of text, each of which appear as a separate title:

> The Dark Ages / The Land was Divided without a King
> Out of Those Lost Centuries, Rose a Legend
> Of the Sorcerer Merlin
> Of the Coming King
> Of the Sword of Power
> Excalibur[30]

The three tones F–F♯–G, heard in the lower strings with a rest in between each note, are synced with the text beginning with the line "Of the Sorcerer Merlin" so that the *fortissimo* chord on which they land accentuates the shimmering title "Excalibur." This opening can come across as comedic to modern audiences, ascribing an epic scope to the legend that can seem pretentious. While this might be seen as the result of a film from the early eighties not aging well, it is worth noting that *Monty Python and the Holy Grail* came out six years prior. It is also worth noting that the music seems to poorly reflect the action on screen, though it does lend itself conceptually to the narrative. As the scene opens on a dark and chaotic battle bathed in smoke and fiery orange light, we hear fanfares that sound heroic and triumphant and seem to contrast with the umbric *mise en scène* that introduces us to Uther (Gabriel Byrne) and Merlin (Nicol Williamson). We see armor-clad knights fighting and killing each other brutally without any indication of whose side anyone is on, or even what the sides are, and while the fanfares make sense in the context of a funeral procession for a fallen hero, it is unclear in the opening chaos of the film whether there is a hero to be found. Given what might be read as comedic hedging (Boorman trying to take himself seriously, but not too seriously) in the pairing of music with opening text and the oddity of heroic fanfares in the midst of a bloody battle shrouded in flame and mist, perhaps the music here is intended to call attention to itself. Perhaps Boorman is using the music not just to set a mood, but also to comment on the mythic significance (and epic scale) of what is begun in this scene—Merlin's support for Uther leads to Arthur's birth. It also emphasizes the importance of the sword Excalibur and the central role that the sword will play in the plot.

The music excerpted from *Götterdämmerung* contains three thematic elements that are lifted out of their Wagnerian context and redeployed throughout *Excalibur* in what might be described as an associative network. The first of these motifs can be seen in Example 29.1. The eighth-note chords followed by the running triplets are generally associated with the betrayal and death of Siegfried in Wagner's *Götterdämmerung*, but Boorman attaches this music to Excalibur.[31] This motif is synced with the title of the movie, as discussed previously, but also with the emergence of the sword from the water when the Lady of the Lake gives it to Merlin (to give to Uther). It returns when Uther plunges the sword into the stone, as well as both times that Arthur draws the sword from the stone, and sounds again when Arthur has Uryens knight him with Excalibur and when Guenevere returns the sword to him just before the battle of Camlann.[32] These scenes establish a connection between the triplet motif and the image of Excalibur; and Excalibur is inextricably linked to Arthur's destiny—he is the only one worthy of wielding it; the only one who can draw it from the stone. Yet every step Arthur takes toward his destiny also seals his fate, as Sterling-Hellenbrand asserts:

> It is always clear in Boorman's film that the sword carries the mechanism and the potential for Arthur's destruction. Arthur's fate parallels Siegfried's; the music draws attention to what one could perhaps call the funerary echo.[33]

EXAMPLE 29.1 "Siegfried's Death and Betrayal" motive from *Götterdämmerung*, used in *Excalibur* to refer to the eponymous sword.

For Sterling-Hellenbrand, the concepts of betrayal and death, which are associated with this triplet motif in Wagner, combined with other narrative parallels between Siegfried and Arthur, suggest that Boorman and Wagner share a similar intent.[34] This leads her to conclude that

> the score works to create a new mythological landscape by combining the ways in which nineteenth-century Germany and twentieth-century America inscribed their "national" heroes in their respective landscapes, seeking to find a heroic past to give an uncertain present the hope of a glorious future.[35]

This conclusion puts the message of Boorman's film at odds with his politics. While the use of the funeral march helps to foreground the connection between destiny and fate, I argue that these elements are wielded by Boorman to yield a rather different meaning than that suggested by Sterling-Hellenbrand. Rather than using these quotations at the beginning and end of *Excalibur* to establish a parallel between the myths of Siegfried and Arthur, I believe that Boorman is signifying the mythic status of the film itself. Quoting Wagner, then, is a sort of self-conscious mythopoetic gesture akin to crediting Malory as a source.[36] Expanding the music beyond the narrative frame of the story also highlights the cyclical nature of Arthurian lore, drawing attention to the similarities between the chaotic battles and death at the beginning and end of the film.

Except for the first time Arthur draws the sword from the stone, the triplet motif is always preceded or followed by at least one other thematic excerpt. To return briefly to the first scene, after the opening described previously, the first fanfare-like figure heard after the triplet motif is seen in Example 29.2 (referred to hereafter as the heroism motif). In Wagner's operas, this fanfare gesture is associated with the strength and heroism of the Volsungs.[37] In the operas it can be heard in association with both Siegmund and Siegfried, often when they are preparing for combat, but it sounds for the last time during the funeral procession in *Götterdämmerung*.

As it appears in the film, this darker-sounding version of the fanfare heralds the arrival of Uther and Merlin. Shortly after this theme ends, the triplets return, and we find the first cut in the music, as it skips over a softer, more mournful melody to set up the entrance of the second fanfare we hear. This more triumphant fanfare, seen in

EXAMPLE 29.2 "Volsung's Strength and Heroism" motif from *Götterdämmerung*, used in *Excalibur* to denote similar concepts.

EXAMPLE 29.3 "Wotan's Redemption/Sword" motif from *Götterdämmerung*, used in *Excalibur* as a "triumphant fanfare."

Example 29.3 (referred to hereafter as the triumphant fanfare), is associated in Wagner's cycle both with Wotan's plan to redeem his mistakes through the Volsungs and with the sword Nothung.[38] The climax of this fanfare is synced so that it emphasizes the first audible dialogue in the film as Merlin calls out to Uther. Functionally, this scene establishes the need for peace, which Merlin attempts to achieve through Uther by granting him the sword Excalibur. Boorman's Merlin is the fullest representation in his films of an archetypal character that he uses regularly. Boorman characterizes Merlin as one who is prescient but limited in power, who can meddle, but not always foresee the results of his meddling.[39] This musical pairing offers another parallel between Wagner and *Excalibur*, one that would match Wotan and Merlin. It is Merlin's meddling to make Uther king that begins the events that lead to Arthur's birth, and it is he who gives Uther the sword that Arthur is destined to wield, just as Wotan leaves the sword for Siegmund in *Die Walküre* that Siegfried will later wield. But the music does more than just allude to the plot of Wagner's operas. When Merlin retrieves the sword from the Lady of the Lake, the heroism motif sounds as the camera is focused on his face, but, as previously mentioned, it is the triplet motif that is synced with the emergence of the sword itself. Boorman and Jones could have chosen to use the triumphant fanfare (which is associated, among other things, with Nothung) to accompany the rise of Excalibur, but instead they chose a motif that calls attention to Arthur's eventual fate. This suggests that Boorman is interested in using the music of Wagner for his own purposes, not just to point to the narrative parallels that exist.

Indeed, once Wagner's music is introduced in the context of *Excalibur*, the referential power it has to the operas can only operate on audience members familiar with the musical source. However, the mood set by the music and the associations mapped onto it by the film should be readily apparent, even if one does not know the works of Wagner. When each of the previously mentioned themes returns, it carries with it associations from earlier in the film. For example, when Uther drives the sword into the stone, we hear the music from the scene when Merlin retrieves Excalibur, though it ends a few measures earlier here to accommodate the editing. The heroic motif is synced with the moment in which Merlin tells the infant Arthur that he will be the one to draw the sword from the stone, and the triplet motif sounds when the camera focuses on Excalibur. This reinforces the earlier pairing and sets up the cue for the second time Arthur draws the sword from the stone. The first time no one was watching, and he retrieved it for Sir Kay (Niall O'Brien), whereas the second time, everyone is there to witness the event, and as Arthur draws Excalibur for himself, we hear the triumphant fanfare, followed by the triplet motif. This same pairing is heard at the end of the first act, when Arthur announces his intention to form the round table, build Camelot, and marry Guenevere. In each of these instances, ending with the more foreboding musical figure reminds anyone in the audience familiar with the story of Arthur that, despite the triumph of the moment, Arthur's path leads ultimately to Camlann and death.

The same logic applies to the other two *Götterdämmerung* excerpts that are paired with the triplet motif. These are longer themes that are each used twice, once near the beginning and once near the end of the film. The first of these themes can be seen in Example 29.4. This is the theme that is edited out of the opening battle scene by the cut mentioned earlier. According to Kirby, it is part of the Volsungs heroism leitmotif that is associated with Siegmund's Wehwalt (woeful) tale.[40] The large-scale semitonal descents in this theme—from A♭ to G in the tenor register and from the D♭ Major harmony to the C-minor ending chord—create an effect of noble sadness, and when this theme occurs in *Excalibur*, its dulcet tones seem to prefigure Arthur's fate. This theme follows the triplet motif during the siege of Cameliard, when Arthur halts the battle by offering Uryens mercy. Uryens refuses, because Arthur is only a squire, at which point Arthur hands over Excalibur, asking Uryens to knight him. The triplet motif sounds as Arthur kneels to be knighted, and the Wehwalt theme enters as Uryens, overcome by the boy's bravery, not only knights Arthur but also pledges fealty to him as king.[41] While this more somber melody fits the sobriety of the moment, in retrospect we can read it as foreshadowing not only the fate that awaits Arthur at Camlann, but also the fate of Uryens (Uryens will be the last of the quest knights to die before Perceval recovers the grail). We hear this same cue (lacking one measure on each end) when Guenevere returns Excalibur to Arthur while he is seeking her forgiveness at the convent where she fled after her tryst was discovered. The common element between these scenes is Arthur showing signs of courage and maturity of character and judgment. In the first instance, he recognized the truth of Uryens's objections and corrected them in a way that won Uryens over. In the second, he not only accepts Guenevere's apology, but also apologizes to her, saying

EXAMPLE 29.4 "Wehwalt" theme from *Götterdämmerung*.

EXAMPLE 29.5 Excerpt from "Siegfried's Funeral March" heard at the opening of *Excalibur* and at the moment Arthur and Mordred mortally wound each other.

"I was not born to live a man's life, but to be the stuff of future memory."[42] While the music enters after this bit of dialogue, the Wehwalt theme is well suited to the somber nature of the scene as Arthur recognizes his role and steels himself for his final battle.

Perhaps the most significant quotation of the funeral march comes in the final battle scene when Arthur and Mordred finally meet each other in combat. For this climactic moment, Boorman repeats the section of the funeral march that he used for the opening credits almost verbatim (it is offset here by a measure, starting one measure earlier to catch the triplet lead-in to the melody and ending a measure earlier as well). In this scene, the music is synced so that Arthur and Mordred slay each other while we hear the four-measure theme (seen in Example 29.5) that opened the movie. The syncing of Arthur's final combat with the four measures that opened the film seems to add credence to the idea that *Excalibur* is indeed Arthur's funeral march, reinforcing the link between *Excalibur* and the *Ring*. But Arthur's march is different from Siegfried's. In the *Ring* cycle, it is Wotan's seizure of power by destruction of the world tree that establishes a linear path toward destruction that culminates in the immolation scene at the end of *Götterdämmerung*. In *Excalibur*, however, Arthur's march is not a steady decline, but rather a journey that follows the circular turn of that popular medieval icon, the *Rota Fortunae* (Fortune's wheel), as we witness the rise and fall of Arthur.

While the *Rota Fortunae* icon may be hinted at by the cyclic nature of the *Götterdämmerung* selections, it requires detailed knowledge of Wagner's score to discover that connection. The iconography is introduced less subtly by the use of "O Fortuna." Orff's piece is a musical depiction of the *Rota Fortunae*. The text bemoans the fickle goddess of fortune and her ever-spinning wheel, the motion of which is echoed by the cyclical repetition of the musical accompaniment.[43] The music builds slowly, and though it maintains a doleful D minor until the last nine measures, a Picardy third and frantic *accelerando* result in an unexpectedly exuberant cadence on D Major. The text, however, maintains a tone of mournful despair over the oppressive cycle of Fortune's wheel, concluding with the idea that we should join together and weep because we are all slaves to fate. In a way, then, the music might represent the upturn of the wheel, which elevates people from the position of *regnabo* (I will reign) to *regno* (I reign), while the text speaks of the wheel's downturn, which topples figures from the position of *regno* to *regnavo* (I reigned) and *sum sine regno* (I reign no more).[44] The iconographic nature of this music translates directly to its deployment in *Excalibur*. Excerpts are used four times in *Excalibur*, and each use corresponds to a character's (usually Arthur's) decision to stop struggling against fate and embrace his or her destiny. The first excerpt (taken from mm. 33–82 of Orff's score) sounds as Arthur steps into his appointed role and rides into battle to save Leodegrance (Patrick Stewart) at Cameliard. This occurs just after he accepts Merlin's testimony that he is the son of Uther Pendragon and that he is destined to wield Excalibur as king. A longer excerpt (mm. 41 to the end of Orff's score) underscores Arthur riding out from Camelot after being restored by the Grail, in an amazing scene where we witness the land come back to life in his wake.[45] Arthur had abdicated his role, but in this scene, he steps into it once again by drinking from the Grail and remembering that the king and the land are one. This reacceptance of his destiny extends to his knights as well, who ride off to battle with a renewed sense of purpose. As Arthur orders Kay to gather his knights for battle against Mordred, the turn of destiny is heralded by the entrance of "O Fortuna." This is also the only time we hear the D Major ending, which is synced with a long shot on Arthur leading his knights down a path lined with cherry blossom trees. Like a festive throng tossing confetti, the trees shower the knights with their petals, lending a celebratory air to the visual climax of the scene. The cherry blossoms in this scene vividly portray renewal while reminding us of the ephemeral nature of life. This visual is appropriately reinforced by "O Fortuna" in the underscore. It is also interesting that the musical signifier of the *regno* position in "O Fortuna" is heard only after Camelot's golden age has passed. Read this way, it not only suggests the ephemeral nature of Arthur's reign, but also might support Aronstein's assertion that Boorman equates the golden age of Camelot with the stagnation of modern society.[46] Interestingly, this also suggests that the health of the land is dependent not on the king staying alive (as Arthur is riding ultimately to his death at Camlann), but on the willingness of the king to follow his destined path. Boorman clarifies his thinking on destiny in *Excalibur* when he tells Harlan Kennedy, "What destiny means is to find your place in life, your stream in the river, to find a wholeness in relation to nature."[47] While Arthur's destiny is interwoven with the land he rules, they share different fates.

The final two times that "O Fortuna" sounds in *Excalibur* occur during the battle of Camlann. As Arthur and his knights ride into action after settling on a battle plan, "O Fortuna" enters (mm. 49–76), and as Arthur's forces begin to be overwhelmed, Orff's music fades out. When Lancelot rides to their aid, restoring morale and turning the tide of the battle in Arthur's favor, "O Fortuna" resounds for the final time (mm. 77–84).[48] The musical silence between these two entrances is curious. To anyone in the audience unfamiliar with Orff's cantata, "O Fortuna" is the music for riding into battle—with its static voices above a more quickly moving accompaniment, it even rhythmically mirrors the image of a warrior on horseback. But it seems odd that once it has faded and the sounds of the battle itself are foregrounded, "O Fortuna" would enter again, especially since we only briefly see Lancelot on horseback. Perhaps it is paired with Lancelot to indicate that his destiny lies with Arthur and his knights as their champion, an interpretation bolstered by the presence of the Grail theme at Lancelot's death, which will be discussed further later.

Based on the way it is synchronized with the narrative, it might be said that "O Fortuna" signifies the acceptance of the inescapable fate heralded by "Siegfried's Funeral

March." This semiotic logic, however, leaves several questions unanswered. For if Excalibur is a symbol of hope, as Merlin claims, the source of that hope is not entirely clear. Arthur dies, and Excalibur is returned to the Lady of the Lake, but are we to hope for the return of a king who can wield the sword, or will that merely restart the same fatalistic cycle that we have just witnessed? For Excalibur to function as a true symbol of hope, that hope must include the possibility of breaking the cycle.[49] In Boorman's myth, though, the realm of Arthur seems doomed from the beginning. Neither king nor realm can escape fate.

The extent to which an audience member is able to articulate the connection between destiny, fate, and the musical use of "Siegfried's Funeral March" and "O Fortuna" would, at least to some degree, depend on the knowledge they had entering into their experience with the film. But even if audience members did not understand all the intertextual references, the centrality of fate in Boorman's film would have been impossible to miss. "The people in this film," complains Roger Ebert in his review of *Excalibur*, "seem doomed to their behavior. They have no choice."[50] While one can arrive at this sentiment without a detailed understanding of the music, the music used in *Excalibur* bolsters the centrality of fate to the narrative, as the above analysis shows.

While Arthur's fate at Camlann is the inescapable terminus of his quest, if his destiny is a matter of him finding his place in the world, is there more to his role than marching toward death? After he tells Guenevere that he is meant to be the "stuff of future memory," Arthur says, "the fellowship was a brief beginning, a fair time that cannot be forgotten, and because it will not be forgotten, that fair time may come again; now once more I must ride with my knights to defend what was, and the dream of what could be."[51] If the "fair time" refers to Camelot, this quote could be read as offering a utopian vision for the future, in which case Arthur's destiny was to unite the land in a time of peace and prosperity, and his legacy is to be a beacon of hope. However, this is said in the context of acknowledging to Guenevere that his destiny prevented him from being the husband she needed. Does this mean Guenevere was not part of his destiny, or is Arthur trying to justify placing his laws and role as king before their relationship? Put another way, is Arthur's destiny linked only to the *regno* position on the wheel, or is it tied fully in with his fate? In the paradigm described above, if he is destined to be king, that brings with it the entire rotation of Fortune's wheel, not just the high point. How we understand Arthur's destiny determines, to a certain extent, how we read the politics of nostalgia in Boorman's film. Understanding Boorman's *Excalibur* as a dramatization of the role of fate de-emphasizes the importance of Camelot and allows a reading of the film as a second-order myth. In this reading, Camelot does not offer escape from the wheel; it is fixed on the top of it. The hope that it offers is both illusory and temporary. If *Excalibur* critiques Arthurian myth by drawing our attention to its mythic properties, then Boorman does not offer a phantasmagoria, but rather illuminates Camelot as a type of *Fata Morgana*. To test the veracity of this reading, an examination of how Boorman treats the rise and fall of Camelot is in order.

The Setup: Two Dance Scenes and a Wedding

The story of Camelot's rise and fall is told through the interactions of three relational triangles in Boorman's *Excalibur*. The Cornwall/Igrayne/Uther triangle marks the birth of Arthur, but also plants the motivational seeds for his destruction by Morgana. Further, Boorman and Jones draw interesting parallels between this triangle and the Arthur/Guenevere/Lancelot triangle, which is the focus of the second act of the screenplay and ostensibly leads to Camelot's fall. The involvement of Merlin, Morgana, and Arthur in both relational triangles constitutes a third triangle of relationships that reveal the motivations that drive the characters who have agency in the rise and fall of Camelot.

We encounter the Cornwall/Igrayne/Uther triangle near the beginning of the film. During the feast celebrating the truce between Uther and the Duke of Cornwall, the Duke commands his wife, Igrayne (Katrine Boorman), to dance for them. He then goads Uther, saying "You may be king, Uther, but no queen of yours will ever match her."[52] Throughout this scene, Igrayne is objectified and dominated by the male gaze. Her husband shows her off as a prized possession. She dances to music provided by the musicians that she has no control over. The music is formally patterned after a thirteenth-century estampie, but with some telling differences. It follows the verse–refrain form of the estampie, but each phrase ends with an open cadence, rather than following the anticipated periodic structure. Constructed this way, the music denies closure and therefore denies Igrayne hope of rest. As the situation becomes more threatening, the lack of cadential closure creates a sense that she is trapped, as incapable of escaping the male gaze as the music is of escaping its tonal cycle—the return of the tonic is also the beginning of the next phrase. During the penultimate refrain, she moves to the lower level of the room, in front of the banquet table, and as the knights begin to pound in a drunkenly uncoordinated unison on the table with the hilts of their daggers, she begins to spin. The last verse introduces a rising chromatic line (which feels uncharacteristic of an authentic estampie, even of the more chromatic Italian variety) that gradually accelerates in tempo as her spinning becomes more frantic. She comes out of the spin, bends over backward momentarily, and then is on her hands and knees, gyrating and rolling her head, as the final refrain enters at twice its normal speed. The music would demand she continue to work herself into a sexually charged frenzy if it, and her dance, were not cut off by a guttural interjection from her husband, after Uther stood and declared, "I must have her."[53] This effectively breaks the truce they had sealed with a blood oath at the beginning of the scene, as Uther and Cornwall take up arms again, leading their armies to war over Igrayne.

Haines labels this scene as representative of the *oriental medieval*. He explains, "Not even the Arthurian world is exempt from the oriental meal-time dance number, as seen and heard in Igrayne's performance in the first act of *Excalibur* (1981)."[54] For Haines, this represents the added commercial value of "scantily clothed women" as it participates in the eroticization of the exotic feminine Other, mapping that onto a fantastic construction of the alterity of the Middle Ages.[55] As mentioned previously, Haines focuses on the fantastic nature of authentic early music performance, using the *Excalibur* scene, among others, to define a *topos*. Since Boorman was intentionally constructing a fantastic world, the pertinent question then becomes how Boorman and Jones are using that *topos* within the film. The instrumentation certainly fits with Haines's observation of the Celtic aesthetic often used in such dance scenes (until an electronic drone joins in near the end), and the choreography is reminiscent of a Bacchanalian dithyramb danced by the maenads.[56] I believe, however, that it does more than just eroticize Igrayne for spectacle. I think the music and visuals draw attention to the lack of agency Igrayne has under the scrutiny of the male gaze in a way that points to the situation as undesirable. In such a reading, it is not Igrayne's transgressive sexuality that breaks the peace, but Uther's transgressive lust and the Duke's treatment of her as a sexual object. It is the male gaze itself that leads to renewed fighting and to Merlin using his magic to satisfy Uther's lust. Igrayne's lack of agency, in contrast, illustrates the extent to which she is a slave to the passions of the men in her world. One might consider, then, that the oriental medieval *topos* is used here to critique its own standard implementation, rather than to merely perpetuate it.

The scenes that immediately follow Igrayne's dance further insinuate the negative results of Uther's lust. As the battle over Igrayne ensues, Uther's army has little success in breaking through the gate to Cornwall's castle, Tintagel. As evening sets in, he orders his army to withdraw to lure the duke out of his castle in pursuit. In the scene that follows, Uther is transformed to take on the visage of the duke so that he can gain entrance into Tintagel and rape Igrayne, who thinks it is her husband returned from battle to lie with her. As Uther approaches the bed chamber, the scene cuts to the Duke of Cornwall riding into battle in search of Uther, and at the exact moment we see him thrown from his horse and impaled on a rack of spears, we cut back to the bed chamber and see the child Morgana (Barbara Byrne) sit up and proclaim, "My father is dead."[57] Igrayne goes to comfort her, then sees Uther, and, accepting the magical transformation, tells Morgana her father is here and it was just a dream. Uther summons her, and she tells Morgana to go to sleep and goes to him. At this point, the audience sees the scenario as Igrayne does—we see her approach her husband, who roughly handles her and partly disrobes her. As they turn to the bed, however, we suddenly see the face of Uther, instead of Cornwall. He looks up and makes eye contact with Morgana, who is staring right at him. There is then another cut to the impaled image of the real duke, dying on the battlefield, before we return to the bedchamber and see the face of Uther transform back into the visage of the Duke, restoring the audience perspective to that of Igrayne. This momentary appearance of Uther's visage puts the audience briefly in the subject position of Morgana, who sees through the magic and knows that her father is dying. This foreshadows the later revelation that Morgana is, herself, a magical being like Merlin, which will be discussed in more detail later. As the rape scene draws to a climax, the vision of Uther (as Cornwall) copulating with Igrayne is cross-cut with images of the real Cornwall's dying breath, aligning the Duke's death with Arthur's conception. Flames burn across the background of both scenes (as torches, the fireplace, and fires on the battlefield), visually representing the passion to which Igrayne is a victim.[58] It is not her passion, but Uther's that plunges the world back into the chaos of warfare. His inability to control his urges costs him his son, whom Merlin receives to raise as he sees fit in exchange for using magic to allow Uther to have Igrayne. It also costs him his kingdom, as the nobles stop trusting him and a handful of them ambush and kill him.

The musical underscore for the rape scene reinforces the problematic nature of Uther's lust and Igrayne's helplessness. A variation of the estampie from Igrayne's dance provides the rhythmic underpinning for Uther's ride across the mist of the dragon's breath, carried, as Merlin states, by his lust, while the electronic wailing of a disembodied female voice signifies the magic that Merlin used to conjure the mist. After a brief lull, the music begins again, with an even clearer reference to the ascending chromatic line of Igrayne's dance underscoring the buildup to the sexual climax of the scene, again paired with the vocal motif soaring above to remind us that it is Merlin's magic that made the fulfillment of Uther's lust possible. Immediately following the moment of Arthur's conception, Boorman cuts to an external shot of Tintagel with Merlin in the foreground. This is followed by a close shot on his face and Merlin's proclamation that "the future has taken root in the present, it is done."[59] But that future goes beyond the birth of Arthur. Morgana witnessed the deception and understood the magic behind it, the trauma of which sets her on the path of vengeance. Thus, the seeds of Arthur's destruction were sown at the moment of his birth.

In contrast to Igrayne's dance, the festive dance celebrating the victory at Cameliard is a social dance scene. The music supplied by Trevor Jones follows the estampie form discussed previously, but this time the refrain follows the expected cadential formula, ending with a closed cadence and lacking the entrapped frenzy of the music that accompanies Igrayne. Near the beginning of this scene, Arthur has to stop dancing with Guenevere because of pain from a wound he received in battle. After this, the verses of the estampie begin to increasingly draw material from the previous scenes involving Igrayne. First, a repeated pitch in the bass line recalls the rhythm of the first verse of Igrayne's estampie—the same rhythm that recurs near the beginning of Uther's ride across the mists (created by the dragon's breath) to Tintagel when he rapes Igrayne. This begins in an interlude, of sorts, between the second verse of the Cameliard estampie and the refrain. The rising chromatic line from Igrayne's dance, in the rhythmic form it took during Uther's ride to Tintagel, then enters above this bass line, followed by the quotation of a half refrain from Igrayne's estampie. This interlude underscores Arthur confessing his love for Guenevere to Merlin and asking if the wizard can make her love him, which Merlin refuses to do. The close-up on Arthur and Merlin in conversation is intercut with mid-range shots of Guenevere dancing, suggesting that the musical reference here is meant to sync with a moment when Guenevere falls under Arthur's gaze. After this, we hear the Cameliard refrain, along with a half verse, but then the interlude music returns, this time underscoring Merlin warning Arthur that both marriage and betrayal lie down that road. This time the cue ends with a return to the Cameliard estampie refrain before the half refrain from Igrayne's estampie is heard. The third time this interlude music sounds is when Guenevere flirts with Arthur, offering him cakes that she baked to help him heal, but refusing to tell him all the ingredients. This time we get the half refrain as Merlin sees Arthur staring at a cake and says, "Looking at the cake is like looking at the future, until you've tasted it, what do you really know, and then of course, it's too late," after which Arthur takes a bite and Merlin quips, "Too late."[60] Interestingly, in this scene, Guenevere seems to have some agency as she flirts with Arthur, but is not endowed with the power of the male gaze, as we are reminded by the quotations of Igrayne's estampie. These quotations also foreshadow the betrayal of Arthur by Lancelot and Guenevere.

In fact, if Guenevere does have a powerful gaze in the film, it is not directed at Arthur, but rather at Lancelot. When Lancelot arrives in Cameliard to escort Guenevere to her wedding, they seem to fall in love at first sight. Their first glimpse of each other is accompanied by the third iteration of the love potion motive from the *Tristan* prelude (mm. 8–11).[61] Indeed, excerpts of the prelude underscore most of the important moments in the tale of Lancelot and Guenevere. Norris Lacy elucidates the connection implicit in this pairing between the "destructive love triangles: Lancelot/Guenevere/Arthur and Tristan/Isolde/Mark."[62] This sentiment is echoed by Alexandra Sterling-Hellenbrand and Brian Hoyle, both of whom further point to the visual parallel between Gottfried von Strasburg's account of Mark's discovery of Tristan and Isolde with a sword between them and Boorman's depiction of Arthur driving Excalibur into the ground between Lancelot and Guenevere when he finds them together.[63] But—as is the case with the quotations from the funeral march that I discussed earlier—consideration of how the music of *Tristan* interacts with the rest of the film moves us beyond the quotidian observations about narrative similarities between *Tristan* and *Excalibur* and redirects our attention toward a more holistic understanding of the film's mythic world.

As the cue accompanying their first meeting ends, the camera cuts to the journey to Camelot, wherein Lancelot pledges his love to Guenevere (in a courtly, unrequited way). Immediately after his declaration, the first climactic point of the *Tristan* prelude (mm. 16–17) sounds, as Guenevere, who had been riding beside Lancelot, falls behind him with a stunned look on her face.[64] This is abruptly followed by a direct cut to the wedding scene and its accompanying music. With this transition, the *Tristan* music is cut in the middle of an elision. We hear the ascending phrase conclude in the upper strings, but also hear the beginning of a new theme in the celli. This theme, identified by Kirby as the glance theme, is interrupted mid-gesture by the intrusion of the music Trevor Jones wrote for the wedding scene. The abrupt nature of the direct cut to the wedding places narrative emphasis on the denial of romantic passion for the sake of fulfilling duty to king and maintaining honor in accordance with a sense of knightly chivalry. However, this narrative message is undercut by several close shots of Lancelot during the wedding and by the underscore.

The wedding music supplied by Trevor Jones stands out from other diegetic cues as the only one that does not show the source of the music on screen—we hear a choir, but do not see monks performing. The acousmatic nature of these choral voices creates an otherworldly, but not celebratory, aura for the opening of the wedding.[65] The lower timbre that dominates the processional and opening of the ceremony provides stark contrast to the brightness of the lights reflected (intentionally) off the shining armor worn by the knights and Arthur. It marks a solemn, rather than celebratory occasion and emphasizes the ritual aspects of the scene. The scene perhaps evokes a comparison to the offstage chorus in Wagner's *Parsifal*, but rather than treble voices from above signifying some sense of heaven, the bass voices in *Excalibur* seem to invert this aesthetic. Indeed, Jones's music here approaches what James Deaville describes as the *topos* of the evil medieval.[66] When the text enters, we hear "Benedicto Jesu Christe" (Blessed be Jesus Christ) underscoring the close shot of the altar where the priest administers communion to Arthur and Guenevere. The priest says, "By the blood of Jesus Christ, I join you in marriage, man to woman, king to queen, and Arthur to Guenevere."[67] When he utters their names, the contrapuntal texture fades away and we hear clearly for the first time the words "Kyrie eleison" (Lord have mercy). This speech is bookended by cuts to close shots focused on Lancelot's face, which, in conjunction with the syncing of "Kyrie eleison" with Arthur and Guenevere's names, foreshadows the eventual tryst between Lancelot and Guenevere. Only after this, when the camera cuts back to a close shot of Morgana (Helen Mirren) turning away from the wedding to beg Merlin to train her in the ways of sorcery, do we hear treble voices, followed by an instrumental passage that lightens the texture and, briefly, the mood of the music. Every time the attention shifts back to the wedding, however, the lower tones of the Kyrie are heard. These textural differences emphasize the conversation between Merlin and Morgana in an interesting way.

In this first appearance of Morgana as a grown woman, she turns away from the wedding and approaches Merlin, asking, "Don't you know me, Lord Merlin?" and identifies herself as "Morgana of Cornwall," which serves an expository function. After Merlin responds with "You have your father's eyes," Morgana ignores his comment, stating, "I remember you. When my brother Arthur was born, you came and took him away."[68] When Merlin queries why Morgana has turned away from the wedding, she replies, "Because I am a creature like you."[69]

The grown Morgana's self-identification as "a creature like Merlin" confirms for the audience what is suspected from her witness of the rape scene, discussed previously. That she is indeed magical is then confirmed by Merlin as he tests her, all while the wedding is ongoing in the background. Merlin then responds to her request for tutelage: "The days of our kind are numbered; the one God comes to drive out the many gods; the spirits of wood and stream grow silent; it's the way of things—yes—it's a time for men and their ways."[70] This quote is immediately followed by the close shot on the altar capturing the end of the wedding. This is accompanied by a final iteration of the Kyrie, leading to the end of the scene. We see Arthur and Guenevere kiss and then a close shot of Lancelot's face, which coincides with the text "Amen," sung only by the bass voices.

By juxtaposing the lighter musical texture (used to accompany Merlin's lament that his ways are dying) with a darker texture for the marriage of Arthur and Guenevere, Boorman inverts conventional expectations in interesting ways. "The Arthurian legend,"

Boorman states, "is about the passing of the old gods and the coming of the Age of Man, of rationality, of laws—of man controlling his affairs. The price he pays for this is the loss of harmony with nature, which includes magic."[71] The music for the wedding scene, then, characterizes the coming age of Camelot in a not entirely positive way. This returns us to the question of Boorman and Jones's use of tropes. John Aberth considers the use of the Kyrie to be an obvious "reference to Christianity," which he sees as an essential element of Arthurian lore, while John Haines associates chant as a trope that can signify mysticism or magic.[72] In this case, both are true. Jones's Kyrie signifies the dawn of Christian civilization while simultaneously lamenting the waning of a mystical connection to nature from which both Merlin and Excalibur derive their power. The wedding scene, then, is another instance pointing to the idea of the cyclic nature of life. Although it has not yet been built, Camelot is symbolically connected to the marriage of Arthur and Guenevere and to the construction of a peaceful society that this marriage makes possible. In this sense, the wedding scene demonstrates how the elements that lead to Camelot's downfall existed from its inception—it is the forgetting of nature and mysticism that allows Arthur to drive his sword into the "spine of the dragon" between Lancelot and Guenevere, which leads to the Wasteland. Additionally, Morgana's training in magic, and bitterness over her past, as well as the feelings Lancelot and Guenevere share for each other, are all established by the music, dialogue, and visuals. This suggests one more possible meaning associated with the Kyrie. To anyone familiar with the translation of the words, the alignment of the text "Kyrie eleison" (Lord have mercy) with every shot of Arthur and Guenevere at the altar might be a subtle reference to the shape of things to come.

The Fall of Camelot and Redemption through the Grail

If both Arthur and Camelot are destined to fall, as I have argued thus far, the idea of Camelot as the source of future hope in a nostalgic construction of Arthurian myth would seem to be at odds not only with Boorman's politics, but also with his mythopoiesis. This is evident, too, in the representation of Camelot during act 2 of *Excalibur*. It is only when seen through Perceval's eyes that Camelot is venerated. Perceval's perspective, however, is marked by naiveté. For the audience, identification with Perceval's awe of Camelot is undercut, not only by the character's lack of knowledge, but also by the court intrigue that quickly overtakes the action of the second act. Upon arrival, Perceval is handed off to Sir Kay, while our attention is drawn to another suppressed moment between Lancelot and Guenevere, as the *Tristan* prelude again accompanies a shared gaze between them. The glance is as far as Lancelot is willing to go, refusing even to return Guenevere's wave and turning to leave Camelot. But Morgana sees the exchange and uses the knowledge she gains to sow discord at the round table.

The central action of the act comes with two parallel sequences that frame the joust in which Lancelot defends Guenevere's innocence by facing Gawain (Liam Neeson). The sequence leading up to the joust begins with a banquet scene, as the knights and their ladies eat at the round table. The table itself exists not as a symbol of democratic egalitarianism; rather, it commemorates the circle of knights formed inadvertently when Merlin interrupts the victory celebration at the end of the first act, warning them to "savor the moment" for it is "the doom of men that they forget."[73] The meal is underscored by a slower, more docile, stylized variation of the first strain of the Cameliard estampie discussed previously, effectively domesticating the lively exuberance of the Cameliard dance. The music is abruptly halted by Arthur asking Merlin, "For years, peace has reigned in the land, crops grow in abundance, there's no want, every one of my subjects enjoys his portion of happiness and justice. Tell me, Merlin, have we defeated evil, as it seems we have?" Merlin replies, "Good and evil, there never is one without the other." Arthur then asks, "Where hides evil then in my kingdom?" To which Merlin replies, "Always where you never expect it. Always."[74] Gawain, goaded by Morgana, takes this to refer to the queen's feelings for Lancelot and, being slightly drunk, says as much to the table. This leads to the decree that the matter will be settled in combat between Lancelot and Gawain. After the meal breaks up, we cut to a scene in which Arthur and Guenevere argue over Arthur's role. As king, Arthur insists, he is bound by his own laws to serve as judge and therefore cannot defend his bride's honor. This scene establishing Arthur's cold adherence to the law is underscored by excerpts from the *Tristan* prelude, which continues as the scene transitions outside where Lancelot prays in the forest, acknowledging that they are "guilty in their hearts" and asking God to purge his desire for Guenevere from him. Again, the music of *Tristan* gets cut abruptly mid-phrase as the camera cuts directly to an image of Lancelot sleeping in the forest. His dream is underscored by a dissonant series of drones and stingers that recalls horror tropes even more directly than the oblique reference of the wedding mass to the *topos* of the evil medieval. This horror music draws the audience into the uncanny moment when Lancelot fights himself and drops out when he reintegrates to discover that he has impaled himself with his sword. Bignell refers to this moment as evocative of masculine "vulnerability and homoeroticism," suggesting that it offers a reprieve from male-dominated society.[75] Whether or not one agrees with Bignell on this point, Lancelot's wound is part of his identity that he must face uncovered and accept before he can reassume the armor-clad masculinity of knighthood and ride to champion Guenevere.

At the joust scene, the slow build of the drums embodies the tension of the spectators (both on and off screen), culminating with Perceval being dismissed as Lancelot's stand-in as the wounded knight sweeps in at the last minute. He defeats Gawain and proves the queen innocent before collapsing from his self-inflicted wound.[76] Interestingly, in the midst of the tense buildup and the ensuing action, Morgana is shown ten times, always standing apart from the crowd, clearly on the side of Gawain. And the fourth, fifth, and eighth of those shots are close or mid-range, allowing us to see her reaction. Her inclusion with Arthur, Guenevere, and the combatants as worthy of a close-up emphasizes her importance and her agency in bringing about the combat.

After the joust, Lancelot is healed by Merlin's magic (at the request of Arthur and Guenevere), and on his return to court, he observes, "We have lost our way, Arthur." Arthur replies, "It's not easy for them without the hard teaching of war and quest. It is only your example, Lancelot, that binds them now." This begins a sequence that parallels the one preceding the joust. Lancelot's conversation with Arthur occurs at the onset of a feast at the round table, with the same subdued variation of the Cameliard estampie in the underscore. Again, the music is interrupted by Arthur asking a question of Merlin. This time, Arthur asks, "Which is the greatest quality of knighthood: courage, compassion, loyalty, humility? What do you say, Merlin?" To which, after some hesitation, Merlin replies, "Ah, ah, ah, the greatest, well they blend, like the metals we mix to make a good sword." Arthur demands a straight answer, and Merlin asserts, "Alright then, truth, that's it, yes, it must be truth, above all. When a man lies, he murders some part of the world. You should know that."[77] As in the previous sequence, the next music to enter is the *Tristan* prelude, this time setting the stage for the tryst, as Guenevere follows Lancelot into the woods and the lovers embrace for the first time. As this moment leads up to the climax, the action gets intercut between the lovers in the forest, Arthur on his way to confront them, and Merlin leading Morgana down into the "coils of the dragon" on the pretense of giving her the Charm of Making so he can banish her into oblivion. Once the characters are in place, the *Tristan* prelude, which had at first only accompanied the clips of the lovers in the forest, plays continuously to the climax when the music is symbolically cut off by Arthur thrusting Excalibur into the ground between the naked bodies of Lancelot and Guenevere. This gesture excises the *Tristan* music from the score and emasculates King Arthur, transforming him into the Fisher King. It also parallels Uther's thrusting of the sword into the stone (and therefore inverts Arthur's pulling the sword from the stone), marking the action as one of symbolic abdication. He also thrusts the sword into "the spine of the dragon," distracting Merlin (visually signified by the momentary appearance of the sword thrust through Merlin himself, indicating his own link to the dragon) just before he finishes magically banishing Morgana. This allows her to gain the upper hand and trick the now weakened Merlin into giving up the Charm of Making, thereby trapping him. This climactic moment is underscored by a strikingly dissonant tremolando effect similar to the cue accompanying Lancelot's dream. While the first sequence led to the joust scene that emphasized Morgana's agency, this sequence leads to Morgana's triumph. She uses the Charm of Making to rape Arthur in the guise of Guenevere, conceiving Mordred, and avenging the wrong done to her mother, Igrayne. This scene is underscored by the same music that accompanies the earlier rape scene. The same upward chromatic line that marked Uther's lust for Igrayne now marks Morgana's lust for vengeance and power. Since Arthur is incapable of seeing through the enchantment, Morgana breaks it for him, revealing her true visage, as she says, "I could kill you now brother, but I want you to live to see our son be king."[78] After this, Arthur collapses, Morgana leaves, and a direct cut jumps us ahead in time to a dark, stormy night filled with lightning. We witness Mordred's birth and then cut to Camelot, where Arthur is struck by lightning during a communion service, adding a physical wound to match his psychic one and bringing the second act to a close.

The music in these two sequences helps create an unfavorable view of Camelot while simultaneously drawing attention to the agents of its destruction. The flaccid underscore for the feast scenes reinforces Aronstein's claim that Camelot is depicted as stagnant. We do not see the prosperity of the land or the happiness and justice Arthur boasts of; we see an idle court that is all too easy for Morgana to push to the brink of collapse. The heavy use of the *Tristan* prelude draws our attention to the suppressed desires that lurk under the surface. Using the *Tristan* prelude to underscore the row between Arthur and Guenevere emphasizes the suppressed passion of Arthur, as his laws and his duties as king do not allow him to be the loving husband Guenevere desires. It also draws our attention to Guenevere's suppressed desire for Lancelot that is awakening as Arthur refuses to be her champion. While these tensions simmer during the joust scene, when the *Tristan* music returns they come to full boil. Lancelot and Guenevere finally consummate their relationship, and Arthur unleashes his passion in the act of abdication. In terms of agency, Morgana works behind the scenes to gain her revenge, but Lancelot, Guenevere, and Arthur share responsibility for the downfall of Camelot. Morgana would have been vanquished by Merlin if Arthur's passion had not driven him to drive *Excalibur* into the spine of the dragon. This spreading of the blame allows Boorman to subvert the normative nostalgic reading of Camelot as the golden age of democracy. Placing the blame on just Lancelot and Guenevere, as other Arthurian movies have done, allows Arthur to be the wise and just king whose reign is brought down by betrayal. The same could be said of blaming only Morgana. But Arthur's powerfully symbolic act of abdication, while not absolving the others, makes him arguably more culpable for the plight brought on his kingdom.

Spreading the blame also opens up the possibility of several different readings of Merlin's pronouncement about the evil near the beginning of the act. On the one hand, it leads some to see Morgana as the "evil" Merlin warned about. Jacqueline de Weever argues that, "by suppressing the love affair of Lancelot and Guinevere as the main cause of the Round Table's fall, Boorman enhances Morgana's role as destroyer."[79] This leads her to conclude that

> *Excalibur's* feminist subtext emerges as readers and viewers ponder its meanings. Men cannot deny women their rightful inheritances and expect the world to live happily ever after.[80]

Similarly, Maureen Fries observes,

> Boorman's version of Morgan serves as no other film has … to restore Morgan La Fey to Arthurian history. For that he has utilized fully the technique of the gaze, his Morgana observing and observed with a malice and a desire always hungry and never fulfilled, and serving eloquently as an objective correlative to the illusion which is her only weapon, as a woman, against a male dominant and hostile world.[81]

While she praises *Excalibur*, her conclusion still yearns for a "more sympathetic version (of Morgana) to match the powerful male-friendly vision Boorman offers."[82] Indeed, even though Morgana has a degree of agency, it still must be exercised within a male-dominated world that condemns her transgressive desire for power and revenge. As Torregrossa rightly asserts, Mordred is "the instrument through which his mother, Morgana, seeks to get revenge."[83] But in the end, it is Mordred who kills her and Merlin's spirit who tricks her into using up her powers to summon the fog that evens the odds at Camlann. In this scene, Morgana's abuse of magic to satisfy her own vanity is the beginning of her downfall. Merlin taunts her in her dreams, inciting her to speak the Charm of Making, which calls forth fog around Mordred's camp and uses up so much power that she can no longer hold the illusion of her youth. Mordred enters her tent, finds her confused and shriveled with age, and strangles her, perhaps out of rage at her summoning the fog, perhaps out of disgust at the sight of her aged body, or perhaps both motivations cause him to realize the only way he will be free of the destructive mother archetype that she represents is by killing her.[84] In short, while Morgana is a powerful character, her agency is seen as excessive and threatening—she is, in some ways, still, the transgressive femme fatale. Yet, she is not solely responsible for the downfall of Camelot, and that leaves one other possibility open in regard to Merlin's warning. If Arthur's act of abdication is as responsible for bringing about the wasteland as it seems to be, then perhaps the evil lies in the "myth of progress" proclaimed by Arthur that Merlin was responding to when he issued the warning. Discussing Camelot in the director's commentary, Boorman states,

> We wanted to give this impression of a kind of you know almost a Roman thing, that they've achieved this power, this strength, this civilization, and to some extent they're incarcerated by it, they're cut off from nature, from the natural world that they sprung from, as happens you know with, in civilization, is that the price we pay for knowledge is the loss of perhaps that primal magic.[85]

In losing touch with that "primal magic," Arthur forgets the essential truth Merlin taught him at the beginning of his reign: that the king and the land are one. It is this transgression that requires redemption through the Grail.

This desacralization of the Grail (and the elision of Arthur with the Fisher King) is, perhaps, the most contentious of Boorman's changes to the legend. Aberth decries Boorman's treatment of the Grail, asserting that "the religious symbolism of the Grail, at least, must be retained in any film about Arthur that aspires to be medieval," though he concludes with a speculation that "Boorman intends his film to be timeless."[86] But Boorman's Grail draws on the work of Jessie Weston and is the "feminine symbol of wholeness and harmony" that allows Arthur to rekindle "oneness with nature."[87] Interestingly, the desacralized Grail is paired with the "Sacrament Theme" from Wagner's *Parsifal*. The hauntingly beautiful rising melodic lines of this theme lend a sense of intimacy and purity to the scene, as we witness Perceval successfully obtain the Grail by discovering its secret: that it serves the king and that the king and the land are one. The music continues through a cut to Arthur's moment of redemption, when he drinks from the cup at Perceval's behest and the music fades as Arthur begins to speak of the wholeness he now feels. We witness the sacrament, but it is a pagan, rather than Christian ritual—a fact that is doubly highlighted by the noticeable departure from common Grail lore and by the use of Wagner's music. In Boorman's mythopoiesis, the desacralized Grail demonstrates that what is lost and longed for in *Excalibur* is not Camelot, but the knowledge of some sort of mystical precivilized age when man was more closely united with nature.

The other two occurrences of the "Sacrament Theme" affirm and further this interpretation. It returns when Arthur remembers his connection to nature and thus rekindles a link with Merlin. Arthur awakens Merlin's spirit, which allows the wizard to exist in the "realm of dreams" and help them defeat Morgana and Mordred at Camlann. It sounds again when Lancelot lies dying of his old wound on the battlefield of Camlann.[88] Taken together, the three occurrences of this theme might be read as symbolizing a regressive redemption. Perceval is only able to retrieve the Grail after stripping off his armor, recalling his roots as a simple child of nature, living off the land in the forest before he became Lancelot's squire. Arthur's healing, as already discussed, involves resuming a forsaken mantle. In his conversation with Morgana at the wedding of Arthur and Guenevere, Merlin indicates that the power of the old gods is waning; the partial restoration of his power near the end of the film thus suggests another kind of regression. Even Lancelot's resumption of fealty to Arthur is regressive, evidenced by the fact that he dies not of a new wound from the battle, but from the old, self-inflicted wound (which also creates some interesting parallels with Amfortas). If the redemption offered by the Grail is regressive, perhaps that is because the characters are being restored to their proper position, on the downward turn of the *Rota Fortunae*. This, in turn (if you will pardon the pun), allows them to fulfill their archetypal roles. If they are destined to be "the stuff of future memory," they are also doomed by this fate.

Conclusions

In *Excalibur*, John Boorman creates an Arthurian myth that deconstructs itself. His characters are archetypal, bound by fate to their destinies, and as such have no hope of escaping Fortune's wheel. They have their own passions and motivations, and limited agency, but are always being guided back to their destined path. Rather than representing a beacon of hope that might be aspired to in the future, Camelot is presented instead as a mythic realm that itself longs for a past time when union with nature was possible. Michel Ciment observes, "Here, as in *Zardoz*, a Utopia harbours the seed of its own destruction, since, being a pure product of reason, it fatally omits to account for either nature or spirituality."[89] Boorman's *Excalibur* occupies the same register as the mythic sources he draws from. But rather than locating the Middle Ages as the "*bon vieux temps*," he uses the visual and aural language of Arthuriana to call attention to the mythic status of the Utopian view typically foist on that period. "According to Jung," Boorman states, "the Middle Ages . . . was a period which, like the unconscious, we ought to study in order to gain a better understanding of ourselves."[90]

In this light, Boorman's medievalism, rather than offering an escape through nostalgic hope or a *Fata Morgana*, instead demands that we engage with the mythic medieval ourselves, in the hope that we might be better for it. He foregrounds the mythic status of his work and by doing so adds a new register to the dialogue of medievalism, a register we might refer to as the Mythic Medieval.

Notes

1. See Kevin J. Harty, "Cinema Arthuriana: Translations of the Arthurian Legend to the Screen," *Arthurian Interpretations* 2, no. 1 (Fall 1987): 95–113. See also Norris J. Lacy, "Arthurian Film and the Tyranny of Tradition," *Arthurian Interpretations* 4, no. 1 (Fall 1989): 75–85. See also the essays in the following two collected editions: Kevin J. Harty, ed., *King Arthur on Film: New Essays on Arthurian Cinema* (London: McFarland, 1999); and Kevin J. Harty, ed., *Cinema Arthuriana: Twenty Essays Revised Edition* (London: McFarland, 2002).

2. See David Williams, "Medieval Movies," in "Literature in the Modern Media: Radio, Film, and Television Special Number," *The Yearbook of English Studies* 20, (1990): 1–32. See also John Aberth, *A Knight at the Movies: Medieval History on Film* (New York: Routledge, 1993). See also Nicholas Haydock, *Movie Medievalism* (London: McFarland, 2008); John Haines, *Music in Films on the Middle Ages: Authenticity vs. Fantasy* (New York: Routledge, 2014); Susan Aronstein, *Hollywood Knights: Arthurian Cinema and the Politics of Nostalgia* (New York: MacMillan, 2005); and E. Jane Burns, "Nostalgia Isn't What It Used to Be: The Middle Ages in Literature and Film," in *Shadows of the Magic Lamp: Fantasy and Science Fiction in Film*, ed. George E. Slusser and Eric S. Rabkin (Carbondale: Southern Illinois University Press, 1985), 86–97.

3. The titles given here are taken verbatim from the end credits: *Excalibur*, directed by John Boorman (Orion Pictures, 1981), DVD (Warner Bros., 2010), 02:20:15. For further discussion of Boorman's collaboration with Jones in making the musical selections for the film, see Michel Ciment, *John Boorman*, trans. Gilbert Adair (London: Faber & Faber, 1986), 200.

4. See Aberth, *A Knight at the Movies*, 23. See also Haines, *Music in Films on the Middle Ages*, 24, 49, 78.

5. Roy Wakefield, "Excalibur: Film Reception and Political Distance," in *Politics in German Literature*, ed. Beth Bjorklund and Mark E. Cory (Columbia, SC: Camden House, 1998), 166.

6. Ibid., 166–176.

7. Jonathan Bignell, "Music and the Politics of Masculinity in Excalibur," originally in *Les aurtres arts dans l'art du cinema* (Rennes: University of Rennes Press, 2007), 141–151, translated into English by the author and available for download at https://reading.academia.edu/JonathanBignell.

8. See Aronstein, *Hollywood Knights*, 145–160. See also Brian Hoyle, *The Cinema of John Boorman* (Toronto: Scarecrow Press, 2012), 117–134.

9. Aronstein, *Hollywood Knights*, 153.

10. See Roland Barthes, *Mythologies*, trans. Annette Lavers (New York: Hill and Wang, 1972).

11. See John Boorman, *Adventures of a Suburban Boy* (London: Faber & Faber, 2003). He also discusses this in various interviews. For a sampling, see Harlan Kennedy, "The World of

King Arthur According to John Boorman," *American Film*, 30–37; Ciment, *John Boorman*, 192; Dan Yakir, "Interview with John Boorman," *The Sorcerer* 17, no. 3 (May/June 1981): 49–53.

12. John Boorman, *Excalibur*, 02:17:45.

13. Ciment, *John Boorman*, 192. See also Hoyle, *The Cinema of John Boorman*, 131.

14. He makes this or similar statements in most of the interviews he has given about *Excalibur*. See also Note 11.

15. John Boorman, "Director's Commentary," *Excalibur*, 01:57:08–01:58:47.

16. Harlan Kennedy, "The World of King Arthur According to John Boorman," 34.

17. Ibid.

18. Norris Lacy, "Arthurian Film and the Tyranny of Tradition," *Arthurian Interpretations* 4, no. 1 (Fall 1989): 75–85.

19. Kennedy, "The World of King Arthur According to John Boorman," 33.

20. See Ciment, *John Boorman*, 185–201; Smith, "Beyond Images," 44–58; and Hoyle, *The Cinema of John Boorman*.

21. Yakir, "Interview with John Boorman," 51.

22. Barthes, *Mythologies*, 135.

23. Ciment, *John Boorman*, 192.

24. Boorman, *Excalibur*, 01:32:17–01:32:45.

25. Alexandra Sterling-Hellenbrand, "Excalibur's Siegfried and the Music of Myth," in "New Research in Medieval Germanic Studies," *Yearbook for the Society of Medieval Germanic Studies* 1, no. 1 (May 2009): 39.

26. Ibid., 43.

27. Ciment, *John Boorman*, 192.

28. Boorman, *Adventures of a Suburban Boy*, 239–240.

29. Ciment, *John Boorman*, 200.

30. Boorman, *Excalibur*, 00:00:00–00:00:55.

31. See F. E. Kirby, *Wagner's Themes: A Study in Musical Expression* (Warren, MI: Harmonie Park Press, 2004), 104–105.

32. These scenes can, respectively, be found at the following time stamps in Boorman, *Excalibur*, 00:03:09–00:03:51, 00:22:28–00:22:58, 00:27:42–00:27:51, 00:29:10–00:29:24, 00:41:22–00:42:06, 01:58:35–01:59:08.

33. Sterling-Hellenbrand, "Excalibur's Siegfried and the Music of Myth," 44.

34. Both involve a sword passed on from father to son that can only be retrieved from where they were thrust into the earth by the person destined to wield them.

35. Sterling-Hellenbrand, "Excalibur's Siegfried and the Music of Myth," 47.

36. In his essay "Star Wars, Music, and Myth," in *Music and Cinema*, ed. James Buhler, Caryl Flinn, and David Neumeyer (London: Wesleyan University Press, 2000), 33–57, James Buhler makes a similar argument regarding the use of the opening music (and the silence in between) to suggest a mythic origin for the saga. The chief difference is that Williams's original score contributed to a Barthian first-order mythic discourse, while I believe quoting music that is already associated with myth is one way that Boorman begins to establish *Excalibur* as a second-order myth.

37. See Kirby, *Wagner's Themes*, 97–98.

38. See Adrian Daub and Patrick McCreless, "Wotan," in *The Cambridge Wagner Encyclopedia*, ed. Nicholas Vazsonyi (Cambridge: Cambridge University Press, 2013), 732–733, 770.

39. See Hoyle, *The Cinema of John Boorman*, for more on Boorman's use of the Merlin archetype. See also Ciment, *John Boorman*, 192–196; and Yakir, "The Sorcerer," *Film Comment*, 49–53.

40. See Kirby, *Wagner's Themes*, 97–98.

41. Boorman, *Excalibur*, 00:40:54–00:42:56.

42. Ibid., 01:56:56–01:59:55.

43. The topic of medievalism within Orff's cantata itself is explored by Kirsten Yri in her contribution to this volume, "Medievalism and Anti-Romanticism in Carl Orff's Carmina Burana," pp. 269–300.

44. Orff explains how he was inspired by the icon itself, which appears at the beginning of the Codex Buranas, just above the text for "O Fortuna" in *Carl Orff und Sein Werk: Dokumentation*, vol. 4, *Trionfi: Carmina Burana-Catulli Carmina-Trionfo di Afrodite* (Tutzing: Hans Schneider, 1979), 38–42.

45. These scenes can be found at Boorman, *Excalibur*, 00:35:56–00:36:58 and 01:55:33–01:56:54, respectively.

46. Aronstein, *Hollywood Knights*, 155.

47. Kennedy, "The World of King Arthur According to John Boorman," 37.

48. Boorman, *Excalibur*, 02:07:48–02:10:33.

49. This, too, is consistent with medieval writings on the *Rota Fortunae*. Boethius, in his *Consolation of Philosophy*, offers the possibility of exiting Fortune's wheel by discovering the grace of Providence, while Machaut carries this further, offering Hope as the *Remede de Fortune*.

50. Roger Ebert, "Excalibur," January 2, 1981, http://www.rogerebert.com/reviews/excalibur-1981.

51. Boorman, *Excalibur*, 01:58:00–01:58:35.

52. Ibid., 00:05:03–00:07:00.

53. Ibid., 00:06:36–00:06:39.

54. Haines, *Music in Films on the Middle Ages*, 78.

55. Ibid., 67–72.

56. Ibid. See also Fiona Macintosh's interesting discussion of Greek dance in modern Britain in her essay "Dancing Maenads in Early Twentieth-Century Britain," in *The Ancient Dancer in the Modern World: Responses to Greek and Roman Dance*, ed. Fiona Macintosh (Oxford: Oxford University Press, 2010), 188–210.

57. Boorman, *Excalibur*, 00:13:36.

58. For more on this imagery, see Muriel Whitaker, "Fire, Water, Rock: Elements of Setting in John Boorman's *Excalibur* and Steve Barron's *Merlin*," in *Cinema Arthuriana*, 44–53.

59. Boorman, *Excalibur*, 00:15:29.

60. Ibid., 00:42:55–00:45:48.

61. See ibid., 00:57:57; See also 00:59:45–00:59:56.

62. Norris Lacy, "Mythopoeia in *Excalibur*," in *Cinema Arthuriana: Twenty Essays*, revised ed., ed. Kevin J. Harty (London: McFarland, 2002), 37.

63. See Sterling-Hellenbrand "Excalibur's Siegfried and the Music of Myth," 37. See also Hoyle, *The Cinema of John Boorman*, 126–127.

64. Measure numbers are taken from Edition Eulenburg no. 905. It is worth pointing out that the contrapuntal nature of Wagner's writing in this section makes a clean cut difficult to achieve. The scene occurs in Boorman, *Excalibur*, 00:59:56–01:03:30.

65. For more on the connection between acousmatic sound and the magical, see Michel Chion's discussion of the *acousmaître* in *The Voice and Cinema*, trans. Claudia Gorbman (New York: Columbia University Press, 1999), 17–48.

66. James Deaville, "The Topos of 'Evil Medieval' in American Horror Film Music," in *Music, Meaning, & Media*, ed. Erkki Pekkilä, David Neumeyer, and Richard Littlefield (Helsinki: International Semiotics Institute, 2006), 26–37. Deaville expands and develops his discussion of this *topos* in his contribution to this volume, "Evil Medieval: Chant and the New Dark Spirituality of Vietnam-Era Film in America," pp. 709–728.

67. Boorman, *Excalibur*, 01:00:22–01:00:46.

68. Ibid., 01:00:54–01:01:18.

69. Ibid., 01:01:26.

70. Ibid., 01:02:51.

71. Yakir, "The Sorcerer," *Film Comment*, 50.

72. Aberth, *A Knight at the Movies*, 22–24; see also Haines, *Music in Films on the Middle Ages: Authenticity vs. Fantasy*, 26–44, 111–132.

73. Boorman, *Excalibur*, 00:55:55–00:56:37.

74. Ibid., 01:08:23–01:15:00.

75. Bignell, "Music and the Politics of Masculinity in *Excalibur*," 11.

76. Boorman, *Excalibur*, 01:15:03–01:20:18.

77. Ibid., 01:22:01–01:30:14.

78. Ibid., 01:32:48–01:33:43.

79. Boorman, "Morgana and the Problem of Incest," in *Cinema Arthuriana: Twenty Essays Revised Edition*, 58.

80. Ibid., 61.

81. Maureen Fries, "How to Handle a Woman, or Morgan at the Movies," in *King Arthur on Film*, 79.

82. Ibid.

83. "Will the 'Reel' Mordred Please Stand Up? Strategies for Representing Mordred in American and British Arthurian Film," in *Cinema Arthuriana: Twenty Essays Revised Edition*, 204.

84. Boorman, *Excalibur*, 02:02:56–02:07:34.

85. Boorman, "Director's Commentary," *Excalibur*, 01:06:36–01:07:20.

86. Aberth, *Knight at the Movies*, 24.

87. "Mythopoeia in *Excalibur*," in *Cinema Arthuriana: Twenty Essays Revised Edition*, 34–43. It is worth noting that the work of Jessie Weston has been dismissed by many in the field of Arthurian scholarship after J. D. Bruce, as Shichtman points out in "Hollywood's New Weston." The original sources for this debate are Jessie L. Weston, *From Ritual to Romance* (1920; repr. New York: Doubleday Anchor Books, 1957), which is noted for its influence on Eliot's *The Waste Land* and James Douglas Bruce, "Miss Weston's Gawain Complex," in *The Evolution of Arthurian Romance from the Beginnings down to the Year 1300* (Baltimore: John Hopkins University Press, 1923) 2:91–103. See also Boorman, *Adventures of a Suburban Boy*, 237.

88. Boorman, *Excalibur*. These two scenes occur at 02:00:25–02:02:22, and 02:11:16–02:12:15, respectively.

89. Ciment, *John Boorman*, 180.

90. Ibid.

....

CHAPTER 30

THE MANY MUSICAL MEDIEVALISMS OF DISNEY

....

JOHN HAINES

ALTHOUGH this essay aims to outline Disney's main musical medievalisms, along the way I will argue for the company's role as one of society's main purveyors of medievalism, as embodied in the ubiquitous Disney Company icon, Sleeping Beauty Castle. The idea of Disney as a force for medievalism may strike some academic readers as odd, given the still common view of medievalism as a primarily academic phenomenon. It will be best, then, to counter this assumption right away. Some thirty years ago, medievalism strutted out on the runway of academic high fashion with a spree of books and articles. This was the nineties, a decade as crucial to the global postsecondary education industry as it was to Disney and other corporate entities. In these publications from the nineties, medievalism was portrayed as an academic thing. The story was nothing short of a grand narrative, one in which learned hermits had groped their way around the medieval elephant and eventually stumbled onto "the Middle Ages," currently the centerpiece of entire university departments, including my own University of Toronto's Center for Medieval Studies. In this narrative of academic medievalism, there were bad guys (Nazi Friedrich Gennrich) and good gals (first woman Anglo-Saxonist Elizabeth Elstob), entrepreneurs ("God's plagiarist" Jean-Paul Migne) and nationalists (French advocate Gaston Paris), preromantic loners (antiquarian Lacurne de Sainte-Palaye) and postromantic ones (independent scholar Leslie Workman).[1] Alternately, medievalism was viewed less as a great enterprise than as a crisis of nostalgia that had given birth to the postmodern Enlightenment.[2] However one looked at it in the 1990s and early 2000s, medievalism was the preserve of academia. It was a conversation among intellectual grown-ups about history and philosophy, an adult conversation that had started in the nineteenth century.

Yet academic medievalism is only a winding trail off a much broader path, the king's way of popular medievalism—pop culture, not literature, in Umberto Eco's words.[3] Still today, the received notion is that the Middle Ages were rescued by academics from oblivion sometime in the nineteenth century.[4] Much the same thing, incidentally, is argued for early music and folk music.[5] As for the beginnings of medievalism, the sixteenth century, it is usually seen as "a period in which the concept of the medieval past was yet unsettled," to quote leading medievalist Richard Utz.[6] Not until the nineteenth century, in other words, did medievalism get started. This assumption is a result of the near dearth of scholarly study on sixteenth-century medievalism. Even David Matthews's exceptionally long view of medievalism, one that ostensibly takes the earliest phase into account, in fact devotes nearly all its pages to the nineteenth century and beyond.[7]

As I have argued for over a decade, however, the sixteenth century is a far more foundational period to medievalism than commonly assumed.[8] It is worth repeating that, long before the sensational 1990s, the Middle Ages were for most of their five-hundred-year existence neither a distinct chronological unit nor the sole province of professors. In fact, the noun *Middle Ages* and the adverb *medieval* did not become standard in English until the mid-twentieth century, at the tail end of the five-century-long reception of the Middle Ages.[9] For early students like William Worcester (late fifteenth century) or Clément Marot (early sixteenth century), the period we now label medieval was just part of antiquity, or at least an extension of antiquity that had the merit, unlike Greek or Roman antiquity, of belonging to each antiquarian's patria: Worcester was after "English antiquities" (*Antiquitates Anglie*) and Marot pined for the "antiquité Françoise."[10] This view of the Middle Ages as a vernacular knock-off of antiquity lasted for most of the modern period, and it is the one that has endured in cinema for over a century. A representative example is Edward Gibbons's *History of the Decline and Fall of the Roman Empire* (1776–1788), which envisions the Middle Ages (not yet so named) as antiquity redux, a descent into Gothic barbarity followed by a revived Eastern Empire that fizzles out with the Saracen taking of Constantinople in the fifteenth century, to paraphrase Gibbons.[11] Thus have the Middle Ages been seen for most of their five-hundred-year existence as a calque of antiquity, as a maternal version of the too distant Greek–Roman father.

Most of the basic preconceptions concerning the Middle Ages prevalent today were established in the 1500s and have remained ensconced in both the popular and the academic imagination for the following five centuries, beginning with the notion of a single thousand-year entity. Over the course of its five-hundred-year reception, the medieval golden age has been consistently associated with a handful of distinct stereotypes that I highlighted in *Music in Films on the Middle Ages* (2014). As I argued then, these stereotypes are less the product of a systematic historiography than the haphazard result of a collective nostalgia for a golden age just out of reach.[12] The six stereotypes are as follows, given here in both chronological and hierarchical order; a few correspond to one of Umberto Eco's "Ten Little Middle Ages." Most fundamental is the chivalric stereotype, which is characterized in musical works by a triumphant horse-riding fanfare and prevalent from the early sixteenth century onward. Next in chronological order are the supernatural Middle Ages, dovetailing with Eco's Middle Ages of tradition or occult philosophy; the main musical associations with this stereotype are various kinds of chant.[13] Third are the primitive Middle Ages (Eco's "barbaric age"), with their rustic folk songs.[14] Next come the pastoral Middle Ages and their trademark hunting horn in stage works and cinema.[15] Fifth are the orientalist Middle Ages, often typified by dance numbers. Last in the history of medievalism are the satirical (i.e., satirized) Middle Ages, which Eco terms *ironical visitation*,[16] a self-parodying universe ideally suited to cinema's time-traveling obsession. Originating in Cervantes's *Don Quixote*, this approached flowered in film with the different cinematic paeans to Twain's *A Connecticut Yankee in King Arthur's Court* and their mashup of cool jazz and European stuffiness.

For nearly a century, Disney has made good use of all six stereotypes. Yet little attention has been paid until now to Disney's medievalism. Only recently has one scholarly volume finally appeared that is dedicated to Disney's medievalism: *The Disney Middle Ages*, edited by Tison Pugh and Susan Aronstein.[17] One reason for this neglect is, as Elizabeth Bell, Lynda Haas, and Laura Sells argued some twenty years ago, that Disney's fantastical worlds are understood by most of us having little to do with the historical period we call the Middle Ages.[18] And yet, Disney has become in our time one of the largest vendors of medievalism, not the narrow academic kind, but the more generic and common type of medievalism that has prevailed over the past five hundred years. Disney, in other words, is the largest provider of medievalism *tout court*, the modern nostalgia for fairy-tale days when brave heroes battled evil monsters and witches, *le bon vieulx temps* (to cite Clément Marot) when chanting priests sang alongside minstrels in the courts of the great kings.[19]

Its medievalism aside, Disney is without contest the most powerful entertainment conglomerate in the world today. Under the direction of chief executive officer and chairman Michael Eisner (1984–2004), the company began a series of aggressive acquisitions that have resulted in its current domination, not only of the global entertainment industry, but also of related and far more lucrative industries ranging from toy markets to vacation resorts. Following Eisner's takeover, the company's burgeoning profits increasingly came not from movies, as one might expect, but from related industries, in particular, theme parks and home videos.[20] Things continued to crescendo in the aughts with Disney's purchase of Pixar (2006) and Marvel (2009), followed in 2012 by the acquisition of the most profitable film franchise of all time, Lucasfilm—already nicknamed "Star Bucks" by Peter Biskind in the late nineties.[21] With the proliferation of Star Wars products in the past few years, Disney has shown just how many more bucks could be bled from George Lucas's franchise. Disney's devouring of the world (to quote Carl Hiaasen's book title) has been achieved thanks to the ruthlessness of its litigation and spin machines.[22] No disaster sticks to the mighty makers of Mickey Mouse, be it Banksy's Dismaland (2015) or Euro Disney's bankruptcy (2017). There is always a happy ending. Following the gruesome alligator killing of a two-year-old boy by the name of Lane Graves at Disney World's Grand Floridian resort in June 2016, a preventable disaster that would have shuttered most other corporations, Disney made its usual swift public-relations recovery. Inexplicably, the mainstream press exonerated the company with sympathetic releases, and a few months later, the toddler's mauling had revolved out of the news cycle entirely. To replace this too-sad story came the latest in syndicated news offerings about Disney, a Hollywoodian conflict–resolution tale. After suffering a "rare stumble in the fiscal fourth quarter," Disney was poised to swing back, stronger than ever! Iger projected "more robust growth in fiscal 2018 and beyond" thanks to an upcoming slate of Marvel and Star Wars movies.[23] Meanwhile, there was not a word about the size of Disney's settlement with Lane's parents, who, it turned out, would not sue the entertainment colossus.

Next to publicity landmines like child-eating alligators, the tiny posse of Disney's intellectual critics may be a negligible threat, but it still merits the company's vigilance. The starting point of the academic critique of Disney remains film critic Richard Schickel's 1968 tour de force, *The Disney Version*, for which Schickel was "banned, for a time, from Disney screening rooms."[24] Not surprisingly, intellectuals' criticism of the company stepped up during the Eisner era, with seminal works like Norman Klein's *Seven Minutes* (1993), Alan Bryman's *Disney and His Worlds* (1995), and Carl Hiaasen's *Team Rodent: How Disney Devours the World* (1998).[25] Around this time, when the editors of a book on Disney wrote to the company's personnel for access to its archives, they were informed that Disney does not allow third-party books to use the word *Disney* in their titles, with the following threat: "All of our valuable properties, characters, and marks are protected under copyright and trademark law, and any unauthorized use of our protected material would constitute infringements of our rights under said law."[26] During the production of my own book on *Music in Films on the Middle Ages* (2014), I was warned by the publisher (Routledge) to not include photo stills from Disney films, even though the reproduction of screenshots in published research is widespread and within the bounds of the law. Apparently, Routledge had learned that no one, fusty professors included, messes with Disney.[27]

Medievalism as Capitalism

If capitalism and medievalism are intertwined in the history of Disney, it is because these two phenomena have grown up together since their common genesis in the sixteenth century. To summarize my argument so far, the phenomenon we know today as medievalism began in the sixteenth century as a longing for an era that had just passed, a chronologically ambivalent "Gothic antiquity" characterized by a strong chivalric code, a supernatural aura, and a strongly primitive and pastoral feel. This distinctive view of the Middle Ages, in place by the 1500s, was reinforced during this five-hundred-year reception in many an opera. As I stated in *Music in Films on the Middle Ages*, "it would take up an entire book to relate the pre-cinematic fascination with the Chivalric" stereotype alone, not to mention the other five.[28] If such a book is ever written, its usefulness would lie in demonstrating the historical connection between musical medievalisms from the sixteenth to nineteenth centuries and the music of cinema in the twentieth century.[29] For the chivalric stereotype, for example, it would be worthwhile to trace the use of brass passages in operas from Purcell's *King Arthur* (1691) to Arthur Sullivan's *Ivanhoe* (1891) and to continue on to similar music in medievalist film. Regarding the supernatural stereotype, a study of the use of relevant choral passages with nonsensical or "demonic" texts in operas such as Weber's *Freischütz* (1821) could compare the Orff–*Carmina Burana* sound of scores from John Barry's *Lion in Winter* onward, a sound nearly ubiquitous in the superhero film genre.[30] With respect to the primitive Middle Ages, the music of the early modern *romancero* and subsequent folk-song movement could shed considerable light on its musical derivative in medieval film. A study of Wagner's stage works in connection with cinematic medievalist pastoral idioms would be helpful in understanding the pastoral stereotype. In the case of the orientalist Middle Ages, an account of precinematic precursors such as Weber's *Oberon* (1826) would be highly relevant to the study of medieval film.[31] As for medieval parodies, one could begin with operatic paraphrases of *Don Quixote* (1605), such as Richard Strauss's 1898 opera by the same name, to properly situate time-traveling medieval parodies in their historical context.[32]

The long view of medievalism from the 1500s to the present that I have just sketched out has an important parallel development: the history of capitalism. In the conclusion to *Music in Films on the Middle Ages*, I summarized this development with reference to German historians, notably Karl Marx and his most famous follower, Werner Sombart, who in the early twentieth century coined the various phases of capitalism that are still in use today: *Vorkapitalismus* (precapitalism), *Frühkapitalismus* (early capitalism or mercantilism), and *Hochkapitalismus* (high capitalism).[33] As later historians have confirmed, it was indeed in the late Middle Ages when emerged the banking system that would become the backbone of modern industry, what Giovanni Arrighi has called "genesis of high finance."[34] The sixteenth century would inaugurate Europe's aggressive global colonization and capitalism's "first systemic cycle of accumulation," in Arrighi's terminology.[35]

It is no coincidence that the crystalizing of the medieval golden age occurred just as the new economic order of transatlantic mercantilism was taking shape, what Immanuel Wallerstein once called the European world economy, in the sixteenth century.[36] As proof of this, one need look no further than the literature of early capitalist (i.e., mercantile) ventures in the Americas, permeated as they were with the notion of a recently lost European past that could be miraculously recovered in the newly invaded Americas. The early modern equivocation of medieval Europe and indigenous America has been discussed by early modern historians.[37] As pointed out by Andrew Hadfield, the most striking case of this, visually speaking, is the parallel engravings of Old World Picts and New World Algonquians in Thomas Harriot's *Briefe and True Report of the New Found Land of Virginia* (1588): each naked, savage, and, most important, innocent of modernity.[38] As another example (sticking with English invaders of the Americas), Humphrey Gilbert's use of Morris dancers for "the allurement of Savages" of Newfoundland in 1583 is one instance of the European assimilation of their own folk dance practices with those of the New World.[39] This view of America ("capitalism's land of promise," as economist Werner Sombart called it in 1906) as a kind of medieval Eden has not only endured since the 1500s, but also become in the past few centuries crucial to American self-perception.[40]

In the history of American cinema, and more broadly the entertainment industry, the Disney Company (as it calls itself today) is one of the oldest companies and arguably the most successful of all.[41] Founded in 1923 by brothers Walt and Roy Disney, the animation studio got its start by producing animated shorts that were distributed by Universal, one of the so-called Little Three of Hollywood. After the release of *Snow White and the Seven Dwarfs* (1937), Disney switched distributors to Big Five member RKO. The latter agreed to Disney's prescient demand for control of all future television rights.[42] It is worth emphasizing that Disney's trajectory for almost a century now has been one of steady ascent, contrary to some narratives (including Disney's own) that portray the company as regularly beset by flops. For example, in his hagiography *The Magic Kingdom: Walt Disney and the American Way of Life*, Steven Watts labels the forties the period of "Disney's descent."[43] While Disney did experience some business challenges in the forties, it also experienced successes (notably *Dumbo* in 1941), the most significant of which were its forays into the untapped markets of war propaganda shorts and live-action films.[44] In fact, Disney's well-oiled merchandising machine, more or less in place by around 1930, has consistently pumped out greater and greater profits over the course of the twentieth and twenty-first centuries thanks to a savvy diversification. Already by the early thirties, Disney products ranged from belt buckles and porridge bowls to chewing gum and neckwear, not to mention the successful Mickey Mouse watch.[45] Franchise merchandise, or tie-ins as they are now called, have been Disney's secret weapon from the beginning.

In the selling of this merchandise, the nostalgia for a medievalist golden age has remained the one indispensable ingredient. As a good example of this point, let us briefly compare Disney's merchandise with that of another prescient image-conscious capitalist, Alfred Hitchcock. Early on, Hitchcock had made his admiration for Disney's business acumen clear in a filmic homage, a scene in *Sabotage* (1936) featuring a theatrical showing of the Silly Symphonies short *Who Killed Cock Robin?* By the fifties, Hitchcock and Disney seemed to be moving in parallel motion. Both had their own distribution companies (Hitchcock's Shamley Productions vs. Disney's Buena Vista).[46] Both briefly dabbled with 3D; Disney even branched out, Hitch-like, into live-action films. Both had tapped the potential not only of television ("Hitchcock Presents" vs. "Walt Disney Presents"), but also of magazines (*Alfred Hitchcock Magazine* vs. *Bulletin of the Mickey Mouse Club*), children's books (*Alfred Hitchcock and the Three Investigators* vs. Disney's Little Golden Books series), LP records (*Ghost Stories for Young People* vs. Disney's many sound-recording versions of its feature films), and even board games (*Why?* vs. *Tomorrowland*). Both were busy harnessing the purchasing power of song—Disney much more successfully, with earworms such as "The Ballad of Davy Crockett."[47] What distinguished Disney's brand from Hitchcock's was a distinctly medievalist touch. While the Englishman's adult world of horror and suspense was epitomized in his trademark nine-stroke silhouette, the fundamental symbol of Disney's medievalism was Sleeping Beauty Castle.

The Many Musical Medievalisms of Disney

At the heart of Disney's success is music, and at the heart of Disney's music, is song.[48] The just-mentioned Davy Crockett ballad from the fifties is exemplary of the company's multimedia marketing strategies that have served it so well for nearly a century. This popular song was used to promote an entire range of goods, not only in the domain of television (the original Davy Crockett television series, 1954–1955), but also in print (the Little Golden Book *Davy Crockett*, 1955), sound recording (both 78 and 33rpm LPs with titles like *Walt Disney's Story of Davy Crockett*), and feature film (*Davy Crockett: King of the Wild Frontier*, 1955). This multipronged approach anticipated Robert Iger's more recent (2013) "tent-pole" approach, wherein one film promotes a whole range of ancillary products peddled by companies other than Disney, a franchise in the true sense of the word.[49]

One of the most commercially successful descendants in recent days of the Davy Crockett ballad has been the hit song "Let It Go" from the medievalist *Frozen* (2013).[50] Disseminated through myriad tie-ins, "Let It Go" won both Academy and Grammy Awards; it has been translated into every major language in the world. Key to the song's global success was its singer, Idina Menzel, whose squeaky-clean image differs from that of other tween stars. Trained on the planks of the Broadway stage, Menzel's decidedly old-fashioned alto conforms to a vocal branding that Disney inaugurated back in the thirties. In contrast to characters like Betty Boop (voiced by Mae Questel) or even Disney's own pre-Code Minnie Mouse, Snow White (voiced by Adriana Caselotti) embodied an emerging conservatism in the wake of the film industry's Production Code (aka Hays Code). Thus, Menzel's Princess Elsa in *Frozen* is but one in a long line of man-cooing Disney heroines.[51] Like Elsa, these ladies harken back to a golden age sometime— anytime, really—prior to the bra burnings of second-wave feminism. Princess Elsa, like Rapunzel in *Tangled* (2011) or Ariel in *The Little Mermaid* (1989), pines just as much for her fantastical kingdom as for a more recent time just out of reach.

This nostalgia for a chronologically ambiguous golden age that characterizes *Frozen* and so many other Disney films has been, as mentioned earlier, a hallmark of medievalism since the sixteenth century. Of the six medievalist stereotypes identified at the beginning of this chapter, *Frozen* makes special use of the supernatural. *Frozen's* plot presents as its central conflict Elsa's abuse of her magical powers in mistakenly freezing her sister, Anna. This womanly excess is corrected with the assistance of men, notably the troll wizard Grand Pabbie and Prince Hans. The movie's medieval kingdom is populated by magical creatures, from trolls to ghostly snow creatures, both threatening (Marshmallow the monster) and benign (Olaf the snowman). It almost goes without saying that *Frozen* is neither the first nor the last of a medievalist trope playing a prominent role in a Disney film. For the remainder of this essay, I would like to briefly run through the six medievalist stereotypes outlined earlier with a view to highlighting some of Disney's many musical medievalisms over the course of nearly a century.

We begin with the chivalric Middle Ages. As I have previously written, the sound most frequently associated with the chivalric medieval mode in film is the brassy underscore that accompanies horse-riding warriors. Examples of this phenomenon abound, both in Hollywood and in global film, as heard, for example, in the Russian movie *Ilya Muromets* (1956, with a score composed by Igor Morozov) and in the Japanese *Rashomon* (1950, score by Fumio Hayasaka).[52] A related musical *topos* is that of the trumpet fanfare in jousting scenes.[53] The tradition of trumpet fanfares in film, medievalist or nonmedievalist, can be traced back to the nineteenth-century music hall, where trumpet calls frequently marked number changes as one act exited and the other entered.[54] Disney provides us with an early example of a medievalist trumpet fanfare in its cartoon short *Ye Olden Days* (1933). At some point in this musical smorgasbord ranging from Wagnerian opera to coon-song jazz, two pig trumpeters announce Goofy the prince and Minnie the princess.[55] Interestingly, in light of later medieval satires, Disney's vaudevillian fanfare in this early short film functions less as a simple homage to the medievalist tradition than as a parody of it.[56]

Nearly a century later, we find an interesting continuation of this vaudevillian medievalism in the form of canned movie music at Disney's theme parks. The medievalist trumpet fanfare comes courtesy of one of high capitalism's most recognizable sounds, John Williams's main theme (the Luke Skywalker theme) from the original *Star Wars* (1977).[57] One might rightly ask, How medieval is *Star Wars*?[58] Indeed, the film that launched the world's most profitable film franchise has elements from cinematic genres ranging from Western to World War II drama. As I argued in *Music in Films on the Middle Ages*, despite this heterogeneity, the film's fundamental medievalism can be seen from its basic outline: "A naive young man, on the way to freeing a princess captured by an evil lord, meets a hermit who turns him into a knight by training him in the art of sword fighting. After many perilous adventures the princess is rescued from the dark lord, and the young knight and his companions are ceremoniously welcomed as heroes by the reinstated princess, to the sounds of a final rousing brass fanfare." *Star Wars* is not as medieval as, say, *El Cid* (1961), a film that could equally be considered as partly belonging to the biblical epic genre, as pointed out by Stephen Meyer, but the film certainly merits the attention it has received from medievalist scholars as being at least a "pseudo-medieval" film, in Kevin Harty's words.[59] As film scholars Kristin Thompson and David Bordwell have put it, when it was first released in 1977, "*Star Wars* offered chivalric myth for 1970s teens."[60]

Disney has come a long way since its first tentative step into the medievalist Star Wars galaxy, the already-mentioned Star Tours at Disney parks in the late 1980s. Since then, the company's $4 billion purchase of Lucasfilm has paid off many times over thanks to an ocean of merchandise ranging from LEGO toys and T-shirts to ice cream and cookies. The most spectacular Star Wars tie-in is Disney Parks' Star Wars lands. At the time of my writing, the company's Star Wars lands, one each in Disneyland (Anaheim, California) and Disneyworld (Orlando, Florida), are scheduled for completion in late August 2019 and, as always with Disney, are poised to beat all expectations for an "immersive inside-the-movie experience."[61] Along with Pandora Land (opened 2017), the Star Wars extravaganza takes aim at Disney's main competitor in the bustling theme park market, Universal's Wizarding World of Harry Potter, which opened on Disney's Orlando turf in 2010. The lead-up since then to the much-ballyhooed Star Wars land is what Dennis L. Speigel, president of the analysis firm International Theme Park Services, has recently called "the greatest armaments war of attractions we've ever seen." Speigel adds, "It's nothing to spend $500 million and up on a new themed area." In fact, Disney will have spent over $1 billion on the two Star Wars parks alone.[62] Once complete, these industrial extravaganzas will resonate with a sound that Disney has been using for three decades since the original Star Tours, one of medievalism's most recognizable musical staples for over four centuries: the chivalric trumpet fanfare.[63]

Like the chivalric Middle Ages, the stereotype of a supernatural Middle Ages goes back to the earliest phase of medievalism. At the turn of the fifteenth and sixteenth centuries, some of the most frequently printed books after the Bible were Arthurian romances such as the *Prose Tristan*, stories that featured supernatural monsters and enchanters beginning with Merlin the magician.[64] Since this time, the enchanter-witch has remained a staple of musical medievalism, from Lully's operas to Wagner's *Gesamtkunstwerken*.[65] The film company that has made the most of the supernatural Middle Ages is Disney's nemesis and one of cinema's oldest corporations, Universal Studios. Back when Walt Disney was just getting started in the mid-1920s, Universal nearly put Disney's fledgling animation studio out of business with its popular cartoon character Oswald the Rabbit.[66] A century later, Disney and Universal are still duking it out, with Orlando, Florida, as their battlefield and Hogwarts Castle's dark towers pitted against the cheery banners of Sleeping Beauty's abode.[67]

This is not to say that Disney has not made good use of the supernatural stereotype once in a while. A good example is the 1996 animated feature *The Hunchback of Notre Dame*, lugubrious by Disney standards. Indeed, the film received parental criticism for its inappropriately scary scenes.[68] Still, *Hunchback* did well enough, with related merchandise flooding outlets from Walmart to MacDonald's.[69] To fit *Hunchback*'s dark theme, Disney stable composer Alan Menken drew on a stock musical association with the supernatural Middle Ages, the sound of Gregorian chant, the most famous example being the Dies irae and its occurrence in Ingmar Bergman's *Seventh Seal* (1957).[70] A related musical medievalism is that of an orchestral underscore accompanying a choir singing in Latin or pseudo-Latin in the style of Carl Orff's "O Fortuna" from *Carmina Burana*. First featured in films such as *Conan the Barbarian* (1981, with music by Basil Poledouris), this kind of choral sound has become the staple of big-budget superhero movies since around 2000.[71] We find both the Dies irae and the Latin-like choral passages in Menken's underscore for *Hunchback*.[72] A related cinematic *topos* or the supernatural, although not found in *Hunchback*, is that of a beam of light accompanied by a voiceless choir.[73] It occurs in Disney's *The Sword in the Stone* (1963).[74]

In both this film's storybook opening and the pivotal scene where Wart (the young Arthur) pulls the sword from the stone, a beam of light shines down as a choir erupts on an extended vocalise.

We next come to the primitive stereotype, the paradox of medieval people as barbaric and backward but as "possessing a primitive purity that had long vanished from modern music."[75] As mentioned earlier in this chapter, the notion of a medieval golden age as preserved in contemporary folk traditions has been regularly evoked in the course of five centuries of medievalism. The oldest and most influential example of this is the folk-song anthology, beginning with the early Renaissance *romancero* and moving seamlessly to the folk-song movement that includes Johann Gottfried Herder's landmark *Volkslieder* (1778–1779).[76] In medievalist cinema, the aural stereotype of the contemporary folk song as a medieval remnant occurs often; Neapolitan tunes in Pasolini's *Decameron* (1971), for example, the Irish campfire song ("Preab San Ól") in *Snow White and the Huntsman* (2012), or the chanting of the Qur'an in *Kingdom of Heaven* (2005).[77] As already noted, the idea of a secret link between present-day folklore and long-lost medieval traditions, a concept foundational to musical medievalism, goes back to the sixteenth century. For Montaigne writing in the late 1500s, the Southern French folk dances of his day had preserved past traditions in a way not possible in writing. The ability of folk poetry and dance to do this, Montaigne insisted, owed to their "naïveté."[78] Following the sixteenth-century medievalist movement, the word *naïf* would come to signify that which was quintessentially medieval, as in the "style marotique" named after Clément Marot (d. 1544).[79] As mentioned earlier, already in the sixteenth century, the idea of a Middle Ages that was preserved in the rustic art of the folk had extended beyond Europe to the Americas. The song and dance of indigenous Americans was deemed naive enough, untainted enough by European literacy, to have in germ form something essential from Europe's own medieval antiquity.

Over the long term, the primitive Middle Ages' most recognizable incarnation has been the wandering minstrel as a singer of folk songs. The generic minstrel of medievalist film is often portrayed as a performer of folkloric traditions that range from American bluegrass (Disney's 1973 *Robin Hood*) to Irish–Celtic folk music (e.g., *Braveheart*, 1995).[80] Whether he is American or European, the folk singer's special cause is the preservation of ancient and medieval song thanks to "oral tradition" passed on "from generation to generation," in the words of one eighteenth-century French scholar.[81] Thus the academic trend of orality in the late 1900s plays into a much older predilection found on the king's way (as I put it earlier) of nonacademic medievalism. The global troubadour is the folk minstrel's most recent incarnation. Not so long ago, English musicologist Wilfrid Mellers defined the American troubadour—the prototype being the recently laureated Bob Dylan—as a marginalized wanderer who sings on behalf of the folk using the simple music of the folk; in other words, a beatnik spin-off of the naive singer of songs in the style marotique.[82]

The primitive troubadour regularly pops up in films on the Middle Ages. The style of his song ranges from Elizabethan, as in *The Flame and the Arrow* (1950), to Irish–Celtic, as in the already mentioned 2012 *Snow White*.[83] The latter example, the dwarf Quert's melancholy song performed around a campfire, illustrates a typically cinematic conflation of the Western and the medieval film that I have recently called the *Medieval-Western*.[84] It's a blend especially suited to the very American Disney Company. Raised in Kansas City in the first decade of the twentieth century, Walt Disney maintained a deep nostalgia for frontier America and for his Southern heritage, as expressed in films such as *The Three Little Pigs* (1933) or *Song of the South* (1946).[85] It comes as no surprise, then, that Disney has often dished up its Middle Ages with a healthy dollop of American folk song. Such is the case, for example, with the theme song from the Disney television series *The Adventures of Robin Hood*. If we compare the aforementioned Davy Crockett ballad to the Robin Hood theme song, the melodies are remarkably alike in their upbeat mood (both use major keys and similar tempos), their simple triadic construction, and their use of repetition: the words "Robin Hood" in the one ("Robin Hood, Robin Hood, riding through the glen," etc.) and the one-line "Davy, Davy Crockett, king of the wild frontier" refrain in the other.[86] Essentially, both songs come out of the same Medieval-Western mold, with one crucial difference: the Davy Crockett ballad swings, while the Robin Hood theme song does not. Another interesting use by Disney of the troubadour *topos* is that of the minstrel narrator.[87] We find a minstrel narrator in the 1952 Disney film *The Story of Robin Hood and His Merrie Men* that inspired the just-mentioned television series. Opening and ending with the Robin Hood theme song, a minstrel frames the film's narrative.[88] The same device is used in the 1973 animated *Robin Hood*, but this time the Medieval-Western conflation is blatant and parodic. The minstrel narrator, a rooster voiced by honky-tonk star Roger Miller, leans into his soft Southern drawl, an homage to the roots of Disney's founder, who had died only a few years before production on *Robin Hood* began.[89]

Next, we have the pastoral Middle Ages. While the primitive stereotype embodies the chaotic and barbaric side of the Middle Ages, the more recent pastoral stereotype represents its orderly natural beauty. This medievalist pastoralism emerges in the eighteenth century and finds its nineteenth-century fulfillment in the musical universe of Beethoven's Pastoral Symphony or in certain scenes from the medieval operas of Richard Wagner, like the swan that carries Lohengrin.[90] A more recent musical expression of the pastoral Middle Ages is the Irish–Celtic sound emerging in the 1990s with the popularity of performers like Enya and Riverdance. The recently deceased James Horner made use of the Irish bagpipe or uillean pipes and bodhran drum in his score for the very popular *Braveheart* (1995), followed by the Irish tin whistle in the even more popular *Titanic* (1997).[91] Later uses of the tin whistle as an aural signifier of the pastoral Middle Ages include Howard Shore's music for the Lord of the Rings trilogy.[92]

In an apparent follow-up of the nineties trend, Disney has made use of the Irish–Celtic sound in productions like *Tangled* (2011), where composer Alan Menken introduces a Celtic band during the dance scene in the first half of the film. A more pervasive use of the Celtic sound occurs in the animated feature film released the following year, *Brave* (2012). In the very first scene, Scottish composer Patrick Doyle introduces the indispensable tin whistle (accompanied by a harp), followed by a fiddle. A few minutes later, the film's second cue completes the Celtic trinity with the sound of the uillean pipes as the young heroine Merida wanders in the woods. From this point onward, these three musical instruments weave in and out of the underscore to confirm that we are indeed in the Scottish Middle Ages. In the film's final scene, fiddle, whistle, and pipes unite in a reassuring cue that all will be well and that Merida's mother, Queen Elinor, will indeed successfully shape-shift from a bear back to herself—even better, to her former youthful self.[93]

Given Walt Disney's aforementioned predilection for Americana in his company's products, it should come as no surprise that orientalism is the least evoked of the six stereotypes in Disney products.[94] To be sure, the oriental Middle Ages are one of the younger stereotypes, first showing up with the orientalist phenomenon at the turn of the eighteenth and nineteenth centuries. The so-called oriental scale (a minor key with a raised flat degree) is an early favorite, as heard, for example, in Weber's *Oberon* (1826).[95] One of the ways in which medievalist cinema updates this particular operatic tradition is by using sound recordings of Qur'anic chant, beginning with the early sound film *The Crusades* (1935).[96] Another orientalist operatic tradition that carries over into medievalist cinema is the solo dance number. By the fifties, it becomes something of a staple in American films on the Middle Ages—and in the biblical epics studied by Stephen Meyer.[97] Examples of the orientalist dance number from this high point of epic film productivity include *King Richard and the Crusaders* (1954) and *The Conqueror* (1956).[98]

The orientalist dance number occurs in a few Disney films, beginning with the already mentioned *Hunchback* (1996), featuring Esmeralda, voiced by Demi Moore. Seizing on Moore's fame as a pole dancer in the film *Striptease*, Disney uses her husky alto as the voice of the gypsy Esmeralda. Further sealing the symbiosis between the real Moore and the fake Esmeralda is the fact that both *Hunchback* and *Striptease* were released the same month, June 1996; both films were often exhibited in the same multiplex theater. Like *Striptease*, *Hunchback* also features a dance number, unusually provocative by Disney standards, that ends with the scantily-clad, barefooted Esmeralda (i.e., Demi Moore) twirling around a spear planted in the ground, a thinly disguised reference to Moore's famous pole dancing in *Striptease*.[99] An interesting Disney variant on the oriental dance number is a parody found in *The Black Cauldron* (1985). Near the beginning of this film, a character is introduced in a tavern located in the castle of the Horned King.[100] In her book *Good Girls and Wicked Witches*, Amy Davis describes this "unnamed, unfeatured character" as "a fat, lascivious dancing girl whose sole function is to entertain the Horned King's human lackeys,"[101] a foil, in other words, to the svelte, young orientalist dancers in many a medievalist film of the fifties and sixties.

This example of a parody leads us to my sixth and final stereotype, the satirical Middle Ages. At first blush, irony would seem ill-fitted to Disney's rosy outlook until one realizes just how much pre-Code Mickey Mouse differed from present-day Disney characters. In his landmark study, *Seven Minutes: The Life and Death of the American Animated Cartoon* (1993), Norman Klein traces the company's transition from its late-twenties jazzy anarchy to the puritanical products of the Depression era. Klein considers the 1937

Snow White a turning point in Disney's transition to the barely tapped children's market, in anticipation of the fifties and its "world of consumer marketing...and television."[102] The "whiteness of Snow White," as Klein puts it, contrasted with a series of animated shorts in which Disney put a decidedly ironic spin on its Middle Ages, beginning with the already mentioned *Ye Olden Days* (1933).[103] Musical tricks in these cartoons include spoofs of the trumpet fanfare and the singing minstrel. Renditions of the medieval joust as a modern-day sports event was something of a Disney favorite, as seen and heard, for example, in *Knight for a Day* and *Wotta Knight*, both from the forties.[104] With the coming of the fifties, this ironic Middle Ages would recede from the Disney palette in favor of something more naive, to use the time-honored word. Subsequently, the satirical Middle Ages only rarely occurs in Disney products, one notable example being the 1979 live action *Unidentified Flying Oddball*, with a score by Ron Goodwin of the Miss Marple series fame. This paraphrase of Mark Twain's popular *Connecticut Yankee* novel may take considerable license with Twain's plot, but of all versions, Kevin Harty considers it the "truest to the humor found in the original novel."[105]

There would be more, in fact a great deal more, to say about the musical medievalisms of Disney, especially in areas outside cinema such as the case discussed earlier of the Star Wars fanfare played at Disney parks. More broadly, there would be more to say about music's role in the Disney universe period. Music, the subject of this essay, is as indispensable an ingredient to Disney's medievalism as it is to the company's overall operation. In one way or the other, the sixth liberal art is heard in each of the five major company policies identified by Alan Bryman in his ground-breaking *Disneyization of Society* (2004): theming (an artificial theme applied it to a range of products), hybrid consumption (the bundling of different forms of consumption in a single setting), merchandising (the promotion and sale of goods bearing copyright images or logos), performative labor (including what Bryman calls *emotional labor* like smiling to create illusions such as the Disney-family or the customer-king, and control and surveillance.[106] As Bryman emphasizes, Disney has led the way in the development of these five policies that are now ubiquitous in present-day capitalist society.[107] Given music's indispensability to Disney's success, it is not surprising to find it being used everywhere nowadays as a means of mind control, from the laptops buzzing in our bedrooms to the mood music used in shopping malls and airports.[108] For this reason, the examples presented in the second half of this essay having to do with Disney are suggestive of a much broader development, namely, music's vital role in the twin developments of capitalism and medievalism and their pining for a golden age, once upon a long time ago.

ACKNOWLEDGMENTS

An earlier version of this essay was presented at the University of Toronto in the spring of 2014 ("Disney's Many Musical Medievalisms") and in the fall of October 2017 at the Université de Tours ("Médiévismes mécaniques: le cas de Disney"). I am especially grateful to Vasco Zara, Daniel Saulnier, Graeme Boone and Philippe Vendrix for their comments.

NOTES

1. Besides the "Nazi twins" discussed by Norman Cantor, *Inventing the Middle Ages: The Lives, Works and Ideas of the Great Medievalists of the Twentieth Century* (New York: William Morrow, 1991), 79–117, the musicologist Friedrich Gennrich should be mentioned; Gennrich dedicates *Die Strassburger Schule für Musikwissenschaft* (Würzburg: n.p., 1940), to Adolf Hitler. On the remaining names in this paragraph, see Helen Damico and Joseph Zavadil, eds., *Medieval Scholarship: Biographical Studies on the Formation of a Discipline*, vol. 1, *History* (New York: Garland, 1995), and vol. 2, *Literature and Philology* (1998); Howard Bloch, *God's Plagiarist: Being an Account of the Fabulous Industry and Irregular Commerce of the Abbe Migne* (Chicago: University of Chicago Press, 1994); and Richard Utz, *Medievalism: A Manifesto* (Kalamazoo, MI: ARC Humanities Press, 2017), 19–21.

2. For example, Kevin Brownlee, Marina Brownlee, and Stephen Nichols, eds., *The New Medievalism* (Baltimore: Johns Hopkins University Press, 1991); Howard Bloch and Stephen Nichols, *Medievalism and the Modernist Temper* (Baltimore: Johns Hopkins University Press, 1996); and Kathleen Biddick, *The Shock of Medievalism* (Durham, NC: Duke University Press, 1998).

3. Umberto Eco, *Travels in Hyper Reality*, trans. William Weaver (San Diego: Harvest, 2002), 61–62.

4. An assumption, incidentally, that also runs through Eco's influential essay on medievalism in Eco, *Travels*, 61–85. Cf. Cantor, *Invention of the Middle Ages*, 28–29: "We owe to the…early nineteenth century the alteration of the image of a 'Middle Age' of barbarism, ignorance, and superstition…invented by fifteenth-century Renaissance Italian humanists…with the shining image of a Gothic culture steeped in idealism, spirituality, heroism, and adoration of women."

5. On the revival *topos* for early music and folk music, see John Haines, "Antiquarian Nostalgia and the Institutionalization of Early Music," in *The Oxford Handbook of Music Revivals*, ed. Caroline Bithell and Juniper Hill (Oxford: Oxford University Press, 2014), 71–91.

6. Utz, *Medievalism*, 70.

7. David Matthews, *Medievalism: A Critical History* (Woodbridge, UK: Boydell & Brewer, 2015). While the back-jacket synopsis promises that the author traces "medievalism from its earliest appearances in the sixteenth century" to the present, the book only presents a handful of English sixteenth-century sources on pp. 46 and 132–133.

8. See especially my *Eight Centuries*, 49–88; "Antiquarian Studies"; and *Music in Films*, 3–10 and 153–158.

9. John Haines, "The Revival of Medieval Music," in *The Cambridge Handbook of Medieval Music*, ed. Thomas F. Kelly and Mark Everist (Cambridge: Cambridge University Press, 2019), vol. 1, 561–581. For a discussion of the topic of periodization (and especially of the division between the Middle Ages and the Renaissance) in early nineteenth-century German historiography, see Laura K. T. Stokes's contribution to this volume, "Medievalisms in Early Nineteenth-Century German Musical Thought," pp. 17–37.

10. William Worcestre [Worcester], *Itineraries*, ed. John Harvey (Oxford: Clarendon, 1969), xi; Haines, *Eight Centuries*, 50.

11. Edward Gibbons, *The History of the Decline and Fall of the Roman Empire*, ed. David Womersley (London: Penguin, 2000), esp. 723.

12. Haines, *Music in Films*, 4–10; see also Haines, "The Revival of Medieval Music." I am less interested in a systematic itemization along the lines of Eco's categories than in situating different medievalist trends in their historical development. Eco's frequently cited ten medievalisms (e.g., Matthews, *Medievalism*, 17–18) are found in Eco, *Travels*, 68–72.

13. Eco, *Travels*, 71.

14. Cf. Eco, *Travels*, 69.

15. The closest Eco comes to this are his "Middle Ages of Romanticism" (Eco, *Travels*, 69).

16. Ibid., 69.

17. Tison Pugh and Susan Aronstein, eds., *The Disney Middle Ages* (New York: Palgrave Macmillan, 2012). See also Haines, *Music in Films*, 40–41, 63–6, 79–80, and 152.

18. This point is also made by Elizabeth Bell, Lynda Haas, and Laura Sells, "Introduction: Walt's in the Movies," in *From Mouse to Mermaid: The Politics of Film, Gender and Culture* (Bloomington: Indiana University Press, 1995), 4.

19. Marot, cited in Haines, *Eight Centuries*, 50.

20. James B. Stewart, *DisneyWar* (New York: Simon & Schuster, 2005), 96. The company's profits went from $300 million to $800 million in Eisner's first three years.

21. Peter Biskind, *Easy Riders, Raging Bulls: How the Sex-Drugs-and-Rock 'n' Roll Generation Saved Hollywood* (New York: Simon & Schuster, 1998), 98–100.

22. Carl Hiaasen, *Team Rodent: How Disney Devours the World* (New York: Ballantine, 1998).

23. Christopher Palmeri, "Disney Expects Renewed Growth in 2017 Following Rare Drop" (Bloomberg), *Toronto Star*, November 12, 2016, B2.

24. Richard Schickel, *The Disney Version: The Life, Times, Art and Commerce of Walt Disney*, 3rd ed. (Chicago: Dee, 1997), 3.

25. Norman Klein, *Seven Minutes: The Life and Death of the American Animated Cartoon* (London: Verso, 1993); Alan Bryman, *Disney and His Worlds* (New York: Routledge, 1995); and Hiaasen, *Team Rodent*.

26. Bell, Haas, and Sells, "Introduction: Walt's in the Movies," in *From Mouse to Mermaid*, 1.

27. See Martha Bayless, "Disney's Castles and the Work of the Medieval in the Magic Kingdom," in *The Disney Middle Ages*, 54n1: "Images of Disney's various castles are readily available online; copyright issues prohibit their inclusion in this volume."

28. Haines, *Music in Films*, 5.

29. The remainder of this paragraph draws on Haines, *Music in Films*, 5–10, where further references are provided.

30. Haines, *Music in Films*, 24, 32, and 129. On a related note, see Jamie Webster, "Creating Magic with Music: The Changing Dramatic Relationship between Music and Magic in Harry Potter Films," in *The Music of Fantasy Cinema*, ed. Janet Halfyard (Sheffield: Equinox, 2012), 193–217.

31. See, most recently, Kirsten Yri, "Inverting the Epic: The Music of Ridley Scott's *Kingdom of Heaven*," in *Music in Epic Film: Listening to Spectacle*, ed. Stephen Meyer (New York: Routledge, 2017), 189–209; and Haines, *Music in Films on the Middle Ages*, 77–78. For the related corpus of fantasy films, see Mark Brill, "Fantasy and the Exotic Other: The Films of Ray Harryhausen," in *Music of Fantasy Cinema*, 22–24.

32. See Haines, *Music in Films*, 163n45; and John Haines, "The Musical Incongruities of Time Travel in Arthurian Film," in *The Legacy of Courtly Literature: From Medieval to Contemporary Culture*, ed. Deborah Nelson-Campbell and Ruben Cholakian (New York: Palgrave, 2017), 151–174.

33. Haines, *Music in Medieval Films*, 154.
34. Giovanni Arrighi, *The Long Twentieth Century: Money, Power, and the Origins of Our Times* (London: Verso, 2010), 97–111.
35. Ibid., 111–130.
36. Haines, *Music in Films*, 154.
37. See especially Jean-Pierre Sanchez, *Mythes et légendes de la conquête de l'Amérique* (Rennes: Presses Universitaires de Rennes, 1996), 93–100; and Andrew Hadfield, *Literature, Travel, and Colonial Writing in the English Renaissance, 1545–1625* (Oxford: Clarendon, 1998), 114–133.
38. Hadfield, *Literature, Travel*, 115–119. The images are reproduced in Haines, "Antiquarian Nostalgia," 73–75.
39. Haines, *Music in Films*, 155; and John Haines, "The Earliest European Responses to Dancing in the Americas," *U.S. Catholic Historian* 30 (2012): 1.
40. Sombart cited in Haines, *Music in Films*, 145 and 191n73. On which, see, for example, Susan Aronstein's *Hollywood Knights: Arthurian Cinema and the Politics of Nostalgia* (New York: Palgrave, 2005); and Kevin Harty, "'The Knights of the Square Table': The Boy Scouts and Thomas Edison Make an Arthurian Film," *Arthuriana* 4 (1994): 313–323 (the remaining essays in this issue are all devoted to King Arthur in America).
41. As found on its official website, accessed August 5, 2019, https://thewaltdisneycompany.com/.
42. Schickel, *Disney Version*, 213–214.
43. Steven Watts, *The Magic Kingdom: Walt Disney and the American Way of Life* (Columbia: University of Missouri Press, 1997), 243–263. As another example of this "poor Disney" *topos*, see the press releases following Disney's acquisition of Lucasfilm in 2012 (Haines, *Music in Films*, 152).
44. Schickel, *Disney Version*, 263–281.
45. Klein, *Seven Minutes*, 53.
46. On Buena Vista, see Schickel, *Disney Version*, 308–309.
47. "The Ballad of Davy Crockett" was often paraphrased, including as the campaign song for Hubert Humphrey in 1960 ("Hubert, Hubert Humphrey, the president for you and me"). On Hitchcock's quest for a hit song, see Jack Sullivan, *Hitchcock's Music* (New Haven, CT: Yale University Press, 2006), chaps. 13, 15, and 18.
48. On the importance of music to Disney early on, see Haines, *Music in Films*, 16.
49. Christopher Palmeri, "Disney Hit as Lone Ranger Misfires" (Bloomberg), *Toronto Star*, August 8, 2013, B6.
50. Incidentally, the success of "Let It Go" also illustrates the point made earlier in this chapter about Disney in the forties, for *Frozen*'s record global profits were buried under syndicated news about 2013 misadventures like *Planes* or *The Lone Ranger*. "Disney Hit as Lone Ranger Misfires," went one Bloomberg release title, followed by an even more dismal subtitle: "Box-Office Flop Shoots Down Entertainment Empire's Third-Quarter Profit" (Palmeri, "Disney Hit"). No word about the billions of dollars generated in a single year by *Frozen*'s hit song.
51. See Elizabeth Bell's essay, "Somatexts at the Disney Shop: Constructing the Pentimentos of Women's Animated Bodies," in *From Mouse to Mermaid*, 107–124.
52. Haines, *Music in Films*, 132–152, the chapter entitled "The Riding Warrior."
53. Ibid., 45–66.
54. Ibid., 48 and 172n20.

55. Ibid., 48.

56. See the context for the famous fanfare in the 2001 *Knight's Tale* in Haines, *Music in Films*, 63–66.

57. On this theme, see Roger Hickman, *Reel Music: Exploring 100 Years of Film Music*, 2nd ed. (New York: Norton, 2017), 352. For the argument for *Star Wars* (1977) being mainly medievalist, see Haines, *Music in Films*, 148–149.

58. Haines, *Music in Films*, 148.

59. Stephen C. Meyer, *Epic Sound: Music in Postwar Hollywood Biblical Films* (Bloomington: Indiana University Press, 2015), 3; Kevin Harty, *The Real Middle Ages: Films about Medieval Europe* (Jefferson, NC: McFarland, 1999), 5; *El Cid* is included in Harty's catalogue on pp. 148–149. See also Tom Henthorne, "Boys to Men: Medievalism and Masculinity in *Star Wars* and *E.T.: The Extra-Terrestrial*, in *The Medieval Hero on Screen: Representations from Beowulf to Buffy*, ed. Martha Driver and Sid Ray (Jefferson, NC: McFarland, 2004), 73–89.

60. Kristin Thompson and David Bordwell, *Film History: An Introduction*, 3rd ed. (New York: McGraw–Hill, 2010), 485.

61. Linda Barnard, "Disney's Pandora Brings Fantasy to Life," *Toronto Star*, June 10, 2017, T4.

62. Sharon Kennedy Wynne (*Tampa Bay Times*), "Taking a Ride on Disney's Dark Side," *Toronto Star*, April 30, 2017, E9.

63. The earliest example of chivalric medieval music cited in Haines, *Music in Films*, 5, comes from Monteverdi's *Combattimento di Tancredi e Clorinda* (1624).

64. Other sixteenth-century literary examples are discussed in Haines, *Music in Films*, 5–6, including Ariosto's *Orlando furioso*.

65. Haines, *Music in Films*, 5–6.

66. Universal's Oswald in the twenties foreshadowed Disney's more famous leporine competition, Warner's Bugs Bunny, who began appearing in cartoons from the late thirties onward; see William Moritz, "Animation," in *The Oxford History of World Cinema*, ed. Geoffrey Nowell-Smith (Oxford: Oxford University Press, 1997), 269.

67. Haines, *Music in Films*, 106–107.

68. Hickman, *Reel Music*, 457; and Haines, *Music in Films*, 81.

69. Haines, *Music in Films*, 80.

70. Ibid., 128. On Menken, see Hickman, *Reel Music*, 452–458; on the 1996 *Hunchback*, see Haines, *Music in Films*, 25 and 77–83.

71. Haines, *Music in Films*, 129. Another famous example is the use of "O Fortuna" in John Boorman's *Excalibur*, discussed by David Clem in his contribution to this volume, "Hope against Fate or Fata Morgana? Music and Mythopoiesis in Boorman's *Excalibur*," pp. 662–689.

72. In addition to the Dies irae, Menken also makes use of the Kyrie. For a summary of the film, see Kevin Harty, *The Reel Middle Ages* (Jefferson, NC: McFarland, 1999), 127–128. See also James Deaville, "The Topos of 'Evil Medieval' in American Horror Film Music," in *Music, Meaning and Media*, ed. Erkki Pekkilä, David Neumeyer, and Richard Littlefield (Helsinki: Semiotic Society of Finland, University of Helsinki and International Semiotics Institute at Imatra, 2006), 26–37.

73. On which see John Haines, "The Musical Incongruities of Time Travel in Arthurian Film," in *The Legacy of Courtly Literature: From Medieval to Contemporary Culture*, ed. Deborah Nelson-Campbell and Ruben Cholakian (New York: Palgrave, 2017), 151–174.

74. On this film, see Harty, *Reel Middle Ages*, 490–491.

75. Haines, *Music in Films*, 7.

76. On this development, see Haines, "Antiquarian Nostalgia and the Institutionalization of Early Music."

77. Haines, *Music in Films*, 71, 108, and 122–123; see Chapter 4 of my *Music in Films* for a discussion of folk song in medieval films. For a fuller discussion of music in *Kingdom of Heaven*, see Kirsten Yri, "Inverting the Epic: The Music of Ridley Scott's *Kingdom of Heaven*," in *Music in Epic Film*, ed. Stephen C. Meyer (New York: Routledge, 2016), 195–215.

78. Haines, *Eight Centuries*, 51.

79. Ibid., 50 and 128–130.

80. Ibid., 110 as well as chap. 4.

81. Le Comte de Tressan, cited in Haines, Eight Centuries, 108.

82. Here paraphrasing Mellers in Haines, "Living Troubadours and Other Uses for Medieval Music," *Popular Music* 23 (2004): 139.

83. Haines, *Music in Films*, 94–96 and 107–109.

84. Ibid., 158; on the campfire scene, see 104–109.

85. Schickel, *Disney Version*, 55–65.

86. Both can be heard on YouTube by searching "ballad of davy crockett" and "theme song to adventures of robin hood," respectively.

87. Another classic example of the minstrel narrator is Burl Ives.

88. On this film, see Harty, *Reel Middle Ages*, 252–253.

89. Haines, *Music in Films*, 90.

90. Ibid., 7–8.

91. Haines, *Music in Films*, 19.

92. I am thinking of the Shire or Hobbit theme, as Hickman calls it (Hickman, *Reel Music*, 499). See also Stephen C. Meyer's contribution to this volume: "From the Music of the Ainur to the Music of the Voice-over: Music and Medievalism in *The Lord of the Rings*," pp. 611–635.

93. The cue occurs at 1:21:00–1:22:00, Mark Andrews and Brenda Chapman, dir., *Brave* (Buena Vista: Disney/Pixar, 2012).

94. On orientalism, see Kirsten Yri, "Thomas Binkley and the Studio der Frühen Musik: Challenging 'the Myth of Westernness,'" *Early Music* 38 (2010): 273–280.

95. Haines, *Music in Films*, 77–78.

96. Ibid., 122.

97. See Meyer, *Epic Sound*, 16, 22, 29, 47, 86, and 93–94. Another example of this *topos* occurs in John Boorman's *Excalibur*. See David Clem's contribution to this volume, "Hope against Fate or Fata Morgana: Music and Mythopoiesis in Boorman's Excalibur," pp. 662–689.

98. Haines, *Music in Films*, 78.

99. Ibid., 82–83.

100. Ted Berman and Richard Rich, dir., *The Black Cauldron (25th Anniversary)* (Buena Vista: Disney, 2010), 19:96–20:19. For a bibliography, see Harty, *Reel Middle Ages*, 43.

101. Amy Davis, *Good Girls and Wicked Witches: Women in Disney's Feature Animation* (Bloomington: Indiana University Press, 2011), 157.

102. Klein, *Seven Minutes*, 106.

103. Ibid., 139–145.

104. Haines, *Music in Films*, 64.

105. Harty, *Reel Middle Ages*, 268.

106. Alan Bryman, *The Disneyization of Society* (Los Angeles: Sage, 2004).

107. Bryman, *Disneyization*, 105–107. The kind of attention currently paid by nearly all institutions—academia included—to branding, for example, was pioneered by the company's theme park. As Schickel relates, already by the sixties Walt Disney's "compulsion to keep the place [Disneyland] perfectly groomed at all times" was "legion," with nightly cleanups and the yearly replacement of hundreds of thousands of plants, all to accommodate the fact that "Disney refused to put signs asking his 'guests' not to trample them" (Schickel, *The Disney Version*, 317).

108. Muzak was purchased in 2011 by Texas' Mood Media, which was in turn purchased by Apollo Global Management and GSO Capital Partners in 2017; David Lazarus, "The Comeback of Muzak," syndicated news article (*Los Angeles Times*) in *Toronto Star*, July 11, 2017, GT9.

CHAPTER 31

....

EVIL MEDIEVAL

Chant and the New Dark Spirituality of Vietnam-Era Film in America

....

JAMES DEAVILLE

IN April 2013, Salon.com posted a blog based on the *Game of Thrones* with the explanatory words: "Think the royals in *Game of Thrones* are wicked? Check out the real-life bad guys of the Middle Ages." After a brief introduction, the blog published a rogue's gallery of medieval rulers (among others, the Visconti of Milan, Pedro the Cruel of Castile, and Edward III of England), all under the rubric "They put the evil in Medieval."[1] The neomedievalism that George R. R. Martin's characters embody is rife with references to "the medieval 'Other' . . . , dark, obscure, and barbaric."[2] This reflects a popular imagining of the distant past as the "Dark Ages," as a period of war, violence, and disease, in a "medieval world characterized by exploitation, ignorance, and barbarity."[3] This version of the Middle Ages contrasts with the romanticized construction of a time when gallantry, chivalry, and courtly love prevailed among humans (e.g., the various Arthurian mythologies) or—in contemporary fantasy—of a fictional place where benign and malevolent creatures coexist in preindustrial naiveté (for example, *The Hobbit* or *The Elder Scrolls V: Skyrim*).[4] It also differs significantly from the more idealized images of the period as they informed the folk-rock revival of the late 1960s and early 1970s.[5] Nevertheless, the neomedievalism of popular culture in the digital era has privileged the dark side of the Dark Ages, to the extent that in *TechGnosis*, Erik Davis could aver that "the phantasms of the Dark Ages form the imaginary bedrock of cyberspace."[6]

This essay will explore one particular aspect of the "dark" neomedievalism that we might call *evil medieval*, a cultural phenomenon of the late 1960s and the 1970s whereby customs and procedures associated with the medieval church underwent resignification as representing evil practices. The semiotic reversal of evil medieval manifested itself most evidently in film, where audiences would come to interpret scenes of robed monks chanting in Latin as signifying the devil's work. In this exploratory investigation, we will first trace the Gothic revival and the rise of satanism in the nineteenth century and then examine in depth the historical moment at which the inversion occurred, with particular attention to the musical manifestations of evil medieval.

The fascination with evil in the medieval had already cast its spell over the European mind long before the forces of neomedievalism took it up with renewed vigor. In his classic text *Gothic*, Fred Botting describes the age of Gothic renewal as a response to the Enlightenment and its texts as "not good in moral, aesthetic, or social terms. Their concern is with vice: protagonists are selfish or evil.... Their effects, aesthetically and socially, are also replete with a range of negative features..., and [they] register revulsion, abhorrence, fear, disgust, and terror."[7] For such products of the arts during the late eighteenth and early nineteenth centuries, the designation *Gothic* seemed appropriate, conjuring up images of "barbarous customs and practices, of superstition, ignorant, extravagant fancies and natural wildness."[8] As such, the Gothic style was a prominent cultural trope of the late eighteenth and early nineteenth centuries, "a powerful and popular discourse system" that attempted to "ritualize, contain, commodify, reify, or displace the sacred."[9] In tandem with architecture and art, Gothic novels by Horace Walpole, William Beckford, Ann Radcliffe, and Matthew Lewis (among others) challenged the Enlightenment rationalism that held to principles of reason, order, and balance.[10] They confronted the church in a literature of anti-Catholicism that was "populated by villainous monks,... sexually perverse devils and nuns, and inquisitions that were the very antithesis of modernity's legal reforms."[11] Thus the traditional institution of holiness became a place for evil, its cultural capital revalued so that the traditional markers of Catholicism such as church buildings became forbidding edifices where the most unspeakable crimes occurred, and the sanctified people of the church—priests, monks, nuns—came to be recognized as the earthly sources of the wickedness.

It stands to reason that the art of music would not be spared from the ubiquitous Gothic (or dark) romanticism of the early nineteenth century, whether in the symphonic realm (e.g., Hector Berlioz's *Symphonie fantastique*) or on the operatic stage (Carl Maria von Weber's *Der Freischütz* or Giacomo Meyerbeer's *Robert le diable*, for example). Long before the style became de rigueur in the evil medieval of cinema, audiences experienced men's voices (monophonically) chanting corrupted Latin texts on stage or in concert, and readers could allow their imaginations to roam in vivid literary descriptions of the music accompanying the Black Mass. The Gothic musical efflorescence would serve as a prelude to the shift observed in the late 1960s and early 1970s, when the church's musical traditions were resignified to connote diabolical practices.

This reversal in the signification of sacred signs and their associated values, a classic semiotic reversal, suggests the principle of parody as theorized by Mikhail Bakhtin and interpreted by Linda Hutcheon, who defines it as follows: "parody... is a form of imitation, but imitation characterized by ironic inversion."[12] In her reading of Bakhtin, Hutcheon distinguishes parody for the purpose of disrespect from that which "signals ironic difference."[13] According to Bakhtin himself, parody is "double-voiced," even though only the parodied voice "is present in its own right"; "the other is present invisibly, as an actualizing background for creating and perceiving."[14] Bakhtin's concept of parody suggests not criticizing a text but rather establishing a dialogic relationship between two texts, thus a case of intertextuality.[15]

The practice of semiotic reversal in evil medieval relies on at least an awareness, if not a more detailed knowledge, of the original text being parodied, whether a church (as a religious site), a sacred writing (as a bearer of epistemic truth), or a chant (as a song in Latin). If the public for evil medieval does not recognize the "host" text, the double-voicedness and dialogic interplay could be lost and the resignification is either absorbed into the mainstream or disappears altogether. Nevertheless, some of the tropes are self-perpetuating, resistant to the temporal distance from the parodied text—this is the case with the practice of chanting in Latin. The Catholic Church abolished this practice from the liturgy in the late 1960s, yet it maintains a presence in screen media (especially horror and fantasy) and music (various dark genres of metal).[16]

It is not superfluous to observe here that, despite the trend of secularization during the Enlightenment and Napoleonic Wars, the Catholic Church remained a presence and retained an authority for citizens of western Europe. That included the living legacy of the Latin chants and the liturgical rituals that dated back to the Middle Ages. Creators and consumers of culture alike knew the traditions that the works of the Gothic revival drew on, and the medieval architecture that figured so prominently in the arts was for many a matter of daily life. Thus the era lacked the distance from church practices to justify what historian Roger Homan has identified as the "dislocation of the sacred" that would characterize evil medieval in the later twentieth century.[17] Indeed, the rejection of Enlightenment rationalism led in general to a deepened engagement on the one hand with established religions and belief systems, in particular Christianity, and on the other hand with superstition, Gothic horror, and vestiges of satanism.

Precursors of the Evil Medieval

As Ruben van Luijk's comprehensive history of satanism explains, at the beginning of the nineteenth century,

> a select number of authors and artists now professed their sympathy with the fallen angel and endeavored to rehabilitate him in some form or another, at least in the artistic domain. Second, and not less significantly, they resurrected him from the burial he had been given by Enlightenment rationalism, which had ridiculed or ignored Satan as an obsolete relic of superstition that was certainly not fit as object of veneration. This double rehabilitation, I like to argue, represents an essential step in the historical emergence of modern Satanism.[18]

Luijk's comments stand in stark contrast to the position of most recent authors on satanism in the nineteenth century, that Enlightenment rationalism had banished the devil and superstition from religious discourse.[19] Yet the rehabilitation that Luijk describes, suggesting a belief in a personal devil, persisted alongside the fictional representations in Gothic literature, art, and—as we shall see—music. As the century progressed, non-fiction histories and documentations about witchcraft, demonology, and even satanism began to appear on the market. A select list would lead from Walter Scott's apologetic *Letters on Demonology and Witchcraft* from 1830, through Thomas Wright's 1851 anthology *Narratives of Sorcery and Magic from the Most Authentic Sources* and Jules Michelet's landmark 1862 study *La sorcière* (subtitled "The Witch of the Middle Ages" in the English translation from 1863), to Joris-Karl Huysmans's scandalous, decadent *Là-bas* from 1891. *Là-bas* appeared only six years before Bram Stoker's *Dracula*, which Isabella van Elferen has provocatively designated as representing "a nineteenth-century epitome of Gothicized Catholicism."[20]

Important to these authors is the recognition that the practices of witchcraft and devil worship date back to the Middle Ages, which in turn sets the stage for evil medieval. For example, Wright's dedication of his book to Albert Denison, Lord Londesborough, argues for the need to bring to light the "viciousness and brutality" of the Middle Ages.[21] Michelet's introduction stresses the "darkness of the Middle Ages," against which back-drop his book paints a vivid picture of witchcraft's rise.[22] Michelet devotes considerable care and space to his description of the Black Mass of the fourteenth century, which he calls "a ritual upside down."[23] He documents the devil's inversive usurpation of elements of the traditional Mass, through mockeries of its components, including the Introit, Credo, and Communion, although he makes no reference to the language or texts used in this Black Mass (or Sabbath).[24] It is with the work of Huysmans at the end of the century that the practice of satanism shifts from the Middle Ages to contemporary life, as the character Durtal attests: "I have heard tell of sacrilegious priests, of a certain canon who has revived the sabbats of the Middle Ages."[25] By authoring what appeared to be an apology for satanism and providing lurid details about its practices, above all the Black Mass, Huysmans' *Là-bas* anticipated the renewed and more culturally pervasive evil medieval of seventy-five years hence.

Music of the nineteenth century did its part in countering Enlightenment rationality on the one hand and the Catholic Church and its clergy on the other, but in music, and especially opera, it took longer for the Gothic and darker influences to make themselves felt, and then in alliance with romanticism. This led to an association that Duggett has provocatively termed *Gothic romanticism*.[26] The elements of supernatural horror and dread that the writers attempted to invoke, their portrayals of Catholic clergy as power hungry and dominated by evil lusts, and of the church itself as corrupted to the core: these and related Gothicisms would find their musical expression in the operas and pro-gram music of western Europe during the 1820s and 1830s.[27] In Germany and France, the predecessors to evil medieval were closely linked to the emergence of romanticism in music, with an emphasis on the rejection of the Enlightenment ideals of rationality and order. The English performance and reception of these compositions brought them into line with the burgeoning anglophone Gothic literature of the time, exploiting and sensationalizing their Gothic elements.

It is impossible to imagine the two leading exemplars of evil medieval in music—Weber's *Der Freischütz* and Berlioz's *Symphonie fantastique*—without invoking the tremendously influential *Faust* by Goethe. As Eric Hadley Denton observes in *The Handbook to Gothic Literature*, "Goethe's reception has been largely Romantic, and three works... [including *Faust*] have proved crucial to the Gothic agenda."[28] While commentators on the play's Gothic elements have tended to focus on the *Walpurgisnacht* scene at the end of part 1, two other passages merit attention as forerunners of the resignification of Latin chant in the spirit of evil medieval: Gretchen's scene in the cathedral and the scene involving Mephistopheles and the student. The evil spirit Gretchen encounters during Mass in the cathedral causes her to seek forgiveness, and this happens as the choir intones the Dies irae about the Day of Judgment. No reversal of meaning occurs, yet the juxtaposition of Latin chant and evil spirit certainly suggests the exploitation of the sacred song for darker purposes. Also, in Faust's study, Mephistopheles has the student recite a Scripture verse in Latin that reproduces the devil's own words of temptation from the Garden of Eden. In fact, the overall narrative and the specific details of Goethe's play—called "the most grotesque masterpiece of Western poetry" by Harold Bloom— inspired generations of "Gothic Romantics from Charles Maturin to Baudelaire... [to take] the side of Faust's Mephistopheles."[29]

These two scenes from *Faust*—the cathedral encounter between Gretchen and Mephistopheles and the scene in Faust's study—undoubtedly influenced early romantic practices of semiotic reversal, in these instances resacralization, in texted or descriptive compositions that in turn foreshadow the re-emergence of musical evil medieval in the later twentieth century. Central to the resignification in musical settings was the substitution of a profane text and context for the sacred original, that is, the introduction of corrupted or perverse Latin as chanted by one or more (male) figures in an ostensibly liturgical scenario. The appearance and sound of this cultural trope in the works of Weber, Berlioz, Meyerbeer, and Marschner (to name only its most historically prominent exponents) may considerably vary, yet the principle remains the same: forces of evil co-opt elements of the liturgical rite of the Catholic Church—its chants and rituals—to promote their own diabolical spirituality.

Although Weber was the first composer to adopt the Gothic (horror) principle to achieve the effect of evil medieval, E. T. A. Hoffmann's "magic opera" *Undine* (1812–1814) anticipates German romantic opera in its text that draws on the fantastic and the supernatural. The composition left an important influence on Weber, who favorably reviewed it after the 1816 premiere in Berlin and started composing his *Der Freischütz* some months thereafter.[30] Yet it was not any specific Gothic romantic feature that attracted Weber, but rather the unified approach to the work as a whole.

It was in the opera premiered five years later that composer Weber and librettist Johann Friedrich Kind would create the conditions for the performance of evil medieval in the musical realm. Although the opera's natural/supernatural binary is shared with the Gothic literature of the time, the finale of act 2, the so-called Wolf's Glen scene, brings dramatic horror to the forefront.[31] The villain Caspar is in league with the forces of darkness, and in this scene he casts magic bullets at midnight in a place permeated by evil powers. As the ritual proceeds to the final bullet, the violence of the evil progressively intensifies, to the speaking (actually, shouting) appearance of the Black Huntsman himself, Samiel. The scene as a whole effectively captures the spirit and letter of Gothic horror, yet in terms of evil medieval, the monotone incantation of a chorus of invisible malefic (male) spirits at the scene's opening subverts monophonic (medieval) church practice to diabolical ends. While it is true that their chanting of malevolent words, beginning with "Milch des Mondes fiel aufs Kraut," is not in Latin but in German and that they do not create an evil contrafactum for a known Gregorian chant, the spirit choir does anticipate the unison monotone singing that would characterize the evil medieval Latin chant of "Ave Satani" from *The Omen* (1976), among other examples. The very lack of melodic inflection infuses the incantation with a primal power that represents the antithesis to the much-vaunted beauty of Gregorian chant. After all, Weber and Hildegard of Bingen (among others) gave the devil speaking rather than singing parts.[32] Moreover, the ritual and chant of the Wolf's Glen scene takes place in the nonliturgical, if not antiliturgical, outdoor setting of the realm of darkness rather than inside the church.

When *Der Freischütz* traveled to London in February of 1824, the opera's kinship with Gothic literature was straightaway recognized and exploited on stage. The English performances "highlighted the sensationalism of the Wolfsschlucht, [and] emphasized the Gothic elements in the plot," as reflected in the translation provided for the title of the work: *The Fatal Marksman or the Demon of the Black Forest*.[33] Mary Shelley, whose *Frankenstein* had appeared three years before the Berlin premiere of *Der Freischütz*, attended a performance that summer and was so impressed by the "incantation scene" that she refers to *Freischütz* in her next novel, *The Last Man*. There the despondent protagonist compares the experience of music to "the demoniac chorus in the Wolf's Glen."[34]

While Weber's subsequent operatic work turned toward subjects of fantasy, the master trope of Gothic horror would maintain its presence on German opera stages for the next decade, although with varying degrees of indebtedness to practices of evil medieval. Heinrich Marschner's *Der Vampyr* (1828) carried on and in some ways intensified Weber's invocation of the trope, highlighting a dark, Gothic spirituality throughout with a vampire (Lord Ruthven) in the leading role. After the overture, the opera opens on the scene of a witches' sabbath: A mixed chorus of "witches and spirits in bizarre forms" greets the proceedings with occasional unison chants.[35] The appearance of the vampire master—again a speaking part—causes Ruthven to take an oath in the style of an incantation. In this scene liturgical customs are parodied, appropriated for evil purposes as they were in Weber's scene and yet, like his predecessor, Marschner does not invoke Latin or Gregorian chant in the rituals of evil. Marschner's other major work, *Hans Heiling* (1833), is more a tale of the supernatural, of the fantasy world of earth spirits akin to *Undine* than one of Gothic horror, with evil and the realm of darkness embodied by Ruthven.

Nevertheless, the trend of Gothic romanticism was powerful in German operas of the 1820s and early 1830s. Even the young Richard Wagner tried his hand at a tragic Shakespearean-Gothic opera entitled *Leubald* that Martin Geck has described as characterized by a "veritable spree of serial killings and by scenes of sexual violence, chuckle-headedness, and ghostly apparitions."[36] Such works obviously reflect the influence from the Gothic horror literature of the time, yet also an awakened interest in German-speaking lands in religion and legends of the *Volk* and a disaffection from the nonmystical, tradition-based church and its servants.[37]

Weber's long shadow extended to France and operas like *La Dame blanche* by François-Adrien Boieldieu (1825) and *Robert le diable* by Giacomo Meyerbeer (1831), even though *Der Freischütz* was only known through a bowdlerized version entitled *Robin des bois*. Above all, in *Robert* one encounters both the supernatural elements of German Gothic romanticism and the evil that manifested itself within the church: In the wake of the Napoleonic secularization, which bears comparison with the reforms of the Second Vatican Council (1962–1965), French opera of the 1820s and 1830s tended to paint the agents of the traditional church in a dark light. In the work of a composer and cultural critic like Meyerbeer, priests, monks, and nuns were presented as corrupt zealots who, if not in league with the devil, at least carried out his work on earth.

Robert le diable represents a particularly salient point in the history of evil medieval, because not only does it connect with the predecessors by Weber and Marschner, but also it serves as one of the earliest grand operas at the Parisian Opéra.[38] Specifically, Robert is aided by a mysterious demonic figure named Bertram, who in act 3 encourages Robert to appropriate a sacred relic to fulfill his lustful desires. With its setting in a ruined monastery, invocation to infernal spirits, and conjuring of a magical object, the act's closing scenes call to mind the Wolf's Glen scene by Weber, only Meyerbeer takes Weber's Gothic romanticism to a new level of evil medieval: Bertram calls forth the spirits of dead nuns, who perform a dance extolling the lusts of life (a bacchanal).

Other operas from later in the 1830s and further into the nineteenth century adopt elements of dark romanticism, in its general outlines as well as specific manifestations. For example, Meyerbeer's *Les Huguenots* (1836) exposes an underlying anticlericalism/anti-Catholicism in the sense of Diane Long Hoeveler's "Anti-Catholicism and the Gothic Imaginary"; this attitude carries over into the composer's subsequent operas *Le Prophète* (1849) and *L'Africaine* (1865) and would strongly influence Verdi in *Don Carlos* (1867).[39] Verdi, who had attended the premiere of *Le Prophète*, portrayed in that work "the Church as a malevolent political entity," which "is rooted in his own anticlericalism."[40] With his *La Nonne sanglante* (1854), Charles Gounod composed the one opera that set a portion of an actual Gothic horror tale, Matthew Lewis's *The Monk* from 1796—however, the work was a failure, closing after only eleven performances, arguably because "the flagrantly Gothic text [was] fundamentally unsuited to the (unconscious) needs of a mid-nineteenth-century libretto."[41]

Goethe's *Faust* continued to fascinate opera composers throughout the nineteenth century and into the twentieth, from Louis Spohr through Ferruccio Busoni; still, the most popular settings reduce Goethe's complex moral and philosophical inquiry to the struggle of good and evil within frail humanity. Moreover, even in its less bowdlerized settings, the narrative of *Faust* stands worlds apart from the devil worship and Black Mass as described by Michelet. Thus, large-scale vocal settings by prominent composers such as Robert Schumann and Hector Berlioz reveal personal interpretations that do not engage in the evil medieval trope. Richard Wagner himself was swept up by the

Faustmania of the mid-nineteenth century, with his *Faust* Overture, and yet his most obvious foray into the realm of the Gothic occurred with the aforementioned early composition *Leubald*.[42] In his mature works Wagner did not engage in the semiotic inversion of sacred terms that characterized the Gothic-influenced operas of the 1820s and 1830s, where the rituals of the Catholic Church become the subjects of parody by the forces of darkness.

It stands to reason that instrumental music could not serve as a fruitful site for the contestation of sacred traditions except when it availed itself of descriptive language. Even in works that were programmatic in character, like Liszt's *Faust* symphony and Wagner's aforementioned *Faust* overture, however, the music merely depicts the narrative rather than exploiting its potential for subverting ecclesiastical practices, including Gregorian chant. Berlioz's *Symphonie fantastique* stands alone as an exception to this principle, to the extent that it progresses beyond the realm of the purely illustrative to participate in the narrative's diabolical inversion of the sacred in the form of the Black Mass (witches' sabbath).

As one of the landmark compositions of the nineteenth century and a major precursor of evil medieval, Berlioz's composition merits closer attention. In performing his semiotic reversal, Berlioz deploys the register of parody, which here involves (mis-) appropriating a well-known Gregorian chant, the late medieval sequence Dies irae. There is a double meaning at work in the symphony's finale, because the sequence was an integral part of the Requiem Mass and almost universally came to signify death during the nineteenth century, as one composer after another cited its melody in morbid contexts.[43] Nevertheless, Berlioz was apparently the first composer to exploit the sequence—and indeed, any Gregorian chant—to signify the infernal (and a victorious infernal at that). Under the influence of a large corpus of romantic literary works, including *Faust* and *Confessions of an Opium Eater* by Thomas de Quincey, Berlioz introduced a shadow side to the sacred realm, which his auditors could hardly have missed, given the bellowing performance of the Dies irae on the serpent and ophicleide in the final movement.[44] Linda Schubert summarizes the impact of this instance of semiotic inversion through instrumental music when she notes how Berlioz "musically depicts the demonic supernatural: in the final movement, the chant is played, distorted and combined with a jig in a figurative 'desecration' to depict the blasphemy of a Witches' Sabbath."[45] It is important to note that in her survey of nineteenth-century reviews of the work, Schubert observes the diversity of meanings assigned to the Dies irae, including the demonic supernatural, death, and—quite important for this study— the remote past.[46]

Despite a spate of later nineteenth-century instrumental works from eastern Europe and Russia that illustrate evil in its various forms, including symphonic poems by Musorgsky (*Witches' Sabbath* of 1867) and Dvořák (*The Midday Witch* of 1896), these compositions did not capture the public's attention like Berlioz's piece.[47] Moreover, in the long run they failed to impact the development of evil medieval in the way that Carl Orff's *Carmina Burana* (1937) did.

Although much of the current popular reception of the work—that it was a product of Third Reich ideology by a Nazi sympathizer—has been contested by scholars, *Carmina Burana* nevertheless remains a landmark composition that enjoys widespread recognition by the public.[48] The primitivist rhythms of "O Fortuna" have resonated across the contemporary mediascape, in countless epic film trailers and—more specifically—in the 1981 film *Excalibur*, the Carlton Draught "Big Ad" for television (2005, with new words), and the first (2009) season of *Glee* (episode 7, "Throwdown"), just to name three divergent examples.[49] The point is that the public knows the sound of the music and has formed associations of it with such topics as epic grandiosity, timeless barbarism, and fleshly overindulgence. The widely disseminated beer commercials for Carlton Draught and Rickard's Red arguably hew most closely to the evil medieval trope in visual terms, because there we see monks and nuns—symbolizing both brewers and consumers—extolling earthly pleasures, albeit singing English-language parody lyrics to Orff's music.

With its strongly anticlerical attitudes, the Third Reich provided a fitting context for Orff's secularizing if not demonizing representation of Christianity/Catholicism in "Fortuna Imperatrix Mundi" and "In Taberna." These sections in particular position the church and its clerics within the timeless, ritualistic discourses of the barbaric, whereby he clad the "perverted" Latin chant in primitivist rhythms. Here was a work that musically articulated and celebrated a fallen (in)version of Christianity, as practiced in the Dark Ages. For our purposes, *Carmina Burana* is not as important in the context of its reception in 1937 as for those later film composers such as Jerry Goldsmith and John Williams, who modeled their own creations on certain aspects of the work—it is hard to imagine Goldsmith's "Ave Satani" without the precedent of *Carmina Burana*.

The Evil Medieval from the 1970s to the Present

The full revelation of the cultural trope of evil medieval nevertheless had to await a unique convergence of historical events and cultural developments in the final third of the twentieth century. At that time, it took hold in popular culture more profoundly and thoroughly than in the manifestations of the Gothic revival in literature and Gothic romanticism in music and even the clandestine satanism of the nineteenth century. The semiotic reversal resulted in a paradigm shift that resignified symbols and practices of the Catholic Church into markers of evil and the diabolical.

The strands from which the fabric of the evil medieval are woven came together in North America in the late 1960s and early 1970s. Broadly speaking, first the power and authority of the traditional (Catholic) church and its sacred symbols and liturgical rituals became seriously effaced during this period, and not only by the secularism of the times. Some of this rejection of historic spirituality arose from the disillusionment of youth over the establishment and its conservative values, mobilizing themselves as the counterculture "around issues of civil rights, poverty, feminism, and militarism that were cresting at the time."[50] Even as the reforms of Vatican II (which, among other changes, banished Latin chant from the liturgy) were taking hold, a dark spirituality was emerging in the United States, in part sparked by the activities of satanist Anton LaVey (founder of the Church of Satan and author of *The Satanic Bible*). The "turn to the dark side" was confirmed through such diverse manifestations as the recording activity of Ozzy Osbourne's occult/death metal band Coven, the murderous spree of suspected satanist Charles Manson and his "family," and a spate of Hollywood horror films. New Age spirituality grew out of the counterculture and flourished after about 1970—it is associated with the revival of Gregorian chant that began in the late 1970s, which forms an ironic pendant to the cultural trope of evil medieval.

Space does not permit a detailed exploration of each of the factors that ultimately led to the semiotic reversal of sacred and diabolical. Nevertheless, it is important to consider the influences specific to the abandonment and devaluation of sacred traditions from the Middle Ages on the one hand and the valorizing of the immoral, the evil, and even the satanic on the other. The convergence of these two lines of development was responsible for the emergence of evil medieval as a trope in North American culture.

The Sacred

The Second Vatican Council undertook its work of spiritually renewing the Catholic Church at a time of decline for traditional Christianity.[51] As religious historian Hugh McLeod observes, "the 1960s were a time when history moved faster, and in which a dynamic of change built up which old institutions and traditions were powerless to withstand."[52] McLeod argues that the most significant catalysts for the devaluation of the church were the reforms of Vatican II and the Vietnam War, which came into convergence in 1968: "The hatred of institutions and structures, the love affair of many radical Catholics with Marxism, and their idealization of the Third World...all had devastating effects on the Catholic Church."[53]

The impact of Vatican II on the Catholic Church and representations of it cannot be underestimated. For many commentators, the effects of its reforms can be summarized in the concepts of modernization and secularization, which contributed to the decline of the Roman Catholic Church through "weakening of the dogmas, the rites, and the moral–ethical proscriptions."[54] As theologian Roger Homan has stated, "Vatican II [stripped] down...religious language, ritual, art, atmosphere and music...in terms of simplicity."[55] With its removal of spoken Latin and Gregorian chant from the Catholic liturgy in North America, as well as other aspects of the church's timeless ritual (for example, the traditional garb of ministering clergy), a gap was created between the medieval past that spawned these conventions and the present. Through its conscious attempt to make itself contemporary and relevant, through modernizing and secularizing, the Catholic Church in America became commonplace, so that Christian ritual and Latin chant were no longer part of the familiar daily or weekly routines of parishioners. Even the rite of exorcism was downplayed, reduced to a simple prayer: "Exorcism is nothing more than a prayer to God...to restrain the power of demons over men and things."[56] For many of its members, especially the youth of the counterculture, the Catholic Church—with its conservative views on birth control and the status of women, among other topics—seemed irrelevant at a time when the civil rights movements was making advances, Marxism was challenging the established political order, and young people were protesting the war in Vietnam.[57] Though the reforms of Vatican II only applied to Catholics, other Christian denominations like the Anglicans and Lutherans followed suit with moves to modernize and secularize.[58]

One of the council's more controversial revisions to the liturgy involved its music. Joseph Peter Swan succinctly summarizes the reform in sacred musical practices: "The Second Vatican Council...banned the singing of liturgical Latin [Gregorian chant] and instead mandated the use of local vernacular languages....It promoted the composition of new liturgical works in popular styles to replace the outmoded Gregorian chants."[59] In the spirit of modernization, chanting in a language unknown to the parishioners no longer had any place within the liturgy of the church, which may help explain why its revival gained such a popular following in the next generation of the 1970s and 1980s, many of its admirers from the ranks of non-Catholics.[60]

The banishment of Latin from the everyday experience of the Catholic enhanced its remoteness and esotericism, so that it became available for "liturgical" use in the semiotic reversal of evil medieval. Like its earlier role in the Gothic imaginary, monophonic Latin chant sung by men took on dark meanings in association with diabolical ritual, above all in the genre of horror in film (and television). And the neomedieval connotations of using chant to invoke ancient spirits were not lost on the screen media, in its ability to evoke the Dark Ages, fashioning a world of barbaric malevolence in which timeless ritual forges a link between past and present.

At the same time as this spiritual transformation, the New Hollywood of the late 1960s by and large avoided Christian themes, other than in the epic genre, and even there the number of films declined.[61] Movie-goers increasingly sought meaning in political movements and alternative religions and the industry eventually abandoned the morality code in the late 1960s, which influenced the long-term trend away from cinematic depictions of the traditional church. When conventional Catholic rituals appeared on screen after the late 1960s, it was to foreground the church's alleged hypocrisy, like the baptism scene in *The Godfather*, where director Martin Scorsese crosscuts between Michael's renunciation of the devil and the mobster assassinations. When removed from the trappings of the church and its medieval customs, the figure of Jesus nevertheless was compelling for certain filmmakers such as Norman Jewison (*Jesus Christ Superstar*) and Franco Zeffirelli (*Jesus of Nazareth*). Still, it is ironic that historic sacred practices of the Catholic Church received more film footage after Vatican II in the genre of horror than in any other cinematic context, which reflects the power of evil medieval as a cultural trope.

The Diabolical

The postconciliar disappearance of Catholic rituals dating back to the Middle Ages created a distance from those practices that enabled their eventual resignification in conjunction with developments on the dark side of spirituality. As already established, satanism and evil ritual had precedents in the Gothic revival and Gothic horror in literature and art of the nineteenth century and the Gothic romanticism of music from the era. Such artistic evocations of evil by nonsatanists kept it at arm's length, betraying a lack of personal engagement with the belief system and its object of veneration. Cornelis J. Roelofse has argued that "there are two categories of Satanists. Those who see this in metaphorical dimensions and those who venerate Satan as a metaphysical being."[62] Still, public engagement with the beliefs and practices remained very much underground at the time: "the authentic Satanist lived rather secretly...and did not advertise their Satanic activities."[63] The fact that certain of its manifestations in literature and music took on parodic tones reflects more of an anticlericalism and anti-Catholicism than a devil-oriented belief system.

The academic literature seems to agree that the counterculture of the 1960s was the breeding ground for developments in society and culture that would lead to the rise of dark religion in its various forms.[64] Thus satanism emerged in the public consciousness through the proliferation of alternative religions during the 1960s, and its rise coincided with the realization of the Vatican II reforms. The central figure in this advancement of the devil was the flamboyant Anton LaVey, who founded the Church of Satan in 1966 and published *The Satanic Bible* in 1969.[65] LaVey and his brand of satanism fascinated Hollywood celebrities, including Sammy Davis Jr., Jayne Mansfield, and Keenan Wynn, who, however, preferred their association with him to remain a secret for fear of a backlash from audiences. It took less than a year for the church to receive national press coverage, however, through LaVey's satanist adoption of a set of Christian rites: marriage, baptism, and last rites.[66] As he himself reports, LaVey may have initially been "performing Satanism, but the media attention brought the man, the church and their beliefs before the American public, at a time when the Catholic Church had abandoned its traditions and rituals and religious exploration had become part of the countercultural experience."[67] Then came the Manson murders, which seemed to confirm for the public that the devil of LaVey was real and that satanic ritual practices were now being carried out by his acolytes, though much of the hype was based on speculation and hearsay.[68]

Satanism readily and quickly found its musical voice. As he was working on *The Satanic Bible*, LaVey produced an album called *The Satanic Mass*, which was recorded in 1967 at the Church of Satan but not released until 1968.[69] The second side features passages from *The Satanic Bible*, set to music by Beethoven, Wagner, and Sousa. Rock bands of the time added their support to LaVey and followers by appearing to promote satanism in their music and lifestyles, beginning in the late 1960s. For groups like Black Sabbath and the Rolling Stones (with their album *Their Satanic Majesties Request*), the initial connections with the devil were more titular and sensational than belief based, though fans and critics positioned such groups as reflecting the principles of satanism. Thus, the BBC well captured the aura of dark spirituality surrounding Black Sabbath when it reported in early 1970 that "their darker lyrical themes of death and references to Satan seemed to resonate with those tired of the 60s optimism and flower power."[70] Jimmy Page's obsession with occultist Aleister Crowley—popularly regarded as a satanist—came to the public's attention in 1970 when he had two of Crowley's sayings inscribed in the run-off grooves of the early vinyl pressings of *Led Zeppelin III*.[71]

However, the clearest manifestation of the discourse of evil medieval in rock at that time occurred in the music of occult band Coven, which recorded openly satanic albums, starting with the curiously titled *Witchcraft Destroys Minds & Reaps Souls* from 1969.[72] The inside of the record's gatefold features the three musicians enacting a satanic ritual while casting the devil horns (the first time the salute was depicted in cover art), while the songs themselves combine infernal lyrics—some in Latin—with chanting ("Satanic Mass") and diabolical-sounding music ("Black Sabbath"). The thirteen-minute "Satanic Mass" presents the quintessence of evil medieval in audio: It begins with tolling bells and chanting in an unknown language and then Latin and English chants and spoken text proceed in alteration, in an inversion of the pre-Vatican liturgical Mass that includes the Lord's Prayer recited backward. The enactment of the Black Mass ends with the call and response: "[priest] Rege Satanas! [congregation] Hail Satan! [priest] Ave Satanas! [congregation] Hail Satan!" Although the album appeared almost concurrently with the LaVey documentary *Satanis: The Devil's Mass* (1970), the two seem to have originated independent of each other, causing a recent commentator to support "the existence of a wider underground Satanic subculture during the late 1960s."[73]

To close the loop and bring the discussion back to Hollywood film, it is important to note that LaVey was rumored to have originally been cast in the part of the devil in the first major horror film of this era, Roman Polanski's *Rosemary's Baby* (1968). However, according to several sources, he had no part in the movie, not even as an advisor—it nonetheless is ironic that one of the victims of Manson's group was Polanski's wife, Sharon Tate. Several newspaper banner headlines on August 10, 1969, the day after the murders, announced them as "ritual," thereby publicly tying them to some form of (dark) religious practice, and although aspects of the forensic evidence disputed that attribution, the popular imagination seemed intent on regarding the slayings as manifestations of an evil spirituality.

Rosemary's Baby was the first major cinematic offering in what James R. Lewis has called "a threshold period for diabolically inspired movies" (i.e., the late 1960s and early 1970s)[74]: the unholy trinity of influential satanic blockbusters from this period is continued and completed by *The Exorcist* (1973) and *The Omen* (1976). *Rosemary's Baby* was the most subdued of the three in its depiction of the practices of devil worship (also in its music), yet it hit American society like a bombshell and—in the words of LaVey—"did for the Church of Satan what *The Birth of a Nation* did for the Ku Klux Klan."[75] The devil worshippers here dressed and acted like regular citizens, with no robed monks, no chanted Latin, no evil medieval: This was a modern satanism that is all the more uncanny because of its mundaneness.[76]

In contrast, the feature-length documentary *Satanis: The Devil's Mass* (1970) about LaVey and his Church of Satan visually presented the inversion of sacred Catholic ritual as the satanic priest and his followers celebrated the Black Mass.[77] The video intercuts the portions of the Mass with interviews of church members and people from the neighborhood, some of them antagonistic toward LaVey. Although it afforded the public first glimpses inside the church, *Satanis* "did poorly at local showings and failed to reach national distribution,"[78] attaining the status of a cult movie by the mid-1970s. Hampered by weak direction (Ray Laurent) and amateurish standards of cinematography and music, the documentary nevertheless centers on the enactment of the Mass, replete with hooded figures, sacrilegious ceremonials, and chanted Latin (e.g., "In nomine Satanas, Lucifer excelsis dei").[79] That the film did not reach a wide audience and that its ritual seemed contrived does not diminish its position as a full-fledged filmic manifestation of the cultural trope of evil medieval.

The Latin here is correct, even though the designations for infernal deities have been substituted for their sacred counterparts in this semiotic inversion of good and evil. However, not all the resignified Latin in audiovisual media after 1970 was accurate: in fact, the choral parts of numerous cinematic epic music tracks contain what has been called *nonsense Latin*. On the one hand, the devil cannot be heard to speak proper Latin.[80] On the other hand, the language is well suited for providing *Gothic gravity*, as Christopher Partridge describes the types of scenes in which evil medieval operates.[81] The author of the *TV Tropes* entry "Ominous Latin Chanting" describes the practice this way: "The actual meaning of the words is unimportant...it's the sound that matters."[82] They proceed to argue that "Hollywood will tell you that nothing can dictate... 'the End of the World' more than potent choir chants in a language most viewers don't know, and that this is the way to give a scene that extra bit of ominous importance."

Latin chanting figures prominently in *The Omen* (1976), but in the hands of gifted film composer Jerry Goldsmith, all hints of a superficial and merely coloristic use of the musical gesture have fallen away. The intoning of the once-sacred language has becomes truly menacing and frightening, as exemplified by the incantation of the film's Oscar-nominated theme "Ave Satani" during the opening titles. As Goldsmith revealed in an interview for the documentary *666: The Omen Revealed* (2000), he drew on the practices of evil medieval when composing the chant: "I got this idea . . . , why don't I make this like a Black Mass?...What if we just twist [the words] around, like instead of hailing Mary...let's hail Satan?"[83] The Latin chant (monophonic, if not fully monotonic) evokes the Middle Ages, which have become the Dark Ages through rhythm, accompaniment, and harmony. The satanic text is sung three times, each with increasing threat accomplished not only by rising dynamic level but also by intensifying textural density and dissonance. This ominous music of the credits sets the bleak, diabolic tone and provides thematic material for the rest of the film, accompanying various scenes of menace and evil ritual. Such is the sound that would influence a generation of moviegoers to associate Latin and chant with the "dark side" and thus would encourage a generation of film composers to perpetuate the musical *topos* in scenes of satanic ritual in movies like those listed in the appendix.

Conclusions: The Afterlife of a Cultural Trope

Evil medieval clearly survived the period of its efflorescence in the 1970s—film and television continued to draw on the cultural trope, in horror and—to a lesser extent—science fiction/fantasy genres. For example, Francis Ford Coppola's *Bram Stoker's Dracula* of 1992 illustrates the industry's continuing fascination over the mutability of the boundaries between sacred and profane, in this case the venerable holy traditions of the church becoming corrupted, reflected through the agency of music. At the beginning of the narrative, Count Dracula discovers the suicide of his bride Elisabetha upon returning home from war. Composer Wojciech Kilar submits a simple, four-note wordless chant-like melody symbolizing the church to a transformation as the count commits sacrilege and renounces the church. As he destroys the liturgical symbols of the (Orthodox) church and drinks blood from the chalice in a new satanic ritual of transubstantiation, while the chant builds to an "O Fortuna"- or *Omen*-like archaic climax, we witness the whole historical process leading to evil medieval in one powerful cinematic scene.

In a scene from *Star Wars Episode 1: The Phantom Menace* (1999), we also encounter a lingering sonic enactment of evil medieval. John Williams has created a Latin-sounding chant (actually in Sanskrit) to accompany the ritualistic final battle between Qui Gon and Darth Maul. Though not monophonically intoned, the ominous, repetitive quasi-chanted chorus resonates in a kind of crude organum, evoking the timeless, barbaric world of dark ritual that the evil Darth Maul inhabits. It stands in contrast with the contemporary-sounding music for Qui Gon used elsewhere in the film and has more than a hint of the choral writing we recognize from "O Fortuna" and *The Omen*.[84]

Nevertheless, as the activism and disquiet of the counterculture faded into memory, the recollection of preconciliar liturgical-musical practices grew dim, and the devil and his works entered the North American cultural mainstream, evil medieval lost its "medieval," its roots in sacred religious practices of the distant past. In the double-voiced, parodying semiotic reversal of evil medieval, the audience needs to have a familiarity with the invisibly present-originating text—in our case, Catholic liturgy and Gregorian chant—for the ironic inversion to have its full effect. The parody of evil medieval's "actualizing background for creating and perceiving" is absent from contemporary representations of the devil, though screen media may still present robed monks chanting in an arcane language.

Returning to our opening example, the neomedievalism in *Game of Thrones* may be both evil and medieval, but it is not evil medieval: The late 2010s are too far removed from the political, social, cultural, and even specifically musical conditions that gave birth to evil medieval's resignification of the sacred into the diabolical. The phenomenon of the evil medieval has become historicized, or rather, it has itself become subject to a process of resignification that is central to the development of both film music and medievalism.

APPENDIX

Evil Medieval in Feature Films: A Selection

- *The Devils* (1971)
- *Vault of Horror* (1973)
- *Satan's School for Girls* (1973)
- *The Cursed Ship* (1974)
- *Race with the Devil* (1975)
- *Carrie* (1976)
- *The Omen* (1976)
- *Jabberwocky* (1977)
- *The Car* (1977)
- *The Shining* (1980)
- *Excalibur* (1981)
- *Sleeping with the Enemy* (1991)
- *Bram Stoker's Dracula* (1992)
- *Eyes Wide Shut* (1999)
- *Star Wars I: The Phantom Menace* (1999)

ACKNOWLEDGMENTS

This chapter represents a substantial expansion and revision of the author's article "The Topos of 'Evil Medieval' in American Horror Film Music," in *Music, Meaning & Media*, ed. Erkki Pekkilä, David Neumeyer, and Richard Littlefield, Acta Semiotica Fennica XXV, Approaches to Musical Semiotics 11, Studia Musicologica Universitatis Helsingiensis 15 (Helsinki: Semiotic Society of Finland, University of Helsinki and International Semiotics Institute at Imatra, 2006), 26–37. My thanks for their assistance in the preparation of this article extend to Stephen C. Meyer, Alexis Luko, Erkki Pekkilä, and Jim Buhler.

NOTES

1. Laura Miller, "They Put the Evil in Medieval," *Salon.com*, April 5, 2013, accessed March 22, 2018, https://www.salon.com/2013/04/05/they_put_the_evil_in_medieval.
2. Kim Selling, "'Fantastic Medievalism': The Image of the Middle Ages in Popular Fantasy," in *Flashes of the Fantastic: Selected Essays from the* War of the Worlds *Centennial*, ed. David Ketterer (Westport, CT: Praeger, 2004), 213.
3. Tom Vercruysse, "The Dark Ages Imaginary in European Films" (PhD diss., KU Leuven, 2014), 53. See also Ceri Jones, "Frames of Meaning: Young People, Historical Consciousness and Challenging History at Museums and Historic Sites," in *Challenging History in the Museum: International Perspectives*, ed. Jenny Kidd, Sam Cairns, Alex Drago, Amy Ryall, and Miranda Stearn (New York: Routledge, 2016), 223–234.
4. Vercruysse, "The Dark Ages Imaginary in European Films," 54.
5. See Edward Macan, *Rocking the Classics, English Progressive Rock and the Counterculture* (London: Oxford University Press, 1997).

6. Erik Davis, *TechGnosis: Myth, Magic, and Mysticism in the Age of Information* (New York: Harmony Books, 1998), 205.

7. Fred Botting, *Gothic*, 2nd ed. (New York: Routledge, 2014), 2.

8. Ibid., 21.

9. Diane Long Hoeveler, *Gothic Riffs: Secularizing the Uncanny in the European Imaginary, 1780–1820* (Columbus: Ohio University Press, 2010), 30, 33.

10. Tom Duggett, *Gothic Romanticism: Architecture, Politics, and Literary Form* (New York: Palgrave Macmillan, 2010), 7.

11. Diane Long Hoeveler, "Anti-Catholicism and the Gothic Imaginary: The Historical and Literary Contexts," in *Religion in the Age of Enlightenment 3*, ed. Brett C. McInelly (Brooklyn: AMS Press, 2012), 2.

12. Linda Hutcheon, "Modern Parody and Bakhtin," in *Rethinking Bakhtin: Extensions and Challenges*, ed. Gary Saul Morson and Caryl Emerson (Evanston, IL: Northwestern University Press, 1989), 87.

13. Ibid., 91.

14. Mikhail Bakhtin, *The Dialogic Imagination: Four Essays*, ed. Michael Holquist (Austin: University of Texas Press, 1984), 6, 76.

15. See James Deaville, "Recut and Re-tuned: Fan-Produced Parody Trailers," *The Journal of Fandom Studies* 4, no. 2 (2016): 209–223.

16. See Simon Trafford's contribution to this volume, "Viking Metal," pp. 564–585.

17. Roger Homan, *The Art of the Sublime: Principles of Christian Art and Architecture* (Aldershot, UK: Ashgate, 2006). Through the dislocation of the sacred, we lose sight (and hearing) of the religious practice's provenance and original meaning—for example, we hear on Classical FM that "Nearer My God to Thee" is the beautiful song from *Titanic*, whereby its setting has been displaced from a place of Christian worship to Hollywood (another site of worship).

18. Ruben van Luijk, *Children of Lucifer: The Origins of Modern Religious Satanism* (New York: Oxford University Press, 2016), 69.

19. Patrick Vadermeersch explains at length the historical and intellectual origins of the myth of the victory of enlightened thought over superstition through the establishment of psychiatry in "The Victory of Psychiatry over Demonology: The Origin of the Nineteenth-Century Myth," *History of Psychiatry* 2, no. 8 (1991): 351–363. See also Darren Oldridge, who traces "Lucifer's long retreat" through the nineteenth century, when "the scepticism about Satan 'in polite society' was accelerated…by new theories in the natural sciences," *The Devil: A Very Short Introduction* (Oxford, UK: Oxford University Press, 2012), 43.

20. Isabella van Elferen, "Music that Sucks and Bloody Liturgy," in *Roman Catholicism and Fantastic Film: Essays on Belief, Spectacle, Ritual and Imagery*, ed. Regina Hanson, (Jefferson, NC: McFarland & Company, 2011) 99.

21. Thomas Wright, *Narratives of Sorcery and Magic, from the Most Authentic Sources* (London: Richard Bentley, 1851), 2:5.

22. Jules Michelet, *La Sorcière; The Witch of the Middle Ages*, trans. L. J. Trotter (London: Simpkin, Marshall, 1863), 2.

23. Ibid., 146.

24. Ibid., 143–156.

25. Huysmans, *Là-bas*, trans. Keene Wallis as *Down There* (Paris: n.p., 1928), 169.

26. See his *Gothic Romanticism: Architecture, Politics, and Literary Form*. Already in 2000, Michael Gamer published the first full-length study to link romantic and Gothic literatures,

Romanticism and the Gothic: Genre, Reception, and Canon Formation (Cambridge: Cambridge University Press, 2000).

27. Among others, see Zaheed Alam, "Treatment of the Gothic Elements by the Early Romantics," *ASA University Review* 6 no. 1 (2012): 303; and Susan M. Griffin, *Anti-Catholicism and Nineteenth-Century Fiction* (Cambridge: Cambridge University Press, 2004).

28. Eric Hadley Denton, "Goethe," in *The Handbook to Gothic Literature*, ed. Marie Mulvey-Roberts (London: Macmillan, 1998), 70.

29. Harold Bloom, *The Western Canon: The Books and School of the Ages* (New York: Harcourt Brace, 1994), 204; and Michael Lowy, "Consumed by Night's Fire: The Dark Romanticism of Guy Debord," *Radical Philosophy* 87 (1998): 33.

30. Ludwig Finscher, "Weber's Freischütz: Conceptions and Misconceptions," *Proceedings of the Royal Musical Association* 110 (1983–1984): 79–90.

31. For a detailed discussion of the opera's plot and plot structure, see Stephen C. Meyer, *Carl Maria von Weber and the Search for a German Opera* (Bloomington: Indiana University Press, 2003), 83–94.

32. The twelfth-century German abbess Hildegard von Bingen wrote a drama with music entitled *Ordo virtutum* in which the devil has a speaking role.

33. Donald Henderson, *The Freischütz Phenomenon: Opera as Cultural Mirror* (Bloomington, IN: Xlibris, 2011), 108.

34. Mary Shelley, *The Last Man* (London: Colburn, 1826), 3:159.

35. "Chor der Hexen und Geister in abentheuerlichen Gestalten." Performance indication from p. 9 of the piano score reproduced in the International Music Score Library Project (IMSLP) (Leipzig: Friedrich Hofmeister, n.d.), which appears to have served as a conductor's copy.

36. Martin Geck, *Richard Wagner: A Life in Music*, trans. Stewart Spencer (Chicago: University of Chicago Press, 2012), 9.

37. See, above all, Todd H. Weir, *Secularism and Religion in Nineteenth-Century Germany: The Rise of the Fourth Confession* (New York: Cambridge University Press, 2014).

38. For details about this opera, see especially Catherine Join-Dieterlé, "*Robert le Diable*: le premier opéra romantique," *Romantisme* 28–29 (1980): 147–166.

39. See Fulcher, *The Nation's Image: French Grand Opera as Politics and Politicized Art* (Cambridge: Cambridge University Press, 1987), 90–101, for an extended treatment of the difficulties Meyerbeer encountered in staging the work. For more on the image of the Middle Ages in grand opera, see Diana Hallman's contribution to this volume: "The Distant Past as Mirror and Metaphor: Portraying the Medieval in Historical French Grand Operas," pp. 109–134.

40. Jean Andrews, "Meyerbeer's *L'Africaine*: French Grand Opera and the Iberian Exotic," *Modern Language Review* 102, no. 1 (2007): 118.

41. Anne Williams, "Lewis/Gounod's Bleeding Nonne: An Introduction and Translation of the Scribe/Delavigne Libretto," *Romantic Circles* (May 2005): §4, accessed March 22, 2018, http://www.rc.umd.edu/praxis/opera/williams/williams.html.

42. About the Faustmania of the period, see Mai Kawabata, "Virtuosity, the Violin, the Devil...What Really Made Paganini "Demonic"?" *Current Musicology* 83 (2007): 90–92.

43. Regarding this phenomenon, see Linda Schubert, "Plainchant in Motion Pictures: The *Dies irae* in Film Scores," *Florilegium* 15 (1998): 207–229.

44. In his orchestration treatise, Berlioz refers to the serpent as "much better suited for the bloody cult of the Druids than for that of the Catholic church." Cited in Richard Sanborn

Morgan, "The Serpent and Ophicleide as Instruments of Romantic Color in Selected Works by Mendelssohn, Berlioz and Wagner" (DMA diss., University of North Texas, 2006), 53.

45. Schubert, "Plainchant in Motion Pictures," 211.

46. Ibid. The Dies irae would reappear as a symbol of the dark supernatural and death in sound film, ranging from *A Tale of Two Cities* (1935) through *It's a Wonderful Life* (1946), to *Sleeping with the Enemy* (1991) and *Rogue One* (2016). Gottfried Huppertz's accompanying score for the silent film *Metropolis* (1927) also uses the Dies irae in this way.

47. Mussorgsky's *Witches Sabbath* was an early version of the *Night on Bald Mountain*.

48. See Michael Kater, "Carl Orff im dritten Reich," *Vierteljahreshefte für Zeitgeschichte* 43, no. 1 (1995): 8; as well as the chapter on Carl Orff ("Carl Orff: Man of Legend") in his *Composers of the Nazi Era: Eight Portraits* (New York: Oxford University Press, 2000), 111–143. See also Kirsten Yri's contribution in this collection, "Medievalism and Antiromanticism in Carl Orff's *Carmina Burana*," pp. 269–300.

49. David Clem's essay in this volume addresses not only the film's use of "O Fortuna," but above all the medieval chant "Kyrie" that accompanies the wedding of Arthur and Guenevere, which, as Clem observes, "is a pagan, rather than Christian ritual." David Clem, "Hope against Fate or Fata Morgana? Music and Mythopoiesis in Boorman's *Excalibur*" in this volume, pp. 662–689.

50. Michael Ryan and Douglas Kellner, *Camera Politica: The Politics and Ideology of Contemporary Hollywood Film* (Bloomington: Indiana University Press, 1988), 17.

51. Hugh McLeod, *The Religious Crisis of the 1960s* (Oxford: Oxford University Press, 2008), 137–139.

52. Ibid., 16.

53. Ibid., 11.

54. Piero Ignazi and E. Spencer Wellhofer, "Votes and Votive Candles: Modernization, Secularization, Vatican II, and the Decline of Religious Voting in Italy: 1953–1992," *Comparative Political Studies* 46, no. 1 (2013): 35.

55. Roger Homan, "The Decomposition of the Sacred," *New Directions* 46 (March 1999), accessed March 22, 2018, http://trushare.com/46MAR99/mr99homa.htm.

56. E. J. Gratsch, "Exorcism," in *The New Catholic Encyclopedia* (New York: McGraw–Hill, 1967), 5:551.

57. Callum Brown, *The Death of Christian Britain: Understanding Secularisation, 1800–2000* (Abingdon, UK: Routledge, 2001), 175–192.

58. Pippa Norris and Ronald Inglehart, *Sacred and Secular: Religion and Politics Worldwide* (Cambridge: Cambridge University Press, 2004).

59. Joseph Peter Swain, *Sacred Treasure: Understanding Catholic Liturgical Music* (Collegeville, MN: Liturgical Press, 2012), 23.

60. Veronica Ortenberg, *In Search of the Holy Grail: The Quest for the Middle Ages* (London: Bloomsbury, 2007), 185.

61. Albert J. Bergesen and Andrew M. Greeley, *God in the Movies* (New Brunswick, NJ: Transaction, 2000).

62. Cornelis J. Roelofse, "Satanism, the Occult, Mysticism and Crime: Perspectives on the Inversion of Christianity," *Internal Security* 18, no. 1 (2016): 227.

63. Massimo Introvigne, *Satanism: A Social History* (Boston: Brill, 2016), 110.

64. See, for example, Sheila Whitely, *The Space between the Notes: Rock and the Counter-Culture* (London: Routledge, 1992); and Jonathon Green, *All Dressed Up: The Sixties and the Counterculture* (London: Cape, 1998).

65. Anton Szandor LaVey, *The Satanic Bible* (New York: Avon, 1960). Regarding LaVey, see, above all, the uncritical, yet firsthand account by Blanche Barton, *The Secret Life of a Satanist: The Authorized Biography of Anton LaVey* (Port Townsend, WA: Feral House, 1990), as well as the scholarly studies by James R. Lewis, "Diabolical Authority: Anton LaVey, *The Satanic Bible* and the Satanist 'Tradition,'" *Marburg Journal of Religion* 7, no. 1 (2002): 1–16, and Per Faxneld, "Secret Lineages and De Facto Satanists: Anton LaVey's Use of Esoteric Tradition," in *Contemporary Esotericism*, ed. Egil Asprem and Kenneth Granholm (Sheffield, UK: Equinox, 2013), 72–90.

66. Arthur Lyons, *Satan Wants You: The Cult of Devil Worship in America* (New York: Mysterious Press, 1988), 107.

67. Barton, *The Secret Life of a Satanist*, 114.

68. Bill Ellis, *Raising the Devil: Satanism, New Religions, and the Media* (Lexington: University Press of Kentucky, 2000), 177–184.

69. Anton LaVey, *The Satanic Mass*, Murgenstrumm MM6660, 1968.

70. "Black Sabbath Release 'Debut,'" *BBC*, February 13, 1970, accessed March 22, 2018, http://www.bbc.co.uk/music/sevenages/events/heavy-metal/black-sabbath-release-debut/.

71. Theodore Schick, "With Flames from the Dragon of Darkness," in *Led Zeppelin and Philosophy: All Will Be Revealed*, ed. Scott Calef (Chicago: Open Court, 2009), 100–101. In her contribution to this volume, "'Ramble On': Medievalism as Nostalgic Practice in Led Zeppelin's Use of J. R. R. Tolkien," Caitlin Carlos examines another aspect of Led Zepplin's appropriation of medievalist tropes, pp. 530–546.

72. Coven, *Witchcraft Destroys Minds & Reaps Souls*, Mercury SR 61239, 1969.

73. Hugh B. Urban, *New Age, Neopagan, and New Religious Movements: Alternative Spirituality in Contemporary America* (Berkeley: University of California Press, 2015), 192.

74. James R. Lewis, "Satanic Ritual Abuse," in *The Oxford Handbook of New Religious Movements*, ed. Lewis and Inga B. Tollefsen (New York: Oxford University Press), 2: 213.

75. Barton, *The Secret Life of a Satanist*, 108.

76. About *Rosemary's Baby*, see Lucy Fischer, "Birth Traumas: Parturition and Horror in 'Rosemary's Baby,'" *Cinema Journal* 31, no. 3 (1992): 3–18.

77. *Satanis: The Devil's Mass*, dir. Ray Laurent, music by Anton Lavey (Sherpix, 1970; rereleased DVD, Something Weird Video, 2003), accessed March 22, 2018, https://www.youtube.com/watch?v=N5Aha-vkkxg&t=22s.

78. Joshua Gunn, "Prime-Time Satanism: Rumor-Panic and the Work of Iconic Topoi," *Visual Communication* 4, no. 1 (2005): 108.

79. The full text of the Black Mass can be found in *Missale Satanicum* (Akron, OH: Libreria Esoterica Editrice Il Reame d'Inverno, 2012).

80. Richard K. Emmerson, "'Englysch Laten' and 'Franch': Language as Sign of Evil in Medieval English Drama," in *The Devil, Heresy and Witchcraft in the Middle Ages: Essays in Honour of Jeffrey B. Russell*, ed. Alberto Ferreiro (Leiden: Brill, 1998), 316–317.

81. Christopher Partridge, *The Lyre of Orpheus: Popular Music, the Sacred, and the Profane* (New York: Oxford University Press, 2013), 44.

82. "Ominous Latin Chanting," TV Tropes, accessed March 22, 2018, http://tvtropes.org/pmwiki/pmwiki.php/Main/OminousLatinChanting.

83. Jerry Goldsmith, interview in *666: The Omen Revealed*, DVD, Directed by J.M. Kenny, Los Angeles: Twentieth Century Fox, 2000, 36:53–37:10, at 6:53–37:10.

84. See Deaville, "The Topos of 'Evil Medieval,'" 32, for selected comments by cinema audience members about their dark associations for this music.

CHAPTER 32

FANTASY MEDIEVALISM AND SCREEN MEDIA

JAMES COOK

THIS chapter focuses on fantasy medievalism on screen and its connection to genres of music that may be seen as equally medievalist in origin and aesthetic: progressive rock, heavy metal, and folk. It gives an overview of the medievalist features of the genres before discussing how they are used in a range of fantasy screen media from *Legend* to *Highlander* and from *Game of Thrones* to *The Witcher*. There has been a historical move from the representation of the fantasy medieval through rock to its representation through folk in more recent years. This representational shift not only relies on changes in the way that medievalist fantasy positions itself for audience but also represents a change in the way that aspects such as power, gender, sex, and social structure are formulated within medievalist fantasy.

Prog Rock, Heavy Metal, Fantasy, and Medievalism

Progressive rock and heavy metal have a history of influence with fantasy (and medievalism more broadly) that is complex, multifaceted, and surprisingly mutual. The mutability of the terms prog and metal adds a further level of complexity to any discussion. In many cases, it may be asked where prog ends and metal begins.[1] For example, Deep Purple, perhaps more commonly thought of as heavy metal (or at least proto–heavy metal) certainly incorporated aspects of prog, and even prog legends King Crimson could be seen to incorporate aspects of heavy metal. A more realistic picture perhaps instead paints this web of associations as a nexus of mutually supportive ideas, drawing from similar cultural trends but also including direct and deliberate borrowing or influence. With this in mind, the generic distinctions drawn below may seem somewhat arbitrary.[2] Nonetheless, for all their interconnectedness, there are clear distinctions in the way that aspects of the medieval are used to construct meanings in each genre, and it is on these distinctions that this essay will ultimately focus. As I will show, both progressive rock and heavy metal (though the reasons for medievalist borrowings are often markedly different) can be seen to draw creatively from the past in a way that presents the medievalist themes as Other while collapsing any sense of chronological distance.

Progressive Rock

Perhaps the most directly obvious associations with fantasy and medievalism come with prog. Both medieval and fantasy elements are seen as essential ingredients of the genre. A wonderful, if tongue-in-cheek, example is Bill Bailey's "Leg of Time," which, as a send-up of the genre, makes frequent allusion to both medievalist and broader fantasy tropes, especially in its opening line: "The jester hops on the leg of time / the curse of wizard nation / Madrigal chanting is no crime / when you're suckled by a blind Alsatian." The question of from where these medievalist aspects are derived has been explored more fully elsewhere in this volume. Nonetheless, for the purposes of this discussion, a few of these aspects require further attention. The first of these is the nationalistic aspect of prog. As an explicitly British phenomenon and one that was enormously influenced by the art music tradition, much of its medievalism could be seen as an exploration of the art music tradition of its ancestral home.[3] Edward Macan has traced Western art influences on the genre back into the medieval period, mediated through the Anglican tradition and the singing of hymns in school.[4] Through the Anglican church, English music of the sixteenth century is often held as a high point of national artistic expression. Similar arguments could be made for the music of England but a few generations earlier, which, in the fifteenth century, reached a level of international renown and spread that would be unsurpassed until the Beatles.[5]

Part of the attraction clearly also came from a broader aesthetic and ideological desire to explore the premodern. As Paul Hardwick has noted, the apparent dichotomy between the romanticized ideals of the nontechnological and premodern on the one hand, and the exploration of the most advanced technological musical advancements of the time on the other, appears somewhat unusual at first glance.[6] Nonetheless, Bill Martin contends, such a combination of past and future was common to the New Left political thought and counterculture with which prog might be connected.[7] Hardwick, for instance, when addressing the same question of paradox, is reminded of artist and socialist William Morris's earlier combination of medievalism, socialism, and forward-looking ideas.[8] According to Macan, such idealization of the premodern was essentially twofold:

> Fantasy landscapes and medieval or Eastern imagery come to present the idealized society—close to the earth, based on mutual dependence and a strong sense of community, linked with the past—to which the hippies aspired. On the other hand,

bizarre sci-fi imagery is often used to represent the oppressive, soulless bureaucracy which the counterculture believed is crushing the life out of Western culture.... This same general dichotomy is evident in the lyrics as well.[9]

Such a formulation, as Charles Elkins has noted, situates medievalism as a reaction against the rationalistic, antiheroic, materialist, and empiricist bent of modern society through escape into a world where old certainties can be reasserted.[10]

Such medievalist associations may present obvious connections between prog and fantasy, and yet further, more explicit, links may be drawn too. As Hardwick has noted, Arthurian legend, and especially the notion of the quest for the Grail, may be seen as a particularly common trope in prog.[11] Arthurian myth does tie many of our current strands together. It is explicitly British, created as part of Geoffrey of Monmouth's great nationalistic legendary history and dealing, predominantly, with the "matter of Britain."[12] It is also doubly medievalist, as a tale drawn explicitly from the "real" Middle Ages (that is initially beginning as a medieval story) and that may represent at least some elements of historical events and including some historical people. Nonetheless, it is clearly fantastical, as a myth that has built up numerous popular accretions as it has traversed history. Hardwick goes further than these associations, however, suggesting that Arthurian legend may stand as a metaphor for artistic endeavor and prog itself, in the minds of its performers. The example of Rick Wakeman's *The Myths and Legends of King Arthur and the Knights of the Round Table* is particularly striking. The album art makes much of the fantasy and medievalist aspects, "housed in a sumptuous, embossed gatefold cover and accompanied by a lavish twelve-page booklet of lyrics illustrated with medieval and pseudo-medieval woodcuts."[13] Wakeman's own discussion of this album emphasized a link between the musicians and King Arthur and his knights and especially, given that the tide of critical opinion had started to turn against prog, between Lancelot's quest and that of the musician. According to Hardwick,

> the musician, then, may be seen as the helmed knight depicted inside the gatefold; victorious, triumphant, and almost—but not quite—within the reach of the Grail, which surmounts the combatants and gives purpose to their endeavors. Indeed, the album itself, in Malorian terms, is a display of "prowess" in order to win "worship."[14]

The allure of the related concepts of fantasy and medievalism are key to the power of prog. They help to give an escape from the social dislocation of modernity, evoking, as Susan Fast has argued, "a time of greater integrity and substantiality than what we perceive to have in the present [. . .] dominated by the warmth of feeling and emotion (which is equated with soul and spirituality) rather than the coldness of reason."[15] Importantly, though, these aspects are divorced from any sense of chronology, becoming part of a larger Other that stands for everything outside the dominant culture. There is, nonetheless, a curious contradiction at the heart of prog in which dominant hegemonic musical structures are both rejected and evoked. Recourse to medievalism allows it to be "radically enough removed from the tradition of classical music making that continues in the present (modern instruments, the tonal system)" to give it a countercultural edge, while borrowings from the heyday of English music and, especially, as Fast has noted, reference to the power of medieval English kings nonetheless imparts a power tied to this dominant culture.[16]

Heavy Metal

Metal's connections to fantasy and medievalism are perhaps less obvious, but direct influence does clearly exist among heavy metal luminaries. Several songs by Led Zeppelin can be seen to be modeled directly on Tolkien, for instance. The 1969 track "Ramble On," from their second album, opens with the line "Leaves are falling all around," aping the opening of Tolkien's *Namárië*, "Ah! like gold fall the leaves in the wind."[17] More obvious allusions come later when both Mordor and Gollum are referenced, even if the broader narrative is clearly not drawn from Tolkien:

> Mine's a tale that can't be told
> My freedom I hold dear
> How years ago in days of old
> When magic filled the air
> 'Twas in the darkest depths of Mordor
> I met a girl so fair
> But Gollum, and the evil one crept up
> And slipped away with her

The 1971 tracks "Misty Mountain Hop" and "The Battle of Evermore" also make clear references to Tolkien, with the name of the former derived from a mountain range in Middle Earth. "The Battle of Evermore" has a somewhat more complex relationship to this source, clearly referencing "ring-wraiths" within the text and sketching a narrative that, more broadly, might be seen to reference some events of *The Return of the King*.[18] All three of these songs were released shortly after *The Lord of the Rings* became a literary phenomenon in the mid-1960s, much the same period that similarly focused prog rock was being written. Indeed, some metal bands drew even deeper influence from Tolkien's world. The band Hobbit (whose name requires no explanation) release music that is exclusively based on Tolkien's world, as a key part of the genre known as heavy mithril, based on the fictional metal found in Middle-earth. Blind Guardian, by contrast, may be considered somewhat less devoted to Tolkien with a rather broader output, yet their 1998 album was based entirely on Tolkien's *The Silmarillion*, as are many works by the Finnish band Battlelore or the Austrian band Summoning. These fantasy borrowings are, in many ways, rather more direct than those seen in prog. Nonetheless, as well as borrowing narrative and lyrical aspects from medievalist fantasy, metal also commonly drew heavily on broader aspects of fantasy aesthetics. While prog borrowed somewhat softer, more overtly medieval, fantastical, and folk-inspired imagery, transferred from the psychedelic hippy culture's interest in Tolkien, most metal (excluding those bands just discussed) generally appeared to draw more deeply on sword and sorcery imagery. In particular, hypermasculinized male warrior figures (such as the muscled Conan the Barbarian, resplendent in loincloth, greased muscles, and carrying serious weaponry) would take center stage alongside sexualized female warriors. Combined with satanic imagery, often borrowing from dark or horror fantasy itself, these images came to dominate the visual side of metal iconography.[19] Such iconography is still very much alive in bands such as Conan, Majesty, and Rhapsody of Fire. As Gibbons has noted in his recent study of early video-game scores (including several fantasy examples), there is a nexus of related media here that cater to the same demographic, with heavy metal, sword and sorcery films, video games, and the Dungeons & Dragons role-playing game "being squarely marketed at the archetypical so-called 'geek culture' typically represented in the 1980s as disenfranchised teenage males."[20] Citing Donovan, he notes the enormous impact of Dungeons & Dragons on the narrative, gameplay, and settings of fantasy video games such as *Wizardry* and *Gauntlet*, alongside the imagery and even sound effects from films such as *Conan the Barbarian*.[21] Certainly, all these related media seem to have drawn scorn from conservative and religious groups because of their associations with rebellion and the satanic.[22]

Robert Walser has famously explored the forging of masculinity and exploration of power dynamics and related anxieties within and through heavy metal.[23] Much of this relates to Fiske's assertion that "our society denies most males adequate means of exercising the power upon which their masculinity apparently depends. Masculinity is thus socially and psychologically insecure; and its insecurity produces the need for its constant reachievement."[24] Such assertions (or negotiations) of power are, according to Walser, multifaceted, ranging from the musical (vocal extremes, power chords, distortion, sheer volume), to the visual (swaggering males, "noisy" clothing, phallic thrusted guitars and mic stands), to the more performative such as "visual enactments of spectacular transgression" through hypermasculinity or androgyny. Many of the "satanic" or mythological aspects are seen by Walser as simply ways of negotiating power. Iron Maiden's "symbolic borrowings" of "Christianity, alchemy, myth, astrology, [and] the mystique of vanished Egyptian dynasties" (all of which might be seen as symbolically relating either to fantasy, medievalism, or both) are "available in the modern world as sources of power and mystery." Importantly, "such eclectic constructions of power … are possible *only because* they are not perceived as tied to strict historical contexts."[25] As with prog, which saw the Otherness of the premodern world as a site for the negotiation of the frustrations with the dominant social norms of their time, metal also explores concepts of the Other. According to Walser, metal is "nearly always concerned with making sense of the world" but does so by exploring the "'other,' everything that hegemonic society does not want to acknowledge, the dark side of the daylit, enlightened adult world."[26] For both genres, therefore, medievalism is a powerful means of constructing meaning. It does not situate something in the past, but rather offers a rich body of material from which new meanings can be forged.

Folk, Fantasy, and Medievalism

Like prog and metal, folk has long had associations with fantasy and medievalism, especially the latter of these two phenomena. Perhaps the most obvious manifestation of this is the increasing degree to which folk music has come to be used as a musical shorthand for representations of the medieval in screen media. Simon Nugent has recently made this point for the subgenre of Celtic folk.[27] His examples are striking, perhaps the most so being Ridley Scott's *Robin Hood*. In one scene, in which the people of Nottingham (then a rather small and rustic village) dance, the underscore is a piece of preexistent music, *Mná na hÉireann* (Women of Ireland), a setting, by Seán Ó Riada (1931–1971), of the poem of the same name by the eighteenth-century poet, Peadar Ó Doirnín (ca. 1700–1769). Though ostensibly about the love of a man for a woman, it is more commonly understood as an allegory for nationalistic love of Ireland. The song is itself rather famous, having been covered by many popular singers and appearing in several films (often explicitly linked to the Irish diaspora). In short, a more obviously Irish song would perhaps be hard to find. Its use to underscore a scene in Nottingham therefore seems at first strange. Indeed, Robin Hood's story and its connection to Nottingham is exceptionally well known and the location of the scene is further emphasized by onscreen text. As Nugent has noted, the film's composer seems to have seen little contradiction, however, stating that "since the film is set in England in the twelfth century, I wanted to pick up on the time period and location by utilizing Medieval and Celtic solo instruments."[28] This concept of Celtic folk coming to stand for "authentic" medieval music is not just limited to historically situated drama. Similar examples may be found in fantasy films that draw on medieval tropes, such as *How to Train Your Dragon* or The Lord of the Rings trilogy. Similar sentiments, linking concepts of Celticness to music of the distant past, are mentioned by Howard Shore, the composer of The Lord of the Rings film score, who stated that

> with *The Fellowship of the Ring* we were trying to design a piece of work that would seem as if it had been written five or six thousand years ago. Celtic music is very old—the ideas and sounds take you back in a historical sense to the very origins of music.[29]

Such links between Celtic folk and the medieval in popular culture, according to Nugent, draw from a number of sources. In particular, they seem to relate to marketing strategies for Celtic folk that sought to portray it as the vestige of an authentic (and international) folk tradition stretching back into premodernity and yet only surviving in the Celtic regions. Such a tradition may well have begun as part of a way to evoke (and capitalize on) nostalgia for a lost homeland within the American Celtic diaspora, but it has since spread far beyond this to those outside this diasporic community.[30] Perceptions of authenticity here are clearly one of the greatest appeals of this kind of folk as a representation of the medieval.

Celtic music may also carry other associations relating to social structure. As Jane Tolmey has noted, fantasy writers such as Gael Baudino and Patricia Kennealy-Morrison turn to pagan Celtic sources as an alternative to what they perceive as the medieval Christian degradation of women.[31] This association between pagan prehistory, matriarchy, and freedom for women seems a common theme in the popular conception of the past, echoed by theorists such as Albert Classen.[32] Colonial narratives seem an important part of the construction of Celtic ideals too; the concept of the Celts being "war mad, high spirited and quick to battle" were, as Barry Cunliffe has argued, revived by colonial powers as a way of explaining the frequent rebellions of occupied Celtic regions.[33] In popular culture, these ideas often intertwine, forming a broad field of ideas that may be freely borrowed.

Fast's discussion of folk makes similar claims, emphasizing the degree to which folk-rock band Steeleye Span constructed an identity based on associations with the archaic, the preindustrialized, the pastoral, and the lower class.[34] Fast also notes that, in their album *Below the Salt*, Steeleye Span make a point of indicating the sources for each of their songs. To me, this seems another clear example of privileging narratives of authenticity, suggesting that folk is the true, unchanged music of the medieval peasantry. Perhaps the best example is Steeleye Span's retelling of the sixteenth-century Latin-texted song "Gaudete." Their performance eschews the traditional pronunciation of Latin (be that the pronunciation used in most modern performances or an attempt at re-creating the original sixteenth-century pronunciation as would have been used in Sweden, where the song originated) and instead uses an exaggerated form of Estuary English, removing the learned/sacred connotations and replacing them with "rustic" ones. Their "translation," too, undermines the religious nature of the song, instead emphasizing its pastoral connections. In essence, folk is presented as early music and early music as folk.

Such an approach to the equating of folk with earlier musical practices has historical precedence. As Edward Breen has shown, David Munrow's pioneering work continuously looked to the folk music traditions of other parts of the world to seek historically informed playing techniques and styles.[35] This has had the effect, through the centrality of Munrow to the historically informed performance practice movement, of placing ideas of folk and world musics at the heart of the debate around authenticity in early music.

Folk's relationship to medievalism is therefore rather different than that of prog or heavy metal. For the latter two forms, medievalism offered something creative with which to play, be that nationalistic nostalgia or communal antimodernism with prog or the negotiation of power dynamics or masculinity in metal. Folk, in contrast, seems to be presented popularly *as* medieval. Rather than drawing associations from popular imaginings about the past, it instead is seen as an authentic and unchanged music of the medieval peasantry, or at least as close an approximation as can be found.

Prog, Metal, and Folk as Fantasy Medieval Score

Janet Halfyard's edited collection *The Music of Fantasy Cinema* traced a narrative for the representation of fantasy, arguing that, from the orchestrally produced fantasy scores of the 1970s, rock and pop became the predominant musical representation from the 1980s onward.[36] There does seem to be a trend in this period toward the representation of fantasy through rock, as shown by many of the examples found in her edited collection such as *Legend*, *Highlander*, *Flash Gordon*, or *Labyrinth* and others, such as *Heavy Metal*, from a similar era, or even the more recent *A Knight's Tale*. Nonetheless, I would argue that this is a trend of limited duration that has more recently been rather overtaken by an interest in using folk or folklike music. We have already seen reference to what Gibbons has labeled "the archetypical so-called 'geek culture' typically represented in the 1980s as disenfranchised teenage males."[37] Might these films simply be marketed to take advantage of this particular consumer group, merging many aspects of their shared interests? Certainly, this is one explanation, but it seems that broader concepts of the changing representations of medievalist fantasy are important here too. Two examples drawn from those discussed in *The Music of Fantasy Cinema* may stand as useful points of comparison here: *Legend* and *Highlander*. As Lee Barron has noted, *Legend* is a rather strange case of a film that has two complete soundtracks, one by the orchestral film composer Jerry Goldsmith and the other by the Electronica band Tangerine Dream.[38] As Barron has discussed, some of the reason for replacing Goldsmith with Tangerine Dream may have come from a desire to replicate the experimentations of films such as *Top Gun* using tie-ins with popular music to bring about a younger audience.[39] Barron himself expresses some doubts as to how effective this strategy may have been given the somewhat niche style that the band promoted. Perhaps one route for understanding this more thoroughly is through precisely the geek culture discussed previously. Certainly, the electronic experimentation of Tangerine Dream may not have been popular to a mainstream pop audience, but it would have been a point of contact with the 1980s geek culture and with prog. Indeed, I would argue that it is through the lens of prog that we might best understand the use of Tangerine Dream in this film score, their electronic experimentation and synthesizers calling to mind prog experimentation and orchestration, and attendant connections with medievalist fantasy. Particularly striking is the use of synthesized harpsichord sounds, which have a clear connection with prog, both harpsichord-dominated tracks such as "Madrigal" by Yes and the broader sound world, which often made of use harpsichords, clavinovas, and other unusual keyboard timbres.

Perhaps the most obviously prog-related track from the soundtrack is "Cottage." The synth and harpsichord combination draw a clear parallel with contemporary prog, but this is further emphasized by the harmonic language. This track, as with much prog, exploits ambiguity between major and minor tonality and makes use of frequent chromaticisms. Many of its harmonic passages are common to prog, such as III–IV(♯3)–I(♯3) (Example 32.1), which play on major/minor ambiguity. In this context, the opening

EXAMPLE 32.1 Prog rock–inspired harmony in soundtrack for *Legend*, Tangerine Dream, "Cottage."

Eb

C minor: III

F

IV

C

I

EXAMPLE 32.2 Prog rock–inspired harmony in soundtrack for *Legend*, Tangerine Dream, "Cottage."

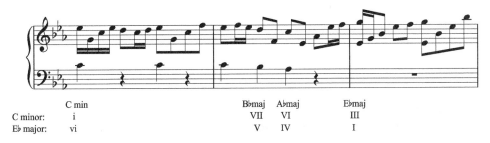

C min

C minor: i

Eb major: vi

Bbmaj Abmaj

VII   VI

V   IV

Ebmaj

III

I

EXAMPLE 32.3 Prog rock–inspired harmony in soundtrack for *Legend*, Tangerine Dream, "Cottage."

C min

D min

G min

A min

i–VII–VI–III (Example 32.2) sounds similarly prog influenced since it could be heard either as i–VII–VI–III in the minor or as a vi–V–IV–I blues turn in the major. The frequent modulations by the circle of fifths, here studiously keeping minor through modulations (Example 32.3), are also particularly common in prog. Interestingly, many of these turns could be viewed as medievalist in their own right, harmonically exploiting the minor/major ambiguity through the imposition of *musica ficta* in pretonal music and orchestrationally exploiting the clear historicizing nature of the harpsichord.[40] Even the chromatically adjusted plagal cadence of Example 32.1 can be seen as a nod to the hymn tune tradition. This is clearly a soundtrack designed to evoke the medievalist prog fantasy world of the songs of Wakeman's *The Legends and Myths of King Arthur* and others of its ilk.

Any connection between this score and prog is clearly strengthened further by the presence of Jon Anderson and Brian Ferry—of Yes and Roxy Music, respectively—both clearly recognizable through their singing. As Barron has noted, the Otherness of this film score may well have been an attempt to capture the fantastical nature of the world here created.[41] Nonetheless, when compared to other scores by the same band, such a connection does not seem fully to explain the situation. Polanski's *Macbeth*, for instance, is certainly not fantasy, but rather an attempt at a gritty, realistic reinterpretation of the medieval source that Shakespeare used for his famous play. Tangerine Dream's score for this film then surely should not be seen as simply an expression of Otherness (though historical distance and unfamiliarity are clearly linked) but rather as an attempt to draw on the medievalist associations of progressive rock (updated for a more modern audience through electronica) and especially those relating to a sense of wonder and free exploration within the premodern world.

Highlander is a rather different film, which draws heavily on metal rather than progressive rock aesthetics. As J. Drew Stephen notes, this connection seems, most obviously, to draw on associations with heavy metal, power, masculinity, and violence, in particular reinforcing "the overtly masculine and violently aggressive nature of the characters with whom they are associated."[42] Of course, much of *Highlander* takes place in the modern day, so it might be argued that the associations drawn here are not with medievalist fantasy, but with more modern representations of gender and power. Nonetheless, as Stephen notes, even when Kurgan (with whom much of heavy metal soundscape is associated) is first introduced as a sixteenth-century warrior, he is still underscored by distorted power chords.[43] Crucially, distortion is recognized as a representation of extreme power.[44] Here, recourse to the medieval is clearly used, as it is in metal, to excuse aggressive masculinity and violence as a way of sidestepping the civilizing effects of modernity.

In both of these examples, the fantasy medieval is represented, at least partially, through rock, especially drawing on associations between both progressive rock and heavy metal and medievalism. While this might partly have been a result of marketing concerns, especially relating to tying the films to the kinds of subcultures of the 1980s most likely to have consumed fantasy, it also seems to relate to broader narrative themes. Importantly, it also demonstrates that, at the time, the intrusion of modern rock sound into medievalist worlds was not seen as disconcerting or temporally incompatible. As I will show, with two long-running small screen series—one a video game, the other a television show—attitudes toward rock as a representation of the medieval of screen have changed extensively in more recent years. Both examples are representative of broader trends that might be seen in shows such as *Vikings* or games such as *World of Warcraft*. Nonetheless, both exemplify these broader trends especially effectively and, *The Witcher* in particular, because of its longevity as a series, may serve as a microcosm of the phenomena here discussed.

Game of Thrones

Game of Thrones, like the similarly popular fantasy screen media such as Lord of the Rings or Harry Potter films, draws on a series of books (George R. R. Martin's *A Song of Ice and Fire*) as its source material. Unlike both of these, however, it was released through the medium of television, rather than film. As a forerunner in what has become known as the golden age of television, it broke new ground in many ways, making full use of the new kinds of epic storytelling made possible by the medium.[45]

The series has an original score by Ramin Djawadi, known also for *Clash of the Titans*, *Pacific Rim*, and *Iron Man*. His score for *Game of Thrones* mixes aspects of postromantic filmic composition, folk, diegetic period-style music, and more ambient horror-type music. For the purposes of this discussion, the most interesting aspect is the way that rock is used within the series. In a way, rock is a constant silent presence throughout many scenes and yet it is never allowed to enter sonically into the tightly controlled world of the score, in the manner of some of the examples discussed previously. Nonetheless, as has been discussed elsewhere,[46] the series makes frequent use of cameos by famous rock musicians. These include Gary Lightbody of Snow Patrol, who plays a Bolton soldier who sings "The Bear and the Maiden Fair" on horseback, Will Champion of Coldplay, who plays a bodhrán at the famous Red Wedding, and Sigur Rós, who perform the "Rains of Castamere" at the wedding of Joffrey and Sansa.[47] In each of these cases, the rock musicians do not play rock music. Instead, they are part of a diegetic group of musicians who play folk-style versions of music (which is described in the books) on period instruments.

The singing style that Lightbody uses for his performance of "The Bear and the Maiden Fair" is clearly drawn from the Celtic folk tradition and seems designed to suggest an authentically medieval setting (as discussed previously). Given the dramatic context of this scene (the characters seem to have a low socioeconomic status and are at the end of a long journey on horseback), instrumental accompaniment would not seem to be appropriate. Performances with instruments offer additional opportunities for medievalist references. In the famous Red Wedding scene, for example, Champion appears as a member of the small band of instrumentalists (an ensemble that includes two lutes, a psaltery, a bass viol—played with a modern cello rather than viol bow hold— a bodhrán, and a portative organ). They play both "The Bear and the Maiden Fair" and "The Rains of Castamere" (this latter being rather important narratively) in a setting that is diegetic, even if the instruments do not perfectly match those heard. Clearly, both the instruments shown on screen and those heard playing are period instruments, helping to situate the sound world in a vaguely (that is, nonspecifically) medievalist past. The same context is found in the Joffrey/Sansa wedding scene, in which Sigur Rós play a deliberately maudlin setting of "The Rains of Castamere" on a portative organ (much to the displeasure of the king). Again, both the sound world and the images are meant to historicize. In each of these cases, rock is present but never heard, other than perhaps in the imagination of the viewers who are sufficiently familiar with the bands in question.

This is not the only use of rock within the show, however, since both songs are heard in the closing credits with explicitly modern rock arrangements. "The Bear and the Maiden Fair" is given an uptempo punk treatment by the Hold Steady while Sigur Rós give their own reworking of "The Rains of Castamere." That each of these rock recompositions is relegated to the liminal space of the credits seems key here. The tightly constructed sonic verisimilitude of the on-screen world is therefore never broken, with only ahistorical postromantic filmic music, folk, and medievalist period pastiche heard on screen.

The fact that these are resettings of the same songs also seems important here. In essence, we have the same song viewed through two different frames. In our world, as represented by the space afforded by the credits—in which the created world of *Game of Thrones* essentially collapses in on itself through the revelation that the characters are actors reading a script—these songs are presented as rock. Within the world of *Game of Thrones*, the same song is heard either as folk or as period pastiche on medieval instruments and, as we have seen, in the popular imagination, folk and medieval music are, in essence, the same thing.

The Witcher

The Witcher is a series of high-fantasy role-playing games that mix action and the kind of branching narrative found in games such as those in the Mass Effect franchise. The series is based on the Polish fantasy novels of Andrzej Sapkowski and, like much fantasy, it is clearly set in a world based on the western Middle Ages. The Polish origin of both the books on which the game series is based and the game developer have clearly also had an impact, with aspects that are clearly redolent of Poland and Polish myth and folklore.

The score for the third game is (by and large) adaptive, relying on layered audio stems that respond to player action. As the composer Marcin Przybylowicz has described in a recent interview with the *Tech Times*, "the cues (that were interactive) are divided into smaller layers, which come together, in the case of a combat cue, only when we are dealing with a very powerful enemy. If the enemy is small ... only the first layer of the piece will play."[48] This form of composition is the norm in video games these days since it enables music to feel responsive to player action. As Przybylowicz has described, these cues are often related to particular situations (such as combat), but may also relate to the presence of characters or ideas. Crucially for us, these layered cues are reorchestrated for each geographical area of the fictional world so as to present and preserve its aural identity. The importance of medievalist tropes for each of these areas of the game has been explored elsewhere,[49] but an overview will be given here. In a separate interview with IC-Radio.de, Przybylowicz described the composition process, and specifically the aesthetic ideas behind each region, as follows:

No Mans (sic.) Land [Velen] is a war ravaged land.... It's also full of slavic references, pagan beliefs etc.... Then, there's Novigrad—the biggest city in northern kingdoms.... I decided music in Novigrad should be more civilized—that's why there are lots of string instruments playing there (dulcimer, bouzouki, guitars, lutes, cimbalom etc.), and overall tone of the music is lighter, [and] reminds [me] a bit music of [the] Renaissance. Finally, [the] Skellige Isles—[a] region with Celtic, Scottish and Norse references, that had to be reflected in music as well. Use of bagpipes, flutes and Scandinavian folk instruments corresponds with that setting. On top of that, I had to think how it would all work together. That's where our themes come in.... We use those themes in every major location... [and] we reorchestrate them with instruments corresponding to a particular region.[50]

This approach gives an extremely effective blend of unity and variety. There is a sense that the world hangs together (sonically) with each part related to a greater whole. Nonetheless, there is also a sense of clear difference between each region that utilizes different types of medievalism to signify deep concepts of social structure. Broadly speaking, the world can be divided into the regions of Skellige, Oxfenfurt/Novigrad, and Velen/White Orchard for the main release game.[51]

Skellige draws deeply on the "Celtic" associations discussed previously. It is an archipelago of Highlands and Islands-esque landscape occupied by clans that form a loose nation but also raid one another. Its occupants dress in tartans and speak with Irish accents.[52] The Celtic elements of Skellige are infused with other markers of "northern" medievalism, in much the same way as is seen in *How to Train Your Dragon*, in which Celtic and Viking/Norse elements are merged. In Skellige, while the occupants wear tartans, they also wear stereotypical Viking helmets, travel in longships, and practice both longship burial and widow sacrifice.[53] The degree to which the landscape dominates the people of Skellige—extraordinarily powerful thunderstorms often dominate the audiovisual landscape when traveling this part of the world—rather than its people dominating the landscape, is also common to this form of medievalism. At a social level, too, aspects of Celtic medievalism are felt in this area. Its people are quick to anger and enjoy battle, but they are also honorable: a rough-hewn but honest folk. Women have a far more equal role here than in other areas of the game world, too, contributing as warriors and even as leaders. Skellige's main religion also relies on female priestesses and emphasizes a commitment to nature, all aspects often found in representations of the Celtic medieval.

Skellige also draws deeply on Celtic medievalism in terms of sound. As the composer has noted, the region makes extensive use of bagpipes and flutes, playing Celtic-style folk melodies. The Hardanger fiddle, a Norse folk instrument often used (such as in The Lord of the Rings trilogy, where it performed most of the leitmotifs relating to the Rohirrim) to connote northern medievalism in general and Celtic medievalism as a subset of this, also appears prominently. The female vocal work in this area is also delivered in a manner that is fast becoming the norm for northern/Celtic medieval representations, using a gentle, high, and metrically free approach that draws obvious comparisons with the soundtrack for the northern parts of the world in another fantasy video game, *Age of Conan*. Notably, in *Age of Conan*, the northern medievalist aspects are made clearer by Norwegian singer Helene Bøksle singing an Old Norse text taken from the Völuspá, the first poem of the Poetic Edda. Perhaps most important, music in Skellige is nondiegetic, as though it is the very sound of the landscape itself.

Velen also draws, to an extent, on folk instrumentation but almost entirely eschews Celtic associations. Instead, it merges two other common medievalist tropes, the pastoral and orientalist. These two ideas are used variously to demonstrate the more idyllic parts of the area and those terribly ravaged by war. The dirty and war-ravaged rusticity of this area particularly draws on microtonal inflection, glissandi, and non-Western instruments such as the kemenche, electric cello, hurdy-gurdy, bowed gusli, gheychak, and the bowed yaylı.

In contrast to both of these regions, the more urban areas of Novigrad and Oxenfurt almost entirely eschew folk connections, focusing more clearly on period pastiche. The music here is far more metrical and makes use of a more Renaissance sound world dominated by plucked and struck strings and percussion. The music here is also clearly both by and for people, with Renaissance dance bands roaming the streets providing clearly diegetic music (to which onscreen nonplayer characters clearly react) that gets louder as the character approaches. One particularly striking scene features a trobaritz who gives a concert performance that, notably, begins with tuning and ends with applause. Unlike most other parts of the game, the player must sit and watch the complete performance. There is a clear attempt at creating a contrast between recognizably medieval and Renaissance areas of the game world. The narrative emphasizes a divide between the fantastical medievalist world and the more rational, urban centers, which also plays out in the score. Religion in the urban centers is also clearly different. Rather than the priestesses of Skellige, the Temple of the Eternal Fire has male priests, who preside over a clear stand-in for Christianity. The temple's inquisitions and burnings of magic users have a clear historical resonance with regrettable periods of Christian history. Musically, as you approach their main temple, the only male voices in the game are heard, with low, textless chanting increasing in volume the closer you get to the building. This clearly draws on another common medievalist trope in which chanting male voices signify the internal space of a church.

In all, folk music is clearly important in the creation of this score. Indeed, the Polish folk band Percival are jointly credited as its composers,[54] having adapted some of their previous releases to fit the soundtrack alongside newly composed works. Folk certainly pervades all aspects of this score, coming to represent the authentic medieval world in those areas of the game that are more rural and rustic. It is clearly and deliberately contrasted with more Renaissance pastiche–style compositions in those areas of the world that have begun to feel the touch of modernity. As with *Game of Thrones*, here folk is used to evoke particularly rural, peasant-filled, and rustic medievalism alongside the period-pastiche aspects that represent more urban or courtly settings. Rock, again like *Game of Thrones*, is completely barred from the on-screen world.

This rejection of rock has not always been present in *The Witcher* game series, however. The first game of the series, released in 2007 and with a score by Adam Skorupa and Pawel Blaszczak, instead blended rock, and particularly heavy metal, into the wider score (alongside the postromantic film score and period pastiche). In particular, heavily distorted guitar and heavy percussion were often heard in fight cues. This is a clear point of contact with *Highlander*, in which sixteenth-century masculine violence was represented through power chords. Arguably, *The Witcher* invokes an early period still (or rather an almost flattened-out temporal world where references to the thirteenth century sit happily alongside references to the sixteenth century). Interestingly, the second game of the series, released in 2011, seems to chart a middle ground. The heavily distorted guitar no longer makes itself felt in the broader soundtrack. It does, however, insert itself into the opening cutscene. This scene is something of a tour de force. It opens with a quintessential scene of medieval celebration, complete with diegetic period music including shawms and a hurdy-gurdy. As this celebration rapidly turns sour because of the attack by an assassin, the scene turns to slow motion, underscored with what has become an almost operatic soundtrack that fairly oozes with dramatic tension. Following the successful assassination, a brief (less than ten-second) distorted heavy metal guitar riff is heard, as the assassin (muscular and garbed in leather, of course) surveys his handiwork. Interestingly, this mirrors the use of rock in *Game of Thrones* in which it is pushed into the liminal spaces such as closing credits or, in this case, opening cutscenes.

Conclusions: Authenticity, Nostalgia, and New Fantasy Audiences

The position of fantasy within popular media has undoubtedly changed in recent years from a genre marketed either at children or at explicitly (or perhaps explicit) adult geek culture to one that is both far broader and transcends the boundary between child and adult audiences. The Lord of the Rings trilogy is often viewed as being instrumental in this. All three films are regularly listed within the top ten (certainly top one hundred) films. *The Two Towers* and *Return of the King* were the highest grossing films of 2002 and 2003, respectively. In fact, the former was, at one point, the fourth highest grossing film of all time and the latter was the second. Another important fantasy film, the first of the Harry Potter series, premiered the same year as *The Fellowship of the Ring* and succeeded in beating it at the box office, becoming the highest grossing film of 2001. While films with a fantasy topic had previously been successful (Disney's *Snow White* is the tenth highest grossing film of all time, if inflation is taken into account), this is arguably the first time that fantasy had made a significant impact on the broader cinema-going public, transcending the idea of fantasy being for children or young adults or for an adolescent geek culture.[55]

The historical trend traced here from representation of the fantasy medieval through progressive rock and/or heavy metal may therefore be seen to relate purely to these marketing concerns, with progressive rock and heavy metal no longer seeming relevant to the new fantasy market. Nonetheless, I would argue that there is more to it than this for the use of heavy metal in particular, though changing demographics must surely have some impact. I would instead situate the importance of this change within an understanding of the way that sex, power, and violence is portrayed within these media. Both *Game of Thrones* and *The Witcher* are notable for their violence and explicit sex and nudity. It could be argued that their popularity rests partly on these aspects, rather than despite them. Renée Trilling certainly sees the violence, pain, and suffering of the medieval world as central to its lure for us, asking,

> Do we seek license to indulge in bloodshed, misogyny, and racism without the attendant guilt? Do we secretly long for an existence that absolves us from challenging social injustice? Do we desire a sense of belonging that transcends the individual with an unquestioned tribalism and nationalism?

Invoking Freud's assertion that "civilization imposes restriction on the most basic of human instincts, teaching us to sublimate our drives toward sex and aggression and to strive for cleanliness and order," Trilling would argue that the answer to these questions is yes, that the premodern world of medievalism offers an escape for our instincts in the face of cultural frustration.[56]

Central to this understanding, though, is a sense of nostalgia, of safety. The medieval is, for us, a space in which such ideas may be navigated without attendant danger and without risk to civilization. For Trilling, the medieval can only stand as the site for objects of "overt revulsion and covert desire" (such as violence, sex, dirt, etc.)[57] because it presents "the past as absolutely and irrevocably separate from the present." "Once situated in the far side of the barrier of time," she writes, "the medieval can operate as a site of projection for fantasies of wholeness and escape from cultural repression, or as a repository for the violence and dirt that are anathema to, and a source of humor for, modern life."[58]

Viewed through this lens, our genres of folk, heavy metal, and progressive rock can be seen to have very different roles to play. When present *as* medieval—that is real, authentic medieval music—folk evokes the sense of temporal distance that is necessary for nostalgia. Separated by this clear temporal divide, *Game of Thrones* may safely stand as a "repository for the violence" of the Red Wedding, for instance. Folk is therefore a distancing feature, placing the events that happen on screen "as absolutely and irrevocably separate from the present." To an extent, the rock cameos of *Game of Thrones* make this process even more explicit. We see familiar musicians who are changed almost beyond recognition. Their music, too, is consciously distorted through a Westerosi frame, becoming no longer rock but instead the authentic medieval of folk or period pastiche. The recognizability of the characters and music, in a sense, increases the sense of distance. In *The Witcher III*, folk and period pastiche perform much the same function, essentially excusing the violence and explicit sex and nudity. Through nostalgic distancing, such aspects therefore become acceptable to a wide demographic, with the medieval being a "site of projection for fantasies" that would otherwise be inappropriate.

But are films such as *Highlander* or *Heavy Metal* really very different in terms of their approach to violence and (particularly in the latter) sex? Both certainly exploit these aspects. Nonetheless, I would argue that they are handled in a very different manner. Both films are very much positioned within a masculinist discourse with regard to power and violence. In both cases, this is supported by heavy metal within the score. Its use, instead of situating the action in a distanced past, serves to collapse the sense of distance. Such a point is perhaps most clearly made in *Highlander*, in which the violence of the opening modern-day wrestling scene is explicitly linked with the flashback of a sixteenth-century battle. As Walser has noted, the medievalist aspects here are presented as "sources of power and mystery" that are not "tied to strict historical contexts."[59] The medievalism exists not to excuse the violence, the dirt, and the sex through positioning it squarely and nostalgically in the past, but to hold them as sources of Otherness, just one aspect of "everything that hegemonic society does not want to acknowledge, the dark side of the daylit, enlightened adult world." The move from metal to folk in the scores of *The Witcher* series can therefore be seen in the same light, as a depriviledging of a masculinist discourse in favor of a new framing of the game's sex and violence. In the first game, notable for its inclusion of metal in the score, players were encouraged to view women as sexual objects through the awarding of cards (which were often explicit in themselves) for every woman successfully seduced. The third game of the series (though certainly not immune to criticism of its representation of gender, sexuality, or race) does nonetheless make a point of featuring strong female protagonists, with sex taking place for somewhat more mutual reasons and, generally, for the furthering of narrative or character development. The move from rock to folk in both *Game of Thrones* and *The Witcher* can therefore be viewed not only as the product of a widening of demographics but also as a factor in the depriviledging of masculinist discourses.

NOTES

1. For a discussion of one example of this metal/prog alloy, see Durrell S. Bowman, "'Let Them All Make Their Own Music': Individualism, Rush, and the Progressive/Hard Rock Alloy, 1976–77," in *Progressive Rock Reconsidered*, ed. Kevin Holm Hudson (New York: Routledge, 2002); for an overview of prog rock, see Edward Macan, *Rocking the Classics: English Progressive Rock and the Counterculture* (Oxford: Oxford University Press, 1997); for rock more generally, see Peter Wicke, *Rock Music: Culture, Aesthetics, and Sociology*, trans. Rachel Fogg (Cambridge: Cambridge University Press, 1990).
2. Similarly, nothing will be said of crossover genres such as progressive metal, exemplified by bands such as Dream Theatre or Fates Warning. There is even overlap between the genres discussed directly below and folk, which will be discussed later. Folk rock bands such as Fairport Convention or Steeleye Span certainly derive much of their material from the

same sources as more traditional folk musicians, but their aesthetic choices, musical influences, and instrumentations often had more in common with prog and even metal. Jethro Tull make an interesting case in point, having begun as more of a blues-oriented outfit, before becoming heavily influenced by prog rock in the early 1970s and then successfully merging elements of folk rock and metal into the late 1970s. A clear delimitation of these styles or an in-depth investigation into their numerous subgenres is beyond the scope of this essay.

3. Susan Fast, "Days of Future Past: Rock, Pop, and the Yearning for the Middle Ages," in *KulturReihe Aktuell*, ed. Dorothea Redepening (Kiel: Wissenschaftsverlag Vauk, 2000), 35–56.

4. Macan, *Rocking the Classics*, 40, 149–151.

5. For a discussion of the importance of English sacred music for Continental musicians and theorists, see James Cook, *The Cyclic Mass: Anglo-Continental Exchange in the Fifteenth Century*. Royal Musical Association Monographs, 33 (Oxford, New York: Routledge, 2019); for an overview of the historiography of the English works from the period, see Margaret Bent, "What Next? Recent Work and New Directions for English Medieval Music," *Early Music* 45, no. 1 (2017): 3–10.

6. Paul Hardwick, "'If I Lay my Hands on the Grail': Arthurianism and Progressive Rock," in *Mass Market Medieval, Essays on the Middle Ages in Popular Culture*, ed. David W. Marshall (Jefferson, North Carolina & London: McFarland & Company, Inc., 2007), 33.

7. Bill Martin, *Listening to the Future: The Time of Progressive Rock, 1968–1978* (Chicago: Carus, 1998), 133–134.

8. Hardwick, "Arthurianism," 33.

9. Macan, *Rocking the Classics*, 73.

10. Charles Elkins, "Approach to the Social Functions of Science Fiction and Fantasy," in *The Scope of the Fantastic—Culture, Biography, Themes, Children's Literature: Selected Essays from the First International Conference on the Fantastic in Literature and Film*, ed. R. A. Collins and H. D. Pearce (Westport, CT: Greenwood Press), 23–31.

11. Hardwick, "Arthurianism," 33–36.

12. For an edition of Monmouth's *Historia regum Brittaniae*, see Geoffrey of Monmouth, *The History of the Kings of Britain*, ed. and trans. Michael Faletra (Peterborough, Ontario: Broadview Books, 2008); for an account of the author, see Michal Curley, *Geoffrey of Monmouth* (New York: Twayne, 1994); for a broader discussion of early Arthurian myth, see Siân Echard, ed., *The Arthur of Medieval Latin Literature: The Development and Dissemination of the Arthurian Legend in Medieval Latin* (Cardiff: University of Wales Press, 2011).

13. Hardwick, "Arthurianism," 34.

14. Ibid., 35.

15. Fast, "Days of Future Past," 36.

16. Ibid., 36–43.

17. J. R. R. Tolkien, *The Lord of the Rings* (Boston: Houghton Mifflin, 2001), 368. For more on the relationship between Led Zeppelin and *The Lord of the Rings*, see Caitlin Carlos's contribution to this volume, "'Ramble On': Medievalism as Nostalgic Practice in Led Zeppelin's Use of J. R. R. Tolkien," pp. 530–546.

18. The exact nature of the relationship between this song and *The Lord of the Rings* still ignites a surprising degree of debate among fans of both Tolkien and Led Zeppelin. The allusions themselves are seemingly left deliberately vague and potentially multivalent. The song itself is clearly indebted to folk-rock crossovers of the period with the central tale told by a narrator. The mutability of the text may itself therefore be a nod to the evolution of stories on central themes within aural story traditions.

19. Will Straw, "Characterizing Rock Music Cultures: The Case of Heavy Metal," *Canadian University Music Review* 5 (1984): 118.

20. William Gibbons, "'Little Harmonic Labyrinths': Baroque Musical Style on the Nintendo Entertainment System," in *Recomposing the Past: Representations of Early Music on Stage and Screen*, ed. James Cook, Alexander Kolassa, and Adam Whittaker (New York: Routledge, 2018), 191–197.

21. Tristian Donovan, *Replay: The History of Video Games* (East Sussex: Yellow Ant, 2010), 53–54, in Gibbons, "Little Harmonic Labyrinths," 192.

22. Staci Tucker, "Early Online Gaming: BBSs and MUDs," in *Before the Crash: Early Video Game History*, ed. M. J. P. Wolf (Detroit: Wayne State University Press, 2012), 216–217; see also Robert Walser, *Running with the Devil: Power, Gender, and Madness in Heavy Metal Music* (Middletown, CT: Wesleyan University Press, 1993), 137–172.

23. Walser, *Running with the Devil*, 108–136.

24. Ibid., 108–109.

25. Ibid., 154.

26. Ibid., 162.

27. Simon Nugent, "Celtic Music and Hollywood Cinema: Representation, Stereotype, and Affect," in *Recomposing the Past: Representations of Early Music on Stage and Screen*, ed. James Cook, Alex Kolassa, and Adam Whittaker (New York: Routledge, 2018), 107–123.

28. Marc Streitenfeld as cited by Nugent, "Celtic Music and Hollywood Cinema," 113

29. Howard Shore as cited by Nugent, "Celtic Music and Hollywood Cinema," 120. For more on the relationship between medievalism and the Lord of the Rings films, see Stephen Meyer's contribution to this volume, "From the Music of the Ainur to the Music of the Voice-over: Music and Medievalism in *The Lord of the Rings*," pp. 611–635.

30. Nugent, "Celtic Music and Hollywood Cinema," 107–123.

31. Jane Tolmie, "Medievalism and the Fantasy Heroine," *Journal of Gender Studies* 15, no. 2 (2006): 152.

32. Albert Classen, "The Defeat of the Matriarch Brunhild in the Nibelüngenlied, with Some Thoughts on Matriarchy as Evinced in Literary Texts," in *"Waz sider sa geschach": American–German Studies on the Nibelüngenlied*, ed. Werner Wunderlich and Ulrich Müller (Göppingen: Kümmerle Verlag, 1992), 92.

33. Barry Cunliffe, *The Celts: A Very Short Introduction* (New York: Oxford University Press, 2003), 11.

34. Fast, "Days of Future Past," 44–47.

35. Edward Breen, "David Munrow's 'Turkish Nightclub Piece,'" in *Recomposing the Past: Representations of Early Music on Stage and Screen*, ed. James Cook, Alex Kolassa, and Adam Whittaker (New York: Routledge, 2018); David Munrow, *Instruments of the Middle Ages and Renaissance* (Oxford: Oxford University Press, 1976); Anthony Baines, *Woodwind Instruments and Their History* (New York: Norton, 1957); and Curt Sachs, *The History of Musical Instruments* (New York: Norton, 1949) each make the case that folk instruments provide the key to understanding early instruments. See also Edward Breen's contribution to this volume, "Medieval Folk in the Revivals of David Munrow," pp. 224–246.

36. Halfyard, *Fantasy Cinema*, 11–12.

37. Gibbons, "Little Harmonic Labyrinths," 191–197.

38. Lee Barron, "Fantasy Meets Electronica: *Legend* and the Music of Tangerine Dream," in *The Music of Fantasy Cinema*, ed. Janet K. Halfyard (Sheffield, UK: Equinox, 2012), 79–94.

39. Barron, "Fantasy Meets Electronica," 84–85.

40. Will Gibbon's assertion that baroque harpsichord came to be associated with the fantasy medieval in videogame, at least partially because of the technological aspects, might provide a further context for a specifically medievalist, rather than merely historicizing impetus behind the use of harpsichord.

41. Barron, "Fantasy Meets Electronica," 84–85.

42. J. Drew Stephen, "Who Wants to Live Forever: Glam Rock, Queen and Fantasy Film," in *The Music of Fantasy Cinema*, ed. Janet K. Halfyard (Sheffield, UK: Equinox, 2012), 66–67.

43. Stephen, "Who Wants to Live Forever," 66–67.

44. Stephen, "Who Wants to Live Forever," 73.

45. See the journalist descriptions of Todd Leopold, *The New, New TV Golden Age*, May 6, 2013, http://edition.cnn.com/2013/05/06/showbiz/golden-age-of-tv/; or John Plunkett and Jason Deans, "Kevin Spacey: Television Has Entered a New Golden Age," *The Guardian*, August 22, 2013, https://www.theguardian.com/media/2013/aug/22/kevin-spacey-tv-golden-age. For more on *Game of Thrones* and the new golden age of television, see James Cook, Alexander Kolassa, and Adam Whittaker, "Music in Fantasy Pasts: Neomedievalism and *Game of Thrones*," in *Recomposing the Past: Representations of Early Music on Stage and Screen* ed. James Cook, Alex Kolassa, and Adam Whittaker (New York: Routledge, 2018), 229–250.

46. Cook, Kolassa, and Whittaker, "Music in Fantasy Pasts," 229–250.

47. When these two songs are used in the television series, they invariably occur diegetically (though "The Rains of Castamere," after its first few diegetic occurrences, becomes used as a nondiegetic leitmotif whenever the Lannisters are on screen) and often use period instruments.

48. Cameron Koch, "Interview: '*The Witcher 3*' Composer Mikolai Stroinski Talks about How Music Helps Bring the Game to Life," *Tech Times*, May 18, 2015, http://www.tech-times.com/articles/53814/20150518/the-witcher-3-wild-hunt-composer-mikolai-stro-inski.htm.

49. James Cook, "Playing with the Past in the Imaginary Middle Ages: Music and Soundscape in Video Game," *Sounding Out!*, Medieval Soundscapes, accessed October 3, 2016, https://soundstudiesblog.com/tag/james-cook/ and James Cook, 'Sonic Medievalism, World Building, and Cultural Identity in Fantasy Video Games', *Studies in Medievalism* 29 (2020), forthcoming.

50. ICO Radio, "Show 78: *The Witcher 3* Komponist im Interview," June 21, 2015, http://www.ico-radio.de/2015/06/show-79-the-witcher-3-komponist-im-interview/.

51. Other areas are introduced in expansion packs. Toussaint, in particular, draws on visual, aural, and social cues from French chivalry, drawing musically on the "Frenchness" of the accordion and the exaggerated "heroicness" of Wagernian brass.

52. The Scottish accent is almost uniformly reserved for Dwarfs within fantasy.

53. Both of these aspects are attested in some Scandinavian Viking sources.

54. The band are a medievalist folk group who have, interestingly, named themselves after one of the characters from the books on which the games are based. Despite their interest in historical re-enactment, they are also clearly interested in broader medievalist ideas, such as their recent medievalist folk and hip-hop collaboration.

55. *Snow White* could be considered a fairy tale rather than fantasy depending on how strictly generic boundaries are being drawn. For a discussion of fantasy's position within the burgeoning field of young adult literature, see Rachel Falconer, "Young Adult Fiction and the

Crossover Phenomenon," in *The Routledge Companion to Children's Literature*, ed. David Rudd (London: Routledge, 2010), 87–88.

56. René Trilling, "Medievalism and Its Discontents," *Postmedieval: A Journal of Medieval Cultural Studies* 2, no. 2 (2011): 216–224.

57. Ibid., 218.

58. Ibid., 219.

59. Walser, *Running with the Devil*, 154.

CHAPTER 33

GAMING THE MEDIEVALIST WORLD IN HARRY POTTER

KAREN M. COOK

WHEN first we meet Harry Potter, he is a young orphan living with his abusive aunt, uncle, and cousin in an ordinary English suburb. On his eleventh birthday, he discovers he is in fact a wizard, like his deceased parents before him, and is invited to begin attending Hogwarts School of Witchcraft and Wizardry. While en route to Hogwarts, he is finally told the truth about his past: that the evil Lord Voldemort murdered his parents and attempted to kill him while he was a baby, but failed, leaving only a lightning bolt–shaped scar on Harry's forehead. Unbeknownst to Harry, he is a legend, recognized by all in the wizarding world as "The Boy Who Lived." Over the course of the seven books in J. K. Rowling's famous series, Harry is faced with a variety of problems and challenges from the magical to the mundane, but none so great as saving wizarding Britain from Voldemort's return.[1]

Medieval (and medievalist) elements in the Harry Potter books have been continuously discussed by fans and scholars alike since the first book was published twenty years ago.[2] As Renée Ward discusses, Rowling incorporates references to and reworkings of the medieval in virtually every aspect of the books: location (the ancient Hogwarts castle; the Forbidden Forest), actions and storylines (quests; feasting; tournaments; membership in clubs, guilds, or confraternities such as the Hogwarts Houses or the Order of the Phoenix; the orphan, outsider, mentor figure, and hero motifs), historical or legendary people (Nicholas Flamel; Merlin), visual accoutrements (ancient portraits; robes; suits of armor; dusty old manuscripts), and even creatures from myth and medieval bestiaries (dragons; centaurs; hippogrifs; unicorns; werewolves; and Fluffy, the Cerberus-like three-headed dog).[3] Each of these elements is drawn not only from medieval history or narrative but also from themes perpetuated as medievalisms since the Middle Ages themselves, what Clare Simmons calls "cultural adaptations" of medieval concepts.[4] Magic, too, has played a major, if fictive, role in medievalist literature and art from the medieval period to today.[5] An obviously central theme, the Harry Potter series draws on this heritage of magic as medievalism: witches and wizards fly on broomsticks, transform into animals, keep pets as familiars, cast spells in pseudo-Latin, brew potions, and even dabble in the Dark Arts.

The film and game versions of the books interpret these medievalisms anew. In typical fashion, the characters and plot lines were trimmed and tightened for the films; the games, while retaining the most prominent characters, excised the rest and developed their own loose narratives around the main story arc of each book. The films and games also provided their own visual interpretations of textually described medievalisms from the book: the geography, people, creatures, and things of Harry Potter's world, giant castle and looming forest, quills and cauldrons, robes and wands and broomsticks. Ward points out that the films further reinforce the medievalist elements of the books via their use of actual medieval locations as sets; Hogwarts, for example, is composed of bits and pieces of the Gloucester Cloisters, Durham Cathedral, and the Great Hall of Christ Church, Oxford, among other buildings.[6] Ward does not include any of the games in her analysis, but as Electronic Arts worked alongside Warner Bros. to model their scenery on that of the films, her statement holds true for the games as well.

Yet missing from Ward's and other studies of the Harry Potter agglomerate is any consideration of the auditory. This is a rather surprising omission, given that in the films and books—the primary objects of study to date—the aural elements play as much of a role in characterizing the Harry Potter world as the visual ones do. The popularity of the John Williams soundtracks from the first three films attests to the fundamental role that music plays in the Harry Potter experience. Music itself is a recurring theme in the books: the Sorting Hat entertains and educates the Hogwarts body at the start of each term, Professor Flitwick leads the school chorus, carolers revel in Diagon Alley. Moreover, Rowling describes the overall sonic environment of Harry's world: the sounds of characters' voices, of the various creatures, of the different buildings and places, of technological devices, even of magic itself. The auditory in the films, like the visual, is both based on these descriptions and fleshed out in a manner in keeping with the books' overall aesthetic. Because this aesthetic is, in no small part, medievalist, an understanding of just how sound and music enhance that interpretation within the films, games, and even the Wizarding World theme parks merits further investigation. Such an investigation would be a monumental one. Therefore, since the games have yet to be approached with a critical eye or ear, this chapter focuses on them, unpacking the relationship between medievalism and sound therein. I argue that the games' auditory content enhances the player's sense of medievalism, not because it stems from a medieval point of origin akin to the sets (which it clearly does not), but rather because it reflects what John Haines calls "an authenticity to the tradition of medievalism."[7] In other words, the sounds and music used allude to and borrow from a wide host of medievalist musical pasts, such as art music, opera, and other films and video games.

Medievalism and Video-Game Music

Much of what I lay out here can act as a preliminary introduction to music and medievalism in the film scores. But the deployment of sonic material in many video games necessarily occurs differently than in film. A film is a linear sonic experience for a passive audience, whereas games require active participation from the player and utilize sonic material to shape that experience, often in nonlinear fashion. The player of the Harry Potter games not only receives information from various types of sonic elements but also actively causes many of these aural cues to take place based on in-game decisions. The auditory in the games thus provides different, functional information to the player in a manner that goes beyond the mood-setting and narrative foreshadowing of the films. Drawing on Haines and others, I propose that the aural elements that create a sense of medievalism in the Harry Potter world are the heroic, romantic orchestral score; the use of certain instruments with medievalist significance, namely the horn, harp, celesta or glockenspiel, and xylophone, and wordless choir; and the ambient environmental sounds, or Foley. The player actively triggers various changes in the musical soundtrack, in the diegetic Foley, and in what I call metadiegetic sounds (auditory cues indicating an achievement), thereby becoming a de facto co-creator of the medievalisms present within this world. Moreover, since the metadiegetic sounds represent magic performed by the player as Harry, I suggest that music itself is employed as a symbol of the magical, and thus the medieval.

As a detailed study of the soundtracks of all of the Harry Potter games (currently numbering over one hundred) would be its own hefty volume, this chapter will focus solely on a small subset, namely the first two games created for the PlayStation 2 console.[8] I concentrate on these games because, like the first two films, they are more closely linked to each other than to the others in the series with regard to game play, visual environment, and approach to sound.[9] These games also serve as an important introduction to the world of Harry Potter, especially for players who might not have read the books or seen the films. From the perspective of gaming the medieval, then, the very beginning is a very good place to start.

Both *Sorcerer's Stone* and *Chamber of Secrets* are third-person perspective action and puzzle games. The player, controlling Harry, re-enacts the basic events of the first two books.[10] In *Sorcerer's Stone*, Harry begins in Diagon Alley, where he learns how to use his wand at Ollivander's; in *Chamber of Secrets*, he goes first to the Burrow, then to Knockturn Alley, before finally reuniting with the Weasleys in Diagon Alley. In both games, Harry then heads to Hogwarts, where he attends classes, interacts with teachers and fellow students, learns spells, and explores the Hogwarts castle and grounds. Along the way, Harry (with the help of other characters in the game) must solve puzzles, overcome challenges, and defeat enemies, many of which are loosely based on the book narratives. Most of this game time is active, meaning that the player directly controls Harry's actions and makes in-game decisions. Both games also feature a number of "cutscenes": sequences in which the player cannot affect the action whatsoever. These scenes, some of which are quite lengthy, often feature voice-over narration or dialogue derived from the books and serve to advance the plot or to give Harry instructions for his next task.

The first chapter of *Sorcerer's Stone* suffices as an example of game play. The game begins with a series of cutscenes that the player watches passively, as if they were scenes in a film. These scenes quickly summarize the first several chapters of the book, explaining Harry's past via narration and dialogue, and then shift to ten-year-old Harry living at Privet Drive with his Muggle family, whom we do not see. An owl delivers Harry's letter of acceptance to Hogwarts, and a second later, he is accompanying Hagrid through Diagon Alley, meeting Professor Quirrell before heading to Ollivander's. The player actively controls Harry in a search for his wand for a few brief seconds before another cutscene interrupts; Ollivander discloses to Harry the secret of his scar, and his wand, before giving him instructions on the first quest of the game. Approximately six minutes into the game, the player finally begins to play. Navigating Harry around a cavernous storage area, the player learns to sneak along walls, jump from ledge to ledge, crawl through tunnels, and climb boxes. Eventually locating the hidden spell book, Harry learns his first spell, which he must then use successfully to defeat the first foes of the game, a group of imps.

These scenes aptly demonstrate the different levels of auditory information present throughout the games. In the cutscenes, the player first hears famed actor Stephen Fry narrate Harry's story, a story continued in the dialogue between Hagrid and Professors Dumbledore and McGonagall. Dialogue is also foregrounded throughout Diagon Alley, including in Ollivander's wand shop, focusing the player's attention on the new information provided about Harry and his world. Foley sounds are heard in every cutscene, from Hagrid's motorbike and flying owls to footsteps, doors, and general crowd noise. Musical accompaniment also dips in and out; the soundtrack plays during Hagrid's arrival at Privet Drive with baby Harry, rising to a climax as this flashback scene ends, but is notably absent as the owl delivers Harry's letter. As Harry reads it, the opening horn-call motive of the theme called "Gryffindor Common Room" plays, acting as a bit of musical foreshadowing.[11] Short themes play at other crucial moments; for example, a brief ethereal theme is heard when Hagrid opens the brick-walled passage into Diagon Alley, marking Harry's entrance into the wizarding world, and a harp plays a startled downward arpeggio when the wand-maker Ollivander recognizes Harry.

During active play, sound occurs in similar fashion. As Harry explores Ollivander's shop, the player hears a harp play a meditative theme called "Trying Wands," which swells joyfully as Harry successfully tests out his new wand. The soundtrack continues beneath the subsequent dialogue and into the first quest of the game: locating the Flipendo spellbook. In this quest, the player hears—and causes—the sounds of Harry's footsteps on wooden platforms, the swish of his robes against the walls, and his voice describing the Bertie Bott's Every Flavour Beans he collects. Each bean collected triggers

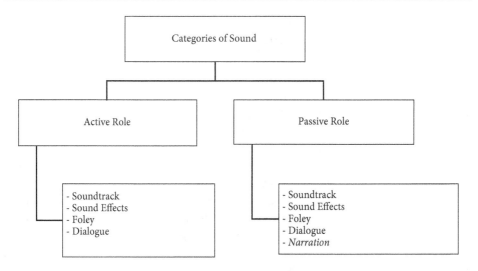

FIGURE 33.1 Categories of sound.

a metadiegetic synth effect, and finding the spellbook prompts a short cutscene complete with a swirling, ascending theme of victory ("Pick Up Spellbook").

Sound in these two games can thus be divided according to the two main roles of the player: active and passive. From there, they can be categorized by type, as shown in Figure 33.1. As the chart shows, narration is the only category of sound that is exclusive to one type of player role, because it is heard only during the cutscenes. The other types of sound occur regardless of whether the player is actively controlling Harry or passively watching.

Whether the dialogue and narration contribute to a sense of medievalism is beyond the scope of this chapter. But the soundtrack itself as a whole, the instrumentation found within it, and the metadiegetic sounds, and to some extent the Foley, all draw on stereotypes molded over centuries of musical medievalism and thus contribute to the games' medievalist aesthetic.

The soundtracks for both *Sorcerer's Stone* and *Chamber of Secrets* are closely tied to game geography. Both games take place predominantly at Hogwarts, and Harry must explore the huge castle and its vast grounds to find objects and complete challenges. Most of the main areas here have their own particular soundtrack themes, though they do not all play continuously. Harry revisits the Gryffindor Common Room, corridors, and stairs daily, and so their themes will be repeated throughout the games. Other areas, such as the Whomping Willow or the various locations in Diagon Alley, are ones that Harry accesses only once for the purposes of a particular quest, and so those themes are heard only during Harry's time there.

Game goals affect the soundtracks in the games. Harry's tasks take several forms: searching for objects such as potions ingredients or spellbooks, collecting beans, solving locked-door puzzles, and battling enemies. As Harry progresses through the game, he will have more objects and spells at his disposal, and the player obtains an ever-growing spatial awareness of Hogwarts and its grounds. When Harry enters a new area, then, a change of soundtrack theme helps to alert the player to the nature of the unfamiliar surroundings. During combat scenes—when Harry battles against imps, ghosts, Voldemort, or the basilisk—the soundtrack theme is loud, bombastic, and continuous. In other situations, in which Harry is more focused on solving a puzzle or finding an exit, the themes might be shorter or play only for a brief time, leaving the player to concentrate on the task at hand.

The soundtrack also reflects the passage of time. Once Harry arrives at Hogwarts, game play is loosely structured around the depiction of the school term in the books. Play takes place over five or six "days," each of which involves tasks based on Harry's classes (Potions, Charms, etc.); the respective nights engage Harry in practicing spells and battling creatures. As Harry begins and ends each day in his dormitory, the repetition of the themes for the hallways, stairways, and Gryffindor Common Room mark not only Harry's return to those areas but also the elapsing of game time. The raucous brass band theme that concludes each game day ("End Day House Points") also plays during the cutscene in which these (completely irrelevant) House Points are tallied, thus articulating the passage of time in the game world.

As mentioned before, Electronic Arts worked directly with Warner Bros. to create game visuals based on those in the films, from the design and decoration of Hogwarts and its grounds to the general appearance of the cast members. Sonic similarities between the earliest films and games, however, are telling but largely accidental. Unlike later games in the series, none of the film's cast members provided voice acting in the first two games, and while composer Jeremy Soule is known as the "John Williams of video game music," he wrote his score for the *Sorcerer's Stone* game before John Williams composed the first film's soundtrack.[12]

Despite the fact that Soule and Williams had no access to each other's scores, their compositional approaches to the Harry Potter world are remarkably similar. Since Soule knew of Williams's commission, in part this can be attributed to Soule's familiarity with Williams's prior work. His scores for films such as *Jaws*, *E.T.*, and the Star Wars, Indiana Jones, and Jurassic Park series are instantly recognizable to many for their sweeping melodies and lush orchestral textures, and Soule repeatedly referred to Williams as a compositional influence long before he was asked to score the Harry Potter games.[13] It is not surprising, then, that Soule approached the games in a deliberately Williams-esque style.

Sounding Medieval: Timbre and Instrumentation

The soundtracks, which were recorded by a full symphony orchestra, including harp and occasional vocals, are thus what viewers and players have come to expect in an epic fantasy. John Williams is often considered the "fountainhead of this film music genre," with others such as Hans Zimmer (*Gladiator*, Pirates of the Caribbean), Howard Shore (the Hobbit, the Lord of the Rings), and Danny Elfman (Batman, *Edward Scissorhands*) contributing significantly to this aesthetic.[14] The use of a large symphony orchestra for such epic tales predates Williams by many years, though. What Elizabeth Randell Upton calls the "imagined medieval sound of romantic music" was created in the nineteenth century, itself drawing on centuries of earlier opera and art music from Monteverdi and Lully to Berlioz, Strauss, and Wagner. The huge nineteenth-century orchestra became indelibly linked to the tropes of the heroic, the fantastic, and the medieval(ist) and thus to the types of scores produced for so many twentieth-century Hollywood films; see, for example, Erich Korngold's score for *The Adventures of Robin Hood* or virtually every film scored by Max Steiner, including the Robin Hood-esque adventure *The Flame and the Arrow*.[15] While this type of orchestral score is not medieval, nor is it inherently medievalist, it has undergone a "medievalizing process," such that in an already established medievalist context such as a Robin Hood movie or a Harry Potter game, it reinforces a tradition of medievalism via its resemblance to soundtracks in other previously established medievalist films, operas, and the like—a resemblance that Haines calls "medieval film's penchant for nostalgia."[16]

Given Soule's admiration for Williams and the tradition on which both were drawing, it is not surprising that Soule and Williams also made strikingly similar choices in instrumentation. As in a heroic film score, the sound of a particular instrument creates a kind of musical–cultural resonance that can transcend the associations of a newly composed melody or modern harmonic approach. Working independently, both Soule and Williams deploy instruments such as the harp, horn, pitched percussion, and wordless choir to leverage stereotypes that each of these instruments or vocal timbres has accumulated over the centuries.

The harp and horn were each present in the western European Middle Ages, though perhaps not in the ways we might imagine them today. Modern art music, film, video games, and other media draw not on their actual sound (whatever that might have been) but on earlier, frequently medievalist, orchestral, and operatic traditions. With regard to the horn, Leonard Ratner and Raymond Monelle discuss its role extensively within pastoral, hunting, and military contexts.[17] John Haines expands on this work, hearing the horn and the horn call as signifiers of the medieval, especially as channeled through the romantic orchestral score in heroic or fantasy film; Isabella van Elferen echoes his statements with regard to fantasy literature.[18] Monelle points out that the horn call was imitated in music as early as the fourteenth century. As a symbol of the hunt, the chivalric, and even a call to battle, it was heard in opera as early as Cavalli and Purcell. It was pervasively used in romantic art music and especially Wagnerian opera, which were later echoed in films such as *The Crusades* (1935), *The Vikings* (1958), and in all of the Lord of the Rings films (2001–2003). The horn as a symbol of the pastoral was already familiar to eighteenth-century audiences, a symbol cemented in works such as Beethoven's "Pastoral" Symphony no. 6 and Carl Maria von Weber's *Der Freischütz*. Wagnerian opera too made frequent use of the pastoral horn, and in such cases as Mendelssohn's *Nocturne* and Weber's *Oberon*, it is specifically associated with magic.[19]

Of all the instruments listed earlier, the horn is by far the most frequently used in the two Harry Potter games. It is practically omnipresent, both in soundtrack themes and in metadiegetic sounds. At times, horns are paired with trumpets for martial fanfares; at others they are foregrounded against an orchestral texture. The horn's long association with the hunt and the military explains its prominence during the themes that play during battle. Take, for example, the theme that plays during the battle with the Whomping Willow in *Chamber of Secrets*. It begins with a loud crush of heavy brass chords, accompanied by swirling string scales and massive percussion, but around eight seconds in, it drops down to a much smaller, quieter texture consisting of strings, bassoon, and pitched percussion. High brass returns for a moment before everything drops out except for horns playing *fortissimo* and crashing cymbals. This massive horn ensemble dominates the rest of the theme, accompanied at times by trumpets, percussion, and strings. While in some lesser battles the horns might be quieter or less active, they are a noticeable accompaniment to the texted choir in the basilisk battle and the central musical element in the first half of the theme for the battle with Voldemort.

For analogous reasons, the horn is heard during Quidditch matches, often alongside trumpets and other brass. In the theme "Quidditch Intro" from *Sorcerer's Stone*, the trumpets play a martial dotted fanfare motif over the more sustained, heroic horn melody. The horns are also foregrounded in the back-to-back themes "Quidditch Anthem" and "Quidditch Attack" from *Chamber of Secrets*, where they play a loud, boisterous melody offset by cymbals, timpani, harp, strings, and winds, before segueing into a *fortissimo* theme in which the horns, low brass, and trumpets aggressively alternate alongside crashing cymbals and a shrieking piccolo.

Scenarios or areas in which Harry is required to be stealthy or to solve a puzzle, such as sneaking past Percy on his way to Fred and George's shop, also make use of the horn, either as the primary instrument or in a notable accompanying role. The horn is most frequently heard in the majestic themes representing the main areas of Hogwarts, the ones that Harry revisits throughout the game. The main motif in each of these themes is a short modal theme emphasizing leaps of fifths and octaves with a lowered seventh scale degree, as shown in Example 33.1.

The horn plays this motif in "Gryffindor Common Room/Happy Hogwarts" and its countermelody in "Hogwarts Wander: Entry Hall/Hogwarts Wander: Grand Staircase/Hogwarts Neutral" and "Gryffindor Common Room." The motif returns as part of Hedwig's game theme in *Chamber of Secrets*, in which the horn again plays its countermelody. The open intervals comprising this motif are reminiscent not just of the stereotypical horn call but also of the preeminence of perfect fifths and octaves within

EXAMPLE 33.1 Opening motif representing Hogwarts.

medieval music; the horn and this melody thus doubly enforce the medievalness of the castle itself.[20]

The themes for areas outside the castle also feature the horn, drawing on its pastoral symbolism. In both games, the horn peeks through the texture with a rising melody in "Hagrid's Hut" and "Hogwarts Grounds (Day)," while it lurks ominously near the surface of the "Hogwarts Grounds (Night)" theme. The horn also takes a turn playing the main motif from "The Burrow" in *Chamber of Secrets*.

Throughout both games, the horn is used heavily in cutscenes, such as the aforementioned short scene that displays the House Points at the end of each day at Hogwarts, which is accompanied by a beer hall–type brass band. Furthermore, the horn is prominent in the metadiegetic sounds created by magical actions. For example, when a door, ladder, or other hidden object is revealed, the horn typically takes part in the short musical phrase accompanying that discovery. The stinger that plays when Harry successfully finishes a challenge features the horn, as does the short congratulatory theme that sounds when Harry finds a spellbook or locates Ginny's belongings in Diagon Alley at the beginning of *Chamber of Secrets*.

In both the soundtrack and the metadiegetic sounds, then, the horn maintains its symbolic representation of the pastoral, the military, the hunt, and the chase. Its presence in metadiegetic sounds, and that of the trumpet to a lesser extent, also plays on the idea of the brass fanfare as an announcement or celebration, a concept that was predominantly developed within medievalist film; see, for example, brass fanfares in everything from Disney's *Ye Olden Days* and *Robin Hood* to *Ivanhoe* (1952) and *A Knight's Tale* (2001).[21] Throughout the games, the horn signals the bucolic grounds, Harry's heroism, and especially the medieval castle itself.

The association of the harp with the wandering minstrel, troubadour, or bard, telling his epic tales or singing songs of courtly love, brings to mind the myth of Orpheus and his lyre. The connection of the harp to a minstrel-type figure has been perpetuated in medieval and modern literature, opera (especially about Orpheus), poetry such as Sir Walter Scott's *Lay of the Last Minstrel*, and games such as Dungeons & Dragons and its video-game cousins, especially *The Bard's Tale*. The harp is also the instrument of choice for angels, whether in heaven or on someone's shoulder (see, for example, the "shoulder angel" in Disney's *The Emperor's New Groove*, who holds a tiny gold lyre), and by extension has become a symbol of purity, otherworldliness, mysticism, and magic.[22] Last, it so frequently signifies a dream sequence or a flashback that it is quite commonly parodied, as in *Monty Python's Flying Circus* and *Frasier*.[23]

The harp is less frequently used here than the horn because of its timbre, which would get lost in the loud, full romantic orchestral portions of the score, and so it is usually reserved for sparser or solo textures. The harp is heard in a few minor or more unusual battles, such as with the Venomous Tentacula in *Sorcerer's Stone*. It also plays during some of the scenes that involve stealth or searching, such as those that take place in the Girls' Bathroom or the greenhouse while collecting potions ingredients.

More commonly, the harp is heard in themes and metadiegetic sounds associated with magic. When Harry finds a Wizard Card or a spellbook, the harp plays a rippling upward arpeggio reminiscent of a dream sequence motif. It is particularly prominent in the aforementioned "Trying Wands" theme from *Sorcerer's Stone*. While Harry explores Ollivander's in search of the perfect wand, the harp performs a chromatic melody against an incredibly subtle string accompaniment; later, after the strings have grown louder, the harp interjects a brief flurry of ascending arpeggios before fading away. A solo harp also interrupts the main ensemble in themes accompanying the Flipendo spell challenge in *Sorcerer's Stone* and the Expelliarmus and Incendio challenges in *Chamber of Secrets*.

The most noteworthy use of the harp occurs during the one scene of *Sorcerer's Stone* in which music itself is diegetic. As Harry, Ron, and Hermione prepare to go down the trap door in search of the Stone, they find Fluffy, the three-headed guard dog, lulled fast asleep by the sounds of a magical harp. In this cutscene, a harp is clearly visible behind the main characters, and the soundtrack is a quirky duet between harp and flute. In this respect, the harp is communicating not only its history as an instrument from the western European Middle Ages, but also its own medievalist symbolism of innocence, delicateness, and dreaming. Overall, the harp's role in these games furthers the previous connection between itself and magic, thus reinforcing the magic of Harry's world—and, more significantly, Harry's own magic—as medievalist.[24]

The pitched percussion, namely the celesta, glockenspiel, and xylophone, have more recent histories than the other instruments discussed thus far.[25] Alongside the harp, the celesta or glockenspiel often signifies a dream sequence or a flashback, as in the transition to the medievalist world of the "Neighborhood of Make-Believe" on *Mr. Rogers' Neighborhood*. The high-pitched ring of these instruments is reminiscent of a music box or childhood toys, thus symbolizing youth or innocence, as in the song "Pure Imagination" from *Willy Wonka and the Chocolate Factory*. But like the harp, this unique sound can easily be parodied, connoting the loss of innocence in many of Danny Elfman's fantasy or neo-Gothic soundtracks, such as in *Edward Scissorhands*. The xylophone, however, typically represents more fantastic, even humorous, things such as skeletons, hard-shelled insects, or scurrying creatures.[26]

In both games, the xylophone is heard in humorous situations, such as when Harry sneaks past Percy into Fred and George's shop. It lends a little of this humor to other more fantastical scenarios, like Harry's battles with imps. There, the association of the xylophone's wooden timbre with bones and crawling creatures paints a picture of these creatures as fast moving, sneaky, and even hard shelled. The dryness of the xylophone further emphasizes the hard, artificial nature of the flurry of flying keys barring the door to the Sorcerer's Stone, whereas its woodenness symbolizes Harry's broomstick and reinforces the Venomous Tentacula and the Whomping Willow as living, organic creatures.

The celesta or glockenspiel strengthens the interpretation of a scenario as magical. While spiders have a real-world counterpart, those in the Harry Potter world are gigantic, and their patriarch Aragog can talk to humans; ghostly gytrashes, a type of dog spirit, stalk humans at night. The themes for Harry's battles with these creatures therefore use the metallic, reverberant glockenspiel. So too do the aforementioned themes for the imps, the Venomous Tentacula, and the Whomping Willow, where the glockenspiel works alongside the xylophone to couch them as extraordinary magical, yet living, creatures. Similarly, the glockenspiel transforms the Leaky Cauldron from an ordinary pub into a gathering place for witches and wizards, the Gryffindor Common Room from a regular dormitory into a magical chamber, and the Girls' Bathroom from a lavatory into a place of hidden secrets.

The glockenspiel also contributes to annunciatory metadiegetic sounds. When Harry collects a magical object, the glockenspiel accompanies the harp with a swirling upward arpeggio; when he successfully finishes a challenge, it plays a fast, ascending scale; when he defeats the Rotating Target in *Sorcerer's Stone*, it finishes the congratulatory sound effect with a short chime-like motif. In this fashion, the player is reminded that each of these tasks, quests, and battles is in fact magical.

The wordless choir is the least frequently used timbre, yet its medievalist connotations are perhaps the most overt. Both Robert D. Reynolds and Jean-David Jumeau-Lafond treat the wordless choir as a compositional phenomenon, noting that it can be traced at least as far back as the medievalist operas of Jean-Baptiste Lully (*Isis* in particular).[27] But the composer who cemented the link between the medieval, the sacred, the supernatural, and the wordless choir was Hector Berlioz, in numerous pieces such as his *Marche funèbre pour la dernière scène d'Hamlet*. Since then, it has been used in dozens of operas, films, video games, and concert pieces and described in Gothic and fantasy literature, in all of which it symbolizes everything from mystery, magic, terror, violence, and death to, as Haines notes in his chapter on chant, evil and the occult.[28]

As with the harp and pitched percussion, the wordless choir is occasionally buried in the larger orchestral texture of the soundtracks, but is used clearly in moments signifying the fantastical, the congratulatory, and combat. In foreboding, even spooky locations such as the Forbidden Forest or the Common Room at night, the wordless choir floats in and out on a hushed vowel. In the theme for the Library Tower, for example, tremolo strings, low bassoon, and rumbling percussion set up an ominous mood, which is compounded by the entrance of the wordless choir (here largely high voices) singing an ever louder "ooh." Similarly, a high-voiced choir sings a tremulous "ah" as Harry and company navigate the chess board at the end of *Sorcerer's Stone*, accompanied only by whispering strings and the occasional percussive strike by brass and snare. This marks these places, and the giant figures, as otherworldly, magical, and potentially dangerous.

The same vowels are heard in the congratulatory metadiegetic sounds that mark Harry's successes, such as when Harry locates Ginny's missing things in Diagon Alley, obtains his wand at Ollivander's, or successfully uses the Lumos spell to find his way out of a challenge area. The sound of the wordless choir within these themes is less intimidating than those already mentioned; rather, the voices sound joyful, exuberant, even heraldic.

The wordless choir takes on a much more pointed, aggressive timbre in combat scenes. Rather than the quiet swells or rejoicing crescendos of other themes, the wordless choir signals the start of battle with Voldemort at the end of *Sorcerer's Stone* with an increasingly loud, high-pitched "oh." It also marks the moment in which Voldemort is defeated with a mournful, lamenting melody accompanied by flute and strings. The choir is even more aggressive in *Chamber of Secrets*; as the basilisk enters the Chamber, the choir lets forth with a *fortissimo* "ah" alongside thundering brass, gongs, and strings. As battle proceeds, the choir, now much more audibly consisting of both deep men's and high women's voices, rhythmicizes the "ah" to match the militant brass and percussion beneath it. At this point, the choir is given text for the first time in the games, a Latin or pseudo-Latin text that the entire choir sings forcefully in unison before splintering into harmony in the manner of Carl Orff's "O Fortuna" from *Carmina Burana*. Once Harry defeats the basilisk, though, the choir returns to the softer, gentler timbre of earlier themes, before a single, vibratoless female voice emerges to perform a wordless melody against low winds and piano; the full choir then returns to end this theme with a single swell on "oh." Pertinent here are the remarks of Haines and James Deaville, who observe that Latin or pseudo-Latin in chant, or in an Orff-like arrangement, regularly marks a sense of battle, evil, or the satanic in medievalist films from Star Wars and *The Omen* to *Conan the Barbarian* and The Lord of the Rings.[29] Certainly here the satanic could only be metaphorical, but the battle with the basilisk, and the presence of its evil, are very much the center point of this scene and are thus marked by this unique sonic moment.

The connotations of a wordless choir are complex, symbolizing the mystical, the fantastic, the eerie, even the occult. Since a wordless choir is often employed in film and art music alike to represent a medieval past, its presence here both instills and solidifies a sense of medievalism in the Harry Potter world. The obvious resemblance between the militant Latinate choir and Orff's "O Fortuna" plays on the familiarity of the latter's medievalist tropes, which have greatly affected both the texts and the timbres of choirs in other epic or fantastical films over the past century.[30] When heard during the final battle against the basilisk in the *Chamber of Secrets*, the player immediately interprets that creature as ancient, dangerous, and obscene, a magical creature but also a profane one, associated with Voldemort and thus anathema to Harry's (and the player's?) goodness and heroism.

Altogether, the tropes in instrumentation used by both Soule and Williams suggest that Harry Potter and his world are heroic, pastoral, and, most important, magical, that it is a place of youth and wonder but also of fear, innocence and its loss, battle, and even death. Given the blatantly medievalist aspects of the books and their visual representation on screen, the presence of these instruments into the soundtrack and metadiegetic sounds suggests as well as reinforces a medievalist interpretation of Harry's world.

Sound Effects

So too does the Foley in both the films and the games. The ambient noises embedded in these media also shape the player's or viewer's understanding of the Harry Potter environment; footsteps on the carpeted stairs of Privet Drive might enhance the feeling of a typical suburban home, but footsteps echoing along the large stone corridors of Hogwarts bring to mind a completely different sense of space and time.

As with the soundtrack, geography determines Foley. Outside Hogwarts Castle, when Harry races across the green grass of the courtyard or its gravel pathways, the sounds of his footsteps change accordingly. When Harry finally learns to ride his broom, little is heard but the sound of wind racing past him as he flies. Other Foley sounds associated with character actions, such as Harry crawling through stone passageways, leaping across wooden platforms, pushing heavy objects across the floor, or opening creaky wooden doors and treasure chests, also heighten the player's sense of space—and spaciousness—in the games. The same can be said of Foley triggered by Harry's explorations but not directly caused by him: As Harry roams the grounds outside Hogwarts, birds chirp and a gentle breeze blows, whereas inside, the magical stairways creak into place, fire crackles, potions bubble, water drips, and so forth. The various animals and creatures throughout the game world have their own particular cries, and if the player is in a more populated area, he or she might hear coughs, whispers, cheers, and other human sounds. Harry also vocalizes throughout his adventures, narrating the discoveries he makes, casting spells, and providing various grunts, sighs, and exclamations; the level of reverberation given to such vocalizations adds another sonic layer to the spatialization of Harry's surroundings.

Since soundtrack themes do not play continuously, Foley is often the predominant source of sonic information for the player in both active and passive play. Regardless of where Harry is, the Foley sounds characterize the nature of his location. Populated areas such as Diagon Alley contain quite a bit of sound generated by people, and the environmental sounds of footsteps and the like are dampened. But the sounds of Hogwarts are quite reverberant, the various sounds of Harry and castle alike echoing through the high-ceilinged hallways. Outside, though, virtually nothing is heard but the sounds of nature: wind, birds, trees, and such. These noises, in their own way, also mark Harry's world as medievalist, because on the one hand they play on the notion of the medieval past as pastoral, environmentally untainted, far removed from industry and its sounds, while on the other hand they tap into the inherited legacy of the sounds of castle and cathedral, the twinned institutional stereotypes of the medieval period as chivalric and Christian.

These sounds are distinctly diegetic—that is, heard by Harry—whereas the sounds I refer to as metadiegetic blur the boundaries between diegetic and nondiegetic sound.[31] The metadiegetic sounds emanate from Harry's magical activities, such as collecting a bean, finding a magical object, or casting a spell. One could reasonably presume that Harry can hear the sound of his own voice uttering a spell, but it is unclear if he can also hear the sizzling hiss that issues forth from his wand. Similarly, Harry likely hears the creaking hinges of the treasure chests he opens, but can he also hear the vaguely metallic pop that sounds when he collects a bean or a pumpkin pasty or the short joyful theme that bursts forth from a spellbook when he finds it? Such metadiegetic sounds occur in both passive and active play, regardless of the presence or absence of the soundtrack, although they are (perhaps obviously) much more prominent during moments in which there are fewer competing sounds. These sounds permeate the game; their utilization of the same tropes in orchestration and instrumentation present in the soundtrack form a cohesive aural world that is rich in medievalist symbolism. As these sounds are specifically linked to magic performed by Harry, the player is directly responsible for causing them. In this fashion, the metadiegetic sounds might create the most conscious link between sound, magic, and medievalism that the games have to offer.

The world of the Harry Potter games is already rendered medievalist via the visual scenery and, of course, the narrative itself. The different aural elements of the games both draw on their own individual medievalist genealogies to further imbue the games with medievalist overtones and are simultaneously "remedievalized" by virtue of their presence in the game. The diegetic Foley, the nondiegetic soundtrack, and the metadiegetic sounds that blur the boundaries between the two thus construct for the player a sense of where and when they are in the game world. More important, all describe for the player not just what that area of the world sounds like to Harry but also what it must feel like to be in that space, as Harry Potter, in Harry Potter's world. It is the sound, perhaps even more than the visual, that fully immerses the player in the believability of this particular world, and in that regard, perhaps music is magic, after all.

ACKNOWLEDGMENTS

I would like to thank Samantha Arten, Graeme Boone, James Cook, Elizabeth Hambleton, and Ryan Thompson, as well as the students in my Medievalism in Contemporary Culture seminar (spring 2017), for their insights on this chapter.

NOTES

1. Space considerations prohibit me from defining all Harry Potter–related terms or people, but I refer interested readers to the Harry Potter Wiki if clarification is needed: http://harrypotter.wikia.com/wiki/Main_Page.
2. The terms *medieval* and *Middle Ages* are here understood to refer to western Europe between the fifth and fifteenth centuries. As the introduction and other chapters in this volume describe, the term medievalism is not concretely defined within current scholarship. See also the overviews given in David Matthews, *Medievalism: A Critical History* (Cambridge: Brewer, 2015); and Clare Simmons, "Introduction," in *Medievalism and the Quest for the "Real" Middle Ages* (London: Frank Cass, 2001), 1–28. I will refrain here from entering the fray but will simply use the term medievalism to refer to the use or reworking of medieval ideas in any later medieval or postmedieval period.
3. Renée Ward, "Harry Potter and Medievalism," in *Medieval Afterlives in Contemporary Culture*, ed. Gail Ashton (London: Bloomsbury, 2015), 263–274; see also M. J. Toswell, "The Tropes of Medievalism," in *Defining Medievalisms: Studies in Medievalism* XVII, ed. Karl Fugelso (Cambridge: Brewer, 2009), 68–76.
4. Simmons, "Introduction," 22.
5. For the relationships between magic and the medieval, see Toswell; also Kim Selling, " 'Fantastic Neomedievalism': The Image of the Middle Ages in Popular Fantasy," in *Flashes of the Fantastic: Selected Essays from the War of the Worlds Centennial, Nineteenth International Conference on the Fantastic in the Arts*, ed. David Ketterer (Westport, CT:

Greenwood, 2004), 211–218; W. A. Senior, "Medieval Literature and Modern Fantasy: Toward a Common Metaphysic," *Journal of the Fantastic in the Arts* 3, no. 3/4 (11/12), The Lost Issues (1994): 32–49.

6. Ward, "Harry Potter and Medievalism."

7. John Haines, *Music in Films on the Middle Ages: Authenticity vs. Fantasy* (New York: Routledge, 2014), 3.

8. *Harry Potter and the Sorcerer's Stone* was originally released in 2001 for PC, PlayStation, Game Boy Color, and Game Boy Advance. *Harry Potter and the Chamber of Secrets* was released a year later for those platforms but also for the new Xbox, GameCube, and PlayStation 2 consoles. These games earned much better reviews, in no small part because of the improvements to play allowed by the three newer, more advanced consoles, and thus in 2003, developer Electronic Arts remade *Sorcerer's Stone* for them as well.

9. As an aside, the vast similarities in game play between the two games caused many to criticize the next-generation remake of *Sorcerer's Stone*, one going so far as to call it a "digital equivalent to a Ron Weasley hand-me-down," accessed April 30, 2017, http://gaming. wikia.com/wiki/Harry_Potter_and_the_Philosopher%27s_Stone.

10. Although her work treats the first-generation version of *Sorcerer's Stone*, see Anna Gunders, "Harry Ludens: *Harry Potter and the Philosopher's Stone* as a Novel and Computer Game," *Human IT* 7, no. 2 (2004): 1–137.

11. The theme names are taken from the official *Sorcerer's Stone* and *Chamber of Secrets* soundtracks, both released in 2006, as listed on the Video Game Music Database, accessed April 30, 2017, http://vgmdb.net/album/5898; http://vgmdb.net/album/5897. As neither contains the sum total of music in the games, I have also relied on supplementary material.

12. yak, "Jeremy Soule—Music in Games 1," accessed April 30, 2017, http://www.yiya.de/reviews/j/jes001e1.shtml.

13. Ibid.; Jayson Napolitano, "Interview with Composer Jeremy Soule at PLAY! San Jose," *Music4Games*, June 6, 2007, accessed April 30, 2017, http://web.archive.org/web/20080620051533/http://www.music4games.net/Features_Display.aspx?id=145.

14. Stephen Meyer, "Soundscapes of Middle Earth: The Question of Medievalist Music in Peter Jackson's Lord of the Rings Films," in *Studies in Medievalism XVIII: Defining Medievalism(s) II*, ed. Karl Fugelso (Suffolk: Boydell & Brewer, 2009), 165–187, 166.

15. Elizabeth Randell Upton, "Coconut Clops and Motorcycle Warfare: What Sounds Medieval?," *Sounding Out!*, September 19, 2016, accessed April 30, 2017, https://soundstudiesblog.com/2016/09/19/coconut-clops-and-motorcycle-fanfare-what-sounds-medieval/.

16. Meyer, "Soundscapes of Middle Earth," 168; Haines, *Music in Films on the Middle Ages*, 24.

17. Raymond Monelle, *The Musical Topic: Hunt, Military and Pastoral* (Bloomington: Indiana University Press, 2006); Leonard Ratner, *Classic Music: Expression, Form, and Style* (New York: Schirmer, 1992).

18. See Haines, *Music in Films on the Middle Ages*, chap. 45.; Isabella van Elferen, "Fantasy Music: Epic Soundtracks, Magical Instruments, Musical Metaphysics," *Journal of the Fantastic in the Arts* 24, no. 1 (87) (2013): 4–24.

19. See Monelle, *The Musical Topic*, esp. chap. 7.

20. See Haines, *Music in Films on the Middle Ages*, 49.

21. See Haines, *Music in Films on the Middle Ages*, 58–66.

22. See van Elferen, "Fantasy Music," for a discussion of the harp's role in fantasy literature.

23. "Flashback Sequence," TV Tropes, http://tvtropes.org/pmwiki/pmwiki.php/Main/FlashbackEffects; "Dream Sequence," TV Tropes, http://tvtropes.org/pmwiki/pmwiki.php/Main/DreamSequence, accessed April 30, 2017.

24. For more connections between music and "otherworldly magic," see van Elferen, "Fantasy Music."

25. Because of the sonic similarities of the celesta and glockenspiel, especially within larger orchestral textures, and their respective symbolic connotations, I do not distinguish between the two here. It must also be said that it is very difficult in some cases to distinguish between the xylophone, glockenspiel, harp, and piano, and so I have tried to discuss only those instances where I feel fairly sure, without access to a score, that I am referencing the correct instrument. Piano is increasingly used in *Chamber of Secrets*, but in ways that mimic the sounds of, or even replace, the harp, xylophone, and glockenspiel or celesta as they were used in *Sorcerer's Stone* and so it will not be treated separately here.

26. "Mood Motif," TV Tropes, http://tvtropes.org/pmwiki/pmwiki.php/Main/MoodMotif, accessed April 30, 2017,

27. Robert Reynolds, "Textless Choral Music," *The Choral Journal* 41, no. 2 (September 2000): 19–34; Jean-David Jumeau-Lafond, "Le choeur sans paroles ou les voix du sublime," *Revue de Musicologie* 83, no. 2 (1997): 263–279.

28. Haines, *Music in Films on the Middle Ages*, 132. Particularly well-known examples from heroic or medievalist films include the Ark theme from *Raiders of the Lost Ark* and numerous examples from the Star Wars series, all composed by John Williams; see also various themes from *The Legend of Zelda: Ocarina of Time*, "Ethereal Choir," TV Tropes, accessed April 30, 2017, http://tvtropes.org/pmwiki/pmwiki.php/Main/EtherealChoir.

29. Haines, *Music in Films on the Middle Ages*, 129–130; James Deaville, "The Topos of 'Evil Medieval' in American Horror Film Music," in *Music, Meaning, and Media*, ed. Erkki Pekkilä, David Neumeyer, and Richard Littlefield (Helsinki: Semiotic Society of Finland, University of Helsinki and International Semiotics Institute at Imatra, 2006), 26–37; "Ominous Latin Chanting," TV Tropes, accessed April 30, 2017, http://tvtropes.org/pmwiki/pmwiki.php/Main/OminousLatinChanting. See also James Deaville's contribution to this volume, "Evil Medieval: Chant and the New Dark Spirituality of Vietnam-Era Film in America," pp. 709–728.

30. See Kirsten Yri's contribution to this volume, "Medievalism and Anti-Romanticism in Carl Orff's *Carmina Burana*," pp. 269–300.

31. John Haines points out that the blurring of diegetic and nondiegetic music is prominent in medieval(ist) film, though he refers more specifically to the horn call and trumpet fanfare motifs. See Haines, *Music in Films on the Middle Ages*, 63.

Selected Bibliography

Aberth, John. *A Knight at the Movies: Medieval History on Film*. New York: Routledge, 1993.

Addison, Agnes. *Romanticism and the Gothic Revival*. New York: Gordian Press, 1967.

Alam, Zaheed. "Treatment of the Gothic Elements by the Early Romantics." *ASA University Review* 6, no. 1 (January–June 2012): 295–304.

Albin, Andrew, Mary C. Erler, Thomas O'Donnell, Nicholas L. Paul, and Nina Rowe, eds. *Whose Middle Ages?: Teachable Moments for an Ill-Used Past*. New York: Fordham University Press, 2019.

Aldrich, Megan. *Gothic Revival*. London: Phaidon, 1994.

Alexander, Michael. *Medievalism: The Middle Ages in Modern England*. New Haven, CT: Yale University Press, 2007.

Apel, Willi. *The Notation of Polyphonic Music 900–1600*. Cambridge, MA: Mediaeval Academy of America, 1950.

Aronstein, Susan. *Hollywood Knights: Arthurian Cinema and the Politics of Nostalgia*. New York: Palgrave Macmillan, 2005.

Aronstein, Susan, and Nancy Coiner. "Twice Knightly: Democratizing the Middle Ages for Middle-Class America." *Studies in Medievalism* 6 (1994): 212–231.

Ashby, Steven P., and John Schofield. "'Hold the Heathen Hammer High': Representation, Re-enactment and the Construction of 'Pagan' Heritage." *International Journal of Heritage Studies* 21, no. 5 (2015): 493–511.

Aubrey, Elizabeth. *The Music of the Troubadours*. Bloomington: Indiana University Press, 1996.

Bain, Jennifer. *Hildegard of Bingen and Musical Reception: The Modern Revival of a Medieval Composer*. Cambridge: Cambridge University Press, 2015.

Bain, Jennifer. "Hildegard on 34th Street: Chant in the Marketplace." *Echo* 6, no. 1 (Spring 2004): n.p. http://www.echo.ucla.edu/Volume6-issue1/bain/bain1.html.

Barber, Richard, ed. *King Arthur in Music*. Cambridge: Brewer, 2002.

Barclay, David E. "Medievalism and Monarchy in Nineteenth Century Germany: Ludwig I and Frederick William IV." In *Selected Papers on Medievalism*, edited by Janet Goebel and Rebecca Cochran, 2:124–135. Indiana: Indiana University of Pennsylvania Press, 1988.

Barclay, David E. "Medievalism and Nationalism in Nineteenth-Century Germany." *Studies in Medievalism* 5 (1993): 5–22.

Becker, C. F. "Literatur: Die Minnesinger des 12., 13. und 14. Jahrhunderts." *Neue Zeitschrift für Musik* 13, no. 28 (October 3, 1840): 111–112.

Bellman, Jonathan. "*Aus alten Märchen*: The Chivalric Style of Schumann and Brahms." *Journal of Musicology* 13, no. 1 (Winter 1995): 117–135.

Bennett, Alana. "Reinventing the Past in European Neo-Medieval Music." In *The Middle Ages in Popular Culture: Medievalism and Genre*, edited by Helen Young, 91–112. Amherst, NY: Cambria Press, 2015.

Bent, Margaret. "*Resfacta* and *Cantare Super Librum*." *Journal of the American Musicological Society* 36, no. 3 (Autumn 1983): 371–391.

Bent, Margaret. "What Next? Recent Work and New Directions for English Medieval Music." *Early Music* 45, no. 1 (February 2017): 3–10.

Bergeron, Katherine. *Decadent Enchantments: The Revival of Gregorian Chant at Solesmes.* Berkeley: University of California Press, 1998.

Bergeron, Katherine. "A Lifetime of Chants." In *Disciplining Music: Musicology and Its Canons,* edited by Katherine Bergeron and Philip V. Bohlman, 182–196. Chicago: University of Chicago Press, 1992.

Bergeron, Katherine. "The Virtual Sacred: Finding God at Tower Records." *New Republic* 212, no. 9 (February 27, 1995): 29–34.

Bernanke, Judith. "Howard Shore's *Ring* Cycle: The Film Score and Operatic Strategy." In *Studying the Event Film: "The Lord of the Rings,"* edited by Harriet Margolis, Sean Cubitt, Barry King, and Thierry Jutel, 176–184. Manchester: Manchester University Press, 2008.

Bernau, Anke, and Bettina Bildhauer, eds. *Medieval Film.* Manchester: Manchester University Press, 2009.

Berns, Ute, and Andrew James Johnston. "Medievalism: A Very Short Introduction." *European Journal of English Studies* 15, no. 2 (2011): 97–100.

Besseler, Heinrich. "Studien zur Musik des Mittelalters: I. Neue Quellen des 14. und beginnen den 15. Jahrhunderts." *Archiv für Musikwissenschaft* 7 (1925): 167–252.

Biddick, Kathleen. *The Shock of Medievalism.* London: Duke University Press, 1998.

Bildhauer, Bettina. *Filming the Middle Ages.* London: Reaktion Books, 2011.

Björnsson, Árni. *Wagner and the Volsungs: Icelandic Sources of "Der Ring des Nibelungen."* London: Viking Society for Northern Research, 2003.

Blackmore, Josiah. "Melancholy, Passionate Love, and the *Coita d'Amor.*" *PMLA* 124, no. 2 (March 2009): 640–646.

Blanton, Virginia. "'Don't Worry, I Won't Let Them Rape You': Guinevere's Agency in Jerry Bruckheimer's *King Arthur.*" *Arthuriana* 15, no. 3 (Fall 2005): 91–111.

Bloch, R. Howard. *Medieval Misogyny and the Invention of Western Romantic Love.* Chicago: University of Chicago Press, 1991.

Bloch, R. Howard. "The Once and Future Middle Ages." *Modern Language Quarterly* 54, no. 1 (March 1993): 67–77.

Bloch, R. Howard, and Stephen G. Nichols, eds. *Medievalism and the Modernist Temper.* Baltimore: John Hopkins University Press, 1996.

Boase, Roger. *The Origin and Meaning of Courtly Love: A Critical Study of European Scholarship.* Manchester: Manchester University Press, 1977.

Bomback, Larry. "Wagner's Access to Minnesinger Melodies Prior to Completing *Tannhäuser.*" *Musical Times* 147, no. 1896 (Autumn 2006): 19–31.

Bonner, Andrew, ed. and trans. *Songs of the Troubadours.* New York: Schocken Press, 1972.

Bontrager, Shannon Ty. "The Imagined Crusade: The Church of England and the Mythology of Nationalism and Christianity during the Great War." *Church History* 71, no. 4 (2002): 774–798.

Bordone, Renato. "Il Medioevo nell'immaginario dell'ottocento italiano." *Bullettino dell'Istituto storico italiano per il Medioevo* 100 (1997): 109–149.

Bordwell, David. *Filmguide to "La passion de Jeanne d'Arc."* Bloomington: Indiana University Press, 1973.

Borghetti, Vincenzo. "Purezza e trasgressione: Il suono del Medioevo dagli anni Cinquanta ad oggi" [Purity and transgression: The sound of the Middle Ages from the 1950s to present]. *Semicerchio* 44 (2011): 37–54.

Botting, Fred. *Gothic.* 2nd ed. London: Routledge, 2014.

Boucher, Louis. *La première fête nationale de Jeanne d'Arc à Rouen en 1920*. Rouen: Defontaine, 1922.

Boyes, Georgina. *The Imagined Village: Culture, Ideology and the English Folk Revival*. Manchester: Manchester University Press, 1993.

Brauneiss, Leopold. "Arvo Pärt's Tintinnabuli Style: Contemporary Music towards a New Middle Ages?" *Studies in Medievalism* 13 (2003): 27–34.

Brauneiss, Leopold. "The Unification of Opposites: The Tintinnabuli Style in the Light of the Philosophy of Nicolaus Cusanus." Translated by Robert Crow. *Music and Literature* 1 (2012): 53–60.

Breen, Edward. "David Munrow's 'Turkish Nightclub Piece.'" In *Recomposing the Past: Representations of Early Music on Stage and Screen*, edited by James Cook, Alexander Kolassa, and Adam Whittaker, 124–138. London: Routledge, 2018.

Breen, Edward. "The Performance Practice of David Munrow and the Early Music Consort of London: Medieval Music in the 1960s and 1970s." PhD diss., King's College London, 2015.

Breen, Edward. "Travel in Space, Travel in Time: Michael Morrow's Approach to Performing Medieval Music in the 1960s." *Studies in Medievalism* 25 (2016): 89–114.

Brendel, Franz. "R. Schumann's Oper: *Genoveva*." *Neue Zeitschrift für Musik* 33, no. 1 (July 2, 1850): 1–4.

Brown, Harry. "Baphomet Incorporated: A Case Study in Neomedievalism." *Studies in Medievalism* 20 (2011): 1–10.

Brownlee, Marina S., Kevin Brownlee, and Stephen G. Nichols, eds. *The New Medievalism*. Baltimore: Johns Hopkins University Press, 1991.

Bruce, James Douglas. *The Evolution of Arthurian Romance from the Beginnings down to the Year 1300*. 2 vols. Baltimore: John Hopkins Press, 1923.

Buehler-McWilliams, Kathryn, and Russell E. Murray. "The Monochord in the Medieval and Modern Classroom." *Journal of Music History Pedagogy* 3, no. 2 (2013): 151–172.

Buhler, James. "Enchantments of *Lord of the Rings*: Soundtrack, Myth, Language, and Modernity." In *From Hobbits to Hollywood: Essays on Peter Jackson's "Lord of the Rings,"* edited by Ernest Mathijs and Murray Pomerance, 231–248. Amsterdam: Rudopi, 2006.

Burns, E. Jane. "Courtly Love: Who Needs It? Recent Feminist Work in the Medieval French Tradition." *Signs* 27, no. 1 (Autumn 2001): 23–57.

Burns, E. Jane. "Nostalgia Isn't What It Used to Be: The Middle Ages in Literature and Film." In *Shadows of the Magic Lamp: Fantasy and Science Fiction in Film*, edited by George E. Slusser and Eric S. Rabkin, 86–97. Carbondale: Southern Illinois University Press, 1985.

Buschinger, Danielle. *Le Moyen Âge de Richard Wagner*. Amiens: Presses de l'Université de Picardie–Jules Verne, 2003.

Busse Berger, Anna Maria. *Medieval Music and the Art of Memory*. Berkeley: University of California Press, 2005.

Butt, John. *Playing with History: The Historical Approach to Musical Performance*. Cambridge: Cambridge University Press, 2002.

Calmel, Huguette, and Pascal Lécroart. *"Jeanne d'Arc au bûcher" de Paul Claudel et Arthur Honegger*. Geneva: Éditions Papillon, 2004.

Cantor, Norman F. *Inventing the Middle Ages: The Lives, Works and Ideas of the Great Medievalists of the Twentieth Century*. New York: Quill William Morrow, 1991.

Capellanus, Andreas. *The Art of Courtly Love*. With an introduction, translation, and notes by John Jay Parry. New York: Columbia University Press, 1941.

Chance, Jane, and Alfred K. Siewers, eds. *Tolkien's Modern Middle Ages*. New York: Palgrave Macmillan, 2005.

Chism, Christine. "Middle-Earth, the Middle Ages, and the Aryan Nation: Myth and History in World War II." In *Tolkien the Medievalist*, edited by Jane Chance, 63–92. London: Routledge, 2003.

Cicora, Mary A. *From History to Myth: Wagner's "Tannhäuser" and Its Literary Sources*. Bern: Lang, 1992.

Cicora, Mary A. "Medievalism and Metaphysics: The Literary Background of *Parsifal*." In *A Companion to Wagner's "Parsifal,"* edited by William Kinderman and Katherine R. Syer, 29–53. Rochester, NY: Camden House, 2005.

Cicora, Mary A. *Wagner's "Ring" and German Drama: Comparative Studies in Mythology and History in Drama*. Westport, CT: Greenwood Press, 1999.

Classen, Albert. "The Defeat of the Matriarch Brünhild in the *Nibelungenlied*, with Some Thoughts on Matriarchy as Evinced in Literary Texts." In *"Waz sider da geschach": American-German Studies on the "Nibelungenlied,"* edited by Werner Wunderlich and Ulrich Müller, 89–110. Göppingen: Kümmerle Verlag, 1992.

Cohen, Jeffrey Jerome, ed. *The Postcolonial Middle Ages*. New York: St. Martin's Press, 2000.

Colton, Lisa. "The Articulation of Virginity in the Medieval *Chanson de nonne*." *Journal of the Royal Musical Association* 133, no. 2 (2008): 159–188.

Colton, Lisa. "Medievalism, Music, and Agency in *The Wicker Man* (1973)." In *Recomposing the Past: Early Music on Stage and Screen*, edited by James Cook, Alexander Kolassa, and Adam Whittaker, Abingdon, UK: Routledge, 2017.

Colton, Lisa. "Medievalism, Renewal and Englishness in the Music of Benjamin Britten." Paper presented at Britten in Context, Liverpool Hope University, 2010. http://hud.academia.edu/LisaColton.

Cook, James. "Playing with the Past in the Imaginary Middle Ages: Music and Soundscape in Video Game." *Sounding Out!* October 3, 2016. https://soundstudiesblog.com/tag/james-cook/.

Cook, James, Alexander Kolassa, and Adam Whittaker. "Music in Fantasy Pasts: Neomedievalism and *Game of Thrones*." In *Recomposing the Past: Representations of Early Music on Stage and Screen*, edited by James Cook, Alexander Kolassa, and Adam Whittaker, 229–250. London: Routledge, 2018.

Cooke, Deryck. *I Saw the World End: A Study of Wagner's "Ring."* London: Oxford University Press, 1979.

Coote, Lesley. "A Short Essay about Neomedievalism." *Studies in Medievalism* 19 (2010): 25–33.

Crane, Frederick. *Extant Medieval Musical Instruments: A Provisional Catalogue by Types*. Iowa City: University of Iowa Press, 1972.

Curley, Michael J. *Geoffrey of Monmouth*. New York: Twayne, 1994.

Damico, Helen, and Joseph Zavadil, eds. *Medieval Scholarship: Biographical Studies on the Formation of a Discipline*. 3 vols. New York: Garland, 1995–2000.

D'Arcens, Louise, ed. *The Cambridge Companion to Medievalism*. Cambridge: Cambridge University Press, 2016.

Daverio, John. "Brahms's *Magelone Romanzen* and the 'Romantic Imperative.'" *Journal of Musicology* 7, no. 3 (Summer 1989): 343–365.

Davis, Kathleen, and Nadia Altschul, eds. *Medievalisms in the Postcolonial World: The Idea of "the Middle Ages" outside Europe*. Baltimore: John Hopkins University Press, 2009.

Davison, Archibald T., and Willi Apel. *Historical Anthology of Music*. Vol. 1, *Oriental, Medieval and Renaissance Music*. Cambridge, MA: Harvard University Press, 1946.

Deathridge, John. *Wagner's "Rienzi": A Reappraisal Based on a Study of the Sketches and Drafts*. Oxford: Clarendon Press, 1977.

Deaville, James. "The Topos of 'Evil Medieval' in American Horror Film Music." In *Music, Meaning, and Media*, edited by Erkki Pekkilä, David Neumeyer, and Richard Littlefield, 26–44. Helsinki: International Semiotics Institute, 2006.

De Geer, Ingrid. "Music." In *The Cambridge History of Scandinavia*. Vol. 1, *Prehistory to 1520*, edited by Knut Helle, 550–556. Cambridge: Cambridge University Press, 2003.

Dell, Helen. "Dying for Love in Trouvère Song." In *Singing Death: Reflections on Music and Mortality*, edited by Helen Dell and Helen M. Hickey, 119–135. London: Routledge, 2017.

Demouy, Patrick. "La liturgie du sacre de Charles VII." *Annales de l'Est*, no. 2 (2015): 111–121.

Dendle, Peter. "'The Age of Faith': Everyone in the Middle Ages Believed in God." In *Misconceptions about the Middle Ages*, edited by Stephen J. Harris and Bryon L. Grigsby, 49–53. Routledge Studies in Medieval Religion and Culture 7. New York: Routledge, 2008.

Desmond, Karen. "Refusal, the Look of Love, and the Beastly Woman of Machaut's Balades 27 and 38." *Early Music History* 32 (2013): 71–118.

Desportes, Pierre. *Fasti Ecclesiae Gallicanae: Répertoire prosopographique des évêques, dignitaires et chanoines des diocèses de France de 1200 à 1500*. Vol. 3, *Diocèse de Reims*, edited by Hélène Millet. Turnhout: Brepols, 1998.

Dillon, Emma. *The Sense of Sound: Musical Meaning in France, 1260–1330*. Oxford: Oxford University Press, 2012.

Dinshaw, Carolyn. *Getting Medieval: Sexualities and Communities, Pre- and Postmodern*. Durham, NC: Duke University Press, 1999.

Dinshaw, Carolyn. *How Soon Is Now? Medieval Texts, Amateur Readers, and the Queerness of Time*. Durham, NC: Duke University Press, 2012.

Dister, Elizabeth. "Inspiring the Nation: French Music about Jeanne d'Arc in the 1930s and 1940s." PhD diss., Washington University in St. Louis, 2015.

Domokos, Zsuzsanna. "Liszt's Connection with the Cecilian Movement in the Light of His Music Library in Budapest." In *Franz Liszt's Estate at the Budapest Academy of Music*, edited by Mária Eckhardt. Vol. 2, *Music*, 76–84. Budapest: Liszt Ferenc Zeneművészeti Főiskola, 1993.

D'Ortigue, J[oseph]. *Dictionnaire liturgique, historique et théorique de plain-chant et de musique d'église au moyen âge et dans les temps modernes*. Paris: Potier, 1854. http://gallica.bnf.fr/ark:/12148/bpt6k6298607m?rk=21459;2.

Dufetel, Nicolas. "Religious Workshop and Gregorian Chant: The Janus Liszt, or How to Make New with the Old." In *Liszt's Legacies: Based on Papers Presented at the International Liszt Conference Held at Carleton University, Ottawa, Canada, 28–31 July 2011*, edited by James Deaville and Michael Saffle, 43–71. Hillsdale, NY: Pendragon Press, 2014.

Duffin, Ross W., ed. *A Performer's Guide to Medieval Music*. Bloomington: Indiana University Press, 2000.

Duggett, Tom. *Gothic Romanticism: Architecture, Politics, and Literary Form*. New York: Palgrave Macmillan, 2010.

Earp, Lawrence. *Guillaume de Machaut: A Guide to Research*. New York: Garland, 1995.

Echard, Siân, ed. *The Arthur of Medieval Latin Literature: The Development and Dissemination of the Arthurian Legend in Medieval Latin*. Cardiff: University of Wales Press, 2011.

Eco, Umberto. "The Return of the Middle Ages." In *Faith in Fakes: Travels in Hyperreality*, translated by William Weaver, 61–85. London: Minerva, 1995.

Edwards, Jennifer C. "Casting, Plotting, and Enchanting: Arthurian Women in Starz's *Camelot* and the BBC's *Merlin*." *Arthuriana* 25, no. 1 (Spring 2015): 57–81.

Ehrismann, Otfried. *Das Nibelungenlied in Deutschland: Studien zur Rezeption des Nibelungenlieds von der Mitte des 18. Jahrhunderts bis zum Ersten Weltkrieg*. Munich: Fink, 1975.

Ehrismann, Otfried. "Reception of the *Nibelungenlied* in Germany." In *The Nibelungen Tradition: An Encyclopedia*, edited by Francis G. Gentry, Winder McConnell, Ulrich Müller, and Werner Wunderlich, 219–224. New York: Routledge, 2002.

Elliott, Andrew B. R. *Remaking the Middle Ages: The Methods of Cinema and History in Portraying the Medieval World*. Jefferson, NC: McFarland, 2011.

Ellis, Katherine. *Interpreting the Musical Past: Early Music in Nineteenth-Century France*. Oxford: Oxford University Press, 2005.

Emery, Elizabeth. "Medievalism and the Middle Ages." *Studies in Medievalism* 17 (2009): 77–85.

Emery, Elizabeth, and Laura Morowitz. *Consuming the Past: The Medieval Revival in fin-de-siècle France*. Burlington, VT: Ashgate, 2003.

Emery, Elizabeth, and Richard Utz, eds. *Medievalism: Key Critical Terms*. Cambridge: Brewer, 2014.

Emmerson, Richard K. "'Englysch Laten' and 'Franch': Language as Sign of Evil in Medieval English Drama." In *The Devil, Heresy and Witchcraft in the Middle Ages: Essays in Honor of Jeffrey B. Russell*, edited Alberto Ferreiro, 305–326. Leiden: Brill, 1998.

Erfen, Irene, ed. *"...der Welt noch den Tannhäuser schuldig": Richard Wagner; "Tannhäuser" und der Sängerkrieg auf der Wartburg*. Regensburg: Schnell und Steiner, 1999.

Evans, R. J. W., and Guy P. Marchal. *The Uses of the Middle Ages in Modern European States: History, Nationhood and the Search for Origins*. Basingstoke, UK: Palgrave Macmillan, 2011.

Evans, Timothy H. "Folklore as Utopia: English Medievalists and the Ideology of Revivalism." *Western Folklore* 47, no. 4 (October 1988): 245–268.

Everist, Mark, ed. *The Cambridge Companion to Medieval Music*. Cambridge: Cambridge University Press, 2011.

Ewert, Hansjörg. *Anspruch und Wirkung: Studien zur Entstehung der Oper "Genoveva" von Robert Schumann*. Tutzing: Schneider, 2003.

Fabre, Joseph. *Procès de condamnation de Jeanne d'Arc, d'après les textes authentiques des procès-verbaux officiels, traduction avec éclaircissements*. Paris: Librairie Ch. Delagrave, 1884.

Fabre, Joseph. *Procès de réhabilitation de Jeanne d'Arc: Raconté et traduit d'après les textes latins officiels*. 2 vols. Paris: Librairie Ch. Delagrave, 1888.

Fallows, David. "Performing Medieval Music." In *The Future of Early Music in Britain: Papers Delivered at the Conference Held in the Waterloo Room of the Royal Festival Hall, London, 14-16 May 1977*, edited by J. M. Thomson, 1–5. London: Oxford University Press, 1978.

Fallows, David. "Performing Medieval Music in the Late-1960s: Michael Morrow and Thomas Binkley." In *Essays in Honor of László Somfai on His 70th Birthday: Studies in the Sources and the Interpretation of Music*, edited by László Vikárius and Vera Lampert, 51–56. Lanham, MD: Scarecrow Press, 2005.

Fernandez-Herrera, Dario. *The Myth of the Andalusian Paradise: Muslims, Christians, and Jews under Islamic Rule in Medieval Spain*. Wilmington, IN: Intercollegiate Studies Institute, 2016.

Feurzeig, Lisa. "Don't Ask: Faith, Magic, Knowledge, and Sources in *Lohengrin*." In *Wagner Outside the Ring: Essays on the Operas, Their Performance and Their Connections with Other Arts*, edited by John Louis DiGaetani, 80–104. Jefferson, NC: McFarland, 2009.

Ficker, Rudolf. "Polyphonic Music of the Gothic Period." *Musical Quarterly* 15, no. 4 (October 1929): 483–505.

Finke, Laurie A., and Martin B. Shichtman. *Cinematic Illuminations: The Middle Ages on Film*. Baltimore: Johns Hopkins University Press, 2010.

Finscher, Ludwig. "Weber's *Freischütz*: Conceptions and Misconceptions." *Proceedings of the Royal Musical Association* 110 (1983–1984): 79–90.

Fischer, Jens Malte. "Singende Recken und blitzende Schwerter: Die Mittelalteroper neben und nach Wagner—ein Überblick." In *Mittelalter-Rezeption: Ein Symposium*, edited by Peter Wapnewski, 511–530. Stuttgart: Metzler, 1986.

François, Stéphane. "The Euro-Pagan Scene: Between Paganism and the Radical Right." *Journal for the Study of Radicalism* 1, no. 2 (Summer 2007): 35–54.

Frank, Roberta. "The Invention of the Viking Horned Helmet." In *International Scandinavian and Medieval Studies in Memory of Gerd Wolfgang Weber*, edited by Michael Dallapiazza, Olaf Hansen, Preben Meulengracht Sørensen, and Yvonne S. Bonnetain, 199–208. Trieste, Italy: Edizioni Parnaso, 2000.

Fries, Maureen. "Gender and the Grail." *Arthuriana* 8, no. 1 (Spring 1998): 67–79.

Fries, Maureen. "What Tennyson Really Did to Malory's Women." *Quondam et Futurus* 1, no. 1 (Spring 1991): 44–55.

Frisch, Walter. "Reger's Historicist Modernism." *Musical Quarterly* 87, no. 4 (Winter 2004): 732–748.

Fulton, Helen. "A Woman's Place: Guinevere in the Welsh and French Romances." *Quondam et Futurus* 3, no. 2 (Summer 1993): 1–25.

Gamer, Michael. *Romanticism and the Gothic: Genre, Reception, and Canon Formation*. Cambridge: Cambridge University Press, 2000.

Ganim, John M. *Medievalism and Orientalism: Three Essays on Literature, Architecture and Cultural Identity*. The New Middle Ages. New York: Palgrave Macmillan, 2005.

Gaunt, Simon. *Love and Death in Medieval French and Occitan Courtly Literature: Martyrs to Love*. Oxford: Oxford University Press, 2006.

Gaunt, Simon, and Sarah Kay, eds. *The Troubadours: An Introduction*. Cambridge: Cambridge University Press, 1999.

Geck, Martin. "Richard Wagner und die ältere Musik." In *Die Ausbreitung des Historismus über die Musik*, edited by Walter Wiora, 123–146. Regensburg: Bosse, 1969.

Gentry, Francis G. "The Politicization of the Middle Ages: Nationalism and Festivals in Nineteenth-Century Germany." *Studies in Medievalism* 3, no. 4 (Spring 1991): 467–488.

Gentry, Francis G., and Ulrich Müller. "The Reception of the Middle Ages in Germany." *Studies in Medievalism* 3, no. 4 (Spring 1991): 399–422.

Geoffrey of Monmouth. *The History of the Kings of Britain*. Edited and translated by Michael A. Faletra. Peterborough, ON: Broadview Editions, 2008.

Girouard, Mark. *The Return to Camelot: Chivalry and the English Gentleman*. New Haven, CT: Yale University Press, 1981.

Glencross, Michael. *Reconstructing Camelot: French Romantic Medievalism and the Arthurian Tradition*. Cambridge: Brewer, 1995.

Gobel, Stefan. *The Great War and Medieval Memory: War, Remembrance and Medievalism in Britain and Germany, 1914–1940*. Cambridge: Cambridge University Press, 2006.

Golden, Rachel May. "Polyphonies of Sound and Space: Motet, Montage, *Voices of Light*, and *La Passion de Jeanne d'Arc*." *Musical Quarterly* 96, no. 2 (August 2013): 296–330.

Goldin, Frederick. *The Mirror of Narcissus in the Courtly Love Lyric*. Ithaca, NY: Cornell University Press, 1967.

Greig, Donald. "*Ars Subtilior* Repertory as Performance Palimpsest." *Early Music* 31, no. 2 (2003): 196–209.

Groos, Arthur. "Constructing Nuremberg: Typological and Proleptic Communities in *Die Meistersinger*." *19th-Century Music* 16, no. 1 (Summer 1992): 18–34.

Günther, Ursula. "Das Ende der Ars Nova." *Die Musikforschung* 16 (1963): 105–120.

Gut, Serge. "Die historische Position der Modalität bei Franz Liszt." In *Liszt Studien 1: Kongress-Bericht Eisenstadt 1975*, edited by Wolfgang Suppan, 97–103. Graz: Akademische Druck- u. Verlagsanstalt, 1977.

Hagen, Friedrich Heinrich von der. *Minnesinger: Deutsche Liederdichter des zwölften, dreizehnten und vierzehnten Jahrhunderts*. Vol. 1. Leipzig: Barth, 1838.

Hagenberg-Miliu, Ebba-Christina. "'… Denn nur der Ruhm des Vaterlandes ist mein Ziel': Zu Erneuerungen des Nibelungen- und des Kudrunepos." PhD diss., Rheinische Friedrich-Wilhelms-Universität Bonn, 1988.

Hahn, Thomas, ed. *Robin Hood in Popular Culture: Violence, Transgression, and Justice*. Cambridge: Brewer, 2000.

Haines, John. "Antiquarian Nostalgia and the Institutionalization of Early Music." In *The Oxford Handbook of Music Revival*, edited by Caroline Bithell and Juniper Hill, 73–93. Oxford: Oxford University Press, 2014.

Haines, John. "The Arabic Style of Performing Medieval Music." *Early Music* 29, no. 3 (August 2001): 369–378.

Haines, John. *Eight Centuries of Troubadours and Trouvères: The Changing Identity of Medieval Music*. Cambridge: Cambridge University Press, 2004.

Haines, John. "Living Troubadours and Other Recent Uses for Medieval Music." *Popular Music* 23, no. 2 (May 2004): 133–153.

Haines, John. *Medieval Song in Romance Languages*. Cambridge: Cambridge University Press, 2010.

Haines, John. "The Musical Incongruities of Time Travel in Arthurian Film." In *The Legacy of Courtly Literature: From Medieval to Contemporary Culture*, edited by Deborah Nelson-Campbell and Ruben Cholakian, 151–174. Cham, Switzerland: Palgrave Macmillan, 2017.

Haines, John. *Music in Films on the Middle Ages: Authenticity vs. Fantasy*. New York: Routledge, 2013.

Haines, John. "The Revival of Medieval Music." In *The Cambridge History of Medieval Music*, edited by Thomas F. Kelly and Mark Everist, 561–581. Cambridge: Cambridge University Press, 2018.

Hallman, Diana R. *Opera, Liberalism, and Antisemitism in Nineteenth-Century France: The Politics of Halévy's "La Juive."* Cambridge: Cambridge University Press, 2002.

Harper-Scott, J. P. E. "Medieval Romance and Wagner's Musical Narrative in the *Ring*." *19th-Century Music* 32, no. 3 (Spring 2009): 211–234.

Harris, Joseph. "'Ethnopaleography' and Recovered Performance: The Problematic Witnesses to 'Eddic song.'" *Western Folklore* 62, no. 1/2 (Winter–Spring 2003): 97–117.

Harris, Joseph. "The Performance of Old Norse Eddic Poetry: A Retrospective." In *The Oral Epic: Performance and Music*, edited by Karl Reichl, 225–232. Intercultural Music Studies 12. Berlin: Verlag für Wissenschaft und Bildung, 2000.

Harty, Kevin J. "Cinema Arthuriana: Translations of the Arthurian Legend to the Screen." *Arthurian Interpretations* 2, no. 1 (Fall 1987): 95–113.

Harty, Kevin J. "*The Knights of the Square Table*: The Boy Scouts and Thomas Edison Make an Arthurian Film." *Arthuriana* 4, no. 4 (Winter 1994): 313–323.

Harty, Kevin J. *The Reel Middle Ages: American, Western and Eastern European, Middle Eastern and Asian Films about Medieval Europe.* Jefferson, NC: McFarland, 1999.

Harty, Kevin J., ed. *Cinema Arthuriana: Twenty Essays.* Rev. ed. Jefferson, NC: McFarland, 2002.

Harty, Kevin J., ed. *King Arthur on Film: New Essays on Arthurian Cinema.* Jefferson, NC: McFarland, 1999.

Haskell, Harry. *The Early Music Revival, A History.* Mineola, NY: Dover, 1996.

Hauer, Stanley R. "Wagner and the *Völospá*." *19th-Century Music* 15, no. 1 (Summer 1991): 52–63.

Haycock, Marged. "Llyfr Taliesin." *National Library of Wales Journal/Cylchgrawn Llyfrgell Genedlaethol Cymru* 25, no. 4 (Winter 1988): 357–386.

Haydock, Nickolas. *Movie Medievalism: The Imaginary Middle Ages.* Jefferson, NC: McFarland, 2008.

Haymes, Edward R. "*Ring of the Nibelung* and the *Nibelungenlied*: Wagner's Ambiguous Relationship to a Source." *Studies in Medievalism* 17 (2009): 218–246.

Haymes, Edward R. "Two-Storied Medievalism in Wagner's *Die Meistersinger von Nürnberg*." *Studies in Medievalism* 3, no. 3–4 (1991): 505–513.

Heinzle, Joachim. "Mythos, Mythen und Wagners Mittelalter." In *Wagner Handbuch*, edited by Laurenz Lütteken, 102–109. Kassel: Bärenreiter, 2012.

Heinzle, Joachim, and Anneliese Waldschmidt, eds. *Die Nibelungen: Ein deutscher Wahn, ein deutscher Alptraum; Studien und Dokumente zur Rezeption des Nibelungenstoffs im 19. und 20. Jahrhundert.* Frankfurt am Main: Suhrkamp, 1991.

Helden, Imke von. "Barbarians and Literature: Viking Metal and Its Links to Old Norse Mythology." In *The Metal Void: First Gatherings*, edited by Niall W. R. Scott and Imke von Helden, 257–264. Oxford: Inter-Disciplinary Press, 2010. https://www.scribd.com/document/48532891/The-Metal-Void.

Heng, Geraldine. *The Invention of Race in the European Middle Ages.* Cambridge: Cambridge University Press, 2018.

Henkel, Nikolaus. "Wagners Vorstellungen von den Nibelungen: Einblicke in das Mittelalter-Gedächtnis des 19. Jahrhunderts." In *Wagners Siegfried und die (post-)heroische Moderne*, edited by Tobias Janz, 135–156. Würzburg: Königshausen und Neumann, 2011.

Henthorne, Tom. "Boys to Men: Medievalism and Masculinity in *Star Wars* and *E.T.: The Extra-Terrestrial*." In *The Medieval Hero on Screen: Representations from Beowulf to Buffy*, edited by Martha W. Driver and Sid Ray, 73–89. Jefferson, NC: McFarland, 2004.

Hibberd, Sarah. *French Grand Opera and the Historical Imagination.* Cambridge: Cambridge University Press, 2009.

Hoad, Catherine. "'Hold the Heathen Hammer High': Viking Metal from the Local to the Global." Paper presented at the International Association for the Study of Popular Music—Australia/New Zealand Conference, Hobart, December 5–7, 2012. https://www.academia.edu/5768762/Hold_the_Heathen_Hammer_High_-_Viking_Metal_from_the_Local_to_the_Global.

Hoeveler, Diane Long. "Anti-Catholicism and the Gothic Imaginary: The Historical and Literary Contexts." In *Religion in the Age of Enlightenment*, edited by Brett C. McInelly, 3:1–31. New York: AMS Press, 2012.

Hoeveler, Diane Long. *Gothic Riffs: Secularizing the Uncanny in the European Imaginary, 1780–1820.* Columbus: Ohio State University Press, 2010.

Holm, Thomas Robert. "Analysis and Comparison of Three Major Vocal/Instrumental Works of Arvo Pärt: *Passio*, *Miserere*, and *Litany*." DMA diss., University of Illinois at Urbana–Champaign, 1998.

Holsinger, Bruce Wood. "The Flesh of the Voice: Embodiment and the Homoerotics of Devotion in the Music of Hildegard of Bingen (1098–1179)." *Signs: Journal of Women in Culture and Society* 19, no.1 (Autumn 1993): 92–125.

Holsinger, Bruce Wood. *Music, Body, and Desire in Medieval Culture: Hildegard of Bingen to Chaucer*. Stanford, CA: Stanford University Press, 2001.

Holsinger, Bruce Wood. *The Premodern Condition: Medievalism and the Making of Theory*. Chicago: University of Chicago Press, 2005.

Huizinga, Johan. *The Autumn of the Middle Ages*. Translated by Rodney J. Payton and Ulrich Mammitzsch. Chicago: University of Chicago Press, 1996.

Huot, Sylvia. *Allegorical Play in the Old French Motet: The Sacred and the Profane in Thirteenth-Century Polyphony*. Stanford, CA: Stanford University Press, 1997.

Hurley, Thérèse. "Jeanne d'Arc on the 1870s Musical Stage: Jules Barbier and Charles Gounod's Melodrama and Auguste Mermet's Opera." PhD diss., University of Oregon, 2013.

Jeanroy, Alfred. *La poésie lyrique des troubadours*. 2 vols. Paris: Didier, 1934.

Join-Dieterlé, Catherine. "*Robert le Diable*: Le premier opéra romantique." *Romantisme* 28–29 (1980): 147–166.

Josephson, Nors S. "*Rodericus, Angelorum Psalat*." *Musica Disciplina* 25 (1971): 113–126.

Jost, Christa. "Die Nibelungen auf dem Weg zur Oper." In *"Nibelungenlied" und "Klage": Ursprung—Funktion—Bedeutung*, edited by Dietz-Rüdiger Moser and Marianne Sammer, 483–505. Munich: Institut für Bayerischer Literaturgeschichte, 1998.

Kaczmarczyk, Adrienne. "Liszt, Lamennais und der *Totentanz*." *Studia Musicologica Academiae Scientiarum Hungaricae* 43, no. 1/2 (2002): 53–72.

Karnes, Kevin C. *Arvo Pärt's Tabula Rasa*. Oxford Keynotes. Oxford: Oxford University Press, 2017.

Kasten, Ingrid. *Frauendienst bei Trobadors und Minnesängern im 12. Jahrhundert: Zur Entwicklung und Adaption eines literarischen Konzepts*. Germanisch-romanische Monatsschrift 5. Heidelberg: Carl Winter Universitätsverlag, 1986.

Kaufman, Amy S. "Medieval Unmoored." *Studies in Medievalism* 19 (2010): 1–11.

Kautny, Oliver. "'Dem Himmel ein Stück näher...': Der neoromantische Mythos 'Arvo Pärt.'" *Neue Zeitschrift für Musik* 163, no. 5 (September–October 2002): 24–27.

Kay, Sarah. "Courts, Clerks and Courtly Love." In *The Cambridge Companion to Medieval Romance*, edited by Roberta L. Krueger, 81–96. Cambridge: Cambridge University Press, 2000.

Kelly, Thomas Forrest. *Early Music: A Very Short Introduction*. Oxford: Oxford University Press, 2011.

Kennedy, Harlan. "The World of King Arthur According to John Boorman." *American Film* 6, no. 5 (March 1981): 30–37.

Kiesewetter, Raphael Georg. "Ueber den weltlichen und volksmässigen Gesang im Mittelalter." *Allgemeine musikalische Zeitung* 40, no. 15 (April 11, 1838): 233–247.

Kirkman, Andrew. "'Under Such Heavy Chains': The Discovery and Evaluation of Late Medieval Music before Ambros." *19th-Century Music* 24, no. 1 (2000): 89–112.

Klante, Wolfram. "Carl Ludwig Amadeus Mangolds *Tanhäuser*-Oper." In *"Tannhäuser" in der Kunst*, edited by Heinrich Weigel, Wolfram Klante, and Ingrid Schulze, 112–132. Bucha bei Jena: Quartus, 1999.

Koehler, Erich. "Observations historiques et sociologiques sur la poésie des troubadours." *Cahiers de civilisation médiévale* 7, no. 25 (1964): 27–51.

Koller, Angelika. *Minnesang-Rezeption um 1800: Falldarstellungen zu den Romantikern und ihren Zeitgenossen und Exkurse zu ausgewählten Sachfragen*. Bern: Lang, 1992.

Kretschmer, [Andreas]. "Freie Aufsätze: Ueber deutsche Musik des Mittelalters." *Berliner allgemeine musikalische Zeitung* 4, no. 17 (April 24, 1827): 129–131.

Kreutziger-Herr, Annette. *Ein Traum vom Mittelalter: Die Wiederentdeckung mittelalterlicher Musik in der Neuzeit*. Cologne: Böhlau Verlag, 2003.

Kreutziger-Herr, Annette. "Imagining Medieval Music: A Short History." *Studies in Medievalism* 14 (2005): 81–109.

Kreutziger-Herr, Annette. "Postmodern Middle Ages: Medieval Music at the Dawn of the Twenty-First Century." *Florilegium* 15 (1998): 187–205.

Kreutziger-Herr, Annette, and Dorothea Redepenning, eds. *Mittelalter-Sehnsucht? Texte des interdisziplinären Symposions zur musikalischen Mittelalterrezeption an der Universität Heidelberg, April 1998*. KulturReihe Aktuell 2. Kiel: Wissenschaftsverlag Vauk, 2000.

Labbie, Erin Felicia. "Pop Medievalism." Studies in Medievalism 24 (2015): 21–29.

Lacy, Norris J. "Arthurian Film and the Tyranny of Tradition." *Arthurian Interpretations* 4, no. 1 (Fall 1989): 75–85.

Lawson, Peter. "Maxwell Davies's *Worldes Blis*." *Tempo* 90 (Autumn 1969): 23–27.

Lazar, Moshe. "Fin'amor." In *A Handbook of the Troubadours*, edited by F. R. P. Akehurst and Judith M. Davis, 61–100. Berkeley: University of California Press, 1995.

Leech-Wilkinson, Daniel. *The Modern Invention of Medieval Music: Scholarship, Ideology, Performance*. Cambridge: Cambridge University Press, 2002.

Lemaire, Ria. "Explaining Away the Female Subject: The Case of Medieval Lyric." *Poetics Today* 7, no. 4 (1986): 729–743.

Lewis, C. S. *The Allegory of Love: A Study in Medieval Tradition*. Oxford: Clarendon Press, 1936.

Lindmayr-Brandl, Andrea. "*Resjois toi terre de France/Rex pacificus*: An 'Ockeghem' Work Reattributed to Busnoys." In *Antoine Busnoys: Method, Meaning, and Context in Late Medieval Music*, edited by Paula Higgins, 277–294. Oxford: Clarendon Press, 1999.

Loges, Natasha. "The Limits of the Lied: Brahms's *Magelone-Romanzen*, op. 33." In *Brahms in the Home and the Concert Hall: Between Private and Public Performance*, edited by Katy Hamilton and Natasha Loges, 300–323. Cambridge: Cambridge University Press, 2014.

Lönnroth, Lars. "The Vikings in History and Legend." In *The Oxford Illustrated History of the Vikings*, edited by Peter Sawyer, 225–249. Oxford: Oxford University Press, 1997.

Lott, Marie Sumner. "Romantic Medievalism in the Piano Romances of Clara and Robert Schumann and Brahms." *American Brahms Society Newsletter* 33, no. 1 (2015): 1–8.

Lupack, Alan. "Popular Images Derived from Tennyson's Arthurian Poems." *Arthuriana* 21, no. 2 (Summer 2011): 90–118.

Magee, Elizabeth. *Richard Wagner and the Nibelungs*. Oxford: Clarendon Press, 1990.

Mann, Thomas. "Richard Wagner and *Der Ring des Nibelungen*." In *Pro and Contra Wagner*, translated by Allan Blunden, 171–183. London: Faber & Faber, 1985.

Marshall, David W. "Neomedievalism, Identification, and the Haze of Medievalisms." *Studies in Medievalism* 20 (2011): 21–34.

Marshall, David W., ed. *Mass Market Medieval: Essays on the Middle Ages in Popular Culture*. Jefferson, NC: McFarland, 2007.

Martensen-Larsen, Britta. "Inspirationen fra middelalderens miniaturer." *Kosmorama* 39, no. 204 (Summer 1993): 26–31.

Martinez, Ann M. "Elvencentrism: The Green Medievalism of Tolkien's Elven Realms." *Studies in Medievalism* 26 (2017): 31–42.

Mathijs, Ernest, ed. *"The Lord of the Rings": Popular Culture in Global Context*. London: Wallflower Press, 2006.

Matthews, David. *Medievalism: A Critical History*. Cambridge: Brewer, 2015.

McGregor, Jamie. "Two Rings to Rule Them All: A Comparative Study of Tolkien and Wagner." *Mythlore* 29, no. 3 (Spring/Summer 2001): 133–153. https://dc.swosu.edu/mythlore/vol29/iss3/10.

Mehler, Eugen. "*Rienzi* und die Dresdener Theaterzensur." *Die Musik*, Bd. 46, 12 Jg., 2 Q. (1912–1913): 195–201.

Mertens, Volker. "Durch Gottes Sieg…—Gottesurteile im *Lohengrin* und anderswo." In "Schwerpunkt: *Lohengrin*." Issue of *Wagnerspectrum*, no. 1 (2014): 61–80.

Mertens, Volker. "Mittelalter und Renaissance." In *Wagner und Nietzsche: Kultur—Werk— Wirkung; Ein Handbuch*, edited by Stefan Lorenz Sorgner, H. James Birx, and Nikolaus Knoepffler, 79–105. Reinbek bei Hamburg: Rowohlt, 2008.

Mertens, Volker. "Wagner's Middle Ages," translated by Stewart Spencer. In *Wagner Handbook*, edited by Ulrich Müller and Peter Wapnewski, translation edited by John Deathridge, 236–268. Cambridge, MA: Harvard University Press, 1992.

Meyer, Stephen C. *Epic Sound: Music in Postwar Hollywood Biblical Films*. Bloomington: Indiana University Press, 2015.

Meyer, Stephen C. "Soundscapes of Middle Earth: The Question of Medievalist Music in Peter Jackson's *Lord of the Rings* Films." *Studies in Medievalism* 18 (2009): 165–187.

Michelet, Jules. *Histoire de France*, 19 vols. Paris, Librairie Internationale, 1876–1877.

Michelet, Jules. *La Sorcière: The Witch of the Middle Ages*. Translated by L. J. Trotter. London: Simpkin, Marshall, 1863.

Miller, Laura. "They Put the Evil in Medieval." *Salon*. April 5, 2013. https://www.salon.com/2013/04/05/they_put_the_evil_in_medieval.

Mjöberg, Jöran. "Romanticism and Revival." In *The Northern World: The History and Heritage of Northern Europe, AD 400–1100*, edited by David M. Wilson, 207–238. London: Thames & Hudson, 1980.

Moore, John C. " 'Courtly Love': A Problem of Terminology." *Journal of the History of Ideas* 40, no. 4 (October–December 1979): 621–632.

Morgan, Gwendolyn. "Medievalism, Authority, and the Academy." *Studies in Medievalism* 17 (2009): 55–67.

Müller, Ulrich, and Oswald Panagl, eds. *Ring und Gral: Texte, Kommentare und Interpretationen zu Richard Wagners "Der Ring des Nibelungen," "Tristan und Isolde," "Die Meistersinger von Nürnberg" und "Parsifal."* Würzburg: Königshausen und Neumann, 2002.

Müller, Ursula, and Ulrich Müller, eds. *Richard Wagner und sein Mittelalter*. Anif, Salzburg: Verlag Ursula Müller-Speiser, 1989.

Munrow, David. *Instruments of the Middle Ages and Renaissance*. Oxford: Oxford University Press, 1976.

Nelson, Victoria. "Faux Catholic: A Gothic Subgenre from Monk Lewis to Dan Brown." *Boundary 2: An International Journal of Literature and Culture* 34, no. 3 (February 2007): 87–107.

Niedermeyer, Louis, and Joseph d'Ortigue. *Traité théorique et pratique de l'accompagnement du plain-chant*. Paris: Heugel, 1857.

Nussbaum, Rachel. "Wagner's *Rienzi* and the Creation of a People." *Musical Quarterly* 84, no. 3 (Autumn 2000): 417–425.

Omont, Henri. *Le livre des merveilles: Marco Polo, Odoric de Pordenone, Mandeville, Hayton, etc.; Reproduction des 265 miniatures du manuscript français 2810 de la Bibliothèque nationale*. 2 vols. Paris: Berthaud, 1907.

Orff, Carl. *Carl Orff und sein Werk: Dokumentation*. Vol. 4, *Trionfi: Carmina Burana—Catulli Carmina—Trionfo di Afrodite*. Tutzing: Schneider, 1979.

Ortenberg, Veronica. *In Search of the Holy Grail: The Quest for the Middle Ages*. London: Hambledon Continuum, 2007.

Owens, Peter. "*Worldes Blis* and Its Satellites." In *Perspectives on Peter Maxwell Davies*, edited by Richard McGregor, 23–50. Aldershot, UK: Ashgate, 2000.

Page, Christopher. *Discarding Images: Reflections on Music and Culture in Medieval France*. Oxford: Clarendon Press, 1993.

Page, Christopher. "The Performance of Ars Antiqua Motets." *Early Music* 16, no. 2 (May 1988): 147–164.

Paris, Gaston. "Études sur les Romans de la Table Ronde: Lancelot du Lac; Le Conte de la Charrette." *Romania* 12, no. 48 (October 1883): 459–534.

Partridge, Christopher. *The Lyre of Orpheus: Popular Music, the Sacred, and the Profane*. Oxford: Oxford University Press, 2014.

Peters, Gretchen. *The Musical Sounds of Medieval French Cities: Players, Patrons, and Politics*. Cambridge: Cambridge University Press, 2012.

Petersen, Nils Holger. "The Medievalism of Carl Maria von Weber's *Euryanthe*." *Studies in Medievalism* 14 (2005): 110–142.

Petersen, Nils Holger. "Medieval Resurfacing, Old and New." *Studies in Medievalism* 20 (2011): 35–42.

Pfalzgraf, Annegret. "Eine deutsche Ilias? Homer und das 'Nibelungenlied' bei Johann Jakob Bodmer: Zu den Anfängen der nationalen Nibelungenrezeption im 18. Jahrhundert." PhD diss., Universität Marburg, 2003.

Piotrowska, Anna G. "Scandinavian Heavy Metal as an Intertextual Play with Norse Mythology." In *Music at the Extremes: Essays on Sounds Outside the Mainstream*, edited by Scott A. Wilson, 101–114. Jefferson, NC: McFarland, 2015.

Pipolo, Tony. "The Spectre of *Joan of Arc*: Textual Variations in the Key Prints of Carl Dreyer's Film." *Film History* 2, no. 4 (November–December 1988): 301–324.

Planchart, Alejandro Enrique. "The Origins and Early History of *L'homme armé*." *Journal of Musicology* 20, no. 3 (Summer 2003): 305–357.

Plumley, Yolanda, and Ann Stone. *Chantilly Codex, MS 564: Critical Study and Facsimile Edition*. Turnhout: Brepols, 2008.

Pospíšil, Milan. "Meyerbeer's *Les Huguenots* in Prague and Austrian Censorship." In *Meyerbeer and* Grand opéra *from the July Monarchy to the Present*, edited by Mark Everist, 107–122. Turnhout: Brepols, 2016.

Pottinger, Mark. "The Staging of History in France: Characterizations of Historical Figures in French Grand Opera during the July Monarchy." PhD diss., City University of New York, Graduate Center, 2005.

"Procès de rehabilitation: Déposition de Jean Pasquerel." SteJeannedArc.net. Updated 2014. http://www.stejeannedarc.net/rehabilitation/dep_jean_pasquerel.php.

"Procès de rehabilitation: V-3—Déposition de Jean d'Orléans, comte de Dunois." SteJeannedArc. net. Updated 2014. http://www.stejeannedarc.net/rehabilitation/dep_dunois.php.

Pugh, Tison, and Susan Lynn Aronstein, eds. *The Disney Middle Ages: A Fairy-Tale and Fantasy Past*. New York: Palgrave Macmillan, 2012.

Pugh, Tison, and Angela Jane Weisl. *Medievalisms: Making the Past in the Present*. London: Routledge, 2013.

Quicherat, Jules. *Procès de condamnation et de réhabilitation de Jeanne d'Arc dite La Pucelle*. 5 vols. Paris: Jules Renouard, 1841–1849.

Ragnard, Isabelle. "Le thème de *L'homme armé* dans le film *Jeanne La Pucelle* de Jacques Rivette." *Le Paon d'Héra* 8 (2012): 23–34.

Ramey, Lynn T., and Tison Pugh, eds. *Race, Class, and Gender in "Medieval" Cinema*. New York: Palgrave Macmillan, 2007.

Richardson, Michael Scott. "Evoking an Ancient Sound: Richard Wagner's Musical Medievalism." Master's thesis, Rice University, 2009.

Richardson, Michael Scott. "Medievalism, Historicism, and Nationalism in Early Nineteenth-Century German Opera," PhD diss., Stony Brook University, 2016.

Robertson, Anne Walters. *Guillaume de Machaut and Reims: Context and Meaning in His Musical Works*. Cambridge: Cambridge University Press, 2007.

Robinson, Carol L., and Pamela Clements. "Living with Neomedievalism." *Studies in Medievalism* 18 (2009): 55–75.

Robson-Scott, W. D. *The Literary Background of the Gothic Revival in Germany: A Chapter in the History of Taste*. Oxford: Clarendon Press, 1965.

Rosenberg, Bruce A. "Kennedy in Camelot: The Arthurian Legend in America." *Western Folkore* 35, no. 1 (January 1976): 52–59.

Rosenthal, Bernard, and Paul E. Szarmach, eds. *Medievalism in American Culture: Papers of the Eighteenth Annual Conference of the Center for Medieval and Early Renaissance Studies*. Binghamton: Medieval and Renaissance Texts and Studies, 1989.

Rothenberg, David J. *The Flower of Paradise: Marian Devotion and Secular Song in Medieval and Renaissance Music*. Oxford: Oxford University Press, 2011.

Rovira, James, ed. *Rock and Romanticism: Post-Punk, Goth, and Metal as Dark Romanticisms*. New York: Palgrave Macmillan, 2018.

Runge, Paul. *Die Lieder und Melodien der Geissler des Jahres 1349, nach der Aufzeichnung Hugo's von Reutlingen*. Leipzig: Druck und Verlag von Breithopf und Härtel, 1900.

Ruskin, John. "On the Nature of Gothic." In *The Stones of Venice*. Vol. 2, *The Sea-Stories*, 151–231. London: Smith, Elder, 1853.

Sachs, Curt. "Primitive and Medieval Music: A Parallel." In "A Musicological Offering to Otto Kinkeldey upon the Occasion of His 80th Anniversary." Special issue. *Journal of the American Musicological Society* 13, no. 1/3 (1960): 43–49.

Säuberlich, Hartmut. "Die Dekorationspläne der frühen Tannhäuser-Aufführungen." *Maske und Kothurn* 8 (1962): 74–84.

Schmees, Iwen. *Musik in der Mittelalter-Szene: Stilrichtungen, Repertoire und Interpretation*. Hamburg: Diplomica Verlag, 2008.

Schubert, Linda. "Plainchant in Motion Pictures: The *Dies irae* in Film Scores." *Florilegium* 15 (1998): 207–229.

Schultz, James A. *Courtly Love, the Love of Courtliness, and the History of Sexuality*. Chicago: University of Chicago Press, 2006.

See, Klaus von. *Europa und der Norden im Mittelalter*. Heidelberg: Universitätverlag C. Winter 1999.

Selling, Kim. " 'Fantastic Neomedievalism': The Image of the Middle Ages in Popular Fantasy." In *Flashes of the Fantastic: Selected Essays from "The War of the Worlds" Centennial, Nineteenth International Conference on the Fantastic in the Arts*, edited by David Ketterer, 211–218. Westport, CT: Praeger, 2004.

Senior, W. A. "Medieval Literature and Modern Fantasy: Toward a Common Metaphysic." *Journal of the Fantastic in the Arts* 3, no. 3/4 (1994): 32–49.

Service, Alexandra. "Popular Vikings: Constructions of Viking Identity in Twentieth Century Britain." PhD diss., University of York, 1998.

Shelemay, Kay Kaufman. "Toward an Ethnomusicology of the Early Music Movement: Thoughts on Bridging Disciplines and Musical Worlds." *Ethnomusicology* 45, no. 1 (Winter 2001): 1–29.

Shichtman, Martin B. "Hollywood's New Weston: The Grail Myth in Francis Ford Coppola's *Apocalypse Now* and John Boorman's *Excalibur.*" In *The Grail: A Casebook*, edited by Dhira B. Mahoney, 561–573. New York: Routledge, 2000.

Shippey, Tom. "Medievalisms and Why They Matter." *Studies in Medievalism* 17 (2009): 45–54.

Siberry, Elizabeth. *The New Crusaders: Images of the Crusades in the 19th and Early 20th Centuries*. Farnham, UK: Ashgate, 2000.

Siegel, Linda. "A Second Look at Schumann's *Genoveva.*" *Music Review* 36 (1975): 17–41.

Simmons, Clare A. *Popular Medievalism in Romantic-Era Britain*. New York: Palgrave Macmillan, 2011.

Simmons, Clare A., ed. *Medievalism and the Quest for the "Real" Middle Ages*. London: Cass, 2001.

Simons, John. *From Medieval to Medievalism*. New York: St. Martin's Press, 1992.

Smilansky, Uri. "Rethinking *Ars Subtilior*: Context, Language, Study and Performance." PhD diss., University of Exeter, 2010.

Solterer, Helen. *Medieval Roles for Modern Times: Theater and the Battle for the French Republic*. University Park: Pennsylvania State University Press, 2010.

Sorba, Carlotta. "*Attila* and Verdi's Historical Imagination." *Cambridge Opera Journal* 21, no. 3 (November 2009): 241–248.

Spencer, Stewart. "The 'Romantic Operas' and the Turn to Myth." In *The Cambridge Companion to Wagner*, edited by Thomas S. Grey, 67–73. Cambridge: Cambridge University Press, 2008.

Spencer, Stewart. "Wagner's Nuremberg." *Cambridge Opera Journal* 4, no. 1 (March 1992): 21–41.

Stephan, Dom John. *The "Adeste fideles": A Study on Its Origin and Development*. Originally published in 1947. Accessed September 14, 2017. http://www.hymnsandcarolsofchristmas. com/Hymns_and_Carols/Images/Stephan/adeste_fideles_a_study_on_its_or.htm.

Sterling-Hellenbrand, Alexandra. "*Excalibur*'s Siegfried and the Music of Myth." *New Research in Medieval German Studies: Yearbook of the Society for Medieval German Studies* 1 (Spring 2009): 34–49.

Stoehr, Ingo R. "(Post)Modern Rewritings of the *Nibelungenlied—Der Nibelungen Roman* and Armin Ayren as *Meister Konrad.*" In *Medieval German Voices in the 21st Century: The Paradigmatic Function of Medieval German Studies for German Studies*, edited by Albrecht Classen, 165–178. Amsterdam: Editions Rodopi B.V., 2000.

Stoessel, Jason. "Symbolic Innovation: The Notation of Jacob de Senleches." *Acta Musicologica* 71, no. 2 (1999): 136–164.

Swabey, Ffiona. *Eleanor of Aquitaine, Courtly Love, and the Troubadours*. Greenwood Guides to Historic Events of the Medieval World. Westport, CT: Greenwood Press, 2004.

Sweers, Britta. *Electric Folk: The Changing Face of English Traditional Music*. Oxford: Oxford University Press, 2005.

Symonds, John Addington. *Wine, Women, Song: Mediaeval Latin Students' Songs First Translated into English Verse with an Essay by John Addington Symonds*. 1884. Reprint, New York: Cooper Square, 1966.

Szabó-Knotik, Cornelia. "Tradition as a Source of Progress: Franz Liszt and Historicism." In *Liszt and the Birth of Modern Europe*, edited by Michael Saffle and Rossana Dalmonte, 143–156. Franz Liszt Studies Series 9. Hillsdale, NY: Pendragon Press, 2003.

Tabbagh, Vincent. *Fasti Ecclesiae Gallicanae: Répertoire prosopographique des évêques, dignitaires et chanoines des diocèses de France de 1200 à 1500*. Vol. 2, *Diocèse de Rouen*, edited by Hélène Millet. Turnhout: Brepols, 1998.

Taga Gabsi, Rim. "Delteil tel qu'on l'ignore: Chantre de Jeanne d'Arc." In *Delteil en détail*, edited by Anne-Lise Blanc, 103–118. Perpignan: Presses Universitaires de Perpignan, 2011.

Taylor, Henry Osborn. *The Medieval Mind: A History of the Development of Thought and Emotion in the Middle Ages*. London: Macmillan, 1911.

Tolkien, J. R. R. *The Monsters and the Critics and Other Essays*. Edited by Christopher Tolkien. Boston: Houghton Mifflin, 1984.

Tolmie, Jane. "Medievalism and the Fantasy Heroine." *Journal of Gender Studies* 15, no. 2 (July 2006): 145–158.

Toswell, M. J. "The Tropes of Medievalism." *Studies in Medievalism* 17 (2009): 68–76.

Trafford, Simon. "Blood, Fire, Death: Bathory and the Birth of Viking Metal." In *Gathering of the Tribe: Music and Heavy Conscious Creation*, edited by Mark Goodall, 302–308. London: Headpress, 2013.

Trilling, René. "Medievalism and Its Discontents." *Postmedieval: A Journal of Medieval Cultural Studies* 2, no. 2 (Summer 2011): 216–224.

Trippett, David, ed. "Liszt on *Lohengrin* (or: Wagner in absentia): Translation from *The Monthly Musical Record*." *Wagner Journal* 4, no. 1 (March 2010): 4–21.

Tsuakmoto, Chihiro. "What Did They Sound Like? Reconstructing the Music of the Viking Age." Master's thesis, University of Iceland, 2017.

Upton, Elizabeth Randell. "Coconut Clops and Motorcycle Warfare: What Sounds Medieval?" *Sounding Out!* September 19, 2016. https://soundstudiesblog.com/2016/09/19/coconut-clops-and-motorcycle-fanfare-what-sounds-medieval/.

Upton, Elizabeth Randell. "Concepts of Authenticity in Early Music and Popular Music Communities." *Ethnomusicology Review* 17 (2012): n.p. http://ethnomusicologyreview.ucla.edu/journal/volume/17/piece/591.

Utz, Richard. *Medievalism: A Manifesto*. Kalamazoo, MI: ARC Humanities Press, 2017.

Utz, Richard, and Tom Shippey, eds. *Medievalism in the Modern World: Essays in Honour of Leslie J. Workman*. Turnhout: Brepols, 1998.

Utz, Richard, and Jesse G. Swan, eds. "Postmodern Medievalisms." *Studies in Medievalisms* 13 (2003).

Van Deusen, Nancy. "Introduction to Part II: Music." In *Medieval Scholarship: Philosophy and the Arts*, edited by Helen Damico et al. Abingdon, UK: Taylor & Francis, 1995.

Van Elferen, Isabella. *Gothic Music: The Sounds of the Uncanny*. Cardiff: University of Wales Press, 2012.

Van Elferen, Isabella. "Spectral Liturgy: Transgression, Ritual and Music in Gothic." In *The Gothic in Contemporary Literature and Popular Culture: Pop Goth*, edited by Justin D. Edwards and Agnieszka Soltysik Monnet, 135–147. New York: Routledge, 2012.

Vercruysse, Tom. "The Dark Ages Imaginary in European Films." PhD diss., Katholieke Universiteit Leuven, 2014.

Verduin, Kathleen. "The Founding and the Founder: Medievalism and the Legacy of Leslie J. Workman." *Studies in Medievalism* 17 (2009): 1–27.

Wack, Mary Frances. *Lovesickness in the Middle Ages: The "Viaticum" and Its Commentaries*. Philadelphia: University of Pennsylvania Press, 1990.

Wagner, Richard. *Die Wibelungen: Weltgeschichte aus der Sage*. Leipzig: Otto Wigand, 1850.

Wagner, Richard. "Über die Aufführung des *Tannhäuser*." In *Gesammelte Schriften und Dichtungen*, 5:123–159. 2nd ed. Leipzig: Fritzsch, 1887.

Wakefield, Ray. "*Excalibur*: Film Reception and Political Distance." In *Politics in German Literature*, edited by Beth Bjorklund and Mark E. Cory, 166–176. Columbia, SC: Camden House, 1998.

Wakefield, Ray. "Middle Ages." In *The Cambridge Wagner Encyclopedia*, edited by Nicholas Vazsonyi, 302–303. Cambridge: Cambridge University Press, 2013.

Ward, Renée. "Harry Potter and Medievalism." In *Medieval Afterlives in Contemporary Culture*, edited by Gail Ashton, 263–274. London: Bloomsbury, 2015.

Warrack, John. *Richard Wagner: "Die Meistersinger von Nürnberg."* Cambridge: Cambridge University Press, 1994.

Wawn, Andrew. *The Vikings and the Victorians: Inventing the Old North in 19th-Century Britain*. Cambridge: Brewer, 2000.

Wegman, Rob C. "Sense and Sensibility in Late Medieval Music: Thoughts on Aesthetics and 'Authenticity.'" *Early Music* 23, no. 2 (May 1995): 299–312.

Weisl, Angela Jane. *The Persistence of Medievalism: Narrative Adventures in Contemporary Culture*. New York: Palgrave Macmillan, 2003.

Weston, Donna, and Andy Bennett. *Pop Pagans: Paganism and Popular Music*. Studies in Contemporary and Historical Paganism. London: Routledge, 2013.

Williams, David. "Medieval Movies." In "Literature in the Modern Media: Radio, Film, and Television." Special issue. *Yearbook of English Studies* 20 (1990): 1–32.

Williamson, George S. *The Longing for Myth in Germany: Religion and Aesthetic Culture from Romanticism to Nietzsche*. Chicago: University of Chicago Press, 2004.

Winick, Steve. "*Eine kleine mittelalterliche Musik*: German Folk-Rock Gets Medieval." *Dirty Linen* 123 (April/May 2006): 40–43.

Winick, Steve. "A Medieval Bestiary: More Folk-Rock from the Middle Ages." *Dirty Linen* 128 (February/March 2007): 24–27.

Winock, Michel. "Joan of Arc." In *Realms of Memory: The Construction of the French Past*, edited by Pierre Nora, English-language edition edited by Lawrence D. Kritzman, translated by Arthur Goldhammer. Vol. 3, *Symbols*, 432–480. New York: Columbia University Press, 1998.

Witts, Richard. "How to Make a Saint: On Interpreting Hildegard of Bingen." *Early Music* 26, no. 3 (August 1998): 478–485.

Wright, Craig. "Dufay's *Nuper Rosarum Flores*, King Solomon's Temple, and the Veneration of the Virgin." *Journal of the American Musicological Society* 47, no. 3 (Autumn 1994): 395–441.

Young, Crawford. "Antiphon of the Angels: *Angelorum psalat tripudium*." *Recercare* 20, no. 1/2 (2008): 5–23.

Young, Helen. "Where Do the 'White Middle Ages' Come From?" *Public Medievalist*. March 21, 2017. http://www.publicmedievalist.com/white-middle-ages-come/.

Yri, Kirsten. "Medievalism and Exoticism in the Music of Dead Can Dance." *Current Musicology* 85 (Spring 2008): 53–72.

Yri, Kirsten. "Medieval Uncloistered: Uses of Medieval Music in Late Twentieth Century Culture." PhD diss., Stony Brook University, 2004.

Yri, Kirsten. "Noah Greenberg and the New York Pro Musica: Medievalism and the Cultural Front." *American Music* 24, no. 4 (Winter 2006): 421–444.

Yri, Kirsten. "Remaking the Past: Feminist Spirituality in Anonymous 4 and Sequentia's Vox Feminae." *Women and Music: A Journal of Gender and Culture* 12 (2008): 1–21.

Yri, Kirsten. "Thomas Binkley and the Studio der Frühen Musik: Challenging 'the Myth of Westernness.'" *Early Music* 38, no. 2 (May 2010): 273–280.

Zegowitz, Bernd. "Die Nibelungen vor dem *Ring*: Zur (Vor)geschichte eines Opernstoffes." In *Getauft auf Musik: Festschrift für Dieter Borchmeyer*, edited by Udo Bermbach, Hans Rudolf Vaget, and Yvonne Nilges, 257–274. Würzburg: Königshausen und Neumann, 2006.

Zeppezauer-Wachauer, Katharina. *Kurzwîl als Entertainment: Das Mittelalterfest als populärkulturelle Mittelalterrezeption; Historisch-ethnografische Betrachtungen zum Event als Spiel*. Marburg: Tectum Verlag, 2012.

INDEX

Note: Tables are indicated by *t*, figures are indicated by *f*, and examples are indicated by italicized number.